John P. Furches

Hill

THE HERITAGE OF WILKES COUNTY 1982

The Wilkes Genealogical Society, Incorporated
North Wilkesboro, North Carolina

Editor
Mrs. W.O. Absher

Published by the Wilkes Genealogical Society, Inc.
in cooperation with
Hunter Publishing Company
Winston-Salem, North Carolina

Copyright 1982
by the Wilkes Genealogical Society, Incorporated
North Wilkesboro, North Carolina 28659
All rights reserved
ISBN 0-89459-189-4
Printed in the United States of America
by Hunter Publishing Company
Winston-Salem, North Carolina

Library of Congress Catalog Card Number: 82 — 83538

All book order correspondence should be addressed to:
The Heritage of Wilkes County
Post Office Box 1629
North Wilkesboro, North Carolina 28659

CONTENTS

Preface   iv

Local History/ Wilkes Communities   1

Family Histories   73

Pictorial Honor Pages   477

Index   511

The old John Parker Mill on Rocky Creek in the Brushy Mountains was the site for family gatherings and baptismals. The flume (shown upper right) brought water to the wheel, seen on the left. 1895.

Preface
The Heritage of Wilkes County

INTRODUCTION

In its official motto, "Imperium Intra Imperio," Wilkes County proclaims itself a "state within a state" and provides an accurate reflection of the civic pride of its citizens.

There can be several interpretations of this slogan. It can refer to the present size of the county, for Wilkes is very large. It can also remind us of an earlier time when Wilkes included all of the northwestern part of the state and some territory to the west, besides. But, in its most profound sense, the state within a state is a state of mind, shared by many persons both here and away.

It is an attitude suggesting that Wilkes is a part of North Carolina, to be sure, but that it is also very much an entity to itself, bearing a proud sense of self-sufficiency that has shaped and colored much of its history.

Because so many of its writers have cherished the strong Wilkes brand of individuality and recognized it in their stories about themselves and their forebears, this book is permeated with its subject's special flavor.

Through recitations of the everyday and the extraordinary, triumphs and tragedies, laughter and tears, a cadence sounds loud and clear of a people who have known what they wanted, sought the opportunity to live as they chose, shared and cared but minded their own business, given little quarter to enemies perceived near or far, taken great stock in their own traditions, wanted the best of both old and new for their children, and shown no surprise that so many others have seen the good life here and come to join it.

By presenting their heritages of family and of community, the writers have identified themselves and their kinspeople, delineated and described occupations, achievements and even personal quirks of those who've gone before. They've preserved the significant and the amusing, the pivotal and the trivial; and they've allowed us today and those yet to come the pleasure of knowing about them, too.

By gathering all this together, this book has served its purpose. The story and the spirit of Wilkes County are perpetuated for all of us who would know of our past, learn from it about ourselves, and perhaps find inspiration therein for the road ahead, as well.

WILKES COUNTY

Wilkes County was formed in the year 1777 from Surry and named in honor of John Wilkes, a distinguished English statesman and member of Parliament. He was ejected by the ministerial party from Parliament on account of his liberal political views, and as often he was returned by the people. He died in 1797.

Wilkes County is situated in the extreme northwest portion of North Carolina, and bounded on the north by the Blue Ridge Mountains, which separate it from Ashe and Alleghany Counties; on the east by Surry; on the south by Alexander and Iredell; and on the west by Watauga and Caldwell.

Wilkesboro is the county seat, which is one hundred and seventy-two miles northwest of Raleigh, North Carolina, the state capital.

The records of the county do not begin until 1778. An account of the first court of Pleas and Quarter Sessions reads as follows: "State of North Carolina, Wilkes County — Agreeable to an Act of the General Assembly, from his Excellency, Richard Caswell, Esq., Governor, Commander-in-Chief of this State, the following gentlemen named for erecting and holding Court for the County of Wilkes at Brown's at the Bent of the Yadkin on the first Monday, being the 2nd day of March One Thousand Seven Hundred Seventy-Eight in the year of Our Lord; and the Second Year of American Independence, each took the Oath of Justice of the Peace, viz: Benjamin Cleveland, Benjamin Herndon, Elijah Isaacs, William Terrel Lewis, Charles Gordon, John Brown, John Parks, Junr., Joseph Herndon, James Fletcher, John Greer, William Lewis, Thomas Elledge, George Morris and William Colvart.

Richard Allen was duly chosen Sheriff, took the Oath of Allegiance to the State and entered into Bond with Samuel Bicknal, Thomas Tanner, Daniel Vannoye, Benjamin Greer and Benjamin Elledge in the sum of One Thousand Pounds, current money of the State. Likewise, the Court proceeded to chose a Clerk of the said County Court of Sessions and William Lenoir was duly chosen Clerk and took the Oath of Allegiance to the State and Oath of Office and entered into Bond with Joseph Herndon, John Brown and John Greer, securities, in the sum of One Thousand Pounds.

Benjamin Herndon was chosen Entry Taker, Joseph Herndon, Surveyor, John Brown, Register and Ranger and Colo. Charles Gordon, Coroner."

In the month of June 1778, John Parks, John Barton, George Gordon, Francis Hardgrave, Rowland Judd, George Morris and John Witherspoon were Commissioners appointed by an Act of the Assembly to appoint (select) a place for erecting a Court House, Prison, Pillory and Stocks in Wilkes County, who considered "where the Mulberry Fields Meeting House stands to be the most Sentral, Suitable and Proper Place this 3rd day of June 1778."

On the 9th September 1778, the commissioners (who included Robert Lanier, Henry Speer and Joseph Herndon) appointed to run a dividing line between Surry and Wilkes Counties gave their report: Beginning in the Rowan County line, half a mile below Daniel Rashes on the head branch of Hunting Creek, north crossing Mulberry Field Road about half a mile below Hamlins old Store House; thence through Solomon Sparks Plantation, leaving said Sparks House in Surry County; thence crossing the Brushy Mountains at the head of the north fork of Swan Creek; thence crossing the Yadkin River a little below Capt. Parkses, through the lower end of Carrolds Plantation on the north side of the said river; thence crossing Big Elkin at Long Sholes; thence crossing the south fork of Mitchels River below John Scotts; crossing the top of Piney Know to the main Ridge of Mountains west of Fishes Peak; thence to the Virginia line. The above line being exactly twenty-six miles west of the Surry Court House, agreeable to an Act of the Assembly." Thus, the county of Wilkes was officially separate and apart from its parent county of Surry.

Naturally, the governing process of the newly formed county of Wilkes was carried on through the courts. The court gave "leave" for griss (grist) mills to be built along the streams; licenses were granted to individuals to keep a Tavern or an Ordinary in their "now dwelling houses"; men over sixty years of age and/or infirm, as well as those in the Continental Service during the Revolutionary War, were exempt from paying a poll tax; juries were appointed by the court to build and keep up roads in their respective neighborhoods; deeds, State grants and wills were recorded and probated; administrators of estates were appointed; civil and criminal cases were tried; veniremen were appointed to attend the Supreme Court at Salisbury; branding marks were recorded; guardians were appointed for orphans and many other affairs were settled in court.

In 1840, Wilkes County produced corn, oats, wheat, tobacco, cotton, and wool. Its population in 1850 was 10,746 whites, 211 free persons of colour, 1,142 slaves, and 11,642 representative population. In 1860, the population was 14,740 persons. There were fourteen Baptist, five Methodist, two Episcopal churches and one Presbyterian church in the county. Wilkes had one hotel (the Wilkes in Wilkesboro), three lawyers, one cotton and one tobacco manufactory, twenty-one merchants, fourteen Baptist, four Methodist, One Episcopal, one Lutheran and two Christian ministers, seven grist mills, four physicians, nine postoffices, two academies (Wilkesboro and Lewis Fork), and the staple crops were wheat, corn, tobacco, rye and oats, with butter, livestock and medicinal herbs as important business concerns, also.

Today, the population is 58,657 citizens; the school system consists of four high schools, one junior high, and sixteen elementary schools, a community college; there is a 141-bed hospital; there are more than a dozen civic organizations, a historical society, a genealogical society, six banking facilities, four electric power suppliers and five communication facilities; and the major crops are apples, corn, tobacco, wheat, soybeans, hay, peaches and home gardens, with livestock and poultry businesses too. There are two mirror manufacturing plants, a machine manufacturing mill, several furniture factories and a foundry. Until recently there was a clay pottery. There are many churches in the county, representing Baptist, Methodist, Presbyterian, Lutheran, Catholic, Mormon, Adventist and other denominations and faiths.

Sources: Original court minutes, *History of N.C.* by Wheeler (1851), Business Directory (1860), Wilkes Chamber of Commerce Publication (1981).

WILKES GENEALOGICAL SOCIETY, INC.

The society was formed on the 21 January 1967 by a group of citizens interested in having a genealogical society in Wilkes County. There were almost sixty people who were considered charter members. They named the organization "The Genealogy Society of the "Original" Wilkes County", a title that soon became burdensome because of its length, and the name was changed to the present title about ten years ago.

The first meeting was held in the public library building on C Street in North Wilkesboro and this is still the meeting place, as well as the depository of the society's materials collection (which may be used by the public during library hours). Several years ago the county commissioners appropriated a given sum of money for the renovation of an unused room in the basement of the library building to be used exclusively for a genealogical research room.

All of the physical operation of the society is carried on through a totally volunteer arrangement. A quarterly bulletin entitled Spring, Summer, Fall, Winter of a given calendar year is published and mailed to between three hundred and fifty and four hundred members in almost every state in the Union.

A few members have abstracted, compiled and indexed the oldest records of the county beginning in 1778, and the society has sold and is selling these publications through the mail. With the proceeds from the sale of these abstracts and from the membership fees, genealogical research material is continually being placed in the genealogy room of the library.

The collection consists of more than two thousand printed volumes, valued at over fifty thousand dollars. Some of these volumes contain abstracts of courthouse records of counties in Maryland, Virginia, Delaware, Pennsylvania, South Carolina, Kentucky, North Carolina and others. There is a section on family histories, including some Wilkes families, some church minutes, war and miscellaneous records.

There is a microfilm collection containing the *Federal Census of the State of North Carolina* from 1790 through 1900. Also, reels of early deeds, wills, court minutes, some newspapers, some church minutes, the Ashe County Wade Eller collection and many other records are included.

People whose roots were and are in Wilkes County are pleased when they come here and use the material. The signatures on the register at the main desk in the library and in the room itself are proof positive that the volunteer efforts of the members of the society have been and are worth the energies put forth.

We are grateful to those people who were farsighted enough to organize the society, to those people who have continued to work and support our efforts and to those members "out there" whom we may never meet personally, but who are foremost in our thoughts when we are selecting and searching for the material that goes in our quarterly bulletins and in the material that is placed in the genealogy room here.

We were given a golden opportunity to sponsor a Wilkes County Heritage Book which has made it possible for everyone who wanted to to include their families and histories in a durable volume. Such a project had long been a dream of members of the society. That it has become a reality does surely "maketh our cup runneth over."

The members of the book committee were hand-picked by the editor because of their abilities and willingness to give their best efforts toward the success of a given project. They all have lived up to the confidence placed in them, some going a bit beyond the "last mile"! Their efforts are greatly appreciated.

We want to thank the "authors" for their overwhelming response, the publishers for their cooperation and praise of our progress, and the people who have made our pre-publication sales proof that the book will sell. We also want to thank Mr. W.O. Absher for his patience and understanding.

There will be errors found; there will be criticisms; there will be people who will be sorry they did not get their family histories in the book, and perhaps a few who will be sorry they did! At any rate, we ask that you overlook the errors, be slow to criticise, and be proud with us that we at last have a book about the real people who have been and are now the Heritage of Wilkes County, North Carolina.

THE HERITAGE OF WILKES COUNTY BOOK COMMITTEE
MRS. W.O. ABSHER, C.G.R.S., EDITOR

MRS. H.D. BALL, MRS. EDWARD P. BELL, MRS. EDWARD BENTON, MRS. JAY CALL, MRS. R.L. ELAM, MRS. GEORGE FORESTER, JR., MISS EVA GERMAN, MR. DON HAYES, MRS. ROBERT K. HAYES, SR., MRS. MILES HELTON, MRS. HARVEL HOWELL, MRS. J.T. HUTCHENS, MRS. HUGH MARTIN, MRS. LOTT MAYBERRY, MRS. TOM OGBURN, MRS. SAMUEL E. SEBASTIAN, MRS. J. ARNOLD SIMPSON, MRS. C.D. SMITHEY, MRS. ROBERT SMOAK AND MR. EUGENE TESTER, MEMBERS OF THE HERITAGE BOOK COMMITTEE.

OFFICERS OF THE GENEALOGICAL SOCIETY AND SOME MEMBERS OF THE WILKES HERITAGE BOOK COMMITTEE: Seated, L to R; Mrs. Edward P. Bell, Mrs. W.O. Absher, Mrs. C.D. Smithey. Standing, L to R; Mrs. J. Arnold Simpson, Mrs. Robert K. Hayes, Sr., Mrs. Hugh Martin, Mrs. George Forester, Jr., and Mrs. Lott Mayberry.

In Appreciation

The Heritage of Wilkes County book committee would like to express their thanks and admiration to Mrs. W.O. Absher, editor of this book and a leader in every sense of the word.

One of the organizers of the North Carolina Genealogical Society, Mrs. Absher has been a mainstay in the Wilkes Genealogical Society (as well as publishing her own research and abstracts on this county), and so it was only natural that she edit this heritage book. Her humor, enthusiasm, ambition and determination kept our progress in line. You could say that Mrs. Absher has a way with people — and we are all the richer for it.

Our appreciation for your time and your dedication,

The Book Committee

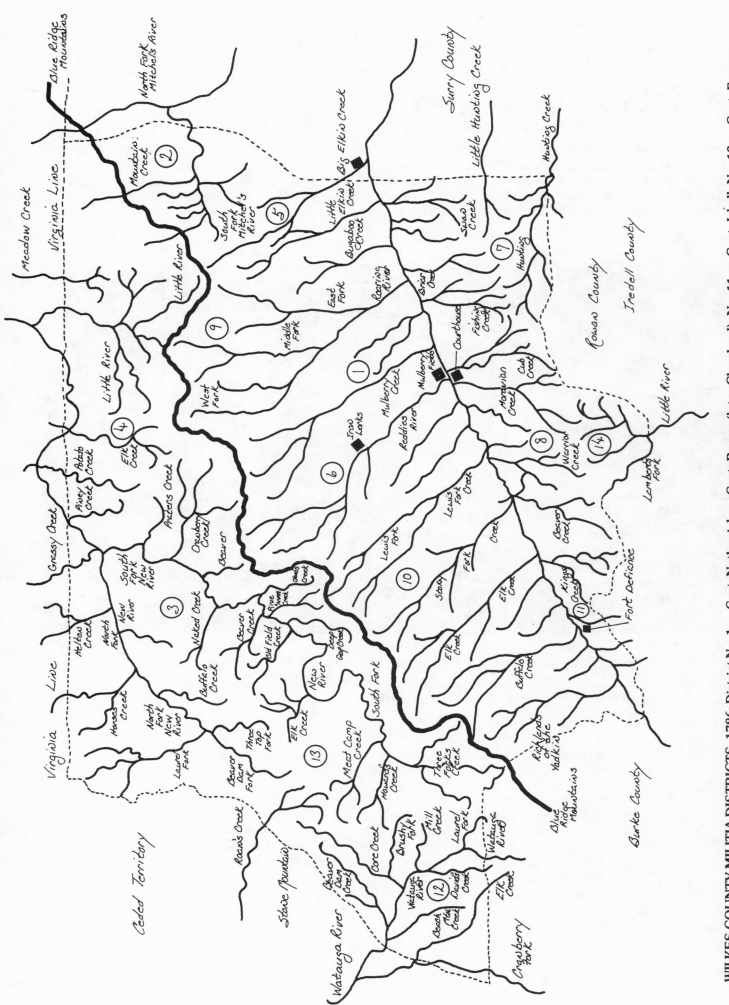

WILKES COUNTY MILITIA DISTRICTS, 1786: District No. 1 — Capt. Nathaniel Gordon; No. 2 — Capt. Hardin (this was taken into Surry in 1792); No. 3 — Capt. Vannoy; No. 4 — Capt. Nall; No. 5 — Capt. Carrel; No. 6 — Capt. Judd; No. 7 — Capt. Alexander Gordon; No. 8 — Capt. Tribble; No. 9 — Capt. Johnson; No. 10 — Capt. Brown (later Cleveland); No. 11 — Capt. Isbell; No. 12 — Capt. Ferguson; No. 13 was established in 1789 and was Capt. Bunyard's District; No. 14 was established 1790 and was Capt. Forester's District.

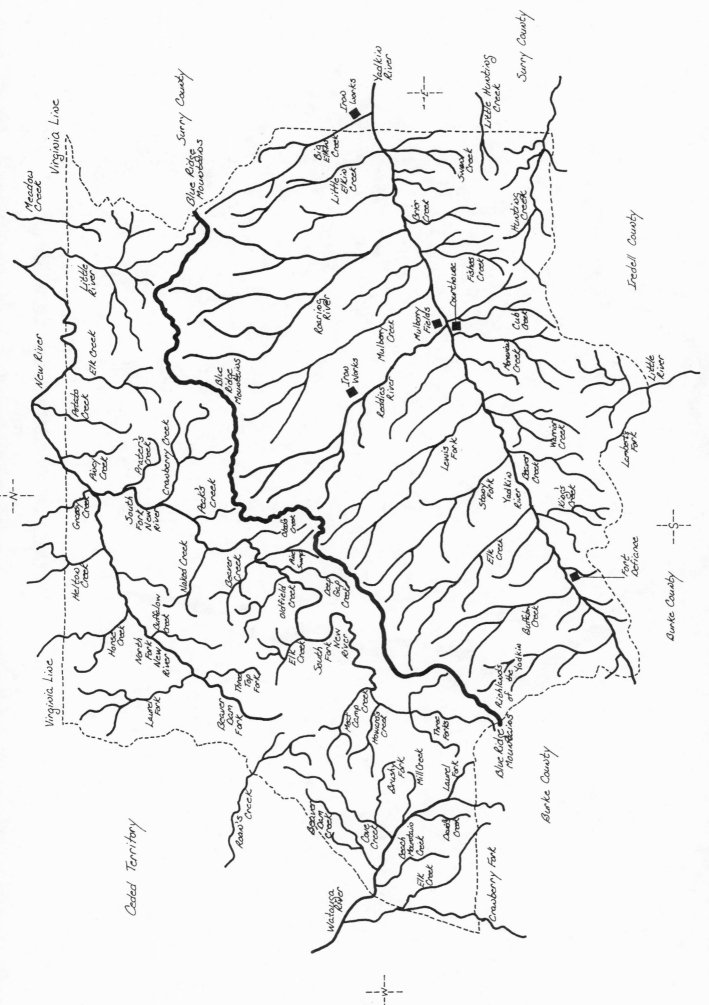

Done by a scale of 400 chains or 5 miles to the inch. The above is a combination of two plats, showing the boundaries of WILKES COUNTY, NORTH CAROLINA in the year 1795. All that plat of land northwest of the BLUE RIDGE MOUNTAINS represents 472,737 acres of land, was surveyed 6 day July, 1795 by H. Rousseau,

C.S. with James and Randolph Williams serving as chain carriers. All that plat of land south of the BLUE RIDGE MOUNTAINS represents 264,680 acres of land, was surveyed 26 July, 1795 by H. Rousseau, C.S. with Daniel Vannoy & John Burke.

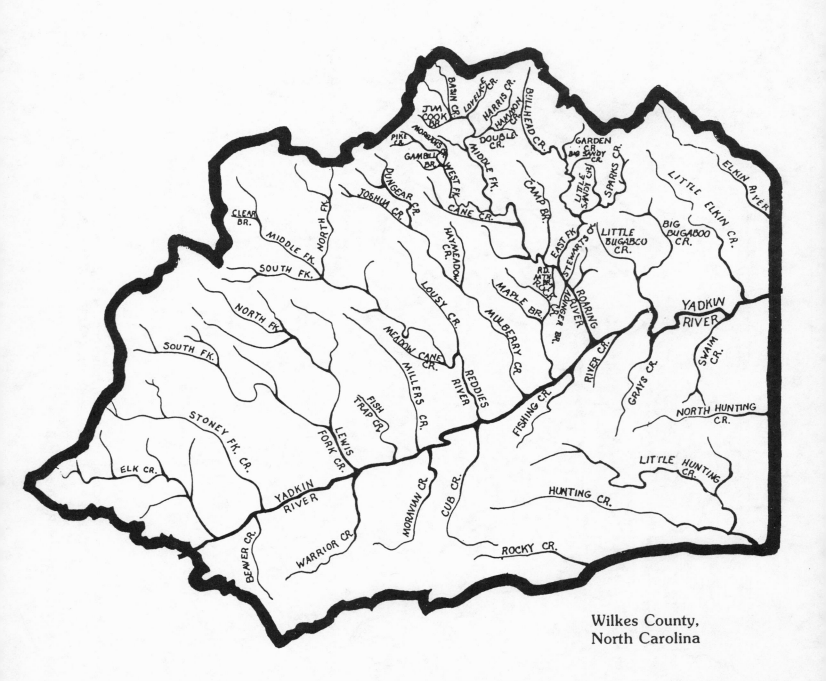

Wilkes County,
North Carolina

Local History
Wilkes Communities

OLD TIMES IN THE HILLS OF WILKES

I was born in 1900 in Wilkes County on a farm which lay on Big Warrior and Little Warrior Creeks. The creeks ran together above a ledge where they spilled over a beautiful falls. Below the falls there was a big, old-fashioned mill which ran an undershot wheel. It ground wheat for flour and corn for meal for the community, and also ran a sawmill. The house we lived in was built from lumber sawed at that mill owned by my father and his brother. I lived in that house until I was married.

From the west side of our home we could see a low range of mountains. This range of mountains seemed to have been cut off from the regular Brushy Mountains at the Caldwell County line. It angled northward and ended in a tall peak which was known as Morris' Knob. It then dropped off sharply from the peak to low hills and valleys which led to the Yadkin River about two miles away.

There were twenty-six families living on this mountain in log cabins. The mountains were thick with game at that time. These people were all good hunters and lived off the game from the mountains. When a mountain boy got ready to marry he would pick a girl from this mountain. Sometimes they moved to the flatlands, but mostly they stayed in the mountains. They would seek out a fairly flat area and cut enough of the large trees to build a one room log house. When the family grew, and it always did, they would add more rooms and space. Usually a kitchen was built off to the side. The kitchen always had a rough table and benches made of split logs. They cooked at the fireplace, since there were no cook stoves back in the mountains in those days.

The main room of the cabin was called the "big house." There were usually three beds to the back and most of the time there would be a loft for the overflo of children. Newlyweds would always burn off and clear a flat place for a garden, which was planted mostly in corn for bread, beans, a few tomatoes, cucumbers, sweet potatoes, Irish potatoes, pumpkins, onions, cabbage and turnips. They raised all sorts of fruit, most commonly apples, cherries, plums and peaches. No one ever heard of a sprayer, but the fruit never seemed to have worms or any other bugs. Of course, they didn't have our wonderful fruit trees such as Stark's Delicious.

There was no such thing as jars for canning, so the women dried apples, peaches and blackberries for use during the winter, when times were hard.

There wasn't a cow on the mountain because there was no place to keep one. If cows were turned loose, they would eat the gardens; so the people drank spiced teas and coffee. They grew the spices or gathered them from mountain plants and trees. Many of them never tasted milk until they were grown and left home.

When I was about seven or eight years old my father sold his mill and used the money to put up a country store. It was long, long miles from this mountain to any other store, so these mountain folks did their trading with my father. Their main source of income was the roots and herbs they gathered from the mountains and foothills all around.

No Schools Nearby

There were no schools anywhere near. It was miles to the only school or church, and the mountain people hardly ever went to either. Every once in a while a few children would make a long walk to the nearest school, but in winter it was impossible since they didn't have any warm clothing. None of them ever learned to read or write.

In the spring when the sap was up and the leaves came out they would take their mattocks and go off to dig the roots and herbs. They gathered and skinned sassafras roots, star root, cohosh, yellow root, poke root (to be sliced and dried) mullen, and many others. They would also cut the bark off the wild cherry trees. Many white pine trees lay and rotted because the people would cut them down and skin the bark. The inner bark was a tannish, thick, dry bark which they would let dry and break, and take it to the store and get four or five cents a pound for it. The king of all roots and herbs was the ginseng. It grew on northern sides of mountain slopes in cool, shady places as a rule, and when these people found a bed of it, they dug every root and every plant, leaving none to reseed itself. Each plant had two roots, more or less the shape of a man. After these roots were dried they would sell for three or four dollars a pound, which the people thought was wonderful. Today, it brings ninety dollars a pound.

Sometime ago, when the ginseng became almost extinct, the government stopped the digging until recently. Now people are only allowed to dig part of each patch, as half of it must be left to reseed itself.

The people would bring a load of roots and herbs to my father's store after they dried the plants. The women grew catnip, mint, and sage which they dried and brought to sell. The leaves of the jimpson weed and mullen were also dried, but you'd better not get the juice of the jimpson weed on your eyes, for it is very poisonous.

Herbs and Other Goods

Each year the store in North Wilkesboro would send a list to my father, telling the price per pound and the name of each root and herb they would buy. All roots and herbs had to be dry. If they weren't they would mold before my father could get them to town. He would always examine the bags of roots and herbs and sometimes find they were not dry enough. Sometimes he would find a rock weighing

A Picnic on Pores Knob (1910).

several pounds stuffed down in the bag, which he would throw out, and tell the seller he didn't buy rocks. If the roots and herbs were not dry, he would have to spread them out on the floor of the room above the store to finish drying.

The mountain people would exchange what their roots and herbs brought for goods in the store, but what they bought first was snuff or tobacco. My father sold Scotch Snuff for a nickel. He also sold Brown's Mule and Apple plug tobacco for a dime a plug. A lot of times they could only afford a nickel's worth, so he would cut a plug in two and sell each part for a nickel.

Papa sold coffee that came in large, burlap bags and was green. It was very cheap and they'd take it home and roast it in a skillet over the fire. When it turned brown it was ready to grind and make coffee, and every family had a little coffee mill which was turned by hand, of course.

He also sold strong yellow lard in buckets which the mountain people used in place of butter. One old mountain man told me that nothing tasted so good as some of that "yaller" lard spread on a piece of bread.

My father always kept a few bolts of cloth. One sort of cloth was called Alamance cloth which nobody now has ever heard of. This cloth was somewhat like gingham, but was much coarser and stronger. The women bought this cloth, which was not much more than ten cents a yard, to make their own and their children's dresses. Unbleached domestic, or factory cloth as it was then called, was also sold at the store. The women used this to make children's underwear.

Other products sold were soda, salt, and other basic necessities. The people always bought a pound or two of fatback, for that was all the meat there was in the stores in those days. We had no refrigeration because we had no electricity.

My father always kept an old wooden egg crate in the store. When the mountain people were lucky enough to find a hen's nest that had been hidden out in the bushes, they brought a few eggs to the store. The crate would gradually fill up — it held several dozen but would sit there a lot of time in the hottest weather for over a month before it would get full, and my father then sold the crate of eggs to a grocery store in town. Since then I've often wondered just how fresh those eggs were that were sold out of grocery stores in town.

About once a month or more, my father would load up his wagon with roots and herbs, chickens (if he had some) and the eggs and drive twenty miles over a muddy, gully road to North Wilkesboro. There wasn't a mile of gravel road in Wilkes County. There were two cars in the county when I was a child, one owned by Leonard Vine in North Wilkesboro and one owned by R. Don Laws of Moravian Falls. If the weather was dry they could drive from North Wilkesboro to Lenoir, if they could get over the big holes in the road. They had many stops along the way and then would have to walk around the front and crank and crank — sometimes it took fifteen or twenty minutes before the motor would start.

A Visit to the Mountain

Early one March day, before the snakes started to crawl, my little cousin, who was about my age (about twelve), and I decided to go to the top of the mountain. Part of the way up the mountain we passed the house of a family we knew well, as the man worked for my father during the wheat harvest. There was a girl in the family who was our age and she said she would go with us to show us the best paths up the mountain. There were no roads of any kind in the mountains, just paths from one house to another.

We got to the mountain and we stopped several times to visit a few houses. On top of the mountain were several acres of rather level land. The people who lived there lived better because they had more land to work with and one or two even had a cow. Some had yokes of oxen with which they plowed their fields. They grew corn and other vegetables, and some had bees which made pure, clear sourwood honey. The families on top of the mountain generally had a cane patch from which they made molasses, as that was all they had to sweeten anything with in those days, except some brown sugar once in a great while.

We rested a while with the people on top of the mountain, started down and came to a high ridge where we could see straight down to the bottom of the mountain. We could see a house down below in a place which looked like a hole with mountains all the way around it. We wanted very much to go down there, so this girl said her oldest brother lived there and she would take us to his home. Only a narrow path led straight down the side of the mountain — the only way to get in and out to their home. When we got down we found a one room log cabin near a spring. There was about an acre of level ground around this little stream. The house was surrounded by lots of peach trees which were budded and ready to bloom. We were invited inside, where we found a very clean floor with two beds in the back of the room, a homemade table, and a few chairs.

The woman was cooking lunch on an open fire, but what amazed us was a pen built about five feet square in the corner of the room, not more than three feet from where the woman was cooking her lunch. The floor of this pen was covered with a thick layer of dry leaves and on these leaves slept a nice, fat pig, where it

The Tulbert and Reid Store which housed the first post office at Spurgeon, NC.

had lived all of its life. There was no odor at all in the room, so they must have cleaned out the leaves every little while. They invited us to stay for lunch, but we decided we didn't want to eat with a pig, though we were hungry.

We went back up the long path to the girl's house on the mountain, and when we got to her house she invited us to go in and eat lunch, or dinner as they called it. As we were about starved after our long walk we decided to go in and eat. What they had on the table was a cake of cornbread made from corn meal and water, a few slices of fatback meat, half fried and floating in a bowl of pure, clear grease, and a few dried, stewed blackberries with no sweetening of any kind. As well as I remember, we ate a few bites while a crowd of hungry children stood at the back of the room and watched us. We got home late that afternoon, tired and hungry. That was my last trip to the top of the mountain for many, many years.

As the children of these mountain families grew up, times got harder and harder. The game had been killed out almost entirely. The roots and herbs were getting scarcer all the time. A few men had jobs with the farmers who lived in nearby valleys, and as soon as the children got old enough they heard of jobs they could get in the cotton mills not too far away. They soon found work, and many of their parents followed them, so they could live.

Soon, no one was left but a few of the very old people. They died out and were buried in lonely graveyards on the hillsides where so many children had died from illnesses and lack of nourishment before thay were very old. The years passed slowly, but before too long not a soul was left on the mountain. The trees grew over the little garden patches and smothered out the fruit trees. The houses rotted and fell down. The only way you could tell that anyone had ever lived there was by a pile of rocks where a chimney once stood. Mother Nature took over once more. The trees grew thick, the dogwoods bloomed white, and many beautiful wild flowers grew over the mountain where people used to go through mountains and valleys. The mountain was once more as it had been in the beginning.

For many years it stood like this. About three years ago, some people from Florida came and found this mountain. They bought land, built roads and are building houses, some on the very sites where the log cabins once stood (although they don't know that). They changed the name of Morris' Knob to Mars Mountain. In time, it is said, there will be a large community of beautiful homes in these mountains, as they bought hundreds of acres.

Source: An article written by Nell S. Carlton, Boomer, N.C. used by permission of the Carltons.

ADLEY COMMUNITY
SHADY GROVE BAPTIST CHURCH

"September 12, 1880, according to appointment, the members dismissed as an arm from Cub Creek Baptist Church met on Laws Hill, four and one half miles above Wilkesboro in order to be constituted into a church. Divine services were held by Elders Benjamin Ashley and Franklin Eller. Then J.W. Kilby was called to sit with the presbytery. The letters of the following were examined: B.M. Pardue and wife Prudence, R.F. Jarvis and wife Martha Ann, Nancy E. Pardue, J.L. Pardue, A.T. Pardue and Emily Childress. They were then examined on articles of faith and found to be orthodox. Their duty was then explained to them. The members above were then constituted into a church in solemn form by the name of Shady Grove. The church elected Elder Benjamin Ashley pastor and A.T. Pardue church clerk. The meetings were ruled to be the second Saturday in each month. It was then decided that this church be attached to the Elkin Association. The presbytery was appointed to write a constitution. The church door was then open for reception of members, when three came forward: Lodemia L. Jarvis W.F. Jarvis and B.G. Pardue and joined by experience and received into fellowship after baptism. The total church membership was then eleven." So states the minutes of the first meeting.

The members first met in a Brush Arbor, with meetings held in the Adley Schoolhouse during cold weather. By April 1887 a building had been erected and the church bought a stove for heating.

The first deacons recorded were H.J. Steelman and J.L. Pardue, who were ordained on Jan. 18, 1885. Robert P. Yates was elected Sunday School supertendent on Mar. 12, 1887. The quarterlies and cards were adopted for the classes in June 1889. The church entered the Brushy Mountain association in 1891.

"The first to walk through the valley of the shadow of death was sister Allie Church who was a consistent member of the church and died in a good old age. Though she was so old and infirm she could feel that her light afflictions were but for a moment."

Shady Grove Baptist Church (1880).

Pastors

Pastors serving the church are as follows: Elder Benjamin W. Ashley; Rev. Milton McNeil; Rev. A.T. Pardue; Rev. R.F. Jarvis; Rev. G.M. Burcham; Rev. J.J. Beach; Rev. George Hamby; Rev. L.B. Murray; Rev. Isaac Watts; Rev. Alfred Foster; Rev. Ed O. Miller; Rev. B.L. Minton; Rev. D.C. Clanton; Rev. Glenn Huffman; Rev. C. Lester Johnson; Rev. Gilbert Osborne; Rev. Albert Pruitt; Rev. Garfield Cardwell; Rev. Albert Byrd; Rev. Garland Reeves; Rev. Wade Phillips; Rev. Floyd Minton; and Rev. Hubert L. Bullis.

Those serving as church clerks have been: A.T. Pardue, P.H. Pardue, R.F. Yates, D.J. Pardue, J.L. Pardue, M.G. Steelman, J.S. Steelman, T.B. Jarvis, Irving Eller, Earl Anderson, Fate Greene, T.M. Faw, Ozelle Faw, I.C. Church, James Wellborn, Mrs. Lillie G. White and Christine E. Walker.

The building of weather board construction has been remodeled twice. The brick veneering was added in 1958. The government took an easement on part of the land in 1960. This small country church now serves over 100 members.

Sources: Church and association minutes, research by Christine E. Walker.

Gladville School.

BENHAM COMMUNITY

Benham is a community in Wilkes between Little Elkin and Big Elkin River.

Littleton Calhoun Carter and his wife, Martha Elizabeth Phillips founded a school called Gladville in 1910 and continued operating the school until 1915. The school was a small brown frame building of simple construction made of forest pine. It was the only school of its kind in the area in that it was actually a summer school that catered to students who wished to prepare for the teaching and business world.

The school and the Carter farm were located near Shoaly Branch Baptist Church in the Benham Community.

Sources: Research, *N.C. Gazetteer* (1968).

BOOMER COMMUNITY

In the early 1700s families began building homes along Warrior Creek about four miles south of the Yadkin River.

A man named Mathison from Alexander County started a small store in the area. He and some other men went to the Blue Ridge bear hunting. The only thing they killed was a boomer, which is a small animal of the squirrel family. When they returned from the hunt some neighbors gathered around and asked about the hunt. Mr. Mathison took the little boomer from his pocket and threw it on the ground. He was nicknamed Boomer. Later when the post office was established it was named Boomer.

The first school in the community was taught in a log building on the farm now owned by Charlie German. Then a larger building was erected near the post office. This became one

Shoaley Branch Baptist Church.

Little Rock School.

Russell Gap School.

of the excellent academies of the county. Students from other places came and boarded in homes of the community in order to attend school here. Some outstanding educators taught in the academy. The building burned.

First Graded School

With the help of contributions by the local citizens a new four-room school building was erected in 1904. This was the first graded school in Wilkes. When the county adopted the school bus system, high school students were taken to Wilkesboro High School.

In 1814 Zion Hill Baptist Church was organized and a log church house was built near the post office. The present building is at the same place. A Methodist church was also near the post office. Around 1912 the membership of this church was moved to the Moravian Falls Methodist Church and the building was sold. The Boomer Christian Advent Church is near the latest school building.

Little Rock Baptist Church is about six miles west of Boomer post office on N.C. Highway 18. Soon after the Civil War, seventeen negro members of Zion Hill Church were granted letters of dismission and organized Thankful Baptist Church. It is three miles west near Highway 18.

Boomer Community Organization has been a great help to the community. The building is on the highway near the post office. It has an excellent baseball field where tournaments are played each season.

The Boomer Volunteer Fire Department is active and efficient.

Source: Research by Eva German.

THANKFUL BAPTIST CHURCH

Zion Hill Baptist Church of Boomer, N.C. was organized on the second Saturday in April, 1814. It adopted strict rules for the order of its business meetings and for the conduct of its members. There seems to have been a large number of charter members, twenty of whom were black.

In May, 1869, Zion Hill Baptist Church granted letters of dismissal to seventeen black members so that they could form their own church.

At first the members went from house to house to hold worship services, but later on they built a brush arbor for these services. They moved from the brush arbor to a schoolhouse that was built of logs and had an open fireplace. It was lit with oil lamps. The seats were made of logs that had been split through the middle and had holes bored for peg-legs. The house had one door and one window. The next building was made of weatherboarding. It was lit with lamps hanging on the walls and was heated by wood stoves. The fourth building was covered with white siding. It was heated by a wood stove and lit by electricity. The present church building is made of brick and has all modern conveniences.

The land for the church was donated by Mr. Thomas Carlton and his wife Mrs. Sallie Carlton.

On March 9, 1897, the name "Thankful" was given to the church because of the thankfulness for the land which had been given.

Zion Hill Baptist Church.

Ministers

Ministers who served Thankful Baptist Church were: Rev. Silver Honeycutt, Rev. Weldon, Rev. Bene Watts, Rev. Francis Parker, Rev. R.B. Watts, Rev. Weldon, Rev. Robert Grinton, Rev. G.W. Fletcher, Rev. L.F. Smith, Rev. K.J. Carlton, Rev. J.A. Parsons, Rev. P. Rowe, Rev. Willie Patterson, Rev. R.W. Barber, Rev. J. Rowe and the present pastor Rev. H.P. Dalton.

Associate pastors were Rev. Willie Rowe, Rev. Fred Carlton and Rev. Roosevelt Carlton.

Those who served as deacons until they were called into the ministry were Brother Lloyd Carlton and Brother Montreal Howell.

One church, St. John, moved from Thankful to Taylorsville. Another church, Piney Grove, moved from Thankful to Moravian Falls.

Source: *The Centennial Year of the Yadkin Valley Missionary Baptist Association* 1880-1980. Research by Mrs. Katherine Denny.

BRIARCREEK COMMUNITY

Wilkes County, one of the most interesting in North Carolina, attains sesquicentennial this year of 1927. In it there is a field of most absorbing interest for historians, technologists, botanists, geologists and mineralogists.

Wilkes was set off from Surry by the North Carolina General Assembly in late 1777. It was created for better convenience of the upper Yadkin settlements. Across this county in a northeasterly direction the beautiful Yadkin, once the Sapons, flows between the Blue Ridge and the Brushy Mountains. The valleys of the Yadkin and its tributaries are fertile, the upland in some parts of the county is good, in some poor, the mountains are rugged and well timbered. The entire county is well watered. From their sources in the Blue Ridge the Yadkin receives the waters of Reddies River, Lewis Fork, Roaring River, Mulberry, Bugaboo, Little Elkin and other streams. From the Brushies come Moravian, Cub, Fishing, Brier, Sales, McBride and other creeks. The scenery in Wilkes is indescribably beautiful.

Colonel Benjamin Cleveland, who was largely instrumental in the formation of Wilkes County, had settled within its territory about 1769. His first home was on Roaring River which rushes, roars and tumbles in cascades down the side of that natural curiosity, Stone Mountain, about five miles southwest of Roaring Gap. Later Col. Cleveland traveled down the valley of Roaring River and four miles below its mouth, located on famous "Round-About" plantation, where the town of Ronda has been built.

The plantation is called Round-About because by a horse shoe curve in its course the Yadkin almost surrounds it. One mile up the

Yadkin, on the same side is the mouth of Bugaboo Creek. Still farther up but from the southern side Brier Creek enters the Yadkin. This particular section of Wilkes has a most interesting history.

During 1775, when Cleveland, neighbors and friends of the upper Yadkin valley had occasion to go to Cross Creek (Fayetteville) to dispose of their surplus productions, and purchase their supplies of iron, sugar, salt, and other necessities, they were compelled, before they were permitted to buy or sell, to take the oath of allegiance to the king. When Cleveland heard of these tyrannical acts, and attempts to forstall the politics of the people, he swore roundly that he would like nothing better than to dislodge those Scotch scoundrels at Cross Creek. Nor was an opportunity long wanting. In February 1776, the Highland Tories of that locality raised the British standard. Captain Cleveland marched down from the mountains with a party of volunteer riflemen, and tradition has it that he reached the front in season to share in the fight and in the suppression of the revolt.

Cleveland's Devils

Cleveland's men were known to the Tories as "Cleveland's Devils," the Whigs called them, "Cleveland's Bull Dogs and Cleveland's Heroes." Most of his men were from what is now Wilkes County, and a number of them came out of old Brier Creek neighborhood.

In the year 1776, after their Cross Creek expedition they scouted on the western frontier of the state, then went against the Cherokee Indians "suffering many hardships and privations; often destitute of provisions, without tents, with few blankets, dressed in clothing made of crude materials derived from hemp, tow and the wild nettle."

In the spring of 1777, Captain Cleveland and his men were sent to protect the Watauga settlements against the Cherokees and served until the treaty of Long Island was made in July of that year when they returned to the Yadkin valley. In the autumn Cleveland attended the North Carolina assembly to use his influence toward the dividing of Surry and forming a new county. In March 1778, Wilkes County was organized. Cleveland was made head of the commission of justices and colonel of the militia. He was also elected to represent Wilkes in the house of commons, and in the state senate.

Old Round-About

"Old Round-About," as Cleveland was often called, claimed that each of his men was equal to five ordinary soldiers. They did their full share toward freeing the colonies from British rule.

When the call came to aid in the campaign against Ferguson, Cleveland gathered his men together on Rendezvous Mountain, in Wilkes County. About 350 men marched to Quaker Meadows, joined other patriots who took part in the campaign, and moved on to King's Mountain. The battle was fought 7 October, 1780, and Col. Ferguson was killed.

On 12 October, 1780, General Gates directed that the prisoners be sent under proper guards to Fincastle Courthouse, Virginia. The Wilkes men were detailed for guard duty. The line of march crossed portions of the counties of Cleveland, Rutherford, McDowell, Burke, moving down the valley of the Yadkin they camped near Fort Defiance, then at Moravian Creek two miles above old Mulberry Fields. The next day they reached Brier Creek and camped on Hagood's plantation.

After several other expeditions, they rendered their last military service during the war of the American Revolution and returned home to Wilkes.

Col. Cleveland lived a few years longer at Round-About, then moved to South Carolina where he died. Capt. Robert Cleveland died in Wilkes County and Lieut. Larkin Cleveland died in Tennessee. They were brothers of Col. Ben, whose son, John was also in the service. Col. Richard Allen died at his home on Bugaboo, Major Joseph Herndon on McBride's Creek, and Col. Benjamin Herndon removed to South Carolina.

Other Wilkes men who served with Cleveland were Gen. William Lenior, Capt. John Bartow, Miner Smith, John Brown, Samuel Johnson, the brothers, David and John Witherspoon, Elisha Reynolds, and Cleveland's neighbor William Meredith. Thomas Bicknell and Daniel Sisk were killed at the battle of King's Mountain.

Oldest Baptist Church

Less than two years after the close of the Revolutionary War, the oldest of all the existing Baptist churches in all Northwestern North Carolina was organized in the Brier Creek neighborhood by John Cleveland of Round-About. At that time there was but one other Baptist church in all the territory now included in the counties of Yadkin, Surry, Alleghany, Ash, Watauga, Caldwell, Alexander, Irdell, Wilkes and other counties to the west. That pioneer center of Baptist faith and order was known as George McNiel's church on Reddies River. It soon ceased to exist.

Brier Creek, the mother Baptist church, was constituted the 8th day of June 1783 by Lewis Shelton, George McNiel and John Cleveland, with the following eleven members: Benjamin Martin, John Parks, Benjamin Toney, Gooding Licking, Jacob Medcalf, Charles Bond, Dianah Martin, Elizabeth Toney, Sarah Thirmond, Hannah Garrison and Mary Calloway.

Benjamin Martin lived and died within one mile of the church. Some of his descendants live near it still, as do the descendants of John Parks. The Toneys, Lickings, Bonds, Medcalfs, and Harrisons have disappeared from the locality.

John Cleveland was chosen pastor of Brier Creek Church 24 July 1783. Andrew Baker served it for four years, resigning in 1787. From 1790 to 1800 the church met regularly but had no pastor. In 1800 Andrew Baker took the work again for two years. Pastors during the years that followed were: Thomas Masten, Jesse Adams, William Franklin Adams, Richard W. Wooten, and William F. Myers. The present pastor is Rev. W.T. Jarvis.

The first clerk, Richard Allen, served 21 years; Thomas Foster, more than 30 years; G.W. Sale has served 25 years or longer.

Some of the churches organized from 'old Brier Creek' are Cub Creek, Cool Springs, Fishing Creek, Covenant, Swan Creek, Antioch, White Plains, Pleasant Grove and Oak Forest.

The oldest Baptist church in North Carolina is Shiloh, in Camden County. On 8 June, 1933, Brier Creek will round up 150 years.

In the years since the centennial many have been laid to rest in Old Brier Creek graveyard,

Boomer School.

Brocktown Community: The Joseph Martin and Delilah Ray Revis Home.

among them Major James H. Foote and several members of his family. It would be interesting if a list of the persons buried there could be made, but that is impossible. Few headstones, in the early days, were anything more than large stones found near the burial places, and such stones bore no inscriptions. As relatives and friends passed away the locations of the individual graves were forgotten, even the names passed from memory. Marble yards were miles away and well-to-do could mark the spots where the bodies of their loved ones await the resurrection. Many were buried in the family graveyards on their own plantation, or that of some near neighbor.

Among the Revolutionary soldiers resting in family graveyards are the Irish brothers, John and Andrew Bryan, who emigrated to America from Armagh County, Ireland. John Bryan was buried on his plantation on Fishing Creek.

Old Brier Creek Church is on the Andrew Bryan place. The Bryan graveyard, where Andrew was buried, is about half a mile from the church. The Yadkin separates this place from Round-About. The Allen graveyard is on Bugaboo, his home place.

There were, and there still remain (1927) other family graveyards within a few miles of the church. Some of these old burying grounds have been cultivated over and all traces of them obliterated. Even tombstones containing inscriptions have been removed and no trace of them can be found. Surely God's Acre should be regarded as sacred.

Because of such vandalism it is customary in this day to bury the dead in churchyards, and Brier Creek graveyard has been enlarged. The rock wall was taken away and the whole burying ground enclosed by a wire fence.

It speaks well for landowners and church people that a deed to the Brier Creek Church property was not thought of until within the last twenty years, when all considered it wise to observe that legal formality, less the plantation should pass into the possession of strangers.

Yadkin Baptist Association

According to state records the Yadkin Baptist Association was formed in 1790. Six ministers were enrolled as members, namely: George McNiel, John Cleveland, William Petty, William Hammond, Andrew Baker and John Stone. This is the oldest association in Northwestern North Carolina.

The Rev. W.F. Adams, that beloved pastor of Brier Creek Church, willed his entire estate to be equally divided among the Oxford Orphans Asylum, Brier Creek Church and Brier Creek Association for mission work.

The minutes of Brier Creek Church state that Brier Creek Association was organized 23 November, 1822, at Brier Creek Church in Wilkes County and was composed of nine churches: Bethel, Fishing Creek, Little River, Mitchell's River, Snow Creek, Roaring River, Zion Hill, Cool Springs and Brier Creek.

Where is the historic church of Brier Creek located? Between Brier and Sales Creek, on the north side of the Boone Trail Highway as this road was first located through Antioch township, Wilkes County.

The first church building was of logs, and stood on the south side of the highway about 250 yards southwest of the present building. In 1820 a second log house was built on top of the ridge, north of the road. This was used for more than fifty years, when the frame building now standing (1927) took its place. After the Boone Trail Highway was opened this church was moved to the site of the old Arbor. It is painted and above the door one reads the legend "Brier Creek Church, constituted in 1783."

Services at Briar Creek Church

The value of Brier Creek Church to the community, the county, the state, cannot be estimated. In its early days people from within a radius of 25 miles around attended the services. Its protracted meetings were annual events of great interest, crowds of people attending. In pleasant weather, services were held under the Arbor. The preacher's "stand" or pulpit, was one third of the distance from the west end of the arbor. White people were seated in front of it, negroes in the rear. Women and children sat on one side of the aisle, men and larger boys on the other. Occasionally a bold brave swain would sit on the women's side. Whole families attended the meetings. No one was upset when a baby cried except the timid little mother. No one grumbled about the hard seats — backless benches of slabs, with peg legs. Some brought chairs from their wagons. From hitching places in the woods, sometimes a horse neighed, a mule brayed. None but children noticed such things and giggling was suppressed. People went to meeting to hear the Word. They had no time for trivialities. "The word of the Lord was precious in those days."

The minister "lined out" the hymns. The congregation sang with heart and soul and voice. What melody in the voices of the negroes. How exemplary their reverential demeanor.

Between the services of the day was an "intermission" of from one to two hours, according to the length of the morning service. During intermission dinner was spread, picnic style, under the trees. Neighbors, friends, kindred and strangers were welcomed at the feast. How kindly the greetings, how hearty the interest in each individual's welfare — how whole-souled and free-hearted the hospitality.

Old time religion had much to recommend it, and Horace Bushnell said, "The capacity for religion is a talent, the highest talent we have."

Sources: Excerpts from an article by Mrs. F.G. Harrill, *Wilkes Journal*, December 15, 1927.

BROADWAY COMMUNITY DAMASCUS BAPTIST CHURCH

Damscus Baptist Church was organized, possibly as early as 1865, the year the Emancipation Proclamation was signed. Rev. Samuel Smith (a white minister) assisted in the organization. Some of the charter members were: Brothers Franklin Parks, Albert Parks, Nathaniel Harris, Irvin Parks, and Sisters Judy Barber, Mariah Parks, and Lucinda Parks.

The first pastor was Rev. B.F. Watts. Other pastors who have served are: Rev. G.W. Parker, Rev. George W. Petty, Rev. A.B. Clark, Rev. R.B. Watts, Rev. V.A. Parks, Rev. Robert Grinton, Rev. L.J. Carlton, Rev. R.W. Barber and Rev. L.R. Howell.

The first church building was a small log cabin near Fishing Creek, called "Noisy Branch." Since then buildings have been located at two other sites. The early church bought a "lot" near what is now known as Old Highway 60, where we still have the church cemetery. In 1935 under the leadership of Rev. L.J. Carlton, in his closing years as pastor, and under our next pastor, the now late Rev. R.W. Barber, this present site was purchased and the sanctuary built.

Church Leaders

Rev. Carlton pastored twenty-six years — walking from Moravian Falls much of the time. Rev. R.B. Watts was the architect of this present edifice fitting the framing one year after it was cut.

Rev. R.W. Barber was a great advocate of the church being built closer to the membership. He taught the members to tithe. His close friend in Christ was the late Rev. Dennis Palmer, who served as deacon, Superintendent of Sunday School. and senior choir director, until called into the ministry. God has called so many to preach from our church. The Reverends Robert Grinton, G.W. Petty, V.A. Parks, J.C. Redmon, T.G. Redmon, Dennis Palmer, C.C. Harris, R.W. Barber, Frank Bailey, Millard Harris, Jr., and Bro. James Barber, Sr. Rev. L.R. Howell served fourteen years. He was a winner of souls and a staunch supporter of the General Baptist Convention. Our Parsonage was built during his tenure.

Twenty acres of land have been purchased by the church at another site. This was done in order to encourage "Home Ownership."

During the last seventeen years, under the leadership of Rev. W.N. Rowe, an educational department with Baptismal facilities and ten classrooms, complete with kitchen and dining room/fellowship hall, have been added. The church is air-conditioned and has an extensive sound system. An organ has been purchased and also a church bus. The parsonage and choirloft have been renovated.

Rev. Rowe conducts revivals in many churches, and is instrumental in winning many souls to Christ. For the past two years, he has taught the adults in the evening session of Bible School. He is president of the Yadkin Valley Sunday School Convention. He has been given a trip to Israel. Rev. Rowe has been awarded the Bachelor of Theology degree from Shaw University, Raleigh, N.C.

Present enrollment is approximately 450 members.

For these blessings and all others that we are enjoying — To God be the Praise, the Honor and the Glory forever and ever. Amen and Amen. By: Sister Loree Harris Anderson, Church Clerk.

Source: *The Centennial Year of the Yadkin Valley Missionary Baptist Association, 1880-1980.* Research by Mrs. Katherine Denny.

BRUSHY MOUNTAIN COMMUNITY

BRUSHY MOUNTAIN'S OUT O'WHACK

There's something wrong on Brushy, so all the people say, the mountain don't look like it did, two weeks ago today.

From Oakwoods to the Pine Hills, Brush is just plumb out of whack, the reason is Aunt Dovie's left, and hasn't yet come back.

A week on Sunday Dovie grabbed her stick and her valise, she hit the grit for Caldwell, where she went to see her niece.

The folks on Brush they hated it, but she was bound to go; now when she's coming back again, is what they want to know.

There's uncle William Hays on Brush, and old Jim Hame Legs, too; there's George at Oakwoods, Doctor White, they're all a feeling blue.

And Mr. Sherman's looking sad, he's got a heavy eye; for fun and jokes, they're dead and gone, since Dovie said good-bye.

What Dovie doesn't know about the moon ain't worth a cent; she knows most every blessed star, in all the firmament.

And when she says the signs are right for puttin' in your stuff, move then just like you meant it, and you'll hit it sure enough.

Aunt Dovie isn't quite as young but yet we hope she may live on, and on, and on, and on, for many and many a day.

And still keep livin' on to tell about the times 'way back; of homemade 'bacca, homemade shoes, and homemade apple jack.

Good luck and health to you Aunt Dovie, we want you to come back; the folks in town they ask for you and Brushy's out of whack.

Just come ahead, Aunt Dovie, quick, Old Wilkes is feeling bad; Brush don't look right without you, so come, we'll all be glad. (Postlude)

Finally Aunt Dovie made the journey to that blissful shore; it filled our hearts with sorrow

Mormon Chapel.

for we'll see her never more.

But now we have another to take Aunt Dovie's place; Bid Williams lives among us and knows all the signs and symbols that benefit the human race.

Source: column by Dwight Nichols in *Journal-Patriot* newspaper. Poem written by "Lonesome Crittur" and Mr. J. Gordon Hackett, June 20, 1912.

MORMAN CHAPEL IN GILREATH BRUSHY MOUNTAIN

Three families built the first Latter-Day Saint (Morman) chapel in Wilkes County. They were the Balls, Marlows and Nances, which formed the backbone of the church there. These families married together so many times they were like one family.

They used Ball land to build the chapel on. It was close to the sawmill and so it was easy to cut the logs, drag them to the sawmill and saw the timbers. The boards were smoothed with hand planes, and the roof was made with shakes or boards stripped from the tree by Byn Marlow and Wilburn Jonah Ball. The chapel was a thirty-by-forty-feet frame building, lit by kerosene lamps which were hung along the wall. It was heated by a pot belly stove which sat in the middle of the room.

By some it was called a schoolhouse, but people in the community called it a Temple. Whatever you call it, it was truly special. "It was a small one room church, a beautiful place, a beautiful church and it was built with love."

The church flourished. For recreation they would have spelling bees at the church. Curtains separated the one room building into different Sunday School Classes. It was a house of the Lord.

A Sunday School was started in Gilreath 19 July 1907. The Gilreath Chapel was dedicated 25 July 1909. When this building became too small, another church was built and when this was outgrown, a large brick structure was built on highway 115 a few miles south of N. Wilkesboro, N.C.

Baptising, July 31, 1921.

Source: Excerpts from a paper: "The Perils of Mormonism in the South;" Bringham Young University; 15 December, 1981; by Karen Boles. Submitted by Ann Transou Ball.

HOTEL LITHIA

Resort hotels at mineral springs flourished during the gay nineties and through the turn of the century. Hotel Lithia was a popular hotel on the Brushies south of Wilkesboro. Besides the change of air and food, and the opportunity to meet old and new friends, the chief attraction was the lithia spring located within easy walking distance down the mountain.

Hotel Lithia had about four years of successful operation before the large, frame structure was destroyed by fire. Quoting from *The Chronicle,* early Wilkesboro newspaper, of the issue of November 23, 1892: "The Brushy Mountain Iron and Lithia Springs Company, which has been in comtemplation for

Hotel Lithia.

some time, was organized the 17th inst. The following officers were elected: president, J. Ed Finley, North Wilkesboro; vice-president, J.T. Ferguson, Wilkesboro; secretary and treasurer, J. George Finley, North Wilkesboro.''

Hotel Lithia was not ready for operation until the summer of 1898. A letter written that summer on Hotel Lithia stationary, giving the name of Mrs. M.J. Brady, proprietress, by Mrs. Augustus Finley to her daughter-in-law, Mrs. T.B. Finley, says, in part, ''I think if you bring Mamie for a nurse when you come, she had better have a quilt or two and sleep in your room. There is a house here for the servants but it is awfully crowded, and they, the servants, carouse nearly all night — Mrs. Mott has a cow here. The milk is very good. Write or phone soon.''

One moonlight night in September 1902, Hotel Lithia burned to the ground. I quote from the Chronicle dated September 24, 1902: ''All was lost except the trunks and clothing of the guests. The provisions, furniture and all were lost. The fire was discovered just before ten o'clock in the garret or lumber room, and was beyond control. It rapidly spread, and soon enveloped the whole building. The origin of the fire is a mystery. No one, so far as is known, had been in that part of the building this summer. The loss of the building is some $6,000.''

The hotel was filled with guests. Members of the R.W. gwyn family were staying there on that fateful night. Needless to say, it was a time of great excitement, and many people from the two towns went to view the disaster, and to offer help. Mr. and Mrs. W.A. Sydnor were proprietors that season.

The hotel was located where the Sykes and Bumgarner cottages now stand.

Sources: Chronicle Newspaper articles, research by Elizabeth Finley

EARLY LIFE ON THE MOORE FARM

Home nestled deep in the Brushy Mountains (then called the Gilreath township). The ol' homeplace . . . well, it's long since fallen in but the memory of the rustic but sturdy log cabin remains. Neighbors and family worked together on the simple construction using hand-hewn logs (anywhere from 10'' to 14'' wide and notched at the corners in a semi-dovetail manner), secured with locust pegs, and chinked with mud. The house was intact.

The covering was made with the use of a ''froe'' for splitting or riving the boards as was the flooring or ''puncheon'' as it was then called, using chestnut logs. The old place was sound but despite all efforts the mountainous windy weather was hard to keep out. Many a'morning a skimmering of snow covered the ladder rungs as the boys drowsily climbed down from the loft. Mamo always saw that there were plenty of thick, warm handmade quilts on hand though so their roughly made beds were cozy and warm. Clothing was all handmade, of course, but they did get one new pair of shoes every year. Berlwyn laughingly recalls Papa saying, ''better take care of 'em boys, that's all you're gonna get.''

Life was simple and hard back in those hills but nobody seemed to mind 'cause that's all they'd ever known. There was an awful lot of love and plenty to eat, and Mamo always believed in cooking a little extra — ''you never know when somebody might come.'' Papa's land covered 100 or a little more acres with about 50 acres in orchards and cultivations and the other in pastures and woodlands. He used mules and horses and occasionally a team of oxen for plowing. Needless to say, there was little left over from the crops to sell after feeding a big family and preserving for

winter.

Income was solely from the sale of apples, dried sassafras bark which was used in medicine and for flavoring, tobacco, crossties, cord wood (a measure of wood cut for fuel — 128 cu. ft.), and tanbark (bark from water oaks containing tannic acid used in tanning hides). So, this called for a trip to town! Papa usually sent a couple of the boys about once a week, generally when it was too wet for plowing. A horse and wagon was their only transportation and the trip took the entire day. In late fall when the apple crop came in, they often had to haul their apples all the way to Statesville or Mooresville and this took two to three days, having to camp overnight along the way. They killed and cured their own meat (mainly pork); some they canned and the rest was purified with salt and put in the meat box in the back of the kitchen. They dried a lot of vegetation and fruit (green beans, apples, etc.) and this was stored in the dry house. I recall when I was a little girl, Mamo still liked to dry green beans for ''leather britches.''

Papa and boys weren't the only ones that worked; there was just as much to be done around the house but Mamo always saw that her family was cared for. There was sewing, washing, making her own butter and soap, not to mention cooking for a houseful of hungry, towheaded boys. When their only daughter Sylvia (Sis) came along, there was soon help in the kitchen! Learning to cook at such an early age, well, it's no wonder she's the marvelous cook she is today. All the family agrees, there's no-one who can get a meal on the table as quickly as Sis.

Fun on the Farm

Life wasn't all work for the Moores however; they played together just as they worked together. Quilting bees, bean stringings, molasses makings, and corn shuckings were hard work for the adults but with all the neighbors working together, why, it meant just a good time with the young'uns gleefully flitting to and fro. The boys also enjoyed 'possum hunts and an occasional trip to the creek. ''We'd work fast as we could all morning trying to get a little ahead, then off we'd go running two miles to the creek, quickly toss our britches onto a nearby bush and jump in. Wow!'' When asked how long they got to swim my Dad answered, ''Swim? the creek wasn't big enough to swim in, we just dabbled around a few minutes to cool off and then back to the fields we ran just as fast as we could go.'' Our love for music comes from those hills too. Supper over, many an evening you'd see a neighborin' friend headed towards the house ready to ''make music.'' Lonnie had somehow acquired an old guitar and a lifelong friend, Chester Marlow, played either the fiddle or banjo and you could soon hear voices begin to blend and echo through those mountains. There was no formal training back in those hills but their voices were strong and clear. This tradition has never stopped for anytime there is a family gathering, we'll all end up around the piano to sing for awhile with Papa (now 99 years of age) joining in. Watch out too for if it's a light lively tune, Papa, eyes twinkling with laughter and merriment, may just begin to shuffle his feet a'bit!

Christmas, though lean, was the happiest time of year for mountain folk. The tree was not aglow with festive lights but simply adorned with mistletoe and strings of popcorn and holly. Santy Clause was sure to come! Stockings were not hung, instead, they simply "set up their hats" or a shoebox if they happened to have one. Scampering up the ladder and into their trundle beds, the endless night began. Morning came! Whooping as they made their way down from the loft to the "big room," Santy had been. There was an orange (maybe two), a handful of raisins on the stem, and some "bucket candy" and Sis might get a little rag doll. Oranges and candy meant Christmas itself; why, after eating their orange, they even saved the peeling to dry to chew on later. A special smile or a tender touch was the only gift Papa and Mamo had for each other — they neither wanted nor expected more. Seeing that special glow in the young-uns' faces was Christmas enough for them. It was a gala time with ringing sounds of laughter, a roaring fire going, and spicy aromas from the kitchen. Mamo usually had pork for Christmas dinner along with big pots of turnips, sweet potatoes, gravy and plenty of big biscuits and butter. Sugar was scarce back then so a molasses cake or gingerbread was desert. My! it was good eatin.' Bundled up in their warmest clothing, off they ran to hitch up the horse and wagon and head to the schoolhouse for the play. It might be snowing or the narrow rough road icy but the play was a part of their day.

Dovie's Chapel in August 1939.

Education and Religion

The schoolhouse was simply one big room, heated with an 'ol pot-bellied stove. It was understood that the boys were expected to keep wood cut and the stove fed. The teacher taught only to the seventh grade so this had a big impact on Papa finally deciding to get out of the mountains and move to town. The teacher was a special and respected person among the mountain people. So, in order for

the children to continue their education, the Moores left their beloved mountain in 1935.

Religion is an important part of Papa's life, just as it was in Mamo's. Papa was one of the founders of Cherry Grove Baptist and the Church clerk and many of his old notes are still stuck away in the family Bible. After their move into town, they joined Hinshaw Baptist where Papa is still a member.

Come Saturday afternoon, you could always find Mamo in her bibbed apron and sunbonnet out in her garden lovingly picking flowers for two "flowerpots" — one for her own dining room table and the other to put in the Church.

Papa attributes his marvelous health and long life to his parents, and a Christian attitude toward others. "The Bible says to 'honor thy father and mother and thy days shall be long upon the earth'." He calls his family the "greatest pleasure in my life." Much of the credit for rearing the children he gives to Mamo, but adds "I love them all as much as I know how. I tried to see that they minded, but if love didn't do it, then I would chastise them, but love goes farther than harsh words."

Papa, ever witty with peppered quaint expressions and always busy at something from working in his garden or with needle in hand mending old hats and gloves, says he's gonna quit when he gets old enough! Papa believes life should be shared with others, both laughter and tears, and he still believes a "handshake seals a deal."

Source: Family knowledge, research by Ann Moore.

THE OLD ELLIS HOME OR WALKER PLACE

The center structure of the house, built of large logs, was built before 1800 by William Ellis — making this one of the oldest homes still standing in Brushy Mtn Community of Wilkes County. William Ellis and his wife, Anna, are buried just a few yards away beneath some old apple trees. William Ellis was a large land owner and obtained much of this land from the state in the form of land grants. Years ago this farm was called Elk Valley Farm. The bottom land was swampy and elk could be seen wallowing in the swamps. The Elk Wallow was noted on an original deed. Indians apparently lived in this area, because arrowheads were often found in plowed fields. Elk, small game and water were plentiful.

This house and the land that surrounds it are owned by the heirs of Clarence Hayes. The heirs of William Ellis sold the house and farm to Stephen Hendren. Stephen Hendren was a brother to William Hendren, Jr. who married Charlotte Ellis, daughter of William Ellis. Stephen Hendren handed down about 140 of the 600 acres he owned to his son, E. Elbert Hendren. Elbert married Charlotte Rufinia Hendren who was a great-granddaughter of William Ellis. After the death of Elbert Hendren, Charlotte and a daughter, "Nolie" (Lenora Delaney Hendren who married Harvey C. Walker), lived in the house for many years. This is how it became to be known as the Old Walker Place. The house and land was later sold to Clarence Hayes and his wife Emma Lee

Old Ellis Home.

Walker Hayes. Emma was a great-great-great-granddaughter of the original owner, William Ellis.

Hundreds of descendants of William Ellis still live in Wilkes County. Through marriage, members of the following families are connected to the Ellis family: Hendren, Call, Moore, Hayes, Johnson and Walker.

Source: Research by Don Hayes.

CLINGMAN COMMUNITY

The *N.C. Gazetteer* (1968) states that Clingman was named for congressman Thomas L. Clingman. Those living in the community at present state that is received its name from James Clingman Green in 1880. When he was a young man he was dating Eliza Gray from Dellaplane. The U.S. Post Office Department was waiting for the community to be named so that a post office could be established there. Eliza suggested it be named Clingman.

A post office was established in a building beside J.C. Green's General Store, and Green was the first Postmaster. This post office existed from 1880 until 1907 when it was moved to Ronda.

Merchantile business has historically been a trademark for J.C. Green and his descendants. In the late 1870s he opened a general store that has continously been operated by the Green family. His sons Harry G., Granville and Click and Harry's sons, Bob and Joe have operated the business, which includes a grocery store, farm supply store, used car lot and a family restaurant.

During the early years of the general store, much of the business was conducted by barter and exchange. People brought chickens, herbs, cow hides, eggs, and other items and exchanged them for staple goods. Business conducted by money exchange was very low until after WW I.

The Greens also operated a small tobacco factory and sold tobacco in N.C., S.C. and Ga. This business quit operating after Reynolds Tobacco factory was established.

T.M. Green operated a general store in Clingman during his lifetime. The last store building was built in 1896 and is still standing adjacent to a store operated by a grandson, Edward Green.

Clingman has been, and continues to be a very progressive rural community. Church life, education, and fraternal organizations have been an integral part of the lives of its residents. A Masonic Lodge was a part of the Clingman community during early 1900.

Pleasant Grove Baptist Church, 1898.

First Clingman School (early 1900s).

Masonic Lodge (early 1900s).

Pleasant Grove was founded as a Brush Arbor and the first building was constructed in 1872. The second frame building was built in 1898 and the present structure was built in 1963.

The first school was built in the early 1900s on land given by Clingman Green. Men in the community gave the timber and labor to build it. The brick school building is used for Clingman Medical enter and a community center. Dr. James Hartye heads the center and pharmacy.

During the late 1800s Dr. Columbus L. Cook was a family physcian who served the community and was also Clingman Postmaster in 1904. He served as coroner, a pastor of a church in Wilkesboro, tobacco manufacturer, and member of the N.C. Legislature.

Sources: *N.C. Gazetteer;* Research, Interviews by William C. Davis, Jr.

CRICKET COMMUNITY
H.C. PENNELL HOMEPLACE

Prior to being demolished in 1981 to make way for the new mall in Wilkesboro, this house, built prior to 1850, was a landmark for wagon travellers between Jefferson and Winston-Salem. It was the only painted house on the wagon trail and people stopped at the spring to water their teams, refresh themselves, and often camp overnight.

DELLAPLANE COMMUNITY
OLD DELLAPLANE SCHOOL

Picture of Dellaplane School taken about 1915. (The building is still standing.) This school began about 1900 and continued until 1930 when the students were sent to Roaring River. The building consisted of one room divided by a curtain — grades 1, 2, 3, and 4 on one side, and 5, 6, and 7 on other. It was located across the road from Oak Forest Baptist Church, down old highway 60.

There was a reunion of students and teachers there on Sunday, May 30, 1982. Erie Mathis, a former student, has her 7th grade diploma from Dellaplane School, and Shirley Johnson has a list of many of those who taught there . . .

Source: research by Shirley Johnson.

DOCKERY

Dockery community, located on the middle prong of Roaring River, about mid way between Mt. View and Traphill, was named according to legend for a Mr. Dockery. The families of Abshers, Alexanders, Billings, Caudills, Ellis, Gambills, Holbrooks, Myers, Staleys, Walkers, Wiles and others made up the early community. Most were farmers and craftsmen.

The community was outstanding for the number of skilled craftsmen. Jackson Caudill, an expert builder of great talent and ability, built many fine homes as well as furniture in this and surrounding areas. Other builders were James Kilby, Robert Walker and Matthew Waddell. Some of Mr. Caudill's and Mr. Waddell's beautiful corner cupboards and desks

T.M. Green Store.

Original store of Clingman Greene.

A Sunday Gathering in the Cricket Community.

still exist in homes in Wilkes. Willis Miles was a maker of cord beds.

Jasper Billings, a blacksmith and a Revolutionary War veteran, owned several hundred acres of land and had one of the first grist mills in the area. He was given a license on July 30, 1792, to build one on Roaring River, where Thomas Billings had formerly had a mill. Other millers were James Walker and William M. Billings. James Walker also had a sawmill. Burlson Waddell and James Walker were listed as wheelwrights in 1884. Colby Alexander was a blacksmith.

George W. Smoot and Joshua Spicer were associates in the tannery business, which was later moved and owned by W. Lewis Sparks. Mr Sparks was also a shoemaker.

One of the first stores, around 1850, was owned by William Wiles, a large landowner. Merchants in 1883 were W.M. Absher and Billings Brothers, followed in 1896 by A.C. Billings Co. and T.P. Hanks and Son. Later merchants were John Myers and Walter W. Gambill.

New Covenant Baptist Church is the oldest church, established before 1839, and was the center of religious activities for many years. People came for miles for the "Big August" meetings, with dinner on the grounds and much preaching and socializing. Mt. Pisgah Missionary Baptist Church was organized on February 14, 1879. Charter members were Mr. and Mrs. Felix Brewer, Mr. and Mrs. Nathaniel Ingool, Mr. and Mrs. Rhesa Lyon, Mr. and Mrs. Jacob Staley, Mr. and Mrs. G. Elihue Myers, Mr. and Mrs. I. Boyden Goss and Mrs. Calvin Walters.

Dockery post office was established in 1872 near the present location of Mt. Pisgah Church. William F. Porter and William H. Absher were the first two postmasters, followed by Eli Grimes who was also a Methodist minister. The post office existed until 1953

Congo Community: William Minton homeplace, 1918. Most of the property is now owned by the government which purchased it for the Kerr Scott Dam.

H.C. Pennell homeplace.

when the area was divided between Traphill and Hays.

Mt. Pisgah Masonic Lodge No. 623 was granted a charter on January 20, 1915. C.M. Caudill was master, R.M. Waddell, senior warden, and J.H. Billings, junior warden. In 1934 Mt. Pisgah Lodge was consolidated with Traphill Lodge N. 483.

Dockery Academy

Mt. Pisgah School was located near the church and existed until 1931, when it was consolidated with Traphill School. The school near New Covenant Church, believed to be Dockery Academy, was the largest early school with well qualified teachers. Early teachers of the area included Colby Alexander and Rhesa Lyon, who taught for many years and was especially known for his mathematical ability. Other early teachers were Felix Brewer, Roxie Billings, Rowan C. Billings, Bud Miles, Elisha L. Billings and R.M. Waddell.

Dr. R. Paul Caudill, well known Baptist minister and author, was born and spent his early years in this community. Dr. Eugene Billings, a heart surgeon, was also a native. Rudolph Emory Walters, who was born and lived in this community for several years, served as Governor of the Province of Mindora Islands in the Philippines and later as postmaster of North Wilkesboro. Franklin J. Alexander, a native of Dockery, and wife, Tabitha Stewart, had children who married into many prominent Wilkes families — Covard, Hubbard, McGee, Lenderman. Conard Alexander, the nationally known newspaper editor, was one of his descendants.

Many families and individuals moved from this area in the late 1800s and early 1900s as there was little money to be made by farming. Many went to the mid-west, some to the west coast and Canada and some to Tennessee and West Virginia. With the coming of the poultry industry to Wilkes and better methods of farming, living conditions have improved. Most are still farmers, raising beef cattle and chickens, but there are a variety of other businesses. These include at least two sawmill operators, a trucking business, Wiles mill, David Whitman's Dairy Nursery and Absher's Super Pan, Inc. as well as the Dockery Grocery operated by the R. Dale Gambill Family.

Sources: Court Records, church records, *Branson's Reports* and research by Alice Billings.

BREWER'S MILL, DOCKERY

Shown in the photograph, this old mill is on the William Burton Blackburn land just below his homesite on the east fork of Roaring River. Possibly built in the late 1800s.

DOUGHTON — GHOST TOWN

Doughton is located on U.S. Highway 21 north of Elkin at the foot of the Blue Ridge Mountains. In the early 1920s before the road was paved, the trail from Elkin to Doughton was a narrow, wagon road coming out through a gap at the top of the mountain directly above Doughton and then continuing through a valley

Old Dellaplane School.

Mt. Pisgah School Class, 1897. Bottom Row L to R: Cynthis Lyon, Cora Billings, Florence Myers, Pearl Waddell, Docia Absher, John Granville Billings, Esquire Gambill, Nathan Gambill, Virgil Billings, Blaine Alexander, Alonzo Holbrook, Bertha Holbrook, Mersey Holbrook, Mattie Holbrook.
Short Row (sitting): Tyre Myers, Ellen Myers, Lura Gambill, Izora Gambill, Dinah Holbrook.
Middle Row: R.M. Waddell, teacher, J. Randolph Gambill, Cessie Gambill, Maud Lyon, Lucretia Billings, Edith Lyon, Nannie Richardson, Lillie Caudill, Lula Holbrook, Nettie Gambill, Minnie Holbrook, Jennie Carrico, Lewis G. Billings.
Top Row: Robert Gambill, Elisha Gambill, Ulysses Walters, Robert F. Miles, Columbus Ellis, John Pinkney Johnson, Liz Pardue, Verlin Alexander, Winfrey Holbrook, Mary Ann Caudill Holbrook, Elizabeth Wiles Alexander, John Alexander.

John Myers' wedding in the Dockery Community.

The William Burton Blackburn Homeplace.

Brewer's Mill.

Old William M. Absher House, built in 1875.

now covered by the lake at Roaring Gap and on into Virginia.

In the early days cattlemen would drive their herds to market along this route from as far away as Kentucky and West Virginia to Winston-Salem, Raleigh, and Wilmington. Johnse Gentry, born about 1869, had a large farm at Doughton, and here the drivers would spend the night. According to Gentry, he had kept as many as a thousand head of cattle for them as long as two weeks at a time.

Since travel through this area in those days was by foot, horseback, wagon, or buggy, it was natural that travelers on their journey northwest would stop here at the foot of the mountain before their climb. It was also logical that services would be set up here to meet the needs of the traveling public. The real boom to Doughton came with the building of the Elkin and Alleghany Railroad from Elkin to Doughton. In 1907 the railroad line was surveyed from Elkin to Sparta with the intent to connect later with the Norfolk and Western line to the coal mines of West Virginia. The Chathams of Winston-Salem and Elkin, the Doughtons of Alleghany, and others were instrumental in getting this railroad built. As it turned out, the town of Doughton became the end of the line for the railroad.

Naming Doughton

Some people say that the town of Doughton was named for Lt. Gov. R.A. Doughton, who was responsible for getting the railroad bill through the legislature, but others say that the mountain was so steep that those who built the railroad doubted they could ever cut the grade to the top of the mountain — hence the name Doubt-on or Doughton.

With the coming of the railroad Doughton became a boom town with a number of businesses. Among these was a depot and post office operated by Wiley Royall, Preston Holcomb's Roller and Saw Mill, Norman and Bivens' Store, C.C. Smoot and Son's Bark Shed, J.A.J. Royall's Fertilizer House, Hardin Blackburn's Store, William F. Royall's General Store, Simmons' Garage, Bryan's Service Station, Esso Bulk and Storage Tanks, Bryan's Rail Fence Factory, J.K. Valley (buyer of acid wood and light poles), H.H. Warren's Store, Snow and Folger's Store, Sanders' Store, and Cicero Bryant's Store.

Each day saw the town full of farmers and lumbermen with their wagons loaded with tan bark and other lumber products to be placed in boxcars for shipment to other parts of the country. Several crews of men were kept busy loading and unloading boxcars six days a week. The stores were also busy as the wagoneers would load their wagons with dry goods, staples, and fertilizer for their return trips.

There was a lot of hustle and bustle, and to a youngster there was a lot of excitement when the train arrived. The train traveled perhaps a mile beyond Doughton to where it turned around. Many young people delighted in walking to meet the train there so that they could ride back to Doughton free.

Granny Holcomb's house, located across from the depot beside William F. (Billy) Royall's store, was also a favorite gathering place for the younger generation. Doughton, to be sure, was lively in its heyday.

There were also solemn moments in the history of Doughton. As a youngster during World War I, one former resident recalls how sad it was when parents from Ashe and Alleghany Counties brought their boys to catch the train. He remembers the tears as they sent their sons to war.

Doughton's Decline

Perhaps the two main factors that contrib- uted to the downfall of Doughton were the coming of a paved road from Elkin through Doughton across the Blue Ridge and the decline of the Elkin and Alleghany Railroad.

In the early 1920s work was begun on the highway by cutting a winding grade northwest of Doughton around the mountain to Roaring Gap. This work was done by a steam shovel, which operated like a steam locomotive. It required a fireman to keep a fire of wood or coal and water for a good head of steam, an operator, and someone to sit on a seat built on the crane and to ride it as it swung around pulling the rope to dump the shovel of dirt at the correct place. Lonnie Royall of Cody, Wyoming, recalls doing the rope pulling job on this grading.

When this road, U.S. Highway 21, was completed it was a winding, narrow, asphalt road just wide enough for one car. When two cars met, it was necessary for both cars to run two wheels off the pavement in order to pass. From Johnse Gentry's house going north into Doughton there was about a mile of this road that was straight. As motorists traveling north toward the base of the mountains looked up toward the top, an illusion was created making the road appear to be on a downgrade, when, in reality, it was a gradual climb. According to Kelly Rose of Elkin, who once operated a service station at Doughton, many people would stop to have their cars checked, thinking something was wrong as they had to accelerate to go what seemed to be downhill. He would explain that there was nothing wrong with the car, since "downhill" was actually in the other direction.

With a railroad and a paved road Doughton, the gateway to the Blue Ridge, continued to thrive as a beginning point for the mountaineers to the outside world.

By the time of the Great Depression it became apparent to the owners of the Elkin and Alleghany Railroad that their plans for continuing the railroad would not materialize. The railroad line had fallen into disrepair and resources from the line were dwindling. By the middle of the 1930s the E. and A. Railroad was liquidated, the rails were removed, and the depot was closed. With the railroad gone store after store closed. The post office was discontinued in 1934. William F. Royall's store, perhaps one of the last stores to operate, closed after his death in 1936. Bryan's Service Station struggled for a few years before closing.

Tragedy always seems to lurk in the shadow of a boom-and-burst town, and Doughton was no exception. The roster of those who met violent death in Doughton could have been taken from any ghost town in the old west. The list includes the following: P. Holcomb — killed at mill, W. Lyon — shot, L. Ayers — killed in wreck, M. Holbrook — shot, R. Holbrook — shot, S. Hutchinson — killed in wreck, Mr. Wall — shot, V. Spicer — killed in wreck, E. Bauguess — killed.

In the 1950s U.S. Highway 21 was regraded from Elkin to Sparta missing Doughton by a hundred feet or so. All that is left of Doughton are the cuts and fills of the old railroad and a few spots of the first narrow, paved road.

Double Creek Community: J.H. Joines' Store, 1905.

Double Creek School, 1907.

There are no businesses. Doughton, like the E. and A. Railroad, had finally reached the end of the line and so deserves its place as a ghost town of Wilkes County, North Carolina.

Sources: *The Elkin Tribune,* Elkin, North Carolina; *The Union Republican,* Winston-Salem, North Carolina; Bray, *The E. and A. Railroad Company;* interviews; and personal knowledge of Hardin J. Royall.

ELKVILLE COMMUNITY
RAILROADING ON THE YADKIN RIVER

This is the story of a man who dreamed of running his own railroad.

In 1912, W.J. Grandin came from Pa. to Wilkes County to build the Watauga Railroad on the banks of the Yadkin River, and for a while his dream became reality.

Wealthy from other business ventures, Grandin brought key personnel from Pa. for his Wilkes venture, including H.C. Landon, surveyor of the roadway and, after completion of the railway, the man in charge of operations. Two others came from Pa., Bert Wilson and A.J. Lovejoy, to be the line's engineers. The other employees were all from Wilkes County. Among them were George Campbell, an extra engineer; J. B. "Bid" Williams, who helped in management and tract maintenance; and Jim Brewer, Bob Bauguss and Charlie Bauguss.

The original intention of Mr. Grandin was to build the railroad from Darby north across Watauga County into Tennessee and to connect with the Norfolk and Western RR. The tract was laid approximately one mile north of Darby, but that part was never used.

Mr. Landon surveyed the roadbed which followed the circuitous Yadkin River. He was warned by the old people of Wilkes about the flooding of the river. One of these, 92 year old Wade Gilbert pointed out the high water marks on rocks beside the proposed roadbed to let him know the risk of building on low ground near the river. Landon scoffed at the old timer saying, "I can stop the water with the heel of my shoe." The flood of 1916 was to prove him wrong.

Construction of the roadbed required one tunnel and 20 trestles. It was built utilizing new 80 pound rail and was of standard gauge. Convict labor, hired from the state, was used to lay track. Guards were required to watch the convicts and camps were erected along the route.

Crossties and rails for the young line were shipped in via the Southern RR to North Wilkesboro. From there they were shoved ahead of the engines of the Watauga on flat cars. The first cars obtained were two red passenger cars and a baggage car. A small engine was also acquired at this time, called a "Dinky."

The new line stretched from a station built on the west side of North Wilkesboro, near Reddies River to Darby. The line passed Brown's Ford over the Lewis Fork on to Goshen and the Marley Ford over Stony Fork. From here it went to Ferguson, Elkville and Elk Creek. A switch was located here, and one section went three miles to Grandin, the other went the 10 miles to Darby.

The railroad was welcomed by many. It provided a means of transportation for themselves as well as their goods, and economic growth was predicted.

After the railroad was built to Grandin, the trains would stay there at night and leave each morning. As soon as this section was operational the line to Darby was built. The train would proceed to Darby, then on to North Wilkesboro, taking empties and passengers back to Grandin. The train made one round trip each day, two on Saturdays and a passenger excursion on Sundays. This was a popular mode of entertainment.

Round Trip — 45¢

The fare from Marley Ford to North Wilkesboro was 25¢. A round trip cost 45¢. To ship a large box car load of lumber cost $60. S.V. Tomlinson, owner of a brick yard near North Wilkesboro, was incensed at paying $10 to have a carload of brick transported the half mile or so into town. Engineer Campbell was reported to make $30 a month, while laborers were paid 15¢ to 20¢ to load a car.

There are many stories and anecdotes related to the Watauga Railroad. One of these happened at Denny, a station between Elkville and Darby. A large crowd had gathered to see their first train. The engineer and fireman decided to have a little fun. As they rolled into the station the fireman put extra coal into the fire box which caused a large amount of black smoke to belch forth from the smoke stack. As this happened the steam pop valve exploded with a loud noise. All of the frightened people started running, leaving a deserted station in a matter of minutes.

Watauga Railroad.

Grandin, N.C., 1979.

Watauga Elkville Railroad Station on Tomlinson Farm.

"A Sunday Train Ride To Darby", 1915.

Along the line were two places in the river known as the Pea Hole and the Granny Hole. These were favorite places for fishing. People would ride the train and the engineer would stop to let them off and pick them up on the return trip.

In Ferguson lived a very interesting person named Greeley Minton. He was jokingly known as the mayor of that community. He met all the trains and, as people got off, they bowed and addressed him as Mr. Mayor, which pleased him very much. His wife was noted for her fine cooking. Many people would go out of their way to dine with them.

At Grandin lived a Dr. Carter. His kitchen was in Wilkes and the rest of the house was in Caldwell. In the winter when someone along the railroad became seriously ill, Mr. Landon would allow Dr. Carter to take the small dinky to visit the sick person and if necessary transport them to North Wilkesboro for better medical attention.

One time a circus came to North Wilkesboro via the Southern and the Watauga took it to Grandin. When the circus arrived there the crew made what is known as a flying switch to get the engine on the other end of the train. In the process the engine was derailed and could not be moved until the Southern sent an engine from North Wilkesboro to rerail it. There was a pouring rain that day, which made conditions difficult for the many people who had come out to see the circus. The derailment and the rain scared the people so badly that when the train was righted they were hanging all over it trying to get back to North Wilkesboro.

The train was never operated in a hurry or on a schedule. They would often stop and raid someone's watermelon patch or take some corn to roast in the fire box. They drank their liquor, did their job, and apparently, loved railroading. Once they saw a house in flames and stopped the train and extinguished the fire, got back on board and continued on their way.

In 1916, the Yadkin River flooded, catching the train at Ferguson. The crew put the brakes on the train and fled to higher ground. The water lifted the passenger car off the tracks, and it was carried down river. The engine was pushed one mile down the tracks, where it was found after the water receded. The train crew slept in a barn that night, and next day walked 12 miles to North Wilkesboro. A majority of the roadbed was destroyed, but the tunnel near Marley Ford was only damaged slightly and amazingly, some of the trestles remained.

Mr. Grandin decided to rebuild. After the rebuilding the line was operated as before with the exception that it began its run from North Wilkesboro and would return there for the overnight stay.

In October 1918, another flood ravaged the railroad. After days of rain the water continued rising. The train went to Grandin, then on to Darby. Mr. Landon called by telephone, which had just been established to Darby, and told the crew to bring the train back to North Wilkesboro. They returned to within a quarter of a mile of town and had to leave the train there, since the water was over the Reddies River trestle. The engine on this trip was the 101. George Campbell was the engineer and Archie Fairchild the fireman.

The railroad had never been a financial success, and because of the 1918 flood it was never rebuilt.

Source: Excerpts from an article written by Norman T. Foster and printed in *The State* magazine and the *Journal-Patriot* newspaper, courtesy of Mr. Foster for the Heritage Book.

TOM DOOLEY (DULA)

On a May day of 1866, gay laughing Tom Dula (often called Dooley) rode atop his coffin, scraping a farewell tune on his fiddle, to the gallows. Convicted of murdering his sweetheart, Laura Foster, he thumbed his nose at fate as always, joked and made merry with the crowd until the end.

Likeable, funlovin', fiddlin' Tom has increased in popularity with the passing of time. For many years there were few persons who would admit kinship with Tom. Now hundreds of people in the hills of North Carolina are claiming him as a great uncle or cousin.

Tom lived in Wilkes county at Elkville and Laura lived six miles from his home at German Hill in Caldwell county. Both communities are in Happy Valley.

The hill folk, as was typical of the day, composed ballads about the notorious crime and hanging. Some say Tom wrote the verses himself; however, it isn't likely since he declared his innocence until the end.

The stabbing of Laura occurred soon after the end of the War for Southern Independence in the spring of 1865. Tom wasn't hanged until the following spring of 1866.

She was the daughter of Patsy Bowman Foster and Wilson Foster. Her father was an affable, friendly fellow, who spent most of his time trapping and hunting. Laura had a happy childhood, roaming the fields and playing about the woodlands with her cousins Ann and Perline Foster.

As the girls grew older, their beauty and charm increased. Ann and Laura were noted for their attractiveness and the number of their beaus. It was inevitable that they would become rivals for neighborhood swains.

Unfortunately both decided that Tom Dula was the man of their choice; and handsome, carefree Tom generously divided his favors equally between the two girls. Well-liked by young and old, he was to be found at most of the social affairs in the valley, scrapin' his fiddle or pickin' his banjo.

Tom enlisted in the Confederate army at Elkville, Wilkes County, March 1862. He joined Company K, 42nd N.C. regiment which distinguished itself in many battles. Often at night about campfires Tom was to be found strumming battle hymns and ballads. Changed from private to musician in Company K, 42nd regiment, he was captured March 10, 1865 at Kinston and imprisoned at Point Lookout, Maryland, where records indicated there was difficulty over the spelling of his name, signed Thomas C. Dooley with "Dula" written above it. Described as being 69 inches tall with dark brown hair and eyes and a fair complexion, he survived the war with no injuries and only a few illnesses which included typhoid fever.

While Tom was away, Ann's love for him faded. Before long she married James Melton. Laura remained steadfast in her devotion to Tom. Though she had many suitors, none mattered to her except Tom. There was one persistant admirer, Bob Grayson (others say his name was Cummings), a schoolteacher, who loved her devotedly and did all in his power to persuade her to marry him. But she would have none of him. Her heart was with young Tom.

When Tom returned, with his gay lovin' ways, Laura's joy knew no bounds. With Ann safely married, she was certain she and Tom would wed. But fate would not have it so. Upon seeing Tom again, Ann's love for him returned and she endeavored to see him on all occasions. It is said Ann grew to believe if Laura were out of the way, things would be clear for her to marry Tom.

The Elopement . . .

The story goes, that a message was sent from Tom to Laura asking her to meet him the next morning to elope with him. Before daybreak, silently, she arose and dressed. Taking a small bundle of clothing with her, she quietly slipped outside, saddled her brown mare, Belle, and quickly departed on the fateful ride to her death.

Laura was only eighteen years old when she disappeared. Her father and brothers searched far and wide for her and then decided that she must have eloped with Tom Dula. On June 10, 1865, three weeks after Laura's disappearance, her horse returned home with a rope halter worn to shreds. The news quickly spread about the neighborhood. Everyone suspected foul play. People began searching the area, especially in the vicinity about the tree, where, it appeared, the horse had been tied. The tree was detected by the gnawed bark and hoof-trodden ground about it.

Two months had passed since Laura vanished. The search was about to be abandoned, when no evidence could be found. It was thought that her body had probably been disposed of in the near by Yadkin River.

At a gathering one night Ann and Perline got into a quarrel. Ann spoke sharp words to Perline, who retorted that Ann should be care-ful or she would tell what she knew. Not heeding the consequences, Ann heatedly replied that Perline was as deeply involved as she was. Suspicion immediately centered on the two girls.

They were interrogated by authorities. Eager to absolve herself of the crime, Perline agreed to tell all she knew. She declared that she knew nothing of the murder except what Ann had told her. Ann had said that Tom Dula had killed Laura. Perline said she accompanied Ann one day to a location near Elkville and waited while Ann went to see it the grave had been disturbed. She said the place she had waited was a hollow which forked between a ridge. She pointed out the location to a searching party. The group, about 75 in all, spread out over the area, combing it thoroughly. In one party were David E. Horton, Walter Winkler, Robert A. Kendall, James K. Isbell, Bob Grayson, and James Melton. As they rode along David E. Horton's horse shied from a spot. James Isbell, noticing it, immediately dismounted to investigate. He found the earth loose and started digging. Two feet deep in the ground was found the body of Laura. By prearranged signal, a shot was fired to summon the others. Dr. George N. Carter was called to conduct an examination. There was a stab wound in Laura's breast and her legs had been broken to fit the small excavation.

Though it was two months from the time of her disappearance, there could be no doubt it was Laura. There was her long chestnut brown hair and a gold tooth on the upper left side of her mouth. Bob Grayson, her devoted beau, recognized the little "homespun and woven dress" she wore and James Melton stated the shoes were the one he had made for her himself. Her apron was neatly folded four times, as a woman might have folded it, and placed over her face. Beneath her body was the small bundle of clothing which she had taken with her.

Laura's body was taken to Elk Creek where it was placed in a coffin made by Calvin Horton and Linville Land and then carried by wagon to Barret field and buried on a hill, known since as Laura Foster Ridge.

A Certain Clue

Bob Grayson noted something which he didn't mention to anyone else at the time. In the grave had been a handkerchief, that he was certain belonged to Ann Melton. Grimly silent he set forth on a determined search which led to Ann's and Tom's imprisonment and eventually to Tom's death.

At the time he disappeared on the investigation, several other young men, Tom Dula, Jack Adkins, Ben Ferguson, Jack Keaton, and others, also left. Speculation ran rife. All those who had associated with Laura were suspected.

On a hot day in July, about three weeks from the time Laura's body was found a strange procession filed into Elkville. Men standing about Cowle's store turned in amazement when they recognized the five horsemen. Solemnly the procession approached. Grayson led the group. Behind him rode Tom Dula and Jack Keaton, prisoners, their arms bound behind their backs, with Ben Ferguson and Jack Adkins guarding them with guns. Grimly Grayson stated that Tom had murdered Laura with the assistance of Keaton and Ann. Grayson confessed that he had faked a writ of extradition and had arrested Tom and Jack unlawfully to bring them back.

Tom sat unconcernedly on his horse, exchanged greetings with the crowd and asked that his hands be untied for a moment. Then in mock ceremony he doffed his hat to the onlookers and played a gay tune on his fiddle. The two prisoners were taken to Wilkesboro where they were placed in jail in custody of J.T. Ferguson. The next day Ann Melton was also imprisoned. Keaton was able to furnish an alibi and was set free. Ann and Tom were bound over to the fall term of court.

Zebulon Vance announced that he would defend Tom since he had been a Confederate soldier. Vance had the trial moved from Wilkesboro, where feeling mounted against Tom, to Statesville. The sensational trial drew great crowds from all over the state. The village was filled with covered wagons of those who had come from far and near. The courthouse was overflowing. The case was tried before Judge Ralph Burton.

Bob Grayson had proved to be such a relentless sleuth that it was his evidence which convicted Tom. From a washerwoman, Betsy Scott, it was learned that she had met Laura on the day she disappeared and that Laura had told her she was going to meet Tom Dula. Betsy appeared on the stand and refused to be changed in her testimony. Evidence was also presented that Ann and Tom were having an affair. (see Tom Dula file N.C. Archives.)

Dula's Trial

From the beginning Tom pleaded his innocence; but when questioned about angles implicating Ann and others, he remained strangely silent. Vance pleaded eloquently and long in his defense. Since the jury was composed chiefly of war veterans, he presented Laura in the light of a woman of low morals and Tom as the brave, dutiful soldier who had been seduced (see Tom Dula file in N.C. Archives).

The jury, however, found Tom guilty and he was sentenced to hang. Vance appealed to the State Supreme Court and Tom was granted a new trial which took place in January of 1866. Once again he was found guilty and another appeal was made. This time another trial was not granted.

On the first day of May, Tom took his last ride. Perched on his coffin, he fiddled jaunty tunes in the sweet sunshine of the spring day, joking with those who walked about the wagon, as he went to the gallows in Statesville. When Sheriff W.E. Watson, who was the executioner, placed the noose over his head, Tom jested, "I'd a washed my neck, if I'd known you were going to use such a nice clean rope."

In a final moment of seriousness when asked if he had a last word to say, Tom held up his right hand and solemnly asked, "Gentleman, do you see this hand? Does it tremble?; Then he declared, "I never hurt a hair on the girl's head." Tom was buried in the family cemetery by the side of the old North Wilkesboro-Lenoir road, about a mile below Elkville.

Ann Melton was also defended by Vance. She was set free, but public opinion condemned her. Uncaring, she continued her bold flirtatious ways. Later she was killed when an oxcart overturned. There were those who declared Satan himself came and got her.

Many ballads have been written. The Kingston Trio's recording of "Tom Dooley" was very popular for sometime. William Thomas Land, the poet, found recorded in the Land Family History, wrote several poems about Tom, Ann and Laura. People have chipped away his gravestone and a play has been written and presented about him. The Tom Dula-Laura Foster-Ann Melton case is one of Wilkes County's tragedies.

Sources: *Tom Dooley* by Nancy Alexander; Copies of documents in N.C. Archives in Tom Dula file; Land family history.

FAIRPLAINS COMMUNITY
PLEASANT HILL BAPTIST CHURCH

Pleasant Hill Missionary Baptist Church Number 1 came into existence almost a century ago. A small group of people led by Brother William Luper decided to establish a church in the Fairplains Community, north of North Wilkesboro, N.C. The work began and a one-room building was erected. It was used for Sunday School and worship service. There is no record of the first organization of the church, the membership or the name of the pastor.

Pleasant Hill was represented in the Yadkin Valley Association, which was also in its infancy. There was a Pleasant Hill Number 1 and a Pleasant Hill Number 2, but in the 1906 minutes of the Association, Pleasant Hill Number 2 failed to present and there was no more mention of that church. Pleasant Hill Number 1 continued to grow.

Sister Sadie Harris was church clerk following Brother Majors. She held that position for fifty years.

Brother William Luper passed away about 1920, and the church property went to his only heir, Sister Mattie Luper Mitchell.

In 1925, the present property was purchased from Rev. E.L. Long, and a new sanctuary was erected. Rev. Long and Brothers S.C. Turner, Robert Thomas, Sr. and C. Watkins labored along with others to complete the proposed new building. In July, 1925, the first service was held in the new building. Pleasant Hill experienced a growing membership and soon the B.Y.P.U., the Missionary Society and the W.F.C. Society were formed.

Pastors

Some of the early pastors were: Rev. John Parsons — 1912, Rev. J.W. Majors — 1913, Rev. T.C. Graham — 1917 and 1918, and Rev. Majors again in 1919. Rev. A.S. Redmon later served for twelve years. Rev. V.C. Burns also served.

Rev. S.B. Stevenson and Rev. William Turner served in later years and were followed by Rev. Eli McEachern and Rev. Eugene Glenn.

In 1961, under the leadership of Rev. Glenn, a building fund was established.

Later, Rev. J.A. Dudley served as pastor and made improvements in the auxiliaries and membership of the church.

Rev. William Turner was called again but later resigned because of poor health. Rev. Coot Gilreath accepted the call to pastor in 1969.

In November, 1971, grading began for the new building. The first services were held in the new church on April 30, 1972, and the dedication was held on May 7, 1972. Rev. J.A. Dudley, now residing in Hammon, Indiana, delivered the message at the dedication services.

Pleasant Hill continues to strive for what the Lord would have her do.

Source: *The Centennial Year of the Yadkin Valley Missionary Baptist Association, 1880-1980.* Research by Mrs. Katherine Denny.

"Elkville", The Howard House — 1809, Ferguson Community. Home of Mr. and Mrs. H.C. Wheeling. (Sketch by Edith F. Carter.)

FERGUSON COMMUNITY
BEAVER CREEK ADVENT CHRISTIAN CHURCH

The Beaver Creek Advent Christian Church, Ferguson, N.C. was organized on Sept. 27, 1879, through the pioneer work of Rev. John A. Cargile of Alabama. There were nineteen charter members: Lowery and Martha Jane Dula, Mrs. Allie Dula, John and Eleander Ferguson, Dicie Ferguson, John and Sallie Dula Foster, Franklin and Sarah Hendrix, Henry and Martha Miller, Edith Ferguson Spicer, Amanda Triplett, Bethania Triplett, Mary Triplett, E.K. and Mira Walsh, and Julia Walsh.

Land for the church was donated by John and Eleander Ferguson and later land for a parsonage was donated by Edith Ferguson Spicer. A wooden frame church was erected by Andy Gould with lumber donated by the church members. The church had two doors in front; one for the men to enter by and one for the women. The men sat on one side of the church and the women sat on the other.

The first pastor of the church was George D. Sherrill, a Confederate veteran of honor, small in stature, but an intellectual giant. He knew the scriptures and was a Godly man. The little group of Christians were a faithful and dedicated group and each Sunday the musical

Beaver Creek Advent Christian Church.

strains of the "Old Jubilee Harp" song book rang out from this little church in the wildwood.

A Great Stabilizer

In his book, *Home on the Yadkin,* Mr. Thomas Ferguson says: "This little church has been a great stabilizer for this whole valley and its influence has radiated out over many parts of the world through its membership and Sunday School students, many of whom were members of other denominations. Through its influence, many other churches and Sunday Schools were established and flourished like the green bay tree. Hundreds of people, now scattered abroad, owe a deep debt of gratitude to this holy sanctuary. Indeed, it has lost itself in the service of humanity and it will live forever, if not materially, then in the heart throbs of those who came within the pale of its consecrated sanctum. Its influence has been wholesome, progressive, and constructive because it was founded on a deep spiritual basis."

In 1910 the Woman's Home and Foreign Mission Society was organized in the church. Some of the first members of this society were: Julia Hartley, Sarah Ferguson, Julia Sanders, Blanche and Beulah Ferguson, Janie Spicer, Alice, Mary and Loula Foster.

This little church continued to grow under the leadership of sincere and deeply religious men like Rufus Cottrell, Robert L. Isbell, Alonzo Downs, Franklin Hendrix, William Trivett, and Willard Preslar. Sunday School rooms were added to the original one room church in the late 1930s and in the early 1940s remodeling was done on the front of the church. In the early 1950's Rev. Hal Vannoy became pastor and the parsonage was remodeled and an educational building was added to the church.

Other pastors of the church who have contributed to the growth of the church are: Rev. G.W. Chapman, Rev. Johnny Carpenter, Rev. Roger Byrd, and Rev. Floyd Boston. During this period of time, the church has grown in number and spiritually. Additional building and improvements have been made. There is an active Sunday School, Youth Fellowship, Junior Action, King's Jewels, Missionary Society, Men's Fellowship.

In 1981 the church became a full time church with a full time pastor, Rev. Floyd Boston. In Nov. 1981, the church was recognized at the "Rural Church of the Year" by the North Carolina State Grange.

Source: Research by Edith F. Carter.

WHIPPOORWILL ACADEMY

The little 'one-teacher school' known as Whippoorwill Academy was erected some time in the 1880s and lasted as a functioning school until 1902 when it was succeeded by Beaver Creek Academy. It is located in a thickly wooded forest about one and a quarter miles southeast of the village of Ferguson in Beaver Creek Township. Still in fair condition, it was originally constructed out of dressed lumber and contains one room with two windows on each side, one door, a portable blackboard and rather rough desks. Being in an isolated area, it was nicknamed Whippoorwill Academy, rather out of derision, but the name remained with it throughout the years.

From the hills and valleys of the Yadkin and its tributaries, came many scholars as the students were known at that time, to attend the noted and historic Whippoorwill Academy. Many of these scholars were good students with enviable records and went on to become famous as teachers, doctors, ministers, farmers, engineers, poets and writers. Approximately twenty-five percent became college graduates while ninty percent of those that remained made respectable citizens and reared fine families. Many of their descendants still reside in the Ferguson Community, in Beaver and Elk Townships.

All these students came from humble homes with highly respected parents who actually contributed the funds for the erection of the Academy. No funds were furnished by the county educational system as funds were quite limited at that time. Teachers were paid from 18 to 20 dollars per month. The school term sometimes started in August with two months off for fodder pulling and corn gathering. The term then reconvened for three months during the winter.

At that time, there were no school buses. Students had to walk to school, many times in mud, snow or slush, as far as three miles. School equipment and facilities were very meager, and students had to furnish their own textbooks, which consisted of First, Second, Third and Fourth Readers together with Geography, History and Arithmetic. Teachers were very strict in discipline and in reality, "Readin', Writin', an' 'Rithmetic" were often "taught to the tune of a hickory stick." For that day, it was a well rounded, scholastic program.

A School Day

A day at the Academy began at eight o'clock the year around. It consisted of a fifteen minute recess (morning and evening) with an hour at noon for lunch which was provided by the students. It was brought in buckets and/or baskets and was usually eaten out of doors on logs or grass. Athletics consisted of Town Ball, Bull Pen and Prisoner's Base for boys. A game known as Tap Hand was played by boys and girls. This game helped to develope fast feet as the boy had to catch the girl who tapped him before he received his reward. Sanitary conditions were primitive. Water was brought from a nearby spring in a bucket and all used the same dipper, cup or gourd. School always closed with commencement exercises with speeches, recitations, dialogues and possibly a noted speaker.

The first teacher was Rev. George Durham Sherrill, a noted minister and an honored Confederate Veteran. He was followed by a list of well known educators, not all college graduates, but well versed in all the fundamentals and who were considered citizens of the highest order. Rev. Sherrill was followed by Commodore Triplett, Betty Spicer, Ref. Alfred J. Foster, Blanche K. Ferguson, Beulah Ferguson, Benjamin Proffit, his brother Judson Proffit and Augustos Cobb.

N.C. Poet Laureate

Perhaps the most noted scholar and product of the old Whippoorwill Academy was the late James Larkin Pearson. He was Poet Laureate of North Carolina for 27 years and was well known not only in North Carolina but all over the nation.

The old Whippoorwill Academy building, no longer used for a school, still stands in its original form except for some sheds which have been added to it by the farmer who owns it and the adjoining land. Much has been said about making a shrine out of the old building and preserving it for future generations to see and admire.

The early 'one teacher schools' were a definite assets to the country, even in their primitive conditions. They formed the fundamental basis of our education today. With our educational facilities in Wilkes County, our School Systems are equal to any in the state of North Carolina. The ten little 'one teacher schools' of the Gay Nineties, have, after a long struggle, been consolidated into one large elementary school known as the Boomer-Ferguson School. It serves Boomer, Beaver Creek and Elk Townships with excellent equipment and a fine faculty.

Source: Personal knowledge — Mr. Tom W. Ferguson.

BEAVER CREEK BAPTIST CHURCH FERGUSON

The history of Beaver Creek Baptist Church was written in 1949 for the 170th year celebration, again in 1956, and recorded in the minutes of the 85th Session of the Brushy Mountain Baptist Association. Since that time three books of the church minutes, believed to have been lost, were found. These records cover the years from 1819 to 1907. The first 40 years of records remain lost. In 1979 the history was again written for the church's bicentennial celebration and is recorded in the minutes of the 180th Session of the Brushy Mountain Baptist Association.

The earliest known record of Beaver Creek Baptist Church is found in Dutchmans Creek Baptist Church records, presently known as Eatons Baptist Church in Davie County. A petition was presented to Dutchmans Creek Baptist asking for help in a constitution for Beaver Creek, dated May 8, 1779. These records show John Barlow as pastor of Beaver Creek

Beaver Creek Baptist Church (Sketch by Edith Carter).

Baptist Church in 1782.

Other records show Beaver Creek Baptist Church belonged to Strawberry Association of Virginia in 1786. Beaver Creek, along with other churches of North Carolina, formed a branch of the Strawberry Association becoming known as the Yadkin Association in 1790.

In 1879, the Advent Christian doctrine caused a division in the church with loss of members and establishing of the Advent Christian Church, Ferguson, N.C.

In June 1865, three men were appointed "to propose a statement of the facts in writing of why the church had no meeting in April". This is a lengthy statement concerning a lawless band of rogues, deserters and bushwhackers roaming the country, insomuch as they were afraid to leave their homes unprotected.

The original building was of log structure with a fireplace, wooden windows, split log benches and a section for slaves. In 1891, a new building was built. Records show the church settled with the carpenters the amount of $199.82, leaving unpaid balance of $78.18. Another building was erected in 1937. There are no records of the cost since records cannot be located from May 1937 to September, 1944. Sunday school rooms were added in 1945. In 1970, the building was remodeled, interior and exterior, at a cost of $15,000.00

A Sunday School was organized in 1861 and called Sabbath School. Other organizations have been a part of the church training and mission teaching since that time. Mission giving was first recorded in 1881, an amount of $.60 for foreign missions. Presently 10% of all tithes and offerings go to the Cooperative Program and 4% to Associational Missions.

Sources: Church Records.

FISHING CREEK COMMUNITY

FISHING CREEK BAPTIST CHURCH

Fishing Creek Baptist Church, located on Old Highway 60, about four miles east of Wilkesboro, North Carolina, was constituted as an arm of Brier Creek Baptist Church pursuant to a petition filed by members of Brier Creek who lived some distance from the church was inconvenient for members to commute for services, since they journeyed by horse and buggy. In 1822, some members of Brier Creek Baptist Church petitioned to found a new church, which would be nearer their residence.

"We the undersigned members of Brier Creek Church being at a distance, and for convenience, do agree to petition our mother church for an arm to be set off at Robert Martins, Esq.: and if granted also petition for the ministerial help to attend us."

The petition handed in and acted on and granted for an arm to set off agreeably to the petition and to meet on the first Saturday in March, 1822. On Saturday, August 4, 1822, the Elders, composed of Rev. Thomas Mastin, William Dotson and William Gilliam, met: and Fishing Creek Baptist Church was this day constituted. The Charter membership was: Joshua Johnson, William W. Wright, William P. Johnson, Rasha Anderson, John Curry, Joel Curry, Green Anderson, "Black Jack", Amelia Martin, Sarah Wright, Amelia M. Mastin, Lyda Wright, Frances Johnson, Elizabeth Anderson, Cloa Hayes, Prisilla Chambers, Mary Johnson, and "Black Sallie." The first deacon, Joshua Johnson, was ordained on the day of the constitution, August 4, 1822; and he was a charter member.

Meetings were held for sometime in the Robert Martin home.

The oldest members think that the original church building was a one-room log building erected near the present church building. It has passed from generation to generation, that the first building contained a pew in the rear of the church building for colored people, and that Black Jack and Black Sallie were two colored slaves that were charter members of the church.

The church house stands today about one-fourth of a mile west of Robert Martin house, now owned by Old Wiles, on Old Highway 60. The Martin and Smith families are burial in the family graveyard within a few steps of the residence.

Sunday School was started Sunday May 7, 1899. This was the first mention of Sunday

Fishing Creek Baptist Church.

Goshen Community: Goshen School, the last one-teacher school in Wilkes County.

School in the minutes.

The cemetery at Fishing Creek began 82 years (1904) after the founding of the church. Uncle Jim Pardue rode a horse to a deacon's residence near Cub Creek to inquire about the possibility of beginning a cemetery at Fishing Creek. The bodies of Mrs. C.H. (Augusta) Holland and Mrs. E.F. (Mary) Anderson were the first two interments in the cemetery. One was interred one day, and the other the following day.

Fishing Creek has ordained four ministers: Revs. Vaughn Brown, Vestal Moore, Hugh Hayes and Dewey Foster.

Sources: Fishing Creek Church minutes.

HAYS COMMUNITY

Located in central Wilkes between Hay Meadow Creek and the head of Camp Branch. The post office was established in the 1890s and named for the first postmistress, Pauline Hays Elledge. This village is also referred to as Mt. View, possibly because of the institute that was there for many years.

Sources: *N.C. Gazetteer* by Powell.

Old store building H.C. Sebastian (1880s), now restored.

Old Mt. View Baptist Church (1920s).

MOUNTAIN VIEW INSTITUTE

Mountain View Institute was established in 1912 by the Stone Mountain, Brushy Mountain and Elkin Baptist Associations. It was founded at the instigation of James S. Kilby and wife, who gave the land and assisted by Abner Caudill, W.D. Woodruff, J.P. Elledge, J.A. Gilliam, Andrew Blevins, Azure Hayes, Cleve Kilby, P.A. Lomax, Milton McNeill, A.G. Hendren and C.C. Wright.

The founders, aided by the other Baptist of this section and by the Home Board of the Southern Baptist Convention, founded and equipped a plant that was valued in 1922 at

Silas M. Shumate Home.

Girl's Dormitory, Mt. View Institute.

Boy's Dormitory, Mt. View Institute.

A.E. Myers Homeplace (1882).

Sam Sebastian Homeplace (1890).

The Administrative Building of Mt. View Institute.

HUNTING CREEK COMMUNITY FRIENDSHIP BAPTIST CHURCH

Friendship Baptist Church was formed on the Thursday before the second Sunday in May, 1875. During this period blacks and whites attended the same church. Brother Edon Weldon, who was later appointed the first minister, offered the first prayer. The church was ordained formerly under the arms of Grassy Knob Baptist Church.

The first deacons for Friendship Baptist Church were Wesley Redmon, a Negro, and Jessie Barber and Thomas Williams, whites. Amos Smith served as the first church clerk. The members first met in an old school house to hold their church services. In March, 1876, the church made up $16.14 to buy Brother Weldon a horse.

On Saturday before the first Sunday in October, 1876, the church met for the monthly church conference. Brother Wesley Redmon was chosen as the first delegate to the Mt. Catawba Association along with Jesse Barber.

On Sunday before the first Sunday in April, 1877, the first Sabbath School was organized. Brother Mike Redmon was appointed head teacher. Sisters Harriet Williams and Violet Redmon, blacks, were the assistant teachers.

In April, 1887, the church record book was forwarded to the black members of Friendship Baptist Church.

In 1894, the Lord touched one of the members, Brother Silas Redmon, a former slave, and he sold the members an acre of land for $5.00 to build a church on. Three different churches have been built on the site. The first church was an arbor. In 1903, the members met and decided to construct a building because of the inconvenience of cold and wet weather.

On September 5, 1903, Brother A.D. Redmon and R.W. Williams were appointed to

$75,000.00.

When the school was built the area was a dense forest. In 1922 there were four modern brick buildings located on a campus which equalled any other in western N.C. Adjoining the campus was a beautiful brick church built by the friends of Mountain View Institute.

The school was located on a ridge midway between the Brushies on the south and the Blue Ridge Mountains on the north and west.

Sources: Mountain View catalogue 1921-1922.

Hunting Creek Community: Schoolchildren in 1932.

oversee the building of the first church.

When the second church was built, the materials were donated by Mr. Preston Sharpe, father of Herman Sharpe. He was not a member at that time but later joined the church. Between 1960 and 1968 the members were successful in remodeling and painting the church by tithes and rallies.

Ministers who have pastored at Friendship are: Rev. John Parsons, Rev. P.C. Adams, Rev. J.C. Redmon, Rev. Watts, Rev. I.P. Rowe, Rev. W.N. Nixon. Rev. J.C. Rowe, Rev. Harrison Flowers, and the present pastor, Rev. James Milsaps.

Many things have changed since our ancestors organized our church in 1875, but records dating back to that time revealed that the church conferences were held on each Saturday before the first Sunday in each month. This tradition is still followed.

It has been a long hard struggle, but the members have kept the faith. The hopes, dreams, and prayers of our foreparents are a reality. We now have a modernized brick church with all conveniences.

The present church membership is sixty-six. Sabbath School is held each Sunday, and morning worship is held the first and third Sunday of each month.

Source: *THE CENTENNIAL YEAR OF THE YADKIN VALLEY MISSIONARY BAPTIST ASSOCIATION 1880-1980.* Research by Mrs. Katherine Denny.

A HEINOUS CRIME

Some ten miles north of Harmony near the spot where the Wilkes, Yadkin and Iredell county lines adjoin stands an old deserted house with the date 1813 scratched on the rock chimney. Intelligent persons have no fear of the old place, but superstitious white and practically all negroes of that section shun the house because of its many "ghosts" and the dozens of tales of death and suffering connected with it.

All the house as it now stands is not the original structure, but part of it is, and in the first buildings. Long before the Civil War, Kut Robbins, a notorious slave drive, tortured an old negro to death by beating and cutting him almost into insensibility and finally pouring hot melted lead into his ears. This actually happened and Kit Robbins, the killer, was tried in Wilkesboro for murder, convicted and hung for the crime. It is said that the tree on which he met his death still stands in historic old Wilkesboro.

Stories and weird folk-lore tales are numerous and popular in all the countryside and opinion differs among the old people as to when the first tragedy occurred at the "haunted house." However, all of them connect a suicide with its early history and misfortunes. The story goes that a man hung himself to an old fashioned bed post in this house and the majority of the storytellers say that this happened before Kit Robbins killed old Jim Beard, his faithful negro slave. The beds of that day were made with hand-carved, high posts and the alleged suicide was no difficult accomplishment. Other stories are told of the early history of the house, but the suicide and Kit Robbins tales are verified by all the old people of the neighborhood.

W.B. York, prominent north Iredell contractor who operates here and in Elkin, was born and raised near this Kit Robbins house. He knows the stories of the place and the fears of superstitious people from Yadkin farm folk who told them around winter fires when he was a boy. J.N. Barron, superintendent of the old Harmony Academy and at present a rural mail carried from this place, knows the story from his father, who witnessed the hanging of Kit Robbins in Wilkesboro.

A Horrible Killing

One hardly wonders at the fear of the house. The story of the killing of the slave, Jim Beard, is as horrible as can be imagined. It is told that Kit Robbins, a descendant of one of the first settlers, was rather well-to-do, but extremely wicked. One day after an election he came home drunk and called on Jim Beard for help in some work he wanted done. Jim was an old negro and practically helpless from too much work already done that day. Robbins decided he would make the negro work. He beat him unmercifully. He cut long lashes in his skin and poured salt in them, according to popular stories in the community today, and then carried him to a shed nearby and poured melted lead in his ears to "wake him up."

Many people went from this section to see Kit Robbins hung for the crime. Wilkesboro was crowded and when the body of Kit Robbins was brought back the people refused to bury it according to the time honored custom and place the body with the head facing the west and the feet east. He was placed in the ground far away from the community graveyard and his body was laid north and south. His remains are supposed to still lie on the side of a small mountain several miles from where he killed Jim Beard. Near the old house where this occurred is a family burying ground, unmarked except for plain stones, but it was not meant for Kit Robbins.

The community for several miles around the "haunted house" is not as thickly settled as formerly. There are many abandoned homes in that section of Iredell, Yadkin and Wilkes. But the people who do live there are the best southern stock of rural folk. There are good farms, and of course, some bad ones. The people are fine, but many strange tragedies have occurred in that section.

Sources: *The Wilkes Journal,* Thursday, July 30, 1925 — by G. Wright Lankford.

KNOTTVILLE COMMUNITY
LIBERTY GROVE BAPTIST CHURCH

On the third Saturday in December 1886, T.W. Paris, I.N. Haynes and J.W. Burchette met in a school house in district number thirty-six, Wilkes County to organize a Missionary Baptist Church. T.W. Parish was elected moderator and I.N. Haynes was elected clerk.

The following brethern and sisters presented letters to become members: A.M. Church, who donated the land for the church to be built upon, Susan Church, E.S. Church, M.O. Church, who all came from the Wilkesboro church, Hiram Wiles, Sarah Ann Wiles, G.M. Woodruff, S.C. Woodruff, K.J. Woodruff, W.D. Woodruff, all from Rock Creek Church, T.W. Parish, J.W. Burchette, Susanna C. Stafford, C.S. Stafford, I.J. Haynes, R.L. Church. A.M. Church was elected the first clerk.

The church records for a period were destroyed by fire. In July 1954, a building committee was appointed composed of F.C. Johnson, Paul Church, Guy Hutchinson and Mesdames Tam Hutchinson, Claude Caudill and Eva Taylor.

In September, 1954, the board of trustees, Kermit Absher, Elbert Johnston, Jim Henderson, were appointed for the purpose of purchasing land from the Pat Anderson heirs to enlarge the church grounds. On January 5, 1956, church services were held in the new educational building.

The church has had pastors: W.W. White, C.S. Fields, I. Prevette, A.T. Pardue, J.W. Burchette, W.W Myers, W.T. Comer, T.E.

Redmon, C.G.M. Burcham, A.B. Hayes, J.S. Elliott, J.A. Elliott, H.A. Bullis, Loyd Pardue, B.L. Temple, Roy Franklin, C.S. Welborn, Leroy Thomas, Howard Laney, Clarence Corbitt and Paul Shoupe, who is presently the pastor.

Church clerks have been A.M. Church, W.N. Alexander, Abner Caudill, R.S. Wiles, J.S. Forester, W.A. Wiles, Charlie Burchette, Charlie Church, R.L. Church, C.F. Johnson, McCager Brown, Paul E. Church, C.E. Burchette, Roscoe Porter, Tam Hutchinson, D.W. Smith, Ben Johnson, Johnny Emerson, Jimmy Brown, Bill Shepherd and Glenn Mitchell.

On November 23, 1941, R. Andrew Call was ordained to the ministry. Charles Pearson, the first deaf person to attend Liberty Grove, joined in 1961, and was ordained a deacon in 1964 and a minister in 1976. Eugene Parker was also ordained a deacon in 1964.

Sources: Existing church minutes. Research by Paul Shroupe.

ones of McNeil, Church, Eller, Hayes, Faw, Pierce, Bumgarner, Kilby, Shepherd, Vannoy and others.

Sources: Research by Mae R. Hayes.

R.D. Hayes Store (1941).

Friendship Methodist Church.

MILLERS CREEK VILLAGE

Millers Creek is a small unincorporated town located five miles west of North Wilkesboro at the junction of the old Boone Trail and highway sixteen. It is near the head of Millers Creek for which it apparently was named. Many residents have not known where the creek was located or if a creek even existed. Others believed the creek ran underground. A well, which is now covered by a paved parking area of a shopping center, convinced some that an underground stream ran through the bottom of the well. The creek bubbles out at the top of the ground on property about 300 yards south of the above mentioned well.

Millers Creek runs from north to south, flowing southward until it flows into the Yadkin River about one mile below the Kerr Scott Dam. Its entire length measures four miles. Several small branches meander from the creek at various locations, one of the largest running behind the United Methodist Church and on to land near Pads Road, from which a view of the creek may be seen.

The old William Calloway Parsons' vine-covered homeplace stands on a ridge on the west side of the creek. Calloway operated a store there and a mill for grinding corn meal. The mill washed away in the 1916 flood.

One of the first mentions of the creek appears in a deed 24 Dec., 1798, when one Benjamin Coffey received a grant from the state for land on the South Fork of the Yadkin River called Millers Creek.

The citizens of Millers Creek are proud of their thriving community. They have kept pace with the times and there have been many changes. In addition to the usual grocery stores and service stations, there are dress shops, a restaurant, beauty shops, ice cream store, air conditioning and heating, and electric companies, TV repair shop, jewelry, hardware and drug stores.

The bank and post office are relatively new assets. At the present time the post office serves 1,500 families.

There are several residential areas around Millers Creek adding new names to the familiar

Millers Creek Village; Delp store and Caudill Dwelling.

Store Building of Turner Nichols (1940s).

J.A. Rhodes Sawmill (1910). Left to right: Steven Rash, Arthur Lankford, Lee Brooks, Roby Brooks, Clate Rhoades, Elijah Brown, J.A. (Bud) Rhoades, Rush Rhoades, C.C. Brooks, Sr.

This is the W.A. (Uncle Bill) Bumgarner homeplace where he raised his twelve children. The house was constructed prior to the Civil War by Nelson Bumgarner. During the war the Stephen Bumgarner family used the new house for storing provisions. The Home Guard raided the house gaining entry by carving a diamond shaped hole in the heavy door. This hole served many purposes through the generations. Not only did the soldiers get their food, but many a young Bumgarner maiden had to compete with a little "shaver tail" brother taking advantage of the "peek hole" while some handsome suitor tried to pay court to her. Only a small part of the building stands today.

Church Store Building.

Cross Roads School about 1900. Presley Brown, Teacher.

Millers Creek Baptist Church.

Old Store Building bought in 1913 from R.F. Wyatt by C.H.M. Tulbert which carried groceries, hardware, coffins, farm tools. Tulbert home on right. (Millers Creek).

R.D. Hayes Home, built ca. 1924, on Old Boone Trail in 1976.

23

Dunkirk Methodist Church (1957).

MILLERS CREEK UNITED METHODIST CHURCH

Millers Creek United Methodist Church stands on a knoll just this side of the heart of Millers Creek. This church results from the merger of Friendship and old Millers Creek Church in October, 1952.

Friendship Methodist Church was organized 1 Dec., 1867, and a log building was constructed on land donated by Mrs. Mary McKee Wright. This building was torn away in 1893 to make way for a frame structure which was erected on the same site. This building burned in a forest fire 3 April, 1909, and was replaced by another frame building which housed Friendship Church until 1953 when it was razed to make way for the present Millers Creek United Methodist Church.

Old Millers Creek Methodist Church located nearby was established 9 January, 1890. The early membership of these two churches came largely, if not entirely, from Charity Methodist Church.

After the decision for the two churches to combine was finalized, services were held at Millers Creek School for about two years. The Rev. C. Jack Caudill, a native of Millers Creek, was pastor when the churches united. The first chairman of the Official Board of the united church was C.S. Bumgarner. The building committee for the new church consisted of A.G. Nichols, Chairman, M.F. Bumgarner, Secretary, Nat Tolbert, Robert K. Hayes, Avery Johnson, G.A. Bumgarner, E.S. Gaither, Lin Bumgarner, J.H. Eudaily, and N.W. Bumgarner.

The present building was completed 1959.
Source: Church minutes.

ARBOR GROVE UNITED METHODIST CHURCH

About 1870 Mrs. Ann Howard Grant Hayes, wife of Joseph Washington Hayes, helped to establish the first of the present church which is located between Millers Creek and Purlear communities. She was assisted by the Rev. Benny Weisner, a pioneer circuit rider from Iredell County.

The first church was built on land owned by J.W. Hayes and was known as Hays' Arbor. It was located about one-half mile from the present church. It was built of upright poles covered with brush. Seats were made of rough, hewn logs. Scaffolds covered with dirt furnished a safe place for pine torches to light the arbor for night services.

The next place of worship was a shed built nearby. Jonas Coles was the pastor.

About 1885 the shed was torn away and a log building was erected. It was built on land deeded to the church by William Berry and Cynthia Roberson Nichols and Mack and Elizabeth Minton. The deed was dated 30 December 1885, and stated that John E. Pierce, Henry Bumgarner, and G.F. Bumgarner, trustees, "should build or cause to be built a house or place of worship for the use of the Methodist Episcopal Church in the U.S.A. according to the rules and discipline, to have and to hold to them the said trustees and their successors in office forever a place to worship for the minister and members of said church. Said property not to be sold or rented or used for any other purpose."

In 1904 a frame structure was built with a seating capacity of approximately 200. Four classrooms were added to the sanctuary during 1946-47. The last service was held in this frame building June 21, 1959.
Sources: Church History

Arbor Grove Methodist Church (1904).

Faculty (1935).

Old Millers Creek High School School Building (1935).

Gym at Millers Creek High School.

Millers Creek United Methodist Church.

Basketball Team 1939; county-wide champions.

Graduation Class (1935).

FIRE DEPARTMENT

On April 2, 1957 the first rural fire department in Wilkes County was organized. Clate Bumgarner, a strong force behind the organization, was elected president and is still serving in that capacity. Other officers included James Graham, vice-president; Mrs. Allen Phillips, secretary, the late Paul Delp, treasurer and Harold Baker, publicity chairman. These officers along with Charlie Bishop and Henseley Eller made up the first board of directors. The first fire chief was Joe Owings.

The first rural volunteer fire department in Wilkes County: Millers Creek Fire Dept.

PLEASANT HOME BAPTIST CHURCH

On the fourteenth day of February, 1880, a group of Christian men and women met for the purpose of organizing a Baptist Church. Meeting in a grove where the cemetary is now located, they heard a sermon by the Rev. L.P. Gwaltney. Twenty-three presented themselves for membership: J.S. Marlow, A.C. McRary, Ellen C. McRary, Amanda Eller, J.E. Bullis, Eliza J. Bullis, Jane Riggs, Polly Miller, Susan McNiel, Harrison Eller, J.H. McNiel, Susannah McNiel, Martha J. Kilby, John G. McNiel, (Polly) McNiel, Louisa McNiel, Elvira McNiel, Annie Nichols, Barbara Kilby, Martha J. Church, Peter Eller, Sarah Jane Eller, and Margaret Eller. These being found to be orthodox in their beliefs, were accepted as charter members and the newly organized church was unanimously named Pleasant Home Baptist Church. According to old records of both New Hope and Pleasant Home Baptist Churches, most of these charter members came by letter from New Hope Church. The presbytery consisted of John Adams moderator, I.T. Prevette, secretary, J.P. Gwaltney, and J.T. Tinsley. A church covenant was adopted.

Preaching services were held under a brush arbor until the erection of the church. The site was given by J.H. McNiel. A second building was erected in 1903 and served as a place of worship until the erection of the present building.

In August of 1900, letters of recommendation were granted a group of members who wished to help to constitute a church at Harmony. As the church there became established, these people returned to Pleasant Home.

In January, 1946, a building committee composed of J.C. Whittington, Clate Bumgarner, and Howard McNiel was appointed by the church to oversee the erection of a new building across the road from the old church. Grading was started in May, 1947. The building was completed in May, 1948.

Sources: Church Records.

Pleasant Home Baptist Church.

McNeil Home at Cross Roads (Miller Creek).

THE VILLAGE OF MORAVIAN FALLS

The village of Moravian Falls had its beginning over 125 years ago. For many years the village was known as the "Forks of the Road," later it took the name of "Petersburg." About 1874, the village became known as Moravian Falls, a Post Office having been established at that time. Prior to 1874, mail for the citizens of the community was directed to Wilkesboro, while at the same time, the citizens of Wilkes-boro came to Moravian Falls to vote in general elections.

One of the early settlers of the village was Mr. William Pitt Waugh of Adams County, Pa. His first building was the "Brick House," which stood in the "Forks of the Road." Tradition has it that the clay for making the brick used in the house was prepared by turning a small branch near Cub Creek into the loosened earth and driving horses around until the clay was mixed for the molding.

Moravian Falls Baptist and Moravian Falls Methodist Churches have always played a strong role in the influence upon the community. The Baptist Church had two front doors. The entrance on the left, complete with banister, was used by the men. The entrance on the right, minus the banister, was used by the women. Once inside, separation of the sexes continued. The Methodist Church had only one front entrance. Once inside, however, separation of the sexes continued, as in the Baptist Church. This practice continued until about 1935.

In the late 1800s and early 1900s, Moravian Falls could boast of having 18 newspapers. Some of these papers were short lived. The most noteworthy of these would be the *Yellow Jacket*. Publication of this anti-Democratic paper began in 1895 by R. Don Laws. From the beginning, the *Yellow Jacket* had for its motto, "To swat all liars and leeches, hypocritics and humbugs, demagogs and dastards." The circulation grew to 100,000.

Moravian Falls has played a tremendously important part in the history of Northwest North Carolina, and especially in Wilkes County.

Source: Local Knowledge, Research by Mary J. Lovette, Thelma Laws.

Left: T.P. Parlier's Store. Right: Yellow Jacket office (1930).

R.A. Spainhour Store (1882).

R. Don Laws driving his Maxwell roadster (Academy in background).

Masonic Hall.

MORAVIAN FALLS ACADEMY

At one time, Moravian Falls was considered to be the literary center of Wilkes County. The first school was known as the Edgewood School. This was a two-room building used until 1875.

In the summer of 1876, the citizens of Moravian Falls community held a meeting and made plans to erect a nice building at Moravian Falls. In the fall of 1876 construction work began. A six-room two story building with belfry was erected, located where the present school now stands. In the year 1877, J.F. Spainhour, who was later an attorney in Morganton, N.C., and Rev. George W. Greene opened the school known as Moravian Falls Academy in the new building.

Fees were charged according to the number of subjects taken. The minimum scholastic fee was one dollar and the maximum was four dollars per month. The fees were paid quarterly.

Professor Greene became principal in 1877 and continued until 1890. He was a native of Stony Fork, Wilkes County, graduated from Wake Forest and Louisville Seminary. After leaving Wake Forest, Greene went to China and became a member of Graves Theological Seminary and died there in 1910.

Professor R.L. Patton of Morganton was the next principal and he was succeeded by W.R. Bradshaw, who was principal for twenty-two years. In 1893, Professor F.B. Hendren became head of the school serving four years, then Professor K.M. Allen was principal for three years.

In 1894 the school was chartered as a military academy and continued as such for five years. In 1897, Professor W.G. Stevenson became principal followed by Rev. S.J. Beaker, Rev. J. Van Beach and W.S. Surratt. It was in 1906 that the school was closed, with the onset of public education.

Benefactors of the school were the

ANNUAL COMMENCEMENT
OF
MORAVIAN FALLS ACADEMY.
FRIDAY, MAY 31st, 1889.

——:o:——

MARSHALS:

E. M. BLACKBURN, Wilkes Co. | W. M. FAW, Wilkes Co.
W. F. REECE, Iredell Co. | J. R. BLEDSOE, Ashe Co.

——:o:——

10:30 A. M.

Anthem—THEY THAT WAIT UPON THE LORD.

Concert Recitation—PSALM XXIII.

PRAYER.

Sacred Chorus—WHAT A GATHERING!

Declamation—MORAL HEROISM.
L. J. Lane, Wilkes Co., N. C.

Reading—THE ARCHERY OF WILLIAM TELL.
Miss Ollie Bledsoe, Ashe Co., N. C.

Round—BIM, BOME, BELLS.

Reading—THE REVOLUTIONARY RISING.
Miss Anna Greene, Moravian Falls, N. C.

Reading—ONLY SIXTEEN!
Miss Stella Puett, Lenoir, N. C.

Solo—HAVE COURAGE, MY BOY, TO SAY NO!

Declamation—SPARTACUS TO THE GLADIATORS.
G. M. Icenhour, Caldwell Co., N. C.

Declamation—SPARTACUS TO THE ROMAN ENVOYS.
R. L. Sherrill, Caldwell Co., N. C.

Reading—WHAT I HATE TO SEE.
Miss Lola Brown, Moravian Falls, N. C.

Solo—MERRY LITTLE BOBOLINK.

Reading—THE EXILE OF ERIN.
Miss Vic. Swann, Iredell Co., N. C.

Reading—THE WONDERFUL ONE HOSS SHAY.
Miss Lella Hubbard, Moravian Falls, N. C.

Concert Reading—TUBAL CAIN, THE FIRST BLACKSMITH.

Anthem—THOUGH YOUR SINS BE AS SCARLET.

Reading—MRS. CAUDLE ON SHIRT BUTTONS.
Miss Dora Pool, Lenoir, N. C.

Declamation—APPEARANCES DECEPTIVE.
Charlie Hix, Moravian Falls, N. C.

Song—BUSY CHILDREN.

Reading—CURFEW MUST NOT RING TO-NIGHT.
Miss Dovie Lane, Moravian Falls, N. C.

Declamation—LIBERTY AND UNION.
W. T. Bobbitt, Moravian Falls, N. C.

Reading—LITTLE JIM.
Miss Ida Howell, Moravian Falls, N. C.

Serenade—STARS OF THE SUMMER NIGHT.

Declamation—THE PYRAMIDS NOT ALL EGYPTIAN.
W. R. Absher, Wilkes Co., N. C.

Reading—THE DEATH OF MINNEHAHA.
Miss Etta Eidson, Iredell Co., N. C.

Sacred Chorus—SHINE ON, O STAR.

——:o:——

2 P. M.

Annual Address—W. W. BARBER, ESQ., Wilkesboro, N. C.

——:o:——

3 P. M.

Annual Sermon—REV. J. C. STOWELL, Statesville, N. C.

Program of the Moravians Falls Academy Annual Commencement (1889).

Moravian Falls Academy.

"The Falls".

Spainhours, Gilreaths, Parliers, Squire Hubbard, the Hixes, Foster, Major Sneed and others. Some of the teachers were Vance McGinnis, W.R. Hendren, Miss Janie Gilreath, Mrs. R.L. Scroggs, Mrs. J.W. Nichols, Mrs. George Kennedy and J.W. Hendren.

Sources: *Wilkes Journal*, 15 May 1924; Personal papers Mary Jo Lowe Lovette.

Old Mill at Moravian Falls, early 1900s.

MORAVIAN FALLS

The land surrounding the falls at Moravian Falls was a part of two land grants made to the Moravian Brethren who settled at Salem, North Carolina. These grants were made in 1752 by Lord Granville, one of the eight Lords Proprietors appointed by Charles II of England. This section was traversed by a creek named "Moravian" by the surveyors sent out by the Moravian Brethren, hence the beautiful cascade on Moravian Creek became known as Moravian Falls. In 1874, the little village, one-half miles from the Falls, was officially named Moravian Falls, at which time the post office was established.

In the early part of the year 1800, Colonel William Pitt Waugh came from Pennsylvania and purchased a large tract of land which included the Falls on Moravian Creek. Colonel Waugh's chief development was centered at

Sunday afternoon at the Falls.

"Moravian Belles" at The Falls (1915).

ders, Wright, Hargrave, Norman, Hamby, Montgomery, Hubbard and others.

Source: An article by the late Lucy Hubbard Critcher in 1974.

MORAVIAN FALLS METHODIST CHURCH

In 1876 the congregations of Sharon and Shiloh formed a union, taking the name Center Methodist Church. Shiloh was located on the Boomer highway. Sharon was located on old N.C. 18. These churches have records dating back to 1833.

Sharon Church had an arbor and natural amphitheater where camp meetings were held. Those camp meetings were the high spots of the religious activities of those days. Folks came from over the area, bringing their families and food cooked over open fireplaces. The campground had permanent posts over which each family stretched a canvas to make a tent for sleeping.

Shiloh Church was a log structure. It was used as a school during the week and was called "A Public Free School".

In 1874, a piece of ground in the village of Moravian Falls was given by R.L. Hix for the purpose of building a Methodist Church in the community. The name of the church, Center was changed to Beulah in 1877, and this name

was used for ninety years. In 1966, the name was officially changed to Moravian Falls Methodist Church.

The original church building was of wood siding outside, with flat wooden inside walls and a very high ceiling. The church was lighted by reflector oil lamps hung on the walls. A big wood stove was used for heating. The first windows were of clear glass. In 1951 stained glass windows were donated by J.R. Hix.

Originally the church did not have a belfry. The church bell was small and hung from a pole in front of the church. In 1908, R. Don Laws donated a large bell, which was placed on a sturdy platform beside the church.

Sources: History of the Methodist Church at Moravian Falls, by Lucy Critcher, 1967.

Moravian Falls Baptist Church, 1886.

the Falls where he built the first burr flour mill in Wilkes County. This flour mill building also housed a corn mill, a linseed oil mill and a wool carding machine. In 1849, Richard L. Hix, from Randolph County, North Carolina, bought the Falls property and carried on the industries started by Colonel Waugh, adding sawmill equipment.

The property changed ownership many times during the following years. In 1911 the property was sold to J.T. Humphries and Smith Coachman of Clearwater, Florida, and an electric power plant was erected. This was the first electric power plant in the county. In addition to furnishing electric power and lights to the communities of Moravian Falls and Wilkesboro, the usual milling operations were carried on. The old three-story mill building was torn away in 1927, and the business activities at the Falls ceased.

Today there is a fish lake, swimming lake, picnicking facilities and a restaurant at the Falls, which offer fine recreational opportunities.

Some of the early families who lived in this area of Wilkes County are as follows: Trible, Greer, Lowe, Hampton, Martin, Isbell, Gilreath, Mitchell, Elledge, Walker, McCoy, Cross, Smither (Smithey), Lovelace, Jones, Morgen, Demoss, Dyer, Donathan, Allen, Hamrick, Gwyn, Barber, Wilson, Keller, San-

Moravian Falls Methodist Church.

Franklin Brown and his sister, Lola M. Brown, beside their home in Moravian Falls. The old house stood for 150 years on the road to Boomer, and three generations of Browns lived there (1900).

THE YELLOW JACKET

An institution of the Moravian Falls community was the newspaper started by R. Don Laws in June 1895, called *The Yellow Jacket.* In a few years it attained national and some international circulation. It gave employment to one or two members of practically every local family and brought in several new families, namely the Abernethys and Hulses who became permanent residents. The business had a book bindery and ran a linotype school. Quite a few young people put out amateur publications: Leonard Laws, Don's brother, started *The Lash* and James Larkin Pearson started the *Fool Killer,* both of which enjoyed wide popularity but did not reach the level of success of *The Yellow Jacket.*

Source: Articles by R. Don Laws.

The Yellow Jacket Building (1917).

Mount Pleasant Community: Robert Jones Home.

MOUNT PLEASANT

Lodge No. 573, A.F. & A.M.

Mount Pleasant Lodge No. 537, Ancient, Free and Accepted Masons, was organized in 1909, operating under dispensation from the Grand Lodge of North Carolina, and received its Charter on January 12, 1910. A number of Masons who were members of New Hope Lodge, located near Millers Creek, and who lived in or near the Mount Pleasant community, desiring a meeting place in their community, petitioned the Grand Lodge of North Carolina and were granted permission to establish a Lodge at that place.

W. Hayes Foster was elected the first Master of the Lodge with W. Harrison Eller as Senior Deacon and Nathan C. Huffman as Junior Deacon. Other members who were elected as Masters of the Lodge during its early history

were U.G. Foster, R.L. Proffit, D.F. Shepherd, P.O. Church and J.C. McNeil. These are only a few of those who have been elected to serve as Master of the Lodge, but they were among those most instrumental in keeping the Lodge operating during the depression of the early 1930s when so many of the Lodges in Wilkes County failed.

New Hope Lodge, the parent Lodge of Mount Pleasant Lodge, no longer exists but Mount Pleasant continues a strong, active Masonic Lodge.

One of the more prominent members of Mount Pleasant Lodge was Dr. James W. Davis, founder and owner of Davis Hospital of Statesville. Dr. Davis was elected to serve as Master of the Lodge during 1945 and commuted from Statesville to attend the meetings as often as possible. Numerous other members of the Lodge were outstanding men in various occupations, serving their Lodge and Country with distinction.

Two members have had the honor of having been elected Master of the Lodge, been appointed District Deputy Grand Master, and have had three sons who have also served their Lodge as Master. These are R.L. Proffit (deceased) and J.M. Joines. Mount Pleasant Lodge has been a consistent supporter of the Oxford Orphanage at Oxford, N.C. and the Masonic and Eastern Home at Greensboro, N.C.

Source: Article by a member from Lodge (information from *Lodge Minutes).*

MULBERRY COMMUNITY
CROSS ROADS PRIMITIVE
BAPTIST CHURCH

Cross Roads Primitive Baptist Church was constituted from Mulberry Primitive Baptist Church on November 8, 1849. The families of Jennings, Elledge, Wyatt, Brown, Owens, Reeves, Adams, Brooks, Tinsley, Absher, Kilby, Shumate, Rhodes and many others attended this church. It is located west of highway 18 going north from North Wilkesboro toward the Blue Ridge Mountains.

Cross Roads Primitive Baptist Church.

SULPHUR SPRINGS ACADEMY

The Sulphur Springs Academy building, located about seven miles north of North Wilkesboro, adjacent to Mulberry school, was built over one hundred years ago. It was erected as a community project for grades one through

seven, and continued to be used as a school until Mulberry school was built about 1935.

The land for the academy was given by Isom and Rachel Dancy. The name was derived from a spring less than a mile away believed to run water containing sulphur.

During the early years, the building was used for community debates, a popular form of pastime and diversion before the days of radio and television. Pie suppers, box suppers, spelling bees, and other activities were also quite popular.

Robert Lee Plummer at one time was a principal of Sulphur Springs Academy. He taught school at North Wilkesboro in 1896-97, and later moved to Ashe County schools. He helped found Healing Springs High School in Ashe County.

Another highly respected principal of Sulphur Springs was Professor W.R. (Roe) Absher. He taught in North Wilkesboro in 1894-95, and was also an outstanding businessman and religious leader.

Oscar C. Dancy, who was mayor of North Wilkesboro 1907-09, received his education at the Academy. He was a soldier in the Spanish-American War and for many years was a judge in Texas.

Another Sulphur Springs student, Archie Elledge, served many terms as a member of the Board of Aldermen in Winston-Salem, North Carolina and was an outstanding lawyer there.

Among the alumni of the school was Dr. Ira S. Gambill, M.F. (Bob) Absher, for several years chairman of the Wilkes County Board of Commissioners, Tom M. Brown, a former commissioner and associated with P.E. Brown Lumber Company, Grant G. Elledge, sheriff of Wilkes in 1922-23 and county surveyor and Presley E. Brown sheriff of Wilkes. Brown also headed field forces of the U.S. Treasury for many years, served as minority leader in sessions of the North Carolina General Assembly in 1925 and 1927, and later owner and operator of the P.E. Brown Lumber Company. He also served on the N.C. State Board of Elections.

Sources: Excerpts from article by Wake O. Tinsley, 1975.

Sulphur Springs Academy.

MULBERRY PRIMITIVE BAPTIST CHURCH

This church is located on the Northeast side of Highway 18 North toward the Blue Ridge Mountains beside Mulberry Creek. It was constituted about 1794 and the building is supposed to be that of the old Mulberry Fields Primitive Baptist Church which was constituted as an arm of Eaton's Baptist Church the 4th of October, 1777: the building having been removed to its present location around 1794. The families of Absher, Adams, Dillard, Tinsley, Jennings, Brown, Shumate, Kilby, Sebastian, Elledge, Harrold, Rhodes, Hall, Owens, Reeves and many others attended this church from its beginning through the 1800s.

Mulberry Primitive Baptist Church.

Old Presley Brown home.

MOUNT ZION COMMUNITY

MOUNT ZION BAPTIST CHURCH

On the 3rd Saturday in May, 1849, a body of Missionary Baptists met on Stony Fork, at what is now Elk Township #1. Elder William Church acted as moderator and a motion appointed Wilson Fairchilds clerk. A motion was made that Thomas Land be appointed a messenger to Lewis Fork Church, Wilson Fairchilds to Beaver Creek and William Adkins to Zion Hill.

On the 30th day of June, 1849, according to

appointment a number of messengers met on Stony Fork. They called for the organization of this body; appointed William Church moderator for the day; selected William Church and William Brown as a Presbytery; and named Thomas Land and William Fairchilds to answer the questions for this body.

As the questions were answered satisfactorily, this body was found orthodox. Thomas Land was chosen to act as deacon and Wilson Fairchilds, clerk. This body was regularly organized as a Baptist Church and named Mount Zion Missionary Baptist Church.

After the organization was completed, members were called for and the following presented themselves: Wilson Fairchilds, Elizabeth Fairchilds, Mary Gray, Mary A. Triplett, Thomas Land, Jane Land, Mary Land, Nancy Land, Unice Miller, John Culler, William Adkins and Sarah Adkins. Being orthodox in the faith of the Gospel, they were received into the membership of Mount Zion Missionary Baptist Church.

The first minutes give no information about a building being erected. From an interview of older members, it seems that this church held services for a while in a school house then erected a log building about one mile east of the present building.

The minutes of the 4th Sunday in November, 1887, state that the church took under consideration the selecting of a site on which to erect a new building. At the December meeting, 1887, the church decided to erect a new building near the school house in District No. 65, J.F. Triplette donated one acre of land; the deed is recorded in Book 98, page 16, in the Register of Deeds office of Wilkes County. The building was to be 24′ by 36″ and to have six windows and one double door in the end of the building. F. West, T.H. West, and G.F. Hendrix were appointed to get up subscriptions and also to act as a building committee. They reported at the January meeting 1888, that $321.00 had been raised and 7 to 8 thousand feet of lumber given. The church instructed the building committee to go ahead; added T.C. Land and J.F. Triplette to the building committee; and ordered lumber from the old building used in the new building and the remainder sold.

Some of the members have stated that the present building was erected in 1924, but the minutes say nothing about it.

Pastors

The church has had pastors as follows: William Church, July, 1849 — April, 1851; Jacob Crouch, 1851-1856; John G. Bryan, 1856-1857; James McNeil, 1857-1860; Linville Land, 1860-1861; John H. Brown, 1861-1862, (Larkin Pipes elected in November 1862, but did not serve) F. Carlton, 1862-1863; Linville Land, 1863-1865; J.B. Brown, 1865-1868; Linville Land, 1868-1870; Larkin Lodges, 1870-1872; John H. Brown 1872-1876; Linville Land, 1876-1877; J.F. Eller, 1877-1879; Linville Land, 1879-1880; Larkin Pipes, 1880-1881; M. McNeill, 1881-1883; Larkin Pipes, 1883-1886; Sidney Carroll, 1886-1887; A.S. Church, 1887-1889; A.T. Pardue, 1889-1890; W.M. Leel, 1890-1892;

James Calvin Land's Home, built about 1880.

Asa Brown, 1892-1909; Dan Wheeler, 1910-1920; Levi Greene, 1920-1929; Ed Hodges, 1929-1952; Raymond Hendrix 1952-1961; Frank Walker, 1961-1967; Alfred Gibson, 1967-1968; Sherrill Wellborn, 1969-1971; Rex Shumate May 1971 — Dec. 1971; Wade Phillips 1972-1974 and Clifford Johnson 1974-present.

Clerks of this church have served as follows; William Fairchilds, June, 1849 — March, 1853; Thomas Land, March, 1853 — June, 1870; William Waters, June, 1870 — Feb., 1889; T.C. Land, Feb., 1889 — July, 1891; G.F. Hendrix, July, 1891 — Dec., 1905; W.O. Barnette, Dec. 1905 — Feb. 1956; Ray Welborn, Feb. 1956 — Sept. 1978; Bobbie Hawkins, Sept. 1978 — present.

Ministers have been ordained as follows: November, 1854, Linville Land; January, 1858, William R. Miller; September, 1859, A.B. West; and August, 1876, L.B. West.

A Sunday School is first mentioned in the minutes in March, 1879, when the church agreed to organize a Sunday School, in February, 1881, the church sent delegates to a Sunday School meeting at Mount Pleasant and on the 4th Sunday in April, 1881, they made a favorable report to the church and reorganized Sunday School. In 1888, T.H. West, was elected superintendent and served until 1899, T.C. Land, 1899-1900; T.H. West, 1900-1902, N.H. Robinett, 1902-1903; C.M. Triplette, 1903-1904; S.J. Barnette, 1904-1908; William Minton, 1908-1910; W.O. Barnette, 1910-1914; N.H. Robinette, 1914-1918; W.M. Minton, 1918-1919; S.J. Barnette, 1919-1925; Mrs. I.S. Walsh, 1925-1927; Lelia Barnette, 1927-1929; W.O. Barnette, 1929-1955; Paul Welborn, 1955-1971; Dickie Welborn, 1972-1977 and Danny Walker, 1977 — present. The Sunday School started in 1879 with 25 students and one office and has progressed until last year the enrollment was 80 students with 14 officers and teachers.

Sources: Church minutes and personal knowledge and memories. Research by Bobbie Hawkins.

NORTH WILKESBORO

A charter was granted for "New Wilkesboro" by the legislature of North Carolina of 1891. Citizens of Wilkesboro objected to the name, so to compromise, the name was changed to "North Wilkesboro", so that an act was passed and ratified on 4 March, 1891.

The following officers were named in the Charter to hold office until May 1, 1892: A.A.

Finley, major, E.S. Blair, M. Joines, G.A. Allison, W.A. McLean, J.R. Finley, commissioners, and J.U. Grant, constable.

Among the first citizens of the town were the Abshers, Allison, Blairs, Brames, Cashions, Churches, Combs, Foresters, Finleys, Gordons, Grants, Gwyns, Harts, Hortons, Joines, McLeans, Moores, Myers, Smoots, Trogdons, Walters and others.

North Wilkesboro is a town in south central Wilkes County, which was named for the county seat, Wilkesboro, across the Yadkin River to the south. The site was described as Mulberry Fields, a former Cherokee Indian area, in a report of the Moravian Surveyors in 1752. It appears as Mulberry Fields on the Collect map of 1770.

There were two old farms in Wilkes County near the junction of Reddies and Yadkin Rivers, with a population, all told owners, renters and laborers of not over thirty souls. About this time there was in the course of construction a railroad from Greensboro by the way of Winston and Elkin, to Wilkesboro, a distance of about one hundred and three miles. This railroad stopped on the north side of the Yadkin River and east of the Reddies River. Around this terminus and on these two farms sprang up the busy, bustling little town of North Wilkesboro, whose population in 1900 was 916 and in 1906, 2,000. The first train arrived on the new railroad 30 August 1890.

One of the founders of the new town was Willard Franklin Trogdon, who was born on his father's farm near Millboro, Randolph County, 5 February 1854, the son of Solomon Franklin and Dorcas Arretta Odell Trogdon. He was well educated and had an excellent business background in salesmanship before he sold his property in Greensboro in 1890 and invested the proceeds in the upbuilding of North Wilkesboro.

In June 1890, while the railroad was being built up along the Yadkin River, Mr. Trogdon began negotiations for the 100 acres of land along the railroad right-of-way at its proposed terminus and the same year became secretary and treasurer of the Winston Land and Improvement Company. He was part owner of several other companies for financing and carrying on the construction work in the building of the new town, and personally at his own expense advertised the town all over North Carolina. He built and owned eleven brick store buildings and the Deposit and Savings Bank building, and several frame stores and dwelling houses. These things inspired confidence in North Wilkesboro and its growth was thus assured.

The Backbone of N. Wilkesboro

Mr. Trogdon's knowledge of the tanning business led to the establishment of the Smoot tanners, which became the backbone of North Wilkesboro and he was one of the publishers of the first newspaper. He organized in 1903 the Deposit and Savings Bank, serving seven years as its president; in 1910 he sold controlling interest in the bank to Congressman R.L. Doughton. He served as mayor and town commissioner and was one of the organizers of the Methodist Church and Sunday School.

Old Brame Drug Store on the Square (1913).

Street Scene, (1900s).

Parade down B Street (1908).

Float in Prade (1908).

High Wheeled Autos (1909).

"A Taxi for Hire, Bill Hart, Driver".

John Spark's Elephant Fair (1908-1916).

Street Scene (1900s).

The J. Gordon Hackett Home was built in 1907 by J.F. Allen Construction Co. for J. Gordon Hackett, a prominent citizen of Wilkes County, who served as Postmaster in North Wilkesboro and on the State Highway Commission. Isaac and Ann Duncan bought the home in 1959.

North Wilkesboro is built on high ground, almost surrounded by the Blue Ridge and Brushy Mountains, overlooking the beautiful Yadkin Valley. After the land was bought by the improvement company, it was surveyed and plotted off into lots and streets and laid out with mathematical precision and regularity, and the first work of the company was to grade and finish up many of the streets, build some large public buildings in the best manner and style, notably a graded school building, an opera house, bank building and others, and then invite the public to buy and occupy. At its first sale of lots, many small investors invested in cheap lots in the western part of the town and erected cheap frame stores and shops and went into business. Today these small purchasers are the most prosperous businessmen in the town and their cheap frame buildings have been replaced by solid brick blocks and the town continues to enlarge its borders.

One of the earliest citizens stated that few board sidewalks had been built and it was twelve or fifteen years before concrete walks and paved streets became realities. He also said that several bar rooms were in the town in its early history and that it was not safe for a lady to walk the streets alone in the day light.

North Wilkesboro is the shipping point for a larger territory than any other depot in the State. The people of more than six counties sell their produce, lumber, grain and fruit here. The town is recognized as a summer health resort from June until October. The Brushy Mountain Iron and Lithia Springs are noted for their curative powers, and are only six miles from the town.

"In 1906, North Wilkesboro had two banks,

twenty-six large brick store houses, three drug stores, wholesale dry goods, grocery and hardware stores, five churches, three hotels, a graded school, a tannery, two large roller mills, a foundry and machine shop, harness manufacturing establishments, ladies hat factory, wholesale lumber dealers, locust pin factory and many other businesses. The town ships more oak and poplar lumber, roots and herbs, green apples, chickens, eggs, dried fruit, leather and country bacon than any other town in the State.''

Sources: Views of North Wilkesboro (1906), *N.C. Gazetteer* by Powell (1968), Remarks by J.E. Finley to Woman's Club Meeting 22 February, 1923, *The Wilkes Journal*, The Wilkes Journal 28 October, 1928, "Life of W.F. Trogdon".

FAIRMOUNT

I consider myself to be very lucky in that my grandmother lived in an interesting old house when I was a little boy — the kind of house with a big attic full of things to look through, a basement with all sorts of hiding places, and a bannister rail going down two storys of stairs to slide on. Now I appreciate her house because it has quite a history to it.

The house, which is now located at 707 Kensington Avenue in North Wilkesboro, was built in the early 19th century and was named "Fairmount" by one of its owners. The original site of Fairmount was on the hilltop which was later cut down and is now the location of the North Wilkesboro Post Office. Fairmount, moved down the hill by sliding it on logs, is now across Kensington Avenue on the north side of the post office and is the oldest house in North Wilkesboro.

On this hilltop, approximately three-quarters of a mile north and east of where the Reddies River joins the Yadkin, early settlers of the region built a kind of fort, known as the Black House. Here they could seek refuge when attacked by the Indians.

The slope of the hill was kept clear of trees and undergrowth so the savages could be shot before they reached the fort. After the Black House was destroyed, possibly by fire, a second house called the Red House was built on the same spot, and parts of it are to be found today in Fairmount.

All of what is now Wilkes County was in the tract of land given by King Charles II of England to John Carteret, Earl of Granville, in 1663. On October 27, 1752 Granville's agent granted a 354-acre section to Morgan Bryan which was later called Mulberry Fields and included what is now downtown North Wilkesboro.

Real estate speculation seems to have been Morgan Bryan's main occupation, and he and his family moved often. This new land granted him by Lord Granville was then the outermost fringe of white civilization.

In 1753 a group of Moravians came from Pennsylvania looking for a place in the Granville holdings for a church community. They started their search on the south side of the Yadkin and upon reaching the river did not cross, according to local legend, because the Indians were having a corn dance where North Wilkesboro now is. The true reason the Moravians stopped at the river is because the Mul-

1890 photograph of Fairmount with private railroad car of Col. A.B. Andrews which was attached to the first train in August 1890.

The center of the city, Kensington Heights, upon which stands Fairmount, the oldest residence in North Wilkesboro.

Dr. W.P. Horton Residence.

berry Fields had already been taken by Morgan Bryan.

The Bryans settled on the forks of the Yadkin in what is now Davie County in 1748, and were joined there later by several other families, including the Boones. Of his nine children, it was Joseph to whom Morgan Bryan willed Mulberry Fields. Joseph's daughter, Rebecca, married Daniel Boone, the famous explorer. I don't believe any of the Bryans or Boones ever lived at Mulberry Fields.

Joseph Bryan sold this tract to Marmaduke Kimbrough in 1865, who sold it to John Payne, who sold it to Charles Gordon in 1775.

Charles Gordon had three sons, all of whom fought in the battle of Kings Mountain, and the youngest, Chapman, met Charity King, whose father owned the mountain. They married and came to Wilkes to live in the Red House, forerunner of my grandmother's house. (Much later, one of their grandsons, John Brown Gordon, was twice governor of Georgia, a U.S. Senator, and a famous Confederate general.)

Meanwhile, sometime before 1845, the firm of Finley and Waugh had bought many tracts of land in Wilkes County, and in dividing them between themselves that year, W.P. Waugh conveyed his half interest in the 300 acres known as the Red House tract or Mulberry Fields to his cousin, Major John Finley. Two

Dr. George Doughton's Residence.

E.S. Blair's Residence.

months later Major Finley conveyed it to his son, Augustus W. Finley, who with his wife, Martha, enlarged the house and named it "Fairmount."

General Stoneman

Near the end of the Civil War General George Stoneman of the Union Army campaigned through this area. Stoneman's army came across the mountains and followed the Yadkin River eastward, and on March 29, 1865, the 12th Ohio Cavalry drove the Confederates from Wilkesboro, capturing their horses and supplies. The 10th Michigan Cavalry and the 15th Pennsylvania Cavalry were moved to the north bank of the Yadkin the next day, under the command of Col. W.J. Palmer. The 12th Ohio followed, leaving a small group led by an officer named Busby to show Stoneman where to ford the river.

In his journal Busby noted: "We are at last come to a wider river, which is running wild, and which we soon found we are about to cross. A large house with a Piazza on it was on the right of where we came out, as I could see a man moving about on it. I took it for granted that Colonel Palmer had taken that house for his headquarters and with his field glasses was looking for the head of Stoneman's command.

"The river rose a foot or more. "How long has it been since they crossed?" Stoneman asked me upon his arrival. "Easily an hour and a half," I replied. (Swearing does not look well in print, so what he said you will not know . . .) The water was coming down in sheets. With the rain coming down in torrents and the mud knee-deep, and the stuff warm in the stills, our brave allies were driven to drink. Stoneman was blaming the officers for this and was calling them down . . . Now as the 2nd and 3rd Brigades camped on the south side of the Yadkin below Wilkesboro and Palmer's brigade on the north, Mallaby opened communications with Palmer by signal. Palmer appeared on the piazza of the house where he was staying, field glasses in hand. All this time Palmer was signaling with flags. At night torches replaced flags.

"The following message came from Col. Palmer March 31, 1865, at 3:30 p.m. "My command will go on from this position to Hickerson's plantation nine miles from here . . . unless I meet courier at Roaring River . . . No enemy is to be seen this side of the river. W.J. Palmer, Col."

The house where Palmer was staying, with its piazza, on the north side of the river and just east of Wilkesboro was Fairmount.

Soon after the Civil War, General Robert F. Hoke sent to Wilkes to put down the bushwackers a group of renegade soldiers who were terrorizing the citizens, also made this plantation house his headquarters.

A New Town

After Augustus Finley died in 1889, his heirs and those of his brother, William, joined together to sell one thousand acres of land to the Winston Land and Improvement Company, which wanted to build a town at the terminus of the new railroad, across from Wilkesboro. During the development of the new town, which they named North Wilkesboro, the land company rented out Fairmount for a long time.

In 1911 Walter Horton purchased ten acres, including Fairmount, divided it into a number of lots and named the hill Kensington Heights. The next year he had the old house placed on logs and moved down the slope about a hundred yards. There he remodeled it for his bride, removing the end chimneys and the full-length front porch.

Then in 1922 the house was bought by my grandparents, Mr. and Mrs. Daniel Jennings Carter, who lived there from then on. My grandfather died in 1945 and my grandmother in 1980.

In 1969 Grier Suttlemyre of the N.C. Department of Archives and History chose Fairmount for study as an historic house and made a professional appraisal of it. Later he wrote my grandmother, "After our investigation of the framing in the cellar and examination of the mantel and the stair, we feel safe in saying that the house is an exceptional and sophisticated example of federal period architecture. Your dating it as prior to 1808 is quite in order with details of construction."

Fairmount has known many interesting occupants and events in its long history. Our family has been privileged to be one of its owners.

Sources: *Happy Valley*, Felix Hickerson; *The Land of Wilkes*, Johnson J. Hayes, Heritage Press, 1962; *Wilkes County Sketches*, J. Jay Anderson, 1976; "The Red House, later Named Fairmount," Miss Elizabeth Finley; "Along the Way," Conrad Alexander; *Dictionary of N.C. Biography*, W.S. Powell, UNC Press, 1979; abstracted deeds of Rowan and Wilkes Counties; notes and correspondence of Mrs. D.J. Carter. Research by Daniel Carter Ogburn.

THE LAND OF THE WATAGIS, 1925

Northwestern North Carolina, the one-time stomping ground of Daniel Boone, Benjamin Cleveland and Montford Stokes, the land of lofty mountains, deep ravines, green pastures and primeval forests; the land of fried chicken, country ham, mountain cheese and cold buttermilk; the summerland of cool breezes in which you pull up the blanket before morning is at last coming into her own. Since the coming of good roads and automobiles this mountain country's beauty is being heralded abroad by tourists and summer visitors from all sections of the United States.

North Wilkesboro, the key to this summer playground, has developed into a thriving city with beautiful homes, furniture factories, corn mill factories, cotton and knitting mills, moulding and flooring factories, lumber finishing mills, the largest herbarium in the

"A Former Mayor and Friends" (1922).

world, the largest tannery in the south, good hotels and boarding houses, good schools and churches, a good hospital, a fine water and light system and with more miles of paved streets and sidewalks than any city of its size in the United States. This city nestles among hills on the north side of the beautiful Yadkin, shut in by the peaks of the Blue Ridge and Brushy Mountains. No better place for spending the summer vacation can be found and the country is fast waking up to this fact. North Wilkesboro, in the no distant future, will be the center of a great summer playground. Real estate values, in this section, especially in North Wilkesboro, have advanced from 200 to 500 per cent within the last five or six years.

North Carolinians or others looking for opportunities to do something for people, for opportunities to make money fast, or for a home in a land where sweet rest is filled with maple syrup and buckwheat cakes, will make no mistake if they head their automobiles toward North Wilkesboro and Daniel Boone's land of the Watagis.

Source: *Wilkes Journal,* 6 August 1925, written by T.G. Perry for the Charlotte Observer.

THE TANNERY

Already much has been written about the C.C. Smoot and Sons Company Tannery which came to Wilkes County in 1895.

It brought in personnel from outside the county who either brought with them or later established families here.

Mr. J.C. Smoot came when the tannery opened, but his family maintained their residence in Alexandria, Virginia for several years.

John N. Ashkettle, originally from Orleans Cross-Roads, W. Va. came early as a bark inspector to determine the supply of wood and bark.

A.R. Sherman, from Berkeley Springs, W. Va. came as the first superintendent. C.P. Walter, also from Berkeley Springs, came with his family in November 1897. Later came H.L. Mechem with his family and J.N. Shockey from the same town.

George Johnson, Sr. came as foreman of the dry-loft from Alexandria, Va. Edwin I. Kendall in 1895 and H.B. Dodson in October 1896 came from Sperryville, Va. where they were previously employed in a Smoot tannery. Also from there came A.K. Pearson, a native of Sweden, and B.F. Estes.

With the exception of Mr. Pearson, Mr. Sherman and Mr. Shockey, all of these persons have present day descendants living in Wilkes.

Eleven years after the tannery began operation the following was written: "North Wilkesboro claims to have not one of the largest, but the largest steam tanneries in the South, a branch of the C.C. Smoot & Sons Company of Alexandria, Va. This enterprise was brought here in 1895, and is a plant covering acres of land with its buildings, and employing from one hundred to two hundred hands, with a large pay roll, and turning out hundreds of thousands of dollars worth of finished leather annually, furnishing a market for all the chestnut oak bark that can be obtained in all the surrounding counties, at prices that go to enlarge the income of the farmers who own the bark lands.

During bark season you can see from one hundred to three hundred wagons daily on their yard, unloading bark and receiving the cash. Besides this, many car loads of bark are

"The Tannery."

"Tanner's Rest."

OPERA HOUSE HOTEL

In the 21 June 1905 issue of the *Chronicle* newspaper, a news item reads: "Mr. Trogdon is having the opera building in North Wilkesboro arranged for a hotel building." This building was completed by 1906 and was erected on the north east corner of D and Fifth Streets, fronting one hundred feet on Fifth and one hundred thirty five feet along D. It was Lots 21, 22, 23 and 24 in Block 51 as shown on Trogdon's Map of North Wilkesboro and was owned by The State Company, W.F. Trogdon, President.

On the 2nd August 1911, The State Company sold the above property to F.D. Forester & Company for $6,000.00 and the deed states "Whereon now stands the large brick opera house building." On the 1st day of November 1922, the property was sold by the F.D. Forester Company to the Vestry of Saint Paul's Episcopal Church of Wilkesboro for $2,800.90, the Vestymen being H.H. Morehouse, C.C. Smoot, 3rd, Clarence Call, J.B. McCoy, and W.W. Barber, Jr. On the 21st of September 1943, St. Paul's Episcopal Church of Wilkesboro, through its Vestrymen, J.B. McCoy, W.W. Barber, Joe R. Barber, Joe E. Johnson, L.B. Dula, Paul Osborne, H.H. Morehouse and R.L. Morehouse, sold the property for

shipped in from Elkin, Mt. Airy, and other railroad points. This company is constantly enlarging its plant and contributing to the improvement of the town in many ways."

On January 1, 1925, the International Shoe Company began operation of the tannery, having purchased it from the original owners. The employees remained the same with the following listed in a newspaper account: C.P. Walter, superintendent; J.C. Grayson, cashier; E.G. Finley, superintendent of bark and wood; Joe Kyellander, manager of the plants in Morganton and North Wilkesboro.

Other persons, with their families, came in time to be employed by the tannery. These included: J.D. Schaefer, Frank Johnson, Carl Wonner, Jeff Rhodes and H.V. Wagoner.

Excerpts from an account of the operation of the tannery written in 1929 by a high school student follows: "As an aid in the study of a health problem in Civics, members of the Civic class of the North Wilkesboro high school visited the Wilkes Tannery here.

The Tanning Process

The process that the leather goes through is very interesting. It takes one hide four months to go through the whole process of tanning. The hides come from the western states and South America.

First, the hides are soaked, then limed, and after that the hair is taken off. Then the flesh is taken off and the hides are cleaned. They are again soaked over night, then tanned and afterwards cut in strips. Next the hides are bleached then oiled and dried again. Then the hides are dipped in water, smoothed and dried again. The hides are sponged and rolled and again dried; then washed and dried again. Next they are brushed, sorted, rolled up and packed. The leather is then shipped to the factory at St. Louis, Missouri, to be used in the making of shoes.

The hair taken from the hides is washed and dried, bailed up and shipped to the mattress and rug factories. The trimmings off the hides are sent to glue factories.

The tanning materials used on the hides are as follows: Chestnut oak bark and chestnut

wood from Wilkes County; Kuebracho from Argentina; Cutch from the Phillippine Islands and Barneo; Myrabalams, from Ceylon and Wattle bark from South Africa.

The tannery generates its own power and lights. River water is used for tanning purposes. Fire and accident prevention is urged and bills are posted over the plant concerning that. The plant is kept clean. The men that work in cleaning, tanning and oiling the hides wear aprons and boots to keep dry. The tannery is also well ventilated by means of fans and windows."

The disastrous flood of 1940 with an accompanying fire damaged the plant greatly. Tanning operation ceased, but the plant, with J.D. Schaefer as manager, continued as an extract plant until 1945.

Sources: "North Wilkesboro Views (1906)"; *The Wilkes Journal*, April 18, 1929; Personal research, by Mary S. Smithey.

The Opera House Hotel (Sketch by Edward Wood).

THE FLUME: The Flume was built in the early 1900s by the Giant Lumber Company and used by the company until the flood of 1916, which destroyed it. The Flume was built in order for the lumber, which was planed at sawmills along its route from trees cut in the mountains, to be sent to the newly founded town of North Wilkesboro. The Flume followed the body of water called Reddies River, was constructed of wood in a trough-like manner and the lumber was floated through this contraption by means of a constant flow of water in the trough. The milled planks were nailed together before placing them in the flume and when the lumber reached its destination in North Wilkesboro, the nails were drawn from the lumber, returned to the various sawmills along the route and used for the next batch that was sent down.

Covered bridge over the Reddies River (end of D Street, 1935).

NORTH WILKESBORO GRADE SCHOOL BUILDING (Sketch by Edward Wood).

$6,500.00 to Mr. and Mrs. C.O. McNiel. It was owned by Mrs. McNiel at the time of her death in October 1981.

The building was built primarily for a place of entertainment, to house business offices and possibly a bank. It is fact that it was used for entertainment, and after the F.D. Forester Company bought it, it was used to store roots and herbs, as well as an athletic underwear factory the company operated. At one time it housed what became the Wilkes Hosiery Mill. There is no record that it was ever used as a hotel.

The opera house building burned on Saturday night, 8th January 1921. Miss Ruth Linney wrote an eyewitness account of the fire in a diary she kept, that of the awesome sight the fire made, the falling of the walls impressed her the most.

Sources: *Chronicle* Newspaper, Wilkes deeds, Ruth Linney Diary.

BLUE RIDGE INSTITUTE

Around 1900 a private preparatory school, the Blue Ridge Institute, was established in North Wilkesboro. Owned by a number of local Baptists, it was, nevertheless, open to all leading denominations. During its first year, the enrollment was recorded as one hundred forty-seven children, many of them room and board students who lived in private homes in the area for $6.50 a month.

Tuition rates for the school were from one dollar to three dollars a month with musical instruction extra at two dollars per month.

Courses were offered for the study of the three "r's" plus Bible, Georgraphy, History, Science, Latin, Physiology and Hygiene, Greek, Botany and Zoology, Roman History, Greek History, Civil Government, Chemistry and Geology.

The first principal of the school was Professor R.P. Johnson and the second Mr. W.R. Bradshaw. The primary teacher was Mrs. Mary Wilborn. Dr. W.P. Horton instructed

North Wilkesboro Grade School Children (ca 1906). Front Row, L to R: Mamie Williams, Nellie Hart, Mamie Jones, Mabel Hampton, Agnes Walter, Beatrice Myers, Della Brewer, Hattie McLean. Back Row, L to R: Annie Robinette, Hattie McNeill, Minnie Brown, Belle Faw, Minnie Turner, Willie Pardue, Flossie Hendren, Estelle Myers.

young men wishing to go into the study of medicine while Dr. L.A. Hauser taught the principles of dentistry. Lawyer F.B. Hendren gave lessons to any pupil desiring to study law.

A description of the location and surroundings of the Institute was included in the catalogue as follows: "The Blue Ridge Institute is admirable located. The town of North Wilkesboro, itself, is notable for its beautiful natural environment. The school building is one of the largest, most modern and best constructed in all this section. It is furnished with good desks. Besides the school rooms, there is a large chapel which will be used for lectures,

entertainments and other activities. Near by the building is a play ground.

The building is located on a knoll, overlooking the Yadkin River, and in full view of the Brushy Mountains and the Blue Ridge (near the present sight of the old North Wilkesboro Elementary School building). We have daily trains. A phone system penetrating adjoining counties.

The health of the town is good. In sending them here, parents run very little risk of endangering the health of their children. The social and religious influences are excellent. No small part of a child's education is derived from the people with whom it comes in con-

North Wilkesboro First Baptist Church (1892-1912).

North Wilkesboro First Baptist Church (1912-1966). (Sketch by Edward Wood.)

WILKES SUFFRAGETTES: A group of Wilkes County women strike a pose for the right to vote, sometime before the Constitutional Amendment of 1920. Among those pictured are: (front row, second from left) Mrs. Dan (Lewis) Carter and (front row, far right) Mrs. Archie (Bernice) Horton. The identities of the others are unknown.

tact. Then we can say that North Wilkesboro is a most suitable location for a school. No place in all this section of our state can afford all the advantages which are found here. Therefore, we ask you to send your children to our school."

The school's Board of Directors was: Dr. W.P. Horton, president; R.L. Church, vice-president; C.P. Andrews, secretary; A.M. McGee, treasurer; D.W. Mayberry, auditor.

Source: Blue Ridge Institute Catalogue, 1902.

THE FRIDAY AFTERNOON BOOK CLUB

The Friday Afternoon Book Club "grew out of a spirit of friendship in the hearts of the women in our little town." Mesdames J.Q. Myers, W.R. Absher, and W.F. Trogdon met at Mrs. Trogdon's home on 15 February 1907 to make plans for the club.

The name of the club was chosen, and the following ladies were invited to be members and all accepted: Mesdames W.F. Trogdon, W.R. Absher, J.Q. Myers, R.M. Brame, Genio Cardwell, M.H. Church, J.L. Clements, Sr., C.D. Coffey, Sr. J.E. Finley, T.B. Finley, J.C. Henry, W.P. Horton, C.W. Moseley, R.W. Gwyn, Matt Palmer Houck and Leonard Vyne. A date was set to meet, select books, and discuss programs.

The Book Club remained a group of twenty members for several years. Through the years others joined and the present club numbers fourteen active and two inactive members. A number of these are daughters of former members.

Programs did not bother the club for awhile

because flinch and rook were played at the meetings. In 1908, the club members entertained their husbands at the home of Mr. and Mrs. J.E. Finley. In 1909, the husbands and members were entertained at the Gordon Hotel with Dr. and Mrs. J.Q. Myers as hosts. All wore colonial costumes and "some of the younger ones did the old Virginia Reel."

When the club was organized in 1907, the ladies wore high collars, long sleeves and skirts which touched the ground, but the attire of present-day members is quite different, perhaps more comfortable, but the varied programs and books shared at the meetings are still being enjoyed.

Source: A history written by Mrs. R.M. Brame, Sr. in 1953

NORTH WILKESBORO FIRST BAPTIST CHURCH

First Baptist Church was organized 17 December, 1892, with fifteen charter members, as follows: Madora Arabella Absher, Nancy Jane Absher, William Matthew Absher, Jane Byrd, A.M. Church, Harvey Church, Mary L. Church, Lilly Church, Mary Octavia Church, Susanna Church, Augusta E. Forester, W.P. Horton, A.M. McGee, Mary C. McGee, H.B. Parker, Jr.

A wooden structure at Sixth and F Streets was used from 1892 until 1912. In January, 1912, the congregation held is first worship service in the new brick building on the corner of Sixth and D Streets. This building served as the place of worship from 1912 until 14 August, 1966, when the new Sanctuary was completed. From 1966 until February 1974 the

older building was used for many activities. On 14 February, 1974, demolition was started. All agreed it was a well-built building, beautiful in architecture, and had served its congregation well through many years.

Source: History of the church.

FIRST BAPTIST CHURCH

The forerunner of First Baptist Church on B Street was "The Church in the Bottom," which was founded by Brothers Simon Davenport, Jake Isenhour, Pink McCurdy and Jim Reynolds. It began near the old Tannery in a house donated by Frank Blair, Sr. This first church had a membership of fifteen.

Under the leadership of Rev. Ford, the church grew in membership and there was soon a pressing need for a larger structure. Land was purchased in the Tannery area at the present site where a church building was erected and named First Baptist Church.

Rev. G.W. Montgomery of Salisbury was the next minister of First Baptist. Others who served were: Revs. Williams, Ramsou, W.H. Sharrell, L.C. Foster, J.W. Hairston, J.W. Caldwell, and J.J. Alexander.

In more recent years pastors who have served the church are: Rev. T.M. Walker who came on March 26, 1946, as a part-time pastor. In June, 1947, he moved into the community and became a full-time pastor. Under his leadership forty-seven members were added to the church roll. The Nunn property next door was purchased and a parsonage was erected.

In April, 1953, Rev. M.R. Silva accepted the call to serve the church. Under his leadership eight new members were added to the church roll and physical improvements were made.

Rev. S.P. Thomas of Troutman was the next pastor. Under his leadership stained-glass windows were installed, Sunday School rooms and a kitchen were added and a Hammond organ was purchased. The cornerstone of the church was laid in a formal ceremony. Twenty-three members were added to the church roll. Rev. Thomas resigned on February 12, 1961.

Rev. C.C. Harris of Wilkesboro served as supply pastor on the first and third Sundays of each month. Rev. J.S. Norris was called in January, 1962, to serve along with Rev. Harris. Twenty-three members were added to the membership under the leadership of these two pastors.

Rev. M.A. Nimmo of Greensboro officially assumed his duties in January, 1963. Several improvements were made to the building and twenty-seven members were added to the church roll during this four years of service.

Rev. E.E. Harris of Newton was called as supply pastor in October, 1967. Under his leadership the church was renovated and the dedication service was held in September, 1973.

Rev. R.W. Barber of Wilkesboro served first as supply pastor and then was installed as regular pastor in June, 1974. Under his leadership central air-conditioning was added and another bus was purchased. Because of Rev. Barber's failing health, Rev. John A. Speaks was called to serve as an assistant pastor in December, 1977.

Rev. Speaks was installed as the regular

COLORED BAPTIST CHURCH
North Wilkesboro, N. C.

pastor in January, 1978. Under his leadership the church has grown both spiritually and financially. New pews, new carpet and a new piano have been added, and the church has been cleared of all indebtedness. Fifteen members have been added to the church roll. First Baptist Church continues to progress under the leadership of Rev. Speaks.

Source: *The Centennial Year of the Yadkin Valley Missionary Baptist Association 1880-1980.*

FIRST METHODIST CHURCH

It was in the early nineties that Reverend E.A. Wiley, Pastor of the Wilkesboro Circuit, canvassed among the few people living in North Wilkesboro at the time and found several Methodists. They were mostly in the families of Presbyterians and Baptists, for the majority of native Christians of Wilkes were one of these faiths. However, Brother Wiley obtained the names of five who agreed that, if enough Methodists could be found to organize a church, they would move their membership from home churches. And so, on November 25, 1892, in an old printing office on the corner of D and Fifth streets at the rear of the Opera House, the First Methodists Church of North Wilkesboro was organized with the following members present: W.F. Trogdon and wife, Lizzie; J.L. Turner and wife Ella E.; Miss Mary Church; Miss Lou Church; T.J. Lowery; John A. Cashion and wife Fannie; W.M. Darlington and wife; James B. Church and wife; and Mrs. W.P. Horton.

During the year of 1894, the Reverend S.P. Douglas was instrumental in leading the congregation in building a small church located on the present property. A four-room parsonage was soon added.

The splendid work done by the women during the building of the parsonage and the church was crystalized in the organization of the Woman's Missionary Society in the year 1897. In 1940, the Woman's Missionary Society became the Woman's Society of Christian Service and expanded its work to all aspects of the church program. As of 1973, the women's organization became the United Methodist Women and still, as in the early days, remain deeply involved in the life of the church.

During the pastorate of the Reverend Parker Holmes (1908-1912), a larger church with stained glass windows and a pipe organ was built. It was during this time that the church became a station.

During the year 1937, the first church kitchen was built and equipped, this room being added to the Scout Hut to which three classrooms for the Sunday School had already been constructed. During the pastorate of Dr. Gilbert R. Combs, this entire building was torn down to made room for the present educational building and chapel, which were occupied in the spring of 1949.

In February, 1953, the old church building was torn down to make room for the new sanctuary. The first service held in the new church was on April 8, 1954, Easter Sunday. The Reverend John H. Carper was the pastor at this time. On Easter Sunday morning, April 1, 1956, upon authorization of J.R. Hix, Chair-

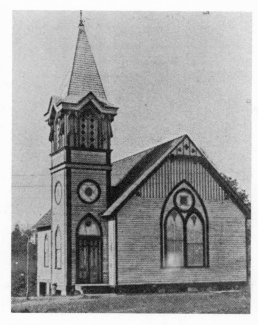

First Methodist Church (1894).

man of the Finance Committee, Reverend Carper announced the liquidation of all indebtedness from the church property.

On Sunday, November 25, 1956, the 64th anniversary of the church's beginning, the First Methodist Church was dedicated by Bishop Noland B. Harmon, assisted by Reverend Garland Stafford, Superintendent of the North Wilkesboro District, and Reverend John R. Carper, Pastor.

In all ways throughout the years since its humble beginnings, the First United Methodist Church has been, and is continuing to be, faithful in its mission for Christ at home and around the world.

Sources: Church Directory and Church History.

PRESBYTERIAN CHURCH

The North Wilkesboro Presbyterian Church was built before the actual organization of the church, which was on July 29, 1893. Eleven persons were received by letter from the Wilkesboro Presbyterian Church. There were two elders and two deacons.

Reverend C.W. Robinson became pastor in 1895, resigned in 1904, called back in 1906. He served forty three years, dying in January 1938.

The Reverend Watt M. Cooper was installed on April 3, 1938. He had been assistant pastor for two years. There were one hundred and seventy members on the roll then.

In January 1940, work was started on new religious education building, a building of native stone to accomodate an eventual enrollment of about 500. By 1942, there were 240 members. Mr. Cooper resigned this year to become Chaplain in the Navy. In 1944 the religious education building was built. The Reverend Cooper returned in December 1945, and in 1947 a new church building fund was growing. On April 11, 1948, the last service was held in the little white frame church building. It had served needs of the congregation for more than 54 years, from 16 members to 300.

North Wilkesboro Presbyterian Church.

Work on the new building began in April 1948, under the supervision of A.A. Cashion, Elder, who gave every day for eighteen months to this work. The first service was held on September 11, 1949. The new church building is Gothic in design and built of native stone. Mr. Cooper left in October to serve another pastorate. A full time director for Christian Education was employed.

The Rev. James B. MacLeod became pastor in September 1950. The church was dedicated on April 12, 1953. A church kindergarten was started in the fall of 1954. Mr. MacLeod resigned December 15, 1956 and Rev. Watt Cooper returned as pastor March 1, 1957.

A new manse was completed October 1958. Mr. Cooper retired August 31, 1970. The Rev. James P. Barksdale was installed as pastor October 18, 1970.

Sources: Church records.

WILKES COUNTY HISTORICAL SOCIETY

Wilkes County Historical Society was organized March 30, 1954 at the City Hall in North Wilkesboro for the purpose of collecting and preserving facts about Wilkes County, and to develop a greater interest and pride in it.

During its twenty-eight years of existence the Society has had many varied and informative programs. From time to time the Society made interesting historical tours, usually inside the county.

Sizable contributions have been made by the Society to Old Wilkes Inc. to help restore and furnish the Old Jail, as well as the public library in North Wilkesboro.

During the early years the Society made successful efforts to have the State Department of Historical Markers erect one at each of these places: site of Col. Benjamin Cleveland's home, "Roundabout", site of Fort Hamby, and the homeplace of Governor Stokes "Mourne Rouge".

During the years 1959-1969 the Society sponsored essays on local history among the high schools and elementary schools of the county. First, second and third prizes of cash were awarded at the April meeting each year. All of these prize winning essays were read by the authors to the Society, and then filed with the curator.

The following presidents served the Society: T.E. Story 1954-Jan. 1968; Leonard Brooks Jr. 1968-1970; Mrs. Annie Winkler 1970-1971; and Jay Anderson October 1971-

Source: The original Minute Book.

LIBERTY GROVE LODGE NO. 407, A.F. & A.M.

(North Wilkesboro Lodge No. 407 A.F. & A.M.)

On January 11, 1888 Worshipful Brother, C.N. Robinson, Grand Master of the Grand Lodge of Ancient Free and Accepted Masons in North Carolina, and by approval of the Grand Lodge of Ancient Free and Accepted Masons of North Carolina, issued a Charter for the formation and constitution of a Masonic Lodge. Brother John S. Forester was named as Master, Brother W.M. Absher was named as Senior Warden and Brother C.N. Hunt was named as Junior Warden. And by virtue of their appointment were empowered to constitute and open a Lodge of Ancient Free and Accepted Masons. The same to be holden in Liberty Grove Baptist Church, Boyles, Wilkes County, North Carolina. The same to be distinguished by name and number as LIBERTY GROVE LODGE NO. 407, A.F. & A.M.

The minutes of the Communications of Liberty Grove Lodge No. 407, A.F. and A.M. from date of constitution until 1899 are almost non-existant and details of the activity of the lodge are sketchy.

The minutes of Liberty Grove Lodge No. 407, dated July 21, 1899, records the Lodge as meeting in the Fraternal Hall, North Wilkesboro, North Carolina. Evidently the location of the Lodge was moved in the 1890's. Also it may be assumed the Lodge was very active due to the mention of the various programs being sponsored by the Lodge as named in the 1899 Communication.

It is interesting to note the progress of the Lodge from the date of 1900 thru 1930. Which progress was made possible under the capable leadership of Brethren too numerous to name. To name a few of these dedicated Brethren as follows: W.M. Absher, A.V. Foote, C.N. Hunt, James E. Deans, James D. Moore, Leonard Vyne, E.W. Trodgon, Eli Marcus Blackburn, Rev. C.W. Robinson, Charles S. Sink, Sr., Charles Preston Walter, Walter P. Kelly, James C. Wallace, James H. Rector, Ira D. Payne, James C. Grayson and John W. Nichols, and many other Brethren.

Depression Times

The economics Depression of 1929 and the early 1930s dealt a almost fatal blow to the Lodge and the huge loss of membership was recorded. At the time of the Depression there were 16 Masonic Lodges operating in Wilkes County. At a Stated Communication of Liberty Grove Lodge No. 407, A.F. & A.M., A Motion made and Seconded and adopted that all the Lodges in Wilkes County consolidate into one lodge for survival. The minutes record that several lodges were consolidated with Liberty Grove Lodge No. 407 and the name of Liberty Grove Lodge was changed to North Wilkesboro Lodge, and that the name and number therafter be distinguished as "NORTH WILKESBORO LODGE NO. 407, A.F. & A.M." The final results of the consolidation program undertaken was that four lodges survived the Depression, namely: Liberty Lodge No. 45, Wilkesboro, N.C., North Wilkesboro Lodge No. 407, North Wilkes, N.C., Traphill Lodge No. 483, Traphill, N.C. and Mt. Pleasant Lodge No. 573, (Champion, N.C.) Rte #1, Wilkesboro, N.C. the survival and progress of the Lodge has to be attributed to the dedicated and devoted leadership of brethren such as William Kent Sturdivant, Gilbert Garret Foster, R. Eugene Sebastian, John W. Nichols, George P. Johnson, D. Elbert Elledge and numerous others.

For the period from 1950 through 1981 North Wilkesboro Lodge No. 407, A.F. and A.M. has been a dynamic and driving force in the successful endeavors of the Masonic Fraternity which is evidenced by the dedicated and devoted service of several Brethren. While they are many there are two Brethren whose long, dedicated and devoted service to Freemasonry are pointed out as Brethren who should merit our esteem. They are Brother Maurice Elledge Walsh and Brother Tam L. Shumaker. These Brethren have served Masonry long and faithful, not only on a local level, but also on County, State, National and International level, which has brought honor and esteem to the lodge by the Offices and positions which they have served, and are continuing to serve, with distinction and honor in the various Bodies of Freemasonry.

Thus at the end of the year 1981, it is recorded that North Wilkesboro Lodge No. 407, A.F. & A.M. largest Masonic Lodge in Wilkes County with an enrollment of 160 members. They now have a permanent home which is the Masonic Temple located at 203 Temple Street, North Wilkesboro, N.C.

Source: Article by Tam L. Shumaker from minutes.

THE WILKES HOSPITAL

The Wilkes Hospital, the first permanent hospital in Wilkes County, was opened April 1, 1923. It was not a gorgeous display of fireworks nor great enthusiasm on the part of the people. It was opened under very modest conditions and was a great risk financially and economically. Nevertheless, the years have proven that is was one of the most important events in the history of Wilkes County. There were many discouragements in the preparation and operation of the hospital in the early days. It is common knowledge, however, that all the great improvements and developments are always hard and associated with many discouragements.

The hospitals in North Carolina at the time of

the opening of the Wilkes Hospital were, with the exception of three or four hospitals in the state, privately owned and operated by individual doctors or groups of doctors. The Wilkes Hospital was on the lower rungs of the pioneer hospitals in North Carolina. The reasons for the establishment of the hospital was that there were no central clinics or hospitals for emergencies and patients were carried to other hospitals out of the county for treatment and hospitalization.

The argument against a hospital in Wilkes County was that there probably would not be enough support to sustain the hospital and doctors. Furthermore, there was division among the local doctors as to the need for a hospital. Many reasons could be given for this.

What prompted the idea of a hospital in Wilkes County was the fact that several leading citizens advised the establishment of the hospital and offered to help with the establishment in a financial way. Another reason was that I had been prepared following my medical course to do special work in surgery and I was looking for a job. Due consideration was given to the plans for a hospital, to the actual need for one and the advantages to the people and the doctors. After giving due consideration, it was decided to take the chance. The matter of help in operating the hospital, the location and the facilities for operating such a facility were considered. For instance, North Wilkesboro had only a light and only fairly dependable power plant so that at night before operating, we had to caution them not to cut off the power. The telephone service was not too dependable and there was no ice plant nor laundry in town. All of these items had been taken care of and considered seriously. The location was another problem but was easily solved by renting the old Tom Church residence from J.T. Prevette on the southeast corner of Eighth and E Streets which was in the center of town and well located.

I was very fortunate in securing good help for nursing: Miss Laura Turner, Miss Norma Stevenson, Miss Witherspoon, Miss Loftin, and Miss Hattie McNeil were among the first nursing help that was available. Miss Laura Turner served as superintendent as there were few, if any people trained as superintendent directors at that time. Fred Hubbard, Jr., after the first few years of operation went to Northwest University in Chicago and took a special course in hospital administration and was one of the first serving in the state.

The building was worked over and rearranged and heated and the very best of hospital equipment including a good x-ray machine and sterlizing plant were installed. It was necessary at that time for the nurses to make the dressings and sterlize them, to make all the plaster bandages, and to make up the glucose solutions because there were no companies of that date preparing these things, as well as many other things that are available today already prepared to make it easier to operate a hospital as well as benefiting the patients.

The first blood transfusions, hysterectomies, cholecystectomies, thyroidecomies, resections of the stomach, as well as many other major operations that were done in Wilkes County were done in the Wilkes Hospital. The charges were $5.00 for a private room, $3.00 for a sem-private room and $2.50 for the ward. The operating room charges were $10.00 and anesthetic was $5.00 These charges were in keeping with the charges in other hospitals in the state.

Expansion

Within the first ten to fifteen years, two additions were added to the hospital building, running it up from a ten bed hospital to start with, to a twenty-five to thirty bed hospital. The work had gradually increased and several new doctors had moved into the county following their interships and were immediately added to the active staff. In 1936 a new fire-proof addition was added with covered walkways to the old building. At the same time the old building was brick veneered and had a sprinkler system installed. The new building was modern in every respect and made it possible to provide for fifty to sixty patients. More doctors, nurses and technicians were added as the demand grew. During all this time, the people in the county had reacted wonderfully to the services rendered by the hospital. The opposition that was shown by some of the doctors to the Wilkes Hospital inside and outside the county finally proved to no avail.

The new Wilkes General Hospital was built as an extension of the Wilkes Hospital. It was funded by the federal government under the Hill-Burton Bill, the state government and the town of North Wilkesboro. It was the only municipally owned hospital in North Carolina because the town of North Wilkesboro voted the local funds which the county had refused to do.

I happened to be on the State Medical Care Commission and when our option came up, the location where the hospital now stands was selected and the funds appropriated. At the same time, I surrendered my interest in the Wilkes Hospital and joined the staff at the Wilkes General Hospital, there by making a great sacrifice. I had always envisioned a public hospital because I felt it was beyond the financial means of a local group to do it and it would be better both for the patients and the doctors. The funds provided for a new hospital of one hundred beds, well equipped. Since that time, a nurses home and a new addition of sixty beds has been added to the Wilkes General Hospital and it is now a large, busy, flourishing and great service to the people of Wilkes County and surrounding counties.

It is a godsend to the people of this section and came as did the Wilkes Hospital at a time when there were no hospitals in the northwest part of the state, Statesville and Winston-Salem being the only contacts for hospitilization before that time. The staff of nurses and doctors have been gradually increased through the years and in recent years, we have had several specialist added including an opthalmologist, a urologist, pediatrician, internist and so on.

The Women's Auxillary of the Wilkes General Hospital has served the hospital magnificently in many ways, not only in actual service but as a publicity agent.

The hospital at present is adequately supplied with well trained nurses and Licensed Practical Nurses and aids. The people are well pleased with the great service being rendered by the Wilkes General Hospital and the future looks bright for extended medical, surgical and health services to the people of Wilkes County.

Sources: Article by Dr. Fred C. Hubbard, founder of The Wilkes Hospital, corner Eight and E Streets (1982).

DEPOSIT & SAVINGS BANK

The Deposit & Savings Bank was established March 2, 1903. The officers were W.F.

Deposit & Savings Bank (1903).

Trogdon, President, W.W. Barber, Vice-President, H.O. Absher, Cashier, Miss Ella Campbell, Teller. The Directors were W.W. Barber, Attorney-at-Law, Col. P.H. Hanes, Capitalist, of Winston-Salem, Spencer Blackburn, member of Congress, John E. McEwen, Ex-Sheriff of Wilkes County, R. Don Laws, Editor Yellow Jacket, F.D. Forester, Wholesale Merchant, J.M. Welbron, Harness Manufacturer, H.O. Absher, President of The W.M. Absher Company, F.D. Hackett, Attorney-at-Law, and W.F. Trogdon, Real Estate and Insurance. Capital Stock paid in $20,000.00, Deposits $60,000.00, Assets, $80,000.00

This bank is three years old and we wish to publicly thank the friends of the institution who are responsible for the steady growth during each day. Its deposits nearly doubled last year and it now looks as if they will more than double this year. The bank was organized and has been developed and conducted on the principle of conservative and economical banking along progressive lines, and on this basis has gained steadily in strength, in scope and in the confidence of the public whose patronage has been freely extended, and we have striven hard to prove ourselves entitled to this gratifying and remarkable growth.

The equipment of our banking house, including the steel fire-proof vaults, burglar-proof safes and burglar insurance, is the most complete and inviting in this section, and every person, firm or corporation desiring the convenience, protection and courteous service of a well regulated bank are invited to favor us with their banking business, whether large or small; all are welcome. Four per cent, per annum compound interest allowed on savings deposits.

Source: Views of North Wilkesboro (1906).

THE BANK OF NORTH WILKESBORO

From nearly nothing to about three millions in resources, that is the fifty year history of the Bank of North Wilkesboro.

Fifty years ago in March 1892, less than a year after North Wilkesboro had been organized as a municipality, the Bank of North Wilkesboro was formed and chartered to serve the infant village and the surrounding countryside.

The railroad from Winston-Salem had just been completed a short time before, and a few forward-looking residents were laying the foundations for a flourishing community. A few residents who had courage to meet the obstacles and problems of that day, and the faith to lay foundations for future developement and growth, wanted banking facilities to finance their promotional activities and commercial life.

They began the bank with capital stock of only $20,000. and with only $10,000. actually paid in. The Dimmette building, one of the town's first brick buildings, was rented as the first banking house. At the time, the available savings of the people of this section were deposited in strong banks in other towns.

However, because of the confidence the people had in the bank's officers and directors, these deposits began to remain at home and to trickle back here in a steady stream.

The late James Edward Finley was born and reared here, but had moved to his farm in Watauga County where he was engaged in stock raising. He gave up his horses and cattle at Meat Camp in Watauga, returned to Wilkes and served as one of the founders and president of the bank until 1923, when ill health dictated his retirement. He died a few months later.

The first cashier was D.W. Greenlee; the first vice-president was J.G. Finley; the first directors were T.B. Finley, Capt. J.T. Pedien, Capt. E.S. Blair, J.E. Finley and W.M. Absher, all of whom were outstanding business and professional men of the community.

When J.R. Finley died in 1898, his brother Arthur A. Finley was elected to succeed him. The latter served the institution for forty years until his death in 1938.

In August 1892 only a few months after the bank was founded, R.W. Gwyn joined the staff and succeeded Mr. Greenlee as cashier. Mr. Gwyn's keen aptitude for banking, his faithfulness through the years, his personal and painstaking attention to details were of inestimable importance in the growth of the Bank of North Wilkesboro and in the growth of Wilkes County. Mr. Gwyn made more loans than any man in the county, probably knew more people in the county than any other man. He completed fifty years of service with the bank in August 1942.

James R. Hix was elected president of the bank in January 1923 succeeding J.E. Finley and was singularly successful.

In 1938, W.D. Halfacre, superintendent of the city schools, went with the bank as executive vice-president.

The junior officers or assistant cashiers were: W.W. Starr, J.G. McNeil, W.B. Gwyn, and J.T. Brame. Directors were J.R. Hix,

R.W. Gwyn, S.V. Tomlinson, R.G. Finley, W.E. Halfacre, Ralph Duncan, J.E. Justice, Jr. and E.M. Blackburn.

Mrs. Louise Carrigan Spruill and Miss Ruth Hubbard were long time employees of the bank. Alfred Barber, the janitor was one of the oldest employees in point of service.

From nearly nothing to about three millions in resources; that is the fifty year history of the Bank of North Wilkesboro.

Source: *Newsworld,* March 19, 1942 "50th Anniversary Observation."

NORTHWESTERN BANK

The Deposit & Savings Bank, founded in 1903, was the forerunner of the Northwestern Bank in North Wilkesboro. In 1906, the Deposit & Savings built its new building on the site of the present Northwestern Bank.

In July 1937, the Deposit & Savings Bank, along with the Merchants & Farmers' Bank of Bakersville, the Bank of Sparta, and the Watauga Bank of Boone consolidated to form The Northwestern Bank. The beginning capital at that time was $150,000; surplus $75,000; undivided profits $50,000, and deposits $2,285,000.

The bank's early leaders included men with long, impressive records of service to their communities, their home state, and their nation. Rufus A. Doughton of Sparta, who had returned home after forty years of government service, became the first president; Edwin Duncan, the first vice-president.

The Northwestern soon embarked on a period of phenomenal growth, expanding both through increased banking services and through mergers with other banks and opening additional offices until in 1981, it was the fourth largest North Carolina commercial bank, with 185 North Carolina banking offices from Raleigh westward.

Source: Newspaper article.

North Wilkesboro Building and Loan Directors. L to R: John Snyder; J.C. Reins; J. Bid Williams; A.F. Kilby; Ed Gardner; W.O. Absher; Frank Tomlinson; C.E. Jenkins, Jr.; J.H. Whicker, Jr.; R.G. Finley; W.H.H. Waugh; John Walker.

YADKIN VALLEY MOTOR COMPANY

Ford Motor Company first produced cars in 1903. The first Model T was produced for sale in 1908. Henry Ford reduced prices continually on the Model T, because of the rising profits of Ford Motor Company due to mass production. He could afford to sell for less money, resulting in more sales. By 1915 the price of a Model T Touring car was four hundred and forty dollars, which was half of it's original introduction price. The demand for an affordable automobile for the masses was so great that a Ford Dealership was considered a gold mine. Because of this attractive available investment, on March 1, 1915 at eight thirty P.M., the first meeting of Yadkin Valley Motor Company Incorporated took place at the residence of C.C. Smoot III. Officers established were C.C. Smoot III as President, his wife Rebecca as Vice President, and F.G. Harper as Secretary. F.G. Harper was the only active officer in the company. His starting salary was fifty dollars a month, later to be raised to fifteen hundred dollars a year in 1917. Between 1915 and 1918 Harper purchased the Smoot's stock.

There have been six different brands of new automobiles sold at Yadkin Valley in the past. Fords and Overlands were sold starting in 1915. In March of 1918 Overlands were dropped from the inventory and Buicks were made available for sale. In 1920 Franklins were available. Fords were better afforded by the local people and so the high priced Buicks, Overlands, and Franklins were eventually dropped for sale. Lincoln Zephyrs were sold beginning in 1937 and Mercurys in 1939.

The first car sold at Yadkin Valley was an Overland, in March of 1915, to R. Don Laws, Editor of the *Yellow Jacket* newspaper.

The first Ford sold was a Touring model and was sold to A. Caudill April 6, 1915.

Model T. Fords were shipped by rail unassembled to be assembled by the dealer upon arrival. It took two men five to six hours to assemble one car.

New Buicks were sold here in 1918. In the early 1920's A.F. Kilby would take Frank Tomlinson, among others, and ride a train to Flint Michigan to receive their new inventories of Buicks. It would take approximately five days to drive back on the rough roads of those days, if the weather was good.

R.W. Gwyn bought the first Franklin sold here on June 10, 1920.

In 1919, after serving in the French Alps during World War I, A.F. Kilby was employed by Gwyn Harper. He managed West Jefferson's first Ford agency, for two years before returning to North Wilkesboro.

Sometime between 1919 and 1929 F.G. Harper sold his stock to C.D. Coffey, and he issued it to his son, C.D. Coffey Jr. In January of 1930 A.F. Kilby purchased the stock of C.D. Coffey Jr. At this time C.B. Lomax and his mother Sarah bought stock in Yadkin Valley.

Sourcew: Records of the Company.

Yadkin Valley Motor Company.

Old Foster Home: This old home was built by craftsmen from England who had helped build Biltmore House in Asheville. While working their way back to Wilmington to sail for home, these men would stop to build a house in order to replenish their funds. The house was constructed for the Foster family, members of whom are standing on the porch.

Parsonville Community: J. Cicero Parsons Home.

PORES KNOB COMMUNITY

Pores Knob Community was named for a man who settled here at an unknown date, probably on the mountain which is called the Pores Knob Mountain until the present time. This man's name was Moses Poore. The first post office for this community was Poors Knob Post Office. During the early 20th Century some fruit growers got the name of our post office changed from Poors Knob to Fruitland and East Fruitland which was a very appropriate name for it considering that almost every patron of the office grew some fine fruits along with their farm crops. After a short time some of the older settlers were not satisfied with doing away with the name of Poors so they got the name of the post office changed back to its original name but spelled it PORES instead of POORS. This community is in the south end of Wilkes County and joins Alexander County at the top of Kilby Mountain. It is in Moravian Falls Township. The Pores Knob Mountain is the highest peak in the Brushy Mountains.

There is a legend about a print found on a large rock in this mountain. It is told that probably one of the Poors men was eloping with his bride on a fast horse and the Indians got after him and ran the horse out on this large rock. When the horse saw the edge of the high rock, he whirled so quickly that he left the print of his shoe in the rock. It can be seen until this day.

Some of the earliest names of the settlers of this community are Laws, Lowe, Broyhill, Joines, Price, Kilby, Fletcher, Smith, Edsel, Brown, Brock, Bentley, Jennings, Wiles, Treadway, Davis, Ashley, Meadows and others.

Walnut Grove Baptist Church is the only church in this community. It was organized in 1845 and has been a beacon to the community down through the years. Some of the most noted Southern Baptist preachers have pastored this church. The Gawltneys, Bumgarners, Pooles, Redmons are among those serving this church during the Pioneer Years.

There was a one or two-teacher school near the Walnut Grove Church and one in the Brocktown section of the community and one on the mountain behind the Poors Knob Mountain. The three were consolidated with Moravian Falls Elementary School in the fall of 1931.

Farming and apple growing have always been the chief occupations of this community. The Meadow Mills were patented and made here by the Meadows family.

There was a Home Demostration Club (now called Extension Home Makers Club) organized in the fall of 1939 and is still a strong club serving the community, making it a better place to live and helping the members to become better home makers. This club has been instrumental in obtaining and building a nice community center known as the Pores Knob Community Center.

Sources: personal knowledge and interviews by Eula Brock Bentley.

WALNUT GROVE BAPTIST CHURCH

Walnut Grove Baptist Church was organized about the year of 1845 as an arm or branch of Little River Church in Alexander County. It was organized at the home of James Price.

After the church was organized, services were held in private homes until a log house was built. This building continued to be used until 1879 when a frame structure was built. The wooden building continued in use until about 1932 when the brick structure was completed. The Sunday school rooms were added around 1947.

Most of the time, the Saturday business sessions was consumed in disciplinary action. Members were cited and excluded for non-

Walnut Grove Baptist Church, Pores Knob by Highway 16.

church attendance, denial of church membership; contempt of the church; improper conduct; patting and dancing; intoxication; swearing; being drunk; profane language and many other charges. An example will show how stern this church was in discipline.

Dr. H.G. Duncan's grandmother was excluded from this church for nonchurch atten-

New Hope School (1897).

dance in May 1868. She lost her oldest son in the Civil War. Her husband had died fifteen months before and her fourth son, ten months before her exclusion. These deaths left her with ten children, the youngest being about three years of age, to care for. To attend church, she had to travel seven miles each way and had no way to go except by wagon, mule back or walk. In December 1882, Old Mountain Church sent a committee and letter to know why she was excluded.

Strict communion and foot-washing were yearly practices in the early history of this church, but we find no mention of foot-washing after April 1876.

Source: Walnut Grove 1970 Church Directory.

PURLEAR COMMUNITY

Purlear is a community in west-central Wilkes County on Cole Creek, named for Isaac Parlier, who settled on what was once known as Isaac Parlier's Creek.

Around 1900 Mr. Alexander operated a store on the north bank of the road that led from Wilkesboro and North Wilkesboro to Phillips Gap in Ashe County, the main artery of travel at that time. All of the travel and transportation was done by wagons pulled princi-

pally by horses and mules and sometimes by cattle.

After the Alexander Store, it was followed by D.V. Nichols and later D.V. Nichols and Sons. Across the road from D.V. Nichols and Sons was J.F. Hayes and C.C. Hayes.

About 1922 the stores were no longer operating profitably and some of those who went from the community to World War I, did not return to Purlear. The families were the W.H. Eller's, the Nichols family, the McNiel families and Vannoy families, the Canters and the Hayes family. Salesmen were called drummers and they usually stopped at Mr. and Mrs. C.C. Hayes' to spend the night and to sell to the merchants. They traveled by buggy.

About 1910, a camp lot was established where people with wagons could camp on their way to Wilkesboro and North Wilkesboro from Ashe and Watauga County. It took travelers by wagon a day to get to Purlear, where they camped for the night, and a day to come to the

James M. Eller Homeplace.

two towns and back to Purlear. Many times as many as 20 wagons would be on the camp lot for the night. Most of them either cooked their meals on an open fire and slept in their wagons or slept at Mr. and Mrs. C.C. Hayes' house. It is a recollection that they got breakfast and a bed for the night for twenty-five cents.

The Purlear Community extended from near the Arbor Grove Road east of the post office, west to the Stanton Township line. Stanton Post Office was about three miles or less from the Purlear Post Office. From about 1900, the large tannery for hides was operated at Stanton. It was known as the Stanton Tanning Company and was dismantled right after World War I.

Loafersville

Up until about 1920, Purlear also had the name of Loafersville. This was because the young men congregated in the stores located at Purlear on rainy days, and days when the weather was not suitable for outside activities. They had a game which they called Cracker-loos, which was pitching pennies at cracks to see who could get the closest to the crack. Whoever came closest won the pennies. They also had a fair baseball team and played baseball when the weather would permit. Christmas parties were given and groups would go out at night to visit the homes, dressed in masks as Santa Clauses. Singings, banjo picking and entertainment of that nature was common place in various parts of the small community.

The first post master who I remember was Claude A. McNiel. The rural carrier out of the Purlear Post Office was N.C. Cooper. In those days the post master and the rural mail carrier apparently changed with the administration. After McNeil, W.A. Hayes was appointed and he was followed by Mrs. Vaughn Church and she was followed by Turner Huffman. R.G. Vannoy carried the rural route for more than thirty years, first with a horse and buggy; but as times changed and roads improved, he carried the mail in a motor vehicle.

Purlear Post Office was moved about one half mile south of its original location on the bank of the old highway 50 as it was called. It was later moved to the north side of what is now old Highway 421, where it now remains.

Source: Recollections of Kyle Hayes.

ROBERT CLEVELAND HOUSE, PURLEAR

An 18th Century log dwelling, this sturdy log house was built by Capt. Robert Cleveland, who fought in the Battle of Kings Mountain, and is regarded as the oldest standing structure in Wilkes County. The house is located on the Parsonsville Road, fifteen miles northwest of the Wilkesboros. It overlooks Lewis Fork Creek. Robert Cleveland reared seventeen children in this house and was living in it at the time of his death in 1812. The property is now owned by Mr. and Mrs. Parks Church.

John and Mary Roberson Home.

Bell's View School (mid-1920s), located on a knob about ¼ mile south of Highway 60 near Purlear. The school is no longer standing. Students, front row l. to r.: Willa Nichols, Cecil Vannoy, Annie Laura Vannoy, Frank McNiel, Holly Greer, Hazel Nichols. Back row: (first unknown), Gwyn Nichols, Bill Nichols, Minnie Pierce, Pearl Nichols.

Robert Cleveland House (Sketch by Penelope Chester).

ROARING RIVER

Roaring River is located in the northeastern part of Wilkes County at the mouth of Roaring River, from where it gets its name, and the Yadkin River. Roaring River heads at Stone Mountain. The community is one of the oldest existing settlements in Wilkes.

The first settlers came from Virginia here. The Parks families and the Bryans and Martin families across the river arrived between 1785 and 1788. They owned 5,000 acres of land and soon homes were established along the river.

The first church in the community was Reeves Chapel Methodist Church established around 1835, which later became Roaring River United Methodist Church, which is still active. The early trustees of Reeves Chapel Methodist were the Parks, Crumpler, Reeves, Laxton, Foote, Martin and Warren families.

In 1908 the Roaring River Baptist church was built, but it had its beginning in 1906 and they held services at the school. Mr. T.J. McNeil instigated the first Sunday School and church. For two years Sunday School was held in the schoolhouse. Rev. N.T. Jarvis pastor of Briar Creek, was elected moderator. The presbytery consisted of R.N. Gorver, J.T. Comer, and T.J. McNeil. Charter members were J.Q. Blackburn and wife, Mattie, Rock Creek, J.R. Boldin, White Plains, R.L. Church and family of North Wilkesboro First Baptist, W.G. Church of Briar Creek, E.R. Felts, Pleasant Grove, L.J. Salmon of Flat Rock, Mr. and Mrs. T.J. McNeill, and Minnie Forester. A new church was built and first services were held in 1910. Pews were bought from First Baptist, North Wilkesboro for $50.

The first public School was begun April, 1908, with committee members E.E. Tharpe, W.S. Alexander, E.R. Felts. The school consisted of two rooms, two front doors and two cloak rooms. First two teachers were Mr. W.T. Comer and Miss Minnie Myers. Teachers salaries were $25 and $32 per month, average attendance 52 pupils. Lunch was brought in buckets. Water carried in a bucket from a spring with only one dipper to drink from. It was heated with a wood stove. Boys carried wood, girls helped the teacher clean the rooms.

The old school building burned in 1942. After consideration a new building was built and the first lunch room started in 1938. Students were allowed to bring food in exchange for meal tickets. All of the schools that had a lunch room helped raise a large garden at Roaring River on six acres of land. When vegetables were harvested they were canned at the lunch room and divided among the schools. Roaring River's share was 1400 jars of food.

In 1954 Roaring River and Ronda High School consolidated to form East Wilkes High.

The first post office was opened in 1874. James M. Parks was the first post master.

Masonic Lodge No. 570 was started in 1911. They met over Mr. Richard Reeves dry goods store. Early members were T.J. McNeil, F.L. Parks, H.E. Parks, Charles Greenwood, J.B. Church, and Richard Reeves.

Early Businesses

Many businesses had developed by 1824. Some of the earliest were J.W. Burchette and John Shipwash, blacksmithing and wheel-wrighting; E. Sparks, building and contracting; J.F. Mahaffery, coopering; J. Dimmette and Sons, millwrighting; L. D. Parks and Sons, R.A. Reeves, Granville Church, J.Q. Blackburn, J.A. Longbottom, and others, general stores; S.J. Greenwood, and W.H. Reeves, distillery; and W.H. Reeves, physician, merchant, and corn, flour, and lumber milling.

In 1911 the cotton mill was built. It went broke and was bought by Bill Palmer. The Grier Cotton Mill firm bought the plant to spin cotton into thread. The buildind was used for machine storage until it burned. The walls are still standing.

The Roaring River Furniture Company was organized on September 5, 1922 by C.J. Lambeth from High Point, but was owned by locals people. It employed 150 workers. The company went out of business in the 1930's. The building burned.

The Parks Lumber Company was organized on October 9, 1909 by L.J. Salmon, H.E. Parks, T.J. McNeil, and R.L. Church. The Damask Manufacturing Company of Roaring River was organized by Ira R. Hayes, R.W.S. Pegra, and W.L. Harper.

In the 1940s and 1950s, W.O. Blackburn & Sons' Building and Supply was developed on the lot where the Holly Farms Mill is today. It manufactured doors, windows, and blocks. Marshall and Wolfe also had a plant during this period. They manufactured cement products, particularly blocks. It was located on the site of G.C. Porter's home.

Roaring River also boasted of a canning factory, a chicken coop and bee-gum factory, later bought by and converted into Roaring River Casket Factory, a box shop, a tobacco press, a fertilize house; the first Staley's Restaurant, and a grape orchard famous for their specially developed pink grape.

Roaring River had their own power supply. The Roaring River Mill had a generator and provided Southern Public Light to anyone who would buy an appliance.

A volunteer fire department was organized April 12, 1958, the best equipped in the county.

Sources: *Happy Valley* by Hickerson; *Roaring River History* by Amanda Porter and Inez Boles; Parks Family Records of Eleanor Elam.

POPLAR SPRING BAPTIST CHURCH

The history of Poplar Spring Missionary Baptist Church is by no means complete. We pause and thank God for the many blessings that have been ours to enjoy. We are still

LINSY LAFAYETTE Church Store Building at Ready Branch, N.C. was built around 1878, operated by owner until 1920. From 1920 until 1945 the store was operated by Mrs. Zora Church Eller. In 1945, the store was purchased by Mrs. Estelle Church McGee and husband, Gerald McGee, who operated the store until 1958. The building is still owned by Mr. and Mrs. McGee.

Dr. A.J. Eller Home.

searching here and there for new information about our church. Poplar Spring Missionary Baptist Church was organized in 1879, 101 years ago, by Rev. Francis Parker and a few dedicated pilgrims who became weary of working White Plains Missionary Baptist Church which is a church of white membership. The first building was a log cabin located on the Aunt Prissie place. Bro. Edelin Allen was the first deacon. An acre of land was donated by Ben Martin for the building of God's house. The name was derived from a large Poplar Tree growing over a spring, the church's water supply.

Since that time many others have come on the scene following in the footsteps of Rev. Parker as pastor; Revs. George Fletcher, Robert Grinton, Bill Bailey, T.C. Graham, L.J. Carlton, J.A. Parsons, J.B. Hampton and our present pastor, Rev. Fred Carlton. Rev. Parsons served the longest, remaining thirty-eight years.

In 1942 with Rev. Parsons as our pastor and with God's guidance and help a new church was built. It was remodeled and an addition was made to it while Rev. Hampton was serving as pastor. In the past few years a baptistry has been added, the fellowship hall remodeled and many other items have been added to beautify God's house.

The church continues to progress under the able leadership of Rev. Carlton even though it

The Zolley Coffer and Rebecca Eller Church house was built in the early 1900s in the Ready Branch community, now Route 1, Ferguson. In the late 1930s their eldest daughter, Estelle Church McGee and her husband Gerald McGee bought the homeplace. It still stands.

Ready Branch Community: "A Little Boy Who Lived at Ready Branch — Early 1900s."

seems sometimes slow and rough. But if we hold to the Faith like Abraham, be above reproach like Daniel, courageous like Joshua, long suffering like Paul, preserving like Moses, bold like Peter and John and above all be God like, like Enoch, we will meet the king in that Great Homecoming in the sky. Yes, we have built a new church but the shadows of the past still linger in our minds when our forefathers said let's build a church.

Presently our church continues her growth both in membership and christian allegiance. To date the membership of Poplar Spring Missionary Baptist Church has increased to 103.

We have two active missionary groups, our music department is composed of a senior choir, gospel choir and a youth choir. To assist our pastor, we have deacons Bros. Howard Adams, Edward Mitchell, Alton J. Allen, James E. Adams, Ronald Whittington, Albert Adams and Ronald Hayes.

Sources: Church records and memories by the church people.

Ronda Community: "Haying Time on the Hendrix Farm."

Ronda, ''Claymont Hill'', home of William Arthur Hendrix (built 1840).

STRAW

Straw community is in the south of Wilkes County near the east prong of Cub Creek. This community is also known as Edgewood, having had an Edgewood School and at present an Edgewood Baptist Church in the community. The post office has long since been discontinued. Five photographs of the Straw Community are shown.

Straw Community: Left: Edgewood Church. Right: Ranse Miller home — first Straw Post Office.

John and Maggie Fletcher Family (1946).

Old Eschol Methodist Church in 1957.

John Fletcher Home (1949) on Highway 115.

Pupils at Edgewood School (1914).

TRAPHILL

In 1887 the Baptists of the village withdrew from Old Roaring River Primitive Baptist Church and organized Trap Hill Missionary Baptist Church, which supported a preparatory school, Trap Hill Institute. In 1895/96 there were 96 students in attendance from 25 locations in the state and three from Virginia. The school closed at the turn of the century, marking the end of Trap Hill's golden age.

Since around 1860 Trap Hill had resident doctors, one or more at a time: Drs. Tyre York, T.W. Smith, Joshua Joines, Charlie Bryan, Robert Thompson, T.H. Higgins, Ira Gambill, and Walter Miles. Dr. Choate was part-time, with an office on second floor of Trap Hill Bargain House, as was dentists in summer especially Dr. C.A. Reeves.

In the 1870s and 1880s a number of local manufactories sprang up: carpenters, R.M. Holbrook and J.C. Lowe; harness and saddle maker, William Cheatwood; wagon maker, Marion McCann; tanners, Hardin and Joshua Spicer; wood carders, Spicer Brothers; and maker of plug tobacco, Joshua Spicer.

Merchants were plentiful in the 1880s: R.J. Bauguess selling honey from his apiary, Hanks Bros., J.D. Hunt, J. McCann, G.R. Reves and J.S. Kilby. Earlier ones had been: Stephen Johnson, J.Q.A.Bryan, Bryan and Carson,

C.C. Crumpler, R.R. Gwyn Co. Later ones were L.A. Harris, C.D. Holbrook, J.R. Pruitt, D.A. Harris, Mostella Yale and Charlie Miles.

Perhaps Trap Hill's most distinguished citizen was Dr. Tyre York, who served five terms in the House of Representatives, two in the Senate, and one in Congress, and campaigned for governor on his faithful mule, Jackson. He along with the colorful J.Q.A. Bryan, also with five terms in the House, A.C. and T.S. Bryan, Benjamin F. Martin, J.S. and John A. Holbrook, all from Trap Hill, served a total of twenty years in legislative halls. Recently Senator T.R. Bryan and Representatives Claude Billings and John Brown have also served.

A red letter day in Trap Hill's history came in 1900 when Aycock made a campaign speech at Trap Hill. He spoke to a crowd of 400, with Dr. Tyre York as master of ceremonies.

The Trap Hill post office was the fifth opened in the county in 1837, with Thomas Crumpler, post-master. It was named for hunter William Blackburn's railpen snare which he set on a nearby hill to catch wild turkeys.

Trap Hill was two words until 1892.

Trap Hill's Fair View College was chartered in 1891, and Traphill's listing as a Historic District in the National Register of Historic Places in 1980.

Elk Spur Settlement

The Elk Spur settlement (later Trap Hill) on the southern tip of Elk Spur, which runs off the Blue Ridge at Roaring Gap, began somewhat later than other scattered settlements "on the waters of Roaring River", on Longbottom and Greenstreet Mountain.

Of the first Elk Spur settlers, William and Sally Blackburn, there remains today on the hill south of the crossroads only their family burial ground of unmarked graves, but descendants of their ten children run into the hundreds.

Still standing are the big white dwelling and the store building (now housing Stone Mountain Crafts) built by the second settler, Joseph T. Bryan, who was the second post master. He and wife Fannie (Spicer) later moved to east Tennessee.

The third settler, Joseph Spicer, son of William, died in 1845, leaving to his son Joseph the mill on Sandy Creek, the Trap Hill mill, evidently built by Joseph or William. It remained in the family for more than a hundred years, owned by H.S. Holbrook and nephews, C.O. Pruitt and Lloyd and Paul Holbrook. It has recently been restored as a residence by the Dean Weatherman.

The first mention of Trap Hill in county records was in 1833 when Benjamin F. Martin, a county justice and state legislator, requested license to retail spirits at Trap Hill for three months. The same man had a legislative act passed to create a town Johnsonville at the "place called Trap Hill", but it was never implemented.

The Siamese Twins

In 1839 the Siamese Twins came to Trap Hill, bought land, built a house, took the name Bunker, married sisters and lived here ten years, until their families had increased so much that they needed two houses, which they built at White Plains. Their former agent, Charles Harris, came the same year, married Fannie Bauguess and became post master in 1843.

Trap Hill was a stage of action in the Civil War, and General J.Q.A. Bryan and Captain A.C. Bryan were chief actors, raising the Union flag and recruiting men to slip through lines to Tennessee. General Hoke's brigade camped here and one man was killed. Family treasures contain papers and pictures of R.P. Brooks, James A. Johnson, W.H.H. Lyons, Jacob Matthew Pruitt, Robert and William Sparks, and Gideon and Joshua Spicer. Dr. Tyre York visited Governor Vance regarding deserters.

Early Baptists had worshiped at Old Roaring River, and Methodists at Antioch, near Roaring Gap. In 1870 the Bryan family, especially J.Q.A., led in organizing Trap Hill Methodist Church, which sponsored Trap Hill Seminary, later chartered as Fair View College which functioned until 1915.

Sources: Research and personal knowledge by Bea Holbrook.

Winfrey Holbrook Mill Seat (mid-1800s) East Fork Roaring River.

Joseph S. Holbrook Home.

OLD ROARING RIVER BAPTIST CHURCH
at
TRAPHILL

The Old Roaring River Primitive Baptist Church was constituted in 1779. The early minutes have been lost, therefore the first members are not listed in any record. The church was first housed in a crude log building for winter meetings, and a brush arbor down near the spring for summer meetings. This brush arbor was replenished from year to year and continued in use until the early 1880s.

The old frame church building was built by Jonathan Gentry and his son-in-law, Levi Burcham.

This church has served continously and is a very active church today. A copy of the church minutes can be found in the church library, giving the names of the many people who have been members of the church.

Sources: Original church minutes.

Old Traphill Mill (mid-1800s) on Sandy Creek.

Traphill Baptist Church (1887).

Old Roaring River Baptist Church.

FAIR VIEW COLLEGE,

W.H. JONES, B.L., PRESIDENT, TRAPHILL, N.C.

January 2, 1894

My dear Emma,

I had not thought of writing to you so soon but we will have to hope you or Miss Cockerham will get one of our students. He is going to board at Kilby's and they are trying hard to get him. He plays well and wants vocal music; round notes, and oh! lots of things I never heard of. I have a class of six worked up. I will take this time and make seven if you will let me.

Will have a young lady from Ashe in about a month. School opened with 30. None of the old boarders are in yet . . . will take the Theological course. Think we will have a large school in a few days.

Prof. C. is not here and I fear he will not come at all, but I ought not to have told you this for now you will not want to come. Do come in by Monday next if you possibly can or Warren will leave us. Tell some of the girls to come with you. Tell Bro. Johnson to come with you, we want to see him. I have one fine looking boy, but I warn you not to get struck on him or I shall be awfully jealous. Warren has supplanted me in Miss A's affections; she will hardly speak to me any more but she and W. are "getting there" . . . I didn't get up a single case Xmas and of course feel like the time was wasted. Miles gave you dead away to me that W. before we left wanted to tease you about it awful bad.

This is the first day of the new year. How calm and beautiful it has been. The old one is gone with all its joys and sorrows. To some it brought happiness, to others bitter pain. Its path is strewn with broken hearts and mildewed with tears. Its background is lined with unkept pledges and violated vows. Still to us it has been kind and I owe it to the new year to be better in every way, at least to try.

May it bring only happiness to you is the wish of one who dearly loves you.

Be here Monday.

s/Will

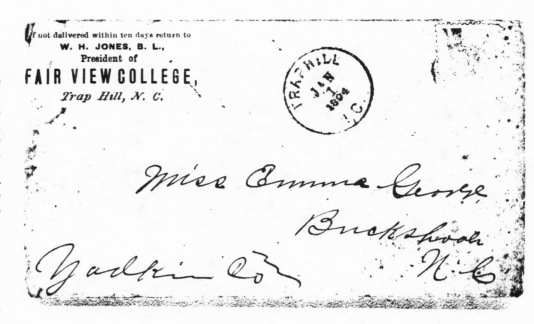

Fairview College Building (1891).

Fairview College Students (1891).

TRAPHILL LODGE #483

The charter for the first masonic lodge in Traphill was granted in 1875. The lodge number was 346. The charter was surrendered in 1896 for reasons which have become somewhat obscure over the years. Therefore, suppositions as to what occurred to cause the charter surrender will not be attempted here.

For twelve years there were sporadic efforts to restore the lodge membership under charter number 483. It was not until November 7, 1908 that a major effort was effectively attempted. On this date Past Master J.S. Kilby installed the following officers: Jas. C. Sparks — Worshipful Master; J.S. Holbrook — Senior Warden; J.T. Bryd — Junior Warden; William Sparks — Treasurer; J.S. Kilby — Secretary; J.C. Sparks — Senior Deacon; A.C.

Fairview College Girl's Dorm.

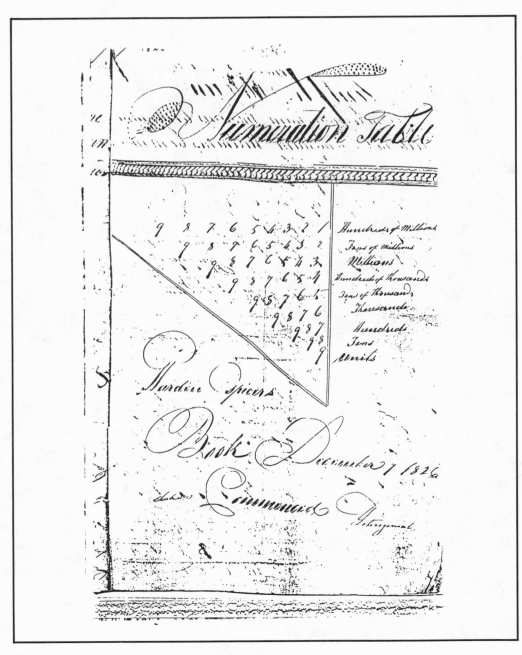

Hardin Spicer's Mathematical Tables.

Billings — Junior Deacon; W.H. Brooks — Tyler.

At this meeting, petitions for the degrees in Masonry were read for eight candidates. It was decided to write Brother R.F. Edwards in Alleghany County to ask his help in conferring the proposed degrees. At this time, regular meetings of the lodge were scheduled on Saturdays — on or before each full moon.

On Saturday morning, December 5, 1908 the lodge convened. The lodge was not officially closed until the following Friday evening while Initiating, Passing, and Raising all candidates through the three degrees.

After this undoubtedly strenuous and tiring week it is interesting to note that the lodge opened again the next day — for no apparent reason other than to vote to accept a waivered petition from another candidate. It might be conjectured that the brethren had become so conditioned to attending lodge that they didn't know what else to do with themselves.

Traphill Lodge #483 is the smallest of the four Masonic Lodges in the 50th Masonic District of North Carolina. However, it now has more members than at any time in its history. The lodge meets on the first and third Tuesdays of each month in the same building the lodge brethren have always met. Years ago the meeting time was changed from the lunar reference — probably because not very many of us calculate our time in that manner any more.

The Master of Traphill Lodge during this year of 1982 is Bergie C. Speaks, Jr.

Source: Research in minutes by Thomas S. Bryan.

STONE MOUNTAIN TRAGEDY

Stone Mountain, of Trap Hill, North Carolina, claimed its first and only victim in 1871, a century after the first settlers came to this area, and approximately a hundred years ago.

On Sunday morning, May 27, 1871, Thomas Alexander "Alex" Atkins, a nephew of J.Q.A. Bryan, of Trap Hill, and Lenora Wiley, his bride of four months, accompanied by five young relatives, including Dave, Monroe and Robert Calloway Bryan and Robert Atkins, set out from the village of Trap Hill for a day's outing to Stone Mountain, five miles away. The trip was arranged as a going-away party for Lenora, who was to visit soon her parents in Guilford County for the first time since her marriage.

After climbing the wooded eastern slope, the party reached the bare rock near the summit. The bride, awed with the immensity of the dome, expressed her reverence for the Creator of all that grandeur. The groom, in his pride at showing her this granite wonder, which he had explored many times, boasted of his intention to go farther down the steep side of the mountain than anyone had ever gone before.

The entire group had gone down some distance to examine a cave called The Big Pot. The others had crossed a wet place on the moss-coated granite below a patch of woods, when Alex, hand-in-hand with Lenora, stepped on the wet moss and lost his balance. Lenora shrieked. Together, they slipped farther and farther down the steep rock. Soon they were

Stone Mountain.

separated by a projecting rock, and Lenora cried, ''God, save him!'' Her light body bounced on the rock as she plunged downward. Alex's weight (175 pounds) caused him to slide down on his back.

The others descended as quickly as possible the west side of the mountain, which is not so steep and which is partially covered with vegetation. In about three quarters of an hour they reached the couple at the foot. They found Lenora ''cold and still in death.'' She had fallen through the branches of a black gum tree, on which her hat ''and veil'' had lodged. Not far away, on a pile of rotten wood, lay Alex unconscious. The flesh from his back and limbs had been worn away to the bone.

Some of the men rushed to the nearest house, that of Emanuel Sparks, to borrow sheets. Finding none, they went to John Hutchinson's, near Wolf Rock, where they quickly improvised stretchers. The companions of the early morning climb became stretcher and pall bearers. The condition of the injured man made it necessary to stop with him at Dick Brown's two miles from the scene of the tragedy.

The body of the deceased was borne on,

MASONIC LODGE #483-TRAPHILL: Front Row, L to R: John W. Wood, A.C. Yale, William Sparks, Thomas S. Bryan, James C. Sparks, C. Millard Caudill, James S. Kilby, H. Gaither Pruitt. Middle Row, L to R: Dave C. Bryan, Bob Stiller, Joe F. Lyon, W.H.H. Lyon, Joseph B. Spicer, John Myers, Major Joines, C.W. Wood, Avery C. Billings (with small son). Back Row, L to R: Chy O. Pruitt, Rob Waddell, Thomas C. DeBorde, Clarence DeLoss Holbrook, J. Gideon Lyon, W.R. Shepherd.

53

Baptising in Sandy Creek, Traphill.

J.S. Kilby Home.

J.S. Kilby Store.

passing old Roaring River Baptist Church, where "meeting" was being held. Among Alex's relatives in the congregation was an aunt, Mrs. Hardin S. Holbrook, who was expecting the couple to spend that night in her home. The "meeting" was abruptly broken up by the cries of the women. The procession moved on to Trap Hill, where the body was placed on the big stone hearth in the home of Dr. T.W. Smith.

Lenora Wiley Atkins was buried in the Bryan family cemetery, northeast of Trap Hill. Thomas Alexander Atkins recovered and was married twice afterwards.

Stone Mountain is now a State Park (1982).

Source: Article by Miss Beatrice Holbrook, based on interviews with local people and an article of 1895 by Walter Bynum Bell.

EXPERIENCES IN WILKES

When at Wilkesboro for the first time, I saw a handsome young fellow, 19 or 20 years old and his eight ox-team. I had just landed in town and secured a room at the quaint old hotel, when I heard an outcry: "Get up there you long horned son of a devil!" I looked out of my top-story window, three or four floors from the ground, but saw nothing. Soon the outburst was repeated. Again I failed to see the author of it. About thirty minutes later the piercing yell broke near me and I looked down and saw four pairs of oxen tugging along the street, drawing two tremendous logs, and standing on them was a real fellow, pink of cheek, husky, and keen-eyed. His whip lash must have been ten feet long. His propelling words rang out clear and loud. He was on his way to North Wilkesboro, across the river, where the logs were being loaded on railway trucks for shipment.

At Wilkesboro I met many interesting people — old man John S. Cranor, a good lawyer and fox hunter; Mitch Vannoy, another hound man. In climbing the mountains between Lenoir and Blowing Rock I passed close to the home of Uncle Rans Triplett, who owned a pack of famous red fox dogs, called the Blue-Ticked Fantails.

While in Wilkes, Richard N. Hackett steered me up against Horace Greeley Minton, a rural

Sidney Lewis Johnson Home, built ca. 1890, Walnut Grove.

mail carrier, and a Boomer township Democrat. Mr. Minton invited me to go on a fox hunt back in the mountains. I went and came as near getting drunk as I ever did in my life.

Having been reared in Providence township, Mecklenburg County, among pious Scotch-Irish Presbyterians I never knew the difference in the strength of corn whiskey, beer and brandy. Somehow I got the impression that beer was just a little more intoxicating than brandy. That proved my downfall.

A Fine Toddy

We drove to Kernel Lunsford's where we were to hunt the next morning. On the way, Mr. Minton told me Mr. Lunsford mixed a fine toddy and he hoped that I would have one as that was a real token of friendship in that part of the country. I promised. Mr. Lundsford had the toddy ready when we arrived. I sipped it and handed it to Mr. Minton, who sipped it and handed it back and told me to drink all of it. I drank it down and twenty minutes later I was heavy-headed. All I recall is that we went into supper and after eating a fair meal, we left the table. I moved away and took the chin of a little waiting girl in my hand.

Next morning Mr. Minton and Mr. Lunsford woke me and we walked about fifteen miles. I believe I would have been drunk until now if I had not walked. To this day, I realize that Kernel Lunsford knew how to make a brandy toddy, and had I been an expert in such things, I would have rested about one-third the way down the glass and not listened to Horace Greeley Minton.

We never found a fox, and the next day we went back down the mountain, dogs and all. On the way we treed a bear. We were driving through a beautiful wooded mountain country. Old Mose, the biggest hound I ever saw, struck a hot trail ahead of us. Every other dog joined him and with a terrific roar the pack swept away. When we caught up with the pack

we found we had run down a Turk and his trick bear, and on the approach of the hounds the Turk had made the bear climb the tree and he was frantically warding off the dogs with a stick.

Sources: article by H.E.C. Bryant, newspaper man and correspondent for *Charlotte Observer* in Washington (Wilkes Journal 1927).

LAST HANGING IN WILKES

In an account for the newspaper, the late W.H. Hurley, in 1956, described the last hanging in Wilkes County. We quote from that article.

"Three score and eight years ago — Friday, July 13, 1888, from early dawn, and even before that, the exodus from the homes began. Men, women and children were hurrying in a steady stream, from hill and dale, from cabins, mountain homes, valley homes, and distant points, from out of the county. There was a thrill in store. So they continued to pour in, singly, by twos, and by dozens; they came by foot, by wagon, and horseback. These were slowly converging on the lot back of the county jail. Some had arrived the night before, in order to get a better view. Many of these slept in their wagons, had their "provisions", and cooked them over a camp fire. A county-wide get-together — the main topic of conversation — the hanging of James (Jim) Byers. There hadn't been a hanging in thirty-three years in the county — there must be one, it mattered little as to the victim.

By noon the crowd was estimated to be 6,000-8,000, every inch of available space, except near the gallows was taken. House windows were filled — people sat, stood, leaned and propped on each other. Many were tired, others almost exhausted, but leave — no sir, these people were curious and serious. They had made a sacrifice to come. Children cried, feet ached, and limbs were cramped, but none thought of leaving.

At 12:25 p.m., the sheriff, Mr. McEwen, and a deputy led the prisoner from his cell and the "last mile" was begun. At the jail door they were joined by a group of twenty-five armed men who had been appointed as guards. (it had been rumored that an attempt of rescue of the prisoner would be made). The group made their way to the back of the jail, and approached the gallows. The group halted, and the sheriff lifted his hand for attention, and said, "My friends, I hope all will remain perfectly quiet. This is a solemn occasion, and I have a solemn duty to perform, but nevertheless, I must not shirk my duty. I hope no man will attempt to prevent me from doing that duty. I have selected to assist me men in whom I have the utmost confidence. My orders are that if any man attempts to rescue the prisoner, that these guards will shoot him down. I trust that there will be no such attempt." No man felt more keenly the unpleasant duty to be performed than did Sheriff McEwen.

The guards, the sheriff and the prisoner moved on to the gallows. The guards circled the stand, and after a few words were exchanged by the troup, two ministers took over their talks with the prisoner. Following the brief but solemn ceremony, the sheriff ascended the steps leading to the scaffold, with the condemned man. The prisoner in a few words, stated that he was innocent of the crime of murder as charged, and asserted his action was in self-defense. The rope was placed about his neck, the noose adjusted, the arms and legs were fastened securely. The black cap was pulled over his head and around the neck. The sheriff grasped the right hand of the prisoner, and said, "God bless you, and goodbye." He stepped nervously to the ground, grasped an axe and swung it, once. The rope which supported the trap door parted as the axe made a dull clank. The door fell silently and the doomed man dropped approximately three feet. The rope "twanged" taut. The doomed body spun clockwise, then counter-clockwise. The shoulders contracted as did the legs at the knees. In this terrifying and nerve straining four minutes, many things happened. The sheriff walked, maybe a score of steps, and stretched himself under a tree in the shade. A man came toward the gallows, waving a pistol and shouting, "Cut the poor man down, for God's sake, don't let him die!" He was quickly caught.

About the time the rope parted, a great sigh escaped from many lips, the tempo increased to whimpers, moans, wails and outright screams. As wave after wave of yells, screams and groans continued, women wrung their hands, tore their hair and pounded others on the back. Brave men turned their backs, strong men were moved to tears. Many fainted and others were hysterical. One man fainted and fell from his perch in a tree. His "better" view paid off, with interest. Maybe the ghosts of Col. Cleveland's Tories were present. Something in the air certainly brought out emotional strains, and etched on the memories and in the minds images that would last a lifetime. People said that all during the summer their mind would suddenly bring this to the front, they

Walnut Grove Community: Walnut Grove School, 1904, Alice Higgins — teacher.

could not escape the horror of these visions — of that doomed man's body as it swayed to and fro.

Nine minutes after the rope was cut, the prisoner was pronounced dead. In one more minute the body was taken down. The neck was not broken. The next day the body was buried about four miles north of Wilkesboro.

A short time before the execution, the prisoner asked to be baptized. So he was led from his cell, with his legs chained together, and taken approximately one-half mile to Cub Creek, was immersed and returned to his cell.

An Eye for an Eye

It had been thirty-three years since a criminal was hanged in the county of Wilkes. Public opinion and sentiment, or should you say inhumanity, clamored for blood. Hangings, it was thought by some, were necessary to keep down crime. "Eye for an eye, and a tooth for a tooth" still ran rampant in the thoughts of many. Many happenings were a long while dated from the hanging of Jim Byers. Ballads were composed and tunes were fitted to renditions of these. These were hummed and whistled, and some sung in wide areas of the county.

The law decreed that Byers should hang, but judged by today's ideas of justice, he should have received more lenient treatment. But I am persuaded that the hanging of Byers was a challenge to citizens to fight for more humane treatment. It was the dawn of a new day. The horizons of social and legal justice were beginning to widen.

For more than twenty-one years there was not a murder committed in Wilkes County. Too, today it is almost impossible to find a jury who will bring in a verdict, "Guilty of murder in the first degree." Who knows, the hanging of Byers may have played a major part of changing opinions of our citizenry in the immediate past as well as our ideas and ideals today."

Background of the Hanging

Around the first of August in 1886, James Byers, borrowed a horse of Henry Edwards, who lived near the Virginia-Carolina line beyond Sparta. Mr. and Mrs. Byers were to visit relatives, southeast of Wilkesboro. Something happened, and the horse was not returned as promised. Mr. Edwards started to find the trouble. Apparently armed with a rifle and a high-strung temper he came into Wilkesboro searching for a "d____ horse thief." At least he asked the people whom he chanced to meet, if they had seen this particular type person. About fifteen miles from Wilkesboro, out Sparta way, Mr. Edwards met the Byerses. Mrs. Byers was mounted on the horse. Several words were passed. The argument grew worse. Threats were made. It is guessed that Mr. Edwards tried to aim or was in the act of aiming the rifle. Byers drew a pistol and fired, probably twice, as there seemed to be a bullet imprint on the stock of the rifle. Edwards was mortally wounded. The Byerses passed on homeward bound. In November, 1886 Mitch Woodie, a deputy sheriff, arrested Byers in Virginia, and brought him to Wilkes County for

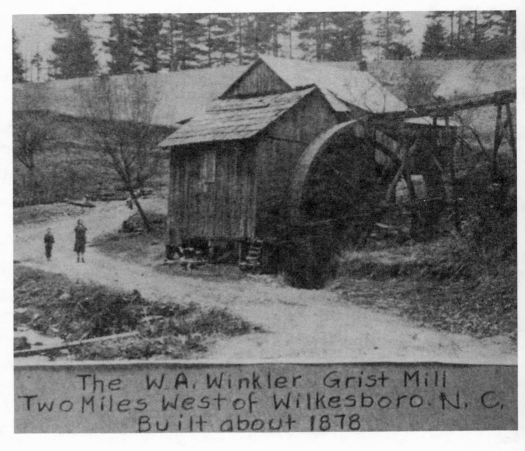

The W. A. Winkler Grist Mill Two Miles West of Wilkesboro. N. C. Built about 1878

"Morne Rouge", home of Governor Montford Stokes (Sketch by Edward Wood.)

Old Restored Jail.

trial as the murderer of Henry Edwards. (An innocent man, one James Stone who had come upon the scene of the shooting was mistakenly accused and convicted of a second degree verdict and sentenced to twenty years in the state prison before gossip and rumor convinced lawmakers that Byers and not Stone had killed Edwards.) Byers came willingly without extradition proceedings. When the hearing came up in the March, 1888 term of court, a young lawyer named Greene was assigned to defend Byers. Court convened at 9:00 a.m.; hearing soon started. Byers pleaded self-defense, but before adjournment that afternoon, he had been convicted, and sentenced to be hanged on Friday, July 13, 1888.

Source: Newspaper Article.

WILKESBORO

Wilkesboro is a beautiful town situated on the south side of the Yadkin River near the center of the county. It was founded in 1778 by

John Parks, John Barton, George Gordon, Francis Hardgrave, Rowland Judd, George Morris and John Witherspoon, who were appointed by the General Assembly to select a county seat for Wilkes County. It is about 175 miles north-west of Raleigh, N.C. the state Capital.

In 1825 the General Assembly directed the commissioners to erect a new courthouse in the public square. The town of Wilkesboro was issued a charter in 1889, providing for a mayor and four commissioners. The town apparently saw no necessity to have the town incorporated until 1889.

The old courthouse had been in use since 1825. The present courthouse was built in 1904 and has been remodeled from time to time with added wings.

The Federal courthouse was built in 1906 but was too small for the big courts that were held during the prohibition era, so courts were always held in the county courthouse. The Federal building now houses the offices of the county Board of Education.

The town first had wells to furnish water to

the town. Then they had a gravity system bringing water from the Brushy Mountains into town. A modern water system is now used.

From 1890 until after World War II, the only brick structures which were made of native brick were the old jail, now designated as an historical site, the Wilkesboro Hotel, now Smithey Hotel building (see separate article in Wilkesboro section), the Ferguson building, Jarvis building, Winkler building, Bank of Wilkes building, Dula Grocery Store and Morrison's Hardware store.

For many years a clay pottery was located in Wilkesboro and was operated by the Kennedy family.

The old Presbyterian Church is a block east of the courthouse. St. Paul's Episcopal Church is located on a hill above town and both date back to the mid-nineteenth century (see separate articles.) Both the Methodist and Baptist Churches are on Main Street and date back prior to 1900.

There are two branch banks, a distribution plant for milk, two glove factories, a shoe factory, a hosiery mill, a large poultry processing plant, furniture and hardware stores, a florist, a dry goods and grocery store now located in the town.

A business administration college was established in Wilkesboro in 1947 and served the community for twelve years. The county community college (see separate article) now serves not only Wilkes, but surrounding counties.

Sources: *Land of Wilkes* by J.H. Hayes; N.C. Private Laws 1889, Chapter 240; Personal Knowledge of Kyle Hayes.

THE TORY OAK

The Tory Oak was a hangin' tree. Over 200 years ago, it was a good sized tree with many sturdy branches. At least a half dozen men, or more perhaps, were strung up on those substantial limbs. They were hanged during the Revolutionary era when differences between mountain patriots and Tory followers of the crown reached a violent pitch.

Chief among those patriots in the area was Col. Benjamin Cleveland, who had established Roundabout Farm about 14 miles from the present site of Wilkesboro.

Cleveland, who had come to this area about 1769 along with his brothers, Absolom, Larkin and the Rev. John Cleveland, and perhaps Robert, was a huge man, weighing around 300 pounds.

He was born a community leader, and was instrumental in the formation of Wilkes County by the North Carolina General Assembly in 1778.

Cleveland's farm and those of his neighbors were victimized by Tory followers, who stole horses and ravaged property. In such instances, he had little hesitation in deciding what to do with the accused marauders when they were rounded up.

"Hang 'em" he said. And hang them, they did. They used ropes when they had them, and grapevines when they didn't.

Through the years, the role of the Tory Oak

Historic Tory Oak.

in the history of Wilkes County has been merged into the current history of later times. A small metal plaque at the foot of the tree identified it only as "The Tory Oak, on which a number of Tory leaders were hanged by Col. Benjamin Cleveland and others."

The Tory Oak has been placed on the North Carolina registry of trees.

Source: 1968 newspaper article from *Journal-Patriot.*

DISCONTINUED POST OFFICES

Abshers, Adley, Antney, Austin, Barlow, Beaux, Benham, Blackstone, Bowles, Brewers, Brier Creek, Bruce, Brushy Mountain, Buck, Bugaboo, Burcham, Byrd, Call, Champion, Chuckle, Church's Store, Claud, Cline, Clingman, Congo, Cowles, Cricket.

Darbe, Darnell, Daylo, Dehart, Dellaplane, Denny, Dennyville, Dimmette, Dinsmore, Dockery, Doughton, Dyer, East Fruitland, Edna, Elder Branch, Elk Spur, Electa, Elkville, Evatin, Fairplains, Felicia, Felts, Fort Defiance, Gilreath, Glass, Gordon, Grassy Fork, Gray, Gunter Hill.

Halls Mill, Hanes, Harley, Harp, Haymeadow, Hendrix, Hicks, Holbrook, Holman's Ford, Hunting Creek, Ilk, Ink, Ira, Isaac, Jarvis, Job's Cabin, Johnlen, Joines, Kendal, Knottville, Laurel Gap, Lester, Lewis Fork, Leyula, Lomax, Lovelace, Lucile, Maple Springs, Marley Ford, Meadow Hill, Mertie, Minton, Mole, Mount Zion, Moxley, Mulberry, Myers, New Castle, Newlife, Oakdale, Oakwoods, Offen, Osbornville, Ozark, Parks, Parsonville, Patriot, Patton, Perry, Phipps, Pore's Knob, Proffit, Purlear's Creek, Purlear, Radical, Ready Branch, Reddies River, Reno, Round Mountain, Sheets, Sherman, Shoe, Sourwood, Spicer, Springfield, Spurgeon, Stanton, Stony Hill, Straw, Summit, Swan Pond, Thrift, Top, Vannoy, Viands, Vox, Walsh, Warrior Creek, Whittington, Wiles, Windy Gap, Woodruff, Yates, Yellow Hill, York, Zebra, Zimmerman.

Source: copied from Microfilm from GSA, National Archives, by Beatrice Holbrook.

WILKESBORO PRESBYTERIAN CHURCH

From the standpoint of organization, the Wilkesboro Presbyterian Church is the oldest Presbyterian church in twenty-one western N.C. counties. Presbyterian services are still being held in the original building.

The Church was organized on June 17, 1837 with six charter members who were admitted by certificate from other churches, namely: John Finley and wife, Ellen Tate Finley, Collin Stevens and wife, Frances Stevens and Alexander Hall and wife Martha Hall.

The church was served for many years by

Wilkesboro P.O., 1850.

Old Presbyterian Church.
(Sketch by Edith Carter.)

circuit riding preachers from Concord Presbytery.

It was the custom for all small churches in the early 1800s to hold services in private homes. However by May 7, 1849, the lot on which the church stands was bought from Joshua Pennell, and the deed states: "for the purpose of building thereon a Presbyterian church."

The original brick building, contracted by "old Dameron" who also built the Episcopal church, is of Greek Revival architecture, built in 1849 and still stands. In June 1967 a historical marker was erected by the N.C. Department of Archives.

Formerly there was a gallery for black people. This gallery was supported by columns similar to the ones outside. The entrance to the gallery was on the east side of the church.

The old pulpit was a high, round type with inside steps. On the church bell is written "Molded in Philadelphia in 1849." A large pulpit Bible donated and inscribed by the donor, Ellen Tate Finley in 1851 is preserved today.

Sources: Original church minutes, Synod's record book.

ST. PAUL'S EPISCOPAL CHURCH

Services of the Saint Paul's Episcopal Church started before a church house was constructed. The present building was started in October 1848 and was finished in July 1849.

Charter members of the church were Mr. and Mrs. James Gwyn, Dr. and Mrs. James Calloway, Miss Fannie Williams and her sister, Mrs. Mary Taylor Peden. The church was consecrated on July 8, 1849.

The first clergyman at the church was the

St. Paul's Episcopal Church.

Rev. William R. Gries. He began his ministry at a discesan convention held in Edenton in 1858.

St. Paul's Episcopal Church was admitted as a parish and the following delegates were seated: James R. Dodge, James Gwyn, James Calloway and Ransom Hickerson.

The vestry was composed of James Gwyn, James Calloway, J.B. Gordon, William W. Barber, John J. Peden and Ransom Hickerson.

The second minister at St. Paul's was the Rev. Richard Wainwright Barber, who became a rector upon the admission of the church as a parish in 1858. He served 45 years, together with the churches at Ronda, Elkin and Statesville.

The present minister Rev. Frank E. McKenzie began his service March 15, 1958.

Source: Facts from *Land of Wilkes* by J.J. Hayes.

THE WILKES CONCERT BAND

As one reminises and gets his nostalgic senses in action, many things and affairs in the history of the community in which he was brought up come to mind. No doubt there are very few people in Wilkesboro and in Wilkes County who remember the Wilkes Concert Band. The band was organized around 1908

and was the main attraction of the town and county for many years. This was, of course, before the days of good roads and modern conveniences and places of amusement. Of course, there were picnics in the summertime, and box suppers and ice cream suppers at times during the year and this was about all that we had to look forward to except our activities in the churches. I can remember very well a magic lantern show in Wilkesboro when I was very young. This was put on by an outside troop in the Wilkesboro Methodist Church and presented motion pictures connected with Bible scenes all of which were very interesting and the attendance was very good. So when the band was organized everybody, particularly the young set, a good many of them took an active part.

Mr. William Martin who was a former member of the famous Lenoir Band, was our teacher. At that time he and his wife lived in North Wilkesboro. He was interested in the lumber business. He was a great band man and all the members adored him and took quite an interest in the development of the band. Of course, like every other organization, some of them made good band men and others did not and there was some dropping out occasionally and others being installed. We had the usual brass instruments of that time, coronets, bass, barotone, alto, tenor's, french horns and drums but there were no reed instruments. The members learned pretty fast how to play certain selections and finally how to play certain of the Sousa productions. After a few months practice, the band was in great demand. We played at commencement exercises, holiday exercises such as the 4th of July, Thanksgiving and Christmas. We also were engaged to play at land auctions and those were frequent at that time over the county. The band performed at the Wilkesboro Fair. One of the most notable engagements was the Ashe County Fair. We attended two or three of

WILKESBORO CONCERT BAND: Front Row, L to R: Lonnie Lunn, Julius C. Hubbard, Sr., Harley Green, Weaver Starr. Back Row, L to R: Earl Davis, Adolphus Bell, Norman Smoak, Charlie Staley, Fred C. Hubbard, Blaine Henderson, John Holman, Robert Starr.

these during our time of activity. The trip to Ashe was a notable thing in the lives of the members of the band. We usually had about 15 members and made the trip to Ashe over old time undeveloped roads. We usually had about two horse drawn vehicles called hacks. This was a large, covered, three seated affair very much in use at that time by people who traveled and especially by drummers or salesmen who traveled over the country to the different stores and had trunks of samples to show their customers.

Added Attractions

We usually spent about three days at the Ashe County Fair and were one of the main attractions. We roomed all together in one room at one of the big hotels and had concerts more or less at night. All of the members being single, made it more and more interesting because there was always a group of good looking girls attending the fair and two or three members of the band really picked out some attractive and beautiful girls to sport around with during the hours of the fair. Probably the only reason we did not pick some of them out for life partners was the fact that we had some very dear girls that we were deeply interested in back home.

The band had practice hours about two days a week in the evenings. In the summer time we practiced under one of the big trees on the courthouse lawn to which we hung lanterns for light. We always had a group of interested bystanders to hear us practice. In the colder months we met upstairs in the old Rousseau store building, which was across the street from the courthouse and stood where the Texaco station now stands. The town also had a lot of box suppers and ice cream suppers in this building.

The really permanent members of the band were; Bill Martin, teacher, Blaine Henderson, Norman Smoak, Tom Hubbard, Fred Hubbard, Charlie (Chunk) Staley, Earl Davis, Julius Hubbard, Weaver Starr, Waverly Morrison, Frank Lunn, Lonnie Lunn, Arlie Green and Rob Starr. I will not enumerate who played the different instruments because occasionally we changed around on these.

All together the Wilkes Concert Band played a very important part in the social life of Wilkesboro from about 1908 until 1920, at which time other developments had taken place and other social amusement had developed. Some of the boys went to college and the band gradually fell apart but not without the very pleasant memories connected with the organization, by the different participants and the community in general. Two or three of the members of the band who went to college enjoyed the membership of the college bands and were very fortunate in being able to perform with these bands.

Another Band

At this point I am compelled to mention with a great deal of pleasure and admiration, of a Negro band which existed at the same time as the Wilkes Concert Band. The members that I remember particularly of this band was Ira Gilreath who was a well trained and great performer on the coronet. I also remember very well Rich Lomax who was a famous bass horn man. I can still remember when he lived over on Harris Ridge back of Wilkesboro and practiced on his bass horn. He filled the horn well and could make grand and effective tones on his bass. The sounds echoed up and down the Cub Creek valley and over the hills in the evenings and one could not help but admire the performance. The Negro band was not as large as the Wilkes Concert Band but it seemed to us that they made awfully good music and we were always glad to hear them in concert.

All the members of both bands are gone. The only two members of the Wilkes Concert Band left are Dr. Hubbard and Weaver Starr. Weaver, for the past several years, has lived in Reidsville, N.C.

And so the years tumble along and leave with those few citizens and members of the band something very pleasant to remember and to cherish in connection with the past history of the town.

Article by Dr. Fred C. Hubbard.

LIBERTY LODGE NO. 45 ANCIENT FREE AND ACCEPTED MASONS

Liberty Lodge No. 45, A.F. & A.M., was instituted in the year 1804 and the charter was issued December 10, 1804 in the town of Wilkesborough, North Carolina. Liberty Lodge is the eighteenth oldest Lodge in North Carolina still active.

William Lenoir was appointed to serve as the first Master of Liberty Lodge.

The names of any of the charter members are not available at this time due to a fire in 1891 which destroyed the building occupied by Liberty Lodge and all the records and furniture.

In the early years, the Lodge regular meetings were held on or before the first full moon in each month, and on Tuesday of each court week, and on the Festivals of the Saints John. The Lodge now meets on the first Thursday of each month.

Three former members of Liberty Lodge were elected to serve as Grand Masters of Masons in North Carolina. Richard N. Hackett served in 1910-1911, during which time the Masonic and Eastern Star home was built in the City of Greensboro, North Carolina. Samuel F. Patterson of Liberty Lodge served as Grand Master in 1833-1834. Charles Harrison Pugh, M.D., served as Grand Master in 1955-56. Brother Pugh held many offices in related Masonic bodies while maintaining a large medical practice.

Since the year 1804 to the present date, there have been seventeen Lodges chartered in Wilkes County. Liberty Lodge is the oldest. Only four of these exist at this date.

Moravian Falls Lodge No. 353 was consolidated with Liberty Lodge in the year 1938. Howard M. Broyhill, deceased, and Brother Shafter R. Laws, former member of Moravian Falls Lodge No. 353 and now a member of Liberty Lodge No. 45, both received Sixty Year continuous membership awards. Ed Crysel of Wilkesboro, who was made a Mason at Liberty Lodge in 1924, is still active and approaching his sixtieth year of service.

In 1973, the members of Liberty Lodge purchased land and constructed a new Lodge Hall on School Street in Wilkesboro, North Carolina, which provides excellent facilities for the holding of meetings and other Masonic functions. This building was erected and completely paid for through the efforts of the membership.

Many outstanding men have passed through the portals of Liberty Lodge No. 45 in the past 178 years whom we are happy to claim as our forebearers in this Masonic fraternity.

Liberty Lodge continues strong and active today with a present membership of 152. Edward D. Welborn is the present Master of the Lodge.

Source: Lodge minutes researched by Page Choate.

GRAY BROTHERS FURNITURE, INC.

Gray Brothers Furniture Company of Wilkesboro, N.C. was founded in 1929 as a partnership between A.R. Gray, Sr. and Lawrence M. Gray.

The business was first located in the N.B. Smithey building on Main Street across from the Smithey Hotel and remained there until about 1932 when it was moved to the Old Calloway Inn and Home on the Southwest corner of Main and Bridge Street. About 1934 the Winkler Building on the Southeast corner of Main and Bridge Streets, together with the range and heater business of Mr. D.E. Smoak, became available and were taken over by Gray Brothers Furniture Company — which then operated on the two corners — The Calloway Building and the Winkler Building — for the next 12 years.

By 1935, L.M. Gray had sold his interest to A.R. Gray, Sr. and A.R. Gray, Jr. became a full time employee of the business. A.R. Gray, Jr. has remained a full partner and manager for 47 years.

In 1937, William C. Gray became a partner in the business and, with the exception of 1 year in college and 3 years in World War II remained a full active partner in the business until his retirement in 1981.

In 1946 the business was moved to the present location at 125 West Main Street where it remains today.

In 1949 A.R. Gray, Sr., founder of the business, died and his interest was left to his wife, Sarah C. Gray and his two sons, A.R. Gray, Jr. and William C. Gray.

In 1970 James R. Gray, son of A.R. Gray, Jr., became the first third generation member of the Gray family to enter the business. James R. Gray became a partner in the business in 1977. In 1981 the business was incorporated and A.R. Gray, Jr. became president and James R. Gray became secretary-treasurer and general operating officer.

A.R. Sherman House, early 1900s.

Gray Brothers Furniture, Inc. has always been located on Main Street in Wilkesboro and is the oldest retail furniture store in Northwestern North Carolina.

SMITHEY HOTEL

The Smithey Hotel located on a corner lot on Main and Court Streets is closed down now but during its forty-seven years of operation, played a significant role in Wilkesboro's history.

In 1891, the Wilkesboro Hotel Company was formed to construct the hotel. The Company believed that a hotel would be profitable next to the court-house. The company hired local masons to build the building, native brick from the North Wilkesboro Brick Company was used in its construction. The members of the Wilkesboro Hotel Company were: W.M. Absher of Dockery, J.R. Combs of Roaring River, J.T. Ferguson, J.C. Hubbard, J.W. White, T.B. Finley, J.A. Cooper of Dellaplane, I.T. Prevette, H.W. Horton, Eller & Starbuck, A.E. Berrington, S.J. Ginnings and W.W. Barber.

The first owner of the hotel was W.S. Welborn and was called the Wilkesboro Hotel. The hotel failed, however, and Welborn went bankrupt. Welborn hunted frantically for someone to buy the hotel. On May 1, 1906, Nike B. Smithey and his father, Isaac, bought the hotel. According to local legend, Welborn had not taken Nike Smithey seriously at first. Nike's only money came from selling beef door to door. However, Nike and his father borrowed $3,800 to buy the hotel. This was the only money Nike Smithey ever borrowed.

After Nike Smithey and his father bought the hotel, he and his parents moved into it and changed its name to Smithey. Later, when Isaac Smithey died, Nike bought the hotel from the other heirs, Mack, Britton, Myrtle Freeland, Jeanette Sherrill, Wanie Shoaf, Vecie Call-Poindexter, and Ney Tomlinson.

The hotel was a three-story building. When Smithey purchased it, the first floor was occupied by a post office, grocery store and drug store. These soon moved to other locations in Wilkesboro.

The hotel quarters were on the second and third stories of the building. It had thirty bedrooms, one large dining room and a kitchen. The second floor had a large hallway with three stairways to the third floor. An outside porch ran around the second and third floors.

The hotel continued operation until 1973. During its last years of operation it became more of a place for roomers than for the traveling public. Several school teachers lived there during the week and a few people who worked in local factories roomed there.

Reasons for its lack of business were commuters and stiff competition from more modern facilities. Electric wires were also exposed throughout the building so the family thought it best to close the hotel completely. Some of the furniture was auctioned off and the rest was given to Crossnore school in Avery County, N.C.

Presently the hotel building is owned by Mrs. N.B. Smithey. It has recently been nominated by the North Carolina Department of Cultural Resources as a potential historical site worthy of restoration.

Sources: a story by Charlene Beshears; Personal knowledge of Kyle Hayes.

TALKING SHOP AT THE OLD WILKES HOTEL

EARLY DAYS OF NASCAR

In 1947 a group of friends — semiformal business partners — playing poker in a room at the Old Wilkes Hotel were idly talking shop.

One seemed distracted, doodling, only occasionally joining the conversation. Finally, he held up a rough drawing, which showed two winged cars apparently on the verge of crashing, head on.

"This is going to be the emblem of our organization, which we're going to call NASCAR", declared the artist, Bill France, Sr.

Charlie Combs, John Mastin, and Enoch Staley sat there and listened to what France was saying, about how people in this part of the country would someday pay to see cars just like they drove, run in a race on a track. Before they knew it, he talked them into building a speedway.

They had been going to races France put on at Charlotte and Greensboro and seeing a lot of Wilkes County people at both places. They figured if they go there, they'll go here, so they got a piece of land and roughed out an oval track, which is now North Wilkesboro Speedway, a ⅝-mile track.

Sources: family records, personal knowledge and memories by Irene Mastin Whittington.

"MISS MAMIE BARBER'S HOME SCHOOL FOR YOUNG LADIES"

Miss Mamie Barber's school played an important part in the education in Wilkes County between the years of 1879 and 1924.

Mary Taylor Barber was the daughter of the Rev. Richard Wainwright Barber, rector of St. Paul's Episcopal Church. Mr. Barber also conducted a school for boys at his home, Cedar Lawn, east of Wilkesboro, now owned by W.K. Sturdivant.

Mary Taylor Barber gave up her position as a member of the faculty of St. Mary's School in Raleigh, where she had graduated, and came back to Wilkesboro and in 1879 opened a school for girls located in the Barber home, Cedar Lawn. The school was soon recognized for its thorough training and christian home atmosphere.

In addition to the boarding students there were always a dozen or more day students, coming from the nearby homes up and down the river. Those who sent their children there were the Cowles, Miller, Harold, Absher, Peden, Hemphill, Barber, Walter, Doughton, Rousseau, and other families. The school usually had an enrollment of about twenty students a year, who in addition to scholarship, learned the finest behavior, and have contributed immeasurably to the moral, cultural and spiritual growth of this area.

Miss Mamie's school was far from being modern. It was a substantial log building with a long porch across the front of two rooms. There were home made desks, split bottom chairs, and a big iron stove in the middle of the room to give plenty of heat. Two cedar water buckets were filled with good fresh water on the shelf with two tin dippers, and outdoor toilets.

There were two fifteen minute recesses and an hour for lunch. Everyone had baskets of food and after lunch there was usually a ball game or other games until time for school to "take up." In addition to other equipment there was a large clock, a black board and a picture of George Washington. School always opened with Bible reading, prayers and a hymn.

Classes from the first grade through high

Pupils of Miss Mamie Barber's School.

Wilkesboro High School Ball Players.

school were taught. Special attention was given to those who needed help. Miss Mamie was an exceptionally fine teacher, who loved her work, and as a History and English teacher she could not be surpassed. Like her father, she was a fine Latin teacher, which is the basis of a good English course.

Friday afternoons we either had a spelling bee, or recitations, compositions or some form of entertainment, and in this we were taught to appear before others with ease and confidence.

Sources: Family knowledge of Mrs. Margaret Barber Moore.

NEGRO SCHOOLS OF LONG AGO

At one time there were eighteen negro schools in Wilkes County. They were Old Academy, Denny's Grove and Parks Grove, in Wilkesboro township; Thankful No. 1, Moravian Falls Township; Thankful No. 2 at Boomer; Lewis Fork, Ferguson, Wilbar, Fairplains, Woodlawn and Rock Creek in North

Wilkesboro township; Union Grove and Roaring River Elementary in Roaring River township; Mount Valley and Piney Grove in Ronda township and Traphill. There was also Lincoln Heights.

All of these schools were one and two-teacher schools. They were eventually consolidated and bused into the Lincoln Heights Union or combination school with the exception of Woodlawn.

Lincoln Heights accommodated all Negro children who chose to take advantage of high school training in Wilkes and many other adjoining counties from 1924 to 1967. For many years, eighth grade students from these outlying communities came into Lincoln Heights until they completed their high school training. The Woodlawn students also came to Lincoln Heights to high school.

In 1954, Sparta (in Alleghany County) had made no preparation for high school training for its Negro youth. A little station wagon bus was bought and those children were bused into Lincoln Heights High School until the school was phased out in 1967.

In 1967-68, the elementary school was housed in the then relatively new high school building, but it too, was phased out in the spring of that year. At this time there is a Day Care Center being conducted in what was old Lincoln Heights and the Wilkes County Vocational center is housed in the new building.

Contrary to the thoughts of many, Lincoln Heights was very near and dear to our people. True, we are law abiding citizens and went along with the "Law of the Land", but I for one had sold brick at twenty-five cents per brick, and I was a fifth grader when the first building was erected. I finished there in the class of 1931. Returned there in 1935 as a teacher and remained there for thirty-three years. Needless to say we miss our school. Please do not read into this bitterness on my part. It was a great

Mrs. John Harris "Aunt Julia" "Jule", 100 years old.

experience and we learned a lot. There was a closeness among our people and a great spirit of cooperation to some extent than I sometimes feel exists now that we attend the schools nearest us.

Much is to be said for the peaceful way in which the schools were integrated in our county. I have worked at Wilkes Community College for four years since the closing of Lincoln Heights and also for four years at Moravian Falls School as Resource Teacher. These, too, were challenging experiences and I feel I am a better person for having been blessed to survive forty-three years as a teacher.

School terms in one and two-teacher schools, in which my father and mother began teaching, were only three and four months long per year. We have come a long, long, way and I personally am looking forward, optimistically, to the future. May God bless and continue to bless us everyone.

Sources: Research by Loree Harris Anderson.

WILKES COMMUNITY COLLEGE

The 1963 North Carolina General Assembly passed the Community College Act creating a system of comprehensive community colleges and technical institutes under the State Board of Education. In September 1964, the people of Wilkes County approved the College through a bond vote of 5000,000. for construction of facilities and up to five cents tax authorization for the operation of the College. Wilkes Community College was approved by the State Board of Education on October 1, 1964.

The first Board of Trustees was sworn into office on January 15, 1965 and the name "Wilkes Community College" was officially adopted on that date.

The first President, Dr. Howard E. Thompson, was elected on March 5, 1965, and he opened an office in the North Carolina National Bank Building in North Wilkesboro on July 1, 1965.

J. Hyatt Hammond Associates was selected as architect on June 4, 1965.

Apprenticeship Training Classes were the first classes to be scheduled and were held in September 1965. Part-time Business Technology Programs began in December 1965. The first one-year diploma program, Practical Nurse Education, began March 7, 1965. On September 15, 1966, students were admitted to full-time status in Associate in Arts and Associate in Applied Science Degree programs.

The new facilities on Collegiate Drive were occupied on April 1, 1969. The college is located in the western section of Wilkesboro.

The 75 acre campus contains five ultra-modern, air conditioned and electrically heated buildings of white poured-concrete construction. These buildings contain more than 150,000 square feet of class-rooms, labs, shops and offices and are equipped with the best teaching facilities available for the programs offered.

Source: Wilkes Community College Catalogue (1979).

Wilkes Community College.

THE WARS AND WILKES
REVOLUTIONARY WAR MEN OF WILKES

In the fall of 1775, a provincial convention was called. Benjamin Cleveland, John Hamlin, Jesse Walton, Benjamin Herndon and William Lenoir represented Wilkes County. Out of these meetings came a group of men determined to resist the British tyranny at any cost. The following are names of those who either fought in the Militia, N.C. and Virginia Continental lines or gave patriotic service during the Revolutionary War, and who lived in Wilkes for a period of time. All were privates unless otherwise stated:

Capt. Richard Allen, b. 1741, d. 1832; William Adams b. 1760, d. 1783; Henry Adams b. 1759, d. 1821; John Amburgy b. 1758, d. 1831; Benjamin Adams b. 1752, d. 1829; William Alexander b. 1749; Travis Alexander; William Anglea b. 1754, d. 1852; Jacob Adams b. 1760, d. 1833; Hezekiah Barker d. 1816; Corp. Benjamin Brown b. 1763, d. 1846; Robert Brown b. 1762, d. 1846; Capt. John Barton d. 1827; Jasper Billings b. 1758, d. 1834; Jasper Billings b. 1766; Thomas Boling, b. 1766; Sgt. Jesse Boling b. 1758; David Benge, b. 1760, d. 1854; George Barker b. 1758; David Burns, b. 1760; Capt. John Bryan, b. 1750; John Baltrip; Robert Bryant b. 1754; Warren Benton d. 1819; Thomas Becknell, killed; Thomas Brotherton, b. 1755; Capt. John Brown b. 1738, d. 1812; Deveroux Ballard; Samuel Burdine; David Burk, Sr.; Corp. John Burk, Sgt. William Blackburn b. 1756; Charles Burns; William Burns; Miller Childers b. 1756; Reubin Coffey b. 1759; Henry Cook b. 1760; George Cook b. 1764; Isaac Cook, b. 1759; John Campbell, d. 1834; George Combs, b. 1761; William Combs; John Chapman b. 1750, d. 1836; Thomas Cargill b. 1762, d. 1847; William Cargill d. 1845; Archelous Craft b. 1759, d. 1853; Ambrose Carlton b. 1763, d. 1832; Lewis Carlton b. 1758, d. 1832; Amos Church b. 1758; John Church b. 1760; Jobe Cole b. 1753; John Childers; Ens. Charles Cranshaw; William Carter, b. 1760; James Caudill b. 1763, d. 1839; Stephen Caudill b. 1663, d. 1839; John Colyer b. 1757; William Cox; Absolum Cleveland; Capt. Larkin Cleveland; Col. Benjmain Cleveland b. 1751, d. 1806; Lt. John Cleveland b. 1760, d. 1810; Jarrott Crabb b. 1751; Capt. Robert Cleveland b. 1744, d. 1812; William Cash; Joseph Chapman b. 1760; Jeremiah Crysel; Wilber Carter; Samuel Castle; Bailey Chandler, Jonah Chandler, Josiah Chandler; Joel Chandler, Joseph Calloway; Henry Carter d. 1799; Mastin Durham b. 1755; Monah Dyer b. 1755; William Dugger b. 1750, d. 1838; William Davis b. 1761; John Darnall, killed 1780; John Duncan; Jesse Duncan; Joseph Duncan; Elijah Denny, Edmond Denny, Isham Dickerson b. 1763; Benjamin Eastridge b. 1761; Abendigo Earp; Thompson Epperson b. 1757, d. 1838; James Fletcher; Sgt. Anthony Foster b. 1758; Thomas Fletcher b. 1759; Francis Fox; Capt. Jesse Franklin b. 1760, Gov. of N.C.; James Gray b. 1763; Jesse Green; Capt. William Gilreath, b. 1752; Alexander Gilreath; John Grant b. 1755, d. 1843; Capt. Martin Gambill; Thomas Grimsley; Capt. Nathaniel C. Gordon b. 1762, d. 1802; Chapman Gordon b. 1743, d. 1800; Charles Gordon, Sr. b. 1830, d. 1811; Capt. Alexander Gordon; Benjamin Hammons b. 1756, d. 1835; Henry Holdaway b. 1740; William Harris b. ca 1735; John Hammons b. 1760; Howell Hunt d. 1793; Joseph Hancock b. 1762, d. 1835; Abraham Hunt b. 1762; Charles Hardiman; Joseph Holeman; Daniel Holeman; Henry Horton; Joshua Horton; John Hill b. 1759; Samuel Heldra b. 1766; William Hampton b. 1742; Robert Higgins; Thomas Hall, David Hall; Samuel Hall, Sr.; Colby Holbrook; William Holbrook; John Holbrook; Joel Hampton; Capt. Fredrick Hambright; Maj. Joseph Herndon b. 1751, d. 1798; Col. Benjamin Herndon b. 1748, d. 1819; Col. Elijah Isaacs; Lt. Thomas Isbell; John English b. 1761; Capt. Pendleton Isbell; John Judd b. 1765; Capt. Rowland Judd; George Johnson, Sr. b. 1748; Ens. William Johnson b. 1753; William Johnson b. 1750; Alexander Johnson b. 1760; d. 1824; Thomas Johnson; John Johnson; Capt. Samuel Johnson b. 1762; Thomas Joines; Major Joines killed S.C.; Thomas Jones; Capt. John Kees; Leonard Kelland; Jacob Lyon b. 1757; John Lane b.

1742; John Love b. 1760; David Laws, Sr. b. 1754; Gen. William Lenoir b. 1751, c. 1839; Capt. Joel Lewis b. 1760, d. 1816; Lt. James M. Lewis b. 1762, d. 1830; Capt. Micajah Lewis b. 1755, d. 1781; Thomas Majors b. 1764; Zach Martin b. 1761, d. 1833; Henry Main b. 1738; Chaplain George McNiel; b. 1720, d. 1805; Capt. William Meredith; Ens. Benjamin Morgan; John Montgomery b. 1754; William Miller b. 1756; Isaac Miller b. 1754; Henry Miller b. 1760, d. 1852; Leonard Miller b. 1755, d. 1845; Thomas McGee b. 1749; John Norris; Barnard Owens; David Owens d. 1822; William Powell b. 1759; John Parmely b. 1762, d. 1848; William Proffit d. 1823; Joseph Pinson b. 1754; George Parks; Lt. John Parks; Aaron Parks; Joseph Pruitt; Henry Pumphrey; Joseph Porter; Pleasant Proffitt; Richard Price; Joseph Phillips; George Pearson b. 1762, Asher Reeves; Corp. Sgt. Sterling Rose b. 1756; Lt. Elisha Reynolds b. 1754, d. 1836; William Roberts b. 1760; Bethil Riggs; William Ross b. 1745, d. 1831; John Redding b. 1755; Charles Reynolds; James Reynolds; Jesse Ray; Abel Rollin; Sgt. Leonard Rice b. 1759; John Smith b. 1760; Capt. Miner Smith; Daniel Sisk, killed; Reubin Smithers; Gabriel Smithers; William Smith; John Sparks b. 1752; James Shepherd; John Swanson b. 1760; Benjamin Sebastian b. 1845, d. 1819; Lt. James Scurlock; James Smoot b. 1763; Winborn Summerlin b. 1761; Montford Stokes, gov N.C.; Robert Smith b. 1762; Jacob Stamper b. 1762, d. 1834; Joel Stamper b. 1755; William Spicer b. 1754; John Thrasher; Rober Turner b. 1759; Richard Taylor b. 1730; John Townsen; Moses Toliver; Jesse Toliver; Elijah Trible b. 1754; Elijah Vickers; Capt. Andrew Vannoy; Capt. John Vickers; John Vickers b. 1758, d. 1834; William Vickers b. 1766; Jacob Wall b. 1748; Jonathan Wall b. 1744; Corp. John Whitaker, b. 1760; Lt. David Witherspoon, b. 1758; John Witherspoon b. 1760; Moses Waters b. 1753; William Whitaker; William Walton; Abraham Wiles b. 1762; William Yates; John Yates; John Yergain b. 1759.

Source: Research by Samuel E. Sebastian.

REVOLUTIONARY WAR GRAVES MARKED IN WILKES COUNTY

This list of Wilkes County Revolutionary soldiers, their ranks, their dates of birth and death, and the site of their grave has been compiled by the Rendezvous Mountain Chapter of the Daughters of the American Revolution of North Wilkesboro.

Richard Allen, Sr., Col., 1741-1832, buried on farm of Jack Hoots in Edwards Township; Jasper Billings, Pvt., 1758-1805, Dockery community near Mt. Pisgah Church; John Brown, Capt., 1738-1812, Brown's Ford Cemetery, four miles west of Wilkesboro; John Bryan, Capt., died 1842, Bryan-Parks Cemetery, Antioch Township; Jeremiah Crysel, Pvt., 1757-1835, North Wilkesboro Township, west on U.S. 421 on knoll on right beyond Winn-Dixie store; Robert Cleveland,

Capt., 1744-1812, on Parsonsville Road at Purlear; William Dula, Pvt., 1755-1835, near Yadkin River; Chapman Gordon, 1764-1811, Pvt., under sanctuary of North Wilkesboro Presbyterian Church; George Gordon, soldier, 1743-1800, St. Paul's Episcopal Church cemetery in Wilkesboro; Benjamin Howard, Sr., Pvt., 1742-1828, Wolf Farm; John Jennings, Patriot, 1706-1811, family cemetery on Mulberry Creek, N.C. 18 between McGrady and North Wilkesboro; Luke Jennings, Patriot, 1748-1839, family cemetery on Mulberry Creek; Samuel Johnson, Capt., 1757-1834, Johnson Family Cemetery near Traphill on Gristletail Road; Jacob Lyon, 1762-1840, Lyon Family Cemetery near Traphill; Banjamin Martin, Ensign, 1746-1821, Brier Creek Cemetery in Antioch Township; George McNiel, Chaplain, 1720-1805, approximately 14 miles west of North Wilkesboro on the Parsonsville Road, one-half mile east of Stony Hill Baptist Church; William Spicer, 1752-1831, Round Hill Church Cemetery in Traphill; Thomas Mastin, Capt., 1749-1828, Brier Creek Church near Dellaplane; John Montgomery, Pvt., 1756-1843, Moravian Falls Cemetery; John Whittington, Civil Service, 1726-1778, Broyhill Farm near King's Creek.

Source: Newspaper account, list of DAR and Smithsonian list at Washington, D.C.

WILKES VALLEY GUARDS (U.D.C.)

The Wilkes Valley Guards chapter of the United Daughters of the Confederacy (UDC), named after the first company of volunteers from the county to the Confederacy, was organized September 19, 1911 with twenty-six members. Mrs. Carrie Finley Pilson was elected the first president. Surnames of these charter members were: Barber, Coffey, Elmore, Ferguson, Finley, Hall, Hackett, Hix, Holman, Pilson, Rousseau and Wilkins.

The chapter honored the memory of those who served and fell in the service of the Confederate states. Markers were erected on Confederate soldiers' graves. These graves received especial attention on Memorial Day. Money was sent to care for the Confederate Cemetery in Raleigh, to the Confederate Woman's Home, and to the Memorial Building fund.

The chapter tried to preserve a truthful history of the War Between the States, and to see that this was taught to children.

Nice Christmas boxes were sent to surviving Confederate soldiers in the county.

In August 1913 the Wilkes Valley Guards had the honor of sponsoring the journal *Carolina and the Southern Cross*, published monthly at Kinston. This was instigated to rescue much of the true southern story that still remained unwritten. Many Wilkes heroes of the Confederacy are written up here. Copies are still preserved. The chapter disbanded in 1966 after fifty-five years of existence.

Sources: Chapter treasurer's book; chapter literature and the August 1913 issue of *Carolina and the Southern Cross*.

JOHN A. FOSTER

CIVIL WAR LETTER

Beaver Creek, Wilkes county, N.C. March 10, 1864

Lt. Thomas J. Foster.

Dear Uncle, we received you kind favor by yesterdays mail dated Jan. 29th. informing us that you and all of our relation in Texas was well which was a service of great satisfaction to us all. We are tolerable well, truley hoping these lines may reach and find you and all our relations in the like enjoyment.

I have nothing of interest to write you. I have been at home 10 days today and will remain at home 14 days yet. I got a furlough for 30 days by furnishing a recuret (Virginia's brother Jesse M. Foster). I have no war news of importance to write you, when I left the army everything seemed to be quite.

I haven't been with my command but very little the last six months. I was wounded at Bristo, Va. in battle on the 14th. of Oct. last, was in the hospital for three months I then rejoined my regiment and staid about three weeks and got a furlough of indulgence for 18 days and came home and staid 8 days and then went back to my Co. Taken brother Jepe back with me to join my company as recruit and staid 2 weeks and got a 30 day furlough. I left my regiment of the Refillion River near Orange County court house, Va. I am going to make my furlough pay me this time. You requested Pa to inform you of the whereabouts of our relation. N.A. Foster is Captain of my Co. and is at this time a prisoner of war. W.W. Carmichael, J.J. Pearlier and J.G. Hall are my Lients. A.E. and J.T. Foster are both in my Co. also John S. Foster (Thomas's son) B.F. Foster is at home on furlough, he has been hauling salt for the government. Dr. Foster and J.E. Foster are both at home (exempt) Pa and Uncle J.J. Foster and A.J. Jones are at home, to olde, Justice of Peace and Post Master. John B. Miller and Uncle Alfred are at home, to olde. All of Uncle Alfred's boys are in the service (in Lee's Army) Wm. P. Miller was Capt. of Co. K 53rd. N.C. Regt. and was killed in battle of Gettysburg, Pa. Thomas Miller is Lie't. in his Co. and is at this time prisoner of war. Henry Miller is in the same Co. and was well when I saw him last. Jep Miller is also in the Co. and a private. E.W. Foster and J.W. Bowman are both privates in the same Co. We haven't heard anything from Uncle Calvin Miller since that county has been invaded. Cousin Henderson and Rufus Jones both joined the army. Henderson is thought to be dead. I saw him last I reckon of any of his relation in the hospital at Petersburg, Va. about 18 months ago. Rufius is in the service yet. Olde Uncle Edmund Foster is living at Rufisus Jones. Little Jep Triplett is in the army. We cannot tell where Ambrose is haven't heard from him since the war broke out. Little Jepe F. Triplett was in the same Brigade that I belonged to, he was orderly Sergt. and was killed in the battle of Gettysburg, Pa. Little Larkin T. Jones died in the army of Disn. Y.C. Land is Lient. in cousin Wm. P. Miller's olde Co. Cousin M.A. Parks is Col. of my regiment, at this time

a prisoner of war. He is a fine man. I have a position in the orderly Co., Sergt. I also stand a chance of promotion, (Lient.)

Well Uncle if you get this I shall expect to hear from you. When you write direct thus; Sergt. John A. Foster, Co. F, 52nd. Regt. N.C. Troops, Kirklands Brigade, Heath's Div., A.P. Hill's Corp. Richmond, Va.

Well, Uncle I am getting very tired of this cruel war. I have been in 8 battles but been very fortunate. I have only been wounded onst. I wish I could write you an interesting letter but I am not prepared for it at this time. I am thinking that we will have some very hard fighting in Va. this spring and summer. Much depends upon the spring campaigns as to the termination of this war. We have all reinlisted for the war. I think it has already had a good effect. It has demoralized the enemy very much I learn. Aunt Sarah is here and sends howdy to you all. Mother and Pa and all the children sends their love and howdy to you all. Give my respects to Lient. Ball and all my aquaintances (if any other) Tell Grandmaw and Aunt Mary and Uncle Thurmand and little children and Uncle Wm. and his lady all howdy for me. Tell them I haven't forgot them, also give my respects to your lady (Aunt Francis) and little girl and boy. I would like to see you all. Write me soon and often and keep us informed and how to direct. I will answer I assure you every letter that I receive from you. Well, Uncle Thomas if I am ever so fortunate as to live to see this war end I shall I think be contented to live any where in olde Wilkes but no where else. Pa will write you enclosed with this. I have enjoyed tolerable health since I have been in the service thought not half as well satisfied as I would be at home, but it is on us and every man should be willing to do his duty. I like the soldier that acts right and honorable. I will close please excuse this badly written and composed letter for I have wrote in haste, Yours Very Respectfully, John A. Foster 1st. Sergt. of Co. F 52nd. Regt. N.C. Troops

LETTERS FROM FRANKLIN M. McGEE CIVIL WAR

Franklin M. McGee was born 13 June, 1834, died 10 July, 1963, form wounds received at the Battle of Gettysburg. He was the son of Holland McGee of Wilkes County. He entered the service 1 October, 1862, in Company I, 32nd Regiment, N.C. Troops. The following are the letters he wrote to his family during his service in the war:

"October 3rd, 1862 — Camp near Drury's Bluff, Chesterfield County, Virginia: My dear Companion & Children, I now take my pen in hand to write a few lines to you by which you will find that I am well at present and I greatly hope these few lines will find you all well and doing well. I will first let you know that I with many others from Wilkes is signed over to the 32nd Regt. N.C.T. and in the same brigade of the 53rd. We got here last evening and this morning I went up to Captain Miller's Compa-

ny and saw them. Our Regt. is close to theirs. We left Wilkesboro on Saturday and got to Statesville on Sunday evening and we left there on Monday evening and went to Salibury that evening and we left Salisbury on that evening at 8 o'clock and we went on about three miles and the car broke down and we did not go any fatther until about 3 o'clock the next morning and then we went on to Raleigh and we staid at Raleigh about one day and we drew out clothes and knapsacks and then we went on to Petersburg on Thursday and we were from there to a place called the halfway station and there we quit the cars and went down to the Rdgt. where we are now; and we have drew fifty dollars bounty today and I will send you forty dollars by Jas. Eller and I sent my black breeches back by John Waters from Raleigh. I want you all to write to me as soon as you get this and let me know how you are getting along with saving your fodder.

Write to me soon and fail not. Direct your letters to Proctor's Creek P.O. Chesterfield County, Virginia, C.O. 0-32nd Regt. N.C. Troops in Care of Capt. London.

I remain your loving husband until death. F.M. McGee to Matilda McGee and children.''

''Dear Father & Mother, I also will write a few lines to you which I hope will find you all well. I will let you know that we was far mistaken about going to any Regt. that we pleased. We had to go just where our officers pleased but I think that we have got under a very good Captain or he appears to be a very smart man. I have no news of interest to write to you at the present. The people about here don't think there will be any fighting about here soon. I am not able yet to tell you anything about how I like camp life but I don't think it will agree with me very well. Write to me soon and fail not. I remain yours truly, F.M. McGee to Thomas Walsh & Family.'' (in same letter)

''I would like to see you all very well if I could but as I can't I send my best regards to you all. s/G. S. Powel.''

''January 2, 1863 — Camp near Drury's Bluff — My dear Companion, It is through the mercy of God that I seat myself down by candle light to write you a few lines which will inform you that I am in tolerable health at this time. I truly hope when these few lines come to your hand it will find you and the children and your father's folks all well and doing well. I have no news to write at this time only we have to start on a march in the morning but I can't tell where we will go. Some say that we are going to Goldsboro and some say that we will go to Blackwater Station but I can't tell, but I am afraid that we will have to right into a fight and if I do I hope that God will be with us. I want you all to pray for me that I may live to come home and see you and our dear little children and all of your father's folks. I had rather see you all than to have all the Southern Confederacy at my own command, but I want you all to do the best you can. If I live I will try to come home about the last of next month, but I don't know whether I can get a furlough or not but I will try, if I live till that time. We will draw two months wages in a few days. I would of got it in the morning if we hadn't had to left here. We have to start at six o'clock in the morning. I

have not got a letter from any of you in two weeks. I wrote to W.L. Walsh and William Church about three weeks ago and I have got no answer from either. Give them my best respects and tell them to write to me and fail not. I will close by saying write soon and often for I love to get a letter from any of you, so no more now only I remain your husband until death. So Farewell. You need not write till I write again. s/F. M. McGee to Matilda McGee''

''January 17, 1863 — Camp near Goldsboro, Miss Matilda McGee My dear Companion, It is through the mercy of a gracious God that I seat myself down to write you a few lines which will inform you that I am in common health at this time and to let you know that I received your kind letter dated the 10th of this instant which I was glad to receive and to hear that you are all well and doing well and I truly hope that when these few lines come to hand they will find you all well and doing well. Matilda, you said that you hadn't had no letter in three weeks. I can't account for it for I have wrote every week. I wrote you and Philip a letter about three weeks ago and I have wrote four since. I think that the letters surely will come better than they have been doing for it was two and three weeks. I have not received no answer from Philip. Matilda, you wanted me to get a furlough and come home but I am afraid there is no chance to get a furlough but I low to try to get one if I live and come home and see you all. You said you sent me some braid. I got the braid and the little bunches of the children's hair. I was glad to get it. You don't know how bad I felt to see how natural it looked and to think that I was so far away from you and no chance to help myself. You said that you got that money that I sent by Willis Waters. I am glad you got it. I would like to know how much money you have got. You said you had found three of the killing hogs. There is two more yet, for there was six of the big ones and six of the shoats which made twelve in all. I hope you will find the others too. You said that the stock all looks tolerable well. I was glad to hear that. I wish you could get shed of the old mare so that you would not have to feed her for the corn will do you more good than she will. I want you to do the best you can for yourself, for when recollections crowd my mind and bygone days I view them as a pleasant dream doth come, sweet thoughts dear friend of you, I hear affection from your lips, I see your lovely smile, your graceful form and laughing eyes though absent yet the while; I cant forget one look of thine though miles apart we be, while life shall last and memory reign, I will remember thee and if on earth we meet no more, ere death the summons brings, to take us to our home above, with angels there to sing; our home in heaven yes, let us strive to meet each other there, where one eternal spring presides, and skies are always clear. I must cose by saying write soon and fail not. So no more at this time, only I remain your husband until death, so farewell for awhile. s/F.M. McGee to Matilda McGee.''

''February 8, 1863, Camp near Kinston, N.C., Mrs. Matilda McGee. My dear Companion, It is through the mercy of a gracious God

that I am blessed with one more opportunity of dropping you a few lines which will inform you that I am well as common at this time and I truly hope when these few lines come to hand they may find you and the children and your father's family all well and doing well. I can inform you that we have left Goldsboro and we are in one mile and a half of Kinston, but I don't know how long we will stay here. I can inform you that I have not had no letter from none of you since William McNeill come down. I want to hear from you the worst in the world. I can inform you that I sent you a letter by Lemuel Watson and a dollar's worth of stamps in it and told him to leave it at pop's for you. I will tell you something about our march. It snowed on Monday night about shoe-mouth deep and it turned cold next day and we got marching orders next morning and we started that evening and marched about 8 miles and took up and we had to make beds out of rails to keep out of the snow, but I had to stand guard that night and I can tell you it was cold the next morning and it commenced raining and we went on through the snow and rain and water shoe-mouth deep till about four o'clock that evening and then we stopped and stayed till Saturday morning for we could not get across the creek, and then we had to take the railroad and cross the bridge and went on till we got to where we are now, but I can tell you that I ruined my feet till I could hardly walk at all. My feet were raw in places as big as dollars. I saw several Yankees graves and where they had camped. I can tell you the way they do destroy things is awful where they go. I want you all to do the best you can and I want all to write and let me hear from you all, for it is more satisfaction to me to hear from home than anything else that I can hear. You can direct your letters to Kinston, the 32 Regt. Com. I, in care of Captain London. I must close by asking you to write soon and fail not. So no more only I remain your husband until death. So farewell. s/F.M. McGee to Matilda McGee.''

''April 29, 1863 — State of North Carolina, Pitt County — Mrs. Matilda McGee, My Dear Companion, It is through the mercies of a gracious God that I am yet spared to live and permitted of this one more opportunity of dropping you a few lines which will inform you I am in common health at this time for which we ought to be thankful to the almight God for his mercies at all times and all places and I do truly hope when thes lines come to hand they may find you and the children and all the rest of the family well and hearty and getting along as well as you could wish. Matilda, I do want to see you and the children the worst of all flesh in this world. You don't know how tired I am of this war. If I live to see tomorrow, it will be seven months since I left you and the children and it seems like it has been twelve, but I do hope and pray to God that the time will soon come when we will all get to come home one more time in life, but if I never live to come home I hope we will all meet in a better world. I want you to write how your corn held out and how you are getting along with the work. I will close by saying, write soon so no more, only I remain your husband until death. From F.M. McGee to Matilds McGee. Matilda, I can say to you that I have give Captain Miller $38.00 to sent home for me for I can't see nobody to send it by and he said he would sent it the first chance to you or his wife, so you can get it. You can write to me when you get it. He was looking for John Miller down, but I don't know whether he has been there or not, for I only get to see them once in a while, so no more at this time."

"June 18, 1863, Williamsport in Maryland, Mrs. Matilda McGee, My Dear Companion, It is through the mercies of a gracious God that I am blest with this one more opportunity of writing a few lines which will inform you that I am in common health at this time and I do truly hope when these few lines come to hand they may find you and the children and all the rest of the family well and doing well. I can say to you that I have not heard from none of you since Jessie Miller came back. I wish I could a heard from you all. I can say to you all that we have had a hard time since we have left our camps. We have driven the enemy out of four towns and they have retreated back across the Potomac and we crossed the river last night and stopped to camp and I wrote a few lines by firelight for I did not expect to get the chance to send a letter any more but there is one more chance to start a letter for they are going to send the most of the wagons back to Richmond and this is all the chance to send a letter for there is no mail route that comes to us. Matilda, I used to think that I see a hard time but if I was there and could stay in peace with you and the children I would be willing to live on dry bread but I see no chance to come home unless the war would stop but it looks like a bad chance. I want Father to write how wheat is and how he made out to get is saved and how corn looks and how he is getting along with his work. I shall have to close by asking you all to write to me and let me hear from you. Direct your letters to Richmond, 32nd Regiment, Company I, Daniels Brigade, so no more, only I remain, as ever, your husband until death. From F.M. McGee to Matilda McGee. I want you all to pray for me that I may live to come home but if not, let us try to meet in a better world."

"September 1, 1863, Orange Court House, Virginia, Mr. Walsh, I seat myself to drop you a few line which will inform you I am well, hoping these few lines may find you well. I received your letter last night. I was glad to hear from you and was glad to know you got the letter I wrote you. You requested me to write you again if I could hear from F.M. McGee. The sad news came this morning that he was dead. Captain London got a letter from a man in our company that was wounded the same day F.M. was and he was in New York and he said F.M. McGee was dead. I don't know whether F.M. died in New York or not. He died from his wounds. I was sorry to hear that he was dead, for he was a good soldier and was respected by all the company. There is four months wages due him the day he got wounded. If you will tend to it, you can get it I think. I will stop for this time. I remain your friend until death. You can write if you see proper. From S.E. Whittington to Mr. Thomas Walsh."

"October 22, 1863 — Mr. Walsh, I seat myself to drop you a few lines which will inform you that I am well, hoping the same of you. I can say to you that I received a letter from you and I was glad to hear from you. I can inform you that we have had a right smart race after the yankees here in Virginia. We taken several prisoners. Out loss was not very heavy. I haven't any news that will interest you much only the yankees is coming back again. Sgt. T.A. Council is going to send the money that he owed McGee in this letter and Lieutenent Enbanks is in comman of this company. He will send you a certificate of what was due McGee, so he said. I understand they are getting all the deserters up in Wilkes. I want them to come and face the yankees a while. One man is no better to face them than another if he is under the law. I must close. I remain your friend. Write soon. From S.E. Whittington to Mr. Thomas Walsh."

Source: family papers of Mrs. Nancy C. Canter.

WAR DAYS IN THE BRUSHY MOUNTAINS

Attention to the Brushy Mountains calls my recollection to a tramp through that section in September 1863, with a detached troop of soldiers — Our mission was to persuade those people to be loyal to the Confederacy — I recall the fine country through which we passed from Statesville. Passing on the west side of Taylorsville, we soon struck heavily laden apple orchards that continued on to Wilkesboro. Brushy Mountain is broad and smooth, rather than abrupt. The south side of the mountain was literally banked with chinquapin bushes, then ripe in their prime. Passing down the north side we found a residence in a flat between two branches. Here we stopped to rest and cook some dinner. The landlord invited us to help ourselves to his cabbage heads and we filled a large wash pot, and dropped in our bits of bacon and we soon had a bountiful feast. He also supplied us with all the brandy we wanted at low cost.

We arrived in Wilkesboro before night and camped in a grove near the church. Our feet were blistered, and we had a few days' rest before combing the big mountains for conscripts and deserters. Many from Lee's army had lodged in that hospitable mountain section. It was court week and I saw a white man branded on the palm of his right hand for manslaughter. Wilkesboro was then a small town with a log house hotel, a bar room and a church. It was a goodly country with milk and honey, fat cattle and buckwheat cakes, and we fared sumptuously. Major Graham's headquarters were at New Hope Academy ... In Wilkesboro I saw barefoot women bring in kegs of brandy on sleds, stand up to the bars and take their brandy straight, enjoying more liberty than they now have. Telling of these incidents to a Methodist preacher who had been located there three years ago, he said, "Those mountain women had tramped up enough red mud with bare feet in Wilkesboro to make brick for a good sized town."

Source: (J.C. Elliott in Charlotte Observer), re-copied in an issue of the Wilkes Patriot in the 1920's.

THE 52ND. REGIMENT COMPANY F

From Wilkes County N.C. Troops Kirkland's Brigade, Heath's Division, A.P. Hill's Corp. The company had 169 privates, the regiment was organized at Camp Mangum, camp of instruction near Raleigh, April 22, 1862 and was composed of ten companies.

Officers; Marcus A. Parks, Lt. Col. Nathanel A. Foster, Captian William W. Carmichael, 1st. Lt. Joseph E. Hall, 1st. Serg. E.R. Vannoy, 2nd. Serg. William A. Foster, 3rd. Serg. James P. Gilreath, 1st Corp. All of the men enlisted from Wilkes county.

The company after organizing was sent to a camp near Lenoir where they went into camp to learn drilling and soldiering, until they were ordered to proceed to Goldsboro, N.C. There they fought a battle with the Federals on Dec. 17, 1862. They were greatly out numbered and were forced to retreat before reinforcements arrived.

Civil War Veterans — B Street North Wilkesboro, (1920).

Civil War Veterans, North Wilkesboro Fairgrounds (1910).

Company F fought at Gettysburg under N.C. General Pettigrew. A monument near the statue of General Lee lists company F. on July 4th., after most of the senior officers had been wounded or killed in the 52nd., Capt. N.A. Foster was placed in command. On the night of the 4th. Gen. Lee ordered a retreat in the direction of the Potomac River. On reaching there at Falling Waters, Md., the river was so swollen because of heavy rains that fording was impractible. Lee's pontoon bridges were partly destroyed and the army had to halt while the bridges were repaired, after which the army started to cross. The 52nd. was ordered to follow. The brigade, which the 52nd. was part of, was assigned to guard the rear while the army crossed the river. While the men were resting the Federal cavalry attacked catching the men by suprise, many of them were killed or wounded before the Federals could be driven off. The loss in killed and wounded in the 52nd. was very heavy. Captain N.A. Foster was wounded and captured and was a prisoner of war on Johnsons Island in lake Erie until the war ended. Afterwards he returned to Jefferson, N.C. and operated a general store with his brother Edmund until his death.

Source: *Volume III of N.C. Regiments in the Confederate Army* by Walter Clark.

FORT HAMBY, WILKESBORO

In March, 1865, General Stoneman left East Tennessee, moving by the turnpike leading from Taylorsville, Tennessee, through Watauga county to Deep Gap on the Blue Ridge. On the 26 of March he entered Boone, N.C. and on the 27 the column was divided, one division under General Stoneman marching towards Wilkesboro, while the other, under General Gillam, crossed the Blue Ridge at Blowing Rock and went to Patterson, and then joined Stoneman at Wilkesboro. Leaving Wilkesboro on the 31st General Stoneman moved over into Surry county, going towards Mt. Airy. During the march through this section of the State, Stoneman's men committed many depredations, and after leaving Wilkesboro a number of the lawless element of his command deserted. Shortly after this a number of men, some deserters from Stoneman's command and other worthless characters, led by two desperate men, Wade and Simmons, completely terrorized a large portion of Wilkes county by their frequent raids.

In order to fully understand the situation, the condition of the country at that time must

Fort Hamby (Sketch by Edith F. Carter.)

World War I Recruits. The young men were known as the "First Twelve", to be drafted to go for encampment in World War I, on September 5, 1917. They are, l. to r. Maurice Shepherd, W. Percy Bumgarner, Charlie Lane, Carl Gambill, Walter Greer, William Miller, Charles Shumate, Archie Rousseau, John Hall, Tal Barnes, Grady Allen and Otto Whittington. They all returned home and Grady Allen was the last one to die in 1980.

be taken into consideration. Almost every man fit for military service was in the army.

These marauders were divided into two bands. One, led by Simmons, had its headquarters in the Brushy Mountains, and the other, led by Wade, had its headquarters near the Yadkin river, in Wilkes county. The bands at times operated together, but it is principally with Wade's band that this article is to deal. The house which Wade had chosen and fortified was situated near the road which leads from Wilkesboro to Lenoir and about a mile from Holman's Ford, where the valley road crosses the Yadkin river. The house was situated on a high hill, commanding a fine view of the Yadkin valley, and of the valley road for a distance of a mile above and a mile below the ford. The house fronted the river on the south, while the rear was protected by the "Flat Woods" belt, in which there were sympathizers, if not aiders and abettors, of the band. From this position the Yadkin valley and the

surrounding country for at least half a mile in every direction could be swept and controlled by Wade's guns. It would have been almost impossible to have chosen a stronger location, both offensive and defensive, than this. The house was built of oak logs, and was two stories high. In the upper story Wade had cut port-holes for his guns, which were army guns of the most improved type, and could command the approaches to the house from all directions, making it indeed hazardous to attempt to reach it. This house belonged to some dissolute women by the name of Hamby, and after Wade had fortified it, the name by which it was known was "Fort Hamby."

Making this their headquarters, they began to plunder the surrounding country, and from their cruelty it appears that their object was to gratify a spirit of revenge as well as to enrich themselves. They marched as a well-drilled military force, armed with the best rifles. It was only a short time before they brought the citizens for many miles around in every direction under their dominion. They plundered the best citizens, subjecting men and women to the grossest insults. A woman was working in a field, near Holman's ford, having a child with her. The child climbed on the fence, and the men began to shoot at it, and finally killed it.

Raid into Caldwell

Emboldened by their success in Wilkes County, they made a raid into Caldwell county on 7th of May. Major Harvey Bingham, with about a half dozen young men from Caldwell and Watauga counties, attempted to rout these murderers from their stronghold at Fort Hamby. On Sunday night, Major Bingham made a well-planned move on the fort at a late hour of the night. Wade and his men were not aware of the approach of Bingham's men until they had entered the house. Wade announced their defenceless condition and begged for their lives. No guns were seen, so Bingham believed his prisoners. They gave Wade and his men time to dress, after which, at a moment when the captors were off their guard, they rushed to their guns which were concealed about their beds and opened fire on them. The result was that Clark, a son of General Clark of Caldwell county, and Henley were killed. The others escaped, leaving the bodies of Clark and Henley.

Being encouraged by the failure to dislodge them, they began to enlarge the territory which they were to plunder. About this time W.C. Green, of Alexander county, who had been a lieutenant in the Confederate army, recieved news from a friend in Wilkes that Wade had planned to move into Alexander county and raid on his father, Rev. J.B. Green and to kill W.C. Green, if found. Green began to fortify his house, barring all the doors with iron. They also took five negroes into their confidence, who promised to assist in defending the house.

Wade started across the Brushy mountains on Saturday, May 13th and reached Green's that evening about dark. W.C. Green saw a number of men stop their horses in the road above the house and notified his father, and mustered the negroes in the dining room. J.B. Green stationed himself at the front door, with a revolver in one hand and a dirk in the other. W.C. Green took his position at a window commanding a view of the front gate and porch. The negrose were stationed in the rear part of the house. Three men with guns approached the house in front, one of them being Wade, who had on a bright Confederate uniform, which he always wore on his raids, posing as a Confederate soldier when necessary to gain admission into the houses he wished to plunder.

A Turn of Affairs

Some of the men had by this time come up from the rear and were trying to force entrance. The Greens rushed to the rear, knocked out a pane of glass, and opened fire on them, wounding one of the men. This unexpected turn of affairs seemed to frighten them and they all began to retire. It was found out afterwards that five of Wade's men had remained at the store of W.C. Linney, below Mr. Green's house and had not taken part in the attempt to make the raid.

W.C. Green went to York Collegiate Institute and informed several men of the raid, and by ten o'clock twenty-two men, almost all of them Confederate soldiers, had gathered, ready to pursue the robbers. Col. Wash. Sharpe was placed in command and they started in pursuit. The first news from Wade was when they reached "Law's Gap" and it was found Wade had camped in the Brushy Mountains part of the night after the attack on the Greens and about sunrise next morning had made a raid on Mr. Laws and forced him to give up his money. The pursurers followed the trail and found that five miles from Wilkesboro Wade's men had left the public road and had taken a shorter route by way of Hix's Mill and Holman's ford to Fort Hamby. The ford was reached in the evening of May 14th, and after crossing the river, and traveling along the public road for a half mile, the pursuing party left the public road and followed a private road which led to a creek at the base of the hill on which the Hamby house stood. In the enthusiasm of the moment all seemed to forget the danger. Col. Flowers' men had gotten within seventy-five yards and Capt. Ellis' men within twenty yards of the house when its defenders poured a volley of minie-balls through the port-holes. James K. Linney and James Brown were killed. Some of the men were compelled to jump from their horses and throw themselves on the ground in order to escape being shot down. Their horses became frightened and breaking loose from them, ran to where Wade's men had their horses.

Under the severe fire the men were compelled to retreat. The force was now divided, part having fallen back across the creek, and part having reached the pines east of the building. There was no chance to re-unite, and after waiting until dark, the men withdrew, some reaching Moravian Falls that night. These met the others at "Squire" Hubbard's the next morning. In retreating the men were compelled to leave the bodies of Linney and Brown. Wade's men buried them near the fort.

These men returned to Alexander county and raised a large company, a strong force having been brought from Iredell county under the command of Wallace Sharpe. On Wednesday the force started towards Fort Hamby. A courier was sent back to Iredell to request Capt. Cowan to raise a company and come to their assistance. Before reaching Moravian Falls, they received a message from Wade, saying "Come on, I am looking for you; I can whip a thousand of you." It was dark when Holman's Ford was reached. A company from Caldwell county was encamped in the woods, and the two companies camped there together that night. The next morning they marched up the river and crossed at a small ford. They came to the house of Mr. Talbert, who lived on the public road, and there they found a woman dying. She had been shot the day before by the men from the fort, while she and her husband were coming to the ford in a wagon on the opposite side of the river from the fort, nearly a miles distance.

Mr. Talbert begged the men to return, telling them that Wade was expecting them, and had sent for re-inforcements. He told them that it was impossible to dislodge them, and to make an attempt and fail would make it worse for the people.

Sharpe in Command

Capt. R.M. Sharpe, of Alexander county, assumed command of both companies, numbering several hundred men. W.R. Gwaltney was sent with a small body of men to reach a high hill overlooking Lenoir's Creek and to remain there, while all the others marched around to the north and east of the fort.

The companies had left their encampment before day, and by daybreak the fort was surrounded, the men being placed about twenty steps apart. The soldiers kept up the fire on the fort during the day and night. Wade's men returned the fire, shooting with great accuracy. The soldiers were compelled to keep behind logs and trees, or out of range of the guns. It seemed impossible to take the fort. Some of the bravest men were in favor of giving it up, while others said death was preferable to being run over by such devils.

This state of affairs continued until the night of the 19th, when the lines were moved nearer up, and about four o'clock in the morning Wallace Sharpe and W.A. Daniel crept up behind the kitchen and set it on fire. The flames soon reached the roof of the fortress, and the sight of the fire seemed to completely unnerve Wade's men. "What terms will you give us?" cried Wade. "We will shoot you," replied Sharpe, from behind the burning kitchen.

It was now about daybreak, and some of the men surrounding the fort began to rush up. Wade made a rush towards the river, through a body of Caldwell men, who opened fire on him, but as it was yet a little dark, he escaped. Four men were captured, Beck, Church, Lockwad, and one unknown. The flames which had caught the fort were extinguished, and in the house was found property of almost every description. Five ladies' dresses and bonnets had been taken from the dissolute women who had occupied the house. About twenty horses were found stabled near the fort. Some of the property was restored to the owners.

The men who were captured plead for a trial according to the course and practice of the courts. They were informed that they would be disposed of as summarily as they had disposed of Clark, Henley, Brown and Linney. Stakes were put up, and on the way to the place of execution they were given time to pray. Their prayer was "O, men, spare us." Wallace Sharpe replied: "Men, pray to God; don't pray to us. He alone can save you."

After the prisoners were shot, the fort was set on fire. When the flames reached the cellar, the firing of guns was like a hot skirmish. Wade's men had stored away a great many loaded guns and a large quantity of ammunition.

Wade was seen in the vicinity several days after. He claimed to have been a major in Stonemen's command and a native of Michigan. He said he had escaped to the Yadkin river from the fort and had hid under the banks until night.

The bodies of Linney and Brown were brought back home for final burial.

Though all the desperadoes were not brought to justice, this completely broke up their depredations.

Source: Article in 17 Nov. 1895 Daily Charlotte Observer, written by Robert L. Flowers, professor of Trinity College, with information obtained from Hon. R. Z. Linney, Col. George W. Flowers, Rev. W.R. Gwaltney, and Dr. W.C. Green, all of whom took an active part in the capture of the fort.

AN EARLY BUSINESS: CRUDE DRUGS IN WILKES

Roots and herbs or crude drugs were an important source of income for many Wilkes County and surrounding area farm families from the beginning of the settlement of this area until recent times. Entire families including small children could busy themselves in the gathering, drying, and bagging of the many varieties of leaves, roots, and barks found in our mountains. In fact, our Appalachians are blessed with a larger variety of plant life than can be found any place else on earth.

Once the herbs were gathered and dried, they were sold to crude drug dealers who accumulated them in large quantities for sale and shipment to manufacturers of medicine throughout this country and abroad. My uncle shipped ginseng and witch hazel to Germany and ginseng to China.

Some of the dealers in this area who bought and sold roots and herbs were my uncle, A.F. Phillips and Company; Carl A. Lowe and Sons; S.V. Tomlinson; E.E. Eller and Son; F.D. Forester; and Scroggs and Company.

During the teens, twenties and thirties, A.F. Phillips became one of the largest independent crude drug dealers in the nation.

The following are a few of the herbs bought and sold and their uses: Ginseng — tea; Black Cohash — beneficial for heart disorders; Witch Hazel — used as an astringent; Ladies Slipper — good for nervous disorders; Tansy — a potent narcotic; Sumach — remedy for sore throat; Blackberry Root — treatment for diarrhea; Slippery Elm Bark — remedy for kidney disorders; Wild Cherry — used in making root beer plus aid for upset stomach; Wahoo — appetite stimulant; Blue Cohash — remedy for deficient labor pains; Black Haw Bark — antispasmodic, diuretic and tonic; Golden Seal — increases flow of bile; Boneset — tea used as remedy for pneumonia.

During the middle twenties A.F. Phillips was buying more than one hundred thirty different roots and herbs. At the present time there are around fifty varieties being bought by Lowe Fur & Herb, Inc. operated by Arthur Lowe and Lowe Hide and Metal Company operated by Elmer Lowe. Decline in number of varieties from the middle twenties to the present time is attributed to the fact that chemists can derive from coal (a relatively cheap and plentiful product) everything that can be found in natural roots and herbs.

Inflation Again

It is interesting to note that inflation is evident in the root and herb business also. Some prices of note: Sassafras Root Bark sold for 10¢ per lb. in 1927; $1.00 per lb. 1982; Witch Hazel Leaves sold for 3¢ per lb. in 1927; .75 per lb. 1982; Lobelia Herb sold for 12¢ per lb. in 1927; .75 per lb. 1982; Ginseng Wild sold for $12.00 per lb. in 1927; $80.00 plus per lb. 1982.

Recently there has been some revival by drug manufacturers in roots and herbs. It may well be that they have decided that antibotics are not the only treatment of any disorders that beset mankind.

Sources: White's materia Medico (1906), A.F. Phillips & Co. 1927 price list of roots and herbs; Lowe Hide & Metal Company 1982 price list; Lowe Fur & Herb price list 1982; personal interviews with Arthur Lowe, Mary S. Smithey, Bruce Phillips.

LAST BUT NOT LEAST . . . THE MOONSHINE INDUSTRY OF WILKES COUNTY

Question: Does Wilkes County deserve its reputation as "The Moonshine Capital of the World?"

Answer: For any one place to be called the world's captial of anything smacks of gross exaggeration but every available record and knowledgeable source indicate that there has been a truly enormous amount of illicit whisky made in Wilkes County. However, if the nickname was ever valid, it would have been in the past, for the heyday of the moonshine industry here was from the nineteen-twenties to the sixties, and very little is being made here now.

Question: Why has everyone, whatever their opinion of the moonshine industry, been so interested in it?

Answers: To many outsiders, it has seemed to be a real-life game of hide-and-seek straight out of the "Snuffy Smith" comic strip, with both the good guys and the bad guys abiding by certain chivalrous rules and not really hurting anybody, which in later years has grown into a bigtime under-cover business with such interesting offshoots as stockcar racing.

To local people not directly involved — for everyone here has been indirectly affected by a major component in the economics development of our community — it has been a somewhat lower-key version of the above going on back in the beautiful hills around us, plus the fun of guessing who the kingpins are or were — and the shame or pride (or both) of answering to That Reputation every time we go anywhere else.

To the members of many local church groups, it has been a disgrace, the root of much misery and, quite simply, a sin.

To law officers, it has been tax revenues unpaid, laws violated and not much of a game at that.

To those who've made their living from moonshining, it has been a family business going back many generations, hard work under difficult conditions, a job when few others were available, and the making of a

product for which there was much demand.

Question: How did Wilkes County get to be such a center for this particular enterprise?

Answer: It started out that way. Whisky has been made in this section since its first settlers arrived over 200 years ago. Many of them were Scotch-Irish, a race who have made whisky throughout their recorded history, and they found here every necessary ingredient to continue their craft — swift-flowing creeks of mineral-free water, abundant hardwood trees for fuel, and broad fertile bottomlands ideal for growing corn. And, for the first hundred years or more, making whisky was legal.

After the county itself was established in 1778, one of its first public records was John Witherspoon's will, in which he disposed of both his grist mill and his whisky still, and it was typical in that the owner of one was often also the owner of the other. Other early county business involved the licensing of taverns and ordinaries in which the offerings included locally made corn whisky at specific prices set down in the record. Inventories of other 18th century estates list whisky stills, hogsheads (large barrels in which whisky was aged) and casks (smaller ones in which it was sold).

Two great advantages in making whisky in those days before highways or even all-weather roads came into this isolated section were its keep-ability and its portability. And, until well into the second half of the 19th century, there was little discernable opposition to the making, selling or drinking of alcoholic beverages, and it would have been an unusual household which was without them.

As Wilkes County grew, its whisky industry grew, too. Distillers had to purchase state licenses and tax stamps; and revenue agents, popularly called "brandy gaugers," went around and collected tax on each distillers' inventory in his warehouse (usually his wellhouse). But, because the whisky's tax nearly equalled its going price, almost always a portion of each run was put back out of sight to be "blockaded" — sold, that is, without benefit of the government tax stamp. And, occasionally, a "blockader" would be caught redhanded moving a stamp from one barrel to another, or apprehended going to market with several unstamped casks concealed under a wagonload of apples.

When Bronson's Business Directory of North Carolina came out in 1884, its Wilkes section listed twelve legal distilleries: W. & E.F. Anderson and William Sanders, both of Wilkesboro; W.V. Adams & J.C. Tinsley of Mulberry; J.R. Combs of Hunting Creek; W.M. Cooper of Osbornville; L. Harris and E.F. Ebs & H. Ebs, both of Halls Mills; S.J. Greenwood and W.& J. Reeves, both of Roaring River; J.L. Hays of Millers Creek; Sparks & Gray of Clingman and J.L. Whittington of Wilbar. There were undoubtedly many smaller distilleries for which no license was ever bought.

The Temperance Movement

The year the directory came out, 1884, was in the midst of a climatic period of a campaign which had been gathering steam nationwide since the end of the Civil War — the temperance movement. Born of the abuse of alcohol, it preached temperance, but what its supporters really wanted was abolition, and what they wanted abolished was the making of all whisky.

Initially a moral issue, the temperance movement developed political muscle by the 1880's and instigated a referendum in North Carolina on statewide prohibition of the manufacture of intoxicating liquor and its sale except in small medicinal quantities by prescription at drugstores.

The high moral tone disintegrated into rabid partisan name-calling, and one result was that a coalition of those most adamantly opposed to the referendum formed themselves into a third party, which they named the Liberal Anti-Prohibition Party, and offered a slate of candidates for state and national office. One of the new party's leaders was a Wilkes County physician, Dr. Tyre York of Traphill, who ran for the U.S. House of Representatives in 1882.

After some more mudslinging, the votes were cast and, among other things, the prohibition referendum was defeated and Dr. York was elected to Congress. Its success in defeating the referendum destroyed much of the Liberal Anti-Prohibition Party's relevancy, however, and when Dr. York sought the North Carolina governorship as its candidate in 1884, he was soundly defeated.

As the 19th century ended, social attitudes toward the drinking of alcoholic beverages, dancing, card playing and other customs earlier considered acceptable hardened, and many church groups put great emphasis upon eradicating such practices within their congregations and their communities.

Political pressure again developed and became partisan. When the state Democratic chairman, Furnifold M. Simmons, pushed into law a measure outlawing the manufacture and sale of spirituous liquors except in incorporated towns, he said the purpose was to get rid of county distilleries, which he called "Republican recruiting stations." Named the Watts Act, as a law forbidding liquor traffic except in incorporated cities of over a thousand inhabitants, it dried up 68 of the 98 counties and all but 80 of the 328 incorporated towns, at least on paper.

Statewide prohibition was the aim of a 1908 referendum. Of the 21 counties which voted against it, Wilkes was one of the five most strongly opposed. It passed overwhelmingly.

The opposition of the majority of Wilkes citizens to statewide prohibition is understandable: it was aimed at their chief money crop. The county's only other sizeable industry at that time was the lumber industry — sawmills, some small millwork and furniture factories and a tannery — which could not absorb nearly all those who would be unemployed if the manufacture of whisky was halted.

So what had been a semi-legal (government stamped liquor) and semi-illicit (blockade) trade, usually located on small streams among heavily wooded hills through which there were few roads, simply and easily took to cover. Whisky making became moonshining.

Longstanding animosities between people of Scotch-Irish and those of English descent, western North Carolinians against eastern North Carolinians mostly Republicans versus mostly Democrats probably eased many local decisions to ignore the law.

Actually, some of the temperance laws of this period helped rather than hurt the now illicit distillers of Wilkes County. For example, the 1913 federal law forbidding the transport of liquor from wet states into dry created a vast new market for moonshine whisky among those who had been bringing theirs in from Virginia and other states.

The helpful stateline barricade was soon followed by a dramatic development at the still itself. Someone discovered that by taking the cooked mash, which they called slop, from a run of corn whisky, putting it back in the fermenting box with sugar, water, yeast and some rye meal, a much larger amount of cheaper secondary whisky could be made. They called it sugarhead, or, sometimes, white lightning; and it revolutionized a moderately profitable enterprise into a very lucrative and commercially attractive business. Moonshine (a nickname resulting from the nighttime nature of the illicit operation) came into its own.

Sugarhead and Secrecy

No longer a legal product made of mostly local ingredients exactly as it had been turned out in Scotland for hundreds of years, most Wilkes whisky now was sugarhead, its ingredients were mostly imported, and its manufacture and sale were wrapped in deepest secrecy.

As the moonshine industry grew, its impact on the overall Wilkes economy was increasingly felt. Gigantic purchases of sugar, cornmeal and jars created profitable accounts at wholesale groceries; the need for many more copper stills, condensers and mash boxes helped hardware stores; and the distillers' increased buying power and need of legal counsel were felt throughout the business community.

When the 18th amendment to the U.S. Constitution was enacted in 1919, prohibiting the manufacture, sale or transportation of intoxicating liquors within the United States, all liquor became illegal and its prices jumped. The moonshiners of Wilkes, already outside the law, made even more money but also got a wider array of adversaries, including federal law enforcement officers.

Law-abiding in other respects and renowned for their conscientious payment of all debts, most moonshiners viewed this latest decree as another instance of the other team changing the rules after the game was underway, and treated it accordingly. Besides, they saw no other way to support themselves and their families in a mountainous region unsuited to most agricultural money crops.

Prohibition finally ended in 1933 but its demise did not automatically allow Wilkes moonshine to come out into the sunshine. It was still illegal to make liquor according to the state, and the federal government sought to ease its Depression woes by imposing a tax upon the manufacturers of all alcoholic drinks.

Enter the revenuers. There had been prohibition agents during Prohibition, there had also been state tax collectors, there had been sheriffs and deputies, there had been brandy gaugers, but when the federal government sent its Treasury Department agents into the Appalachian Mountains from West Virginia to Georgia to destroy all those hidden-non-tax-paying stills, moonshining entered its most colorful and widely know era.

Even though making whisky was exceedingly hard work and even though the federal tax agents, called revenuers, were quite serious of purpose, there remains an undeniable aura of little boys playing games about the manuevers between the two groups. As Junior Johnson, who went on from hauling illicit whisky to national fame as a stockcar racer, says, "We tried to outslick them and they tried to catch us at it."

The best known of all the revenuers was Charles S. Felts, a Wilkes native who spent thirty years tracking down and "cutting" stills, and many of the stories moonshiners and revenuers tell are about him.

A true one, according to his wife, was about the time a stillhand, unaware he was being watched, got the mash to cooking and then spoke into an imaginary telephone: "Hello, Charlie! Here we are. Come and get us!" To his great surprise and chagrin, the real Charlie Felts stepped into the light and announced "Here I am!" Another time, while the song, "If I'd A'known You Were Coming, I'd A-baked a Cake," was popular, he came to a stillsite and found a little storebought cake on a stump with a note saying, "I knowed you were coming, Charlie, so I bought a cake."

Sometimes there have been humorous aspects to the ingenuity with which moonshiners tried to conceal their product — as when a cache of whisky was discovered under a hog-pen, in one case, or in the girls' bathroom of Ferguson Elementary School, for another. And, to others, there was some fun in the plight of the fellow caught, convicted and given a probationary sentence for operating a still on his kitchen stove.

For the most part, however, moonshining was very serious business. Certain parts of Wilkes County got the name of being moonshine centers — Windy Gap, Traphill, the Call community, Boomer and Ingle Hollow are on most lists, with the Brushy Mountain known for its apple brandy after harvest season.

Most of the people in these neighborhoods, if not involved, were careful not to stumble onto a suspected stillsite, but this was not always the case. One woman who found a still stood guard while her husband went for the law. When three hapless stillhands showed up, she held them under citizen's arrest and the nose of her gun until the officers came. Another "dry bone", as the moonshiners called them, made seeking out and reporting stills practically a fulltime career, and among Charlie Felts' souvenirs was an unsigned Christmas card on which, above the holiday greetings, was carefully printed, "They is a still place between So-and-So's and So-and-S-s place on the branch."

The revenuers were assisted by such free tips, paid undercover agents and sometimes even followed their noses after catching a pun-

Charlie Felts "cuts" a still at Alder Gap, while fellow officers look on, June 1951.

gent whiff of cooking mash.

In most concentrated still areas every stranger was suspect. Dwight Nichols recalls going with Dr. Harold Smith to the Call community to make a house call. When they reached a certain crossroads, Dr. Smith stopped the car and a man came up out of the woods, got in and directed them on to the patient's house.

Cutting Stills

Cutting stills — which usually consisted of chopping holes in the big equipment with mattocks, shooting the jars with shotguns — and then dynamiting the whole place — was not all the Alcoholic Tax Unit officers did to eradicate the illicit whiskey business. They also checked wholesale grocers' records to see who'd been buying large amounts of sugar (a clue as to who might be making sugarhead) and whether the grocer was keeping the required records.

They and state Alcoholic Beverage Control officers also chased moonshine haulers as they transported the whisky to wholesalers in nearby cities. Often the younger sons of moonshine makers, easily the best known of the former haulers is Junior Johnson, who went on to win 50 NASCAR Grand National races and then to become a race car team owner and innovative mechanic whose cars

have won a record 79 races in ten years and earned him a spot in the North Carolina Sports Hall of Fame.

A member of a three-or-more-generations-in-the-moonshine-business family, Robert Glenn Johnson, Jr., began hauling liquor at the age of thirteen, making three runs a night, each time carrying 150 gallons to a nearby city. He developed his extraordinary driving skills and mechanical ability in order to outrun any intercepting officer, who would most likely be driving a similar car — usually a '39 or '40 Ford — not weighted down by all that whisky!

One of the most famous raids in Wilkes moonshine history took place at Junior Johnson's home when he was a young child. Many Ingle Hollow moonshiners brought their whisky to Glenn Johnson, Sr., to sell and the Johnson home served as their warehouse. Because it was 1935 and the Great Depression was on, sales were slow and the whisky accumulated to such an extent that the entire upstairs was filled. When the revenuers arrived, they got what was termed the largest inland seizure of strictly blockade liquor in the entire country up to that time. They found 7100 gallons of whisky, 9150 pounds of sugar, four copper condensers, five complete distilling plants and more than $1000 worth of fruit jars. Federal taxes

and penalties on the liquor seized were estimated at $28,000.

Other raids were smaller but collectively they yielded enough offenders to justify two two-week terms of federal court in Wilkesboro annually for nearly fifty years. Local attorneys recall several occasions on which the government chartered two or more large buses to take all the sentenced moonshiners to federal prison after a term of court here.

Youthful offenders (those under thirty) were sent to the special facility at Chillicothe, Ohio, while the more mature went, for the most part, to Atlanta penitentiary, or sometimes to Leavenworth, Kansas, or to Petersburg, VA. A-year-and-a-day was a typical first timer's sentence; repeaters might get three-to-five years, or even more.

The federal judge most associated in the public mind with the trying of moonshiners was a Wilkes native, Johnson J. Hayes. Son of a licensed distiller, Johnson Hayes took a vow as a teenager never to drink. Deeply religious and sincerely convinced that drinking was sinful, he was a prominent layleader of the Baptist church and, after he became the first federal judge of the Middle District of North Carolina in 1926, he presided over hundreds, perhaps thousands, of liquor violation cases. Judge

Hayes won the reputation of a fair but stern dispenser of justice while on the bench, and as a man who also considered it almost a personal crusade to rid his native county of the curse of the whisky business.

The heyday of the moonshine industry, sometimes called "the white liquor busines," was also the height of the local "red liquor business," although the products were different and the people involved were seldom the same. The red liquor trade was the illegal importation of legally made, bonded and sealed whisky for local consumption. It also was a large volume business, particularly during World War II, when one local bootlegger, who had customers in several states, was relieved of over thirty thousand dollars' worth of red liquor by state officers one morning and had replaced it with an equivalent amount by nightfall of the same day. The advent of state ABC stores spelled the doom of the red liquor business.

The post-World War II period brought new ways of doing things to both the revenuers and the moonshiners. The revenuers took to the air, flying small planes at low altitudes over the thickly-forested countryside to spot the telltale smoke of a still in operation. The moonshiners switched from burning wood to coke, which is practically smokeless. They also went subterranean — removing the stills from back on the creek and setting them under a barn or chicken house, pumping the water to them as well as bringing in the other components. Some of the subterranean stills were enormous — capable of making 500 to 1000 gallons of liquor in 24 hours — limited only by the space necessary to accomodate enough boxes of "beer" (fermenting mash), at a ratio of one gallon of whisky from each ten gallons of beer, and the problem of disposing of the leftover slop without attracting attention. Blowing enough fresh air into the underground quarters was also difficult.

Silver Clouds

But the biggest problem of all was some-thing which was happening to the whisky itself. Many moonshiners had changed over from copper stills to "Silver Clouds," which were cheaper and easier to obtain, but which were joined together by lead solder, which leached into the whisky and could be poisonous to the drinker. By the seventies, according to former ATU agent Bob Powell, as much as half of all confiscated whisky tested out to have lead salts in it, and half of that was in dangerous amounts.

The attention of outsiders to the moonshine business — particularly when it appeared in print — was deeply resented by many Wilkes Countians. As far back as 1906 a local newspaper editorialized against "the great amount of free, undesirable and unmerited advertising ... because of the amounts of spiritus fermenti made (or supposed to be made) and consumed within (our) borders."

Public outrage climaxed when Vance Packard wrote "Millions in Moonshine" for the September 1950 issue of American Magazine. Belittling other facets of Wilkes life and industry, exaggerating the moonshiners' influence and sensationalizing the illegality of a native trade, the article managed to inpuriate almost everybody. The Chamber of Commerce took exception, several state papers charged foul play, and Packard was forced to respond with a lengthy letter of explanation and justification.

One of Packard's contentions, in both the article and letter, was that the Wilkesboro post was the number one ATU group in America in terms of number of illicit stills seizures.

Today, 32 years later, there is no ATU post here, no federal court has been held in Wilkesboro in five years, and knowledgeable observers doubt if there are more than a handful of moonshiners left. The industry has almost completely faded away.

What happened to it? Several things, apparently, with one clearly predominent. Legal liquor became more available, and people's tastes and social customs changed. Fear of lead poisoning was poor advertising. The treasury department, which also had gun control responsibilities, changed emphasis after the political assassinations of the sixties — all contributing to the decline of moonshining and revenuers in pursuit.

But, far and away more important than all of that, an alternative way to make a living arose. More profitable and without the risk of arrest and prison, it was the poultry business. "Millions in Chickens" might not be a very sensational article but its subject would be about a multi-million dollar business here and, according to those who know, many of the oldtime moonshiners are now in it and doing exceedingly well. The majority of these observers say that yesterday's moonshiners are not today's marijuana growers, by the way. The poultry business is where most of them are now, above board and legal.

Final question: But how big was the moonshine industry in Wilkes County when it was at its height?

Answer: When Charlie Felts retired in 1961 after thirty years as a revenuer, he compiled some statistics on his own career: over 2500 arrests, over four million gallons of mash and seventy thousands gallons of illicit whisky confiscated (representing over five million dollars in unpaid taxes), and over 500 vehicles seized.

That was one man's career record, and while it covered most of the moonshine heyday, there were other raids and other seizures. And the statistics are on the ones who got caught.

That's BIG.

Sources: *The History of a Southern State*, Lefler and Newsome, 1973; *The Land of Wilkes*, Johnson J. Hayes, 1962; *Wilkes County Sketches*, J. Jay Anderson, 1976; Wilkes court records, newspaper accounts; interviews with Mrs. Charles Felts, Kyle Hayes, Junior Johnson, W.H. McElwee, Sr., Dwight Nichols, G.R. Powell and Phillip Yates.
Research by Jane Carter Ogburn.

Wilkes County Free School Teachers Meeting around 1900.

The People of Wilkes:
Family Histories

ADAM ABSHER
300

Adam Absher, son of William and Elizabeth (Absher) Absher, was born in 1830, died 10 September 1864 in Richmond, Virginia, while serving in the Civil War. He was in the 52nd Regt., Company F., Infantry, entering the service on the 22 September 1862.

He joined Mulberry Primitive Baptist Church, 2 July 1848 and married 30 July 1851, Letes Jane Brown, daughter of Wesley and Letes (Jennings) Brown of Mulberry. "Letty" was born 15 October 1835, died 25 June 1891. She is buried in the Cross Roads Primitive Baptist Churchyard and Adam is buried in the Hollywood National Cemetery, Richmond, Va. After the death of Adam, "Letty" married John A. Brown. It has been told in the family that she only married him to "tote & fetch" for her! This may be true, for her tombstone reads: "Letty, the wife of Adam Absher, second husband, John A. Brown".

Adam and Letes (Brown) Absher had six children: (1) Candace Rebecca, born 28 October 1852, died unmarried 29 August 1888, (2) George Winfield, born 12th September 1853, died 28 June 1891, married 1st. 18 March 1876, Amelia Ellen Buttery, born 13 June 1854, died after 1880, daughter of John Thompson and Winnie Matilda (Wiles) Buttery, 2nd. 11 December 1887, Alice Joins. No issue. (3) Lewis William, born 22 August 1855, died 22 August 1892, married 27 October 1884, Octavia C. Deal, daughter of Miles Deal of Alexander County. (4) Mary L., born 11 February 1857, died 8 August 1886, married 7 August 1883, P. Elmore Dancy. (5) William Lundy, born 22 December 1859, died 23 October 1909, married 7 May 1885, Roxie Miller from Alleghany County. (8) Virginia, born about 1861, married Council Brown.

George Winfield Absher, son of Adam and Letes (Brown) Absher, was a country merchant at Obids in Ashe County when he was first married. At the time of his death, he was postmaster at Abshers postoffice in the Traphill community of Wilkes County and is buried on his land near the site. He and Ellen had two children: (1) Martha Geneva (called

Mattie), born 10 March 1877 Obids, Ashe County, died 4 August 1892, of typhoid fever in Wilkesboro at the home of her uncle, Lewis William Absher. She is buried at Abshers beside her father in unmarked grave. (2) Minnie Matilda Absher, born 18 February 1879, Obids, Ashe County died 27 October 1961 in Burke County, married 1 September 1902 by Rev. W.R. Bradshaw, Henry Oliver Absher, her second cousin, son of William Matthew and Nancy Jane (Reynolds) Absher.

Minnie also lived with her uncle, Lewis William Absher in Wilkesboro after the death of her mother. Her uncle died of typhoid fever soon after the death of her sister, Mattie. She was then sent to Oxford Orphanage, being the first child going there from Wilkes County. After she returned to Wilkes County, she taught school in Rock Creek township before she married H.O. Absher in 1902.

Sources: Civil War burial records, National Archives, *Moore's Roster, Vol III* N.C. Archives, Wilkes marriages, Federal Census, *Chronicle* Newspaper, gravestone inscriptions, personal knowledge.

— Mrs. W.O. Absher

ELISHA M. ABSHER
301

Elisha M. Absher was one of the six children of Alfred J. and Martha (Patsy) Johnson Absher. He was born 8 May 1854, died 28 February 1924. He was twice married. He is buried at Cross Roads Primitive Churchyard beside his second wife.

His first wife was Sarah A. Sebastian, born 4 December 1849, died 2 March 1904, daughter of Lewis and Rachael Adams Sebastian. They were married about 1872. Sarah A. is buried in the Alfred J. Absher family cemetery in the Mulberry community.

Elisha M. and Sarah A. were the parents of four children: (1) Freeland Alexander, born 17 October 1873, died 29 July 1930, married 20 August 1892, Irene C. Jennings; (2) Sue Ellen born 1877, died 1886 and buried in Alfred J. Absher family cemetery; (3) Chromodore D. born 1 June 1879, died 23 November 1941, married first, Martha Victoria Johnson, and

second, Ida Roberts; (4) Mollie Clementine, born 28 December 1880, died 25 January 1964, married 22 June 1899, William Avery Brown.

Elisha M. Absher married, as his second wife, Mary Jane Shumate on the 6 June 1904 and had two more children, Eleanor and Otcheus Odell. In his will, Elisha named his five living children and his wife, Mary Jane.

Chromodore D. (Commie) Absher and his first wife, Martha Victoria Johnson, were married 29 October 1900. Martha Victoria was born 23 March 1882, died 21 January 1910, daughter of William Martin and Frances Janie Long Johnson. Her father, William Martin Johnson, was born 23 February 1856 and died in 1934. Frances Janie Long was born 14 October 1861 and died 22 March 1922 in North Wilkesboro at the home of a daughter, Mrs. J.E. Caudill, whom she had come to visit from her home in Bel Air, Maryland.

Chromodore D. and Martha Victoria were the parents of three children: (1) Clarence E. Absher, born 20 October 1901, died 4 August 1978 in Helena, Montana and is buried in the V.A. Cemetery in Twin Bridges, Montana, who never married; (2) Numma Lee Absher, son of Chromodore D. and Martha Victoria, was born 17 May 1903, and married 24 August 1927 in the North Wilkesboro First Baptist Church, Irene E. Kilby, born 2 July 1907, daughter of Cyrus C. and Viola Pierce Kilby.

Numma went to Maryland with his Johnson grandparents to live in 1918. He returned to North Wilkesboro and worked as a funeral director for over fifty years. He is now retired. He and Irene were the parents of three children:

Marvin Martin Absher, a twin, born and died 20 March 1929, Martha Viola Absher, born 20 March 1929, married 8 October 1949 Worth C. Cuthbertson, who was born 8 November 1920, son of I.J. and Lena Helms Cuthbertson of Guilford County, N.C.

Martha is employed by the Wilkes Community College in Wilkesboro. Worth "Cubby" served in the Army during World War II, played professional baseball and now works at the Oakwoods Country Club. They have a daughter, Victoria Lee Cuthbertson, who was born 22 August 1951, married 9 August 1969 in North Wilkesboro First Baptist Church, Roy Alfred Spainhour, Jr., son of Roy Alfred, Sr. and Hazel Taylor Spainhour.

Vicky owns and operates her own craft store and Al is in the retail mercantile business in Elkin, North Carolina, where they reside.

The third child of Numma and Irene is Numma Lee Absher, Jr. who was born 31 January 1936, married 12 June 1960 in the North Wilkesboro First Baptist Church, Barkley Moore, daughter of Larry S. and Dorothy Wallace Moore.

Lee served in the Army in Germany for eighteen months. He was associated with Hubbard's clothing store for several years and now he and Barkley own and operate a ladies and men's clothing store in West Jefferson, Ashe County, N.C.

Lee and Barkley have three sons, Larry Mark Absher, born 30 December 1960 who now operates a store for his father in Boone, Watauga County; Phillip Lee Absher, born 5 August 1964; and Michael Scott Absher, born 29 April 1968.

(3) Ivan M. Absher, son of Chromodore D. and Martha Victoria Johnson Absher, was born 1 June 1906, died 20 May 1974. He married 11 December 1937 in Grayson County, Virginia, Gladys Jean Bare, born 13 December 1914 in Ashe County, N.C. They lived in Wilkesboro.

Ivan M. worked for the North Wilkesboro Coca-Cola Bottling Company for many years. Jean worked with the Wilkes County Welfare Department. They had one daughter, Rita Ann Absher, who was born 10 April 1947.

Rita Ann Absher married 6 June 1969 in the Wilkesboro Baptist Church, Tony R. Wingler, son of Mr. and Mrs. N.A. Wingler. They now reside in Greensboro, Guilford County, N.C. They have two sons, Matthew Evan born 11 May 1976 and Adam Scott, born 22 October 1979.

Sources: Absher Family Bible, records of Mrs. W.O. Absher, C.G.R.S., personal knowledge.

— Martha Absher Cuthbertson

JOHN ABSHER, SR.
302

John Absher, Sr., William Absher and Sarah (Absher) Rhodes were children of an Absher who left his family in Virginia and returned to Ireland, reason unknown. The mother "managed" to marry a man by the name of Hall. This story is according to legend. It is believed that Mr. Hall and this Absher family came to Wilkes County about 1785 from Bedford County, Virginia and settled on Mulberry Creek.

John Absher, Sr. was a farmer. He married about 1790, Eleanor Brown, a daughter of Walter and Mary (Pilgrim) Brown of Mulberry Creek. He was born about 1771 in Virginia and died 6 June 1846 in Wilkes County. Eleanor was born about 1773 and died 21 June 1857. Both are buried in unmarked graves in a family graveyard near Mulberry Primitive Baptist Church on Mulberry Creek. They had twelve children: (1) Elizabeth, born 1791, died 1870,

married 25 July 1812, Elijah F. Jennings, son of Luke, Sr. and Letes (Townsend) Jennings. They are buried at Mt. Zion Churchyard, Mulberry township, (2) William, born 1793, died 14 January 1848, married 10 February 1820, his first cousin, Elizabeth Absher, born 1795, died 13 February 1883, daughter of William and Nancy (Jennings) Absher, who lived on a branch of Roaring River. Both are buried in unmarked graves in a family graveyard near Mulberry Primitive Baptist Church on Mulberry Creek.

(3) Keziah, born 1795, died December 1847, married 10 August 1826, Walter Brown, son of Aaron and Sarah Brown, (4) Ezekiel, born 1797, died April 1883, married 1st. 1 November 1824, Jane Brown, daughter of William and Mary Brown, 2nd. 29 January 1833, Elizabeth Brown, daughter of Aaron and Sarah Brown, (5) Walter Matthew, born 1799, died 19 February 1863, married 7 July 1821, Nancy Brown, daughter of Aaron and Sarah Brown. (6) Jane, born 1803, died 31 July 1892, married 3 May 1822, her first cousin, Gowan Absher, son of William and Nancy (Jennings) Absher.

(7) Nancy, born 1805, died after 1870, married 3 May 1822 John A. Holbrook (8) Mary, born 1807, died 2 August 1894, married Caleb Church, son of William and Martha Church. (9) Jacob, born 1809 died 24 July 1888, married 9 April 1831, Sarah Hall, daughter of Robert, Jr. and Mariah (Hammon) Hall. (10), Phebe, born 1812, married 23 August 1831 William Woody, Jr., son of William Sr., (11) Susannah, born 1813, died 22 March 1889, married 12 December 1833, William Brown, (12) John A., Jr. born 1815, died 12 October 1906, married 16 November 1836, Mary Vannoy, daughter of Andrew Vannoy.

William Absher, the oldest son of John and Eleanor (Brown) Abhser, was referred to as Junior in order to dintinguish between his uncle William and himself. He was a farmer. After the death of his father, William bought the shares of real estate of his father from his eleven brothers and sisters.

He and Elizabeth had seven children: (1) John L. Absher, born ca 1820, died 24 June 1883, married 1 February 1842 Amelia Shumate, daughter of William and Amelia Ann (McMillan) Shumate. It is believed he is buried in the Wiley P. Absher family cemetery, Haymeadow, in an unmarked grave, since he died at the home of his brother, Wiley Patterson Absher. One of their children was William Roe Absher, who married Kate Feltcher of Ashe County and who was a school teacher and a clothier in North Wilkesboro.

(2) Mary Absher, born 1 February 1823, died 13 January 1894 in Alleghany County, married 29 October 1840, John R. Long, son of Jonathan and Susan (Stamper) Long of now Alleghany County. (3) Alfred J. Absher, born 14 October 1824, died 24 February 1885, married 22 February 1847, Martha Johnson, daughter of Eli and Sarah (Wheatley) Johnson.

(4) Nancy E. Absher, born 1826, died in Galia County, Ohio, married 28 November 1844, Dr. Solomon Long, son of Jonathan and Susan (Stamper) Long of now Alleghany County. It has been told in the family that

Nancy E. Long would get so homesick for relatives in N.C. after she moved to Ohio, that she would ride horseback alone from Ohio to come to see them!

(5) Wiley Patterson Absher, born 2 July 1828, died 3 December 1905, married 1850 Sarah Lucinda Walker, born 14 November 1830, died 7 December 1897, daughter of Willis and Elizabeth (Rhodes) Walker, They are both buried in the Wiley P. Absher family cemetery on original Absher land in the Haymeadow community.

(6) Adam Absher, born 1830, died 10 September 1864 while serving in the Civil War. He married 30 July 1851, Letes Jane Brown, daughter of Wesley and Letes (Jennings) Brown. She was born 15 October 1835, died 26 June 1891. Adam is buried in Hollywood National Cemetery, Henrico County, Va., and "Letty" is buried in Cross Roads Primitive Baptist Churchyard, Mulberry Community.

(7) William H. Absher, born 1832, died September 1863, married 20 October 1850, Mary Jennings, daughter of Daniel and Rebecca M. (Powell) Jennings. William H. is supposed to have been shot in the back during the Civil War.

Wiley Patterson Absher, son of William and Elizabeth (Absher) Absher, was a country merchant and justice of the peace in the Haymeadow Community of Wilkes. He joined Mulberry Primitive Baptist Church 1 January 1889 and soon thereafter became church clerk. He stood up in church one day and announced that he did not think people were friendly enough, suggesting that the staid rules of the church be changed. He was soon divested of his clerkship!

Wiley Patterson and Sarah Lucinda (Walker) Absher had three children: (1) William Matthew Absher, born 20 May 1852, died 6 December 1903, married in September 1871, Nancy Jane Reynolds, daughter of William Elisah and Susannah (Adams) Reynolds. They are buried in the North Wilkesboro Cemetery. (2) Willis Mack Absher, born 10 June 1854, died 26 March 1900, married 6 March 1879, Julia Emaline McNiel of Ashe County. They are buried in the North Wilkesboro Cemetery. They had children, but none of them remained in Wilkes County. (3) Sarah E. Absher, born 18 February 1856, died 27 December 1882, married 21 May 1876, Henry Harrison Reynolds, a brother of Nancy Jane Reynolds. She is buried in the Wiley P. Absher Cemetery, Haymeadow Community.

Sources: Wilkes County deeds and marriages, old family papers, Church minutes, tombstone inscriptions, Federal Census.

— Mrs. W.O. Absher

RUBY TUTTLE ABSHER
303

Ruby Tuttle Absher, my mother, is an attractive woman with dark brown, expressive, large eyes. She has a lovely fair complexion which needs little make up. She wears her dark brown hair very neatly and occasionally has it sprayed gray to make her a more glamourous 'granny'. Her medium height frame carries a pleasingly plump build that has always been an excuse for joke telling for her family.

It is much harder to describe her personality. She is an extremely sensitive person, which makes her more emotionally aware than many other persons. According to her horoscope she is a "Libra" which means "the scale". Although she doesn't hold any store in astrology, she certainly supports her star sign. Everything in her home must balance from pictures on the wall to flower arrangements. She is stubborn by nature and once she makes up her mind, whether the matter is trivial or of great importance, absolutely nothing can change it.

Akin to her stubborness is her one-track mindedness. Once she starts anything, she finishes that particular task before beginning another, stopping only for the necessities. This particular characteristic includes ironing everything in the house to any of her numerous hobby projects and may last in length from ten minutes to ten weeks.

She has a wonderful sense of humor, which has always made her appear a very jovial person. One of my fondest memories is of hearing her laughter, which is extremely infectuous to everyone.

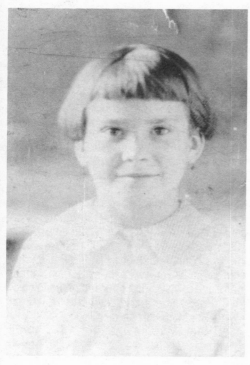

Ruby Tuttle Absher.

As we were growing up, she was a professional mother and homemaker. My brother and I agree wholeheartedly that she had a successful career. She was definitely cut out to be a mother. She was stern and a strict disciplinarian, but at the same time affectionate, praise-giving and trusting. Even at the worst moments we always knew that we were loved. We often called her a "mean old mother," when she made us do things we didn't want to do, or when she denied us permission, or punished us. We used this term partly meaning it and partly as an endearment because we were old enough to realize she was doing these things for our own good. She was a wizard at child psychology when she left notes on our piles of dirty clothes on the floor or unmade beds, stating that these chores would remain undone until we did them. Eventually we learned our lesson.

In addition to her talents as a mother she is also very creative and artistic. She has excellent color sense which shows in her wardrobe, her yard and flowers, her needlework, and her home decor. Her sense of order and balance helps here too. One of her hobbies is hooking rugs. They are truly more beautiful than professional hooked rugs and give her home a unique decorating touch. She also has made cross-stitched bed quilts and samplers which further exhibit her artistic ability. Her family and friends consider these items future heirlooms.

Another talent, and part of her total personality, is her cooking talent. Another childhood memory is that of the Christmas Open House parties my parents would give. Although they would often invite over a hundred guests, Mother always made all the party food with very little help. Everything would look and taste as if a caterer were close by. After the parties it would be the family's turn to sample the goodies and stay up even later at night. She indulged us in everyday meals too, by fixing our favorites. However we would tease her unmercifully when she baked biscuits, because she made them so rarely. We would make our point by yelling, "Mama made biscuits" and promptly lie on the floor pretending to faint. Then we would all convulse into laughter. Another of her culinary tricks was to make 'bird sandwiches' which taught us at a very early age to eat our breakfast. These sandwiches would consist of bacon and eggs on toast in bite sizes which she fed to us like baby birds. This sounds rediculous, but as tiny children we loved it. Even today when we visit her on our birthdays, she alway fixes something special for us and for each member of our families.

Some of her favorite things are apple pie, country ham, green beans, the color of brown, yellow and especially green, flashy, chunky costume jewelry, pretty shoes, snow, bird watching, genealogy, talking and her grandchildren. Among her pet peeves are snakes, baths, and Republicans, especially Richard M. Nixon. Her likes and dislikes are usually intense and she is definitely not middle-of-the-road on any of her opinions. (20 July 1969)

My mother came to North Wilkesboro on the 5th of July 1923, a year after the death of her mother in Rockingham County, N.C. She lived with her sister, Luella Tuttle McNiel, grew up, attended Woman's College, was secretary in the Wilkes County Board of Education office, met my father, William Oliver Absher, and married him on the 19th March 1939.

She has been president of the North Wilkesboro Junior Woman's Club, registrar of the Rendezvous Mountain Chapter of the DAR, was one of the organizers and first directors, and a life member, of the State Genealogical Society, and for the past several years has been a professional genealogist, certified in genealogical records searching. She has been voluntarily involved in the Wilkes Genealogical Society, Inc. for over ten years, an interest that has taken precedence over all other activities. (11 April 1982).

Sources: personal knowledge.

— Mary Elizabeth Absher Brooks

TROY D. ABSHER FAMILY

304

John Abshire and his wife Eleanor Brown were among the early families to settle on the head waters of Mulberry Creek. To this union were born William, Nancy, Keziah, Elizabeth, Ezekiel, Walter Matthew, Jane, Mary, Jacob, Susannah and John, Jr.

William Absher (Abshire) son of John Abshire, married Elizabeth Abshire February 10, 1820. She was the daughter of William Abshire, who was a brother of John Abshire. Their children were John L, Mary, Alfred J., Nancy E., Wiley P., Adam and William H.

Alfred J. Abshire was married to Martha Jane (Patsy) Johnson on February 22, 1847. According to minute of Cross Roads Primitive Baptist Church in Mulberry township, Alfred was one of the origanizers of this church. On November 8, 1849, Alfred J. Abshire was appointed church clerk. His wife joined by letter. To this union were born America, William Frank, Elisha M., Leander, Felix and Dock Solomon.

A grand jury presented a list of people who aided and abetted deserters during the Civil War. In the fall of 1863, Polly Church and Nancy Walker, who with force and arms did arrest and take one Eli Walker, a confederate Prisoner from Alfred Abshire and others as witnessed by Alfred Abshire and John A. Abshire.

Elisha (Eli) M. Absher was born May 8, 1854. He was first married to Sarah (Sally) Sebastian. Their children were: Freeland A., Louella, Chrommodore and Molly C.

Eli's second wife was Mary Jane Shumate, whom he married June 6, 1904. Their children were: Elinore, and O.O. Absher.

According to old land deeds in the Wilkes County Court House, Eli must have owned large acreages of land in Wilkes. On February 9, 1888, he sold to Henry C. Sebastian 363 acres. In 1906 he bought three tracts of land totaling 843 acres. In 1911 Eli deeded an acre of land to the Wilkes County Board of Education for the sum of one dollar. On this property now stands Pine View Baptist Church.

On January 1, 1912 Eli Absher along with other landowners who lived along the Reddies River, signed a right of way to the Wilkesboro and Jefferson Turnpike Company giving them the right to survey and locate, construct and maintain a turnpike road and electric car line through their land. This right of way beginning from the bridge in North Wilkesboro, up the Reddies River to A.M. Whittington's.

In 1922 Eli sold a tract of land to J.R. Hincher. He sold other tracts, but the above shows that he was a businessman of ability.

On August 22, 1884, Eli M. Absher received a Magistrates Commission from the Clerk of Superior Court, I.S. Call. This office had been filled by Alfred J. Absher before Eli was appointed.

My grandfather, F.A. Absher (Freeland) was born 7 October 1878, married Alice Eugenia Jennings August 20, 1892. Their children were Maie, L.D., Callie, Spencer and Max. This is the couple whose picture in on the Wilkes Heritage Book flyer.

F.A. was educated at Fairview Academy at Traphill, N.C. After completing his education he taught at Sulphur Springs. Shortly after this he went to work for the U.S. Postal Service. He and Royal Prevette were two of the first rural mail carriers out of the North Wilkesboro Post Office. At first, he carried the mail by horseback.

L.D. Absher, my father, was born January 2, 1898. He married Gertrude Eller Rhodes. The first two children of L.D. and Gertrude were born in Winston-Salem, N.C. They were twin boys Troy and Roy. Later two other sons were born, Bueford and F.A. L.D. Absher spent most of his life in Wilkes County.

During the first World War he worked in army camps and later did some work in the coal mines in West Virginia. During World War II, he worked on defense work as a carpenter. L.D. was also a cabinet worker in the furniture plants of Wilkes County. L.D. married Mary Lou Adams, after the death of his first wife.

Troy D. Absher, along with his twin brother Roy, was born in Winston-Salem. Shortly after our births our parents moved back to Wilkes County, where I grew up. I went to Mulberry Elementary School, and North Wilkesboro High School.

I went to work for Payne Clothing Comapny in North Wilkesboro in 1945. On November 24, 1951 I joined the U.S. Air Force during the Korean conflict. The following four years were spent in Texas and Florida. Following my discharge November 24, 1955, I came back to dear old Wilkes County, enrolled in Clevenger Business College for night classes and went to work for Belk Department Store.

On September 20, 1959 I married Lee Mathis. We have two sons, Blake and Keith.

Sources: Old letters, Wilkes County deeds, marriage bonds, church minutes, Research of Mrs. W.O. Absher, C.G.R.S., personal knowledge.

— Troy D. Absher

WILLIAM ABSHER, SR.
305

William Absher, Sr. was born about 1769 in Virginia, died 2 September 1842 in Wilkes County. He married about 1788, Nancy Jennings, daughter of John, Sr. and Ann (Burton) Jennings. She died before 1820. William Absher, Sr. was a son of the widow Absher, who "managed" to marry a man by the name of Hall. He was a farmer. His will is recorded in Wilkes County in WB 4, p. 277. He named a wife, Katherine. It is believed that after the death of Nancy, he married a daughter of Walter and Mary (Pilgrim) Brown of Mulberry Creek. His second wife was dead before 1850.

William, Sr. and Nancy (Jennings) Absher lived on a branch of Roaring River. They had seven children: (1) Jeremiah born about 1789, died April 1816, unmarried, leaving a will. He was in the War of 1812. (2) John, born about 1792 removed to Barren County, Ky. (3) Elizabeth, born 1795, died 13 December 1883, married 10 February 1820, her first cousin, William Absher (Jr.) (4) Gowan (called Going), born 1797, died June 1869, married first 29 January 1818 Sarah Wheatley, second 3 May 1822, Jane Absher, his first cousin, daughter of John, Sr. and Eleanor (Brown) Absher of Mulberry Creek. (5) Mary Absher, born about 1798, died about 1821 unmarried. (6) Edmond Absher, born about 1799, removed to Barren County, Ky. (7) Allen Absher, born about 1801, removed to Barren County, Ky.

Gowan Absher, son of William and Nancy (Jennings) Absher died of a heart disease and is supposedly buried in a family cemetery where North High School now stands. He first married Sarah Wheatley by whom he had (1) Susan Absher born about 1819, married 17 July 1834 Ephraim Osborne. By his second marriage to Jane Absher, he had nine other children (2) William, born about 1823, died 31 January 1896, married 6 September 1847, Milly Jennings, daughter of Elijah F. and Elizabeth (Absher) Jennings, (3) Phebe, born about 1837, married 17 July 1847 Caleb Holbrook, son of John H. and Nancy (Absher) Holbrook. (4) Allen, born about 1828, died 19 September 1863, while in the Civil War. (5) Ezekiel Absher, born October 1832, died 23 April 1908, married first 18 November 1858 Elizabeth Crouse, second 8 March 1870 Nancy Gentry. Ezekiel was in the Civil War. (6) Edmond Absher, born 1835, married Katherine Holbrook. (7) Abraham Absher, born about 1838. (8) Jacob, born about 1840, died January 1862 while serving in the Civil War. (9) Isaac, born about 1842, married 13 January 1866, Miranda Eskew. Isaac fought in the Civil War and removed to Johnson County, Tennessee. (11) Millie, born about 1846.

Records reveal that this family suffered hardships and sorrow. Four sons fought in the Civil War, two of them being killed. By 1869, just before the death of Gowan, both he and Jane were released from the poor house to live with Caleb Holbrook and Ezekiel Absher. In July 1873, William Absher was given an allowance by the warden of the poor, for taking care of Jane Absher. In the 1880 Federal Census of Wilkes County, Jane Absher was again living in the poor house.

Sources: Wilkes County will, deeds, marriages, poor house book, old family papers.

— Mrs. W.O. Absher

WILLIAM MATTHEW ABSHER
306

William Matthew Absher was born 20 May 1852 in the Haymeadow Community of Wilkes County, a son of Wiley Patterson and Sarah Lucinda (Walker) Absher. He died suddenly 6 December 1903 at his home on E Street in North Wilkesboro. He married in September 1871, Nancy Jane Reynolds, born 12 July 1849, died at the 26 May 1916, daughter of William Elisha and Susannah (Adams) Reynolds. Both are buried in the North Wilkesboro Cemetery, Sixth Street.

W.M. Absher bought land in the Dockery Community of the county, built a house patterned after the one his father lived in and became a country merchant and farmer. He was a member of New Covenant Baptist Church, located only a few hundred yards from his home. He continued to live at Dockery until the town of North Wilkesboro began to build up around the railroad, at which time he bought a lot on the NE end of E Street, built a house and moved his family into it in the new town.

Nancy Jane Reynolds Absher.

W.M. Absher served as county commissioner 1882-1891, was chairman of the Wilkes County Board of Education in 1895, organized the W.M. Absher Company 9 December 1896, was one of the organizers of the Forest Furniture Company, was vice-president and director of Wilkesboro Telephone Company, president of the Wilkesboro Hotel Company 16 July 1891, was Mayor of North Wilkesboro 1900-1903, a charter member of the First Baptist Church of North Wilkesboro 17 December 1892, and owned a great portion of the town of North Wilkesboro and many acres of land in Wilkes County when he died.

William Matthew and Nancy Jane (Reynolds) Absher had seven children, all born at Dockery, Wilkes County: (1) Henry Oliver, born 12 December 1872, died 31 March 1937, married 1 September 1902, Minnie Matilda Absher, born 18 February 1879, at Obids, Ashe County, died 27 October 1961 in Burke County, daughter of George Winfield and Amelia Ellen (Buttery) Absher, (2) Lucinda Clementine, born 12 July 1874, died 5 September 1896, unmarried. Clementine attended Miss Mamie Barber's school at Cedar Lawn in 1888. She is buried in the North Wilkesboro cemetery, (4) Nancy Sophronia, born 18 March 1878, died 2 March 1909, married 1st. 20 February 1896, William Thomas Paisley Ward, son of S.M.D. and Mary Ann (Hutcherson) Ward of Donnaha, Forsyth County, N.C. "Nannie" attended Miss Mamie Barber's school at Cedat Lawn in 1888. After the death of W.T.P. Ward, "Nannie" married, as his first wife, Clude B. Gentry. (5) Shober English, born 6 August 1880, died 6 February 1966, married 1st. 11 September 1901, Cora Gray, 2nd. Beulah Bollinger, 3rd. Mrs. Felcie Whitaker Beaver. He had children by the first two wives, but none remained in Wilkes County. He is buried in Durham, N.C. (6) Madia Varina, born 26 February 1882, died 23 October 1901, married 25 August 1900, Charles A Bowles. No issue. She is buried in North Wilkesboro Cemetery. (7) Garland Lamra, born 13 September 1889, died 1 July 1968 in Baltimore, Maryland, unmarried. He is buried in Mt. Carmel Cemetery in Baltimore.

When Henry Oliver Absher, son of W.M. and Nancy Jane (Reynolds) Absher, was a young man living at Dockery, he attended Moravian Falls Institute in 1888. He moved to North Wilkesboro with his father and was active in the early growth of the town. He was one of the organizers of the W.M. Absher, Company, the North Wilkesboro Drug Company in 1908 (later Horton's Drug), the Deposit & Savings Bank and was its first cashier. He was considered one of the best book-keepers of his time. He owned the first typewriter in Wilkes County, an Oliver.

Henry Oliver Absher.

H.O. and Minnie (Absher) Absher had five children: (1) unnamed male born and died 27 June 1903, (2) unnamed female born and died 20 March 1905, (3) Virginia Inez, born 17 July 1906, married 20 April 1938, Wilford Jones Bowles, born 11 August 1905, died 25 March 1978. No issue. He is buried in North Wilkesboro Cemetery. She is living. (4) William Oliver, born 16 January 1909, married 19th March 1939, Ruby Tuttle, born 22 October 1915 in Forsyth County, daughter of John Gray and Louretta (Ward) Tuttle of Stokes and Rockingham Counties, N.C. (5) George Woodrow, born 9 August 1911 died 15 February 1942 unmarried. He is buried in North Wilkesboro cemetery.

William Oliver Absher, son of H.O. and Minnie (Absher) Absher, was affiliated with the

Minnie Matilda Absher Absher.

Dodge Automotive Agency for thirty-six years, selling his half interest and retiring in 1971. He is a life deacon of the First Baptist Church, a director of the North Wilkesboro Federal Savings & Loan, chairman of the Board of Trustees of Wilkes General Hospital, a Scottish Rite Mason, a Shriner, past president and long-time member of the North Wilkesboro Lion's Club, one of the founders and charter member of Wilkes Chamber of Commerce, a former city commissioner and mayor pro tem of North Wilkesboro, and a life long resident of the town of North Wilkesboro, having been born in a house on the corner of Third and C. Streets.

William Oliver and Ruby (Tuttle) Absher have two children: (1) Henry Gray Absher, born 21 December 1939, married 24 June 1962, Sarah Jane Payne, born 23 April 1940, daughter of Ira Dewitte and Annie Cline (Barnhardt) Payne of North Wilkesboro. Henry graduated from U.N.C. Chapel Hill in 1962 and is a partner with the international accounting firm of Deloitte, Haskins & Sells in the Atlanta, Georgia office. They have two children: (a) Elizabeth Barnhardt Absher, born 7 February 1965 in Mecklenburg County, (b) William Gray Absher, born 8 February 1968 in Mecklenburg County. (2) Mary Elizabeth Absher, born 25 December 1944, married 17 April 1966, Leonard Lawrence Brooks, Jr., born 9 May 1942, son of L.L. Sr. and Mildred Tate (Finley) Brooks of Wilkes County. Libby attended Greensboro College and is a homemaker. They have two children: (a) Laura Elizabeth Brooks, (b) Matthew Niel Brooks. They live at Breeze Hill Farm, North Wilkesboro, N.C.

Sources: Wilkes County deeds, marriages, tombstone inscriptions, Family Bibles, personal knowledge, old family letters.

— Mrs. W.O. Absher

JOHN A. ABSHIRE, JR.
307

John A. Abshire, Jr. son of John and Leanner (Brown) Abshire was born 18 May, 1817,

in Wilkes County, N.C., died 12 Oct. 1906, and buried in Abshire Cemetery, Scottville community, Ashe County, N.C., married 16 Nov. 1836, Mary "Polly" Vannoy, born 11 Oct. 1814, in Wilkes County, died 5 Mar. 1903 and buried in same cemetery as husband John. John and Mary were the parents of nine children, all born in Wilkes County, N.C.: (1) Levi Abshire (1838-1920); (2) Susannah Abshire Handy (1841-1905); (3) Nancy Abshire Caudle (1843-?); (4) Leanna Abshire Owens (1845-?); (5) Isaiah Abshire (1848-1905); (6) Tobias Abshier (1850-1900); (7) Phebe Abshire Abshire (1853-1935); (8) Fanny Abshire Brown (1856-1876); (9) Elizabeth Abshire Lanier (1895-?). John was a farmer probably in Halls Mill Community, Wilkes County, N.C., for at least sixty years of his life, but about 1881 he and Mary moved to Ashe County, N.C., with one of their daughters and husband Phebe and Lewis W. Abshire.

Phebe Abshire, the seventh child of John and Mary married her first cousin Lewis W. Abshire, 3 May, 1873, in Wilkes County, N.C. Lewis was born 13 Mar. 1848, the seventh and youngest child of Walter Matthew and Nancy (Brown) Abshire. According to story passed down by mouth, Lewis went "out west" and stayed a few years. When he returned to Wilkes County, his first cousin, Phebe, had grown into a "young lady" to whom he was attracted, thereto their courtship and marriage.

Lewis and Phebe were the parents of eight children, the two older ones being born in Wilkes County and the last six born in Ashe County, N.C.: (1) Flora Absher (1874-1904); (2) Mary Emma Absher (1876-1963); (3) Maud Absher Richardson (1884-1947); (4) Walter M. Absher (1886-1968); (5) Cora Absher Richardson (1890-still living); (6) Nora Absher, twin to Cora (1890-1890); (7) John Absher (1892-1903); (8) Cox Absher (1895-1978). The spelling changed from Abshire to Absher with this generation in recorded records.

Mary Emma Absher was the mother of three children: (1) Elbert Absher (1901-1972); (2) Hazel Absher Trivett (1905-1980); (3) Thomas John Absher (14 Mar. 1907 — 16 Nov. 1972). All three were born in the Scottville community, Ashe County, N.C., and lived their early days before marriage in Scottville.

I knew Emma (Granny Absher) in her late 70s and early 80s, and at that age she could walk up and down stairs just as a 20 year old. She was short in height and very very neat, always wearing a pretty brooch or jewelry, silk stockings, never heavy cotton stockings; very careful of her appearance.

Thomas John Absher, known as "Tom" attended school at Scottville's one room schoolhouse. The building is still standing on Jimmy Maines' land. In later years it was used as Scottville Baptist Church, but at present is unoccupied. Before his marriage he served a short tour in the U.S. Army in the late 1920s and worked a period of time in the coal mines of West Virginia. After marriage Tom was timekeeper while the Scenic Parkway was being built, a sawmiller, foreman at Oak Flooring Plant, Jefferson, and in the latter years, part owner of sawmill in Ashe and Alleghany Counties. He was a man of friendly and likeable disposition and had a great knowledge of timber and kinds of woods and trees. He was ordained and served as a deacon at Cranberry Baptist Church, Ashe County in 1955 until poor health kept him indoors most of the time a few years before his death. Tom many times told of remembering the winter being so cold and severe until New River at Scottville Community froze so thick that wagons and horses were driven across without accident in his boyhood years (around the 1920s).

Tom married Sybol Pollard (1913-1974), daughter of John "Press" Pollard (1882-1949) and Sarah Jane "Jennie" Sawyer (1889-1976) of Chestnut Hill Community, Ashe County on 27 June, 1931. Tom and "Syb" were the parents of seven children, all born in Ashe County: (1) Charles R. Absher, born 1932; (2) Thomas Jack Absher (1934-1980), married Bonnie Zue Hash (Grassy Creek, N.C.); (3) Erban Dean Absher, born 1936, married Mary Lois Woodie (McGrady, N.C.); (4) Jesse J. Absher, born 1942, married 1. Merle Bezold (Wisconsin) 2. Arlene Heath (New York); (5) Virginia Absher Brooks, born 1943, married Bobby Brooks (Glade Valley, N.C.); (6) Jerry W. Absher, born 1947, married Rebecca Coldiron (Jefferson, N.C.); (7) Debra Absher Neal, born 1957, married Pete Neal (Jefferson, N.C.).

Charles Roger Absher, is the oldest child of Tom and "Syb". He attended Nathans Creek High School, N.C., graduating in 1951, entering the U.S. Air Force immediately. In 1971, he retired from the Air Force after having duty stations in Texas, Georgia, Newfoundland, Germany, Florida, Massachusetts, Thailand, and Alabama. While stationed at Robins AFB, Georgia, he met his wife, Wylene Wood Absher, the daughter of Wiley E. Wood born in 1908 in Laurens County, Georgia, and Cleo Daniel Wood (1916-1978) born in same county. Wylene is the oldest daughter of Wiley and Cleo, born in 1935 at Dexter, Ga. Charles, being known in Scottville, N.C., as Roger, and in Georgia as Charles, was married 1 Apr. 1956, to Wylene. They have three children, who reside at present with them in Wilbar Community, Wilkes County, N.C.: (1) Charles Roger Absher, Jr., born 24 Nov. 1958 (Robins AFB, Ga.) graduated from Wilkes Community College, Wilkesboro, N.C. and presently employed with the Northwestern Bank Regional Operations Center, N. Wilkesboro, N.C.; (2) Carlton Edward Absher born 22 Mar. 1962 (Bitburg AB, Germany), a student in second year at Wilkes Community College; and (3) Joy Cheree Absher, a "late comer", but such a "joy" born 1 Apr. 1978, at Jefferson, N.C.

All of Charles R. Absher's family are members of, and have different jobs of service at, the Glendale Springs Baptist Church, Glendale Springs, N.C.

Sources: Federal Census Records, Court House Records, family Bible. Records, personal knowledge and memories.

— Wylene Wood Absher

CHARLES ADAMS
308

Charles Adams appears on the 1771 tax list for Surry County, but lived on Reddies River when Wilkes was formed from Surry in 1778. He had land grants for 150 acres. He had one brother, William Adams, but the relationship to the other Adams families living in Wilkes County has not been proven.

Charles was indicted for failure to report for jury duty in July 1780, but when his case was called it was discovered that he had died in the Revolutionary War sometime before.

The name of his wife is unknown. The following children are believed to be his: (1) Henry, born about 1760, died 1821; (2) George, born 1764, (3) Spencer, born 1778; (4) Charles, born 1770; (5) Elizabeth, (6) Frances; (7) Nancy; and perhaps other children.

All of the sons of Charles except Henry left Wilkes County sometime after 1800. No records have been found concerning the daughters.

Henry lived on the land of his father Charles until his death in 1821. His wife was Susannah whose last name is unknown. She filed for a widow's pension for Henry's service in the Revolution but her records were imcomplete and she failed to get a pension. Henry and Susannah had ten children, all of whom are named in the settlement of his estate:

(1) Elizabeth, born about 1784, married in 1800, Benjamin Bullis, who had several children: (2) Charles, born 1787, died 1872, married Nancy Stamper (?) born about 1784, died after 1850, believed to be the daughter of Joel and Nancy Cannaday Stamper, who had nine or more children; (3) Abigail, born November 7, 1793, died June 13, 1849, married 1813, John Adams, son of Jacob and Mary Stamper Adams, who moved to Johnson County, Missouri and had ten children, Abigail died in Johnston County and John remarried; (4) Margaret, born 1794, died January 3, 1843, married 1813 Spencer Adams, son of Jacob and Mary Stamper Adams. They also moved to Johnston County, Missouri. They had eight or more children; (5) Nancy, born 1791, died February 2, 1867, married 1807 her cousin William H. Adams, who lived in the Reddies River area and had thirteen children; (6) Fannie, born 1801 and never married; (7) Jane, born 1800, married 1819, Henry Hays; (8) Susanah born about 1805, married Solomon Owens; (9) Debbie, born 1809, married 1827, Charles Hawkins; (10) Sarah, born 1800, married John Rhodes.

To return to the Charles and Nancy Stamper Adams family: Charles and Nancy were members of the old Mulberry Primitive Baptist church. Charles was active in the church with his support in service and finances. Their children were:

(1) Rachel, born 1809, died 1893, married 1833 Lewis Sebastian, son of William and Elizabeth Carter Sebastian, who had nine children; (2) William born 1812, married Elizabeth; (3) Willis, born 1815, married Rosamond Huffman; (4) King David, born 1819, married Rachel Handy; (5) Nancy, born 1820, married Joel Brewer, son of John and Kesiah Johnson Brewer, who lived in Rock Creek township near the forks of Roaring River; (6) Mary, born 1824, married King E. Shumate, who lived in the Mulberry area; (7) Delphia, born 1816, married 1833, Noel Richardson and lived in Alleghany County; (8) Joseph H. born 1826, married 1854, Catherine McGrady and lived in Haymeadow; (9) Susannah, born 1828, died 1878, married 1849 William Elisha Reynolds, who lived in the Haymeadow community.

Sources: Bible Records, Family members, Wilkes County records.

— Samuel E. Sebastian

ELIZABETH HOLBROOK ADAMS FAMILY
309

Elizabeth Holbrook Adams was the second of thirteen known children born to Ezekiel Holbrook and his two wives. Elizabeth's mother was the first wife, Susannah Gross (Grose, Crouse). Born in 1823, Elizabeth was busy during her youthful years helping her mother care for and ever expanding family. There is no doubt that Elizabeth became the number one helper in this home.

Characteristic of the women of her day, Elizabeth received very little formal education. In fact, Elizabeth was eighteen years old before the first public school was organized in Wilkes County. The Wilkes County School Census of 1841 and 1842 show that Elizabeth, as well as six brothers and sisters, were enrolled both years in School District number sixty-two, which was located at Dockery. Since she was eighteen years old when she enrolled in school, she had little time to learn the basic educational skills taught in that day.

Elizabwth Holbrook was married to William Rufus Adams 2 April 1850, the ceremony taking place in the Adams home. Her husband, born 15 May 1828 to Sally Higgins and Chapman Adams, attended school in District number twenty-seven. Since school sessions were never more than three months in any given year prior to the Civil War, it seems reasonable to assume that a working knowledge of the three R's was about all the education that both Elizabeth and Rufus were able to get during those difficult years.

Elizabeth and Rufus lived to see nine of their eleven children reach maturity. They were (1) Martha Jane Adams, born 4 May 1851, died 4 November 1924. She married William Johnson and had Cromie, who married Ennice Dowell; Plutina, who never married; Martha, who married Jim Felts; Mary, who married John Billings; Jane who married Curtis Burcham; Rhoda, who married Dock Harrold; and John, who married Minnie Hall Shumate.

(2) Celia Ann Adams was born 22 April 1852, married William Franklin Gregory (see William Franklin Gregory family). (3) Susie Adelaide Adams, born 2 April 1954, died 3 July 1929. She married Smith Ellis and had two children, Claude who married Etta McCarter, and Sherman. (4) Rubin Oliver Adams, born 24 April 1858, married Selina Blackburn,

daughter of James and Diana Waddell Blackburn. Their children were Shover, who married Millie Whitley; Ila, who never married; Wheeler who married Lollie Whitley. Rubin Oliver Adams died 11 December 1940. His wife, Diane died 7 February 1948 and both are buried at New Covenant Church.

(5) Franklin Verlin Adams, born 1860, married Launa Waddell and had the following children: Hester Ann who married Shober McQuary; Ivy who married Janie Maynard; Melvin who married Edna Taylor; Cuba, who married Kathrine Spangler; Talmage who married Roxie Harmon; Leavy, who married Willis Mahaffey; and Vert, who married first John Scott and second, Thurman Martin. All members of this family moved to West Virginia, except Hester Ann.

(6) Huanzy Adams, born 26 October 1861, died 19 July 1953. He married Mary Ellen Hutchison, daughter of William E. and Martha Hall Hutchison and had the following children: Lona who married Monroe Billings; Ella who married Timothy Elledge; Walsie who married Iredell Watkins; Arthur who left the state; Mattie and Luellen who died young.

(7) William Ansel Adams born 29 October 1863, died 3 January 1936. He married Martha Handy, daughter of Noel and Emily Waddell Gregory Handy and had the following children: Dona, who married a Mr. Craven and lived near Flint Hill; Tarnie who married Gertie Byrd, daughter of George and Polly Byrd and lived in Bluestone, West Virginia; Dewey who married and lived in Detroit; Odell, who married Laura Martin and lived in Bluestone, West Virginia; Lessie who married Lynn Bauguess; Lora, who married Ernest Brewer; and Coy, who married Alma Gregory, daughter of John Franklin and LouEllen Shepherd Gregory.

(8) John Quincy Adams, born 1866, died 1960. He married Emma Miles and had no children. They lived and died in or near Statesville.

(9) Mary Pauline Adams, the last child born, arrived 9 September 1869 and died 3 May 1953. She married Everette Hutchison, son of William E. and Martha Hall Hutchison and had the following children: Ronda, who married Grace Church; Hillery, who married Mae Bauguess; Crommie, who married Mattie Brown and was subsequently killed by Lewis Johnson; Mack, who married Rosa Adams; and Etta who married Laude Bowers and had nine children.

Elizabeth Holbrook Adams and her husband, William Rufus Adams were hard working middle-class citizens. They lived on Shumate Mountain and spent their lives there conjuring out a living from the hills and valleys which surrounded their home. Both Elizabeth and Rufus were very religious and both were active member of the church. Rufus joined Round Mountain Baptist Church 3 October 1896 where his membership remained until his death. His obituary, written in 1907, gives some of his last words, and they speak of the faith of this Godly man: "I have fought a good fight. I would not give the hope I have for ten thousand such worlds as this. I am going away to that Glory Land where friends will part no more."

Elizabeth Holbrook Adams died quietly in her home 24 February 1907 and her husband died 28 February 1907, just four days after his wife had passed away. Both were buried in the Miles Cemetery on the middle fork of Roaring River near the home of Reid Miles.

Sources: Family Bible, personal interview with Ila Adams, grand-daughter; Wilkes County marriage records, census records, Grave markers and personal knowledge.

— Paul W. Gregory

GIBSON ADAMS

310

Gibson Adams was born January 3, 1786. It is not known if he was born in Wilkes County, North Carolina or not. On the records where he appears his name is spelled Gibson or Gipson. By the year 1801, Gibson's parents must have been dead.

The Wilkes County Court of P's and Q's minutes of May 5, 1801 lists Gibson, age 15, as being bound out to Menoah Dyer to learn the hatters trade. Also, at the same time there were two other children bound out with the name Adams. They were Molly Adams, age 10, bound to Henry Adams. Rebeckah Adams, age 12, bound out to Reuben Hays. They could have been sisters to Gibson.

When the war of 1812 was declared, Gibson enlisted for the term of six months, from September 1814 to March 1815. He was in Captain Ambrose Carlton's company of Detached Milita from Wilkes. His pay was eight dollars per month. Along with his company, Gibson rendezvoused at Wadesboro on the 28th of February 1815, where they received orders on the 1st of March to return to their place of residence. When they arrived on the 9th of March, they were discharged.

On August 11, 1815, Gibson meet with Isaiah Hampton to post a bond for 500 pounds, stating that there was no just cause to obstruct the marriage between Gibson Adams and Susana Hampton. Susana Hampton was the daughter of Turner Hampton, a lawyer in Wilkes County. Gibson and Susana were married on August 17th, 1815 in Wilkes County, North Carolina. Isaiah Hampton was a brother to Susana. Gibson was 29 when he was married.

Gibson was described as being six feet tall. He had dark hair, blue eyes and tolerable fair skin. He was listed as a farmer.

Gibson and Susana Adams had at least nine children. They were: William Harper, John, Byrd, Jessie, Tillie, Polly, Manda, Besta and Elizabeth. All are believed to have been born in Wilkes.

Gibson first appears in Wayne County, North Carolina in 1820. In 1830 in Wilkes County, Gibson appears with a Steven Gentle, who also appeared with him in Wayne County. In 1861, Gibson's son William Harper married Martha Ann Gentle, daughter of the same Steven Gentle.

Gibson made his will in August 1833. He left all his possessions to his wife. He died in 1835 in Wilkes County. He and Susana are buried at Moravian Falls, North Carolina. In 1878, Susana filed for Gibson's service pension. She was 80 years old and was able to sign her name on the form. Gibson was 49 when he died.

The children of William Harper and Martha Gentle Adams are; Henry Clay, Franklin (Dock) Hackett, Marcus L., Pantha, Julia Ann, James Gordon (grandfather), Mary Ellen, and Alice. All were born in Wilkes except James and Mary who were born in Ashe County, North Carolina.

Sources: Wilkes and Wayne County Census, Death, Marriage Records, Wills and old letters.

— Jere Gordon Adams

SPENCER ADAMS

311

Spencer Adams was born ca 1750-60, died 1829 in Dallas County, Alabama. He was the son of John Adams of Virginia. He had brothers, John, Jacob, Benjamin, and perhaps other brothers and sisters. His wife was Nancy Ann Townsen or Caudill. Spencer was a prominent farmer, minister, and businessman. He lived in the Traphill area of Wilkes County as early as 1784 and was very active in religious, political and business activities in the county for the next twenty years.

Sometime before 1803, he went to eastern Kentucky and ran a series of revival meetings in the Regular Baptist churches there. He returned to Wilkes County, where he organized a wagon train, and in the fall of 1803, with his family, his brothers John and Benjamin, their families and some of his neighbors, set out for Kentucky. They went by way of the Holston and Clinch Rivers to Pound Gap, Virginia and turned left down to the north fork of the Kentucky River where they camped. A big snow fell that night, and after a conference they decided to settle there.

Shortly thereafter, Spencer was appointed a Magistrate and later a deputy sheriff. He was a Captain in the War of 1812 and in 1817, was elected high sheriff of Floyd County, Kentucky. He was a real estate and livestock dealer. He also served as pastor of Indian Bottom church, the Sand Lick church and the Castlewood church in Russell County, Va.

In 1821, he sold his holdings in Kentucky and with his sons and sons-in-law moved to Dallas County, Alabama. In Alabama he acquired a large amount of land and slaves. He disposed of his slaves in his will, which was probated in 1830, giving each of his children two. The rest of the slaves were not to be sold out of the Adams family.

Spencer and Nancy Ann were the parents of the following children: (1) John A., born 1780, died 1861, married 1803 Rachel Fletcher. Rachel died and John married second, Sarah Smith McElroy. He married a third time to Artie Carson. They died in Dallas County, Alabama. (2) Benjamin, born 1785, married Elizabeth Caudill in Wilkes County, N.C. They lived in Alabama. (3) Jesse, born February 12, 1796, died 1875, married Rhoda Martin in 1817 and moved to Alabama. (4) Irwin, born 1798, married in 1818 Levica Ellis, daughter of Benjamin and Hannah Ellis. They moved to Mississippi. (5) William married a Caudill and had children Hannah and Spencer. (6) Elizabeth, born 1791, died 1855, married Sampson Caudill, son of James Caudill, Jr. They moved to Cedar County, Missouri. (7) Jane, born 1787, died 1860, married first an Adams. They had a son Spencer, who married Tacy Johnson in Wilkes County and had a daughter. He divorced Tacy and went to Dallas County, Alabama and married his cousin, a daughter of John A. Adams. After the death of her first husband, Jane married Abner Caudill about 1804.

Abner Caudill was the son of old James Caudill, Sr., of Lunenburg County, Va. Abner had brothers Mathew, Stephen, James Jr. and Thomas. Abner and Jane Adams Caudill had the following children: (1) Mary, born 1808, died 1850, married Eli Blackburn, born 1806, died 1900, son of William and Sarah Blackburn (see Blackburn story). Mary is buried in the family cemetery east side of Roaring River below Bethany Ford bridge. Eli A. is buried at Bethany Baptist Church Cemetery. (2) Thomas, born 1810, died October 2, 1898, married 1838 Elizabeth Matilda Holloway, born 1821, died 1898, daughter of John Holloway. They had eight children and lived near Bethany Ford on Roaring River. They are buried in a family cemetery. (3) Jane born 1818, died 1907 married 1846; a McCrary is a possible daughter (4) Matilda born 1825, married 1845 Enoch Johnson, is also a possible daughter.

Sources: Wilkes County, Kentucky, Alabama, Virginia records and family members..

— Samuel E. Sebastian

ALEXANDER FAMILY
312

William Munsey Alexander (Munse) was born in Wilkes County, but his family moved to Walla Walla, Washington where he lived until grown and then moved back to Wilkes. Later he worked as chief clerk in an office for the coal companies of West Virginia. While there he volunteered for the army and stayed in until the Armestice was signed in 1918. Later, back in North Wilkesboro, he worked in the office of S. V. Tomlinson. He had an inventive mind and worked on may different projects, including principle of the jet engine in 1935.

Mary Linwood Greene and he were married in June 1922. After marriage he worked as office clerk and manager for the Johnston Mills Company of Charlotte, moving to Monroe, N.C. to one of their mills there. Ten years later he moved his family back to Wilkes where he built a home on the Yadkin River and was office manager for Greer Cotton Mills until retirement.

William Munsey and Mary Linwood Alexander have four children, two girls and two boys, all married. (1) Mary Charles, married to Dr. Robert H. Griffin of Asheville, who have three daughters: Susanne Hamilton, now married to Mickeal Bowman of Charlotte, Joan Alexander Griffin, not yet married, Mary Charles (Molly) married to Peter Bockman, now living in California; (2) Elizabeth Wellborn (Libby) married to C. Jack Caudill, now a minister in the Methodist church and also a government counselor, who now live in Marion, N.C. and have three girls,: Elizabety Gray (Betsy) with a Masters degree in German, Mary Lynn, married to Dave Melton, a minister, and Jenny Louise,

the youngest; (3) William Munsey Alexander, Jr. in Social Service work, married to Betty Sue Haynes; (4) Robert Linwood Alexander, has two daughters, Laura Louise and Leslie Dianne, both in school.

Sources: family knowledge.

— Mrs. Mary Greene Alexander

ANGUS ALEXANDER
313

Angus Alexander, whose name labels him as Scotch-Irish, settled at the head of the middle prong of Roaring River, claiming the rich bottom land and foothills before there was a Wilkes County, just in time for him and Woenifred (Fugate) to be counted in Surry's first List of Taxables for the House of Burgesses in 1771.

In 1772 his settlement was put on the map when Surry's Court of Pleas and Quarter Sessions ordered a road laid out "from Thomas Jones (Joines) at Longbottom on Roaring River to Elkin Creek", the location of iron works. On the 12-man jury were names of his close neighbors, Joseph Graves, father-in-law of Benjamin Cleveland, and William Nall.

The next year neighbor Benjamin Cleveland witnessed a technical violation by "planter" Angus — selling two pints of Rum and one bowl of Toddy, when for protection of tavern operators the law required a license to sell less than a quart of spirituous liquor. Court was held at Gideon Wright's on the Yadkin.

In 1775 and 1778 two sons, Willis Fugate and Jesse, were born to Angus and Woenifred.

Angus barely lived to see Wilkes County formed and was not able to file entries for the land he had improved. He died sometime before September, 1778, without a will, and was buried in an unmarked grave on the plantation.

The letter of administration to Woenifred was signed by Benjamin Cleveland and Jesse Alexander, who is believed to be the father of Angus. Jesse was named as a son of Angus Alexander, of Lancaster County, Virginia, in 1742.

The sale of the perishable part of the estate of Angus amounted to 378 pounds, 3 shillings 9 pence. A pair of compasses indicated that he was surveyor as well as a "planter".

Woenifred received land grants in 1781 and deeded 350 acres to her sons the upper area to Willis . . the lower to Jesse. The brothers did not get along well and went to court later over debts and land.

In 1783 Woenifred married Samuel Warner, with Solomon Alexander as witness.

Willis, the older son of Angus and Woenifred, married on May 1, 1789, Susan, called Sukey, Holbrook, daughter of Randolph and Mary with Ralph Holbrook as bondsman.

In 1790 Willis was licensed as an attorney and served as county attorney at the October term of court.

Jesse married two Woolfolk sisters, Nancy and Fannie, daughters of Joseph, Jr. Of the marriage to Nancy in the late 1890s there were ten children. Susanna (1799-1862), who married in 1816 Samuel Broomfield Johnson (1790-1852) and moved to Georgia; Joseph Woolfolk, born about 1800, who bought the

the Little River iron forge in Ashe (later Alleghany) County, near Gap Civil, and because of heavy debt in 1841, hanged himself. Two moved to Indiana: Mary, called Polly, was married to a Burton; and Elizabeth, to William Gambill. Three migrated to Cherokee County; Winny, who was married to Elijah Herbert sometime before 1834 (after a first marriage to William Billings in 1816); Fannie, in 1834 to Robert Martin; and Nancy, in 1836 to John H. Johnson. Louisa and Sally died in infancy. John (1802-1885), who married in 1832 Mary, called Polly (Thompson) remained at the homeplace. (See The Family of the First John Alexander.)

The marriage bond of Jesse and his second wife, Fannie (Woolfolk) on April 27, 1814, was signed by Reuben Sparks, who performed the ceremony. Their children were Jesse, Jr., of whom nothing is known, and Sarah, born about 1821, who married first William Thompson and moved to Cherokee County about 1853.

The children of William and Sarah were: Robert, born about 1840; Alex B., born about 1841; and Katherine, born in 1844. Both Alex and Katherine were married to cousins from Longbottom, Martha, called Matt. and Jesse T. Alexander, daughter and son of John and Polly. Alex and Matt lived in Clay County and Jesse and Katherine, at Longbottom.

After the death of William Thompson, Sarah returned to Wilkes and married a widower Hardin Spicer (See The Family of Hardin Spicer.)

Sources: Ashe County wills; Surry County court minutes and tax lists; Wilkes County court minutes and marriage records; Lancaster County, Virginia, wills; Bible records, interviews.

— B. Beatrice Holbrook

THE FIRST JOHN ALEXANDER
314

The first John Alexander, born April 8, 1802, was the only one of the ten children of Jesse and Nancy (Woolfolk) to remain in Wilkes County until 1850.

On October 29, 1832, he married Mary (called Polly,) Thompson, born January 10, 1812, to Robert and Catherine (Herbert of Gap Civil, Ashe County, now Alleghany, a descendant of William Herbert who built iron forges on his 3000 acre bounty land grant on New River and Little River.

Johnny Alexander Farm, "Long-Bottom", 1930.

Through the years the Alexanders have intermarried with families in Ashe and Alleghany because of proximity ever since 1779, when the Wilkes court ordered that "there be a good

Bridle Way opened and continued from the mouth of Peak Creek at New River to the county road at the Long Bottom on Roaring River''.

John and Polly inherited the Alexander homeplace located on a beautiful and productive plantation of 725 acres, valued at $2,410. in 1824, with grazing land extending beyond the top of the Blue Ridge. In 1839 John had no slaves but five people employed producing 850 bushels of corn, 200 of oats, 50 of rye and 60 of potatoes. His livestock consisted of four horses, 35 cattle, 29 sheep, 100 swine and only six poultry.

John was on the first public school committee of Walnut Grove district #35, with Hardin Spicer and S. J. Gambill, Sr. Later he supported the Double Creek Academy, at which the Rev. Hugh Stokes, brother of the governor, taught several years around 1850.

John and Polly were members of Old Roaring River Baptist Church, he since 1828, until an arm was set off at Double Creek. There he was often a messenger to the Association and served on committees.

Between 1802 and 1847 five daughters and two sons were born to John and Polly. It was a happy family until the eve of the war. Bettie, 24, had eloped to marry William B. Reeves in Ashe County in 1858; Emaline, 24, had gone to Jonesville Academy and was teaching in Rocky River in Cabarrus County when she met and married Matthias Laird Harris, and later moved to Charlotte.

At home Nannie, 22, was waiting for her prince, one of the California '49ers to return in his covered wagon as he promised; Fannie, a petite girl of 20, and Martha, in her early teens, were dreaming; Jesse, 19, and Freel, 13, were hardly aware of war clouds.

But suddenly their joy was turned to grief at the loss of their mother, February 8, 1860. Bits of her wedding dress and of embroidery done by her, one slipper with leather still soft, and even a piece of face cloth used in the casket have been kept for 122 years in memory of her.

A tradition was to give each daughter when she married a corner cupboard and each son land.

During the war, responsibility was heavy on the girls at home, with Brother Jesse in the First Regiment — Infantry, Company B, and Brother Freel in for a while later. They had buried some treasurers, but when a raid by bushwhackers was expected they hid others under a feather bed on which one sister pretended to be seriously ill. The raiders, having respect for her, left the bed alone.

After the war more marriage vows were said: Nancy Adeline (1837-1924) to her prince, Shubill Lunceford, much older than she; Fanny Caroline (1839-1937) to Joseph S. Holbrook, in 1886; Jesse T. (1842-1933) to a cousin Katherine Thomson, in 1867; Martha Jane (1844-) to a cousin Alexander Thompson, in 1868; Freeland Huysen (1847-1928) to Sarah Spicer, in 1876.

John Alexander, 83 years old, died September 28, 1885, at the residence of his son-in-law, J.S. Holbrook, and was ''buried among those who have gone before in the old home . . .'' (from obituary). A pine settee made to be used as a ''cooling board'' for him is now a treasured piece of furniture restored.

Sources: family Bibles; church minutes, U.S. census; Wilkes court minutes; interviews with relatives, personal memories.

— B. Beatrice Holbrook

ANDERSON FAMILIES
315

Samuel Anderson, born 1767, was the son of John Anderson. He was married to Martha Ellis. . .Sam's will contained several hundred acres of land, which was given to the following children: William N., Cornelius, Evan, Ellis, Robinette, Wesley, Sophia, Mary, Samuel W., and John.

In our research we followed his son Robinette, who was born 1810, in the Hunting Creek Township. He seemed to do quite well for himself. During his life time he obtained a number of acres of land besides his inheritance. He was married first to Rebecca Curry on March 26, 1828. To this union were born four children, who were; Ambrose, born 1829; Malinda, born 1832; William, born 1833; and Martin born 1834. Rebecca died around the year 1842.

Robinette then married Keziah Hayes, born 1830. She was the daughter of Harvel and Chloe Johnson Hayes. They had ten children: Noel R., born February 1850; Oliver, born 1851; Leland, born 1854; Sidney, born 1856; Mary, born 1858; Lucreasy, born 1864; Lettie, born 1866; Harrison McKinley, born January 4, 1868; and Eli J., born 1870. Robinette died January 4, 1871, while several of the children were very small.

Granny Keziah, as she was called by many, raised the children, and she lived to be 90 years of age. During her last years she lived with her son Harrison M.

Harrison McKinley and Carolina Love Anderson (1950).

Harrison M. married Carolina Love February 5, 1889. Carolina was born February 15, 1873. Harrison bought, as well as inherited, 148 acres of land on hunting Creek where he was born. He then purchased a number of acres on the Little Brushy Mountain, where he built a home, and raised 14 children who were: Bessie Lee, born March 14, 1890, died February 2, 1963, wife of Aaron Call; Gertrude, born

January 13, 1892, died July 22, 1966, wife of Andrew Johnson; Clyde Turner Sr., born April 6, 1893; Tina, born April 24, 1894, wife of William Wesley Anderson; Robert H., born May 4, 1896; Ethel, born May 30, 1898, wife of Luther Johnson; Florence, born April 17, 1900, died April 14, 1967, wife of Wilson Hayes; H. Lester, born November 12, 1902, died December 21, 1939; Christene L., born December 25, 1904, wife of Dewey Parker; Alma S., born February 10, 1907, wife of Raymond Parks; Sherman T., born December 14, 1908; Lora M., born September 23, 1910, wife of Harry Shore; Fones S., born December 10, 1912; and Vecie S., born June 22, 1917, wife of George Dancy.

Harrison owned one of the largest farms of that time in Wilkes County. He bought property along the Yadkin River, just off the Armory Road. He and Carolina moved there, leaving a son Turner and his family on the Little Brushy at the homeplace, where Turner and his wife still live today. Later on in life, Harrison sold the River property and bought on up the Armory Road where both he and Carolina died. Harrison died February 26, 1954, Carolina died March 13, 1968 at the age of 95. At her death she left 324 descendants. Ten of her children were living, along with 88 grandchildren, and 203 great-grandchildren, also 23 great-great-grandchildren. Both Harrison and Carolina were buried at Fishing Creek Baptist Church Cemetery in Wilkes County.

Source: Bible, census, marriage records, family information.

— Gracie F. Call

ANDERSONS
316

Sally Anderson, daughter of Ransom and Mary Anderson, was born in Ireland of Scotch Irish ancestry. The 1880 census records of Wilkes County, N.C. list Sally as being 70 years old. She died August 1, 1881 on Stony Fork and is buried in the lower Mt. Zion Church Cemetery.

The Anderson family left Ireland and landed at Wilmington, N.C. After living in Orange County for several years, the family moved west, planning to join the Boone Colony in Tennessee. On the way Ransom Anderson became ill and died. He is buried near Greensboro. Mary Anderson and Sally came to Wilkes County and settled at Hunting Creek. It was believed that they were related to Billy Anderson, who owned the whole valley at that time. Mary Anderson is buried at Hunting Creek.

Sally and her family moved to Elkville and lived there until after the Civil War; then they moved to Stony Fork and she lived there until her death. Sally had six children: Rebecca, Celia, William, Geroge Washington, Eliza and Selina.

Rebecca was born 1835 and died August 21, 1913. She is buried in the lower Mt. Zion Church Cemetery. She had two sons: James and Sidney. James had four children; Will Bost, Rosa and Nancy. He is buried in the lower Mt. Zion Church Cemetery. Sidney Anderson was born June 10, 1861 in Wilkes County, died March 11 1942 and is buried at

lower Mt. Zion Church cemetery. He had six children: (1) Millard, born Oct. 20, 1899 in Wilkes County, died Oct. 20, 1980 in Watauga County and is buried in Mt. Zion Baptist Church Cemetery. He married Jennie Anderson and had four children: Marvin, Ruby, Mabel and Myrtle. (2) Effie, born April 10, 1902 in Wilkes County, died July 9, 1938 in Wilkes County and is buried in the lower Mt. Zion Church Cemetery. She married Doughton Hamby and had one son, Earl. (3) Avery born Jan. 5, 1904 in Wilkes County, died Feb. 12, 1982 and is buried in Mt. Zion Baptist Church Cemetery. He married Willie Teeters and had 5 children: Jack, Noah, Carl, Hazel and Paul. (4) Roxie, born, Feb. 26, 1907 in Wilkes County and married Clyde Adkins. She has 5 children: Mildred, Ruth, Sidney, Ray and Bruce. (5) Nellie, born June 10, 1913 in Wilkes County. She married Howard Brown and had 2 children: Prentiss and Jolene. (6) Annie, born Sept. 9, 1915 in Wilkes Co. She married Casper Hawkins and has 2 daughters: Etta Lee and Bobbie.

Celia Anderson was born 1838 in Wilkes County, died Jan. 8, 1929 and is buried at Mt. Pleasant Baptist Church Cemetery in Wilkes County. She married James Scott and had one son James Pinkney Scott, born May 4, 1862, died April 8, 1952 in Wilkes County and is buried in Sinkler Cemetery at Beaver Creek, N.C. He married Sally Pearson June 8, 1889 and had six children: (1) Estella, born Aug. 8, 1890, died Dec. 2, 1929, married John Edmiston. She had 9 children: Jim, Joe, Helen, Clint, Codie, George, Hazel, Dare and Elizabeth. (2) Nathan was born Sept. 16, 1892 and had seven children: Jess Willard, Juanita, Hubert, Odell, Topsie, Louise and Holbert. (3) Howard Scott was born Aug. 16, 1894. (4) Homer Scott was born April 6, 1898. He married Pansy Hamby and had 7 children: Novella, James Ford, William, Fred, Fair, Connie Lucille, Willa Dean and Ruby Ann. (5) Jettie Florence Scott was born Aug. 25, 1900. She married Stogue Laws and has 2 children; Ray Vaughn and Gwyndolyn. (6) Hobert Hayes Scott was born Nov. 29, 1904. He has 3 children: Corrina, Hayes Edward and July Carol.

William Henry Harrison Anderson was born Dec. 1, 1840, in Wilkes County, died Dec. 25, 1923. He married Eda Carolina Dula Dec. 3, 1865. He had 9 children: (1) Alice Virginia was born Oct. 22, 1869 and died May 24, 1887. (2) Lindsey Bryant born April 4, 1872, and died Aug. 9, 1939. He married Mollie Hawkins and had 2 children: Collis and Alice. (3) William Jones, born Mar. 20, 1877, died Oct. 22, 1960. He married Callie Harris and had 9 children: Clara, Elizabeth, Mildred, Annie Mae, Edith, Alfred, Edward, Hope and Audrey. (4) Alphus Kelly was born Dec. 1, 1879 and died Nov. 15, 1928. He married Roxie McGee and had 6 children: Ernest, Virginia, Howard, Ruth Carolyn, Eugene Ray and Irene Lee. (5) Carrie Gertrude Anderson, born Nov. 9, 1874, died Jan. 21, 1878. (6) Joe Coleman born May 1, 1883 died Jan. 21 1964, married Coleen McGhinnis and had 2 children: Joe, Jr. and Lonnie. (7) Wade Cloyd, born Oct. 10, 1886, died July 15, 1975, married Cora Walker and had 3 children: Jack Cloyd, Hellen and Mar-

garet Wade. (8) Leila Mae, born Jan. 28, 1890, married William Lee Alexander, had one child, William Ervin. (9) Mollie.

George Washington Anderson, born 1849, died Aug. 23, 1913, buried lower Mt. Zion Cemetery. He married Mary Brown and had 7 children: (1) Phennie, born 1879, died Jan. 4, 1940, married Sidney Anderson and had 6 children: Millard, Effie, Avery, Roxie, Nellie and Annie. (2) Sally Anderson, married Robert Hamby and had 6 children: Calvin, Mae, George, Wade, Blain and Versie. (3) Roxie Anderson, born Oct. 12, 1884 Job Triplett, had one son Arley. (4) Hattie, married Green Shell and had 5 children: Ben, Nellie, Augustie, Bervin and Bryant. (5) Frank Anderson, married Kiter Marley and had one child Rose Emma. (6) George, married Beulah Adkins and had 5 children: Alma, Burley, Faye, Roy and Alta. (7) Ed married Mellie Walker and had 4 children: Belva, Lula, Mary and Helen.

Eliza Anderson, born 1854 in Wilkes County and buried in the lower Mt. Zion Cemetery. She had 3 sons: (1) Gaither, born Feb. 22, 1880, died Jan. 12, 1952 and buried in Charlotte Co. Va. He married Elizabeth Laws and had 6 children: Kelly, Virginia, Clyde, Wade, Callie and Zedar. (2) Simpson, born May 1, 1873, died Jan. 10, 1939 and buried in the lower Mt. Zion Cemetery. He married Laura Hodge and had 5 children: Alice, Leonard, Amanda, Ira and Clinard. (3) Alverta, married Mart West and had 9 children: Nellie, Charlie, Kiter, Bessie, Annie, Ernest, Luther, Frances and Me.

Selina Anderson was born 1857 in the Reedy Branch Community of Wilkes County. She is buried in the lower Mt. Zion Cemetery on Stony Fork.

Sources: Family memories, the family Bible, Wilkes County marriage and birth records, grave stones, and census records.

— Bobbie Hawkins

THE CORNELIUS ANDERSON and ETTA M. QUEEN FAMILY
317

Cornelius Anderson was born in April of 1822, in Wilkes County, North Carolina. He was the son of Samuel Anderson.

On August 4, 1840, Cornelius Anderson married Etta Mittie Queen, in Wilkes County, N.C. James Queen was the bondsman. They had a family of seven children: (1) Arrel, born 1842, Wilkes Co.; (2) Martha Lou, born 1845, Wilkes Co.; (3) Joseph, born 1849, Murray Co., Ga.; (4) Margaret Lucy Caroline, born 29 April, 1851, Austell/Marietta, Ga. Margaret was first married to Ezekial Staggs, March 27, 1877, in Prairie Co., Ark. and second to Robert Franklin Waters, December 30, 1888, also in Prairie Co., Ark.; (5) Alice Pernelia Ann, who married L.O. Jackson, Prairie Co., Ark.; (6) Joel; (7) Name unknown; Martha Lou died sometime during the Civil War, of typhoid fever.

Cornelius Anderson purchased 50 acres of land on Grape Vine Branch, in Wilkes Co. from Levi Brotherton, July 14, 1847. Witnesses were James and Hugh Queen, brothers of Etta. January 29, 1848 Cornelius Anderson sold 50 acres on Grapevine Branch. July 1, 1848, the Sheriff sold James Queen land adjacent Jeremiah Gilreath and Samuel Anderson, deceased. (Court action against property of Cornelius Anderson, son of Samuel Anderson.)

By 1849 Cornelius had moved his family to Murray Co. Ga. They stayed there until after 1850 then relocated to the Austell/Marietta (Cobb Co.) area. Francis Queen (brother to Etta) and wife, Lucey (Anderson — sister to Cornelius) also went to the same area.

Cornelius served in the Confederate army — Company A 9th Georgia Artillery from 1861-1865 and he spent some time in a "Yankee" prison near Memphis, Tennessee. His wife, Etta made a trip from Atlanta to Memphis by a freight train and spent the entire trip sitting in the only available space which was a sack of salt.

The first record of the Anderson's in Arkansas was the 1880 in Prairie Co. with Cornelius and Etta living in the household of their son, Joel and his family. Their first meal after arriving in Arkansas consisted of rabbit, rice, sweet potatoes, and white oak acorns that they used to make coffee. November 24, 1884 Cornelius Anderson bought 40 acres of land in Prairie Co., Ark.

Cornelius Anderson had a long white beard. Stories remembered and told by his grandchildren state that when he would go swimming the beard would float out in front of him in the water. Cornelius and wife, Etta attended Walters Chappel Baptist Church and would drive to the services in a surrey with fringe on top drawn by a pair of matched bay horses.

Cornelius drew a Confederate Pension from the state of Arkansas. He and Etta died in 1908 and are buried in the Walters Chappel Cemetery. His grave has a Confederate headstone.

Sources: Wilkes County, NC deeds; marriages; Murray County, Georgia Census records; Confederate records; Interviews with family members; Prairie County, Ark. deeds and marriage records.

— Kay Waters Sakaris

ROSA HENDREN CHAMBERS ANDERSON
318

Rosa Anderson was born January 5, 1909, in Wilkes County. She went to Mt. Sinai school, just a small country school with two rooms.

She married Charlie Chambers September 20th. Charlie was born December 18, 1908, died 1933. He went to Fishing Creek Arbor school. Their children were:

(1) Rosla born December 31, 1928, attended school at Mt. Sinai and married Archie William Moore, son of Richard and Maggie Parker Moore. Archie worked at Coble Dairy for 28 years, is semi-retired and works for Mathis Brothers Construction Co. Rosla is employed at the *Journal-Patriot*. They had (1) Helen Rosla, born February 12, 1945, who graduated from Wilkes Central in 1963 and married Larry Ernest Eller August 2, 1963, son of Ernest A. and Geneva Faw Eller. Larry is employed by Central Telephone Co., and Helen

is secretary at the First Methodist Church in North Wilkesboro. They have Tammy Renee, born November 7, 1967 and James Larry born April 7, 1971. (2) Madgaline (Maggie), born September 10, 1949, graduated from Wilkes Central and Draughn's Business College, and married Billy Mathis February 14, 1970. Billy is the son of Mont and Mattie Johnson Mathis and is co-owner of Mathis Brothers Construction Co. Maggie is a homemaker. They have Berry William born March 6, 1971 died March 5, 1972; Bridgett Dawn born July 27, 1974 and Bart Christopher born March 27, 1976.

(2) Pansy Mae born April 29, 1930 and went to school at Wilkesboro. She married Lonnie (Bud) Moore, son of Gent and Ruey Moore. He attended Spurgeon School and is self-employed. Bud was one of the original founders of the Wagon Train. Pansy is employed at Carolina Business Machines. They have (1) Becky born December 27, 1952 who went to school at C.C. Wright and Wilkes Central. She is a Key Punch operator and married to Randy E. Mabe, son of Roy and Mae Mabe. They have April, born July 4, 1974 and Jason born January 12, 1980. (2) Charlie Lee born February 11, 1954, went to C.C. Wright and Wilkes Central and in the construction business. He married Frances Queen, daughter of Thomas and Carrie Lee Rash Queen. She is a florist. They have Chad born January 3, 1979. (3) Nancy born November 28, 1955, went to school at C.C. Wright and Wilkes Central, is an Expense Clerk and is divorced. She has Monica Steelman born June 3, 1974 and Nella Steelman born June 9, 1975. (4) Wanda, born May 6, 1957, attended C.C. Wright and Wilkes Central and is a school bus driver. She married Herbert Gary Nab, son of Herbert B. and Mary Nab from Wendell, Idaho. They have Douglas born November 4, 1974 and Traci born October 27, 1979. (5) Tommy born October 6, 1961, attended C.C. Wright and Wilkes Central and is in the construction business.

Rosa Chambers married as her second husband, Reuben Anderson, June 30, 1936. Reuben was born March 13, 1913. They had the following children: (3) Betty Sue, born September 15, 1936. She was 3 years old when she had spinal meningitis which left her unable to hear. She graduated from the School for the Deaf at Morganton. She married James Franklin Lovette November 14, 1955, son of Robert Elmore and Pearl Rosa Laws Lovette. Betty Sue is employed at Modern Glove and Frank is self-employed. They have (1) Patricia born March 11, 1956, who attended West Wilkes High School, married Cecil Kermit Holbrook September 20, 1975. Pat and Cecil are employed at Northwestern Bank and have Cecil Kevin, born June 1, 1979. (2) Victoria Rose born March 21, 1958, attended West High, married Randy Allen Roten July 3, 1976. Vickie is employed at Modern Glove and Randy works at Carolina Mirror.

(4) Ernest born April 21, 1938, attended school in Wilkesboro and married Delores Anderson. They have Ernest Reuben, Cynthia Rosa and Crystal. Ernest and Delores divorced and he married Bobbie and has Cheryl.

(5) Jimmy Anderson born July 9, 1940, attended Wilkesboro School, married Betty

Earp February 24th. He works for General Motors in Michigan. They have Jimmie, Jr.

(6) Bobby born January 22, 1944, died March 15, 1955 at a result of an accidental gunshot wound. (7) Jerry Dean born October 18, 1946, was killed in an automobile accident in his early years. (8) Christine born February 18, 1949, married Tommy Morgan June 17, 1981.

Sources: Personal information.

— Helen M. Eller

ARLEE BROYHILL ANDREWS
319

Julie Arlee Broyhill, daughter of Issac Jefferson and Ada Belle Carlton Broyhill, was born September 5, 1919. She graduated from Wilkesboro High School and attended Appalachian State College. On August 23, 1939, she married John William Andrews, son of Nelson Coles and Ollie Earp Andrews. He graduated from Wilkesboro High School and is a farmer, orchardist and cattleman. They live on a large farm in Boomer.

Mary Elizabeth Andrews, daughter of Arlee and John Andrews, was born March 18, 1951. She graduated from Wilkes Central High School in 1969, Wilkes Community College with an A.A. degree in 1971 and East Tennessee State University with a B.S. degree in Elementary Education in 1973. In 1981 she was certified in Reading Education from Appalachian State University. She teaches reading at King's Creek Elementary School in Caldwell County. On August 7, 1976 she married Charles Stephen Hendrix, son of Jack Kelly and Frankie Mode Hendrix of Granite Falls, North Carolina. He graduated from Hudson High School and Appalachian State University with a B.S. degree in Industrial Arts. He is employed by Data Forms and Systems, Inc. of Hickory, North Carolina. They live in Boomer.

Robert William Andrews, son of Arlee and John Andrews, was born June 1, 1954. He graduated from Wilkes Central High School in 1972, U.N.C. Chapel Hill with a B.C. degree in Zoology in 1976 and received his M.D. degree from the Bowman Gray School of Medicine in 1980. He is now a resident in surgery in N.C. Memorial Hospital, Chapel Hill.

Sources: Personal knowledge.

— Arlee Broyhill Andrews

NELSON ANDREWS
320

Nelson Coles Andrews was born July 5, 1889, to William Coles and Martha Matilda Swanson Andrews in Little Rock Community. When he was a young man of 22 he purchased 120 acres of land from Levi L. Walker for $1,650. That was July 6, 1911. On December 17, 1911 he married Margaret Ollie Earp. She was born February 24, 1889 to John and Nancy Earp of Little Rock community. Together they shared the joys and hardships of farming in the southern part of the Brushy Mountains.

Having a large family was an asset to a farmer and nine months after Nelson and Ollie were married they were blessed with their first

Nelson and Ollie Andrews, 1911.

liam was born June 1, 1954 and is in medical school residency in Chapel Hill. John has been an active farmer all of his life. He managed the family farm after his father's death and the farm grew and prospered. Taking advantage of the excellent location in the Brushy Mountains the farming specialized in orchards, forestry management and beef cattle. John is retired and enjoys traveling and fishing. He serves on the following boards: Northwestern Bank, Wilkes County Planning Board, Farm Bureau, and Extension Advisory Leadership Committee for the year 2000. In 1965 John was award the North Carolina State Farmer of the Year award from the Soil and Water Conservation Commission. He is also an active member of Little Rock Baptist Church.

Edna Genevieve Andrews graduated from Wilkesboro High School in 1937, and Davie Hospital School of Nursing in 1942. She served three years in the Navy Nurse Corps during World War II. She married William Carlyle Weston of Iredell County March 5, 1948. They were blessed with three children. Gloria Kay born December 17, 1955, married Jerry Kilby, has one child, Sara, and lives in Little Rock. Dan Carlyle born January 30, 1958. Glenn Orenn born September 12, 1960. Dan and Glenn live with their parents on the Andrews' old homeplace. Dan, Glenn, and Carlyle manage the family farm started by Nelson in 1911. Edna was inactive in nursing for thirteen years in order to raise her children but started part time nursing in 1966. For the past twelve years she has been Supervisor in the Surgery Department at Blackwelder Hospital in Lenoir. She is an active member of Little Rock Baptist Church and a member of the Woman's Missionary Union. She enjoys working in the vegetable garden during summer months.

Mary Gozelle graduated from Wilkesboro High School in 1943, and A.S.T.C. in 1947. She married Charles Austin Ham of Iredell County October 27, 1951 and they were blessed with four children. Martha Louise born December 21, 1954, married F.W. Townes, IV, and lives in Little Rock. Karl Andrew born May 11, 1957, and lives and works in Charlotte. Margaret Ollie born September 19, 1961, and is in Nursing School at Chapel Hill. Rose Marie born June 25, 1966 is an honor student at Wilkes Central High School. Gozelle worked as a librarian at Mooresville High School for six years after college graduation. She was a full time mother for sixteen years and returned to work in 1969 as librarian at Wilkes Central High School. In the summer she enjoys working in the vegetable garden and excells in growing beautiful roses. She is also an active member of Little Rock Baptist Church.

Sources: Family Bible, Little Rock Baptist Church Cemetary, personal interviews, and Wilkes County records.

— Martha Ham Townes

MARVIN ASHLEY FAMILY

321

Coleman Marvin Ashley, Sr., was born May 25, 1903 in Wilkes County, son of John Hamp-

child, Ruby Nancy, born September 16, 1912. Four other children were born as follows: John William, March 8, 1916, Edna Genevieve, November 9, 1920, infant son born and died August 4, 1922, and Mary Gozelle, November 26, 1926. All of the four children grew up with an understanding of the importance of the work ethic, moral values, and education. Nelson and Ollie were active members in Little Rock Baptist Church and they are buried there. Nelson was a prosperous farmer and a community leader. He served on the Little Rock School Board in the 1920s.

In the summer months Nelson and Ollie would sell produce to customers in Lenoir. On one such trip in July of 1959 they had an accident in their farm truck and Ollie was fatally injured. She died July 16, 1959. Nelson died March 30, 1964 from emphysema at the age of 75.

Ruby Nancy Andrews graduated from Wilkesboro High School in 1931. She Married Roy McGee of Caldwell County, August 19, 1931. They made their home in Lenoir and had three daughters. Betty was born August 25, 1933, married Delbert Teem, has three children; Mike, David, and Carol, and lives in Raleigh. Pat was born February 1, 1938, and lives and works in McLean, Virginia. Jean was born April 24, 1947, married Bill Benfield, has two sons; Scott and Brian, and lives in Lenoir. Since retirement Ruby has enjoyed needlework and quilting. She is quilting each grandchild a quilt with a special design.

John William Andrews graduated from Wilkesboro High School in 1934. He married Julia Arlee Broyhill, also of Little Rock, August 23, 1939. They have two children. Mary Elizabeth was born March 18, 1951, married Chuck Hendrix, and lives in Little Rock. Robert Wil-ton and Vina Elvira Lowe Ashley. He was a brother to Lydia Elizabeth, Thomas Roosevelt, Joe William and Jay Gordon, all of whom are deceased and buried in Walnut Grove Baptist Church cemetery except Roosevelt who is buried at Spring Lake, N.C.

Marvin graduated from Wilkesboro High and attended Ives Business College. He was ticket clerk at Wilkes Hosiery Mill for 25 years and since retirement had done orchard work.

In high school, his drawing of a N.C. map won him a blue ribbon at the county fair. He pitched baseball on the hosiery and cotton mill teams; sang in a quartet; played a tenor banjo and guitar for square dances; sings bass in the church choir at present and has been choir leader.

He married July 19, 1930, Nellie Mae Brock, daughter of Charles Parks and Nora Dell Coone Brock. Nell was born December 1, 1905. They live at the homeplace of his parents which he inherited. They raised the following children:

(1) Coleman Marvin, Jr. was born 1931, and after high school joined U.S. Air Force. He now sells insurance in S.C. In 1950 he married Mildred Broyhill. They had: Thomas Edward, born at St. Johns, Newfoundland in 1953, married Lynn Cason in 1975 and they have Joy, born 1977 and John born 1980. Karen Elaine born 1955, married David Peters in 1974 and had Brian, born 1976 and Brent born 1979.

Marvin, Jr. and Mildred were divorced in 1958 and he married Janet Haynes in 1958. They have William Coleman, born 1960, a student at Columbia University, and Stephen Haynes born in 1964 in England.

(2) John Charles, born 1933, joined U.S. army after high school graduation and spent 2½ years in Japan. He attended Clevenger's College and Wilkes Community College. He worked for Holly Farms before retirement on disability. He married Reba Shumate in 1953 and they had: Gerald Charles born 1956, graduate of N.C. State University with a degree in Science, married Marlene Settle 1979; Timothy Lee born 1958, worked in Alexander County; Evelyn Mae born 1960, married Donald Staley 1981 and has Michael born April 26, 1982.

(3) Mary Nell, born 1931, married William Carroll in 1959. He was a field engineer in Cape Hatteras and Puerto Rico. While in Puerto Rico they had: Nancy Susan born 1960, who married Jeffrey Barnes 1981 and had Jeffrey, Jr. 7 March 1982; Donald Alan born 1963, is in U.S. navy; Stewart Ashley born 1964.

Bill Carroll works at the Pentagon.

(4) Betty Sue, born 1936, has been a secretary for twenty-seven years, married Bob Smith in 1958. They have Annette Lynn, born 1960, who married Michael Whisenhut May 1, 1982.

(5) Robert Wootson born 1938, attended Wilkes Central H.S. and is employed by American Drew. He married Kay Childers in 1960. They have Robert, Jr. born 1963 and is in the Navy; Richard Len born 1964, attended Alexander County H.S. and works for a furniture company; Alden Clay, born 1940, married Jeanette Robinson 1961 and they have Ricky Clay, born 1962, married Lori Marie Prevette;

Lisa Ann born 1966; Melany Lynn born 1970; Devin Dale born 1973.

Marvin and Nell celebrated their 50th Wedding Anniversary July 19, 1980 with a reception given by their six children in the fellowship hall of their church. Nell taught school for five years in a one-teacher school before her marriage. She taught the Wilkesboro Trainable Retarded Class for eight years before her retirement. She was church clerk for seventeen years, and a charter member of the Pores Knob Extension Homemakers Club, where she has forty years perfect attendance.

Sources: Bible, personal knowledge and memories.

— Nell Ashley

MARY BEATY (BAITY)
322

The earliest records of the Beaty (Baity) Family in Wilkes Co. are found approximately 1827, at which time Mary Beaty purchased land from Abner Caudill. Mary (Polly) Wilson Beaty was the daughter of John and Agnes Wilson and had married John Beaty, Jr., son of John Beaty, Sr. and Leah ? Beaty. They were married in Mecklenburg County May 22, 1806, and to this writer's knowledge there were only four children born of this union: John W., Samuel Harvey, Mary Elizabeth, and Martha. After the death of John Beaty, Jr., Polly began the move presumably to Ashe County. Upon arriving at the old Call's mill, she stopped her horses and wagon for the night. During the night the horses were stolen and she could continue no further. According to family tradition, she moved onto the property of the parker family nearby before purchasing property of her own. The 1850 census shows the name spelled Beaty. Tax lists show the name spelled Baty. Then in the 1860 census the name was spelled, evidently by the census taker as Baity and this spelling has been carried by the clan in Wilkes County ever since. Polly is listed as being 75 years old in the 1860 census. I do not know the exact date of her death, but it was before the next census and family tradition has it that she was buried in the Parker family cemetery on Hwy. 115 across from the rock quarry.

Samuel Harvey married Elizabeth Call, daughter of Daniel and Anna Eller Call, on the 15th of February 1851.

Mary Elizabeth married Newland (Newburn) Parker, son of Richard Parker of Virginia and ? Smoot Parker of Wilkes County.

Martha was still living with Samuel Harvey's family in the 1880 census and was 66 years of age at that time. Apparantly she never married.

No records on John W. Beaty have been located at the present time.

Mary (Polly) Beaty's husband, John Beaty, Jr., was the grandson of Francis and Martha Beaty of Mecklenburg County. Francis was a very wealthy man, a farmer and surveyor and owned thousands and thousands of acres of land in the Piedmont section of the State. He had moved from the Augusta County, Virginia area and his first land grant was in 1754 in old Tryon County.

Source: Personal knowledge.

— Betty Jean M. Baity

PAUL BAITY FAMILY
322A

Paul Monroe Baity was born 22 June 1886, the son of William Adolphus Baity and Rhoda Emma Moore and the grandson of Samuel Harvey Baity and Elizabeth Call. He was born in Wilkes County, the sixth of twelve children. His brothers and sisters were: Isaac Samuel, Authur Kynderd, William Jakers, Stephen Elias, Sanford Swim, John Wilson, Alice Elizabeth, Lodema, Leathend, Cora and Mary Myrtle.

Pearlie Eva Hayes was born 10 May 1884 in Wilkes County. She was the daughter of Jefferson Tedder and Mary Irene Hayes, the granddaughter of William P. Hayes and Mary Elizabeth Moore. Pearlie had one sister named Dina Mae Hayes. Her mother was married on 6 Dec. 1887 to Wilborn Turner. Wilborn Turner and Mary Irene Hayes then had eight children who were half brothers and sisters to Pearlie. They were: Wiley E. Turner, Paris Vaughn, Simeon Purvis, Winston, Dewey, Texie (girl), Vierdie (girl) and Arvie (girl).

Paul and Pearlie were married on the 20 October 1906. Their first child, Edgar Roosevelt, was born 26 May 1908. He was a blue baby and died 14 July 1908. Edmond Vaughn was b. 12 Aug. 1909; Albert Andrew, 29 Sep. 1911; Lola Maybell, 12 May 1913; Minnie Lee, 14 Oct. 1914; Stella Elizabeth, 10 Sep. 1916; Howard Fred, 31 Dec. 1919; and Frank Friday, 7 Aug. 1925. Their house is described as having three rooms in it; it was a planked up house. When it snowed, the beds would be lined with snow that would blow in under the roof. It also had an upstairs where the children all slept. The house had a fireplace in the living room where Pearlie did her cooking; she would bake her bread in a skillet over the coals.

One day Paul had borrowed a horse from Mr. Davis so as to sow his rye. He had told Stella to stay home from school and take care of Howard, and if she would do that then he would let her go to school the next day. The older children had gone to school. She was six years old. Pearlie was out digging Irish potatoes, and she came into the house to build a fire to cook dinner. Later, Stella and Howard were playing foxy geesy gander. The game is where you call out how many geese you got, and the answer is more geese than you can catch in a week and then you would start running. Stella was wearing a long flannel gown and got too close to the fireplace. Her gown caught on fire and she ran out on the front porch, but she couldn't get off. There were no steps at the front porch and it was higher than your head. She ran out there thinking either her mother or father would see her, but they didn't. Then she ran back to the other door. There was only one door that you could get out of the house with. The door entered the kitchen. It was steep behind the house. She was burned very badly. The older children were met coming home from school by Martin Moore with his mule. They were just messing along eating simons and didn't know of the tragedy at home. Stella died as a result of her burns on the 30 Nov. 1921, twenty-one days

Paul and Pearlie Baity, 20 Oct. 1906.

later.

The children tell of many good times when they would swing on grapevine swings, of swimming in the creek, fishing with a tow sack, homemade sliding boards, and with all the hills, there were lots of places to slide, mainly in the cow pastures. All the children attended the Mountain Crest School. There were no gloves or book sachels, and lunch was carried to school in a half gallon tin bucket. The children would crawl under the schoolhouse and eat their lunch; bread and milk tasted good in the winter.

Pearlie was a good hand with the maddock and she used to dig for sasafras bark, which was dried and sold. When it is dried it is used in medicine and for flavoring. The money for the bark was hers.

Pearlie was partially blind for thirty-five years. She was totally blind for the last five years before her death. Her blindness was caused by glaucoma, and the cataracts on her eyes. None of the children could fool her, even with her blindness; she could tell them by their walk just as soon as their feet hit the porch. She loved company.

Paul ran a country store and was robbed twice. One of those times was 16 July 1964. The news article in the *Greensboro Daily News* read: A 78 year old man in the Brushy Mountain community was robbed of about $150 at 2 A.M. this morning. Paul Baity, who operates a country store at his home near Mountain Crest School reported the robbery to Sheriff Fred Myers. Baity was quoted as saying he was sleeping in his store when a knock on the door awakened him. Two men were at the door, one saying they wanted a flashlight to see how to fix their car. When he opened the door, Baity said, one man grabbed him around the neck, choking him to the point of helplessness, and he held him in such manner that he could not get a good look at his assailants. He said the men demanded his money, and took the store's money, amounting to about $50 from a

box. Then they demanded his billfold, which contained about $100.00; they took overalls, billfold and all. Following this act, they marched him, unclothed, out of the store a distance of several yards, turned him loose, ran back to the front of the store and drove off in an automobile which they had parked there on the road.

Paul was an orchardist of apples and peaches. He also hauled milk for eighteen years. Paul died on 1 April 1972. Pearlie had died on 21 December 1968. They were both buried at New Hope Baptist Church.

Sources: Children and personal knowledge of the author, president of the Surry County Geneological Association.

— Wanda Baity Lewis

SAMUEL HARVEY BAITY
323

Samuel Harvey Baity was born in March of 1817 in Mecklenburg County, the son of John Beaty, Jr. and Mary (Polly) Wilson Beaty. He married Elizabeth (Betsy) Call, daughter of Daniel and Anna Eller Call on the 15th day of February, 1851, and of this union were born nine children, to wit: William Adolphus, born July 26, 1852; Zennis Pinkney, born Nov. 24, 1857; James, born in 1864; Mary A.; Martha A. (Nettie), born 25th of August, 1970; Remus, born 1858; John E., born 1854; Adelaide E., born Nov. 18, 1871; and Alice E., born 8 June 1861.

Harvey and his family lived in the Hunting Creek area of Wilkes County and his mother and sister lived with the family for a number of years also. The earliest deed shows Harvey purchasing land from Circus Parker of 50 acres at the fork of Hunting Creek. He was a farmer and loved his family and church.

William Adolphus married Rhoda Emeline Moore, daughter of Wilson and Mary Hayes Moore on the 26th day of November, 1874.

Zennis Pinkney married Mary L. Barnard,

daughter of F.L. and Matilda Wright Barnard, on the 29th day of December 1899.

Mary A. married James C. Brotherton on the 27th day of October, 1878.

Martha A. (Nettie) married Eli D. Barnett, son of James and Martha Call Barnett, on the 5th day of January, 1904.

John E. married first Josephine M. Staley, daughter of Enoch Staley, on the 27th day of February, 1888. Josephine died giving birth to twins. He later married Nelia Miller on the 27th day of January, 1890.

Adelaide E. married Jessie Dotson, son of William and Susie Chatburn Dotson, on the 28th day of February, 1897.

Alice E. married James Shepherd on the 30th day of January, 1892.

James and Remus evidently died as young children.

Harvey died around 1916 and his definite grave site is not known by this writer. Elizabeth died January 4, 1916 and is buried at Fishing Creek Arbor Baptist Church in Wilkes County.

Source: personal knowledge.

— Betty Jean M. Baity

STEPHEN EDWARD BAITY
324

Stephen Edward Baity was born Oct. 10, 1889, the son of William Adolphus and Rhoda Emaline Moore Baity in Wilkes County. He married on the 16th day of July, 1910 Nancy Isabelle Campbell, daughter of Noah Alfrod and Elizabeth Campbell Campbell. They were married while the family was living in Alexander County, but moved back to Wilkes County where their children were born with the exception of Beulah Mae.

They lived on the corner of J and 7th Street and the children loved to pull each other in their little red wagon up and down the hill.

Stephen died the 8th day of November, 1918 in Wilkesboro after a bout with the flu. Due to the young age of the children, the family encouraged Isabelle to take her young children back to Alexander County where her family lived. Being large with child and unable to work, she did as they bid and moved the family over to Alexander County, first on Rocky Creek. The children attended school when possible at Shady Grove, walking to and from school.

Children born of this union were: Roosevelt Lee; Homer Albert, Walter Holman; Cora Belle; Beulah Mae; William Mack and a still born son that was not named. William Mack and Cora Belle had also died as young children and both are buried at Bethany, old cemetery, in Wilkes County.

The others married as follows: Roosevelt Lee to Zula Millsaps on the 24th day of December, 1930; Homer Albert to Mattie Jeanette Reavis on the 25th day of December, 1932; Walter Holman to Ethel Reavis on the 5th day of December 1938. Mattie and Ethel were sisters and the daughters of William Regulis and Dorothy Mae Estep Reavis both of Wilkes County also. Beulah Mae married first to Claude Foust and then to David Chapman.

Homer Baity is a Baptist minister and has

supplied for Cherry Grove Baptist Church and Lewis Baptist Church both in Wilkes County. He is currently the oldest practicing minister in Iredell of Alexander County. He pastors Friendly Chapel Baptist Church in Iredell County and lives in Alexander County. Homer is my father-in-law.

Source: Personal knowledge.

— Betty Jean M. Baity

WILLIAM ADOLPHUS BAITY
325

William Adolphus Baity, son of Samuel Harvey and Elizabeth Call Batiy was born July 26, 1852, in Wilkes County. He married Rhoda Emaline Moore, daughter of Wilson and Mary Hayes Moore on the 26th day of November, 1874. William Adolphus (Dawfie) was a farmer and miller. He ran an old mill on the Brusy Mountains for a number of years before moving his family over to Alexander County. When he left, he left the mill with his son Isaac and his new wife. While in Alexander County he also operated a mill on the Vashti Road.

Rhoda was an active midwife and assisted in the birth of a number of children.

William and Rhoda were very active church members and attended Hunting Creek Baptist Church. William died April 17, 1930, and Rhoda June 12, 1941, and both are buried in the old abandoned cemetery at Hunting Creek Baptist Church.

Twelve children were born to this union, to wit: Isaac Samuel, born 12 Nov. 1876; Arthur Kynderd, born 11 Sept. 1878; Alice Elizabeth, born 28 April 1881; William John, born Jan. 20, 1883; Lodianna, born Oct. 2, 1885; Paul Monroe, born June 22, 1886; Leathend (Leathy), born 22 March 1888; Stephen Edward, born 10 Oct. 1889; Sanford Swin, born 26 Aug. 1892; Cora, born 15 March 1894; John Wilson, born 7 Feb. 1895; and Mary Martha, born 31 May 1898.

Three of the children, William John, Cora and Sanford died as young children.

The other children married as follows: Isaac Samuel, first to Martha Emma Call and then to Mary Ann (Nelia) Miller; Arthur Kynderd to Nancy M. Brooks; Alice Elizabeth to Iredell Tedder; Paul Monroe to Pearl Hayes; Leathend (Leathy) to Floyd Tedder and then to Roman Bentley; Stephen Edward to Nancy Isabelle Campbell; John Wilson to Josie Kerley; and Mary Martha Baity to Simon Johnson.

A number of the descendants of William Adolphus and Rhoda Baity are still living on the Brushy Mountains.

Source: personal knowledge.

— Betty Jean M. Baity

RUFUS BALDWIN FAMILY
326

Andrew J. and Mary Jane Stone Baldwin were my great-grandparents. They were married March 8, 1866, by A. Wiles, J.P. The children and years of birth are: Frank — 1867; John W. — 1869; Louella (Dink) Wood — 1877; Robert Edwin — 1878; Rufus (my grandfather) — 1881, Arthur — 1887; and Charlie — 1893. Andrew died soon after being hit in the head by a long, sharp rock. He died when the rock was removed.

A tombstone in the Rock Creek Baptist Church Cemetery has these names: Andrew J., Elizabeth, Arra (Mary ?) and the date 1894.

My grandparents, Rufus and Mary Ann Burchette Baldwin were married February 11, 1906, by C.G. Bryant in Roaring River. Witnesses were J.F. Parks, J.N. Burchette and F.L. Parks. Despite the fact that Rufus was almost totally blind, they reared five sons and five daughters. They are: Annie Sue, who married Will Ward (deceased); Walsie, who married George King (deceased); Rex, my father, married Dessie Mae Hall (deceased); Sally (deceased) married John Creed; Sam (deceased) married Maggie Johnson; Lottie married Charlie Creed (deceased); Christy married Hazel Mastin; Ara married John Brannon; Conrad married Sarah Ruth Flinchum; and Bob married Betty Pearce.

The family moved to Ronda several times, at least once with the help of Uncle John Childress and his steer and wagon. Daddy said that one time, Uncle John's wife had made a stack of pumpkin pies for the moving day. He kept giving Daddy pies, not realizing that Daddy didn't like them and was throwing them between the wagon wheels. Daddy said he didn't want to hurt his feelings.

In 1926, the family built a home on the White Plains Church Road in Roaring River. The curved road around the house became known as Baldwin's Curve. Grandpa and Daddy cut wood off the land, and would heat bricks to keep warm in the wagon used for hauling. My aunts, Walsie and Annie Sue, say they remember helping put on the roof.

The family moved to Fries, Virginia in 1931 for three months. They moved in two trucks owned by Barney Jordan. Daddy said he was coming back to Wilkes County, and the rest of the family came too.

Daddy was in the CCC Camp at Mortimer, North Carolina, along with other family members. The cotton mill was the main employer of the community, with family members from Wilkes employed there. I was born in the old hotel (boarding house) run by my Grandmother Biddix. When the mill and community were almost completely destroyed by the 1940 flood, the family members came back to Wilkes County. Almost all the children of Rufus and Mary Ann worked in the cotton mill at Roaring River, except the younger children and my Aunt Ara who had been blind since the age of three.

The children moved on to other jobs. Some have been, and others still are, self-employed.

Grandpa farmed the bottom lands in Roaring River. One of the crops was sugar cane, which was then made into molasses at Judge Smithey's home. Grandpa was stricken with a heart attack while in the fields and died the same day at Wilkes General Hospital. Grandma lived until 1971, having passed away in Greensboro where she lived with Ara.

The Rufus Baldwin Family now numbers around 125 descendants. The majority still live in the Roaring River community and surrounding Wilkes County.

Sources: N.C. Archives, Raleigh, N.C.; Wilkes County Library Genealogical Section; Mrs. W.O. Absher; Family Interviews; Rock Creek Baptist Church Minutes; Personal Memories and Louise and Bill Bryant.

— Mary Helen Baldwin Robbins

JOHN K. BALDWIN FAMILY
327

In the estate papers of Wilkes County, in the State Archives, in Raleigh, there is a John Baldwin who died by the 7th of November, 1794, in Wilkes County. Elisha Baldwin was the executor of his estate.

Elisha Baldwin is listed in the 1790 Census as being in the 10th Company of the Morgan District, which included Wilkes County. Elisha Baldwin (supposedly the same) lived on Potatoe Creek in Ashe County (now Alleghany) adjoining Grayson County, Virginia. Most of Ashe County was taken from Wilkes in 1799. Elisha is listed on both the 1800 and 1810 Census for Ashe County. He died before 1813 in Ashe County. Deeds show he had sons Elisha, Jr., William, Stephen, Joseph D., Jacob and Enoch. Census records show he had two other males and six females listed. Research leads me, and a professional researcher, to believe one of the unidentified males to be John K. Baldwin.

John K. Baldwin is listed on both the Ashe County, North Carolina and the Grayson County, Virginia 1850 Federal Census. He married Polly Porter on March 5, 1829. She was a daughter of Joseph Porter, Jr. On March 10, 1829, a charge of bigamy was brought against John K. Baldwin. No record has been found of this earlier marriage. Apparently, this matter was cleared up, because Polly is listed on the 1850 Census role as his wife. She must have died soon after 1850, for on February 18, 1854, John K. Baldwin married Sarah Warren.

Children from the marriage to Polly Porter are as follows: Jane, Sarah, Delphia, Joseph, Robert, Susannah, Julia, Mary, Andrew (my great-grandfather), and John K., Jr. Children from the marriage to Sarah Warren are Frances and Elizabeth. There is more about Andrew in the Rufus Baldwin story.

John K. Baldwin joined Rock Creek Baptist Church by letter on October 9, 1858. During the night service, the church agreed to liberate (to preach) Brother John K. Baldwin to use his gift of public preaching wheresoever God may cast his lot. He served the church in many positions and was ordained as a deacon November 10, 1862. He served as clerk, elder, and on August 8, 1863, agreed to serve as part-time pastor. He is last listed in the church minutes of August 8, 1868, as leading the singing and having prayer to open the business conference as he had done many times before.

The business conferences were always held on Saturdays, and were sometimes called off because of rain or poor attendance.

Members were often called before the church body for infractions and dismissed from the body. John K. Baldwin had the job of seeing that the church was in fellowship before the conference could begin. Some interesting infractions as taken directly from the church minutes are, *"sum verry vulger; unbecumming language; drinking too much spirits; getting out of temper; and saying more then he wished to say; and telling fortunes by turning coffee cups."*

Written in the front cover of the church minutes book are these words by J.K. Baldwin. *"When this you see Remember me, Tho in this life, I may not be this 20th August 1863."*

Sources: N.C. Archives, Raleigh, N.C.; Wilkes County Library Genealogical Section; Mrs. W.O. Absher and Rock Creek Baptist Church minutes.

— Mary Helen Baldwin Robbins

BALL FAMILY
328

Over the years many searches in different records have been made to obtain more information about the Ball family heritage and the early life of these fine people, our progenitors.

An early deed for William Ball is a land grant, three hundred acres, waters of Hunting Creek near Surry line, signed by James Brandon 16 Jan. 1780 — No. 2346 Rowan County. (This is Iredell, Wilkes land now). A history sent to me showed a William Ball who married a Betty Debord, had children: Daniel, Osborne, William, who married Sarah Campbell, John, Benjamin, Mary, m. Daniel Freeman, Elsie, m. Aaron Freeman, and Elisabeth, m. Moses Freeman. In checking Iredell County Deeds, we find these names there and in early census. The Debord name is on Ball deeds as witnesses or buyers of land.

In checking deeds for John Ball (b. abt 1768) for Iredell County, N.C., we have found several deeds and ascertained the location of the land as being near the Wilkes County and Surry County line. While trying to locate land mentioned in deeds, we talked with Isom Cambell, age 90 years, who lives in the region. We got to his home by crossing over Hunting Creek and Osborne Creek, going up a hill on a winding dirt road. He pointed out to a field, saying the old Surry line (now Yadkin) was out there and the Wilkes County line, not too far away.

A deed in Surry Co. for a John Ball or Bull was bought from a Charles Johnson and sold to Charles Coleman who was related to William Ball's wife Sarah Campbell according to a Campbell family history, land on Osborne Creek, Surry line. John Ball sold Iredell Co. land in this area in 1812 as a resident of Wilkes Co. His son Javen Ball signed as witness to one deed, another deed signed by James Ball, deed registered in 1819.

John Ball is listed in 1810 Census as over 45 and in 1830 John Ball is between 60-70. He is not in Wilkes in 1840, but Nancy Ball is — age 50-60. In 1812 John Ball was the highest bidder for the sale of land owned by William Ball. Later John Ball sold one hundred acres for $200 to William Ball. Later, John Ball got a land grant in Wilkes County and sold it in 1831.

Javen Ball, born 1797, a son of John Ball, served in the War of 1812, being drafted in Wilkes County in July of 1814. He was discharged March 9th, 1815, at Wadesboro. He served with Charles Vickers and Hiram Smoot

(whom his sister Gincey married November 13, 1816). Javen married a daughter of a Elijah Vickers, Revolutionary War soldier, Elizabeth Vickers, on August 4, 1815 (born 1788).

Javen Ball left North Carolina after 1840, and was living in Wayne Co., Indiana, and later in Tipton Co., Ind., in the 1850s. In 1851 he applied for Bounty land, given to those who had served in the War of 1812. Javen and Elizabeth are listed in Tipton Co., Ind., in 1860. A deed has been located, dated Dec. 29, 1868, where Javen Ball bought 40 acres in Madison township, Tipton County, subject to a for-life estate clause. According to an August 19, 1871 deed, this land was transferred, indicating that Javen Ball had died before 1871.

Sources: Wilkes County and Indiana Records.

— Sandra Ball

JAMES ARTHUR BALL
329

My name is James Arthur Ball. I was born in Wilkes County, the 6th of November, 1904. My father was Daniel Wesley Ball, dying when I was two; my mother was Lennie LoDelia Ball.

We went to an old log school on the other side of the creek, when I got old enough to go to school. We had to cross on rocks and boards so we would have something to walk on. As I grew, I remember one of the first presents that I ever got; my uncles gave me for Christmas, a little old cap-buster. I thought that was one of the greatest things in the world that I had ever seen. We only got one pair of shoes a year for the winter; whenever the weather got cold, we would get some homemade shoes that would last us til the spring of the year.

James Arthur and Gladys Ball.

I guess we went to school about a mile or three quarters of a mile. I was seven when I got to go to school. If it was bad weather, mother wouldn't let me go. I went only in the early fall and spring. In the snow and wintertime, I had

to stay home.

My brother Bryan and I run around not too much. He wouldn't let me go, he'd run me back every time when I started after him. We got along pretty good. We would have some fights. It wasn't much of a fight, he'd give me a whipping.

Mother married Joseph Obey Marlow on 22 March 1913, in Wilkes County they had six children: Ethel Maybell, Albert, Mortis, Lue Ellen, Hebert Wilborn, and Mary Lo Demie.

I was about thirteen, when my folks decided to move down to Moore County. My uncle had a large farm. I left early in the winter to help him build a house for us all, so we could all move down there and work on the farm. We got the house ready, and my grandpa, Jonah Ball, when it got time to go said he wasn't going. He'd stay up there in Wilkes with some of the other children. He said that he enjoyed staying with mother, but he didn't want to leave home and go somewhere else to go to die. So when he said that, mother wouldn't go; they never left there.

I stayed in Moore County and worked there in the summer and for several summers after that. I quit school early. Later, I come back to school for a year and a half. Then I left home. I worked in Wilkesboro in the coffin shop for a while. Then I got a job in Lexington in a veneering plant. I stayed with Aunt Nellie Cross. Me and one of her boys ran around a lot together. He had a car and always out on the weekend going somewhere. I worked in the chair factory after I left the veneering plant.

Then I went back home. I stayed at home while my grandfather, Jonah Ball, was bad off sick. I stayed at home for a few months, helping my mother wait on him as long as he lived.

After I worked down in the sandhills, for my uncle, I stayed with one of my other uncles for a year. I left and went to Florida and worked in the winter on the railroad. Then I came back and got a job in the mill and worked there for a while. Then I went back home to the mountains. Then later on, I went back to Kannapolis and got a job in the cotton mill. I worked over there ever since, about 36 years.

Since retiring from Cannon Mill in Kannapolis, I bought a mobile home, and set it up next to my son, Charles Willis, and his family. My wife Gladys, and I work in our garden. We are able to attend church regularly. We celebrated our 50th Wedding anniversary on April 11, 1980, with our family and friends.

Source: Tape recording.

— James Arthur Ball

JAMES CALLOWAY BALL
330

James Calloway Ball, son of John Wesley, was born January 17, 1843. He was called Doc because he was named for Doctor James Calloway. He married Asenith Marlow. In the year 1886, he made preparations to leave N.C. and remove to Colorado. When he and his family left, they went to Hickory, N.C. in wagons and took a train to Chattanooga, Tennessee. Here they boarded big immigrant trains especially prepared with beds built along the insides.

In Kansas City the train stopped for a break, and James got off the train to get his youngest child a cup of milk. He went over to the hotel, and in the meantime, the train pulled up to a tank. He was told the train was going to back up, so James waited, and lo and behold, that train didn't back up at all, but pulled right off and left James there with his cup of milk. James had to take the next train out to catch up with his family.

To people from the south, Colorado proved a cold and desolate country. The town of Manassa was built up by the time James Calloway Ball got there with such things as a saw mill, school, and an irrigation company. There were many cattle and sheep herds on the vast land. The land was plentiful and ran about one dollar and twenty five cents an acre. This land was said to look bleak and forbidding.

It took James, his wife Asenith, his children, and his brothers and sisters with their families five days to reach the town. In the Manassa area they found jobs and started homes. After two years James and some of the other Ball families moved north to Kaysville, Utah, leaving the rest of the family behind.

Asenith died in Manassa. James returned to Wilkes for a short time, after corresponding with his future wife, Sarah Emeline Moore. They married and returned to Utah to his children, who were staying with his sister Louise and her husband, John Marlow.

Here James and some of his brothers found jobs and homes again. James stacked grain and worked on the railroad. He lived in a big brick house for four years. Again he left his family with relatives and went to Idaho to make a home on Snake River Valley. On his way he met a man coming back, and was told the valley was not worth going to so James settled in Marsh Valley where his sons could build homes close to him.

Sources: The personal history of James Calloway Ball.

— Karen Boles
and Sandra Ball

JOHN WESLEY BALL FAMILY
331

John Wesley Ball, son of Javin and Elizabeth Vickers Ball, was born 15 May 1817, died 11 October 1899, married 6 February 1836 Ary Melvina Stanley, who was born 13 May 1812, died 6 August 1906, daughter of Charlotte Stanley.

When they were married, John Wesley had land in Iredell County near the Wilkes line, but he bought land and moved over into Wilkes. The land was mountanous and sloped off into rolling hills with greenery everywhere. The soil was for the most part, red clay, and there was a great deal of pine and hardwood trees. The soil was also very rocky, the rocks so large the farmers had to plow around them to plant their corn and grain crops. The main crop was fruit trees. They sold eggs and milk to the people in town.

Ary Ball was an active lady. She often rode her horse into town to get something she needed. She was a religious woman, a faithful Baptist, remembered for carrying her Bible, reading and studying the scriptures and having

Ary Ball.

a deep love for the Lord. She was troubled by the inconsistencies in teachings. She had been praying for some answers about the time the Mormon missionaries came to the Brushy Mountains.

When Ary met the missionaries she was already seventy-three years old and had eleven children that lived around her with their families. After spending some time with the missionaries she was baptised on the 18 June 1885 into the Mormon faith.

John Wesley Ball was bitter about the church at first and was furious with his wife for joining. He would not even stay in the same house with her. For awhile he slept out by the grist mill, but finally came around and was baptised 27 March 1898, about a year before he died on the 11 October 1899.

Eventually all of their eleven children joined the church. Nine of the children moved west, but Wilburn Jonah and Nancy Ellen remained in Wilkes County. The eleven children of John Wesley and Ary Stanley Ball were as follows:

Marinda F. born 10 January 1834, married Alexander Moore; Louise M., born 25 January 1837, married Hardy Estep; Jerusha Bartine, born 8 February 1839 unmarried; William Javin, born 26 April 1841, married Fatine Nance; James Calloway born 17 January 1843, married Asenith Marlow; Mary Clementine, born 9 September 1845, married James Young "Bud" Nance; Wilburn Jonah, born 27 April 1847, married Mary C. Anderson; John Wesley, Jr., born 11 April 1849, married Mary Lodemie Ball; Ary Melvina, born 11 March 1851, married General Francis Marion Nance; Amanda Fatine, born 20 February 1853, married William Hamilton Nance; Nancy Ellen, born 19 December 1857, died 18 March 1936, married William Bynum Marlow.

Wilburn Jonah Ball, son of John Wesley and Ary, was born 27 April 1847, died 17 February 1925 in Wilkes County. He married Mary (Polly) Anderson, who was born 10 December 1852, died 17 August 1907 in Wilkes County,

Jonah Ball and wife Mary Polly Anderson.

daughter of Elias and Biddy Tedder Anderson.

Wilburn Jonah joined the church 3 July 1905 when he was helping build the Gilreath Chapel. While the chapel was being built Nancy Ellen and Wilburn Jonah alternated having Sunday School in their homes.

Wilburn J. loved the land and the Brushy Mountains. He also loved to dance, which sometimes embarassed his children. He was honest and industrious, owned and operated a grist mill with a saw mill attached to it. The mills were powered by water. The Mormons in the area were baptised in the pond which powered Wilburn's mill.

Wilburn Jonah and Mary C. were the parents of ten children: William A., born 9 June 1870, married Julie Kissa Moore; Rebecca Nettie, born 11 March 1872, married Johnny Moore; Elvis Wesley, born 1 July 1874, married Ary K. Ball; John Avery, born 7 June 1876, married Laura Marlow; Thomas Welborn, born 22 June 1878, married Doria Ball; Enie I., born 19 August 1881, married Arlie Barns; Lennie Lodelia, born 21 March 1884, married Joseph O. Marlow; Matthew I. born 23 September 1886, married Getsy Edna Dixon; Mitchell Andrew born 20 February 1888, married Mary Marlow; Augustus Young, born 15 December 1890, married Bessie Bridge.

Enie I. Ball married Arlie Barnes, lived in the Gilreath Community, on the Ball's Mill Road. Enie and Arlie had one son Hansford Durant. Enie was a farmer, owned a apple orchard and a small country store, and operated a corn mill. Enie was the first Branch President of the church of Jesus Christ of Latter Day Saints (Mormon) Church, in Wilkes County.

Enie's son Hansford, was also Branch President of the first and second Latter Day Saint Church, on the Ball's Mill Road. Hansford married Anna Madonna Transou. They own and operate the Thrift Super Market with the help of their two daughters, Brenda and Kay. Hansford and Ann have four children and ten grandchildren. (1) Hansford Jr.; (2) Linda

Ann; (3) Brenda Kay; (4) Zonda Kay.

Hansford Durant Jr. married Lucia Eager, and they are parents of three children; (1) Kathryn Ann; (2) Julia; (3) Daryl. Linda Ann married David Edsel Dancy, and they are parents of seven children; (1) Mark Kevin; (2) Lisa Ann (3&4) Twins, Chad Edward, and Brad Phillip; (5) Chere Dawn; (6) Andrea Leigh; (7) Michael David.

Sources: Exerpts from paper: "The Perils of Mormonism in the South;" Brigham Young University, 15 December, 1981, by Karen Boles; family research, Wilkes County records.

— Ann Transou Ball

WILBURN JONAH BALL
332

Wilburn Jonah Ball was born on 27th of April, 1847, in Wilkes County, son of John Wesley Ball and Ary Stanley Ball. He loved the land and Brushy Mountains of his home. He married Mary (Polly) Anderson daughter of Elias and Biddy Tedder Anderson. They had ten children: William Aswell, Rebecca Genetta, Elias Wesley, John Avery, Thomas Wilburn, Enie Israel, Lennie LoDelia, Matthew Isaac, Michael Andrew and Augustus Young.

In business Wilburn Jonah was honest and industrious. He owned and operated a grist mill with a saw mill attached to it. The mills were powered by water. He loved his work and his family. In his latter years, he lived with his daughter, Lennie LoDelia, and her family. A grandson, Arthur, helped him grind cornmeal.

Jonah and his wife, Mary, were baptised on 3rd of July, 1905, and became members of The Church of Jesus Christ of Latter-day Saints. Many baptisms for years were held in the shallow area near the pond which powered Jonah's mill.

Jonah Ball was religious and loved to have fun. He loved to dance and would often dance in his home when the children brought their friends in to have a dance; when the music started, Jonah was the first to dance.

He helped care for some of his grandchildren and would often take one or more of the children with him to work at the mill or as he helped to build the little Church nearby. After work he always washed his face and his beard. Then he sat down and combed his long beard til it suited him. This ritual is remembered with love by the lucky grandchildren. Jonah's wife, Mary, died on 17th of August in 1907, before the chapel was dedicated by President Robert Andrus, 25 July, 1909.

Jonah had the opportunity to move to the sandhills in Moore County, years later. His sons, Matthew and Gus had built a home for him. His love for his Mountain was too great and he refused to leave. He died in the place that he loved, near his work, near his Church, on 17th of February, 1925.

Sources: Recollections of family members and family records.

— Sandra Ball

BARBER
333

The ancestors of the Barber family in Rowan

Wilburn Jonah and Mary Anderson Ball and Family.

and Wilkes County came from Yorkshire, England.

Dr. Luke Barber, the progenitor of the Barber family of Yorkshire, came to America in 1654. Dr. Barber was a surgeon and a member of the Cromwell Court. This is not to be taken as meaning he was sympathetic with Puritanism for Dr. Barber was a loyal churchman. For his bravery in the battle of the Seven and his help throughout the Puritan rule in Maryland, Lord Baltimore presented him 1,000 acres of land on the Wiconico River in St. Mary's, Maryland. This land is still in the Barber's name according to information in 1927.

Dr. Luke Barber married Elizabeth Young. Their great, great grandsons, Elias and Jonathan of St. Mary's, emmigrated to North

William Wainwright Barber.

Carolina in 1794. They settled near what is now Cleveland, N.C.

Elias married Elizabeth Wainwright and Jonathan married Elizabeth Swann, both of St. Mary's County.

Elizabeth Wainwright was born near the mouth of Thames in England. She was a woman of unusual power and a remarkable gift of mind. It is to her, perhaps more than any other person, that Christ Episcopal Church of Rowan owes it existence. The deed to the church land in Rowan was given by Elias, John E., and Luke Barber.

Elias and Elizabeth had nine children, the oldest being William, born in 1783. He married Margaret Hughey. To this union was born Richard Wainwright Barber on June 18, 1823, in Rowan County. He was educated in Rowan County schools and with Bishop Davis of Salisbury. He completed all courses at Valle Crucis, an Episcopal school. He was made a deacon by Bishop Ives May 12, 1850. His first church was in Plymouth, N.C., but on account of the climate he moved to the mountains and became the second Rector of St. Paul's Episcopal Church in Wilkesboro. He served continuously for 45 years, not only in Wilkesboro but in churches in Elkin, Statesville and Lenoir whenever needed, always riding horseback to the church.

Mr. Barber had a private school for boys at his home "Cedar Lawn" from 1863-1895 (see schools). Mr. Barber married the widow of John P. Peden. Her children by Mr. Peden were: John T. Peden, a prominent business man in Wilkesboro; Fannie Williams Peden, who never married; and Joseph William Peden, unmarried. After this marriage, Mr. and Mrs. Barber lived in the Peden home on Main Street known as the Waugh-Peden home (recently torn down). Later, Mr. and Mrs. Barber moved to their home on the Yadkin River known as "Cedar Lawn," now owned by W.K. Sturdivant.

The Rev. Richard Wainwright Barber, and Joseph Richard Barber.

Moore II. Their children are Margaret Wainwright, Mariana Worth, and William Carroll III.

William Wilcox married Zola Gage. Their children are Mary Gage and Elizabeth Worth. Elizabeth Worth Barber is unmarried. Joseph Richard married Nell Somers. Their children are Joseph Richard II, and Saran Ann.

Sources: Family records, personal knowledge.

— Margaret Taylor Moore

"MAMMY" JUDITH BARBER
334

There are still many Wilkes County Citizens who recall the black slave, "Mammy" Judy Barber. She was born 1820 in Yadkin County, North Carolina and was brought to the county of Wilkes by Mr. Richard W. Barber to begin servitude when she was about 12 years of age.

Accounts of the past or storytelling have always held a fascination for me, especially those that afforded an opportunity to ask questions and get answers that would help me understand more clearly how one person, namely, "Mammy" Judy, served as a beginning for hundreds of us — now counted among her descendants.

Relatives of the late Mr. Richard Barber, have given us valuable assistance in compiling information needed for research into our heritage. From Bible recorded records of the St. Paul's Episcopal Church, Cowles Street, Wilkesboro, we were able to find copies of births, baptisms, weddings and deaths of some of Mammy's offspring. This and additional information is shared during a July 4th Memorial Day celebration, now held yearly in her honor.

Vivid descriptions of this lady have been voiced by some who personally knew her. She was small of stature, personable, and neat. The mental picture I had drawn was in close harmony with the photo that I was later given. (See inset). Her long black cotton dress with mutton-like long sleeves, was gathered at the waist around which was tied a crisp white cotton floor length apron. Tucked inside the apron pocket was "that" handkerchief. A tiny white skull-cap completed her daily garb. Many ancestors are wearers of unusual head coverings and bearers of pretty handkerchiefs, with or without approval of fashion.

Job assignments were many, for "Mammy" Judy, in the Barber household. Having become adapt in the art of housekeeping, she taught and required the 9 of her 13 daughters, who reached maturity, to strive for excellence in whatever the task. Her lessons to them covered, to name a few, cooking — she was the head cook, and a good one — the laundress, keeper of the meat and milk houses, maker of hominy and soap, seamstress, nursemaid, and rendered her services as midwife.

Many of us are probably benefactors of some of those "home remedies" made and issued out to the sick relations — such as: bone-set tea for croup; mountain tea for hives, milkweed for poison oak, snuff was dampened and rubbed on stings, warm breast milk, dropped in ear for ear ache — the list could go on and on — concerning survival. That's the

The Barbers had two children: William Wainwright Barber, born October 14, 1855, and Mary Taylor Barber, born January 6, ? (see schools).

William Wainwright was educated by his father and by Col. George N. Folk. He also studied law under Col. Folk. He was admitted to the bar in 1879. In 1882, he formed a partnership with Col. W.H.H. Cowles for the practice of law. When Col. Cowles was elected to Congress, the partnership was mutually disolved and Mr. Barber practiced law alone in Wilkes and adjoining counties. He was interested in politics and served as chairman of the County Executive Committee of the Democratic party several times. He served eight years as a member of the executive committee for the judicial district, four years as chairman.

For ten years he was a member of the Congressional Executive Committee. He was clerk to the committee in Washington of which Col. Cowles was chairman, but resigned after two years to take his seat in State Senate in 1889.

In 1898, Governor Thomas M. Holt appointed Mr. Barber as Solicitor and he served in that position for a term. During his lifetime, he filled many important and influential positions, one of which was vice-president and director of Deposit and Savings Bank.

In 1891, William Wainwright Barber married Mariana Martitia Wilcox, daughter of Dr. Joseph O. Wilcox and Martitia Worth of Ashe County. To this union were born four children: Margaret Taylor, William Wilcox, Elizabeth Worth, and Joseph Richard.

Margaret Taylor married William Carroll

way it was!

My mother, Mrs. Josephine Speaks, a great-granddaughter of Judith, would take me as a child, to the site where Mammy's log cabin sat. (See picture). It was located near the present North Wilkesboro Municipal Park. Mom pointed out to me a pile of stones, partially covered with earth, that once was the fireplace and chimney of the cabin. I also remember flowers such as tiger-lillies, thorny red japonica, bubby-roses and short double ground lillies, still growing wild about the place. Some relatives salvaged cherry and walnut tree rootlets that still grow in our neighborhood.

Judith Barber.

The Honorable Judge J.J. Hayes wrote in his book, *The Land of Wilkes*, page 126 — #975.6 (H) that along with others, four slaves — Bynum, Phoebe, Detsy and Judith (our Judith), were confirmed Sunday, July 8, 1849, at St. Paul's Episcopal Church. Later, I've read, Judith, along with two others began their own church which became the present New Damascus Baptist near Noisy Branch.

Having had a keen desire to learn, Mammy prayed for a chance to have her children gain "book learning", and began early teaching them to be honest, trustworthy, dependable, prompt, patient, faithful and wise in judgment — to respect God and help one's fellowman. Achievements and blessings have come to us because she cared. In many walks of life you'll find us — some as government employees, homemakers, public workers, educators, preachers, seamstresses, beauticians, farmers and performers in the arts.

"SUNSET" indicates the close of a day; the "FINAL CURTAIN" ends the show, "FINIS", the book is finished; thus: my great-great-grandmother Judith's journey through this life was over September 8, 1912.

The following article of her demise was taken from an old copy of the *Wilkes Journal*.

Judith Barber's Cabin.

Faithful Colored Woman Dead.

Died, September 8, 1912, at the home of her granddaughter, Annie Jones, Aunt Judy Barber, aged 92 years, 4 months and 29 days. She was born in Yadkin County, April 9, 1820, and moved to this county in 1844. She is survived by nine daughters, forty-three grand-children, a large number of great grand children and two children of the fourth generation. She was highly esteemed by all who knew her, as she always responded to every appeal for help in time of sickness or sorrow. Fidelity was the keynote of her character, and the universal testimony of her friends and employers that she never neglected or abandoned a case of sickness committed to her care. In ante-bellum days she was a member of the Episcopal church, having been comfirmed by Bishop Ives. In 1866, she connected herself with the colored church of Damascus, of which she was a member at the time of her death. She was regular in her attendance as long as her strength permitted, and when unable to go would request her pastor to hold a service at her house. She loved the Old South but the decadence of the stately dignity and lavish hospitality of the Southern homes was always deplored by her. Her relatives and friends have this assurance that she has now the blessed encomium, "Well done, good and faithful servant, enter thou into the joy of thy Lord." — Contributed.

Sources: Personal knowledge.

— Elizabeth Ann P. Grinton

THE BARE FACTS

335

The B.J. Bare family includes B.J. (Billy Joe) born 2/3/35 at Jefferson, North Carolina; Dareleen Bowers Bare born 9/24/36 at Jefferson, North Carolina; Stephen Mark Bare born 8/9/59 at Knoxville, Tennessee and Allison Jo Bare born 11/5/60 at Knoxville, Tennessee.

We have lived in Wilkes County since 1964, and are descendants of the Bares in Ashe County, as are all the Bares we have ever known.

My parents were Jess (no middle name) Bare, Jr. (5/14/1885 — 11/26/55) and Chessie Bare Bare (8/13/1892 — 7/12/81). They were married 2/9/11. Jess Bare was a hardware merchant, a farmer, a miller, a lumberman, and a trafficer and a trader. His parents were Bart and Lois Coldiron Bare. Chessie Bare was the daughter of Reid and Missouri Kansas Halsey Bare.

Dareleen is the daughter of James Paul Bowers (4/20/08 — 9/7/60) and Cora Hartsoe Bowers (9/9/10). James Paul was born in Ashe County to John and Lou Hurley Bowers, and Cora Hartsoe was born in Ashe County to David and Emma Ashley Hartsoe. They were married on December 12, 1934. She is now a patient at Britthaven Nursing Home in Wilkesboro, NC.

Steve and Allison Bare both attended North Wilkesboro Elementary and Wilkes Central High Schools. Steve graduated this year (1982) from Gardner Webb College with a BS in Business Management. Allison is a Senior

Education Major at Wake Forest University.

Our family is very close. We enjoy each other's company and do many things together. All are members of First Baptist Church in North Wilkesboro where I have served as a Deacon, and Steve and Allison both sing in the choir and are also active in the Single Young People's Group. Steve and Allison were both in "The Highlighters", a choral group at Wilkes Central High School. Both were also members of the award winning Wilkes Central Band. Steve played the trumpet and Allison played the flute.

Other family interests include traveling, spectator sports, golf, tennis, fishing, hunting, walking and jogging. I am a licensed private pilot. My other activities have included the Rotary Club, Commissioner for the Town of North Wilkesboro, Board of Directors of the Wilkes Chamber of Commerce, North Wilkesboro City School Board, Board of Directors and Member of the Wilkes County Home Builder's Association.

B.J. Bare, Mrs. Dareleen Bare, Allison Jo Bare, Stephen Mark Bare.

I attended Jefferson Elementary and High School, Lee's McRae College and North Carolina State College. I served two years in the United States Army, and then began a career with Lowe's Companies, Inc. I am Manager of Lowe's of North Wilkesboro and have seen the chain grow from six stores in 1956 to the present 230.

Dareleen attended Healing Springs Elementary and High School and Draughon Business College. She worked as a bookkeeper and secretary before devoting full time to being a Homemaker.

Probably the most interesting family member was my Dad. He left the family farm on the Boggs Road in Ashe County around 1909. He, his brother Will, and a neighbor went to the state of Oregon to seek their fortunes. The others found jobs in lumber camps, but Dad chose the solitary life of a sheep herdsman. He tended a flock in the high mountainous meadows and did not see another person for weeks at the time. His brother became ill, and all the group returned to Ashe County. Shortly afterward, he and Mother were married.

Dad was a self-taught musician. He played the banjo and fiddle with some proficiency. He was playing the fiddle at a dance in the Glendale Springs Community when a fight broke out, and he broke the fiddle over someone's head. So far as we know, he never played the fiddle again. I never had the opportunity to hear him play, but fondly remember his leading the small Orion Baptist Church congregation in singing their favorites from the song books.

Dad never cared much for the hard labor of farm work. After their marriage, his occupation was "traffickin' and tradin' ". He would make the rounds to nearby farms and purchase any livestock that might be for sale; consolidate these offerings from various farms and then drive the animals to markets in North Wilkesboro, NC or Abingdon, VA.

Turkeys were driven to market in North Wilkesboro, and the trip took two days. Dad said he had little choice as to where he camped for the night. As soon as the internal clocks told the turkeys it was time to roost, they began flying into trees, and this place became the campsite.

Sheep were one of the area cash crops. Wool was sold to the woolen mills at Mouth of Wilson, VA. Sheep were slaughtered on the farm on Saturday morning and sold to the waiting city dwellers in Jefferson.

Dad operated a sawmill in the mid 20's. His leg was broken in a logging accident in 1925. When the leg healed, it was shorter than the other, and he had a limp for the rest of his life.

He and his youngest brother Ambrose operated a rolling mill until World War II begun.

Then Dad opened Cash Hardware in West Jefferson where he worked until his death.

Sources: Family Bible, family traditions, and personal knowledge.

— B.J. Bare

THE MEREDITH BARKER FAMILY
336

Meredith Barker was the son of Nathaniel and Amelia Cockerham Barker. On October 21, 1851, Meredith married Mary Ann Cockerham, the daughter of James Cockerham.

Meredith and Mary Ann had children as follows: Mollie, William, Betty (died in their youth), John N. (1855-1945), and James Hampton (1852-1924).

John N. married Sarah Laster (1856-1923) and their children were as follows: Dora (1881-1906) m. R. C. Waddell; W. David (1885-1955) m. Cora Hicks; Thomas C. (1896-1965) m. Ida Belle Luffman and Mollie Wilmouth; Charlie H. (1900-1968) m. Lexie Cockerham and Mary B. Brown; Joseph I. (1892-1961) m. Mary E. Harpe (1895-1958); Carrie (1887-1968) m. J. Arthur West (1886-1965); Nancy (1890-1970) m. Edd Smith (1894-1968); and

Benjamin Harrison and Bertha Pruitt Barker.

Johnny W. (1883-1939) m. Mary McCann and Mary Belle Lyon (1896-1972). John N. later married Linney Hincher after the death of Sarah, his first wife.

James Hampton Barker married Nancy Jones Laster (1850-1941), sister to Sarah, John N.'s wife. Hampton and Nancy Jane had children as follows: Laura (1888-1964) m. A. Huston West (1888-1979); Tyre D. (1884-1949) m. Susie Handy (1885-1949); M. Franklin (1882-1966) m. Sadie Bauguess (1886-1966); Ambrose J. (1886-1947) m. Eva Cockerham (1893-1947), and B. Harrison (1890-1965) m. Bertha Pruitt (1894-1977). Hillary and Charlie died as children in 1880.

After the death of Mary Ann, Meredith married Luvicie Cockerham Luffman. They had twin children, Noah and Oma. Noah (1893-1980) m. Maude Cockerham (1892-1972). Oma married William Jordan.

Meredith Barker was a very colorful character. Uncle Huston West told me that Meredith usually wore black clothing and a big, black hat. He wore a full beard which was snow white in color. He owned a large, white horse which he proudly rode as he journeyed through the countryside. Meredith was apparently a "ladies' man", as evidenced by the fact that he was married to four different women. Two wives not previously mentioned were Carrie J. Willey and Mary Ann Settle. Meredith must have been a dashing figure of a man as he made his way through this world.

Meredith Barker died as he sat by the fire in his open fireplace. My brother, Cecil Barker, was a witness to his death. Meredith fell out of his chair and hit his head against the rocks of the fireplace as he expired. A sudden heart attack had apparently taken his life. Meredith Barker rests in the Charity Methodist Church Cemetery.

James Hampton and Nancy Jane Barker were my grandparents. We are told that both Hampy and Nancy Jane were very kind and gentle people. The demise of these two is a touching revelation. Hampy had been sick for some time and apparently knew he was soon going to die as he asked for all his children to come to his bedside. Shortly after all the children had gathered around Hampy, he peacefully departed this life.

Nancy Jane was a strong woman, both physically and spiritually. At an old age, she would take a chair and move herself about as she gathered vegetables from her garden. The day before she died, Nancy Jane asked those present to sing hymns. My grandmother then sat up in her bed and helped sing hymns only hours before she passed away.

My father, Benjamin Harrison Barker was the youngest child of James Hampton and Nancy Jane Laster Barker. The Rev. B. H. Barker was a beloved Baptist minister and farmer. His life was an inspiration to all who knew him. His entire being was devoted to our mother, his children, relatives, and friends. Dad left with us a legacy of kindness, compassion, and respect for our fellowman which shall remain forever.

B. Harrison Barker married Bertha P. Pruitt on May 15, 1910. Their marriage was bountifully blessed with thirteen children: Cecil I., b. 1911, m. Vena Holbrook; Mary Ethel, b. 1913, m. Herbert Durham; Grace F., b. 1914; Pansy A., b. 1917; Ermal W. (1919-1980), m. Mary Cheek; Luther M., b. 1921, m. Georgia Holloway; James R., b. 1923, m. Eva Warren; Flora C., b. 1925, m. James Pardue; Mary L., b. 1927, m. Pless Welborn; Hazel M., b. 1929, m. Oscar Blevins; Kenneth R., b. 1932, m. Betty Flynt; Benjamin A., b. 1934, m. Donna Vestal, and G. Rex, b. 1939, m. Nancy

Woodward.

Glenn Rex Barker, the writer of this article, married Nancy E. Woodward on July 5, 1963. This marriage has been wonderfully blessed with three sons to carry forth the Barker name: Jeffrey W., b. 1964; Eric M., b. 1968, and Craig G., b. 1971.

Sources: Personal knowledge and interviews with family members.

— G. Rex Barker

THE NATHANIEL BARKER FAMILY

337

The first Barker to reside in Wilkes County was evidently George Barker, Sr. George, Sr. was born about 1723 and is listed as paying poll tax in Wilkes County for the years of 1771, 1774, 1775, and 1779.

The 1784, 1786, and 1788 tax listings show George Barker, Sr. as being the father of three sons, 21 or more years of age. These three sons were Hezikiah, who first appears in the 1790 census, John, and George, Jr. All three of these sons appear in the 1792, 1793, 1795, and 1800 census. The Barker families lived in the "Yellow Banks" section of the county which is located between present-day Hays and Mulberry.

The first Barker to make his home in eastern Wilkes County was Nathaniel Barker. Nathaniel is the common ancestor of all the Barker clan now residing in the eastern community of the county commonly referred to as "Barker Town." Nathaniel was born about 1808 and died as a young man in the 1830s.

"Nathan" Barker, also called "Nattie," appears in the 1830 census. In 1830, the census states that Nathan Barker is married, has no children, and both he and his wife being between 20 and 30 years of age. A partial listing of this same census also includes the families of Humphrey Cockerham and Samuel Pratt living near Nathan Barker in the Bugaboo section of the county. Humphrey Cockerham's daughter, Amelia, married Nathaniel Barker on November 14, 1829.

The appearance of Samuel Pratt living near Nathan Barker in 1830 lends strong support to the story that our "original" Barker was once a Pratt. My father, Harrison Barker, and my uncle, Frank Barker, both told me and others that our Barker ancestor changed his name from Pratt to Barker.

Prior to 1830, the other Barkers in the county were all living in Yellow Banks. One of these Barkers, possibly one of George, Sr.'s sons, was apparently Nathaniel's father. Therefore, based upon the "Pratt to Barker" story, and upon the fact that Samuel Pratt lived near Nathan Barker and Humphrey Cockerham, it is most likely that Samuel Pratt's daughter was, indeed, Nathaniel Barker's mother.

Nathaniel, being the illegitimate son of Miss Pratt, was called Nathaniel Pratt until he reached manhood. Upon learning that his father was a Barker, he then changed his name from Nathaniel Pratt to Nathaniel Barker.

All of the Barkers disappeared from Wilkes County in the early 1800's with the exception of Nathaniel and Lewis, who was Hezikiah's son. Those Barkers who died are buried in a Barker cemetery at Yellow Banks. We are told that remnants of this cemetery still remain. The surviving Barkers, including Lewis, left Wilkes County and moved to either Kentucky or Virginia. Because of his family ties to the Cockerhams and Pratts. Nathaniel remained in the county until his death.

Nathaniel Barker is not listed in the 1840 census which indicates his demise before 1840. Amelia Barker, Nathaniel's wife, is listed as head of the family. Several children are included in the 1840 census of which only two can be positively identified. These two are Meredith Barker (1830-1919) and Adeline b. 1831. Meredith Barker married Mary Ann Cockerham, the daughter of James Cockerham, and granddaughter of Humphrey Cockerham. Nancy Adeline married Jordan Gentry.

Sources: Personal knowledge, and interviews with family members, Wilkes County census and tax records.

— G. Rex Barker

BARLOW

338

The surname Barlow was found to have had its beginning in Derbyshire, England. In this section of England there was an area where the wild boar ran over the ground loose. From this "Boarground" came the name of Barlow. The following variations in spelling all belong to this origin — Barley, Barlee, Barlowe, Barloe, and Barlow.

Scattered among the pages of history you will find the name of Barlow. It is definitely true that our ancestors took part in the founding of our great country. We do not have the exact date on which the Barlows came to North Carolina nor the path they traveled to get here. We do know that a John Barlow settled in Wilkes County sometime between 1775 and 1800. He received a grant of land in 1787, but we are not sure that this was his first grant. The first white man came to Wilkes County in 1750, therefore we know that John Barlow came sometime after that year but before his land was recorded. He and his son, John, Jr., received other grants of land in the Beaver Creek and King's Creek section in 1790 and 1791. Eliphalet Barlow also received a grant of land in 1797. From this time until now Barlows have lived in the King's Creek and Beaver Creek area of North Carolina. This is located in the southwestern part of Wilkes County and northwestern part of Caldwell County. John Barlow may have been one member of a large family or he may have been the head of a large family. This John Barlow is recorded in the book, *The Land of Wilkes,* as having been a delegate to the August 28-30, 1790, meeting of the Baptist Churches forming the Yadkin Association in NC. He is later listed as an active member in the association's progress as forerunner of the Baptist State Convention. In 1822 a Thomas Barlow married Sarah Kilby and bought the Abraham Kilby estate on Reddies River in 1829. We assume that the Thomas Barlow owning land in the southwestern Wilkes area was the same Thomas to move to Reddies River. It is only logical that he was related to John Barlow of Beaver Creek. Records were not well kept but we believe that Thomas Barlow was the father of John B. Barlow who married Nancy Kilby in 1842. Thomas Barlow was the only Barlow recorded as owning land on the Reddies River at this time. John B. and his brother Linville were raised on the north fork of the Reddies River. John B. enlisted in the Civil War in 1861. He died December 23, 1862, leaving Nancy Kilby Barlow with a small three year old son, Rudolphus Emanuel, to raise. Linville Barlow was burned to death in a fire that destroyed his home some years later.

Rudolphus Barlow married Nancy Dancy in 1879 and they had ten children. After her death he married Sara Roberts and they had five children. Rudolphus Emanuel Barlow was the father of the following clan: (1) John A. Barlow married Minnie E. Burke; (2) William A. Barlow married Mary Joines; (3) James Monroe Barlow married Nancy Staley; (4) Joseph H. Barlow married Lillie Surbaugh; (5) Thomas H. Barlow married Dallas Tugman; (6) Luemma Barlow married Mitchell Vannoy; (7) Hester Barlow married Pete Dancy; (8) Elizabeth Barlow married Walter Whittington; (9) Avery Coy Barlow married Alam Goff; (10) Golda Barlow married Crommie Adams; (11) Clate Barlow married Caroline Wilkerson; (12) Vallie Barlow married Jess Dunn; (13) Anna Barlow married Ralph Deitz; (14) Blanche Barlow married (a) Marvin Ball, (b) V.C. Potter; and (15) Howard Barlow married Johnsie Sherrill.

Sources: Personal knowledge.

— Mrs. Elbert McPhaul

JOHN STACEY BARNES FAMILY

339

John Stacey Barnes was born in Alexander County, N.C. in 1865 to John G. and Jane Smith Barnes. He came to Wilkes County in 1890 and married Eugenia E. Felts, daughter of James Wesley and Martha Woodruff Felts, that same year. The Barnes family were Bap-

John Stacy Barnes.

tist, being early members of Liberty Grove Church. When they moved to North Wilkesboro they were active members of First Baptist Church. Stacey's brother, Lloyd E. Barnes, remained in Alexander County and was a well-known Baptist minister.

Stacey Barnes held the position of foreman at Forest Furniture Company from the time of the organization until his death in 1922. According to family legend, he set up every piece of machinery in that plant.

The Barnes family lived on the east end of E Street, and all of their children were born there. Allie Wesley, born 1892, moved to Florida when a young man and worked as a salesman for Swift and Company. He married Margaret Bryant of Brevard. He died in 1936 leaving no children.

Tallie Stacey Barnes, born September 1893, became a pharmacist and owned the "Rexall Store" on B Street in North Wilkesboro. This was a popular meeting place for young and old in the 1920s and early 1930s. Tal was in poor health for many years because of a heart prob-

Ruby, Al and Tal Barnes.

lem and this necessitated his selling the business while still a young man. He sold his interest to Jay H. Johnson, a local pharmacist. A very young niece who had enjoyed special treats at the soda fountain said, "Uncle Tal, please don't sell the half that has the ice cream in it."

Tal married Ethel M. Dix, daughter of J.W. Dix, of Mount Airy, in 1922. They built a house further down the block on E Street and lived there many years. They had two children: Billie Dix Barnes and Tal S. Barnes, Jr. Billie married Dr. Livingston Johnson and they had five children: Janet, Donald, Wingate, Nancy and Duncan. Tal, Jr. married Lea Walsh, and they had two daughters, Patricia and Pamela.

The elder Barnes had one daughter, Ruby Grenell, born in 1896, who married R. Neal Pendley on July 4, 1916 and they had one child, Marcella Louise Pendley. Neal and Ruby built a house between her parents and Tal. This

was a pre-cut frame house, the first one of its kind erected in North Wilkesboro.

The Pendleys moved to Greensboro in 1927 and lived there until Neal's death in 1932. Ruby and her daughter returned to North Wilkesboro where she married Winfield Scott Fletcher in 1939. She died in 1963 and is buried beside Neal Pendley in Greenwood Cemetery.

Ruby was an artist, painting mostly oils and hand-painted china. She had an art studio in downtown North Wilkesboro for many years. She spent the last year and a half of her life with her daughter, Marcella and her husband, Parks, and their daughters, Martha Neal and Elizabeth in Ypsilanti, Michigan. She was active in Senior citizens then and was appointed Art Director. That group installed a drinking fountain in their center in her memory following her death.

All the Barnes family were Baptists except Ruby. She and Neal Pendley joined the North Wilkesboro Presbyterian Church shortly after their marriage. At her death she was a member of the First Presbyterian Church in High Point where she had worked for several years for W.P.A. as Recreational Director.

Sources: Family Bible, Grave markers, Census records, personal knowledge.

— Marcella P. Church

THE BAUGUESS FAMILY
340

The Bauguess family has lived in Wilkes County, N.C. since before 1790. Prior to that the family resided in Loudoun Co., Va. Richard Boggess, the progenitor of the Wilkes Co. Bauguess family last appears in the records of Loudoun Co. in 1785, then appears on the 1786 tax list for Wilkes Co., N.C.

Richard was married twice, fathering twenty two children. His first wife, an Irish emigrant, was Nancy McCarty. She was one of the first people to be buried in Old Roaring River Baptist Church Cemetery in Traphill. Richard is believed to be buried in a family graveyard on the old Osborne Bauguess farm near Traphill. The will of Richard Boggess is dated 1809 and was probated April 1822. It names wife, Kezia who is presumed to have been Keziah Rose.

Known children are: Vincent; James; Emmanuel who married Amelia Sparks in 1817; Jane who married an Edwards; Fanny who married a Higgins; Sarah who married Zachariah Brooks in 1821; Phoebe who married a Southard; Lydia who married a Cockerham in 1829; Mary (Polly) who married Isaiah Rose in 1826; Jemima who married William Spicer; Nancy who married a Murphy; Richard, Jr.; Henry; Robert who married Mary Sparks, and Elijah Harrison. The latter is possibly two sons.

Rockford Bauguess of Seattle, Charles Ivan Bauguess of Woodbridge, Va. and Ruth Bauguess Pruitt of Traphill descend from Richard Bauguess. These are the children of John Perly and Ella Yale Bauguess. The maternal line descends from Robert and Mary Sparks Bauguess.

A family Bible shows Robert to have been born June 12, 1777 in Virginia, son of

Richard. Mary was born in Surry Co., N.C. to John and Sarah (Shores) Sparks. Robert and Mary Sparks Bauguess had the following children, all born in Wilkes County, N.C.: Nancy, married Thomas Bryan; Robert Jr. who married Nancy Sparks; Solomon; Samuel who married a Yates; Mary, Jane (Jennie) who married John Holbrook; Lewis who married Mary Frances Holloway; Richard who married a Hurst; Sarah who married a Rousseau; Lydia; David who married a Hall; John K. who married a Forrester; and Fanny.

Lewis, of the above children, was born December 1, 1828 and married February 28, 1847. His wife, Mary Frances, born November 28, 1830, is thought to have been the daughter of Daniel Holloway, son of Edgewood.

It is said that shortly after the Civil War Lewis picked up his rifle one day and walked over the mountain to Kentucky, leaving behind his wife and at least six children. He was never heard from again. There is no further record of his wife. It is known that his brother, Robert and his wife, Nancy, raised one son, John A. Bauguess. It is possible that they took the other children too. Robert was known in the community as "Bee-Bob" because of his interest in raising bees.

John Andrew Bauguess, the youngest son of Lewis and Mary, was born in 1858. He married Susan Childress, born 1861 or 1862 to Willis and Sally Pardue Childress. John spent much time in the west tending sheep. The wind in the western pastures affected his eyes and he was known most of his life as "Red-eye" Bauguess. The children of this family were: Alverda who married a Joines; Flora who married John Arlie Brooks; John K.; De Ette who married a Holbrook; Lewis who married Nora Holbrook and moved to Idaho; Sherman; Armfield; Etta; Mary Jane who married Elihu Yale; and Robert.

Mary Jane Bauguess was born September 12, 1880 and married on October 28, 1894 in Traphill. She and Elihu Yale had three children: Ella, Mostella and Fanny. Elihu died Nov. 13, 1966 and his wife died Dec. 5, 1962. Both are buried in Old Roaring River Baptist Church Cemetery. Ella, the only surviving child of this marriage, still makes her home in Traphill. She was married to John Perlie Bauguess on Oct. 29, 1916.

The paternal Bauguess line of this family goes back through John Perly Bauguess, born October 20, 1866, to John Bauguess and his wife, Letty Jane, daughter of John and Mary Blackburn Brooks. John Bauguess was born March 15, 1855 in Traphill and was known for the water wheels he built. In 1912 he erected a mill on Sparks Creek. This mill remained in operation by the family until the early 1940's, turning out quality, custom ground mill, grain and flour, often on a "toll" or barter plan with so much of the finished product for the mill operator. John and his wife, Letty, were the parents of the following children: Rosie; Ettie B.; John Perly; William; Carl; Matt; Nan and Delia.

John was born to James Madison Bauguess and his wife, Elizabeth, born 1828, to Christopher and Priscilla Edner. This family was also known as Mc Crary. James and Elizabeth were parents of the following children: William; John; Oscar; Horton; Sarah; Elizabeth; Martha; James M.; Nancy; Fanny and Joe.

The earliest ancestor in this line is William and his wife, Sally, believed to have been Sally Waddell. If so, William's marriage is recorded in Wilkes County on February 19, 1819. William's children were: John born May 23, 1821; Susanna born May 30, 1824; Elizabeth born December 24, 1828; James Madison born June 20, 1830. As yet, William has not been identified as a son of the original Richard of Wilkes County.

The Bauguess family has lived in Wilkes County, mostly in the Traphill area, for generations. They primarily made their livings as farmers and were closely associated with the Baptist Churches of that area.

Sources: Court records, cemetery records, Bible records, family knowledge.

— Wilmetta Bauguess
(Mrs. Rockford Bauguess)

HENRY and LYDIA (SPARKS) BAUGUESS
341

Henry Bauguess was born, probably in Virginia, between 1784 and 1790. There was a Bauguess family in northern Virginia as early as 1671 and genealogists have tried, with little success, to link Henry Bauguess with the earlier family. Tradition, however, indicates that the parents of Henry Bauguess were immigrants from England or Ireland. Henry was probably a son of Richard and Nancy (Mc Carty) Bauguess. Richard Bauguess was supposedly born in England. Shortly before the Revolutionary War, he settled in Loudoun Co., Va., after which, in about 1790, he moved to Wilkes Co., N.C. His will was written May 27, 1809, but according to the recollections of his grandson, he lived to over 100 years of age. Tradition also has it that Richard Bauguess came from Ireland. Perhaps this confusion over the origin of the Bauguess family developed because Richard Bauguess, an Englishman, might have settled first in Ireland, married Nancy Mc Carthy, who was supposedly of Irish birth, and then moved to America. Nancy (Mc Carthy) Bauguess was supposedly the mother of 22 children.

Henry Bauguess was described by his son, Bryant, as a typical Irishman — red-haired, raw boned, 6'2'' in his stocking feet and very strong, competing in feats of strength until he was known as the strongest man in several states. Henry Bauguess married Lydia Sparks shortly before 1810. According to the *Sparks Quarterly* (Vol. XV No. 3), Lydia Sparks was born in 1804. However, the 1850 census of Owen Co., Ind. reported her age as 65, suggesting a birth year of 1785. The 1810, 1820, and 1830 censuses of Wilkes Co. suggest a birthdate between 1790 and 1794. Lydia Sparks was the daughter of Reuben Sparks (1755-1840) and Cassa Buttery (1765-1842), who were married in 1783. Reuben Sparks was the son of Solomon and Sarah Sparks. Cassa Buttery was probably the daughter of John Buttery and Ann Allen.

Henry Bauguess lived near Traphill, N.C.

His son, Bryant, passed on stories of the good eating grey squirrels, mistletoe growing on the oaks, smilax, sumac, and many flowers of the region. He spoke of a perpendicular rock in the area near his old home.

Henry Bauguess was martyred between 1830 and 1840. According to his son, Bryant, Henry Bauguess left Virginia because of the feuds so common then. As his roots did not go down into colonial times, he did not want to be drawn into one or the other factions. One time at the polls in North Carolina, two different factions told him how to vote. He refused to be intimidated and voted as he thought. He was waylaid and beaten by both factions on his way home and died as a result. Henry Bauguess supposedly made a will, in which he freed his slaves.

Henry and Lydia (Sparks) Bauguess had at least nine children: a son and daughter (born 1810-15), a daughter (born 1815-20), Cassa (born 1819), Nancy (born 1821), Bryant (born Mar. 29, 1823), a son (born 1825-30), Eli P. (born 1828), and Fanny M. (born Dec. 13, 1830). The unidentified children of Henry Bauguess were probably: Lafayette, "One Eye," Vincent, Lydia, and possibly John. Most of these children, along with their mother, moved to Marion Twp., Owen Co., Ind., where they were listed in the 1850 census.

Cassa Bauguess married Luke Jennings, who purchased land in Owen Co., Ind. in 1838. Their children were: Lydia (born 1841), William (born 1844), Henry (born 1848), and Bryant (born 1849).

Nancy Bauguess married Andrew Johnson. During the 1840s and 1850s they lived in Owen Co., Ind. Later they settled in Bourbon Co., Ks., where Nancy died before 1900. Among their children were: Ambrose (born 1841), Elizabeth (born 1843), Lydia (born 1845), Loess (born 1847), John (born 1849), Eli (born 1857), and Henry (born 1861).

Bryant Bauguess married Mary Elizabeth Holliday on Dec. 6, 1848. In 1855, they settled in Drywood Twp., Bourbon Co., Ks. In 1905, Bryant moved to Sultan, Snohomish Co., Wash., where he died on Feb. 6, 1913. His children were: Agnes (1850-1916), Lydia (1852-1873), George Washington (1854-1875), William Henry (1856-1931), Irene Matilda (1860-1882), Ely Lincoln (1862-1882), Ulysses Grant (1864-1935), Bryant Jr. (1867-1918), and Elizabeth Ellen (1871-1945).

Eli P. Bauguess married Mary A. They settled in Monroe Twp., Anderson Co., Ks. before 1856, where Eli died before 1870. Their children were: Minerva (born 1849), Sarah (born 1851), William (born 1856), John F. (born 1859), and Mary M. (born 1862).

Fanny M. Bauguess married Alexander Malcolm Eagleton on Jan. 17, 1853 in Crawford Co., Ill., where they lived until after the Civil War. They moved to Arcadia, Crawford Co., Ks. in 1866, where they lived until 1880, when they moved to Rich Hill, Bates Co., Mo., where Fanny died on April 6, 1926. Their children were: a daughter (born 1853, died young), John H. (1855-1930), Sarah Adaline (1857-1881), Reuben (born 1860- died young), Abram L. (born 1865, died young),

Lydia Margaret (1868-1949), Mable Etta (1871-1959), Fanny Ethel (1875-1960) and two others that died in infancy.

Sources: Census records, family tradition, *Sparks Quarterly*, "Bauguess Background," and "Buttrey Bits," both by Orella Chadwick.

— Timothy E. Peterman

THE RICHARD BEAMON FAMILY
342

James Richard Beamon (son of William Bart and Rhoada Louise Brooks Beamon) and Ruth Etta Anthony Beamon (daughter of Thomas Elwood and Mary Catherine Bradley Anthony) were married in Independence, Virginia on June 5, 1937. Rich spent all of his life in Wilkes County, and tough Ruth was born in Surry County, she grew up in Wilkes County.

Bart Beamon worked at Forest Furniture Company, but his grandchildren remember him as a lovable grey-haired man who loved to sit on the front porch of his home in the Fairplains community and watch his grandchildren play, always seeing the humorous side of life. Although his activities were hampered by asthma in late life, he never appeared bored and always found something to keep his mind occupied. Rhoada Louise, whom he married on April 7, 1907, was the daughter of a founder of Fairplains Baptist Church. At the time of her death, "Lula" was the last surviving charter member of that church. She was an avid reader of the Bible and actively gardened throughout every growing season of her life. In addition to their oldest son Richard, Bart and Lula have five daughters: Venie Lucinda, Edith Mozelle (Mrs. Granville Kilby); Margie Camille (Mrs. Lawrence Walsh); Grace Marie (Mrs. Jimmie Palmer); and Virginia Dare (Mrs. Arlie Jennings).

Thomas Elwood Anthony was a life long tobacco farmer and his wife Mary Catherine "Katie" was a wonderful cook and housekeeper. Her grandchildren still treasure the array of delicious recipes she left them. She made beautiful quilts-piecing them by hand and quilting them in a frame in the living room of their farm home in the Ronda community. In late life she made each of her grandchildren a special quilt and these are treasured to this day. Their home had a back porch that extended around two sides of the kitchen, and grapevines covered the edges of the porch. During September it was a special treat to sit on their porch and eat large bunches of white sweet grapes. Tom read his Bible from cover to cover several times during his life. Both he and Katie were born to Quaker families in Surry County and moved to Wilkes County after Ruth's birth. Ruth had two older brothers: James Elmer, and Hoyle Elwood Anthony who still live in eastern Wilkes County. Tom and Katie were married for sixty-four years.

Rich and Ruth have lived in their home at 162 Sparta Road since their marriage. Rich has been an upholsterer by trade and specialized in reworking precious antique chairs for people all over the country. Always a hard worker who did not believe in retirement, he has been devoted to his family, teaching them survival skills and self discipline early in life. Ruth is a devoted housewife, mother, and grandmother, gifted in gardening, sewing, and embroidery which she taught to her daughters. They took care to give their children an education and strong religious backgrounds. Training was tempered with fun activities like trips, music, scouting, and investment in civic affairs. Rich serves on the Board of Directors of the Junior Order Home in Lexington, N.C. and both Ruth and Rich are active in the Hilltop Baptist Church where Rich is Chairman of the Board of Deacons. They have three children.

Dorthy Ruth is a professional social worker, having served as the County Director of the Mental Health Program since 1973. She graduated from Appalachian State Teachers College and earned her Master's Degree in Psychiatric Social Work from the University of North Carolina at Chapel Hill. She serves as a consultant to nursing homes and hospitals and on many boards and committees devoted to human betterment.

Catherine Louise (Kaye) married John E. Hall, a native of Eden, N.C., and became a wife and mother on the same day. John's four year old son (born by a previous marriage to Peggy Measmer who had died when John Elbert Jr. was two years old). Bert quickly endeared himself to all the family by becoming the first grandchild. Kaye always loved needlework and homemaking, her husband is the senior partner in the Hall and Brooks Legal Agency in Wilkesboro. Kaye worked in civic clubs, and after Bert grew up and graduated from Patterson School, Kaye went into partnership with her sister-in-law running the Carol-Kaye Clothing Store for Women in North Wilkesboro. Bert works for Dermox Vending Co.

James Richard Beamon Jr. (Jim) married Caroline Knox, a native of Creston, N.C., whom he met while they were both students at Wilkes Community College. They live on "Long Branch" farm in the Fairplains community where they farm and raise horses. Their two beautiful daughters Marianne Elizabeth, age 8; and Christina Katherine, age 4, are presently preoccupied with growing and learning. Jim owns Beamon's Welding Co. and with John Hall co-owns Bermachris (named for the three Beamon grandchildren) which trades as E. Lowe Iron and Metal Co. Caroline, an avid reader, is Kaye's business partner and Jim and Caroline love outdoor life, teaching their children to love learning, caring for animals, and how to ride and show horses.

Sources: Family records, Bibles and personal knowledge.

— Dorothy Ruth Beamon

BERTHA MAY BELL
343

Bertha Maine May Bell was born 14 January 1889 in Yadkin County to Sarah Jane Willyard and Mathan Stanley Chaffin May. She was one of eight children and was educated in the Yadkin County schools. Mrs. Bell was married to William A. Bell and they had no children.

After her husband's death, Mrs. Bell entered Long's Hospital in Statesville, N.C., where she studied to become a nurse. After graduation, she began her duties in Wilkes County as a public health nurse in 1929. She served in that capacity for twenty-five years. Mrs. Bell served during the latter years of Dr. J. W. White's service as Health Officer and through the many years when Dr. A. J. Eller headed the department. She continued to serve the department when it was without a health officer.

Mrs. Bell was genuinely interested in people she served, especially the children, whom she dearly loved. She worked faithfully in connection with the crippled children's clinic and made numerous trips to carry crippled children to Gastonia and Charlotte for corrective surgery and hospital treatment. Nothing pleased her more than to observe the good results of her work which often made an able-bodied person of a cripple.

The children whose lives were affected by the work of Mrs. Bell will never forget her kindness, her interest, and her efforts to make them well. Her career in Wilkes County was one of faithful and loyal service.

She retired in 1954 because of ill health. She died 9 November 1955 in Wilkes General Hospital and is buried in Forsyth Memorial Park in Winston-Salem, N.C.

Sources: Bible records and personal knowledge.

— Josephine B. Smith

EDWARD P. BELL
344

Since 1945 Edward Parker Bell has been a resident of Wilkes County. He was born 20 March 1918 in Wilkesboro to Louis Selig and Allie Benjamin Rives Bell but his family left soon after. His father was associated with the local newspaper during his two-year residency here. Edward is the second of six children and the only one born in Wilkes County.

Edward grew up in Pasquotank County

Edward P. Bell.

where he was graduated from the Elizabeth City High School, attended business college and became associated with First and Citizens National Bank. In 1940 he was the first young man drafted for one year under the Selective Service Act from his home county. However, he spent five years in the U.S. Army — two at Fort Bragg, two in New York City and one in the Pacific Theater. He was commissioned in Artillery in December 1942.

While at Fort Bragg, he married Helen Louise Bumgarner of Wilkesboro 4 April 1942 in the Reception Center Chapel. She is the daughter of the late James Marshall and Emma Pennell Bumgarner. They had three daughters: Helen Frances, born 14 July, 1944 in New York City, died 22 June 1956 from leukemia; Mary Elizabeth and Martha Ellen.

Mary Elizabeth, born 18 October 1956, was graduated from the U.N.C-G in 1978 with a B.S. Degree in Home Economics Education, which prepared her well for the role of homemaker. On 12 June 1977 she and Peter Michael Thomas Southwell, also a U.N.C.-G. graduate, were married and are the parents of Edward Michael and Philip James Southwell.

Martha Ellen, born 4 January 1960, was graduated from U.N.C.-G. in 1982 with a B.S. in Home Economics (Clothing and Textiles) with a concentration in Fashion Merchandising. She enjoys working with people and always spreads sunshine wherever she goes.

Edward became associated with The Northwestern Bank following his discharge in December 1945. He attended NABAC School at the University of Wisconsin and several other schools related to banking. He was Vice President and General Auditor for many years prior to his retirement.

Scouting has always been his principal outside interest. He joined the Boy Scouts of America at age twelve and has been involved continuously, having attained the rank of Eagle while in high school, and he will have fifty years of service in 1983. He received the Silver Beaver Award, which is the highest award given to an adult scouter, and he has also received numerous other awards. He is a member of the Order of the Arrow and is presently Vice President of Scouting of the Old Hickory Council.

During the past thirty-six years, Edward has been an active member of the North Wilkesboro Lions Club, having held many offices on both local and District levels and has served as District Governor of 31-B. He is a past director and president of the Wilkes Chamber of Commerce, is a member of Liberty Lodge 45, and is secretary-treasurer of the Blue Ridge Shrine Club. He is an active member of the First United Methodist Church in North Wilkesboro where he has been a Sunday School teacher, a member of the Administrative Board and is presently serving on the Board of Trustees. He is also President of the Dr. Fred C. Hubbard Scholarship Fund, Inc., and has served as chairman of the North Wilkesboro Zoning Board of Adjustment.

Helen, a graduate of Woman's College of the University of N.C., now U.N.C.-G., has been involved in many church and community activities, has taught in Wilkesboro High

School, North Wilkesboro High School and was associated with Clevenger College of Business Administration in an executive capacity for more than five years. She was with the State Department of Public Instruction in Greensboro prior to working almost four years with the F.B.I. in Charlotte and New York City. However, her favorite role has been that of homemaker and mother for the past twenty years and now a grandmother for three years.

Sources: Bible records and personal knowledge.

— Helen B. Bell

THE BENGES and MYERS
345

The Benge and Myers have been a part of Wilkes County since the early 1800's. Family records indicate that the father of Joseph Myers was born in London, England, and came to Wilkes from there. Joseph was 23 in 1850. In 1860 his son Wiley was age 10. Wiley Myers, one of six children, was my Great-Great Grandfather. He married Rebecca Sprinkle who died on October 17, 1926 in Wilkes County.

Wiley and Rebecca's daughter, Suzanne, one of four children, was married to Joe Benge on September 18, 1898. Marriage records in Wilkes County state that Joe Benge was age 21 and Suzanne was 19 at the time of their marriage. They had 11 children, one of whom is my grandfather, Bryant Benge.

Joe Benge was a sawmill worker and made liquor. His son Bryant was married to Evie Anderson, daughter of Lee and Ettie Anderson, in July 1936. Bryant is fourteen years older than Evie and knew her as a baby. He waited for her to grow up so he could marry her. Bryant, just as his father, was a sawmill worker and made liquor for which he served time in prison. It seemed to be something that thrilled him. He used to laugh when he told of running from the law. His greatest pride was the still he built underground, and has never divulged the whereabouts of that still. One of his best liquor-making buddies is now a minister.

Bryant and Evie had nine children, one of whom is my Mother, Minnie. Minnie married Ronnie Lee Millsaps on October 22, 1960. Ronnie is from Iredell County. She and Ronnie had two children, Cindy and Randall. They now live in a rural area in Wilkes County. Ronnie is a minister and has been the pastor of Central Baptist Church for 14 years.

Sources: Personal knowledge, 1850 and 1860 Census, Wilkes Co. Marriage Records.

— Randall Millsaps

JAMES MACK and EULA BROCK BENTLEY
346

James Mack Bentley was born in Pores Knob, NC, April 28, 1897, to James Enoch and Josephine Brown Bentley. James E. was a son of Joel Johnson and Margaret Mitchell Bentley. He was born in Alexander County, NC, November 4, 1852, and came with his parents to the Pores Knob Community, Wilkes

County, in 1862, where he spent the remainder of his life. He died June 29, 1930. Josephine Bentley was a daughter of Thorton A. and Lucinda (Lucy) Lane Brown. She was born September 6, 1859, and died June 22, 1943.

James Mack Bentley was married to Eula Brock, May 29, 1926. They lived at the homeplace of his parents where they raised three sons: James Mack, Jr., Charles Parks, and Franklin Brock Bentley. At this time, 1982, Eula, the widow of James Mack, Sr., still lives at their old home and all three sons are married and have homes in Wilkes County. James Mack, Jr., was born Feb. 8, 1932, and is married to Doris Kerbaugh. They have three children: James Roger, Beverley Ruth, and Gracia Len Bentley. Charles P. was born Sept. 13, 1936, and is married to Lois Dempsey. They have three children: Laura Lea, Lecia Lynn, and Lizabeth Loraine (Beth) Bentley. Franklin Brock Bentley was born April 6, 1943, and is married to Paula York. They have three children: Crystal Lynette, Tina Paulette, and Gina Annette.

James Mack, Sr., was a farmer and lumber man. He was a member of Walnut Grove Baptist Church. He died Nov. 20, 1975, and was buried in Walnut Grove Cemetery. Eula Brock Bentley is a daughter of Charles P. and Nora Coone Brock and was born at Pores Knob, NC, March 7, 1908. Besides being a homemaker and helping with the farm, she taught school two terms, was manager of lunchrooms at Moravian Falls Elementary school and Wilkes Central High School for several years. She was a charter member of the Pores Knob Home Demonstration Club, now the Extension Homemakers Club and is the current President of the club. She is a member of Walnut Grove Baptist Church.

Sources: personal information and family records.

— Eula Brock Bentley

JOEL JOHNSON BENTLEY FAMILY
347

Joel Johnson Bentley, born 24 September, 1820, died 26 April, 1906, was the son of James Bentley and Elizabeth (Betsy) Laws, who had married 25 February, 1806. Joel Johnson married Margaret Mitchell, born 29 November, 1820, died 30 July, 1893. They had the following children: (1) John, who married Josephine Russell; (2) Katherine, who married Andy Laws; (3) Rebecca, who married Pickney Laws; (4) William, who married Violet Lane; (5) James Enoch, who married Josephine Brown; (6) Franklin, who married Adelaide Hartley; (7) Jane, who married Larkin Hartley.

James Enoch, the fifth child of Joel Johnson Bentley, married Josephine V. Brown, whose ancestry can be traced through her father, Thornton Asbury Brown and Mary Lucinda Lane. Josephine's paternal grandparents were Elijah and Wilmoth Cordellia Church Brown. Her maternal grandparents were Thomas and Betsy Crysel Lane.

James Enoch and Josephine V. Brown Bentley had nine children, but only six lived to

adulthood: (1) Jessie Margaret who married R. F. Campbell; (2) Sallie Lucinda, who married J. Floyd Parlier; (3) Grace Jane, who married William S. Reavis; (4) Ethel Octave, who married T. J. Haigwood; (5) Luther Parks who married Margie Broyhill; and (6) James Mack, who married Eula Brock.

Luther Parks Bentley, born 20 September, 1894, married Margie Idell Broyhill, born 11 May, 1900. Parks and Margie had seven sons: (1) Joel Johnson, born 5 November, 1921, married Edna Absher; (2) Fredrick Claude, born 13 December, 1922, married Katherine Irvin; (3) James Worth, born 22 August, 1924, married Linda Earp; (4) Clint William, born 1 March, 1927, married Miron Carey; (5) Lee Winfred, born 1 March, 1927, married Betty Harwell; (6) Keith Lambeth, born 21 October, 1930, married Joyce Aileen Joines; (7) Ralph Luther, born 29 August, 1935, married Caroline Hayes.

Keith L. Bentley and Aileen Joines were married 2 August, 1958. They have two children: Milton Keith born 22 December, 1959, and Myra Joyce born 3 July, 1961.

Sources: Public records; personal interviews.

— Peggy Martin

THE BESHEARS FAMILY
348

It seems appropriate to begin the Beshears story with the first immigrants to America. Robert Brasseuir and spouse Florence along with a brother Benois and his spouse Marie immigrated to America by way of the Isle of Thanet near Kent, England in 1637.

Robert and Benois were born in France; the family originating in the old French providence of Champagne. Robert, Benois, and families settled in the new world along the Nansemond River in Virginia. The brothers, having a difference of opinion with the other settlers about their religious beliefs, decided it was too crowded there. With Robert disposing of 1900 acres and Benois 300 acres, they went up the Chespeake Bay to Calvert County, Maryland.

Robert died in 1665 leaving a daughter Margaret Brashear Jordan, who was married to Thomas Jordan in 1662 at Isle of Wight Virginia.

Benois became the progenitor of the Brasseuir family of America, each generation using a different spelling of their French surname. In the year 1662, Benois and wife Marie was granted citizenship and their names were anglicized Benjamin and Mary Brashear.

In this period of time the pronunciation of the name lent itself to various phonetic spellings. Even in official documents there was a great deal of reckless independence in spelling.

The diversity of the Brasseuir spelling took on several different forms such as Brashear, Brashears, Beshears, and others. Even today there's not complete agreement on spelling.

Benjamin, making his move to Maryland, contracted for and moved onto the 1,150 acre plantation known as upper Bennett in Calvert County. The farm already had servants, cattle, and hogs, having previously been owned by

Parks and Margie Broyhill Bentley.

Richard Bennett. The three-hundred twenty four year old brick and clapboard structure is reportedly still standing overlooking Chespeake Bay.

Prior to 1663 Benjamin died leaving the parcel of land and dwellings known as the Brashears purchase to Mary, his wife. Mary later married Thomas Sterling, whose transportation Benjamin had paid from Virginia to Maryland. The tract of land later became known as "Sterlings Nest".

The year 1800 saw the spelling Beshears as is now used by some branches of the original Brashear family. The name was first recorded on the tax list of Bourbon County Kentucky.

By 1810 a branch of the Beshears family had stopped in Wilkes County while heading west. It seems a lot of Wilkes residents had been "squatters" waiting for a grant to their land. Aaron Beshears was no different; his grant was issued in the mid 1880's for land in Wilkes. In this "wilderness" as described by some Wilkes residents of that period, records were not kept as they are today. Some of the family moved on to other parts of the county and records on them are ubobtainable. By the early eighteen hundreds, Aaron was head of the Beshears family of Wilkes.

Aaron Beshears and Alia Ownes were married in 1843. To this union were born several children, one of whom was Cornelius C. Beshears, born 1860, married Sarah Owens, born 1856. Marshal Clinton Beshears 1887-1978, grandfather of this writer, was born of that union. I asked grandpa several years before his death if times were hard in his boyhood years, "We had plenty back then. Chickens, hogs, corn, and sheep, we raised everything we ate; at one time dad had a hundred stands of bees, We lived good."

From the days of that pioneer spirit to the present, America has been good to all of us.

Sources: Va. Land Patents. Hall of Records of Maryland. Maryland Archives. Tax List Bourbon County. Personal knowledge and interviews with family members.

— Morris L. Beshears

ADDISON BILLINGS FAMILY
349

Addison Billings, son of William M. Billings and Sarah Childers, was born around 1834. He was married first on March 12, 1854 to Susan Holbrook, daughter of Ezekiel Holbrook and Elizabeth Adams. Susan was born 1839 and died in 1879. They had 6 children: James Oscar, William Oliver, John Irving, Sarah Elizabeth, Ida Jane and Susan Valeria. On the death of his wife Susan, Addison married second Betsy Ann Blackburn, daughter of Reubin Jordan Blackburn and Paulina Douglas. Betsy Ann was born around 1860 and died between 1890 and 1900. They had 3 children: William Tyre, James Lloyd, and Romulus. Addison died on Jan. 16, 1900 on the day his grandson Frank Billings was born. He lies buried with other members of his family on the forested ridge near the river not far from the Jesse J. Billings old homeplace.

1) James Oscar Billings, the oldest of Addison's children, was born March 4, 1857 and acquired substantial acreage of land on the Camp Branch of Roaring River between the Greenstreet Mountains and Rice's Knob, including the land deeded to him by his grandfather William M. Billings when he was only 18 months old. James Oscar married Phoebe Cansadie Smoot, daughter of Granville Smoot and Asenith (Susan) Phillips, born Feb. 24, 1862. They chose the location of their home near a huge spring. This house, built by local craftsman Robert Walker, still stands and is presently occupied by his youngest son, Lonnie G. Billings. Oscar and Cansadie had 8 children: Avery, Lucretia, Hillery, Cora, Granville, Vaughn, Bruce and Lonnie. Cansadie died shortly after they celebrated their golden wedding anniversary in 1929.

Avery Arthur, oldest of the children of James Oscar and Cansadie, was born Aug. 1, 1880 and spent most of his life in Hibbing, Minnesota. Ellen Lucretia, born March 26, 1882 married Joseph Huanza Holbrook, son of Patterson B. Holbrook and Wadie Pruitt, and they had a large family in the Traphill area. A granddaughter, Lois Rae Royall, married Thomas Monroe Huffman and is an officer in the Northwestern Bank in North Wilkesboro. James Hillery, born May 14, 1886 married Martha Bowers, daughter of James Bowers and Julia Walker. He moved to Win-

James Oscar Billings Family. Seated: L to R: Avery Arthur, James Oscar and wife Phoebe Cansadie Smoot, Lucretia. Standing L to R: James Hillery, John Granville, Bruce, Vaughn, Cora, Lonnie Grant.

ston-Salem in the early 1940s and most of their children work for R.J. Reynolds Tobacco Co. there. One grandchild, Linda Gail Swaim, has won a mass of medals and trophies in her unusual recreation of speed skating, attending meets all over the world. Cora, born Jan 12, 1888 married first on April 3, 1908 Manley R. Holbrook married second on Jan. 28, 1933 Elliott P. Bowers, son of Giles Bowers and Louisa Holbrook, and she and "P" lived in Independence, Va. and are buried at Salem Methodist Church there. John Granville, born March 16, 1891 married Beatrice Wiles, daughter of Robert Wiles and Angeline Wheatley and they had 7 children. Granville was a teacher, merchant, and farmer and also served as Postmaster of Offen. Vaughn was born Sept. 30, 1898. He died early on Feb. 23, 1933 while on a trip to Montana. Bruce was born March 12, 1894. He married Maud Lyon, daughter of Rhesa Lyon and Elizabeth Blackburn and they reared their 3 daughters in the Dockery community. Bruce was the master farmer nominee for Wilkes County in 1927 and was among 66 farmers in the State so honored that year. He utilized the most progressive methods of farming to improve his acreage, and in 1950 joined the ranks of corn growers who reached a yield of over 100 bushels per acre. He was also active in his church and was a Deacon and Treasurer of Mt. Pisgah Baptist Church for over 25 years.

Lonnie Grant, the youngest child of this family, was born Aug. 31, 1905. He is a member of the Wilkes Agricultural Stabilization and Conservation Service, which administers farm programs in Wilkes County, and is on the Board of Directors for the Mt. View Medical Center. He is a Deacon of Mt. Pisgah Baptist Church and has served as Church Clerk there for 52 years. He married Joyce Mayberry, daughter of J. W. Jones Mayberry and Josephine Sparks, and they have 2 children: Eva Sue and James Oscar. Sue taught home economics for several years in the Surry Co. schools, married Ralph C. Cooke, Jr. and they own a solar house industry in Mt. Airy. Jim works for the State Park Service, currently being stationed at Morrow Mountain State Park near Albemarle, N.C., and his wife Juanita, daughter of Arthur Howard Osborne and Helen Riggsbee, is a registered nurse.

2) William Oliver Billings was born March 20, 1859 and married on Sept. 4, 1887 Martha Elizabeth Combs, daughter of Zadock Combs and Nancy Ann Edwards. They had 10 children. Martha Elizabeth was born March 15, 1869 and died May 22, 1955. They lived and are buried in West Virginia and most of their children live in that area. A great grandson, Stephen Jerome Smith, is presently studying at Harvard Law School and hopes to do his early practice in N.C.

3) John Irving Billings, born Feb. 13, 1863, married Emma Bowers, born July 21, 1871, daughter of Giles Bowers and Louisa Holbrook. Their children Rance and Ida were brought up in Grayson Co., Va. and many of their descendants live in that area.

4) Sarah Elizabeth Billings, born March 7, 1869 married Thomas Billings, son of Abel Billings and Kiziah Blevins. They had 9 chil-

dren. One son Frank Billings married into another line of Billings, Bessie Mae Billings, daughter of William Billings and Charlotte Samantha Pruitt.

5) Ida Jane Billings born Jan. 1874 married John D. Shaver, son of Aubrey Shaver and Nancy Dudley. John was born in April 1865 and died May 20, 1941. They had 3 children: Carl married Edna Faye Overcash, Jettie married Archie Pruitt, and Ruby married Joseph Johnson.

6) Susan Valeria Billings was born March 22, 1879, married Hugh M. Walker born Nov. 2, 1874. He was the son of Robert J. Walker and Mersia Ann Stamper. Their 4 children, Alma, Augusta, Georgia and Ella moved to the Winston-Salem area.

7) William Tyre Billings, first child of Addison by his second wife, Betsy Ann Blackburn, was born July 9, 1884. He married Janie Holbrook, born Jan. 10, 1879 who was the daughter of Patterson B. Holbrook and Wadie Pruitt. Tyre operated the Brewer mills for years. Tyre and Janie had one child, Claude Dean who married Lilly Triplett, daughter of William Hardin Triplett and Pearl Waddell. Dean continues to live on the land owned by his Holbrook ancestors for over 100 years.

8) James Lloyd Billings, born July 14, 1888, married Winnie Poe Brown who was born July 30, 1896. They had 8 children: Okie Lee, Wallace, Virginia, Maden. La Vern, Lawrence, Iva Lee and Betty Ann. A son, Wallace, operates a dry cleaning shop in North Wilkesboro.

9) Romulus, the last of Addison's children, was born April 20, 1890 and married Catherine Billings, daughter of Eli Billings and Elizabeth Brooks. Catherine was born Aug. 6, 1894 and died Sept. 22, 1977. They had an even dozen children, most of whom still live in the Offen area.

Sources: Family Records and Information, Cemetery Records, Census.

— Naomi B. Gordon

JASPER BILLINGS
350

Jasper Billings was a soldier in the Revolutionary War, serving as a Private in the N.C. Militia. He was born April 3, 1759 in Pittsylvania Co., Va., but moved to N.C. with his father when he was 15 years old, and in Aug. 1776 while still a teen enlisted as a volunteer under Lt. Martin Davenport to fight the Cherokee Indians, who were troublesome at that time. He served about 6 weeks, and again in the fall of 1780 he volunteered for 3-months service under Capt. William Hewlett and Lt. John Parker, most of which time he spent guarding prisoners taken at the Battle of King's Mountain. During his third tour of duty, beginning in July 1781 for 3 months, he was under Capt. Alexander Gordon and participated in the Battle of Eutaw Springs in S.C. He mentioned Thomas Joines as being in his group in this last service, and gave James Bauguess as reference in his application for pension.

Jasper was a large land owner, holding lands in the Reddies River area as well as the

homeplace in Dockery. He is listed in Capt. Judd's District in the 1797 Taxables with 390 acres of land, and Elisha Richardson is also listed in this same group. An order dated July 30, 1792 gave "him leave to build a griss mill on Roaring River at the place where Thomas Billings formerly had a griss mill." On June 14, 1795 he was married in Wilkes County, N.C., where he had returned to live after the Revolutionary War, to Elizabeth Richardson who was born around 1774. Elisha Richardson is given as surety on their marriage bond, so it appears he was probably related to Jasper's wife.

Jasper and Elizabeth Richardson Billings had several children. In the 1820 Census he was listed with 6 males under 20 and 3 females, but only 4 children have been definitely identified: Elisha, Thomas, Hiram and Abel. Alpha and Bethane are possible children of his.

Of his four known children, Elisha was born around 1804, married first on Nov. 4, 1831 to Nancy Hawkins, married second on Nov. 9, 1837 to Malinda McCrary, and married third to Susan Sabrina Wheatley. He had at least 16 children. Hiram, born 1805, married on March 20, 1828 to Rosannah Minton, born about 1810. They had 10 children. Thomas, born 1815 married 1. on Sept. 26, 1845 to Nancy Wiles, dau. of Abraham Wiles and Winnie Aubrey, married second on Sept. 16, 1864 to Frances Bowers and married third on Jan. 28, 1867 to Sarah Ellis. At least 14 children were born to him and his wives. Abel, the last child born to Jasper and Elizabeth, was born on May 10, 1825. He married Keziah Blevins and they had 8 children. Abel died on Feb. 12, 1917.

Jasper Billings died on Nov. 12, 1835 and is buried with other members of his family in a family plot on land now owned by Alice Billings in the Dockery community. The peak just above this graveyard bears his name, Jasper's Knob.

Sources: Archives Report, Census Records, Cemetery Records.

— Naomi B. Gordon

PETER BILLINGS and DESCENDANTS
351

Peter Billings was born before 1774, and his place of birth was South Carolina according to his son, William. In 1797, Peter was living in the Roaring River Settlement in Wilkes County, and his name is on a petition for water rights presented by that community. Then in 1800 he is listed on the census for Wilkes County as married but with no children. His age is given as 26-45, and the age of his wife was 16-26. Wilkes County land records show that he bought 20 acres on Roaring River from William Holbrook in 1803, and in 1805, he bought 100 acres from William Manard. Peter is next found in 1811 in White County, Tennessee. At this time he bought 109 acres of land from James Cole. This land was located on Post Oak Creek, and was apparently in that part of White County which later became De-Kalb County where Peter died in 1838. The disposition of his property after his death lists the following children: William, John, Bird, Peter, James, Rebecca, Rhoda, Gibson, Elizabeth, Elsie and Mary.

William Billings, a son of Peter, was born in Wilkes County January 31, 1801. In White County, Tennessee about 1822, he married Mary Davis and his first five children were born here. In 1828, he moved to Lawrence County, Indiana, where Mary died in 1840. The children of this marriage were: Rebecca and Elizabeth, twins, Peter, Nancy, John, Jesse, Aaron, James, Lucinda Jane and Joseph.

On February 1, 1843, William married Sarah (Elkins) Schaufner. The family continued to live on their farm in Lawrence County until 1852 when they moved to Richland County, Illinois, and settled on a farm near Noble. William and his family remained here until about 1865 when he moved to Missouri and lived near Appleton City in Bates County. Sarah died here September 1, 1871, and she was buried at Round Prairie Cemetery. The children of this marriage were: William D., Mary A., Lucinda E., Bird Franklin and Lydia Catherine.

August 31, 1873, William married Sarah E. Hall at Appleton City and they had two children: Rhoda E. and Abraham. Abe died at Sheridan, Wyoming, April 11, 1966. William died in Bates County September 22, 1880, and he was buried at Round Prairie Cemetery.

Peter Billings, a son of William, was born in White County, Tennessee March 18, 1825. November 24, 1842, he married Mary Murray, a daughter of Timothy and Catherine (Finger) Murray, in Lawrence County, Indiana. This marriage resulted in five children: Timothy (b Sept. 6, 1843 d Dec. 29, 1929), John William (b May 11, 1846 d Dec. 8, 1854), Catherine (b Jan. 25, 1856 d Oct 15, 1858), Lewis Elijah (b Aug. 13, 1859 d Apr. 27, 1949) and James Marion (b July 23, 1863 d Nov. 18, 1949).

Peter Billings was a prominent citizen and a successful farmer in Richland County. He built one of the first brick homes in that area and owned several hundred acres of land north of Noble, Illinois.

Mary died April 16, 1890, and was buried in North Freedom Cemetery North of Noble. Peter married Matilda Speigal January 11, 1891, and moved to Texas. He lived near Houston and died there January 30, 1914, and was buried in Hollywood Cemetery. He and Matilda had a daughter, Ethel, who married George F. Brosius.

Lewis Elijah Billings, a son of Peter Billings and Mary Murray, was born near Noble, Illinois, August 13, 1859, where he grew to manhood. He received his education in the common schools and graduated from Olney High School in June 1880 — one of the first of the Billings clan to accomplish this. December 29, 1896, he married Pearl Chapman in the home of her father at Hanson, Texas. Their children were: Hazel Norrine (b Oct. 13, 1897 d Dec. 27, 1979), Myrtle Ruby (b June 1, 1899, d April 16, 1969) and Claude Earl (March 12, 1901 d Oct. 15, 1981).

Lewis Elijah Billings taught school at Freedom Schoolhouse near Noble for a few years. He worked on the Noble newspaper, was postmaster at Noble and a successful merchant. He owned and operated four apple evaporators and shipped dried apples all over the U.S. and to foreign countries. About 1914, he moved to Arkansas where he continued in the grocery business for several years. He and Pearl were divorced, and December 4, 1917, he married Margaret India Jenkins of Newton, Illinois. She was the daughter of W.H. and Gertrude (Miller) Jenkins. This marriage was productive in four boys: Lewis William (b Oct. 31, 1918), James Jenkins (b July 20, 1920), David Neal (b June 14, 1924), and John Wesley (b Jan. 13, 1931). Lewis E. Billings died at his home south of Little Rock, Arkansas, April 27, 1949, and Margaret Billings died November 15, 1975. They are buried at Landmark Cemetery.

Lewis William Billings, a son of Lewis E. and Margaret Billings, was born at Newton, Illinois October 31, 1918. He graduated from Mabelvale High School in May 1938 and joined the C.C.C. While in camp near Russellville, Arkansas, he met and married Martha Berry, a daughter of Charles W. and Beulah (Rachel) Berry, December 19, 1941.

After serving in the USNR during WW II, he completed his college work at Arkansas Tech at Russellville. In 1957, he received his masters degree in education for the University of Arkansas at Fayetteville. He has taught school for thirty years: sixteen years at Crossett, Arkansas, and fourteen years at Russellville High School.

Lewis and Martha Billings have two children: Lewis W. Jr. who married Patricia Boyd, the daughter of Frederick and Betty (Harold) Boyd. Their children are: Lewis W. III, born at Shreveport, Louisiana, July 12, 1968, and Matthew C., born there November 10, 1969. Martha Anne Billings married Peter Dennis McCarthy, the son of Edward and Mary (Pender) McCarthy. Their daughters, born in Memphis, Tennessee, are: Carol Michelle, born April 26, 1974, and Mary Kristen, born April 9, 1981.

Sources: Family records, family Bible records, county records from the counties mentioned and family tradition.

— Lewis W. Billings

WILLIAM M. BILLINGS
352

William M. Billings was born around 1784 in Wilkes Co. married first Winifred Alexander on April 10, 1816, possibly married again, and on April 8, 1831 married Sally Childers, born 1795. He was a miller and farmer, owning lands near the Jesse J. Billings place on the middle prong of Roaring River in the Dockery community. On the 1840 School Census he is listed with the following children: Amelia, Susan, Jesse, Addison and Wilburn. Jackson was listed with the family in the 1850 Census.

Little is known about the two girls, 1) Amelia born around 1822 and 2) Susan. Amelia was living with her father in 1870, apparently still unmarried.

3) Jesse James Billings, born Jan. 4, 1824, married on Jan. 17, 1851 Emily Elizabeth Buttrey, daughter of John Abraham Buttrey and Sarah Barker. He started the Billings School near his home to educate his and neighbor children in those early years. He died on June 6, 1906 and is buried with his wife on the family plot overlooking the river near his home. Emily Elizabeth was born Dec. 31, 1831 and died Feb. 10, 1888. To Jesse J. and Emily were born six children: Rowan, Avery, James, Roxie, Ellen and Leander.

Rowan C., born Oct. 23, 1853 married 1. Mary I. McNeill then moved to Tennessee, where he remarried after the death of his first wife. Avery Columbus, born Sept. 27, 1856 married first Mattie Alice Kilby, daughter of James Kilby, and on April 24, 1907 after her death on July 29, 1906, he married second Ida Ann Higgins, daughter of John T. Higgins and Alice Jennings. A son, Eugene, became a prominent surgeon, pioneering in open heart surgery in Philadelphia, Penn. James E. (Jeemes) was born May 13, 1859 and married on May 1, 1899 Carrie Jane Gambill, daughter of William D. Gambill and America Holbrook. Carrie was born March 21, 1880 and lived until Feb. 1, 1972, rearing 4 children. A daughter, Pearl, became a nurse; granddaughter Henrietta Burchette works for a newspaper and her sister Virginia Dare Burchette, wife of William Morris, is a school teacher in New Jersey. Sarah Roxie Ann was born May 13, 1862 and lived with her sister Ellen, born Dec. 7, 1866, on the old homeplace in Dockery until her death on Feb. 29, 1940. Known affectionately as Miss Roxie to her many students, she taught more than 50 years as a public teacher in Wilkes County. Ellen died on June 22, 1955. Leander born in 1855, died young.

4) Addison Billings, first child of William M. Billings and Sarah Childers, was born around 1834. He married first on March 12, 1854, Susan Holbrook, and married second Betsy Ann Blackburn. (See Addison Billings)

5) William Wilburn Billings, born about 1836, married Catherine Holbrook, born 1835, daughter of Ezekiel Holbrook and Elizabeth Adams. They had 5 children: Andrew Jackson, Susan Emily, Robinson Crusoe, Nancy Caroline and Lewis Gilmer. Catherine died around 1899.

Andrew Jackson was born on March 15, 1859 and married Dousie A. Smoot, daughter of Galomiel Leonard Smoot and Nancy Clementine Walker. Dousie was born Jan. 17, 1861 and died Feb. 3, 1936. They lived in the Moxley area and had 7 children: Esta A., Claude E., Metta L., Clementine, Retta I., Challie G. and Rose Ellen. Esta A. married a well-known Baptist preacher, Rev. Louis Baxter Murray, who helped organize several churches in Wilkes County. Claude E. married Laura Elledge and lived in the Mt. View community. Their son Claude served as Wilkes Co. Sheriff during the years 1950-58. Clementine married William Clyde Brewer and reared a fine family in the Moxley area. Metta L. died early. Retta I. married first Burr Bowers and married second John Ivey Myers. Challie Gilmore married Grace Armstrong and they moved to Michigan. Rose Ellen married Anderson Mitchell Church, Jr., son of A.M. Church and Lillie Staley.

Susan Emily, born Feb. 24, 1860, married John Wesley Brown who became a well-known Baptist preacher. John W. was born May 1,

1859 and died March 17, 1952. They had 2 children: Nannie Sara who married Joseph D. Brinegar, son of Joseph S. Brinegar and Louisa Billings, and Avery Columbus, who married Martha Jane Holbrook, daughter of James Calloway Holbrook and Alsie Cleary.

Robinson Crusoe was born June 6, 1862, married on Dec. 3, 1890 to Laura E. Childress, born April 22, 1875. They moved to Tennessee and many of the descendants of their 10 children still live in the Rockwood, Tenn. area.

Nancy Caroline was born in 1867. She married first Nov. 29, 1890 James Soots, by whom she had 3 children: Mitchell married Kate Whitlock, Minnie died young, and Lelia married V. Cooper Pardue and had 10 children. Nancy Caroline married second Elisha Childers and married third Frank Bowers.

Lewis Gilmer, born Aug. 17, 1868 married first Jennie Belle Carrico Gambill, born Aug. 26, 1869 daughter of Aaron K. Carrico and Rousie Emeline Cornette and widow of Nathan H. Gambill, and later moved to Missouri. Their children were: Virgil Emerson married Nettie Cohen, Howard Quay married Gladys E. Robertson, Lillian Mayo married first Mr. Adams and second Arthur Hudson, and Lillie Mae married Freeman Roloson. After the death of Jennie Belle on Oct. 9, 1903 and her burial in Pattonsburg, Mo., Lewis returned to N.C. and married second Minnie Cook, by whom he had 2 more children: James Montgomery who married Etta Crabb and Robert Hillery who married first Hilda Jane Burchette and second Velna Pruitt.

6) Jackson T. Billings was born Feb. 1, 1830 and married Margaret Clementine Porter, oldest child of Andrew Porter and Mary Cooper and sister of W.F. Porter. Margaret was born in 1832 and died June 7, 1907. They lived in the Mulberry section of Wilkes County, where they had 12 children, 4 of whom were dead by 1907. They are believed buried in a family plot on Chestnut Mountain. The children of Jackson and Margaret were: Martha, Jesse F., William Francis, Sarah Ann, John, Emily, Joseph, Doxanna, Roxanna and Alice.

Martha E. born 1855 married McDaniel Absher, son of Jacob Absher and Sarah Hall. Jesse F. born Aug. 20, 1858 married Polly Shumate, dau. of King Shumate. William Francis "Yank" was born June 16, 1862, married first Samantha Shumate, married second Cloie E. Shumate, daughter of Esley Shumate and Nancy Kilby. Sarah Ann, born March 9, 1863 married Nathan Alfred Wyatt, son of Lewis Wyatt and Phoebe Brown. John A. was born March 5, 1865 and married first Elizabeth Absher, married second Martha Handy and third Sarah Shumate. Emily, born in 1868, died Dec. 12, 1890. Joseph Columbus "Birch" was born Sept. 25, 1872, married Lura Elizabeth Coffey, daughter of Asberry Coffey and Sarah Wingler. Doxanna and Roxanna, twin girls, were born June 5, 1875. Doxanna died young. Roxanna married Silas M. Shumate, son of Hugh A. Shumate and Candis M. Absher, who was a prominent farmer in the Mt. View area. Alice Octavia, born April 8, 1880 married James Gilbright Myers, born Oct. 31, 1877. Their son Fred Everette Myers was Wilkes County Sheriff for several years in the late 1950s.

Sources: Census; other Public Records; Newspapers.

— Naomi B. Gordon

BENJAMIN BINGHAM
353

Benjamin Bingham was born in 1756. He resided in Culpepper County, Virginia, until he entered the Revolutionary War in 1776. He served with his brother, Robert, but they became separated during their service.

According to A History of Watauga County, "It is a family tradition that Benjamin Bingham, who came from Virginia to Reddy's River, fired the last cannon at Yorktown. This Benjamin was a giant in his day, and it is related of him that a noted fighter, wishing to test his strength as a wrestler, came to Reddy's River and lay in the shade of some trees and watched Benjamin lead the reapers in the wheat harvest till sundown, when he made his business known. It was then that Benjamin, without resting or eating, girded his loins and threw his opponent as often as he wished to try conclusion with him."

It is believed the following were his children: (1) Anne, who married James Wiles on Jan. 10, 1810 in Surry Co., (2) Edney, who married Joshua Jones on Aug. 31, 1815, (3) Jane, who married William Iles on Dec. 11, 1813, (4) Stephen N. born about 1796 in Virginia, married Synthy Pritchard in Surry County on Dec. 20, 1817, (5) Jemima, born Feb. 8, 1798 in Virginia, married James Arrington Proffitt on May 21, 1816. Jemima died Nov. 29, 1881 in Greene Co., Mo. Jemima and Arrington also lived in McMinn Co., Tenn., moving there about 1824.

Another probable son is Benjamin, who married Nancy Proffit in 1818 with that marriage bond being in Wilkes County.

Our early Benjamin Bingham moved on to Blount Co., Tennessee, where in 1832, he states in his Rev. War Declaration that he is 76 years old.

Sources: A History of Watauga County, Rev. War Papers, Marriage Bonds and Census Records.

— Mrs. J. Arnold Simpson

GEORGE M. BINGHAM
354

George M. Bingham was born July 20, 1805, on Reddies River, Wilkes County, North Carolina. About 1833, he was married to Mary Ann Davis, born in 1813, and believed to be the daughter of Golston and Elizabeth Whitlow Davis.

The children of George M. and Mary Ann were: (1) William G., born in 1835, and married to Roxanna Presnell. (2) Louisa, born about 1837, married Marshall Miller in 1856, and lived on Cove Creek until about 1837. At that time, she moved to Idaho. Her husband had died during the Civil War. (3) Harvey, the next child, was born February 13, 1839 and died March 17, 1895. In 1861, he married Nancy Ann Miller, the daughter of John B. and Mary Triplett Miller. (4) Harrison died in infancy. (5) Violet Emeline was born about 1843

and died at an early age. (6) Thomas, born on February 3, 1845, was married twice, to Sarah Ann Farmer in 1870 and to Laura E. Combs in 1885. (7) Elliot was born about 1847 and was killed during the Civil War on Beech Mountain. (8) Marshall, who was born about 1849, died at age 34, unmarried. (9) Isidor was born about 1851 and died at age two. (10) Nancy Carolina was born about 1853 and married E.L. Presnell.

George was prominent in the Methodist Community of Henson's Chapel. His mother-in-law, Elizabeth Whitlow Davis, is believed to be the first Methodist in that area. George is also credited with offering his home as a meeting house for a couple of Missionary Baptists about 1854.

George M. was the first elected Clerk of Superior Court in 1852 but resigned during his first term because of a speech impediment.

He died on January 20, 1880 in Watauga County.

Sources: A History of Watauga County and Census Records.

— Margaret Somers

JOSEPH TERRY BINGHAM
355

Joseph Terry Bingham, born 20 Oct. 1818, married 23 Nov. 1846 Minerva Adline Lewis daughter of David and Mary (Polly) Hendrix Lewis. They lived in the part of Wilkes which later became Watauga County. They were the parents of six children: Stephen, Jerusha, Mary Caroline, Devalt, Robert Lewis and Cynthia Bingham.

In the year of 1877 Joseph T. Bingham was appointed Postmaster at Pine Run in Watauga County. He was a land owner, a farmer, and operated a dry goods store and a mill. His wife, Minerva Adline, died 28 Feb. 1877 and was the first person to be buried in the cemetery at Rutherwood in Watauga County.

Joseph T. Bingham married second Lou S. Brown and they had three children: Joe, Edna and Grace. He died 28 Sept. 1897 and is buried with his first wife at Rutherwood.

Mary Caroline Bingham, the third child of Joseph T. and Minerva Adeline Lewis Bingham, is remembered for the beautiful quilts she made on a spinning wheel. She married David Marshall Winkler. (see The Ancestors of Mary Elizabeth Winkler Carroll.)

Sources: personal knowledge.

— Gayle C. Benton

MAJOR HARVEY BINGHAM
356

Harvey Bingham was the third child of George M. and Mary Ann Davis Bingham. He was born on February 13, 1839. In 1861, he married Nancy Ann Miller, daughter of John B. and Mary Triplett, who was born in Wilkes County on January 12, 1840. Their children were: (1) Mary Laura (1865-1947) who married William Johnson; (2) Lunda Louisa (1868-1937) who married Charles H. Somers, (3) Eudora L. (1870-1949) who married Albert R

Major Harvey Bingham.

Sherman; (4) Lenora Viola (1873-1934) who married L.C. Lewis; (5) C. Plato (1876- ?) who married Mattie St. John and practiced medicine in Bristol, Tennessee; (6) Robert K. (1878- ?) who married Jennie Norris and practiced medicine in Boone, North Carolina; (7) Martha L. and (8) Mertie W., twins born in 1880 who died in childhood and (9) Annie (1885-1971) who married Walter S. Harwell.

During the war, Harvey enlisted in Young Farthing's Company, 37th N.C. Regiment, was wounded twice, and was discharged in the latter part of 1862 because of bad health. He then became Major of the Home Guard Battalion at Camp Mast. On May 7, 1865, he led a group of men from Watauga and Catawba Counties in the first attack on Fort Hamby.

After the war, he and Nancy Ann went to Haywood County by horseback. He taught school at the Ford of Pigeon River, now Canton, and attended school at Sand Hill, Buncombe County, under the instruction of a Presbyterian minister named Hood. In 1869, he was admitted to the Bar and practiced law in Watauga County until 1881 when he moved to Statesville. There he continued in active and successful practice and also conducted a school of law. Many young men came to live in the Bingham home while they read law with "Major Harvey". An 1828 unabridged edition of Webster's Dictionary used in that school is now on loan to Old Wilkes Jail Museum in Wilkesboro. In 1876, he was elected to the N.C. State Senate.

Harvey Bingham died on March 17, 1895 and is buried in Oakwood Cemetary in Statesville. Nancy Ann Miller Bingham lived another nineteen years and died while visiting her daughters in Wilkesboro.

The letter quoted in its entirety was written to the seventeen and nineteen year old sons of Major Harvey Bingham upon receipt of the news of his death by his brother Thomas Bingham.

Amantha, N.C. April 9, 1895. Messrs. Plato and Robert Bingham; Dear Boys, I have been intending to write to you all for several days, but have not felt like doing so until now, and this letter is intended for all. It is very hard to realize that your Pa is dead, and while I had but little hope of his recovery, still the news of his death was a great shock to me and fills me with sadness. In my father's family there were six boys all of whom are gone but myself. For your Pa I always entertained a very strong brotherly affection because of moral and intellectual superiority. From his early youth his life was entirely free from the vices so common among young men. No profane language ever polluted his lips and he looked with disgust on the use of ardent spirits. At your age boys he had perhaps not as much learning as either of you, but he valiantly charged the citadel of ignorance and her mighty bulwarks were demolished before his wonderful intellectual industry. I write this of him that I might awaken in each of you a determination to emulate his example. Boys if you have been sowing wild oats, sow them no longer and may this sad bereavement bring you to reflect and may seek like your sainted Pa the pearl of great price and then you can truly say . . . .

Of his legal ability and success as a lawyer I shall not speak. He was the preceptor of a large number of young men while preparing them to enter the profession of law. As to his efficiency as instructor of law quite a number of his old students doubtless would testify. My deceased brother was a good scholar, a splendid historian, and well up on current literature of the day. Of his moral and religious life I wish to refer. The record of his life was never stained by the use of a single profane expression nor in the indulgence of any of the vices so common to depraved and fallen humanity. From his youth he was a close Bible student and its divine teachings he ardently sought to introduce into practice. During his long illness he bore his affliction with Christian resignation and expressed perfect submission to the will of a kind providence.

On the 13th. inst. he wrote me referring to the uncertainty of his condition. "Things look a little squally but I possess my soul in patience calmly awaiting the result. If I die I would love to repose with my father, mother and other kindred and accompany them to the judgment at the sound of the last trumpet, buy my finances are too nearly exhausted to expect that."

My late Bro. had strong political convictions, but tolerance and kindness for those who from honest motives differed from him . . . .

I presume from what the girls write you all intend to stay where you are for the present and I hope you will be successful. If not before, I hope you will come up after the crops are laid by. I know so little about your affairs that I can hardly venture even a suggestion. Your Ma has many friends capable of giving advice in the management of her business. If your property could be sold at a fair price and invest in a farm it would seem the wiser course. Your Pa's law library ought to be worth a great deal and if you could sell it that would be of much advantage.

I fear from what the girls write that Caldwell has not acted a man in the partnership and if not I should ask the advice of legal friends. I want to hear from you at once. Let me know how you are getting along and what are your prospects and intentions.

I have written this letter to you boys for the first time and hope it will be somewhat appreciated. Tell your Ma and the girls to write. Laura sends love to all. Jimmie's leg is a little better. We have taken fractured bones out of his big toe.

Very truly,
Tho Bingham

Sources: *A History of Watauga County, Land of Wilkes,* Johnson J. Hayes Obituary Notices, Census Records, Family Records and letters in my possession.

— Margaret Somers

THE ROBERT BINGHAM FAMILY
357

The earliest known Bingham in Wilkes County was Robert Bingham. Robert, born between 1755 to 1765, came to Wilkes County from Virginia, probably Culpepper Co., Virginia. He appears on the 1784 Tax List return with no property. By the 1786 Tax List, he is in Capt. Judd's District (#6) with 200 acres of land.

This time in his life must have been very busy. The Revolution was going on and he and his brother, Benjamin, both served in the war. He also found time to propose to Elizabeth McNeil. She was the daughter of the Reverend George McNeil from Scotland and was born about 1767, probably in Virginia. Elizabeth accepted his proposal and they were married by Andrew Baker, a Baptist Minister of the Gospel on Dec. 7, 1785, in Wilkes County.

Robert acquired additional land and by the 1787 Tax List, he is shown in Capt. Brown's District (#10) with 300 acres of land. He, as the other men of his time was assigned to a jury to view roads. In 1789, he was assigned to view the road below Capt. Cleveland's to the branch below his father-in-law's, George McNeil, field. This was the area in which he lived.

By 1790, Robert and Elizabeth are the parents of two daughters. The 1800 Census adds another daughter and two sons, while the 1810 Census indicates another son and three more daughters have been added. This makes a total of nine children. It is believed the following were their children. (1) Nancy, born about 1790, who married Joseph Miller in 1807. (2) Sarah, who married twice — first, to Thomas Proffit and next to William Case. (3) Joel, who married (Lydia?) Miller. (4) George M., born 1805, married Mary Ann Davis. (5) William, born 1795, who married Frances Case. (6) Jemima, who did not marry and possibly died when about grown. (7) Elizabeth, born about 1810, married David Miller and lived in Watauga County. The other two girls names are not known at this time.

Robert died on March 26, 1811 in Wilkes County. Elizabeth remained a widow until her death. She states that she in ninety when she applies for a Revolutionary War Pension in 1857. She was living in Watauga County with her daughter and son-in-law, Elizabeth and David Miller in 1850.

The land that was owned by Robert was on Naked Creek near the path and on Buck Bull Branch of Lewis Fork Creek with William Ellison's line and Peter Ragans line.

The minutes of the Reddies River Baptist Church indicate that Bingham's were members of that church at one time.

Sources: Tax Lists, Marriage Bonds, Church Records and Census Records.

— Mrs. J. Arnold Simpson

MINNIE SELINA McEWEN BISHOP
358

Minnie Selina McEwen Bishop, born December 31, 1882, was the daughter of John Elam and Nannie Catherine Bledsoe McEwen. Her parents came to Wilkes County from Iredell County in 1866. She attended Miss Mamie Barber's Academy, which was a boarding school in Wilkesboro. Minnie taught school in Wilkes County for several years.

Minnie married Charles Turner Bishop, the son of Will and Anne Parsons Bishop. She and Charles had three children: Paul Bledsoe, Nannie, and Minnie Kathleen. Minnie passed away on October 28, 1948 and is buried in Mountlawn Cemetery. Charles passed away on March 18, 1970. He also is buried in Mountlawn Cemetery.

Paul Bledsoe Bishop married Mary Thelma Bumgarner. Thelma was graduated from Wilkesboro High School and attended Meredith

College in Raleigh, N.C. Paul was a farmer, a self-educated man, and a great teller of tall tales. In his later years, he ran Brown's Ford Grocery, and people came from far and wide to hear his tales. Paul and Thelma had three daughters and one son: Mary June, Carol Jean, Bill, and John Peter.

Mary June Bishop Gambill, Office Manager for Cashion, Inc., is married to Buel G. Gambill, Jr., who is Vice-President of Gambill Bros. Construction and one of the developers of the new Wilkes Mall. They have one 10-year old son, Jerome Stevenson Gambill. He is in the fifth grade at Wilkesboro Elementary School and attends the Wilkes Karate Academy, where he has attained the rank of Green Belt.

Carol Jean Bishop Bullis is employed at Ithaca Industries in Wilkesboro and is married to Glenn Bullis, who works at Church's Used Cars. They have six children: Teresa Gail, Vickie Lynn, Jeffrey Glenn, Patrick Jason, Scarlette Mariea, and Shannon Bledsoe.

Teresa is married to Kimmie Childress, who is in the U.S. Navy, stationed at Norfolk, Virginia. Teresa and her sister, Vickie Lynn live in Stanley County, N.C. Teresa works for an accounting firm in Charlotte. Vickie is employed by Stanley County School System as a Media Center Co-Ordinator. Jeffrey Glenn, a student at Wilkes Central Senior High School, is presently empolyed part-time at the Western Steer Steakhouse in Wilkesboro. Patrick Jason is a student at Woodward Junior High. The two youngest Bullis children, Scarlette Mariea and Shannon Bledsoe, are students at Wilkesboro Elementary School.

Bill Bishop Griffin is Secretary to the Secretary-Treasurer of Lowe's Food Stores, Inc. She is married to William Lindsay Griffin, owner of Blue Ridge Engraving and Griffin's Locksmith Shop. She has one son, Richard (Dick) Stevenson Powell. Dick is married to the former Linda Faye Minton. They have a son, Nicholas Stevenson, the youngest Wilkes County descendant of the Bledsoe-McEwen union. Dick is employed by Security Forces of Charlotte, Blue Ridge Engraving and Griffin's Locksmith Shop.

John Peter Bishop, the only son of Paul and Thelma, lives on the Bishop homeplace and is a farmer. He is married to the former Betty Porter. They have one daughter, Sandra Kaye, a student at Wilkes Central Senior High School and a part-time employee of McDonald's in Wilkesboro.

Paul passed away on September 19, 1978, and is buried in Mountlawn Cemetery. Thelma now makes her home with her son, Pete.

Nannie Bishop was married to Clayton Davis. Soon after the birth of a stillborn daughter, Nannie passed away on September 19, 1933. They were buried together at St. Paul's Episcopal Church in Wilkesboro. Their bodies were later moved to Mountlawn Cemetery.

Minnie Kathleen Bishop, the youngest daughter of Minnie and Charles Bishop, was graduated from Wilkesboro High School. She is married to William Morgan Roope. Morgan was a furniture retailer for forty years, during which time he was part owner in the Wilkes Furniture Exchange located on 10th Street in North Wilkesboro, The Ideal Furniture Store located on B Street in North Wilkesboro, and Mark-Down Furniture Company in Wilkesboro. Kathleen and Morgan have one daughter, Nannie Morguenya (called Butch). She is married to Richard (Dick) Tipton McNeil, Jr. Butch was graduated from the Woman's College of the University of North Carolina (now UNC-G), and taught at North Wilkes High School for six years. Dick is Secretary-Treasurer and Manager of The North Wilkesboro Coca-Cola Bottling Company. Butch and Dick have one daughter, Jacqueline Elizabeth (called Jackie), who has just completed her sophomore year at Meredith College in Raleigh, N.C. Next year, she will transfer to North Carolina State University, where she plans to major in Chemistry and Animal Science. Jackie owns and shows registered quarter horses.

Sources: Personal knowledge, grave markers.

— June Bishop Gambill
Jean Bishop Gambill
Bill Bishop Griffin
Morguenya Roope McNeil

E. M. BLACKBURN

359

E. M. Blackburn was born October 18, 1864, and died 27 November 1949, being a lifelong resident of Wilkes County. His father was E. Spencer Blackburn and was called Squire. He was a prominent Wilkes County citizen, having served a number of years as a justice of the peace, deputy sheriff, church leader and a member of the home guard during the Civil War. He was a man of strong convictions and principals from whom E. M. Blackburn received his many characteristics.

Mr. E. M. Blackburn was educated in public schools and attended Fairview College at Traphill and Moravian Falls Academy, where he later became an instructor. As a young man he also taught in the public schools. He later became a businessman, churchman, and civic leader. His career and influence figured largely in the building of North Wilkesboro from a village into a thriving city.

Soon after the founding of North Wilkesboro, Mr. Blackburn entered the mercantile business here and opened a store by the name of Absher, Hayes, and Blackburn Department Store. This store later became Absher and Blackburn clothing firm and for a period of more than thirty-five years was a widely known clothing firm.

In addition to the mercantile and real estate business, Mr. Blackburn was associated with other successful business enterprises and for a quarter of a century was a director of the Bank of North Wilkesboro, now the North Carolina National Bank.

Being one of the best known citizens of Wilkes County, Mr. Blackburn held a number of positions of leadership. In 1896 he was elected register of deeds for the county. He served in that office for two terms. Later he was mayor of North Wilkesboro and here he also served on the City Council and was a member of the city board of education as secretary.

In the First Baptist Church, Mr. Blackburn was for more than thirty years Sunday School Superintendent. He was a member of the

Mr. and Mrs. E.M. Blackburn.

board of deacons for several decades, being made a life member of the board.

He was also active in fraternal groups, being a Mason, Shriner and a member of the Knights of Phythias over a long period. He was also a charter member of the North Wilkesboro Kiwanis Club.

Mr. Blackburn was married to Miss Myrtle Edwards, daughter of David Robert Edwards of Wilkesboro. To this union five children were born: Robert Spencer, Ruby, Jeter, Margaret and John K., all of whom have died except the daughter, Ruby, who lives at the homeplace.

Sources: Family records, personal knowledge.

— Ruby Blackburn

SPENCER BLACKBURN

360

Spencer Blackburn was born 1831, died 1919. He was the son of Eli A. and Mary Caudill Blackburn. and married February 10, 1853, Elvira Wiles, born 1835 died 1927, daughter of Evan and Mary Prevette Wiles. Both are buried at Rock Creek Baptist Church Cemetery east of Hays.

Spencer served as a deputy sheriff, tax collector, census taker, justice of the peace, merchant and was a certified school teacher by the State of North Carolina. He was a member of Rock Creek Baptist Church and served for many years as church clerk. He owned a large tract of land on the south side of Roaring River in the Rock Creek community and some of his descendants still own some of it.

Spencer and Elvira had the following children: (1) Mary, born December 15, 1853, died March 4, 1913, married February 1872 Samuel Sebastian, born April 4, 1852, died June 13, 1901, son of Lewis and Rachel Adams Sebastian. In June 1901 Samuel was kicked by a mule he was working and died shortly afterwards. Mary was a very compassionate person, always doing things to help someone. She died of the measles in the winter of 1913. Samuel was a staunch supporter of the Baptist Church. They are buried at Rock Creek Baptist cemetery; (2) Sarah E., born 1855, married Patison Wood, son of Reubin and Nellie Johnson Wood, and lived near the fork of Roaring River; (3) Melinda Jane, born 1858, married John Henderson; (4) Nancy L. born 1860, married Jim Jordan and moved to Indiana; (5) Eli M. born October 18, 1864, died November 27, 1949. E. M. married Myrtle Edwards and lived in North Wilkesboro. (6) Z. G., born March 21, 1869, died November 30, 1891 in Bristol, Tennessee. He was buried there but his family removed his remains to Rock Creek Baptist Church. He was not married; (7) John, born 1872, married Mattie Jordan, lived awhile at Roaring River and moved to Indiana; (8) Alfonsa, born 1877, died 1879; (9) Clementine, born 1874, married Rev. John Burcham; (10) Rebecca, born 1879; married J.A. Sebastian, son of Zack and Caroline Shepherd Sebastian. J.A. and Rebecca lived in the Rock Creek area at the foot of Round Mountain.

J.A. and Rebecca Sebastian had two chil-

dren: Nilta, who taught school in the Wilkes County school system for many years, and Eugene, who worked with Holly Farms Poultry, but is now retired.

J.A. was very active in Rock Creek Baptist Church. He taught the men's Sunday School Class, served as a deacon and was clerk for several years.

Sources: Church records, Wilkes County records, Family members and records.

— Samuel E. Sebastian

WILLIAM BLACKBURN

361

William Blackburn was born in Virginia about 1764 and died in Wilkes County after 1850. His wife was Sarah. He is buried at Traphill behind the old homesite.

He first appeared in Wilkes County on the 1789 tax list. He was one of the first settlers of Traphill. Legend has it that Traphill got its name from it being the place where William set his traps to catch turkeys. He was a farmer-trapper and also had a tar kiln. His home was near the old Clarence Holbrook store.

In 1810, he was fined ten pounds for failing to report for jury duty.

It would seem that William's father was Augustine Blackburn, who lived in Wilkes County before William was here. William named a son Eli Austin, Austin being a short name for Augustine. There has been an Austin Blackburn in Wilkes for five generations.

In a letter written by Eli A. Blackburn, son of William, in 1877, he states that he had four brothers and four sisters. The nine children of William and Sarah were probably the following: (1) John, born 1788, married first Catherine Manard; second, Winnie Prevette; and third, Charlotte Hendrix. (2) William Burton, born March 26, 1896, died June 17, 1870, married Catherine Hannks. (3) Lambeth T. born 1804, died 1840, married Nancy Hanks. (4) Eli A., born 1806, died 1900, married first Mary Caudill, born 1812, died 1850, daughter of Abner and Jane Adams Caudill. Eli was a farmer and livestock dealer. He is buried at Bethany Baptist Church Cemetery. Mary is buried in the old Caudill family cemetery. Eli was in the Civil War and signed a Pledge of Allegiance to the Union after the war was over. Eli A. and Mary had nine children, and after her death he married Mrs. Mary Winfrey Holbrook, widow of Caleb Holbrook. (5) Mary, married Alexander Lyon (6) Nancy born 1791, married 1814, Joel Sparks. (7) Pheaby, born 1807, married Reubin Sparks, Jr. (8) Polly, born 1790, married 1808 Samuel Hanks (9) Sarah, born 1812, did not marry.

Eli A. and Mary Caudill Blackburn had the following children: (1) Thomas born 1829, died June 7, 1888, married Mary Holloway (2) Spencer, born 1831, died 1919, married February 19, 1853, Elvira Wiles, born 1835, died 1927, daughter of Evan and Mary Prevette Wiles (3) Sarah, born 1834, died 1908, was never married. She was called Aunt "Puss" by all her nieces and nephews. She was a seamstress and made tailor made men's suits. She is buried at Bethany Baptist Church. (4) William Calloway, born 1837, married 1963, Susan-

nah Brewer, born 1845, died 1904, daughter of Joel and Nancy Adams Brewer. Both are buried near New Light Baptist Church. (5) Martha, born 1839, married 1864 William Hampton Wiles. (6) Jesse, born 1843, married Mary Wood, daughter of John Wood. (7) Austin, born 1846. (8) Nancy, born 1848, married C. F. Childress (9) Eli, Jr. born 1851, died 1889, married first, Mary Jane Alexander and second, Sarah Alexander, her sister.

Eli, Jr. and Sarah had two children: Rhoda who married Lin Blackburn, and Marcus. They are buried at Bethany Church.

Sources: Wilkes County records, family members.

— Samuel E. Sebastian

ELIJAH STEELE BLAIR

362

Elijah Steele Blair was born in Caldwell County June 14, 1838. He came to Wilkes County from Watauga, where his family had moved, shortly after serving in the Confederate Army with rank of Captain. He was thereafter always known and called "Cap'n Blair".

He shortly thereafter married Sara Corinna Finley, May 17, 1870, daughter of William Waugh Finley. Her grandchildren enjoyed stories she told of Stoneman's raid when they marched through Wilkes destroying and burning everything in their path. She was sixteen at the time and is credited to saving much of the furniture in the home which they burned. One of the most valued pieces is a sofa which is being used today by one of her grandchildren. She often told the writer that she had no idea how she was able to get the heavy piece outside to safety.

The Blairs had seven children: Nellie, Cora, Tate, Frank, Walter, William and Henry.

Walter went to Texas as a young man, married Lucille Gibson and died young with no children. Cora died while still a young woman.

Nell married J.L. Clements and she died young also leaving two children, Corinne and a young baby, Gwyn, who died before he was a year old. Corinne married Howard Price, a druggist from Mooresville and they had two children, Blair and S. H. Price, Jr.

Tate married R. W. Gwyn who came as a young man from Elkin to be cashier of Bank of North Wilkesboro. For quite a while he was the youngest bank cashier in the state. It is said he could be compared to the modern computer as he was able to tell at a glance the total of several columns of figures.

The R. W. Gwyns had seven children: twins who died when a few months old and Frances who died at one year. Margaret married Carl Coffey, who was killed in a plane accident. He was an early plane enthusiast and owned and piloted his own all over the U.S., but was killed when his plane went down and burned near Ronda, N.C. They had two children, Carl Gwyn who married twice, Mary Bryson and later Patty Hawkes. Blair, who married Robert Yale.

Nell, married R. M. Brame, Jr., and they had three children: Nell Gwyn who married J.C. Parker, Jr. of Winston Salem, R. M. Brame III who married Bonnie Rhinehardt, and Richard Gwyn Brame who married Sheila Bondurant of Lincolnton, N.C.

Richard Walker Gwyn, Jr. and William Blair Gwyn were the second set of twins born to Tate and R.W. Gwyn. Richard married Suzanne Sauvage of Paris, France, they had two sons, Richard Gwyn III and Robert Paul, both single. Blair Gwyn married Florence Guigou from Valdese. They had four children: Carolyn, William, Roslyn and Mike; Carolyn married and later divorced Sam Bell; Roslyn married Peter Schmidt; Bill a lawyer in Wilson, N.C. and Mike a banker in Texas, both single.

Soon after moving to Wilkes "Cap'n Blair" bought all the land from Blair's Island in the Yadkin River to the land that is now the Fairplains section. His plan was for the town of North Wilkesboro to be located there. He thought the land was prettier there as well as more heathful, and it is said that it actually is. However, when the railroad was built that changed the plans for the location of the town.

The railroad provided a big bonus for the unmarried ladies of the community as it brought quite a few single men to Wilkes, several of whom became prominent lawyers in the town.

"Cap'n Blair" built his first home in the block where Carolina Business Machine is now located. He established a small private school on the grounds and the teachers lived in the home. The first teacher, Miss Mamie McElwee was an aunt of W. H. McElwee, Sr. The school closed when his children were grown. Later, when he needed a larger home, he cut the original house exactly in half and had each part moved about two or three blocks away to the site near the Bryce Caudill's home now on C Street one on each side of the street. He gave each of his two daughters a half, and they used these for rental property for several years.

The Blairs' three sons were: Frank who married Estelle Davis and had one son, F. P. Blair, Jr.; Will who married Alma Wright and no children; Colonel Henry Blair who never married.

"Cap'n Blair" died at St. Leo's Hospital in Greensboro, Jan 13, 1911. His wife died Jan. 2, 1924.

The Blair home was burned about 45 years ago and as it burned, two of his great grandchildren who were living there were also burned to death. The house was renovated and used again as a home for several years, but later demolished.

When it was new and being furnished, all the furniture was ordered from Baltimore, including a grand piano which has been rebuilt and is in use today by one of the great-great-grandchildren. The home which included a large barn, wood house, smoke house, ice house, well house, corn crib, schoolhouse and other farm buildings was the scene for many years of social gatherings, house parties and a steady stream of guests, some of whom visited for months. It witnessed a way of life which is completely foreign to today's world, and still there are some who sigh for those days that are gone forever.

Sources: Family Lore; Finley Book of Wilkes 1804-1981, City Cemetery.

— Mrs. R.M. Brame, Jr.

BLANKENSHIP

363

Mack Beech, Blankenship was born June 19, 1898, the son of William Pool and Lillie Novella Wiseman Blankenship. He married Bertha Estella Clanton Nov. 4, 1918. In 1921 or 22, Beech, his wife & 2 small children moved to N. Wilkesboro. His father and sister Darius, drove two wagons bringing their household items. Beech went to work for Mr. Clanton in the Cafe Business. He later bought the business and was sucessful until his death Aug. of 1964. Beech and Estella had 6 children: (1). Mary Beatrice, b. July 19, 1919, Albert Dixion Chandler June 2, 1941. They have one child, Marjorie Kay, b. Aug. 25, 1942, m. Bennet Edward Napier, April 20, 1968. They have one child, Bennet Edward Jr., b. July, 19, 1969. Mary Beatrice was widowed Dec. 30, 1968, and then m. Henry Hazel Clodfelter Oct. 1, 1976. They live in High Point, N.C.

(2). Wayne Q., born July 22, 1921, m. Ruth Kathleen Cook, April 1941. They have 5 children, Barbara Ann, b. April 9, 1942, and she m. a Handy. Virginia Sue, b. May 11, 1943, m. an Alexander. Mary Lucille, b. July 8, 1944, m. a Vannoy. Margaret Jane, b. July 23, 1945 m. a Stubbs. Stella Ruth, b. Aug. 3, 1946, m. a Church.

(3). Radford Harold, b. Sept. 15, 1923, m. Opal Ella Church on Dec. 28, 1941. They have 2 sons: Radford Harold, Jr., b. Jan. 30, 1943, m. Martha Jo Cabe, July, 1965. They had 2 sons, Nathan Keith, b. May 23, 1971, and Matthew Alan, b. June 1, 1973. Radford and Mary Jo have a Chiropractic Clinic in Statesville, N.C. Mike Church b. July 16, 1951, m. Rhonda Singleton. Mike is a dentist. Harold and Opal own Harold's Cafe' on 10th street in N. Wilkesboro;

(4) Helen Margaret, b. Aug. 9, 1926. She m. Francis Eugene Andrews on Oct. 25, 1947, and they had 2 children, Nancy Patricia, b. May 4, 1949, m. Robert Ashley Sept. 7, 1969. He is a newspaper editor and she is a psychologist. Robert Marvin, b. Mar. 25, 1959, m. Bennie Renee Felts, Aug. 3, 1980. Robert is a engineer;

(5) Marion Louise, b. Feb. 1, 1929, m. Wade Hamilton Palmer Mar. 7, 1947. They had one son Steven Wade, b. Jan. 31, 1953, m. Laura Ann Holbrook and had one son Joseph Wade. Louise and Wade work at City Florists in N. Wilkesboro, N.C.;

(6) Mack Beech Jr., b. Aug. 27, 1931, m. Mary Jo-Anne Sloan, Dec. 26, 1951. They had 3 children: Mack Beech III, born Mar. 20, 1957, Mark Sloan, b. Jan. 21, 1960, and Malinda Ann b. Oct. 1968. They live in Greensboro, N.C.

Q.B. Blankenship was b. in Alex. Co. Apr. 8, 1879, son of William Thomas and Catherine McIntosh Blankenship, m. Lara Warren Dec. 5, 1894. They have one child Elsie Mae, b. Nov. 7, 1896. In the early 20's he went to N. Wilkesboro from Montana. He then m. Gertrude Canner and they have one child Ruth. Q.B. was successful in the Cafe' business until his death Feb. 26, 1944.

Hunter Maude Blankenship b. July 7,

1896, m. Bertha Bowers Jan. 26, 1917. Hunter was a brother to Beech, Quez, and Walter. He went to N. Wilkesboro in 1938. He ran a cafe and farmed in Wilkesboro. Hunter and Bertha had 10 children: Vera Evelena, b. Nov. 13, 1918; William Pernell, b. Mar. 28, 1919; Mildred, Sept. 22, 1920; J.C., born Feb. 19, 1922; Odelia, b. May 20, 1924; Francis, b. June 10, 1927; Rachel, b. July 22, 1929; Rebecca, b. Oct. 11, 1933; Lillie Mae, b. Nov. 13, 1934; and Boddy, b. Mar. 14, 1936. When Hunter and Bertha moved back to Alex. Co. Pernell remained in Wilkes Co. with his wife Wilma Higgins and 4 children: Earnest William, Brenda Kay, Jimmy Gwyn, and Danny. Pernell died May 6, 1974, and Danny died Mar. 29, 1978, in Wilkes Co.

Quez Waitsel, b. Mar. 3, 1891, brother to Beech, m. Julie Barnes. They moved to N. Wilkesboro in the early 20's. Quez went to work with Q.B. and then Beech later opened his own cafe. Walter could play any musical instrument and his aunts, Darius and Daphne had a string band until Pool died in 1931. Then, Walter and his family moved to Belmont, N.C. In 1944, Quez's health was poor and he asked Walter and his family to help in the cafe. So in Dec. of 1944 William Walter, b. Oct. 11, 1904, moved to N. Wilkesboro with his wife Letha Mae Stewart, b. Nov. 4, 1901, and m. June 18, 1925. Quez died in Apr. 8, 1945. Walter and Letha's children are Lucille Virginia, b. Mar. 5, 1926, and Betty Sue, b. Feb. 4, 1929.

Lucille m. Frank Theodore Kaczor, Aug. 5, 1944. He was born Sept. 27, 1917. (Polish descent). Their children are: (1). Anna Mae, b. Sept. 9, 1945, m. Wyndell Alfred Hollar Nov. 2, 1963. They have 3 children: Sharon Renee', b. May 8, 1966; Kathryn Ann, b. Jan. 18, 1970; & Brian Wyndell, b. Nov. 13, 1971; (2). Frank Theodore, Jr., b. June 24, 1947, d. June 28, 1969. (3). Joseph, b. July 25, 1950, d. July 25, 1950; (4). Lucille Virginia, b. Mar. 22, 1952, m. Willard Briggs Sept. 22, 1977. They have a son Frank Alan b. Dec. 7, 1980; (5). Rose Marie, b. Jan. 8, 1955, m. Paul Stephen Lail Dec. 23, 1972. They have 2 daughters, Stephanie Marie, b. Nov. 3, 1973, & Paula Annette, b. Aug. 14, 1975; (6). Richard, b. Jan. 25, 1958, m. Cathy Ann Loving on Sept. 16, 1978. They have one daughter, Erica Ann, b. Mar. 21, 1981.

Betty Sue Blankenship m. William Gaither (Jack) Treadway Sept. 2, 1945. He was born Feb. 21, 1925, the son of Rufus and Alma Kerley Treadway of Wilkes Co. They have 2 sons: William Gaither, Jr., b. May 2, 1947, d. June 16, 1964. Gary Vinson, b. Dec. 3, 1950, m. Kathy Suzanne Johnson Aug. 29, 1971. They have 1 son Chad Johnson, b. April 10, 1979. They all live in Wilkes Co.

Sources: Interviews with family members, gravestones, and personal knowledge.

— Lucille Balnkenship Kaczor

BLEVINS-GAMBILL

364

Since the year 1901, few families have had a wider or better influence in Wilkes County than that of Oliver Franklin Blevins and wife Sarah

Oliver Franklin and Sarah Ann Gambill Blevins.

Ann Gambill Blevins. It was in that year that the couple moved from their mountain farm in Walnut Grove township to Wilkesboro so that their children could attend better schools.

Both Mr. and Mrs. Blevins descended from Colonial settlers of the county. The first Blevins emigrated from Wales. Mr. Blevins, the son of the Reverend Calloway Blevins and Lucinda Caudill Blevins, was a descendant of the Joines and Caudill families. His ancestry included many ministers of the Gospel.

Oliver was born in Alleghany County March 19, 1867. He spent his early manhood in the mountains of northern Wilkes, where his father pastored many Baptist churches. He was a farmer, lumberman, and a teacher of singing schools. After moving to Wilkesboro he suffered the loss of a leg in an accident at the A.M. Church Lumber Plant, where he was employed. He, as time moved along, held many positions of trust: Deacon in the Wilkesboro Baptist Church, Register of Deeds of Wilkes County for eight years, assistant Cashier at the former Deposit and Savings Bank, a member of the Wilkesboro School Board, assistant to Postmaster Rev. W.E. Linney, Clerk of the Town of Wilkesboro. He was influential in securing better schools and the first Federal Court House in the county. Though always laboring under a physical handicap, Mr. Blevins had a happy disposition, a fine musical talent and an infinite faculty for making friends. He died December 23, 1935. His funeral was on a snowy, sleety Christmas Day. The church was filled to overflowing with people from all walks of life, attesting to their great love and respect for him.

Sarah Ann Gambill Blevins was a daughter of William Bourne Gambill and Elizabeth Brown Gambill. She was a direct descendant of Captain Andrew Vannoy, Thomas Joines, and Captain Samuel Johnson of Revolutionary War Fame. Her father served in the Civil War, and members of her family served in both World War I and World War II. She was a justly proud patriot. An honest Christian, she spent her life rearing her eleven children and four of her grandchildren. She was intent on education and all but one of these fifteen children had some education on the college level. The oldest son, the Reverend R. Presley Blevins, graduated from Wake Forest College and received further degrees from the University of Pennsylvania and Crozier Theological Seminary at Camden, New Jersey. The Blevins home became a "place to stay" to attend high school in Wilkesboro for quite a few young men and women, children of former neighbors in Walnut Grove Township. Mrs. Blevins died November 14, 1946. The Reverent Howard Ford, minister at her funeral, said her "price was far above rubies."

There are now about one hundred descendants of Mr. and Mrs. Blevins. They include teachers, dentists, church leaders, nurse, engineers, bankers, artists, authors and musicians. Surely the good works of Oliver and Sarah Ann "do follow after them."

The four surviving members of the immediate family are Mrs. Norman O. Smoak (Savannah), Mrs. Oliver McNeil Proffit (Ursula), Mrs. William T. Ritchie, Jr. (Elizabeth), and Mrs. Lloyd Pardue (Helen).

Sources: *"The Ancestry Of Della Blevins Graham:,* in Genealogical Branch of State Library, Raleigh, N.C. in Library of NSDAR, Nat. DAR numbers: 335930, 326910, 463194 and 463193; Letters of Allen Poe to Della Blevins Graham, 1958.

— Ursula B. Proffit

EDMOND BOAZ

365

Edmond Boaz, son of Thomas and Agnes Boaz, was born 1745 in Ireland. He emigrated to America with his parents and four small siblings in 1748. His father, Thomas Boaz was born in Scotland September 27, 1721, died September 13, 1791, in America. Young Thomas grew to manhood in Scotland and became a Presbyterian Dissenter. Thomas left his native Scotland and went to Ireland where he met and married Agnes, who died July 1823. Thomas and Agnes and five young children sailed for America, landing in Virginia about 1747. They settled in Pittsylvania Co., Va. where they lived out their lives.

Thomas Boaz gave his means and services as a surveyor and juror during the Revolutionary War. Six of his sons fought in that war. Thomas is listed as a patriot of Pittsylvania County. Thomas and Agnes were the parents of twelve children, the first five being born in Ireland. They were: Thomas, Jr, Archibald, Edmond, Daniel, Gemima, James, Shadrack, Meshack, Mary, Abednego, Agnes and Nellie.

Edmond Boaz I, son of Thomas and Agnes, grew to manhood in Pittsylvania County, Va. and was a young farmer with landed property of his own when he decided to move to Wilkes County, N.C. by 1778, when he sold some of his land to his brother, Shadrack. On September 20, 1787, he received a land grant from North Carolina for services rendered in the Revolutionary War.

Edmond I, was married twice, his first wife unknown, but they had at least one child, Thomas, born May 25, 1785, in Wilkes County. In the 1790's Edmond I returned to Pittsylvania Co., Va., where he married his second wife, Sallie Thurmon, daughter of John and Nancy Thurman on October 3, 1796. Their children were: Edmond A., born 1797, died in Tennessee, married September 24, 1821 Elizabeth Booker. They pioneered to Tennessee and settled on his father's Military grant; John, born 1800, married Mildred Breedlove January 4, 1826; James, born April 17, 1804, died 1878, married first Sarah Booker in 1823, and second Elizabeth Prince; Mary married Corbin H. Francis.

Sources: *Thomas Boaz Fam. in America* by Hiram A. Boaz; gravestones, DAR magazine; Pittsylvania Co, Va. and Wilkes Co. N.C. records.

— Ruth Cunningham Morgan

THOMAS and FANNY PARKS BOAZ
366

Thomas Boaz was born May 25, 1785, in Wilkes County, N.C. He was the son of Edmond Boaz I, and grandson of Thomas Boaz I and wife Agnes. Fanny Parks was born May 27, 1791, in Wilkes County. She was the daughter of Aaron and Oney Stubblefield Parks. Thomas and Fanny were married November 22, 1814, in Lincoln County, Tennessee where both the Boaz and Parks families had migrated.

In Wilkes County the Parks and Boaz families were neighbors. They settled together in Tennessee. The Aaron Parks family came to Tennessee in 1809. It is believed that Thomas Boaz came with them or came soon thereafter.

Thomas and Fanny reared a large family. They were farmers and member of Mt. Olivet Primitive Baptist Church. They had the following children: (1) Elizabeth P., born September 15, 1815, married John G. Broadaway October 18, 1931. Elizabeth died in 1868 in Lincoln County; (2) Edmond A., born February 3, 1817, died September 16, 1882, married February 4, 1840, Elizabeth Hoots, born September 12, 1820 in Surry County, N.C., daughter of Jacob and Mary Renegar Hoots; (3) Aaron, born November 25, 1819, died January 25, 1848, unmarried; (4) Oney born August 1, 1821, died September 28, 1827, unmarried; (5) Sarah, born October 21, 1823; (6) Martha Ann, born November 7, 1825, died November 2, 1838, unmarried; (7) Parthenia, born December 12, 1827; (8) Robert M., born July 8, 1831, and was in the Civil War (9) Mary Jane, born March 28, 1834, died December 9, 1857, unmarried.

Edmond A. Boaz was my great-grandfather. His wife, Elizabeth Hoots, came to Lincoln County with her parents in 1821 and settled near the Parks and Boaz families. Edmond A. had orchards and vineyards and many bee hives. He and Elizabeth had the following children: (1) William Newton, born 1841, died November 8, 1916, married May 4, 1865 Lucy Thurman. He was a Confederate soldier; (2) John W., born April 25, 1842, died July 29, 1917 during the flu epidemic, married Susan Largen, and was a soldier of the Confederacy; (3) Thomas Aaron, born December 1843, died April 8, 1818, married March 14, 1864, O'Leatha Ann Thompson. He was the family historian; (4) James Archibald, born October 23, 1845, died February 7, 1931, married Jennie Allen; (5) Henry Doak, born September 24, 1849, died August 17, 1923, married August 15, 1872, Louisa Buntley.

Henry Doak Boaz was a well read man, served as deacon in his church, was a farmer, a Democrat and a Baptist. Louisa Buntley was a daughter of Jacob B. and Elizabeth Forrester Buntley. They were my grandparents. They had the following children: (1) Mattie E., my mother was born May 18, 1873, died in 1957, married August 26, 1893 John Wilson Cunningham. She belonged to the sixth generations of my Boaz ancestors. My father was a farmer. They were Baptist and Democrats. My mother became totally blind in her last few

Mattie Boaz Cunningham.

years. During her widowhood she lived with her daughter Ruth C. Morgan.

Mattie E. and John Wilson Cunningham have the following children:

(1) Ottie Franklin, born 1894, died 1974, married 1918 Lizzie D. Warden; (2) Alma Lee, born November 1895. (3) John Henry, born February 27, 1897, married Elton Waggoner in 1919. He is still living; (4) Charlie Wilson born January 27, 1902, died in 1979, married Elise Rives in 1924; (5) Ruth Mae, the compiler of this story, born November 2, 1906, in the community where I still live. I have a B.S. degree from TCW, taught 32 years and worked for Tennessee agencies. Married 1941, Charles Windle Morgan of Overton County, Tn. We had one son Robert Morgan, who met his death in a automobile accident leaving a small son.

Prior to his marriage to Barbara Ann Brown, Robert attended M.T.U. We are Presbyterians. My hobbies are painting, sewing and genealogy. Have been regent of the King's Mountain Messenger Chapter DAR through Thomas Boaz I, my ancestor.

(6) Georgie Lillian Cunningham, born June 10, 1908.

Sources: Hiriam A. Boaz book; Bible of Thomas and Fanny Parks Boaz; Bible of Henry Doak Boaz; family knowledge.

— Ruth Cunningham Morgan

PETER JOYNER BRAME
367

Although Peter Joyner Brame was a comparatively late-comer to the town of North Wilkesboro, arriving in the year 1919, he and his family made a large contribution to the business, civic, religious, and cultural life of the community.

He brought his large family to North Wilkesboro from Winston-Salem by way of the "new" Southern Railway, even bringing along the cow "Daisy". He bought a large house on

E Street from Mr. Genio Cardwell and established his family there. After Mr. Brame's death in 1964 the property was bought by the First Baptist Church, the house was razed and the land became a church parking lot. During the years that the Brame family lived there the home was always a center of family gatherings and offered unusual hospitality to friends and neighbors.

Peter Joyner Brame was born May 25, 1868 in Franklin County, son of William Anderson Brame (1826-1894) and Ella Oschia Joyner (1837-1926). His early life was spent in Franklin County. During his boyhood the family moved to Trinity in Randolph County where the boys attended Trinity College (now Duke University at Durham), and both parents taught at Trinity College. His father was also a minister of the Methodist Episcopal Church.

When he was about 18 years of age Mr. Brame came to Winston-Salem and worked in the tobacco business of T.L. Vaughn. Later he joined the Owen Drug Co. and after the death of Mr. Owen, the original owner, he bought the company and operated it very successfully until he sold it in 1919 when he moved to North Wilkesboro to join his brother Marvin in the Brame Drug Co.

Peter Joyner Brame and Mary Gertrude Watson were married in Winston-Salem on Nov. 17, 1892. Mrs. Brame was the daughter of Cyrus Barksdale Watson (1844-1916) and Amelia Henley Watson (1846-1907). Mr. Watson was an eminent lawyer of Winston-Salem. He ran for governor of North Carolina and was defeated by a close friend, Robert Glenn. Mary Watson Brame (1872-1947) was educated at Salem Female Academy and College and received a degree in music. Mr. and Mrs. Brame celebrated their Golden Wedding with a reception for family and friends on Nov. 17, 1942.

Mr. Brame was a business leader in the town of North Wilkesboro until his retirement in 1946. He served on the town Board of Commissioners and on the Welfare Board for many years. He remained active in his retirement, giving attention to his farm property and other interests.

In early life Mr. and Mrs. Brame were members of Centenary Methodist Church in Winston-Salem where Mr. Brame was Sunday School Superintendent for many years. After the move to North Wilkesboro they were faithful members of the First Methodist Church there, sharing their musical talents with the congregation and were leaders in the church organizations. Mr. Brame served on the church Board of Stewards and for many years was the teacher of the Ladies Adult Bible Class.

The following children were born to Mr. and Mrs. Brame: Peter Joyner, Jr. (died 1946), William Anderson, Dorothy Dillard (died 1968), John Thomas (died 1970), Cyrus Watson (died 1978), Joseph Wilson (died 1976), and Ella Cassandra.

Peter Joyner, Jr. married Grace Thomas Price of Charlotte. Their daughter, Nancy Ann, married James Murray Dumbell of Charlotte. There are two great-grandchildren, James Murray Dumbell, Jr. and Grace Elizabeth Dumbell. James, Jr. married Elizabeth Ann Griffin. There are two great-

Mr. and Mrs. Peter Joyner Brame on their Golden Wedding, Nov. 17, 1942.

great-grandchildren, William Griffin Dumbell and James Brian Dumbell.

William Anderson married Rebecca Pfohl Landquist of Winston-Salem and their children are: William Anderson, Jr. and Mary Ann Brame. William, Jr. married Vanya Lee Forehand of North Wilkesboro and Mary Ann married Michael Neil Finger of Jonesville. There are four great-grandchildren: William Anderson Brame, III, Elizabeth Michelle Brame, Angela Rebecca Brame, and Michael Neil Finger, Jr.

John Thomas married Virginia Porter Hix of North Wilkesboro and their children are: Virginia Hix Brame, Marticia Folger Brame (died 1942), John Thomas Brame, Jr. and Peter Joyner Brame. Virginia married William Robert Story of Wilkesboro. There are two great-grandchildren: William Robert Story, Jr. and Dorothy Cassandra Story.

Cyrus Watson married Mary Lina Forester of North Wilkesboro and their children are: Linda Forester Brame (died 1980), Cyrus Watson Brame, Jr., Gerald Forester Brame (died 1949). There are three great-grandchildren: Karen Elizabeth Brame, Cyrus Watson Brame, III, Amanda Christine Brame.

Sources: Family Bible, Family Records, Personal Knowledge.

— Virginia Hix Brame

THE ROBERT MARVIN BRAME, SR. FAMILY

368

Dr. Robert Marvin Brame was born on May 14, 1876 in Franklin Co., N.C., the youngest child of William Anderson and Ella Oscia Joyner Brame. Both parents were teachers, and W.A. Brame was also a circuit rider in the Methodist Episcopal Church. Dr. Brame attended Trinity College, Randolph Co., where his family was living, and then Dr. Simpson's School in Raleigh from which he received his degree in pharmacy.

Dr. Brame was working in Winston, N.C. at Dr. V.O. Thompson's drug store when he met Lula Gwyn Hester. She was born May 17, 1882, the second child of John William and Elizabeth Tesh Hester of Lewisville, N.C., where John Hester was a farmer and livery stable operator. She was educated at West Bend Academy and Salem Girl's School. She was an excellent horsewoman and enjoyed riding (side-saddle, of course!) all her life.

Dr. and Mrs. Brame met when he went to her family farm to hunt. He was an excellent shot and enjoyed quail and duck hunting all his life. It is family legend that Mrs. Brame really captured Dr. Brame's attention during a hunt at her family farm, when she accidently almost shot him in the leg!

The couple were married on May 2, 1902 and lived in Winston for two years, during which time their first child was born.

Dr. Brame began traveling to Wilkes Co. for Dr. Thompson in 1900, and in 1902 he bought

Dr. Robert Marvin Brame, Sr.

a drug store here. After commuting for several years he moved his family to North Wilkesboro in late 1904 and operated Brame Drug Store for the remainder of his life, in later years with his sons. He also operated Brame Wholesale Drug Company for many years, manufacturing such popular remedies as *Brame's Vapomentha Croup and Pneumonia Salve, Brame's Cream Linament* (''good for man or beast''), *Brame's Baby Bowel Medicine* and *Brame's Pain Knocker.*

Dr. and Mrs. Brame were always active in their community and in their church, First Methodist of North Wilkesboro. Dr. Brame was a life-long Methodist, but Mrs. Brame was reared in the Baptist faith, and joined the Methodist church with her husband. Dr. Brame was a community leader and was an early advocate of municipal waterworks and paved streets in North Wilkesboro. Mrs. Brame was a charter member of the Friday Afternoon Book Club, organized in 1907, which is the oldest club in North Wilkesboro.

Dr. and Mrs. Brame were the parents of nine children!

Elizabeth Oscia — born June 4, 1903. Lib attended Salem and Queens Colleges and the University of Virginia. In 1926 she married Eugene Sydnor Spainhour of Wilkesboro. They have lived in Elkin, N.C. for many years. They have no children.

Lula Hester Brame (Mrs. R.M., Sr.).

Robert Marvin, Jr. — born January 26, 1906. Bob attended UNC and worked with his father before opening Red Cross Pharmacy in North Wilkesboro in 1937. He married Nell Blair Gwyn of N. Wilkesboro in 1930. They have three children: Nell Gwyn Parker (Mrs. James C., Jr.) of Winston-Salem, Robert Marvin III and Richard Gwyn Brame, both of N. Wilkesboro. Bob and Nell have five grandchildren. Bob is semi-retired.

Mary Cassandra — born April 26, 1908. Mary attended Davenport College before marrying Richard Wright Sloop in 1926. They had two sons: Richard Brame Sloop of Dunn Loring, Va., and Roger Hester Sloop of Rural Hall,

R.M. Brame Family, l. to r., front: Bill, Phil, Becky. Middle: Mrs. R.M. Brame (with Lula Hester on her lap), Dr. Brame (with Ella Joyner on his lap), Mrs. Ella Joyner Brame, mother of Dr. Brame and Mrs. Cassandra B. Albea, sister of Dr. Brame. Back: Mary, Ruth, Lib and Bob.

N.C. Mary and Dick were divorced in 1933 and she married George Gale Vlk in 1942. They lived in Washington, D.C. for many years but are now retired and living in Enfield, N.C. Mary has seven grandchildren.

Ruth Hester — born June 1, 1910. Ruth was educated at West Hampton College and married Sloane Waller Payne of Taylorsville in 1937. She has made her home there ever since. Sloane died in 1970. There are three children: Barbara Brame Nanney (Mrs. Donald) of Miami, Fla., Sloane W. Jr., of Moretown, Vt. and Robert Clinton of Chapel Hill, N.C. Ruth has three grandchildren.

William John — born February 19, 1913. Bill was educated at ASU, George Washington University and Springfield (Mass.) College of Pharmacy. He served in the US Navy, CPhm, from 1942-45. He married Martha Reed Warlick of Newton in 1951 and they have one daughter: Elizabeth Brandon Brame of Chapel Hill, N.C. Bill is semi-retired from Brame Drug, which he operated with his brother Phil.

Phillip Augustus — born January 30, 1915. Phil received his degree in pharmacy from UNC-CH. He served in the US Merchant Marines as a Lt. from 1942-45. He married Earline Weisner of Waldo, Fla., in 1945 and they have three children: Dr. Phillip Marvin and Arthur Weisner Brame, both of North Wilkesboro and Susan Earline Brame of Winston-Salem. Phil is still a practicing pharmacist.

Rebecca Louise — born August 28, 1917. Becky is a retired teacher. She received her degree from Salem College and, in 1941, married William Preston Ingram of Taylorsville, where they have always made their home. They had two daughters: Elizabeth Brame Ingram, who died in 1972, and Molly Preston Ingram, a pharmacist, of Greensboro.

Ella Joyner — born December 24, 1919. Ella attended Salem College and USC. She married Lawrence Richter Toburen of Manhattan, Kan., in 1942. She and Toby live in Win- ston-Salem and have four children: L.R. Toburen, Jr. of Winston-Salem, William Brame Toburen of Raleigh, Luanne Taylor (Mrs. Leonard) and Gwendolyn Horn (Mrs. Larry), both of Winston-Salem. Ella and Toby have five grandchildren. Ella is a realtor.

Lula Hester — born August 26, 1921. Lula attended Greensboro College and served in the WACS from 1943-45. Lula (Harrison) is divorced and lives in Morganton, N.C. where she is retired after working there many years as a receptionist and bookkeeper. She has no children.

Sources: Family Bibles, gravestones, interviews with family members, newspaper clippings, family tradition and personal knowledge.

— Mrs. William J. Brame

JOHN BREWER

369

John Brewer was born in 1789 in Randolph County. His wife, Keziah Johnson was born in Chatham County, also in 1789. They moved to Wilkes Co. and lived about one-half mile from the Rock Creek Rd. on the Bethany Ford Road. It is said that they both are buried on the old Zoah Myers' homestead. He was at one time clerk of Rachel Baptist Church and later was clerk of Rock Creek Baptist Church, a position he held until his death.

John and Keziah's children were: (1) Joel, (2) Mary (3) Jane, (4) John Andrew, (5) Nathan, (6) James, (7) Eli, (8) Henry, (9) Josiah.

I am a decendant of Joel Brewer who was born in Wilkes County in 1818 and Nancy Adams Brewer born also in Wilkes County in 1820. Nancy could not read nor write, yet she and Joel owned approximately 200 acres of land. They reared their children in the Rock Creek community on the Little Mountain Road or some folks call it the Greenhorn Road.

Their children were: (1) James, (2) Dianah, A., (3) Saryan M., (4) Susanah, (5) Charles L.N., (6) Mary Jane.

James, born December 9, 1840, died in 1862, was my great-great grandfather, and he married Malinda Wiles, born 1837 — died June 6, 1891. Her parents were Evan Wiles and Mary Prevette. They only had two children, both boys; one named Ambrose born July 2, 1858 — died February 24, 1935, and Joel who married Nancy Shipwash.

James at the age of 21, eager to serve his country went off to fight in the Civil War as a Confederate. He left behind a young wife and a son aged two years and another son aged six months.

During the month of December, 1862, he wrote a letter home to his parents telling of his recuperation from the measles and of the hardships of war. Also he wished "the worst I ever did" to be able to meet at Rachel Church before he died. He never made it through, because he never completely recovered and died somewhere in an army hospital.

His wife, Malinda, found it difficult to rear two children on her own so she entrusted their welfare to their Grandfather, Joel Brewer. Later, she married John W. Emerson. But Joel Brewer reared his two young grandsons.

On April 15, 1880, Ambrose Brewer married Mary Alice Emerson, born June 5, 1860 — died January 5, 1938. He was a teacher and a County Commissioner and also served as a Deacon at Rock Creek Baptist Church. They lived on the Brewer Farm on the Greenhorn Road. Their children were: (1) Dora Belle, (2) Willie Alexander, (3) Mary Elizabeth, (4) Nancy Malinda, (5) James Nathan, (6) John Walter, (7) Everette Olin, (8) Bertha Estelle, (9) Ambrose Clifton.

My grandparents, Ambrose Clifton, born March 28, 1900 — died October 31, 1970, and Lola Haynes, born June 2, 1903, were married on April 19, 1924. She was the daughter of William Augustus Haynes and Cornelia Sebastian. They lived with his parents for several years, and all three of their children were born there on the Brewer Farm.

The names of their children are: Marjorie Alice born January 23, 1925, William Ambrose born September 5, 1926, Charles Max born September 6, 1932.

In several years they moved to Cleveland, Ohio for a while and Pa Pa Brewer worked in a defense plant up there. Later they moved back home for a while and finally settled in Walnut Cove in Stokes County where Pa Pa worked for the state as a bridge foreman, and later operated a small country store.

But before Grandmommie and Pa Pa moved to Walnut Cove, my parents were married. William Ambrose Brewer and Elna Mae Coe, born September 30, 1928, were married on December 10, 1946, here in Wilkes County. She is the daughter of Numa Adrum Coe and Lily Irene Campbell of Wilkes County.

Then my parents moved away to Stokes County, where we children were born, and in later years moved to Salem — Roanoke, Virginia.

First to be born was Deborah Denise, born December 23, 1948; second, myself, Tresa Mae, born January 4, 1951; and last, Jolene born December 10, 1955.

We lived in several places. Dad is a tool and die craftsman. Mom worked in a hosiery mill for a while, and later when we moved to Wilkes Co. in 1965, she went to work for Reynolds' Tobacco Company.

I met Barry Eugene Splawn, born June 19, 1950, in November, 1965, and three years later, on September 8, 1968, we were married at Bethel Branch Church of Christ. He is the son of James Robert Splawn and Texie Louella Harris.

We are now living on the old homeplace of my Great Grandfather William Augustus Haynes. (See his history.)

Also we have three children: Charity Jo born October 30, 1970; Yancey Luke born October 20, 1973; and Hannah Kathleen born August 15, 1978.

Barry is self-employed as an insulation and a guttering contractor. I am a homemaker. Some of our interests are archery and fishing.

Sources: Family Bible, census records, gravestones, interviews with family members, personal knowledge.

— Tresa Brewer Splawn

BROCK FAMILY

370

Raney Wootson Brock was born about 1765 in Virginia, bought land near Warrior Creek in Wilkes County in 1798. In 1805 he purchased land along Cub Creek and moved to the area that has come to be known as Brocktown, near Moravian Falls.

The early Federal Census lists him as being the only Brock family in Wilkes. He and his wife, Nancy, who was born in Virginia, had one daughter and several sons, the youngest of which was Raney Wootson Brock, Jr. born in 1817. He married Agnes Ragsdell in 1848, and lived near his parents on one hundred and fifty acres along Cub Creek which he purchased from his father in 1852.

Raney, Jr. and Agnes reared three sons: John M., Raney Wootson, "Bud", and William, "Billy", and two daughters, Nancy Anne and Mary Jane.

Raney served on the side of the Confederacy in the Civil War.

His middle son, Bud, was born in 1851 and married Edith Lane in 1874. They lived along Cub Creek and reared ten children: Thomas Jefferson, Charles Parks, Joseph E., Isaac C., Gertrude, Reiney Wootson, James F., Bessie, Mary Jane, and Clementine.

Thomas Jefferson Brock was born 1876, married Hattie Arbelle Revis in 1896, and after living awhile in Illinois, they settled in Wilkes County and reared five children in the Brocktown area: Fred Revis, Mable Clementine (Yarbrough), Fleet O'Day, Joseph Shafter and Thomas Mack.

Sources: Personal knowledge.

— Agnes Craven Brock

CHARLES P. and NORA COONE BROCK

371

Charles Parks Brock was born Dec. 26, 1877 to Reiney Wootson Brock IV and Mary Jane Bebber Brock at their home in the heart of the Brocktown section of Pores Knob. The home still stands and is now occupied by the widow of the youngest son of R.W. IV, Isaac C. Brock. They were farmers, and R.W. did some carpenter work. R.W. IV (Bud) was born Dec. 27, 1851 and died July, 1937. He was born near where he spent his entire life to R.W. III and Agnes Ragsdale Brock. Mary Jane Brock was born Jan. 18, 1856 to John and Rebecca Irene Joines Bebber. She died in Aug., 1938. They were buried in Walnut Grove Cemetery. They were members of Walnut Grove Baptist Church as were their parents.

Charles P. Brock was married to Nora Coone, Dec. 28, 1904 at the home of one of Nora's sisters, Mrs. P.F. Lenderman in Wilkesboro. She was the youngest child of Henry A. and Mary Maria Childress Coone. She was born in Alexander Co., July 1, 1885 and came with her parents to Wilkes Co. in 1888. They were farmers.

Charles and Nora Brock raised five daughters: Nellie Mae (Mrs. C.M. Ashley), Eula Blanche (Mrs. J.M. Bentley), Miss Bessie Leona Brock, Mary Edna (Mrs. J.B. Parlier), and Nora Pauline (Mrs. Edmon Edsel).

Charlie bought his grandmother Bebber's land and built his home in 1904 where he and his wife spent the rest of their lives. The home is now owned and occupied by a daughter, Miss Bessie Brock.

He farmed, raised fruit and was in the lumber business. He was a deacon in Walnut Grove Baptist Church for many years. He died Dec. 28, 1937. Nora C. Brock died Jan. 11, 1967. They were buried in Walnut Grove Cemetery.

Sources: Personal knowledge and family records.

— Mrs. Eula Brock Bentley

William Thomas and Dovie Jane Brock Joines.

RAINEY WOOTSON BROCK FAMILY
372

According to the Quaker Records of Virginia, Rainey (Rany) Brock, born ca 1765, and Nancy Rich, born ca 1777, the daughter of Nimrod Rich, were married 6 November 1795 in Hinshaw, Virginia. Why they migrated and settled in Wilkes County is not known, but in 1800, Rainey Brock is listed in Wilkes County. There are two known children: (1) Nancy, born 4 April 1816, died 15 February 1898 and (2) Rainey Wootson III, born ca 1820, married Agnes Elizabeth Ragsdale 28 December 1848 and died in 1863.

Rainey and Agnes Brock had five children: (1) John M., born 4 January 1850, married Nancy Louisa Hood, died 16 September 1916 (2) Rainey Wootson IV, born 27 December 1851, married Mary Jane Bebber 27 August 1874, died 22 June 1937 (3) Nancy Ann, born 1857, married George Pearson (4) Mary J., born ca 1859, married Frank Wallace (5) William V., born ca 1862, never married.

John M. Brock, the eldest son, and Louisa Hood Brock were my great grandparents. They had four children: (1) John Columbus, born 21 March 1875, married Almedia Lowe, died 10 November 1952, (2) Dovie Jane, my grandmother, born 12 September 1882, married William Thomas Joines 18 April 1909 (See Ezekiel Joines Family.), died 12 April 1962, (3) Lizzie, married first a Duncan and then Arthur Earp, (4) Ila Lou, born 8 May 1888, married Lee Edsel, died 6 June 1920.

My grandmother, Dovie Jane Brock Joines, had a beautiful soul and has achieved immortality in a sense because she lives in so many of us who knew her. She was a fine Christian woman in the purest sense: she refused to gossip, visited the sick and shut-ins, attended church each time the doors opened and had a patience and love that endeared her to us in a special way. Though not well educated, she was able to sort through the trivial and discover what was important in living a full life. My grandmother's faith in God comforted her and she, like Paul, fought a good fight and finished the course.

We still miss her.

Sources: Quaker Record of Virginia, records in Wilkes County Courthouse and the Wilkes Genealogical Library, grave markers, interviews with family members.

— Peggy Joines Martin

LEE S. BROOKS
373

Lee S. Brooks was born March 17, 1850 in the State of Tenn., died Jan. 28, 1922. In early manhood he came to Wilkes County, met, and married Rachel Sophronia Rash, daughter of Wm. (Billy) and Margaret (Peggy) Kilby Rash. To this union were born seven children: Mattie, married C.W. Wallace; Roslyn (Rosa), first married, Gaither Farrington, second marriage, Ed Pearson, third marriage, Will Holcomb, and fourth marriage, Jim Eller; Mary, first married Needham Ingram, second marriage, William Craven; Florence, married Ralph Gaither; Roby, married Roxie Bumgarner;

Lee S. and Sophronia R. Brooks.

Anna, married C.W. Wallace; (Anna died in early life and her widower married Mattie); Claude, married Cilla Rhoades. Lee was a farmer and a digger of wells. He was a devout Christian, having taught Sunday School for many years.

Source: Family Bible, gravestones, family inquiries.

— Sidney Johnston

WILEY MATTHEW BROOKS
374

Wiley Matthew Brooks, son of Rev. John N. and Susannah (Jennings) Brooks, was born 15 December 1889 in Wilkes County, died 13 November 1970, married on the 17 October 1909, Maggie Marie Jennings, born 6 August 1890, died 28 April 1972, daughter of Rev. Samuel Smith and Rhoda (Elledge) Jennings. Both are buried in Mt. Lawn Memorial Park cemetery, just across the road from their home north of North Wilkesboro on highway no. 18.

Wiley Matthew Brooks was a cattle farmer and automobile dealer, a career which began with the Yadkin Valley Motor Company in 1921. From 1929 until 1832 he was associated with C.D. Coffey and Sons. In 1932 he established the Motor Service Sales Company, Chrysler & Plymouth dealer in North Wilkesboro, N.C. He was a charter member of the Fairplains Baptist Church, where he served as

Wiley M. and Maggie Brooks.

deacon. Maggie was very active in her community through her church and through the home demonstration club. She was known for her handiwork. They had five children: (1) Kenneth Clayborn, born 29 April 1910, married Dossie Hayes. They have one child, Barbara Carol Brooks, born 12 July 1933. She is married to Bill Hubbard. (2) Bruce Weldon, born 29 October 1911, married 23 March 1940 in Grayson County, Virginia, Alta Sales, born 18 February 1920, died 23 January 1964. They are buried in Mt. Lawn Memorial Park Cemetery. They had two daughters, Vickie Marie, born 9 June 1950, and Angela, born 22 August 1956, married in October 1980 Dennis Joines. (3) Doris Elizabeth, born 14 November 1913, married 7 June 1947, Julius Barnette. They have no children. (4) Branford Wiley, born 11 September 1916, died 5 April 1966, married 2 August 1941 Lottie Anderson. They had four children: Brenda, born 23 January 1943, married 7 November 1970 Roger Pruitte; John Matthew, born 25 October 1947, married 26 July 1968 Barbara Shumate; Deborah Ann, born in June 1951, married 10 May 1975 Stephen Palmer, and Alan Leroy, born 23 December 1954, is unmarried. (5) Leonard Lawrence, born 18 April 1919, married 5 July 1941 in York, South Carolina, Mildred Tate Finley, born 31 July 1921 in Norfolk, Virginia, daughter of Fred Tate and Mildred Hope (Whitney) Finley of North Wilkesboro, N.C.

Leonard is the owner of the Motor Service Company, started by his father, and he and Mildred are members of the North Wilkesboro Presbyterian Church. They live on a part of the Wiley Matthew Brooks farm north of town. They had two children: (1) Leonard Lawrence, Jr. born 9 May 1942, married 17 April 1966 Mary Elizabeth Absher, daughter of William Oliver and Ruby (Tuttle) Absher. Len graduated from Wake Forest University in Winston-Salem and is a Microbiologist at Holly Farms, Inc. They are members of the First Baptist Church in North Wilkesboro and live at Breeze Hill Farm, east of North Wilkesboro. Their two children are: (a) Laura Elizabeth Brooks, born 14 October 1969, a seventh grade student at Woodward Junior High School and (b) Matthew Niel Brooks, born 25 January 1980. (2) William Finley, born 12 June 1953, graduated from Lenoir-Rhyne College in Hickory and from Wake Forest Law School in Winston-Salem. He is a lawyer in North Wilkesboro and lives the life of a bachelor.

Sources: Family history, tombstone inscriptions, personal knowledge.

— Leonard Lawrence Brooks, Jr.

JOHN N. BROOKS
375

Stokes H. Brooks was born 6 January 1802 in Halifax County, Virginia, died 12 June 1886 in Wilkes County, married 1 January 1822, Clarissa H. Reynolds, born 15 October 1801, died in 1878 in Wilkes County, daughter of John Ashley and Nancy (Cleveland) Reynolds.

Stokes H. and Clarissa joined Brier Creek Baptist Church in 1829. Stokes H. Brooks became a Baptist minister. He and his family

Rev. John N. Brooks Family.

were members of the Old Roaring River Primitive Baptist Church at Traphill, Cross Roads Primitive Baptist Church in Mulberry community and were constitutional members of the Zion Baptist Church in Haymeadow community where they remained for eighteen years.

Stokes and Clarissa had ten children: (1) Larkin G., born 2 November 1822, died 25 June 1904, married 15 November 1843 Mary Brown, (2) Hardin, born 1 June 1824, died 1903 in Alleghany County, married Keziah Sparks, (3) William E., born 13 August 1826, died 5 January 1900, married Rebecca E. Brown, (4) Nathan Matthew, born 1828, killed in the Civil War, married Jane Abigail Stutz, (5) Permelia, born 14 March 1830, died 28 August 1914, married 29 May 1852 William Harrison Adams, Jr. They were divorced in 1860, (6) Mary, born 1833, (7) unidentified male, (8) Robert P., born 1836, died 12 May 1862 in Civil War, (9) Jesse, born 1842, died 12 May 1862 in Civil War, (10) John N., born 15 October 1844, died 29 December 1921, married Susannah Jennings.

John N. Brooks was licensed to preach while a member of Zion Baptist Church in the Haymeadow community. He was superintendent of the Wilkes County Poor House for sixteen years. His obituary states: "The sudden death of this good man occurred at his home on North Wilkesboro, Route one last Thursday following an illness of several years. He had reached the ripe old age of 77 years and two months and fourteen days. Death came unexpected and threw the entire neighborhood into gloom. He married Miss Susan Jennings of this county on December 27, 1866, and to this union were born ten children, five boys and five girls . . . The funeral services were conducted at the church by Rev. W.W. Myers and Rev. Milton McNeill, his life-long friends and co-workers in the ministerial field."

Susannah Jennings was born 4 May 1848, died 1 March 1940, daughter of Luke, Jr. and Elizabeth (Bullis) Jennings, survived her husband by several years. They are both buried in

the Baptist Home Churchyard, Mulberry community of the county. They were the parents of the following children: (1) Martha E., born 10 November 1867, died 6 September 1917, married a Johnson, (2) Robert Levi, born 20 November 1869, died 3 June 1877, (3) Luke Gaither, born 19 July 1872, died 20 January 1923, (4) Clarissa Elizabeth, born 12th May 1875, died 16 June 1929, married 15 February 1903, Charles Shepherd, (5) Sarah Ellen, born 4 July 1878, died 25 August 1916, (6) Millard Filmore, born 26 September 1879, (7) Minta Alice, born 3 January 1882, married John Warren, (8) Nancy Jane, born 11 May 1884, died March 1908, married A.P. Grant, (9) Wiley Matthew, born 15 December 1889, died 13 November 1970, married Maggie Jennings, (10) Spurgeon, born April 1893.

Sources: Wilkes County Federal Census, marriage records, Bible Record, and Carter's Weekly newspaper.

— Leonard Lawrence Brooks, Jr.

WILLIAM ROBY BROOKS
376

William Roby Brooks (3-7-1889 — 11-15-1958) was the son of Lee S. and Sophronia Rash Brooks. On April 10, 1910, he married Roxie Bumgarner, daughter of William Amon and Myra Camilla B. Bumgarner. This union had one child, Sidney.

Roby was quite a large man — large in physique and large in character. He was a farmer, a carpenter, and construction worker, and an old fashion country horse doctor (not licensed). He was known for his exceptional physical strength and his ability to do hard work over long periods of time. He took great pride in his work and in his properties. His farm animals (horses and mules) had to be the best, his crops the most carefully cultivated.

He was very independent and firm in all his standards. His word was his bond. He would not hesitate to say "no" to his closest friend if he was sure "no" was the right answer. At the

Roby and Roxie B. Brooks.

same time he was the first to offer a helping hand to a neighbor, and he was never too busy to do a favor for someone in need. Despite his "stubbornness", to know him was to call him friend.

His image is best perpetuated in his grandson and only descendant, Wm. E. (Eddie) Johnston, son of Lonnie and Sidney Brooks Johnston.

Eddie, like his grandfather, is a farmer. He attended Berea College, Berea, Ky., and Wilkes Community College, where he majored in agriculture science. He is married to Denise Hoyle (Johnston), daughter of Rev. Edward and Arbutus Hurley Hoyle.

Denise was educated at Berea College, Wilkes Community College, and Caldwell Community College and Technical Institute, where she graduated as a Registered Nurse. She is employed at Wilkes General Hospital.

Eddie and Denise reside at the old Brooks homeplace.

Source: Family Records and Personal knowledge.

— Sidney Johnston

NOAH and SARAH MILLER BROOKSHIRE
377

Noah B. Brookshire was born in 1840, the son of William and Nancy Triplett Brookshire. He married Sarah Miller on August 5, 1861 in Wilkes County. Sarah was born July 22, 1844, the daughter of John B. and Mary (Polly) Triplett Miller.

Noah and his wife, Sarah, are listed on the 1870 Watauga Census in the Blue Ridge Township with three children. By the 1900 Census, Sarah had died, leaving Noah, at age 60, in a household with his son Sherman who was 17 years old and a granddaughter Doris

Green who was 9 years old.

Sarah and Noah's children are: (1) Mary E., born about 1862, (2) Nancy O., born about 1865, (3) Juna S., born about 1870, (4) Frances L. O., born about 1872, (5) William C., born about 1874 and (6) Sherman, born about 1883.

A granddaughter of Noah's and a daughter of his son, Juna Brookshire was Mary Brookshire, a dedicated and much loved nurse at Davis Hospital in Statesville.

Sources: Census, Marriage Bonds and Family History.

— Mrs. J. Arnold Simpson

JANE BROWN
378

Jane, or Jensey Brown as she was always called, was born around 1840. She was the oldest daughter of Eli Brown. Her mother's name is not known by this writer. She was the second wife of Hix Combs.

Jane Brown Combs.

Faced with a family, she had a hard task of housework, weaving, sewing and cooking. She was said to have been an excellent cook. Her dress consisted of a long skirt, mostly black, a shirt waist and a bonnet. I can recall my mother saying that her father, Felix Combs, said his mother had pierced ears. She wore earrings only on Sunday. During the week she put broom straws in her ears to keep them for growing shut.

The following is an account of Jensey talking to her granddaughter, Maie Combs Johnson, after the death of Hix Combs. "Hix was a home guard during the Civil War. He and another homeguard had a prisoner tied up in their home. Both Hix and the man fell asleep." The prisoner began to beg Jensey to free him. He said if he didn't return home, his family would surely starve. She felt sorry for the prisoner and allowed him to go. She gave him a couple of hours to escape before awakening

her husband and the other homeguard. She exclaimed, "I have awakened to find our prisoner escaped!" They jumped on their horses and searched for the prisoner to no avail. This was an act of treason so she had to remain silent or face the possibility of being hanged.

Shortly after the death of her husband, she and her youngest son, Felix, moved to Iredell Co. She remained here until her death on June 10, 1910. She was taken back to Wilkes Co. to the home of her son, Robert Combs, to be prepared for burial. She was buried at Lewis Baptist Church.

Source: family tradition.

— Barbara A. Jordan

JOHN MILTON BROWN
379

John Milton Brown was born February 8, 1824, the son of Presley Brown and his first wife, Elizabeth Vannoy, who was the daughter of Susannah Shepherd and Captain Andrew Vannoy, Revolutionary War officer from Wilkes County. John Milton was the grandson of William Brown and the great-grandson of Walter Brown, one of the first settlers of Wilkes County.

On March 28, 1854, John Milton married Pheroby Joines, daughter of Sarah Caudill and Major Joines and granddaughter of Thomas Joines. To this union were born three children: Elizabeth Jane Brown, Julia Ann Brown and Millard Fillmore Brown.

On Thanksgiving Day, November 25, 1869, Elizabeth Jane Brown married her schoolteacher and neighbor, William Bourn Gambill, who had returned to his family home after serving with the Confederate Army during the Civil War. Six boys and six girls were born to their union.

Julia Ann Brown married Terrellius C. Myers and Millard F. Brown married Alice Holbrook.

John M. Brown acquired through inheritance and his own efforts a considerable amount of property in Wilkes County He was a respected leader of his community and county in religious and civic affairs. Though remote from the outside world, he was interested in events taking place therein. He subscribed to newspapers and periodicals and possessed a valuable library. He would call community meetings and confer with his neighbors on the issues of the day. He and his wife, Pheroby, upheld the high standards of conduct and living which had been brought to the wilderness by their ancestors.

John Milton Brown died June 28, 1890. He was buried at the site of the first Walnut Grove Baptist Church beside the Roaring River in the Springfield Community.

Sources: Family Bible Records, Wilkes County Marriage Bonds, Ancestry of Della Blevins Graham.

— Elizabeth McNeill Forester

PRESLEY E. BROWN
380

Presley Elmer Brown was born in Wilkes County on March 2, 1879, the son of Millard F. and Alice Holbrook Brown. His father moved to

Presley E. Brown.

Virginia but Presley stayed in the Mulberry community, living with his Aunt Susan Brown. He attended grade school at Mulberry, known then as Sulphur Springs Academy. In 1895, he graduated from Fairview College in Traphill. The building is still standing. During the summers he was in college, he supported himself by driving cattle to Virginia to fatten them up and then selling them when school was about to begin again. He used the money for his tuition and to support himself. After graduation, he taught school for several years before entering the field of politics, in which he was eminently successful.

In 1911, he married Rosalie Walding of Dothan, Alabama. They lived at the Smithey Hotel in Wilkesboro until purchasing what is now referred to as the "Old Brown Home" in Wilkesboro.

In 1906 at the age of 26, Presley Brown was elected Sheriff of Wilkes County on the Republican ticket and for the rest of his life was known to most people as "Sheriff Brown". While Sheriff, he was also county tax collector. Once a year, he would ride in his buggy throughout the precinct for several weeks. There weren't many cars then and he would travel throughout the county so the people could pay their taxes and not have to travel so far into town. He rode his horse everywhere he went and on the first day of the county fair, rode a white horse to officially open the fair. Once, on Christmas Day, he had to ride his horse into what was known as the Duck Creek area, along with a deputy on horseback, to bring back a man who had killed another.

Presley Brown was well thought of throughout the county and community. He served four two-year terms as sheriff before voluntarily retiring from office, after which he returned to the lumber business in which he had been engaged to some extent prior to becoming sheriff.

For a number of years he headed field forces of the U.S. Treasury Department's revenue agents in North Carolina. When the income tax law was passed, anyone making over $5,000 had to pay taxes and Presley's job was to audit questionable returns. Once he went out to see a man who had fudged a little on his taxes. The man was scared to death. Presley helped him refigure his taxes and the man was so relieved, he called Presley "The greatest man I have ever known."

In 1916, Presley was the Republican candidate for congress. He was a delegate to the Republican Convention in Chicago in 1920, in Kansas City in 1928, and in Philadelphia in 1948. He was a member of the State Board of Elections in North Carolina for two years. For a number of years he had been a member of the Republican Executive Committee and State Republican Executive Committee of which he remained a member until his death.

He appeared with a group of leading citizens to secure an appropriation of $6500 toward procuring and establishing the armory for the 112th Battalion for the National Guard.

Throughout the greater part of his adult life, Sheriff Brown was engaged in the lumber business as a wholesale dealer. In 1928, he established an industrial plant here for manufacture of finished lumber and building materials. This plant and several million feet of lumber were extensively damaged in the disastrous flood of 1940 and again totally by a fire in 1950. From both disasters, he made a rapid recovery and his business grew constantly.

Presley Brown was a member of the Wilkesboro Methodist Church. He gave active and material support to many movements and projects in the interest of progress.

Judge Johnson J. Hayes wrote the following message of tribute upon the death of Presley E. Brown on October 30, 1858:

"In the passing of Sheriff Presley E. Brown today, the state of North Carolina has lost one of its most outstanding citizens. In early life, Sheriff Brown taught school and then while still a very young man, was elected Sheriff of Wilkes County in 1906, which office he held until 1914, being as long as any man had held the office in the county and was not a candidate to succeed himself. Later he was in charge of the income tax agents of the state of North Carolina, having been a member during the Morrison administration when the "good roads program" arose and was one of the staunchest supporters of North Carolina's road building program. He was a great advocate of better roads and any movement looking to the progress of our state. He was an extensive dealer in lumber products right on up to the time of his death and employed great numbers of men in the manufacturing of lumber and lumber products. He was beyond doubt, the foremost citizen of Wilkes County."

Della Graham Blevins had this to say about Rosalie and Presley Brown's home in Wilkesboro: "They had no children of their own, but their home was a place where all children were welcomed. They owned and lived in the old Brown home in Wilkesboro, one of the most comodious of the historic homes in that town. Rosalie was a beautiful woman, a charming hostess, and was well beloved not only by her husband's kin but by her friends and neighbors as well."

They raised their nephew James Osborne, as well as Presley's brother Mac, seeing to their educational needs and bringing them up as their own.

Sources: *The Journal Patriot* Newspaper, Personal knowledge.

— Paul Osborne

THE PRESLEY BROWN ANCESTRY

381

John Brown from England was the first Brown to settle in Wilkes County. He came up the Yadkin River around 1790 and settled in Mulberry Fields, which was the old name for Wilkesboro. John's son William was the father of ten children, one of whom was the first Presley Brown. Presley settled near the Mulberry Post Office and had extensive land holdings, much of which is still in the family today.

Presley Brown was first married to Elizabeth Vannoy. They had two children, John M. and Susan Brown. After Elizabeth died, Presley married a widow Kilby. This marriage produced four children, none of whom live in the area today. John M. married Pheroby Joines and lived near the present Walnut Grove Baptist Church. He gave the church the land on which it stands. He acquired much land in the area and was a respected leader of his community in religious and civic affairs. Early in life he freed all his slaves although labeled an "abolitionist" by other slave owners. His wife Pheroby was born in 1835 and died in 1912. The desire to care for the sick and suffering was a ruling passion in her life. She had a natural flair for medicine and traveled by horse to visit and practice medicine among her kin and neighbors nearby and in the surrounding communities. She cared for all in need of her assistance and many of her descendants became doctors and nurses.

John and Pheroby had three children, Millard Fillmore, Julia, and Jane Brown. Julia Brown married Trelie Myers. Their son, John Quincy Myers became a well-known doctor in the area and as a young boy, traveled with his grandmother as she administered to the sick. He was a graduate of Davidson College, practiced medicine here in Wilkesboro and organized the first Wilkes County Medical Society. He was a physician in World War I and he held many positions in the N.C. Medical field. He later moved to Charlotte. He was held in high esteem by his church, community, and profession.

Jane Brown married Billy Gambill and lived near the old home place, raising eight children. Millard Fillmore Brown married Alice Holbrook and lived in the Mulberry community during the early part of their marriage. He owned a large amount of land in the community and was a respected leader in the county in religious and civic affairs. He farmed and also ran a store in the Mulberry community until around 1895. Since there was no train in Wilkes County, he had to take a covered wagon to go to Satesville to get his supplies and goods for the store. He and Alice were the parents of four children: Presley Elmer Brown, Nancy Maude Brown (Osborne), Bessie Brown (Neal) and John McKinley Brown.

Around 1895, Millard Brown moved to Tazewell County, Virginia, after swapping farms with a legal bootlegger, Mr. Bowman. Mr. Bowman had run into difficulty with the law and wanted to swap his land with Millard. Millard operated the still and farmed until the state of Virginia voted in prohibition. After this, he came back to Wilkes County (around 1924).

Millard and Alice's son Presley Elmer Brown stayed here in Wilkes County except for summer visits back to Virginia and lived with his Aunt Susan who had never married. Susan had inherited a good amount of land and lived at the old homeplace. Presley went to school at the Sulphur Springs Academy at Mulberry and graduated from Fairview College in Traphill in 1895. He married Rosalie Walding of Dothan, Alabama in 1911 and they lived in Wilkesboro in the old Brown home. Presley became the youngest sheriff of Wilkes County in 1906 and was thereafter known to everyone as "Sheriff Brown".

Millard and Alice's daughter Nancy Maude married James Madison Osborne in Virginia at a young age. To them were born ten children, five of whom settled in Wilkes County. These five were: James, Paul, Howard, Archie Lee, and Ruth Osborne (Necessary). Bessie Brown married James Neal from Virginia. They had one daughter Elizabeth who is married to Arthur Lowe and lives in Wilkesboro.

John McKinley Brown, the last son of Millard and Alice Brown, was born in Virginia while his parents lived there. He went through grade school but since there was no high school in Tazewell County, he came back to Wilkesboro to live with his brother Presley in order to continue his schooling. He graduated from North Wilkesboro High School, and then went on to college, receiving his law degree from Wake Forest University and came back to Wilkes to practice law. He married Edith Foster and they had one child, Nancy who is married to Jim Jenkins and lives in Wilkesboro. Mac, as he was known, practiced law in partnership with John R. Jones until his death in 1940. This was one of the largest law firms around at that time and was located over what was then the Bank of Wilkes. Mac was much respected in the community.

Sources: Genealogy book by Della Graham Blevins.

— Paul Osborne

THORNTON A. BROWN
382

Thornton A. Brown was a resident of the Pores Knob community. His occupation was that of shoemaker and he also engaged in farming. Thornton was born in the Mulberry section of Wilkes County on April 21, 1832. He was possibly an apprentice of Lewis Lineback of the Pores Knob community as his name is listed in that household in the 1850 census of Wilkes County. He married Mary Lucinda Lane (the daughter of Thomas and Elizabeth Christey (Crystal) Lane) on March 25, 1851. When they were newlyweds, they lived at the old

Bentley place (now owned by James Broyhill) in the Pores Knob section. Later they moved to Mulberry. Their final move was to a tract of land in the Pores Knob community near one branch of Cub Creek. This property is now owned by the Phineas Marlowe family, a direct descendant of Thornton.

Thornton was a descendant of Walter and Mary Pilgrim Brown who came to America from England. Their son Thomas William Brown was Thornton's grandfather. Thornton's parents were Elijah and Wilmouth Church Brown. Elijah Brown was born in 1806 and died August 22, 1861. All this family lived in the Mulberry section.

Thornton and Mary had nine children listed below: (1) Mary Elizabeth, born April 22, 1853 — died October 11, 1902, married to James Senter Jennings. (2) Sarah Matilda (Sally) born November 27, 1857, died August 5, 1941, married Leander C. Jennings. (3) Josephine, born September 6, 1859, died June 22, 1943, married James E. Bentley. (4) Julia — twin sister to Josephine, born September, 6, 1859, married John Bentley of the Sugar Loaf section of Alexander County. (5) Delia, born October 22, 1861, died September 6, 1927, married Vance Marlowe. (6) Wilmouth, born March 2, 1864 and (7) his twin John A., born March 2, 1864, died January 23, 1929, married Clementine Hendren. (8) William Allen, born May 30, 1867, died January 28, 1917, married Elizabeth Pennell (a sister of R. Vance Pennell). (9) Laura, born August 16, 1871, died December 14, 1942, married R. Vance Pennell.

Thornton Brown died on October 5, 1912. His wife died on June 20, 1909. Both are buried in Walnut Grove Baptist Church cemetery in the Pores Knob community.

Sources: Family Bible, Wilkes County records, census.

— Virginia Jennings

WALTER BROWN
383

According to the book, *Annals of Haywood County* by Allen, "the Browns were transplanted almost directly from England to North Carolina. Walter Brown, the progenitor of the Haywood County line, as well as others who have settled at numerous places in North Carolina and the South, came from England to Wilkes County before the Revolutionary War. Before leaving England, he was married to Mary Pilgrim who lived in London. She was the daughter of a wealthy Londoner who was very opposed to his daughter's choice, which fact may have decided the coming of this couple to America, although this is not definitely known. It is quite authenic however, that they both espoused the cause of the Americans in their struggle for independence."

Walter Brown, who was born about 1750 and died 1821-22, had two brothers, John and Francis, who were in Wilkes before 1800. Some believe they were of German descent. John's will recorded Jan. 1785 in Wilkes, names wife Elizabeth and children: John, Rubin, Lyda, Joanna, and Rebecca. Francis Brown went to Greenville Co., S.C. about

1790. Walter settled on Mulberry Creek and at one time owned several hundred acres of land.

There was a John Brown buried in a Brown cemetery in the Joines area who may be related in some way to Walter's family. He was called, "John, the Dutchman" and his tombstone says he was born in Germany (born 24 Jan. 1761, died 2 June 1833). He apparently came to Wilkes from Maryland.

The mentioned book has confused and omitted some of the children born to Walter and Mary Pilgrim Brown. Judging from census schedules and other recorded data, the known children of this couple are as follows: (1) Susannah married Michael Kilby 10 Sept. 1781 and they had several children. A son, Henry Kilby married Mary Harmon and they moved to Haywood County. After Michael died, Susannah married Thomas Tinsley 27 Jan. 1800. They had at least two daughters, Margaret and Rachel Tinsley. (2) Katherine married William Abshire whose first wife, Nancy Jennings Abshire, was deceased prior to 1820. William and Katherine did not have children. There is some indication that Katherine may have married first a Haynes, but there are no available records to substaniate this.

(3) Aaron who died in 1816, married Sarah (surname unknown) and they had seven children: Elizabeth, Jane, Eli, Wesley, Larkin, Nancy, and Walter Brown. (4) Thomas William Brown married about 1790 Mary (surname unknown). He died in 1836 and his will names the following children: Presley, Ezekiel, Whitfield, William H. (Billy), Thornton, Elijah, Elizabeth, Soloman, Phebe, and John Allen R. Brown. (5) Ezekiel married 17 Jan. 1800 Rachel Harman and the moved to Haywood Co., N.C. Known children include William, John, Mary, Ezekiel, Walter, Nancy, Isaac, Rebecca, Aaron and Jesse Brown.

(6) Leanner married John Abshire about 1790 and they had twelve children: Elizabeth, William, Keziah, Ezekiel, Walter Matthew, Jane, Nancy, Mary, Jacob, Phebe, Susanna, and John A. Abshire. (7) Mary, daughter of Walter, married Joseph Wheatley (Whitley). I have no further data on this couple (8) Phebe married Elijah Sebastian 23 Feb. 1801. Martin Chandler, age 2, was bound to them by the court in August 1801 and was known thereafter as Martin Sebastian. They moved to St. Francis, Mo. where Phebe died about 1812. (9) It is believed that Walter and Mary had a son, Benjamin, who moved to Hall Co., Ga.

Sources: Wilkes County Wills, Marriages, Census Schedules, Deeds, etc.

— Mae R. Hayes

THE BROYHILLS
384

For a long time the surname Broyhill baffled those who attempted to trace the family history. It did not show up at a time more than three or four generations earlier; then came the breakthrough.

The name James Brayhill, born 1760 or 1761, appeared in a pension claim for Revolutionary War Service. In his deposition, his son James supplied the name of his mother,

James Sr.'s wife, as Rebecca Bailey. James Sr. apparently had lived in Tennessee, Virginia, and Illinois and also for many years in Wilkes County, N.C. He seemed to be the head of the family using the Broyhill name.

James Sr. indicated that during the Revolution his name had been listed as Brayhill and sometimes simply as Bray. Further study indicated that the name originally was Broughill.

Since it is a clouded situation, I will limit my attention to the descendants of John Norman Broyhill who married Martha (Polly) Davis on September 15, 1810.

My mother, whose mother was Frances Lucinda Broyhill, had always understood that John Norman Broyhill was her great-grandfather. The same relationship had been told to Marvin, grandson of Squire William, and to William of Peoria, Illinois.

John Norman and Martha (Polly) had four boys and two girls: Thomas, William A., James, John, Alvira, and Serena. Of these, Thomas married and lived in Iowa; William A. (Squire) married Annie Earp, November 16, 1848, and reared six girls and two boys; John married Alvira Bebber and had a son Isaac who had two sons, Tom and Ed, who were successful furniture manufacturers in Lenoir. Ed has a son James who has been a U.S. Congressman for many years.

Squire William's daughter, Frances Lucinda, married S. Franklin Wallace and had one daughter, Dora Ann Caroline, who married R. Don Laws. William's son Thomas married Sallie Gilreath. They had a son, Marvin, who was a big building contractor in Virginia, in the D.C. area. Marvin's son Joel was for many years a U.S. Congressman in Virginia.

The many Broyhills not mentioned in this article will please forgive me for the omissions. We have gained a firmer hold on future research because one 18 year old Revolutionary War soldier gave us information we had long thought was unavailable.

Sources: Revolutionary War Pension, Personal Knowledge.

— Thelma Laws

Burtle McKinley Broyhill.

BURTLE M. and ETHEL LOWE BROYHILL

385

Burtle McKinley Broyhill (1894-1965) son of Wm. Andrew and Delia Price Broyhill; he had five brothers — Herman, Mack, Howard, Dewey and Irdell, and three sisters — Bertha (Mrs. John Crisp), Vetra (Mrs. J.P. Marlow), and Margie (Mrs. Parks Bentley).

Burtle married Ethel Lowe (1894-1975) in May 1921. She was dau. of Caney and Nancy Smith Lowe of Pores Knob, NC. She had four brothers — Mack, Perry, Glenn and Clayton, also two sisters — Grace (Mrs. Frank Freeze) and Gay (Mrs. Monroe Blevins).

He was a World War I veteran serving in France; returned with a medal of honor. Also a Mason of many years receiving the 25 year certificate. Other than a short time as rural mail carrier and a short period working for the Rockafellow Estate near Fayetteville, NC, he spent his years in the Pores Knob area of Wilkes growing apples. For many years he worked in partnership with his father-in-law Caney Lowe, and then having acquired orchards of his own, went into business for himself.

To this marriage three daughters were born: Nola (Mrs. Howard Frazier); Grace (Mrs. Don Fraizer) and Zelma Broyhill Smith (Mrs. Miles Helton).

They had four grandchildren; Gail Frazier (Mrs. Keith Walsh), North Wilkesboro, NC; Eric Frazier (wife Nancy Freeman) Nashville, TN; Robert Frazier (unmarried) Lincolnton, NC; Gary Smith Helton (wife Shirley Israel) of Long Beach, CA.

Also, five great-grandchildren: Lisa and Burton Walsh of North Wilkesboro; Jackie Frazier of Nashville, TN; Gary Steve Helton II and Chad Helton of Long Beach, CA.

Burtle and Ethel were both members of Walnut Grove Baptist Church on the Taylorsville Road, supporting it in everyway they could. They both enjoyed doing anything possible to help someone else. He always kept extra cans of gasoline for anyone traveling the highway who would run out of gas. This happened many times a month because of the distance between gas stations.

After his death, Ethel was in a wheel chair as an amputee. People would visit to cheer her up, and go away amazed that they indeed had been the one helped and encouraged.

For ten years she cooked, cleaned and maintained her home with always a smile and welcome for anyone that came to the door. No self-pity, nor did she want any from anyone

Ethel Lowe Broyhill.

else.

Before the hospitals, when someone was sick she was always willing to give of her time and energy to help care for them. When food was needed she would be among the first to share. When clothes or household goods were needed by someone, she shared of the best she had, not something that she herself could not use.

She was an encourager, a helper and an inspiration to know.

Their home was always open to friends and relatives. It was never an inconvenience to prepare a meal for anyone at anytime or to get a bed ready for unexpected guest.

Their lives radiated love and concern for every individual that came their way.

Sources: Personal knowledge.

— Zelma Broyhill Helton

THE ISAAC BROYHILL FAMILY
386

Isaac Broyhill was born June 1, 1850 at Moravian Falls in Wilkes County. He was one of ten boys and three girls born to John E. and Mary Bebber Broyhill. His ancestors migrated to Wilkes County from Virginia about 1798.

While working as a carpenter in Boomer, Isaac met Margaret Parsons, daughter of Harvey Parsons who was a farmer and veteran of the Confederate Army. Margaret was born February 1, 1857.

Margaret and Isaac were married April 23, 1876 by Magistrate Squire Hubbard in Moravian Falls. They rode up to the magistrate's home on horseback and had the ceremony performed while seated on their horses. They returned to the Pores Knob area where they lived in a small cabin.

Shortly after the birth of their first son Thomas Hamilton in 1877, Margaret and Isaac moved to a farm near Boomer which Margaret had inherited upon the death of her father. Here Isaac had a sawmill and a mill for grinding wheat and corn. He also kept bees. Margaret kept cows and sold cream and butter. She also raised chickens and sold eggs to the hatchery in North Wilkesboro.

Isaac was very religious and spent many hours reading his Bible. He helped build the first Little Rock Baptist Church.

His formal education was limited to brief studies at a school near Pores Knob. Isaac enjoyed quoting poetry and singing hymns to his grandchildren.

Isaac and Margaret had eight children: Thomas H. (1877-1955), Gordon, A. (1879-1956), John M. (1883-1964), William C. (1885-1968), Mary Lou (1887-1973), Isaac Jefferson (1889-1960), James Edgar (1892-living), Nancy Victoria (1894-1896), and Myrtle Mae (1898-living).

Of the children, only Mary and Jefferson spent their life in Wilkes County. The others moved to Caldwell County where Tom and Edgar were co-founders of the Broyhill Furniture Industries.

Isaac died Christmas Day 1935. Margaret died October 29, 1938. Both are interred in the Little Rock Church Cemetery.

Sources: Family traditions, family memories, Anvil of Adversity by William Stevens.

— Naomi Broyhill Parks Triplett

THE ISAAC JEFFERSON BROYHILL FAMILY
387

Isaac Jefferson, known to his friends as Jeff or I.J., was born February 9, 1889, near Boomer in Wilkes County. He was one of nine children born to Isaac and Margaret Parsons Broyhill.

Jeff attended school under Vance McGhennis for a few years and learned to read, write and do math. He was especially good in mathematics.

As a young man Jeff worked on his father's farm and at the sawmill with his brothers.

Jeff married Ada Belle Carlton, daughter of Daniel Milton and Julia Brookshire Carlton, September 25, 1918. The couple were married at the home of the bride in Caldwell County with family and close friends in attendance.

Ada attended school in Caldwell County. She enjoyed reading, writing and geography.

Jeff purchased a farm from Solomon Barnes which joined his father's farm. He increased the size of his farm as the years passed by. Additional purchases as the land became available. Jeff spent his life on the farm growing wheat, corn and apples. He also kept cattle and raised chickens.

Jeff was an active member of Little Rock Baptist Church. He was a deacon of the church and a teacher in the Sunday School for several years.

Being interested in serving the people of Wilkes County, Jeff ran for County Commissioner and was elected in 1944 and served three terms.

Born to Jeff and Ada were: Julia Arlee, 1919; Naomi Mae, 1922; Jessie Evelyn, 1924; James Lloyd, 1926; and Vernon Carlton, 1929.

Jeff died February 27, 1960, in Caldwell County and is interred in the Little Rock Baptist Cemetery.

Ada resides at the home in Wilkes County.

Sources: Personal knowledge and family traditions.

— Naomi Broyhill Parks Triplett

JAMES BROYHILL FAMILY
388

James Broyhill was born in Caroline County, Virginia 29 April, 1760 or 61, married Rebecca Bailey 25 September, 1785, died in Tazewell County, Illinois, on 7 January 1842. James's father was probably John Broughill and his grandfather William Broughill of Ireland. James served in the Revolutionary (File #S. 32136) under the name of James Bray.

James and Rebecca came to Wilkes County around 1790 and established a family here, but in 1829 they migrated first to Monroe County, Tennessee, and because they were opposed to slavery, left there and went on to Tazewell County, Illinois. In all they had seven children: (1) John Norman, born ca 1887, married Polly Davis 15 September 1810; (2) Polly, born ca 1787; (3) William, born ca 1792, married Nancy Johnson 22 March 1816; (4) Sarah, born ca 1895, married Isiah Hampton 23 September 1815; (5) Frances, born ca 1796, married Elijah Hampton 12 October 1814; (6) James, Jr., born ca 1798, married Clarissa Harlowe Johnson 28 June 1820; (7) Ann, born ca 1802. The four older children were probably born in Virginia, and the youngest child Ann was probably born in Wilkes County. Since James and Rebecca left Wilkes County in 1820, the older children were married and had established families here. The only son to remain here was John Norman; the Broyhills in western North Carolina all descended from him.

John Norman Broyhill, who had married Polly Davis 15 September, 1819, remained here since he had established his family. He also served in the second war for independence — the War of 1812. Norm (as he was called) and Polly had four children: (1) William Allen, who married Annie Earp 16 November, 1848, (2) Johnny E., born ca 1820, married Polly Bebber, sister of John Bebber (3) Elvira, born ca 1815, married John Wesley Joines 11 January, 1834 (See Ezekiel Joines Family.) (4) James H., born ca. 1812, married Rody Hampton 2 March, 1835.

Sources: records in Wilkes County Courthouse, censuses of 1790 to 1880, interview with family members, files in Wilkes County Genealogical Library.

— Peggy Joines Martin

JAMES LLOYD BROYHILL
389

James Lloyd Broyhill, son of Issac Jefferson Broyhill and Ada Belle Carlton Broyhill, was born December 17, 1926 in Wilkes County. He graduated from Wilkesboro High School. He was drafted into the Army in 1945 where he worked in the Generals office in Washington, D.C. After he got out of the Army he started farming with his father on his parent's estate. He grows apples and raises cattle. He is active in the Little Rock Baptist Church and the Republican Party.

He married Mary Sue Hendren on June 23, 1951. She is the daughter of Weddy Clyde Hendren and Mae Sue Phillips Hendren. She graduated from Wilkesboro High School and Appalachian State Teachers College where she received a Bachelor of Science Degree in Primary Education. She taught in the Wilkes County School Systems for twenty-two years until a stroke left her disabled in 1974.

They have three children: (1) Brenda Sue was born on September 13, 1952. She graduated from Wilkes Central High School in 1970 and Mars Hill College in 1974 where she received a B.A. Degree in Primary Education. She is employed by the Wilkes County School Systems. On June 23, 1978, she married Larry Wayne Anderson son of Clyde Turner and Sina Anderson. He graduated from Appalachian State University with a degree in Management and Information Systems. (2) William Clyde was born October 7, 1957. He graduated from Wilkes Central High School in 1975 and Wilkes Community College in 1981, where he received a degree in Restaurant Management. He is manager of Wendy's in Wilkesboro. (3) Diana Lynne was born February 23, 1961 in Wilkes County. She graduated from Wilkes Central High School in 1979. She is a senior at Appalachian State University where she is majoring in Primary Education.

Sources: Personal Knowledge.

— J.L. Broyhill

VERNON C. BROYHILL FAMILY
390

Vernon Carlton Broyhill, son of Isaac Jefferson Broyhill and Ada Belle Carlton Broyhill, was born February 2, 1929. He graduated from Wilkesboro High School in 1947 and North Carolina State College in Raleigh, North Carolina in 1952, with a Bachelor of Science degree in Furniture Marketing and Management.

With ROTC training, he entered the army as a lieutenant and served twenty-four months during the Korean conflict with ten months in Korea. When he returned home from the army he worked for Broyhill Furniture Industries in Lenoir, North Carolina in the upholstry division. He was later transferred to plant number 5 in Taylorsville as Plant Manager. He is active in the Republican Party and served as County Commissioner for four years in Alexander County.

He married Patty Louise Canter on August 7, 1954, daughter of Hubert Canter and Edith Elledge Canter of Millers Creek. She graduated from Millers Creek High School and Appalachian State Teachers College with a Bachelor of Science in Home Economics. They have three children: (1) Janet Louise, born March 13, 1958, graduated from Alexander High School and from the University of North Carolina at Greensboro with a Bachelor of Science in nursing. She works at Moses H. Cone Hospital in Greensboro. (2) Gary Carlton, born September 17, 1956, graduated from Alexander High School and attended North Carolina State University in Raleigh. He is working in Washington, D.C. (3) Sandra Lee, born March 15, 1960, graduated from Alexander High School and attended two years at the University of North Carolina at Chapel Hill. She transferred to North Carolina State University in Raleigh. She is studying Furniture Manufacturing.

Sources: Personal Knowledge.

— Vernon C. Broyhill

WILLIAM A. and DELIA PRICE BROYHILL
391

The first record of the Broyhill name that we have found is William, Broughill, Carolina Co., VA. (1732), son John Broughill; listed tax (1773) Carolina County, Va.; son James Broyhill (wife Rebecca Baily of Carolina Co., Va.; lived here during the time of the Revolution War 1775-1783; moved to Wilkes County 1810. James Sr. and wife with sons Wm. and James, Jr. moved to Tennessee around 1820, then to Illinois around 1842. Leaving here in this area daughters Sally, Polly Anne and sons Frances and John Norman.

John Norman married Polly Davis 1810. To this marriage four children were born, James H., William A., Johnny E. and Elvira.

William A. (1826-1902) married Anne Earp and to this union was born six children; Thomas, William Andrew II (Andy), Martha, Frances, Pantha, Dovie.

William Andrew II (Andy) (1859-1913) married Delia Price (1861-1948) and to this union was born Bertha (1884-1958), husband John Crisp, Beaverdam, Va.; Herman (1890-living) wife Bertha of Oklahoma; Mack (1888-1964) first wife Sue Brown, second wife Mae Lowe of

Andy and Delia Broyhill.

Children of Andy and Delia Broyhill: Dewey, Burtle, Herman, Margie, Howard, Vetra and Mack Broyhill.

Wilkes Co.; Howard (1891-1979) wife Mae Lowe of Alexander County; Burtle (1894-1965) wife Ethel Lowe, Moravian Falls; Verta (1895-living) husband Phineas Marlow of Moravian Falls; Dewey (1897-1973) wife Janie Lowe of Moravian Falls; Margie (1900-1973) husband Parks Bentley, Moravian Falls; Irdell (1902-living) wife Zelda Howard of Dallas, Texas.

Andy Broyhill died in 1913 from fever, leaving a wife and nine children. His wife Delia with the help of the children kept the home together, making a livelihood. They were a committed Christian family and their lifestyle supported this.

Aunt Delia, as everyone called her, was loved and respected her for her faithfulness to the Biblical truths. She lived the truths out in her daily life. Occassionally she would shout at church, this was not show; for her it was in all sincerity. This brought more response at a revival than most any sermon could. Anyone today that remembers her, does so with admiration for the inspiration she gave. She had 53 grandchildren as listed:

Bertha and John Crisp: Ray, Nola, Alda, Roy, Ralph, Rom, Eula Mae, Louise, and Robert of Virginia.

Mack and Sue: Carmine and William Allen (Bud) of Moravian Falls, N.C.

Mack and Mae: Homer and Ruth of State Road, N.C.

Howard and Mae: Infant Son, Alma, Vaugh, Everett, Kenneth, Mary Belle, Pauline, Cling, Alda and Clyde of Moravian Falls, N.C.

Burtle and Ethel: Nola, Grace and Zelma of Moravian Falls, N.C.

Phineas and Verta Marlow: Infant Son, Julia, Infant Dau., Andrew, Jimmy, Grace, Blanche, Glenn, Edwin, Ruth of Moravian Falls, N.C.

Dewey and Janie: Anne, Mildred, Herbert, Walter, Francis, L.C., Linda of Moravian Falls, N.C.

Parks and Margie Bentley: Joel, Claude, Worth, Lee, Clint, Keith, Ralph of Moravian Falls, N.C.

Irdell and Zelda: Eloise, Kent and Clara of Dallas, Texas.

Herman and Bertha: No Children.

Sources: Personal Knowledge.

— Zelma B. Hilton

BRYAN FAMILY

392

The three brothers, John, Andrew and Henry Bryan came to Wilkes County shortly before 1788 from Virginia. Previously they had lived and entered the Revolutionary army in Chester County, Pennsylvania, where their father, Andrew Bryan, Sr. had come from Ireland accompanied by his wife, three sons and two daughters. The name was originally O'Brien.

Major John Bryan (1753-1842) of the Revolutionary army, known as Col. Bryan in Wilkes, was described by Rev. William Barber as possessing unswerving integrity and candor. He married in 1788, Nancy Robbins of Gloucester County, Virginia. Their children were: (1) Elvira (1790-1863) who married in 1806 Col. James Martin (1777-1863); (2) Matilda who married William Parks, parents of Col. Felix Parks who lived just east of the John Bryan home and on the original tract; (3) Mary who married James Parks, parents of Col. Marcus and Col. Lyndolph Parks, who lived where the Village of Roaring River stands; (4) Felix, married first Miss Shields, and second Miss Burney in Georgia where they lived; (5) Cynthia, married Col. Frank Petty; (6) Nancy who married George Bower of Ashe County; (7) John Andrew.

Col. John Bryan settled on the south side of the Yadkin a few miles east of Wilkesboro. Here he built in 1803, one of the country mansions of that day. In later years it came into possession of the Parks family through the marriage of his daughter Matilda to William Parks. In 1927, the old home was burned. The Bryan plantation extended several miles eastward along the Yadkin to the land of Benjamin Martin.

Andrew Bryan, Jr. (1756-1808), brother of Col. John Bryan, married in 1790, Delphia Garnett Jones. Their children were: (1) Edmund, born 1791, married Ursilla Hampton, descendant of Col. A. Hampton of King's Mountain fame. He lived in Rutherfordton where he was known as Gen. Edmund Bryan, a fine example of the old school gentleman, handsome, stately in bearing, and displaying a generous hospitality.

(2) Nancy married William Hampton, son of Henry Hampton of Hamptonville, lived at "Swann Pond" on the south side of the Yadkin five miles east of Brier Creek; (3) Fanny, married Abner Carmichael, lived in the Brier Creek section and were parents of Mary L. Carmichael who married Dr. James Callaway and Phebe Caroline Carmichael who married Dr. Lawson Harrill of Rutherfordton, whose daughter Miss Jettie Harrill is now living in Statesville, N.C; (4) George; (5) Phebe, who married Thomas Kelly and moved to Dalton, Georgia; (6) Leander, moved to Alabama; (7) Betsy Lemira, who married Miller Irvin of Burke County, and moved to Georgia; (8) John Jones, married a Miss Duncan; (9) Larkin.

The children of Gen Edmund Bryan and Ursilla Hampton Bryan of Rutherfordton were: (1) Rufus who married Sue McCampbell and lived in Tennessee; (2) Eliza who married first William Mills and second, Ambrose Mills; (3) Louise who married Gen. Collett Leventhorpe (1815-1889), C.S.A., born in England, lived at "Holley Lodge" in Happy Valley; (4) Mary who married William Davenport Jones, lived at the "Fountain" in Happy Valley; (5) Edmund who married Lavallett Pierce of Abingdon, Virginia.

Source: Excerpts from *Happy Valley* by Felix Hickerson.

— Eleanor Parks Elam

BRYAN FAMILY

393

Francis Bryan was born in Virginia June 25, 1770. His family supposedly came from Culpeper County. He came to the Galax County area and hired or bound himself to work at Blair's forge. When age 21 he removed from Virginia and settled in what is now Alleghany County, N.C., on Glade Creek.

He erected a cabin of chestnut saplings, made his crude furniture and married Pheobe Woodruff, born 22 August, 1777, died 9 March, 1856. Francis lived to be 97 years of age, dying 10 February, 1863.

He and Pheobe had the following children: (1) Morgan, born 9 August, 1795, died 26 March, 1882, married Susan Hale; (2) Gideon, born 5 January, 1798, died 29 August, 1878, married 5 August, 1818, as his first wife Mary Johnson; (3) Thomas, born 15 March, 1880, died July, 1863 in Wilkes County, married Nancy Bauguss (4) Jinnet (Jane), born 20 October, 1802, died in infancy; (5) Sampson, born 4 April, 1805, died in infancy. (6) John, born 20 November, 1807, married first, Nancy Thompson; second, Lydia Jeffries. (7) Solomon, born 1 August, 1810, died in infancy; (8) William, born 3 August, 1811, married Charlotte Woodruff; (9) Francis, Jr., born 6 October, 1914, married as his first wife Margaret Carson; (10) Abraham M., born 13 June 1817, died 18 February, 1877, married Mrs. Celia Carter Woodruff; (11) Joseph, born 13 June, 1817; twin, died in infancy; (12) Phebe, born 30 December, 1819, married Hugh Roberts.

Thomas Bryan, son of Francis and Pheobe, married Nancy Bauguss 27, July, 1818, in Wilkes County, daughter of Robert and Mary Sparks Bauguss. They settled at the foot of the Blue Ridge Mountains near Traphill. He was a farmer, a Justice of Peace and a leader in the Methodist Church.

He and Nancy had eleven children: (1) Robert B., born 3 April, 1820, died 2 February, 1890, married Jane Carson, born 11 September, 1820, died 1 January, 1905; (2) Cinderella, born 22 November, 1821, married Jonathan Greenberry Atkins 23 April, 1843; (3) Sarah, born 11 August, 1823, married Shadrack Bryan; (4) Francis, born 18 August, 1825, died 2 January, 1890, married first Charlotte Hale Atkins, 1 August, 1847; second, Elizabeth Moore, 4 September, 1861; and third Sena Brown; (5) Emily, born 8 July, 1827, died young; (6) Mary, born 17 September, 1829, married Meshack Couch 8 January, 1850; (7) Phebe, born 3 February, 1832, married 26 November, 1851, Zadock Wright; (8) John Quincy Adams, born 10 October, 1833, died 11 October, 1905, married Martha Bryan, a cousin; (9) Thomas Jefferson, born 25 July, 1836, died in young manhood in Nashville, Tennessee; (10) Nancy Dawson, born 15 July, 1837, married Hardin S. Holbrook 30 December, 1856; (11) Abraham C., born 13 September, 1839.

I descend from Francis and Charlotte Hale Bryan through their son, Robert Calloway Bryan who was born May 20, 1851, married August 10, 1872, Lydia Elizabeth Wiley of Guilford County and died in Randolph County, N.C.

My family had lost track of the origination of the Bryan clan in Traphill and Glade Creek. The only lead we had for twenty years was a voting form filled out by Robert Calloway Bryan around 1900 stating his father was Francis Bryan. Through research and personal contact with the Bryans of Wilkes County, we now know we descend from Francis and Pheobe Woodruff Bryan.

Sources: Francis Bryan Bible in possession of John Wesley Bryan in 1955; Wilkes records, personal knowledge.

— Larry Wayne Bryan

MARY BRYAN

394

Mary (Polly) Bryan was born near Traphill, N.C. Sept. 27, 1828, the daughter of Thomas and Nancy (Bauguess) Bryan. She was the granddaughter of Francis and Phoebe (Woodruff) Bryan of Alleghany County.

In 1839, her grandfather Robert Bauguess sold land to the original Siamese Twins, Chang and Eng Bunker. In 1843, Mary and her sisters helped their mother cook the wedding dinner when the Siamese Twins married the Yates sisters.

In 1848, Meshach Couch, a mechanic from Guilford County came to Wilkes. He courted the beautiful, red-haired Mary and they were married Jan. 10, 1850. Their eldest son, William L. Couch was born Nov. 20, 1850. Other children born in North Carolina were: Quincy, 1854; Thomas Abe, 1857; Mary Dawson, 1860; Joseph, 1863; and John, 1865. Other children born in Kansas, Charles, 1869 and Alice, 1871.

In the War Between the States, Traphill community was half North and half South. The Bryan and Couch families believed in the preservation of the Union. Jeff Davis gave an order to conscript every man able to carry a gun. Meshach Couch had no choice. He left his wife and children to live near her kin. Meshach hid in a cave in the Blue Ridge foothills. Thirteen-year-old William took him food and fresh clothing. One day Meshach was sick. William hurried home for medicine. Upon his return he called into the cave but heard no answer. He forced himself into the cave, the hardest thing he ever did in his whole life. He lit a sulphur match and found a note. The men of the underground had come to take his father through to the North.

Mary Bryan Couch lived near her parents with her children: William, 13; Quint 9; Abe 6; Mary 3; and infant Joseph. Her father Thomas Bryan and grandfather Francis Bryan both died in 1863. Mary's horses were stolen and locked dresser drawers slit open and her home vandalized. Her brother J.Q.A. Bryan became an officer in the Union army. He came home to visit his family. The Confederates intended to capture him when he left. Every morning before daylight hogs went into the hills to feed on acorns. J.Q.A. Bryan crawled out with the hogs.

Mary's eldest son William Couch and his cousin Billy Bryan decided to run away from home and join the Union Army. The Union Army would not accept them on account of their age, so they were obliged to return home. They walked all one day asking for food along the way and received none. Finally, late in the day a woman told them she had no food. William said, "We'll see about that." They forced their way past the woman, opened the food "safe", pulled up chairs and filled their shrunken stomachs with cabbage, vegetables and cold cornbread.

Early in 1865 near the close of the War, Meshach Couch returned to North Carolina. Mary and Meshach settled up their affairs, sold their land and in the spring of 1866 left for Kansas in covered wagons, driving their livestock. They were three months on the road. They bought a farm half a mile south of Douglass, Kansas. In 1889 Mary and her whole family moved to Oklahoma in the great land opening. Meshach Couch died in 1895. In May 1907, Mary Bryan Couch was present at the first of a long succession of consecutive annual picnics now numbering seventy-six. The

family meets for a picnic twice a year, Easter Sunday with an egg hunt and on the Fourth of July.

In October 1908, Mary Couch went to get a velvet quilt she had entered in the Oklahoma State Fair. She sat on her front porch and a neighbor came over to talk. She asked the neighbor to rub her back. "Mary do you feel better?" the neighbor asked, but Mary did not answer. Mary had died peacefully after a long and useful life far from her Traphill birthplace.

Sources: *One Pioneer Family* by Eugene Couch, John Wesley Bryan in 1957, family stories, Bible records and Census records.

— Edna M. Couch

THE FAMILY OF PASCHAL and CYNTHIA RASH BUCKNER

395

Paschal Buckner was born in Virginia, in 1795, a son of Henry Buckner, Jr. and Elizabeth Womack. It is the theory, Paschal was the brother of John and James Buckner.

On 6 April 1816, in Granville County, North Carolina, Paschal married Medda Bowers. No known issue from this marriage.

Paschal's second marriage, was to Cynthia L. Rash, in Wilkes County, North Carolina, on 22 May 1830. Cynthia was born 1810, North Carolina. Parents not known.

Both Paschal and Cynthia were members of the Reddies River Church. She was baptized in 1831, and he in 1832.

Paschal Buckner, died 1845, in either Meigs or Overton County, Tennessee. Cynthia L. Buckner, died, 20 March 1877, at age 67, in Polk County, Missouri, and is buried in the Payne Cemetery, near Polk, Polk County, Missouri. Their children include the following:

John A., born March 1831, in Wilkes County, North Carolina. In 1850, he married, Lurana Swift (1827-1837-1910), daughter of Franklin Swift and Elizabeth Norris. John died in Greene County, Missouri, after 1900, and is buried near Ash Grove, Greene County, Missouri. The issue from this marriage: Andrew Jackson (1852-1921), George W. (born 1858), Isabella (born 1861), Martha (born 1864), Permelid "Thulie" Towe (1867-1938), Jacob Leander (1870-1952), William (born 1872), Fannyel Mettie Reynard-Erwin-Bacala (1874-1946), Minnie Fram (born 1877).

George Washington, born 8 April 1833, in Washington County, Tennessee. On 8 Feb. 1855, in Overton County, Tennessee, he married Martha L. Copeland (1839-1893). George died, 18 October 1913, in Polk County, Missouri, and is buried in Payne Cemetery. The children from this marriage were: Margaret E. (born 24 Feb. 1856), Julia A. Hutcheson (1857-1930), Mary A. Kitt (1858-9-1922), Viola L. List (1860-1907), Alta L. Payne (1862-1899), James C. (born 1866), twin of, Rev. William Paschal (1866-1937), Henry S. (born 1868-9), George M. (born 1870), Lela A. "Ida" Whittaker (born 1872), Venna Alba Barnett (1882-1952).

Polly, born 1839 in Tennessee, believed to be twin of Jacob A.

Jacob A., born 1839, probably in Meigs

County, Tennessee. He first married, Nancy L.?. No known issue from marriage. His second marriage was to Eliza J. ?. Jacob died after 1907, in Jackson County, Arkansas. Children from this marriage were: Susan A. Hudson (1876-1960), Marietta (born 1879), William G. (1880-1954), Lillie (born 1885), Alice, Ruth, (and another daughter ?).

Elizabeth A., born 29 October 1840, probably in Meigs County, Tennessee, as Paschal and family were there in the 1840 census. Elizabeth, married Green Samuel Wilson, 8 September 1861, in Carroll County, Arkansas. Green S. Wilson (1840-1913), was the son of Samuel Houston Wilson and Cynthia Gibson. Elizabeth died, 6 June 1917 in Polk County, Missouri, and is buried in the Mt. Olive Cemetery. The children from this marriage were: William Henry (1862-1938), Joseph Green (1864-1944), Emma E. Bridges (1865-1951), George Thomas (1867-1935), Elizabeth (1870-1882), Martha Hood (born 1870 ?), Samuel Houston (1872-1932), Maggie (born about 1872, d. 1887-9), Catherine Barnes (born about 1876), Julia List (1878-1957).

Jesse Franklin, born 17 November 1842, in Meigs County, Tennessee. Jesse first married, Martha L. Brooks, she died, September 1868, in Polk County, Missouri, and is buried in the Payne Cemetery. One child from this marriage: Columbus ''Toby'' (1867-1870-1). Jesse's second marriage was on 7 February 1869, in Cedar County, Missouri, he married, Mary Ann R. Mitchell (1846-50-1923), daughter of Wiley Blunt Mitchell (1827-1904) and Sarah B. Looney (1826-1918). Jesse died, 28 October 1914, in Polk County, Missouri, and is buried in the Payne Cemetery. Issue from this marriage were: George (1870-1870-1), Martha A. Birdsong (1871-1928), Charles F. (1873-1893-4), Sarah E. Richter (born Feb. 1877), Julia E. Bailey (1878-1908), James Henry (1879-1955), Maggie M. Perry (1881-1946). Jesse Blunt (1882-1954), Rodo Belle (1884-1885), Everett Austin (1886-1966), Christina Stewart (born 25 December 1887), Jacob Golden (1889-1903-4), Eva D. Keithley (1890-1912), Murtle Mae Kelly-Tedder (born 8 December 1891), Alpha O. (1893-1975), Isaac ''Ike'' (1895-1978).

Nancy M. born 1843, probably Meigs County, Tennessee. On 4 October 1873, in Polk County, Missouri, she married Chesley Neeley. Nancy died, 1886-1888 at Smithton, Clark County, Arkansas. No issue from this marriage.

Henry, born 1846, in Tennessee.

John A., George W. and Jesse F. Buckner were farmers, and owned land in Polk County, Missouri.

George W. and Jesse F. were Civil War veterans, and received Civil War pensions.

Sources: Polk County, Missouri Courthouse records, 1820-1900 census records, marriage records, death certificates, tombstone inscriptions, newspaper obituaries, Civil War pension records, wills, and family traditions.

— Artie Marie (Bailey) Pastrick

CARL WARREN BULLIS
396

Carl Warren Bullis was born in Millers Creek, N.C. on January 11, 1896, the first of six children of Roby Johnson and Mary Lou Wright Bullis. He grew up on the family farm and attended Millers Creek School.

He is a Veteran of World War I, enlisting in the Army on October 5, 1917, spent eleven months in Camp Jackson, S.C. and served in France from August 5, 1918 to June 9, 1919. He was Chief Mechanic of the 316th. F.A., 81st. Wildcat Division. After the war he moved with his family to a tobacco and cotton farm in Sanford, N.C.

He was married to Arpha Louraine Foster (born June 10, 1894 — died May 30, 1981) on December 26, 1920. She was the daughter of Absolem and Martha Hubbard Foster of the Mount Pleasant community in Wilkes County. They lived in Sanford, N.C. where their only child, Roena, was born on October 27, 1921. They later moved to Hamlet, N.C. where they resided for eight years before moving to Wilkesboro, N.C. on July 3, 1930.

He is a member of the Mount Pleasant Baptist Church and a Mason. He built and donated furniture to the Wilkesboro, North Wilkesboro and Mount Pleasant Masonic Lodges. He served 35 years in the Wilkesboro Fire Department, 27 of which he was Fire Chief. He was employed by the N.B. Smithey Department Stores and Buster Forester Beverage Company before becoming self-employed as a custom cabinet builder. After retiring, he developed a hobby of designing and building grandfather clocks, most of the work and finishing done by hand. As of this date, he has completed 15, each one different and most of them given to members of his family.

Daughter Roena was married to Petro Kulynych of Smithmill, Pa. on December 11, 1943. They had two daughters, Brenda Gail, born November 30, 1946 and Janice Lynn, born July 25, 1953. Brenda married Dale Kenneth Cline on August 15, 1970. They live in Hickory, N.C. and have three children: Laura Kristin, born May 26, 1972; Adam Kenneth, born March 3, 1974; and Luke Kulynych, born February 4, 1977. Janice married Thomas Edgar Story, III on September 3, 1977, and they reside in Atlanta, Georgia.

Carl Bullis' parents, Roby Johnson Bullis (born August 26, 1873 — died February 26, 1938) and Mary Lou Wright Bullis, (born July 7, 1872 — died December 1, 1948) were married March 14, 1895 in Millers Creek, N.C. where they lived until 1919, when they moved to Sanford, N.C., bought a tobacco farm and remained there until their deaths.

His maternal grandfather, Joseph Wright (born May 13, 1836 — died September 19, 1888), son of John Wright and Mary McKee Wright, grew up on his father's farm and was married in 1870 or 1871 to Mary Rebecca Forcume of Harmony, N.C. (born April 10, 1843 — died September 20, 1920). Joseph and Mary had four children: Mary Lou (1872-1948), John (born May 4, 1874 — died July 28, 1941), William E. (born April 3, 1876 — died July 19, 1968), Ila (born April 23, 1878 — died October 4, 1956).

Great-grandparents John Wright (born March 6, 1800) and Mary McKee Wright (born September 23, 1803) were married in the Cathedral of Armagh on August 10, 1831 in Derrycoose, Ireland, Parish of Laughgall, Armagh County. They had four children, the first three born in Ireland; Ann E., (born May 30, 1832), Mary Jane (born November 29, 1833) and Joseph, (born May 13, 1836). John and Mary, their three children and Mary's father, John McKee, left Derrycoose, Ireland on May 10, 1839 and landed in Philadelphia July 6, 1839. They traveled to Wilmington, N.C. and Fayetteville, N.C. and then to Wilkesboro, N.C. in September, 1839 and settled on a farm containing 640 acres at Millers Creek, N.C. on the south side of the stage road leading from Wilkesboro to Jefferson. The youngest child of John and Mary, Frances Terressa, was born in Wilkes County on March 13, 1845.

The deed to land containing seven and one half acres on which the Friendship Church at Millers Creek was built (now known as Millers Creek United Methodist Church) was given to the church as a gift by Mary McKee Wright.

Sources: Family Bibles, grave markers, family papers.

— Roena Bullis Kulynych

JAMES ELBERT BULLIS
397

James Elbert Bullis was born 15 September 1844 and died 13 February 1906, the son of Samuel Wesley Bullis, born 1814, died 20 March 1863, and Mariah Bumgarner, born 1815. James married Eliza Jane McNiel, born 20 April 1844, died 27 December 1929, on the 16 May 1866 in Wilkes County. Eliza's parents were William Squire McNiel born 14 March 1805, died 22 February 1875 and Mary (Polly) Wilcox born 8 February 1817, died 24 May 1888, who were married 24 December 1833. Their marriage bond was dated 23 December 1833.

James Elbert Bullis served four years in the Civil War, had a farm on Millers Creek, where he operated a roller mill. Before moving to Millers Creek he and his wife lived in Watauga

Eliza Jane McNiel Bullis.

County for a short while.

Eliza was my great grand-mother, who was blind for twenty-two years. Being a widow, she lived with her youngest daughter, Pansy. She always wore a black dress and white starched apron. When my mother and I visited her, she would want to feel my arms and face to tell how much I had grown. She was sweet and thoughtful to everyone who came to see her.

To the union of James Eliza the following children were born: James Andrew, born 16 January 1867, died 17 January 1867; Mary Ann (Molly), born 18 February 1868, died 29 May 1946; married Leander Bobbit Pierce; William Alexander, born 29 November 1870, died 9 June 1954, married Helen Compton and served as mayor of North Wilkesboro for several years; Roby Johnson, born 26 August 1873, died 26 February 1938, married Mary Lou Wright and lived in Lee County, N.C. all his adult life; Dora Evaline, born 1 March 1876, died 18 January 1958, married Otis Campbell; John Reigner, born 23 February 1879, died 11 November 1953, married Maude Lenderman. Both died the same day and are buried in Salem Cemetery in Winston-Salem, N.C.; Lizzie Ellen and Alice Virginia were twins, born 1 May 1882. Lizzie Ellen married Rupert Harold and Alice Virginia married Charles Horton; Mayrah Leaner, born 2 August 1884, is living, the widow of J.C. Wallace. Walter Cowles, born 19 April 1888, died 5 August 1958, married Dora; Pansy Bell, born 27 January 1892, died 16 July 1969, married Robert Parker.

The eldest daughter of James E. and Eliza Bullis was called "Molly" and her grave marker bears her name as such. She was my grandmother and I remember her as being a wonderful cook, good housekeeper. When her house work was finished, she would have her knitting in her hands. She made all the children a knit bedspread and all her grandchildren enough lace for a large table cloth. All her work was superb with lasting beauty.

Mary Ann (Molly) Bullis and L.B. Pierce were married 5 November 1885. They lived near Millers Creek until their home burned. They made their home in North Wilkesboro for the remainder of their lives. Their children were: Viola, born 8 October 1886, died 27 November 1951, married Cyrus Kilby; Dora Bell, born 24 June 1888, died 3 May 1927, married Wiley Thomas McNiel; Ella Vetra, born 17 May 1892, died 4 June 1958, married Zollie O. Eller; Ruel Shafford, born 4 August 1897, died February 1972, married Fanny Watts; Pansy Vistula, born 29 September 1900, is living, married Paul Rogers; Fred Marvin, born 12 August 1903, died 26 June 1972, married Fay; Jennie Gwyndolyn, born 20 November 1907, died 29 August 1951, married Retired Army Major Smith; Eliza Lucille, born 11 December 1910, died 4 July 1975 unmarried.

Sources: *McNiel Clan*, by J.H. Hayes, Bullis family Bible.

— Dare Eller Howell

BUMGARNER
398

Although it has not been proven, research suggests that Michael Bumgarner, who was exempted from taxes in Rowan County in the late 1700s and who married Mary, was deceased or had left North Carolina prior to 1800, could have been the parents of Leonard Bumgarner, Sr., who married Catharine, and Daniel Bumgarner, who married Elizabeth.

Leonard Sr. and Catharine were parents of nine children: (1) Female (2) Female (3) Lydia (4) Leonard, Jr., who married Elizabeth Houck (5) Michael, born 1789, married Elizabeth (Betsy) Church (6) Daniel, born 1793, married Sarah (Sally) Kilby (7) Henry, married Phebe Kilby (8) Male and (9) Mary (Polly), married John Bullis(on).

Leonard, Sr., Catharine and Lydia are buried on the farm, long known as the "Wash Nichols' place" (but for many years owned by the late W. Percy Bumgarner, a descendant of Michael) which now belongs to his widow and heirs.

Michael, born 1789, and Elizabeth (Betsy) Church Bumgarner, born 1792, married 30 June 1813 and were the parents of seven children, namely: (1) Amos, born 1814, died 4 May 1884, married Matilda Church, 25 March 1841; (2) Henry, born 1816, married 13 February 1843, Amelia (Millie) Church, born ca 1820, daughter of Gabriel and Sallie Beshears Church; (3) John Elam "Buck", born 1824, married Emeline Church 16 December 1847; (4) Elizabeth, died 7 March 1881; (5) Mary (Polly), born 1825, died 17 June 1907, married Thomas Jefferson Church the 29th of January 1846; (6) Allen, born 1830; and (7) Myra, born 1834, single.

Henry and Amelia (Millie) Church Bumgarner were the parents of one daughter and three sons: (a) Elizabeth Jane (Betsy), born 1846, married William Curtis, 6 July 1866. (Legend is that they left soon after they were married via covered wagon for Missouri and there is nothing more known about them.) (b) John (c) Michael, who died in his teens; and (d) Henry, born 6 August 1857, married in August 1876 Minerva Angeline Milam, born 27 April 1857.

Amelia (Millie) Bumgarner died sometime prior to 1870. Henry Bumgarner married a second time Elizabeth (Betsy) Billings Lovette, on 6 January 1873. She was born 28 June 1836 and was the widow of A.H. Lovette. They were the parents of Mary Lou(ise), born 1877, married 20 April 1890 Arthur U. Billings, died in 1955, and Lily Bumgarner, born 1878, married Numa Hayes, and died in 1957.

Henry Bumgarner died 28 March 1896 and Betsy died 10 November 1906. She is buried in the Baptist Cemetery on Sixth Street in North Wilkesboro.

Sources: Census, cemetery listings and Bible records.

— Helen Bumgarner Bell

ARTHUR GARFIELD BUMGARNER
399

Arthur Garfield Bumgarner was born November 23, 1884, son of Alexander and Belverlee Hays Bumgarner. He grew up on a farm near Reddies River which was part of the Stephen Bumgarner land (his grandfather).

He attended school in the Cross Roads area when it was in session. His schooling was limited but he was an avid reader and gained a lot of knowledge through that and the experiences of life. He was married to Hatava Nichols August 10, 1905. He settled his own home on this farm on which he grew up and lived there all of his life.

To this union were born ten children: six sons and four daughters. Only seven grew to adulthood. The oldest son, Blake, died at the age of twenty-four years leaving two small sons who finished college at Appalachian. The eldest, Bill B. works in social services in Wilkesboro, and Claude teaches business at West High School in Millers Creek. Ruth, the eldest daughter, married C.O. Lovette and made her home in Millers Creek. Clate also lives in Millers Creek. Guy lives in Wilkesboro. Clate is a retired Holly Farms employee. Guy is still employed at Holly. Byrdie, Mrs. C.S. Goddard, still lives on the original homeplace. Her husband is Postmaster at Millers Creek. Claire, Mrs. W. H. Burnett, lives in Falls Church, Virginia near Washington, D.C. She is a retired government office worker. The youngest son, Jack, also lives in Woodbridge, Virginia and is a government employee.

Arthur raised his family on the farm and in his spare time hauled by wagon team various commodities to market in surrounding towns. Later, he grew broilers for the poultry market, and also kept some cattle and other livestock. He was one time a Justice of the Peace. He also served on the jury often and would be called many times on a special case when jurors were needed in an emergency. He was interested in politics but was not an extremist. He could always see the other side's point of view.

He joined Pleasant Home Baptist Church in early life where he was a faithful member until his death. He was very active in church work and was a deacon for over sixty years. He was always at the services except when sickness prevented.

He loved people, enjoyed conversation with others, enjoyed newspapers, the state paper, and any historical reading. He had read the Bible through numerous times and was quite a Bible scholar.

He always enjoyed reasonably good health and was able to attend church until about four months before his death.

In early life before there were many doctors, nurses, or a hospital in the area, he would help the neighbors take care of their family illnesses. Many times, he would get up at midnight to go and relieve someone who was sitting with a sick person, come home at daylight, and plow all day. Such were times in his early life.

At his passing he had twenty-two grandchildren, twenty-four great-grandchildren, and two great-great-grandchildren.

His wife passed away February 28, 1951. He never remarried. He died on March 21, 1978 on the same land he had lived on all his life, and was laid to rest by the church he loved so well. He was a good Christian, a good citizen, a loyal neighbor, and a good family man.

Sources: Personal Knowledge.

— Ruth B. Lovette

Arthur Garfield Bumgarner.

Mary married Henry Bumgarner, and Eva who was the mother of Archie Bumgarner. Eva first married Bill Nichols and second, James Perkins.

(3) Henry M. Bumgarner married Lamira Apoline Wilcox(en), the daughter of William C. and Lamira Robbins Wilcoxen. They were the parents of Martha who did not marry, Mary who married Tom Bishop, Sarah Almedia who married Hackett Nichols, William Jones who married Maggie Bishop and Thomas Farr Bumgarner who married Kate Dancy.

(4) Matilda Bumgarner was probably a daughter of Daniel and Sarah Kilby Bumgarner. She was the mother of Nancy, Mary, James C. and William. James C. Bumgarner married Bethania Minton 1 June 1867 and they were the parents of James Rufus who married Mary Wyatt and Mary E. (Mollie) who married Arthur Eller.

Sources: Wilkes County Wills, Marriages, Census Schedules, and Family Bible.

— Mrs. Robert K. Hayes, Sr.

GENE BUMGARNER

401

Robert Eugene Bumgarner, son of Wm. Amon and Myra Camilla Bumgarner was born June 18, 1902, and died June 3, 1978. He married Violet Absher, daughter of Samuel and Myrtle Brown Absher. Their children are Thomas Lee, who married Mary Elledge; Kathleen married Gene Chappell; Reba married Bob Fender; and Jo Ann married S.D. Eller.

By trade, Gene was a skilled carpenter. No job was too big or too small for him to tackle as long as it had to do with putting wood together. He loved to hunt and was a great teller of tall tales when it came to how great his dogs were.

He was a good neighbor and a man that many called friend.

Sources: Family Bible and consultation with family members.

— Sidney Johnston

DANIEL and SARAH KILBY BUMGARNER

400

Although I cannot furnish documentary proof, I believe this Daniel Bumgarner, born about 1793, was the son of Leonard and Katherine Bumgarner who are buried on the Percy Bumgarner farm above Millers Creek.

The sale of Leonard Bumgarner's estate appears in Wilkes Will Book 3, page 187, November term, 1818. The administrators of Leonard's estate were Katherine and Daniel Bumgarner. Katherine died between 1820 and 1830.

Daniel Bumgarner married Sarah (Sally) Kilby, bond issued 25 Oct. 1813. According to census schedules, they were the parents of several children. Daniel Bumgarner, Jr. who married Elizabeth McNiel 16 Aug. 1837, may have been their son. However, I only have definite data on the following: (1) Adam Bumgarner, my husband's great-grandfather, was

born 6 Dec. 1818. Adam was a farmer, school teacher, and a very good shoemaker. Miss Bessie Bumgarner, who lives in the New Hope Church community remembers her mother saying that Adam "was a pretty little man, always neat as a pin." He married Mary Louise (Polly) Brown, 24 Dec. 1861. She was the daughter of W.H. (Billy) Brown and his wife, Julia Stout Brown. Adam and Polly had two daughters: Martha Cornelia born 28 Sept. 1865, married James N. Vannoy; and Sarah Julia born 7 Feb. 1869 married Davie Vance Nichols. Adam and his father-in-law, W.H. Brown, were among the original members of New Hope Baptist Church.

(2) William E. (Chipaway) Bumgarner married Lewiza Hines, bond issued 28 Dec. 1854. They had eight children: James Madison (Matt) who married Elvira McNeil; Thomas Jefferson, twin to Matt, married Barbara Nichols; William A. (Boat) married Alice McNeil; Uriah married first Mertie Faw and second Amanda Whittington; Minerva married Leland Taylor,

HENRY and MINERVA ANGELINE MILAM BURMGARNER

402

Henry Bumgarner, a tall, thin young man, and Minerva Angeline Milam, a very sweet, soft-spoken young lady, who had been friends for some time, decided in the summer of 1876 to get married. Both of them were nineteen at the time, and they chose the month of August for their wedding.

They became the parents of four sons and three daughters: (1) James Marshall Bumgarner, born 19 May 1877, died 26 March 1937, who married Emma Louise Pennell 17 December 1911. They had one daughter, Helen Louise Bumgarner Bell, and they are buried in Mt. Lawn Memorial Park, North Wilkesboro. (2) Linville Melvin Bumgarner, born 1 October 1878, died 27 December 1956, married Eliza Dula, 3 January 1904. They had no children and they are buried in Pleasant Grove Church

Cemetery. (3) Martha Elizabeth Bumgarner, known as Mattie, born 25 October 1881, died 3 October 1936, married William Seth Dula, 29 July 1906. They were the parents of Maud Angelin Dula Luffman and John Walter Dula (deceased). They are buried in Shady Grove Church Cemetery near the Kerr Scott Resevoir. (4) Carrie Louisa Bumgarner, born 8 March 1885, died 3 October 1957, married James Arthur Jenkins in 1909. Their children are Edith, Melvin (deceased), Presley, John, Willard, a Baptist minister, and Valerie (deceased). They are buried in Drexel, N.C. (5) Nelia Octavia Bumgarner, born 2 November 1887, died 5 October 1970, married John William Kilby, 5 January 1907. They had two daughters — Emma Connie Chandler and Clara Zealy, and they are buried in Shady Grove Cemetery also. (6) William Percy Bumgarner, born 4 July 1890, died 27 December 1977, married Belva Lou Triplett, 25 December 1920. They are the parents of Howard Charles, Rex Coolidge (deceased) and Jene Clinton Bumgarner. Percy is buried in Mt. Lawn Cemetery and at this time Belva is the last living member of her generation in this family. (7) Harley Thomas (or Thompson), born 15 March 1896, died 28 September 1972, married Rebecca Leora Walsh, and they had one son, James Roland Bumgarner. They are buried in Mt. Lawn also.

Several years after the death of his first wife, Henry Bumgarner married Kate Bumgarner, who outlived him a number of years.

Though most of his life was spent on a farm in western Wilkes County, several moves brought Henry Bumgarner and his family nearer to Wilkesboro. Henry, the son of Henry and Amelia Church Bumgarner, was born 6 August 1857 and died 24 August 1937, five months after the death of his eldest son. Minerva Angeline Milam Bumgarner, born 27 April 1957, died 28 May 1928, was the daughter of William Jason and Martha L. Minton Milam. They are buried in Pleasant Grove Cemetery.

One of my fondest memories is our weekly visits, usually on Sunday afternoon, to Grandpa and Grandma Bumgarner's home where there was almost always a gathering of relatives and neighbors and many children, often cousins, with whom to play. Being an only child, this was a real treat for me and one to which I looked forward. I also remember popping corn over the coals in the large fireplace in the dining room, where the outside door was usually open on the coldest day — yet no one ever seemed to have a cold.

Another fond recollection is my Grandpa's trips to town (Wilkesboro) in his one-horse wagon to buy necessities and to visit in our home. When he was ready to leave, I was permitted to ride in the wagon with him as far as the corner of Cherry and Main Streets. I usually ran all the way home from this exciting experience. These are childhood memories never to be forgotten, and the kind of memories our children never had.

Sources: Bible records and personal recollections.

— Helen Bumgarner Bell

JAMES CLAYTON BUMGARNER 403

James Clayton Bumgarner, the son of Arthrur Garfield and Hatava Nichols Bumgarner, was born May 20, 1915. He was the great-grandson of Stephen Bumgarner of German descent.

Many times his grandmother, Hatava Nichols Bumgarner, had told her children of her elopement; throwing a flour-sackful of clothes out the window and running through the woods to marry Arthur Bumgarner.

Just before his 20th birthday, Clate stole his childhood sweetheart from the Jim and Bessie Martin farm, went by the Wilkes County courthouse, to their pastor's home, Rev. Finley Watts, and he married them, knowing they had run away. Clate and Piney (Alpina Martin) became one on March 2, 1935, but not totally unprepared! Clate had rented two rooms from Jim and Mary Nichols where Lovette's Shopping Center is now in Millers Creek, N.C.

Henry and Minerva Bumgarner.

James Clayton Bumgarner (1980).

He had spent a whole hundred dollars to furnish it and had a month's salary in his pocket, for you see, he was making a dollar a day driving a produce truck for Tom Gritchellis (Greek) of Charlotte, N.C. Their son, Max Edward, was born 31 Dec. 1935 and married Carolyn Vannoy, They gave Clate and Piny three grandchildren: Alisa Carolyn born Jan. 20, 1956, Eric Max Edward born Feb. 6, 1959, and Kirk Clayton born June 26, 1961. A fourth child, Mitzi Alice died at birth Dec. 20, 1956.

Being a God-fearing man and very optimistic, Clate has always made the living, and I've made the living worthwhile. Very early he was ordained a deacon in Pleasant Home Baptist Church, serving then as Sunday School superintendent and as chairman of the Building Committee in 1948.

About this time he had established his own produce and chicken business.

Sports-minded, he picked up an idea and ran with it. Having square dances in the Wilhelmena Triplett gym raised $1900.00 one summer which bought seven acres of land behind Millers Creek High School so that we could have football at Millers Creek. The Redskins were the first County School in Wilkes to play football In 1957 Millers Creek and Mt. Pleasant High Schools were consolidated into West Wilkes High School.

An avid hunter, Clate was soon hunting for a community project. The idea became evident with the need for a fire department. The first fire department was organized in 1956 followed by twenty-three others in the county by 1982; Millers Creek being the first. Clate has been the president for 25 years. Since he thought of it, he had to be it!

Seeing twenty children playing on Knothole Street on Sunday mornings, (and at Sunday School time too!) Clate approached his pastor, Rev. Clate Brown, and Pleasant Home Church gave birth to a church; yes, in the Fire Station. In 1958 a Sunday School was started and the next year, Millers Creek Baptist Church was organized. Stop! No — a building was necessary: Clate already Chairman of Deacons was now Chairman of the Building Committee.

By now his business had merged into Holly Farms and he still stays quite busy.

Still a hunter, Clate with son, Max and grandsons Eric and Kirk, all sports-minded and hunters, camp in the mountains a week each year to hunt deer and to fish. "Paw Daddy" is the cook.

Only the granddaughter, Alisa is married, to Douglas Eller. She teaches Math and Science at Millers Creek Intermediary School. The grandsons are still looking.

Clate's hobbies are gardening, making baskets, and barbeque sauce.

It has been said "that behind every good man there is a good woman." Written by "Clate's Behind."

Source: Personal knowledge.

— Alpina Martin Bumgarner

JAMES LINVILLE BUMGARNER
404

The Reverend James Linville Bumgarner was the eldest son of Stephen and Rebecca Nichols Bumgarner, born in Wilkes 7 Oct. 1832. He was a farmer and Methodist "circuit rider," or more accurately, circuit "walker." He worked hard on the farm all week, and at noon on Saturday he would come in, eat and dress, and set out on foot to one of the points on his circuit. Arriving there, he would spend the night with one of his parishoners, preach on Sunday morning, and walk back on Sunday afternoon to be ready for the farm on Monday.

During the war, in 1863, Jim was commissioned by Gov. Zeb Vance as 2nd Lt. in the 68th Battalion of the North Carolina Militia for Home Defense.

Jim married Phoebe Ann Hincher (1835-1914), daughter of William and Charlotte Carroll Hincher, who were married in Orange County, N.C. in 1827 before coming to Wilkes to live and rear their children, all of whom were born in Wilkes County.

Of the seven children born to Jim and Phoebe, only three reached maturity. In 1863 an epidemic took the lives of Mary and Emily, and in 1879 a similar tragedy took Carrie and Grant. The eldest, George Washington, married Mary Elizabeth Nichols, and they built a home and lived on land deeded to her by her father, John Wilburn Nichols. Maria married Tom Cole and they built and lived on land deeded to her by her father, downstream and cross Buck Branch from her childhood home. Linville married Bessie Ryan McNiel, and they first lived across the creek and on the hill south of his father's place, but later moved to Wilkesboro where they lived for the remainder of their lives.

Jim's work did not end with farming, preaching, and serving in the Home Guard. In winter he used a team of big oxen to haul lumber from Tom Broyhill's mill in the Millers Creek area to North Wilkesboro. And a community service was to go to the home and bathe, dress, and "lay out" the body whenever a man died.

He was an expert producer of sweet potatoes, and he grew an abundant crop every year. There were sweet potatoes for the family, for neighbors and friends, and for seed the following year. People would come for miles around to buy seed potatoes in the spring.

Sources: N.C. State Archives and Writings of Millard F. Bumgarner.

— Flora B. Friend

JAMES M. and EMMA P. BUMGARNER
405

James Marshall Bumgarner was born in a log cabin near the Yadkin River in Wilkes County, 19, May 1877, the oldest child of Henry and Minerva Angeline Milam Bumgarner. To his family and many friends he was fondly known as "Jim".

He and Emma Louise Pennell, born 16 August, 1888, were married at the Methodist Parsonage in Wilkesboro on 17 December, 1911, by the Reverend A.T. Bell and the witnesses were Mr. and Mrs. Presley E. Brown and Earnest Bell. Emma was the daughter of

Emma P. Bumgarner.

William Thomas and Jessie Julia Warren Pennell of Wilkesboro.

When "Jim" was sixteen years old, he went to East Tennessee and lived with his Uncle Thomas Lovelace Milam in Milligan College for whom he worked for room and board and fifty cents a day for two years. He returned to Wilkes County with his father and brother Percy who had come to Tennessee in their wagon. He often said he loaned one hundred dollars of his earnings at six percent interest and got his "start."

In 1898, Sheriff John Henry Johnson asked Jim Bumgarner to be his "Chief Deputy." At twenty-one years of age, he became the youngest deputy in the history of Wilkes County. He continued to serve in this capacity for thirty years. From 1906 to 1914, he served under Sheriff Presley E. Brown; from 1914 to 1922, under Sheriff William D. Woodruff; and from 1922 to 1928, under Sheriff General Grant Elledge.

Soon after leaving the court house, Mr. Bumgarner was appointed one of two Deputy Marshals in Wilkes County by Marshall J.J. Jenkins of the United States Middle District of North Carolina. At the time he was sworn into office, Marshal Jenkins commented, "at last I have a Marshal whose handwriting I can read." (Jim had a beautiful and flourishing handwriting and at that time all local records and all reports sent to the Marshal were written in long-hand.)

After leaving the Marshal's office three years later, Jim opened a collection agency which he operated from his home. This proved to be a lucrative business for the remainder of his life.

Even though he never had the opportunity for further his education beyond the schools in Wilkes County and to fulfill his dream of becoming a lawyer, many persons felt he was so widely read that he knew as much law as many of the lawyers of his day. He was often said to be known by more people and to know more persons by name in Wilkes County than any

James M. Bumgarner.

other man of his generation. He was a friend to every man — poor or rich — and the number of persons who attended his funeral on Easter Sunday, the 28th of March, 1937, attested to this fact. His untimely death on 26 March at the age of fifty-nine ended a life of great belief in and devotion to Wilkes County.

Emma Bumgarner was a lady of strong beliefs and deep convictions. She never found fault with others nor passed judgment upon them but accepted persons at face value. She believed everyone should exercise his or her right to vote, but she was for the person not the party and often remarked that she was sure she had "killed" her husband's vote. How she voted was a very personal matter. She was a happy person who was young at heart and who smiled a great deal. Her most important calling was that of "homemaker" and she was an ideal one in the eyes of her family, being an especially good old-fashioned cook. When her health and a broken limb prevented her attending church, she listened to the services on the radio.

Jim and Emma Bumgarner were the parents of one daughter, Helen Louise Bumgarner, born 20 December, 1918, who married Edward Parker Bell of Elizabeth City, North Carolina. Emma continued to live with her daughter and family until her death at age eighty-five on 5 November, 1973. Mr. and Mrs. Bumgarner are buried at Mount Lawn Memorial Park in N. Wilkesboro, N.C.

Sources: Family Bible, obituary, personal knowledge.

— Helen Bumgarner Bell

JAMES RAY BUMGARNER
406

James Ray Bumgarner (b. Jan. 20., 1906, d. June 11, 1968) was the great-grandson of Steven Alexander Bumgarner and his wife Rebecca Nichols Bumgarner, Enoch Cooper and his wife Elizabeth Caroline McGlamery Cooper, Abraham C. Nichols and his wife Harriet Evaine McNeil Nichols, John G. McNeil and Polly Nichols McNeil.

He was the grandson of William Amon Bumgarner and his wife Nancy Caroline Cooper Bumgarner, Gaither Alexander Nichols and his wife Louisa McNeil Nichols.

He was the son of Roby Enoch Bumgarner and Deborah Virginia Nichols Bumgarner.

He was born at Millers Creek, North Carolina, and lived there all his life.

His father was killed while cutting timber to build a home when a tree accidentally fell on him twelve days before Ray was born. Ray and his mother lived in her parent's home.

After Ray learned to drive he drove for his Uncle who was blind. Later he sold cars and taught driving for a short time for a business in North Wilkesboro.

Later he got a license to be a barber and operated a barber shop in Wilkesboro for 25 years until he had to stop because of bad health. His first shop was in the basement of Gray Brothers Furniture Store and his second was in the rock building on courthouse square.

He attended Crossroads Elementary School and Millers Creek High School in Millers Creek.

In 1936 he married Cornelia Gilreath from Alexander County. Her parents were originally from Wilkes. She was a teacher for 35 years in Alexander and Wilkes counties.

They had one daughter, Virginia Ann Bumgarner. She is a teacher in Wilkes County.

After Ray retired he enjoyed horseback riding with his friends, going on the Blue Ridge Wagon Train to Ashe County and rabbit hunting. All his life he enjoyed fox and rabbit hunting.

Sources: Genealogical research and family knowledge.

— Ann Bumgarner

JAMES THOMAS and GRACE W. BUMGARNER
407

James Thomas Bumgarner was the son of Linville and Bessie Ryan McNiell Bumgarner of the Millers Creek vicinity in Wilkes County. He married Mary Grace Wilson, daughter of Arch Leslie Wilson and his wife from Iredell Co., N.C., on 29 Dec. 1938.

A.L. and Ella Lee Scott Wilson were the parents of seven children: Annie Belle who married Albert Arnold and lived in Wilkesboro; Jamie who married Mason Holt and lived in Mebane; Grace who married Tom Bumgarner and made their home in Wilkesboro; Sarah who married John Wiles and lived in Wilkesboro; George who lives in Florida; A.L., Jr. lives in Sough Carolina; and Delbert Wilson who is chief of police in Wilkesboro at the present time. These children were all born in Iredell County near Harmony before the family came to Millers Creek where Mr. Wilson owned and operated Wilson Milling Company. The children attended Millers Creek School until sometime after the fire which completely destroyed the mill, and the family moved to Wilkesboro.

James Thomas (Tom) Bumgarner was employed by Duke Power Company until his death on 27 May 1959 at the age of 49. He had been with Duke Power for almost twenty-five years when he died. Grace worked at Peoples Drug

Store in Wilkesboro for about 11 years and was librarian in the Library at the Old Jail for about eight years.

Tom and Grace had two sons: Thomas Grant (Tommy) married Bobby Jean Parsons in 1969 and they have one son, Jacob Thomas. James Donald (Donnie) married Patsy Arlene Wingler in 1970 and they have one son, Jonathan Ryan.

Sources: Personal knowledge.

— Grace W. Bumgarner

JOHN LINVILLE ASBURY and MARGARET EDNA PATTON BUMGARNER
408

John Linville Asbury Bumgarner was born June 30, 1878, to George Washington and Mary Elizabveth Nichols Bumgarner near Millers Creek, N.C., the oldest of eleven children. He was married to Margaret Edna (Maggie) Patton on June 12, 1907. Six children were born to this union, one of them dying in infancy and another in young adulthood Dr. James Irvin Bumgarner. The four remaining are Rosemary (Mrs. J.W. Tysinger), Dr. John R. Bumgarner, Doris (Mrs. J. Allie Hayes), and Rev. G. William Bumgarner.

Dad was taught the value of education in the church and school at a very early age and spent the remainder of his life teaching and preaching and helping others to learn this valuable lesson. His first school was called Mud Hunker which was located in the Millers Creek vicinity and indeed, he did go by foot through a lot of muds, snows, etc. to get there. From there he went to Moravian Falls Academy after which he went back to Mud Hunker for a four month term, teaching at $18.00 per month. Then he taught at Reddies River for two years followed by more study back at Moravian Falls Academy for another term.

Dad always felt a strong attachment to the church, was baptized at an early age, and joined the church at Friendship (now Millers

J.L.A. Bumgarner.

Creek United Methodist) at age 12 or 13. He seemed to perceive his need for training in this field and pursued it diligently for his lifetime.

In 1901 he spent a year at a Methodist school, Aaron Seminary at Montezuma in Avery County, N.C., where he continued his studies and did some of his first preaching. He was admitted to and ordanied by the Blue Ridge Atlantic Conference of the Methodist Episcopal Church during his year there. Learning to preach did not come easy for him, but he never quit studying toward his goal and working for self-improvement. From Montezuma he went to Athens College (now Tennessee Wesleyan) at Athens, Tenn., where he studied, worked for room and board, etc., taught and preached some in the small churches nearby. He had some experience in speaking in the debating society also. Dad was at Athens for five years, along with Uncle M.F. Bumgarner, Uncle C.S. Bumgarner, and other members of his family. During the last two years he was there, my mother, Margaret Edna (Maggie) Patton was also there in school. Their acquaintance ripened into love and led to marriage on June 12, 1907.

Their first year together was spent teaching and preaching at Baileytown and Rogersville, Tenn. In 1908 they returned to North Carolina where he received "full connection and appointment" from the Blue Ridge Atlantic Conference of the Daisy Circuit at Walkertown, N.C. (Forsyth County). After two years there, he felt the need for still more education, so, in 1910, he and mother, and by then one child, Rosemary, moved to Chattanooga, Tenn. to the university there, where he completed his work for the A.B degree and secured his high school teaching certificate. He was now 32 years of age and little Rosemary was old enough to cry "Daddy!" when he marched down to receive his diploma.

Dad was ordained Elder in 1910 at Bethel Methodist Church near Asheville, N.C., and was appointed to the Lansing Circuit in Ashe Co., N.C. My mother's parents, Rev. and Mrs. W. A. Patton lived here and Grand-daddy Patton was also a Methodist minister and was a great influence on my father. During the Lansing appointment, a son John Reed Bumgarner, was born. He is now medical internist and cardiologist in Greensboro, N.C. The next appointment, in 1913, was to Fairview College in Wilkes County where he served as "head" and teacher until 1916. Two more additions blessed the family during this time at Traphill: Doris (now Mrs. J. Allie Hayes) and George William (Bill) who is presently a retired Methodist minister living in Winston-Salem.

In 1916 Dad started serving as District Superintendent of the Asheville District which covered most of the mountainous end of the state. We lived at Clyde, N.C. Dad had to travel 6,000 miles each year to visit all the churches, but he always had a good report for conference in the fall. In 1918, James Irvin Bumgarner was born. He became a medical doctor, but died at the age of 39, a sad loss to family and community.

We rode in Dad's brand new, second-hand, T Model Ford to Walkertown, N.C., in 1921 for his second appointment there. In 1925 he was moved to Wilkes County and was pastor of Friendship, Arbor Grove, Charity, Antioch, Dunkirk, Eschol, and other churches there. He acted as principal of Millers Creek School 1925-1928 and as math and science teacher at Wilkesboro High School for the following eleven years. He also served churches in Yadkin and Ashe Counties. He and mother worked together in the church, school and home to help make a better future for their family and for mankind. Their sacrifices were many and great in educating their children and in helping other members of the family, but the word "discouragement" wasn't in their vocabulary.

Dad was retired by conference in 1946 but continued to serve until 1958 when his health failed at age 80. He entered The Methodist Home in Charlotte in May 1961 where he found opportunity to serve in his God given calling and to help found and support Plaza Methodist Church. He died on Oct. 2, 1967, at Charlotte Presbyterian Hospital and was buried in the Millers Creek United Methodist Cemetery beside mother who preceded him in death in January 1956.

Sources: Personal knowledge and a history compiled by Rev. Bill Bumgarner from data given by Dad himself and from church records.

— Doris B. Hayes

LINVILLE and BESSIE BUMGARNER
409

Linville Bumgarner was born July 7, 1867 in a log cabin approximately one mile north of the Millers Creek Methodist Church in Millers Creek. He was the son of the Reverend James Linville Bumgarner, Methodist Minister, and Phoebe Hincher Bumgarner. Linville Bumgarner died in the Wilkes Hospital November 1, 1941 at the age of seventy-four years.

He joined the church in his early youth and became one of the stalwart Sons of the South in the midst of its reconstruction from a devastating Civil War. He used every opportunity and all his strength in his own promotion to a high and intelligent Christian life, which he maintained faithfully until his death.

Linville Bumgarner was educated in the public schools of Wilkes County. He later completed three years at Moravian Falls Academy in the heyday of that institution under Dr. George W. Greene. After completing his education, Linville Bumgarner married Bessie Ryan McNeil at Millers Creek on January 20, 1889.

Bessie Ryan McNeil was born February 15, 1870 approximately one half mile south of West Wilkes High School in Millers Creek. She was the daughter of Thomas Winslow and Martha Jane Nichols McNeil. She also attended the public schools of Wilkes County available at that time and after her marriage remained in the home to love and nurture her children while her husband farmed and took an active role in the political and economic life of the community and area. Bessie Bumgarner was a well loved and respected lady and a member of one of the best known families in this part of the state at the time of her death on

Linville Bumgarner and wife Bessie Ryan McNeil Bumgarner, around 1918 near their home.

November 27, 1938.

Linville and Bessie Bumgarner first lived in Millers Creek with his parents after marrying. Later, they moved into a house of their own and in the fall of 1898 they moved to Wilkesboro. This home was located on Bridge Street.

It was after moving to Wilkesboro that Linville Bumgarner's involvement in the political and economic life of his community grew and matured. He began his professional career as a public school teacher and later clerk in a store. He became Clerk of Superior Court of Wilkes County for four years and farmed.

A second home in Wilkesboro was purchased from R.A. Spainhour for $1,200 about 1900. This house was located on Cherry Street. At the time this house was a small, five room, single story dwelling. However, the home was remodeled by T.M. Foster of Foster and Allen Contractors about 1912, and a second story was added along with one additional room downstairs. It was here Linville and Bessie Bumgarner were to remain and rear their children until their respective deaths. This home was to become known as the Linville Bumgarner homeplace and stood intact until destroyed by fire on March 8, 1981.

Linville Bumgarner was one of the founders of the Oak Furniture Company in North Wilkesboro and worked there as a bookkeeper. He later was an alderman for the Town of Wilkesboro and was elected to the North Carolina Legislature. He represented his county two terms in the Lower House and one term in the Senate. He was Director of the Wilkesboro Building and Loan Association and Clerk of the Wilkesboro Baptist Church for seventeen years. At the time of his death, he was Deputy Clerk of the U.S. Court for the Middle District of North Carolina which was then located in Wilkesboro.

Sources: family records, interviews with family members, personal knowledge, newspaper articles, and grave stones.

— Donnie Bumgarner

CHILDREN OF LINVILLE and BESSIE BUMGARNER

410

Linville and Bessie Bumgarner had fourteen children. Twelve lived to adulthood and two died in infancy. Their first child, Bertha Olena Bumgarner, born May 1, 1890, lived only thirteen months and died June 21, 1891.

Pedie Isabel Bumgarner, born January 7, 1892, died September 6, 1962, graduated from Appalachian State Teacher's College in Boone and taught school all her adult life in eastern Wilkes County. She married Robert O. Poplin, merchant, who later managed Smithey's Department Store in Elkin. They had two children, Robert O. Poplin, Jr. and Hazel Poplin. Each had two sons. Robert O. Poplin, Jr. graduated from Wake Forest College and received a Masters Degree from Appalachian State Teacher's College. He was principal of North Surry High School in Surry County before retirement.

Plato Settle Bumgarner, born September 13, 1893, died January 26, 1952. Married Mitzie Mehavolic, of Hungarian decent, while in U.S. Army. They settled in New Jersey near her family. He was a shipping clerk for Merck and Company. They had three daughters, Ruth, Blanch, and Mitzie Bumgarner.

Pearl Blanche Bumgarner, born Feburary 22, 1895, died September 2, 1973, graduated from Appalachian State Teacher's College in Boone. She took numerous courses at the University of North Carolina at Chapel Hill and taught school all her adult life at Mt. Airy, High Point, Albemarle, North Wilkesboro, and Wilkesboro. She never married and was affectionaly referred to as "Miss Pearl"

Edgar Eugene Bumgarner, born October 26, 1896, died January 11, 1968, began work at R. J. Reynolds Tobacco Company in Winston-Salem in 1916. He served in the U.S. Navy. He retired from R. J. Reynolds Tobacco Company as Personnel Manager. He first married Alma Preston and had five sons: Eugene, Jack, John, James, and Bobby Bumgarner. His second marriage was to Brown Phillips and they had no children.

Romulus Linville Bumgarner, born September 10, 1898, died August 28, 1962. He ran away to Tennessee at age fourteen. He married Annie Hunter and had three sons, Eugene, James, and Harold Bumgarner, and two daughters, Aileen and Ruth Bumgarner.

Mary Louise Bumgarner, born October 18, 1900, died December 20, 1970. She took nurses training in Tennessee and while there, married Charles M. Hart. He was in the foundry and iron business. They had one son, Edward (Ted) Hart.

Ruth Bumgarner, born March 24, 1902, died January 21, 1973, married J.V. Jennings, newspaper publisher. They had one son, James Allen Jennings who graduated from Wake Forest College. A writer and salesman for newspaper machines and parts, he married Charlotte Boone. They had one son and two daughters.

Abagail Bumgarner, born May 18, died January 24, 1972, was a Deputy Register of Deeds for Wilkes County, Justice of the Peace, and

married over five hundred couples. She married Bryan Gilreath who was a freight agent for Southern Railway Company. They had two daughters, Martha Jane and Rebecca Gail Gilreath. Martha Jane married Walter Bishop and had two sons and a daughter. Rebecca's second marriage was to Jack Rich and they had two daughters.

Tyre Bumgarner, born January 24, 1906, died June 4, 1957, was a merchant and operator of Two-Way Service Station in Wilkesboro. He married Doris Laws and they had one daughter, Linda Carole Bumgarner who graduated from the University of North Carolina at Greensboro, is a school teacher, and has never married.

Charlie Grant Bumgarner, born October 29, 1907, still living; Served in U.S. Army; worked at Wilkes Hoisery; served as Commissioner for the Town of Wilkesboro; Wilkes County Tax Collector and Mayor of Wilkesboro from 1953-1973. He married Sue Lyon of Eastern Wilkes County. She was Deputy Clerk of Superior Court for Wilkes County and Deputy Clerk of the U.S. Court for the Middle District of North Carolina. They had a son, Charles Ryan Bumgarner, born May 17, 1943 and a daughter, Janet Sue Bumgarner, born October 6, 1947. Charles Bumgarner graduated from North Carolina State University and received his law degree from the Woodrow Wilson School of Law in Atlanta, Georgia. He flew 201 bombing missions during Vietnam War and is a pilot for Delta Airlines. He married Mary Kennedy of Massachusetts. Janet Bumgarner graduated from East Carolina University and married David Dail of Winterville, N.C. They have two daughters, Jennifer Susanne Bumgarner, born August 28, 1974 and Rebecca Whitney, born February 19, 1977.

Bessie Byrd Bumgarner, born July 14, 1909, still living, completed her nurses training at the New Charlotte Sanitorium. She nursed all her adult life in Chapel Hill and Raleigh area. She married Walter Hillman Riley, who was an engineer for the N.C. Department of Water Resources in Raleigh.

James Thomas Bumgarner, born May 24, 1911, died June 27, 1959. Tom Bumgarner worked for Duke Power Company in North Wilkesboro. He married Mary Eunice Grace Wilson from Iredell County. She was the first Wilkesboro Branch Librarian. They had two sons, Thomas Grant, born February 27, 1941, and James Donald Bumgarner, born July 30, 1946. Tommy Bumgarner married Bobby Parsons. They had one son, Jacob Thomas Bumgarner, born August 8, 1978. Donnie Bumgarner graduated from Campbell College and received a Master of Social Work Degree from the University of North Carolina at Chapel Hill. He worked for the Baptist Children's Homes of N.C., Inc. two years and has worked for the Wilkes County Department of Social Services ten years. He married Patsy Arlene Wingler who graduated from the University of North Carolina at Greensboro and also received a Master of Social Work Degree from the University of North Carolina at Chapel Hill. She worked for the Wilkes County Department of Social Services ten years and was Director of the Skyview Child Development Center. They

had one son, Jonathan Ryan Bumgarner, born September 1, 1978.

Joseph Hope Bumgarner, born February 8, 1915, died February 10, 1915.

Sources: family records, interviews with family members, personal knowledge, newspaper articles, and grave stones.

— Donnie Bumgarner

MILLARD FILMORE BUMGARNER

411

There were powerful influences for good in the background of M.F. Bumgarner. His parents were well educated, and they were deeply committed Christians of the Methodist faith. They encouraged and assisted their children in their school work, read the Scriptures to them regularly, and had daily family prayers. They were scrupulously honest, and charitable toward their neighbors. Millard absorbed all those virtues and made them a part of his life for ninety and a half years.

Millard was the third of ten children born to George and Mary Nichols Bumgarner. Except for his five years at Wesleyan College in Athens, Tenn., and a few teaching terms at other places, he spent his life in the Millers Creek community, serving and elevating the lot of his people. He and his brother, John made a pact with each other as they started out to get their college education, that they would return and give their homefolks the benefit of their experience.

While he was a student at the Moravian Falls Academy, Millard asked and was granted permission to take the teachers examination. His score qualified him for a second grade (class) certificate, but he was not satisfied with that. A while later he took it again and was awarded a first grade certificate. With his new credentials he accepted his first teaching position at age nineteen, on top of the Blue Ridge, at Loggins School.

The school district lay across the Ashe-Wilkes line, and the students came from both counties. Teachers had to be certified in both counties and were paid by both. There were some ruffians in the community who made it their business to harass anyone who came to teach, and they had succeeded in scaring several away. But this time faith, determination, and the belief that right makes might, foiled their efforts, and the gentle, unpretentious teacher stayed — the full term.

One of Millard's outstanding characteristics was his love of challenge. He entered spelling bees and debating contests, and took civil service examinations just for the joy of winning, which he habitually did. He was not only the best speller, and one of the top debaters, but most of the time he made the highest scores on the exams. On those, however, he had two strikes against him. Other examinees were given points for prior service, which brought their scores up, or the opposite political party was in control of the appointments. Thus, the reward most often won from his efforts was the glory — not the (material) gain. In spite of this, on two occasions he was appointed postmaster in Wilkesboro. In 1920 and again in 1940 he was appointed to that office, serving two and then thirteen years, a total of fifteen. This, plus his thirty-two years of public school work, added up to forty-seven years of service to his people. He was in each profession long enough to receive a small retirement benefit, a pittance by today's standards.

As an educator, Millard's career was varied. His lifetime, blanket certificate permitted him to teach any subject and any grade for the rest of his life. He taught in one-teacher schools, multi-grade classes in two or three teacher schools, all high school subjects from Science and Math to English and Latin. He was principal of several different schools, assigned in 1908 to open the high school in Ronda and he taught college classes in the summer.

His term in Ronda brought him the greatest of his life's rewards — his lovely wife, Pansy. She had already taught a year or two, and had returned to school for more training. She was not only bright, but beautiful and talented, just the kind of girl he had hoped to find. They were married on 2 June 1910 at the home of her parents, Peter and Mary Smith Pardue (see Pardue-from Bevel to Pansy).

Throughout his life, Millard was an ardent church member and leader. He taught Sunday School classes, was superintendent of the Sunday School, and held the office of church treasurer for many years. He performed his duties with honest and strict adherance to the church disciplinary code. But his most cherished religious calling was that of licensed lay minister. He could have chosen, but did not choose, to become a licensed preacher, because, he said, "I did not feel worthy." But he spent his life proving that he was!

There were eight children born to this couple, seven of whom reached maturity and had families. They are: Olive Prevette of Athens, Ga.; Flora Friend of Millers Creek; Pauline Cannon of Burlington, N.C.; Henry Grady Bumgarner died at age three; Bonnie Mary Lewis of Ashe County and Jacksonville, Fla.; Iris Carol Pitts of Ormond Beach, Fla., Millard Filmore Bumgarner, Jr., of Burlington; and George Smith Bumgarner of Grand Prairie, Tx.

Pansy died in 1959 at age seventy. Millard died in 1973 at age ninety and a half. They are buried side by side in the Millers Creek United Methodist Cemetery.

Sources: Family Bible, Writings of M.F. Bumgarner, and personal knowledge.

— Flora B. Friend

MONROE MANSFIELD BUMGARNER

412

M.M. Bumgarner was born at the forks of Reddies River and Maiden Cane Creek, on Oct. 14, 1885, and died Dec. 18, 1978. He was the fifth child of Andrew and Cornelia Sturgill Bumgarner. He spent his entire life within three miles of his birthplace.

Andrew became disabled when Monroe was only 12 years old; when he was 16 years old his father died, leaving him with the full responsibility of his mother, his sister, and younger brother. Two sisters died in infancy and his older brother, Billy, died in young manhood.

The family was advised by a physician that if they didn't move away from the river they would continue to have serious respiratory problems. Whereupon, when Monroe was 17 years old he went on the ridge, cleared the land, sawed the timber, and built a new home for his folk. That building is standing today and is occupied.

He first married Dora McNeil, daughter of Alfred and Mariah Bullis McNeil. Dora was a school teacher, and Monroe was, among other things, a substitute teacher. They had been married 8 years when Dora contracted pneumonia and died. Their children are: Mazie, married Turner Faw; Ivie Dean, married Isaac Royal; and Dennis, married Izell Faw. The fourth child, Mack, died only months after his mother's death.

Several years after Dora died, Monroe married Lula Rash. Lula sustained a serious injury in her youth, leaving her affected with seizures. She lived only 6 years after they were married.

Again Monroe and his children were left alone. After keeping the family together until they had all graduated from high school and married into homes of their own, Monroe decided to take a third wife, and whom did he choose but his second wife's sister, Bessie Rash. She too preceded him in death.

Despite all his misfortunes and hardship Monroe led a full and active life. He was a Justice-of-Peace for many years. He was also an acting Deputy Sheriff.

For years he and his family walked six miles, round trip to attend church service every Sunday. In going over some old church records sometime ago the writer found that Monroe Bumgarner, had at sometime in his life, held every Office except choir director and pastor in Friendship Methodist Church (now Millers Creek United Methodist) where he was a member for 77 years.

Source: Family records, contact of living family members and personal knowledge.

— Sidney Johnston

NETA M. CHURCH and NEWTON W. BUMGARNER

413

Neta Mary Church was born May 8, 1905 to Annie Bumgarner and Commodore W. Church in Wilkes County. She was the first of eight children born to her parents. Her five brothers and two sisters are: Tam Welborn, Troy Manus, Annie Mae Dwight Charles, Ina Jean (deceased), James Auburn and Dale Pernell.

Neta was married to Newton Wiley Bumgarner Aug. 28, 1921. Newton's parents were Cornelia and Andrew Bumgarner. He had one brother, Monroe and one sister Tennessee Bumgarner Whitson, all of Wilkes County.

Newton served his country during World War I until he was wounded and sent home to recuperate. Later he became a postal clerk at the North Wilkesboro post office where he worked until his retirement in October 1960. He died June 18, 1962.

After her marriage to Newton, Neta worked for several years at the Wilkes Hosiery Mills. But being ambitious and capable, she directed her boundless energy to developing a business of her own. She was owner and operator of the Millers Creek United Insurance Agency, a thriving business that she built from the ground up. She sold the business to her brother Dale when she retired in 1972.

Neta has been very active in community affairs and in the Millers Creek United Methodist Church where she has been a member since she was a small girl.

Neta and Newton have one daughter, Marianne Jean Bumgarner, who was born August 22, 1945. Marianne now lives in Norwood, N.C., and is working on her Doctorate Degree in Social Studies at the University of North Carolina at Chapel Hill. In addition to her studies, she is doing part time teaching there.

Sources: Personal knowledge, Family Bible, and information from family members.

— Mae Church Johnson

STEPHEN BUMGARNER

414

Stephen Bumgarner was born in Wilkes 8 May, 1811. During his early years he lived on the headwaters of Maiden Cane Creek. As a young married man he built a home at the conflux of Maiden Cane and Reddies River. He acquired several tracts of land, some by grant and some by purchase. When he deeded land to his children, he did it in such a way that it could not be sold during his lifetime without his signature. It was said that because of this arrangement, some had homes who otherwise would have had none.

Family tradition describes Stephen as a large and powerful man, strong enough to carry a buck home on his shoulder after the hunt. He did everything in a big way. He raised plentiful farm and garden crops, kept bees, swine, poultry, and cattle, and did much fishing and hunting to provide food for his large family, and many guests. His hospitality was expansive, and people came from miles around to spend weekends with him and his son Andy, who had a house close by.

Stephen married Rebecca Nichols, daughter of William and Elizabeth Holdaway Nichols, and granddaughter of WWI veteran, Henry Holdaway.

Seven of the ten children of this family lived to have families of their own. The eldelst, Rev. James Linville Bumgarner, was in itinerant Methodist minister, and a 2nd Lt. in the Home Militia. Simeon Nelson died in prison in Petersburg, after serving in the 52nd Infantry Regiment. Nancy Caroline married Andrew Bullis and moved to Tennessee. Lydia Matilda married Joseph Rash and settled in Wilkes. Wesley Levi was captured at the Battle of the Wilderness and died in prison. Stephen Alexander married Belle Hayes and settled near his father's home. Absolom Bobbitt married Sarah Miller and settled east of Millers Creek. Fanny Rebecca died at age 13 in an epidemic.

William Amon married first Nancy Cooper, and second, Myra Camilla Bumgarner, and built a home across the hill from his father, to the east. Andrew Jackson stayed at home to look after the old folks, as the custom was for the youngest child. He married Cornelia Sturgill who was living with his parents at the time.

Among Stephen's grandchildren there were several of note. Rev. J.L.A. Bumgarner was a well-known Methodist minister. M.F. Bumgarner was a prominent educator and postmaster. Charlie Bumgarner, son of Linville, was for many years mayor of the town of Wilkesboro. Willard Cole was editor and publisher and Pulitzer Prize winner. Others include artists, businessmen, dentists, doctors, educators, farmers, musicians, nurses, salesman, and scientists.

Sources: Tombstones, Stephen Bumgarner Cemetery, Wilkes Marriage Records, Family Bible, and Family Tradition.

— Flora B. Friend

WILLIAM AMON BUMGARNER
415

William Amon (Bill) Bumgarner, was born at the Forks of Reddies River and Maiden Cane Creek in Wilkes County, on Aug. 25, 1853, and died Aug. 22, 1934. He was the youngest child of Stephen and Rebecca Nichols Bumgarner. He spent his entire life within three miles of his birthplace.

He was first married to Nancy Caroline Cooper, daughter of Enoch and Caroline McGlamery Cooper. This union was blessed with seven children: Mary, married, J.A. (Bud) Rhoades; J.F. (Jim) married Valeria Warren;

William A. and Camilla Bumgarner.

Rebecca, married, D.J. Brookshire; Caroline (Callie) married Welborn Kilby; Roby, married Deborah (Debbie) Nichols; and Mattie married Ira Rash.

After Nancy died when Mattie was born, he married Myra Camilla Bumgarner, daughter of Amos and Matilda Church Bumgarner. This union produced five children: Roxie, married Roby Brooks; Veada married Luther Nichols; William Isaac (Willie) married Mamie McNeil; DeWitt, married Blanche Warren, and Eugene married Violet Absher.

"Uncle Bill" was an unusual man in many ways. He was quite knowledgable in the field of astronomy. He could not only name the stars, but could locate and point them out. He was an exceptionally good Biblical scholar, despite the fact that he only attended school three weeks in his entire life; and that was during a time that he had a severely cut foot and could not work in the fields. His text books were the Bible, Pilgrims Progress, and Blums Almanac.

By trade he was a farmer, a soapstone miner, a hunter, and in his last years a weaver of baskets. Everything he did had a purpose. He didn't know the meaning of such words as passtime and hobby. His hunting was for the purpose of putting meat on the table, while he made baskets to provide a small cash income. A few of his soapstone fireplaces can still be found in the old houses in the community. His baskets are in the homes of many grandchildren and great grandchildren. But more perpetual than the soapstone and baskets is the stalwart strength of character that lives on in those fortunate enough to be his descendants.

Source: Family Bible and personal knowledge.

— Sidney Johnston

WILLIAM PERCY and BELVA LOU TRIPLETT BUMGARNER
416

One of the first twelve young men to leave Wilkes County on September 5, 1917, for encampment and training in World War I was William Percy Bumgarner, third son of Henry and Minerva Angeline Milam Bumgarner. He was born the 4th of July, 1890, and prior to being drafted, he operated a small general store. He returned from France in July 1919 with many interesting and exciting stores of the French people and his military experiences.

On December 25, 1920, Percy was married to Belva Lou Triplett, born 8 November 1894, daughter of William Cicero and Susan Jane Foster Triplett of the Lewis Fork community. Belva attended Appalachian State Teachers College in Boone and taught school several years prior to her marriage. Had she continued in the field of education, I am sure she would have become an outstanding educator. In 1970 they celebrated their golden wedding anniversary and then had their 57th just two days prior to Percy's death.

Percy and Belva became the parents of four sons, the youngest, William Cline, died in infancy. The other three sons all served in World War II at the same time and all returned home safely.

W.P. and Belva T. Bumgarner.

Howard Charles, born 24 January 1922, entered military service in September 1943 as a mechanic in the U.S. Air Force and since his discharge has lived on the family farm where he raised chickens for many years and still has many head of cattle. He was married 3 June 1961 to Nancy Kate Craven and they had two sons, Charles Howard, born 10 July 1962, and Johnny Randall, born 13 January 1966.

Rex Coolidge, born 12 January 1924, joined the U.S. Army in January 1943. He married Alma Dillard, 25 January 1942, and they had twin sons, Billy Rex and Bobby Rex, born 27 July, 1943, while their father was in service. A third son, Donald Ray, was born 27 December 1947. Bob married Rebecca Greer Stout, 26 July 1969, and they have two children, Rebecca Gwyn and Will. Bill Married Karen Hayes, 22 August 1970. They are the parents of Bryan Beth (deceased) and Casey Blake. Donald married Kathy Parsons, 1969, and they have one son, Carey Matthew. Rex was in the grocery business for many years and prior to his untimely death on 31 December 1981, he was employed by the Wilkes County Schools.

Jene Clinton, born 24 June 1925, joined the Marines in June 1944 and served in the Pacific Theater, having been at Iwo Jima. He is a licensed electrician and is presently Wilkes County Electrical Inspector. He was married on 16 April 1949 to Mary Brewer and they have two children, Kenneth Jene, born 7 December 1953, married Laurie Schnackenberg in August, 1975, and they have two children, Erin and Ashley. Deborah Jo, born 30 January 1957, married Robert Taylor, 30 June 1979.

During the years following his return from World War I, Percy worked for the State Highway Department and later spent two years in Quantico, Virginia in government construction work. From 1930 to 1932 he worked in Washington, D.C. In the late twenties he purchased the "Wash" Nichols farm at Millers Creek and was a farmer, a cattleman and a chicken grower. He died 27 December 1977 and was buried with Masonic rites at Mt. Lawn

Memorial Park. He and his three sons all became members of Mt. Pleasant Masonic Lodge 573.

Sources: Family Bible, personal recollections.

— Howard C. Bumgarner

BUTTERY

417

John Buttery (Buttrey) appeared in Surry County, N.C. in 1775, with the Allens. It is possible he was the step-father of Richard Allen, first sheriff of Wilkes County. Richard Allen's father, John, died in Baltimore County, Maryland, and his mother, Ann (Rhodes) Allen married a man by the name of Buttery. It is believed she moved to Frederick County, Virginia, lived several years, then came to Surry County, North Carolina with her husband and her Allen and Buttery children about 1770. Richard Allen is on the 1771-1777 Surry tax lists. Timothy Buttery was a chain carrier in 1778 in Surry County when land was surveyed for one David And Thomas Allen. He was on the Surry 1781 tax list as a single man.

In 1787, Richard Allen, his wife, Nancy Allen, Ann Buttery, Timothy Buttery, his wife, Mary Buttery, Keziah (Buttery) Sparks and her husband, Reuben Sparks joined Old Brier Creek Baptist Church. In 1792, Timothy and Mary Buttery and the Sparks were members of the Old Roaring River Primitive Baptist Church at Traphill; Timothy as a deacon. Timothy had bought land on a branch of Roaring River called Camp Branch near Traphill. It is believed a third Buttery child named Abraham belonged to Ann (Rhodes-Allen) Buttery. He was on the 1791 tax list of Caswell County, bought land in Surry County on Hunting Creek in 1802, but sold this land and remained in Caswell County.

Timothy Buttery owned 450 acres of land when he died in Wilkes County in 1802. Jesse and Richard Allen were bondsmen for Mary Buttery when she was appointed guardian of her minor children. Jesse Allen was co-administrator with Mary of the estate of Timothy Buttery.

Timothy and Mary (who was possibly a Jones) Buttery had seven children, six of whom have been identified: (1) Elizabeth, born 1784, died after 1860, married 19 March 1808 in Surry County, Wiley Jones, (2) Sarah, born 1786, married 18 May 1805 in Wilkes County, Edward Turner and removed to Kentucky, (4) William, born 1790, removed to Morgan County, Kentucky, (5) John Abraham, born 1792, died 7 March 1862 at Dockery, Wilkes County, married about 1818, Sarah Barker, (6) Mary Jones, born 1796, married 19 April 1826 in Wilkes County, Peter Brown, lived and died in Wilkes County, (7) unidentified female, born 1796, perhaps died young. After the death of Timothy, Mary (Jones) Buttery married on the 4 May 1806 in Wilkes County, the widower, Joseph Thompson, Sr. of Surry County. She outlived him by about twelve years and died in 1832 in Wilkes County, possibly at the home of her son, John Abraham Buttery, who was appointed the administrator of her estate by the court of Wilkes County in 1832.

John Abraham Buttery was a farmer and slave owner. He lived in the Dockery community near Traphill. It is of record that he was sometimes reluctant to pay his taxes! He married Sarah Barker about 1818 and they had six children, all born at Dockery: (1) John Thompson, born 1817, died 25 April 1912. He first married Winnie Matilda Wiles, born 1822, died 1879, daughter of Elizabeth Wiles. They are buried in unmarked graves on the homeplace at Dockery, (2) Timothy, born in 1823, possibly died young, (3) Sernetta P., born 27 March 1821, died 4 September 1900 at Dockery, married Jacob Staley, (4) Julianna, born 1823, (5) Nancy J. born 1825, married Joseph Staley, lived and died at Dellaplane, Wilkes County, (6) Columbus, born 1828, died or left Wilkes County before 1850, (7) Emily Elizabeth, born 30 January 1830, died 10 January 1888 at Dockery, married 17 December 1851, Jesse J. Billings, lived at Dockery.

Family tradition has it that the Buttery family objected to the courtship of John T. Buttery and Winnie Matilda Wiles, so much so, that they would lock John T. in his room. This did not prevent this couple from becoming the parents of eleven children, all born at Dockery: (1) John McClelland, born 9 March 1843, died 25 February 1917 in Utah, married 17 November 1870, Barbara E. Owen, (2) Lodemia, born 15 August 1846, died in Wilkes County, married 17 February 1867, Josiah S. Walker, (3) Sarah Evoline, born 5 June 1849, died in Wilkes County, married 27 February 1866, Isaac Boyden Goss, (4) Rachael Sylvania Jane, born 6 September 1852, died 14 March 1929, married 20 March 1881, James F. Waddell, (5) Julia Ann, born 12 April 1854, died 23 August 1883 in Shelby County, Alabama married John Andrew Walker, (6) Amelia Ellen, born 13 July 1854, died after 1880, married 19 March 1876, George Winfield Absher, (7) Samantha, born 4 May 1856, died 25 November 1938, married 1877 James Dolphus Walker, (8) Abraham Vance, born 8 November 1859, died 21 July 1940 in Ashe County, married 15 October 1880 Lodemia Wiles, (9) Sernetta B., born 16 July 1860, died 1930 in Ashe County, married 10 September 1880, Freeland Miller, (10) James Floyd, born 8 April 1864, died 3 October 1919, married 1st. Ann Beane, 2nd. Lou Stringer, (11) Carrie Belle, born 25th July 1866, died 24 January 1918, married 3 February 1886, Hardin Joines.

John T. Buttery lost his eyesight in his later years. He married as his second wife, Nancy Triplett, who was much younger than he. He was a fastidious man and was constantly concerned that Nancy was not keeping his appearance in a neat and tidy fashion. There were no children by the second marriage.

Sernetta P. Buttery, daughter of John Abraham and Sarah (Barker) Buttery, was born 27 March 1821, died 4 September 1900 at Dockery, married 26 January 1847, Jacob Staley, born 18 March 1826, died 25 April 1903, son of Jacob and Nellie (Childress) Staley. Both are buried in the family cemetery south of Traphill, N.C. Their children were: (1) Sarah who married John W. Myers and lived in Virginia. They had several children. (2) Ellen M., born 4 June 1850, died 11 October 1933, married J. Oliver Brewer. Both are buried at Mt. Pisgah Baptist Church at Dockery. They had no children. (3) Mary Roxana, born 23 May 1854, died 17 May 1934, married George E. Myers, brother to John W. they had seven children. Both are buried at Mt. Pisgah, (4) Sernetta, born 1861, died 10 March 1936, married Adolphus J. Myers. They are buried at Rock Creek Baptist Church east of Hayes. They had six children.

Sources: Old family papers, tombstone inscriptions, Wilkes and Ashe Marriages, Church Minutes, Surry and Wilkes tax lists, Wilkes deeds, information from descendants, Land Grant Office, Raleigh, N.C.

— Ruby Tuttle Absher
and Samuel E. Sebastian

THADDEUS CLINGMAN BYRD FAMILY

418

The Byrd family is an old one, having descended from the first known ancestor, Sir Hugo le Bird, who was a knight in the time of William the Conqueror in England. The spelling "le Bird" was used in certain branches in England, but some migrating into Virginia and North Carolina adopted the spelling "Byrd" The ancestry of the Byrd family has been traced in English records prior to the year 1100.

This account relates to the family of Thaddeus Clingman Byrd who was the sixth child of Thomas Byrd and Elizabeth Thornton Byrd. Thaddeus Clingman Byrd was born on September 2, 1855, and married Sallie Sale on February 15, 1876. Sallie Sale Byrd died on January 20, 1920, and he was married the second time to Martha Jane Richardson of Iredell County. He died on December 11, 1932, and he and both of his wives are buried in the Pleasant Hill Baptist Church Cemetery near Elkin, N.C. The children and lineal descendants of Thaddeus Clingman Byrd born to his first marriage are:

Thomas Luther Byrd, the eldest child, was born March 8, 1877; he died on August 7, 1965. He married Nelia Fields, a daughter of Rev. C. F. Fields, a well known Baptist minister. She died on May 8, 1965.

William Walker Byrd was born on March 4, 1879, and he died on December 4, 1945. He was married to Nannie Hare on February 14, 1906, in Yadkin County, and they resided all of their married life in the town of Elkin, Surry County, at a home on Elk Spur Street which he had purchased prior to their marriage.

Hilary Fletcher Byrd was born July 8, 1882; he died March 3, 1978. He was married to Sallie Fields, a sister of Luther Byrd's wife. She died on November 27, 1973. They spent their entire life in Wilkes County.

Ella Franklin Byrd, the only daughter of Thaddeus Clingman and Sallie Sale Byrd, was born September 8, 1884, and died on January 6, 1977. She married Charles Holcomb of Yadkin County and with him spent the rest of her life in Yadkin County.

Silas Sanford Byrd was born January 20, 1887, and was married to Etha Mae Goforth of Iredell County. Shortly after their marriage they migrated to the State of Iowa where they lived for the remainder of their lives. Sanford, as he was called, died in the 1960s and his wife died March 15, 1981. Both are buried in Orchard Cemetery, Orchard, Iowa.

Thomas Luther Byrd and his wife had ten children, namely: Charlie Byrd, born October 18, 1901; married Metta Hoots. Charlie was a school teacher until his retirement, and he also has extensive farming interests. Viola Byrd was born July 12, 1904, and married John Hurt; Fannie Byrd, born April 17, 1906, married Paul Melton; Ella Byrd, born October 6, 1907, married Elmer Anthony; Vance Byrd was born December 19, 1909, and married Maude Reece Mastin; Charity Byrd was born January 25, 1912, and married Odell Couch; Nell Byrd was born May 9, 1913, and married Ralph Beane; Louise Byrd was born November 10, 1916, and married Samuel Bray; Avery Byrd was born October 5, 1917, and married Opal Bray; and Ralph Byrd was born July 6, 1920, and married Estelle Freeman.

William Walker Byrd and his wife had two children: Blendon Reece Byrd, born August 9, 1907, and married to Zeno Dobbins; Hazel Byrd, born May 24, 1914, was their only other child.

Hilary Fletcher Byrd and his wife, Sallie Fields Byrd, had eleven children, three of whom died young: Susan Ina, born May 3, 1908, Robert Fields, born September 12, 1916, and Walter Edward, born June 20, 1920. Their other children are: Dewey Columbus Clingman Byrd, born March 7, 1907, and married to Hazel Hicks; Ernest Montgomery Byrd, born February 4, 1912, married Annie Barker; Fletcher Otis Byrd, born May 30, 1914, married Iris Sexton; Marvin Mayford Byrd, was born June 11, 1919, and married Ruby Cockerham; Everette Watson Byrd, born October 30, 1920, married Etta Mathis; Javan J. Byrd, born June 20, 1922, and died October 24, 1973; Nancy Lois Byrd was born December 28, 1925, and married Amos Lyons; Sallie Joyce Byrd, was born July 1, 1928, and married Claytus Cothren.

Ella Franklin Byrd Holcomb and husband, Charles Holcomb, had two children, namely: Laura Lee, born January 24, 1923, and married to Sidney Shore; Arthur Clingman Holcomb was born September 14, 1924, married Dorothy Adams.

Silas Sanford Byrd and wife, Etha Mae Byrd, had five children, all born in the State of Iowa, and they are: Kersey Byrd, born August 10, 1912, married Mildren Wentworth; Pauline Byrd, born August 6, 1914, married Merle Roloff; Carroll Byrd, born August 16, 1918, married Hila Hansen; and twins, Ernest Walker and Elaine Byrd, born October 1, 1923. Ernest married Janice Garrison and Elaine married Harlan Hansen.

Thaddeus Clingman Byrd was a farmer and all of his children with the exception of William Walker Byrd, who became a merchant, spent their lives on the farm. Some of his grandchildren pursued farming while others have been engaged in various business enterprises, teachers, employees in industry and in the private sector.

Sources: Family Bible records; *The Byrd Family History* (by Luther N. Byrd), personal knowledge and memories.

— Blendon Byrd Dobbins
and Hazel Byrd

AARON and BESSIE CALL
419

Aaron Conley Call, was born May 25, 1889 and died July 9, 1954. He was the son of John and Jane Johnson Call. He had one brother Daniel born September 1, 1901, died August 5, 1934. Their father died at an early age, leaving their mother with no means of support. Jane took the two boys and lived with her parents. Aaron, was very grateful to his grandparents, John and Fannie Inscore Johnson, for their contribution to his early life.

Aaron was married September 27, 1908 to Bessie Anderson, she was born March 14, 1890, died February 2, 1963. She was the daughter of Harrison M. and Caroline Love Anderson.

Their life together began on the Little Brushy Mountain in Wilkes County. They were both members of Mt. Sinai Baptist Church. Aaron was the Church Clerk for several years. Part of the children were born at the first home on the mountain. Others after they moved to North Wilkesboro, where Aaron worked for American Furniture Company. Some years later, around 1926, Mr. Call purchased some property just outside the City limits. He cleared the land, built a house and moved his family there. They had one last child, Jay Conley Call. Aaron soon left his job at American Furniture Company and built poultry houses for raising broilers, and did some small grain farming.

Aaron and Bessie raised seven children, two died at the age of a month. They were; Everette Call, born July 7, 1909, died May 2, 1967; Ennis Call Hutchinson, born March 14, 1911, died August 16, 1976; Rev. Robert Andrew Call, born December 10, 1914; William Harrison Call born, October 29, 1912; Otha Call, born June 15, 1920; twins, Silvia Fay and Lillie May born March 2, 1918. Silvia died April 3, 1918, Lillie died April 27, 1918. Calvin Hayes Call born July 14, 1924; Jay Conley Call born January 31, 1928. This family of children has contributed much to Wilkes County, in many ways.

I have many fond memories of Aaron and Bessie Call. While Jay and I were living in South Carolina, we would come home for a visit on wekends. If we were later than expected, Mrs. Call would keep the food warm on the wood cook stove for us. Almost everytime she would have a large plate of fried apple pies, she knew I liked them so well. She was always busy with her hands, if sitting around she was crocheting. Most of the things she made, she would give away. She taught me the basic stitches of crochet, and how to read the patterns. For this I am very grateful. I can also pass this handcraft down to my daughters.

Most of us awake to a radio, or an alarm clock in the mornings, but when we were at Mr. Call's house we would awake to hear him singing. He would start the fire in the old wood range, put the coffee on to perk and help Mrs. Call with breakfast. He did all of his work with a song on his lips, smile on his face, and a kind thought in his heart. He was a good neighbor, always there when needed.

I would like to end my story with a poem in their memory: Around the house the buttercups are bright, Someone peeps through the curtins of white, Welcome doors are open as you come into sight, Visiting Mother and Dad was always a delight. We liked to listen to the stories they would tell, of the people who doeth all things well.

Source: Bible records, Personal knowledge.

— Gracie F. Call

Aaron Conley and Bessie Anderson Call (1940).

CLARENCE CALL
420

My grandfather, Clarence Call, was the son of Isaac Slater Call and Martha Caroline Mastin Call. He was born April 7, 1869, in Wilkesboro, of pioneer ancestry.

Having obtained his preliminary education in the public schools of Wilkesboro, Clarence Call entered the Moravian Falls Academy.

Beginning life for himself as a clerk, he was first employed in a drug store at North Wilkesboro, and later in a general store. Changing his occupation, Mr. Call became a commercial traveler, dealing first in hardware and afterwards selling hats for a Norfolk firm.

Clarence Call.

In 1894, Mr. Call was elected sheriff and treasurer of Wilkes County, and, having been re-elected to the same offices in 1896, served two full terms in each position. In the meantime, in 1895, Clarence Call opened a mercantile establishment in North Wilkesboro C. Call's 5¢ & 10¢ Store — Ladies Ready-to-Wear & Millinery and C. C. Clothing Company — Clothing, Shoes, and Gent's Furnishings and carried on a substantial and successful business in that line. He was actively associated with various other enterprises, being a director and Vice-President of the Bank of North Wilkesboro, the principal stockholder and president of the Oak Furniture Company, and the president of the new Williams Mill Company, manufacturers of corn mills. He also established the Call Hotel in North Wilkesboro.

Mr. Call married, in December 1901, Miss Sallie Green Cook, daughter of Thomas A. and Gozeal Rhoades Cook of Guilford County. They had three daughters, namely Gozeal (Mrs. John E. Justice, Jr.), Madeline (Mrs. Orton A. Boren), and Dorothy (Mrs. James Bain Carter).

Not only was Clarence Call a large real estate owner, merchant banker, but he was a recognized leader in the Republican party. At the time of his death, he was the representative of his district in the State Senate, a district composed of Wilkes, Yadkin and Davie Counties. For 16 years, he represented the Republican party on the State Board of Elections. The first time he was appointed by Governor Aycock, and later by Governor Bickett. He also served as a member of the State Republican Committee and as Chairman of Congressional Committee of his district. Intelligently interested in political matters, Mr. Call attended the Republican National Conventions of 1896, 1908, 1912, and 1916.

Clarence Call was a member of Saint Paul's Episcopal Church in Wilkesboro. He was very active in the church serving as vestryman and treasurer.

Clarence Call died very suddenly of a heart attack on July 3, 1927, at the age of 58. He is buried in Mountain Park Cemetery in Wilkesboro. His wife, Sallie Call, who died in 1946, is also buried in Mountain Park Cemetery.

Sources: *Wilkes Journal* — July, 1927, *Charlotte Observer* — July, 1927, *History of North Carolina* — Volume IV, *Winston-Salem Journal* — July 5, 1927.

— Celia Carter Dickinson

JAY and GRACIE CALL
421

Jay Conley Call, was born January 31, 1928, in North Wilkesboro, NC, the son of Aaron Conley and Bessie Anderson Call. He was married July 12, 1952, to Gracie Francis. They moved to Columbia, SC, where Jay spent two years in army, stationed at Fort Jackson. In May of 1953, he spent two weeks at Camp Desert Rock, Nevada, to witness the Atomic Bomb test. After he recieved his honorable discharge September 12, 1954 they returned to North Wilkesboro, NC.

In 1955 he went into business with Tam Hutchinson, forming a partnership company called Chick Haven Poultry, he remained with this company until he sold his share in 1964. That same year he started his own poultry and cattle operation. In 1970 he also started a retail store named Call's Farm and Garden, both businesses are still in operation at this time.

Gracie, is the daughter of Kennie and Jettie Church Francis. She was born March 7, 1932 in Ashe County where she grew up. She graduated from Healing Springs High School at Crumpler, NC. She was first team basket ball player all four years of high school, and won the All-Tournament Award her senior year.

Jay and Gracie are active in community affairs. They are members of Liberty Grove Baptist Church. Jay, is a member of the Elks Club, Home Builders Association, and Member of the Horticulture advisory board of Wilkes Community College. He is also on the board of directors for Rileys Livestock Market, where he is part owner. Gracie, is a member of theWilkes Genealogical Society, Secretary and Treasurer of the Call Family Organization, and Office manager for Call's Farm and Garden.

Jay and Gracie have two daughters, Myra Gail Call Pickard, born July 13, 1954 in Columbia, South Carolina. Marcia Dawn Call, born October 23, 1959, in North Wilkesboro, North Carolina.

Myra was active in High School and Church affairs. At Wilkes Central she was president of the Future Home Makers Club, president of the Health Careers Club, Secretary of home room, member of Interclub Council, Academic Editor of the Year Book, and member of the National Honor Society. She was junior Choir pianist and assistant Senior Choir pianist at Liberty Grove Baptist Church where she is a member.

Myra, graduated with an associate degree in

The Jay Call Family (1980). Marcia Dawn, Myra Gail, Gracie F., and Jay Conley.

Nursing from Gardner Webb College in 1976. In 1979 she returned to graduate school at the University of North Carolina at Charlotte. She graduated in May 1980 with a Bachelor of Science Degree in Nursing. On June 14, 1980 she married Robert Holt Pickard. She is presently employed at the Mechlenburg County Health Department as Staff Nurse.

Marcia, was active, at Wilkes Central High School where she was a member of the Student Council, French club, Talon Staff, Green Key club, secretary of the Sophomore Class, Secretary of The Future Business Leaders of America, Teachers Assistant for four years, and member of the National Honor Society. In 1976 she was awarded the Certificate of Membership in the Society of Distinguished American High School Students. Marcia, is also a member of Liberty Grove Baptist Church.

Marcia ,is presently a senior at Greensboro College. She is secretary of the senior class, and will graduate May 9, 1982 with a major in Business and Legal Administration.

Source: Personal knowledge.

— Gracie F. Call

The Harrison Call Family. Front row: Gary, Lula Swaim Call, Harrison, and James. Back row: Maynard, Andrew, William Harrison, Jr., Willie Call Miller, Callie Call Chatham, Bessie, and Sylvia Call Brown.

WILLIAM HARRISON SR. and LULA CALL

422

William Harrison Call Sr., was born October 29, 1912, in Wilkes County. He was the son of Aaron and Bessie Anderson Call. He spent the first eight years of his life in the Little Brushy Mtn. community where he attended Mt. Zion School. In 1920 his parents sold their home on Little Brushy and bought a home in downtown North Wilkesboro, where he attended North Wilkesboro School for two years. In 1925 his parents again sold their home and purchased some land and built in the Fairplains community. He then attended Fairplains school, after that he helped his father farm until he was married.

He was married November 17, 1928, to Lula Mae Swaim. Jobs were hard to find, so he did miscellaneous work until 1929 when they moved to Mayberry, West Virginia where he was a logger for a mining company. They lived in a two room house, which was shared with another person.

I have heard my father say that cabbage soup was one of the main meals. Around 1930, Harrison and Lula moved back to North Wilkesboro where he went to work for Greer Cotton Mill located on Old 421 just above where Wilkes General Hospital is today. Having no transportation, he walked seven miles to work, put in a ten hour day, and walked back home for fifty cents a day. He did this for six months until he was laid off because of a new law called the minimum Hourly Wage Act (approx. 30¢ per hour). Again jobs were hard to find and for the next few years he did odd jobs to support his family until he went to work on the W.P.A. program. When World War II began, he helped build the camps at Blackstone, Wilmington, Goldsboro and Eden. Later he went to work for F.C. Johnson as a sawmiller and thrasher. During this time, he

would sawmill in the winter and go from house to house thrashing wheat in the summer. He also found time to work his fields and tend other fields for other people. In 1949 he went to work for American-Drew Furniture Company, where he worked for twenty six years and retired.

Harrison joined Flint Hill Baptist Church in 1960 and is presently a Deacon and Sunday School teacher. Lula Mae Swaim, was born January 8, 1911, to Hollie Mae and Clementine Brown Swaim in North Wilkesboro, N.C. She attended Flint Hill School and at age sixteen went to work for Wilkes Hosiery Mill until she was married. She was a member of Liberty Grove Baptist Church untill 1960 when she joined with her husband at Flint Hill Baptist Church.

Since their marriage in 1928 they have had twelve children, nine are still living. They are: Sylvia, born May 8, 1929, married to C.B. Brown; Bessie Lee born April 27, 1931; Callie born February 17, 1935, married William Fredrick Chatham; Willie born February 20, 1937, married Robert Glenn Miller; William Harrison Jr. born January 4, 1940 married Ruth Boggs; Buster Andrew born February 20, 1942 married Angie Hawkins; Maynard born December 3, 1945 married to Edna Ward; James born January 31, 1948 married Pauline Miles; and Gary born July 14, 1950, Married Doris Johnson.

Harrison and Lula, also has sixteen grandchildren and twelve great-grandchildren.

Source: Family Bible and Personal knowledge.

— James Call

WILLIAM SHERMAN CALL

423

William Sherman Call was born June 15, 1908, near the old Call post office six miles east of Wilkesboro, North Carolina. He was the oldest son of Darius Call (1889-1932) and Nora Curry Call (1886-1966.) The brothers and sisters were: Henry Clay (1912-1917); Clarence B. (1915-1917); Hubert Franklin (born 1919); Laura Lucille (1921-1980); James Hafford (born 1924); Charlie Eugene (born 1927); and Ruby Alice (born 1929).

In 1918 the family bought a large water-powered grain and lumber mill located four miles west of Wilkesboro by the Yadkin River where the Kerr Scott dam is now. After graduating from high school at Wilkesboro in 1929, William Sherman spent two years in Ohio learning watch and jewelry repairing. When his father died in 1932, he returned to Wilkes County in the Great Depression. While working for Carl Steele's Jewelry Store in 1934, he married Delta Christene Phillips, born June 26, 1917. That year he moved to Boomer, North Carolina, and worked with James Larkin Pearson in his print shop. At that time, James Larkin was publishing a monthly paper called "The Fool Killer." This paper had a nation-wide circulation.

In 1941, William Sherman moved to Alaneda, California, and set up and operated a school to train aircraft instrument mechanics for the Navy. In 1950 he was appointed by President Truman to serve as an auditor on the Hoover Commission.

While in California, he was active in business and civic organizations.

Returning to Wilkes County in 1965, he worked with the N.C. Mental Health Department and helped organize the Wilkes County Council on Alcoholism and served for two years as its Executive Direcotr. While working with the Alcoholism Program he helped organize the New River Mental Health Program, after which the alcoholism program became part of the Mental Health Program.

He is a Charter Member of the Wilkes County Genealogical Society. He helped organize the Call Family Organization and has served as its president since 1979.

Darius Call's father was Benjamin Franklin Call (1863-1946), and his mother was Laura Cornelia Call (1868-1946). Ben and Laura had eight children who lived to adulthood: Darius, Fielander, Athos, Winford, Audie, Claude, Harvey and Zilla.

"Ben" Call was a millwright who owned and operated a water-powered sawmill and grain mill. He built mills for other people. Laura Call was aked by one of her grandchildren why the Calls sometimes married their cousins. Her reply was, "To keep the wealth in the Call family."

Benjamin Franklin Call's father was James Martin Call (1823-1902). His mother was Emily Call (1827-1918). James and Emily had nine children. They were: Mary Anngenetta, America Elizabeth, Martha Caroline, David Elkanah, Jane Fidelier, Jonathan Silvester, Benjamin Franklin, Acenath Clementine, and Matilda Eveline.

James Martin Call was a school teacher. He was an official in the Methodist Church and helped organize the Eschol Methodist Church, one of the oldest Methodist Churches in Wilkes County.

James Martin Call's father was Isaac Call, born 1794. His mother was Sarah Elizabeth Slater (born 1796). They had six children, who were: Nancy, Josephine, James Martin, Isaac Slater, William Berton and Daniel H.

Isaac Call's father was Daniel Call, Sr., born January 23, 1761 died May 21, 1845. He was married to Margaret Smith on 16 February, 1791, at the Forks of the Yadkin in Rowan County. They had three boys born in Rowan County before they moved to Wilkes. They were: Daniel, Jr., Isaac, and David. They settled on a plantation five miles east of Wilkesboro near the Wilkes County race track. Many members of the family are buried in the cemetery near the old homesite.

Sources: family Bibles; Gravemarkers; Census Reports; Deed Books; Wills, Marriage Records; Other family records.

— William Sherman Call

THE CALLOWAY FAMILY
424

It often happens in many towns and counties where prominent families existed previously, their names are no longr heard. Their memory is often forgotten and engulfed by time. Such is the case in the name of the Calloway family, a member of which was Dr. James Calloway and family which lived in Wilkes County for many years.

To begin with the history of the Calloways, it should be said that they migrated from Virginia to Ashe as early as 1740. They located on the south fork of the New River, on the banks of which is the old Calloway Cemetery in which the older members are buried.

Dr. Thomas Calloway came to Ashe County about 1712. He was a captain in the French and Indian War and was a great friend of Daniel Boone and went with him from North Carolina to Kentucky. Some of the Calloway's followed Boone into Missouri. Captain Thomas Calloway's grave is marked by a long, slim stone, probably six to eight feet long, with the date of his death on it. It was supposed to be the stone that marked Daniel Boone's camps and was treasured by Daniel Boone as a result of the fact that he found it unexpectedly when he killed a deer that fell across the stone close to the Calloway's home.

Elisah Calloway married Mary Cuthbert in 1760. She was a niece of Daniel Boone's. Elisah Calloway came from Virginia early in the 18th century. As stated before, he settled on the south fork of the New River and was my great-great-grandfather.

Eligah Calloway, who was my great-grandfather, built in the same general area of the New River. He built the first brick house which had glass windows in Ashe County and had eleven children including his son James Calloway, around whom this story is being written. He was born at the old home place in 1806. He died in 1878 in his 72nd year. Dr. Calloway was educated in the schools such as existed at that time close to his home. He was studious and had a very receptive mind. He was sent to the N.C. State Senate in 1820, 1830 and 1834. He was 21 years of age when first elected to the Senate. It is interesting to note that there were Calloways from Ashe County in the State House or Senate continuously from 1800 to 1850. There have been other members related to the family in these bodies since that time.

Early in the 1830's, James Calloway was admitted to the University of Pennsylvania as a medical student. At that time, it only took two years to finish the course. It has been said that he attended some lectures also at the Jefferson Medical College. I have instruments that Dr. Calloway used with ebony handles which were used in the pre-aseptic and anitseptic days in surgery; of these I am very proud.

In 1835, Dr. Calloway married Mary Carmichael, daughter of Captain Abner Carmichael of Wilkes County and a sister of L.B. Carmichael, a man familiar to the bar in this judicial district and in the legislature of North Carolina. To this marriage there were four children: Mary Virginia, Frances Caroline, Abner Sydenham and Mary. All of these children were well educated with college degrees and married well. Abner was a graduate of the University of North Carolina and fought all the way through the Civil War, first as a lieutenant and then as a captain. Mary Carmichael Calloway, his wife, died in 1846.

In 1852 Dr. Calloway married Annie Perry Yeakle of Hagerstown, Maryland and Philadelphia. When the doctor met her she was visiting with an aunt in Ashe County. She was a student at Peace College in Raleigh. To this couple were born six children: Harriet Hoge, Elizabeth Charlotte, Annie Yeakle, Ruth Bowie, Jane Alice and a baby who died in infancy. All of these girls were well educated and married well. My mother was Annie Yeakle. During all these years, Dr. Calloway was a very busy man. He practiced in the horse and buggy days and covered seven counties extending into Virginia. He was gone at times for several days being held up frequently by swollen streams which kept him in the house of patients overnight or for several days. Dr. Calloway was the only regularly bred physician in the whole country between Statesville, N.C. and Wytheville, V.A. He was violently opposed to secession when the Civil War developed, but in 1861 he was elected to the convention by Governor Vance and voted for the ordinance of seccession and strenuously supported it during the war.

Dr. Calloway was a great student of the men and participants of the Revolutionary War and gave a great deal of help to the soldiers of the revolution and Civil War in working out their pensions. He had a great deal of correspondence with Governor Vance regarding the state and about the soldiers and other matters. Although at one time he was said to control more votes than any man in the county, he took very little interest in politics after the war and suffered many set backs and had many problems as a resutl of legislation passed following the Civil War.

He was a large land owner in Wilkes and Ashe County as well as in Kansas. As he had great interest west of the Mississippi River, he moved to Kansas where he owned extensive areas of real estate in 1870. His health failed him out there and he came home and died in about three years, in a new home which he built in Wilkesboro, about 1875, and is the place in which I was raised.

He was responsible for bringing the Siamese Twins to Wilkes County which is explained in detail in *The Two,* by Irving and Amy Wallace written about 1875. This book covers their lives and travels as showmen all over the world.

According to a long statement concerning Dr. Calloway in the *Wilkesboro Witness* paper and the *Raleigh Observer*, the following statement was made at its end:

"The Common judgement of those who knew Dr. Calloway well is that he was a man of extraordinary natural strength of mind, sharpened and improved by extensuve professional and business association and of an inflexible purpose in the prosecution of his aims. He had collected a vast amount of traditionary matters connected with the war of the revolution and hence was generally interested in such subjects, and especially useful to those entitled to pensions as soldiers, and all descendants. He was thirty years of his life, a member of the Episcopal Church which he helped build and organize in Wilkesboro. The administrations in his sick room during his long and painful illness by the church gave him the greatest comfort."

Sources: Private files of the Calloway History.

— Fred C. Hubbard, M.D., F.A.C.S.

JOSEPH ALEXANDER LAFAYETTE CAMPBELL
425

Joseph Alexander Lafayette Campbell was born April 17, 1833, in Alexander County, North Carolina, the son of James Campbell and Betsy Bowles Campbell.

He married Sarah E. Meadows on December 21, 1859. They had two children, Quince and Jane. After Sarah's death, he married C. Jane Gwaltney on March 31, 1869, daughter of

Howell Gwaltney and Elsie Hendren. Their children are as follows: (1) Leb, (2) Rhemous Carl, (3) Minnie, (4) John, (5) Kelsey, (6) Florence.

He was a miller by trade and making a very good living until his family grew so large that he could not support them all very well at the mill. He decided to rent a farm so his family could help make the living. In 1887, J.A. "Fate" Campbell and Jane G. Campbell rented a farm and brought their family to Wilkes County to live and work.

Their son Rhemous Carl Campbell, born January 21, 1874, died December 6, 1956, married Lethia Etta Dowell born January 5, 1881, died July 7, 1956, in 1897. She was the daughter of Leander and Annie E. Dowell.

They made their home approximately seven miles east of North Wilkesboro on highway 268. Papa and Granny were hard-working, God-fearing people and certainly raised their family in a Christian home. If ever there was a woman who knew how to manage and care for her family, Granny did, and she simply would not tolerate laziness.

Papa Campbell walked to North Wilkesboro every day to the Turner-White Casket Company and back home each night. Even on snowy mornings, Papa would have Granny bind his feet with rags, and you could hear the snow crunch long after he got out of sight.

Twelve little "strangers" were born to them. (I use this word because of a little book that Papa wrote in his later years telling of his and Granny's courtship and marriage. He wrote "and one day a little 'stranger' came to live with us", referring to their first baby.)

Their children's names are: (1) Vella, (2) Elnore, (3) Annie, (4) Fred, (5) Lav, (6) Paul, (7) Melvin, (8) Viola, (9) Irene, (10) Selma, (11) Helen, (12) Inez, Selma is my mother.

My parents, Selma Kathleen Campbell, born February 20, 1913, and James Burette Wiles born March 21, 1908, died July 27, 1975, were married on November 2, 1933. He was the son of John Avery Wiles and Nancy Melinda Brewer Wiles.

They lived with Daddy's parents for a while and in a short time were able to build a house on the land that Papa Campbell willed to mother. They had a hard life but always had plenty and were very happy when their first baby came along. Born on August 14, 1934, was Patsy Anne, followed by Francis Louise, born January 14, 1936, Harold James born October 28, 1942, and myself, Aundra Jeneane, born February 7, 1947.

On February 11, 1968, I married Kenneth Bryce Absher, born January 25, 1945, son of Hansel Absher and Maude Vannoy Absher. We have made our home on land that my parents gave us which was part of the tract of land that originally belonged to Papa Campbell. We have two sons, Kenneth Brandon, born November 27, 1969, and Gregory James born October 22, 1971. They are students at Roaring River school.

Kenneth served in the army in Viet Nam in 1966 with the 1st Infantry Division. He is employed at Abitibi — Price Corp. In Roaring River and I work for Modern Globe.

Sources: Personal knowledge, interviews with family members, death certificates.

— Aundra Wiles Absher

THE CARLTON FAMILY
426

The family of John and Elizabeth Wallace Carlton came to Virginia prior to the Revolutionary War and settled in Albemarle County. Various members of the family later relocated to Wilkes County, N.C. by the time the county was formed. It has been said that John was lost overboard enroute to the colonies about 1766. It is believed that John and Elizabeth were married in England about 1750. Elizabeth died in Wilkes County, N.C. before 1800.

There were at least five children born to John and Elizabeth: (1) Elizabeth who died about 1810 in Scott County, Ky. (2) John, Jr. (3) Thomas born about 1756, died in 1844 in Wilkes County; (4) Lewis born September 12, 1758, died March 13, 1827 in Wilkes County, near Boomer; (5) Ambrose born March 28, 1763, died December 14, 1832 in Lawrence County, Indiana.

Thomas Carlton, son of John and Elizabeth first married about 1777 a lady by the name of Mary. They must have moved to North Carolina about 1778 from Albemarle County, Va. They had at least nine children as follows: John, Mary, Henry, Cynthia, Thomas, Jr., Jane and three other unidentified daughters. Mary died in 1796.

Thomas Carlton married as his second wife, Catherine Livingston, born about 1775, died after 1800, daughter of John C. Livingston. The marriage bond is dated February 6, 1799. To this union were born eight children: Livingston Leroy, Ambrose, Wyatt, Louenda, Dennis, Silas, Charlotte, Pickens, all born in Wilkes County. Thomas Carlton, Sr. is recorded in history as a Tory during the Revolutionary War.

Wyatt Carlton, son of Thomas and Catherine, was born about 1804, died in Watauga County, N.C. He married Nancy Livingston December 11, 1823. They moved to Caldwell County and later to Watauga. Their children were Finley, Calvin, Elvira, John R., Daniel, Alan, Lindsey, Thomas, Cornelius and Martha.

John R. Carlton, son of Wyatt and Nancy, was born 1835 in Wilkes, died after 1880 in Kentucky. He married March 15, 1854 in Wilkes County, Frances (Frankie) Gold born 1830, in Wilkes County. He is supposed to have become a Baptist preacher before moving to Kentucky. They had children Mary Jane, Wyatt Finley, Darah L., Charlotte, Drury S., John L. and Don Thomas.

I descend through Wyatt Finley Carlton by way of his son William Culbey born May 20, 1895 in Wilkes County, and his grandson, Everette L. Carlton who lives in Gastonia, North Carolina.

Sources: Family research, personal knowledge.

— Linda C. Grant

GLENN BURTON CARLTON FAMILY
427

The Glenn Burton Carlton family, of Boomer, is descended in a direct line from John Carlton, whose father, also John Carlton, drowned accidentally while sailing from England to America with his wife and children in early 1700s. His wife and children settled in Virginia, and the son, John Carlton, married Elizabeth Wallace, a Virginian. They lived on the Staunton River in Virginia before moving to North Carolina between 1777 and 1780, although there is one version which says John died in Virginia before his family moved to North Carolina. There were four sons and one daughter, and the four sons served in the Revolutionary War at the same time. It has been told that the four sons returned from the War at the same time. Their mother was in the potato patch digging potatoes for dinner and was so shocked and surprised to see them that she threw up her arms and lost her knife, which was never found.

Their son, Thomas Carlton, was born in Virginia in 1756 and was living in North Carolina in 1780, where he settled on a 375 acre farm near Boomer and lived there all his life. Part of this property is still owned by his descendants. His first wife, Mary, died after having eight children, and he later remarried and died in 1844.

Their oldest son, John Carlton, was born in 1778, married first Elizabeth Barlow who died after having three children. John later married Susanna Smith in 1813 and had five children. Susanna Smith's mother was Susanna Berryford Smith, who was born at Casebury Town, Chester County, England, the daughter of a marble sculptor. Her mother died when she was very young. She and her brothers and sisters stayed at home alone while their father was at work.

When Susanna Berryford was five years old a strange man and woman came to the home several times, and one day brought another man with them. They gave little Susanna candy and persuaded her to go riding with them. They took her to a port, placed her on a ship and took her to America. She was sold in Virginia or Maryland to a family to do housework. When she was eight years old she was doing the work of an adult and was cruelly treated. Tradition tells that when she did the washing if it did not please her mistress she would beat Susanna with wet sheets. In winter she was forced to iron the sheets at night to have the beds warm for the family.

When she was fifteen years old she ran away to be free from the cruel treatment and married Mr. Smith, with whom she had a slight acquaintance. They moved to Stokes County, North Carolina, and later to Wilkes County. She never heard anything of her family in England after she was kidnapped. Her daughter, Susanna Smith, married John Carlton.

Charles Carlton, the third child of John and Susanna Carlton, was born at Boomer, Wilkes County, in 1819. He married Sarah Catherine Saner, a neighbor girl, and they built a large log house on the homestead land on Warrior

Nell and Glenn Carlton (1978).

Creek at Boomer, and had eight children. He was a teacher, justice of the peace, deputy sheriff, clerk and leader in the Baptist Church, and lived in the home he built for the rest of his life until he died in 1880. The house still stands and was used as a homeplace for several generations. Several of his children went west when young and settled in Texas, Kansas and California.

One of the sons of Charles and Sarah Catherine Carlton, Samuel Smith Carlton, born 1853, remained at Boomer and lived in the log house on the original homestead all of his life. His first wife died at age 23, leaving four small children. His second wife, Eliza Carlton, a distant cousin, had three children. He died in 1926, age 73. The children of Sam and Eliza Carlton were Nora Carlton, Royster Carlton, and Glenn Burton Carlton. Nora married Adonis Howell, had one son, Don Howell, and lived in the old log house all her life. Royster married George Laxton, had no children, and lived in Caldwell County.

The son, Glenn Burton Carlton, married Nellie Caroline Swanson, a distant cousin from a neighboring home, and built a house on part of

the original homestead land. He was born in 1893, was a Rural Mail Carrier from Boomer to Caldwell County, active in Zion Hill Baptist Church, and in all community affairs. He died in 1979 at age 85. His wife is still living in the house built in 1918 and is 82. Glenn and Nell had three children, Carolyn Nell Carlton, Glenn Burton Carlton, Jr. and Vernon Pete Carlton.

Of the three children of Glenn and Nell Carlton, two are living in Wilkes County. Their daughter, Carolyn Nell, born in 1918, married Francis Marion Cross, now deceased, of Wellman, Texas, and lived in El Paso, Texas, for several years. She now resides in Moravian Falls, Wilkes County. Glenn Burton Carlton, Jr. born in 1921, served in the SeaBees in World War II, married Etta Gray Mayberry, of Hays, Wilkes County, deceased, lived in Richmond, Virginia for many years; later married Lee Neilson, and lives in Port St. Lucie, Florida. Vernon Peter Carlton, born in 1926, married Lael Carlton, a distant cousin, of Casa Grande, Arizona, and lives on part of the original homestead in Boomer.

Carolyn Carlton Cross and Francis M. (Chris) Cross, had two daughters, Julia (Judy)

Nell Cross and Frances Carolyn Cross.

Judy Cross married Bobby G. Barnes, of Taylorsville, deceased, and had two children, Christina Rae Barnes and Edward Glenn Barnes, and lives in Wilkesboro, N.C. Frances Carolyn Cross married Clyde McCoy Hunt, Jr., of Winston-Salem, lived in San Diego, California, and Chesapeake, Virginia, for several years, and now lives in Chapel Hill, N.C. They have two daughters, Caroline McCoy Hunt and Sarah Cross Hunt.

Glenn Burton Carlton, Jr. and Etta Gray, his first wife, had one daughter, Linda Kaye, who married Darrell Cranfill, now divorced. She has one son, Nathan Cranfill, and lives in Moravian Falls, N.C.

Vernon Peter (Pete) Carlton and Lael, had one daughter, Cynthia Louise, who married Ernest Winslow. They live in Tappahannock, Virginia, and have one daughter, Brooke, born in 1981.

Sources: The *History of the Carlton Family in Wilkes County*, (written by Luther F. Carlton, of Los Angeles, California) family tradition.

— Carolyn Carlton Cross

ROY ED CARLTON

428

My grandfather, Roy Ed Carlton, was born Janurary 1, 1900. He was raised in Wilkes County, in a small community called Boomer. When asked how Boomer got its name, Roy Ed always said, "This place used to be jammed with Boomer squirrels." People came from miles around to hunt, some even settled here. Later on in the century Boomer became divided into several communities. Roy Ed lived in one of these communities called Thankful.

Roy, like many other blacks at this time, had limited educational skills. The main type of education was the church. Many blacks learned to read there. Thankful Baptist Church is the oldest Negro church in Wilkes County on record. The church type of education lasted until 1935. Roy Ed, superintendent of the church, along wih other staff members, decided to build a school. It took a year to complete and opened in September 1936. Black students in the community attended the school, some parents in the county even moved to Thankful so that their children could attend the new school. Thankful School was the first Negro public school in the county. All of it's teachers have passed on except one, John Barber, who is presently teaching at Woodward Junior High.

The school closed down in 1965. All of Roy Ed's children attended school and graduated. His eldest son, Howard Lee Carlton, went on to complete his education at N.C. State in Raleigh to major in sales management.

Roy Ed had 10 more children: Mary, Tina, Lula, Roy Ed, Jr., Robert, Ralph, Dorothy and Dutch. Roy Ed died in October 12, 1981 at the age of 81. He had 36 grandchildren, and 4 great-grandchildren.

Sources: Personal knowledge, interviews.

— Joseph Randolph Carlton

THE FAMILY of MARY CARROLL

429

Mary Carroll of Wilkes County had four known sons: Thomas, Cleveland, Gasaway, and Dennis. Her husband was thought to be John Carroll, Deed Book I in Wilkes County Courthouse shows that on Feb. 19, 1847 Mary owned 40 acres of land on the Laurel Fork of Elk Creek.

One of her sons, Cleveland Carroll, was born in 1811. In 1840 he was married to Charlotte Triplett, daughter of Lewis and Betsy Triplett. To this union was born Lewis William, James Elijah, Julia A., Sidney Thomas, Smith Ferguson, Nancy, George W., Mary, and John Colbert Carroll. One reminder of this family is a solitary chimney which stands at the site of the old Cleveland Carroll homeplace.

Lewis William Carroll married Rachel L. Hayes. He was a medium-sized man with black hair and blue eyes. He wore a long beard. During his service in the Civil War he told the story of a comrade who had his knapsack strap shot in two by a Yankee bullet. Circumstances were so tense and food in such short supply that the soldier, in the midst of a heated battle, had the forethought to kneel down and pick up his piece of dry bread which had rolled out on the ground.

Lewis William Carroll's six children were: George Washington, James Noah, P. Gasaway, Isabel, Gertrude, and Anna. James Noah and Anna moved to the state of Montana. He spent several years herding sheep on a ranch near Butte, Montana. His sister, Anna, settled nearby and made this area her permanent home. Isabel had a flair for storytelling and was a very entertaining person. She loved to travel and in her last years she would take a bus or airplane and visit her relatives throughout the United States.

P. Gasaway Carroll was born July 17, 1876 and was married to Mary Elizabeth Winkler on January 21, 1907. Their children, all born in Watauga County, were Eula Doyce, Molly Ann, Ward Gurney, and Norma Virginia. Gasaway had an interest in education and after attending school as much as possible in the late 1800's, he took advantage of community singing and penmanship schools which were common at this time. He taught himself to "pick" the five string banjo and enjoyed joining with neighbor musicians to pick and sing. His children used to ask him to play a song, "All Night Long," and he would play a line of the song on the banjo head. He was also the community barber at one time. Besides being a farmer, he served as deputy sheriff and road supervisor. He liked to keep abreast of all county functions and was school committeeman for 22 years, bank director, attended board of education meetings, agriculture meetings and was chairman of his political party in his community.

All of the children were sent to what was then Appalachian State Teachers College. Eula became a teacher and school principal in Watauga County. She and her husband, Mack A. Cowles, taught from 1942 to 1971 in Wilkes County; she was a teacher and he was principal at Ferguson, Roaring River and Millers

Norma Carroll and Leander H. (Nick) Collins.

Creek Schools.

Molly Ann married Claude P. Jackson and lived in Hampton, Virginia as a homemaker for her husband and daughter Carol Ann. Carol Ann graduated from William and Mary College, received her M.A. degree from Old Dominion College in Norfolk and her doctorate from the University of Kentucky. She taught American Literature at Iowa State University and is now residing in Chicago, Ill. She has two daughters, Cynthia Carol and Deborah Kay Verser.

Ward Gurney Carroll served in World War II, was in the lumber business, and became sheriff of Watauga County in 1966 and is still serving as sheriff in 1982. He and his wife, Elsie Elizabeth Baker have two children, Johnny Baker Carroll who serves as deputy sheriff with his father, and Kathy Ann Carroll Main is drivers license inspector for Watauga and Ashe Counties.

Norma Virginia graduated from ASTC, B.S. and M.A. degrees. She was married to Leander Hollister Collins of Egan, South Dakota. She started her teaching career in Watauga County, then went to Caldwell County where she met her husband. Following World War II she went to South Dakota with her husband and resumed her teaching career in Moody County there. Their only child, Norma Gayle, was born in Flandreau, S.D. on April 10, 1947.

Norma returned to North Carolina and came to teach school in Wilkes County at Millers Creek School in 1947 where she remains as second grade teacher. She and her husband moved to Millers Creek in 1952. Her husband, Leander H. Collins, worked as an insurance agent, managed a service station, and was director of the West Wilkes High School Band. They joined Millers Creek Methodist Church; Leander and Norma both sang in the choir for many years. Leander worked as counselor of Youth Fellowship, taught Sunday School, and Norma has taught the primary class since the merger of the church in the 1950's and served in many capacities on the official board, and in the United Methodist Women.

Sources: Wilkes County Deed Books, Census Schedules, and family knowledge.

— Norma C. Collins

MARY ELIZABETH WINKLER CARROLL

430

Mary Elizabeth Winkler was born in the Rutherwood community of Watauga Co., N.C. She was born May 27, 1885 and died May 4, 1962 in Wilkes County. She married P. Gasaway Carroll on Jan. 27, 1907 at the home of her parents. This couple were the parents of four children: Eula, Molly, Ward, and Norma.

Mary Elizabeth Winkler went with her brother Roby and her sister Martha to further their education at Watauga Academy in Boone, N.C. She studied with a professor Frankum. It was her intention to become a teacher but she married instead.

Through the years she made a home for people who were travelling in the community. Teachers and workers boarded in the home. She spent spare time knotting bedspreads to mail to a lady in Poughkeepsie, New York. She earned more than $3,000 from her bedspreads in the 1930s.

After she broke her hip in 1954, she came to live with her daughter, Norma Carroll Collins, in Millers Creek. She lived there until her death from cancer of the jaw and throat.

Mary Elizabeth Winkler was the daughter of David Marshall Winkler, born April 4, 1847, and Mary Caroline Bingham Winkler, born Oct. 15, 1851.

David Marshall Winkler's five children were: Vilene who married Floyd McNeil and had one daughter, Melissa; Benjamin Roby, born July 21, 1877, married Blanche Purlear and had two sons, Gardner and Dorman; Martha Adeline, born Feb. 13, 1884, married George Washington Carroll; Mary Elizabeth (described above); and Avery Crawford, born Feb. 4, 1888, married Rose Wilcox and had several sons and daughters.

David Marshall Winkler's father was Isaac Winkler, sometimes referred to as Joshua, born about 1808. He was married to Mary (Polly) Greer, born 1812. Their children were: Nancy H., born 1842; Sarah A., born 1844; Elizabeth E., born Nov. 9, 1845; Thomas Calvin, born 1848; David Marshall, born Feb. 15, 1849; and Micaja A., born 1855.

Isaac Winkler was believed to be the grandson of Thomas Winkler of Burke County, now Caldwell County, N.C.

Sources: Information from family members, Wilkes County Wills and Census Schedules.

— Norma C. Collins

MR. and MRS. DANIEL JENNINGS CARTER

431

Dan and Lewis Carter were active members of the Wilkes community for many years.

Daniel Jennings Carter, who could trace his connection with Wilkes County back to two great-grandfathers, Edward Carter and James Jennings, who lived here for several years during the Revolutionary War period before moving on to Buncombe County, came here himself in 1911. He had been born on December 10, 1883, in Burnsville, Yancey County, the son of Daniel Ginnings and Ophelia McGimsey Carter. After his father's death when young Dan was eighteen months old, his mother took him and his two sisters back to her previous home, Canoe Hill, in Burke County. They lived with her sister, Mrs. William M. Avery, and went to school there and later at Barium Springs Orphanage.

Daniel Jennings Carter.

Prior to coming to North Wilkesboro, Dan Carter was employed by Asheville newspapers and shortly after arriving here he established the Carter Printing Company. In 1917 he founded the *Wilkes Journal* newspaper, changing its name to *Carter's Weekly* in 1920, and then back to the *Wilkes Journal* in 1923. In 1924 he sold his interest in the *Wilkes Journal* and conducted a commercial printing business until 1932 when he and J.C. Hubbard combined the *Wilkes Journal,* the *Wilkes Patriot* and the commercial printing business into Carter-Hubbard Publishing Company, of which D.J. Carter was president until his death on December 1, 1945.

During the thirty-four years Dan Carter lived in Wilkes County he participated in a variety of church and civic activities. He was an elder and building committee member of the North Wilkesboro Presbyterian Church, a member and then chairman of the North Wilkesboro Board of Education, a member and president of the

N. Wilkesboro Kiwanis Club, on the board of directors of the N. Wilkesboro Building & Loan Association, on the advisory committee of the proposed Wilkes YMCA, and a member of the Knights of Pythias and the A.F. & A.M. Lodges.

His wife, the former Hattie Mae Lewis, was also involved in the business and civic life of the community. Born March 31, 1895, in Sampson County, she was a daughter of Boaz and Jane Parker Lewis. Growing up in Dunn, she received her education there and at Massey College in Richmond, Va. She came to North Wilkesboro in 1915 as bookkeeper of the Forest Furniture Company. She and Daniel J. Carter were married on December 26, 1917.

Mrs. Carter continued her association with Forest Furniture Company until 1950, at which time whe was vice president and director. After her husband's death she served as secretary of Carter-Hubbard Publishing Company and co-publisher of the *Journal Patriot* until 1963. She

Mrs. D.J. (Lewis) Carter.

was a charter member of several community organizations — the N. Wilkesboro Woman's Club, the Musical Arts Club, the Oakwoods Country Club, the Wilkes Chamber of Commerce, the Wilkes Art Guild and the Blue Ridge Women's Golf League. She served in many capacities in the North Wilkesboro Presbyterian Church and was the first treasurer of the Winston-Salem Presbyterial, and area organization of Presbyterian women. She died on October 25, 1980.

The Carter home for over fifty years was at 707 Kensington Avenue in North Wilkesboro, in a house which had been built in 1840 on the hilltop where the present post office stands and which had been named "Fairmount."

The Carters had one daughter, Jane Lewis, who was born September 30, 1930. She was educated at North Wilkesboro High School, Sweet Briar College and the University of North Carolina at Chapel Hill. She was employed as director of information by Old Salem restoration and as a reporter by the Winston-Salem Journal prior to her marriage on September 21, 1957, to John Thomas Ogburn, a native of Smithfield and a Wake Forest College graduate.

The Ogburns have lived in North Wilkesboro since 1959, where he is city executive and senior vice president of North Carolina National Bank. They have two sons, John Thomas, Jr., born July 18, 1960, and Daniel Carter, born December 27, 1962. At this time John (Jack) is a student at Appalachian State University and Dan is a student at Guilford College.

Sources: Personal recollections, newspaper obituaries, family Bible and genealogies, county deed books.

— Jane Carter Ogburn

HENRY CARTER FAMILY
432

Henry Carter was born in Va. ca.1745, died Wilkes County 1799. His wife was Millinder, last name unknown. After Henry's death, Milly married James Right or Wright of Surry County, N.C. Henry was a large landowner and considered a wealthy man for his time. Henry and Milly lived on the north side of the Yadkin River about 5 miles below Wilkesboro where Rock Creek runs into the Yadkin River. Henry is thought to be buried on the old homeplace in a family cemetery. He was a soldier in the Revolutionary War, served under Captain William Lenoir, and fought at the Battle of Ramseur's Mill.

In 1797 he deeded all his land and personal property to his son in law, William Sebastian, Sr. After Henry's death, William Sebastian, Sr. divided all the land and personal property between his children. The children later sold the land to John Foster and John is buried beside the river road on the old Carter farm. It has been suggested that Henry Carter of Wilkes County was the son of Henry Carter of Spotsylvania County, Va., who died in 1773. Henry and Milly's children were: (1) William, born ca. 1776, went to Scott County, Ky; (2) Tanda, born ca. 1782, was in Crawford County, Missouri in 1830; (3) Nancy, nothing further on her after the 1810 Wilkes County census; (4) Martha (Patsy), born ca. 1778, married Richard Stamper, son of Joel and Nancy Cannaday Stamper. They went to Breathitt County, Ky. They had several children; (5) Adelphia, born ca. 1787, married Thomas Johnson, a Revolutionary soldier. They had 4 children. Thomas died 1828, and Adelphia then married Siemon Justice in 1834. Adelphia was a school teacher and Siemon was a Judge. No children to this marriage; (6) Reubin A., born ca. 1780, married Elizabeth Whitley of Wilkes County in 1803. They were living in Crawford County Missouri in 1840. One known child. (7) John, born ca. 1789, married Lucinda Stewart. They were living in Crawford County Missouri in 1840. They had 10 children. (8) Sarah (Sallie), born 1795 and died after 1870. She was never married. She made quilts and did fancy needlework. She lived with the Sebastian families and is buried in the Sebastian family cemetery at Haymeadow.

(10) Elizabeth, born ca. 1775, died 1866, married William Sebastian, Sr., son of Benjamin Sebastian and lived in the Haymeadow community until her death.

Elizabeth was a charter member of old Cross Roads Church and a charter member of Zion Church, both primitive Baptist churches near where where she lived. She was buried in the Sebastian Cemetery at Haymeadow. William Sebastian, Sr., is the progenitor of all the Sebastians living in Wilkes County today in 1982.

Elizabeth and William's children were: (1) Wesley, born 1796, married a Pennington and lived in Ky. and Mo. They had children; (2) Ellen, born ca. 1797, married a Turner and went to Ky; (3) Henry, born 1802, married Nancy (last name unknown). Was living in Johnston County, Mo., in 1850 with 4 children; (4) Nancy, born 1804, married David Call and lived near Hays, N.C. She died after 1870 and is buried in the old Call cemetery near Hays, N.C. 2 children; (5) Benjamin, born 1806, died Grayson County, Va., married Elizabeth Adams daughter of William H. and Nancy Adams Adams of Wilkes County; (6) Lewis, born 1808, died 1864, married Rachel Adams, the daughter of Charles and Nancy Stamper Adams. They lived in Wilkes County. Lewis and Rachel had 9 children; (7) Sarah, born 1817, married William Brown and lived in Wilkes County. They had several children; (8) William, Jr., born 1814, died 1864, married Eliza Grimes and lived in Haymeadow. They had 9 children. Both are buried in the family cemetery.

Sources; Wilkes County Records, Ky. Records, Mo. Records and family sources.

— Samuel E. Sebastian

JAMES BAIN CARTER
433

My father, James Bain Carter, was born July 7, 1899, at Warrensville, North Carolina. He was the son of James Monroe and Celia Teresa Wright Carter.

His wedding to my mother, Dorothy Rhoades Call of Wilkesboro, took place on June 15, 1929, at the Little Church Around the Corner in New York City. When they settled in North Wilkesboro in 1933, having moved from Greensboro, they bought the old Landon home at 612 9th Street and lived there together for the next 31 years.

My father was Secretary-Treasurer of the Oak Furniture Co. from 1933 until the firm was destroyed by fire in 1955. He was a Charter Member of the Board of Trustees of the Wilkes General Hospital and a Charter Member of the Board of Directors of the Wilkes YMCA, where he also served for a number of years as Treasurer. He served also as a member of the Board of Directors of the North Wilkesboro Savings and Loan Association.

Dad was a Past President of the North Wilkesboro Kiwanis Club and an active Kiwanian for nearly 28 years. He was active in Scouting and was a recipient of the Silver Beaver Award presented by the Old Hickory Council of the Boy Scouts of America. He was

James Bain Carter.

also a member of the Knight of Pythias.

He was a great lover of horses and, for many years, rode Tennessee walking horses, always attending the National Tennessee Walking Horse Celebration in Shelbyville every September. In his later years, he was an avid golfer and member of the Oakwoods Country Club.

A member of the First Methodist Church of North Wilkesboro for many years, he served several times on the Board of Stewards, in addition to being Treasurer of the Building Committee for the new church which is presently located on 6th Street. He became a member of St. Paul's Episcopal Church in Wilkesboro in 1964.

James Bain Carter passed away December 1, 1964, and Mrs. Carter continued to live in the 9th Street home in North Wilkesboro until her death on March 2, 1974. Both parents are buried in the cemetery at St. Paul's Episcopal Church.

Two children survive: James Call Carter, born September 3, 1932, (now residing in Montclair, New Jersey); and Dorothy Celia Carter Dickinson, born February 5, 1936 (who now resides in Raleigh, North Carolina). There are three grandchildren: James C. Carter, Jr., born November 24, 1960, presently a Junior at Southern Methodist University in Dallas; Teresa Lynn Dickinson, born November 28, 1966; and John Michael Dickinson, born August 4, 1970, both of Raleigh.

Sources: Personal knowledge.

— James Call Carter

THE JERRY DEAN CARTER and LESTER PAULINE JONES CARTER FAMILY
434

The Jerry Dean Carter and Lester Pauline Jones Carter Family moved to Wilkes County to work in the educational system in Aug. 1957. As of 1982 they are completing their twenty-fifth year at North Wilkes High School where Jerry teaches Mathematics and Pauline works as Media Coordinator. Degrees were received from ASU, Boone, North Carolina.

Jerry was born September 3, 1934 and Pauline was born April 12, 1935 in Ashe County, N.C. They were married March 30, 1956 in Ashe Co. by the Rev. Donley Hart. One child, a daughter Linda Rosetta, was born June 19, 1957 to the Carters. Linda attended Mountain View Elementary School, North Wilkes High School and received her degree from Lenoir-Rhyne College in 1979. Linda married Kenneth Warren Seamster in Mecklenburg Co., VA. on January 31, 1980. She teaches hearing impaired students in the Mecklenburg Co. School System. Guy Warren Seamster was born to Kenneth and Linda in Mecklenburg Co., VA on June 3, 1981.

Jerry's father and mother are Gaither William Carter (Feb. 11, 1900 — Mar. 30, 1956; m. Aug. 30, 1925) and Martha Malinda Darnell (July 3, 1905 — July 29, 1974). His grandparents are Wiley Cicero Carter (Nov. 2, 1870 — Mar. 22, 1939; m. Dec. 16, 1890) and Ettie Ball (Feb. 27, 1874 — May 7, 1948); Johnson Avery Darnell (Jan. 16, 1874 — Mar. 26, 1962; m. June 25, 1898) and Sina Emeline Caudill (July 12, 1878 — July 30, 1960).

Great-grandparents are Joel James Carter (1847-1903) and Amanda Carter (1838-1905); Benjamin Ball (1846-) and Mary Blevins (born 1844); Sylvester Darnell (1849-1925) and Martha Elizabeth Weaver (1845-1877); David Caudill (1852-1933) and Martha Holloway (1853-1943).

Jerry's great-great-grandparents who have been traced and authenticated are: Solomon Blevins (born 1816) and Nancy Sturgill (born 1816); William Darnell (1824-1907) and Sarah York (1825-1905); Andrew Weaver (1822-1843) and Melinda Weaver (1825-1909).

His great-great-great-grandparents were Francis Sturgill, Jr. (1782 — Aug. 1846) and Phoebe Weaver (Oct. 15, 1783 — June 13, 1855); William "Surry Bill" Darnell (1785-1870) and Elizabeth "Betty" Wood (1790-); Isaac Weaver (July 25, 1797 — Aug. 1870) and Mary "Polly" Francis (Jan. 11, 1797-1863); Isaac Weaver, Jr. (born 1780) and Jane, (born 1780).

Pauline's parents are Lester Hasque Jones (Dec. 14, 1889 — June 5, 1970; m. April 1, 1932) and Millie Rosetta Blevins (May 10, 1909 — still living).

Her grandparents were Jesse Ballard Jones (Jan. 26, 1855 — Mar. 28, 1934; m. Apr. 9, 1881) and Louansa Alice Caroline Pennington (Jan. 18, 1864 — Mar. 14, 1947); Robert Johnson Blevins (Sept. 25, 1881 — Jan. 30, 1967; m. Sept. 30, 1901) and Eva Elizabeth Perry (Mar. 30, 1886 — May 18, 1953).

Pauline's great-grandparents are Sandrus Jones (born 1821) and Areany "Rena" Smith? (born 1827); Elisha Pennington (1832-1922; m. Jan. 23, 1859) and Tobitha Jane Anderson (Jan. 19, 1838 — Sept. 14, 1899); Francis M. Blevins (Nov. 1845-1933) and Mary Ann Blevins (June 10, 1838 — Sept. 7, 1907); Solomon Perry (1805 — Nov. 1891; m. Dec. 23,

L. to R.: Jerry D., L. Pauline Carter; Guy Warren Seamster, Linda Rosetta Carter Seamster, Kenneth Warren Seamster. (June 6, 1982).

1863) and Tobitha Ham (June 6, 1848 — April 3, 1933).

Her great-great-grandparents who have been traced and authenticated were Samuel Pennington (1820 census — age 26-45 — 1862?) and Elizabeth Anderson (1820 census — wife-age 26-45 — 1846?); Jesse Anderson (born 1795) and Nancy, (born 1798); Solomon Blevins (born 1816) and Nancy Sturgill (born 1816); Andrew "Andy" Blevins and Charity Wyatt.

Pauline's great-great-great-grandparents were Francis Sturgill, Jr. (born 1782) and Phoebe Weaver (Oct. 15, 1783 — June 13, 1855).

The Sylvester Darnell Family and Martha Holloway Family lived in Wilkes County many years ago before moving to Ashe County.

Jerry and Pauline have a common line through their great-great-grandfather Solomon Blevins (born 1816). Mary Blevins in Jerry's line and Francis M. Blevins in Pauline's line were brother and sister, Solomon Blevins' children. Solomon's wife Nancy's line can be traced back from Frances Sturgill, Jr. to Francis Sturgill, Sr. (died — 1807). Nancy's mother's line can be traced from Phoebe Weaver Sturgill to William Weaver, Sr. (before 1755 — ca 1836) and Joshua Weaver.

Sources: Personal knowledge.

— Jerry and Pauline Carter

ANDREW HARRISON CASEY
435

Andrew Harrison Casey, born September 2, 1888 in Somers township, was a son of J.W. and Sarah Myers Casey of Cycle, N.C. He died December 27, 1942.

He attended Wake Forest College, studying law. At the advent of World War I, he entered the army and was commissioned a second lieutenant. He served in the army nineteen months.

After the war he worked in Washington, D.C. and studied law at night at George Washington University. He later returned to Wake Forest College, where he graduated in August 1922, and was licensed to practice law. He established a law office in North Wilkesboro in September, 1922.

Attorney Casey was a leader in church work. He was chairman of the board of deacons of the First Baptist Church of North Wilkesboro.

He was active in the Kiwanis Club and the Masonic Lodge, and a member of the Wilkes Post of the American Legion.

Over a period of several years Attorney Casey was president of the Wilkes Bar Association. He was an officer of the North Wilkesboro Building and Loan Association. For eight years, he was chairman of the Wilkes County Republican executive committee.

Andrew Casey married Vera Eller, daughter of Dr. and Mrs. A.J. Eller, on June 28, 1919. To this union were born three children: Annie Lucille, William Eller and Mary Ann Casey.

Annie Lucille Casey was born January 23, 1926. She graduated from Meredith College and on September 3, 1949, married George Campbell Wilson, a N.C. State graduate in Textile Engineering. They now live in Charlotte, N.C.

They have two sons, Andrew Casey Wilson, born October 4, 1950, graduated from N.C. State University May 18, 1974, married Valerie Joanne Forvendel, born July 15, 1952. They have a daughter Jennifer Parker born November 5, 1979.

George Campbell Wilson, Jr. born August 23, 1953, graduated from N.C. State University. Married Susan Marie Sheets, born May 12, 1953. They have a son, Jeffery Thomas born August 13, 1979.

William Eller Casey, born August 30, 1928, graduated from Wake Forest College in 1950, served in the army in Korea, entered the life insurance business in 1952. He married Frances Louise Harris, daughter of Lee Edward and Louise Gaither Harris and a graduate of the University of N.C. at Greensboro.

Born to this union were Ellen Harris Casey, born January 30, 1959, a graduate of the University of N.C. at Chapel Hill; Sarah Catherine Casey, born July 22, 1961, a student at the University of N.C. at Chapel Hill, and William Andrew Casey, born October 5, 1963, a student at N.C. State University.

Mary Ann Casey, born January 21, 1931, graduated from Meredith College and married Algernon Festus Sigmon August 4, 1957. He was born March 11, 1925, and graduated from Lenoir-Rhyne College in 1955. He served in the U.S. Air Force and was seriously wounded in service. He is employed by the N.C. Department of Correction and they live in Raleigh, N.C.

Two children were born to this union, Algernon Robert Sigmon, born August 15, 1959, a student at the University of N.C. at Wilmington and Michael Casey Sigmon, born July 8, 1961, a student at N.C. State University.

Sources: Personal knowledge.

— Chelsie Baird Eller

THE JAMES HENRY CASEY FAMILY
436

James Henry Casey was born July 8, 1886 in Windsor's Crossroads area of Yadkin county. He was married to Sarah Clementine Myers of Somers Township on December 24, 1884. They were farmers and established a home in the Union Church community of Somers Township in 1889. Their children were: John William, Andrew Harrison, Robert Preston, Tyre Gwyn, Addie Blanch, Paul Wadsworth, and Silas Burns. Jim died in April, 1936 and Sarah in May 1949.

John was born September 30, 1886, was a farmer and lived at the farm for 80 of his 88 years. He married Maude Howard who still lives at the farm. Their children were: Alma Lee, Sarah LaRita (Tink), and James Henry who died at age 6 months. Alma attended Mars Hill College and A.S.T.C. She is married to James Wright Winkler of Boone where they now live. Alma is currently a student in Housing and Interiors at A.S.U. Their children are Pamela Jane, Judith Ellen, James Casey, and John David. Tink married Billy J. Wilkinson of Mooresville and they live there. Their children were: Lou Ann, (Melissa Lynn died at birth), Billy Scott, and Casey Michelle.

Andrew was born September 2, 1888. He walked to boarding school in Boone and graduated from A.T.S. and Wake Forest College. After discharge from Army in 1919, he worked in the Treasury Dept. in Washington, D.C., and attended law school at Georgetown University. He married Vera Faustina Eller and, after passing the bar, he established a law practice in North Wilkesboro. Andrew died in December 1942, and Vera began working for the Dept. of Social Services and continued until her retirement. Vera lives in their home. Their children were: Annie Lucille, William Eller, and Mary Ann. Lucille is a graduate of Meredith College and married to George Campbell Wilson of Belmont. They live in Charlotte. The Wilsons have two sons: Andrew and George. W.E. (Bill) is a graduate of Wake Forest College and in 1956 married a teacher, Frances Louise Harris from N. Wilkesboro. Their children are Ellen Harris, Sarah Catherine, and William Andrew. At this time (1982) Bill and his family are the only direct descendants of Jim and Sarah Casey who reside in Wilkes County. Mary is a graduate of Meredith College and married to Algernon F. Sigmon from Hickory. They live in Raleigh and have two children: Robert and Michael.

R.P. (Bob) was born May 2, 1891, attended A.T.S., served in the Army, was a graduate of Atlanta Dental College, and practiced dentistry in North Wilkesboro until retirement. Bob married Lillian Cochran of Mecklenburg County. She was a nurse. Both are deceased. Their children are Doris Cochran and Barbara Sue (Bobbie). Doris is a graduate of Meredith College, attended University of Arizona, and is a teacher. She and husband Ben Thompson from Tennessee live in Charlotte. Bobbie attended University of Arizona, is married to Jim Levy from Arizona, and lives in San Ramon, California. The Levy children are: Mark, Erin, and Steve.

Tyre was born May 24, 1893. He was a traveling salesman for much of his life. For several years he was Wilkes County Surveyor. In December, 1948, he married Maud Mast Spainhour of Watauga County. They built a house on his part of the family farm and lived there. Tyre died October 17, 1961, and Maud died May 26, 1968.

Addie was born January 17, 1895. She did not marry. She was a gradutae of A.T.S. and taught first and second grades in the public schools of Wilkes and Yadkin Counties until her retirement. Addie died June 29, 1964.

The twins, Paul and Silas, were born December 24, 1901.

Paul graduated from A.T.S. and became Manager of Southern Furniture Exposition in High Point where he met and married Helen Long of High Point. He died November 6, 1966. There were three children: Charles Long, Mary Elizabeth, and Alexandra (Sandra). Charles L. attended the Citadel, Charleston, S.C. During the Korean War, he was a paratrooper in the Marines and was killed in Korea. Charles Long was not married. Mary E. attended Marjorie Webster, in Washington, D.C. and is married to Lynwood Weaver of Martinsville, Virginia. They live in Martinsville. Three of their four children are: Woody, Helen, and Elizabeth. Sandra also attended Marjorie Webster. She lives in High Point. Sandra married Edward D. Taylor. They have four children: Edward Donald, Charles Henry, Crystal Brooks, and Michael Alexander.

Silas is the only surviving child of Jim and Sarah Casey. He is a graduate of A.T.S., & Wake Forest College law school. Until ill health forced retirement, he practiced law in High Point. His wife is the former Ruth Farlow of High Point. Silas is a patient at Presbyterian Nursing Home in High Point. Ruth lives in High Point. They have one daughter, Carolyn Ruth who attended Stratford Hall, Danville, Virginia. Carolyn married Robert Doll of Florida. They have two children: Andrew and Ann. The Dolls live in Concord, N.C.

Sources: Casey family records, personal knowledge and interviews with family members.

— Alma Casey Winkler
and Bill Casey

THE CASHION FAMILY
437

Burrell Cashion (or Binwell Cathon) was born in 1758 in Chesterfield County, Virginia. He enlisted in Chesterfield Co. Virginia, in 1777 and served under Capt. Francis Goods. He served in Capt. Barkham's company, and was in the battle of Petersburg and the seige of Yorktown. He continued to live in Virginia until 1800, when he moved to Mecklenburg County, North Carolina. He and his wife, Judith, had one son, John (born 1874) and one daughter, Minnie. John married Wilmouth Loftis and raised two girls and four boys, one of which was named James A. Cashion (born Dec. 27, 1827). James A. Cashion and Mary Ann Archer were married July 17, 1851. Children of this marriage were:

(1) Sarah I. — Born May 15, 1852. (2) William H.E.W. — born Feb. 20, 1854 (died Sept. 3, 1854). (3) John A. — born Oct. 1, 1855 (died April 17, 1934). (4) James T. — born July 20, 1857. (5) Margaret E.M. — born Nov. 24, 1859 (died Dec. 12, 1860). (6) David M. — born Dec. 10, 1861. (7) Mary A.R. — born Feb. 20, 1866. (8) Daniel N. — born Sept. 23, 1868. (9) Martha C.E. — born March 25, 1871. (10) Alma L. — born March 11, 1875.

John A. Cashion, son of James A. and Mary Cashion, came to Wilkes County around the turn of the century (1900). He and his wife raised the following children: Joseph Estes; John A.; Andrew Archer (Dick); Lindsay North; and Janie.

During his early years in Wilkes County, John Cashion contributed much to the new town. He was the first person to buy a town lot when much of the territory which is now North Wilkesboro was mapped and broken up into lots by the Winston Land and Improvement Company. He was a charter member of the North Wilkesboro Methodist Church. An interesting story about John Cashion is that he was the first to cross a new bridge built across the Yadkin River. It is reported that Mr. Cashion was obliged to wait more than three hours for the completion of the bridge before crossing. His employment in North Wilkesboro ranged from construction supervisor for Smoot & Sons Tannery in North Wilkesboro, a venture in the grocery business, and the construction industry.

Of John's four sons, only A.A. (Dick) Cashion chose to remain in North Wilkesboro. He and his wife, the former Clara Grist, raised seven children; John, Frances, Paul, Roy and Ray (twins), Elizabeth and Neil.

Dick Cashion was a pioneer service station operator and tire merchant in North Wilkesboro. He served as construction supervisor during the construction of the North Wilkesboro Methodist Church. His time and knowledge were donated as a memorial to his daughter Frances and his parents, who were all members of that church. He later served in the same capacity during the construction of the North Wilkesboro Presbyterian Church. This service was again donated. Overall, approximately 4½ years of work was donated to the two projects. Dick later served the town of North Wilkesboro as Mayor for three terms. Of his seven children Paul, Roy, and Neil chose to remain in North Wilkesboro to raise their families. Paul continues to operate the Cashion Oil Company which was founded by Dick. He and his wife, Mary Elizabeth, raised two daughters. Roy was killed in 1958 while fighting a fire as a volunteer fireman in the North Wilkesboro Fire Department. His wife, Ardena, raised their three daughters and one son. Neil and his wife Mary raised one son and

Cashion Family. Front Row: L. to R.: Elizabeth; Neil; Roy; Ray. Back Row, L. to R.: Frances, Clara Grist Cashion; John; A.A. "Dick"; Paul; John A. Cashion.

two daughters. Neil Cashion, Jr. is currently (1982) serving as Mayor of North Wilkesboro.

Sources: Family Bible, personal records, and *A History of the Cashion Family* prepared by Leonardo Andrea.

— Marie Cashion Ray

DEWEY CLINTON (RED)CASTEVENS FAMILY
438

Dewey Clinton (Red) Castevens was born June 7, 1899, on a farm in Marler, Yadkin Co., N.C., son of Willis Franklin and Nancy Mahalie Wagoner Casstevens. He spent nine years of his life on the farm until the death of his father in 1908. The death caused the family to move in early 1909, to the Benham Hotel in Jonesville, Yadkin Co. The hotel had been converted into apartments and here Nancy lived until her death in 1932. She kept roomers in order to support her family of seven children.

Red received little or no education after the death of his father, having to quit school to go to work to help support the family. His ambition even as a young boy was to have his own business. His philosophy, "it is better to work for yourself than for someone else and it is better to be your own boss than to have a boss," was often repeated to his two children as they grew to adulthood.

As soon as he was old enough to leave home, he went to Detroit, to work in the automobile industry. There he saved money so he could start his own business after returning to N.C. In Winston-Salem he rented and operated the Southern Hotel and Cafe.

Beulah Holbrook was born April 30, 1904 in Traphill, the daughter of Joseph Preston and Frances Louise Johnson Holbrook. Beulah was one year old when her mother died and was raised by her grandparents, Ralph Calloway and Sarah Ann Holbrook Holbrook. When her father remarried she choose to remain with her grandparents. At age 16 she went to Winston-Salem and was employed by the R.J. Reynolds Tobacco Company. Here she met Red at his cafe. They were married on December 31, 1921; he was 22, she was 17. Their first child, William Clinton Castevens, was born in their apartment on the second floor for the hotel.

In 1924, they decided to move to Traphill. He felt a economic depression was coming in the next five years, and remembering his first nine years of life on a farm, he wanted his children to grow up in a country environment. The hotel and cafe were sold and the move was made in the spring of 1925. Their second child, Beatrice Louise Castevens, was born in Traphill in the fall of 1925.

Shortly after arriving in Traphill, he opened a general store and cafe in partnership with Von Pruitt. The cafe was the first in Traphill. In

1929, he sold his interest to Von and had a large building constructed on an 20 acre tract of land. The front part of the building contained a general store, living quarters for the family were in the back. It was opened in 1930, stocked with all types of merchandise including groceries, clothing, hardware, farm supplies, etc. He also raised hogs, cattle, chickens, bought and sold country hams, beef, eggs, butter, and any other type of farm products. The store was operated from 1930, until sold in 1945.

In late 1945, in partnership with John Wesley Bryan, he opened and operated the Traphill Lumber Company. In 1947, he became the sole owner of the business and adding a general store, operated it as the Castevens General Store and Lumber Yard. A few years later, ill health forced his retirement and the closing of the business. He died on May 15, 1956, and is buried at the Traphill Baptist Church.

Red was very active in the civic and fraternal affairs of the Traphill community. For over thirty years he was a member of and later Chairman of the Traphill School Board consisting of the Traphill Grade and High Schools. He was a Trustee for over 25 years of the Traphill Baptist Church and was instrumental in having the church building moved. He was a member of the Traphill Masonic Lodge 483 for over 28 years, holding many positions of responsibility.

After his death, Beulah worked for a short time at the Traphill School Cafeteria. In 1956, she was appointed as Wilkes County Librarian. After over 14 years of service as librarian, she retired on June 30, 1971, at age 67.

Red and Beulah have two children, William Clinton and Beatrice Louise Castevens; two grandchildren, Michael Clinton Castevens and Ralph Samuel Holbrook; three great grandchildren, Tamara Yvone, Michael Hardin and Clinton Ray Castevens.

William Clinton (Bill) Castevens was born August 24, 1923, in Winston-Salem. He is married to Rosa Lee Triplett, born December 4, 1925, in Traphill, daughter of William Hardin and Pearl Waddell Triplett. Bill attended Mars Hill College, The University of Tennessee, and Chapman College. He enlisted in the U.S.M.C. June 14, 1941, and retired July 1, 1973, with over thirty years service. He was promoted to the rank of Master Gunnery Sergeant in 1962. Since retiring he has become an avowed golfer, genealogist, and is the writer of this family history.

Bill and Rosa have one child, Michael Clinton (Mike) Castevens, born February 17, 1948, in North Wilkesboro. He was married in Las Vegas, Nevada to Sharon Marie Lies, born July 31, 1949, in Oceanside, California, daughter of Ray and Betty Lies. Mike and Sharon have three children; Tamara Yvone, born January 28, 1970, Michael Hardin, born December 22, 1972, and Clinton Ray Castevens, born September 7, 1979. Mike lives in Huntington Beach, California and is in the construction business.

Beatrice Louise Castevens was born November 19, 1925, in Traphill. She was married first to Hardin Samuel (Sam) Holbrook, born January 24, 1915, in Traphill, son of Clarence

144

Delos and Eudra Elizabeth Spicer Holbrook. To this marriage was born one son, Ralph Samuel Holbrook. Sam died March 8, 1967, and is buried at the Charity United Methodist Church, Benham. Beatrice's second marriage was to James Winfrey (Jim) Holbrook, born March 23, 1929, In Sunburst, Toole County, Montana, son of Manley Patterson and Kern Finke Holbrook. Jim was a farmer and rancher at Ontario, Oregon prior to moving to Wilkes County in 1963.

Beatrice graduated from A.S.U. and taught school in Wilkes Co. for several years. She was employed by the Appalachian Library Region from 1961 to 1973. She and Jim own and operated the Holbrook Motel and Package Store, on Highway 421 West, and in 1973, she resigned from the Library Region to devote full time to private business.

Ralph Samuel Holbrook, son of Beatrice and Sam, was born September 1, 1948, in North Wilkesboro. He is married to Karen LaRay Long, born May 23, 1949, in Wilkes Co., daughter of Robert and Laura Taylor Long. Ralph attended A.S.U. and is a registered land surveyor. Karen attended A.S.U. and is employed as a secretary at Carolina Mirror Corporation.

Sources: *Descendants of Thomas Casteven, A Genealogical History,* by William Clinton Castevens and Frances Harding Casstevens, (1977), Yadkin and Wilkes County Courthouse Records, personal knowledge, family Bible records.

— William Clinton Castevens

THE CAUDILL FAMILY of MILLERS CREEK WILKES COUNTY

439

Sanford J. Caudill, son of Rev. J.J. Caudill, a Baptist Minister, was born March 25, 1848, and spent his entire life in the Millers Creek community. He married Nancy Elizabeth Wyatt April 11, 1868, and to this union were born the following children: William Victory Caudill (my father), John F. Caudill, James W. Caudill, Sallie Caudill, Thomas C. Caudill, Wiley C. Caudill, and Charlie C. Caudill who died in infancy.

Sanford J. Caudill was a farmer and grew most of what was needed to feed his family, both vegetables, fruits and meats. He was well liked by all his neighbors and helpful in time of need. He was somewhat of a carpenter, and was called upon to build coffins for most of deceased in the neighborhood, and for this reason kept on hand the proper type of lumber for use in building coffins. He was a charter member and deacon of Pleasant Home Baptist Church.

My father, William Victory Caudill, married Clarissa Virginia McNiel, daughter of James Harvey and Sasannah McNiel, of the Millers Creek community, on December 8, 1898, and moved to the Mulberry community to live with and take care of his maternal grandparents, Vickery and Sallie Jennings Wyatt. Having cared for them in their declining years, he inherited their land.

My father and mother had four children:

James Sanford Caudill, Cora Alice Caudill, Edgar Finley Caudill, and Gwyn Albert Caudill.

My father never had the opportunity to go to school beyond the Blue Back Speller, but he was interested in his children and the children of the community getting whatever education they were financially able to get. He served on the School Committee Board of Sulphur Springs Academy (now Mulberry School) as long as it operated as a District School; and he saw to it that his own children were in school every day possible, as well as encouraging neighborhood children to attend.

Father was interested in the betterment of the community in all areas, and served as County Road Commissioner during the time the County had charge of the upkeep of the roads. He, like Grandfather Sanford, was a member and Deacon of Pleasant Home Baptist Church.

Father operated a very profitable country store until the advent of the automobile, when his customers began going to town to do their trading. During the years before the automobile, father took in things grown and produced on the farm and garden, chickens, eggs, butter and herbs, in exchange for items purchased. There was very little cash in our community, and he took the produce to a North Wilkesboro wholesale merchant and received cash for the part not needed to pay for restocking his store.

My brother, James S. Caudill, married Ollie Parlier Brown and they went to the village of Mulberry, where he operated a country store for a number of years. He sold his store at Mulberry and went with Jenkins Hardware in North Wilkesboro as a salesman, where he worked for many years. He then purchased the Morrison Hardware in Wilkesboro and operated that for several years, as Farmer's Hardware, until his death in 1956.

I, Cora Caudill, after having finished a business course in Greensboro, did office work for Brame Drug Company for two years, during World War I. In 1922 I went to Raleigh and worked with the Internal Revenue Department until the middle of 1934, when I was replaced by reason of change of Administration. In March 1935 I went to work for Mr. C.C. Hayes, newly elected Clerk of Superior Court, and worked for him during his entire tenure in office, sixteen years. At his retirement I ran for the office and was elected to four consecutive four-year terms, one of the first two women to hold this particular office in North Carolina.

Edgar F. Caudill was one of the early Bus Drivers in Wilkes County, driving for Camel City Coach in Winston-Salem and for Greyhound Lines. He was married to Jettie Brookshire, and they lived in Charlotte, N.C., the first years of their married life. Later they moved back to North Wilkesboro and went into business for himself, operating C. & S. Motor Express hauling freight until his retirement. During his working years he ran for the office of County Commissioner and was elected to four two-year terms.

Gwyn A. Caudill attended N.C. State College one year and studied electrical engineering. He worked with auto parts companies for many years. He was married to Clara Owens August

3, 1935. He enlisted in the U.S. Army Air Force, serving in World War II. He returned home to care for his father in his declining years. He worked with Wilkes Welding Company as a machinist for 22 years until retirement.

Source: Family Bibles, personal knowledge.

— Cora Caudill

JOHN CAUDILL

440

John Caudill was born about 1805 and died after 1880. He was the son of Jerimiah and Sarah Adams Caudill. He married Levica Smith who was born 1808. They were married on December 17, 1825, and lived near the head of Big Elkin Creek in Wilkes County. He was a farmer and they were of the Baptist faith. His brothers and sister were: William, Pheraby, Sarah, Johnson, Lucy, Cynthia, Jospeh and Riby.

John and Levica children were: William Riby, Margaret, Emily, John, Eleya, James H., Nancy, Thomas, Rufus and Ansel. Thomas was born in 1844 and was married to Sarah Jane Holloway and lived on Basin Creek in Northwestern Wilkes County. He was a carpenter and blacksmith. He and his brother James Harrison owned a mill together on Basin Creek. At one time they were at odds and each one had his own shaker to regulate the grain flow into the mill. About 1908, he and his family moved from Basin Creek to the Hays community where he lived until his death. He was a deacon and his wife a deaconess in the Primitive Baptist Church. Their children were: Mary F. who married L.W. Higgins, Tyra B. who first married Sallie Hendrix and later married Ida Johnson, Joel Daw married Arthosie Henderson, Martha E. married Dan Henderson, D. Colombus married Martha (Mattie) Prevette, Ambrose never married, Jane married Gaither Taylor.

Joe D. was born February 18, 1878, and died September 3, 1955. He married Arthosie Henderson the daughter of Jackie and Julie A. Henderson. They lived two miles East of Hayes on a farm. He was a builder of houses, a blacksmith and a farmer. He and his wife were members of Round Mountain Baptist Church and both are buried in the church cemetery.

Their children were: Minnie, born 1896 and married Charlie Myers; Tyra, born 1898, died young and buried near the head of Basin Creek; Claude E., born 1901 and died 1969, married Essie Harrold, the daughter of Emanuel and Mary Ann Ballard Harrold; Verna, born 1899, married Manley Bryd; Flossie, born 1908, married Newton Blackburn; Gran, born 1911, married Clara Johnson; Paul, date of birth unknown, married Annie Dowell; Silas, date of birth unknown, married Reeta Wiles. There were eight children.

Claude and Essie had nine children: Edwin Joe, married Annice Collins. Their children are Randall, Janet, Beth and Scotty; Grady Claude never married and was killed in an auto accident in 1949; Von married Marzelle Welsh. Their children are Reggie, Linda and Karen; Betty Ann, married Billy Johnson and have one child, David; Jerry W., married Virginia Anderson. Their children are Sandra, Dennis and Richard; Lucy J., married W.M. Walker and have one son, Jeff; Harold D., first married Ida Hutchinson and had one daughter, Crystal. He later married Jean and they had no children; Lynn D., married Connie Cothren and have one daughter, Vanessa; Nancy, married Raymond Seagle. They had a daughter Kimberly who is deceased and a son Rusty.

Sources: Wilkes County Records and Family Member.

— Edwin Joe Caudill

JOHN FRANKLIN CAUDILL
441

This family can be traced back several generations: (1) Stephen and Jane Dehart Caudill, (2) David and Sins Walker Caudill, (3) David and Winny Shumate Caudill, (4) John Jackson and Mary Lafoon Caudill, (5) Sanford J. and Nancy Wyatt Caudill, and the subject of this sketch, (6) John Franklin Caudill.

The six children of Sanford J. and Nancy Wyatt Caudill are William Victory who married Clarissa Virginia McNeil; Thomas C. who married Cassie Stout; John F. who married Callie Faw; James A. who married Dora Faw; Wiley C. who married Mamie Nichols; Sally who married Richard Crysel.

John Franklin, born May 31, 1872, grew up to be a hard-working, fun loving, highly respected young man of his day. He and his brother James made music for many of the family gatherings and community functions. John played the drum and James the fife.

On the 16th day of February 1896, John Franklin and Callie Faw were united in marriage. Callie was the daughter of Thomas H. and Mary Elizabeth Rash Faw. They built a home in the Millers Creek community on a farm which they inherited from Thomas Faw. They bought and added more acreage as the years went by until they owned a large farm in this area. John was not only a good farmer but also a good carpenter and a mover of houses. He worked hard, managed well and became a much loved and highly respected Christian gentleman.

John and Callie were the parents of three children: (1) Herman Dewey married Ethel Long and they lived in the Millers Creek community. To this union was born H.D., Jr., John, Jack, Virginia, Jim and Harvey Caudill. Some time after Ethel's death, Dewey married Cora Sebastian and moved to Winston-Salem. They had one son, Clifton. (2) John Van married Agnes Eller and they had one son, John Alvan. (3) A little girl who died at birth.

In those early days their farm produced almost everything they needed except salt, sugar, clothing and oil for the lamps. Fruits and vegetables were canned, pickled, and preserved. Meat was cured. Cows, chickens and pigs were tended for food while a good pair of horses were well fed and cared for to do the work on the farm as well as help in house moving. When they thought they might need extra corn, more than they could raise on their upland farm, with the Finley family they would share-crop bottom land along the Reddies and Yadkin Rivers near North Wilkesboro.

John Franklin Caudill.

It usually would take at least two days to work these fields. Since they had to travel five miles by wagon, they would camp out overnight giving them longer hours in the field. There were usually one or two hired hands, John and his two boys who made this trip four times each season; one time to plow and plant and three times to work the corn crop. This meant that Callie had to prepare and send enough food along to feed five hungry men.

It was told years later by their youngest son, Van, that working these long rows of corn in these huge fields helped him to decide to go to college!

I have said that John was a good carpenter. He helped to build many homes including his own and those of his two sons. He also put this trade to good use by working in the Florida ship yards during World War I.

John was always interested in the welfare of the youth of his community. He gave his time and labor to see that they had a good school to attend. He served for most of his married life as a member of the local school committee which selected the teachers in their school. Along with others, he gave his time and talent to see that the school building got its needed repairs.

Millers Creek Methodist Church and its activities were a big part of their family life. However, during revival season, they would attend all the churches for miles around. After a hard day at work they would hitch the horses to the buggy, or wagon if neighbors wanted a ride, and make their way to a church for the night service.

We have had, and still have from this family, civic, community, educational and business leaders, administrators and public servants who have been an asset to our county and country.

Sources: Personal knowledge of family members.

— Agnes E. Caudill

JOHN VAN and AGNES E. CAUDILL
442

John Van Caudill was born November 19, 1909 in Wilkes County to John F. and Callie Faw Caudill of Millers Creek.

Van's early education was in Millers Creek Elementary School. His first three years of high school education were also in his home community in Millers Creek High School, but he transferred to Wilkesboro High School his fourth year to graduate. He was a popular member of his classes and an outstanding member of the basketball teams of both Millers Creek and Wilkesboro High Schools.

In preparation for his teaching career, Mr. Caudill attended Appalachian State College which is now Appalachian State University. In order to keep attuned with the best in educational methods throughout his many years of service, he continued his education at Lenoir Rhyne and Catawba Colleges, The University of North Carolina and Appalachian State University.

His career as an educator in Wilkes County schools spanned forty-two years, including positions of classroom teacher, school principal, and schools' supervisor for eighteen years. He retired June 30, 1972.

Mr. Caudill was a member of Millers Creek United Methodist Church where he served in many ways; — as a teacher in the Church school, church school superintendent, member of the Administrative Board, a registered lay speaker, and a delegate to the annual conference. He was a member of the New Hope Junior Order of United American Mechanics.

In the year 1934, Van was married to Agnes Eller, the daughter of William Hamilton and Mertie Lee Haire Eller. Both being teachers, they worked together as a team until Van went into supervision.

To this couple God gave one son, John Alvan Caudill, and three grandsons, John Thomas, James Alex, and Charles Christopher Caudill.

Life ended for Mr. Caudill at 9:45 A.M. July 7, 1975, when he was fatally injured in an accident on his farm. He and his son were constructing a farm pond when a tractor operated by Mr. Caudill overturned down a thirty foot embankment. He is buried in the cemetery of Millers Creek United Methodist Church located on Highway #16 where the former Millers Creek Methodist Church once stood.

— Agnes E. Caudill

MAMIE WALLACE DEAL CAUDILL
443

Mamie Frances Wallace Deal Caudill was born to Frances Matilda Ward and Elbert "Dixie" Wallace on August 17, 1881. She was the second and the last of their children. Her brother was James Calloway Wallace who lived in North Wilkesboro and served as register of deeds for eight years.

Mamie's father Elbert Wallace, ran a store in

John Van and Agnes Caudill.

her husband and family.

To Mamie Wallace and R.A. Deal were born five children. Elbert Franklin was born Dec. 8, 1900. Mamie Estelle was born October 28, 1901. Robert Fred was born Dec. 4, 1902. Mildred Frances was born Feb. 19, 1905, and their last child, James Wallace was born July 29, 1906.

Mamie's oldest son, E. Frank Deal married VanDalia Lowe on May 22, 1922. They lived in Ashland, Kenturcky for awhile and then Wyco, W.Va. where they were living when he died August 12, 1942. He is buried in Sunset Memorial Park, Beckley, W.Va. Frank and Joe (his nickname for Vandalia) had six children: Dorothea Dixie (Apr. 10, 1923), Robert Avery (May 8, 1925), Frances Estelle (April 8, 1927), Willian Franklin "Buddy" (July 2, 1932), Janet Sue (July 6, 1935), Charles Elbert (June 6, 1938). Janet Sue died Sept. 22, 1941. Dorothea Dixie, Estelle, and Charles live in California as does their mother. Robert "Bob" lives at Bogue Inlet, N.C., and Buddy lives in Huntington, W.Va. Robert "Bob" has four children, two girls and two boys. Buddy has

Wilkesboro which was moved to North Wilkesboro sometime after his death and managed by his son. Elbert Wallace was a veteran of the Civil War and first came to Wilkesboro as a salesman. He was born in Salem, Va. to Sarah Kent and George Wallace. He met Frances Matilda Ward on one of his sales trips, and they were married July 9, 1873.

Mamie's mother, Frances Matilda Ward Wallace, was lovingly known as "Little Wally" by her friends. She was tiny in stature, but had an impish personality that drew all to her, young and old alike. Her parents were Mary Susan Foster and Nathan Ward. She had been born, one of eight children, to them at Roaring River, N.C. Nathan Ward was from Rowan Co. and was thought to be the son of Martha Stevens and John Ward, Sr. Mary Susan Foster was the daughter of Ann Vannoy and John Foster.

Mamie's Great-Grandmother Ann Vannoy Foster's father was Nathanal Vannoy. Mamie's great-grandfather's parents were Frances Jones and Thomas Foster, Jr. Thomas Foster's parents were Ann Garnett and Thomas Foster, Sr.

Mamie Frances Wallace (Deal Caudill) was a beautiful woman about 5'4" tall with black hair and blue-grey eyes. She first met her future husband, R.A. Deal, while she was still a little girl. She and her school friends used to stop in the news office on their way home, and the editor would give them old print type to play with. Family stories tell that he used to tease her and tell her that when she grew up, he was going to marry her. And marry her he did when she was eighteen and he was thirty-seven on Feb. 7, 1900.

She attended public school and later Miss Mamie Barber's Finishing School near Wilkesboro. She had a kindergarten in her home for a short time. She worked in her father's store some and helped her husband with the newspaper. Sometime during Wold War I, she worked several months at an ammunition factory in Penniman, Va. Mostly she attended to

Mamie Wallace Deal Caudill.

147

three, two girls and one boy, and Charles has two sons.

Mamie's daughter, Estelle, married Joseph Paul Caudle from Randleman, N.C. on November 26, 1924. They resided in Greensboro, N.C. where their only child, a daughter, Bette Jane, was born Jan. 20, 1925. Estelle moved to W. Va. to live close to her brothers Frank and Fred after her divorce in 1937. She worked for the Wyoming Co. board of education until her retirement, and died in Mullens on March 20, 1972. She is buried in Mountain Park Cemetery, Wilkesboro, beside her mother, Mamie Wallace Deal Caudill. Her daugher is married to Russell McKinney, lives in Greensboro, N.C., has one son and two daughters.

Robert Fred Deal, Mamie's second son, lived in W.Va. and first married Eula Humphries. One daughter, Mary Jacqueline, was born May 9, 1925. After his divroce, he married Grace A. Brooks March 19, 1931, and they had three sons: Robert Edward (Nov. 7, 1931), James Fred (Sept. 14, 1933), and John Richard (June 15, 1939). Ed Deal lives in Dayton, Ohio with his wife, twin daughters, and a son. Jim Deal lives in Beckley, W. Va. with his wife, three sons and one daughter. Dickie lives in New Mexico with his wife, son and daughter. Robert Fred Deal died Sept. 28, 1970. He is buried, as is his wife, in Mt. Park Cemetery.

Mildred Frances Deal, Mamie's other daughter, married Charles L. Holden of Greensboro, N.C. Feb. 4, 1935. She is the only surviving child of Mamie Wallace and Robert Avery Deal and lives in Greensboro.

James Wallace Deal, Mamie's last child, married Mary Elizabeth Devereau June 19, 1937. They lived in Michigan and had four children: James Robert (Mar. 20, 1943), John Avery (Oct. 25, 1945), Janet Sue (Aug. 31, 1948) and Charles Edward (Nov. 21, 1950). Bob lives in Michigan with his wife, son and daughter. John lives in Iowa with wife, daughter and two sons. Janet is married to Max Gibbs, has two girls and two boys and lives in Grand Rapids, Michigan. Charles lives in Alaska. James Wallace Deal died May 4, 1967 and is buried in Howell, Mich.

After the death of her husband, Mamie Wallace Deal married W.A. Caudill on Jan. 5, 1920. She died of cancer on Feb. 17, 1921 and is buried beside her first husband in Mountain Park Cemetery.

Sources: Family Bibles — Court Records — older Family members — newspapers — personal knowledge — grave stones.

— Bette Caudle McKinney

STEPHEN CAUDILL
444

The name Caudill has been spelled several ways, viz: Cordill, Cordil, Caudle, Coddle, Cordle and Caudill. Stephen Caudill of Scotch-Irish descent first appeared in Surry County, Virginia, August 5, 1731 on a land grant from King George II. The 195 acres of land, though listed in Surry County, was later Brunswick and then Lunenburg County. Stephen Caudill appears on the Lunenburg County tax list for 1752 with son James, paying two tithes. There were no other Caudills listed in the county.

James Caudill disappears from Lunenburg County, Virginia and shows up in Rowan County, N.C. on the 1778 tax list.

On the 1787 census for Wilkes County, N.C., James, Sr., Stephen, James, Jr. and Thomas are listed. Thomas and James, Jr. are the sons of James Caudill, Sr. It is believed James Caudill, Sr. had other sons, Benjamin, Mathew, Abner, Stephen and possibly other children.

In the pension application of James, Jr. and Stephen Caudill, both give their birthplace as Lunenburg County, Virginia, James as being born in 1753 and Stephen in 1763. Stephen Caudill served nine months in the Revolutionary War from Wilkes County, N.C. James Caudill also served.

Stephen Caudill, born 1680-90, starts as the first generation. His wife is unknown. In the second generation, James Caudill, Sr. born 1725, died in Wilkes County after 1800. His wife is unknown.

The third generation, Stephen Caudill, born in Lunenburg 1793, died in Kentucky July 26, 1839. Stephen married first Jane Dehart in Wilkes County April 3, 1784. Thomas Caudill was the witness. To this marriage were born three children (1) David, born 1787, died after 1850 in Wilkes County, married Lucinda Walker in 1806; (2) Mary, born 1785, died 1862 in Missouri, married Abraham Adams, who had at least eight children; (3) Fannie married an Adams.

Stephen Caudill married second Sarah Adams and moved to Kentucky. They had ten children. In 1816, Stephen deeded for $5.00, 140 acres of land on Harris Creek of Wilkes County, indicating that he may have been deeding the land to a son.

The fourth generation, David Caudill, born 1787 in North Carolina, died after 1850 in Wilkes County, married in 1806, Lucinda Walker, born in Wake County in 1787, to who were born eight children: Daniel, Matilda, Stephen, Josiah, Mary, Samuel, William and Sarah.

The fifth generation, Daniel Caudill, born August 27, 1807, died July 27 1877, married December 15, 1826, Winifred Shumate, born 1809, died September 10, 1894. Both are buried in Alleghany County at the old home place on Prather Creek. Their children were: John Jackson, Lydia, Linda, David, Josiah, Mahaley, Mark, Calvin, Polly and Hardin.

The sixth generation, John Jackson Caudill, born September 26, 1826, died August 13, 1899, married April 24, 1849, as a first wife, Mary Lafoon of Surry County, born November 29, 1827, died May 7, 1868. To them were born nine children: Sanford, Mark, Winfred, Sarah J., Daniel, William M., Wilson, Cynthia and Mary.

John Jackson Caudill married as his second wife, Nancy Emoline Rash, born October 30, 1842, died February 17, 1834, both of whom are buried at New Covenent Baptist Church cemetery north of Hays, just off the Traphill road. To them were born five children: Reubin, Lilly, Roberta, Maude, and Calvin Millard.

Seventh generation, Calvin Millard Caudill, was born in Wilkes County January 10, 1873, died in Crew, Virginia, September 19, 1952. He married Lucina Myers December 8, 1894,

who was born March 16, 1876, died 1964. Both are buried at Mount Lawn Cemetery beside Highway eighteen north of North Wilkesboro. Lucina was the daughter of George E. and Mary Roxana Staley Myers.

The children of Calvin Millard and Lucina were the eighth generation and were (1) Clara, married Arlie Sebastian, who lived in Crewe, Virginia, where Arlie worked for the railroad, and had a family; (2) Jacob V., born July 12, 1899, died October 18, 1979, married 1922 Ola Kilby, and had children Jacob V., Jr. and Helen; (3) Nell, married William Playor and lived in Alexandria, Virginia, and had a family; (4) Bess, married Louis Pryor and lived in Virginia and had a family; (5) M. Von, born July 1913, married Lucinda Myers Lichty, who live in Norfolk, Virginia but have no children. M. Von served twenty-five years in the U.S. Navy, retiring as a C.P.O. He was diving in the harbor at Naples, Italy during world war II, when the German planes bombed it. He lost part of his hearing because of it; (6) R. Paul, married Fern Alderton, whose children are: Robert Paul, Jr., David Alderton, Nettasue, and Mary Fern.

Dr. R. Paul Caudill got his BA from Wake Forest University and earned his Master of Theology from the Baptist Seminary at Louisville, Kentucky. In 1842 he received his Doctor of Philosophy from Louisville Seminary. In 1944 he became Pastor of the First Baptist Church in Memphis, Tennessee. He is now Pastor Emeritus and is living in Boone, N.C. He is a fifth generation Baptist minister: David, born 1787, Daniel, born 1807, John Jackson, born 1826, Calvin Millard, born 1873 and Dr. Paul.

Sources: Virginia, N.C., Wilkes County records and family sources.

— Millard Von Caudill

CHURCH FAMILIES
445

William Church, was born 1790 in Reddies River Township in Wilkes County. His wife was Martha. In our research thus far, we found three children: Caleb, Jackson and Nancy.

Caleb, was born 1807, in Wilkes County. His wife's name was Mary Absher, but was called Polly. They had thirteen children: Lindsey b. 1833; Jane b. 1835; Martha b. 1837; John b. 1840; Leander b. 1842; Calvin b. 1845; Millie b. 1847; William b. 1848; Tobias b. 1858; Jean b. 1862; Susan b. 1866; Polina b. 1869; and Emily b. 1871.

Their son John had two thumbs on the same hand. He became known as "Double-Thumb" Church. He was inducted into the Army December 8, 1863, and served in Company G. 38th. Infantry. He fought in Georgia, where he met and married his wife Jane Adams. She was a Cherokee Indian, born October 28, 1848.

After serving in the Army, they came back to Wilkes County, raised nine children: Nancy, Martha, Linville A, Caleb Riley, Carolina, Oma, Ellen, Lillie, and Laura. The story goes that Laura drank red devil lye and died when a young girl. After some of the children were married, John and Jane moved to Alleghany

County, Prathers Creek Township. They lived in a one room log house with three of the girls, Oma, Ellen, and Lillie. These girls were never married and lived in the home until their death. Oma was the last one to die, the mail man noticed she wasn't getting her mail, and told the people at the next house. They found her, and she had been dead several days. John died December 11, 1930; his wife Jane died May 4, 1924. Both were buried at Mt. Zion Methodist Church Cemetery in Alleghany County.

Our story now follows one of John's son, Caleb Riley (called Bud). He was born November 1871 in Wilkes County. He was married Emline Stone in 1891. She was born February 1865 in Wilkes County the daughter of Felix and Millie Inscore Stone. They had six children: Jettie Mae, Nola, Luther, Bena, Guy and Callie. They moved to Ashe County, Chestnut Hill Township, where they raised the family. Caleb Riley, died April 7, 1933, Emline died June 4, 1932. Both were buried at Liberty Hill Cemetery at Nathens Creek, NC.

Jettie Mae Church, the oldest daughter of Caleb Riley, was born August 27, 1893 in Wilkes County. She married Kennie Lester Francis, of Ashe County September 25, 1916. He was the son of Malinda Francis. They had six living children who are: Orben Lester, Frederick Orwin, Edward Earl, Virginia Lee, Jay D, and Gracie.

Times were very hard because of the depression. Jettie made most of the clothing for the childrne, even to their shoes in winter time. Her youngest daughter, Gracie, still has a pair of the baby shoes she made for her. Jettie died while still a young woman on April 14, 1933. She was buried at Scott Blevins Cemetery in Ashe County.

Kennie never remarried. He gave the baby girl Gracie, to his brother, Luther Francis and wife Minnie. She was only thirteen months old when her uncle and aunt became her foster parents. They had no children of their own, so they felt that Gracie was a blessing from God. She was with them until her marriage to Jay Conley Call of North Wilkesboro, NC., on July 12, 1952.

Kennie, moved from Ashe County to Kentucky in 1934. There he left Fredrick, Virginia, and Jay D. with another brother. He set up house keeping with the other two boys Orben and Earl. After the children all were grown, their father moved to Towson, Maryland, where he died January 20, 1952. He was buried alongside his wife, Jettie, at Scott Blevins Cemetery in Ashe County.

Sources: Census records, Marriage, Death and Bible Records also personal knowledge.

— Gracie F. Call

ALIE ELIZABETH YATES CHURCH

446

Alie Yates was born on April 11, 1883 in the Purlear community of Wilkes County. She lived with her mother, Laura Anne Yates, and her grandparents who raised her. When she was sixteen years old, she married Finley Horton Church on March 18, 1900. He was also born in the Purlear community on July 19, 1876. They traveled on horseback to West Jefferson where they were married by Esquire Phillips, a Justice of the Peace, at his home.

Alie and Finley set up housekeeping on the bank of Purlear Creek near her mother's home and at the foot of the Blue Ridge mountains. They had seven children, six of whom lived to adulthood and one died in infancy.

On May 11, 1913, Finley Church died at the age of thirty seven and left Alie, age thirty, with six little children, the youngest being born five days after the father's death. In order to pay the doctor who had treated her husband during his illness, Alie worked in a neighbor's field until every bit of the debt was paid.

After their father's death, the children would have been expected to be sent to the orphanage. For those days, before any welfare aid, it was the only course open to a mother bereft of her husband and without any means of support. But Alie gatherer her children around her and explained what they would do. Her children remember her saying, "They want to take you to the orphanage, but we are going to stay together. We will all work and pull together and we'll make it. I will never eat anything myself if we don't have enough for us all."

The children were Ethel (Mrs. Fred Bare), Vernon, Newton, Carl, Ina Nell (Mrs. Philip Yates) and Dare (Mrs. Adolph Crump).

When the weather was good they worked in the neighbors' fields. Alie bound wheat for a neighbor working two days for the privilege of getting part of a day's share of the wheat for her family's bread, and she and her children hoed in the neighbors' fields to get a small part of the corn to make cornmeal for bread. Bread was such an important commodity to them because it composed the greatest part of their diet. Sometimes they would be without bread for a period of time when the crops were lean. Bread and molasses and potatoes comprised

Alie Elizabeth Yates Church.

their food. They set rabbit gums and snares to catch small animals to eat, and this was their source of meat.

When the weather was rainy and field work impossible, they all went up into the mountains to gather herbs and bark to sell in Wilkesboro — sassafras root, wild cherry bark, beedwood leaves and others that Alie showed her children how to gather and which were salable. They gathered these in sacks carried on their backs. Chestnuts grew in abundance in the mountains before the blight and the children like to gather them. They would dearly love to have eaten one occasionally too, but they dared not, for chestnuts sold for one fourth cent a pound, and that made them very dear. When the blight struck the chestnut trees in Western North Carolina, chestnuts became a dearer commodity and sold for a whole cent a pound!

Her good name was a valued possession, and Alie zealously guarded her reputation. She was highly respected for her industry and her sterling character. She always impressed upon her children that their greatest asset was a good name and the right to hold up your head anywhere. She would say, "Even if you are poor, you can work and you can behave and cause no fault to be said."

In the flood of 1916, their house washed away, and they went to live at the grandmother's house. Alie built a "lean-to," which housed the family, of logs and planks that they found in the woods and fields. In that flood, the family suffered much. Their potato rows were washed away, and they had to dig up the whole bottom land to find the potatoes.

Smallpox often struck families in that day, and so it came to this family. Newton and Vernon contracted the disease. Alie recognized it and knew that she had to get the doctor to vaccinate the rest of the family as well as to treat those who were sick. However, two of the other children took smallpox. All this sickness added to the hardships of the family for a long time.

Alie had taught herself to read and to spell from going through the Blue Back Primer and from studying words printed on flour and meal sacks. She would read the Bible to her children at night, and they also sang together. Alie read by the light of the fire, made bright by burning pine knots gathered during the day. They could not use any precious pennies for kerosene for lamps to see by. She wanted her children to go to school, and they all atended some at the Purlear neighborhood "first school." Alie often went barefooted herself so the children could have shoes to go to school. They did not wear shoes when it was not absolutely necessary.

In later years when welfare leigislation came into being, Alie finally had a source of help. She put her enterprising spirit to work, bought chickens and built a chicken house herself. She built a little furnace of rocks and mud to provide the warmth they needed, and was indeed a forerunner to show what chickens have come to mean in the economy of Wilkes County!

Alie's six children were and are good and substantial citizens in the communities where they live. The three girls married and have reared fine families. Carl was a teacher in Wilkes County schools, Vernon was a worker in a chair factory in Hickory, and Newton was a coal miner in West Virginia.

In her last years, Alie made her home with her daughter, Ina Nell, and her husband, Phil Yates, in the Purlear community. She has twenty three grandchildren and fifteen great grandchildren, among whom is a great granddaughter and namesake, Alie Elizabeth Yates, daughter of Mr. and Mrs. Rex Yates, a beautiful tribute to a lovely lady.

Alie Yates Church died on April 23, 1962 and is buried beside her husband at New Hope Baptist Church Cemetery at Purlear.

Sources: The Yates Family Bible and interviews with Mrs. Ina Nell Yates, a daughter.

— Douglas McEwell

ANDERSON MITCHELL CHURCH, SR.

447

Alexander Church, son of Aaron and Nancy Owen Church and grandson of John, Sr. and Jane Church, was born 1 August 1805 in Kentucky where his father lived for awhile. He died in Wilkes County 5 June 1860. Alexander married on the 28 February 1825 Mary Eller, born 17 February 1810 in Ashe County, died 11 June 1898 in North Wilkesboro, daughter of John and Susannah Kerns Eller. Alexander is buried in New Hope Baptist Churchyard and Mary is buried in North Wilkesboro Cemetery.

In 1836, Alexander Church was appointed a Justice of the Peace to take a list of taxable property. In 1841 he was appointed a district superintendent of common schools.

He lived in Lewis Fork township on a farm of some 800 acres. He was a member of New Hope Baptist Church and was a Baptist Minister.

Alexander and Mary were the parents of eleven children, all born in Wilkes County: (1) Nancy Martha, born 1826. (2) Jesse F. born 1838, married 7 October 1848 Sarah Adelaide Miller; (3) Sarah Jane, born 1830. (4) Calvin born 1832. (5) Henry Harrison, born 1835, died January 1897, married Mary McGlamery. (6) Leander married 4 January 1861 Mary Eller. He was killed in the Civil War. (7) Anderson Mitchell, born 29 December 1839. (8) James B., born 1842. (9) Mary Ann, born 1843. (10) America Caroline, born 1844. (11) William, born 1847.

Anderson (Anson) Mitchell Church, son of Alexander and Mary Eller Church, was born 27 December 1839 in Lewis Fork Township, died 30 November 1919 on his three hundred and twelve acre farm four miles east of North Wilkesboro, where he had moved his family from their home on E. Street in town.

He first married August 1861, Mary Susannah Eller, born 2 November 1836, died 31 March 1898 in North Wilkesboro, daughter of Absalom and Sarah Reynolds Eller of Lewis Fork Township. To this union was born eight children: (1) Alice Virginia, born 1864, married Noah H. Robinette 16 March 1882. She lived and died at Mt. Pleasant Tennessee. (2)

Louisa Cornelia, born 5 November 1865, died 16 June 1919, married John Ivey Myers 14 February 1884. (3) Ellen Salena, born 7 June 1867, died 4 June 1920, married John O. Gragg 8 June 1890. (4) Mary Octavia, born 16 April 1869, died 23 October 1954, married Elias Franklin Stafford 3 May 1893. (5) Robert Lee, born 26 September 1871, died 6 September 1946, married Mary Jane Woodruff 17 February 1892. He married as his second wife, Cornelia J. Haynes. (6) Thomas W., born 3 November 1873 died 20 December 1931, marriee Julia R. Forester 23 December 1896. (7) William Harvey, born 1878, died 1931, married Sue Edwards. (8) Beulah Lillian, born 21 February 1881, died 25 September 1894 of typhoid fever. A.M. and Mary Susannah Eller Church and most of the above children are buried in the North Wilkesboro Cemetery.

Anderson Mitchell Church was a pioneer educator of Wilkes County, a sheriff (one of the few Democratic sheriffs elected in Wilkes), a deputy collector of internal revenue, a member of the board of county commissioners several terms, and a leading merchant in North Wilkesboro, operating under the firm name of A.M. Church.

He was made captain of the home gaurd during the Civil War and was active in suppressing the outlaw gangs infesting this section.

He was a member of New Hope Baptist Church. In 1875 he was one of the organizers of Mt. Pleasant Baptist church, donated the land upon which it was built and served as the first clerk and as a deacon. In 1880, he helped organize Wilkesboro Baptist and he and his

Anderson Mitchell Church, Sr.

wife were charter members. In 1886, he donated the land upon which Liberty Grove Baptist was built. He, his wife and three of his children were charter members of the North Wilkesboro Baptist Church. He also gave the land upon which Liberty Grove School was built.

A.M. Church was married on the 21 December 1898 to Lillie Cornelia Staley, born 24 July 1873, died 18 December 1943. She was a daughter of Esley and Mary Jane Porter Staley and, through her Staley line, was a descendant of Col. Benjamin Cleveland.

To this union was born five children: (1) Alma Mae, born 21 August 1899, died 10 September 1978 in North Wilkesboro, married 21 October 1923 Murphey P. Hunt, son of Charles N. and Rebecca Camilla Stokes Hunt, and a great grandson of Governor Montfort Stokes. They had two sons, Joe and Pat. (2) Lola Bertha, born 29 December 1901, married 11 July 1934, J. Quincy Adams, son of Vickory and Elizabeth Whittington Adams. (3) Anderson Mitchell, Jr., born 6 December 1904, married 22 October 1938, Rose Ellen Billings, daughter of Andrew Jackson and Dausie Smoot Billings. They had a son, Anderson Mitchell III., and a daughter, Cornelia Ann. (4) Rufus Bradshaw, born 26 October 1906, died 12 December 1966 in Iredell County and is buried in Statesville. Rufus married 23 October 1925, Clara McNeil, daughter of Banner and Emily Pardue McNeil. They had three children, Ralph, Betty Gray and Dan. (5) Ennis Grace, born 18 July 1908, married 31 October 1931, Claude Ray Johnson, son of Freel and Carrie Miller Johnson. They had a son Thommy Ray.

Sources: History of N.C. by Lewis Publishers; Wilkes County census; Land of Wilkes by J.J. Hayes; Research by Mrs. W.O. Absher, C.G.R.S.; Family Bibles, Tombstone Inscriptions; Obituary of A.M. Church; personal knowledge.

— Anderson Mitchell Church, Jr.

ANNIE C. BUMGARNER and COMMODORE W. CHURCH
448

Annie Cansada Bumgarner was born January 6, 1885 and was married to Commodore Welborn Church September 20, 1904 in Wilkes County, North Carolina.

Annie was the oldest daughter of Mary Nichols and George Bumgarner, one of eleven children. Her brothers and sisters were: J.L.A., M.F., Jim, Lizzie, Quincy, Charlie, Vincent, Phoebe, Maro, and Gaither.

Annie and Commodore had eight children: Mary Neta, Tam Welborn, Troy Manus, Annie Mae, Dwight Charles, Ina Jean, James Auburn and Dale Pernell. They lived and reared their family on the Sawmill Road, near Millers Creek.

Annie was very active in church and community affairs during her long lifetime. She will be fondly remembered as an Avon lady for many years. She was 89 years of age when she died, November 4, 1974.

Commodore Welborn Church was born in Ashe Co., N.C. on December 10, 1887 to Mary Saphronia Pierce and Leonard Bynum Church.

Commodore W. and Annie Bumgarner Church.

Commodore was the fourth in a family of ten sons and one daughter: Robert, Jarvis, Julia, Commodore, Wiley, Eugene, Dillard, Avery, Fayette, Jessie and one who died in infancy. Commodore Welborn Church died December 3, 1967 at the age of eighty.

Sources: Memory and information from family.

— Mae Church Johnson

JARVIE BYNUM and ILA WARREN CHURCH
449

J.B. Church was born in Wilkes County May 5, 1882, at Millers Creek. He was one of eleven children born to Leonard Bynum and Mary S. Pierce Church.

J.B. came to Roaring River to work in the lumber business with his brother Bob Church where he met and married Ila Warren, daughter of William Franklin and Nancy E. Ginnings Warren. Ila was born in Wilkes County March 10, 1887. J.B. and Ila were married October 13, 1905 and lived at Millers Creek for five years.

In 1910 they moved to Roaring River and bought property from Granville Church, a cousin. J.B. was owner of a general merchandise store. They raised five children: Rex B. Church, Mrs. Edwin (Pauline) Deshazo, Mrs. Robert (Elizabeth) Lankford, William W. Church, Samuel G. Church.

J.B. Church became a successful merchant, industrialist and lumberman during the years that followed. He was active in civic and church affairs, becoming a Methodist and remaining faithful through out his life. He died January 18, 1957.

Ila was a faithful and encouraging person; always willing to help others and reach out to new tasks. She made brick by hand to help remodel the Methodist Church in Roaring River. She read the Bible through several times. She always enjoyed cooking and having her children and grandchildren home for Sunday dinners. She was always cheerful, loved people, and had a good sense of humor. She died February 19, 1968.

J.B. and Ila's oldest son, Rex and wife Gladys, live at the old home in Roaring River. Rex has many fond memories of growing up there.

Rex and Gladys have one son, Larry Church who is in the carpentry business.

Sources: Family knowledge.

— Rex Church

LINSY LAFAYETTE CHURCH
450

Linsy Lafayette Church was born August 22, 1852, and died May 19, 1920. He married Elizabeth Simmons who was born June 24, 1849 and died April 7, 1922. To this union were born three children: Zolley Coffer Church, born December 2, 1871; Nancy Zora Church, born March 28, 1875; and Alice Church, born July 7, 1878, died in infancy.

Nancy Zora married Dr. Albert Johnson Eller, son of James Madison and Louise Vannoy Eller September 2, 1894.

Zolley married Rebecca Eller, daughter of James Madison and Louise Vannoy Eller May 23, 1900.

My grandfather was an outstanding citizen and community leader. He operated one of the largest country stores in Wilkes County. He sold the basic items available, such as, salt, sugar, coffee, seasoning meat, patent medicine, tobacco, snuff, hardware, harness for work animals, horse shoes, cloth, clothing, shoes, etc.

He purchased chickens, eggs, butter, corn, wheat, dried apples, roots and herbs, chestnuts and cured hams.

My grandfather served as postmaster of Ready Branch Post Office. The post office was in a section of the store.

On his farm he grew chiefly corn, wheat, oats and hay. He raised beef cattle, hogs and milk cows to produce plenty of milk and butter for home use.

Our home was just a short distance from my grandparents; so I spent a lot of time with my grandfather in the store or with my grandmother helping her with her chickens and yard work.

Later I did some driving a team to a covered wagon hauling produce and herbs to market in North Wilkesboro and bringing goods back for the store.

When the Watauga railroad was built up the Yadkin River my grandfather built a warehouse

Linsy L. Church.

Elizabeth Simmons Church.

at Marley Ford Station that was approximately three miles from his home and store. The building was washed away by the 1916 flood.

My grandparents entertained the traveling public in their home. They were chiefly sales people, known as drummers. Many of these salesmen would rent a horse and buggy, a team of horses or a hack and driver in North Wilkesboro and travel for days or a week visiting stores over a large area. Their home was one of the main stops between North Wilkesboro and Boone.

Grandmother kept domestic help. She always had a large garden and she canned vegetables, fruits and made jelly and preserves. She always kept plenty of chickens for eggs and meat, cured hams and bacon and kept leavened buckwheat flour ready to cook buckwheat cakes. In the fall homemade molasses were made.

On the farm was a deep tunnel dug in the side of a hill that would keep sweet potatoes from harvest in the fall almost until new potatoes were large enough for use in the summer.

The dining room table was a large round lazy susan table. No one left my grandmother's table hungry or was denied a meal if hungry.

My grandfather was progressive and ahead of his time. He subscribed to newspapers and kept up with what was happening. He was a supporter of education, his church and anything progressive and good for the area and country. He was widely known as "Fate" Church.

Sources: Information from parents, personal knowledge.

— Chelcie B. Eller

ROBY ROBERT CHURCH
451

Roby, as everyone affectionately knew him, was born in 1889 in Adley Community of Wilkes County which is now partly covered by the waters of the W. Kerr Scott Reservoir. He was the only child of Ann Triplett Church, postmistress of Adley, and W.M.R. Church, farmer, teacher and Methodist preacher, who always welcomed the chance to advocate high moral standards.

At an early age, Roby learned well the values and high standards that he maintained throughout his illustrious life. He was always so innovative and farsighted when championing all causes that would make for a better community.

While a young man, Roby left Wilkes County for Winding Gulf, West Virginia, and was Postmaster there for several years. While there he met Juliet Herndon of Richmond, Va. From that union were born two sons, Roby Robert Church, Jr., and Forest Herndon Church, both deceased, and one daughter, Margaret (Peggy) Pearson Speas, presently a resident of Wilkes County.

Roby returned to Wilkes County in the mid-1920's and a few years later became associated in the automobile business. Upon establishing an impeccable reputation in the industry, he became associated as a partner in Midway Pontiac Co. Several years later he sold his automobile interests to become associated with his son Forest in a chain of consumer finance companies.

Throughout his industrious life Roby never forgot his duties to his church and community. He was a continual staunch leader and supporter of the little Methodist Church in Adley until the congregation there was merged with the Wilkesboro United Methodist Church. He became a most effective church lay leader and worked strongly in that capacity until his death. He also served his church in many other official positions as well as being a member of the choir for many years. He also enjoyed singing lead tenor in many religious quartets.

When it came to community service, Roby Church could be counted among the first to instigate and innovate new ideas. Some of those civic causes that he so strongly advocated are in effect today and make for a better

Roby Robert Church.

Wilkes County for all present citizens. He served on the Wilkes County Board of Education for 25 years, the last five years of which he was chairman. During this long tenure, he was a very strong believer and advocate of school consolidation, realizing that such a move from having so many small schools scattered over the wide areas of the county, would enrich the programs for a much more effective system. When consolidation was accomplished with his guidance, school programs — educational and vocational — became strengthened thereby making them strongly effective for all the youth in the county. His interest in education did not wane after his retirement from the Board of Education. His continued strong interest in quality education was in part rewarded by the establishment of the Wilkes Community College of which he was so proud.

Roby also made his deep mark in the civic annals of Wilkes County. In 1946 he became one of the founders of the Wilkesboro Business and Professional Men's Club and served as President and a member of the Board of Directors of the club for many years. His service in this club was influential in having an Apple Festival which we enjoy every year. The podium which the club uses today in the Wilkesboro Community Center was the pulpit from the Adley Methodist Church, which was torn down, and donated by Roby in 1978.

The North Wilkesboro Kiwanis Club was one of Roby's favorite gatherings. He was honored on various occasions by the Kiwanis during his more than thirty years as a member. He was a past president of the Kiwanis Club and at various times served on most of its committees. When named to a position or on a committee, Roby always served to the best of his ability and his example was very instrumental in inspiring others.

He served as a member of the board of directors of the Northwest North Carolina Development Association and several of its committees, one of which was instrumental in establishing the present Vocational Sheltered Workshop which continues to have a most helpful and effective program. He also served as President of the Wilkes Chamber of Commerce in 1959.

Roby Church was a Mason and held all the offices from Steward to Master.

It has been said by many of his peers that the impact of his life and career will be in evidence in Wilkes County for many years to come. He served as a symbol of all that is good and right with this world. A man of uncommon humility and towering integrity, he shall forever hold our greatest esteem for setting examples we would all strive to follow. He was a kind and unselfish leader among men and we are all much better off for having shared his life.

At age eighty-eight, he maintained his physical vigor and his optimistic, cheerful outlook until his fatal illness only five days before his death in 1978. His elderly years were an inspiration to many and an example that age does not necessarily mean the end of a person's career or usefulness.

Sources: Friends and personal knowledge.

— Peggy Speas

SHOBER A. CHURCH FAMILY
452

Francis Shober Alexander Church was born July 12, 1872, son of Hiram and Martha Payne Church. His grandfather, John Church, lived to be 90 years old and with his wife, Sarah, had raised a large family.

Shober married Kate McNeil, daughter of Jesse and Julia McNeil (see McNeil). Both Shober and Kate were from large families but they had only two children, namely, Ellen V. (the "V" didn't signify a name but was added because she was born February 14, 1908, Valentine's Day); Robert Parks was born on November 16, 1909. Both children were born in a log house that stood on the home site until it was razed in 1949.

Shober Church.

The elder Churches lived all of their lives in the Purlear community. They were members of New Hope Baptist Church and attended regularly. Shober was a member of the Jr. O.U.A.M., New Hope chapter. Their livelihood was derived from farming. Kate was a very good seamstress and was always busy with some handiwork.

The Church family was saddened by the early demise of their daughter at age thirty-one. She was survived by her husband, Ruff Dockery and two small daughters Eulaine and Marlene. Eulaine married Robert G. Vannoy, Jr. of Millers Creek, and Marlene married James M. Moore of North Wilkesboro.

Parks left Wilkes County during World War II and worked in a bomber plant at Willow Run, Michigan. He married Marcella Pendley, daughter of Neil and Ruby Barnes Pendley, in 1944, and they lived in Ypsilanti, Michigan, for 30 years.

Parks and his wife were employed by Federal Public Housing Administration for several years. When a municipality bought the housing project, where Parks was employed, he was transferred to a water plant. At his retirement in 1974, he had been plant operator for 20 years.

Kate Church died in 1945, and when Shober became seriously ill in 1947, Parks and family moved back to Purlear to care for him. They lived here for several months and then returned to Michigan following his death. While in Wilkes County, their second daughter, Elizabeth was born. Their elder daughter, Martha, was born in Michigan. Both girls live in Atlanta, Georgia.

Following retirement, Parks pursued his hobby of woodworking. He exhibits and sells at the annual "Day in the Park", sponsored by the Wilkes Art Gallery, and the "Apple Festival", sponsored by Brushy Mountain Ruritan Club.

Parks joined New Hope Church as a lad but since his return to Wilkes County, he has attended Presbyterian Church in North Wilkesboro and has won several awards for perfect attendance at Sunday School.

Sources: Family Bible Grave markers, personal knowledge.

— Marcella P. Church

THOMAS BINE CHURCH FAMILY
453

Thomas Bine Church was born January 3, 1887, died June 17, 1971. He was the son of John Wesley Church.

John Wesley Church was the son of Bill and Nancey T. Church. John Wesley was born in 1828 and died in 1924. He first married Nancey Jane Tomlinson November 16, 1848. To this union was born thirteen children. Nancey died while giving birth to twins. John Wesley then married Margaret Annie Welch, daughter of Calapin and Stephanie Holder Welch. Margaret was born November 16, 1839, and died in 1918. To this union was born nine children, including one set of twin girls. Thomas Bine was the youngest child.

One of Thomas Bines brothers, Worth Church, was firing a steam boiler close to the home of Radford Eller of Purlear, when it blew up. Worth was killed.

Thomas Bine Church was married in 1911 to Rola Ruth Blankenship, who was born October 15, 1896. Ruth was the daughter of Harrison A. and Elizabeth Lawrence Blankenship. Harrison A. was born August 10, 1861, died October 27, 1941.

Harrison A. Blankenship's parents were Alec and Adeline Church Blankenship. Alec came from the English Country. He was Irish and his real name was Monday. He changed it to Blankenship here in the United States. Elizabeth Lawrence's parents were Andrew and Sarah Tatem Lawrence. Her mother's name was Salle Swede Tatem and her father was Joseph Taten.

Bine and Ruth's children were: (1) Howard Paul, born May 20, 1913, married Nellie Faye Goforth, daughter of Wilburn and Dicie Ayers Goforth; (2) Silas Clarence, born June 19, 1915, died 1976, married Bessie Mae Holman, daughter of Everette and Lou Annie Graham Holman; (3) Flossie Betra born August 20, 1917, married J. Henson, son of Charlie Hen-

Bine and Ruth Blankenship Church.

son of Albemarle; (4) Annie Mae, born May 5, 1919, died 1941, married Cleophas Worley, son of Napolean P. Worley of Winston-Salem; (5) James Albert born 1921, died 1923; (6) Carnes Harrison, born December 20, 1924, died 1965; (7) Bessel Raye born May 15, 1927, married Daniel Alexander Shumate; (8) Dena Faye, born March 19, 1930, married Everette Poteat, son of Tom and Mae Johnson Poteat; (9) Buster Ulysess, born May 22, 1932, died 1964, married Vera Price; (10) Gracie Lee born April 25, 1934, married Richard Craven who was killed in a car wreck. They had one son, Michael. Gracie married Worth Poteat, son of Bronson and Dorothy Hayes Poteat; (11) Kathleen born August 5, 1937, married Franklin Byrd who was killed in a car wreck. They had a son David. Kathleen married Talmadge Wyatt.

Daniel and Bessel Shumate were married July 29, 1950, by Rev. Thomas Bine Church, at Bines home in Purlear. Daniel Alexander Shumate was born October 9, 1927. He was the son of Doc Martin and Vertie Mae Adams Shumate. Doc was the son of Hugh Ander and Candace Absher Shumate. Vertie Mae was a daughter of Hugh Calvin and Caroline Hayes Adams.

Born of the union of Daniel A. and Bessel Shumate were: (1) Ronald Ray born April 16, 1941, married Cathy Ann Nichols February 18, 1972. To this union was born Candi Lee, born September 8, 1974; (2) Donald Day, born December 8, 1959, married Darlene Anderson June 8, 1980. Darlene is the daughter of Kenneth and Martha Costiner Anderson; (3) Daniel Alexander, Jr. born November 5, 1965.

Sources: Memory of Rola Ruth Church and Family Bible.

— Bessel Church Shumate

Zolley Coffer Church (1871-1907).

Rebecca Eller Church (1878-1959).

THE FAMILY OF ZOLLEY COFFER and REBECCA ELLER CHURCH

454

Zolley Coffer Church was the son of Linsy Lafayette Church and Elizabeth Simmons Church of Ready Branch in Wilkes County. He was born December 2, 1871, and died September 27, 1907. Zolley married Rebecca Eller, daughter of James Madison Eller and Louise Vannoy Eller of Purlear, N.C., May 23, 1900. Rebecca was born January 23, 1878, and died November 29, 1959.

Zolley and Rebecca built a home in the Ready Branch Community. This home still stands today in what is now known as the Ferguson Community and it is owned by their oldest daughter, Estelle and her husband, Gerald McGee.

Zolley operated a general store in the Beaver Creek Community for his father and assisted him on his farm.

Three daughters were born to this union: Estelle (See Family of Gerald and Estelle Church McGee), Beatrice (See Family of Worth and Beatrice Church Vannoy) and Florence (See Family of Dick and Florence Church Thompson).

After Zolley's death, Rebecca was determined to see that her daughters received a good education. In addition to being a homemaker, she gardened, sewed and helped her father-in-law in the L.L. Church General Store.

One outstanding way that she earned extra income was by making knotted bedspreads for Mrs. Jean Nelville owner of the Hand Loom Shop in Whitefield, New Hampshire, and for shops in Charleston, S.C. Knotted bedspreads were a handicraft that has placed a mark in our cultural heritage of the Appalachian Mountains. Today one will find the Fry Collection of knotted spreads on exhibit at the Belk Library on the Appalachian State University campus in Boone, North Carolina.

Thus Rebecca obtained her goal as the three daughters were educated and became teachers.

Sources: Family Bible, personal letters and personal knowledge.

— Kay Thompson Carpenter

ARTHUR and PANSY CLARK

455

Arthur Samuel Clark was born to Isaac Alfonso Clark and Margaret Elizabeth Lowdermilk, December 18, 1894, in Burke County. I.A. Clark was a carpenter. Arthur's mother died December 4, 1899. Arthur was only five years old. He was raised by his sister, Mrs. Mary C. Steel. At twelve years of age he went to work in a textile mill at Brookford (now Hickory) in Catawba County for A.D. Juliard.

He married Arlie Crews in 1912; son Theodore R. born December 1914, died March 1915. Arlie died in December 1914.

On February 19, 1916, he married Pansy McGlamery, daughter of David McGlamery and Hester Eller.

Arthur bought property in Wilkes County in 1920. He moved his family to Wilkes County, but continued to work in Catawba County. He set out an apple and peach orchard in Wilkes County in 1926.

He moved his family back to Newton, N.C. in Catawba County in 1926 and remained there until 1940. He worked as an overseer in the Mid State Silk Mill. While working there, he continued to buy property in Wilkes County, including a Roller Mill in the Purlear section. He hired help to run the mill.

After moving back to Wilkes County in 1940, he had a home built in Millers Creek. This home was completed in 1941. He then went to work at his Roller Mill. There he operated a 14'X17' steel overshot water wheel and ground wheat, corn and mix grain for feed. This old mill was very fascinating to us chil-

dren. It was located on the Lewis Fork Creek and remains standing on the corner of Old Highway 421 and the Parsonville Road in the Purlear Community. There were large rocks out in the middle of the creek. We often had weiner roasts out on the rocks. We also went swimming in the mill pond. He operated the mill until 1948.

During the time he was running the Roller Mill he had a grocery store built in Millers Creek. He ran the store from 1948 until 1963 when he retired. After he retired from his store he went to work in his orchard and worked until 1980. He is still working, making a garden in the spring and hand weaving in the winters. He loves to work, he never believed one had to take a vacation.

Pansy stays busy with her many crafts. She baked and designed her own cakes for many years, but had to give that art up as her eyesight began to fail. She sewed for her family and also outsiders. Now she stays busy making quilts and hand weaving.

Arthur and Pansy are members of the Pleasant Home Baptist Church in the Millers Creek Community.

Arthur and Pansy Clark.

Pansy enjoyed cooking. On Sunday she would want all her children and grandchildren to come to their home to eat. Today, we all take a dish in on special occasions and eat with them. We are still a very close family.

Arthur and Pansy raised nine children:

Wade Hampton, born November 3, 1916, died January 1, 1915, buried in Wilkes County.

Helen Ollo, born March 24, 1919, died November 10, 1949, buried in Wilkes County. She was married to Robert Paige. Their daughter, Barbara Lyn, married David Spires and with their children Timothy and Randall live in West Columbia, S.C.

Mary Hester, born February 23, 1921, married John Lawson Eller and with their sons John and James, live in Millers Creek, NC.

Fred Rex born May 14, 1923, married Joyce Welborn Pearson born November 28, 1915, died July 31, 1980. On May 8, 1981, he married Aleida Bermorda Gessing, they live in Charlotte, N.C.

Carl Wake, born September 29, 1925, married Dorothy Lee Gabriel; they live in Millers Creek, N.C. Their son William Arthur, married Brenda Triplett and with their son Christopher live in Wilkesboro, N.C. Their daughter, Phyllis, married Steve Crews and with their children Andy and Jamie, live in Charlotte, N.C.

Billy Samuel, born April 17, 1928, married Mary Ellen Phillips. Their daughter, Leslie, lives in North Wilkesboro, N.C. and their son, Kevin, lives in Moravian Falls, N.C. Bill and Mary were divorced in 1978. On August 26, 1978, Bill married Jacqueline Eason Rasmussen. They live in Wilkesboro, N.C.

Jamie Ethel, born September 12, 1930, married Jimmy J. Tolbert. Their son, David Clark, born October 7, 1956, died December 23, 1959. Jamie and Jim live in Millers Creek, N.C.

Shirley Ann, born August 4, 1935, married Perry R. Lowe, Jr. They live in Moravian Falls, N.C. Their son, Perry R. Lowe, III, attends college at N.C State in Raleigh, N.C. A daughter, Tammy, born February 25, 1967, died February 25, 1967.

Phyllis Kate, born September 10, 1937, married Wayne G. Miller, divorced in 1975. Their daughter Katrina lives in Charlotte, N.C., and Mary attends college at Central Piedmont Community in Charlotte, N.C. A son, Michael, lives with Kate in Wilkesboro, N.C.

Sources: Family Bible, personal knowledge.

— Mary C. Eller

THE FAMILY OF JOHN ANDREW CLARY
456

John Andrew Clary (1837-1864) was one of the eight children of Alexander and Alice Harris Clary. His parents (born 1809 and 1810 in Rowan County, N.C.) lived in Davie County when the children were born and were in Wilkes County, N.C., by 1850.

An interesting family story tells that Alexander moved his family to Wilkes after a band of Indians, who crossed the Clary farm periodically to reach their hunting grounds, saw young Andy playing outside and simply carried him along with them because his bright red hair was so pretty! Of course the Indians were followed and the child returned peaceably, but his mother never felt safe there again.

The eight children were William (b. 1832), David (1834), John Andrew (1837), Nathan (1838), Thomas (1840), Mary S. (1841 — married John A., son of Robert and Celia Bourne Johnson), Elizabeth (1845) and Rachel (1849).

John Andrew, so recorded in the Robert T. Johnson family bible, was called Andy. His Confederate Army record shows Andrew J. or A.J. Clary, Clarry, and Cleary! He married Ellen "Nellie" Richardson, b. 1842, daughter of Drury Richardson of Grayson County, Va. A farmer, Andy Clary lived in Wilkes County next

to his parents. Daughter Mary Ann arrived Nov. 7, 1859; Evaline was born Aug. 12, 1861. On 29 March 1862 Andy went to Taylorsville and joined the Confederate Army. He was assigned to Co. B, N.C. 46th Regiment. The first of several recorded furloughs was Oct. 4, 1862, for forty days, probably to harvest his crops. Then in 1864 the last recorded: "Absent on furlough of indulgence since 15 Feb. for 18 days by order of Gen. Lee."

Perhaps he never saw his third daughter, Sarah Jane, born 17 April 1864, for he died in Winder Hospital, Richmond, Va., Sept. 29, 1864, of acute "dysenteria."

Times were truly hard for Nellie and the three little girls. Mary Ann said later that she never remembered seeing white bread until, after several years, her mother married William M. Adams of Wilkes County. He came for Nellie and her daughters in a wagon and took them to his home. There a party of well-wishers awaited with a wedding supper including, most impressive to the children, white bread!

Nellie and Mr. Adams had three children: Julie Ann (who married Wiley Johnson); John (who married Sidney Johnson's daughter) and Martin.

Of Andy Clary's three daughters, on 30 Nov. 1876 Mary Ann wed Robert Thomas Johnson (20 Feb. 1850 — 15 March 1914), son of William Bourne and Frances Ellinor Foster Johnson. They lived in Ashe County where Mary Ann died 9 July 1944. Mr. Johnson was a merchant, farmer and school teacher. Their children were: Edward Eubanks Johnson, b. 11 June 1877 (m. 1st Alice Graybeal, 1 son, 3 daughters, 2nd Lilly Hurley, 3 daughters); Caroline, b. 6 Jan. 1880, d. 7 Sept. 1959 (m. Walter Carson, 1 son, 1 daughter); B. Orrin, b. 25 Oct. 1884, d. 9 Sept. 1885; Arthur Gordon, b. 15 June 1886, d. 5 March 1940 (m. 5 Feb. 1913 Claudia Madeline, daughter of Prof. William H. and Emma George Jones, 1 son, 6 daughters); Emma Jane, b. 23 June 1889, d. 4 July 1962 (m. Rev. Dorrus Ballard, 2 sons, 2 daughters); John Anderson "Anse," b. 12 April 1892, d. 8 Dec. 1960 (m. 26 Oct. 1912 Bessie Kate, daughter of William Green and Martha Elizabeth Burkett Warren, 3 sons, 5 daughters); Ada Mae, b. 9 Nov. 1894, d. June 1971 (m. Elbert Warden, 3 sons, 2 daughters); and Robert Glen, b. 26 Oct. 1901, d. 19 Feb. 1964 (m. Elizabeth West, 2 sons).

A.J. Clary's second daughter, Evaline, married Bynum Eubanks Gambill (b. 12 Jan. 1857, d. 10 Oct. 1939) and lived in Wilkes County until her death 15 Jan. 1944. Their children were: Chloe E., b. 2 Dec. 1875; Samuel T., b. 15 May 18, Nere N., b. 15 April 1882; Martisha, b. 21 Sept. 1886; Robert L., b. 6 Aug. 1887; Wiley, b. 6 Oct. 1889; William S., b. 2 March 1892; Lilly A., b. 28 March 1894; Hobart, b. 6 Sept. 1896; Buel G., b. 22 April 1899; Mack, b. 4 March 1906, d. 8 June 1906; and Gwen V., b. 17 Jan. 1907.

Sarah Jane Clary married (10 Feb. 1884) Burrel Calloway Richardson. They lived in Renick, W. Va., where she died 24 Sept. 1922. Known children are: Alice, b.   , d. Nov. 1969, Winston-Salem N.C. (m. Jesse Adams); Ulysses S. Richardson, b. 16 March 1885, d. 14 Dec. 1954 (m. 23 Nov. 1905 to Rhoda Melissa Halbrook, eight children); Ira Joseph Uriah Richardson, b. 27 May 1890, d. 14 Nov. 1967 (m. 1st Cara Wagoner — divorced, no issue; 2nd Lula Lyall who died in Ohio, five children; 3rd Caroline L. Nelson, seven children).

Sources: Mary Ann Clary Johnson; Johnson Family Bible; Ada Harris Warden; Wilkes County, N.C. Census Records, Marriages, Wills; Confederate Records from National Archives; Gwen Gambill, and Ruby Richardson Shumate.

— Mrs. John M. Richards, Jr.

CLEMENTS FAMILY
457

Joseph Lee Clements was born in Wake County, North Carolina July 18, 1872, and died in North Wilkesboro on September 14, 1932. His father was William G. Clements and his mother was Annie Eliza Moring Clements.

Mr. Clements came to Wilkes County as Agent for the Southern Railway after being educated in the schools of Wake County and Elon College. He was active in the civic affairs of North Wilkesboro, serving as mayor, Chairman of the school board and in many other organizations. He was very active in the North Wilkesboro Presbyterian Church as deacon, elder, Sunday-School teacher and superintendent. He first married Nellie Blair, daughter of E.S. and Sarah Corrine Finley Blair. Nellie Blair Clements died in 1911. They had three children, two of whom died at an early age. One daughter, Corinne Finley Clements Price, who died in 1970, is survived by a son and a daughter. In 1915 he married Martha Clyde Watson.

Martha Clyde Watson Clements was born in Wilson County, North Carolina, on April 27, 1886, the daughter of Kinchen and Susan Rice Watson. She was educated in the Wilson schools, Atlantic Christian College, Peace College and the National Kindergarten Institute in Washington, D.C. She came to North Wilkesboro as a first grade teacher and met her future husband, Joseph Lee Clements. They were the parents of three children.

In 1930, Mrs. Clements opened the first kindergarten in Wilkes County which she taught for twenty-five years. During this time she taught and influenced many of the present business and civic leaders of Wilkes County. In 1954, at the request of the First Methodist Church, North Wilkesboro, she came from retirement to organize and teach the kindergarten there.

Mrs. Clements was a member of the North Wilkesboro Presbyterian Church and was active in many of its organizations. She was also active in the civic and social life of the town. She died November 3, 1975.

Sue Moring Clements was born January 30, 1917, the daughter of Joseph Lee and Clyde Watson Clements. She was educated in the North Wilkesboro schools, Flora McDonald College and Woman's College of the University of North Carolina (UNC-G). She recently retired to North Wilkesboro after residing in Charlotte, North Carolina, for a number of years. During this time she was employed as executive secretary to the Resident Partner, Deloitte Haskins & Sells, C.P.A.'s, and later as executive secretary to the Treasurer of Duke Power Company.

Mary Louise Clements was born October 3, 1922, in North Wilkesboro, second daughter of Joseph Lee and Clyde Watson Clements. She was educated in the North Wilkesboro schools, Woman's College of the University of North Carolina (UNC-G) and Peabody College of Vanderbilt University. She taught public school music in the city schools of Wilson, North Carolina and Shelby, North Carolina and North Wilkesboro. After twenty-nine years in the North Wilkesboro and Wilkes County schools she has recently retired.

Joseph Lee Clements, Jr., was born June 14, 1925, only son of Joseph Lee and Clyde Watson Clements. He was educated in the North Wilkesboro schools and North Carolina State University. He served in the United States Navy in the South Pacific during World War II. He married Mary Gage Barber of Wilkesboro and they are the parents of two daughters and a son. Mr. Clements is associated with E.I. DuPont de Nemours as Senior Technical Specialist, Textile Fibers Department, in Charlotte, North Carolina, and resides in Matthews, North Carolina.

Sources: Family Bible and personal knowledge.

— Mary Louise Clements

BENJAMIN CLEVELAND
458

The history books have long ago told of Benjamin Cleveland's many services during the Revolutionary War, while living in Wilkes County, North Carolina. The sketch that follows will deal with his family genealogy.

Benjamin Cleveland, son of John and Martha Elizabeth (Coffey) Cleveland, was born 26 May 1738 in Virginia, died on his plantation on the Tugaloo river in now Oconee County, S.C., in October 1806, and was buried on his farm. He married before 1764 in Orange County, Virginia; Mary Graves, daughter of James Graves of Culpeper County, Virginia.

Benjamin Cleveland came to then Rowan County (later Surry-Wilkes) just before the creation of Surry in 1771, where he was tax collector for the part of Surry that became Wilkes County. He was by trade a house carpenter and builder. After the Revolution he was the Surveyor of Wilkes County. He was very corpulent. An impediment in his speech prevented his entering political life. He owned several hundred acres of land in Wilkes County, living near the present town of Ronda.

Benjamin and Mary (Graves) Cleveland were the parents of only three children: (1) Jemima, born 1765 Culpeper County, Va., died about 1810 in Louisanna, married James Wyley, (2) Absalom, born 1767 in Culpeper County, Va., died 1838 Oconee County, S.C., married 14 November 1782 in Wilkes County, N.C. Martha (Patty) Harrison. Absalom served in the Revolutionary War. (3) John H., born 1769 Culpeper County, Va., died 1810 Oconee County, S.C., married 9 January 1781 in Wilkes County, N.C. Mrs. Catharine (Slone)

Montgomery. He also served in the Revolutionary War despite his being very young.

Absalom Cleveland, son of Benjamin and Mary (Graves) Cleveland and his wife had six children, one of whom was John Harrison Cleveland. John Harrison married 20 July 1805 in Wilkes County, N.C. Amelia Eliza Martin, daughter of Benjamin and Dianah (Harrison) Martin of Wilkes County, N.C. John Harrison died in Clarkesville, Habersham County, Georgia in 1858, having been divorced by Amelia Eliza (Martin) Cleveland in 1825.

John Harrison and Amelia Eliza (Martin) Cleveland were the parents of eight children; (1) Benjamin Martin, born 1806, died in Mississippi, (2) Milton Absalom, born 1809, married Sarah Evans, died in Indiana, (3) Robert Harrison, born 1811, married Harriet Cooper, died in Marietta, Georgia, (4) Mary Lamira, born 1813, died in Missouri, married 19 December 1829, William W. Wheatley, (5) Sarah Caroline, born 1815, died in Clay County, Missouri, married Rev. Zachariah B. Adams, son of Rev. Jesse Adams, a pastor of Brier Creek Baptist Church in Wilkes County, N.C., (6) Dianah Elmira, born 1819, died in Wilkes County, N.C. and supposed to be buried at Antioch Church, married 2 December 1846, Alfred Staley, (7) Martha Amelia, born 9 September 1823, died 15 January 1884 in Wilkes County, buried in the old Presbyterian cemetery, Wilkesboro, married 15 August 1843 Esley Staley, one time sheriff of Wilkes, (8) Paulina Elizabeth, born 1825, died 18 August 1905 in Ashe County, buried in the Calloway graveyard in Ashe County, married Shadrack Calloway.

Many of the above Staley descendants live in Wilkes County today.

Sources: *Cleveland Genealogy,* Vol. III. by E.J. & H.G. Cleveland (1899), *Surry-Wilkes Tax Lists* (1771-1777) by W.P. Johnson, Wilkes County deeds, court minutes, marriage bonds, church minutes, census.

— Mrs. W.O. Absher

ROBERT CLEVELAND
459

Alexander Cleveland, the ancestor of the Clevelands who settled in Wilkes County, N.C., was born prior to 1620 in England, came to America and settled in Prince William County, Virginia. He had at least one child, Alexander, Jr. born 1659 in England or Virginia, died 1770 at the home of his son, John Cleveland, on Blue Run in Orange County, Virginia at age 111. It is believed his wife was Milly Presley, who died in 1770 at the age of 103.

John Cleveland, a house builder, was born 1695 in Virginia, married Martha Elizabeth Coffey, daughter of John and Jane (Graves) Coffey. They both died in 1778 on Blue Run, Orange County, Virginia. John and Martha Elizabeth were the parents of at least eight children, all born on Blue Run, Orange County, Va., five of whom removed to then Rowan (later Surry-Wilkes) County, N.C.: (1) John born 1730, died 1829 Tugaloo, S.C., married Mary McCann. Rev. John Cleveland was a chaplain in the Revolutionary War and pastor of Brier Creek Baptist Church while living in

Wilkes County, (2) Mary, born 26 May 1731, died January 1828 in Surry County, N.C., married Bernard Franklin, (3) Elizabeth, married David Gillespie of Virginia, (4) Benjamin, born 26 May 1738, died October 1806, Tugaloo, S.C., married Mary Graves. Benjamin served in the Revolutionary War while living in Wilkes County, N.C., (5) Robert, born 8 January 1744, died 10 April 1812 in Wilkes County, married, 1st Alice (Alley) Mathis, 2nd. Sarah Johnson, (6) Jeremiah born 1746, died 1806 Albemarle County, Virginia, married Mary Gentry, (7) Larkin, born April 1748, died 9 July 1814 Lincoln County, Tennessee, married February 1773 in Bedford County, Va., Frances Wright. He owned land in Wilkes County during the Revolutionary War and served in that war, (8) Martha married 9 November 1775, James Smith.

Robert Cleveland, son of John and Martha Elizabeth (Coffey) Cleveland, was born 8 January 1744, Orange County, Virginia, died 10 April 1812 on Lewis Fork in Wilkes County, married 1st about 1769 Alice (Alley) Mathis, born 11 December 1750, died 18 December 1791 on Lewis Fork. They are buried in the family graveyard within 150 yards of the old Cleveland homestead, which is still standing and supposed to be the oldest house in Wilkes County, being built about 1781.

Capt. Robert Cleveland, one of the heroes of Kings Mountain, came to Wilkes County about 1775, bought land and settled on Lewis Fork Creek. He was involved in many daring deeds of his brother, Benjamin, during the Revolutionary War. He was prominent in his community and was one of the five Clevelands who served in the Electorial College and was the first one of the name to be chosen to that distinguished and responsible position. He was elected for the 6th Presidential election in 1809. His will is recorded in Wilkes County.

Robert and Alley (Mathis) Cleveland were the parents of thirteen children, the first three possibly born in Prince William County, Virginia; (1) Mathis, born 30 September 1770 in Virginia, died unmarried in Charleston, S.C., (2) Larkin, born 31 October 1772 in Virginia, died 19 April 1852 in Coosa County, Alabama, married 1803 Sarah Buchanan, (3) Jeremiah, born 7 December 1774 in Va. died 2 December 1845 in Greenville County, S.C., married 31 August 1801 Sarah Vannoy, (4) Nancy, born 9 March 1777 on Lewis Fork, Wilkes County, died 1 February 1846 on Mulberry Creek, married 1795 John Ashley Reynolds, Sr., son of John Francis and Anne (Blackburn) Reynolds, (5) Presley, born 16 September 1779, died 31 May 1861 in Monroe County, Tennessee, married 1814, Elizabeth Johnson, (6) Eli, born 1 October 1781, died 23 November 1859 in Monroe County, Tennessee, married 29 December 1803 Mary Regan. Eli Cleveland was a Baptist Minister, lived and owned land in Ashe County, N.C. before removing to Tennessee, (7) Elizabeth, born 15 July 1783 on Lewis Fork, died 4 November 1850 on Lewis Fork, married 13 May 1803, John Yates, Jr., (8) Jesse, born 8 February 1785, died 3 November 1851 Spartanburg, S.C., married 4 August 1814, Mary Blossimgame, (9) Martin, born 7 January 1787, died 17 June 1849 in Grainger

County, Tennessee, married 1st. 1808 Mary Gambill, 2nd. 9 October 1832 Mrs. Anna Petters, (10) Sarah, born 10 November 1789, died after 1855 in South Carolina, married Jesse Rector, (11) Alice (Alley), born 2 November 1790, married 10 June 1807 Morton Jones, Jr., removed to Tennessee, (12) Mary, born 2 December 1791, died 11 October 1850 in Greenville, S.C., married a Robbs, (13) female infant, born 2 December 1791 (twin to Mary), died 18 December 1791 Lewis Fork.

After the death of his first wife, Alley, Robert Cleveland married Sarah Johnson of Wilkes County, who died in 1812 at the home of her daughter, Fanny, in Monroe County, Tennessee. Four children were born to Robert and Sally (Johnson) Cleveland: (14) James Harvey, born 10 January 1796, died 13 July 1842 in Mendin, Louisanna, married 16 May 1822, Mrs. Sarah Waddy Thompson, (15) Fanny born 11 October 1797, died 2 April 1884 in James County, Tennessee, married 1st 15 June 1812 Edward B. Watkins, 2nd. 28 September 1835 Caleb Isaac Parker, (16) Alfred, born 27 November 1800, died after 1837 in Texas, unmarried, (17) Benjamin Franklin, born 2 January 1804, died in Laurens, S.C., married Tabitha Saxon.

Only two of the children of Robert Cleveland lived and died in Wilkes County. Nancy (Cleveland) Reynolds, whose home was on the north side of the Yadkin River at the mouth of Mulberry Creek, and Elizabeth (Cleveland) Yates, who lived in her father's old homestead on Lewis Fork Creek. They both have many descendants living in the county today.

Sources: *Cleveland Genealogy,* Vol. III, by Edward J. and Horace G. Cleveland (1899), Tombstone Inscriptions, Wilkes County deeds, wills, marriage bonds, old family papers, Bible Record.

— Mrs. W.O. Absher

MARTIN COCKERHAM FAMILY
460

Martin was the son of Humphrey. Humphrey was one of four brothers which were the first Cockerhams to settle along the Buggaboo in Wilkes County.

Martin (1802 — unknown) married Lydie Bauguess. They had thirteen children. Four of the sons died in the Civil War. They were Thomas, Calvin, Lafayette, and Richard. James "Buck" also fought and was wounded in the war. He carried the bullet in his neck until his normal death. The other children were Eliza, Phoeba, Elijah, Roby, Matilda, Fannie, Colby, and Madison.

James "Buck" Cockerham (1831-1912) married Mary Ellen Darnell (1842-1892). They had nine children: Haywood (1858-1947) m. Martha Jane Darnell; Charity (1860-1864); Lindolph (1866-1947) m. Isabell Gentry; Troy (1868-1885); Dulsie Louduska (1874-1917) m. Charlie Agnew Dimmette; Roxie Ann (1871-1904) m. Thomas Billings; James Tyre (1876-1952), m. Lena Cockerham, they were cousins; Mary Ellen (1879 — unknown), m. Frelyn Handy; Charlie (1863-1940), m. Nancy Emaline Bauguess.

Charlie Cockerham was the Post Master for

Lester G. and Marie Tilley Cockerham.

Austin during his lifetime. He and Nancy Emaline had nine children.

For some fifty years John Ivory (1887-1953) who married Maude Jenkins was a well known barber in Elkin. They had one daughter, Juanita.

Eulah (1889-1930) married Thomas Poplin. Their children were Lawrence, Denver, Berneice, Bonnie, Clyde, Grady, Otis, Ivan, and Lucille.

Marvin Arthur (1891-1935) married Alice Nixon. He was also a barber. Their children were Odel, David, Flora, Irene, and Marvin Lee.

James Otis (1893-1950) married Minnie Brooks. He was a barber in Washington D.C. and was buried in Arlington Cemetery.

Carl Clyde (1895-1972) married Tessie

Durham. He was a well known Baptist Minister and school teacher. Their children were Ralph, Ruby, Grace, Virginia, Nell, and twins, Geraldean, and Ivadean.

Berlie Audrey (1897-1961) married Ina Durham sister of Tessie Durham. He was also a barber. Their children were Virgil, Wonza, Geneva, Audrey, and Karol.

Tyre Wayne (1900-1902) died as a child.

Beulah Ellen (1902-1968) married Roy Brown. They had six children, Gilbert, Lee, David, Betty, and twins Donald and Douglas.

Lester Glendo (1905) married Marie Tilley. My grandfather has been a well known farmer and merchant who has been active in the Agriculture Stabilization Conservation Services for 27 years and won several awards in soil conservation. He has also served his community and county by being active in church, Grange, Farm Bureau, and Volunteer Fire Department activities.

His children were: Estaline, b. 1926, married Clyde Draughn. They had three children: Luther, Janice, and Zana; James, b. 1927, married Gladys Durham. They had one daughter, Betty; Louise, b. 1932, married Linville Barker. They had two daughters, Wilma and Barbara.

Lester and Marie had one infant son which died at birth in 1930.

The Cockerham family has been well known in the eastern part of Wilkes County for their friendship and services rendered to their community in church, work, and social events.

Sources: A Genealogy Brief compiled by Dewey E. Cockerham, Family Bible, Personal Interviews.

— Barbara Barker Swaim

MRS. SARAH BOWERS COCKERAN
461

My great-grandmother, Mrs. Sarah Bowers Cockeran, was one of the strongest persons that ever lived. She was better known to her grandchildren as "Mama Sir."

She was the sternest person I have ever known. She believed in strict discipline, and spanking unruly children fell right down her alley.

She was the mother of ten; however, she practically raised three generations. Once there were twenty-eight living in her five-bedroom house, the same house she and her husband built, with help from neighbors.

Though she gave me many wonderful and memorable experiences, the one that really stayed with me was the time that she made Sally and me fight for an entire hour. Sally was her son's daughter. Sally and I never really got along and one could usually find us fighting. We averaged about six fights a day. Once we fought and Mama Sir caught us. Mama Sir never allowed fighting amongst her younguns.

As she marched the two of us into the house, she followed with a big hickory and the neighborhood children. After a quick spanking she made us fight. Every time either of us slowed down she would cut us a lick with that hickory and say, "You wanted to fight, so fight!" After an hour of fighting and several licks from her hickory she let us stop.

Mama Sir left this earthly place in body February 8, 1978. I am very grateful that her spirit lives on.

Sources: Personal knowledge.

— Letitia Fletcher

COFFEY'S FROM WILKES
462

My husband's great-grandfather, Jesse S. Coffey, was born 17 July, 1798, in Wilkes County. He lived there until he married 22 December, 1821, Winneford Crumpton, born 20 November, 1801, daughter of Jezekiah and Jane Crimpton of Wilkes County.

Jesse and Winneford moved to Jasper, Georgia. They both died there and are buried at Long Swamp Church. Jesse died 8 October, 1858, and Winneford died 11 November, 1863. Jesse received land lottery in 1832 in Gwinett County, Georgia.

Jesse and Winneford had the following children: Larkin D., Lewis Elbert, Thomas W., William R., Eli C., Martin Van Buren, and John Gordon.

The father of Jesse remains a mystery but some believe that Thomas Coffey, born in Virginia 7 March, 1742, and moved to Wilkes County by 1780, was his father. This Thomas was mentioned as having a son named Jesse.

The last child of Jesse and Winneford was John Gordon Coffey, born 24 August in Pickens County, Ga., married Mary Monroe Pettitt, born 15 September, 1840, daughter of John and Hettie Mooney Pettitt. They were married 21 August, 1859. He died February 1920, and Mary died 19 February, 1915. Both are buried at Long Swamp Church, Jasper, Ga. John Gordon Coffey was in the Civil War.

John Gordon and Mary Pettitt Coffey's children were: (1) James Elbert, born 24 May, 1860, married Frances Crow; (2) Mary Ellen, born 30 October, 1861, married Tom Hamilton. (3) Martha Emiline, born 8 August, 1864, married Thomas Pendley (4) Millie Angeline, born 14 March, 1866, married John Fields. (5) Amanda Jane, born 29 May, 1868, died October 1868 (6) Fannie Permelia, born 5 October, 1869, married William Lafayette Dilbeck; (7) Raymond Lucious, born 12 December, 1871, married Fannie Mullinax; (8) Willie Eleanor, born 12 August, 1874, married Robert S. Hammontree; (9) John Pettitt, born 14 March, 1877, married Susan first and married second Addie Lindsay. (10) Thomas Masterson, born 14 March, 1877, twin, married Dora King (11) Martin Dewitt, born 15 November, 1881, married Mary Laconia Hamilton; (12) Effie Susannah, born 2 July, 1884, married James Fann. (13) Dillie Pearl, born 17 August, 1887, married Berry Reeves.

Martin Dewitt Coffey, son of John and Mary, was born 15 November, 1881, in Georgia and married 23 March, 1905, Mary Laconia Hamilton in Lawrence C., Ala. Mary Laconia was born 16 October, 1883, daughter of Thomas N. and Barbara A. Blaxton Hamilton.

Martin Dewitt died 6 September, 1943. Mary Laconia died 14 February, 1964. They are buried in Lawrence Co., Ala. Martin Dewitt was a farmer and active in the Baptist church.

The children of Martin and Mary were: (1) Clarence Jackson, born 21 June, 1906, married Mable Darnell. He died 10 June, 1970; (2) Edna, born 17 November, 1907, died at birth; (3) Clifton Thomas, born 6 December, 1909, married Sadie Thompson; (4) John Clayton, born 15 November, 1911, married Mary Elizabeth Cornelius; (5) Elbert Carl, born 19 December, 1813, married Louise Smith; (6) Corilla Norean, born 15 January, 1915, married first to Minor Sherril, and second to Sherman Roden; (7) Raymond Paul, born 11 April, 1917, married Edna Martin. Paul died 15 May, 1972, buried in Decatur, Ala.; (8) Martin Dewitt Jr., born 21 February, 1919, killed in Germany 17 July, 1945; (9) Cecil Mark, born 20 September, 1923, married Eva Campbell,

The children in this family loved music. They spent their time after evening meals making music. Martin Dewitt was a singing teacher.

John Clayton Coffey, son of Dewitt and Mary, was born 15 November, 1911, in Lawrence County, Alabama. He began school in a one-room cabin. He remembers this one room well because there were so many wasps the children were afraid they would get stung.

During the Depression John Clayton worked as a farm laborer for fifty cents a day and sometimes would only receive one gallon of mollasses for a day's labor. In 1932 he began dating Mary Elizabeth Cornelius, born 18 April, 1917, the daughter of John Rowland Cornelius and Susie Elizabeth Corum of Decatur, Ala. On 10 February, 1934, John and Mary were married.

By this time John had a job and Mary was also working. This seemed to be a happy beginning, but Mary became ill with typhoid fever and almost died. She recovered, and John took a course in ship building and worked for Ingills Ship Yard where he worked during World War II. After the war he started his business of Home Building in which he was successful.

In 1962 John Clayton's health began to fail, and he was advised to leave the climate of Alabama. He moved to Dallas, Texas where he now lives and has as his hobby the building of grandfather clocks.

John and Mary had two sons: (1) Clayton Douglas, born 12 November, 1939, died with cancer May 27, 1978 and is buried in Decatur, Ala. He married 29 April, 1960, Marjorie Waters. (2) David Anthony, born 1 December, 1946, married Nobuko (Judy) Kobayashi, born 16 April, 1940, in Manchuria (Japan) China.

Sources: Family Bible, Family Memories, Personal knowledge, Census.

— Mary E. Cornelius Coffey

BENJAMIN COFFEY
463

Benjamin Coffey was born in 1747 in Spotsylvania County, Virginia. He was a resident of Wilkes County, North Carolina for nearly thirty years. Benjamin's parents were Jane Graves and John Coffey. John died in Albemarle County, Virginia before March 1775, after his death Jane lived near her children in Wilkes County. Benjamin's grandparents were Ann Powell and Edward Coffey of Essex County, Virginia. Edward died in 1716 and Ann died in 1726.

Benjamin first served the Revolutionary cause for five months from Burke County in 1776. He volunteered and was sent to the frontier, scouting and helping to build Crider's Fort because of "mischief being done by the Cherokee Indians." He married Polly Hayes and moved over to Wilkes County where in 1780 he volunteered again. Benjamin was at the Battle of Kings Mountain as were several of his kinfolk. He did not actually do any fighting in this battle. As a result of losing his horse the evening before, he had to join the foot soldiers, the fighting was all over by the time the foot soldiers got there. He was sent to guard the prisoners on the march to Moravian Town, whereby he developed "pains in his ankles." He was furloughed home for the duration of the war.

Benjamin Coffey with his family moved to Hawkins County, Tennessee and bought two hundred acres of land on the north side of Clinch Mountain on Big War Creek on March 24, 1809.

In September 1833, when Benjamin gave his declaration for a pension, he was eighty-six years old and so old and infirm for the last four of five years that he had not been able to attend the Baptist Church where he was a member. He died January 4, 1834 in Hawkins County, Tennessee.

While still living in Wilkes County, Benjamin and Polly's son, John Coffey (Oct. 15, 1776 — Mar. 15, 1845) married March 1, 1804 to Elizabeth Rucker (Jan. 6, 1787 — Mar. 22, 1855): she was the daughter of Sarah Roberts and Colby Rucker. Elizabeth and John were living in Grainger County in 1810, he served in the War of 1812 from Tennessee. The list of their children is not complete: Ausburn (Jan. 14, 1805 — Dec. 31, 1876) (married Matilda Dalton); Benjamin (Feb. 8, 1808 — May 8, 1867) (married Nancy Hayes); Elizabeth (married George Hayes); Nancy unmarried; John Jackson (Jan. 12, 1812 — Oct. 15, 1877) (married Alicia Nash); Margaret (married Issac Bullen); William born Oct. 31, 1828 (married Ellen Nash); Catherine born Aug. 10, 1834; Sarah Lucinda (married William Coffey, a first double cousin) and Jesse.

Elizabeth and John's oldest son, Ausbon (family spelling), was a blacksmith. After the Civil War, when his brothers, Benjamin and John, and some of their children moved to Rockcastle County, Kentucky, Ausbon and Matilda loaded their wagon, tied the old cow and hound dog to it and moved also. The trip took about a week, two weeks later the old hound dog was waiting at the door to the blacksmith shop in Thorn Hill. Ausbon and Matilda did not stay in Wildie, they returned to Tennessee. Ausbon is buried in the Rucker Family Cemetery northeast of Thorn Hill on the road to Coffey's Chapel Cemetery.

Benjamin didn't live long after moving to Kentucky, he and Nancy (Hayes) are buried in the Maret Cemetery near Wildie. Through their son, Ransome, there are seven generations of Coffeys buried in the Maret Cemetery.

Nancy and Benjamin had nine sons: John; William; Richardson (married Serene Coffey); Ransome (married Delphia Cox and Mary Jane Coffey Wolfe); Calvin; Calton (married Martha Campbell); Perry; Marvel (married Abigail Jordan); Ausbon (married Nancy Ann Phillips Barnett on Feb. 20, 1869); and one daughter, Elizabeth (married Caswell Coffey). At least six of their sons served the Confederate States of America: Richardson, Calvin, Calton, Marvel, Perry, and Ausbon. Ausbon was only seventeen when he joined after becoming angry over federal troops destroying their spring beet crop. Calvin, Perry, and Richardson died before the end of the war. Their cousins, William W. and Simeon, also died as results of wounds received in battle. After his twin, Calvin, died,

Calton was wounded and deserted. Marvel was there when Calton was told to walk slowly and get his leg wound seen about. Marvel said that was the last the family heard of Calton until he was living in Oklahoma nearly forty years later, via Missouri, Arkansas, and Texas. Ransome and his cousins that were living in Kentucky when the war began fought on the Union side.

Ausbon's wife, Nancy, (part Cherokee Indian, passed as Black Dutch) was born in Laurel County, Kentucky. She moved to Missouri with her first husband, who died there. She walked back to Wildie with her small son, Andrew J. Barnett. Nancy and Ausbon's oldest son, William Ransome Shadrick Coffey (Rance) (Dec. 20, 1869 — Dec. 20, 1932) on May 3, 1889 married Lou Mina Jane Clark (May 24, 1869 — May 1, 1939). Their youngest son, Thomas Calvin (Tom) (Dec. 8, 1877 — Feb. 14, 1962) on April 18, 1901 married Mary McGuire. Mary was a cousin to the Mary McGuire that was Andrew Barnett's first wife; Joan Shouse was Andrew's second wife.

In September 1903, Lou Mina and Rance with their six surviving children moved to Red Fork, Indian Territory. Tom helped them to cross the mountain by horse back to board a train in Wildie. Mary and Tom also moved to Oklahoma in 1904 and lived for twenty years, where most of their ten children were born. Gracy, Arch, Luther, Athel, Lawrence, and Rosie Mae lived to be adults. Their return trip to Kentucky began Oct. 1923 by wagon took six months. They worked and camped out along the way, arriving in Wildie in April 1924.

Lou Mina and Rance had twelve children: McClellan; Wallace Ausbon; Celia T. (married S.R. Cross); Nancy Ann; Mary Elizabeth (married A.J. Self); Martha Susan (married J.H. Smith); Flora Mae (married H.K. Sorrels); Teddy B. (married A.L. Rose Capehart); Julius Walter (married E. Harris Holland); Richard Leslie; Lena Jane; and William Benjamin (married Lou Ellen Simcox of Kiowa, Oklahoma).

Sources: Census, court house, military and family records, cemetery markers and Bible records.

— Bennie Lou Coffey Loftin

CHESLEY and JANE (CLEVELAND) COFFEY

464

The existence of Chesley Coffey and Jane Cleveland has never been proved by public records, Bible records, or any other standard means of genealogical proof. The only scrap of evidence that hints at their existence was a note left by Eliza (Coffey) Porter during the 1890s. She wrote of her father, Nathan's family:

"Nathan Coffey was the son of Joel Coffey and Martha Step Coffey, was grandson of Chesley and Jane Cleveland Coffey, natives of Virginia. But the grandparents removed to North Carolina in an early day and settled on the Yadkin river where the parents of our subject was born and raised and married . . . "

Mrs. Porter's knowledge of her family's background was good, as evidenced by the

fact that the names of the children of Joel and Martha Coffey, listed in his will of April, 1789, were identified to those named in her recollection of the children of Joel Coffey and Martha Step.

Joel Coffey was part of a Coffey family that moved from Wilkes Co., N.C. to what is now Russell Co., Ky. during the 1790s. Family members usually lived in close proximity and frequently used Joel, Nathan, Salathiel, Cleveland, and Nebuzaraden as given names.

Joel Coffey was, according to D.A.R. records, born in 1730 and married to Martha Sealey. According to Mrs. Porter's notes, Martha Sealey was actually Martha Step. She was expecting a baby in 1789, as mentioned in the will of Joel Coffey, and was therefore, probably born no earlier than 1744. Joel Coffey was probably born much later than 1730. He died in Wilkes Co., N.C. in July 1789. Joel Coffey was not the father of Nathan Coffey (ca. 1760-1823). Joel Coffey's children were: Joseph (probably died before 1789), Cleveland (born 1765-8, died 1814), James (1774-1826), Joel, Nathaniel (1788-1834), Nebuzaraden (1789-1867), Katherine, Jane, and Celia.

It seems quite likely that Joel Coffey was a brother to: Salathiel (died 1784, Wilkes Co., N.C.), Chesley Jr. (1755-1818), Nebuzaraden (ca. 1757-1797), and Nathan (ca. 1760-1823).

Information on Salathiel Coffey can be found in the story on Eli and Mary Coffey.

Chesley Coffey was born on Nov. 19, 1755. He married Margaret Baldwin. They moved to near Knoxville, Tenn. during the 1780s. They moved to Adair Co., Ky. between 1800 and 1802. In about 1812, they moved to Maury Co., Tenn., where Chesley died on Sep. 18, 1818. Their children were: Nathan (born 1780), Polly, Isaac (murdered 1799), Gracie (ca. 1782-1859), John, Joel, Felicia (1787-1865), Jake and Landon (born 1794).

Nebuzaraden Coffey was born in 1757 or earlier. In 1780 or earlier, he married Elizabeth Hayes. In 1794, he moved to Madison Co., Ky., where he died before March, 1797. His children were: Joel, Sarah, Polly, Fielding, Salathiel, Amanias (1785-1828), Hayes (1793-1860), Betsey, Ruth, and possibly Louis and James.

Information on Nathan Coffey can be found in the story on Nathan and Mary (Saunders) Coffey.

Sources: Eliza Porter's notes, wills of Joel and Nebuzaraden Coffey, letter written by Isaac J. Ross.

— Timothy E. Peterman

ELI and MARY COFFEY

465

Eli Coffey was born in what is now Wilkes Co., N.C. on May 8, 1775. He married Mary "Polly" Coffey, a first cousin according to tradition, on Mar. 22, 1801, in what was then Green Co., Ky. and what is now Russell Co., Ky. Eli Coffey was probably a son of Salathiel and Elizabeth Coffey. Salathiel Coffey died before July 28, 1784 in Wilkes Co., N.C. His widow, Elizabeth, was administrix of his estate. Eli Coffey and Newton Coffey (1773-

1858) were brothers. Their sister was probably the Elizabeth "Graney" Coffey who married Rutherford Coffey on Mar. 17, 1801 in what was then Green Co., Ky. Another brother might have been the Salathiel Coffey who married Polly Blair on Oct. 25, 1808 in Adair Co., Ky. and who was supposedly born in 1781 in Wilkes Co., N.C. Salathiel Coffey (died 1784) was probably a son of Chesley and Jane (Cleveland) Coffey.

Mary "Polly" Coffey was born on Dec. 7, 1785 in Wilkes Co., N.C. A typed copy of the entries made in her husband's Family Bible listed her birth year as 1780. However, considering that her youngest son was born in 1830, the 1785 date is more likely. Mary was the daughter of Nathan and Mary (Saunders) Coffey and probably the granddaughter of Chesley and Jane (Cleveland) Coffey.

The parents of both Eli and Mary Coffey left Wilkes Co., N.C. during the 1790s and settled in that part of Green Co., Ky. that became Adair Co. in 1802 and Russell Co. in 1826.

Eli and Mary Coffey were members of the Baptist Church and must have worked hard to instill their Christian faith in their children, because at least two of their sons became Baptist ministers. Eli Coffey died in Russell Co., Ky. on July 18, 1833. Mary Coffey died there on Mar. 10, 1872.

Eli and Mary Coffey had 12 children: Mariah, Willis, Elizabeth, Nancy, Salathiel, Sirena, Nathaniel, Stanton, William, Newton, Mary Ann, and Reuben.

Mariah Coffey was born on Jan. 17, 1802. She married a second cousin, Elijah Coffey, on May 18, 1826. She died in Russell Co., Ky. in Oct. 1855.

Willis Coffey was born on May 2, 1804. He married Violetta Haynes on Mar. 23, 1828. He died in De Kalb Co., Mo. in 1893.

Elizabeth Coffey was born on Aug. 14, 1807. She married Jacob Wolford on Dec. 19, 1826. She died in Collin Co., Texas on Jan. 21, 1891.

Nancy Coffey was born on Oct. 14, 1809. She married a cousin, Fielding Coffee, on Jan. 17, 1842.

Salathiel Coffey was born on Apr. 20, 1812. He married Nancy Dunbar on Aug. 20, 1835. He married Mrs. Mary Ann (Mc Farland) Ballew, a widow, in 1854. He died in Collin Co., Tx. on May 29, 1892.

Sirena Coffey was born on Aug. 9, 1814. She married Darias Campbell on Sep. 21, 1834. She died on Nov. 23, 1868.

Rev. Nathaniel J. Coffey was born on Jan. 3, 1817. He married Mary H. Carter on Jan. 17, 1842. He died in Illinois.

Stanton P. Coffey was born Dec. 5, 1819. He married Mary C. Saufley on June 27, 1842.

William S. Coffey was born on July 10, 1821. He married Martha Johnson on Sep. 4, 1845.

Rev. Newton Eli Coffey was born on May 2, 1823. He married Martha Louise Vermillion on Apr. 13, 1843. He died in Christian Co., Illinois on Jan. 14, 1890.

Mary Ann Coffey was born on July 4, 1827. She married Joseph E. Hayes on Mar. 25, 1854. She died on May 24, 1869.

Reuben Coffey was born on Feb. 12, 1830.

He was a bachelor.

Sources: County Court minutes of Wilkes Co., N.C. and the Eli Coffey Family Bible.

— Timothy E. Peterman

NATHAN and MARY (SAUNDERS) COFFEY

466

Daughters of the American Revolution records report that Nathan Coffey was born in 1760, that Mary Saunders was born in 1770, and that the two were married in 1785. However, considering that one of their sons was born between 1770 and 1780, it seems likely that they were born several years earlier. Mary was supposedly the daughter of William Saunders. Although D.A.R. records show Nathan as a son of Joel Coffey and Martha Sealey, he was probably a son of Chesley and Jane (Cleveland) Coffey.

Nathan Coffey was either born in what is now Wilkes Co., N.C., or else he moved there with his parents from Virginia, while he was still a youngster. He was a private in the North Carolina Militia during the Revolutionary War. During the 1790s, Nathan Coffey and a number of his relatives settled in Green, later Adair Co., Ky. Shortly after 1820, he moved to Jackson Co., Ala., where he died in 1823. Mary (Saunders) Coffey supposedly died in 1838 in Kentucky.

Nathan and Mary (Saunders) Coffey had 9 children: Rutherford, Elizabeth, Mary, Absolem, Joel, Grace, William, Nancy, and Catherine.

Rutherford Coffey was born between 1770 and 1780. He married Elizabeth "Graney" Coffey on Mar. 17, 1801. He settled in Jackson Co., Ala.

Elizabeth Coffey was born on May 12, 1781. She married her first cousin, James Coffey. She died in 1837.

Mary "Polly" Coffey was born on Dec. 7, 1785. Information on her family can be found in the story on Eli and Mary Coffey.

Absolem Coffey was supposedly born in 1788. He married first to Mary Lusk and second to Nancy Chadwick. He probably settled in Jackson Co., Ala.

Joel Coffey was supposedly born on Aug. 3, 1790. He married Mary Knox in 1817. He died in 1850.

Grace Coffey was supposedly born in 1793. She married a Marlow.

William Saunders Coffey was supposedly born in 1795. He married Elizabeth Schuyler.

Nancy Coffey was supposedly born in 1797. She married Richard Lockett.

Catherine Coffey was supposedly born in 1799. She married John Baxter.

Sources: D.A.R. records, census records, and the James Coffey Family Bible.

— Timothy E. Peterman

COLEMAN

467

The family of Elson B. Coleman and wife, Lula Jackson Coleman, would like to dedicate this story in memory of our wonderful father, the late Elson B. Coleman, and to our loving mother. Our father was born February 15, 1903, in Wilkes County, NC and died March 28, 1973. His wife, Lula J. Coleman, was born April 24, 1909, in Forsyth County, NC and is living in Winston-Salem, NC, at the present time.

The Colemans of Little Hunting and Osborne Creeks:

Our father was one of six children born to Henry Clinton Coleman who was born July 28, 1861, and married October 25, 1888, to Margret Elizabeth Dowell who was born in May 1869, and to their marriage were born the following children: David, born May 20, 1891, died in 1892; Jettie, born June 29, 1894, died November 9, 1917; Ero. L., born March 1, 1897; Clarence, born July 31, 1900, died August 1925; Walter P., born March 25, 1906; and our father, Elson B. Coleman.

Henry Clinton and wife Margret lived in North Wilkesboro until Margret died August 21, 1909, and then Clinton took his family to Mooresville, NC, where he spent his remaining years and died July 16, 1916. Here he left with his oldest daughter, Jettie, his remaining family. One son, Clarence, stayed in Mooresville and learned the shoemaking trade and later opened his own shoe shop in Harmony, NC. The other two sons, Walter P. and Elson B., jumped a train and came to Winston-Salem, in search of a job at Reynolds. When they got off the train they went to apply for a job, the man asked them what color they were, due to their faces being black from the train smoke.

The next step back in Henry Clinton Coleman's life is through the Sommers and Lovelace districts. Where his father and mother, Robert and Mary Ann Coleman, raised their family. Robert was born in 1826 and married September 29, 1845, to Mary Ann Jones, born in 1827. To this marriage were born the following children: Marion "Missa," born 1847, married Hiram Privette; Amos, born 1853, married Almeda Anderson; Bettie Elizabeth, born 1858, married Robert Houston Elliott; John, born 1862; marriages of the next five unknown — James, born 1864; Sally, born 1866; Annie, born 1868; Susie, born 1869; and our grandfather, Henry Clinton Coleman.

The next step back in Robert Coleman's life begins on Little Hunting Creek. He was one of eight children born to Robert H. Coleman and Betsy Elizabeth Rash. Robert H. Coleman was born in 1785 and married June 2, 1805. Betsy Elizabeth Rash was born 1782, and they had the following known four children: John B., born 1808, married Rebecca Brown, August 28, 1828 who was born in 1807; Marion, born in 1821, marriage unknown; Archy, born 1828; and our great-grandfather, Robert Coleman. The rest of his children are unknown at the present time. Robert H. Coleman and wife were large landowners on both sides of Little Hunting Creek. Robert H. Coleman served in the War of 1812 and died in 1846; his wife Elizabeth died in 1873 at age 91.

Now we go back to the beginning of the Coleman Family line in Wilkes County, NC. It all started at the middle fork of Hunting Creek, where the first Charles Coleman owned 460 acres of land and started his family. He was born in 1760 and married Mary (maiden name unknown) in the year 1780 or 1781. Her date of birth is unknown. To this marriage were born Nancy, born 1782, married Asa Rash, November 12, 1800; Beverly, born 1788, married Rebecca Nicholson, December 29, 1808; Phobe, born 1790, married Lazrus Nicholson, March 11, 1809; Archibald, born 1792, married Elizabeth Mooreman, September 6, 1812; John H. Coleman, born 1796, married Susannah Felts, December 26, 1818; and our great-great-grandfather, Robert H. Coleman. Charles Coleman and his wife Mary were large landowners in Wilkes County, NC. They bought land up at Osbornes Creek. In 1808 it is said he owned a mill just below the present site of Sweet Home Church. At the time of his death in 1826, the inventory of his estate showed him owning one plantation where he lived upon his death. His son, Robert H. Coleman, gave bond in sum of $4000.00 as the administrator of his estate. Then upon the death of Mary, his wife, she left in her will that her son John receive her liquor stills, gun and covered wagons, with the rest of her estate going to granddaughter Mary Rash, daughter of Nancy Rash, granddaughter Mary Coleman, and daughter Phobe Nicholson. The oldest descendants of these Coleman lines are as follows: Evan, Avery, and Ralph Coleman from the John B. Coleman line, and Mrs. L.D. Spaugh, Sr., and Mrs. Dolly White, descendants of the John H. and Susannah Felts Coleman line.

This covers 199 years of Colemans from the beginning in Wilkes County, NC to the present.

Sources: Wilkes County Public Library and Courthouse; Forsyth Technical Core Collection on Wilkes County; Forsyth County Public Library; and State Archives, Raleigh, NC.

— Mr. Emory L. Coleman

MEREDITH COLLINS
468

Meredith Collins was born in Virginia in 1760, and was an American Revolutionary War soldier in Montgomery Co., Virginia. A monument which includes his name was unveiled in Pike Co., Ky., May 30, 1929 by the Pikeville Chapter DAR. The name of his first wife is not yet known. The only known child of this first marriage was a son named Bradley. His second marriage was to Polly Holloway between 1790 and 1800. The children of his second marriage were: Archibald, James, and William. Meredith lived for a while in Wilkes Co., N.C. and appears on the 1796 Wilkes Co. Tax List. He migrated to Russell Co., Va. after 1796. About 1809 he settled in Floyd Co., Ky. Meredith Collins was among the white pioneer families of Floyd Co. in 1810. About 1822 he moved on to Pike Co., Ky. and died there in the latter part of 1841. The known children of Meredith Collins are: Bradley, Archibald, James, and William.

Bradley Collins (1787-185?) was born in N. Carolina, possibly in Wilkes Co. He was a farmer by occupation, but also followed other pursuits. He migrated to Russell Co., Va. with his parents between 1796 and 1799. About 1811 Bradley followed his father, Meredith, to Floyd Co., Ky. The Floyd Co. 1820 Census shows that Bradley, in addition to himself and his wife, had one male and two females under the age of fourteen in his household. The male was his son Andrew. Later census records show additional children. The name of his first wife is not yet known.

About 1825 Bradley moved to Clay Co., Ky. While in Clay Co., Andrew married Betsy Ann Sizemore Mar. 31, 1838. He sold his land in 1839 and shortly afterwards he and his family, Andrew and his wife and son Lewis traveled by flatboat down the Kentucky and Ohio Rivers to Missouri. They were in Carroll Co., Mo. in 1840, but later settled near Keytesville, Chariton Co., Mo. It was here that Bradley received a land grant in May of 1841. Bradley and Andrew raised and sold crops of corn, cotton, and tobacco.

About 1844 Bradley and Andrew sold their land in Missouri and moved to Centerville, Appanoose Co., Iowa on the Chariton River. They farmed in addition to running a ferry across the Chariton River. Andrew (1811-c1873) was living in 1850 in Appanoose Co., Iowa Census, with his family Betsy Ann (wife), Lewis, Samson, Archibald, and Polly Ann, and his father Bradley, age 63, born in North Carolina.

Bradley died in either Appanoose Co., Iowa or Hancock Co., Illinois. About 1856 Andrew moved to Warsaw, Hancock Co., Ill. where Polly Ann, his daughter, attended her first year in school. About 1859 Andrew moved to Marion Co., Mo. The 1860 Census shows the following additional family members: Eliza age 9 and Eli age 5. They were both born in Iowa. Andrew and Betsy's sons Samson, Lewis, and Archibald were veterans of the Civil War.

Archibald Collins (1800-c1886) born in Russell Co., Va. He married Margaret (Peggy) Coots on May 18, 1824 in Pike Co., Ky. He engaged in agriculture in Roane Co., W. Va. and he possibly died there between 1882 and 1890. His children were: Matilda, John Wesley, Euorkia, Henry Newberry, Jenny, Washington, Lucinda, and Reece.

James Collins (1804-?) was born in Russell Co., Va. He married Susan Holloway on Oct. 15, 1824 in Pike Co., Ky. He migrated from Pike Co. prior to the 1830. His whereabouts is still unknown.

William Collins was born Apr. 13, 1806 and became a "Jack of all trades." He was a lumberman, gun smith, owner and operator of a dry goods store and a minister of the Primitive Baptist Church. On Mar. 22, 1829 William married Mary (Polly) Mullins. Their children were: William, Pricy, Lucinda, Louisa, John, Arvid, Floyd, Arminda, and Samson. On Nov. 25, 1860 he married Mary A. (Molly) Hatfield. The children of this marriage were Samuel, Tobias, Archibald, Nancy Jane, Aaron, Levi Ancel, and Louemma. William died in Nicholas Co., W. Va. on March 30, 1896.

Sources: Research in Public Records.

— John D. Young

VARDY (VARDI-VARDE) NAVARRAH COLLINS
469

Vardy Collins, born 1764 in N.C. listed on the tax list of Wilkes County during the 1790s, married Margaret (Peggy) Gibson, born 1773 in Virginia. Vardy married Peggy in N.C. and came to what is now Hancock County, Tennessee. He is listed as a taxpayer 1809-1812 in Hawkins County.

They had the following children, all born in Hawkins County, except the oldest, who was born in N.C.: (1) Lottie, also called Letitia or Peggy, born 1791, married Timothy Williams, born 7 November 1808, N.C., son of Charles; (2) Morgan, born 1798, married Minta Gibson, born 1825 in TN.; (3) Allen, born in 1802, married 1st. Rachel Reed, born 1804 TN., 2nd. Rachel Nichols, born 1831 TN., died 1921 in Hancock County; (4) Alford, born 1810, married Elizabeth Mullins, daughter of James and Clarah (Martin) Mullins; (5) Ethie or Effie, born 1812, married Alexander Gowins, born 1815, TN.; (6) Clarkia, born 1813, married Isum Biggs, born 1813, TN., son of William and Elizabeth (Collins) Biggs; (7) Varda, born 1817, married Elizabeth "Betty" Maxey.

The 1830, 1840, and 1850 census of Hawkins County, TN. and the Tennessee Land Grants show Vardy Collins to be living there. These land grants were all in what is now called Vardy, Hancock County. The land extended from the Virginia line to the Mulberry Gap-Sneedville road. It included land from the top of Newman's Ridge to the top of Powell's Mountain.

Where they received the money for this much land is open to speculation. Possibly it was for military services; possible, but improbable is that Vardy was a pirate. Some sources say that Peggy was descended from the rich pirates who plied the North Carolina waters. Whatever the source of his funds he was considered one of the wealthier men in the area.

Vardy and Peggy operated a hotel-boarding house at the foot of Newman's Ridge where a big sulphur spring is still running. After his death, his descendants owned and operated the hotel until the early 1900's. Vardy and Peggy's descendants can be found in all walks of life.

Alford Collins, son of Vardy and Peggy, born 1810, married Elizabeth Mullins, born 1819, daughter of James and Clarah Martin Mullins. Alford and Elizabeth had a large family. One of their children was Batey (Bata) Collins, born 1844 Hawkins County. He married Cynthia Collins, born 1843, daughter of Simeon and Frankie (Bunch) Collins. Frankie was born in 1805 in N.C., died 1885 in Hancock County. She was a daughter of Benjamin and Mary (Dotson) Bunch.

Batey and Cynthia Collins owned and operated the Collins Boarding House at the foot of Newman's Ridge. They had children: (1) Noah, born 1878, married Alice Lovin Bales. Her first husband, Morgan Bales was drowned in Powell's river in Lee County, VA. Noah was a farmer, stock trader and owned a general merchandise store in Vardy. They had three children, Charlie, Mary Edith and Vardy. Vardy remained single. (2) Frankie Collins married Harrison Collins and had a large family; (3) Adelaide Collins married Daniel B. Horton. He also owned and operated a general merchandise store in Vardy; (4) Nancy Collins, born 15 August 1881, died 5 December 1961, married Logan Miser, son of Hamilton and Amelia (Collins) Miser.

Nancy and Logan Miser had 14 children, viz: Grace, Lillian, Roy B., Mae, Edith, Oppie, Walter, Clarabel, Gladys, Ernest, Florence, Cecil, Chester Carl and Chester Logan. The last two died before the age of two.

Lillian Miser, daughter of Nancy and Logan, was born 8 April 1901, died 8 November 1973, married William Paul Grohse, born 19 November 1906 in New York City. They were married in Rhine Township Presbyterian Church, Eldorado, Ill., 10 October 1931. One son, Willie Paul Crohse, born 2 May 1934 in Pennington Gap, Virginia married Mattie Mae Norton, born 20 August 1936 in Sneedville, TN. on 21 June 1953.

Willie and Mattie Mae has issue: Michael Wayne Grohse, born 31 August 1954 in Sneedville, TN. is single; Janet Lynn Grohse, born 17 June 1957 in Sneedville, married Michael Roy Clonce in the Sneedville Methodist Church 31 December 1977. Michael Wayne Grohse and his sister Janet Lynn Clonce are both graduates of Eastern Tennessee State University, Johnson City. They are both presently employed with the Hancock County Board of Education, Sneedville, as teachers. Janet's husband is a registered real estate agent for the State of Tennessee.

Michael Roy and Janet (Grohse) Clonce have a daughter, Leslie Brooke Clonce, born 21 April 1981 in Morristown, Tennessee.

Most of the present day descendants of the original Vardy Collins are school teachers. Some have branched out and became bankers, doctors, college professors, and just name it and you will find some of Vardy Collin's descendants in the occupation. Many of the early descendants of Vardy were also hunters, fisherman, explorers and so on.

It is impossible to write a short story of an ancestor and do it justice. Suffice it to say, most of them can be proud that North Carolina was their state in the beginning.

Sources: Wilkes County Tax lists, Hawkins County, Tennessee tax lists, land grants, and census.

— William P. Grohse

COLVARD

470

One William Colvard and wife Rachael Berry Colvard came from Prince William County, Va., and settled in Wilkes County, Reddies River Community, about 1775. They had a large family of sons and daughters. William Colvard was very active in county affairs. One son was named Wade Colvard. He married Phoebe Vannoy and they had a rather large family. One son was named Rufus Winfield Colvard, who was a schoolteacher, Sunday School teacher, and was very active in county affairs. At the time of his sudden death, he was

chairman of the County Board of Commissioners. While holding this office he was instrumental in getting the Southern Railway to come here. The contract stipulated that it come within one mile of the courthouse, in Wilkesboro. It so happened that it stopped on the north side of Yadkin River, and the town of North Wilkesboro grew up around it. One of his sons was killed in a train wreck in West Virginia. Another one died of an illness when he was a young man. Two other sons — Ben Hamilton Colvard and William Edgar Colvard lived in North Wilkesboro for a number of years. William Edgar married Sue Taylor and they had one son and one daughter. The son is now deceased and the daughter is Mrs. Dean McMillan of West Jefferson. Ben Hamilton Colvard married Cora Taylor, and they had one son and two daughters. The son, Ben Hamilton, Jr. was killed in France during World War II. The daughters are Mrs. William R. Richardson who, with her husband, is on the faculty of Wilkes Community College and Mrs. Buddie Sprinkle of Hickory, NC.

Other descendants of Wade Colvard were: Thomas R. Colvard, long deceased, but lived with his family in North Wilkesboro. Only two of his children are still living — Ruth Colvard, who has worked in office of Meadows Mill Company since 1924, and Frank Colvard of West Jefferson. He and his wife have no children but almost everyone who knows them call them "Uncle Frank and Aunt Lillie Mae." Charlie Colvard, descendant of Wade Colvard, married Elizabeth Vannoy (better known as "Lillie") and they had a rather large family. One son, Evan Colvard, was a prominent schoolteacher in the county schools for a number of years. Now deceased. Another son, Howard Colvard married Sadie Fowler and they had two children: daughter, Allie, who is Mrs. Everett Solomon, Jr. They have one son, Howard Colvard, Jr. (known as "Buddie") who is a very promising young lawyer in North Wilkesboro. He is married and has one son.

Two other descendants of Wade Colvard are: (1) Dr. D.W. Colvard of Charlotte, NC, first Chancellor of UNC in Charlotte, now retired but very active and has travelled extensively. (2) Charles Deward Colvard of Raleigh, N.C. Retired vice president of the N.C. Cooperative Council. In paying tribute to him Gov. James B. Hunt, Jr., called him "one of the greatest advocates that rural North Carolina has ever had and one of the most distinguished citizens of this state."

Sources: Family records, personal knowledge.

— Ruth Colvard

CHARLES HAMPTON COLVARD

471

Charles H. Colvard was a large man, in stature, heritage and foresight. He was born 26 January 1872, the first child of Thomas Jefferson and Mary Ann (Whittington) Colvard. His death was 28 November 1938.

His only sister was Queen Colvard Hutchinson, who proceeded him in death, leaving numerous survivors. His half-brother, Wiley Pinkney Colvard, was born 22 November 1881

and died in 1958, after having been married to Mary Shepherd of Ashe County on 30 March 1910 and becoming the father of seven children.

Early in life Charlie Colvard acquired the old family plantation in the Wilbar community, formerly owned by his great-grandfather, William Colvard. The original deed to this property, dated 17 October 1803, has been given to the Wilkes County Historical Collection, as have documents for grants from North Carolina Governor Tod R. Caldwell for adjoining properties. Some of Charlie Colvard's farm continues to be owned by his direct descendants.

He was married 16 June 1897 to Elizabeth (Lizzie) Vannoy, daughter of Lewis and Louisa (Burkett) Vannoy, and their offspring numbered ten.

(1) Quincy Ethan Colvard was born 13 March 1898 and died 5 March 1958. He was married to Gilie James 31 August 1923 and their three children are (1) Mildred Colvard Gregory, (2) Elizabeth Colvard Cantrell, and (3) Jean Colvard Morris. There are ten grandchildren.

(2) Ella Colvard was born 18 November 1899 and died 13 September 1910.

(3) Evan Lewis Colvard was born 7 January 1902 and died 22 April 1953. He was unmarried.

(4) Sherman Thomas Colvard was born 4 February 1905 and married Ruth Tryon 11 May 1936. They have no children. He is the only surviving child.

(5) Plato Colvard was born 31 December 1906 and died 21 March 1907.

(6) Carl Franklin Colvard was born 22 March 1908 and died 28 May 1962. He was married to Ella Sue Vannoy 6 October 1934. Their only child is C. Frank Colvard, Jr., unmarried.

(7) Howard Charles Colvard was born 7 March 1910 and died 7 November 1970. His marriage to Sadie Fowler was 15 October 1936. Their two children are (1) Allie Colvard Solomon and (2) Howard C. Colvard, Jr. There are two grandchildren.

(8) Dora Belle Colvard was born 6 February 1912 and died 30 November 1974. She was married 7 February 1937 to Howard Norman. The three children are (1) Charles Norman, (2) Nancy Norman Austin, and (3) John Norman, who lives on the site of his grandfather's homeplace.

(9) Clara Elizabeth Colvard was born 6 December 1913 and died 30 June 1975. She married Robert Calloway 12 December 1940. Their children are (1) Mabel Calloway Mast, (2) Mary Calloway Spears, and (3) Bobbie Calloway Blevins. Their grandchildren number three. A son, (4) Sam Colvard Calloway, proceeded his mother in death.

(10) Wade Hampton Colvard was born 11 May 1916 and died 13 July 1923. When asked about his large family and how many offspring there were, Charlie Colvard would reply, "I have no children of whom I am ashamed."

Charlie Colvard had three basic interests: family, Wilkes County, and the Baptist church. He gave the acreage for the Union Baptist Church and Cemetery in Wilbar.

Around the turn of the century, he was

elected to the Wilkes County Board of Commissioners. Prior to and after that time, he served as the County Surveyor.

His chief profession was farming, although eventually he became owner of the Cardwell Lumber Company in North Wilkesboro.

Education was his avocation, and Charlie Colvard, himself, taught many of his children at early ages. His good influence was responsible for many of them obtaining college degrees, during a time when such an achievement was difficult.

Charlie Colvard was proud of his heritage and could trace his paternal lineage back to Sir George Calvert (original spelling), First Lord Baltimore, a title bestowed by King James I of England. The family initially settled in Ireland and eventually in the colonies of Maryland and Virginia, before a branch migrated to North Carolina.

Little has been said about his wife, Elizabeth Vannoy Colvard, because her biography may be found elsewhere in this book.

Charles H. Colvard has been remembered as a gentleman and a scholar, who looked toward the future. This description compliments him well, even to be remembered and discussed at all, since his death was forty-four years ago.

Sources: O'Gorman, *Descendants of Virginia Calverts*; family records and memories.

— C. Frank Colvard

ELIZABETH VANNOY COLVARD
472

A good and true woman was Elizabeth (Lizzie) Vannoy Colvard. She strongly believed in the fine virtues of being a helpful sister, loving wife, and devoted mother. Her values were developed early in life, undoubtedly from the strict upbringing of her parents, Lewis and Louisa (Burkett) Vannoy.

She was born 13 May 1876 and died 30 January 1961. She was the mother of ten children and the grandmother of thirteen. Her birthplace was Reddies River.

As a young woman, her responsibilities were many, an experience she carried with her through later life. She had two sisters and four brothers. They were (1) Mary Jane Vannoy was later married to John L. Whittington. They had nine children and nine grandchildren. (2) Henry Neil Vannoy eventually married Sallie Virginia Colvard. Their children numbered four. There were no grandchildren. (3) Wiley J. Vannoy died unmarried. (4) James Franklin Vannoy was later married to Viola Minton. There were two sons and no grandchildren. (5) Elizabeth Vannoy came next and was married to Charles H. Colvard. Their children are discussed later and also in the biography of their father.

(6) Thomas H. Vannoy was married to Mamie Cosby. There were two daughters and six grandchildren. (7) Dora E. Vannoy married Robert L. Miller, and they had five children and several grandchildren.

Lizzie Colvard's mother died around 1885. Her father, Lewis Vannoy, then married Mrs. Mary (Whittington) Vannoy, widow of his

nephew, James Vannoy. They were the parents of six children.

(8) Roby Vannoy was first married to Ettie Kilby. There were two children and grandchildren. He was later married to Mary Brown. (9) Julia Vannoy was married to Walter S. Cox. There were no children. She and her brother, Roby, were twins. (10) Sallie Vannoy was married to Charles E. Jenkins. There are two sons and three grandchildren. (11) Fanny Vannoy married Frank Alderfer. There are two sons and grandchildren. (12) Minnie Vannoy was married to D. T. Trivette. There is a daughter and two grandchildren. (13) Ethel Vannoy married Dr. E. James Moore. There is a son and two grandchildren.

The only direct survivors of Lewis Vannoy's are Sallie Vannoy Jenkins and Ethel Vannoy Moore, Lizzie Colvard's half-sisters.

Nancy Elizabeth Vannoy married Charles Hampton Colvard 16 June 1897. They located not far from her father's farm, on the original William Colvard tract in the Wilbar community. She carried on in the tradition of her father in having ten children in eighteen years: (1) Quincy Ethan Colvard, (2) Ella Colvard, (3) Evan Lewis Colvard, (4) Sherman Thomas Colvard, (5) Plato Colvard, (6) Carl Franklin Colvard, (7) Howard Charles Colvard, (8) Dora Belle Colvard Norman, (9) Clara Elizabeth Colvard Calloway, and (10) Wade Hampton Colvard.

"The lady of the house," as Charlie Colvard called his wife, was a stern disciplinarian and often carried a hickory switch under her apron to administer deserving punishment when she could get hold of a youngster.

She fostered a yearn for learning in her children. Most of those who survived to adulthood had some higher education. Four of her children were college graduated, and at sometime in their lives they were involved in teaching.

Aside from family, her love was the Baptist church. With her husband she gave the land for the building and cemetery of the Union Baptist Church. Lizzie Colvard was a founding member of this congregation.

Her ancestory was French, six generations removed. But the "old country" attitude prevailed with her in homemaking and in searching for wisdom.

It would bring pleasure to Lizzie Colvard to know some of the contributions her grandchildren and great-grandchildren are attempting to make. Or perhaps there would be a reprimand for their possible "unplanned judgement," as she would often say.

Lizzie Colvard's legacy was wholesome and pure. Only one child, Sherman Thomas Colvard, survives.

Sources: Hook, *George Michael Eller, Descendants of His in America*; family records and memories.

— C. Frank Colvard

HIX OR HICKS COMBS
473

In various records, we have found his name spelled both ways. Hix was born around 1820, and was a son of William and Elizabeth Marlow

Combs.

Hix was a farmer and lived in the Hunting Creek area of Wilkes Co. his entire life. He raised all of his food and grew cotton and sheep for clothing. There was also a blacksmith shop on his farm. As it was a custom to have two dwelling houses during the period of Hix's life, his homestead consist of two houses, one for cooking and eating and one for sitting in and sleeping.

Hix's first marriage was to Elizabeth Lewis on Oct. 9, 1840. His brother-in-law, Wessley Anderson, signed his marriage bond. There were five children born to this union: first was John W. Combs (1844-1916), married Nancy Lewis, a daughter of Joshua and Caroline Chamber Lewis. John and Nancy are buried at Lewis Baptist Church. Second, a daughter, Susannah Combs (1845-1910), married William Love, a son of Ingram and Hallie Parker Love. William and Susannah are buried at Mt. Sinai Baptist Church; third child was James Rufus Combs (1847-1923), married Julia A. Johnson, a daughter of Peter and Flora Padgette Johnson. Rufus is buried at North Wilkesboro Baptist Cemetery; fourth was Enzah Combs (1850-1923); married Elizabeth (Bettie) Lewis, a daughter of Joshua and Caroline Chamber Lewis. Enzah and Bettie are buried at Lewis Church; Last a son, Hicks Jr., was born (1853-1888), married Nancy Elizabeth Bottoms. Hick, Jr. is buried at Lewis Church. A death date or place of burial, have not been found for Elizabeth Lewis Combs.

Hix Combs.

On March 25, 1858, Hix was married to Jane (known as Jensey) Brown, a daughter of Eli Brown. In the 1900 Census, Jensey stated she was the mother of eleven children but I only known of nine children born to this union. They were: (1) Bynum Combs (1858-1938), married to Marth Jane Nance, a daughter of Wilborn and Amanda Nance. Martha Jane and Bynum are buried at Rose Chapel Methodist

Church, Iredell Co.; (2) Elizabeth (Betty) (1859-1899), married to William Vance Somers, a son of William and Rebecca Brown Somers. Elizabeth is buried at Lewis Church; (3) Scennie Combs (1864-1956), married to William Augustus (Gus) Elliot. Scennie is buried at Concord Presbyterian Church in Iredell Co.; (4) Robert Lee Combs (1865-1923), married to Nancy Caroline Alexander a daughter of Jerry and Caroline Porter Alexander. Robert and Nancy are buried at Lewis Church; (5) Nancey Combs (1868-1938), married to Thomas Nelson Jarvis, a son of Nancy Jarvis. Thomas and Nancy are buried at Edgewood Baptist Church; (6) Frankie Combs (1869-1951), married Abel Cass, Jr.,a son of Abel and Rachel Mitchell Cass. Abel and Frankie are buried at Sweet Home Baptist Church; (7) Kizzie Combs (1872-1938), married Osborne M. (Dick) Johnson, a son of James and Dicey Anderson Combs. Dick and Kizzie are buried at Lewis Baptist Church; (8) Minda Combs (1875-1953), married Columbus (Dock) Anderson, son of William and Emily Smithey Anderson. Minda and Dock are buried at Lewis Church; (9) Felix William Combs, my grandfather (1877-1957), married Nancy Matilda Anderson. Felix and Nancy are buried at Rose Chapel Church.

When the Civil War broke out, Hix, with a new bride and several small children, chose to stay home and serve as a home guard.

Hix died on Feb. 7, 1904, and this article appeared in the *Wilkes Chronicle*. "Mr. Hix Combs of Hunting Creek, died last Sunday and was buried at the home graveyard. He was eighty-four years old and had been in feeble health ever since his arm was broken some years ago. He was the father of Mr. Rufus Combs, North Wilkesboro and grandfather of our townsman, A.L. Combs."

My grandfather, Felix Combs, hired Mr. Transou, to build a rock wall around his father's grave. Maie Combs Johnson later marked his grave with the tombstone there now.

The following is part of an epitah used at his funeral and engraved on his tomb.

"IN LOVING REMBRANCE OF HIX COMBS. DIED FEB. 7, 1904 AGED 84 YEARS. GONE BUT NOT FORGOTTEN, A PRECIOUS ONE FROM US HAS GONE, A VOICE WE LOVED IS STILLED, A PLACE IS VACANT IN OUR HOME WHICH CAN NEVER BE FILLED."

Sources: Wilkes co. marriage bond; Federal Census Records, death certificates; and family tradition; *Chronicle Weekly* newspaper.

— Barbara A. Jordan

WILLIAM COMBS OF HUNTING CREEK

474

William Combs was born ca. 1790. His parents, brothers, or sisters are unknown to this writer.

His claim for bounty land under "Act proposed Mar. 3, 1855, and filed Mar. 22, 1855, states he was aged sixty-five years, a resident of N.C. and served in a company commanded by Capt. Ambrose Carlton in F Regiment of N.C. Militia. He was honorably discharged Dec. 1, 1814."

His first marriage was to Elizabeth Marlow on Dec. 17, 1813. According to family information and his will (Book 6; pages 132-133) dated Oct. 10, 1856, three children were born to this marriage. First was Dicey Combs, born ca. 1815, and she was married to Wessley Anderson Jan. 29, 1833. Her death date is unknown. She was buried in the Anderson-Johnson cemetery on land owned by Ruth Johnson Propeck with a field stone for a grave marker. Second child was John Combs, known as Capt. John Combs. He was born ca. 1816 and was first married to Elizabeth (maiden name unknown, but family tradition said she was a Combs, also). His second marriage was to Mary (Polly) Love, a daughter of Ingram and Hallie Parker Love. John's date of death and place of burial are unknown. Hix Combs, the third child, was born ca. 1820. His first marriage was to Elizabeth Lewis on Oct. 9, 1840. His second marriage was to Jane (Jensey) Brown, daughter of Eli Brown, on mar. 25, 1858. He died Feb. 7, 1904, and was buried on land he owned.

William Combs second marriage was to Matilda Lewis on Feb. 8, 1854. To this union two daughters were born: Margery Franky and Mary Elvaria Combs. Nothing else is known about Margery Franky and she doesn't appear in any of the census records. She must have died as a child. Mary Elvaria married William Riley Johnson. She died on Mar. 30, 1926, and was buried in the old Hunting Creek Cemetery.

William Combs died on July 2, 1876, according to his widow's pension record. It also stated that he lived in Wilkes Co. on Hunting Creek. His burial site is unknown.

Sources: Wilkes Co. Will Books; marriage bonds, war claims of 1812 W. C. 15242, Federal Census records and family tradition.

— Barbara A. Jordan

MARY MATILDA COOK

475

My great grandmother, Mary Matilda Stansbury, was born in Wilkes County in 1814. She was the daughter of John H. Stansbury and his wife, Ann Earnest. She married David Cook, the son of Michael Cook of Watauga County, North Carolina. Mary and her husband David were members of the "Three Forks Baptist Church" near Boone, North Carolina, where David commenced preaching in 1838. In 1841 David Cook bought 60 acres of land on the North Fork of New River in Ashe County.

David Cook died in 1850 at an early age of thirty six. At the time of his death he was the minister of the Cranberry Primitive Baptist Church, which is now located in Alleghany County. A memorial was written for him on September 20, 1850 by the Mountain District Baptist Association. A short biography of his early life was entered into the minutes of the Three Forks Baptist Association in 1851.

After the death of her husband, Mary Cook was left with six young children. Her land was sold for money to raise her family. Later she lived with her children after they were married. At the time of her death in 1906, she was living with her daughter, Elizabeth, at White Top, in Grayson County, Virginia. She is buried at Bowers Cemetery at White Top.

The children of David and Mary (Stansbury) Cook were: Emiline born in 1836. Married (1) Harrison Taylor. He died in Civil War. Married (2) Jackson Lewis. Children: Mary Susanne Taylor, born of first marriage, who married John Roberts. Of the second marriage she had a daughter Laura Lewis who married William Arnold and a son William who died young.

Elizabeth born 1838. Married Franklin Dolinger. Their children: Mary Matilda (Polly) married Robey Cook: Edith married Enoch Hart; Emiline married Abraham Stamper; William married Celah Edmondson; Charles married (1) Cordia Barker (2) Emma Powers; Jesse married Lida Blevins; Tom who married (1) Lida Farmer (2) Ida Price (3) Dellie Blevins (4) Ethel Cox; Wesley married (1) A Blevins (2) Alice Pruitt; Harrison (name of wife unknown).

Edith born 1840. Married (1) John Taylor, he was killed in Civil War. They had a son Cicero Taylor who married Alzina Lewis. Married (2) Harrison Baker Miller, a well known Primitive Baptist Minister. Their children were: Dora Malissa Miller married (1) Claborn Pickel (2) James Barkley; John Luther Miller married (1) Etta Bolt (2) Sarah Crabtree.

John Henry born 1842. Married Evaline Miller. Children: Candas married (1) Wiley Ham (2) Will Bolt; Robey married Mary Matilda (Polly) Dolinger; Mary Leona married Daniel Caudill; Edith married Ambrose Anderson; David and Harrison died in infancy.

Harrison G. born June 14, 1846. Died May 12, 1926. Married Mary Ann Tucker on August 24, 1866. She was the daughter of David and Mahala (Blevins) Tucker. Children of Harrison and Mary Ann (Pollyann) were: Sarah Catherine married James Lee Thompson; David Alexander Cook married Laura Tucker; Laura Matilda married (1) ? Blevins (2) Jesse L. Davis; Mary married Solomon Blevins; and Grover Cleveland (changed his name to John Cleveland) married Mary Easter Perry, daughter of Emanuel and Effie (Sheets) Perry. John Cleveland and Mary Easter (Perry) Cook were my parents.

Jesse born 1849. Married Matilda Phipps. Three children died young of typhoid fever.

John Henry and Harrison G. Cook both fought in the Civil War from Ashe County, North Carolina. Company A 37th Regiment (Infantry). This company, along with the other units of the 37th, saw plenty of action. Historian Moore reports deaths in battles, deaths from wounds, deaths from disease in prisons. The company saw bloody fighting at Manassas, Cold Harbor, Hanover Courthouse, Ox Hill, Second Manassas, and Gettysburg. John Taylor, first husband of Edith Cook and Harrison Taylor, husband of Emiline, also fought in the 37th Regiment Company A.

Sources: Family Recollections; Ashe and Wilkes County Records; Three Forks Baptist Church Records, Library of W.F.U.; Roster of North Carolina Troops.

— Violet (Cook) Bohnert

MUMFORD and JULIA McNIELL COOPER

476

My parents were from Wilkes County, but they moved away and lived in High Shoals, N.C., with eight of their children. My brother, Horace Wade, was a baby.

My mother and Dad had been planting a late garden. A good distance from the house was a wide, deep branch. As my parents walked back to the house by the branch, they could hear Fannie singing at the top of her voice. George, my brother, was standing in the branch with baby Wade in his arms, preaching and baptising the baby. My mother had to turn the baby upside down and massage his lungs, as he had almost drowned. Incidentally, my brother George did become a preacher.

George Mumford Cooper (1859-1946).

Mother told me another experience she had with the children. All of the children each had a cat and the cats had litter after litter of kittens. Mother told the children she would give each of them a nickle if they would rid of the cats. One day she came back from milking and saw something was wrong. My brother, Walter, and sister, Fannie, were holding the cats and kittens on the chopping block while my brother, Wylie, cut their heads off. She got them stopped before they killed too many.

On my parents' 50th wedding anniversary, most of the children came home to Charlotte. The men got to telling about the mean things they'd done while growing up. They said George would tell my Daddy everything each of them did. When Clayton, the second oldest boy, knocked out a window light, they all swore each other to secrecy. A couple of days later at the dinner table, George told my father that Clayton did it. Clayton was too big to be whipped, so my Dad made him stay in the house and help my mother with the washing

and housework for two weeks.

The rest of the boys and my sister, went off to the field the next morning while my Mother and Dad went to the mercantile store. They took quart jars and filled them with tobacco worms. When they got to the row of tobacco where George was hoeing barefooted, and with no shirt on, one of the boys held George down while the others poured the worms on him. My mother said he had one big whelp where the worms stung him. George blushed and said he had it coming.

I, Edith Cooper Spurlin, was born in High Shoals in 1912, the baby of nine children — seven boys and two girls. All the older children were so mad at my mother because I came along that they wouldn't speak to her for some time. They still talked to my Dad and ignored Mother completely. As I grew older, they were

Julia E. McNiel Cooper (1869-1948).

lovely to me, and spoiled me, but would do aggravating things to me. My Dad told me to start taking up for myself, rather than crying. I did this and the aggravating stopped.

I loved all of them. My sister was sixteen years older than I, and married when I was a youngster. As we grew older we became very fond of each other. She and I are the only two children living at present.

Sources: Own experiences.

— Edith Cooper Spurlin (Mrs. Boyd)

MY COOPER GRANDPARENTS

477

Grandpa and Grandma both were from the Purlear section of Wilkes County. Grandma was Julia Emma McNiell, daughter of James

John Wesley and Mary A. Eller Cooper.

Calvin and Mary Adlaid Dancy McNiell, who was born about 1832 and died after 1880. Her paternal grandparents were Oliver McNiel, born 1808, and Delilah Eller, born 1812. Her maternal grandparents were Edward (Ned) J. Dancy and Nancy McNiel, born 1813.

Grandpa's parents were John Wesley Cooper, born 1819, and Maryanne Eller, born 1825. His paternal grandmother was Aness W. Hunt, born 1798, died 1850, granddaughter of Jonathan Hunt, born 1716, died 1782 in Rowan County. His maternal grandparents were Peter Eller, Jr., born 1778, died 1851, and Mary Anne Pennington born 1782, died after 1870.

Grandpa was a wonderful tale spinner. My brother, Ken, and I, and our cousins loved to see him coming, always walking. He was thin and spritely with a shock of white hair over his brow. Whenever he sat down he always took out a whittling knife, a piece of soft wood, and went to work while he talked.

A story that Aunt Edith tells, was that when Grandpa was five years old in 1864, he and his brother, Zion, were at the woodpile. Zion chopped Grandpa's foot badly. Their mother, Mary Anne, got out her cat gut and a needle and sewed up Grandpa's foot while the older children held him.

This tells me much about the stamina and fortitude of these Wilkes County women. Away from medical emergency help, these sturdy, pioneering women had to be prepared to take care of their own, and did so with strength and determination.

Source: Cooper Family Bible, Rowan County Records and family books; Research by Mrs. W.O. Absher; word of mouth.

— Colleen Cooper Stoioff

JOHN HARM COSTNER

478

John Harm Costner (April 14, 1840 — March 8, 1918), son of Absalom and Fanny Pinner Costner, was born in Mecklenburg County. He married Margaret Kiser (January 27, 1840 — December 28, 1915), and to this union was born seven children. John and Margaret moved to Wilkes County in 1884. Their children are:

(1) Mink Costner remained in Mecklenburg County; (2) Cindy Costner, married Eli Campbell and had one child; (3) Lulu Costner married John Mitchell; (4) Nannie married Coot Daniels; (5) Jonas Alexander Costner (December 25, 1876 — January 8, 1950), married Etta Barnette (March 22, 1887 — October 31, 1977).

(6) Charlie L. Costner (June 14, 1879 — November 9, 1926) married Cora Baker (January 20, 1882 — April 12, 1958). This union was blessed with 3 children: Icie married Neal Manus; Floyd married Rochell Williams; and Julia Mae married W.C. Clark. Charlie died at age forty-seven in an elevator accident.

(7) Monroe Costner (January 5, 1883 — March 25, 1966) married Elizabeth (Lizzie) Moore (November 28, 1880 — August 1, 1965). They had ten children, seven of whom lived: (1) Etta Bell, married Gather Grieder and had Roy and Cornelia; (2) Homer married Gay

Childress and had Betty Lou who married Cecil Green, Mari who married James Brown, and Mabel who married Wayne Jones; (3) Perry, married Millie Massey and had Ann; (4) Mildred, married Albert Frazier and had A.M., Jr., who married Treva Johnson and had a daughter Sabre Lynn; Cleda who married Wayne Brown and had Anita and Wayne, Jr. Wayne was killed in an automobile accident March 19, 1970, and Cleda married Rev. Coy Walker; Johnnie married Shirley Huffman; James married Shirley June Diamond. (5) Beulah Mae married Hubert Gryder; (6) Thieda married Daniel Tedder and had Daniel, Lois Ann who married David Smithey and had Margaret, Lee Edward and Atwell; (7) Carl married Virgia.

Jonas Alexander Costner, son of John Harm and Margaret, married Etta Viola Barnette February 7, 1906. They had one son, John Dixon, who was born August 12, 1916, and married Stella Ree Hayes 27 December, 1939. John is an orchardist, a member of Bethany Baptist Church, serving as a deacon and church clerk. John and Stella's children are: (1) Martha Sue, born September 27, 1941, married Kenneth Marlow Anderson, a veteran of Korean War, December 25, 1959. They had Darlene Annette, born May 25, 1961, married Donald Day Shumate June 8, 1980. Darlene has finished her third year at A.S.U. where she had made the Dean's List for two years; Tammy Lynn born May 9, 1963 and had finished first year at Community College; Robin Denise born July 28, 1964, and is a 1982 graduate of West Wilkes High. (2) Helen Marie, born June 7, 1946, married Rex Lee Church September 10, 1966. They have two children Regina Marie born March 24, 1970 and Amy LeeAnn born June 11, 1977. (3) Phil Dixon born June 19, 1951, is confined to a wheelchair and lives with his parents.

Sources: Personal knowledge, interviews with family members, family Bibles, grave stones.

— Martha Anderson

THOMAS COTTRELL
479

Thomas Cottrell was born in Scotland and came to Virginia where he lived prior to coming to Wilkes County. He married a Miss Allison. A search of the records indicates a Land Grant to him dated 20 June, 1795.

Thomas Cottrell's will, recorded in the Wilkes County Court House reveals the following children: (1) John Cottrell (2) Rosannah Cottrell (3) Edy Cottrell who married William Curtis (4) Nancy Cottrell who married Joshua Curtis (5) William Cottrell born ca 1779, married Lucy Day, born 1781, on 14 April, 1804, witnesses were Hugh Day and William Lenoir. (6) Susannah Cottrell who married on 11 March 1788 Samuel Curtis, born 1756. Susannah died 8 October, 1844, and Samuel died 6 February, 1852 or 1853.

Samuel Curtis, son-in-law, was appointed executer of Thomas Cottrell's Last Will and Testament, dated 11 March, 1825. Thomas Cottrell died sometime prior to November 1828.

Sources: Census records and will of Thomas Cottrell.

— Helen B. Bell

WILLIAM LEWIS COUCH
480

William Lewis Couch was born 20 Nov. 1850, near Traphill, N.C., son of Meshach H. Couch and Mary (Bryan).

His heritage was a strange mixture, the firey rebellious blood of his Irish Mother's Bryan family and the placid calm of the "Thee and Thou" side of his Quaker ancestry.

Toward the end of the war, Meshach Couch returned from a stay in Kansas where homestead land looked good to a father with a house full of boys. In 1866 the Couch family sold their land and moved to Kansas by covered wagons. William was the eldest of six children.

Sixteen year old William was shy but he spelled, debated, composed and recited doggerel verse at the local school entertainment.

In 1870, he filed on homestead land, built a two-room unceiled box house and in February 1871 married Cynthia Gordon, a native of Guilford Co., N.C. Life was happy but hard and two children were born. In 1875 they moved to the new town of Wichita where William had a general store and later traded in livestock. He prospered and bought land.

February 1, 1883, William Couch was appointed wagonmaster for the longest wagontrain ever to enter Indian Territory, 119 wagons and 600 persons, some women and children. The temperature dropped to 12 to 15 degrees below zero. The settlers camped for a day then moved on south and went into camp east of present Oklahoma City. The U.S. Army arrested the leaders and sent the others back to Kansas. Cattlemen grew rich grazing their herds, free, on the land the farmers hoped to homestead.

William Couch was arrested five or six times for bringing more settlers into the Oklahoma lands. Couch was elected Colony president in 1884 and continued the planned Stillwater settlement.

Beginning January 1886, Couch and others were in Washington, D.C. working for legislation to open the Oklahoma lands. William Couch, his father and five brothers were ready to stake homestead claims. Finally, March 1889, President Harrison signed the proclamation that opened the land, April 22, 1889.

William Couch staked a claim adjoining Okla. City. Five other men claimed the same land. They all settled down to await the decision of homestead authority. At the end of six months, Mayor Couch resigned, moved wife and five children into a two-story house. He fenced forty acres and planted wheat. In January, he and others went to Washington City trying to obtain territorial status for Oklahoma. Early in April he returned to find his fence posts chopped down and horses grazing. William Couch and his eldest son were replacing the fence when an irate claimant shot him in the knee. Blood poison developed and his funeral was April 22, 1890, the first anniversary of the famous Oklahoma Run.

In the last ten of his short thirty-nine year life, William Couch made his place in the history books of Oklahoma.

Sources: Oklahoma history, family knowledge, Bibles.

— Edna M. Couch

WILLIAM HENRY HARRISON COWLES
481

William Henry Harrison Cowles was seventh in descent from John Cowles (1598-1675) who emigrated to New England in 1634. He was born to Josiah and Nancy Carson Duvall Cowles April 22, 1840, at Hamptonville N.C. It is known that he studied at the Jonesville Academy, and that he loved hunting and horseback riding. He was nearly six feet in height; had brown hair, large blue eyes, and was of fair complexion.

At age twenty-one he entered Confederate service as a private in Co. A, First N.C. Cavalry, and served from the spring of 1861 to the close of the Civil War with the Army of Northern Virginia, rising to the rank of Lieut. Colonel. He was twice wounded severely, once through the body, and again on the head. While wounded, he was taken prisoner into Petersburg, where, as soon as he was able to travel, he was paroled and sent home, this being at the close of the war.

One can well imagine the discouragement felt by Cowles and all returning Confederate soldiers with their patriotic enthusiasm crushed and with their having to face economic disaster at home. In Cowles's case he faced the additional sadness that his mother had died during the war and could not welcome him home. On the bright side, he had an enterprising father who soon enrolled him as a boarding student at Judge Pearson's law school, "Richmond Hill" in Yadkin County. (The main building is being restored).

After obtaining his law license, W.H.H. Cowles moved to Wilkesboro, in 1871 and bought the former Hamilton Brown home, just east of the courthouse and the Wilkesboro Hotel. His law office, now remodeled, still stands in the home's front yard on Main Street.

His political life follows: reading clerk of N.C. Senate in sessions 1872-73 and 1873-74; solicitor of tenth judicial district 1874-78; United States congressman (democrat), 4 March 1885 until 3 March 1893.

In 1897 he retired from his law practice and removed his family to a country home one and one half miles east of Wilkesboro on the south side of the Yadkin River, where he devoted his life to his family, his private business and his books. It was here that he died December 30, 1901, of pneumonia, and was buried in the cemetery near the Presbyterian Church in Wilkesboro, (neither of his wives being buried beside him). His heirs continued to own the house in Wilkesboro until 1912. After his death his widow moved to Statesville in order that her children might secure a better education. They continued to spend the summer vacations on the farm until the farm house burned down in 1918.

Cowles was intensely patriotic. He once wrote "Only cowards fear death; good and brave men fear only God and keep his commandments." He was a strong democrat although some in his immediate family were republicans. He would loved to have lived in the days of the automobile, because he always

William H.H. and Cora Worth Cowles.

wanted to get places in a hurry.

His values in life are well expressed in a preserved letter to his oldest son, David, on the occasion of David's ninth birthday. The 1880 letter reads: "When I ask your Heavenly Father for the best thing for my little boy I ask him to enable you to grow up a good man and worthy of his love, I earnestly desire this more for you than all the wealth and honors of this world, for if you had all the honors, all the land, all the horses and carriages, and everything in this world that makes men rich, you would have to die and leave it all. The crown and glory of a well-spent life is more desirable than all these things, and will endure throughout eternity."

Col. Cowles was twice married (1) on June 1, 1870 to Rosamond Corinna Worth (Cora) from Ashe County, whose father David was first cousin to Jonathan Worth, Governor of N.C.; and (2) on Oct. 16, 1883 to Mary Lura Bost, whose mother descended from the German Ramseur family that settled in Lincoln County in the mid 1700s.

From the two marriages came eleven children, most of whom lived to maturity. Two sons, Miles Andrew and Stuart Lee were graduated at West Point and became career army officers; Miles married Anne Kales from Chicago and served in the North Africa-Italy area as brigadier-general; Stuart, the only child now living, married Ethelyn Temple and retired as colonel to live in Asheville, N.C.; Another son, William Henry Harrison, Jr., served in WWI and became professor of mathematics at Pratt Institute. Cowles's oldest daughter Carrie Lizzie married Thomas B. Finley of North Wilkesboro; Sarah married R.O. Self of Raleigh; Esther (Essie) married the Reverend Sydney S. Bost of Durham; and Mary Loretz married J. Neeley Kincaid of Statesville.

Sources: Family papers, family traditions, newspapers and U.S. Congressional Directory.

— Elizabeth Cowles Finley

BRUCE and CAROL CRANE
482

Thomas Crane, born 30 Oct. 1852, died 25 Feb. 1923, was the son of William and Mary Crane. He married Delphia Bumgarner (Bullis or Minton) and they had six children: Jimmy, Landon, Bina, Daisy, Tip and Lunia. Thomas and Delphia are buried at New Hope Baptist Church at Purlear.

Landon Crane, born circa 1873, died 1 Dec. 1944, married Martha Geneva Church, born 18 Sept. 1881, died 16 Feb. 1953. She was the daughter of Wesley (born 8 May 1861) and Candis (born 10 Oct. 1859) Church.

The six children of Landon and Martha Geneva Church Crane were: (1) Rommie married Mollie Church and they had three children, Johnson, Junior and Verlie Crane. (2) Gentry married Eleanor Atkins and they were the parents of Ruth and Lee Crane. (3) Cornice, born 12 June 1909, died 16 Jan. 1980, married Winnie Triplett on 29 June 1929. She was the daughter of Sherman J. and Nancy Foster Triplett who are buried at Lewis Fork Baptist Church. Winnie was born 22 Nov. 1906 and lives on Prospect Drive in the Cricket community. Cornice and Winnie were the parents of four children: Josephine, Willard, Bruce and Jeanette. (4) Sanford Crane married Ella Greene. Their children were Boyce and Marie. (5) Mamie married Doughton Foster and had seven children: Arlie, Veron, Zela, Juanita, Ocie and Arville Foster. A daughter, Madeline died when she was about 15 years old. (6) Zola married Rommie Whittington and they a son, Kermit.

Bruce Stanley Crane, son of Cornice and Winnie, was born 27 Oct. 1935. He is a graduate of Millers Creek High School where he played football and received the Babe Ruth Sports Award. At present, he is a used car salesman.

Bruce married Carol Bumgarner (see sketch on James Bynum Nichols) on 4 July 1953.

Carol graduated from Millers Creek High School and had a year of secretarial training at Clevenger's Business School. She has been employed as a secretary by Ithaca Industries, Inc. for the past thirteen years. They live in the Millers Creek community and are active members of Millers Creek United Methodist Church.

Bruce and Carol have two children: (1) Patricia Carol, born 15 Sept. 1954, graduated from West Wilkes High School and earned a BA degree in studio art from UNC at Greensboro. She is employed by the Department of Social Services as a day care teacher at the Wilkes Child Development Center. Patti was married to Claude Wayne Ashley, son of Charles Benford and Opal Ashley, on April 24, 1982. Wayne is employed by Lowe's Companies as a plant manager of the Wilkes Millwork Division. (2) Ricky Bruce was born 29 November 1956. He is a graduate of West Wilkes and received automotive training at the Fiatt School in Jacksonville, Fla. He is in charge of automotive repairs for Myers Tire store at Millers Creek. Ricky's wife, Ora Kathleen Spears, also a West Wilkes graduate, is the daughter of Ransom and Etoy Griffin. She is employed in the Accounts Payable department of Lowe's Companies.

Sources: Wilkes Marriages, Death Records, tombstone inscriptions and family knowledge.

— Carol B. Crane

THE CRANOR FAMILY
483

One of the earliest records of the Cranor family was of the two brothers, Moses and Thomas, who came to this part of the country from England in the 1700's.

Later Moses was married to Jane Trotter, and settled in Rowan, Salisbury District (this is now Guilford County) on a land grant, in 1789. In 1795, Thomas Cranor became ill, and in his will left his land to his wife, Hannah, with his brother, Moses, as executor of his estate. Both brothers had several sons and daughters. One of these, Emanuel was born to Moses and Jane on Aug. 9, 1813. He married Catherine Elizabeth Swan on March 15, 1834, at Waughtown. In the 1850 N.C. Census, Emanuel Cranor was listed as the over-seer of the jail and the poor-house — also, the stage station, in Rockford (Surry County). Later he was the postmaster there for a brief period. There were six children at this time and our grandfather, John Samuel Cranor, was two years of age. When he was ten years old, his father, Emanuel moved his family to Wilkesboro, to operate a hotel there. When he was about seventeen, John S. Cranor joined Company B of the Confederate Army and received his training at Camp Vance. He was captured by Colonel Kirk's Federal forces and was a prisoner of war in a Chicago prison where he suffered severe exposure and deprivations for about a year. After his parole, he returned to his home in Wilkesboro, to take up the study of law, and was admitted to the bar in 1868. On Nov. 27, 1872, he was married to Miss Sarah Taylor, who was born in Fayetteville,

The Cranor Home.

Sept. 15, 1844 to William Taylor (born in Manchester, England on Oct. 18, 1810) and Elizabeth Babcock Taylor (born in Middletown, Conn., May 22, 1813), and she was a descendant of the John Howland who was dramatically rescued at sea, after having been swept overboard, on the Mayflower's voyage to America.

There were nine children born to John S. and Sarah Taylor Cranor, all of whom they raised and educated. Their earliest schooling was in the home, by tutors. One of these was Miss Kate Cameron of Harnett County. She was employed in 1880 and stayed in their home for several years, prior to her marriage to Mr. Arthur A. Finley of N. Wilkesboro.

The first child, Katherine Cranor was to become a teacher, too. She started her own school in her home in the 1890's. She later taught in other private schools, the Finley School and the Yadkin Valley Institute, as well as the public schools that only operated for a few months of the year, so this didn't interfere with her private teaching. At the time of her retirement, she was a professor at Iowa State College, in Ames, Iowa. She did research abroad for the college, and on a tour of the Orient, in 1923, she survived the terrible earthquake of September in Japan. Her personal accounts of her harrowing experiences there were published later in our local papers.

The second child was Hugh Armfield Cranor, who followed in his father's footsteps to practice law in Wilkesboro. He was educated at the University of N.C. Hugh was first associated with his father's firm for six years and, like his father, (who was Register of Deeds from 1884 to 1886, a State Senator in 1893, a U.S. Commissioner, and Mayor of Wilkesboro), he had a colorful public career. He was elected to Legislature in 1930, the first Democrat sent to the General Assembly in about 50

years, and certainly, by mule-back (For in his campaign, he'd vowed to ride a mule to Raleigh, if elected.).

The next child was Edith, and she became a designer of ladies' fashionable hats. She lived and died in Los Angeles, where she had her millinery shop for years.

William was the fourth child, and he was a butcher and meat market operator for the greater part of his life.

Sarah Elizabeth (Bess) was married to William Henry McElwee and lived in Statesville, where she became the mother of three, one of whom is Atty. W.H. McElwee, Jr., of N. Wilkesboro.

Fannie Susan (Fan) was a very talented artist and entertainer. She helped raise the two small children of her younger brother, John, after the early death of his first wife. John was a salesman who lived in Maryland.

Frank Taylor was next to the youngest, and most of his life he was employed as a Federal Employee at the North Wilkesboro Post Office.

Charles Moses (Charlie) was the last child, and was a salesman, an antique dealer, and a hotel operator in No. Wilkesboro.

In the accompanying photograph of the Cranors, at home in Wilkesboro, all members of the family were present. This house is still standing and occupied, east of the Court House location. Frank and John are on the upper porch rail. Will is on the horse (the Cranors have always loved horses throughout the years). Charlie is astride the goat. The Cranor girls are in the yard, below their mother and father who are seated on the porch.

Sources: Mormon Genealogical Research Library; National Archives and various census index books and microfilm; *Historical Sketches of Wilkes County*, by John Crouch; Babcock Genealogy; *Lest We Forget: Education in Wilkes County*, by Mr. & Mrs. Paul Gregory, and Mary Cranor Higgins' research.

— James T. Cranor
and John W. Cranor

THE REV. RUFUS ROY CRATER FAMILY

484

Rev. Rufus Roy Crater was born in Yadkin September 27, 1892, and died December 31, 1978. He was a rural mail carrier and an ordained Baptist minister. He served churches in Wilkes and Yadkin counties for thirty-four years.

He was the direct descendent of Jacob Greter, born in 1708 at Gumbartshofen in Lower Alsace, Germany. Jacob came to Pennsylvania in 1731. He was a Lutheran. He came to North Carolina in 1774. He died October 26, 1788. His son, Jacob, Jr. born April 16, 1764 and died June 1, 1834, was the father of Rufus Weisner Crater grandfather of Rufus Roy Crater. His grandmother was Mary Ann Mayberry Crater. (Greter is the German spelling for Crater.)

His parents were James Mayberry Crater and Delia Ann Myers Crater, daughter of the Rev. W.A. Myers and Lemirah Jennings Myers of Yadkin County.

Rufus Roy had three sisters; Annie Lee Crater Hinshaw, Joyce Crater Dobbins, and Bertha Crater Stout; three brothers: Sherman G., Wm. Parks, and James Bruce. All his brothers and sisters preceded him in death.

He married Gertrude Gray, daughter of Wm. A. and Mary Ann Armstrong Gray on May 3, 1917. He taught school in Yadkin and Wilkes Counties. He received an appointment to carry mail on a Ronda, N.C. rural route in 1919. He carried the mail for forty years, retiring in 1959. They had four children.

Edith Gertrude Crater was born June 14, 1918 in Yadkin County. She attended the public school of Wilkes County, Mars Hill College and Appalachian State Teacher's College. She taught Primary Education in Wilkes County Schools twenty seven years. She married Wm. Warner Miller, Jr. of Wilkesboro, N.C. April 20, 1941. Warner served in the Air Crops during World War II. They have three daughters — Ann Crater Miller was born March 5, 1943 in Wilkes County. She married Thomas Gene Arnold August 24, 1962. They have two daughters — Lorrie Jane Arnold was born October 3, 1969 in Salisbury, Md. Amy Elizabeth Arnold was born January 10, 1975 in Salisbury, Maryland. The Arnolds now reside in Monroe, N.C. Mary Jane Miller, daughter of Edith and Warner Miller was born April 27, 1945 in Wilkes County. She married Barry Kelly Mims March 29, 1967. They have one son, William Brian Mims born May 9, 1971 in Iredell County. They reside in Winston-Salem, N.C. Marjorie Lorraine Miller was born November 18, 1949 in Wilkes County. She married Z. Russell Golds March 18, 1972. They live in Wilkes County, and have two sons, Andrew Ryan Golds was born March 19, 1979, and Wesley Adam Golds was born July 3, 1981. They were both born in Iredell County.

Gladys Lorraine Crater was born July 20, 1921 in Wilkes County. She was educated in the Wilkes County Schools and Appalachian State Teacher's College. She married David Franklin Johnson June 28, 1941. She is Payroll Person for Vulcan Materials, Inc. in

Winston Salem, N.C. where she and Frank now live.

Roy Gray Crater was born in Wilkes County August 19, 1923. He attended schools in Wilkes County. He served his country in a Tank Division during World War II. He married Ruby Church June 5, 1949. Ruby died in 1963 and Roy Gray died July 25, 1967. They had no children.

James William Crater was born February 3, 1930, in Wilkes County. He attended schools in Wilkes County and Elkin City School in Surry County. He graduated from Emory Riddle Aeronautical College in Miami, Florida, and is an Executive Pilot for Columbia Gas Co., Inc. Columbus, Ohio. He married Joanne Darnell in Surry County April 30, 1947. They live in Westerville, Ohio. They have two children. Donna Gray Crater was born August 30, 1950 in Surry County. She married Bradley David Sallee January 1, 1972 in Surry County. They now live in Fort Lauderdale, Florida. They have two children — William Chad Sallee, born July 29, 1974, and Carrie Jo Sallee born December 3, 1977. Both children were born in Fort Lauderdale, Fla. James Michael Crater was born October 27, 1960, in Surry County — Elkin, N.C. He attended schools in Columbus, Ohio and he has finished his Junior year at the Emory Riddle Aeronautical University at Daytona Beach, Florida. He's following in his daddy' footsteps, and plans to graduate in 1983.

Sources: Death Record in First Church Register of Moravian Congregation of Friedsberg. Family history, and knowledge of the Crater family.

— Edith Crater Miller

CRAVEN FAMILY
485

Aaron Yancy Craven, son of Joshua Craven and Sarah Lambert, was born January 2, 1835, died 1880. After serving in the Civil War on the side of the Confederacy, he married Eliza Elmina McCollum in 1867, and they moved from Randolph County to Wilkes by covered wagon in the 1870s. They settled on Reddies River where Aaron Yancy operated a mill, not far from where the town garage, former city pump station, stands today.

Five children were born to Aaron Yancy and Eliza Elmina: Ada, Samuel Joshua, Franklin Yancy, James Edward and Annie. His son, Samuel Joshua, born in 1871, married Flora Delilah Sloop in 1896, who was christened Matilda Myrtle.

They lived near the dam of the old North Wilkesboro Pump Station, which Sam Craven operated for thirty-eight years. Nineteen children were born to them, fourteen of whom they reared: William Atlee, Paul Aaron, Samuel Jefferson, Henry Edward, Ted B., Joseph Allen, Louise Craven, Marion Miller, Marie Patterson, Agnes Brock, Donald Wilson, Florine Foster, Edith Earp and Ralph Lindbergh Craven.

Sources: Personal knowledge.

— Agnes Craven Brock

THE JOSHUA CRAVEN FAMILY
486

Joshua and Sarah Lambert Craven are the ancestors of many of the Cravens in Wilkes County. Joshua Craven was born in 1785 in Randolph County and is believed to be the son of William Craven and a descendant of Peter Craven. In 1810 he married Sarah Lambert, who was born in 1789, the daughter of John and Mary Hackney Lambert. Joshua was a farmer and reared a rather large family. He lived to about the age of 85 and died in Randolph County in 1870.

The following are believed to be their children: (1) Evelina (Lina), who married Traverse Brown, (2) Jeremiah, (3) Soloman, (4) Patsy, who married William Gillerland (?), (5) a son (maybe Peter or William) born about 1817, who married Jane   , (6) John Alston, born about 1820, who married Elizabeth Brady in 1838, (7) Polly, born about 1822, who married a Moltase (?), (8) Henry, born about 1824, who married Jane Henson, (9) Wincy, born about 1830, (10) Sarah, born about 1833, who married Daniel Jones, (11) Aaron Yancy, born in 1835 and who married two times — to Elizabeth Jane Jenkins and Eliza McCollum, (12) Nancy L., born about 1839 and married Page Brown.

Sources: Estate Records, Census Records and Marriage Bonds.

— Mrs. J. Arnold Simpson

THE CRAWFORD-KENDALL ANCESTRY
487

Sidney James Crawford, a descendant of Sarah Foster Kendall of Wilkes County, was born in Boone County, Arkansas, 5 June, 1897, married Isabelle Jane Hufft and died 19 June, 1965, in Bakersfield, California. He served in World War I in the 129th Battalion of Regiment of Machine Gunners. Isabelle was born in Laclede County, Missouri, the daughter of Thomas Franklin and Ara Palmer Hufft and was a descendant of Ratliff Boon and Robert Harris, early settlers of Surry County, North Carolina.

Children of Sidney James and Isabelle Jane Crawford: (1) Sidney Glenn Crawford married first Betty Constance and had Robin, Alan, Kitty and Bonnie; second Marie and had Wayne and Winona;

(2) Barbara Lou Crawford married Robert E. LeDoux and had Robert E. LeDoux who married Marianne Kleinsmith, and Barbara M. LeDoux who married Clark G. Sherwood and had Aaron; Tudy A. LeDoux married Mark Schiveley and had Steven, Geoffrey and Gregory; Thierry J. LeDoux married Marilyn Bruno; Angela I. LeDoux married Lee A. Brenden and had April, Tanya and Jennifer, twins; Elizabeth LeDoux; Michele C. LeDoux married Steven N. Sakurai and had Catherine; Andre' P. LeDoux married Denise Carothers; D'Arcy A. LeDoux;

(3) David Crawford married first Anne Downing and had Sheryl and Telisa, twins, second Ethelyene and had Shandra;

(4) Rosalie Crawford married Joseph R. Mott and had Pamela Mott; Peggy Mott who married Paul Petersen and had Anaise and Paul Jr.; Joseph R. Mott, Jr. who married Deanna Dunmore and had Sarah Beth; Patricia Mott who married William Randall Dickey;

(5) Mary Jane Crawford married first Ottice Brannon and had Kenneth and Scott, second William Blanset and had William and Tammy.

Sidney James Crawford was the son of Thomas Smith Crawford, born 25 March, 1861, Fannin County, Georgia and Barbara Jane Edwards who was born in 1870, Taney County Missouri. She died in 1905 and Thomas died in 1908, both are buried in Boone County, Arkansas. The parents of Barbara Jane Edwards Crawford were William and Sarah Plumlee Edwards of Taney County, Missouri, and later of Boone County, Arkansas. Their children: Towney Crawford married Vera Heckenlively; Jesse Crawford; Iverson Crawford, married (1) Daisey Denning and (2) Lera; Sidney James Crawford, see above; Thomas Crawford married Helen Hunt; Wayne Crawford; and Rosalie Crawford.

Thomas Smith Crawford was the son of William S. Crawford, born 3 February, 1833, North Carolina, married Christina Kendall and died after 28 June, 1864. He served in the Confederate Army as a teamster in Co. "A", 37th Regiment, Georgia Volunteers, died during the war and is buried in the Antioch Cemetery in Fannin County, Georgia. Christina Kendall was born in Wilkes County, North Carolina on 19 February, 1832, and was the daughter of John Dula Kendall and Nancy Kendall of Wilkes County.

John Dula Kendall was the son of James Kendall and Mary Dula who were married 13 October, 1795, in Wilkes County. John D. Kendall married his cousin Nancy who was the daughter of William Kendall and Elizabeth Hagler who were married in Wilkes County on 28 October, 1793. Elizabeth was the daughter of John and Elizabeth Hagler, both of Wilkes County.

The children of John Dula Kendall and Nancy Kendall were: Sarah Elizabeth (Caroline) born 1825, married Walton Cox of Wilkes County; James P. born 1827, married Martha Crawford, sister of William S. Crawford; Christina married William S. Crawford; Martha Kendall; Nancy Kendall married John M. Crawford; William Smith Kendall married Mary Crawford; Thomas Harrison Kendall married Elizabeth Emeline Crawford; and John Larkin Kendall. All of the Crawford spouses were children of John and Mary Styles Crawford of Fannin County, Georgia.

James and William Kendall were the sons of William and Sarah Foster Kendall. Sarah Foster, as the widow of William, was granted 202 acres of land in Wilkes County on 20 December, 1971. Sarah was the daughter of Thomas and Elizabeth Smith Foster of Essex County, Virginia. Children of William and Sarah Foster Kendall: Sarah Kendall, married Robert Shearer; William Kendall married Elizabeth Hagler; John Kendall; Elizabeth Kendall; Thomas Kendall, married Rebecca Holdman; and James Kendall, married Mary Dula.

Thomas Foster, father of Elizabeth Foster

Kendall was born 1720 in Essex County, Virginia, and married Elizabeth Smith 23 May, 1743, in Middlesex County, Virginia; died after 1779 and served under George Washington in the "Battle of the Meadows" in 1754. Elizabeth, born 19 April, 1723, whose birth is registered in Christ Church, Middlesex County was the daughter of Thomas and Ann Smith.

Thomas Foster was the son of Anthony Foster, born 1693, died 1763; son of Robert Foster, born 1651, died 1718 and married Sarah Biggs. Robert was a Planter who settled in Essex County, Virginia in 1692. He patented land 14 August, 1672, as 2100 acres in Northumberland County, Virginia.

Sources: Virginia marriages; Middlesex, Orange and Essex Co., Va. records; Wilkes County, N.C. census; Georgia census; Boone Co., Ark. records; Bible records.

— Barbara Crawford LeDoux

THE ROY L. CREASMAN FAMILY
488

Roy Creasman was born in Hot Springs, N.C. to Alice and Charles Creasman on May 5, 1902. He was the youngest of three children, having a sister Florence Creasman Clark, and a brother Oscar Creasman. Florence was married and lived most of her life in Hendersonville, N.C. She died in May 1958 of cancer. Oscar married Addie and they lived in Thomsaville and had two sons, Harold and Cecil. Oscar died in 1956 of a stroke. One of his sons, Harold and his wife and family live in High Point, and Cecil and his wife and family live in Thomasville.

Roy grew up in the Western Mountains of N.C. His father died when he was only five years old. Then Roy had to move in with relatives. He had to work for his board and keep. He went to school when it was possible. He never felt like he had a real home or a family to call his own after his father's death.

When he grew up, he worked his way through Coyne Electrical School in Chicago, Ill. After his graduation from Coyne Electrical School in 1921, he moved to Thomasville to work. While living in Thomasville he met the young girl he would later marry. Her name was Pauline (Polly) Kindley.

Polly was born to Jessie Thomas and Sally Caroline Bean Kindley, on Dec. 9, 1905 in Davidson County N.C. She had three brothers and one sister. One brother Olin Taft Kindley who lived and died in Thomasville in 1939, Clyde Wilson Kindley who lives in Greensboro, Arthur Lowe Kindley of Thomasville and one sister Mary Ruth Kindley Harper who lived in Orlando, Florida and died there in 1978.

Polly went to school and grew up in Thomasville. She and Roy met and they were married in July 1932. They had one daughter, Peggy Pauline Creasman, born on April 8, 1933. In 1939 they moved to Wilkesboro and stayed there till World War II broke out. Then they moved to Newport News, Va. where Roy worked in the shipyard wiring ships. In 1947 they moved to N. Wilkesboro, where Roy opened Creasman Electric. He managed this business with the help of his wife Polly until

1966. At this time he and Polly planned to retire and travel, so he sold his business to Mr. Isaac Duncan who owned Duncan Electric. Roy was still working in the business at the time of his death on Sunday, August 20, 1967. He had not completely retired at that time.

Polly stayed on for a while and worked for Mr. Duncan before retiring. Even though she is retired, she is a very active person. She works in flowers and has all the wild flowers native to N.C. She spends many hours wild flower hunting in the woods around her home in the Boone and West Jefferson Mountains, or just anywhere she might be at the time. She is a volunteer worker for The Ladies Auxiliary at the Wilkes General Hospital and is also their Historian. She works several days each week at The Outlet House. Her handmade quilts and dolls are real masterpieces of art. She also makes pillows for newborn babies. Her handwork is really to be treasured.

Their daughter Peggy graduated from N. Wilkesboro High School in 1952 and then attended Woman's College U.N.C., now known as U.N.C.G. She then came home and lived with her parents until Feb. 18, 1956, when she married Frank Day, son of Sally Gantt and Walter Miller Day. Frank and Peggy were married in the chapel of The First Methodist Church in N. Wilkesboro. They had two children, Timothy Franklin Day born June 15, 1958, and Melody Lynn, born March 2, 1960.

In 1957 Roy and Polly built a home in Ken Acres in Wilkesboro. Later in 1966 they built another home next to Frank and Peggy's home on Colonial Drive in N. Wilkesboro. They lived there till Roy's death. In 1968 Polly sold her home to John and Annette Battle and built an apartment onto Peggy and Frank's home. This is where she lives now.

Sources: Family Bible, personal knowledge.

— Mrs. R.L. (Polly) Creasman

THE CREEKMORE FAMILY
489

The Creekmore family originated in England, and by means of the emigration in 1650 to Virginia of only one of its members, Edmund, the family was established in America. All modern-day Creekmores (and other spellings) are descended from Edmond.

Caleb Creekmore, a descendant of Edmund, was born 1775 and married Olive Keeter, daughter of James and Mary Keeter in Norfolk County, Va. on 8 May 1797. From there they moved to Halifax County, N.C. In 1820 they migrated to Wilkes County, N.C.

Caleb and Olive Creekmore had one son, Nicholas, who married Elizabeth Hinshaw 13 March, 1828, in Surry County, a daughter of Joseph Hinshaw. Nicholas and Elizabeth had children: Columbus, born 1829, Caleb, born 1834, Lucinda, born 1835, Almeda, born 1840 and Josephus, born 1843.

Josephus (later changed to Joseph) Creekmore married Sarah Jane Brown in Wilkes County, on 24 February, 1865. Joseph was baptized 1 December, 1870, at Brier Creek Church, Wilkes County. Both he and his brother Caleb served in the Confederate Army

in Co. B. 38th N.C. Infantry Regt. Sarah Brown Creekmore died 4 February, 1908. Joseph died 31 May, 1926. Both are buried in Elmwood Cemetery, Mecklenburg County, N.C.

Their children were: (1) Columbus F., born 8 December, 1865, died 12 September, 1888; (2) Cora Lee, born 1868, died 1946, married George Keller. Their children were Richard Columbus, Zanah Ruth, and Hampton Vibin. (3) Mary Ella, born 1870, died April 1921, married Enoch West. Their children were Verla, Mildred and Grace.

(4) James Millard, born 1872, died 1949, married Anna May Johnson, born 7 June, 1882, died 22 April, 1960, daughter of Robert Toombe and Edna E. Bowers Johnson. Their children were: James Roy, Bowers Otto, who married Augusta Danielson, daughter of August M. and Lula Bendenbaugh Danielson; Robert Bolton, and Martha. The children of Bowers and Augusta are Barba, who married Lamar Smith, Robert Roy, who married Jean Allison, and Mary Lynn, who married Michael Watson.

Robert Roy and Jean Allison Creekmore are the parents of Kimberly Ann, born and died 2 April, 1963, and Robert Todd, born 17 June 1965. Robert Roy is volunteer organist at First Baptist Church, Old Fort, N.C.

Sources: Halifax and Norfold Co., Va. and Wilkes Co., N.C. records; N.C. Archives; Family Bible; Family knowledge.

— Robert R. Creekmore

CULLER
490

John Benjamin Culler was born March 12, 1810 in or near Orangeburg, S.C. where the first Cullers settled in 1735. He was a great hunter and loved to walk. In or about 1840 he walked to Wilkesboro, N.C. He married Nancy Lane from Brushy Mountain area in 1841 and they had the following children: Govan, Elizabeth, M.J. and John S. He helped make the brick that went into the building of St. Paul's Episcopal Church in Wilkesboro.He lived a long life, being one hundred and two years old when he died April 12, 1912. All the children moved to Watauga County except Govan who lived in Wilkes County all his life.

Govan Culler was born in 1842 and served in the army during the Civil War. While serving in the army, he and others were captured, put in a boat on the Mississippi River, the anchor dropped and left to die. They all took turns and finally chewed the anchor rope in two and got to safety. Returning to Wilkes after the war, he married Salena Bumgarner of the Millers Creek area and they had the following children: Robert, Frank, William (who died very young), James, Nancy and John Elam. Govan died in 1919 and was buried in the Wilkesboro Cemetery.

Robert married Sally Crysel and they had three sons. They lived and died in High Point, N.C. Frank and James (Jim) both married and lived in Lenoir, N.C. Frank came back to Wilkes later and died here in 1959. Jim moved to Winston-Salem and died in 1948. Nancy

Culler went to Winston-Salem as a young girl, married and had three daughters. She died there in 1958.

John Elam Culler was born in Wilkes County November 7, 1882, and lived here all his life. As a young man he was an employee of Meadow's Mill Company. Then for some years he had his own milling business, selling it in 1944. In 1946 he went into the grocery business on Main Street in Wilkesboro on the corner of the Culler home property. He married Helsie Beth Minton on January 1st, 1905. She was a charter member of the Wilkesboro Methodist Church and remained active in that church until her death on September 28, 1968. They were good, honest and friendly people to everyone. John Elam died April 24, 1957, being 74 years old. They had the following children and all of them attended Wilkesboro School.

Wrenn Culler was born Oct. 1905. He left Wilkesboro as a young man and became a salesman with a tobacco company, then a hardware company. He married Betty Hendrix of Kernersville, N.C. and moved to Bluefield, W. Wa. where they still live. They have three children, Betty Jean, Robert and Jimmie, and eight grandchildren.

John Elam Culler, Jr. was born Feb. 9, 1908, he owned and operated Culler's Gulf Service, North Wilkesboro until his death November 17, 1978. He married Ressie McLean. They had three children, JoAnne (died an infant), Johnnie (Mrs. Robert Vaught) and Shirley (Mrs. Harry Steele) of Winston-Salem and five grandchildren.

Irene Culler was born July 17, 1910, and died July 29, 1962. She was active in the church, community affairs and being part owner of Culler's Grocery worked there until her death. She did beautiful sewing and made handmade articles.

Lena Culler was born April, 1913. She is a Registered Nurse, a graduate of City Hospital, Gastonia, N.C. She spent her early nursing years in Tennessee, as an employee of Tenn. Valley Authority. There she met and married E.H. Fritts in 1946. They had no children. After his death in 1971, she returned to North Wilkesboro and operates a small flower shop in her home.

Clegg Culler was born January, 1916, and served in World War II in Italy. He returned to Wilkesboro in 1946 and went into the grocery business with his father and sister Irene which he still operates. He married Dessie Hanks in 1951. They have two daughters, "Billie" (Mrs. Larry Watson) of Washington, D.C. who attended Brevard College. "Cindy" Mrs. Steve Kastelburg) of Raleigh, N.C. received her B.S. Degree in Nursing from UNC-Greensboro, N.C. They have three grandchildren.

Lucille Culler was born July, 1919. She worked in the office of Duke Power Co. during World War II, while her husband T. Ed Norman served in the army overseas, having married in November, 1939. He returned in 1945 to his job at Duke Power Co., retiring in 1980 with forty years service. They have three daughters and one grandchild. Beth (Mrs. James Barnes) of Raleigh, N.C. received her B.S. Degree in Nursing from UNC-Chapel Hill, N.C. in 1969.

Nancy Anne teaches Special Education in Jamestown, N.C. receiving a M.A. Degree from UNC-Chapel Hill in 1975. Laurie Jane is now a Senior Industrial Relations Major at UNC-Chapel Hill. In 1973 Lucille returned to work as Assistant Clerk for the Town of Wilkesboro. The family is active in the Methodist Church and community affairs.

Don Turner Culler was born January, 1926. He attended Wilkesboro School until World War II. Joined the Air Force and served in the Pacific Theatre as a crew member of a B-24 Liberator. At the end of War, he returned home and attended National Business College in Roanoke, Virginia. In 1948, he began his working career with Carolina Mirror Corporation. In 1949, married Mary Lee Gardner, born 1927 in Galax, Virginia. Mary Lee attended North Wilkesboro School, Virginia Intermont Junior College, transferred to Greensboro College and graduated with a B.A. Degree in elementary education. She later taught the second grade in North Wilkesboro School. They have two daughters: Donna Lee, born April, 1953, and Patricia Ann, born January, 1959. Both daughters attended Meredith College, graduating with B.A. Degrees. Donna married Peter Hurd of Freeport, Maine, and she operates an interior decorating business. Patricia married Mark Pegram from the Winston-Salem area, and she is a home maker. Don worked at Carolina Mirror Corp. until July, 1961. At that time, he and E.F. Gardner, his father-in-law, resigned and organized Gardner Mirror Corporation. Over the next 20 years, Gardner Mirror Corporation grew to be one of the largest mirror manufacturers in the United States. Peter Hurd and Mark Pegram joined Gardner Mirror and are employed with the company. The entire family resides in the North Wilkesboro area and has always been very active in The First Methodist Church as well as community and civic affairs.

The Wilkesboro Town Hall and Fire Department on the corner of Main and West Street now stands on the Culler property which the Town purchased from the Culler heirs in 1969.

Sources: Family History and personal knowledge.

— Lucille C. Norman

SAMUEL CURTIS

491

Joshua Curtis of English descent served as an Ensign and later as Lieutenant during the Revolutionary War. He was born about 1732 and died 28 November, 1818, in Davidson County, Tennessee. His wife was Mary Clark and nothing else is known of her.

Their children were: (1) Samuel Curtis, born 1756, married Susan Cottrell; (2) Joshua Curtis, married Nancy Cottrell, died in Indiana; (3) William Curtis, married Edy Cottrell; (4) Rebecca Curtis married a Mr. Cottrell; (5) Anna Curtis, married a Mr. Ward; (6) Susanna Curtis, born 1 May, 1784, married Ezra Stonecipher 2 September, 1803; (7) Rachel Curtis, unmarried; (8) Mary Curtis, unmarried; (9) Nancy Curtis, married John H. Stonecipher; and (10) Phoebe, believed to have married a Samuel Stonecipher.

Samuel Curtis received a Land Grant for 100 acres, dated 20 June, 1795. He had married Susannah Cottrell, daughter of Thomas Cottrell on 11 March, 1788, and lived in that part of Wilkes County which is now Caldwell.

They were the parents of Susan Curtis, born 1792, married John Pennell, and died 6 October, 1882; Edith (Edy) Curtis, born 15 October, 1801, married John Roane 27 January, 1831; James Curtis, born 15 July, 1799, married a Miss Hughes; Joshua Curtis, born 14 February, 1803, married Salley Coffey. They moved to Owen County, Indiana, where he died 12 July, 1892; William Curtis, born 7 April, married first a Coffey and second, a Cottrell; Jennie Curtis, married first, Franklin Berry and later a Mr. Aloway; Samuel, deceased; and Hezekiah Curtis, born 15 May, 1810, married Celia Coffey.

Samuel Curtis lived to the ripe old age of ninety-six. A chair, known as the "Samuel Curtis chair" was passed to his son Hezekiah, who gave it to his son Finley Patterson Curtis when he moved to Tennessee. Finley Patterson willed it to his son, Finley Paul Curtis of Butler, Tennessee. When Finley Paul Curtis died in June 1980, he left this chair to Mrs. Edward Bell of North Wilkesboro, a direct descendant of Samuel Curtis.

Sources: Bible records, letters.

— Helen B. Bell

HEZEKIAH CURTIS

492

Hezekiah Curtis, known to everyone as "Uncle Iskie" was born 15 May 1810, the son of Samuel Curtis and Susannah Cottrell Curtis. He was married 26 December, 1833, to Celia Coffey, born 29 June, 1813. She was the daughter of William Coffey and Anna Boone, daughter of Israel Boone and the niece of Daniel Boone.

They moved to vicinity of Wilkesboro and owned many acres of land on the south side of the Yadkin River. They built the large white house now known as the "Sheriff Johnson homeplace" in Wilkesboro and the bridge nearby across the Yadkin was named for Hezekiah Curtis. It is called the Curtis Bridge.

Their children were (1) Larkin Junius, born 29 April, 1835, in Wilkes County. He was an officer in the Civil War and was killed on May 10, 1864, in the Battle of Spottsylvania Court House in Virginia. His body was returned by train to Statesville and brought by wagon to be buried in the family graveyard; (2) Adoninam Judson, born 2 April, 1837, married first Rhoda Wancock Higgins, 8 October, 1868, and secondly, Molly Starnes. In 1866 he moved to Spencer, Indiana, and he died there 1 May, 1926. He had no children of his own; (3) Julia, born 26 January, 1839, died 15 February, 1901. She was unmarried; (4) Finley Patterson, born 20 May, 1841, moved to Butler, Tennessee, in January 1871. On 21 May, 1884, he was married to Selma Florentine Rosenblat, born 2 November, 1861, in Greenville, Tennessee. He died 26 August, 1922, and Selma died 12 December, 1939; (5) Caroline L. (Connie), born 26 November, 18--, and on 10 May, 1866, married William Columbus Coffey. She died 24 June, 1893; (6) Mattie Gertrude (known as "Aunt Mat") was born 23 August, 1846. She never married and resided in Wilkes County until 1905. She died 20 January, 1931, and is buried in Tennessee.

Celia Coffey Curtis died the 12 of July 1899, and Hezekiah Curtis departed this life 20 January, 1901. They too were buried in the Curtis Family Cemetery which was located in that part of Wilkesboro now known as Ken Acres. The remains and tombstones of this graveyard were moved to Mountain Park Cemetery and the iron fence around the area was removed to Tennessee by Curtis descendants.

Sources: Curtis Family Bible, personal knowledge.

— Helen B. Bell

DANCY — SHEPHERD — WHITTINGTON — VANNOY
493

In 1802, Edward Dancy purchased a parcel of land on the headwaters of Reddies River in Wilkes County. At this time, he was 33 years old, having been born in 1769 to John and Ann Morgan Dancy. Edward's first wife, Susan Vannoy, had died in 1799, leaving three children: John, Elizabeth and Sarah.

On 8 July 1802, Edward took Amelia (Milly) Vannoy as his second bride. Milly was the daughter of Francis Vannoy and the granddaughter of John Vannoy who was in Wilkes County at the time of his death in 1778. Edward and Milly had thirteen children: William, Jesse J., Isham, Abraham J., Temperance, Anna, Noah, Edward J., Obediah, Susanna, Thomas J., David E., and Lucinda. Edward died in 1856, followed in death by Milly in 1858.

Abraham J. Dancy, the fourth child of Edward and Milly, was born 3 Nov. 1807. He grew up to become a minister. The name of his first wife is not known, but to the union were born six children: John, Joseph, Wilson, Abraham, William H., and Obediah. On 14 Oct. 1845, he married Sarah Ann Brown, and over the ensuing years fathered eight more children: Melvin, Susan, Edward Taylor, Thomas S., Louisa Ann, Meshack, Sarah Ann and Rufus A. The date of Abraham's death is not known to this writer. His name last appears in the census of 1860. The 1880 census shows that his widow, Sarah, was living with their daughter Susan, who had married Thornton Staley.

Obediah Dancy was the sixth child of Abraham, born 15 Oct. 1842. He married his cousin, Alva Shepherd, who was the daughter of James and Susan Dancy Shepherd. Alva was born 8 Dec. 1844. The known children of Obediah and Alva are: Reece, Noah, Bill, Norman M., Maro (31 May 1872 — 15 Mar. 1890), Clate 8 Oct. 1880 — 26 Oct. 1901), Edward K. (28 Sep. 1882 — 11 Sep. 1901), Obediah served in the Confederate Army during the Civil War. He died 24 Mar. 1922 and is buried in the Reddies River Baptist Church cemetery. Alva lived to be almost 95 years old, dying 3 July 1939. Her grave is beside that of Obediah.

Norman M. Dancy, son of Obediah, was born 6 Feb. 1866. He married Mary Ann Whittington, whose family roots in the Reddies River area of Wilkes County were already almost a century old. She was born 18 Sep. 1870, the daughter of John Lynn Whittington (8 Jul. 1847 — 29 May 1932) and Henrietta Vannoy Whittington (9 Feb. 1847 — 15 May 1882).

John Lynn Whittington was the son of William and Ann Gilreath Whittington. William was the son of Leonard and Sarah Kilby Whittington. Leonard was the son of William and Catherine Whittington. William first appears in the 1782 Tax List of Wilkes County. Leonard's wife, Sarah, was born 20 Oct. 1780, the daughter of William Kilby, who lived in the Reddies River section as early as 1784.

Mary Ann's mother was the daughter of Enoch and Nancy Walters Vannoy. Enoch was the son of Rev. James and Sarah Shepherd Vannoy. James was the son of Andrew, and the grandson of John Vannoy, who died in Wilkes County in 1778.

Mary Ann's grandmother Vannoy was the daughter of John Shepherd, Jr., and the granddaughter of John Shepherd, Sr., who arrived in Wilkes County about 1776 and purchased land in the Deep Ford Hill section.

Norman and Mary Ann made their home along the Reddies River slightly upstream from the present New Light Baptist Church No. 2. Their home was damaged by the 1916 flood; part of it washed away. They later purchased a home and land along what is now the Vannoy Road. Their children were: Ira Gilbert (24 Jun. 1891 — 9 Mar. 1940), Isaac (ca. 1893 — 14 Jun. 1918), Estel, Dewey (10 Oct. 1898 — 15 Apr. 1939), Otho (ca. 1901 — ?), Clyde (ca. 1905-1980), and Annie (ca. 1910 — now living at Chapel Hill, N.C.)

Norman died 15 May 1943. Mary Ann died 30 Dec. 1946. Both are buried in the Reddies River Baptist Church Cemetery.

Ira, the eldest son of Norman, served four years in the U.S. Navy prior to World War I. Upon his discharge, he joined the westward migration and homesteaded in Whatcum County, Washington. At the outbreak of World War I, he enlisted in the Army, serving in France where he was injured by poison gas.

He returned to the Reddies River section in 1918, and met Ella Nora Phillips, whose parents, John Wesley and Rachel Woodie Phillips, lived just across the mountains at Obids, in Ashe County. They were married 25 Nov. 1920. Their children are: Pansy (21 Dec. 1921 — married Robert Maurice Jones, son of Robert and Bessie Church Jones); Gilbert E. (18 Sep. 1923 — married Ora Lee Church — now divorced); M. Katherine (18 Sep. 1925, married C. Blake Hayes, son of Clarence and Emalee Walker Hayes); Philip W. (1 Mar. 1930, never married, served in the Air Force during the Korean conflict.); Norman R. (18 Apr. 1933, married Lola Byrd, daughter of Evan and Elsie Wiles Byrd); Joyce B. (20 Aug. 1937, married George Franklin McNeil, son of Commodore C. and Eva Clary McNeil, and who lineage is traced to Rev. George McNiel, another early Wilkes County settler.

Ira operated an automobile garage in Jefferson for a few years. He later moved with his family to Wilkes County and was a mechanic with the Wilkes County School System before he died 9 Mar. 1940 in the Veterans Hospital in Johnson City, Tenn. from complications arising as a result of being gassed in World War I. He is buried in the Reddies River Baptist Church Cememtery. Ella Phillips Dancy is currently a resident in a local nursing home.

Sources: Early Wilkes County records, family memories and family records.

— Mrs. Joyce Dancy McNeil

THE FRANKLIN GANTT DAY FAMILY
494

Franklin Gantt Day, was born January 8, 1934 to Sally Gantt and Walter Miller Day in North Wilkesboro Hospital. He is the youngest of three children, with a sister Virginia Day Kelly, and a brother James Walter Day. He grew up in a big old house on C Street with his parents, his brother, sister and a lively wire-haired terrier named Jiggs; attended North Wilkesboro Elementary School and belonged to the First Methodist Church.

In the eighth grade he met Peggy Creasman who was born in Thomasville, N.C. at her grandparents' home, Mr. and Mrs. Jessie Thomas Kindley. An only child, she was born on April 8, 1933 to Mr. and Mrs. Roy L. Creasman. When she was six years old, she moved to Wilkesboro with her parents. There she attended Wilkesboro Elementary School. At age ten she moved to Newport News, Va. with her parents where her father Roy Creasman worked in the Newport News Shipyard during World War II. When she was fourteen they moved to N. Wilkesboro in 1947 where her father opened Creasman Electric.

She attended N.W. Elementary School where she and Frank were in different rooms. Peggy was in Miss Sale's room and Frank was in Mrs. Helms eighth grade. Each night on the radio station WILX Jay Anderson was a disc jockey for a request program, and Frank heard boys call in and request songs for Peggy. This made him curious and he wanted to meet her. He did, and he asked her for a date. They dated all through high school and college. They both graduated from N. Wilkesboro High School in 1952. Frank attended Lenoir Rhyne College in Hickory N.C. and Peggy attended Woman's College U.N.C. in Greensboro, N.C. After finishing there Peggy came home to live with her parents and worked as a secretary and bookkeeper for Wilkes Auto Sales. Frank graduated from Lenoir Rhyne in Jan. 1956 with a degree in business.

Frank and Peggy were married on Feb. 18, 1956 in the chapel of The First Methodist Church. Frank worked for his father at Day Electric. They both attended First Methodist Church.

In Oct. 1957 Frank was drafted into the Army. He was stationed at Ft. Bragg, Ft. Jackson, then at Ft. Benning, Ga. Peggy lived at home with her parents until Timothy Franklin Day was born June 15, 1958. After two months Peggy and Tim went to live at Ft. Benning with Frank. There they lived almost two years, and then returned to N. Wilkesboro. Frank went to work for his father at Nancy King Textiles where he is vice-president and designer of sleepwear. Peggy also works there.

On March 2, 1960 in a snow storm a second child, Melody Lynn, was born to Frank and Peggy at Wilkes Gen. Hospital.

In Sept. 1963 they built a home on Colonial Dr., Frank taught the Open Door Sunday School Class for many years in the First Methodist Church. The family attended the First Methodist Church until April 1980, at which time Frank and Peggy moved their membership to the Assemblies of God Church.

Tim and Melody attended N.W. Elementary School and graduated from Wilkes Central High School. Tim graduated in 1976 and attended Appalachian State University where he received a scholarship in Physics. He graduated in 1981 with a degree in Physics and Computer Science. While in college Tim worked for Southwestern Book Co. each summer. After graduation Tim went to work for Sperry Univac in Atlanta, Ga. as a Systems Analyst. Melody graduated from U.N.C.G. in the summer of 1982 with a degree in Fashion Merchandising.

Frank and his brother Jim became private pilots in Oct. 1979. Frank's father bought a four passenger Cessna Plane and Frank and Jim were delighted. Now they could fly almost everywhere, and Mr. W.M. Day is ready to go anytime for he loves to fly. Frank and Jim received their Instrument Rating in 1981.

Frank is also interested in photography. This he puts to good use, doing all the photographs for the Nancy King Catalogue which comes out twice a year.

Frank and Peggy are partners with Frank's brother and his wife, Pat and Jim in Day Inc., Co., which includes mini-storage units and The Outlet House.

Source: Personal knowledge.

— Frank and Peggy Day

CHARLES GRAY DAY FAMILY
495

Charles Gray Day was one of the leading furniture merchants in Wilkes County 1927-1945. He was born in Wilkes 25 February 1891 to Fred Ford and Sarah Jane Carter Day. His early life was spent in Elkin where he worked at a shoe plant, a grocery and hardware store. He moved to North Wilkesboro where he worked for Jenkins Hardware Company until Rhodes-Day Furniture Company was organized by Carl Coffey, Jack Rhodes and Charles G. Day.

Charles G. Day was interested in the improvement and development of the community. He was a member of the First Baptist Church and Sunday School. He was a member of the Junior Order, Knights of Pythias, Kiwanis and Better Business Bureau, serving as the first president of the latter. He was chief of the North Wilkesboro Fire Department for many years.

On September 5, 1915, he married Stella

Charles Gray Day.

DeEtta Hampton (2 January 1899 — 8 October 1928), daughter of Mattie Castevens and John Hampton. To this union were born: Charles Hampton, born 13 August 1916; John Frank, born 9 July 1918; James Edward born 11 April 1921; Ella Louise born 25 September 1922; Bobby Fred born 15 February 1925; and Jack Gray born 8 October 1928.

Charles Hampton Day graduated from National Business College, Roanoke, Va. He married Christine Brown of S.C. 27 February 1943. They had one son, Charles Samuel born 22 November 1944. Sam graduated from U.N.C. Chapel Hill. He married Lynne Welborn, who attended E.C.U. Their children are Chris (1973) and Josh (1975).

John Frank Day (Bill) attended Elon College. He served with the U.S. Armed forces during World War II and married Edwina Pearl Waugh 6 September 1941. They had three children: John Frank, Steven Waugh who attended Clemson Univ. and Judy Edwina, graduate of Clemson University. Steven Waugh has children Stephanie and Matthew.

James Edward Day served with U.S. Infantry during World War II, was wounded and a recipient of the Purple Heart award. He graduated from National Business College and married Rebecca Saunders of Bedford, Va., a graduate of National Business College. She is an executive secretary. Their children are James Timothy, who attended UNC, Chapel Hill, a Viet Nam veteran and married to Ann Babgy. They have one son, Matthew Edward; Susan DeEtta graduate of Peace College and UNC Chapel Hill, married to David Gray. They have children David Adam and Seth.

Ella Louise, graduate of Watts Hospital School of Nursing, married Clyde Miller Waugh, who served as a Navy Pilot during World War II, graduate of NC State. Their children are: Clyde Miller, Jr. graduate of A.S.U. served in U.S. Navy, is married to Cheryl Bivens; Rebecca Louise graduate of A.S.U., married Arthur Lowe, Jr. Their children are Laura Beth and Myra; Martha Elizabeth (Beth) graduate of E.C.U. now employed in Wilkes Co. Health Department.

Bobby Fred Day attended National Business College, served with U.S. Marines during

World War II, married Patricia McNeil 9 October 1948. Their children are Laura Catherine, Frank and Danny.

Jack Gray served with U.S. Navy during World War II, married Alene Ingram. Their children are Mark, now in the Navy, and Amy.

On May 3, 1931, Charles G. Day married Emma Beaman, a teacher from Stantonsburg, N.C. They had two children:

Jerry Beaman, a graduate of Duke University with a Masters Degree in Political Science. He works for IRS in Raleigh area office. He married Joan Sprinkle, daughter of Joe and Louise Sprinkle, a graduate of UNCG with a masters degree, Georgia So. Uni. Their children are: Darren Jeffery, a Magna Cum Laude graduate of Embry-Riddle Aeronautical University, and Jerry Beaman, Jr. who is attending Georgia Tech.

David Eugene, a graduate of A.S.U. with a B.S. Degree, teaches in the Thomasville High Schools, and is married to Sharon Suzanne Morgan of Charleston, W. Va. She is employed with Thomas School Central office. They have no children.

Sources: Family records, Bibles and grave markers.

— Emma Beaman Day
and Louise Day Waugh

THE ANCESTORS OF EMMA BEAMAN DAY
496

The Beaman family dates back to or before the Revolutionary War as do the Speight, Cook, Wood, Vines and many other families who were closely connected. The earliest of these people came to Virginia, later spreading into North Carolina, South Carolina, Georgia, Tennessee and Mississippi and westward to the West Coast also into Texas. The Speight family, came to the New World in 1634 followed about the same time by these other families.

Emma Beaman Day is the great-great-granddaughter of Seth Speight, Sr. who moved to Greene County with his parents from Chowan County. According to records he was a big landowner. The landing on Contentnea Creek, Speight's Landing, was named for the Speight family. From here goods were shipped down stream on the way to England and goods from England were brought back to Speight's Landing. Seth Speight, Sr. was Captain in N.C. Militia during the Revolutionary War.

According to his will (1800) he had the following children: William Vines, Seth, Jr., Henry, Thomas, Lemon, Polly Vines, Nancy Howe, Fanny Bright. Seth Sr. married Elizabeth Vines, daughter of Samuel Vines and Elizabeth Blanchard Vines. It is evident that most of the Speight family were Methodist with several Methodist ministers among the group.

Lemon Speight (20 February 1791 — 11 June 1830) married Charity Cook 6 May 1817. Charity (12 June, 1796 — 19 November 1830) was daughter of Jacob and Celia Cook. The Lemon Speights were my great-grandparents. The Lemon Speights had only two daughters to live to adulthood. They were: (1) Nancy

Howe, wife of John Derring. (2) Celia Evaline married George Joyner.

R.C.D. Beaman and Mary Cook Speight Beamon had only 2 children: Romulus Eugene 12 February 1867 — 23 June 1940; and Charity Speight Beaman who married William A. Darden.

Romulus Eugene married 9 September 1890 to Bettie Agnes Wood 12 February 1869 — 28 May 1955. Their children were: (1) Kenneth Dorsey — never married. Buried in Greene County. (2) Infant daughter — died at birth — buried in Speight Cemetery. (3) Derwood Eugene — Buried in Durham, Lucille Hundley Beaman, his wife, living in Durham. (4) Mary Christine, married A.R. Darden, no children; died of cancer. Both buried in Stantonsburg. (5) Cecil Wood married Annie Skinner. Cecil Wood had heart trouble. He is buried at Tabernacle Church.

(6) Mildred, married Logan Harris Scarboro. Logan died January 1980; is buried in Wendell. They had only one child: Beaman Harris Scarboro married to Ruth Elizabeth Stenguist who have two children: Mark Harris and Lynne Ashley Scarboro. Ruth and Beamon are divorced.

Emma B. Day graduated A.B. Degree from N.C.C.W. now U.N.C.G. She taught for 24 years. She married Charles Gray Day of North Wilkesboro 3 May 1931. Their two children are: Jerry Beamon and David Eugene Day (See Day story).

Sources: Family Records, Bible Records, Grave Markers.

— Emma Beaman Day

THE D. VERNON DEAL FAMILY
497

D. Vernon Deal was born October 24, 1907 to Quintus M. and Bessie Mae Coble Deal.

His banking career started April 1924, upon graduation from Stony Point High School. He attended Lenoir-Rhyne College 1925-1927 and U.N.C. Chapel Hill 1927-1928.

From May 1928 until 1931 he was Assistant Cashier of the Bank of Stony Point, worked with the N.C. Banking Department as Liquidating Agent 1931-1933 and was Assistant Cashier of the Merchants and Farmers Bank, Taylorsville from October 1933 to December 1938.

Moving to North Wilkesboro, N.C. February 1940, he was Assistant Cashier of the Northwestern Bank. He held this office from 1938 to 1942 when he became Vice-President and Secretary. He held this office until 1958 when he was named Chairman of the Board and held this office until 1974. He was Chairman of the Board, member of Board of Directors and Executive Committee, Northwestern Financial Corporation from 1973 until 1977. From 1938 until 1977 the Bank grew from $2.5 million to over $1 billion in assets.

Vernon Deal was a past member of the Small Business Administration; N.C. Advisory Council, with a speciality in community development loans; member of Governor Dan Moore's 168 Blue Ribbon Highway Study Commission; member of several State of N.C. Missions to Canada to invite new business to North Carolina and was one of the incorporators and officers of Wilkes Mountain Poultry Products, which is now Holly Farms Poultry Products Company, and has been a member of several N.C. Agri-Business groups to study and solicit industry from all over the United States to come to North Carolina.

He was a member and Chairman of the Finance Committee of the Board of Commissioners of the Town of North Wilkesboro 1953-1977 and has held many positions in North Carolina Bankers Assoiation 1940-1977 and a member of its 50 year Club.

D. Vernon Deal Family: D. Vernon; Mary Lou; Louise, David.

From 1964 to 1979 he was N.C. Chairman of the Delegation of National Rivers and Harbors Congress; Past Chairman of Wilkes Chamber of Commerce; Old Hickory Council of B.S.A. earning Silver Beaver award on Council Camp Financing. He has also been a member of Wilkes Community College Symphony Board; a past president and member of Wilkes Y.M.C.A. board since it started, member of Wilkes Airport Authority since its origin; member of Wilkes Flood Control Committee which was instrumental in getting Kerr Scott Dam; and Director Wilkes Community College Endowment Fund.

Vernon has traveled extensively with his wife in United States, Europe, Scandinavian Countries, Moscow and Leningrad, the Orient, except China, South Africa, Mexico, South America and around the world in 1979. He is a Methodist, a Lion and a member of the Elks Club.

His wife is Louise Lentz from Stony Point. She graduated from U.N.C. in Greensboro in 1930, taught in the North Wilkesboro Elementary School, was a past president of the P.T.A., appointed by Governor Bob Scott to an unfinished and a consecutive term on the N.C. Arts Council and was instrumental in getting the first grants for the Wilkes Art Gallery.

They have a son David V. Deal, Jr., who is vice-president of Northwestern Bank, and City Executive in Taylorsville, N.C. He has a daughter Heather. Vernon and Louise also have a daughter, Mary Lou, who is a potter in Ashland, Virginia and has one daughter Raasa Leela.

Sources: Deal-Staffer Family, Personal Knowledge.

— D. Vernon Deal

Robert Avery Deal.

ROBERT AVERY DEAL
498

Robert Avery Deal, owner and publisher of *The Chronicle* (weekly newspaper published in Wilkesboro), was the first born of the eleven children born to Frances Hill Blair and William Franklin Deal of Caldwell County. He was not the first born of his father, as this was the second marriage for W.F. Deal. His first wife, Mary Caroline Thompson, died in childbirth with their fifth child, a daughter named Mary Caroline. This daughter lived about a year. Only two children from this first marriage lived to maturity, a son, William Thompson Deal and a daughter, Sarah E. Deal.

R.A. Deal's half-sister, Sarah, married his mother's younger brother, Hartwell Spain Blair. This made his Uncle Hartwell his brother-in-law also. (H.S. Blair and Sarah Deal were not blood related.) The lives of R.A. Deal and H.S. Blair were further intertwined as he worked for his uncle in Lenoir in 1883 when he established *The Chronicle* and later purchased it from him when it was moved to Wilkesboro around 1890-1891.

R.A. Deal's first known American ancestor was Jacob Diehl who sailed from Amsterdam by way of Rotterdam aboard the ship *Glasgow,* with his son William, and probably his wife (women were not listed) and arrived Philadelphia, Pa. Sept. 9, 1738. They were followed by two other sons, John and Jacob, Jr. in 1740 and 1741. R.A. Deal's great-great-grandfather was this William who was born around 1730 who married Susannah Ichard and migrated first to Doylestown, Pa. and then to Newton, N.C. They were both of the "Palatinate Immigration" and had fled Germany because of religious persecution and because their homes had been devastated by many years of wars. They married around 1750 and had at least ten children. Their son, William, born in 1774 became R.A. Deal's great-grandfather. They are buried in the cemetery of Old St. Paul's Lutheran church in Newton, N.C.

R.A. Deal's great-grandfather married Mary Herman 1797 and they had at least nine children. Mary was born in 1780 of German immigrants in Pennsylvania. Mary and William's oldest son was named William and was born in 1798 at Conover N.C. where they had their farm and home. They are buried in the cemetery of St. John's Lutheran Church at Conover.

William Deal, son of Mary and William, married Catharine Smyre, whose lineage was also German, (Smyre's migrated on ship *Neptune* into Philadelphia in 1753) and they established their home at Cedar Valley near Granite Falls, N.C. in Caldwell Co. This Billy Deal and Catharine were very industrious and well situated for their times. They owned a very large farm, a distillery, a tannery, a harness and saddle shop, a blacksmith and woodworking shop in which he made wagons and other needed equipment, a saw mill and a grist mill. He was Postmaster of Deal's Mill Post Office from 1839 until its closing in 1866. Married in 1824, their oldest son was born in 1825 and named William Franklin. They are buried in the cemetery of Cedar Valley Methodist Church very close to their home. They are surrounded by many of their family and families that married into their own.

William Franklin, son of William and Catharine, married Frances Hill Blair in 1861 (his first wife died in 1860) and they became the parents of eleven children, ten of which grew to adulthood. Robert Avery Deal was born to them Dec. 6, 1862. This William and wife Frances were prosperous and he owned a large farm and a mill. They were careful to see that their children were educated. Three of their sons were newspapermen — either owners or editors. One son was a fine violinist who taught and performed in Asheville, N.C. One daughter an artist and one an expert seamstress and needlecraft artist. Their youngest child, Henry Lee Deal, lived to be almost 98. He died in January of 1982. William Franklin and Frances Hill Blair Deal are buried in the cemetery of Ebenezer Methodist Church near where they had their home.

R.A. Deal's mother, Frances Hill Blair, was descended from Colbert Blair who came to Caldwell County in the early 1770's. His father was thought to be James Blair of Old Orange Co., Va. and later of Augusta Co., Va. Colbert married Sarah Morgan and their son, John Blair married Frances Hill and they became the grandparents of Frances Hill Blair Deal. Her parents were John Blair, Jr. and his wife Abigail McRary. These ancestors of Frances Hill Blair Deal are buried in adjacent plots to the William and Catharine Deal's plot at Cedar Valley Methodist Church. Frances Hill Blair Deal lived until 1923 and is buried beside her husband, William, and four of their daughters.

R.A. Deal attended public schools and at least two years under Prof. R.L. Abernethy at Rutherford College. He taught school before he went into the newspaper business with his uncle, H.S. Blair. When he purchased *The Chronicle* and moved to Wilkesboro, he was a handsome young bachelor and much sought after by the parents of the eligible young ladies as a very suitable match. He was about 5' 10'' tall, with dark brown hair and light hazel eyes. He often sported a mustache, as was the custom. He possessed a beautiful tenor voice and sang, not only in his own church choir, (Wilkesboro Methodist) but was also much in demand to sing in other churches and for various other functions.

He fell in love with Mamie Frances Wallace of Wilkesboro and they were maried at her home on Feb. 7, 1900. To them were born five children, three sons and two daughters. (Their names and data listed in Mamie Deal Caudill's biography). He contracted tuberculosis and spent some time in the hospital at Oteen, but he returned home and died February 12, 1916. He is buried in the Mountain Park Cemetery, Wilkesboro, N.C.

He was held in high esteem by all who knew him. He was quite accomplished and his news items are much enjoyed by those who read them even today.

Sources: Family Bibles, Court Records, Older family members, newspapers, Fern Deal Book on Deal geneology — *The Land of Wilkes* by Judge Hayes, personal knowledge, church records, grave stones.

— Bette Caudle McKinney

JAMES E. and PAULINE ELLIOTT DEANS

499

James E. Deans, son of Thomas and Kate Howell Deans, was born June 3, 1864 in Hobbsville community of Chowan County, N.C. These families were late 1700 settlers of Chowan. The Deans family home was a 160 acre farm on the banks and swamp land of the Chowan river. His father was a farmer, lumberman and the community undertaker.

In the case of all small farm families in this section, every family member had to work the farm. Papa, as we affectionately called him, contracted malaria at an early age and did not get rid of it as long as he lived in eastern N.C. This continual illness caused him to be unable to farm or do sawmill work, and he had no taste for undertaking, so he learned lumber grading and measuring and watch and clock repair. He accepted a job with the Roper Lumber Co. of Roper, N.C.

While at work during the summer of 1895, a lumber buyer from N.J. came to the mill to buy long leaf pine and cypress lumber to be shipped north. Mr. Deans was so sick with the

Deans: l. to r. — Marjorie P., J. Elliott, Thos. Richard, Julian S. Back — James E. Deans.

malaria he could hardly finish the order. Being a sympathetic man the buyer asked about the illness. He was informed that it was malaria, and it came from mosquito bites. The customer asked, "Why don't you get out of this country and go where there are no mosquitos?" Papa asked, "Do you know of such a place?" The buyer had just come from Wilkes County on a hardwood buying trip, so he replied, "Wilkes has no mosquitos." The next spring, in 1896 with bag and baggage, Mr. Deans departed from the swamplands for Wilkes County and the mountains.

Upon arrival in North Wilkesboro, he found space in the E.L. Hart Hardware Co. to start the Deans Jewelry business. Already in the same store building was a young fellow, W. Roe Absher, who was starting his clothing business. The two men were to remain very close friends and neighbors the rest of their lives. His business prospered and he recovered from his illness. Wilkes was a lifelong cure for the malaria.

By 1900 he had saved enough money to buy a lot for a home, and go back East and marry THAT GIRL, who was Pauline E. Elliott of the Cross Roads community in Perquimans County. She was the daughter of Richard and Martha Goodwin Elliott, who gave them for a wedding gift the money to build their home on the corner of Ninth and F Street in North Wilkesboro. The house was moved onto another lot in later years and is now a duplex.

With continued improvement in health and growth of business, the Deans family were active members of the community. They were early members of the then new Methodist church. Mr. Deans was a loyal member of the Masonic Lodge, having served among the first Past Masters. He continued a member throughout his life.

July 1902 was a banner time for the Deans. Son, J. Elliott, was born and the building of the Deans Building at 902 B Street was begun. The business grew with the times. Out of this store came Wilkes counties first Kodak, Edison

Phonograph, Waterman self filling pen, Singer Sewing machine, alarm clocks and dollar watches.

There were four children born to the Deans: J. Elliott July 19, 1902; Julian S. January 20, 1904; Thomas Richard September 16, 1905; and Marjorie P. August 1, 1908.

J. Elliott graduated from U.N.C. with a BS in business, with a major in Chemistry. He was active in the jewelry store until 1939 when he accepted a position with Dow Chemical Co. in Freeport, Texas. In 1940 he married Lura Finley Coffey, daughter of Mr. and Mrs. C.D. Coffey, Jr. They located in Houston where he had his own business. They have one son, J.E. Deans, Jr. Ph.D., who has a position with Texas Instrument Co. He is married and has two children.

Julian S. Deans graduated from Penn. State College of Optometry, O.D. Until then his most notable accomplishment was captain of the first fielded football team in Wilkes County in 1921. In 1926, Dr. Deans passed the N.C. State Board and opened his practice of optometry in North Wilkesboro. For four years the practice remained in the jewelry store, since optometry was no longer a business but a profession, the practice was moved out of the store into an office of its own. For the next 48 years it was an ethical professional practice and remains so today under the guidance of Dr. Danny J. Payne.

Dr. Deans married September 2, 1930 Rebecca Blackwell of Statesville, N.C. They made their home for forty years on Sixth Street, but now reside "on the Brushies." They have two children: M. Carolyn, a graduate of Duke U. who married Dr. James I. Gillean, Ph.D. graduate of N.C. State, who has his own business in Winter Park, Fla. They have three daughters.

J. Stuart Deans, a graduate of W.C.C. and Catawba Tech. He has been with Lanier Business Products for over ten years, with his office in Hickory.

Rebecca and Jule are loyal Methodists and

active in civic and social affairs.

Thomas Richard Deans attended Elon College and N.C. State. He operated the jewelry store until it closed in 1974. Richard never married. He was a Mason and a member of the Lion's Club. As a young man he was quite active in sports and the social life of the town. Richard died July 4, 1979.

Marjorie P. Deans, who was a graduate of U.N.C.G., married Wm. H. Kelly, who had a long and active life as Superintendent of Alexander and Stanley County and Bunn High Schools before retiring to their hotel at Wrightsville Beach. He was a Davidson graduate, with post-graduate work at U.N.C. and N.C. State. They had three daughters: Pat, wife of a retired U.S. Army officer; Nancy, married and living in Greenville, S.C.; and Alicia who lives in Boston and is secretary to the president of M.I.T. Mr. Kelly died April 1982 and Marjorie continues to live at their hotel.

Sources: Own knowledge; relatives.

— Dr. J.S. Deans

DILLARD — FOSTER
500

Vergie Dillard, one of eleven children of Ollie and Lura Smoot Dillard, married Walter James Foster, one of three sons of Walter and Ida Haynes Foster, on 7 June 1934. They have four daughters, four granddaughters, and one grandson. Their daughters and their families are as follows: (1) Christine married Bob L. Myers and their two daughters are Melissa and Sherry. (2) Delores married William Donald (Bucky) Horton and they have three children: Donna, Diane and William Donald, Jr. (Bill). (3) Gayle is married to Jim Clemens. (4) Teresa Ellen is the youngest daughter of Jim and Vergie.

Walter James Foster's maternal grandparents were the Rev. Isaac Haynes and Nancy Madison Haynes.

His paternal grandfather, Hugh A. Foster, married Virginia Leckie of Iredell Co., N.C. They had four children: (1) Meta married William Kinyoun who was killed in a railroad accident in 1909. Their oldest child, Hugh Kinyoun, fell from a tree near his home in Dellaplane at the age of ten and broke his arm. Gangrene set in and Dr. William Horton drove his horse and buggy to the home and amputated young Hugh's arm on the kitchen table. The operation was a success and Hugh lived to marry and raise a large family. His widow, Stella, lives in Winston-Salem. Meta and William Kenyoun had three more children, Zelma, Merle, and Bill, Jr. (2) Gertrude Foster married Mr. Carter and they lived in Winston-Salem. Gertrude gave birth to one child who died in infancy; she died soon thereafter. (3) Walter married Ida Haynes and they had three sons, Hugh who died in infancy; Walter James who married Vergie Foster; and Dwight (now deceased) who married Hazel Adams. Dwight and Hazel had a daughter, Nancy, who married Clayton Bumgarner. (4) Charlie married Lora Reins and they made their home in Kernersville. They are both deceased. They had three sons, Olen who died young; Howard (deceased) married Lucille Peoples; and Norman, unmarried, lives in Kernersville.

The eleven children of Ollie and Lura Smoot Dillard are as follows: Varina who married Norman Reynolds; Mae who married Alonzo Rhoads; Clemmie who married Dewey Rhoads; Minnie who married Austin Reynolds; George who married Pearl Hall; Clifton who married Flora Sebastian; Vergie who married Jim Foster; Metta who married Robert Hogan; Eula who married Harland Billings; Grant who married Nannie Dillard, and Johnny who is unmarried.

Ollie Dillard was a hard-working man who from early boyhood made his own way and having only a few months of schooling, showed considerable initiative. When a young teenager, he hired himself out as a day worker and would drive teams of mules or horses, hauling lumber and grain.

By the time of his marriage when he was 27 years old, he had accumulated a good sized farm on which he raised wheat, rye, corn, cane for molasses, and of course, an orchard of fruit trees.

About the year 1915 he bought a small farm on Mulberry Creek which had several acres of bottom land. The family moved there and put out a large crop of corn. This being the year 1916, the flood came and deposited several feet of sand on the bottoms and the crop was ruined.

Back at the farm where they had lived previously, they had raised a large crop of wheat. After going through the back-breaking job of cutting the wheat with a cradle and the women-folk binding it by hand, lightning struck the stacks of wheat and all were destroyed.

After the flood the family moved back to their old farm and sold the farm on Mulberry Creek to P.E. Dancy, known as "Second-gear Dancy." This farm is owned today by George and Pearl Dillard, son of Ollie and Lura. George's son, Olen and his wife, Sherry, operate a large chicken farm there and raise beef cattle.

Sources: Personal knowledge of family members.

— Vergie D. Foster

ELIJAH H. and EMMA WATSON DOCKERY FAMILY
501

Elijah H. Dockery was born Sept. 17, 1840 a son of John S. and Delphia Roberts Dockery. John S. was born (ca. 1811) in Burke County, N.C. and was a shoemaker by trade. John and Delphia were married on Dec. 21, 1831. Elijah's grandfather was also named Elijah Dockery (ca. 1783-1869); his wife was named Susan. The Dockerys lived on the north side of the Yadkin River, in an area known as Red Top, near the Davis Memorial Baptist Church.

Elijah H. had two brothers and a sister. (1) Susan Dockery (1834-1892) married Ephraim Davis, Jr. They are the grandparents of Dr. James W. Davis, founder of the Davis Hospital in Statesville, N.C. (2) Richard and (3) James Dockery.

Elijah H. Dockery enlisted in the Civil War on April 4, 1862. He was a private in the Fifty-third Regiment-Infantry. During the Civil War Elijah and Richard were on a hill side as a cannon ball came rolling and bouncing down the hill. Richard stuck his foot out to try to stop the cannon ball, but his foot was taken off and the cannon ball continued rolling down the hill. Elijah had to carry his brother to an area where he could get help.

Elijah H. Dockery married Emma Mariah Watson, daughter of James and Rachel Powell Watson. They live in a house which was partly made of logs. Their eight children were: (1) Vennie (ca. 1872) first married a Mr. Davis and had two children Crate and Emma Rae D. Spry. Vennie's second husband was known as "Pink" Foster. They had two children "Doc" Foster and Helen Foster. (2) Martha Evelyn (1874-1925) married Edmond C. Foster and had nine children — Hobart, Alva E., Lela Ann F. Barns, Katie Fay, Bernice F. Eller, Max, Verna F. Laws, Chalmer, and Shirley F. Crawford. (3) James L. Dockery (1877-1946) married Cora Selina Hamby. They had a family of six children — Clifford Emitt, Gladys Pearl D. Barnette, Ernest Kyle, James Clarence Elijah, Lillian D. Royall and Hubert Clinton Dockery. (4) Richard Martin Dockery (1879-1966) moved West and was engaged in ranching until he retired and returned to Wilkes County. (5) Olon M. (1881-1909) married Dora Ellis and had three children — Ralph, Ruby, and Ruff Dockery. (6) Sophronia Irene (1883-1942) married Charles Spurgeon Walker and lived in the Boomer community. Their children are listed in a different family. (7) John W. Dockery (1885-1907) went West with his brother Richard, but became sick and returned home where he died. (8) Rachel Emma (1888-1969) married Peter J. Ferguson. Their children are Richard, Raymond, Wheeler, Clinton, Mae, Lucille and Ruth.

Sources: 1850 and 1860 Wilkes County census, Civil War records, tombstones and interviews with family members, family records.

— William G. and Christine Eller Walker

Emma Watson Dockery.

ANCESTRY of the DULA FAMILY

502

Captain William Dula, the ancestor of this branch of the Dula family in North Carolina, was quite a prominent man in this section, accumulating a fortune which at the time of his death, was said to be the largest in Western North Carolina. His landed estates covered a distance of twelve or fifteen miles along the Yadkin River Valley, in addition to a large slave property. It is said that at least a thousand slaves held by his family were freed at the close of the war.

Thomas J. Dula, N.C. Senate 1901.

Three brothers, Thomas, John and Bennett, along with one sister, came with him from Virginia to North Carolina. Thomas moved shortly thereafter to Georgia, and was probably the eldest of the brothers. From him is descended the Georgia branch of the Dula family. Incidentally, they spell their name "Dooley." It is a matter of conjecture why the difference in the spelling. At one time in the history of Ireland, Spanish Colonists settled in Ireland and their names have been transmitted among the Irish people.

According to the best information, William Dula was a man of striking personal appearance, being of large physique, fair complected, blue eyed and having a prominent Roman nose. A hat, which is preserved in the family, shows that his head must have been of an unusual size.

No knowledge of the ancestry of William Dula is known, except that he was of Irish descent and enlisted in the Patriot Army when but seventeen years old, serving the entire war.

Captain William Dula, born in Patrick County, Virginia, in 1759, was in the Revolutionary War, and saw seven year's service under General Washington. Returning home after the war, he married Theodosia Beasley, a widow, and emigrated soon after to North Carolina, settling in what was then Wilkes County, now Caldwell, on the Yadkin River.

Descendants of Captain William Dula are Thomas Beasley Dula, William, Elizabeth, Nancy, Amelia, and Sarah. Thomas Beasley Dula was the father of William Hulme Dula who in turn was the father of Thomas Joshua Dula. Thomas Joshua was born April 22, 1831 and died in 1906. He was married to Mary Emma Howell on April 10, 1859, in Mocksville, North Carolina. She died in 1914. Their children were: Jessie, Thomas, William, Susan, Mary Louise, Louis, John, Ralph, and Annie.

Only Louis and John remained in Wilkesboro. Their father, Thomas Joshua was born at Cedar Hill in Patterson, Caldwell County. Colonel Thomas J. Dula studied law at Emory and Henry College under Judge Anderson Mitchell of Virginia. Admitted to the bar in 1855, he practiced law in Caldwell County and while there, he built Cherry Hill where he lived for many years. In 1860, he represented Caldwell County in the House of Representatives. Colonel Dula, in 1862, became Captain in Company H, the 58th N.C. Regiment, 5th Company that lead one of the seven companies of men from Caldwell County to fight for the Confederacy. He was seriously wounded in the battle of Chickamauga. In 1864, he was made solicitor of Caldwell County. He was a member of the Constitutional Convention of 1875, and later became U. S. Commissioner.

A relative of Thomas Joshua Dula, James B. Dula of Lenoir, relates the following story about Col. Dula. While at Appalachian College, James B. Dula was showing some old Confederates around. A Mr. Cook asked James if he were related to the old man? "Which old man?" "Colonel Thomas Dula," said Mr. Cook. "He was a good man and a fine officer and always saw that we were well provided for. He tried to get everything we needed. I saw Col. Tom roll over a dead Yankee, pull his watch out to see what time it was and put it back into his pocket." When Mr. Cook said, "Many a fellow would have kept that watch," James Dula replied, "Maybe he was looking for a better watch."

Colonel Dula moved to Wilkes County in 1871. He represented Wilkes in 1872 in the House of Representatives and also in the State Senate. In 1884, he was appointed to consult with the Atlantic, Tennessee and Ohio Railroads in regard to building a railroad to Wilkes County.

He and his wife are buried in the Presbyterian Cemetery in Wilkesboro, North Carolina.

Sources: Personal knowledge, Family record, *Bibles*, gravestones.

— Louise Dula Smith
and Marjorie Dula Osborne

ETHEL LENA and LOUIS BROWN DULA

503

Ethel Lena Dula was born on December 21, 1884, the daughter of Ann Rebecca Harshaw Dula and Julius Abram Dula of Caldwell County. She was their twelfth and last child.

She lived most of her life in Wilkesboro where she died on August 17, 1965.

She was a woman of keen intellect and much ability. She was a member of St. Paul's Episcopal Church in Wilkesboro and was always interested in the affairs of her church. She was president of the Auxiliary and held other offices in the church group.

She was the first president of the Parent Teacher's Association and was a strong supporter of education. She was a charter member of the Wilkesboro Woman's Club and also president of this organization at one time. She belonged to the United Daughters of the Confederacy. For some time she served on the Library Board in North Wilkesboro.

Ethel Dula was educated at Davenport College in Lenoir where she excelled in art and won a medal for her excellence in painting. At one time, she taught art classes in her home in Wilkesboro.

She was married to Louis Brown Dula and to them were born seven children, all now living except one.

Ethel Lena Dula's father was Julius Abram Dula. He was born at Patterson, North Carolina on August 3, 1834, and died on August 17, 1915. He was a merchant, teacher, farmer and orchardist, originator of the Dula beauty apple, which is still being grown on the Brushy Mountains today. He served in the army during the war between the states. He was married to Ann Rebecca Harshaw who was born in Caldwell County on May 12, 1884 and died May 1, 1928. To this union were born twelve children.

Louis Brown Dula was born on February 4, 1875 and died on November 18, 1951. He was the son of Thomas Joshua Dula and Mary Emma Howell Dula and was married to Ethel Lena Dula on November 14, 1906.

He was a member of St. Paul's Episcopal Church in Wilkesboro, where he lived most of his life.

Ethel L. Dula.

He was a Mason, member of the Town Board, and Chairman of the Draft Board.

For some years, he worked in the old Deposit and Savings Bank which was located in the building now known as People's Drug

Store. At the time of his death, he was assistant County Accountant.

He belonged to the Republican Party and was interested in town and county affairs.

The children of Ethel and Louis B. Dula are as follows: (1) Harry Louis, was born in August 1907. He first married Mary Grace Baldwin, and had one son, Harry Armond Dula. He is now married to the former Myrtice McNulty and they have two sons, Thomas McNulty Dula and Terrence Dula. Harry and his wife Myrtice live in Lafayette, Louisiana.

(2) Ethel Louise Dula, born in 1909. She is married to Richard Ivy Smith, Jr. and they are the parents of Marjorie Ann (married to Robert Anderson Starling, with two daughters, Teresa Louise and Mary Kathryn Starling.), Richard Ivy Smith, III, and Robert Dula Smith (recently married to Jennifer Hale.)

(3) Thomas Harshaw was born in 1910 and is married to the former Lucille Noell. They have two sons, Thomas Hunter Dula and Harry Sutton Dula who is married to the former Shirley Ann Kleinschmidt.

(4) Alfred Preston was born in 1912 and died on July 24, 1946. He married Numa Dagenhart. They had one son William Howell Dula.

(5) Marjorie Stewart Dula was born December 14, 1915 and is married to Kelly Paul Osborne. They have two sons and two daughters. Paul Brown Osborne, first married to Brenda Byers. Later he married Jennifer Beshears and they have two children, Mike and Jessica Osborne; Judge Samuel Louis Osborne, was first married to Katharine Ricks. They had one son, Samuel Alan Osborne, born in 1968. Samuel Osborne is now married to Loretta Johnson. Their children are Melissa Osborne and Louis Kelly Osborne; Marilyn Louise Osborne was born in 1942 and is married to James Eric Payne. Their two daughters are Ellen Camille Payne and Stephanie Susan Payne; Ethel Susan Osborne.

(6) Helen Corpening Dula, born in 1917 and married Guy Kingsbury Gregg, now deceased. Their children are Guy Jr., married Mary Stimart with one child, Melissa Gregg, and Peter Witherspoon Gregg.

(7) Louis Brown Dula was born in 1926 and is married to the former Mary Susanne Williams. They have three children, Louis Brown Dula, III, Mary Susanne Dula and Michael Williams Dula.

Sources: Personal knowledge.

— Marjorie Dula Osborne
and Louise Dula Smith

JOHN WITHERSPOON DULA
504

John Witherspoon Dula was born on April 20, 1877 and died on June 23, 1946. He was the son of Thomas Joshua and Mary Emma Howell Dula. He was known to most people as Judge Dula.

He served as U.S. Commissioner for around forty years, but his main occupation was the operation of his grocery store on main street in Wilkesboro for many years. He was a member of the Presbyterian Church there and a member of the Masonic Lodge.

In 1924, he married Mettie Lowe Smoak who died when their daughter, Mary Elizabeth Dula was very young.

Mary Dula married Edsel Whittington and they reside in Wilkesboro in a home built on the original homeplace.

They have four sons, the eldest being twins. They are Stephen Lynn Whittington, Stanley Paige Whittington, who is married to Jenny Howard. Stanley and Jenny have two daughters, Erica and Alisa Whittington. The third son is Mark A. Whittington, followed by John Scott Whittington who is married to the former Pamela Tharp.

Sources: Personal knowledge.

— Mary Dula Whittington

DUNCAN FAMILY
505

John Kesler, who died in 1807 in Rowan County, had a son Christian whose children married into Wilkes families. Christian's daughter Christina married James Canter; his daughter Rachel married Ben Duncan; and son Cornelius married a Miller.

Mary Canter married Jesse Duncan and had Effner and Ralph. Eliza Catherine, known as "Tine," married Daniel Duncan and had Julius E. and Hannibal G. and others.

Cornelius Kesler had a son Samuel, born in Rowan but lived near Statesville. Samuel had a daughter Keziah who married J.F. Gilreath.

Elizabeth, daughter of George Kesler (1794-1844) married Chapman "Chap" Duncan as his second wife. Chapman is believed to be the son of Nathan Duncan and possibly his first wife, Susannah. Nathan's second wife was a Tomlinson.

Nathan Duncan evidently came across the Brushies in the early 1800s. He bought small tracts of land until he acquired 217 acres. In 1847, Nathan sold his land to Chapman Duncan.

The Duncans claimed to be Dutch and had a peculiar accent. One Kesler group claimed to be Lutherans from Germany.

Contrary to opinion, the Duncans were not violent abolitionists. Chapman apparently had no need for slaves. The Canters kept their slaves only a short while.

Chapman Duncan was twice married. First to Nancy Hampton. After a long courtship they were married December 8, 1833 and divorced in 1835, a divorce that was finalized just before his married to Elizabeth Kesler.

After the divorce Nancy Hampton Duncan gave birth to Orilla under an assumed name. Nancy remarried John J. Bryan in 1845 as Nancy Hampton. In the settlement of "Chap's" estate, the Duncans gave daughter Orilla Byrd, wife of James Byrd, a share.

Chapman Duncan, born 4 March 1812, died 20 August 1865, married in Rowan County as his second wife, Elizabeth Elvira Kesler on the 8 March 1842. She was born 28 October 1821 Rowan Co., died 27 February 1905 in Wilkes.

A tale has been told that the couple were horseback riding and were almost home when they came to a creek and let their bridles down

Dr. H.G. Duncan (1885-1950).

so the horses could drink. "Chap" broke the dreaded news that he was previously married. She jerked up her bridle and rode around for awhile. Finally she reined up and said, "Let's get going." They were the parents of thirteen children!

(1) Eliza Jane born 18 February 1843, married Matthew Fletcher and is buried at Edgewood cemetery. (2) Alford Wilson born 1 June 1844. (3) Jesse Gwyn born 9 October 1845, died 5 September 1914, buried in family graveyard, married Mary Elizabeth Canter. They were divorced. (4) George Massey born 1 May 1847, died 8 June 1848. (5) Barbara Elizabeth born 24 March 1849, died July 1913, married 11 February 1869 Lytle Harris. (6) Charles Gordon born 3 October 1850. (7) Daniel Scroggs born 27 May 1852, died 31 March 1930, is buried at Moravian Falls, married Eliza Catherine Canter. (8) Christina Adline, born 19 March 1845, died 8 November 1923, buried in family graveyard. The newspaper stated she was the wealthiest woman in the county when she died. (9) Wilson Washington born 18 March 1856. (10) Amelia Susannah born 22 July 1858, married 3 April 1881 William Soffetus Smithey and is buried at Cub Creek. (11) Thomas Binum born 13 January 1860, died 4 March 1928, is buried Cub Creek, married Louise Miller. (12) Chapman Denny born 6 November 1861, died 9 June 1928, is buried Moravian Falls, married first in 1882 Sallie Miller, and second 5 May 1892, Carrie Smithey. (13) Laura Elvira born 14 April 1865, married Cleve Lowe.

The older Duncans were farmers, and good ones at that. They were always experimenting for better soil, seed, cultivation and harvesting. While not all became farmers, the love of growing things remained in them. In different ways they played an important role in the economy of their places of residences.

Jessie, Daniel and Effner were sweet potato growers. Denny was the grape grower, introducing a special white type of grape. Eliza Jane's family turned to orchards. Will Duncan, son of Jesse, grew and marketed truck melons and strawberries. Several branched off into cattle raising.

Barbara Harris's family were at one time or other engaged in merchandising. L. Andrew Harris was a merchant for more than forty years; first at Traphill, then in North Wilkesboro with son-in-law, E.T. Hackney. His son Lee Edward Harris is also a merchant.

The family of Amelia (Millie) Smithey, alone and in conjunction with the Nike Smithey stores, sold goods.

Ralph Duncan, son of Jesse, had a successful business career. He was instrumental in getting phone facilities to Wilkes and founded Duncan Electric Company.

Clate Duncan, son of Denny, established Duncan Insurance Company in North Wilkesboro.

Although Daniel Duncan attended school only two days, his sons head the list of professional men. Hannibal G. Duncan held two doctoral degrees, Th.D and Ph.D. Julius Edgar held an M.D. and practiced until his death in 1930.

Sources: Family *Bibles;* grave markers; Wilkes records; personal knowledge.

— Mrs. Winnie L. Duncan

MISS ANNE MAE DUNCAN
506

Miss Anna Mae Duncan was born July 9, 1904 and reared in Wilkes County. Her parents were William Madison Duncan and Rosie Lou Ferguson Duncan of Moravian Road, Wilkesboro, N.C. Early in life Anne joined the Moravian Falls Baptist Church but later moved her membership to First Baptist Church of North Wilkesboro.

After graduating from Wilkesboro High School, Anne attended for two years Woman's College of the U.N.C. at Greensboro. Holding a Grammar Grade Certificate, she then tried teaching for a very short time but that was not her field. Her advice to young people always was "Be sure to choose a profession you really like or change until you find the right one." Then she took a business course and was secretary for several years with the Deposit and Savings Bank in North Wilkesboro until the merger of this bank in 1937 with the banks in Sparta, Boone, and Bakersville formed The Northwestern Bank, North Wilkesboro, N.C. Under the leadership of President Edwin Duncan, Sr. of Sparta, this bank made phenomenal growth.

One of the few women to become a bank executive in North Carolina at this time, Anne held the position as Assistant Cashier with The Northwestern Bank until her retirement in late 1971. She served in many departments in the bank from keeping the general ledger by hand to consolidating the branch reports. Anne's honesty and pleasing personality gained many friends for both her and The Northwestern Bank. She loved her work and was always ready to serve her customers — rich and poor, black and white — no matter how many extra hours without pay she had to work. This was before the "over time" labor laws. Anne was a

Miss Anne Mae Duncan.

member for many years of The National Association of Bank Women, Inc. and attended many of their conventions.

Since her retirement Anne has traveled extensively touring nine countries in Western Europe, Canada, Mexico and all the U.S.A., except Alaska and Hawaii. Anne has been very active in the North Wilkesboro Woman's Club, having served as Treasurer.

Sources: Family *Bible* and documents, personal knowledge and memories; interviews with family members.

— Anne Duncan

ISAAC PREVETTE DUNCAN
507

Isaac Prevette Duncan was born August 18, 1914, son of Ralph and Pearl Prevette Duncan and brother of Elizabeth Duncan Pittman.

Ralph was a son of Jesse and Mary Canter Duncan. In Wilkes County, Ralph was a leading business man and banker. At one time he was the Manager of Central Telephone Company and in 1906 founded Duncan Electric Co. Friends in the community were always welcomed as they would come in the store seeking his advice on various business matters. Pearl, a daughter of the Rev. Iredell and Alice Call Prevette, has always been well known for her gracious manner and her delicious cooking, especially her pound cakes.

On April 22, 1939, Isaac married Ann Coffey Hartley, a daughter of Frank James and Elizabeth Steele Hartley. Frank was a son of James H. and Julia Ann Coffey Hartley. Before moving to Wilkesboro from Elkville, Frank operated a General Store and Post Office. Lizzie was a daughter of John Calvin and Laura Powell Steele, prominent land owners and farmers of Caldwell County. "Nannie," as she was called by her grandchildren, will always be remembered as a loving and caring person.

Isaac was a graduate of North Carolina State University in Raleigh and Coyne Electrical School of Chicago. Isaac and Ann moved to

St. Louis, Mo. in 1940 with baby daughter Malinda. While in St. Louis, Isaac was connected with White Rogers Electric Company in making airplane controls during World War II. During their residence in St. Louis a daughter, Annette was born. The Duncans returned to North Wilkesboro after the war, when Isaac became associated with his father in the Electrical Construction business, which is now in the 3rd generation of management. Two more daughters arrived at the Duncan home, Nancye Laurice and Susie Jana.

Isaac was widely known for his contribution to the Boy Scouts of America. He was a Life and Eagle Scout and received the Scoutmasters Key and Silver Beaver awards. From 1953 to 1962 he served as District Commissioner in Wilkes County and was active in the Old Hickory Council.

Ralph and Pearl Duncan.

Isaac lived the Scout Motto of Service to God and country. As a member of First Baptist Church, he was a Sunday School teacher, Deacon and served on numerous committees. In his civic contributions he was a past president of the Chamber of Commerce, Kiwanis Club and served on the Board of Directors of Northwestern Bank and Northwestern Financial Corp.

In 1959 Isaac and Ann purchased the Gordon Hackett home at 1102 E. St. North Wilkesboro and began restoration of this historical home. It was completed in 1961, and they were residing there at the time of Isaac's death, March 2, 1978.

Friends and neighbors will remember him for his enthusiasm in organtic gardening and his love of the outdoors. He referred to himself often as "A City Farmer."

The four daughters of Isaac and Ann have varying interests and talents. Malinda Duncan Mori attended Mars Hill College and was a graduate of Wake Forest Univeristy. She received her Master's degree in Social Work from the University of North Carolina at Chapel Hill. Before her marriage to Jason Y. Mori she

Ralph Duncan

The standard question of talk-show hosts is to ask: "How did you choose your profession?" Owen Duncan, Dr. Duncan's eldest son, gave this explanation: Being first born of hardworking farmers, Julius turned to birds and animals for playmates. One day he noticed a young bird had fallen from its nest and broken a wing. He whittled a splint and with a sewing thread bound up the fracture. Carefully he nursed his patient, feeding it a diet of insects and protecting it from marauding cats and dogs. Then came a period of testing until the wing healed. At length after a few wobbly efforts, it was able to rise and fly away. As Julius watched it disappear, he clapped his hands and exclaimed: "I am going to be doctor and mend fractured bones and bruises and bodies."

On Sept. 23, 1908 Dr. Duncan married Minnie Owen of Richmond, Va. Thomas Wolfe once contended that one can never really come home again. Julius did and was contented and happy in his work. He located around 1907-08 in North Wilkesboro. For some years he was associated with Dr. E.M. Hutchens in joint practice. During World War I he volunteered for service and engaged in health work in Eastern North Carolina. During the 23 years of his medical career, he was an integral part of medical practices in Wilkes County. He served as examiner for the Home Guard, served also as a member of the Board of Health and Pension Board.

Dr. Julius Edgar Duncan.

attended the University of Hawaii. Jason and Malinda live in Alexandris, Va. They have two children Jennefer Ann age 14 and Daniel Walker age 9.

Annette Duncan Battle attended Western Carolina College at Cullowee, N.C. and graduated from Patricia Stevens Fashion School, Atlanta, Ga. She married John Bascomb Battle. They reside in North Wilkesboro and have three sons, John Isaac, age 16, Brian Christopher age 13, and Jeffrey David age 8.

Nancye Duncan Johnston attended Mars Hill College, majoring in music and graduated from Dallas Fashion Merchandising College, Dallas, Texas. She is married to Joseph Andrew Johnston, and they live in Wilkesboro, N.C.

Susie Jana Duncan received her BA degree from Appalachian State University in 1981, majoring in Art Marketing. She is currently living in North Wilkesboro, N.C.

May the attributes that characterized Isaac live on in his children and grandchildren.

Sources: Family Records —*Bible* and Memory.

— Mrs. Ann Duncan

DR. JULIUS EDGAR DUNCAN
508

The ancestral roots of Dr. Duncan lie deep in the soil of Wilkes County and deeper in that of Rowan County. Several closely related Kesler women married Wilkes husbands. From these unions came outstanding men as Attorney Charles Gilreath, Dr. Frank Gilreath, Ralph Duncan, Dr. Julius Duncan and Dr. Hannibal Duncan.

In a cabin on a site near what is now Wilkes Country Club, Julius Duncan was born to Daniel Scroggs and Eliza Catherine (Tine) Canter Duncan on Nov. 10, 1875.

For Julius the time was auspicious. Moravian Falls Academy, founded in 1875-76, was in its heyday headed by men the caliber of J.F. Spainhour and Dr. George Green. After graduating here, Julius entered Vanderbilt Medical School at Nashville but later transferred to the University of Medicine at Richmond Va. from which he graduated with honors. His studious habits and his prodigious memory had served him well.

Dr. Duncan's health began to fail in 1929. Despite the fact that all the known practices for fighting cancer were employed, he passed away Aug. 15, 1930. An impressive funeral was held at the First Methodist Church and burial took place at Moravian Falls Cemetery.

It is difficult to estimate the character and human worth of this man; his character had so many facets. His love and consideration for the birds was matched for the solicitude for the horse that had carried him on horseback or by buggy over muddy roads through weather fair and foul.

He was always on call day and night. Once Attorney Gene Trevette cautioned "You won't get a penny for this trip." The answer "Maybe I can be of some help. She needs me." When a generic counterpart would suffice, he prescribed it instead of the brand-named medicine. He was the wealthiest physician in the country.

It was claimed a visit from Dr. Duncan was in itself a boost. His out-going personality made him a good bedside doctor. He had time to listen to a long recital of aches and pains and a bit of conversation. Yet he was known for his careful diagnosis of diseases and the accuracy of treatment.

Although Dr. Duncan had long practiced the tenets of religion he had never committed himself to formalized religion. On March 16, 1930 he united with the First Methodist Church of North Wilkesboro.

There was a lighter side to his personality; he had a passion for playing checkers. Although he dressed in a manner befitting his profession, he was not adverse to shucking off his coat, loosening his tie and rolling up his sleeves for a hard game of checkers. Nor did he mind the appearance of some of his partners.

Perhaps Dr. Fred C. Hubbard sums up Dr. Duncan's career best in his Physicians, *Medical Practices and Development of Hospitals in Wilkes County, 1830 to 1975:* "He had a very active practice and was recognized as one of our outstanding citizens and an excellent doctor."

After her husband's death, Mrs. Duncan resumed her career and served as secretary to Duke Power until her retirement. She was always much interested in her church. For many years she taught an adult class of women in Sunday School. Often she brought one or both of her boys with her. They sometimes added a little levity by improvising pranks when her attention was elsewhere. She passed away March 4, 1954 while reading her *Reader's Digest.*

Two sons survive. Owen married Doris Weat and has two sons — Daniel Edgar and Gary Morrow, and lives in Pageland, S.C. Charles Stuart married Doris Warhold and has four children — Alan Craig, David Owen, Scott Owen, and Janice Lynne. They live in Pittsburgh, Pa.

Sources: Personal knowledge.

— Winnie L. Duncan

WILLIAM MADISON DUNCAN
509

The oldest son of Jesse and Mary Canter Duncan, "W.M." was born on the banks of Cub Creek in Wilkes County, between Oakwoods and Wilkesboro on May 12, 1871. This pioneer family's ancestors had lived in this area for about a hundred years. As a boy he showed aptitude for learning and an intellectual curiosity which remained with him till death. When he tired of the "same things" at the Village School, he asked his mother to help him to attend Moravian Falls Academy. The

Mr. and Mrs. W.M. Duncan (1899).

first installment on the tuition was a bushel of turnips which they carried with them. After graduation from the Academy, he went (on the train) to Lexington, Ky. to enter the Commercial College of Kentucky University where he graduated in June, 1891.

He returned to North Wilkesboro, where he kept books for Sandy McLean and taught school in the Brocktown Community for three years, but decided on a business-like approach to agriculture and horticulture as his life's work.

On December 18, 1898, he married Roxie Lou Ferguson, youngest daughter of Chapman Coffee and Sara Elizabeth Roberts Ferguson of Boomer. Soon after they built a large 2-story white house on the Moravian Road. Together, they operated orchards, wheat and tobacco farms, and a "truck" farm. Before trucks brought in produce, Mr. Will, through experi-

mentation and scientific procedures, was able to supply the two grocery stores (Lenderman's & Dula's) on Main Street in Wilkesboro, and the two (Miller-Long's & Blair's) on Main Street in North Wilkesboro with fresh cabbage, beans, peas, tomatoes, cantaloupes, watermelons, boysenberries, raspberries and strawberries by the basket or crate. His merchandise was always guaranteed. Honesty was his watchword. All five of their children as well as many hired hands and tenants helped in this prosperous farm operation. After supper Will often worked on his accounts and studied farm magazines and government bulletins while Roxie sewed, canned, or ironed. The rewards for the family's diligent work were shopping trips to town, friends in to spend the night, visits to the Circus, church picnics, and whatever "cultural" event came to Wilkes County, as well as the purchase of an organ, surrey "with the fringe on top," a piano, an RCA cabinet radio, a telephone, electric lights, a T-Model Ford, etc.

W.M. was the second clerk in the Moravian Falls Baptist Church, where the entire family attended Sunday School and church services. The children were brought up on the Golden Rule "Do unto others as you would have them do unto you" as well as on the proverbs "Idleness is the devil's workshop" and "Drink (alcohol) leads to destruction."

W.M. and Roxie's standards paid dividends in the five outstanding children they reared: (1) Nellie Elizabeth (Mrs. Rawley M.) Baldock of Roanoke, Va. (2) Miss Anne Mae Duncan of North Wilkesboro (3) Vern (Mrs. Clarence A.) Moser of Lewisville, N.C. (4) Miss Wren Ferguson Duncan of Wilkesboro (5) William Morse Duncan of Wilkesboro.

After Roxie passed away on July 30, 1944, W.M. remained at the old home, reading, gardening, trying out new varieties of fruits and vegetables, taking long walks in the woods, conversing with friends — always urging conservatism in government. Almost 95 years old, he died in his sleep on March 22, 1966.

Sources: Family *Bible* and documents, personal knowledge and memories, and interviews with family members.

— Wren Duncan

WILLIAM MORSE DUNCAN, SR.
510

Born on January 13, 1912, the fifth child of Will and Roxie Duncan was a boy to the great delight of his parents and older sisters. Although a happy and delightful boy, Morse, because of frequent sore throat and diseased tonsils, failed to grow physically. Dr. J.E. Duncan, a cousin, advised removal of tonsils at Dr. White's Clinic in Wilkesboro. Then growth and development were normal until he was, at age eighteen, a handsome six-footer.

Beth Duncan.

Morse Duncan Family. Front: L. to R.: Shaun; Brent. Back: L. to R.: Morse, Sr.; Bill; Mary.

At this age he graduated from Wilkesboro High School. Later he studied poultry farming at State College in Raleigh.

Morse went to work at The American Furniture Company during the "Great Depression" years, becoming the foreman of the finishing department. His work here was interrupted by 3½ years of service with the U.S. Army in the Pacific Theater.

Just after entering the U.S. Army, he was married in July, 1942 to Mary Caldwell, oldest daughter of Johnson and Pearl Yates Caldwell, of Boomer. Their son, William Morse Duncan, Jr. (Bill) was born August 25, 1943, just before Morse left for the Pacific.

Upon his return, he resumed his work at the American Furniture, and he and Mary soon began building their home (near his father's) on the Moravian Road, near Wilkesboro. There their daughter Mary Beth was born August 22, 1949.

A few years later, Morse & Mary bought part ownership in the Blue Ridge Furniture in Wilkesboro. But since his great ambition had always been to have a cattle and poultry farm, he built his poultry houses nearby and resumed the farm life that he had always loved. He was very successful at it too.

Morse's greatest interests in life were his home, wife, two children, and four grandchildren. His second interest was sports. Early in life, he played baseball with the Moravian Team and others. Later he encouraged his children and his grandchildren, Shaun and Brent Duncan and Gam Bates III and Brittain Bates, to participate in sports. "Not just for the exercise," he said, "but for the character lesson in learning to lose without grumbling and win without boasting." Morse and Mary were both active in promoting the Boomer Civic Center.

Because Morse was always ready to lend a helping hand to relatives, neighbors, and friends, never gossiped about anyone, and rejoiced at other's good fortune; he was loved by everyone who came in contact with him. He died suddenly of a heart attack at home on September 13, 1981.

Sources: Family *Bible* and documents, personal knowledge and memories, and interviews with family members.

— Wren Duncan

WREN FERGUSON DUNCAN
511

As a little girl of preschool age, Wren was fascinated by the teaching experiences of her father, W.M. Duncan. After graduating from Moravian Falls Academy and passing the State Teacher's Examination, he taught one year in Wilkes County. Then he graduated from the Business College of the University of Kentucky. After a few more years, he ended his teaching career in the Brocktown Community in 1900 because, to quote him, "I could not make enough money to support my family by teaching three months in the year at $20 — $30 per month. Furthermore, the truck-farming business I had chosen was a year-round job."

In 1915, on the eve of her sixth birthday, Wren asked her parents to let her walk the mile to Moravian Falls School. "You are too small, and besides you don't know your ABC's," they replied. Within the hour she had mastered the ABC's and was permitted to attend school for the first time on her sixth birthday.

After ten years of diligent study she graduated from Wilkesboro High School in 1925, the Valedictorian of her class. In 1929, she earned her AB Degree from the University of North Carolina at Greensboro, having made the Dean's List every year. Later studies were at Northwestern U. and Appalachian State U.

For three years she taught English, French, Latin, Algebra, General Science, Civics, Geometry, and World History, always emphasizing most morality and citizenship. The biggest job there was the cataloging by the Dewey Decimal System of all the library (left over from the Baptist School). This involved reading and discarding all books of theological doctrine. Her work was praised by Dr. J. Henry Highsmith, the State Superintendent of Public Instruction.

In those days the chief amusements were also sources of income for the schools; community plays (which Wren often directed), basketball games, and box suppers.

During the Great Depression of the '30's, many teachers received little or no pay for the 7th & 9th months, because local taxes were not collected. As financial conditions worsened here, Wren accepted a position as a French and English teacher at Fairmont High School, Fairmont, North Carolina.

After six interesting and happy years in that town, she was offered a job in Winston-Salem City Schools. Moreover, when her mother suffered a heart attack, she decided to return to Mountain View for the year 1938-39.

During 1940-41 she taught various subjects in Wilkesboro High School until 1942 when she accepted 8th grade work, a position she held until 1956. Here the physical conditions were often unpleasant, but the school work and the relationships with the students and school personnel were most rewarding.

In 1957 she transferred to Mountain View where one of her first students, Paul W. Gregory, was Principal. She liked the work there so much that in 1960 she moved to North Wilkes High, as a teacher of French and English. At this school she had a good physical plant, the respect of the students (many of whose parents she had previously taught), friendly co-workers, and an excellent principal, who always tempered strictness with fairness and sympathy.

Since her retirement in 1973, Miss Duncan has visited Europe, Mexico, the Western Coast of the United States, and Canada. But the best part of all is returning home, where she encounters former students — lawyers, doctors, nurses, teachers, college professors, electricians, factory workers, business executives — all of whom greet her with a pleasant smile and an enthusiastic, "Miss Duncan, do you remember me?"

Wren is no longer teaching, but she is still an active member of her community, having recently been President of the North Wilkesboro Woman's Club. She also retains an avid interest in the school system.

Sources: Family *Bible* and documents, personal knowledge and memories and interviews with family members.

— Wren Duncan

NATHAN EASTRIDGE FAMILY
512

Nathan Eastridge born 1775, probably a descendant of Abraham Eastridge, pioneer settler of Granville Co., N.C. Nathan appeared in Wilkes County in 1800, in Iredell in 1810, and in Wilkes again in 1820. His homeplace was on Brushy Mountain in the Gilreath community. Nathan sold this farm in 1827 and moved to Ashe Co., where he was living in 1840.

By 1848, Nathan had followed his daughter Elizabeth to Lee Co., Va. where he purchased a 200 acre farm on Cotterell's branch and was living there in 1850.

The children of Nathan and Elizabeth were: (1) Polly born 1798, married Squire Parker 22 March 1819; (2) Winney, born 1800, married Zachariah Tedder 7 Feb. 1817, died 1834, buried on Brushies; (3) Mahalea born 1802, married Benjamin Tedder 6 June 1821, died 1884, buried on Hunting Creek; (4) Delphia born 1811, married Henderson Hubbard 6 Dec. 1827, divorced him 20 Sept. 1850, married Nance Stanley a native of Wilkes and was living in Lee Co., Va. in 1860. In her old age, Delphia returned to Wilkes and lived out her life in a small house on the Brushies.

(5) William born 1812, married Sophia Fender. He was a schoolteacher in Perry Co., Ky. in 1850; (6) Ephriam born 1814, married Susan, moved from N.C.; (7) Elizabeth born 9 Dec. 1818, married William M. Estep; (8) Hiram born 1819, married Katherine, moved to Lee Co., Va.; (9) Frances (Fanny) born 1820 never married, lived with her parents in Lee Co., Va. Left a will dated 8 July 1858. (10) Noah, born 1824 married Milly. Noah died before sister Frances wrote her will.

Sources: Iredell, Wilkes and Ashe census; Lee Co., Va. records; personal contacts.

— Raymond Estep

EDMISTON (EDMONSTON)
513

The Edmiston family settled in Wilkes County before the Civil War. Many of the men fought in the battles and some lost their lives. They were farmers and sawmill operators. Having large tracts of land in western part of Wilkes around Elk Creek, timber was their main business. Each September, John Edmiston's descendants gather for a reunion near Ferguson. Their families are as follows:

John Thompson Edmiston, born 9 June 1802, died 1883, was married three times. His first wife was Susannah Hayes who died in 1842. He married Matilda Minton 5 February 1843 and married her sister Susan Minton Nichols 16 April 1862. His children were: Lousetta; William; born 1838, James Abram born 1825, died 31 October 1863, who married Eleanor Minton 23 July 1853; Margaret (Peggy) who married Joel Church 28 February 1854; Susan who married Deck Joines; Nicie who married Calvin Church 18 February 1851; John, born 21 December 1842; Hannah Martha born 11 August 1844; Minton, born 9 June 1846; Sarah Belinda, born 24 October 1848; Elizabeth Jane, born 8 November 1850; Jessie Franklin, born 16 March 1853, died 13 October 1939; and Delphia Angeline born 28 March 1855.

James Abram Edmiston, Sr. born 1825, died 31 October 1863, married Mary Eleanor Minton 23 July 1853. She was the daughter of Alfred Minton and Betsy Love Minton. James Abram volunteered in the Confederate Army 12 June 1861 at age 36 years. He and Mary Eleanor Minton had children: Alfred, Henderson who married Clarinda Minton 24 February 1880 and James Abram, Jr. born 15 October 1863, died 1941, married Mary Elizabeth Church 2 February 1884, who was the daughter of James Gabriel and Mira Bullis Church.

Children born to James Abram, Jr. and Mary Elizabeth Church Edmiston were: Robert Gaither born 24 July 1885, died 15 October 1952, married first, Belle Watts, second Isabel Church 27 December 1904; James Monroe born 7 October 1887, died 20 May 1954, married Mary Marley 11 May 1907; John Devenreau born 14 April 1890, died 19 August 1959, married Estella Virginia Scott 5 November 1910. She was the daughter of James Pinkney and Sarah Josephine Pearson Scott. Estella was born 9 July 1890; died 2 December 1929.

James Abram, Jr. was raised in the Yadkin Valley in the Goshen community. He was a farmer, cut timber, hauled lumber with a team of horses and worked at a government still.

John Devereau was a sawmiller and farmer all of his life. All his sons helped at one time or another with his work. He was an honorable man and well-thought of in the county. His only hobby of sorts was trading horses and tractors. He took pride in having a fine team of

John D. Edmiston and sons at their log home on Elk Creek.

John D., Annie and their son Dan.

big work horses. Later he enjoyed having a good tractor to work with.

From the background of sawmilling Mr. Edmisten shared with his sons, his eldest son James Howard revolutionized the sawmill industry in N.C. and surrounding states.

John Devereau and Estella Virginia were the parents of nine children: James Howard, born 11 May 1911, married first Beautrice Walsh on 10 June 1930, and after her death, married Nina Triplett 18 December 1977; Joe Fritz, born 24 July 1913, married Dixie Hall 16 December 1933; Vera Helen, born 26 September 1915, first married Fred Russel 25 February 1933. After his death, she married Boone Mikeal 15 April 1978; John Clint, born 2 August 1917, married Opal Walsh 2 October 1940; Hazel Ophelia, born 28 November 1919, married Chester A. Triplett 27 July 1940; William Cody born 18 August 1923, married Edith Triplett 23 October 1923; Virginia Dare, born 31 October 1925, married Chelcie McNeil 20

May 1944; George Scott born 29 January 1928, married Charlotte Marley 9 September 1949; Sarah Elizabeth, born 20 October 1929, married Lester Zelotze Walsh 25 April 1948.

John Devenreau's second wife was Annie Bell Wellborn, born 7 September 1902. They were married 22 October 1930. She was the daughter of Daniel L. and Martha Elizabeth Green Wellborn. They had three children: Mary Lee, born 13 June 1931, who married Thomas Holt 5 November 1962; Daniel Wellborn born 31 March 1934, who married Linda Dare Howell 5 August 1962; and Robert Dean born 23 December 1935 who married Patsy Beatrice Faw 22 July 1961.

James Abram Admiston, Jr.'s fourth child was Charlie born 23 February 1893 and died 10 May 1963. He married Margaret Russel 31 January 1911; the fifth child, Mary never married; sixth child Dora never married; seventh child Floyd born 8 September 1897 married Lydia Golds 21 December 1921; and the last

child, Tom, never married.

Sources: Family records, personal knowledge of Dan and Linda Edmiston.

— Dare Eller Howell

ELLEDGE FAMILY

514

The records show that the Elledge family lived in the present day Warrior Creek section of Wilkes County, North Carolina as early as the 1700s. Due to poor record keeping, little is known of some of the first families.

One of the first well-recorded Elledges was John. He was born in the late 1700s probably in Wilkes County and possibly the son of Jacob Elledge. John was the first Elledge to come to the Mulberry area of Wilkes County. The records state that North Carolina granted John Elledge 150 acres on Mulberry Creek. The transaction was recorded on November 28, 1812. John married an Elizabeth prior to 1800. Their two children were Joseph Ad. and another child (name unknown) who died at an early age.

Joseph Ad. Elledge had two wives during his lifetime. The first was Margaret Roberts whom he married on December 20, 1822. Elizabeth Hawkins, daughter of William and Nancy Adams Hawkins, became Joseph's second wife on October 3, 1843. Joseph and Elizabeth had nine children: (1) Joseph, Jr. — 1839; (2) Benjamin — 1842; (3) James — June 17, 1844; (4) Sarah — November 3, 1845; (5) Nancy — October 2, 1847; (6) Jemima Jane — December 13, 1849; (7) Jacob C. — November 25, 1851; (8) Rhoda — December 9, 1853; and (9) Delilah — March 31, 1856.

Joseph Elledge, Sr. may have had extensive landholdings in the Mulberry area during his lifetime. The records show that between 1849 and 1860 Joseph sold almost 300 acres of land to several of his sons and sons-in-law. Joseph, Sr. also gave one acre of land to Cross Roads Baptist Church to build the church which still stands today in the Mulberry community. The third child of Joseph, Sr. and Elizabeth was James. James married Sarah Ann Sebastian on February 25, 1867 after the Civil War. Sarah was born July 14, 1847 in Wilkes County to William and Eliza Grimes Sebastian. James and Sarah had one son, Abernathy. James fought in the Civil War on the Union side. Many families in Wilkes were split by the Union and the Confederacy during the Civil War as were the Elledges. Sarah's brother, Lewis W. Sebastian, fought for the Confederacy as a Private, Company F, Third Regiment, North Carolina. However, James served in the Union Army, Company H, Tenth Regiment, Tennessee Calvary until the close of the Civil War. During his enlistment, he was wounded in the left arm and carried the bullet the rest of his life.

James and Sarah's only son Abernathy (August 31, 1868 to August 29, 1940) married Martha Jane Hall (March 4, 1871 to April 7, 1964). They were members of Haymeadow Baptist Church in Wilkes County and are buried there. They had a large family of ten children:

Florence Isadoria (b. May 22, 1893, m. 1 Todd Burke, 2. Manley Wiles); James Spencer (b. March 24, 1895, m. Lura Harrold); Nora Weyler (b. October 3, 1897, m. Sam Rhoades); Rheo Doshie (b. February 3, 1900, m. Pedro Brooks); Ransom McKinley (b. March 1, 1902, m. Alice Monday); Ada May (b. November 15, 1904, m. James Rhoades); Winfrey (b. September 20, 1907, m. Marbelle Rhoades); Ira Elmer (b. September 18, 1910, m. Mariann Church); Robert (December 31, 1912 to January 1, 1913); and Charlie Wayne (b. October 16, 1914, m. Opal Pender). Many families in Wilkes can trace their roots to the children of Abernathy and Martha Jane.

Ira, the eighth child of Abernathy and Martha Jane Elledge, married Marian Church on March 30, 1940 and at that time moved from the Mulberry community where he grew up, to Millers Creek where Mariann's family lived. Ira was in World War II from April 1943 to October 1946 and was stationed in England. The war ended one day before he was to be shipped to Japan.

Ira Elledge (Jack is used as a nickname) worked for the Home Chair Company of Wilkes County from 1928 to 1976. At that time he retired as an upholsterer in the furniture industry and began to pursue his long-time nursery business at home. Ira has worked all his life with plants, shrubs, and trees. He and Mariann have run Elledge Nursery in Millers Creek for 36 years. They sold the first shrubs in 1946. He is well known today in Wilkes and surrounding counties for the shrubs and trees which help to make Wilkes so lovely. Ira continues, at the age of 71, to sell shrubs at his home in Millers Creek.

Mariann Church Elledge, wife of Ira, is the daughter of Albert Johnson and Vira Rhoades Church. She is also the granddaughter of Calvin Columbus and Annie Elizabeth Nichols Church, and James Andrew and Mary Jane Bumgarner Rhoades. Mariann is a valuable asset to Ira at home in the nursery business. Also, she worked for Wilkes Hosiery from 1936 to 1953. She has many fond memories of friends and good times there. She has been employed by various other companies in Wilkes County throughout the years and will soon retire from Crawford's Clothing Company of North Wilkesboro.

Ira and Mariann have two children: Nila Jean (b. November 25, 1953, m. James Vernon Johnston on March 2, 1973); and Dennis Wade (b. February 20, 1956, m. Laura Lenoir). The grandchildren are Caleb Matthew Elledge (b. June 10, 1976); Jarrett Alan Johnston (August 4, 1980 — August 6, 1980); and Jeremy Scott Johnston (b. August 7, 1981).

Sources: John Elledge will, family *bible*, census, marriage bonds, and Mrs. W.O. Absher.

— Mrs. Nila Elledge Johnston

GRANT G. ELLEDGE

515

Grant G. Elledge was born July 23, 1872 at the foothills of the Blue Ridge Mountains to Alfred and Elizabeth Rhodes Elledge.

He was a farmer and surveyor for many years, and a deputy sheriff under Clarence Call. In early manhood he took an active interest in church, community, and public affairs. He was a member of Center Baptist Church. He was interested in the schools of Mulberry township and was a school committeeman. He attended Sulphur Springs Academy. He had a great personality and loved people in all walks of life. He did not talk about anyone and called everybody brother and sister. He belonged to the Odd Fellow and Masonic Lodge.

In 1922 he was nominated by the Republican party for sheriff and elected for two terms and served until 1928. He held this office with honor and distinction.

He married Gertrude Jennings on March 3, 1894. To this union were born ten children, one of whom was Coyd M. Elledge who was born July 10, 1895 in Mulberry township.

During Coyd's lifetime, he worked as a surveyor, was county jailor, a candidate for sheriff of Wilkes and was employed in the Veterans Administration Office from 1950 until his retirement in 1970. He married Verna McGrady and they had five children: Edwina, John Grant, Madge, Francis and Sherwin. Coyd M. Elledge died September 1977 of a heart attack.

Grant C. Elledge was ill only three weeks and passed away at Davis Hospital September 12, 1935. His funeral was held and he is buried at Center Baptist Church.

Sources: Personal knowledge, family information.

— Wake Tinsley

THE SHUBA THOMAS ELLEDGE FAMILY

516

Shuba Thomas Elledge was born May 15, 1904, in Wilkes County, N.C., the son of George Washington and Palien Eller Elledge.

He was married March 26, 1932, to Eula Johnson in Mt. City, Tennessee. Eula is the daughter of Thomas Felix and Maude Baldwin Johnson. She was born November 16, 1914, in Wilkes County.

Thomas and Eula were blessed with three children and four grandchildren. Their first born, Wilma Rose born in 1933, married

Arther (A.G. Foster).

Geraldine (Jerry) their second daughter was born in 1940. Jerry married David Vance Nichols. David attended UNC in Chapel-Hill. Jerry, my mom and David, my daddy, had two daughters. Melissa Jayne, born December 2, 1962 and Beverly Lynne, born June 19, 1964.

Thomas and Eula's third child, Robert (Tommy) Thomas, born 1944, in Wilkes County, married Ann Foster. Tommy was drafted to fight in Vietnam. Tommy was injured, but not in combat, and had to return home. Tommy and Ann have two children, Kristi and Darren.

Thomas and Eula moved to Virginia in 1944 for about two years. They returned to Wilkes County and continue to live there. They are known as dependable, trustworthy, caring and hard working people. Thomas and Eula and their children have known times that were good and bad. They all had hardships but also knew how to deal with them. Together they worked the land, did their chores, and always looked out for each other.

Most of their food came from the land. They gathered vegetables from the garden that was well tended. They canned and pickled corn, beans, and cucumbers. Eula is always being praised by her tasty canned fruits, such as preserves and jellies. Pigs are raised for hog killing time. Chickens and cattle are also grown on the farm for food.

There is a small apple orchard near the house with a large garden behind it. The land is covered with tall white pines. You can always find just about every kind of plant, tree or bush around the house.

My grandparents, Thomas and Eula, have and always been good to me, and all of us in and out of the family.

Sources: Family *Bible*, interviews, and personal knowledge.

— Beverly Lynne Mayberry

CHELCIE BAIRD ELLER

517

Chelcie Baird (C.B.) Eller, son of Dr. A.J. and Zora Church Eller, was born December 14, 1900. He attended the local one-teacher school, then attended Mt. View High School, Mars Hill College and North Carolina State College (now North Carolina State University) in Raleigh, N.C. graduating in 1925.

He began teaching and coaching athletics in Warsaw High School in Duplin County in 1925. He moved to Thomasville High School for the school year 1927-28, returning to Warsaw High School as high school principal and athletic coach.

Mr. Eller married Cora Elenoir Holland, daughter of Gideon Gaines and Della Stroud Holland, August 2, 1928.

Mr. Eller was elected superintendent of Wilkes County Schools in June 1933 and served in that capacity until 1966. In 1933, the Wilkes County school system consisted of ninety elementary and nine union schools. (Union schools were schools serving students from beginners to high school graduates.) Of the ninety elementary schools, forty-eigh were one-teacher schools and thirty were two-teacher schools and ten were three-and-four-teacher schools. Of the ninety-nine school, eighty-six served white students and thirteen served black students.

Superintendent Eller realized and was convinced that to improve the educational advantages for the children of Wilkes County, schools must be enlarged and better facilities provided.

This period being in the depth of the great Depression, it was very difficult to secure funds to operate, much less to improve. With a dedicated Board of Education supporting the superintendent, a program of consolidation and improvement was advanced. As fast as space could be provided, roads improved and busses secured, small schools were consolidated with union schools or combined with other elementary schools. Wilkes County was one of the first counties in North Carolina to affect a high school consolidation program.

In 1952, Ferguson and Wilkesboro Union schools were consolidated with North Wilkesboro to form Wilkes Central High School in the North Wilkesboro Administrative Unit. In 1954 Roaring River and Ronda Union schools were consolidated forming East Wilkes High School. In 1956, Mt. Pleasant and Millers Creek Union Schools were consolidated to form West Wilkes High School. In 1957 Mt. View and Traphill Union Schools were consolidated to form North Wilkes High School. During 1965-66, twenty-three schools were operated, three high, one union and nineteen elementary schools.

It is generally conceded that C.B. Eller had a part in more school consolidations than any other educator in North Carolina History.

Mrs. Eller taught fourth grade in Duplin and Wilkes County for twenty years until health conditions forced her retirement. She was very active in the Baptist Church where she taught a lady's Sunday School class for twenty-five years.

C.B. Eller is a Deacon Emeritus in the First Baptist Church of North Wilkesboro, an active Kiwanian, Mason, treasurer of Old Jail, Incorporated, and Secretary-treasurer of the C.O. McNiel Memorial Scholarship Fund.

Sources: personal knowledge.

— Chelcie Baird Eller

THE CLEVELAND ELLER FAMILY

518

Cleveland Eller was born 30 June 1861 to Anderson and Elvira McNeil Eller. They had six children: James Calvin, Simeon, Ambrose, Thomas Cleveland, Rufus Cicero, Carrie and Margaret. Cleveland Eller was married to Mary Jane Church who was born in 1861. He was a blacksmith by trade and died 29 Dec. 1902 at the age of 42, apparently by typhoid fever.

To Cleveland and Jane Eller was born one son, Troy Albert 14 June 1889. He married Bessie Irene Rash on 25 Oct. 1905. She was the daughter of John Clark and Mary Elizabeth McNeil Rash. Troy worked as a furniture and cabinet maker, especially corner cupboards. He was also well known county-wide as a traveling music — singing schoolteacher. He conducted "singing schools" at night in various churches throughout the county. He taught notes and scales using a tuning fork and charts on paper. He died 10 March 1955 of cancer.

Bessie Irene Rash was born 7 July 1886. She was a tiny woman about 5 feet 2 inches tall, weighing about 95 pounds. She had black hair which stayed dark until she was old. She was a very energetic and cheerful woman. She always had a "well starched" look about her. She always wore a fresh, clean apron that stayed clean whether she was hoeing corn or sitting chatting with neighbors.

When I got married she gave me a partial setting of green cherry blossom depression glass. I also inherited the corner cupboard built by my grandfather. She died 27 Jan. 1976.

To Troy and Bessie Rash Eller were born 6 children: Thomas Cleveland, 18 June 1907; William Glenn, 14 April 1909; Russell Johnson; Mary Virginia died at birth; Ella Sue Jane, 28 Feb. 1920; and Troy Albert, Jr., 29 July 1923.

Thomas Cleveland Eller married Myrtle Opal Stoltz on 16 Feb. 1927. He worked as a truck driver for many years before taking up carpentry and brick mason work. He laid the brick on most of the buildings in Millers Creek including the old Millers Creek School, fire department, postoffice, Lovettes and Arbor Grove Methodist Church where he was an active member and Sunday school teacher until his health failed. He was an avid fisherman and hunter. He trained bird dogs for many people as well as himself. Thomas Cleveland Eller died 16 May 1982 and is buried at Arbor Grove United Methodist Church.

Myrtle Opal Stoltz was born in Forsyth County 23 Sept. 1909 to Julius Ulysses Stoltz born 22 Sept. 1867, died 2 Dec. 1943 and Ann Eliza Merrit born 6 April 1873, died 1 March 1937.

Julius Stoltz, son of Rev. Thomas Stoltz, was a German. He originally owned and operated an emporium in Salem, N.C. He and Ann had three children: Irlene, Opal and Bud. They lived in Salem until they sold their store and moved to Millers Creek in Wilkes County, N.C.

At the age of 16, Opal Stoltz went to a revival meeting at the old Millers Creek Methodist church. When Thomas Eller walked in the door she commented to the girl sitting beside her, "There comes the man I'll marry." The girl sitting beside her was Tom's cousin, Daisy McNeil, who after the service introduced them. Six months later they were married.

They had 8 children: (1) Thomas Cleveland Eller born 3 Feb. 1928 married Frances Dillard. They have 5 children: Geraldine, Patsy, Lynn, Tereasa and Lisa, deceased. (2) Richard Glenn Eller born 27 June 1929 married Betty   ? and they had four children. (3) Rose Ellen born 13 April 1931 married Warren Ellis and they have three children, Angel, Bill and Melissa. (4) James Roosevelt born 25 April 1933 married Dare Wingler and they had one daughter, Linda. (5) John Clinton born 15 May 1937 married Shelby Wade and they have two children, David and Mark. (6) Troy Albert III born 14 June 1940 married Twila Church and they had a daughter, Gail. (7) Cynthia Anne born 16 Feb. 1945 married Sam Elledge and they have two children, Tamara and Sheri. (8) Cecil Clayton born 31 August 1947 married Judy Brown and they have two children, Vicki and Wendy.

Sources: Genealogical research and personal knowledge.

— Anne Eller Elledge

ERNEST A. ELLER

519

It is believed that George Michael Eller arrived in America from the Palatinate of Germany and took his Oath of Allegiance on October 7, 1743. George Michael Eller died in Frederick County, Maryland before August 25, 1778.

George Michael Eller had a son, Peter born about 1746. He married about 1766, Elizabeth Dick, daughter of Conrad and Katherine Dick of Frederick Co., Maryland. Peter died in 1799 in Ashe County, N.C.

Ernest and Geneva Eller.

Peter had a son John who was born about 1767. John married Susannah Kerns on November 5, 1792. Susannah died April 10, 1853. John died in 1823. John and Susannah had 8 children. One of the children was Absolom Eller who was born February 17, 1803. He married Sally Reynolds on March 1, 1824. She was born February 16, 1805. The farm of Absolom and Sally Eller was located on Parlears Creek.

Sally died March 6, 1875 and Absolom died February 7, 1879. Absolom and Sally had ten children. One of whom was James Madison Eller born June 17, 1840. James married Nancy Louise Vannoy. James and Nancy ran a store where they hauled merchandise by horse and wagon from Statesville, N.C. James and his family were very interested in education. They let young men and women live with them so that they could go to New Hope Academy. They had eight children. James Madison Eller died July 15, 1920.

One of James' sons was William Thomas Eller born August 29, 1869 at the old home place. He went to school at New Hope Academy, then taught school a few years. He married Nora Robinette from the Stoney Fork Creek Community October 2, 1902. Tom and Nora moved to a farm near New Hope Church in 1917. Tom died on December 4, 1936. He was buried in the New Hope Cemetery. They had six children, the first 3 at Roaring River.

(1) Vernon was born on April 29, 1904, married Bessie Lovette in 1923. He was ordained a Baptist Minister in 1936. Five children were born to this union: Mabel, born 1923, died 1972; Frances, born October 21, 1925; Gilbert, born June 29, 1928; Rex, born December 22, 1930; and Glenn, born 1933, died in 1958.

(2) Viola was born November 6, 1905. She attended college at Boone, N.C. for one year and received a teacher's certificate. She married Charles Combs in 1929. Eleven children were born to this union: Marie, born January 20, 1930; Blanche, born November 6, 1931; Nora, born June 22, 1932; Tommy, born in 1933; Roberta, born July 16, 1935; Sarah, born May 3, 1937; Louise, born May 12, 1941; Patsy, born June 15, 1943 — died at birth; Lewis, born June 21, 1944; Barbara, born April 10, 1947; and Steve, born July 14, 1949.

(3) Clyde was born May 7, 1907. He married Nora Belle Faw in 1929. Thirteen children were born to this union: Ernestine, born in 1931; Franklin, born in February, 1933; Philmore, born in May, 1934; Willie, born September 27, 1935; Lorene, born November 7, 1937; Richard, born September 7, 1939; Christina, born August 18, 1941; Marvin, born March 29, 1943; Jimmie, born December 19, 1944; Arlene, born September 22, 1946; Harold, born January 5, 1949; Max, born November 20, 1950; Maxine, born February 5, 1953.

(4) Electra born October 2, 1913 at Beaver Creek. She graduated from Mount Pleasant High School in 1931. She married Clifton Goodwin in 1935. Two children were born to this union: Betty Jean born February 18, 1939 and R.C. born March 5, 1937.

(5) Edna was born October 12, 1920 at Purlear, N.C. She graduated from Millers Creek School in 1937, and married Joe McNeil. One daughter was born to this union: Juanita, born October 16, 1939. Edna and Joe were divorced and she married Ernest Martin on September 12, 1945. Three children were born to this union: Bronda, born September 17, 1946; Judy, born May 15, 1949; and Pat (son) born on February 21, 1957.

(6) Ernest A. was born September 28, 1915 at Beaver Creek. He grauated from Mount Pleasant School in 1934, and married Geneva Faw on September 15, 1942. She is the daughter of James T. and Ettie Faw. They went to Camp Cook in California where he was stationed in the U.S. Army. They came back to Wilkes County in 1943. Ernest is a retired poultry farmer. Geneva worked at Wilkes General Hospital for 13 years. Three sons were born to this union: Larry Ernest; Earl Thomas; and David James.

Larry Ernest Eller was born on August 6, 1944. He graduated from West Wilkes High School in 1962. Since November, 1962 he has been employed by Central Telephone Company. On August 2, 1963 he married Helen Moore, daughter of Archie William and Rozella Chambers Moore. Helen has been secretary at the First United Methodist Church since 1969. Larry is Fire Chief at the Millers Creek Volunteer Fire Department. Two children were born to this union: Tammy Renee, born November 7, 1967 and James Larry, born April 7, 1971.

Earl Thomas Eller was born March 28, 1946. He graduated from West Wilkes High School, and from Mars Hill College. He majored in physical education and for several years was head football coach at North Wilkes High School, but is now Athletic Director. He was married in 1969 and a daughter, Kristy Jane Eller, was born on January 7, 1976.

David James Eller was born October 21, 1949. He graduated from West Wilkes High School and joined the U.S. Army on September 17, 1969. On October 21, 1970, he was sent to Viet Nam. He married Susan Woods October 21, 1978, daughter of Carroll M. and Betty Ernest Woods. Since 1976 David has worked at Hayes Print and Stamp Company. Susan is a secretary at the Abitibi Corp.

Sources: Eller Family History, by Mrs. Nora Robinette Eller.

— Helen M. Eller

JAMES MADISON ELLER
520

James Madison Eller was born June 17, 1840, the son of Absalom Eller, who was born February 17, 1803 and died 7 February 1879, and Sally Reynolds Eller, who was born February 16, 1805 and died March 6, 1875. James Madison married Nancy Louise Vannoy. Eight children were born to this union: Albert Johnson, Thomas, Matilda, Rebecca, Ethel, Mae who died young, John G., and Sally who died in infancy.

The family lived on a large farm on the north prong of Lewis Fork Creek in Stanton Township near New Hope Baptist Church and the early New Hope Academy. James Madison operated a tannery that produced leather for shoes and harness for work animals. He also operated a retail store.

He was very much interested in education, a strong supporter of the New Hope Academy, and kept most of the teachers that came to the community to teach in the school. James Madison died July 15, 1920 and was buried in the family cemetery on a high hill facing the family home.

Albert Johnson Eller, the oldest son of James Madison Eller, was born December 2, 1867. He attended New Hope Academy and studied under other teachers in the county. He graduated from College of Physicians and Surgeons, Baltimore, Maryland in 1893 and began general practice of medicine at Ready Branch Community in Lewis Fork township in western Wilkes County.

He married Nancy Zora Church September 2, 1894, the daughter of Linsy Lafayette and Elizabeth Simmons Church.

For many years his mode of travel was by horse back, but in spite of this he served the people over a large area of western Wilkes County. To serve as many people as possible, he would travel to an area on a specific day. For example, he would go on Monday to the Stony Fork area and on Tuesday, the Congo area. The people knew his schedule and would leave word for him at key places in the community or homes of critically ill people where they knew he would be visiting.

At that time there was a considerable amount of typhoid fever and other contagious diseases. He realized the need and importance of vaccinations to prevent contagious diseases so when these vaccines became available he promoted, encouraged, and administered them. Mrs. Eller learned how to administer some of these vaccines and was a big help with the program.

The closest dentist was in North Wilkesboro, thirteen miles away, so he pulled a lot of teeth. Mrs. Eller helped him. So many came to

James Madison and Nancy Louise Vannoy Eller.

Dr. Albert Johnson Eller.

his office and home that she began to pull teeth. For years she pulled more aching teeth than he did.

With drug stores also thirteen miles away, it was necessary for him to keep a supply of medicine in his office and to carry a supply in his saddle bags as he visited patients.

In 1931 he accepted the position as Wilkes County Health Officer and served in that capacity until his retirement in 1950. As health officer he joined forces with "an angel of mercy," Mrs. Bertha Bell, public health nurse. They promoted inoculations of students and adults against contagious diseases. They screened children for defects and literally combed the county for crippled children. With the help of the Kiwanis Club and other agencies, they were able to get many children in orthopedic hospitals for corrections.

Born to Dr. and Mrs. Eller were a daughter, Vera Faustina Eller, born September 10, 1895, a son, Chelcie Baird Eller, born December 14, 1900, and a son, Wayne Vannoy Eller, born November 24, 1904.

Vera attended Appalachian Training School at Boone, and Meredith College in Raleigh, N.C. She married Andrew Casey June 28, 1919, after he returned from military service. They went to Washington, D.C., where she worked in the Registered Mail department of the Postal Service. When they returned to North Wilkesboro, she taught in the public schools for four years. After Andrew's death she accepted a position with the Wilkes County Department of Social Services, primarily in child welfare work, and continued in that position for 24 years until her retirement in 1967. She lives in North Wilkesboro and will be 87 years old her birthday in September, 1982.

(See Chelcie Baird Eller and Wayne Vannoy Eller in separate story).

Sources: Personal knowledge.

— Chelcie B. Eller

THE JOHN ELLER FAMILY
521

John Grover Eller, son of James Madison and Louisa Vannoy Eller, was born Jan. 4, 1886. He married Ethel Beatrice Jones on Dec. 24, 1906. Ethel Beatrice Jones was born Dec. 20, 1890. She was the daughter of Robert and Mary Elizabeth Hall Jones. They spent their entire lives (John died Jan. 1, 1953; Ethel on Oct. 6, 1964) near his birthplace on the North Prong of Lewis Fork Creek. After teaching in the public school system of Wilkes County for one year, John was engaged in the lumber industry, cattle raising and farming.

They reared a large family — fourteen children who survive at this writing: (1) Gwyn Jones b. Feb. 24, 1908, married Ola Staley. They have two children — Gwendolyn married West Nickelow and they have three children (Celeste, Wendy and Christie), and Colbert who married June Rhyne and they have one daughter, Melody. (2) Charles Clinton, b. July 31, 1909, married Connie Scott. They have one daughter Patsy. Patsy married Athel Phillips and they have two children. Alisa, who married Ricky Pierce and Kevin, a student at Appalachian State University. (3) Ruth Irene, b. June 3, 1912 married Joe Mikeal. They had three daughters. Betty, single; Wilma who married James Fairchild and they have three boys — Jeffery, Mark, and Anthony; Shirley married Dean Brown. They have two boys, Mikeal and Eric. After the death of Dean, Shirley married Bill Johnston and they have a daughter Tonya. After the death of Joe Mikeal, Ruth married Raford Triplett. They had four children. Roy Triplett married Pansy Bowman and they have two children, Dora Lee and Lynn. Roy is presently married to Shirlyn. Clay Triplett married Christine Kokot. They have one daughter, Darlene. Clay is now married to Lois Prine. They have a daughter Heather. Johnny Triplett was killed in Vietnam. Linda Triplett married James C. Morrison. They have two children — Kenneth and David.

(4) Ruby Lee, b. Aug. 2, 1913, married Joe Greer. Their son, Billy Joe married Ruth Reeves. They have three children — Clara Joe, who married Tommy Earp, had one son Thomas Stuart. Clara Joe is now married to Tommy Miller. Diane married Johnnie Childress. Charles is single. After the death of Joe Greer, Ruby married Clate Greer, now deceased. (5) Florence Vivian, b. April 15, 1915, married David Reddish. After his death, she married Hyman Hagopian. (6) Lucy Marie, b. Feb. 22, 1917, married Javan Byrd. They had a daughter Janet who was killed in an automobile accident. Later, Marie married Harris Brewer, now deceased. (7) Myrtle, b. April 20, 1918, is single and lives at the homeplace. (8) Edna Beatrice, b. Oct. 6, 1919, married Edd Hipps. They have two children — Dean, who married Lavitta   with two children, Scotty and Tiffany, and Elenor who married Edd Franklin, with two children, Paige and Ross. (9) Mattie Lou, b. Feb. 15, 1921, married Herbert Minton. They have four children: Herbert Jr., Virginia (single), Kenny who married Holly Wilkerson and had one child (Emily), and Barbara. (10) Fred Forrest, born Aug. 21, 1922, is

single. (11) James Robert, b. July 15, 1926, married Nancy Yates. They have three children: James Robert, Jr. (single); Gary, who married Candice Crosby (they have a daughter Laura); and Christal. James is presently married to Frances Lovette Hinshaw. (12) Edythe, b. April 10, 1928, married Richard Levine. They have a daughter, Stephanie. (13) John Lester, b. Jan. 30, 1929 married Helen Ford. They have three children — Clara Lee married John Ullrich and has one child, John Christopher; Ruby married Allen Perry; and John married Sheva Heff and has two children, Johnny, III and Tommy. (14) Albert Grayson, b. Oct. 18, 1933, married Velma Brown. They have three children: Nita who married Tex Simmons and has one child, Elizabeth; Tena who married Kurt Noel; and Timothy who is single.

Sources: Personal Knowledge.

— Mr. Clinton Eller

JOHN W. ELLER
522

John W. Eller was born September 29, 1875, the son of Mary Ann Eller. On November 5, 1899 he married Cora Bell Kilby, born December 15, 1879, who was the daughter of John Jackson Kilby and Martha Jane McNeil Kilby. They lived their entire lives in Wilkes County at Millers Creek. They had ten children, Nellie, Albert, Dessie, Arlie, Belva, Conrad, Lawson, Eula Mae, Clara and Ernest. All the children were delivered by the same physician, Dr. J.M. Turner, who drove a horse and buggy for seven miles and some time had to spend the night before his mission was accomplished.

John had a farm, which the children mainly tended, while he ran a country store and also a livery stable and camp ground for travelers who could not make it into the Wilkesboros in one day.

In 1918 three of the family died of influenza only a few days apart. Many Dessie born January 18, 1904 died October 19, 1918; John, October 24, 1918; and Eula Mae born July 20, 1913, died November 8, 1918. It was an uncertain year, families dying all around. None were able to attend funerals, so memorials were held after the flu died down.

After John's death, Cora had a hard time raising and keeping the rest of the family together. She had pride and managed without asking for help. Work was not plentiful and most of her living was made on the farm. Cora had some very good years after she raised her family. On July 8, 1950 she died with cancer at the age of 71.

Conrad Manus born May 25, 1909, died in 1935. He joined the Navy in 1927 and was discharged in a year or so with tuberculosis. He came home for a short time, then decided to go to New Mexico for his health. He only lived a short time and never married.

Albert Vester born October 5, 1902, died July 2, 1968. He was married to Agnes Pearson, September 27, 1937. They had three children: Kenneth who married Nancy Rhodes; Catherine married Robert Anderson, Jr.; and Phillip, who was killed in an automobile accident, September 25, 1968, the same year his father died.

Ernest born January 7, 1918, died August 10, 1977. He married Ila Church April 12, 1941. They had five children: Jack who married Shirley McNeil; Steve married Sandra Eller; Peggy married Jim Murry; Tony lives with his mother in North Wilkesboro and Neil, who died in a sleighing accident at the age of 13.

Five of the children are still living. Belva and Lawson, still live on the farm land in Millers Creek where the family was raised.

Nellie VeNora (Nell) born February 22, 1901, married Ruffus Luther Hendren August 20, 1920. They had one daughter, Margaret Rebecca. On June 20, 1943, Nell married Thomas M. Green and now lives in Charlotte, N.C. Margaret married Carr L. Miller; they were divorced. She later married Cecil H. McEachin; now divorced.

James Arlie born January 16, 1906, married Theresa Beck, October 28, 1933. They had six children: James Arlie, Jr., who married Emma Ann Smith; Patricia, Rose married Walter Mason King; Andrew married Wynona Jones; Timothy and Anthony. Arlie joined the Navy at age 21 and remained there until he retired after 30 years of service. Norfolk, Virginia has been the family's home.

Belva Dean born August 9, 1907 was married May 8, 1927 to Nat K. Tolbert from Stokes County. They were married in High Point, N.C. and lived there several years. They came back to Wilkes County in 1936 and built a home on part of the Eller farm. They had four sons: Jimmy married Jamie Clark; Max married Linda Jean Hayes; William (Bill) married Alan Bumgarner, and Gary married Deborah Miller.

John Lawson born April 21, 1911, married Mary Hester Clark February 19, 1957, who is also from Wilkes County. They have two sons John and James. Both are living at home. Lawson built a home on the same spot where the first Eller home stood.

Clara Luzell, born June 13, 1915, married John R. Prevette of Wilkesboro September 3, 1966. They live in Charlotte, N.C.

Having grown up in a community where homes were so far apart, the Eller family was very close. Communication was very difficult because of the distance between families. Although the family is scattered, today the family is still close.

Sources: Family *Bible,* personal knowledge.

— Belva Tolbert

THOMAS GAITHER ELLER FAMILY

523

Thomas Gaither Eller is a fifth generation descendant of George Michael Eller, who at the age of 20 arrived in America on the ship *St. Andrew* or *Pheonix* from Rotterdam in 1743. The descending family line developed through: (1) Peter and Elizabeth Dick Eller; (2) Peter, Jr. and Mary Ann Pennington Eller; (3) Nancy Eller; (4) James Madison and Eliza Camilla Roberson Eller; to (5) Thomas Gaither Eller.

Thomas Gaither and Martha Walsh Eller.

Gaither was the oldest of the seven children of James Madison and Eliza Camilla Eller. His brothers and sisters were: Sophia Elmira (1867-1953) married Thomas J. Walsh and lived in the State Road area of Wilkes County. William Hamilton (1870-1949) married Mirtie Lee Haire and lived in the Purlear community of Wilkes. Lloyd Eller (1872-1941) married Doshie Walsh and lived in the Beaver Creek area of Wilkes. They had no children and are buried in the German family cemetery. Malona V. (1876-1943) married John F. German and lived in the Beaver Creek area and buried in the German family cemetery. John was born 1878, married Nellie Jones and lived in Jonesville, N.C. Green More (1882-1974) married Martha Walsh, a sister of Lloyd's wife Doshie.

My grandfather, Gaither Eller, was born May 19, 1866 and died February 19, 1937. He was married on March 20, 1898 to Martha Ann Walsh, the daughter of Bennet Hall and Sarah Ann Melton Walsh. Gaither and Ann lived and farmed in Beaver Creek, Stony Point in Alexander County, Butner, Virginia and returned to a Wilkes County farm of Mr. Sankie Steelman, where he died of pneumonia after thrashing out grain that had been covered with soil during a flood of the nearby Yadkin River. This farm was in the community known as Adley, in the area where the W. Kerr Scott Dam was built. The Adley post office, Methodist Church, Adley school and the house where Grandmother Eller sold candy and other treats to the community children are now gone. Gaither and Ann were blessed with eight children:

Sophia Camilla (1899-1964) married Jesse A. Walsh, who was a carpenter. They were active workers in the Goshen Baptist Church where he was a deacon and church clerk; they are buried in the church cemetery. Their children are William Warren, Annie Ruth W. Hori, Wade Terrill, Grace Edith W. Boyd, Helen Irene W. Spaulding, Fannie Faye W. Walker, Sophia

Pauline W. Kilby, Jesse Alonzo, Jr., Jerry Thomas, and Homer Calvin Walsh.

Sarah Arizona, born November 11, 1899, married Grover C. Johnson from Alexander County, N.C. They lived in Wilkesboro. Their children are Mildred J. Woodruff; Devola J. Walsh, Edward Johnson, Ernest Johnson and Marjorie J. Garner.

Thomas Irving, born April 23, 1903, married Sally Severt and lives in Moravian Falls. Irving was a brick mason. Sally and Irving have been faithful workers in the Moravian Falls Baptist Church where he has been a deacon for many years. They have two sons, Thomas Irving, Jr. and Robert Calvin Eller.

Tempa Lucinda, born March 13, 1905, first married Robert DeGueere and second George Borland. She works as a beautician and lives in Elkton, Maryland. Tempa has a daughter, Roberta DeGueere Wallace.

Annie Evelyn, born December 1, 1906, married Thomas R. Goodson. She worked for a furniture company and Tom worked for the Southern Railroad. They live in Hickory, N.C.

Willard Rayvaughn, April 16, 1909 — June 8, 1978, was a brick mason. He married Gertrude Mae Johnson, his childhood sweetheart. Gertrude taught school for 36 years in Wilkes County. They lived in the Brown's Ford area west of Wilkesboro. They had a daughter Jewell Christine, wife of William Glenn Walker, and a grandson Glenn Rayvaughn Walker.

Lafayette Bennet "Fate," born November 15, 1911, served in the U.S. Army during World War II and later married Elmina Roope. They have a son, Kenneth Doyle, who married Judy Goode. Fate and his family live in Lenoir, N.C. where he worked as mechanic, drilled wells and sold office equipment.

Edgar Eugene Eller, born February 6, 1919 and served in the U.S. Army during World War II. He also became a brick mason. Edgar is married to Marie Joines and they live in the

Goshen community of Wilkes. Their children are Danny, Dianne, Wayne and Michael Eller.

The three brothers — Irving, Willard, and Edgar — spent many hard working, but happy hours together as brick layers. Most of their work was in Wilkes County building schools, churches, business offices and many homes.

Sources: Wilkes County census, family memories, family *Bible*, grave markers, interviews with family members.

— Christine Eller Walker

VIRGINIA VANNOY ELLER
524

William Albert Forester served two years in the Civil War. At the end of the war, he returned to Wilkes County and married Sarah Virginia Forester, whom he had met before leaving to enlist in the army. Their children were: Fidel (F.D.), who married Geneva Adams; Dianne Addieline, who married William Allen Vannoy; Virgle Dean who married Eva Tulbert; Ida Isabell, who married Brevard Raymer; Floyd (Tom) Commodor, who married Line (Mamie) McLean; and Cora Alverde, who married Ben Colvard first. Ben Colvard married Cora Taylor second after Cora Alverde died.

Dianne Addieline Forester was born 22 May 1873, died 21 April 1923. She married William Allen Vannoy, who was born 4 April 1868 and died 21 March 1927, and had two children, Virginia Elizabeth and William Albert.

Virginia Elizabeth Vannoy was born 4 November 1903, married Isaac Milton Eller, Sr. on 6 January 1922. Isaac Milton was born 9 July 1900 and died 10 May 1941, the son of Osco Freeland and Amy Elvira McNiel Eller. Virginia's second marriage was to Zollie Osco Eller, brother to Isaac Milton, who was born 4 April 1895 and died 16 September 1960, after being a widow for nineteen years. Virginia is a good businesswoman as well as a devoted mother to her five sons. Both of her husbands were well known merchants.

Born to the union of Virginia Elizabeth Vannoy and Isaac Milton Eller, Sr. are the following: (1) Isaac Milton Eller, Jr. born 17 February 1923, married Frances Mozeal Crawford 7 December 1940, daughter of James M. and Eula Burgess Crawford. They have two sons, James Milton and Thomas Latham. (2) Jack Vannoy Eller, born 15 May 1925, married Edna Bell Miller 10 June 1946, daughter of Rufus John and Stella Miller. (3) Mack Allen Eller, born 1 January 1928, married Vida Alice Joines 21 April 1945, daughter of Frank and Eva Joines. Their children are Michael Allen, Robin Camille, and Kelly Gray. (4) William Osco Eller, born 28 October 1929, married Nancy Sue Absher, 29 June 1948, daughter of O.O. and Della Rhodes Absher. They have two children, Nancy Claudia and William Absher. (5) Joe Thomas Eller, born 19 October 1931, married Carol Delores Wilson 3 June 1957, daughter of Floyd and Flossie Wilson. Their children are Dianne Carol and Glenn Thomas.

Sources: Vannoy and Eller *Bibles*.

— Dare Eller Howell

W.H. and MERTIE HAIRE ELLER
525

William Hamilton Eller, who was born 24 April 1870, was the son of James Madison (Matt) and Eliza Camilla Roberson Eller, daughter of David and Temperance Peasley Roberson.

William Hamilton Eller, better known by his friends as "Ham," was married 5 April 1896 to Mertie Lee Haire, daughter of James M. and Susan Walters Haire. The marriage ceremony was performed by Rev. W.H. Hamilton for whom William Hamilton Eller was named. James Mumford Haire, a Civil War veteran, was the son of Perry Haire who was killed during the Civil War. Susan Walters was the daughter of Lewis and Chloey Walters of Ashe County, N.C. It is believed that Chloey's family came to the United States from Holland.

"Ham" and Mertie Lee first lived on Beaver Creek near Ferguson, N.C. where their first two children, Phinas Hamilton and Katie Susan were born. They bought a large farm in the Purlear community from J.H. Johnson, sheriff of Wilkes County at that time, and they raised their family and lived out their lives on this farm.

To this union was born three more children: a son, William Walter, and two daughters, Maymie Camilla and Mertie Agnes Eller.

(1) Phinas Hamilton married Cecil Teague and they were the parents of Evelyn, Clarence, Tracy, Mertie Lee, and Georgia. (2) Katie Susan married J.F. Hayes. Their children were Hazel and Joan. (3) William Walter married Beatrice Parsons and they had one son, Billy. (4) Maymie married Robert Kerr and they had two sons, Robert, Jr. and Tommy. They live in Durham, N.C. (5) Mertie Agnes married J. Van Caudill and they had one son, John Alvan.

New Hope Baptist Church at Purlear and its functions was a big part of this family's life along with all sorts of games and activities that took place in the home. Their home was a place where the young people in the community liked to gather to sing, play and just have a good time.

Love and respect were taught in Ham and Mertie's home and it was known as a place where anyone needing help, a place to stay or food to eat was welcome.

The people of Purlear began to see a need for another church in their settlement. The community was growing and it was a four mile walk to New Hope Baptist Church (walking was the only way most people had to travel). Ham along with many of the neighbors gave materials, money, time and labor and in 1932 the Purlear Baptist Church came into being. Ham, Mertie, and some of their children were among the charter members of this new church.

Ham died 2 October 1949 and Mertie Lee followed him in death 1 August 1952. They are buried in the cemetery at Purlear Baptist Church.

Sources: Family *Bible* and personal knowledge.

— Agnes E. Caudill

WAYNE VANNOY ELLER
526

Wayne Vannoy Eller, born November 24, 1904, was the youngest child of Dr. and Mrs. Albert Johnson Eller of Ready Branch, N.C. He attended Mountain View School, Appalachian Training school and N.C. State College, class of 1928. He worked for Reynolds Tobacco Company for thirty-three years beginning in 1931, as a salesman in Bluefield, West Virginia. In 1936, he became division manager in Evansville, Indiana. From 1941 to 1943 he was assistant department manager of the Winston-Salem department and in 1943, he became departmental sales manager for New York City, New Jersey, Pannsylvania, Delaware and part of Maryland and Ohio. He maintained offices in Philadelphia and New York.

In 1952 he returned to Winston-Salem to do general staff work and travelled throughout the United States for Reynolds. He became field sales coordinator for them in June of 1956 and continued working in that capacity until his death June 23, 1964.

Wayne Eller was a member of the Masonic Order, Phi Pi Phi Fraternity, the Presbyterian Church, Oldtown Club in Winston-Salem, and was active in the Chamber of Commerce. His hobbies were sports, woodworking and gardening.

He was married to Julia Thelma Holland of Warsaw, N.C. on December 19, 1931. She was born October 30, 1908, the younger daughter of Gideon Gaines and Della Stroud Holland. She was an alumna of Peace College and East Carolina Teachers College and was an elementary school teacher at the time of her marriage. She was active in the Woman's Club, her church work and enjoyed music, bridge, gardening and antiques.

Wayne and Thelma Eller had two daughters: Elizabeth Ann Eller, born July 26, 1934, and Martha Eleanor Eller, born July 17, 1940.

Elizabeth (Libby) graduated from Duke University in 1956 and was married to Henry Maddrey (Penny) Booke on December 27, 1955. He was born November 9, 1933, was a 1956 graduate of N.C. State College in industrial engineering. After a year of graduate training at the University of Michigan, he served for two years as a lieutenant in the U.S. Army in Germany.

In 1959 following army service the Bookes returned to Winston-Salem, N.C. where Penny began work with Wachovia Bank in the area of data processing. In 1972 he joined the family firm of Booke and Company, where he has established a Defined Contributions Division of the pension service company.

Community affairs have been a major interest of the Bookes. Libby has served on the boards of several arts organizations and has been president of the children's Theatre Board and the Arts Council of Winston-Salem. She is also active in church, civic and school activities. The Bookes are members of the First Presbyterian Church, Old Town Club and the Twin City Club.

They have two children, Henry Madrey Booke, Jr., born November 2, 1963 and Martha Eller Booke, born May 13, 1966.

Martha Eleanor Eller graduated from Duke University in 1962 and was married to Lewis Sterling Kunkel, Jr. of Harrisburg, Pa. on March 23, 1963. Lewis Kunkel was born July 4, 1937 and was a 1958 graduate of Princeton University and a 1961 University of Pennsylvania Law School graduate. He is a partner in the law firm of Pepper, Hamilton and Schutz of Philadelphia.

After living in Philadelphia for several years they moved to Harrisburg in 1969 when Lewis opened a branch office for the firm in the state capitol.

The Kunkels are very active in community affairs in the Harrisburg area. Martha has worked with the regional council of the Governor's Justice Commission, the Junior League, the Y.W.C.A. and the Family and Children's Service. Lewis has been chairman of the Board of Trustees of the Harrisburg Academy, and serves on the Harrisburg Hospital Board and other professional organizations.

The Kunkels have three children: Lewis Sterling Kunkel III, born October 14, 1964, Lucy Forsythe Kunkel, born October 1, 1966, and Elizabeth Holland Kunkel, born November 30, 1967. The family belongs to the St. Stephens Episcopal Church, and they live in an old restored farmhouse in Mechanicsburg, Pennsylvania.

Sources: Eller history, personal letters, and clippings, personal knowledge.

— C.B. Eller
and Libby Eller Booke

ZOLLIE OSCO ELLER
527

Zollie Osco Eller (1895-1960), a descendant of George Michael Eller, was the first son of Osco Freeland Eller (1874-1939), grandson of Jacob Eller.

Zollie Osco Eller and Ella Vetra Pierce Eller.

Zollie Osco Eller married Ella Vetra Pierce (1892-1958) 24 December 1914. Their material worth consisted of one good wagon and a pair of mules named France and Maude; cash asset of $60.00. They started housekeeping in a one room log cabin near Millers Creek. Their only child was born 7 February 1916, and was named Vetra Dare. Being the only able bodied man to work the farm, my daddy was excused by the draft board as World War I was in full swing. When cold weather came, he went to the coal fields of West Virginia to make extra money. After three weeks of digging coal, he became home sick for his wife and baby, so he returned to the farm. In 1920, the three of us moved to North Wilkesboro. My mother was a good cook, seamstress, civic worker and dedicated to church work. Daddy drove an oil truck for several years, later owned and operated a grocery store and hatchery. One of his hobbies

was taking his beagles out to hunt rabbits when he came in from work. He and Mother also enjoyed traveling.

My grandmother, Amy Elvira McNiel Eller was the daughter of Thomas Winslow McNiel (1836-1886) and Martha Jane Nichols (1841-1880). Thomas Winslow McNiel, who lived on Fish Dam Creek, was the son of George McNiel (1802-1878) and Susanna Vannoy (1804-1880). George McNiel was a son of James McNiel (1773-1850) and Mary Shepherd (1773-1850). All the above born or died in Wilkes County near Millers Creek, Reddies River and Purlear townships.

James McNiel was one of nine children born to Rev. George McNiel, who was born in Glasgow, Scotland in 1720. He and his brothers, Thomas and John, came to America. He was married to Mary Coats in Virginia. After coming into North Carolina, he settled on the north

Front Row: Zollie Osco Eller, Isaac Milton Eller and Novella Jane Eller. Back Row: Osco Freeland Eller, Amy Elvira McNiel Eller, Jacob M. Eller, Elizabeth Jane Church Eller.

fork of Lewis Fork Creek. He was educated in the Presbyterian ministry in Scotland, but soon after his arrival in America, he was ordained as a Baptist minister so that he might reach more people. He marched with the forces of Colonel Benjamin Cleveland as their Chaplain. He was one of the organizers of the Yadkin Baptist Association in 1786 and served for many years. He served in the Battle of King's Mountain under Colo. Cleveland during the Revolutionary War. This battle is said to be the turning point of the war.

Rev. McNiel died 7 June 1805 and is buried in Stoney Hill cemetery near Parsonsville. A marker was placed at his grave in June 7, 1905 by his descendants. The committee included the names of brethren Milton McNiel, Irvin McNiel, Oliver McNiel, J.M. Eller and George W. Welch.

Sources: The McNiel Clan by J.J. Hayes, Family *Bible*, George Michael Eller and his Descendants in America, by Hook.

— Dare Eller Howell

ELROD and MIKEAL
528

Adam Elrod was born July 20, 1786, married 9 April 1806 in Wilkes County, N.C. to Nancy Phillips, born August 3, 1788. They lived in the Summit area of the county. They had the following children: (1) Elizabeth born March 11, 1807 (2) Sally born December 20, 1808 (3) Coonrad born November 30, 1810 (4) Selah born December 7, 1812 (5) Rebecca born November 27, 1814 (6) Ezra born July 16, 1816, died December 24, 1818. (7) Calloway born March 3, 1818 (8) Hiram born November 10, 1820 (9) Polly born April 7, 1823 (10) Rachel born August 9, 1825. (11) Ally born August 2, 1827 (12) Nancy born August 10, 1829. Adam died February 19, 1875 and Nancy died October 17, 1879.

Selah Elrod, daughter of Adam and Nancy, was born December 7, 1812, died December 21, 1897. She married (March 5, 1840) David Mikeal born February 3, 1818, died May 15, 1905. They are buried at the Mikeal Cemetery at Fall Creek. They had the following children: (1) Ally B. born January 30, 1841 married October 14, 1864 Triplett Hamby. (2) Alexander born September 17, 1842, married A.J. Phillips May 20, 1859. (3) Asa L. born January 1, 1845, married Sarey E. Brown, born September 14, 1843. (4) Rhoda born February 5, 1847, married George Finley Blackburn, born December 26, 1847. (5) Eliza born January 16, 1849, married William M. Lee, born March 6, 1847. (6) Reed, born February 28, 1851 (7) Olive born March 16, 1853 (8) Willborn B. born September 10, 1855.

Olive Mikeal, daughter of David and Selah, married Shadrack Greer Baker, December 1, 1870. He was born November 30, 1845. They had the following children: (1) Laura E. born September 25, 1871 (2) David E. born May 25, 1873 (3) Thursa Matilda born March 26, 1875 (4) William Henry born November 25, 1878 (5) Rhoda Alzora born December 28, 1880 (6) Selah Jane born July 10, 1883 (7) James Asa born June 12, 1885 (8) Granville Maxwell born May 16, 1887 (9) Milton Greenwood born October 11, 1890.

Willborn B. Mikeal, son of David and Selah, was born September 10, 1855, married January 6, 1881 to Martha C. Phillips, daughter of Fannie Caroline and Hugh Phillips. Martha was born October 20, 1862, died January 22, 1955. Willborn died October 7, 1939. Both are buried at Yellow Hill Church Cemetery, Summit, N.C. They had the following children: 1) Emit W. born January 21, 1882, died March 13, 1882. (2) Enoch Reeves, born February 10, 1883, died June 19, 1956, married Winnie Mae Church. (3) Noah Cleveland born April 1, 1885 (4) Fannie Caroline born March 1887 (5) Eliza Elizabeth born November 5, 1890 (6) William Daniel born April 19, 1895, died May 4, 1895 (7) Cicero Call born February 4, 1899.

Enoch Reeves Mikeal married March 26, 1905, Winnie Mae Church, who was born May 22, 1890, daughter of Harrison and Catherine Church. They had the following children: (1) Loy Martha Catherine born March 27, 1907, married Bledsoe Blackburn. (2) L.E. born March 1, 1908, died May 25, 1959, married Linda Rosser. (3) Scott Tillman born June 17, 1909 married Laura Leo Hung (4) Belle Boyd born August 2, 1911, married Charles Stansbury first and married second Fred Simmons. (5) Fannie Pearl born July 18, 1916, married Lonnie H. Parker (6) Ruth M. born February 16, 1918, married Vernal E. Lawrence (7) Asa Burton born February 18, 1920, married Annette B. McRorie (8) Enoch Reeves, Jr. born August 22, 1922, married Lucille Haulk (9) John Willborn born May 19, 1924, married Betty Jo Turner (10) Coy B. born September 23, 1925, married Alice Powers (11) Betty Nell born May 9, 1930, married first, David Knight and second Carroll Byrd (12) Max born February 3, 1933, married Julia Ann Phillips.

Sources: *Bible* of Adam Elrod.

— Linda R. Russell

ESTEPS (EASTEPS)
529

Jacob Estep is the first of the clan in Wilkes County. He was born ca 1794 in Rowan County. His first appearance in the county was approximately 1816 with his father-in-law, Sterling Moore. The land purchased by Sterling Moore was conveyed 15th November 1826 to Jacob Estep. The land was described as lying on the Brushy Mountains adjoing Shadrack Standley and others. This property continued to be the residence for many years.

Jacob Estep and Nancy Moore were married Jan. 3, 1816, in Rowan County. He and Nancy has issue as follows: Elizabeth, born 4-5-1823, died 8-27-1895, married James H. Hayes, son of Henry and Frances Johnson Hayes; Harden, born 2-21-1834, died 7-1-1863, married Louise Malissa Ball, daughter of John Wesley and Ary Melvin Stanley Ball; William M., born Sept. 25, 1816; Reuben, born ca 1831; Polly, born ca 1836; Doctor Calloway, born 2-11-1840, died 12-3-1872, married Amanda Duncan daughter of John and Rebecca Duncan.

Doctor Calloway Estep married Amanda Duncan on the 23rd day of February 1858 in Wilkes County. Their issue is as follows: David Brian, born 3-12-1871, died 6-9-1917, married Sarah Jeanette (Nettie) Marlow; Elza Jones, born 10-25-1868, married Dora Lucinda Reavis; James Haywood, born 1-26-1863, died 11-15-1940, married Mary Moore; Ruah J., born 2-27-1867, married Jay Hayes; William, born 1859, died as a very young child; George, born 4-27-1861 died 10-12-1887, after a fall from a train, never married; John, born 6-4-1860.

Doctor Calloway was in the Civil War and was held as a prisoner of war for some time. He contacted tuberculosis while in the prisoner of war camp. Family tradition has it that three Union soldiers were killed by family members, due to the treatment of Doctor and their looting as they came through Wilkes County.

David Brian, son of Doctor Calloway and Amanda Estep, was born 12th day of March, 1871 and married Sara Jeanette (Nettie) Marlow, daughter of Lafayette and Rena Hayes Marlow, on the 25th day of August, 1893. Their issue were as follows: Dorothy Mae, born 5-4-1894 died 4-10-1950, married William Regulis (Bill) Reavis; Mary Elizabeth (Lizzie), born 11-9-1895, never married; Frank D., born 2-8-1908, married Virgie Smith; Ruie Virgie, born 2-12-1900, married Alonzo Anderson; Julia Lucinda, born 5-11-1910, married Ed Johnson; Leora Amanda, born 9-27-1903 died 10-1-1950; Charity Rene, born 8-24-1894 died 4-6-1908; Iva Jeanette, born 5-1-1905, died 8-14-1969, married Edmund Anderson; Claude Roosevelt, born 4-30-1913, died 1-27-1945 during World War II and never married; Blaine Calloway, born 12-13-1915, died 4-4-1946 during World War II and never married.

Even though the family has spread into other counties, a number of the descendants of Jacob Estep still live in the Brushy Mountains and still own land that was previously owned by Jacob. The old family cemetery, Duncan-Estep, is located on Wildcat Road in a pasture and is in very bad condition at the present time.

Source: Personal knowledge.

— Betty Jean M. Baity

JACOB ESTEP FAMILY
530

The first Estep to settle in Wilkes County was Jacob who arrived about 1816 on Hunting Creek. Jacob was born 1792. On 3 Jan. 1816 he married Nancy Moore, daughter of Sterling and Elizabeth Moore of Rowan County. On 15 Oct. 1826, Jacob and Nancy purchased the Brushy Mountain holdings of her father, consisting of 200 acres on Crane's Creek. They lived at this place until Jacob died 23 June 1869.

Because of his slight stature, Jacob was known as "Little Jakie." In contrast, Nancy grew to a large size, and in later life was said to have weighed almost 300 pounds. After the death of Jacob, Nancy moved to Ashe Co. to make her home with a daughter Rhoda Jane Chappel, wife of William. Nancy died in the

Tuckerdale community January 1885 and is buried in the Bauguess cemetery. In Sept. after her death the settlement of Jacob's estate was initiated in Wilkes court by Hiram John Estep, son of Berry G. Estep of Alleghany Co.

To Jacob and Nancy were born the following children: William M. (25 Sept 1816 — 3 Mar 1902), married Elizabeth Eastridge; Berry G. (6 Oct 1820 — Jan 1911) married first Elvira Smithy 10 Oct 1838, second Louisa Edwards, third Mrs. Ruth Crouse Oct. 1893; Elizabeth (5 Apr 1823 — 27 Aug 1895) married James H. Hayes 8 Feb 1843; Samuel (13 Oct 1828-1913) married first Temperance Marlow, 5 Mar 1850, second Mary J. Hunter; Rhoda Jane (1 Dec 1830 — 18 Sept 1900) married first Rev. William Tedder 11 Feb 1846, second Rev. William Chappel; Rudisil (Rudy) (1832-1850) married Sarah A. Johnson 21 June 1852; Hardy (21 Feb 1834 — 1 July 1863) married Louisa Malissa Ball 1855; Mary (1836-1859) married Harold Hayes 1856; Doctor Calloway (11 Feb 1840 — 3 Dec 1872) married Amanda Duncan 23 Feb. 1858.

Sources: Wilkes Co. records, Confederate service records; Union Army pension and records files.

— Raymond Estep

WILLIAM M. ESTEP FAMILY
531

William M. Estep, son of Jacob and Nancy Moore Estep, was born 25 September 1816 and grew up on Brushy Mountain in Wilkes County; married Elizabeth Eastridge, daughter of Nathan and Elizabeth Eastride in 1837.

Their first two children were born on the Brushies. Malinda born 12 Aug. 1838 and Burrell Harrison born 9 June 1840. They then moved to Ashe Co. where Granville Alexander was born 1 July 1843.

In the spring of 1844 the couple set out in a two-wheeled, ox-drawn cart on a move to Ky. Near Cumberland Gap, Lee County, Va. the vehicle broke down, and William decided to remain there for that year and make a crop.

In Lee Co. Samuel was born 28 September 1845, and Jacob Nathan born 18 Jan. 1848.

Sometime thereafter, William moved his family into Claiborne Co., Tenn. In 1855 he purchased a 100 acre farm which was to be the family home for almost half a century. In Tenn. Nancy Evaline born 15 Dec. 1849; Martha I. born 1 Dec. 1851; Mary E. born 15 Oct. 1852; Lucy A. born 6 June 1854; William born 1 March 1857; John A. born 12 May 1862; James Brownlow born 5 Aug. 1865.

In 1900, William and Elizabeth, by now in their 80's and feeble, were living with son Burrell. Later they moved to Lee Co., Va. and lived with son Granville. There Elizabeth died 6 Feb. 1902 and William died 3 March 1902.

Granville and Burrell served in the Union Army. William, John, and Mary Estep Brown moved to Whitley Co., Ky, then to Oklahoma, where they were joined by James Brownlow. In later years, Evaline and husband James Campbell, a Baptist minister, also settled in Oklahoma. John moved to Texas about 1920.

Sources: Wilkes Co. N.C. and Claiborne Co., Tn. records; Military and Pension records; personal contacts.

— Raymond Estep

THE FAW FAMILY
532

Elijah Calloway, a son of Captain Tom Calloway, married Mary Cutbirth, a grand niece of the great explorer, Daniel Boone. Two of the daughters of Elijah and Mary Calloway married into the Faw family. John Faw married Nancy Calloway, and Jacob III married Mary Calloway. Therefore, those Faws who descended from John or Jacob III can trace their ancestry back to Squire Boone, the father of Daniel Boone, and to seventeenth century England. When he died, Jacob II was buried in the Calloway cemetery situated very near the point at which highway 163 crosses the south fork of New River. The stone which marks his grave is adjacent to the famous field stone shaft which bears the initials, TC, carved by Daniel Boone. This shaft marks the spot where Captain Tom Calloway was buried in his dugout canoe in the year 1800.

It is not known exactly who or how many of the Faw descendants, migrated from Ashe County to Wilkes, but some of those who did are listed here. Absolom Faw, the fifth son of Jacob II, moved to Wilkes County and married Caroline Whittington. He was living in Reddies River Township when the 1860 census was taken. He had six sons and one daughter. One of his sons, Thomas, lived at Millers Creek, and was the father of Claude C. Faw.

Benjamin Faw was the son of John and the grandson of Jacob II. He lived in Ashe County near the ancestral home on New River. One day while he was unhitching a team of work oxen from a wagon, one of the oxen struck at a worrisome dog and accidently caught Uncle Ben in the abdomen with his horn, disemboweling him. This tragic event is well remembered by many people of Ashe County. Ben's son, Emmet, lived in North Wilkesboro where he operated a general store at the head of Trogdon Street for many years. (One of the fond memories of this writer's childhood when he lived on Trogdon Street is the frequest visits to "cousin" Emmet's store.)

Martin Faw, born November 25, 1821, was the oldest son of Jacob III. He married Matilda Kilby and most likely lived in Wilkes. His oldest son, William Harrison Faw, born in 1846, was the father of Iredell Faw who lived on Reddies River. Iredell was the father of nine children, all of whom settled in Wilkes County. These Faw descendants were: Ruth (m. Fred Brown), Ila (m. Ray Pierce), Emily (m. Louis Adams), Ben, Joseph, Garfield, Ancil, May (m. Sylvian Kilby), and Graham.

Martin's second son, Levi, had two sons: Ham and Zeb. Ham lived near Piney Ridge Baptist Church on the road to Jefferson, just south of the jumping-off place. He had two sons, Thurman and Gurney, both of whom still live near Millers Creek. Thurman is the father of J.C. Faw, head of Lowes Food Stores, Edgar and Ozelle who married Pete Williams and lives next door to her father.

John Wesley Faw, the third son of Martin, had three sons and one daughter, all of whom lived on Reddies River. They are: Jonathon, Ada Faw Hoffman, Millard, Fillmore, and Charles.

Jacob Judson, the fourth son of Martin married Luvina Bare and lived near Millers Creek. Jacob and Luvina had seventeen children: Monroe, Doley, Oscar, Carrie (McGlamery), Minnie (Nichols), Chal, Haggie, Krumal, William, John, Lester, Vestal, Edward, Hattie (Pierce), Chessie, Mattie (Grittie), and Rena (Alsby). Many of the Faws of Wilkes County can trace their ancestry to this family.

Henry Judson Faw was the son of Reuben Coffey Faw and the grandson of Jacob Faw III. He spent a large part of his life in Wilkes and is buried in the cemetery at Center Baptist Church. His oldest son, Reuben Estel, was a pioneer well driller, having owned and oper-

William M. (1816-1902) and Elizabeth Eastridge (1818-1902) Estep.

ated one of the first well drilling machines in western North Carolina. The business which he founded continues as Drillers Service Inc., serving well drillers throughout the southeastern states under the able leadership of H. Jack Faw. Henry Judson's second son, Jacob Heggie, lived near Mulberry. He died in May 1981 at the ripe old age of 94½ years. He left behind two sons: Conley and Robert; four daughters: Ruth (Eller), Georgia (Harrold), Ruby Faye (Johnston), and Mable (Rhoades); nineteen grandchildren; twenty-three great-grandchildren; and five great-great-grandchildren, most of whom still call Wilkes County their home.

Sources: Amy and Linda Faw, Tom and Lois Faw, and family records.

— Wendell Faw

FAW FAMILY

533

Jacob Pfau came to America in 1749 from Basil, Switzerland. He was born 3 Oct. 1723 in Basil and married Catharine Disslin before coming to America. His parents were Johannes and Rebecca Spaar Pfau. Catharine died in 1756. His second wife was Anna Magdalena Yount and they had three children: Jacob II married Elizabeth Hire whose father was Rudolph Hire. Jacob II came to Stokes Co., N.C. in 1778 and later moved to Ashe Co., N.C. They had nine children, one of whom was Jacob Faw III, born 29 Jan. 1799.

Jacob III married Mary Calloway, born 7 March 1803 to Elijah and Mary Cutbirth Calloway from Ashe County. They had 12 children, the oldest of whom was Martin, born 25 Nov. 1821.

Martin Faw married Nancy Matilda Kilby in 1845. They had 7 children, the youngest being Jacob Judson Faw, born in 1858. Jacob Judson Faw married Louise (Lou) Bare, born 15 April 1863, the daughter of Henry Cleveland and Barbara Louise Bare from Ashe County. Jacob Judson and Lou Faw had 16 children, many of whose descendants are living in Wilkes County today. Those children were Monroe, Dola, Oscar, Carrie, Minnie, Chal, Heggie and Kramal, William H., John, Lester, Vestal, Edward, Hattie, Chessie and Mattie.

Sources: Research by Mary Schertz.

— Mary Edna Gaither Faw

THE FAMILY OF CLAUDE C. FAW, Sr.

534

The earliest descendant of our branch of the Faw family was Jacob Faw (Pfau), who was born in Basel, Switzerland in 1723. Jacob was a saddler by trade. Early in his life he married Catherine Disslin and had four children, three girls and one boy. In 1749 due to the economic conditions of their country, they left Switzerland and came to America by way of Holland and England. The youngest daughter, Magdalene, died while the family waited on the ship in London for a favorable breeze. Jacob and

Claude Faw I.

his family arrived in America in the latter part of 1749 after a nine week voyage and eventually settled around Frederick County, Maryland with other Swiss families. In 1756, Catherine died, unable to withstand the hardships of the new world. That same year Jacob remarried Anna Magdalene Yount (Yunt) another Swiss emigrant who came to America in 1752. She cared for Jacob's existing children and raised three of her own including Jacob Faw, II born in 1765 who was the ancestor of my grandfather, Claude C. Faw. In 1778, Jacob Faw, I sold his tract of 100 acres in Maryland to his son Abraham. Abraham later became a very prominent homebuilder in Alexandria, Virginia, a member of the Maryland legislature and a candidate from his district to the first U.S. Congress. Jacob, I moved to Stokes County in North Carolina, which is now Forsyth County. According to the tax lists he died there around 1790.

Jacob, II married a daughter of Rudy Hyre of Stokes County and moved to Ashe County in 1806. He bought some land along the south fork of the New River and raised a large family. One of his sons was Absalom, who though born and reared in Ashe County, migrated to Wilkes County and married Caroline Whittington. They lived at Millers Creek and also raised a large family. Details of his life are sketchy, but according to reports he was thrown from a wagon and killed around 1867. One of his sons was Thomas who also settled in the Millers Creek area where he kept a general store and post office. He married Elizabeth Rash and had three children; Thad who died at a young age, Callie Faw Caudill, and my grandfather, Claude C. Faw. My grandfather was born September 17, 1887 and reared in the Millers Creek community and later attended Moravian Falls Academy. He then taught school for thirteen years from 1905 to 1919. He is still remembered by some of the residents of Millers Creek as a wonderful teacher. He married Edna McLean in 1915 and they raised five children. These children are: Mrs. Elizabeth Faw Lewis

of Farmington, Connecticut, Mrs. Margaret Faw Fonvielle of Wilmington, N.C., Mr. Claude C. Faw, of North Wilkesboro, Mrs. Corinne Faw Sink of North Wilkesboro and Mr. Thomas Faw of Mt. Airy, N.C.

My grandfather was always interested in education even after his teaching career. He served as chairman of the Wilkes County Board of Education from July 9, 1919 to October 1, 1928. Later in the 1950's he served for four years as a trustee for the then Appalachian State Teachers College in Boone, N.C. He was also keenly interested in politics and served for several years on the State Democratic Executive committee where he was helpful in improving the roads of Wilkes County. In addition to all of the mentioned he helped found Faw Insurance Agency, Inc. in 1924. This independent insurance agency has been in business continuously ever since and is now managed by my father, Claude C. Faw, Jr. Claude C. Faw died of a heart attack on October 24, 1960 and is buried in a small church cemetery in Millers Creek that his father helped found. He was remembered in newspaper articles of that time as a great friend of education and good businessman. His greatest legacy however is the number of people in the Millers Creek community and Wilkes County in general who still remember him today.

Sources: The Faw Family Record compiled by Amy and Linda Faw — June 4, 1955; newspaper Accounts of death of Claude C. Faw — 1960; article on Claude F. Faw by Mrs. Carolyn Faw Upshaw; conversations with relatives.

— Claude C. Faw, III

JACOB PFAU (FAW) and DESCENDANTS

535

The name FAW is not widely known in this country. Most likely there are fewer than 500 families having that name in the entire U.S.A. Where did the name come from and why are so many members of the family living in Wilkes County?

Those of us who are interested in the answers to these questions are indebted to two cousins, Amy and Linda Faw, of Chillicothe, Illinois. In 1928 they came to North Carolina and started a search which was to occupy most of their spare time for many years to come. They invaded trunks and attics, interviewed many older relatives, and corresponded with "cousins" all over the country. The following brief summary of Faw history is based almost entirely on the work of these people.

Jacob Pfau was born in 1723 in Basel, Switzerland. He was a saddler by trade. He was married to Catherine Disslin. In 1749 he left Switzerland with his wife, Catherine, and four children to seek the good life in America. They made their way down the Rhine and across the channel to England. While waiting there for passage to the new world, their youngest daughter, Magdalena, died of small pox. The child was buried on land just before they set sail. After a long and arduous voyage, they finally landed in Maryland and were safely settled near Frederickstown by the spring of

195

1750. In September 1750, Jacob wrote a letter to his folks back home in Switzerland urging them to come to this wonderful land of opportunity.

The rigors of frontier living proved to be too much for Catherine who died in 1756, leaving Jacob with three small children: Elisabeth, Anna Catharina, and Abraham. Soon thereafter he married Anna Magdalene Yount (Junt). Jacob and Magdalena had three sons: Jacob (1765), Isaac (1773), and Adam (birthdate unknown).

The name Pfau in German means peacock, but the name was soon anglicized to become FAW. In 1768 Jacob Pfau was listed on the quit rent rolls of Lord Baltimore as Jacob Faw. He was then the holder of 100 acres of land in Frederick County, Maryland, near the present town of Johnsville. In 1778 he sold this land to his son, Abraham, who later lived and was buried in Alexandria, Virginia.

Jacob Pfau (Faw) I then migrated with his sons Jacob II, Isaac, and Adam to North Carolina where he settled in Stokes County. No record of his death has been found, though it is thought to have occurred around 1794. Jacob Pfau is shown on the tax rolls of Stokes County as the owner of 274 acres of land from 1790 to 1794. In 1795 the land seems to have been divided between Jacob II (170 acres) and Isaac (104 acres).

Isaac remained in what is now Forsyth County, living just south of the present city of Winston-Salem. He had eight children, and is the ancestor of the Faws now living in the Winston-Salem area.

Adam was a landowner in Ashe County at one time. In 1810 he sold 100 acres of land at the head of Grassy Creek to Alex Smith. Little else is known of him.

Jacob II married a daughter of Rudy Hire. He moved to Ashe County, North Carolina about 1806. He and Elizabith Hyre settled on the south fork of New River near the mouth of Beaver Creek. One of the very first settlers of this area was Captain Tom Calloway. Jacob II bought land from the Calloway family and from others until he became one of the large landowners of the area. The large, two-story log house which he built on the bank of the New River was known as one of the finest houses in that part of the country at the time it was built. He had a large family of nine children, all of whom grew up in this pioneer settlement. Almost all the Faws now living in Wilkes County are descendants of this family.

The children of Jacob II were: John (1792-1875), Jonathan (1793-1868), Jacob III (1799-1859), Rudolph (b. 1806), Absolom (b. 1809), and four daughters, Cloe, Mary Polly, Anne, and Nancy.

Sources: Amy and Linda Faw, Tom and Lois Faw, and family records.

— Wendell Faw

JAMES THOMAS FAW
536

James Thomas Faw, son of Thomas Kenneth and Gertie Church Faw, was born April 14, 1901 in Ashe County. His brothers and sister are: Euria Faw Higgins, born March 5, 1903; Carl Faw, born March 19, 1908; Eugene Faw, born March 26, 1921; Esther, born April 19, 1911; Celia, born October 30, 1905; Vainer, born March 4, 1914; Isabelle, born April 16, 1918; and Evezella, born September 7, 1924. James married Ettie Bare, daughter of Rome and Ida Miller Bare on August 1, 1922. She was born February 8, 1903. Her brothers and sisters are: Glenn, Charlie, Jessie, Hester, Artie, Birtha, Dallie, and Lesie. James is a retired electrician. Seven children were born:

James T. and Ettie B. Faw.

(1) Virginia Dare, born February 15, 1925 in Ashe County. She went to school at Glendale Spring and Millers Creek. She married Joseph Clayton Diviney on March 26, 1947. She is a porcelain finisher. Three children were born: Thurmond Ray, born January 26, 1950, married Josephine Huggins on June 20, 1981; George Marshall, born January 4, 1952, married Gwen Bogle on March 26, 1972. They have two sons: Clayton Marshall and David Edward; Evelyn Louise was born March 18, 1955, married Kenneth Eugene Walsh on June 9, 1973.

(2) Thomas Clifford was born September 13, 1926 in Wilkes County. He went to school at Millers Creek, married Iris Raye Miller on March 26, 1948, and is an upholsterer. Three children were born: Linda Gail was born September 6, 1949, married Clebert Leger, Jr. on November 27, 1981. She has three children: Ricky Steven, Matthew Scott, and Michael Clay. Jerry Dale was born April 29, 1951, married Mary Crystel McGlamery on June 9, 1972. They have one daughter, Jeria Dawn. Sandi Denise Faw was born December 7, 1962, married Roger Alan Chamerlain on May 23, 1982.

(3) Mazella was born August 22, 1929 in Ashe County. She went to school at Millers Creek, married James Earl Bumgarner on October 11, 1947. She is a beautician. They have three daughters: JoAnne was born October 6, 1949. She is divorced, and has two daughters:

Angela Dawn Miller born August 2, 1974; Kendra Jean Miller born September 17, 1979. Delores Kay was born January 13, 1953, married Stephen Edward Kijek March 16, 1973. They have three children: Tyana Rosalina born October 11, 1973; Heather Deanne was born in September, 1975; and James Stephen was born October 12, 1978. Debra Lynn was born August 26, 1955, married Cecil Hamilton Barlow March 17, 1974, and has two children: Cecil Hamilton II (deceased), and Eric Hamilton.

(4) Prichard Greer Faw born August 16, 1933 in Ashe County, went to school at Millers Creek, and married Julia Nell Brown December 23, 1949. He is a metal worker and welder. They have five children: (1) Steven Leonard born July 29, 1951, married Francis Kaye Myers in 1970. They are divorced and he is married to Terri West. He has three children: Stephanie Lynn, born April 12, 1973; Andrea Michelle born June 18, 1976; and Monique Roxanne, born April 20, 1980. (2) Iris Sharon born December 15, 1953, married Kenneth Martin Church June 29, 1975, and has one daughter: Christy Lynn, born January 19, 1976. (3) Keith James born November 21, 1956, and is a welder, carpenter and car dealer. (4) Blake Prichard born June 3, 1960, married Patricia Ann Billings in 1976. They are divorced. He has one son, Christopher Blake, born March 30, 1976. (5) Melony Julia was born June 13, 1964.

(5) Louise was born May 6, 1936, went to school at Millers Creek, and married Glenn D. Livingston June 26, 1954, son of Cowles and Marie Livingston. Louise and Glenn have one son: Thomas Dale, born October 17, 1963. Louise is a homemaker.

(6) Vivian Christine, born September 25, 1938 in Wilkes County, went to school at Millers Creek and West Wilkes High, and married Clarence Everette Hamby on April 4, 1959. They have three children: Elizabeth Christien born January 29, 1960; Anthony Everette born October 15, 1965. Julie Ellen born August 1, 1967. Vivian is a teacher's aid.

(7) Geneva born June 18, 1923, went to school at Millers Creek, married Ernest A. Eller, son of Tom and Nora Robinette Eller, on September 15, 1942. Geneva worked at Wilkes General Hospital as a Nurses' Aide for 13 years. They have three sons: Larry Ernest born August 6, 1944; Thomas Eller, born March 28, 1946 and David James Eller, born October 21, 1949. (see Ernest Eller story).

Sources: From personal information obtained from individuals named.

— Helen M. Eller

FELTS FAMILY
537

There is a legend about the first Felts (Phelps) who came into Wilkes County, N.C. and from records found, it is truly legend. "Aaron Felts, English Episcopal, was born about 1737, and at the age of fifteen he was kidnapped and forced into the British Army, the hardships suffered there and the heavy accoutrements of war carried at this age, made him round shouldered. He was with Washington at Braddock's defeat. He despised the British because of their cruelty to him, and fought against them under Washington during the Revolutionary War.''

Aaron Felts is supposed to have married about 1760, Mollie Collier, born about 1740, the daughter of William and Rebecca (Rothchild) Collier; William born about 1710, English Episcopal, married in Scotland about 1736, and his wife Rebecca, English Jewess, causing the couple to be disowned by both families. Aaron Felts was living in Wilkes County in 1810 and Mollie died 7th January 1823 in Wilkes County. They lived in the Hunting Creek area of the county. Seven of their children have been identified: (1) Elisha, (2) Mary, (3) Sarah, (4) William, born 1767, married about 1790, Susannah Oliver, (5) Aaron, Jr. born ca 1769, married Rebecca Reynolds, (6) John, born 19 February 1770, died 23 September 1866, married Mary Walker, (7) Elizabeth.

John Felts, son of Aaron, Sr. and Mollier (Collier) Felts, married about 1788, Mary Walker, born 1 January 1771, died 27 June 1852 in Wilkes County. In 1820, John Felts owned 29 slaves, so it is assumed he owned quite a large tract of land in the Hunting Creek area. He and Mary had eight children: (1) Joel, born 11 September 1790, (2) Martha, born 4 March 1792, (3) Wilie, born 10 September 1795, died 27 June 1860, married 17 September 1817, Matilda (last name blank on marriage), (4) Elizabeth, born 28 April 1802, married a Bohans, (5) Massey, born 23 February 1804, died 3 December 1829, unmarried, (6) John Lindsey, born 3 May 1807, died 20 June 1851, married Ruth Sprinkle, (7) Rebecca born 23 May 1810, died 12 August 1869, married John B. Madison, (8) Harrison Carmichael, born 30 July 1813, died 8 February 1880, married 25 March 1837, Sarah Tulbert.

John Lindsey Felts, son of John and Mary (Walker) Felts, married 20 January 1830 in Wilkes County, Ruth Sprinkle, born 1818 in Surry County, died 1877 in Wilkes, daughter of Samuel and Ruth (Norman) Sprinkle. They were the parents of ten children, all born in Wilkes County: (1) James Wesley, born 1830, died after 1880, married Martha A. Woodruff, (2) Elza M. born 1833, married Martha McBride, (3) Sarah born 1833 (possibly twin to Elza) married J.F. Somers, (4) Harrison C. born 1836, (5) Rebecca born 1839, married James R. Welborn, (6) Mary A. born 1840 was unmarried in 1880, (7) Lewis F. born 17 July 1842, married Nancy D., died 19 May 1921 Wilkes County, (8) Minerva J. born 23 Dec. 1844, married Calvin A. Roberts, died 23 May 1932, Wilkes County, (9) Louisa Ann born 25 June 1847, died 24 July 1932, married John T. Roberts, (10) Thomas L. born 1848, married Martha.

James Wesley Felts, son of John Lindsey and Ruth (Sprinkle) Felts, married 4 November 1857, in Wilkes County, Martha E. Woodruff, born 1838, died after 1880, daughter of David and Elizabeth (Davis) Woodruff. They lived in Rock Creek Township, in the Liberty Grove Baptist Church community. They had six children: (1) Lindsey B. born 1859, married Julia

A., (2) Robert H., born 1861, (3) James Wesley, Jr., born 1863, (4) William E. born 1868, (5) Florence Hattie born 1868, married a Smith, (6) Eugenia E., born 1873, died 26 February 1926 at the home of her daughter, Ruby Pendley, married 25 March 1890, J. Stacey Barnes, Sr. They are both buried in the North Wilkesboro Cemetery, Sixth Street.

Sources: Old family papers, Federal Census, Wilkes marriage records, tombstone inscriptions.

— Marcella Pendley Church

AARON FELTS FAMILY
538

The first Aaron Felts to come to America was born about 1737 of Scotch-Irish descent. At the age of fifteen, he was forced into the British Army. Aaron was still serving under a forced draft, supposedly, when he met and married Mollie Collier in 1760 in the Tidewater Area of Virginia. It was around this time that Aaron escaped the British militia and joined the Continental Army. Aaron was with Washington at Braddock's defeat during the Revolutionary War.

Aaron Felts.

Several generations later another Aaron Felts was born on June 25, 1840 to Joel and Elizabeth Norman Felts at Hays, North Carolina. Aaron had nine brothers and sisters: Rebecca, John, Nancy, Martha, William, Jasper, James Newton, Mary, Calvin, and Sarah.

Aaron was wounded at Gettysburg, July 1, 1863 and was captured and imprisoned in Elvira, New York. It was said when the war was over he walked and hitched rides from New York State to Wilkes County eating berries and leaves and anything eatable along the way.

After coming home from the Civil War, Aaron married Sarah Elizabeth Reynolds in December, 1863. To this marriage eight chil-

dren were born: Martha Adelaid, Sarah Jane, Ellen, Nancy Elizabeth (Betty), James, Calvin, William H., and Alice. Sarah died June 13, 1887 at the age of forty-four, and Aaron married Julia Clementine Wood, August 10, 1890. Julia and Aaron had four children; Charles Sylvester, Cornelia A., Mary J., and Millard E.

By trade Aaron was a shoe cobbler. The tools that he used for making shoes were inherited by his son Charles. The tools are still being looked at and enjoyed by his children and grandchildren in the home of Mrs. Charles S. Felts.

It is also known that Aaron was a "horse doctor", going to his neighbors with his special treatments.

Aaron Felts died February 16, 1931 at the home of his son, Charles S. Felts. He was buried at Oak Ridge Baptist Church where he was a member. He was affiliated with the church almost all his life. He joined the Antioch Baptist Church in 1858 at the age of 18, and was also a member of the New Covenant Baptist and the Round Mountain Baptist Church.

Several heirlooms that belonged to Mr. Felts are still being used by the family. Mrs. Charles S. Felts has a corner cupboard, corded bed, Seth Thomas Clock, egg basket, Bible carried by Aaron Felts in the Civil War, and a blanket chest that was owned by Elizabeth Norman Felts, Aaron's mother. There is also a document asking Joel Felts, Aaron's father, to release his slaves after the Civil War if he was the owner of any.

Other members of the family have pieces such as a flax-spinning wheel and a chest-of-drawers that are near or over one hundred years old.

Sources: Peggy Atkinson, Broomfield, Colorado; James Felts, Sun City, Florida; Mrs. C. S. Felts, North Wilkesboro, N.C., Family records and interviews with family members.

— Freida Felts Matthews

CHARLES SYLVESTER FELTS
539

Charles Sylvester Felts, Aaron and Julia Woods Felts oldest son, was born May 20, 1891 at Hays, North Carolina. Charles had a very interesting, exciting, and satisfying life. He was a most diversified person having served humanity as an educator, veteran, farmer, revenuer, and magistrate.

From the time he was six years old, Charles was either in school as a student or as a teacher until he was thirty-three years old, with the exception of the year he was in France during World War I after which he took a job with the federal government.

Mr. Felts taught school mostly in two-room schoolhouses for eighteen years in Wilkes County. Teaching and serving as a principal in most of the school districts in Wilkes County. The school districts he served were Oak Grove, White Plains, Rock Creek, Oak Ridge, Sulphur Springs, Mountain Veiw, Cricket, and Flint Hill.

Charles S. Felts joined New Covenant Baptist Church, at Hays, North Carolina at an early age. He later joined Oak Ridge Baptist Church where he served as church clerk and Sunday School teacher.

In 1919, during World War I, Charles served his Country in Chatteraux, France with the 221st Military Police Company, 81st Division.

On September 7, 1927 he married Elsie Wiles and their marriage produced five children: Nancy G. Felts Williams, Suitland, Maryland, Julia E. Felts Byers, North Wilkesboro, N.C., Reba Felts Humphries, Kings Mountain, N.C., Freida Felts Matthews, North Wilkesboro, N.C., and Charles A. Felts, Hays, N.C.

Mr. Felts was the owner of several acres of land in Wilkes County and he farmed a small farm where he lived. He also operated a cattle farm at Hays, N.C. at his old homeplace.

In 1931 Charles became an agent of the Alcohol, Tobacco, and Firearms Division of the U.S. Treasury Department, and he was assigned to the enforcement of federal liquor laws. He served in this capacity in Wilkes County with the exception of a short period in Greensboro, N.C. in which he was assigned the duty of apprehending people suspected of hauling illegal alcohol. He was twice involved in serious accidents while chasing cars. Charles was assigned to the group of officers based in Wilkesboro, and for eight years was in charge of the group.

Charles Sylvester Felts.

During his career as an officer, he made or participated in 2,500 arrests and in those investigations over five million gallons of illicit liquor were destroyed. His career was colored with many humorous incidents which occurred during service to the ATU. On one such occasion a man tending a still deep in the woods accidentally burned his hand. Unaware that Charles and his agents were hiding within earshot, he remarked to his companion, "I wish Charlie Felts would come on and take me in so I could get this hand taken care of." His wish was promptly granted.

He retired at the age of seventy from federal service in 1961, and a banquet was given in his honor at that time which was attended by many officials in federal service.

Charles enjoyed his retirement for ten years until he was called back into service at the age of 80 when he was chosen to serve as Magistrate of the District Court at Wilkesboro, N.C. and serving in this capacity when District Court was first established.

At the age of 81, just one day after he had been re-appointed for another term as Magistrate, Charlie Felts passed away. On December 9, 1972, Mr. Felts was doing what he loved most as he fed his cattle at his old homeplace at Hays, N.C. when he suffered a heart attack and died a few hours later.

The Prohibition Era will always contain the name of Charles Sylvester Felts and his memory will live on in the thoughts of those he served during his life as an educator, veteran, farmer, revenuer, and magistrate.

Sources: Mrs. Charles S. Felts, *The Journal Patriot*, 1961 and 1972, family memories.

— Freida Felts Matthews

ELISHA REYNOLDS FELTS FAMILY

540

Elisha Reynolds Felts was born in the Clingman Community of Wilkes County to Elza and Nancy Tulbert Felts. Elza, my great-grandfather, was born April 3, 1813 and my great-grandmother was born September 8, 1818. They were married June 4, 1835. He died August 2, 1887 and she died May 15, 1901. They are both buried in the Felts family cemetery near Clingman.

Elisha Felts, my grandfather, married my grandmother Theodocia Ann Haynes (born April 8, 1856) March 16, 1873 and had seven children. Lytle McLean, Nancy Cornelia (Salmons), Almeda Hasseltine (Warren), Tyra Glen, James Thomas, Lelia Jane (McNeil and John Finley. Most of his early life was spent farming. He was also a cobbler. One of my sisters has his cobblers bench he used for many years to make shoes for his family and neighbors. He moved his family from Clingman to the Foote farm, across the Yadkin River from the village of Roaring River and farmed the land there for several years. Some of my older sisters remember when they were children they would walk to the bank of the river and call "yoo hoo" and Grandpa would come down and bring his rowboat over and carry them to the other side. In the early 1900's they moved to the Roaring River village and spent the remainder of their lives. She and Grandpa were perfectionist. I've heard my older sisters tell of hoeing the corn he had plowed and of how each hill had to be completely clear of weeds and the dirt pulled around each stalk just so. You didn't dare cut a stalk off or you would be reprimanded.

When a death occurred in the neighborhood, Grandpa and his sons made pine coffins which Grandma and the girls lined. They they bathed the corpse and "laid them out". In other words they prepared them for burial.

They were of strong Baptist faith and along with seven members of the family and eleven others organized Roaring River Baptist Church in 1906. This group met in the one-room school house until a boundary of timbers was bought and the building built. Grandpa loved to smoke a pipe and once when a revival was held at the church by Rev. Mardecai Ham, a well known evangelist, Grandpa said "Rev. Ham how do you feel about using tobacco?". Rev. Ham replied, "Brother Felts, the Bible says, He that is filthy be filthy still," and that closed the conversation on tobacco.

I remember their home was one of routine. There was a place and time for everything and unless something unusual happened it all went like clockwork. Rising at 5:00 a.m. the animals were fed, milking done, etc. Breakfast at 6:00, arriving for work by 7:00, dinner was at 11:30 and supper at 5:00. Monday was wash day, Tuesday ironing, etc. In those days the doctors were few. I remember stepping on a nail once that went through my shoe sole and into my foot Grandma put some yarn rags into a metal bucket and set fire to them. It made a great smoke and I had to hold my foot over it for ever so long. Apparently it was to keep any infection out and it worked for I had no further trouble.

In those days there were no refrigerators and not so far from their house was a big spring. Grandpa built a spring house with troughs in it to set the milk, butter and anything else that needed to be kept cool. Just before each meal someone had to go to the spring house for the milk and butter. I remember any food left from any meal was kept until the next meal lest someone should come to their house hungry.

Despite the hardships of those days they lived long and fruitful lives. The Golden Rule was a guideline and they lived by it. They were kind and gentle people and were loved and respected aby the community. Grandpa died in June 1927 and Grandma died June 1938. They're both buried in the church cemetary they helped organize and loved dearly.

Sources: Family Records, interviews with family members and personal knowledge.

— Inez M. Boles

THE FERGUSON FAMILY

541

Below we give you a brief history and genealogy of the Fergusons, Tripletts and Hagler families of Wilkes and Caldwell Counties and also make reference to more comprehensive records of the Clan Ferguson, Society of North America organized in 1972.

The three original imigrants from Scotland who first came to Pennsylvania then to Virginia, finally settled on the Yadkin River in the vicinity of Ferguson are as follows: John born 1749, and died about 1835, Thomas born 1751 and died 1842, and Richard, born 1753 and died about 1846, all buried in the Yadkin Valley. It is thought that the three brothers were born near Edinburg, Scotland, came to America as young men 18 to 20 years of age and upon arriving in the Yadkin Valley acquired several thousand acres of land much of which is still owned by their descendants. The three brothers married into the Triplett and Foster families. John married Frances Triplett, daughter of William Triplett and Eleanor Harbin original immigrants from Ireland; Richard Ferguson married a sister of Frances, Verlinda Triplett and Thomas married Edith Foster, one of the six daughters of George and Sarah Childers Foster of Burke County, North Carolina. It will be noted here that Sarah Childers might have been the aunt of Sarah Childers who was the wife of President James K, Polk, who lived in the adjoining county of Rutherford to Burke County. All three Ferguson immigrants now have several thousand descendants scattered far and wide over Wilkes and Caldwell Counties as well as over many states, as recorded in the 329 page family history of the Fergusons compiled by Mrs. Hortense Abbott, whose address is 410 Railer Way, Bemet, Calif. Mrs. Abbott is a descendant of John Ferguson, daughter of the original John Ferguson, who married Thomas Triplett. John and Frances had seven children and lived on Stony Fork Creek, tributary of the Yadkin. Their 200-year-old Log House has just recently been dismantled.

Thomas Ferguson, one of the original three who married Edith Foster, settled at Ferguson, on land possibly granted from the King. They had three sons and four daughters, William, John F. and Thomas Jr., Charity, Betty, Polly and Sallie all of whom settled near Ferguson, except William who married Eliza Dula and removed to Englewood, Tennessee. They have descendants living there today and elsewhere. John Foster Ferguson, who married Elender Triplett, grand-daughter of the original William Triplett had a family of six sons and three daughters. Edith Ferguson, who married Johnson Spicer, Confederate Veteran and they have many descendants living in Sumpter County, South Carolina., Lindsay Carson Ferguson, named for Kit Carson, first married Heloise Ferguson, one of the several daughters of William Ferguson. They had four daughters who married Carltons, Fergusons, parliers and Hemphills. Heloise died during the Civil War and Lindsay married Sarah Virginia Kendall, one of six daughters of William and Sarah Hagler Kendall. They had three daughters, Blanche, Beulah, Jessie (Mrs. Jas. R. Hix), John, William, Thomas (The writer of this history) and Clyde. John Foster and Elendar Ferguson also had another daughter who married Obb. Howell, who was a descendent of the original John.

Richard Ferguson, one of the original three married Verlinda Triplett and they had ten children, boys and girls. One daughter married James Swanson, and they had many descendants including Swansons, Carltons, Andrews and McGhinnis. A son, Jeremiah, who married a McGee, are the ancestors of James Larkin Pearson, late Poet Laureate of North Carolina; also of the Zachary and Billy Ferguson and Barlow families. Richard owned the adjoining farm to John Foster Ferguson. It will be noted that the Great Pioneer Daniel Boone, had two log cabins on the lands of Thomas Ferguson, and therefore was a contemporary of the Boones. Boone launched his campaign into Kentucky from one of these cabins and the

Boone family lived here for several years and have many descendants living in Wilkes and Caldwell Counties today. The Ferguson Books can all be found in the Wilkes County Library.

The Caldwell County Fergusons sprang from Sir James Ferguson, native of Scotland who married Elizabeth Smith and they had six children, the most noted one was a son, Rev. Smith Ferguson, who has many descendants in both Caldwell and Wilkes County. He was a noted Baptist minister. Mrs. Abbott records many of the progeny of Sir James and also of the Triplett family. The Hagler family was also closely intertwined with the Ferguson and Triplett families. John Hagler came from Switzerland and married Elizabeth Van Noose, native of Holland about 1750. He first came to New York, then to the Yadkin Valley. They had six sons and the youngest was William Hagler, who married Ellizabeth Mullens, said Elizabeth was the daughter of John William Mullens, who married a niece of William Triplett. William Hagler and Elizabeth had ten sons and three daughters. The youngest daughter was the grandmother of the writer of this history, who married William Kendall.

It is said that all Fergusons are of Scottish descent. The Scottish Highland Games have been in progress at the Grandfather Mountains, Linville, N.C. for some 25 years, at which about 100 Scottish Clans assemble each year in July. In 1972, the Clan Ferguson Society of North America was organized at Grandfather Mountain, with about seventy-five members. The membership today has grown to about 1,000 from far and wide. The president of the Clan is Dr. Malcom Stuart Ferguson, 3522 Twin Branches Drive, Silver Spring, Maryland. The late Sir James Ferguson, who died in 1973, was for many years the Ferguson Scottish Chief, whose home and castle known as Kilkaron, is located at Argyle, Scotland. His son is Charles Ferguson, now Chief and the Chief is always a Lieutenant of the Queen.

Sources: personal knowledge, Publication *The Beeline.*

— Tom W. Ferguson

CARL CHAPMAN FERGURSON
542

The ancestry of Carl Chapman Ferguson takes us back to James and Elizabeth Fergurson of Franklin County, Virginia. Their first four children were born in Virginia. James was called "Sir James" in Wilkes County. James and Elizabeth had six more children born in Wilkes County. All their children were married in Wilkes County, except their last child. "Sir James'" eighth child Smith Ferguson was born March 8, 1791. He married Sarah Cox on March 8, 1821. Smith was a soldier under "Old Hickory" Jackson in the British and Indian War of 1812. After the restoration of peace he entered the ministry and became a noted Baptist minister. The Reverend Smith Fergurson was Moderator of the Lewis Fork Association for more than a quarter of a century. Before his death he wrote the inscription he wished placed upon his marker which was done as follows, *Smith Fergurson, A Sinner Saved By Grace.* He died March 12, 1878.

Smith and Sarah had seven children who were born in Wilkes County. Their first son Chapman Coffey Fergurson was born June 7, 1822. He married Elizabeth Minerva Thompson in 1843. They had three children born in Wilkes County. After Elizabeth died, Chapman married Marie Elizabeth Roberts in July of 1856. They had seven children born in Wilkes County. Both Chapman Coffey and Marie are buried in the Zion Hill Cemetery in Boomer. Their son Benjamin Franklin, a twin was born October 2, 1858. Benjamin married Laura Lucretia Ellis on March 4, 1880. They had twelve children, all born in Boomer. Benjamin and Laura are buried in the Zion Hill Cemetery. Their second child was Roby Smith Fergurson who was born January 6, 1883, and married Julia Ann Pennell on May 13, 1906, in Boomer, They had seven children born in Boomer. Roby and Julia's second child was Carl Chapman Fergurson. He married Gennity Gay Fortner in Boomer. They had nine children all born in Boomer. Christine was born September 25, 1939, and married Garvin Foster. They had two children — Brenda and Steve. Nellie Virginia was born May 22, 1931, and married Verne Katz. They had one son, Gary Kenneth, who was born May 15, 1935, and married Virginia Smith in 1955. They have three children — Anthony, Kenvian, and Jennifer. Lawrence Smith (Jack) was born March 9, 1937, and married Betty Lou Auton in 1967. They have four children — Mark, Monica, Michael and Meredith. Ella Sue was born August 11, 1939, and married Sidney Carlton Swanson in 1958. They have one daughter Karen. Larry Dean was born May 3, 1942, and married Billie Sue Walsh in 1962. They have two children — Kimberly and Michelle. Charles Garner was born May 10, .1944, and died November 10, 1944. Terry Paul was born October 4, 1945, and married Nancy Parlier in 1962. They have two children — Julie and Matthew. Janice Gail was born October 25, 1947, and married Roby Smith Earp, Jr. in 1966. They have two children Robbie and Jelynn. All of Carl's children still live in Wilkes County except Kenneth in Caldwell County, Janice in Louisville, Kentucky, and Larry who lives in Greensboro. Carl Chapman Ferguson died Sunday January 2, 1972, and was buried at Little Rock Baptist Cemetery in Boomer.

Sources: Family *Bible*, pamphlet of the Brushy Mtn. Baptist Association. The Taylorsville Times newspaper, family memories of descendants of Fergurson Families.

— Mrs. Betty Fergurson

CHAPMAN HARVEY and NORA RACHAEL WATSON FERGUSON and DESCENDANTS
543

Chapman Harvey (July 23, 1878) and Nora Rachael Watson Ferguson (Dau. of Martin and Sarah Ann Watson) were married in 1910 under an apple tree on the farm. Both were schoolteachers.

When Harvey was only six years old, he had an illness believed to be polio which left him crippled for life. The use of crutches allowed him to get around to pursue his many interests.

Among his occupations were County Treasurer, insurance salesman, County Tax Collector, and photographer. He also owned a farm. He was a Republican and a very influential man in Wilkes County Government.

Charles Watson was born on September 16, 1911. His mother died when he was only twelve days old.

Charles Watson married Winifred Ferguson (dau. of Robert and Rose Higgins Ferguson) on July 5, 1935. They had eight children: (1) Charles Jerry (June 20, 1937) married Shirley Temple Holman. Jerry is a registered surveyor and works for the Highway Department; (2&3) Twins, Nora Ann, married to Mack Gregory. Nora is a homemaker in Wilkes Co. Vivian Rose has a Master Degree from Applachian. Both girls were born January 16, 1940; (4) Susan Winifred (Dec. 2, 1947) married Howard Barefoot. They are living in Raleigh where Susan is presently working on her PhD. at N.C. State University; (5) Elizabeth Joan (Jan. 25, 1949) married Roy Ray Johnson. She is a Media Specialist in Taylorsville, NC; (6) Mary Judith (Oct. 13, 1951) is presently working on her Masters Degree in Industrial Arts at Applachian; (7) Martin Harvey (Dec. 14, 1952) graduated at Fruitland Bible Institute and has made several missionary trips to various places. He plans to go to Alaska as a mission volunteer; (8) Margaret Frances (Aug. 3, 1955) works as an X-Ray Technician at Ashe Memorial Hospital.

Charlie and Winifred are Baptists. Both are active in the Republican Party. He is a farmer in the Ferguson community and grown small grains such as wheat, corn and soy beans. Winifred is a homemaker. Both have been active in the Beaver Creek Baptist Church. Charlie has served as deacon and both have been Sunday School Teacher. The family is also active in the Ferguson Community Organization, and in the Extension Homemakers Club.

Until the sixties, Charlie and Winifred lived in the Goshen Community. When the Kerr Scott Dam and Reservoir were built, they moved to the Ferguson Community.

They have seven grandchildren at the present. Jerry's children are: (1) Edward Jerry, born 1961; (2) Andora Sue, born 1964; (3) Paula Nadine, born 1966; (4) Belinda Yvette, born 1968. Susan has one daughter, Rebecca Marie, born Feb. 17, 1968. Joann has two children: Michael, born June 16, and Kristy Raye, born Dec. 11, 1975.

Sources: Family *Bible*, County Records and personal knowledge.

— Mrs. C.W. Ferguson

GARRETT COLIN and LELIA BARNETT FOSTER
544

Our daddy, Colin Foster, born in Wilkes County, September 9, 1899, to James Rutherford (Rell) and Ina Eugenia Elledge Foster. He was a brother of Arlie Roscoe, Simon Sacasta, infact boy (Holt), Edith (Mrs. Arlon) Triplett and Avis Muriel (Mrs. Sib) Turner. Their home place, located in the Mt. Pleasant Community, and land is presently owned by their direct

descendants. The Foster ancestry has been traced to Thomas Foster, Lord of Etherstone, England. Thomas died in 1415.

Daddy attended Dick's Hollow and Mt. Pleasant Schools.

In those days, times were hard on the farm. Daddy at an early age began hauling with a team of mules from Stony Fork and Lewis Fork to North Wilkesboro having to camp out over night at the tannery. He later worked on building roads in Wilkes and Alexander Counties.

Dad met our Mother, Lelia Rebecca, daughter of Gaither Franklin and Mary Jane Ball Barnett. She was born July 1, 1902. Mama grew up in the Mt. Zion community of Wilkes County and attended Mt. Zion School and Mtn. View Institute. She later taught school in Caldwell and Wilkes Counties.

On April 28, 1928, with Dad dressed in his blue serge suit and Mama wearing a blue silk dress, they were married at Wilkesboro, N.C.

Mama and Daddy purchased their first farm from the Lee Hamby Heirs on Stony Fork Creek in the Adkins Shop Community. They spent many hours working together in the fields.

Mama and Daddy were blessed with their first child, James Gaither, on April 7, 1929. James married Norma Lee Bartlett, daughter of Otie Thurman and Bonnie Wright Bartlett of (Old Town) Galax, Virginia. Norma was born June 2, 1937.

They have a son and daughter: Ronald James, born October 26, 1960, and Bonnie Rebecca, born December 21, 1963.

Mama and Daddy's second child, John Colin, was born May 4, 1932.

Their third and last child, a daughter, Nancy Lee, was born July 9, 1935. Nancy Lee married Clate Arlie Dillard, son of the Rev. Daniel Monroe and Mollie Reynolds Dillard. Clate was born September 18, 1931.

Due to poor conditions of the roads, the mail box being about a mile away and the children having to walk about one-half mile and wait for the school bus in all kinds of weather, never knowing if the bus would show-up or not, and no electricity, we moved in January 1945 to a farm that joined Grandpa Foster's in the Mt. Pleasant Community. This was during the war and it was nearly a year before we had electricity. But, the mail and school bus was only a few steps away.

We have many wonderful memories of our growing up days. Our favorite being of mama telling us stories, not out of a book, but about things that happened when she was growing up. Daddy told lots of tales about his trips to town.

Daddy died on November 24, 1981, and is buried beside his brother, Arlie, in the Mt. Pleasant Baptist Church Cemetery in the Champion Community of Wilkes County.

Mama is still living at the home place, and cooking Sunday dinner for us.

Sources: Family memories and personal knowledge.

— Nancy Lee Dillard

JAMES HARVEY FERGUSON
545

James Harvey Ferguson was born Feb. 16,

1826 in Wilkes County. He was the son of Smith and Sarah Cox Ferguson. He first married Nancy Minerva Howell on June 26, 1847. She was born Mar. 30, 1832 in Wilkes Co. They had four children:

(1) Frances M., born Feb. 14, 1849 who remained single; (2) Nancy Abigail, born Nov. 15, 1851, married Hezekiah Minton. They had 6 children; (3) James Shufort, born Feb. 13, 1852, married Martha Triplett. She was born in 1842 to Thomas and Theodocia Carolyn Dula Triplett. They had 4 children. Martha died in 1876. He then married Fannie Thomson in 1877; (4) John Smith, born July 13, 1856, married Sarah Lucretia Phillips Dec. 30, 1880. They were cousins as she was the daughter of Elisha B. and Mary P. Ferguson Phillips. She was born Apr. 17, 1850. They had 4 children. John died in 1903 and Sarah in 1934.

James Harvey married Sarah Frances Phillips on May 13, 1868 after the death of his first wife. She was 22 years younger than James, being born June 17, 1848 the daughter of William and Frances Pearson Phillips. They had 6 children born in Wilkes Co. She died May 31, 1916 and James Harvey died Oct. 19, 1920 at age 94. Both are buried in the Mt. Zion cemetery in Boomer.

Their children were: (1) Dora Alice, born Apr. 4, 1869, married Wm. H. Higgins in 1887; (2) Jasper Peter, born June 30, 1873, married Emma Rachel Dockery in 1907; (3) Wheeler William, born Sept. 1, 1877, married Alice Laws; (4) Chapman Harvey, born July 23, 1878, married Nora Watson in 1910; (5) Robert Gerlad, born July 10, 1881, married Rose Lee Higgins on Oct. 9, 1900; (6) Erby Victoria, married Leander Fox.

James Harvey was an outstanding farmer in his day and won a Corn Grower's Award. He believed in the Advent Christian religion.

During the Civil War, James Harvey hauled salt for the Confederacy. When Wade's Bandits were preying on the farmers around the Fort Hamby area by stealing their cattle and crops, James Harvey outsmarted Wade and his henchmen. Wade's men were notorious for shooting men in the back who refused them their cattle, but were not so brave when confronted by James Harvey with a double-barreled shotgun. The robbers usually went away from him empty-handed.

James Harvey's uncle was "Wild Bill" Ferguson. He helped to fight Indians. As "Wild Bill" stood guard duty, he heard a wild hog coming closer and closer. He shot the animal only to find that it was an Indian dressed in a hog skin. This explained why so many of the men that stood guard duty went out to hunt wild hog and never returned.

Often the men would go out to shoot wild turkeys. When they heard them gobble, they would follow it and disappear. After this happened a number of times, "Wild Bill" circled around the section of the woods where the sound of the turkey was. In a tree he saw an Indian gobbling like a turkey. Wild Bill shot and killed him.

These stories were told to my father, Robert G. Ferguson and were handed down to us.

James Harvey lived a long, life. He died October 19, 1920 at the age of 94. He is buried with his second wife in the Mt. Zion Cemetery.

Sources: *Descendants of the Ferguson Families* by Mrs. Hortense E. Abbot, Family Stories, Delight Payne Research.

— Mrs. Charles W. Ferguson

RICHARD and LINNIE TRIPLETT FERGUSON FAMILY
546

This article quotes James Larkin Pearson: Richard Ferguson was born in Scotland March 1, 1765. He came to America with his brothers, John and Thomas Ferguson. I have never learned the date of their coming to America. He married Linnie Triplett, but I don't have the date of the marriage. Richard died in Wilkes County, North Carolina, on May 24, 1854. His wife, Linnie Triplett Ferguson, died on December 10, 1858.

Richard Ferguson located on a farm on Beaver Creek in Wilkes County, North Carolina, later known as the Harrison Brown farm. He and his wife, Linnie, raised a family of thirteen children — four sons and nine daughters, as follows:

John T. Ferguson, known as "Uncle Jack." He apparently became the head of the house for some time after Richard's death, but he never married.

Jesse Ferguson, who married Polly Brown, and they had at least eight children, maybe more. Jesse and his family moved to Georgia many years ago and it seems that they must not have kept in touch with the home folks. The eight children whose names are known must have been born before they left North Carolina. Their names were: Clara, Barlett, Linnie, Betty, Annie, John, James, Joel.

Jerry Ferguson married Louise McGee, and they had eight children as follows: Eliza, Appeline, Rebecca, Amanda, Ann, Martha, Zachary, William.

Nancy Ferguson married John Brown, commonly known as Jack Brown, and they had four children as follows: Hamilton, Harrison, Nellie and Polly. (There has been a question as to whether it was Sally (Sarah) or Nancy who married John Brown. I have always had it Sally on my records, but lately there seems to be proof that it was Nancy.)

Rebecca Ferguson married Joel Waters and they had eleven children as follows: Willis, William, John, Louis, Caroline, Ann, Betsy, Millie, Alie, Polly and Leah. (Leah Waters married Larkin Kendall and was the mother of Amelia Kendall who married Harrison Brown and of Josephine Kendall who married Patrick McShane.)

Sally (Sarah) Ferguson, who must also have been known as Frankie, married Daniel Holman and they evidently had children, but I have not been able to get any record of that family. This is very regretable, since the names of all the others are known. There must be some record of this family which might yet be gotten.

Elizabeth Ferguson married James Swanson and they had ten children, as follows: Anderson, Calvin, Nancy, Frankie, Susan, Annie, Hiley, Caroline, Clara and Nellie.

Nellie Ferguson married Larkin McNeil and they had four children: Frank, Louise, John and Milton. (Louise McNeil married William T. Pearson and was the mother of James Larkin Pearson).

Jordan Ferguson never married. In his old age he became more or less mentally deranged.

Polly Ferguson never married. Her real name, of course, was Mary. She lived to an advanced age, along with three old-maid sisters and a bachelor brother, at the old Richard Ferguson home, which was later known as the Harrison Brown Farm. This was where Amelia Kendall (sister of Josephine) came to live when she married Harrison Brown. Harrison was a first cousin to Amelia's mother. Harrison was a middle-aged bachelor and Amelia was a young girl when they were married. They had three children, two sons and a daughter: Raldo, Metro, and Carrie. Raldo lives at 1515 Ninth St., Boulder, Colorado. Metro is in New York. Carrie married John Fletcher and lived at High Point, North Carolina. She died a few years ago.

Priscilla Ferguson never married. She was one of the four old-maid sisters. She was known as "Aunt Prissy."

Elviry Ferguson never married. She was one of the four old maid sisters. She was known as "Aunt Viry."

Delphia Ferguson never married. She was one of the four old-maid sisters, and in her old age she became more or less mentally unbalanced — harmlessly crazy.

It will be seen from the above that the known grandchildren of Richard Ferguson numbered 45, and it is quite likely that there were others that should be included, particularly the Daniel Holman family, if any. It will be seen, also, that six of Richard Ferguson's children never married.

I lived near the old Richard Ferguson home for several years and was well acquainted with the four old-maid sisters and one bachelor brother, Jordan Ferguson. Harrison Brown was a nephew of these old people, his mother, Nancy Ferguson Brown, having been one of the nine daughters of Richard Ferguson. There is room for a great deal of genealogy work that has not yet been done. Most of the younger generations have never been recorded. Harrison Brown, the nephew, became the head of that rather dismal unmated household and he needed a wife to help him take care of the situation. And that's where Amelia Kendall came in.

Sources: a letter written to my uncle, Daniel Edward McShane, Sr. (1905-1968) by James Larkin Pearson (1879-1981) dated April 7, 1967.

— Nina Joan Cobb

ROBERT GERALD and ROSA LEE HIGGINS FERGUSON
547

Robert Gerald, (born July 10, 1881, died March 20, 1954) and Rosa Lee Higgins, (born August 28, 1884, died 1970) were married on October 9, 1900 in Wilkes County.

Their children were: (1) Pansy Lee (Oct. 18, 1901 — Oct. 21, 1967); (2) Williard Winfield (Jan. 9, 1903 — July 26, 1961) married Mattie Land. Seven children — Williard, Robert, Harry, Edward, Charles, Karen Jean and Joe; (3) Robert Howard (June 8, 1905 — 1980) married Emma Walker. Two children — Linda and Donald Ward; (4) Erby Estelle (Oct. 17, 1909 — Dec. 4, 1976) married Orrin L. Baxter. One son, Robert (Bob); (5) Mary Louise (July 7, 1911 — Feb. 13, 1960) married Troy Redding. One daughter, Olivia, who married Fred Barker; (6) Winifred Vivian (March 22, 1914) married Charles W. Ferguson. Eight children; (7) Paul Varner (July 10, 1916) married Lena Doggett. Paul lives in Chattanooga, Tenn. He has a Doctor of Divinity Degree. He is an Evangelist and minister. They have three children — John Paul (a minister in New York), Timothy (a school teacher in Georgia) and Mark (works in Georgia); (8) Verna Mae (Feb. 27, 1920) married James Claude Church on May 25, 1940. They have one child, James Paul Church born June 23, 1941 and married Barbara Keener in 1963 in Maryland; (9) Margaret Frances (March 15, 1925) married John Frank Crawford. Margaret lives in Hickory and has two children — John Frank Jr. and Steven.

Robert Gerald, known as Bob, hauled lumber with a horse and wagon. He helped build the Old Highway 268. He often pulled logs from the woods with steers. In addition to all of this, he was a farmer.

Being devout, faithful Methodist, Bob and Rose went to the church services held once a month at Lebanon Methodist Church at Goshen. They took their nine children to services with them.

Like his father, Howard was a loyal Republican. When he was only nine, Howard drove a wagon load of ladies in their bonnets to vote at Boomer. The men walked behind the wagon.

Rose Ferguson was kind and generous to her own family and to the neighbors as well. She helped those who were sick and gave food to the hungry as well as giving devoted attention to her family. She had great faith in Jesus Christ as God, Redeemer and Friend.

Sources: Family *Bible*, County Records and personal knowledge.

— Mrs. C.W. Ferguson

SIR JAMES and ELIZABETH FERGUSON
548

James Ferguson, came from Franklin Co. Virginia. He was born between 1750 to 1755, the son of John and Elizabeth Ferguson of Pigg River. He married Elizabeth Smith in Virginia and their first four children were born in Virginia. He was called "Sir James", but his descendants did not know why. He left a will that was probated in the November term of court in 1837.

Ten children were listed in his will: (1) Elizabeth, born in Va. about 1773 married Philip Davis March 9, 1791; (2) Sarah, born 1775, married Edmund Tilley July 22, 1796; (3) John, born about 1778, married Sarah Umphrey on March 27, 1812. They were parents of six children, born in Wilkes County.

John died in 1829. (4) James, Jr. was born in 1781 in Franklin Co., Va. He married Mary Castevens on March 29, 1821. Their six children were born in Wilkes Co. (5) Mary, born about 1782 in Wilkes Co., married John Carrol on Oct. 18, 1800; (6) William, born about 1784 married Marie Elizabeth Holderman on March 4, 1809; (7) Jane, born in 1785, married William Bradley on Jan 26, 1812; (8) Smith, born Nov. 4, 1791, married twice: #1 Sarah Cox on March 28, 1821, #2 Martha Parsons on Oct. 25, 1861; (9) Martha, born 1797, married Briant Merrymon in 1818; (10) George, born 1802, married Mary Estes in Burke County in 1829.

James and Elizabeth lived on a one hundred acre tract of land in what is now the Boomer Community. He left this land and an additional ninety-seven acres to his son George in his will.

Sources: *Descendants of the Ferguson Families* by Mrs. Hortense E. Abbot.

— Mrs. Charles W. Ferguson

SMITH FERGUSON and DESCENDANTS
549

Smith Ferguson was born Nov. 4, 1791 in Wilkes County, the son of James and Elizabeth Smith Ferguson. He was very religious, even as a child. When he inherited slaves from his father, Sir James Ferguson, he believed that it was wrong to own slaves and freed them. The freed slaves worked for wages. He donated the land on which the Thankful Church of Boomer, N.C. stands today. Smith served in the war of 1812 and received a pension.

On May 21, 1821, Smith married Sarah Cox. Sarah was born in 1796. Smith was ordained as a minister by the Kings Creek Baptist Church. After living in Taylorsville for a while, he established the United Baptist Collegiate Institute.

Smith and Sarah were the parents of 7 children. It was said that at one of Smith's revivals, Sarah, not wanting to stay, left, and, on the way home, the horses ran away, overturning the buggy and killing her.

Their seven children are: (1) Chapman Coffey, born June 7, 1822, married #1. Elizabeth Minerva Thompson in 1843. #2. Elizabeth Roberts in 1856; (2) John Milton, born about 1824, married Amelia Mathis; (3) Mary P., born about 1824, married #1. Elisha B. Phillips in 1848. #2. Mr. Childers (Childress?); (4) James Harvey, born Feb. 16, 1826, married #1. Nancy Minerva Howell on June 26, 1847. #2. Sarah F. Phillips on May 13, 1868; (5) J.F.; (6) Samuel F., who moved to Missouri; (7) Nancy, born about 1837, married N.A. Russell in 1862.

After Sarah's death, Smith married Martha Parsons on Oct. 25, 1861. He was seventy years old at the time of this marriage, while Martha was 26. They had 5 children: (1) Thomas Jefferson (1862-1866); (2) William Leroy, born in 1864; (3) Burton Pomroy, born Nov. 13, 1867, died Jan. 2, 1917. (He was known for enjoying playing tricks on his father); (4) Henry Flowers, born in 1873, mar-

ried Minnie Brinkly in 1897; (5) Smithey Ann, born Feb. 9, 1878, married Sylvanus A. Moore in 1898 in Caldwell Co. She died April 23, 1925. Both Smithey and her father Smith are buried in the Dudley Shoals Cemetery.

Smith organized the Little River Association in Alexander Co. in 1852 and was moderator for fifteen years. He came to Wilkes County with a group of people and organized the Brushy Mt. Association. He organized and pastored several churches in Wilkes and other counties. He was pastor of the present day Beaver Creek Baptist Church. He helped many young men get started in the ministry before his death in March, 1878.

Sources: *Descendants of the Ferguson Families* by Mrs. Hortense E. Abbot and Family Legend. Delight Payne, who has done research on this family.

— Mrs. Charles W. Ferguson

ARTHUR A. FINLEY FAMILY
550

Arthur Augustus Finley was born the seventh child and third son of Augustus Washington and Martha Gordon Finley on October 26, 1859. He was baptised in the Wilkesboro Presbyterian Church on April 29, 1860, and educated at the Finley High School in Lenoir. The tale is told that when Arthur rode out to go "a-courtin'" the girls would line up to gaze at his handsome beard! On October 8, 1890, Arthur married Kate Cameron, a teacher in a private school in Wilkesboro.

Kate was born in Harnett County, N.C. on August 7, 1866, to John Atkins and Lucy Martin Cameron.

Arthur and Kate resided in the town of North Wilkesboro in a large frame house on E Street near the Reddies River known as "Riverview". Here they were blessed with five lovely children: Lucy, Grace, Bess, A. Gordon, and Arthur. They were both active in the North Wilkesboro Presbyterian Church; she serving as choir director and he as an elder. As the town grew, Arthur became one of it's leading citizens, serving as the first mayor, a town commissioner, and chairman of the school board. He was also active in the business community, founding the Wilkesboro Manufacturing Co. in 1896, which he headed until his death, and as vice president of the Bank of North Wilkesboro.

Arthur Augustus Finley died March 16, 1938, and is buried in Greenwood Cemetery. His wife, Kate Cameron Finley, died on July 23, 1939, and is buried beside her husband.

Lucy Lenoir Finley, their oldest child, was born on October 7, 1892. She was one of the earliest children born in the town of North Wilkesboro and was the first child to be baptised in the North Wilkesboro Presbyterian Church on June 16, 1893. After being educated at the Finley School and Southern Presbyterian College, she took a nurses training course at Stuart Circle Hospital in Richmond, VA. After working in New York City as a nurse for several years, Lucy returned to "Riverview" and became her father's bookkeeper at the Wilkesboro Manufacturing Co. She was active in the North Wilkesboro Presbyterian Church, the local UDC chapter, and the Ron-

dezvous Mountain Chapter, DAR. Lucy Lenoir Finley died unmarried on November 1, 1958, and is buried with her parents at Greenwood.

Grace Martin Finley was born on March 28, 1894. She was educated at the Finley School and Flora Macdonald College. She returned home to live where she did much of the cooking for the family. She also enjoyed children and worked with them at North Wilkesboro Presbyterian Church Sunday School. Grace died unmarried on August 13, 1951, and is buried in the family plot in Greenwood.

Bess Cameron Finley was Arthur and Kate's third child, born November 24, 1895. She too attended Finley School and Flora Macdonald College. She taught for a time at the Roxboro, N.C. high school. Bess died a fairly young (32) unmarried woman on July 1, 1927, and is buried with the family at Greenwood.

Allen Gordon Finley (Sr.) was born on July 1, 1898. (See the Gordon Finley, Sr. Family.) Arthur Cameron Finley was the fifth and youngest child of Arthur and Kate Finley, born on March 11, 1901. He was educated at the Finley School, North Wilkesboro High School, and Davidson College. Arthur served two years in the National Guard in Wilkes. For many years, he worked as a textile machinist technician for the Soco-Lowell Co. in the Southeastern United States. After World War II, the Soco-Lowell Co. sent Arthur to war ravaged France and Belgium to supervise the reconstruction of the devastated textile mills. He spent several years thus aiding his European counterparts.

On December 9, 1973, Arthur married Mrs. Lucile Woodall Blair in Eatonton, GA. She was born to Sam and Henrietta Turner Woodall on January 15, 1909. She was an avid gardener. Lucille died on June 24, 1978, and is buried in Eatonton Memorial Cemetery, Eatonton, GA. After his wife's death, Arthur returned to North Wilkesboro to live with relatives.

Sources: The Arthur A. Finley Family *Bible*, *Finleys of Wilkes 1804-1981,* and personal knowledge.

— Karen B. Binter.

EDWARD GORDON FINLEY
551

Edward Gordon Finley was born in Watauga County, N.C., September 9, 1884. He was the oldest son of James Edward and Julia Elizabeth (Gwyn) Finley.

He received his education at Horner Military Academy, Oxford, N.C., and Davidson College. After spending some time in California with relatives, he returned to North Wilkesboro, N.C., where he was first employed as Assistant Cashier with the Bank of North Wilkesboro. Later, he became Land and Timber Manager for C.C. Smoot and Sons Company Tannery of North Wilkesboro.

In 1924, with his brother, R.G. Finley, and others, he organized the Meadows Mill Company, manufacturers of grain grinding and wood sawing machinery. He served as Secretary-Treasurer and General Manager of that firm until his retirement on October 1, 1954, due to ill health.

He was active in a number of business and

civic affairs in North Wilkesboro and Wilkes County. He served as a member of the Town Board of Commissioners, had an interest and helped organize the North Wilkesboro Hotel Company, was charter member and past President of the North Wilkesboro Kiwanis Club, leader in the formation of the Wilkes County Public Library, and was active in the Wilkes Chamber of Commerce and Boy Scout program.

In 1911, he married Sibyl Harriet Smoot, daughter of James Clinton and Frank Wood Smoot of North Wilkesboro. Mrs. Finley, who was born in Alexandria, Virginia, received her early education at Miss Chandler's Arlington Institute in Alexandria and later at Goucher College in Baltimore, Maryland, where she was a member of Delta Gamma Sorority.

She was active in many church and community affairs being a member of the North Wilkesboro Presbyterian Church where she held poistions of leadership including Sunday School Teacher, Librarian, President of the Women of the Church as well as various Presbytery activities and work of the Church Young People's Organizations.

In civic life, she was active in the formation of the Wilkes Y.M.C.A. and Parent Teacher Association. She had blue eyes and dark hair and had many varied interests. She died in North Wilkesboro on October 18, 1962 and is buried in Mount Lawn Cemetery.

Children of Edward Gordon and Sibyl (Smoot) Finley: Julia Gwyn (Mrs. Chalmers F. McCutchen) b. 1912; Edward Smoot, b. 1916; and Robert Wood b. 1920.

Edward Finley's religious affiliation was with the North Wilkesboro Presbyterian Church where he served as Elder, Clerk of Session, Sunday School Teacher, and Chairman of the Building Committee.

He loved outdoors, enjoyed fishing and wild flowers. He was 6'1'' tall, had dark hair, and a keen sense of humor. He died in North Wilkesboro on January 5, 1962, and is buried in Mount Lawn Cemetery.

Sources: Family Records, ''Finleys of Wilkes''.

— Edward S. Finley

EDWARD SMOOT FINLEY
552

Edward Smoot Finley b. 4/6/16 in Alexandria, Virginia, son of Edward G. and Sibyl Smoot Finley, was the grandson of James E. and Julia Gwyn Finley.

He grew up in North Wilkesboro where he attended the North Wilkesboro public schools. College education at Davidson College where he graduated in class of 1937; member of Kappa Sigma Fraternity. Afterwards, he returned to North Wilkesboro where he was employed by Meadows Mill Company from 1937 to 1941 working in various capacities and travelling over seven southern states until being ordered to active duty with Army Air Force in June 1941.

On May 2, 1942, he married Elizabeth Stewart Heath in Monroe, N.C., daughter of William Joseph and Elizabeth English Heath. Elizabeth (Lib) received her early education in

Monroe City schools and later at Queens College in Charlotte. In North Wilkesboro where they settled after World War II, she became active in Church and social affairs, serving as Deacon and President of Women of the Church, also as Secretary-Treasurer and Choir Member. She is 5'2'' tall, has brown hair and eyes; likes bridge and needlework.

During World War II, Edward S. Finley served in American and China Theaters of operation, attaining the rank of Lt. Colonel. Returning to civilian life in 1946, he was again employed by Meadows Mill Company and is currently Secretary-Treasurer and General Manager of that firm.

Active in Church and Civic life, he served as member and Chairman of the North Wilkesboro Board of Education from 1957 to 1967; President of Wilkes Jaycees; North Wilkesboro Lions Club; Vice President of Wilkes Chamber of Commerce; Treasurer of Friends of the Wilkes County Library. In North Wilkesboro Presbyterian Church, he has served as Deanon, receiving treasurer, Elder and Clerk of Session. He is 6'2'' tall, 140 lbs. brown eyes and dark hair. Interests: farming, forestry and travel.

Children of Edward S. and Elizabeth H. Finley: Edward Smoot, Jr. b. 3/24/49 and Ann Heath, b. 3/12/52. Edward S. Jr. married Virginia P. Doughton and they have one son, Edward Doughton Finley, b. 2-23-81. Ed Jr. graduated from UNC Law school and is a practicing attorney in Raleigh, NC. Ann Heath graduated from UNC Pharmacy School, married Fairfax C. Reynolds and they have one daughter, Elizabeth Heath Reynolds, b. 9/12/81. Ann and Fairfax currently live in Charlotte, N.C.

Sources: Finleys of Wilkes

— Edward S. Finley

FRED TATE FINLEY
553

Fred Tate Finley, son of William Tate and Nancy Jettie (Martin) Finley, was born 25 November 1893 in Wilkes County, died 9 September 1980, married 27 August 1919 at the Spurgeon Memorial Baptist Church, Norfolk, Virginia, Mildred Hope Whitney, born 26 August 1902, daughter of Joseph McBride and Neppie Leigh (Beamon) Whitney, of Norfolk, Virginia. Fred is buried at Mt. Lawn Memorial Park and Mildred is living east of North Wilkesboro, N.C. on the Yadkin River.

Fred Finley worked in Norfolk during world War one, where he met and married Mildred. They lived in Norfolk until after their first three children were born, before moving to Wilkes County. They were active members of the North Wilkesboro Presbyterian Church, where Mildred is still a member. Fred worked for the Meadows Mill Company and was a farmer. They had eight children born to them: (1) Mildred Tate, born 9 January 1921, married Leonard Lawrence Brooks. They had two children, Leonard Lawrence, Jr.and William Finley and are included in the Brooks family history, (2) Norma Frances, born 8 July 1925, married 8 November 1942 Glenn Dancy, Jr. Their children are Glenn Dancy III, born 26

September 1943, married 24 August 1963 Linda Lou Smoot; Susan Lee Dancy, born 14 May 1947, married 19 March 1965 Donald Richard Blevins; Sandra Lynne Dancy, born 12 October 1960, married 7 January 1978, Dewey Vance Cleary, Jr. (3) Mary Garden, born 20 October 1927, married 31 July 1962 in Hickory, Bob Barton. Their children are Vanessa Elaine, born 26 February 1963 and Bob, Jr. born 17 July 1964. (4)Virginia June, born 4 April 1931 in Wilkes County, married 11 November 1952 James Wright Cain. Their children are: James Wright Cain, Jr. born 27 August 1953, and Janice Rebecca, born 26 May 1956, married 23 August 1980 Thomas Edward Sampson in Colorado Springs, Colorado where the Cains live. (5) Fred Tate, Jr. born 19 September 1933, married 30 May 1959 in Berea, Kentucky, Nina Elizabeth Marable. Their children are: Gail, born 8 March 1965 and Fred Tate, III, born 20 May 1967. (6) Franklin McBride, born 22 January 1937, married 1 July 1963 in Morganton, N.C. Marie Johnson. They have one child, Richard Lee, born 17 January 1971 and adopted 1 January 1980., (7) Richard Whitney, born and died 2 October 1938, (8) Linda Diane, born 20 October 1942, married in 1965 in Berea, Kentucky, Barry Ward Elledge. They have children: Barry Ward, Jr., born 28th September 1962, Northampton, Mass.; Michael Scott, born 20 July 1965, Raleigh, N.C., and Julie Camille, born 9 June 1970 in Boone, N.C. where they now live.

Sources: Family history, Family *Bible* records, personal knowledge.

— Leonard Lawrence Brooks, Jr.

GORDON FINLEY, SR. FAMILY
554

Allen Gordon Finley (Sr.) was born on July 1, 1898, the fourth child and older son of Arthur Augustus and Kate Cameron Finley. He was educated at the Finley School, North Wilkesboro High School, and graduated from Davidson College in 1918, with letters in football and track. He served in the army during World War I.

On June 21, 1922, Gordon married Annie May Barnes in Kitrell, N.C. She was born October 7, 1895, the oldest daughter of Guy Vernon and May Ella Williams Barnes of Kitrell. She was educated in Kitrell High School and taught at the Episcopal Mission School near Tarboro and at Wilkesboro Elementary School. Gordon and Annie May moved ''up the hill'' from his home, ''Riverview'', where they lived and raised three children: Katherine May, Mary Elmore, and A. Gordon, Jr.

Gordon was employed as an engineer for the state highway commission before joining his father in the Wilkesboro Manufacturing Co., where he became president in 1938. He served as a town commissioner and was active in the American Legion and the Kiwanis Club. Gordon also served as a deacon, elder, and treasurer of the North Wilkesboro Presbyterian Church. He was extremely active in the Boy Scouts and received the Silver Beaver Award. On January 27, 1952, Gordon died of a heart attack. He is buried in Greenwood Cemetery.

Annie May also became active in the community, belonging to the American Legion Auxiliary, the local DAR, and the Musical Arts Club. She taught piano for many years at home and in the Wilkes County schools. She was extremely active in the North Wilkesboro Presbyterian Church as organist, choir member, Sunday School teacher, and Junior choir leader. On April 8, 1971, Annie May died at Wilkes General Hospital of a stroke. She is buried beside her husband in Greenwood.

Katherine May Finley was born on July 3, 1924, in North Wilkesboro, oldest child of Gordon (Sr.) and Annie May Finley. She was educated in North Wilkesboro city schools, Flora Macdonald College, and Virginia Commonwealth University. She worked as a lab technician in Burlington and Charlotte. On April 10, 1948, Katherine married Wilson Mathias Blatt; they were the last couple married in the old frame sanctuary of the North Wilkesboro Presbyterian Church.

Wilson was born November 6, 1923, in Milford, VA., the older child of Jacob Augustus and Stella Mathias Blatt. He was educated in Caroline Co., VA. schools and Benjamin Franklin University, Washington, DC. He is the owner-operator of Blatt's Store, a general merchandise and building supply business in Milford, VA. Katherine and Wilson are very active in the Milford Presbyterian Church, teaching Sunday School, as choir members, and serving as officers. Katherine also worked as a social worker and school librarian in Caroline County, VA.

Karen Gordon Blatt, daughter of Katherine Finley and Wilson M. Blatt, was born May 22, 1952, in Richmond, VA. After graduating from Appalachian State University, she worked as a librarian in Virginia and New Jersey. On August 24, 1974, in Milford, VA., Karen married Randolph Kimbell Binter, second son of Frederick Carl and Evelyn Kimbell Binter of Moorestown, NJ. He was born in Philadelphia, PA., on November 17, 1949. After graduating from Appalachian State University, Randolph became a technical consultant in chemical sales for his family owned Independence Chemical Co. Karen and Randy live in Cinnaminson, NJ., with their two daughters, Ashley Katherine (b. 3/11/78) and Rebecca Ann (b. 6/19/80).

Mary Elmore Finley, second child of Gordon and Annie May Finley, was born March 19, 1927, in North Wilkesboro. She was educated in North Wilkesboro city schools, where her graduating class of '44 was the last class of the eleven year school era. She then attended Salem College and Appalachian State University. Mary Elmore worked as a classroom teacher in Winston-Salem and Wilkes County before assuming librarian positions, first with the laboratory school for Western Carolina University and presently for the Wilkes County school system. She is active in the North Wilkesboro Presbyterian Church, in the choir, director of the children's choir, and as church librarian. Mary Elmore now resides in her parents' family home on E Street in North Wilkesboro.

Allen Gordon Finley, Jr. was born June 16, 1930, to Gordon and Annie May Finley. Please see Gordon Finley, Jr. Family.

Sources: The Arthur A. Finley Family Bible, Finleys of Wilkes 1804-1981, and personal knowledge.

— Karen B. Binter

GORDON FINLEY, JR. FAMILY 555

Allen Gordon Finley (Jr.), the third child and only son of A. Gordon (Sr.) and Annie May Barnes Finley, was born June 16, 1930, in North Wilkesboro. He was educated in North Wilkesboro city schools, Lees McRae College, and National Business College, Roanoke, VA. Gordon served in the US Navy in the early fifties. He returned to North Wilkesboro following the death of his father to take over management of Wilkesboro Manufacturing Co. On August 8, 1956, at Ferguson, N.C., Gordon married Carolina Ferguson.

Carolina was born May 3, 1936, the youngest of four daughters, to Thomas Wiley and Edith Kyles Ferguson. She was educated in Wilkes County schools and Greensboro College, where she reigned as May Queen her senior year.

During his years in Wilkes, Gordon has been active in community affairs, serving as a scoutmaster, a past-president of the Wilkes Camp of Gideons, and the Y's Mens Club. He is also active in the North Wilkesboro Presbyterian Church as superintendent of Sunday School, a deacon, an elder, and a choir member. He is presently a realtor for Century 21 — Sherrill — Faw Real Estate.

Carolina has taught art, both privately and for the Wilkes County school system. She also teaches a pre-school program at the Church School of the North Wilkesboro Presbyterian Church. She is active in the church Choir, the Musical Arts Club, the Wilkes Art Guild, and the Grange. She has served as a deacon of the church.

Gordon and Carolina lived for a time in his grandfather's homeplace, "Riverview" before moving out to their "chalet" on the Brushies where they presently live. They have six children: Allen Gordon III, Thomas Cameron, Kathrine Ferguson, Ann Kendal, Carol Kyles, and Mary Rebecca.

Allen Gordon Finley, III, older son of Gordon and Carolina Finley was born September 25, 1959, in North Wilkesboro. He is a graduate of Wilkes Central High School and Central Piedmont Community College, Charlotte. Following in the family tradition of Scouting, Allen is an Eagle Scout and a member of the Order of the Arrow. Allen presently resides in Charlotte where he is an Assistant Art Director of Southern Shows.

Thomas Cameron Finley, second son of Gordon and Carolina Finley, was born in North Wilkesboro on August 26, 1961. He is a graduate of Wilkes Central High School and Wilkes Community College. Like his brother, Cam is also an Eagle Scout and a member of the Order of the Arrow. On June 14, 1979, Cam received the Govenor's Award for Bravery and Heroism after saving the life of a drowning boy. Cam is associated with Knollwood Landscaping, and is presently attending Appalachian State University.

Katherine Ferguson Finley, third child of Gordon and Carolina Finley, was born on May 8, 1964, at Georgetown University Hospital, Washington, DC. She is an honor graduate of Wilkes Central High School where she was a member of the band, Executive Council, and Student Council. Katie was also a member and director of the Interact Club, and a member and president of both the Latin Club and the National Honor Society. A member of the North Wilkesboro Presbyterian Church, she is a member of their Pastoral Nominating Committee and a representative to the Presbytery Youth Council. Katie is presently attending Appalachian State University.

In North Wilkesboro, on February 3, 1970, Gordon and Carolina Finley were blessed with twin daughters, Ann Kendal and Carol Kyles. Kendal and Carol share a love of animals, books, and dance, and have successfully passed the Royal Academy of Dance Exam for two consecutive years.

Mary Rebecca Finley joined the family of Gordon and Carolina Finley on October 3, 1973, in North Wilkesboro. Like her twin sisters, Mary enjoys dancing and has successfully passed the Royal Academy of Dance Exam for two consecutive years.

Sources: The Arthur A. Finley Family Bible, Finleys of Wilkes 1804-1981; and personal knowledge and interviews.

— Karen B. Binter

JAMES EDWARD FINLEY 556

James Edward Finley was born in Wilkes County August 8, 1850. He was the son of Augustus Washington and Martha Lenoir (Gordon) Finley.

He received his education at Bingham School near the village of Mebane in Orange County, N.C. As a young man, he moved to Texas where he was employed as a telegraph operator for several years. Later he returned to North Carolina and to Watauga County where he operated a large farm at Meet Camp.

In 1883, he married Julia Elizabeth Gwyn, daughter of Richard Ransome and Mary Caroline (Dickenson) Gwyn from Elkin, N.C. She was medium height, had brown eyes and dark hair and enjoyed cooking. She died at the age of fifty and is buried in Greenwood cemetery, North Wilkesboro, N.C.

Children of James Edward and Julia Elizabeth (Gwyn) Finley: Edward Gordon b. 1884; Mary Louise b. 1887; and Richard Gwyn b. 1895.

In 1891, he moved to North Wilkesboro where he became involved in many business activities of the town and county. He was founder and President of the Bank of North Wilkesboro, had an interest in the Forest Furniture Company, North Wilkesboro Building and Loan Association, New Williams Mill Company, as well as other enterprises. In addition, he served as Town Commissioner, being elected May 1, 1893 and reelected May 1894.

His religious affiliation was with the North Wilkesboro Presbyterian Church of which he was a charter member, served as Elder in 1896, Superintendent of Sunday School in

1914, and was one of the Trustees of this church.

He was tall, had gray eyes, dark hair, and wore a beard. He enjoyed horses. He died in North Wilkesboro on October 30, 1923 and is buried in Greenwood Cemetery.

Sources: Family Records, "Finleys of Wilkes".

— Edward S. Finley

JOHN FINLEY
557

John Finley, called Major John Finley by many, first bought land in Wilkes in 1804, and began to live in Wilkesboro. He was the ancestor of all Finleys in the county.

John was a twin son born September 2, 1778 to Michael and Mary Waugh Finley of Pa., and later of Augusta County, VA. His grandparents were William and second wife, Catherine Culbertson Finley of Pa.; great-grandparents, Michael and Ann O'Neill Finley, immigrants to America in 1734 from coun-Armagh, Ireland; great-great-grandparents Robert and M. Lauder Finley of north Ireland and Fife, Scotland, John of Wilkes was nineteenth in descent from Macbeth who reigned 1039-1057 in Scotland. Among John's noteworthy lateral kin in America: Samuel Finley D.D., president of Princeton College 1761, great-uncle; and Samuel's grandson, Samuel Finley Breese Morse, noted artist and inventor of the telegraph.

John came directly from Augusta County, Virginia, to Wilkesborough, and immediately bought stock in the mercantile and real estate firm of Waugh and Finley. His partner, William Pitt Waugh, a bachelor cousin from Pa., first lived near the courthouse, later at the Forks of the Road (Moravian Falls). Waugh and Finley operated a chain of stores from 1804 until 1845 in N.C., S.C., Tenn., and Ala.

As early as 1810 Finley was a county trustee, and a justice in 1836 and 1861.

Soon after John's arrival in Wilkes he began buying town lots and tracts of land, a practice he continued throughout his life. In his 1865 will he listed the Wilkesboro Hotel that stood on the lot just east of the courthouse. He owned this property, but leased it to various proprietors to operate. The present brick hotel building was erected later on. Finley bought Lot 12 in 1816 on which he later built his brick home on North Street.

Finley was a strong religious leader. In 1837 when the Presbyterian Church of Wilkesboro was organized, John Finley became a leader in the founding of the Presbyterian church in northwest North Carolina. At that time no Presbyterian church existed in 21 northwest counties of the state. He was a charter member, one of the original elders, and remained faithful and loyal to this church for the remainder of his life. It is said that in his old age someone asked him, "Since you have become so deaf, why do you continue to go to church?" he replied, "I go because of the example". Often it was recorded that a session was held and that John Finley was the only elder present. The First Presbyterian Church of Winston was not organized until 1861, and the

John Finley.

name of John Finley of Wilkesboro is duly recorded as a contributor then.

Not only in the field of religion was Finley a leader, but also in the area of education. He was a trustee of Wilkesborough Academy of 1819, a trustee of the Seminary of 1837, and in 1841 a member of the board of superintendents of common schools in Wilkes. These facts show that he believed in helping to build up the area where he chose to live. He believed in the importance of education for his children and his neighbor's children when many people did not. A receipt is preserved showing that he paid $180 Nov. 20, 1822 to Salem Female Boarding School for his daughter Clarinda's

board, room and instruction.

On April 4, 1807 Finley married Ellen Tate, daughter of John Tate Jr. of Augusta County, Va., a trustee of Staunton Academy, and a soldier in the American Revolution.

In his last days on earth Finley witnessed the rise and fall of the Confederate Government (which he had supported with money), including the devastating visit by Yankee troops to Wilkesboro in 1865.

After his death Nov. 4, 1865 John Finley was buried beside his wife in Wilkesboro's oldest cemetery near the Presbyterian Church. She had preceeded him to the grave by 13 years.

Children reaching maturity were: Clarinda J.E. who married Dr. Thomas Slater Bouchelle; Augustus Washington, who after marriage to Martha Lenoir Gordon, lived on hill where N. Wilkesboro post office now stands; William, who after marriage to Martha Caroline Horton, lived on land that is now the eastern part of N. Wilkesboro; and John Tate, who, after his marriage to Sarah Ann Gordon (sister of Martha L.G.), lived on hill where the Wilkes hospital now stands.

Sources: Family records, county records, family traditions.

— Elizabeth Cowles Finley

JOHN TATE FINLEY FAMILY
558

John Tate Finley was born August 9, 1817. He was married to Sarah Ann Gordon and after marriage lived in Brown-Cowles house in Wilkesboro, east of the courthouse. He was in mercantile business with his brother-in-law, James B. Gordon.

He moved to Alabama in the 1850s but returned to Wilkes to live at "Oakland", (where Wilkes Hospital now stands) where he farmed land north of Yadkin and west of Reddies rivers.

His wife had attended Salem College where records show she studied German, French, drama, art, painting, ornamental needlework, piano, guitar, melodian, in addition to basic courses.

They attended Wilkesboro Presbyterain Church and are buried behind the church. He died in 1896, and she in 1907.

They had the following children:

Walter Gordon, born November 8, 1847 and died 1888. He was married to Annie Elizabeth Van Eaton. He was a surveyor in Texas and owned a cattle ranch near Fort Worth. Three children died young, but two survived, Ellen Tate Finley and William Walter Finley.

Ellen married Archie Reid Ogilvie and they had six children: Clara Finley, Gordon Finley and Jeanie Forsyth (twins), Samuel Reid, Kate Cameron and George MacDonald.

William Walter married Sue Rebecca Miller and when she died, he married Melissa Hoover. By his first marriage he had four children: Annie Elizabeth, Fielden Miller, John Gordon and Martha Sue. By his second marriage, he had six: Dorothy Caldwell, Robert Van Eaton, Malcolm Gwyn, Hannah Stevens, William Walter, Jr. and Allen Brown.

Louise Florence was second child of the John Tate Finley, and she was born December 9, 1849 and died four years later.

Ellen Tate was born in 1852, married David William Greenlee, a banker of Marion, N.C. They had two children: John Harvey and Mary Gordon. John Harvey, born in 1885, married Loto Quinn. She died and he married Claudia Harbison. Harvey was banker and farmer in Marion, and he and Claudia had two children, Charles Harvey and William Gordon. Mary Gordon Greenlee was born in 1888 and married Bernard F. Pollard and they lived and died in Marion.

Martha Clara Finley was born September 15, 1856. She was unmarried and the first teacher of a private Finley school in Lenoir, N.C. She was active in United Daughters of Confederacy, Woman's Christian Temperance Union and work of the Presbyterian Church.

Annie Mary Finley was born June 1, 1860; taught music at the Finley school and like her sister was active in UDC, WCTU, and in church work.

John Thomas Finley was born April 10, 1862. He was unmarried, lived with his sisters, and operated a livery stable in N. Wilkesboro.

James Robert Finley was born May 29, 1864. He and Fanny Turpin were first couple married in first N.W. Presbyterian Church. He was N. Wilkesboro's first Postmaster and one of the first merchants, president of Kiwanis Club, secretary-treasurer of Forest Furniture Co. and very active in his church, as was his wife.

They had three daughters: Bess Gordon, Fanny Eloise and Kate Cameron. Bess Gordon was born June 27, 1894 and married William C. Grier. She was active in Daughters of Confederacy and member of American Legion Auxiliary. She died in 1948. Fanny Eloise was born October 18, 1899 and married Samuel Phillips Mitchell who was a civil engineer. They had one child, Samuel Phillips, Jr. born in 1930. Kate Cameron was born February 27, 1903. She worked in the library system of New York City and in Wilkes County Library for many years, working with the Bookmobile. Kate loves the out-doors and driving friends and relatives around to see the changes of season, wild flowers and deer.

Samuel Gwyn Finley, the youngest child, born March 9, 1867, was educated at Chapel Hill; became a lawyer and lived in Spartanburg, S.C. He married Ruth Caldwell Cofield, and they had four children: Samuel Gwyn II, Ruth Caldwell, Anna Clementina, Margaret Gordon. (1) Samuel Gwyn II was born September 12, 1906; married Ena Clodaine Lambeth and they live at Alamance. They have three children: Ena Ruth, Samuel Gwyn III and Betty Anna. (2) Ruth Caldwell was born January 26, 1908, married George C. Weiterer; no children. (3) Anna Clementina was born September 5, 1909, was in civil service, Washington, D.C. and Spartanburg, S.C. Retired now, she lives in Southport. (4) Margaret Gordon was born in 1918, married Charles Bynum Atwater, Jr. He died, and she now lives in Charleston, S.C. They had five children: Charles Finley, Harvey Gordon, John Cofield, Sarah Clementina, and Robert Dillard.

Sources: Finleys of Wilkes (1804-1981) and personal knowledge.

— Kate Cameron Finley

RICHARD GWYN FINLEY
559

Richard Gwyn Finley, b. 1-26-1895, m. (1) Apphia Jackson; (2) Mary Porter Jackson Gentry. Born in Wilkes County, son of James Edward and Julia Elizabeth Gwyn Finley; attended Finley School (a small private school near his home), North Wilkesboro High School, Fishburn Military Academy and Davidson College, graduating in class of 1916, Phi Beta Kappa. He was a member of Kappa Sigma fraternity.

He served as secretary and treasurer of New Williams Mill Company prior to army service during W.W.I in France. In 1918, he returned to North Wilkesboro and was employed as asst. cashier of Bank of North Wilkesboro for two years. Then he went back as secretary and treasurer of New Williams Mill Company. In 1924, this company was consolidated with two others, Meadows Mill and W.J. Palmer Manufacturing Company. The resulting company was called Meadows Mill Company, and he became President of this firm retaining the title until the present.

In 1929, he was state President of the Izaak Walton League of America; was also vice-president and director of Bank of North Wilkesboro, and later director and chairman of the board of North Wilkesboro branch of N.C. National Bank. On the selective service board (draft board) of Wilkes County during WWII; served three terms as commissioner of Town of North Wilkesboro and one term as county commissioner fo Wilkes County where he was also chairman of the board.

In Kiwanis Club, he served as director for a number of years and President for one term; president and director of both Oakwoods and Blowing Rock Country Clubs. Served as secretary-treasurer of Wilkes General Hospital for 14 years; served as director of North Wilkesboro Savings & Loan Association since 1925 and President of that association since 1979.

In North Wilkesboro Presbyterian Church, he has served as deacon, treasurer, Sunday School teacher, and trustee.

He makes his home in North Wilkesboro and Blowing Rock and is an accomplished golfer whose scores have matched his age numerous times.

Sources: Personal knowledge.

— Mary Porter Finley

JUDGE THOMAS B. FINLEY
560

Thomas B. Finley, Judge of N.C. Superior Court 1918-1934, was born Nov. 6, 1862, the youngest of eight children born to Augustus W. and Martha Lenoir Gordon Finley at their home "Fairmount" (located where the North Wilkesboro post office now stands). His father's plantation beginning in 1842 comprised all the land between Seventh Street and the Reddies River. He was a brother to J. Edward, J. George (unmarried), Arthur A., and Mrs. C.G. Pilson. His mother was a sister of Brigadier James B. Gordon, CSA, Ann and Caroline Gordon, wives respecfully of John Tate Finley and Dr. R.F. Hackett.

As a boy Thomas roamed the woods on his father's land, checking his rabbit gums and hunting. He was sent to Finley High School in Lenoir, afterwards to Davidson College where he was a member of Kappa Alpha social fraternity and won a declaimer's medal. Next, he studied at Col. Folk's law

Judge Thomas B. Finley.

school in Caldwell County. He began the practice of law in Wilkesboro, his first law partner being J.C. Cranor, for one year. Later partners were Herbert Greene and F.B. Hendren. It is not known exactly when he began to occupy the law office just east of the courthouse that is still standing.

Finley was not married until he was almost thirty-one years old. Before marriage he enjoyed parties and dances given by the Hortons in Happy Valley and trips to Blowing Rock. A Wilkesboro newspaper wrote an account of an accident he experienced while taking a visiting young lady friend, Miss Liz Thomas, buggy riding on the Moravian Falls road. It seems that his horse became scared in the exact spot in the road where W.W. Peden had been murdered. in 1844. The buggy overturned, throwing out the occupants. A passing friend drove Miss Thomas back to town, while Finley hunted the nearby woods for his horse.

Finley was known as constant, enthusiastic booster of Wilkes County in all his speeches. He worked vigorously to secure the first railroad to Wilkes, the greatest step this section has ever taken; was chairman of committee that secured rights-of-way for the Watauga Railroad that ran westward from N. Wilkesboro prior to the 1916 flood. In 1916 he was presidential elector, voting for President Wilson. In 1919 he was a member of 16 corporations and committees, president or chairman of nine and director of most of the others; was first vice-president of N.C. Bar Association in 1918; and served as Superior Court Judge of N.C. 1918-1934.

Not only did he work on industrial growth, but he helped to promote better schools (chairman of No. Wilkesboro school board 1914-18.) and better agriculture, as president

of the first Wilkes County Fair prior to the 1916 flood.

In 1893 T.B. Finley married Carrie Lizzie Cowles, daughter of W.H.H. Cowles of Wilkesboro in the Wilkesboro Presbyterian Church. This was a formal public ceremony with bridal attendants. The vows were made to the Reverend Mr. Crawford. Immediately afterwards the bridal couple was accompanied to the railroad station by many well-wishers who wanted to see them off on their honeymoon to Niagara Falls and the World's Fair in Chicago.

In his home, Finley was a good husband and father. For many years the entire family traveled by horses and a three-seated carriage to the Watauga Inn in Blowing Rock for summer vacations. In 1913, before the day of public tennis courts, he built a tennis court on top of a hill behind his residence (on northeast corner of E and Eleventh Streets). The tennis court, surrounded by high wire, was in his cow pasture lot, and became a social gathering spot for his children and their friends.

T.B. Finley died April 3, 1942 preceding his wife's death by five years, and was buried in Greenwood Cemetery in North Wilkesboro.

To select from many written expressions of admiration received about him, a May 1982 note from former Senator Sam J. Ervin of Morganton was: "I had many occasions when I had the opportunity of appearing before

Judge Thomas B. Finley, who was one of the finest men, and one of the greatest judges I have ever been privileged to know.''

Children in this family (all five of whom were college graduates) were: Martha Lura, married C. Don Coffey, Gulf Oil distributor; Thomas Augustus, married Grace Cochran of Huntersville; Corinna Worth, who died at Queens College in Charlotte during the 1918 influenza epidemic; Ellen Lenoir, married Lewis M. Nelson, Sr.; and Elizabeth Cowles, a teacher in the North Wilkesboro primary school for forty-two years.

Sources: Family records, newspapers and personal knowledge.

— Elizabeth C. Finley

WILLIAM TATE FINLEY
561

William Pitt Waugh Finley, son of John, the pioneer, and his wife, Sarah Ellen (Tate) Finley, was born in Wilkes County, N.C. 26 June 1815, died the 3 March 1874, married about 1847, Martha Caroline Horton, born 15 January 1827, died 17 July 1865, daughter of David Eagles and Sarah (Dula) Horton, from what is now Caldwell County. William P.W. Finley was named for a kinsman and partner in business of John Finley, William Pitt Waugh. W.P. Waugh Finley was a farmer and lived on a farm in the eastern part of what is now North Wilkesboro, it being one of the farms that was bought for the town of North Wilkesboro to be built upon. His house stood on the corner of C and Third Streets. It is of interest that my father-in-law, William Oliver Absher, was born in a house on the exact spot, for William Pitt Waugh Finley was my great, great grandfather.

W.P.W. and Martha Caroline (Horton) Finley had seven children, as follows: (1) John Horton, born 16 December 1848, died 25 November 1907, married Rebecca Malinda McGlamery, (2) Sarah Corinna, born 10 August 1849, died 2 January 1924, married 17 May 1870, Elijah Blair, (3) Jane B., born 1853, died 1930 in Mecklenburg County, N.C. married 24 February 1880, Isaac Teeters, (4) Julia A., born 1856, died 7 May 1928 in Morganton, unmarried, (5) Martha Edith, born 12 May 1857, died 6 September 1945, married A. David Reece. (6) David Theodore, born 1 January 1860, died 29 October 1939, unmarried. (7) William Tate born 5 March 1863, died 6 December 1937, married Nancy Jettie Clementine Martin. W.P.W. Finley, his wife and some of his children are buried in the Horton Family Cemetery on the Yadkin River in Caldwell County, not far from the Wilkes County line.

William Tate Finley, son of William Pitt Waugh and Martha Carolina (Horton) Finley, married on Tuesday, 18 October 1892, Nancy Jettie Clementine Martin, born 29 April 1870, died 22 April 1967, daughter of Esq. John Britton and Mrs. Susannah Elizabeth (Sale-Parteete) Martin. Elizabeth was the daughter of John, Jr. and Lemirah (Gray) Sale and the widow of John Parteete, of Brier Creek, Wilkes County, N.C.

William Tate Finley, Fred Tate Finley, and Jettie Martin Finley.

William Tate Finley attended the Buckeye school east of town near the lower bridge, ran a livery stable and later farmed, owning a large acerage of land on the Brushy Mountains, where he lived and died. William Tate and Jettie Finley had only one child, Fred Tate Finley, my grandfather.

Sources: family history, obituary in Chronicle Newspaper (1890-1911), gravestone inscriptions.

— Leonard Lawrence Brooks, Jr.

WINFIELD SCOTT FLETCHER
562

Winfield Scott Fletcher was born October 8, 1885, the youngest child of William Columbus Fletcher and Alpha Jane Eller Fletcher. He spent most of his life in the Purlear community of Stanton Township.

He received his early education at New Hope School, later attending Whitsett Institute near Greensboro. There he won Whitsett's highest honor, a gold medal for oratory, in 1910. He was graduated in 1911.

His first assignment in the Postal Service was to deliver mail on horseback up Lewis' Fork Creek. He transferred to Railway Postal Service and before retirement in 1945 had been promoted to Chief Clerk. During his early years in the postal department he studied law and was admitted to the bar on August 23, 1926. Although he never practiced law, he served as Justice of the Peace for many years and was a Notary Republic.

He was an avid Republican and one of the highlights of his life was attending a national convention. The only time he sought public office, he was an unsuccessful candidate for Clerk of Court. He was a Mason and an active member of the Jr. OUAM, New Hope chapter.

Following his retirement, he became a surveyor and was actively engaged in this vocation until his death. Among his papers are copies of many deeds and plats.

Mr. Fletcher was a history buff and often opened breakfast table conversation citing historical dates, i.e., ''If William Howard Taft had

lived, he would be ninety-seven years old today.''

He regularly attended New Hope Baptist Church but never became a member. Speculation regarding his refusal to associate himself with the church is that he felt that the boundary lines were not clearly drawn on the church property. Others think that he was emulating Abraham Lincoln who, also, never joined a church.

He remained a bachelor until age fifty-five when he married a widow, Ruby Barnes Pendley of North Wilkesboro April 9, 1939. She was the widow of Neal Pendley and the daughter of Stacey and Eugenia Felts Barnes. Mrs. Pendley had one child, Marcella, who made her home with them until her marriage.

The Fletchers traveled by train to California for their honeymoon where they attended the 1939 San Francisco Exhibition. Later that year,

Winfield Scott Fletcher.

they attended the New York World's Fair.

They resided in a large, two-story white frame house in the Purlear community that Mr. Fletcher had built several years prior to their marriage. His brother, Eller, and his family had lived with him prior to his marriage to Mrs. Pendley.

He also owned property on Lewis Fork Creek on which stands the Robert Cleveland House, the oldest house in Wilkes County. It is a two-story log building with rock chimneys on both ends of the house.

In addition to its age of over two hundred years it is historically significant because it was the dwelling of Capt. Robert Cleveland whose brother, Col. Benjamin Cleveland, led the forces from Wilkes County to the Battle of King's Mountain.

Mr. Fletcher died on March 1, 1961 and is buried in New Hope Church cemetery. He was survived by his widow, her daughter, Marcella P. Church, his sister, Lizzie Yates and numerous nieces and nephews. Mrs. Fletcher died a year and a half later.

Sources: Personal knowledge.

— Marcella Pendley Church

FOOTE FAMILY
563

Maj. James Henry Foote (1825-1909), father of Rear Admiral Percy Wright Foote, was born in Wilkes County. When a young boy he attended Peter Stuart Ney's school at Hunting Creek and later, in 1852, graduated at Wake Forest College. In 1861, while holding the position "Professor of ancient and modern languages at Wake Forest" he left with a band of students to join the C.S.A., as captain. Later he was promoted to major, then in 1863 to assistant adjutant general when Zebulon Vance became governor of North Carolina.

Maj. Foote was in Raleigh at the time of Stoneman's raid. He jumped out of a window to escape capture and got together a detail of soldiers to protect the Wake Forest buildings from being burned.

In 1870, Maj. Foote was appointed assistant deputy U.S. marshal, and while holding this position, during the reconstruction period, he had the unique experience of placing General Kirk under arrest.

The ancestors of Maj. Foote came from Warrenton, Fauquier County, Virginia, to Warrenton, North Carolina. They were descended from Judge Richard Foote of old Stafford County, Virginia and from Richard Foote of Cornwall, England. His mother's ancestor, John Wright, was born 1728 in Prince William County, Virginia, was a captain of the Virginia Colonial Militia in Fauquier County. In 1750, he married Anne Williams of Virginia, and in 1774, they moved to Surry County, N.C. where he served in the American Revolutionary army.

Among their children were: Thomas, grandfather of James Henry Foote; Amelia, who married Dr. Robert Martin; Lucretia who married Eli Petty, grandfather of Mrs. Joe Edwards of Ronda and Mrs. Lyndolph Parks of Roaring River.

Charles C. Wright, the superintendent of schools of Wilkes County for so many years was of this Wright family. They were directly descended from Major Francis Wright and his wife, and from John Washington, the great-grandfather of George Washington.

Maj. Foote was married three times. He first married Mary Ann Williams, second to Cynisca Hunt and third to Susanna Clemmons Hunt who was born in 1845.

One child was born of the first marriage: (1) Lillian (1845-1922) who married Julius C. LeGrand and were parents of Mrs. Cora LeGrand Steventon, Eugene LeGrand and Anne Sue LeGrand of Winston-Salem.

There were two children of the second marriage: (2) James H. Foote, Jr. remained unmarried and (3) Vance of Chicago, Illinois who married Carrie Wellborn of Wilkesboro.

Five children were born of the third marriage: (4) Percy Wright who married Genevieve Clary of Great Falls, Montana. (5) Electa who married first Durand Cooper and second, William A. Thomas of Statesville, N.C. (6) Stella who married Carl S. Young of Oak Hill, Virginia. (7) Zera Cleveland who married Charles H. Greenwood of Wilkes County. (8) Ovid Clemmons (1888-1940) at Lt. Commander, Medical Corps, U.S.N., Washington, D.C. who first married Eleanor Potter, and second, Mrs. Florence Boyd Brodrick of San Francisco. During the World War, Ovid Clemmons Foote was chief surgeon at the U.S. Naval Base Hospital, Brest, France.

In 1872, when Maj. James Henry Foote returned to Wilkes County from Raleigh, he built the brick home called "River View" on a hill overlooking the Yadkin Valley south of the village of Roaring River. The plantation surrounding this house was part of a grant to Col. John Bryan, Mrs. Foote's ancestor. In 1909, this house, together with a large and valuable collection of books was destroyed by fire. A second house, built along lines similar to the original structure, remained in the possession of the family until a few years ago when it was sold.

The children of Percy Wright Foote, Rear Admiral, U.S. Navy, retired, and his wife Genevieve Clary Foote are: (1) Capt. Thomas Clary Foote, U.S. Army, (2) Diana Harrison Foote.

Capt. Percy Wright Foote was retired in 1936 and promoted to rank of Rear Admiral in recognition of distinguished service during World War I. He commanded U.S.S. President Lincoln in engagement with German submarine U-90, 1918, served as aide to Secretary of the Navy, Daniels 1918-1921, decorated with the Order of the Crown in person by King Albert of Belgium in 1919, also decorated D.S.M., by president Woodrow Wilson.

In 1937 he was appointed as the Commissioner of the Pennsylvanie Motor Police Force by Governor Earle, and performed the duties of that office with conspicuous success. In recognition of his services in the highway safety program, he was awarded the Meritorious Service Medal of the State of Pennsylvania.

In the 1940s Admiral Foote and wife were residing at Chapel Hill where their daughter Diana was an honor student in the University of

North Carolina.

Sources: Excerpts from *Happy Valley* by Felix Hickerson.

— Eleanor Parks Elam

JAMES and RUTH FORD
564

Ruth and Jim Ford came to North Wilkesboro in May, 1946. All they knew of North Carolina or North Wilkesboro was what they saw on the road map. Two towns, Wilkesboro and North Wilkesboro, so near on the map, they thought unusual. Jim represented Belknap Hardware and Manufacturing Company (now Belknap, Inc.) and the center of his territory was North Wilkesboro.

They found the people friendly and welcoming. The community seemed to be divided by churches — and since Jim was Presbyterian and Ruth, a Methodist, and they lived in the home of a Baptist, they were fortunate to be visited by each group. They later joined the North Wilkesboro Presbyterian Church and told their other friends that the Presbyterians "out-visited" them.

James Kinnaird Ford was born March 11, 1918, in Lancaster, Kentucky (Garrard County) the first son of Elijah Evans and Patsy McKee Kinnaird Ford. He was named for his maternal grandfather, Dr. James B. Kinnaird, who practiced medicine in Garrard County for many years and wrote a history of the county. Jim graduated from Lancaster High School, attended Centre College in Danville and the University of Kentucky. He represented Belknap Hardware of Louisville as a salesman in Kansas City, Missouri before entering the U.S. Army in 1942. While stationed at Camp Campbell (now Fort Campbell) he met and married Ruth Annette Burke April 22, 1944.

Ruth was the youngest of nine children born to Mary Belle Bartlett and Allen Burke in Christian County, Kentucky, July 29, 1922. She grew up at the family farm at Oak Grove and was graduated from Bethel Woman's College in Hopkinsville, Kentucky in 1941. She taught in one of the few remaining one-room schools for one year before becoming a clerk-stenographer at Camp Campbell, where she and Jim met.

Jim and Ruth have four children, all born in North Wilkesboro, and attended North Wilkesboro Elementary School and graduated from Wilkes Central High School.

James Kinnaird Ford, Jr. was born January 6, 1947. He served in the USAF in Viet Nam and later was graduated from East Tennessee State University at Johnson City. He met and married Lorraine Day Jacobs, of Sag Harbor, New York on August 13, 1976.

Anita Burke Ford was born February 21, 1949. She was graduated from University of North Carolina at Greensboro and taught in Fayetteville, N.C. where she met and married Joseph Frederick Springer of Pineville, Louisiana on July 22, 1972. They have two daughters: Sarah Elizabeth, born November 8, 1973 in Fayetteville, and Rachel Ford, born in Raleigh, N.C. August 29, 1977.

Patsy McKee Ford was born January 26,

1953. She was graduated from Appalachian State University. She taught in Charleston, S.C., earned a Masters Degree from The Citadel there, and was married to John William Eads, Lt. USN from Princeton, Indiana on February 17, 1979.

Their fourth child, Douglas Hatton, was born March 31, 1962. Following graduation from Wilkes Central, he accepted a football scholarship at East Carolina University, Greenville, N.C. where he has just completed his second year.

Jim continues to sell hardware for Belknap and Ruth returned to the schoolroom, when their youngest child was seven, as a teacher's aide at North Wilkesboro Elementary School, where she has worked for fourteen years.

Sources: Personal knowledge.

— Ruth Burke Ford

CHARLES FORESTER
565

The Charles Forester family left Virginia to settle on the Lower Little River of the Catawba during the Revolutionary War. It was then Burke County. Part of the area became Wilkes in 1778, and remained in Wilkes until Alexander was formed fifty years later. The sixty or so families that lived along the tributaries of Lambeth fork, Grassy Fork and until 1793, Muddy fork, were separated from the rest of Wilkes by the Brushy Mountains, from Walnut Knob to Cove Gap. Roads were eventually established at Boone Gap and Kilby Gap, but getting over to the courthouse could not have been easy. Until after the war, when settlers started to come from Virginia and more eastern N.C. counties, neighbors were few, but helpful. James Reed sent a note to Henry Reed marking the Forester arrival in 1778, "Give Salt to Charles Forester & oblige."

Charles Forester became Captain of a company that engaged in constant skirmishes with the Tories. The company marched out for Fayetteville and S.C. and were active until after the Battle at Guilford Courthouse.

In 1790 Charles had four male and five females. Seven years later the Foresters left Wilkes and the Lower Little River for less appealing Dry Creek, Smith County, Tn. Charles died there in 1825.

Charles Forester was born in Richmond County, Va. on Northern Neck about 1750 to Robert Forester (1716-1783) and Bridgett Lovelace. Robert was one of four children born to William and Frances Bryant Forester, who were married 13 July 1715. Frances died in April 1723 and seven months later on 5 November 1723, William Forester was murdered by Thomas Glascock. His inventory lists a servant maid to serve three years, the usual animals, iron pots, yards of fine broad cloth, books and "a parcell of Doctors Meme".

Bridgett Lovelace was the daughter of Charles Lovelace (1696-1755) and Bridgett McLaughlin, eldest daughter of Manus and Elizabeth Woodbridge McLaughlin. The last Elizabeth was the daughter of Paul (1631-1691) and Bridgett Fitzherbert Woodbridge.

One of the Lovelace boys took his family to Halifax, Va. in the 1750s and it may be that Charles and his wife, Elizabeth Brown, joined them, for when they came to Lower Little River neighbors included George Brown and his nephew, Edwin Brown who had come from Halifax, Va. a decade earlier.

Charles Forester did not name all of his children in his Smith County will; he omitted Robin born 1778 in Va. and the girls. Bridgett Forester, born 1780 married George Barnes, and Charles Forester, Jr. married Barbara Hays. After Charles Jr's death at the Battle of New Orleans, Barbara married John Vannoy. James, Richard and John Forester and the children of Charles Jr. were given land and other items as well as a still. Charles' wife, Elizabeth Brown, survived him by four years.

Sources: Personal research.

— Priscilla Cummings

FIDEL D. FORESTER, SR.
566

F.D. Forester was born in Wilkes County, November 1, 1870, in the times immediately following the readjustment period of the Civil War, the son of Albert and Sarah Virginia Forester Forester. He died April 2, 1925, at the age of 54.

In 1887, Mr. Forester, in anticipation of the arrival of the railroad, began on a small scale and with limited means, a mercantile business at what was later to be known as North Wilkesboro, and developed it into a wholesale business which was considered to be one of the largest in the state. He was a civic minded businessman who gave freely of his time and his best judgement and unselfish efforts to promote the interests of his town. For 10 years he was a member of the Town Commission, and, at the time of his death, in addition to that position, was also president of F.D. Forester and Company, vice-president and director of the Deposit and Savings Bank, president of Forester-Prevette Insurance Company, Inc., and a member of Forester, Prevette and Forester, Real Estate. He was a director of the North Wilkesboro Hotel Company, a charter member of the North Wilkesboro Kiwanis Club, as well as a loyal supporter of other civic organizations.

On April 25, 1897, F.D. married Alva Geneva Adams, daughter of John Henry and Sarah Caroline Hincher Adams. To their union were born the following children:

Nellie, who married John Davis; Patsy, married (1) Malcolm Rousseau (2) Joe Ivey (3) Robert Boyd; George Stewart, married (1) Harriet Augusta Lenoir (2) Anna Atkinson; Kate, married James M. Anderson; Louise, married William Frazier; Billie, married Henry L. Moore; Rachel, married (1) William F. Absher (2) Thomas Morris; F.D., Jr. married Ina Lorene Caudill; James Herbert, married Josephine Preysz; Alva Caroline, married (1) John Edward Koontz (2) Ralph Singletary. Alva Geneva Adams Forester died December 17, 1960.

George Stewart Forester and Harriet Augusta Lenoir Forester, daughter of Walter James and Harriet Augusta Horton Lenoir, were married June 24, 1924. Their children were:

Nancy Joyce, married December 24, 1946, to Arthur Dwight Miller. Nancy and Dwight have three children: Judith Forester, Carolyn Lenoir and Arthur Dwight, Jr.

George Stewart, Jr., married to Elizabeth Louisa McNeill, daughter of Charles Poole and Hattie Simpson Gambill McNeill, August 28, 1949. Their children:

Charles Stewart, born November 7, 1951; married May 20, 1972, Claudia Jean Hayes, daughter of J. Everette and Nancy Caudill Hayes. Charles and Claudia have one daughter, Morgan Lenoir, born November 6, 1981.

Isaac Gambill, born December 10, 1954; married June 24, 1979, Tamara Joan Burcham.

Elizabeth Lenoir, born September 9, 1957; married May 30, 1981, William Thomas Walsh, son of Lawrence Harold and Marjorie Beamon Walsh.

Walter Lenoir Forester was married October 13, 1962, to Katherine Susan Burchette, daughter of Mr. and Mrs. J.P. Burchette. Walter and Susan have two children: Gregory Lenoir, born March 6, 1963 and Anna Lynn, born February 21, 1971.

Sources: Bible records, newspaper accounts, family records.

— George Forester, Jr.

WILLIAM R. FORTNER
567

William R. Fortner, believed to be the son of Ethdrid Fortner, was born in N.C. in 1816. His wife, Armieo Low, was born in N.C. in 1812. Following their marriage, they continued to live in N.C. until sometime after 1852 when they moved to Fannin County, Ga.

William Fortner apparently died during the 1860s. She died after 1870. The children of William and Armieo were Levi Franklin, born April 24, 1838 in Wilkes County, N.C. died April 18, 1922, married October 5, 1865 Louiza Jane Howard born December 3, 1846, died June 13, 1929; John born 1840; William born 1842; Elijah born 1845; Rosanna M. born 1848; Sarah H. born 1850; Thomas Edward born 1852 and Tyrus Smith born 1860.

Levi Franklin Fortner, was born April 24, 1838 in Wilkes County. During the Civil War he served with the Union Forces as a member of the 9th Tenn. Cavalry. Following his discharge in 1865, he married Louiza Jane Howard in Bradley County, Tennessee.

Levi died April 18, 1922 and Louiza died June 13, 1929. They are buried in Maloney Springs Cemetery in Marietta, Georgia. Their children were: Elijah L., William H., Emma L., Ada M.J., Levi Franklin, Jr. Mary Ann, John N., Robert M., James L., Charlie S., Thomas Edward, Martha Resetta and George Clifton.

Sources: Personal research.

— J.W. Knighton

THE FOSTER FAMILY
568

Achilles Foster Jr.'s family were decendants

from England and the most exact records are at the Orange County Courthouse at Orange, Va.

Achilles Foster was born 1784, the fourth son of Thomas and Francis Jones Foster. He was married to Lavina Goforth. They lived and died in the Lewis Fork section of Wilkes County. They had five children, Achilles Foster, Jr. born 1831, a confederate veteran married to Delpha Rose Foster 1845-1901.

They had seven children: Cara Foster married Rufas McNeil; Amelia married Henry Church; Nancy Foster married Sherman Triplett; Adeliade Foster married Lee Hamby; Mary Foster married John Frazier; Wyatt Foster married Luna Crane; and Thomas Foster unmarried.

Wyatt and Luna Foster had three sons. Raymond Foster married Pearl Cox and had three sons: Kenneth, Charles, and Stanly Foster; and one daughter, Alda Ann married Bill Triplett. Chelsie Foster married Verna Bullis and their children are Paige Foster, Kay Foster, and Mona Gay Foster Hamby (she had two children, Sheldon and Barry). Kelcie Foster born January 27, 1901, died December 4, 1976. Kelcie married Maie Watson who was born April 10, 1906. Their children are: Garvin Foster married Christine Ferguson — born to them were Brenda, who married Raybur Johnson (born to them a daughter Christy Rae, 1973); Steven married Jennie Pipers, had two children Lisa and William John, divorced and second marriage, 1977, Evezelle Tart, two children, Scotty and Pamela.

Coila and Morrison Foster, twins. Morrison Foster died August 18, 1924. Coila Foster married Dale McNeil December 7, 1946. Their children are Gail McNeil, born March 1, 1949, and Dennis McNeil, born June 12, 1956.

Waldon Foster married Edith Triplett and had one son, Larry Foster, born September 17, 1947. Larry married Mickey Lankford, and they had one son, Tommy Foster born October 24, 1969, divorced and then married Cathy Church, had one son, Alex born August 19, 1981.

Claxton Foster, born June 11, 1929, married Zora Moody and their children are Gregory, born January 5, 1955, Timothy, September 24, 1958, and Jeffery, March 30, 1957.

James Curtis Foster, December 11, 1930, married Dorothy Hayes, born on March 12, 1937. Born to them a daughter, Sherry Lynn, March 25, 1956. Sherry married Perry Dancy, born to them Jeremiah Ross, October 5, 1981.

A.K. Foster, Jr. born October 9, 1932, married Arlene Benge, born to them one son, Leslie and one daughter, Teresa.

Rex Garner Foster born May 17, 1936 married Joanne Latham, born to them Deborah Carolyn, March 7, 1961, Ricky, January 30, 1970, Christy Dawn, July 29, 1975.

Etheline Foster, March 25, 1938, married Ralph Jones born to them Peggy, Kathy, and Douglas. Divorced and married Max Eller.

Colon Foster, born January 23, 1944, married Linda Bunton. They have no children.

Source: Family *Bible*.

— Mrs. Waldon Foster

FOSTER
569

The Fosters of Wilkes county have been traced back to Orange county, Virginia in the early 1700s, then to the coast of Virginia, from there to London, England in the early 1600s, and to the N.E. part of England to Bamburgh Castle in the 1200s, from there to what is now the Neatherlands in the 800 a.d.

The first definite connection was a Thomas Foster in Virginia who served in the French and Indian War. His son, also named Thomas was in the Revolutionary War and received a grant of fifty acres of land for his service, the grant signed by Patrick Henry.

Soon after the Revolutionary War three of his sons moved to Wilkes county, N.C. They were; Akillis, Ambrose and John. Akillis settled in the Mount Pleasant Church community and his many decendants have a reunion at the church each year. Ambrose operated wagon trains to Charleston, S.C. and died in Camden, S.C. in 1833 on one of his trips. His wife, with relatives moved to Texas and settled near Canton which is about forty miles east of Dallas. John married Ann Vannoy. They owned a large farm part of which according to tradition was bought for a "muzzle loading rifle and a bear dog". They also owned 30 slaves. John and Ann had fifteen children and adopted another. The youngest of which was thirty years old before there was a death in the family.

In the 1830s three of the sons moved to the S.W. part of Missouri and helped start the town of Marshfield. They were: John, Ambrose and Jesse. Three of the daughters; Elisabeth, Sara and Jane after the War Between The States moved to Texas in a wagon train with their families and about fifty others. They settled East of Dallas near the other Fosters. Now there are so many descendants they publish a Foster Newsletter that is sent all over the U.S.

The other children of John and Ann settled in Wilkes and Allegany counties.

East of N. Wilkesboro in the community known as the Quarry there is an old abandoned cemetery where John and Ann Foster are buried. Also their daughter Mary and her husband Nathan Ward. One of their sons, Thomas Foster and his wife Barbara Fyffe are also buried there.

Thomas Foster, who married Barbara Fyffe was a Justice of the Peace, school teacher and clerk of the Brier Creek Church for thirty-one years. He and his wife had three sons and two daughters: John S., William A., and Hugh A. who served in the 52nd Regt. in the Confederate army.

John S. married Emma Summers and lived in Statesville, N.C. William A. married Lucy Johnson and lived in Wilkesboro. Hugh A. married Virginia Leckie and lived in the Dellaplane community. Caroline married William Ward and lived in Roaring River and Elizabeth married William Campbell and lived near Taylorsville.

Hugh Akillis Foster and his wife Virginia Leckie farmed after he returned from serving in the Confederate army. He also did carpenter work and was a Baptist minister. They had four

children: Meta who married W.J. Kinyoun, Mittie G., who married Robert Carter, Walter L. Foster who married Ida Hanes and Charles Thomas who married Lora Mae Reins.

Charles Thomas and Lora Foster had three sons: Olin born 13 February 1911, died 11 December 1918; Howard Reins born 30 July 1918, died 26 February 1981 and lived near Kernersville, N.C. Norman Thomas born 28 July 1920 and lives near Kernersville.

Howard Reins Foster married Lucille Peoples and had three children: Linda who married Van McGlamery, Loretta who married Glenn Griggs and Stephen who married Jill Umplett. Linda and Van had Roland, Lean and Laura. Loretta and Glenn had Glenn, Jr. and Jonathan. Stephen and Jill had Hollie, Chuck, Carrie and Sarah.

Sources: *Bibles*, tradition, N.C. Archives, Raleigh and Richmond Archives, Wilkes Courthouse, Library of Congress, Washington.

— Norman T. Foster

THE FOSTER FAMILY
570

The name "Foster" is a very common one in England. Old historical records trace the name to King Fergus II of Scotland, 404 A.D.

The most exact records of the Fosters, after they came to America, are in Orange County, Virginia. They show that Thomas and John Foster purchased 1000 acres of land May 25, 1738. Also recorded in Orange County is the will of Thomas Foster taken from Spotslvania county in 1734.

The Fosters of this family are descendants of Thomas Foster and Elizabeth Featheratonhough, who lived in Bamburgh, England. Their grandson, Sir Robert Foster, married a Miss Isham. According to tradition he came to America for a time, but returned to England. He is buried there.

Major Richard Foster, son of Sir Robert and wife, married Sussannah Garnett in 1642 in Northampton, Virginia. Major Foster was a member of the House of Burgesses, Virkus.

Thomas Foster, great-grandson of Richard and Sussannah Garnett Foster, was born in 1720. He first married Elizabeth Smith in 1743, then married Anne Garnett. He served in the French and Indian War. They reared eleven (11) children. His oldest son, Thomas Foster, Jr., born in 1753, was a soldier in the Revolutionary War. He received a certificate granting him 100 acres of land for three years' service in the Contential Line. (Grant recorded in Wilkes county courthouse, book F and H, page 464, entered April 2, 1799.)

Thomas Foster, Jr. married Frances Jones in 1777. They reared a family of nine children. The Fosters were considered prosperous in that time and owned large farms and had many slaves.

John Foster, third oldest son of Thomas and Frances Jones Foster, married Ann Vannoy in 1809.

Ambrose Foster, fifth son of Thomas and Frances Jones Foster, married Mary Miller December 16, 1816. He died September 1832; she died on August 30, 1878. She is buried in Phalba Cemetery outside Canton, Texas. Her faithful servant, Miss Fanny Grinton, is buried at her feet, as she requested.

Ambrose Foster owned an overland freight line and ran teams and freight from Charleston, S.C. to interior areas. He died in Camden, S.C. in September 1832 while on one of these trips. His father-in-law, William Miller, was a member of the N.C. legislature and was a man of some prominence and influence.

Alfred Miller Foster, born September 22, 1817, in Wilkes County, was the second child of Ambrose and Mary Miller Foster. He married his first cousin, Elizabeth Foster (daughter of John Foster, brother of Ambrose) January 21, 1843. They lived in the Beaver Creek community of Wilkes County. Elizabeth is buried in Old Bethel Cemetery near Canton, Texas. Alfred Miller Foster served in the N.C. legislature. After the Civil War he became very despondent over the outcome of the war and died April 9, 1867. Elizabeth later moved to Texas, near Canton. She made the trip by wagon train, taking all of her children, except her oldest son, John Ambrose, with her. John Ambrose remained in the Beaver Creek area.

John Ambrose Foster, oldest son of Alfred Miller and Elizabeth Foster Foster, who remained in Wilkes County lost his right leg in the very last days of the Civil War. He married Sarah Dula December 26, 1867. They were parents of four children, Alice E. Foster, born January 1871, died June 22, 1967; Mary E. Foster, born August 27, 1875, died April 22, 1956. The daughters remained single and lived on the homeplace until their deaths.

Alfred Jefferson Foster was born July 7, 1873, died October 28, 1950. He was a schoolteacher and Baptist minister. He lived on part of the farm owned by his grandfather, Alfred Miller Foster. This land is now owned by Alfred's daughters, having been in the family for over one hundred fifty years. Alfred J. Foster married Buena Jane Ferguson June 6, 1911. She was born September 18, 1888, died July 1, 1969. Their son, Alfred Ferguson Foster, was born January 24, 1926, died May 25, 1936. Delight Foster, born March 3, 1912, married Wake Payne June 21, 1934. Wake was born July 12, 1912. Joy Belle Foster, born April 11, 1919, married John Payne, Wake's brother, June 24, 1937. John was born June 17, 1914. Brent Evan Payne is the adopted son of Wake and Delight Payne. Dwight Gary Payne is the adopted son of John and Joy Belle Payne.

John Edmund C. Foster, second son of John A. and Sarah Dula Foster, was born November 28, 1877, died May 13, 1945. He married Mary Louisa (Loula) Ferguson December 25, 1904. Mary Louisa Ferguson Foster was born April 26, 1886, died February 27, 1980. To this union four children were born.

Sarah Elizabeth Foster, born July 9, 1911, married William John Henry Smithey November 30, 1933. He was born January 16, 1910, died April 18, 1974. Two children: William Smithey was born February 16, 1935. He married Giovanna Chilsa. They have one daughter, Anna Jo Fulcher, and one granddaughter, Tabitha Fulcher. Alice Ann Smithey was born October 10, 1946. She married Albert Richard Johnson, Jr. They have two children: Edith

Elizabeth Johnson and Andrew William Johnson.

Edward Bryan Foster, born January 30, 1913, died May 4, 1977. He married Lois Walsh January 25, 1931. Lois was born May 19, 1914. Their children are: Eva June Foster, born January 21, 1932, and Dr. Jack Foster, born July 5, 1934, died March 28, 1974. Jack had one son, Edward Brian Foster.

John Conway Foster, born December 14, 1914, died May 15, 1963. He married Dorothy Raymer August 1937. Four children: Richard Conway, born February 28, 1938; Jerry Lee, born August 5, 1939; Philip Keith, born August 13, 1943; Elizabeth Louisa (Betty Lou), born September 4, 1948. Richard Conway (Dickie) has four children, Keith has two, and Betty Lou has one.

Robert Lee Foster, born November 18, 1917, married Lillian Catherine Linney July 16, 1941. Their daughter, Mary Florence Foster, was born April 20, 1943, and married William C. Brady October 9, 1965. Two children: Jan Brady (step-daughter) born August 21, 1957, married James Franklin Critz, Jr. and has one child, James Franklin Critz III; Patrick Scott Brady, born April 14, 1972.

Robert Lee Foster, Jr., born March 8, 1947, married Deborah Marshall July 22, 1967. Children: Heather Leigh, born April 5, 1971; Courtney Page, born September 27, 1973. They live in Charlotte, N.C.

Twins.

Thomas Lindsay Foster, born March 8, 1947, married Suzanne McGuirt August 14, 1971. Three children: Jason Godfrey, born May 6, 1976; Jessica Linney, born October 5, 1979; Jonathan Paul, born July 30, 1981. They live in Charlotte.

Sources: Family *Bible*, Texas family records, recorded wills, land grants, grave stones, personal knowledge, interviews with family members in Wilkes County and Texas.

— Delight Foster Payne

ACHILLES FOSTER, SR.
571

Son of Thomas Foster, Jr. and grandson of Thomas Foster, Sr., Achilles was born and raised and lived and died in Wilkes County. As was the case with an older brother Anthony, Achilles married a Goforth, Lavina Goforth. It is interesting that his Aunt Mildred married Thomas Goforth. With travel presenting almost insurmountable problems, it was a mountain way of life for several marriages to take place between families such as the case mentioned above and later between the Fosters and the Walsh family.

Little is known of the life of Achilles Foster and of Lavina Goforth Foster. It is a known fact, however, that life in the outer reaches of Wilkes County in the late afternoon shadows of the Blue Ridge mountains was extremely demanding and difficult beyond our present-day comprehension. Yet despite the problems and the hardships, families such as this did grow and survive. There were three sons and two daughters born of this marriage. It is reasonable to assume that all family members shared the burdens of raising the crops and tending

the cattle for beef and for milk and the hogs for pork. They also shared the joys of survival and of the faith in God that sustained them. The Holy Bible was THE BOOK and it was to it that the mountain people went for that inner peace that is, even today, so often seen on the faces of those who believe and commune with God and Nature. Achilles and Lavina Foster were buried within a mile or so of the Mount Pleasant Church in a family cemetery.

Sources: Personal research.

— Ray Foster

ABSOLEM (ADNEY) FOSTER FAMILY
572

Achilles Foster, born 1784, the fourth son of Thomas and Frances Jones Foster, died 1843. He married Lavina Goforth in 1830 and they had five children: Achilles, Jr., born 1831, Edmond W., born 1834, Mary, born 1835, John Thomas, born 1840, and Louisa, born 1841, died in 1850.

Edmond W., born 1834, died 1911, married Nancy Jane Eller, born 1838, died 1915. They had thirteen children: N.J., born 1855, died young; Absolem (Adney), born 1857; Mary A., born 1859, died young; Achilles Frank, born 1861, died 1945; Janie, born 1864, died 1930; Ailey Naire (Tencie) born 1866; C. Lula, born 1868, died 1939; U. Grant, born 1871, died 1939; Martha, born 1874, died 1949; Edmond C., born 1876, died 1955; Releford (Rel), born 1878, died 1950; Rachel Octavia, born 1880, died young; and Rozilla, born 1882, died 1909.

Absolem (Adney) Foster, born 1857, died 1937, married Martha Ann Hubbard, born 18 July 1865, died 2 September 1909. They were the parents of the following children: (1) Susan Jane, born 1877, married 25 December 1893 William Cicero Triplett, born 1871, died 5 March 1954. (See story William C. Triplett and Susan J. Foster Triplett for their children.) (2) William Hayes, born 11 April 1879, died 7 March 1938, married Dorothy Walsh, born 1881, died 26 September 1957. They were the parents of Charles, Roy, Veva, Halsey, Nola, Shelton and Lutrelle. (3) Arthur Garfield, born 3 April 1881, married Roxie Fairchilds. They had Gilbert, Zola, Raymond, Arnold, Collette, Hazel Wayne, Vincent, Dorothy Deane, Hope and Arthur Garfield, Jr. (4) Gilbert Monroe, born 15 February, 1885, married Dora Bell Shepherd, born 21 October 1887, died 21 December 1968. Their children were Garley Wayne, Troy, Frances, Venver, Verlee Marie and Clara Sue. (5) Furches Olin, born 11 April 1887, died 1 January 1952, married on 24 March 1907, Elizabeth (Lizzie) Walsh, born 4 June 1889. Their children were Veonia, Sterlie, Arvin, Richard, Zella, Mildred, Olin, Ellena, Harold, Harry, Billy Gene and Betty Ann. (6) Beulah, born 7 July 1889, married in November 1911, Commodore Eller, who died 3 November 1934. They had five children: Travis, Leola, Radford, Vensley and Hensley. (7) Kinsa, born 21 November 1891, died 21 November 1978, married on December 26, 1916,

Jesse F. Ellis, born 14 February 1893. Their three children were Chelsie, Velvaree and Faye Netta. (8) Arpha, born 10 June 1894, died 30 May 1981, married Carl Bullis, 26 December 1920. He was born 11 January 1896, and they had one daughter, Roena, born 27 October 1921.

Adney M. Foster was married a second time to Lilly McNeil Eller and they were the parents of one daughter, Irene. Adney was the owner of a general "country" store in Lewis Fork Township and for many years it housed the Dyer, N.C. post office which has long since gone out of existence.

Sources: Family *Bibles* and "The Foster Book."

— Belva Triplett Bumgarner

ADNEY FOSTER
573

Adney Foster was born in the same general area as were the three generations of Fosters immediately preceding him. After a boyhood of hard work tempered by the pleasures of such natural pastimes as fishing, hunting and exploring the hills, mountains and streams all around, Adney married Martha Anne Hubbard. Martha Anne's father, William Hubbard, owned and ran Hubbard's Mill on Lewis Fork Creek near the Mount Pleasant community. This mill continued to be an important economic, social and political factor in that area of Wilkes County until its destruction by flood in 1916. Adney and Martha Anne lived about ½ to ¾ mile upstream from the mill site.

In addition to farming and timber cutting, the Foster couple opened and ran a small general store nearby their home. They sold whiskey as well as general merchandise, and their place thereby became a very important meeting place in the community. Monroe, one of their sons, told many stories of happenings along the creek. He also told of the strict enforcement of the Adney Foster rule of moderation involving the whiskey. Those who could not abide by this rule could not buy from the Fosters. There are stories also of supply trips to Wilkesboro and North Wilkesboro where Adney would take his wagon to replenish inventories. Typically, Adney would make the trip to town in one day with a short rest stop at his son William Hayes Foster's place in the Congo community. After an overnight stay in the town camping grounds where others from around the area would gather to barter and exchange information and tell stories and make some mountain music, Adney would load his wagon for the trip home. With the additional weight of his cargo, the return trip could not be made as quickly as was the inbound trip. Adney would therefore camp overnight in the yard of Hayes and Dorothy. These overnight stops gave the older sons of Hayes and Dorothy — Charlie and Roy — a very good opportunity to become acquainted with their grandfather and enjoy his stories and the songs and camaraderie that took place on these occasions. The sons of Adney and Martha Anne were William Hayes, Arthur Garfield, Gilbert Monroe, and Furches Olin. Daughters of this marriage were Susan Jane,

Beulah, Kinsa, and Arpha. After Martha Anne's death, Adney married Lillie McNeil, and they had a daughter, Irene, who now lives in Akron, Ohio.

Adney and Martha Anne have hundreds of descendants living now in Wilkes and throughout the South. They rest in the peace that prevails in the Mount Pleasant Cemetery.

Sources: Personal knowledge.

— Roy Foster, Jr.

Edmond W. Foster.

EDMOND W. FOSTER
574

In his late teens, Edmond Foster married a nearby mountain girl of fifteen, Nancy Jane Eller. As was the case with his father, Achilles Foster, and his grandfathers and great-grandfathers, Thomas Foster, Sr. and Jr., Edmond elected to live his life in the area now known as Lewis' Fork Township with the Lewis' Fork Creek running nearby. His oldest son, Adney, grew up with him, since only 20 years separated the two, and it was from Edmond that Adney learned to work and pray and to fish, hunt and play. This comradeship between father and son was ended for a time when Edmond joined the Army of the Confederate States and went off to war. It is ironic that many of the mountain folk disapproved wholeheartedly of slavery, but felt bound by the ties of kinship, friendship and tradition to support the Confederacy. Edmond Foster was one of the lucky soldiers who limped home with a rifle ball in his knee, but at least made it home.

He and Nancy Jane had 6 sons and 7 daughters. The sons, in addition to Adney, were N.J., Achilles Frank, Ulysses Grant, Edmond C., and Releford (Rell). The daughters were Mary, Janie, Tencie, Lula, Martha, Rachel, and Rozilla. Edmond and Nancy Jane Foster lie at rest in the Mount Pleasant cemetery — a spot from which they gazed often at the

beauties of Nature before, during and after their times of giving thanks to God for His blessings.

Sources: Personal knowledge.

— Roy Foster Jr.

FANNY FOSTER and WILLIAM BOURNE JOHNSON
575

Frances Ellinor Foster was born 20 July 1818 into a prosperous plantation family. She was one of the 15 children of John Foster, son of Thomas and Frances Jones Foster, and Ann Vannoy, daughter of Nathaniel and Elizabeth Ray Vannoy. Her father's six-page will gives ample evidence of a comfortable station in life. The seventh, or "middle child" of such a large family, she was an out-going, cheerful, generous child, and never lost those attributes. Fifty years after her death (30 Jan. 1904) she was still described with great affection to her younger descendants. It is said that after her marriage she would ride side-saddle from her home in (new) Alleghany Co. to visit her parents, passing the cabins of the former slaves. When they saw her coming they ran to the road, crying with joy and begging her to visit with them. She was loved by all who knew her.

At the age of 20 she married (29 Oct. 1838) William Bourne Johnson, first son of Robert and Celia Bourne Johnson. His grandparents were Capt. Samuel and Mary Hammons Johnson of Wilkes Co. and William and Rosamond Jones Bourne of Grayson Co., VA. He was born 22 May 1818, Wilkes Co. and died 1 April 1856 in Ashe Co.

Fannie, as she was called, and Wm B. Johnson were members of the Methodist Episcopal Church. They moved to the section of Ashe Co. that would become Alleghany in 1859 and carried out the activities of a farm family. Their children were: Mary Ann Johnson, b. 1839, m. Walker; Samuel Johnson, b. 1840; John A. Johnson, b. 1842, m. Mary S. Clary, daughter of Alexander and Alice Harris Clary of Wilkes Co. She was an aunt to Mary Ann Clary, and this couple was fondly known as "Uncle Johnny and Aunt Pop!" Their children were Caroline, Charles, Vance, James, John, Thomas, Walter and Rebecca Jane, who married Harvey Ashley; Selinda Johnson, b. 1844, m. Sherman Myers; Lewis Johnson, b. 1848, m. Elizabeth Weaver, daughter of William and Mary Miller Weaver. Robert Thomas Johnson, b. 20 Feb. 1850, d. 16 March 1914, m. 30 Nov. 1876 to Mary Ann Clary of Wilkes Co. (Their children are named in the John Andrew Clary family story.) Caroline Johnson m. Elcana "Canie" Francis — no issue. She died 12 Oct. 1930; Edmund Foster Johnson m. 29 Nov. 1879 Nancy "Nanny" Childress. Their children were Joseph, m. Lilly Gambill, daughter of Bynum and Evaline Clary Gambill of Wilkes Co.; Ranson, m. Alice Shoaf; Robert Elcana "Canie," m. Minnie Johnson and 2nd Ruth Hartsoe; Lilly, m. James Isom Weaver; a son who died early; William B., who married Mabel Shepherd, daughter of Ed Shepherd; Mary, who never married but was dearly loved by those who knew her.

In those days (mid 1800s) blood-letting, or bleeding, was a common remedy for certain illnesses. Following such a treatment William Bourne Johnson died at the age of 38, when a vein re-opened as he slept that night. He died at Laurel Springs in Ashe Co. Some years after his death, "Fannie" married Mr. Silas Brewer, who had been a childhood sweetheart. She died in Ashe Co. at 86 Jan. 30, 1904, and is buried in a family cemetery near Warrensville, on land that belongeld to "Canie" Johnson.

Sources: Johnson Family *Bible* and knowledge; Wilkes Co. and Ashe Co. Records.

— Mrs. John M. Richards, Jr.

GEORGE PINKNY FOSTER FAMILY

576

George Foster (15 Feb. 1779 — 18 July 1858) was the son of George I and Sarah Foster. He married Amy Grey (15 Sept. 1779 — 14 July 1853) daughter of James and Sarah Grey on 21 June 1800. They had seven children: Rebecca born 3 Apr. 1801 who married first Thomas Davis and second Amos Church; Mary born 22 May 1805; Thomas Harven (27 July 1807 — 25 June 1891); Annes born 3 Aug. 1809 who married Ephriam Davis; Emeline born 18 May 1813 who married Gabriel Church; R.B. Foster (15 Feb. 1816 — 21 Sept. 1910) who married Mary Church; and Matilda born 15 Feb. 1819.

Thomas Harven Foster was thirty-two years older than his wife Martha Jane Church, daughter of Amos and Vicy Minton Church. He took care of his parents until their deaths before beginning a life of his own. Grandmother Martha Foster was born 10 Dec. 1839 and on that day grandfather stopped by to see the "new baby." He said she was so pretty that when she grew up he would marry her. That is what he did on 23 Sept. 1858. They had five children: Margaret (9 Oct. 1859 — ca. 1906) who married Gorden Church; Mirah Jane (13 Oct. 1862 — 20 Mar. 1938) who married Zeb Vance Church; Rebecca Emeline (20 May 1866 — 27 June 1903) who married Newton J. Fairchilds; George Pinkny (13 Apr. 1869 — 7 Feb. 1952) who married Etta Minton (30 May 1876 — 30 Aug. 1946), daughter of Zackery and Sarah O'Rilla Minton on 22 Nov. 1892; Isabell (1874-1932) who married Washington Nichols. Grandmother Martha Jane died 14 May 1933.

Pinkny and Etta had three children: Albert Floyd (19 Feb. 1896 — 10 Nov. 1918) who gave his life for his country during World War I; Walter McKinley Foster (5 Oct. 1899 — 19 Apr. 1955) who married Ada Florence Parsons, daughter of Greely and Isabell Nichols Parsons, on 21 April 1928. A daughter Shirley was born 2 Dec. 1935 and was married 24 Nov. 1953 to James Thomas (J.T.) Hutchens; and Nellie Izola "Zola" (17 June 1904), now lives in Atlanta, Georgia, and married Garvy C. Foster 18 Aug. 1920, son of Grant and Frances Summerlin Foster.

Sources: Family *Bible* of Martha Jane Foster and family records.

— Shirley Hutchens

Pinkny Foster Family (l. to r.): Walter, Zola, Pinkny, Etta, and Floyd.

JOHN EDMUND FOSTER

577

John Edmund C. Foster, son of John A. and Sarah Dula Foster, was born November 28, 1877, in the Beaver Creek area. He died May 13, 1945.

Ed married Mary Louisa (Loula) Ferguson December 25, 1904. Mary Louisa was born April 26, 1886 in Joliet, Ill, where her parents Leander and Elizabeth (Bettie) Ferguson had moved. Elizabeth died there and the family moved back to Wilkes County.

Ed and Loula attended schools in the Ferguson area, one of which was the historical Whippoorwill Academy. Ed prided himself on his penmanship, having received a diploma for special courses in penmanship, and taught penmanship classes.

Ed was a merchant for a time in the Beaver Creek area. He became a rural mail carrier for the Ferguson postoffice and for twenty-eight years braved the changing weather and conditions over twenty-eight miles of rough, hilly rural roads. He went first on horseback, then by horse and buggy, and finally by car. One horse, "Old Joe," was driven over 54,000 miles, but was retired when Ed bought his first car in 1925, a T Model Ford touring car. By whatever means of travel, Ed carried a large tub full of stones to fill the holes and ruts and repair the roads. He made the statement that he had carried enough rock to fill the Wilkes County Courthouse. He also carried hole diggers, mattock, shovel, hammer and nails. He needed these to repair or replace old mail boxes (often buying new ones himself) and to paint the unsightly ones. Each summer, during his week's vacation, he would hire a crew of men to rework and repair the roads on his route, paying them out of his own pocket. Ed loved children, and they him. He kept a supply of candy, gum, fruits, and other goodies to hand out to children who met him at their mail boxes. Needless to say, there were always waiting children. He also gave each family on his route presents at Christmas.

Another service offered by Mr. Foster developed out of need — that of pulling teeth. It started with one person coming to his mail box asking for help. When word got around the practice snowballed. Mr. Ed bought a pair of professional pullers, carried medical supplies for sanitation purposes, and said later that he had probably pulled enough teeth to fill a large washing tub. He asked for none and got no remuneration for this work and gave it up when the practice became too big a risk.

Mr. Foster loved the people on his mail route and they him. They were family and when he retired emotions ran high. It was as sad as a final farewell. His health was not good and his son, Robert Lee, who was his auxiliary carrier, was called into the service of his country. Therefore retirement came a bit early. He had cards printed with a final message for each family.

Ed was a colorful character. He was a natural wit and humorist, and musician. Ed and Loula's home was always open to family, friends, and strangers, and their hospitality was widely known and appreciated. Loula was an excellent cook and a student of good nutrition. Music was a very real part of their family. Loula played the piano, Ed the violin, flute, guitar, and any number of small musical instruments. James Larkin Pearson, Ed's personal friend from boyhood, called him a musical genius. Ed's homespun philosophy was enjoyed by all with whom he came in contact and he always left them with an optimistic outlook on life.

Sources: Family records, personal letters, family *Bible*, interviews with family and friends, school records, and public records.

— Lillian Linney Foster

FOSTER-JONES
578

When Robert Foster and his wife "Miss Isham" came from England to Va., before 1666, and the immigrant ancestor of Hugh Jones came from Wales to Md., they set the stage for several remarkable family romances in the 1760s and 1770s. The Fosters' great-great-grandson, Thomas Foster, b. 1720 in Essex Co. Va., d. 1791, Orange Co. Va. married (23 May 1743, Middlesex Co. Va.) to Elizabeth Smith who was born 19 April 1723, the daughter of Thomas and Anne Smith of Middlesex Co. Thomas and Elizabeth Foster lived in Orange Co. Va. after 1754 when he served under young George Washington in the French and Indian War. They had a family of which 1 son and 3 daughters married 1 daughter and 3 sons of Hugh and Catey Jones also of O. Co. All 4 couples moved to Wilkes Co. N.C., as did the remaining 7 Fosters; both Jones and Foster parents remained in Va. Elizabeth S. Foster d. before 1780, and Thos. m. 2nd Anne Garnett.

The Foster children were: Phoebe Foster married 10 Jan. 1769, George Jones (b. 13 June 1743, d. 3 Dec. 1828). They lived in Wilkes Co. N.C. til his death in 1828 and hers, 1830. They had 13 children: Edmund (m. Ann Lenoir); George (m. Elizabeth Mills); Larkin (died at 30); Catlett (m. Nancy Dula); Thomas (m. Sarah Lenoir and 2nd Thompson of S.C.); John (d. 1813); Elizabeth (m. Sam'l Downs of S.C.); Nancy (m. Ambrose Mills); Lucy (m. Hilliar Gilreath); Delphia G. (m. Andrew J. Bryan, Jr.); Phoebe (m. her 1st cousin, Benjamen Jones, son of Col. Benj. Jones); and Matilda, (born 1794, died young).

Frances Foster m. 13 Nov. 176-, Morton Jones (b. 10 Aug. 1747, d. 8 Nov. 1841). They moved from Wilkes to Franklin Co. Tenn.

Elizabeth Foster m. 12 May 1774, Benjamen Jones (b. 1750, d. 27 Dec. 1820). They lived near Wilkesboro and had Benj. Jr. (m. Phoebe Jones); Phoebe (m. Allen Robinett); Elizabeth (m. Willis Thurmond); Lucy (m. Moses Cass); Ann Mildred (m. John Martin) and Fanny (m. Jesse Robinett).

Thomas Foster, born 4 July 1750, d. 21 Mar. 1811; m. 25 Feb. 1777, Frances Jones, b. 3 June 1757; d. 4 Dec. 1803. They had 7 children.

The remaining Fosters, who did not marry Joneses, were: Anthony, b. 1756, m. 4 April 1776, Elizabeth Price had 4 sons and 1 Dau. by 1787; Nancy Ann who married John Robins and had Lucy (m. Henry Bryan); Nancy or Ann (m. John Bryan, brother of Henry); Peggy (m. Thomas Lenoir); and Franky (m. Hagler).

Mary "Polly" Foster m. 24 Dec. 1775, Thomas Robins.

Sarah Foster m. William Kendall. Her will in Wilkes Co. names 6 children: John, James, Thomas, William, Betsy Barlow and Sarah Shearer.

Mildred Foster m. Thomas Goforth.

John Foster never married. He died in Wilkes Co. Feb. 1824.

Lucy Foster died in Wilkes, 1834, unmarried.

Hugh & Catey Jones of Va. had 7 children.

The 3 who did not marry Fosters were:

Hugh Jones; who moved to Ga., Col. Catlett Jones who married "Miss Crew" and was made a Justice in Wilkes in 1820 later lived in Ohio; and Elizabeth Jones who never married.

All the Jones sons served in the Revolutionary War, as did their Foster brothers-in-law. Their wives never hesitated to set their hands to any work necessary to keep the farms (called plantations then) going while the men were at war. Afterwards the Joneses and Fosters who had come from Va., their children and grandchildren participated in all activities of a rapidly growing and developing area, and served with honor in the county and state they had chosen as home.

Sources: Orange Co. Va. Records; Published Genealogies; *Wilkes County N.C. Records* and *The Foster Family*, by Norman T. Foster.

— Mrs. John M. Richards, Jr.

MONROE FOSTER
579

Monroe Foster was the son of Adney and Martha Hubbard Foster. He lived within sight and sound of Lewis Fork Creek for his lifetime. He married Dora Bell Shepherd, and they raised a fine and talented family. Their sons were Garley, Troy, and Venver, etc. Their daughter(s) were Frances, Verlee, and Clara Sue. Monroe was deacon and faithful member of Lewis Fork Baptist Church, and in its beautiful cemetery, he and Dora Bell were laid to rest.

It was a great pleasure to talk to Monroe and enjoy his recollections of the earlier years of Wilkes. "By hecky doodle" was the full extent of his slang or swearing to the best knowledge of those who knew him best.

When Monroe was 15, his father, Adney, sold whiskey by the drink or by the pint. He would not, however, sell to those who had demonstrated an inability to handle liquid spirits. On one occasion, according to Monroe, he developed a rather severe toothache and was extremely anxious to get relief. He was at home alone when Lee Walsh from across the mountain in Goforth Hollow came to the house seeking a pint of whiskey. At that time Lee was not on the list of approved buyers so Monroe could not sell to him. Now here we had Lee Walsh wanting to buy whiskey and young Monroe Foster with a terrible toothache. Mountain resourcefulness came to the fore. Lee told Monroe he would remedy the toothache if Monroe would sell him the pint. The deal was struck. Lee gave Monroe a plug of chewing tobacco and told him to hold it on the affected tooth. Monroe did so and the tooth was relieved, though the stomach might have suffered a bit. Lee Walsh got his pint so both parties gained their wishes. Monroe Foster continued to chew tobacco for his lifetime, and was one of Nature's real noblemen. Lee Walsh did not continue drinking and spent most of his remaining years in Christian sobriety.

Sources: Personal knowledge.

— Roy Foster, Jr.

ROSA BELL REINS FOSTER
580

After her death at the age of 92, her grand-daughter's college roommate called Rosa Bell Reins Foster "the first liberated woman." Feminist to the core, she firmly believed that girls had a harder time in the world than boys. She always voted, partly because she regarded voting as an obligation and partly because she was interested in the candidates and the issues being debated. To the very end of her life, she was interested in people's personal lives and in what they thought. Working in the office of her husband's business, she liked to meet the people there. She loved a good joke. The Ila Holman Sunday School Class was Mrs. Foster's main interest in the Wilkesboro Baptist Church, where she was a member for many years.

Seeing new places was a great attraction all Mrs. Foster's life. At the age of 77, she, with her husband, brother, and sister-in-law, set out on a train trip across the country. Undaunted by a fall which broke her back the first night on the train, she kept going and saw the sights in the western part of the USA.

Dink, as she was called, was born January 23, 1883 and died February 17, 1975. Her parents were William Franklin and Elizabeth Hall Reins. There were eight children in her family: William Edward, James Calvin, Robert Franklin, Charles C., and Ralph Randolph Reins, and Lora Mae (Mrs. Charles T. Foster), and Maud (Mrs. Bill) Minton. She married Thomas M. Foster on March 23, 1904.

Family was exceedingly important to her. Some of her brothers and sisters were her closest friends. The most tragic event of her life was the untimely death of her daughter, Edith Foster Brown, at the age of 38. As a result, Mrs. Foster reared her granddaughter, Nancy, who was twelve at the time of her mother's death.

Making and re-making her clothes was one of Mrs. Foster's recreations. She especially enjoyed sewing for great-granddaughters, Nancy Jo and Becky Jenkins, and was vitally interested in their upbringing and activities, as well as those of her great-grandsons, Robert Thomas, Bill, and Mike Jenkins.

Stubborness and pride characterized her thinking. Proud of doing the right thing, she was slow to change her opinions. She could hold a grudge for a long time, but eventually her thinking would change. Adjusting to the changes in her life was difficult, but finally she did adjust without losing her "joy of living." As the years of her long life emcompassed many changes in society, community, and country, she was not a bystander, but always an integral part.

Sources: Personal knowledge, Family *Bibles*, Family Records.

— Mrs. Jim Jenkins

ROY G. FOSTER, SR.
581

This son of Dorothy Walsh and William Hayes Foster grew up along the Lewis' Fork Creek and in the Congo community and later in

Wilkesboro. While justifiably proud of his mountain heritage, there was probably a wide vein of defensive feeling in this mountain boy moved to town. The net result of this was one old-fashioned rock'em and sock'em hell raiser of the first degree. Roy Foster grew strong because he had committed himself to a way of life requiring strength. He worked as a boy in the local drugstore and as a young man for the railroad and in a Norfolk shipyard. He drank some whiskey and spent a lot of time with friends, such as Harvey Laffoon, later owner-editor of the Elkin Newspaper; George Forester, still in the furniture business in North Wilkesboro; Bill Brame, a lifetime friend and still an active member of the North Wilkesboro insurance, church and social scene; J. Bid Williams, who early on pointed the way for Wilkes residents to the beautiful Brushies where he lived until his death. Roy and George Forester attended Oak Ridge Military School together, maybe because they were too tough to tame at home. Roy still says that George Forester could get more fights started than anyone he has ever seen.

There was one particular night in Wilkesboro when Roy and some friends had been out on the town and suffice to say had taken a number of drams. Roy finally went home with his hob nail boots making quite a clatter on the hardwood floor. His father, Hayes, was aroused from his sleep and asked to be sure if this was his son. Confirming it was, he asked the time. Roy replied it was a little past eleven, but just then, as fate would decree, the family clock loudly announced the hour was three. Hayes, with a touch of father's anger now, sat up and said with some despair: "Drunk again!" Nothing was left then for Roy to say except for the answer that lives on till today: "So am I, Papa, so am I."

Roy married a school teacher up from Georgia in 1921. She was Lula Lee Stokes, and they were married in the parlor of the Smithey Hotel, where she lived while teaching in Wilkes. As a part of their courtship, it is reliably learned that Roy beat off other challengers for her pretty hand with fists in lieu of finesse for that was the way of it then.

As a young man Roy was scourge of the area with automobile or motorcycle. He was known to almost induce heart failure of the checker players and bystanders down at Linderman's Store in Wilkesboro by breezing through the very narrow opening between the store and the posts that supported the canopy out front at full speed in his roadster. There were only inches to spare, and great was the consternation of Mr. Linderman, who exiled Roy from the cracker barrel and canned tomatoes at one point for disciplinary purposes. It was Roy's misfortune, however, to be spotted standing on the seat of his motorcycle, by his bride Lula Lee, while traveling at high speed. Lula Lee avowed that Roy could decide which would go — the motorcycle or the bride — and that ended the motorcycle career of young Mr. Foster.

In the same year of their marriage, Roy began his career as a bridge and highway contractor. He designed and built many of the steel bridges then used along the Yadkin and

Roy, Sr. and Lula Lee Stokes Foster (1948).

other rivers of western North Carolina. One of his first such bridges was only recently replaced and removed from its crossing of Reddies River just north of North Wilkesboro. Roy Foster moved throughout the Southeast and built Interstate highways and major military installations amounting to millions of dollars worth of construction. He involved himself in the Republican Party and served as Georgia State Chairman of that party for eight years. He was a friend and confidant of Senator Bob Taft of Ohio, and supported Taft's presidential campaign vigorously. He served as Mayor of his adopted town of Wadley, Georgia for eighteen years — an all first for a Georgia Republican. Roy joined the Methodist Church after marriage since Lula Lee was Methodist and was raised in Methodist parsonages throughout South Georgia by her parents, Reverend Freeman L. Stokes and Virginia Proctor Stokes. Roy became deeply involved with many Methodist projects throughout South Georgia and became a close friend of Bishop Arthur J. Moore. He serves now on various church boards and was instrumental in the building of much of the facilities of the Epworth-by-the-Sea Methodist Center at St. Simons, Georgia. He also led the way for provision of an adequate retirement program for Methodist ministers. This was of particular interest to him since he had observed first hand the difficulties experienced by his in-laws during their retirement years.

Roy and Lula Lee had two daughters: Virginia Lee Foster (Thurston) and Elizabeth "Betty" Foster (Plexico then Fulghum), and one son: Roy G. Foster, Jr. Lula Lee Stokes Foster died in the prime of her life in 1949. Her passing came on the night following the marriage of her daughter Virginia, and it is good to report that she was extremely happy at the time. This family continues to treasure Wilkes County as their real home and spends as much time as possible in the Brushy Mountains. Roy now

lives with his wife Virginia in Wadley at age 80.
Sources: Personal knowledge.

— Roy Foster, Jr.

ROY G. FOSTER, JR.

582

Roy was born 9 Oct. 1926 in North Wilkesboro. He was the son of Roy G., Sr. and Lula Lee Stokes Foster, and grandson of W. Hayes Foster and Dorothy Walsh Foster.

After years of traveling throughout the Carolinas and Virginia, Roy grew up in Gordon, Georgia and in Wadley, Georgia. Roy attended several educational facilities, but graduated only from high school. He served in the U.S. Army of Occupation in Germany in 1946-47. His marriage to Parkie Leigh Camp Foster of Newnan, Georgia brought four children: Roy G. Foster III of Savannah, Terri Leigh Foster of Savannah, W. Hayes Foster II of Wilkesboro and Parkie Camp Foster of Savannah. It was during this marriage that this family lived in Columbus, Georgia; Albany, GA; Savannah, GA; Atlanta, GA and mostly in Wadley, GA. Roy served as city councilman and as the first and only Republican State Senator from a rural area of Georgia. He was National Treasurer of the National Federation of Young Republicans and served in such other capacities as PTA president, member of his County Board of Education and as member and chairman of the Official Board of the Methodist Church of Wadley. He was also a Sunday School teacher and president of the local Lion's Club.

Roy worked with his father in airport and highway construction for years. He amassed between six and seven thousand hours of flight time as pilot in command of their company planes as a way of traveling throughout the Southeast to bid on and construct those jobs upon which their bids were successful.

Roy is presently living in Savannah, Georgia

with his wife Gail VanLooven Foster. They own property in the Brushies and get back to Wilkes at every reasonable opportunity.

Roy's older son, Roy G. Foster III, was graduated from Wadley High School and later attended North Georgia College and Middle Georgia College. He joined the Georgia Army National Guard, and presently holds a captain's commission in the guard where he pilots heliocopter cranes, which are tremendous machines. He is in the life insurance business and works with his father and sister, Terri. Terri, older daughter of Roy and Parkie, graduated from the University of Georgia and the Katharine Gibbs Business School of Boston. After several years in Atlanta and Washington, where she was a White House staff member, she returned to Savannah where she works with her father and brother and is also employed by the Merrill Lynch brokerage firm. Younger son W. Hayes Foster II is a graduate of the University of Georgia and of the Walter F. George School of Law at Mercer University, Macon, Georgia. Hayes has returned to Wilkes where he practices law and lives on that Brushy Mountain ridge that overlooks Wilkesboro and North Wilkesboro. Younger daughter Parkie graduated from Savannah High School and attended the University of Georgia. She is now working in Savannah at a beautiful and charming restaurant named "Elizabeth's of 37th St." and is continuing her education at Armstrong State College.

Roy also presently has two grandchildren — Jennifer Paige Foster of Baton Rouge, Louisiana and Roy Zachry Foster of Savannah. His hope is that his grandchildren will grow to love and respect the lessons of Wilkes as did he during the summers of his youth that he spent with his grandmother in her Wilkesboro home that overlooked the Yadkin Valley and North Wilkesboro.

Sources: Personal knowledge.

— Roy Foster, Jr.

THOMAS FOSTER, SR.
583

According to family records, Thomas Foster was of the tenth generation of Fosters that began with another Thomas Foster who was married to Elizabeth De Etherstone, thus becoming Lord of Etherstone. The original Thomas Foster was born sometime around 1350 and lived until 1415. The ensuing generations were Thomas — Thomas — Thomas — Robert — then Sir Robert who lived from 1587 until 1666. His son Richard was a British Army Major who was born in 1615. It is thought that Major Foster was either assigned to the Colony of Virginia during the middle years of the seventeenth century or that he possibly came to the colony after leaving the army. Robert Foster lived from 1651 to 1718, and Anthony Foster lived from 1693 to 1763. Anthony was father of our subject Thomas Foster, Sr.

Thomas Foster, Sr. was father of three sons and eight daughters. It is believed that his son Thomas, Jr. was born to his second wife, Anne Garnett, on July 4, 1750, exactly 26 years prior to the signing of the Declaration of Independence.

Thomas Foster, Jr. lived from 1750 to 1811. He married Frances Jones, and they had eight sons and one daughter.

It is believed that Thomas Foster, Sr., having become disenchanted with what he considered to be repressive British rule, moved his family from Virginia to Wilkes County sometime between 1745 and 1760. One of his grandsons, Achilles Foster, Sr., remained in Wilkes during his lifetime, and it is to Achilles, Sr. that the roots of a large number of present-day Wilkes residents are traced.

Sources: Personal research.

— Roy Foster, Jr.

THOMAS M. FOSTER
584

Thomas M. Foster of Wilkesboro, pioneer building contractor, hatcheryman, and business leader, was born in Wilkes County, April 8, 1880. His businesses were very dear to his heart. A man of integrity, he had no patience with shoddy dealing of any kind.

For many years he was a member of the building firm, Foster and Allen, which erected many commercial and residential buildings in the Wilkesboros and also the Chatham Manufacturing Co. in Elkin. He would point with pride to the Bank of North Wilkesboro Building (now NCNB) and the Hotel Wilkes as examples of his craft. After he went into the hatchery business, he would keep remodeling his house, so great was his interest in building.

In 1933 he established the Blue Ridge Hatchery behind his home in Wilkesboro. It was one of the early firms which spearheaded the poultry industry in Wilkes and one of those which combined to form Holly Farms Poultry Industries.

Mr. Foster was a hard worker all week, but Sunday was set aside for church and for visiting family and friends. Only business emergencies were dealt with on Sunday. For 50 years he was an active member of the Wilkesboro Baptist Church, where he served as deacon. He was generous with his money in support of church and civic endeavors.

Mr. Foster also served in civic capacities, such as Town Commissioner of Wilkesboro, Director of Wilkes Savings and Loan (now Surety), and School Board Member. He was especially proud of his service in World War II on the District Appeals Board of Selective Service (known as the Draft Board).

One of Tom Foster's most cherished possessions was the sword of his father, William A. Foster, who was wounded five times at Gettysburg while serving as Captain in Company F of the 52nd Regiment of the Confederate Army. This sword is now in the possession of Mr. Foster's grand-nephew, Dr. Thomas Foster of Hickory. Mr. Foster's mother was Lucy Franklin Johnson Foster. Brothers and sisters were Burette F. (married Bessie Ogilvie), Edmond C. (married Maude Bentley), Cora (married T.M. Crysel), Grace (married John Tevepaugh), and Mae.

He married Rosa Bell Reins, daughter of

Thomas M. Foster.

William F. and Elizabeth Hall Reins, and had one daughter, Edith, born September 11, 1906. Edith married John McKinley Brown, Wilkes lawyer, and had one daughter Nancy, born August 3, 1932. Nancy grew up in her grandparent's home because of the early death of her parents. She married James R. Jenkins of Sylvester, Georgia, on October 2, 1954. One of the joys of Mr. Foster's old age was his great-grandchildren; Nancy Jo was born October 8, 1955, Rebecca Edith, born February 19, 1957, and Robert Thomas, born April 3, 1958. Two more great-grandchildren, William Asa and Michael John, were born after his death on March 26, 1963.

Sources: Personal knowledge, Family Interviews, Family Bible, Family Records.

— Mrs. Jim Jenkins

THOMAS and FRANCES JONES FOSTER
585

When this couple came to Wilkes Co. N.C. from Orange Co. Va., they had much work and change ahead, but they were not among strangers. Thomas' three sisters Frances, Elizabeth, and Phoebe had married Frances' three brothers Morton, Benjamen, and George. They were already here. In Wilkes Co. also were Thomas' brothers Anthony with his family, and John, who never married. Eventually his sisters Nancy (m. John Robins), Mary "Polly" (m. Thomas Robins), Sarah (m. William Kendall), Mildred (m. Thomas Goforth) and Lucy who never married would all be settled there. So they were part of a large family group, which must have been a source of comfort and pleasure.

The will of Thomas Foster's father (Thomas Foster Sr.,) recorded 28 February 1791, in Orange Co. Va. tells us that Thomas Jr. and the other children excepting Ann Robins and the 3 who were still unmarried (John, Lucy, &

Milley or Mildred) had already received their parts of his estate, so Thomas Jr. was able to purchase land and necessities. Also, he received 100 A. of land in Va. for his service (3 years) in the Va. Continental Line, Revolutionary War. The Warrant (certificate) for land was signed by Patrick Henry and Thomas Meriweather. Despite their relative affluence, however, it was a life of hard work — trees must be cut and trimmed into logs for house and outbuildings; land must be cleared and planted; crops and livestock tended. The men served as jurors to "lay out" roads and conduct other county business. The ladies were seldom idle. They spun, wove and sewed, dried and stored fruits and vegetables, cured meats for winter meals, utilized and improved everything. There were always children to care for and houses to "keep". But Wilkes' folk were sociable, and along with church and school activities there were corn shuckings, quilting bees and just going to visit. There was news of family and friends to share, quilt patterns (called 'shapens') to exchange, babies to admire — no time for boredom. They helped each other through times of trouble and times of happiness. Their spirit can never by sufficiently appreciated.

Thomas and Frances Jones Foster had 8 (known) children. Their son Thomas married Nancy Case (Cass); Anthony m. 30 April 1813 Lucy Goforth, his cousin. John, b. 9 July 1782 in Va., d. 14 June 1860 in Wilkes Co. N.C., married 8 Jan. 1809 Ann Vannoy. They had 15 children. Akilles, b. 1784, d. 1843, married 12 June 1830 Levina Goforth, a cousin; Ambrose m. 16 Dec. 1816 Mary Miller; Benjamen m. 4 Dec. 1816 Phoebe Case; Hugh Edmond married ? and lived in Tn., and Mary Foster never married.

Frances Jones Foster died Dec. 4, 1803, and her husband Thomas Foster died March 21, 1811, both in Wilkes Co.

Sources: Family knowledge and traditions, Orange Co. Va. records, N.C. and Tennessee pension Records, Wilkes Co. N.C. records.

— Mrs. John M. Richards, Jr.

TROY C. FOSTER-GILBERT MONROE FOSTER
586

Gilbert Monroe Foster was born February 15, 1885, died November 20, 1975, married Dora Bell Shepherd, born October 21, 1887, died December 21, 1968. He was a farmer.

They had six children: 1) Garley Wayne Foster, born January 10, 1905, died October 5, 1968, married Charlie Lee Pennell, born April 27, 1908, died June 17, 1978. Their children were: William Wayne, Terry, and Gregory. (2) Troy Cicero Foster, born October 10, 1906, died September 22, 1963, married Gladys M. Cardwell. (3) Frances Foster, born May 24, 1909, died November 5, 1972, married Richard Riggs, born March 28, 1903, died October 11, 1970. They had children: Argill, Wanda Ann, Ruby Ann (twin to Wanda), Evelyn, Margaret and Garley. (4) Venver Damon Foster, born December 30, 1911, married Novella Eller, born September 14, 1912.

Their children were: Clyde Damon, Helen Kate and Judy Gray. (5) Verlee Marie Foster born December 15, 1914, married Jake Eller, born June 6, 1908. They had Forrest Wayne and Floyd Land. (6) Clara Sue Foster, born February 10, 1930, married Curtis Robertson, born July 17, 1928. They have a daughter, Janice Sue.

Troy Cicero Foster, son of Gilbert M. and Dora Bell Shepherd Foster, married Gladys M. Cardwell, born March 22, 1905. Troy was the Register of Deeds of Wilkes County for many years. They had the following children:

(1) Fern Foster, born August 28, 1925, married Jackson Whistant, born August 27, 1923. They had Jackson Cameron Whistant, born August 16, 1950, married Sandra J. Tarlton, born 1950. They have J. Cameron Whistant, Jr. born October 12, 1973; Celia Dare Whistant, born January 10, 1952; and Donna Whistant, born January 12, 1954, married Steve Powell.

(2) Doretta born September 10, 1926, married Dewey Ivey, born September 8, 1925. Their children are Dewey Franklin Ivey, born May 10, 1954 and William Ray Ivey, born November 11, 1956.

(3) Thurman Thomas Foster, born June 12, 1928, married Frances Michell, born June 6, 1931. Their children are: Ella Marie Foster born April 12, 1953, married Jack Steelman and they have John Scott born 1970 and David born 1974; Steven born November 26, 1954; Thomas born January 1964.

(4) Dainard Foster, born September 17, 1929.

(5) Alean Foster, born March 23, 1931, married Thomas Johnson Smith, born December 26, 1929. They have a son, Thomas Troy Smith born November 2, 1953.

(6) Troy Cicero Foster, Jr. born January 17, 1933, died August 25, 1981, married Ina Parsons, born January 6, 1936, daughter of Walter Parsons. They have children: Terry Lynn, born August 16, 1956 who married Dan Murray. Terry Lynn and Dan have Kristen Micheal, born March 31, 1982.

Sources: Family research.

— Ina Parsons Foster

WILLIAM HAYES FOSTER
587

This son of Adney and Martha Hubbard Foster was born within easy hearing of the rushing waters of Lewis-Fork Creek. He grew up there in the late years of the nineteenth century when life was tough beyond our present-day comprehension. In order to be educated, Hayes Foster had to walk from his home to Moravian Falls once a week with a return walk home for the weekend. There was no other way in those days so that is what the boy Hayes Foster did.

At an early age, Hayes married Dorothy Walsh, daughter of Lee and Dinah Walsh from a nearby hollow. They have five sons — Charles C., Roy G., Percival, Halsey B., and Shelton B. Foster — and three daughters — Veva Foster Teague, Nola Foster Barnhardt and Lutrelle Foster Cranor.

Hayes Foster served as Register of Deeds

for Wilkes County for several years. Examples of his excellent handwriting may still be seen on the records still on file at the Courthouse. He also served as Superintendent of the Wilkes County Road System during years in which there was precious little that could be done due to lack of money, equipment and materials with which to improve the system. Everything at that time had to be done with raw man and mule power.

Hayes was also brandy gauger for a time. This entailed traveling throughout the county to the various whiskey stills in order to determine proof and quality of the finished product. Many were the stories of open-armed hospitality afforded this congenial man by citizens of all parts of Wilkes who looked forward to his visits as a means of acquiring information concerning the rest of the county and beyond.

Hayes and Dorothy moved their family first to Congo and later to Wilkesboro, where they lived in the large house overlooking the Yadkin Valley and North Wilkesboro. The house is presently owned and occupied by Attorney Joe Brewer.

Hayes Foster became a power in the Republican Party of Wilkes County and the State of North Carolina. As secretary and effective operating officer of the State Party, he was responsible for the appointment of a number of Federal judges during Republican administrations of the 1920s. One of his proudest achievements was the appointment of Judge Johnson J. Hayes of Wilkes County to the Federal bench. Equally important to Hayes were appointments which he was able to secure for numbers of young Wilkes citizens to positions within the government.

In his later years, Hayes Foster lived in several locations throughout the Carolinas and Georgia. He was involved in highway and bridge construction (with his son Roy G. Foster in Georgia) at the time of his death in 1938.

Even with his busy schedule, Hayes Foster still found the time and had the patience to give of himself to his grandchildren and others. Once he took two grandchildren, Virginia Lee Foster (later Thurston) and Roy G. Foster, Jr., to ride on the Greensboro street car system all the way to the end of the line and back. They remembered and appreciated the occasion for the rest of their lives. He is remembered by all who knew him for the sweetness of his character, his patience and good humor with family, friend and acquaintance and his unfailing kindness and consideration.

Hayes and Dorothy are at rest in the Mount Pleasant Church cemetery.

Sources: Personal knowledge.

— Roy Foster, Jr.

REV. WILLIAM HUGH FOSTER
588

William Hugh Foster born 24 January 1870 Caldwell Co. N.C. married, 25 June 1895 Susan (Susie) Greer, died, 12 March 1920, Cherryville, N.C. Susan Greer Foster, born 12 June 1877, died 10 February 1919 at Casar, N.C., Cleveland Co. Both William and Susan Foster are buried at the New Hope cemetery in Casar. He was the founder of the New Hope Church where a stain glass window is dedicated to them. Susan's parents, Charles W. Greer and Mary Lowrance died when she was young. She lived with the Uncle Joe Clarks at Blowing Rock, and attended school at the Skyland School for young ladies. William Foster attended Mt. Bethel School, Traphill College, then was ordained a Minister in the Methodist Church. He had a circuit of small churches.

At first he rode horseback, but as roads improved he had a buggy and horses. The night before he left on a trip, if the weather was cold; a large stone was put on the hearth, near the fire to warm. It was then wrapped in heavy material, and used to keep his feet warm.

When father was expected home, we would watch, and when his buggy came in sight, mother would run to meet him and they would walk up the path arm in arm. The oldest boys would take care of the horses while we younger children would stand on the porch and wait our turn for a hug. There were nine children: John, Charlie, George, Mary, Spencer, Paul, Nan (Nancy), Edith and William Jr. We could have been poor, and didn't know it; we were a close happy family.

Rev. William Hugh Foster.

Father held large Evangelistic meetings, in tents, the ground covered with saw dust. People would come from miles around, the singing free, loud and joyous. During the sermon to show approval amens could be heard. Sometimes father spoke softly, then, to stress a point he would shout. During a sermon on what a Christian should do to bring souls to God, he shouted, "What are you doing." My brother Paul, thinking he was getting after him, spoke up, "I am just a sitting here." Father answered, "Thats right, we are not out working, we are just sitting here."

On Baptism Sunday ladies brought baskets of food, for a dinner on the grounds. I enjoyed everything except the kissing kin. Crowds would stand on the banks of the river, and sing hymns during the Baptism.

Father had a study, with shelves of books, desk and typewriter, also an organ. When he closed the door it meant, silence, keep out. Sometimes, although he had never had a mu-

sic lesson and couldn't carry a tune; he played and sang; usually we could tell what hymn it was.

Mother kept a scrap book about father. I remember names; a newspaper named "Yellow Jacket," a church Dunkirk, New Hope, Fosters Chapel. etc.

Once mother's missionary group was meeting at our home. Father overheard some of the ladies gossiping. So, he joined the ladies — they asked him to pray. He prayed for God to forgive sinners who used evil gossip to hurt others. That was the only time I saw my mother angry with him.

Every night before retiring, he would take a walk to relax. He said when looking at the stars and heavens he felt near God. One night while away from home, he returned from a walk and said, "Something is wrong, I must go home." He left immediately, a short time later a messenger arrived, saying Mother was very ill. Telephones were scarce then. He got home a few hours before Mother died.

Although he continued to preach after her death, the old vigor and strength seemed to be gone. He still visited the ill, sat up all night praying with the dying — preaching funerals, performing marriages. A year after Mother's death he died at age 50.

Sources: Family *Bible*, older relatives, personal knowledge.

— Nancy Lawson

WILSON FOSTER

589

Wilson Foster, born ca. 1808 died 1883, married 9 February 1842, Martha (Patsy) Bowman, born 1812 Wilkes Co. N.C. died 1863-4. She was the daughter of James A. Bowman and Elizabeth Webb Bowman. Wilson and Martha Foster had five children: 1. Laura 2. James Thomas 3. Elbert 4. John 5. Elizabeth.

In the mid 1800s tragedy struck. In 1863-4 Martha Bowman Foster, John and Elizabeth all died in an epidemic, which was common in those days. On May 20, 1865 Laura disappeared; her body was found two months later. Tom Dula, a local boy, was convicted and hung for her murder — a tragedy that caused great pain to two good families. So beloved was Laura in the community and so sensational the trial, that the story has been told and retold by word and song, for over a hundred years.

In ca. 1870 Elbert Foster, remaining child at home, married Eliza J and moved to Buncombe Co. N.C.

In 1875 James Thomas Foster had married Mary Callie Adkins and had a home of his own. Wilson now lived with James and family. James had a large family; 1. William Hugh 2. Beverly Arnold 3. James Elwood 4. Marshell, 5. Mary Louisa 6. Elizabeth 7. Emmo.

My father Rev. William Hugh Foster was the oldest child, and remembered his grandfather Wilson well. Wilson was a small man, with hazel blue eyes, wavy dark brown hair and enjoyed playing the fiddle and clog dancing. He was a soft spoken gentle man. The home he

shared with Martha and his children he left as it was, and never let anyone else live there. Wilson seemed happiest when alone in the forests, trapping and hunting. Sometimes he would be gone in the woods for days.

Wilson Foster was moderately well-to-do for his time and place. He worked hard as a farmer and blacksmith, supporting his family well. He owned land and his home. In Caldwell Co. deed book 27, pg. 541 — December 1848 Wilson received a State land grant for 100 acres, on Henry's Branch and Laytown Creek, waters of the Yadkin River; entered 25 January 1847. And in deed book 15, page 37 on 27 August 1853, State grant for 90 acres, on the Yadkin River below Thomas Jones Ford. There are three deeds by James Foster, involving Wilson's land. He sold Calvin Triplett 30 acres on Laytown Creek on 14 January 1886 and on 11 May 1886 he sold 160 acres to Newton Corpening known as the Wilson Foster entry, now known as the Lewis German tract. James sold A.S. Abernathy 30 acres on 14 August 1887.

James moved to Blowing Rock, N.C. in 1884, and was in business with William Alexander. James was a well known rock mason and did much of the masonry in Blowing Rock, including the Mayview Manor Hotel. Like his father, James played the fiddle, liked to square dance and clog.

Souces: Caldwell and Wilkes Co. Census and Deed Books, older relatives, personal knowledge.

— Nancy Lawson

THE GAITHER FAMILY

590

John Gater (I) was born in 1599 in Lamberhurst, Kent Co., England and came to America on the ship George in 1620, even before the Mayflower came. He owned a land grant of 800 acres in what is now Norfolk, Va. His son John II (1620-1652) married Mary Walters and they had a son also named John (III) (1646-1702). In 1649 they sold their land in Virginia and moved to Frederick Co., Md. John III married Ruth Morley and they had a son named John (1678-1739). This John IV married Elizabeth Duval and their son was named John (1722-1751). John V married Anne Ruley and they had a son named Benjamin (1744-1788). By this time the name Gater had changed to Gather and then to Gaither, its present spelling.

Benjamin Gaither married Rachel Jacob and they moved from Frederick Co., Md. to North Carolina in 1781. Benjamin fought in the Revolutionary War. His will was the first Gaither will probated in North Carolina (1788, Davie Co., N.C.).

Benjamin and Rachel Gaither's son, Zachariah (23 Nov. 1772 — 14 Oct. 1843), married three times. His third wife was Sarah Taylor. One son from this marriage was Alexander Gray Gaither (4 April 1832 — 22 April 1885). He married Ann Elizabeth Wright (30 May 1832 — 27 May 1891), daughter of John and Mary McKee Wright who owned a large farm in Millers Creek, Wilkes Co., N.C. They built their home on a part of the Wright farm and she was later a school teacher there in the years following the Civil War. Their children were John W. (1862-1947), Joseph Milton (25 Nov. 1864 — 10 Aug. 1943), Mary, and W.E. Gaither.

John W. married Mamie Pennell, Mary married James W. Nichols, and W.E. (Ed) married Hattie Faw.

Joseph Milton Gaither married Mary Elizabeth Crysel (10 Jan. 1873 — 2 July 1949), daughter of Jeremiah and Susan Pennell Crysel after waiting for several years for her to become old enough to marry him. They were married on 11 Feb. 1894. Their farm was on the original Wright tract also.

Joseph Milton (Mit) Gaither built a general store about 1895 at his home on what is now old highway 421 between Millers Creek and North Wilkesboro. This store stocked items from medicine, candy, clothing and foods, to farming tools and anything else needed by the people of the community. Across the road from the store was a camp ground for persons traveling from Ashe and Watauga Counties to stop and spend the night before traveling to North Wilkesboro and Statesville the next morning.

Their three sons Ernest S., born 8 April 1895, Fred Grey born 16 Sept. 1897, and J.M., Jr., born 8 April 1900, enjoyed growing up on their large farm where many horses and cattle were raised. All of their food was grown there also.

The boys attended school at "Mud Hunker" near what is now Hensley Eller's Lumber Supply, walking the distance of about one mile twice a day, even during the winter.

Ernest Samuel Gaither (1895-1980) married Virginia Parker (1914-1979) on 22 Oct. 1935. They had one son, Ernest Samuel, Jr. (Sam) on 19 May 1945. He presently lives in Kingsport, Tenn. with his wife, Janice. They were married in May, 1980.

J.M. Gaither, Jr. married Sarah Bagley on 1 June 1928. They had two sons, J.M. Gaither III, born 30 Dec. 1931 and Henry Bagley Gaither, born 30 March 1934.

When Fred finished school he began working at North Wilkesboro at Boone Trail Motor Company riding a horse five miles to and from work every day. In 1925 he began working in the North Wilkesboro Post Office where he remained until his retirement some 33 years later. It was while working in the Post Office in 1927 that he met Blanche Bodenheimer from Thomasville, N.C., who had recently graduated from Greensboro College, Greensboro, N.C. She was born 16 Feb. 1906 in Davidson County and had come to Wilkes to find a teaching position. During her years in Wilkes County, she knew many students, especially in the Millers Creek community. Her parents were G.V. and Edna Turner Bodenheimer. G.V. Bodenheimer was sherriff of Davidson County for a number of years and at his retirement was a representative of Durham Live Insurance Company. They were both very active members of their church, Unity Methodist, in Thomasville.

Fred and Blanche were married on 21 June 1931 and built a home near the J.M. Gaither store. Their only son, Fred (Sonny), Jr., born 8 Feb. 1936, was unable to attend school

regularly, but dreamed of graduating from high school. With the help of his parents and C.B. Eller, he was able to accomplish this dream and graduated from West Wilkes High School in June, 1960. He was an avid reader and at the time of his death 16 Feb. 1979, he was enrolled as a student at Wilkes Community College. His beautiful smile and his devotion to his church (Millers Creek Methodist) were an inspiration to all who knew him.

Mary Edna, only daughter of Fred and Blanche, was born 27 July 1946. She was named for her two grandmothers. She graduated from West Wilkes High School as an honor student and attended North Carolina State University where she was on the Dean's List and joined Sigma Kappa Sorority. She married John Alfred Faw (born 8 Nov. 1940) on 27 June 1965, and has two sons, Michael Eric, born 26 Jan. 1967, and Randall Scott, born 5 Aug. 1970. They are active in 4-H Club work and Mary Edna is a member of the 4-H Honor Club. She has been active in dairying, both locally and statewide, and is presently serving as President of the North Carolina Guernsey Breeders' Association.

Sources: Data researched by Mr. and Mrs. James Melford Gaither, Family *Bible,* personal knowledge and family memories.

— Mary Edna Gaither Faw

MARY PENNELL and JOHN W. GAITHER

591

Mary Pennell Gaither and her husband John W. Gaither are two persons who touched and enriched many lives in Wilkes and adjoining counties. Having no children, they opened their hearts and home to Albert W. Wellons who was such a blessing to them. He became a minister in the Western North Carolina Conference of the Methodist Church. Albert's tribute to his adopted mother at her passing expresses so well the home atmosphere he and so many others were blessed with. The following is quoted from his tribute:

"For the one word which best characterizes her is friend. Scores of people, all who knew her from far and near, could say of Aunt Mamie, 'She is my friend.' Her heart was large enough to embrace everybody. She was a friend in need; this made her a friend indeed. When a neighbor lost everything in flames, she was among the first in helping refurnish the home. To the sick she carried cheer and hope and material assistance. To the bereaved she conveyed comfort and encouragement. The poor and needy received generously from her hand. No sacrifice was considered too great if the need were sufficient.

The pride of Aunt Mamie's heart was her flowers. Everyone associates flowers with her memory. Her entire front yard was a veritable flower garden. Year by year she labored lovingly with her flowers that she might have a refuge of beauty. And she shared them liberally with everyone. This helped to make her whole life as beautiful as the prettiest flower in her garden."

Aunt Mamie was born 27 April 1861, the

Mary Pennel Gaither

ninth child of Harvey Calvin and Rachel Louise Curtis Pennell of Wilkesboro. Uncle John was born in 1862 and they were married 12 July 1891. They celebrated their golden wedding anniversary in July 1941 just eighteen months prior to her death. Friends and relatives came from near and far and it was truly a gala occasion. Aunt Mamie died 26 January 1943 and Uncle John passed away in 1947. They are buried in Millers Creek Methodist Church cemetery just across the road from their home of many many years.

Theirs truly was a "home by the side of the road" and they were friends to everyone who passed their way.

I remember visits there. Her meals there were so outstanding that words would do a disservice to them. Everything was prepared from their farm. They had such pride in their animals and the crops they raised. The dining room was kept dark by shutters until everything was on the table and ready to be eaten. This was done to keep it cool and to prevent the flies from taking over. Once the bountiful meal was finished, the shutters were closed again and the table cleared in the dim light which found its way through the cracks. All this was an apparent labor of joy and pride with not a single complaint or apology.

Another thing I remember in that lovely home is the feather beds — what an experience to sink into at least a foot of feathers which before my invasion was as smooth as any bed we see today.

Molasses-making time was the big event of the year with the old mule going 'round and 'round to squeeze the juice from the cane. Family members and neighbors were always there to "sop" the boiler regardless of the time of day or night.

Aunt Mamie was a "Woman's Libber" of her time and how Uncle John enjoyed responding to her desires with a chuckle and a twinkle in his eyes. He had asthma and smoked some concoction for it but not in the house!!!! They loved each other and what a

Sources: Family *Bible*, newspaper clipping, personal knowledge.

— Mildred Farthing Wright

WILLIAM BOURNE GAMBILL
592

In the Walnut Grove Township of Wilkes County, on October 27, 1844, William Bourne Gambill was born, the son of Samuel Johnson and Elizabeth Shumate Gambill. He lived his entire life in that pleasant little valley, nestled at the foot of the Blue Ridge Mountains.

As a boy of seventeen, he was carrying the mail between Wilkesboro and Lenoir when the Civil War commenced. He enlisted in the Confederate forces, a member of Company F, 52nd North Carolina Regiment, McRae's Brigade, Heth's Division, Army of Northern Virginia. On March 25, 1865, he was wounded in the battle of Hatcher's Run, Virginia, and taken to the hospital in Richmond. A few years ago I visited the little hilltop there which was the location for the hundreds of tents which served as that hospital complex. It was quiet, and green, and beautiful, and I wondered how very different it must have appeared to him so long ago. When Richmond fell, William was transferred to Newport News, Virginia, as a prisoner of war and remained there until Lee surrendered to Grant on April 9, 1865. He and his companions were released to make their long hard journeys homeward on foot.

Soon after his return to Walnut Grove, William organized a small private school and among his students was a friend and neighbor of earlier days, now a grown up young lady, Elizabeth Jane Brown. William and Elizabeth, daughter of John Milton and Pheroby Joines Brown, were married on Thanksgiving Day, November 25, 1869, traditionally "so that he could teach school in peace!" They made their home first at the spring near the present Walnut Grove Baptist Church and then built their permanent home on the hill above the road which runs along the head waters of the Roaring River.

To William and Elizabeth was born a large family of six boys and six girls: Sarah Ann (1870-1946) married Oliver Franklin Blevins; Edward Franklin (1872-1874); Susan Fredonia (1874-1938) married Elmore Handy; son, stillborn, December 25, 1875; Theodosia Caldonia (1876-1951) married Dr. Tobias H. Higgins; Isaac Calloway (1879-1901); Rebecca Victoria (1883-1961) married Robert L. Higgins; Ira Samuel Milton (1886-1950) married Nancy Gentry; Alda Viola (1889-1966) married Robert A. Shropshire; Carl Montgomery (1893-1936) married (1) Archie Rhodes (2) Alma Lugar; Abraham Lincoln (1897-1952) married Dessie Adams; Hattie Simpson (1900-1968) married Charles Poole McNeill.

William was a church and community leader and a kind and loving husband and father, who was deeply interested in seeing that his family received a good education. Several of his children went to Wilkesboro to school, then to academies in Traphill and Mulberry. Susan, Theodosia and Hattie became school teachers.

William Bourne and Elizabeth Brown Gambill.

Viola became a nurse and served with the Army overseas with the occupation forces after World War I. She had the distinction of being the only World War I woman veteran from Wilkes County. Ira graduated from Oak Ridge Academy and North Carolina Medical College in Charlotte and served the people of Wilkes and Surry counties as a doctor for many years.

Several years ago when a cousin and I were talking "family", we remarked that, although neither of us actually remembered either "Pappy" or "Mammy" Gambill, we felt we knew them intimately, through the stories their children and grandchildren told about their lives — keeping alive the happy memories of a close and loving family.

William Bourn Gambill died on Sunday, March 28th, 1927. Realizing that the end was near, he expressed the desire to return home from Elkin, N.C., where he had been in the home of his son, Dr. Ira Gambill, during an illness of several weeks, so that he might be with lifelong friends and neighbors for his remaining days.

Sources: Family records, *Bible* records.

— Elizabeth McNeill Forester

GARDNER
593

Originally from the Hillsville, Virginia area Edd Frank Gardner and Gertrude Webb Gardner moved to North Wilkesboro December, 1936 with their son and daughter.

As organizer of Carolina Mirror Corporation, Edd began production in 1937 with twenty employees on B Street, North Wilkesboro. Ten years later a larger facility was constructed on highway 268 east. By the year 1961, Carolina Mirror Corporation was one of the industry's largest manufacturers.

After resigning from Carolina Mirror Corporation in 1961, Edd and his son-in-law Don Culler organized Gardner Mirror Corporation. Under their guidance, this company has become one of this country's largest manufacturers of mirrors and fabricated glass products with branches in Phoenix, Arizona and Dallas, Texas.

Edd is active in the first United Methodist Church as well as other civic and business organizations. He has served as president of the Kiwanis Club and as a director of the Northwestern Bank. Currently he is a trustee of Wilkes General Hospital and a director of North Wilkesboro Federal Savings and Loan Company.

Becoming involved in the First United Methodist Church in 1937, Gertrude has assumed various responsibilities. She served as president of the United Methodist Women, superintendent of Sunday school, and teacher. In addition, she was instrumental in organizing a daily kindergarten for five-year-old children. Gertrude has been elected to many leadership positions in the community as well as on the district and state level. With her guidance, the hospital auxillary was organized. While president of the North Wilkesboro Woman's Club, she organized the Senior Citizen's Club. Currently she is serving on the Wilkes County Library board of trustees.

William Edward Gardner, Edd and Gertrude's son, graduated from McCallie Preparatory School for Boys in Chattanooga, Tennessee. Bill attended Davidson College and the University of North Carolina. He joined the Air Force and served until his death in 1952.

Their daughter, Mary Lee, graduated from Virginia Intermont Junior College and Greensboro College. Upon graduation she taught elementary education in the North Wilkesboro City School system. In 1949 she married Don Turner Culler from Wilkesboro.

Born January, 1926, Don attended Wilkesboro school until World War II. He joined the Army Air Corps as a aviation cadet and served in the Pacific Theater as a crew member on a B-24. At the end of World War II he attended National Business College in Roanoke, Virginia. In 1948, he began his business career with Carolina Mirror Corporation. After his resignation as vice president of that corporation in 1961, he organized Gardner Mirror Corporation with his father-in-law E.F. Gardner. Don remains involved in various civic and business organizations. Concisely, he has served as director for the Northwestern Bank, Northwestern Finance Company, Wilkes Chamber of Commerce, and president of the North Wilkesboro Lions Club. In relation to his business career he has been a director of the National Association of Mirror Manufacturers and later became president of that organization. Presently, he is serving as a member on the board of trustees of Wilkes Community College. In addition, Don has held various positions in the First United Methodist Church including chairman of the official board and member of the board of trustees. He has also been greatly involved with the Methodist Children's Home where he has served on the board of trustees.

Don and Mary Lee have two daughters; Donna Lee and Patricia Ann. Donna, born April 1953, graduated from Meredith College with a B.A. degree in home economics. She is co-owner of Grey Gables Interiors, Inc. in Wilkesboro. Donna married Peter Wing Hurd from Freeport, Maine. Peter is a graduate of the University of Maine. He is employed by Gardner Mirror Corporation.

Patricia, born January 1959, is also a graduate of Meredith College with a B.A. degree in home economics. She married Mark Edward Pegram from Clemmons, North Carolina. He is a graduate of North Carolina State University. Mark is employed by Gardner Mirror Corporation.

Sources: Personal Knowledge.

— Donna Culler Hurd

JAMES LEMUEL and ANNIE CARRIGAN GARWOOD
594

My grandfather, James Lemuel Garwood, was born October 13, 1879, to David and Mary Hilton Garwood, in Davie County, North Carolina. He came to Wilkesboro in 1906 and opened Garwood Piano Company, which he operated nearly half a century. During this time he was very active in the Wilkesboro Methodist Church, serving as Sunday School Superintendent and a member of the Board of Stewards. A handsome and intelligent man, he was, as the Wilkes Journal-Patriot said in an editorial following his death on April 14, 1955, "honest and trustworthy, sincere and with integrity of character which made his life a valuable asset to his church, his community and to all who knew him."

On April 10, 1912, James Lemuel (or Papa Garwood) married my grandmother, Annie Lura Carrigan. Annie (or Mama Garwood) was born March 24, 1891, to John Henry and Ida Moose Carrigan, in Wilkesboro. She was working at the Post Office in Wilkesboro when she met my grandfather, and after they were married they moved to Raleigh for a year before returning here and beginning what was destined to be a very large, happy, and successful family. Nine children were born to their marriage, and there are today 14 grandchildren and 12 great-grandchildren.

The first of Mama and Papa Garwood's children, Lucile, was born January 16, 1913. Lucile married Jimmie McFerrin on July 6, 1947, and settled in Austell, Georgia, where Jimmie founded the Austell Natural Gas Company and served as its President until his retirement in 1974. They have one child, James Garwood McFerrin (Jim), born July 22, 1948, who married Martha Lovill on December 7, 1974, and they have Jamie Elizabeth, born June 27, 1977.

The second of Mama and Papa Garwood's children, James Franklin (Sonny), was born December 13, 1916. He served in the United States Armed Forces in World War II, was wounded in action in Germany in 1944, and was awarded the Purple Heart in the same year. Sonny married Rena Walsh on June 28, 1969. He works for Lineberry Foundry & Machine Company.

The third of Mama and Papa Garwood's children, Albert Sidney, was born October 18, 1919. He served in the United States Armed Forces in World War II and worked for

Annie Carrigan Garwood.

James L. Garwood.

Lineberry Foundry & Machine Company, serving as its President until his retirement in 1979. Albert married Anna Laura Hulcher on March 9, 1941, and they have three children: Albert Jr. (Abbie), born March 11, 1944; Marilyn Inez, born August 25, 1948; and Robert Hulcher, born September 19, 1954.

Abbie married Linda Combs August 21, 1965, and they have four children: Jerry, born August 3, 1967; Beth, born November 2, 1969; Jennifer, born May 27, 1979; and Jason Albert, born May 14, 1981. Marilyn married Jimmy Hayes January 28, 1966, and they have one child, Laura Hayes, born August 29, 1967. Robert married Joyce West on February 23, 1974. They have two children: Chris West, born October 20, 1971; and Robyn Michelle, born August 1, 1974.

The fourth of Mama and Papa Garwood's children, Charles Edward, was born March 30, 1922. Charles, served in the United States Armed Forces in World War II, having been a Seabee with the Navy, and later went to work with Lineberry Foundry & Machine Company. On March 5, 1947, he married Ann McNeil, and they have two children: Mary Ellen, born October 8, 1947; and Charles Edward Jr., born March 24, 1953. Mary Ellen married to Tom Mikell on May 31, 1980.

The fifth of Mama and Papa Garwood's children, Edna, was born June 18, 1924. Edna's first child, Robert Allen Parlier, was born June 9, 1941. He married Sandra Bradshaw January 19, 1964, and they have three children: Jeff, born November 5, 1965; Melissa, born August 3, 1969; and Sean, born November 19, 1974. Edna remarried December 6, 1947, Gorman Johnson, who died in 1976. One child was born to Edna and Gorman: Sharon Elaine, born September 7, 1948. Sharon married February 20, 1967, Wayne Arnold, and they have two children: Andrea, born October 1, 1973; and Eric, born November 7, 1974. Edna married Doyle Hutcheson on July 27, 1979.

The sixth of Mama and Papa Garwood's children, Anna Jean (Jeanie), was born March

9, 1927. Jeanie worked for many years with Reins-Sturdivant Funeral Home in North Wilkesboro, and she currently resides with and helps care for Mama Garwood, who is now in her 90's, and yet retains the same intelligent mind, sharp memory, and kind heart by which she has always been known.

The seventh of Mama and Papa Garwood's children was my mother, Nancy Jane, born April 23, 1930. She married my father, Ray Triplett, on January 27, 1951, and they have three children: Anthony Ray (Tony), born October 22, 1955; Nancy Lynn, born January 22, 1957, married David William Brooks II on Aug. 3, 1980; and Elizabeth Ann (Beth), born April 23, 1962. My father joined Lineberry Foundry & Machine Company in 1966.

The eighth of Mama and Papa Garwood's children, John Allen, was born July 8, 1932. John served as Vice-President of Lineberry Foundry & Machine Company for many years before becoming President upon Albert's retirement in 1979. John has in addition pursued a very active and successful role in the Wilkes County Republican Party, having been its Chairman from 1975 to 1980, and in the NC Republican Party, from which he was a delegate to the 1980 Republican National Convention and in which he currently serves as Chairman of the 5th Congressional District. In 1973 he was appointed by Governor Holshouser to the Board of Trustees of A.S.U. and has served as the Board's Chairman. John married Wanda Bandy on August 3, 1957, and they have three children: John Bandy, born December 8, 1961; David Allen, born December 7, 1963; and Susan Elizabeth, born May 15, 1969.

The youngest of Mama and Papa Garwood's children, Joseph Lemuel, was born May 28, 1935. Joe was an outstanding athlete at Wilkesboro and Wilkes Central High Schools and at A.S.T.C., and he later joined Lineberry Foundry & Machine Company. Joe was possessed of a very gifted voice, and for years he sang in the choir of the Wilkesboro United Methodist Church. On August 10, 1968, he was married to Wanda Hincher, and they resided together in Wilkesboro until Joe's unexpected death on February 20, 1982, at the age of 46. Joe's death was a very sad and tragic event for all of us.

Sources: Family records and remembrances, Wilkes Journal-Patriot, personal diary.

— Tony Triplett

GERMAN FAMILY

595

Charles German and his bride, Katherine Kaylor as of November 14, 1777, settled on a land grant located on the water of the Long Fork of Beaver Creek two miles off the Yadkin River in what is now the extreme western area of Wilkes County. The land in question was to remain to the present time in possession of their descendants.

To the German-Kaylor union were born five sons and three daughters: Wilborn, James, John, Lewis, Hubbard, Polly, Elizabeth and Betsy.

James German and Nancy McGuines were married August 27, 1922. To this union were born Elizabeth on May 14, 1940, Aner born 1943, James Sidney born July 29, 1948 and John Finley born April 30, 1953.

John Finley German and Mary Haire were united in marriage June 5, 1892. To this union were born John Clinton September 23, 1895, Gladys Leota June 12, 1898, James Irving January 19, 1903, Grace Gertrude April 21, 1905. Following the death of his wife, John Finley and Malona Victoria Eller were married December 18, 1907. To this union were born Finley Lafayette May 30, 1910, Luty Camilla January 31, 1912, Sidney Worth February 3, 1914, Mamie Tate May 18, 1916 and Malona Myrtle August 18, 1918.

Sources: Personal knowledge.

— F.L. German

THE FAMILY OF HAMILTON GERMAN

596

Hamilton German (1834-1910) was born at Beaver Creek in Wilkes County. He married Martha Carlton, dau. of Burton Carlton near the beginning of the Civil War. He bought a farm on Warrior Creek from Wilson Laxton. This was in the section which became Boomer Community. On the farm was a seven room house, the first house in this vicinity built of sawed lumber.

He rented part of the house to a family named Ayers so that his bride would not be left alone and then he went off to war. When he returned home he started farming. Hamilton and Martha had four children. Sarah married Sidney Elrod and they reared a family of three sons and one daughter in San Francisco, California. Nelia married Nelson Laxton of Caldwell County. They had one son, Bruce. Monroe married Mary Carlton from Georgia. Their children were Lucile, deceased, Carlton, deceased and Nancy Elizabeth who married Lester Bodenhamer and lives in Kernersville.

Charlie married Nell Hendren and lives at Boomer, Annie Ruth married Roby Greer of Boone, Leora married Gus Nan and lives in Texas, Roberta married Jim Britton and lives at Myrtle Beach, and Mildred married Worth Jackson and lives in Raleigh.

Edgar married Belle Laxton of Caldwell County. Their children were Eva German a retired school teacher, John, deceased, Earle married Wilma Mae Jones of Boomer, Blanche married Connor McGee and lives in Lenoir, Atwell married Violet Frazier of Caldwell County.

Edgar and his wife lived on the farm his father owned. He was a grain and vegetable farmer. He and his sons Earle and Atwell established Woodside Dairy.

Monroe bought the adjoining farm on the opposite side of Warrior Creek; he and his son Charlie established Montview Dairy.

The two dairies furnished a large part of the residents of the Wilkesboros with milk until the large dairy companies moved into the county and purchased the two small dairies.

Earle and Atwell own the original Hamilton German farm and raise broilers and beef cattle.

Charlie and his son Monroe own the Monroe German farm and raise broilers. Charlie has a daughter, Mrs. Kay Brooks.

Earle German has a son John who lives at Boomer and a daughter Mrs. Glenn Wellborne, who lives in Raleigh.

Atwell German has a son Ed and a daughter Mrs. Steve Osborne. They both live at Boomer.

Blanche German McGee has two daughters; Mrs. Jack Murdock of Raleigh, North Carolina and Mrs. Tom Harville of the U.S. Air Force.

Through the years the German family has been active in Zion Hill Baptist Church of Boomer.

Sources: Family records, personal knowledge and memories.

— Eva German

JAMES MONROE GERMAN

597

Jsmes Monroe German was born January 10, 1871 as the eldest son of Hamilton German and Elizabeth Carlton German in the Boomer Community. He later made his own home there and reared a large family of eight children. He inherited his large dairy farm (Montview Dairy) from his father and started a retail milk route in the Wilkesboro's in 1926. It had a daily route that required him to employ six men. Through good management and hard work, he built up a good trade and was well known throughout the county. In 1936, he was named "Master Farmer of North Carolina" in the *Progressive Farmer* magazine, through the direction of the County Agent and Clarence Poe, editor of the magazine. He was the first Grange Master in Wilkes County and was an officer in the State Grange. He was a member and a deacon of Zion Hill Baptist Church in Boomer, N.C. About the time he reached retirement age, he was asked to serve on the Wilkes County Board of Education where he served for four years.

He was married to Mary Alice Carlton on September 21, 1898, who was a native of Georgia and a school teacher until she got married. To this union was born Mary Lucille on August 21, 1900. She was a graduate of Appalachian State Teachers College, taught in grammar school for 30 years and later died of a blood clot in 1953. She never married.

Monroe Carlton German was born February 18, 1902, graduated from N.C. State College where he majored in Farm Management. He married Ruth Goodnight from Kannapolis, N.C. They later moved to Virginia where he worked on a tree farm. He later died in a farm accident in 1945. His wife, Ruth, now lives in Kannapolis, N.C. with her family. They never had any children.

Nancy Elizabeth was born February 23,

James Monroe and Mary Carlton German.

223

1904 and later attended Appalachian State Teachers College, became a teacher and taught in the following schools: Boomer, Mt. Pleasant, and Moravian Falls in Wilkes County; Kings Creek Elem. School in Caldwell County; and Wake Christian Academy in Wake County, N.C. She married Carl H. Hendrix, son of George and Martha Hendrix, June 1, 1935. He attended ASU receiving his BS Degree and Class "A" High School Certificate in 1931. He became principal of Traphill High School. He died November 9, 1936. Nancy Elizabeth remarried in 1975 to Lester Bodenhammer of Kernersville, N.C. where they now reside. She never had any children.

Charles Hamilton German was born February 14, 1906, later following in his father's footsteps in the dairy trade. He delivered milk in the Wilkesboros and became well known by all. He married Nell Reed Hendren, daughter of Jehue Jones Hendren, Brushy Mountain, on March 24, 1938. They had two children; James Monroe German II, February 17, 1939, who still resides at home running a large poultry farm; and Kay Hendren German, December 20, 1940 who has been a secretary for B & R Sheet Metal Inc. for 17 years, now married to Marshall Edward Brooks who works for Northwestern Bank.

Annie Ruth German was born April 15, 1908, attending Appalachian State Teachers college in Boone, majoring in Home Economics. She married Roby T. Greer of Boone, N.C. where she still lives with their only daughter, Mary Ann Greer.

Leora German was born April 5, 1910 and graduated ASU, majoring in Social Studies and married Alfred Toerne DDS of San Antonio, Tex. They had one son, Alfred Toerne who later became a Lutheran minister. Leora was named to Who's Who of America.

Roberta Alice German was born July 12, 1912, graduating from ASU with honors majoring in Home Economics, becoming a Home Economic teacher both in Wilkes and Horry counties for 40 years. She married Jim F. Britton of Whiteville, N.C. later moving to Myrtle Beach, S.C. where he owned and operated Britton's Electric for the remainder of his life. Jim died in 1976. Roberta still resides at Myrtle Beach, S.C.

Mildred Fern was born September 26, 1914, graduated from UNC and was secretary to Mr. Kerr Scott for years before he became governor of N.C. She later became a teacher at the school for the blind in Raleigh, N.C. She married Worth H. Jackson of Raleigh, N.C. where they still reside. They had four children: Worth Carlton Jackson, Alan and Nancy, twins, and Mary Alice Jackson. Worth Carlton Jackson is married and lives in Arlington, Texas. Alan Jackson is married and lives in Luggoff, S.C. Nancy (Mrs. Connie Watkins) is married and lives in Raleigh, N.C. Mary Alice (Mrs. Jerry Walters) is married and lives in Wake Forest, N.C.

I remember my grandfather, James Monroe German, as being a very stern gentleman, not taken in by little girls, but he died September 12, 1951 when I was still small and probably very rowdy. He was a great man and well remembered by all of his eight grandchildren.

Sources: Family *Bible*, personal knowledge, memories, and interviews with family members.

— Kay German Brooks

THE ROBERT SHUFORD GIBBS FAMILY

598

In April 1939 I attended a Duke Power Company meeting in Charlotte. Back home in Hendersonville the following day I read in the paper that two men had been killed on their way home from that meeting. They were Malcolm Butner and Arthur "Red" Forester of North Wilkesboro. Later that day my best friend from high school days, Dr. Gurney T. Mitchell, phoned from Wilkesboro and asked why I didn't come and take Malcolm Butner's place as manager of Duke Power. I told him we went where the boss told us to go. Later that same day I had a call from the "boss," E.C. Marshall, president of Duke Power, setting up a meeting for the next day. Subsequently I came to North Wilkesboro as manager of the Duke Power office, where I remained until my retirement in 1967.

I was born February 4, 1902 in Mars Hill, the third child of Robert Shuford and Sallie Kate Jarvis Gibbs. My father, a trustee of Mars Hill College, owned a country store. When electricity came to Mars Hill in 1919 I helped wire our home, the store and several of the college buildings. I graduated from Mars Hill College in 1921 and, with a B.S. degree in electrical engineering, from Georgia Tech in 1925. While working for General Electric in New York City, I met Isabella Frances Gamble, who was studying music at Julliard, and we were married on February 22, 1929 at her parents' summer home on the side of Grandfather Mountain.

Isabella, born February 24, 1906 in Athens, Ga., was a daughter of John and Mable Hodgson Gamble. Her father was an attorney and her mother came from a family of musicians. She had graduated from Lucy Cobb College in Athens before attending the Julliard School of Music. After our marriage we moved to Charlotte and later to Asheville, where the G.E. project on which I was working was abandoned in the wake of the 1929 stock market crash. I then went to work in Hendersonville in September 1936 for Duke Power and we lived there until 1939.

We have six children, including one who died in infancy. Our eldest, John Gamble, was born in 1930 and is a graduate of Davidson College and the Union Theological Seminary in Virginia. After his graduation from the seminary he had the privilege of studying with the renowned Protestant theologian, Carl Barth, in Switzerland. Later John earned his Ph.D. in religion at Princeton University and he is now a professor in the department of humanities at the University of Minnesota. He and his wife, Karen, and youngest child, Anne, live in Moorhead, MN. John's other children are: Elizabeth, who is studying law; Suzanne, who is working on her doctorate in chemistry; and Ian and Patrick who live in Minneapolis. Our second child, Isabella Frances, was born in 1932

and attended Maryville College and later studied art at the University of Georgia. She is unmarried and lives with us. She has been active in the North Wilkesboro Presbyterian Church, the Musical Arts Club and has worked extensively with the Senior Girl Scouts.

Roberta, born in 1936, graduated from Maryville College and is a school librarian in Gallatin, Tennessee. She is married to Kendall Pafford and they have three children: Melanie, who is studying nursing, and Kent and Mark, who are in high school. Roberta and her family have been very active in 4-H work, in which they have won many honors. Our next child, Hyatt, was born in 1938 and attended Mars Hill College and N.C. State University. Later he earned a Ph.D. in physics from the University of California at Berkeley. After working 13 years as a research physicist with Bell Labs, Hyatt is now a professor at the University of Arizona, where he and his wife, Lethia Archer, live in Tucson with their children, Alex and Vanetta. Hyatt has lectured at many U.S. and European universities and spent a year in the Netherlands as an exchange scientist. In 1982 he was elected a fellow of the American Association for the Advancement of Science.

Our youngest child, Mary Turner, born in 1942 in North Wilkesboro, received her RN degree from Watts Hospital and is presently a cardiovascular nurse clinician at Duke Hospital. Under the auspices of the American Heart Association she has lectured to nursing groups around the country about the care of and instruction of patients using pace makers. Mary Turner is married to Kenneth Manwaring and they have three children, Kate, Ami and Eason. Sara A. Dixon, formerly of Hendersonville and a Presbyterian missionary in Mexico since 1951, also made her home with us and has many friends here. Sara was educated at Southeastern State College in Oklahoma and received a masters degree in religious education from the Presbyterian School of Christian Education in Richmond, Va.

All of us have been active members of the North Wilkesboro Presbyterian Church. I have served as teacher, deacon and elder; Isabella is a teacher, longtime choir member and holder of various offices in the Women of the Church group. She has shared her love and knowledge of music through the teaching of piano and voice and has dedicated much of her time and interest to the Girl Scout organization of the community. Her interest in her students and Scouts has followed them as they grew up and she has helped many to find scholarships, where needed, for college and to pursue their chosen careers.

Isabella was the first president of the Wilkes Music Teachers Association, a charter member of the Musical Arts Club, and also a member of the DAR. I was a charter member of the Wilkes YMCA Board of Directors and am a past president of the Wilkes Chamber of Commerce, the Kiwanis Club and the United Fund. I have worked with Boy Scouts in many capacities, receiving the Silver Beaver Award in 1950. After my retirement in 1967, I helped organize and, for two years was executive director of, the Wilkes County Vocational Workshop.

Hiking and camping have been an important part of our lives. In 1974 I completed hiking the Appalachian Trail. The first lap of this trek had been taken when Isabella and I hiked through the Smoky Mountain National Park in 1937.

Wilkes County has been wonderfully good to our family. We have tried to express our appreciation and love for this community through our participation in its cultural, church and civic life.

Sources: personal knowledge and recollections.

— Robert S. Gibbs, Jr.

THE GILREATH FAMILY
599

Cornelia Gilreath Bumgarner followed in the family tradition — her Grandfather taught in Iredell and Wilkes Counties for over 50 years. He only missed one year. During that year he served as superintendent for the county as the superintendent was ill. His name was Thomas Joel Gilreath. He also taught music schools as well as led the choirs at different churches.

Thomas Joel's two daughters taught also. They were Alice Gilreath who taught in Iredell and Wilkes. (She was taken to Richmond, Va. in 1907 where Dr. Stuart McGuire removed her breast. She had cancer. She was the first Wilkes County person to undergo this surgery. She later died of cancer.) Florence Gilreath taught for many years in Alexander, Guilford, and Wilkes Counties.

Thomas Joel's sons Charlie and Clarence taught several years. Clarence paddled a boat across the Yadkin River the years he taught across from his home at Adley. When the river was frozen he walked across. Charlie became an attorney and was mayor of Wilkesboro for several years. One of his sons and his only daughter were teachers.

Cornelia Gilreath Bumgarner's parents left Wilkes before she was born. She was born in Alexander County. Her father James E.C. Gilreath became a master in growing tobacco and taught others how to grow and cure it.

Cornelia Gilreath attended Taylorsville Elementary and High School. She graduated in 1926 in a class of 14. She attended summer school at Appalachian Teachers College for two sessions. She then taught at Oxford one year. The next year she took Teacher Training and did her student teaching at Stony Point High School. She taught at Bethlehem for eight years. After her marriage in 1936 she taught one year at Ellendale. She then moved to Wilkes County and taught at Ferguson for two years, Millers Creek two years, and after a seven year absence to have and raise her daughter she taught at Union for twenty-one years.

Sources: Personal knowledge.

— Cornelia Gilreath Bumgarner

THE EARLY GILREATHS
600

The following relates about the Gilreaths who came to Wilkes County before the Revolutionary War. Many have lived here, but today there are few living here with the Gilreath name, even though there may be relatives about whom the writer has no knowledge. Many have died or moved to South Carolina, Kentucky and Missouri.

There is information that the line between Wilkes, Alexander and Iredell counties has been changed several times. Therefore, the Gilreaths in those areas next to Wilkes are supposed to be descendants of the same family.

The name Gilreath, according to research, can be Gilbraith, Gilbreath, Gibreth or Culbreth.

Traditionally the Gilreaths came to North Carolina from Virginia about 1750 into Bute County. There were two brothers, Alexander and George, who were of Scottish descent. Granville, Franklin and Warren counties comprise that area now.

William Gilreath, Sr. was the son of one of the brothers, Alexander or George, and was born in Bute County about 1730-33. He came to Wilkes County before the Revolutionary War. Knowledge from private papers states he was supposed to have fought in the war along with his sons William, Jr. and Alexander from Wilkes County.

His wife was Mary (Arrington?) who was born about 1734 and whom he married about 1751.

His will was dated October 2, 1794 in Bush River, Newberry, South Carolina and Wilkesboro, North Carolina.

The first record showed he was granted 600 acres of land Feb. 1761 in Bute County by John, Earl of Granville, the last Lord proprietor in England to retain his share of land in North and South Carolina.

The next record found is in Wilkes County where he owned property along Cub Creek. This land was granted by Governor Richard Casewell who was the first governor of North Carolina after its independence. He served seven years in all, 1776-1780 and again 1784-1787.

In 1788 William Gilreath bought land in Newberry County, South Carolina. There are descendants in that area and contact has been made with them and North Carolina relatives. A John Gilreath, Greenville, S.C., has written a book on his family there.

In his will, William Gilreath provided for his children in South Carolina because he had already settled property for the ones who remained in North Carolina. The North Carolina children were John, William, Jr., Alexander and Sarah Thompson.

It seems he had 400 acres of land in North Carolina of which he gave one-third to son George and one-third to daughter Nancy. The remaining third was probably given to another child or his wife in South Carolina.

His children, as listed in his will, were George, James Hall, Jesse, Mary and Nannay Turner (Nancy). The North Carolina children have previously been listed.

According to information from various sources, William, Sr., followed his old Revolutionary War Commander, Col. Benjamin Cleveland down to South Carolina after the close of the war. It is said Col. Cleveland was greatly loved and respected by those who served with him and some of his comrades followed him to his new home in South Carolina.

Two sources state the Gilreath home was supposed to be two miles south of Wilkesboro and the family cemetery is on the plantation called "Oakwood."

Sources: Personal knowledge.

— Mrs. Fred G. Gilreath

CHARLES GENTRY GILREATH
601

Charles Gentry Gilreath was born March 12, 1875, on the family farm near Moravian Falls. He was the youngest of six brothers. When he died in February, 1952, he was living in Wilkesboro, N.C. where he had practiced law for fifty years.

He began teaching around 1895 and taught for seven years. His education was received at Moravian Falls Academy and Wake Forest Law School. On September 1, 1903, he was licensed to practice law.

His first wife, the former Mary Fidelia Moore, from Brushy Mountain, taught school three or four years around 1900. She was born on the farm belonging to her parents, Mr. and Mrs. Enos Moore, October 7, 1879. Mr. Moore's family had lived for several generations in that area. His father was James Moore. Enos Moore married Alcey Hendren, whose father was Stephen Hendren. The Hendren family had resided in the Brushy Mountains for many years also. Mary Fedilia (Delia) received her education at Moravian Falls Academy and Blue Ridge Institute in North Wilkesboro.

Charles G. Gilreath and Delia Moore had two children: Fred Gulley and Grace Moore, both of whom were teachers.

Fred, the oldest child, was born in Wilkesboro, June 2, 1905, and died there July 12,

Charles Gentry Gilreath.

1963. All of his early education was in Wilkesboro Elementary and High School where he graduated in 1924. In 1929, he graduated from the University at Chapel Hill and began teaching in Guilford County. After having taught twenty-three years in Wilkes and Iredell Counties, his total years of teaching amounted to thirty. Fourteen years he served at Trap Hill High School and Mulberry Elementary as principal. He was teaching at Wilkes Central High School when he died. He receeived his Master's Degree at Appalachian State University in 1952. He considered the small Brushy Mountain farm he had inherited from his grandfather, Enos Moore, as home for eighteen years even though he was away most of the time during the school year. He loved the farm and the people in the area. During the administration of Governor Kerr Scott he saw the advantage of getting a hard-surfaced road placed where it would be helpful to the most people. He helped to establish the Brushy Mountain Road. He spent many hours during the summer obtaining right-of-ways for the Rural Electric Association, thus showing his interest in the people and the community.

He and Sallie Olivia Deans were married in Goldsboro, June 2, 1933. She was born October 22, 1907, in Goldsboro, N.C., Wayne County. Her father was Sidney Deans. She began her education in Goldsboro and later continued it in Greene County, N.C. the home of her mother, Irene Joyner Deans. After graduating in 1925, from Snow Hill High School in Greene County, she entered the University of N.C. at Greensboro and after graduation in 1929 went back to Snow Hill to teach for four years before her marriage.

Charles Sidney Gilreath, son of Fred and Sallie, began his first years in education at Piney Grove School, a one-teacher school on the Brushy Mountains where his great-grandfather and ever generation of his family, including his mother, had taught.

Charles Sidney Gilreath attended the various schools wherever his parents happened to be teaching, Coal Spring in Iredell County and Traphill in Wilkes County, graduating from the high school there in 1953. He entered the University at Chapel Hill and remained two years after attending Mars Hill for a year.

After working with Reynolds Tobacco Company in Columbia, S.C. for two years, he went to National College of Chiropractic in Chicago for three 12-month terms. He graduated as a doctor of chiropractic. He now practicces in that profession in Elkin, N.C.

He married Lelia Cooper, daughter of Dr. and Mrs. E.S. Cooper of North Wilkesboro in 1958 and they have two daughters, Teresa (Terri) and Holli. Charles and Lelia were in Chicago the first three years of marriage where Terri was born December 20, 1959.

Grace Moore, the second child of Charles and Delia Gilreath, was born in Wilkesboro October 14, 1907. She graduated from Wilkesboro High School in 1924 and from the University of N.C. at Greensboro in 1928. She taught English in Wilkesboro High School, Mt. Pleasant in Wilkes County, McDowell and Gaston Counties.

In 1933 she married Charles Cowles

Mr. and Mrs. Charles G. Gilreath, Fred G. and Grace (1912).

Elledge, son of Mr. and Mrs. Elbert Elledge. He was born in Champion, Wilkes County, March 18, 1808, attended Millers Creek High School, and graduated from the University at Chapel Hill in 1932. Later he received his Master's Degree at Appalachian State University. He was a teacher at Mt. Pleasant, Wilkes County, and Rutherfordton, later going to Marion High School as principal, finishing his last years before retiring as principal in Gaston County. His avocation was dramatics, including a leading role in the "Horn in the West" outdoor drama in Boone, N.C., television commercials, speaker at various meetings and others.

When Charles Gilreath's wife Delia died in 1914, he married her sister, Ola. They had two sons, Charles Franklin, who died as a small child and Edwin Moore who now lives in Weaverville. Edwin Moore Gilreath was born November 20, 1924, in Wilkesboro. He graduated from Wilkesboro High School in 1943 and from a Photography College in Los Angeles, California. He owned and operated a sutdio in North Wilkesboro before moving to Asheville. On December 19, 1953, he and Eloise Williams were married in North Wilkesboro.

Sources: History of N.C. (1919), Private Papers; Mrs. E.J. Kling Butler, and DAR Records.

— Sallie D. Gilreath

WILLIAM GILREATH, JR.
602

William Gilreath, Jr. was born April 28, 1753 in Bute County, N.C. and died in 1835 in

Dr. and Mrs. Charles Sidney Gilreath, Terri and Holli. (1969).

slave labor.

His son, Hugh, married Elizabeth Barker whose father was Joel Barker. Her mother was a Miss Stevenson from Iredell County. Joel died at age 60 and his wife died at 83. They lived on a farm near Moravian Falls. Their children were Thomas Joel, James Purvis, Elizabeth, and Martha.

Thomas Joel Gilreath was born on a plantation on Rocky Creek in Iredell County in 1831. His wife was Keziah Kesler who was born at Monbo in Iredell County, N.C. She was descended from Samual Kesler and grandfather Cornelius Kesler of Rowan County. She died at age 69.

As a young man, Thomas Joel began teaching in 1856 and that became his life's occupation. He became one of the founders of Moravian Falls Academy and continued teaching for forty years. He bought a farm two miles from Moravian Falls and that furnished him a home and occupation for his leisure until his death at the age of 77.

Judge Johnson J. Hayes paid a tribute to him in his book *The Land of Wilkes*. This is the quotation: ''On January 12, 1909, school teacher Joel Gilreath died at age of 77. From early youth and until his health failed, he taught various schools in Wilkes County. He was the father of Dr. F.H. Gilreath and attorney Charles G. Gilreath, who were widely known throughout Wilkes County. He was a man of sound judgement, spotless character, and wrought mightily for the good of the country.''

Mr. and Mrs. Joel Gilreath had eight children: James E., Alice, William S., Franklin H., Clarence H., Thomas Cicero, Charles G., and Florence.

Keziah Kesler Gilreath was the daughter of Samuel Kesler and Matilda Miller. Matilda's parents were John and Catherine Miller of Pennsylvania. Keziah's grandfather was Cornelius Kesler of German ancestry whose wife was a Miss Wallace.

Sources: Personal Research

— Sallie D. Gilreath

WINONA WALTERS GOONDOW'S STORY

603

I am the last of my family living in Wilkes. My four brothers and I were all born here. My brother 'Ted' died young and my brother, Burette passed on several years ago in Pennsylvania. My other two brothers are Vernon and Paris. Paris graduated from high school at age fifteen, and so was young when leaving home for college. He played the piano for his college band, and eventually played with other well known bands, including the Kentucky Nighthawks. The first time I heard him play with them was on a live radio broadcast from Louisville. It was also on the first radio I'd ever heard. My brother, Burette, had built the set.

My father was Ulysses B. Walters. He had ''The People's Clothing Store'' in the building on Tenth Street that eventually became the Red Cross Pharmacy location for many years. He later moved to Main Street, and was there for several years. One of the business men in town

Wilkes County. He married Sarah (Sallie) Jones on December 3, 1779. She died by 1834.

In his application for a pension which he made October 30, 1832, he states where and when he was born, also that he came to Wilkes County in 1779 at the age of 26.

He entered service in the Revolutionary War as a lieutenant under the command of Captain John Robbins and later succeeded him as captain. He served with Captain William Lenoir and Captain Jesse Walton at the Battle of Kings Mountain October 6, 1780.

In his will, May 1836, in Wilkes County, N.C., he names his children and his bequests to them, including household items, land and slaves. These children were William Hillaire, Rebecca, Susanna Triplett, Martha, Henry, Hugh, grandson Hiram McCoy, Delilah McCoy, and Hardee.

Rebecca Gilreath married Joel Triplett. Their daughter, Sara Elizabeth Jones Triplett married Montford Sidney Stokes, son of Governor Montford Stokes. They had two children, Dr. Lawrence Cain Stokes and Camilla (Minnie). Both of them died young — she from a serious illness and he during the Civil War, leaving two orphaned children. Minnie married Charles N. Hunt and has some descendants.

Henry Gilreath was the first son of William, Jr. and was born in 1786. He married Lavinia Parks who was born in 1790 at Roaring River, N.C.

In his will he listed his children: Sally L. Brown, Hugh M., Thomas G., Rebecca Ellis, William B., Martha, and Mary E. His will was dated March 12, 1841.

He was born three miles south of Wilkesboro and bought a plantation about three miles from his birthplace which he operated with told me that Father was the first merchant in town to use a full page advertisement in the newspaper. (I have in my possession one of those ads which a friend found in an old "Carter's Weekly" and brought to me.) He was a Mason, and a member of the First Baptist Church of North Wilkesboro, where he was a deacon and teacher of the Baraca Men's Class. Soon after coming to town to finish his schooling, he was called into a play production to replace a sick actor. At a rehearsal in the old opera house he caught the eye of a fair maid and offered her an apple. This pretty girl, Ursula Ashkettle, became his wife.

In 1928, for health reasons, Father moved to Pennsylvania with his family, including his parents. He became a dairy farmer. The Mason-Dixon Line crossed through the farm. Once my brother, Vernon, teased my youngest brother, Ted, into digging to find the Line.

Mamma had come to Wilkes with her parents, John and Elizabeth Ashekettle, from Berkeley Springs, West Virginia. Grandfather was bark inspector for the Smoot Tannery. He wisely built on C Street rather than live in Smoot Park, and thus avoided the flooding. One of my early memories is of being held up, at age four, to look at the 1916 floodwaters from an upper back window of that very house.

Mr. and Mrs. Ulysses B. Walters, March 2, 1904.

My paternal grandparents were James Paris Walters and Winnie Wiles. Winnie's father was William. William's father was Ambrose, his father was Abram who came to North Carolina at the time of the Revolutionary War. My grandparents had seven children, including my Uncle Rudolph. He served as a military governor in the Phillipines where he knew 'Black' Jack Pershing and William Howard Taft. He also served in North Wilkesboro as both Chief of Police and Postmaster. Grandfather, due to a lack of catalogues, was known to return home from town and sketch the current dress styles he had seen. Grandmother would then turn the drawings into their daugh-

ters' wardrobe. She also knew how to spin, dye, weave, knit and tailor for the family's needs.

Grandfather taught school, and also "Singing School'. His father, John Calvin, came here from Kentucky to 'get a (second) wife'. John Calvin's father, Israel, who married Elizabeth Holbrook was probably the first Walters in Wilkes. Israel's father Ezekial was from Virginia; they were both Baptist preachers.

In 1967, I came back to Wilkes with my late husband, Delbert Goodnow, after he retired from the employ of the government. We also brought our son, John, now an actor. I now live on Sixth Street, in North Wilkesboro, sometimes visited by John when he is between acting engagements. Nearing seventy years of age I still love to sing and praise the Lord. He has let me live to see Wilkes from a time of dirt roads and horseless carriages to a time when, in my own living room, I could watch men step out on the moon.

Sources: Family and personal records, memories, documents and geneology files.

— Winona Walters Goodnow

BRIGADIER GENERAL JAMES B. GORDON
604

James Byron Gordon, Brigadier General, Confederate States of America, was born November 2, 1822 at his family homestead, "Oakland", situated where the Wilkes General Hospital now stands, to Nathaniel and Sarah Gwyn Gordon.

On his paternal side, his grandparents were George and Sarah Herndon Gordon. George, a soldier in the American Revolution, came with his older brother, Charles Sr., to Wilkes in 1775 from Spotsylvania County, Va. and bought land just north of the Yadkin River at the confluence of the Reddies and Yadkin Rivers. This land was not tied up with the Moravian tract on the south side where later the county seat was established. The parents of Charles and George were John George and Sarah Chapman Gordon, born 1707. Sarah died in Wilkes in April 1795 at age 88. Sarah's parents were Jonathan and Jane Chapman.

On his maternal side his mother was the daughter of Richard Ransom and Martha Lenoir Gwyn, the latter being the daughter of Thomas Lenoir.

In childhood James attended Rev. Abner Gay's school taught in the older courthouse after a newer courthouse had been built, and the school of Peter S. Ney in Iredell County. Afterwards, he studied at Emory and Henry College in Virginia.

Later, Gordon engaged in the mercantile business in Wilkesboro, and sat in the North Carolina legislature in 1850.

At the first organization of Confederate troops in 1861 he became a lieutenant in the Wilkes Valley Guards, a company that first marched to Statesville, then took the train to Raleigh. Gordon belonged to Company B First North Carolina Regiment that fought in the Army of Northern Virginia, and was commissioned brigadier general in September 1863.

In the desperate fighting to save Richmond, Gordon was mortally wounded, and died in a Richmond hospital on May 18, 1864. His remains were brought home and buried in the cemetery of St. Paul's Episcopal Church in Wilkesboro. He had been a vestryman in this church. His half-brother, Tom Brown, being killed previous to this time in another state, made the death of James the second loss sustained by his mother, Sarah Gwyn Gordon Brown, wife of Hamilton Brown.

Sources: North Carolina and the Southern Cross and family papers.

— Elizabeth C. Finley

JOHN GRANT
605

John Grant was born in Somersetshire, England about 1755. He went into the Revolutionary Army from Wilkes County, N.C. when he was 18 years of age.

John married Margaret (Peggy) Sale, daughter of William and Ann Sale, in Wilkes County — bond issued 13 April 1784. William Sale's will (Oct. 1788) is recorded in Wilkes Will Book I, page 245 — the original will is in State Archives, Raleigh, N.C. among others, he named his daughter, Peggy Grant.

John Grant died about 1835 and in his will he mentions wife, Margaret, and three children: Robert, Elizabeth Mitchell, and Ann Howard. Elizabeth Grant married Moses Mitchell in 1801 and Anna Grant married John Howard, Jr. in 1806.

A paper found in the desk which had belonged to Joseph Washington Hayes indicates that Robert Grant probably married Jane Gibbs, the daughter of John Gibbs. It is believed that Robert went to Garrard Co., Ky. about 1814 and returned to Iredell about 1819. The above mentioned paper is headed "John Gibbs Garred County, Cantucky" — the next line reads "Jane F. (?) Grant was born July the 15th day 1797." The account goes on to list the following: "John E. Grant was born April the 21 Day 1815; William B. Grant and James S. Grant was born August the 7th Day 1817 (1816?), Elizabeth F. (?) Grant was born September the 13th Day 1818, Marget Grant was born January the 18th Day 1820, Ann H. Grant was born February the 5th Day 1822, Isaac X Grant was born May the 27th Day 1824, Robert G.M.D. (?) Grant was born December the 28th Day 1825." The eight children whose birthdates appear here were the children of Robert Grant; therefore it is theorized that Robert Grant's wife was Jane Gibbs, daughter of John Gibbs.

John E. Grant, first son of Robert was in Surry Co., N.C., listed on the 1850 census, age 35, a carpenter; Catherine age 22, and Robert W. age 4, Hannah J. age 2, and Mary E. age 3 months. John E. Grant died 5 June 1885 and is buried in the cemetery of Union Grove Methodist Church in Iredell County. Catherine Grant died 9 July 1898 and is buried beside her husband.

William B. Grant was on the 1850 Iredell census, age 34. Amanda F. (presumably his wife) was 21 years old.

James (Sylvester) Grant, twin to William, appeared on the Surry Co., N.C. 1850 census, age 33, manufacturer of cotton machinery; Jane age 34 and William H. age 5. A Mary A. Evans, age 16, was living in the home at that time.

It is believed that Margaret Grant, daughter of Robert, married a Templeton and resided in Iredell County. Belle Templeton who was born 27 Sept. 1883, married Will D. Pharr 15 March 1903, was a descendant of Margaret Grant Templeton. This writer visited Mrs. Pharr a few months before her death on 15 April 1966. The Pharrs were living on land which at one time belonged to J.W. and Ann Howard Grant Hayes.

Ann Howard Grant (apparently named for her father's sister, Anna Grant and Anna's husband, John Howard) married Joseph Washington Hayes 23 January 1845. The ceremony was held at the home of her father, Robert Grant, in Iredell County.

This writer has been unable to learn anything about the remaining three children of Robert Grant: Elizabeth, Isaac X., and Robert McD. Grant. (It would appear that R. Duff Hayes, grandson of J.W. and Ann Hayes, may have been named for his grandmother's brother whose name was probably Robert McDuffy Grant.)

Sources: Military records, Wilkes Co., and Iredell Co. Will Books; Wilkes, Iredell, and Surry Census Schedules; Wilkes and Iredell Marriage records, and family papers.

— Mae R. Hayes

THE GRAY FAMILY
606

In 1920 Dr. A. Russell Gray moved to Wilkesboro along with his wife and eight of their pre-adult thirteen children and opened his medical practice. Being in poor health, by 1922, the local climate forced the Grays to leave and return to Virginia. During these same years some of their grown children came to Wilkes and remained for the rest of their lives. In 1921 A. Russell Gray, Sr. (born October 2, 1896, in Virginia died May 29, 1949) the oldest son moved here with his wife, Sarah Campbell Gray (born Dec. 10, 1894 in Wilmington, Virginia, died May 13, 1982) and two sons, A. Russell Gray, Jr. (born June 1, 1919, Palmyra, Virginia) and William C. Gray, Sr. (born July 24, 1920, Palmyra, Virginia) A. Russell Gray, Sr. engaged in various business enterprises and co-founded Gray Brothers Furniture in 1929 which he ran until his death.

In 1920 Dorothy Virginia Gray, the oldest child (born Dec. 15, 1894, died April 3, 1978) came to Wilkes. In 1918, she married Charles Cranor (born Jan. 28, 1887, died Aug. 7, 1940), a Wilkes native. They met in Hopewell, Virginia and were married there. It was their return to Wilkes that encouraged her parents and family to move here. There was one child who died in infancy. Dorothy became the first dietician at Wilkes General Hospital and devoted the remaining working years of her life to this position.

In 1920, Lawrence M. Gray (born Aug. 14, 1900, died Sept. 26, 1974) made his home in

Wilkes. He co-founded Gray Brothers Furniture Company in 1929. In 1950 he married Mamie Witherspoon (born April 19, 1899 in Catawba County, died July 5, 1974).

A. Russell Gray, Jr. married Annie Vannoy (born in Wilkes County May 17, 1917, died July 4, 1977) on March 31, 1941. He has been associated with Gray Brothers Furniture since 1934 and now serves as President. They had three children: A. Russell Gray, III (born June 13, 1943). He resides in Wilkesboro. James R. Gray (born May 12, 1946) married Mary Iva Reinhardt (born Feb. 23, 1945, Northhampton County, N.C.) June 28, 1969. Two children, David Christopher Gray (Feb. 26, 1974), Martha Elizabeth (born Jan. 27, 1978). James, a graduate of U.N.C.-Chapel Hill, served as an officer in the U.S. Navy during the Vietnam War years. He became associated with Gray Brothers Furniture Company in 1971 and became general operating officer in 1981. Sarah Ruth Gray, (born May 27, 1950) received her AB Degree from U.N.C.-Greensboro and her Masters Degree from ASU. She was a teacher in the Wilkes County Public Schools.

William C. Gray, Sr. married Dorothy Powell (born Feb. 11, 1928) September 10, 1949. He served in Europe during World War II and was a partner in Gray Brothers Furniture from 1945 until his retirement 1981. They had two children: William C. Gray, Jr. (born March 3, 1951). He graduated from U.N.C.-Chapel Hill and Wake Forest University School of Law. He is a partner in the Wilkesboro law firm of Ferree, Cunningham and Gray. Married Katherine Myers (born Wilkes County Nov. 5, 1952) December 28, 1975. They have one child, William Campbell Gray, III (born Sept. 27, 1979).

Elizabeth Powell Gray (born Dec. 27, 1952) is a graduate Meredith College, and married Clarence A. Ferguson (born Feb. 27, 1950) June 21, 1976. They have two children, Mary Elizabeth (Jan. 25, 1979) and David Gray (Jan. 22, 1982). The Fergusons reside in Garner, N.C.

Sources: Personal knowledge.

— James Gray

GRAY-GARNER-JARVIS
607

In 1799 James Gray bought a tract of land containing five hundred acres from the State of North Carolina and paid fifty shillings for every hundred acres. It is located at the headwater of Brier Creek, known as the Cranberry community. His granddaughter, Julia Ann Gray was first married to Hillary Thomas Garner who was born in 1834 and died in 1862 at Camp Mangran near Raleigh from wounds in the Civil War. Lines from the family Bible: "Hillary Thomas Garner lived as a soldier, died as a Christian in perfect mind, age 28, leaving three small sons." He is buried in the family cemetery on the Jarvis farm with relatives and slaves and by the side of the Rev. William Garner who died in 1868 and who has the only legible marker left. Her sons by Garner and her children by James McBride Jarvis were all one

Rev. Robert N. and Letitia M. Garner.

family.

The oldest was John Eli Garner, born 1858, lived in Sheridan, Wyoming, who was successful in oil and coal business. He had no children and is buried in the Masonic side of the cemetery in Sheridan.

Rev. Robert Newton Garner (born in 1860) lived near Big Hunting Creek on Statesville Road. After a few years out west, he returned to marry Mary Ann Staley in 1880. He was pastor of Cub Creek Church from 1916 to 1926. He was also pastor of Pleasant Home Church, Harmony Church, Cranberry and others.

They had one son and two daughters. The son, Robert, Jr., was a surgeon and co-owner of a hospital in northern California. He had one son, Robert, III, who lives in Sacramento.

Following the death of his first wife, Mary Ann, Robert married Letita Martin, Letita was a school teacher and boarded with the Jarvis family for several school terms. She named Mansfield's third daughter, Letita Pauline, as her namesake, and was her first school teacher. "Uncle Bob" came to Mansfield's home many times courting Letita and they returned to visit often after they were married. He was tall, dark and handsome with a good voice and education and is remembered as being very loving.

The youngest of the three Garner boys was William C. (born 1861). He lived in Indiana, worked with a railroad company and is buried in Newcastle. He was a humble, quite man and had two children.

The Garner family had lived in the Liberty Grove community on the Garner family farm.

Sources: Family records, deeds and memories.

— Pauline J. Clark

JOHN and ANN GRAY
608

The Grays were one of the early families who lived in Wilkes County. They owned one hundred acres of land on the mouth of Reedy Branch on Stony Fork. On the 1782 Tax List they owned 1 horse, 4 head of cattle and 100 acres. By the 1790 Census there were 5 males and 5 females living in the household.

We have very little information concerning Ann. John died about the 20th February in 1808 leaving two minor children — John, Jr. and Nancy. Eight children are named in his estate records. (1) James, (2) William, (3) Elizabeth who was married to a Miller, (4) Amy, b. ca. 1780 and married 21 June 1800 to George Foster, (5) Dicey, b. ca 1787 who married Jesse Triplett, (6) Molly (Polly) b. ca. 1793, (7) John, Jr. and (8) Nancy.

James was probably the oldest son and was named guardian to John Jr. and Nancy. Amy, Dicey and Mary (who never married); are known to have remained in Wilkes County, while others in the family may have moved further west.

Sources: 1782 Tax List and other Tax List, Census Records, Estate and Court Records.

— Mrs. J.A. Simpson

GREENE
609

Dr. W.C. Greene was one the older outstanding citizens of Wilkes County. He was originally from Alexander County, N.C. A graduate of old Wake Forest College, and as valedictorian of his class, he described himself to his grandchildren, and deservingly so, as a "scholar and a gentleman." He first studied to be a practicing physician and later studied to be a dentist with his office in the front yard of his home in Wilkesboro, still standing.

He married Laura Ann Gray, daughter of a plantation owner, who was also valedictorian of her class at Woman's College in Greensboro, N.C. Her father, William Gray, then owned the Governor Stokes place on the Yadkin River, which has since been destroyed by fire.

Dr. and Mrs. W.C. Greene had two children. Herbert Linwood Greene was a graduate of North Carolina at Chapel Hill and practiced law in Wilkesboro, at one time a partner in law with Judge T.B. Finley. Their daughter, Ida Maie Greene, a graduate of Woman's college in music, taught piano and voice in Wilkesboro and was instrumental in getting up concerts and programs which was the main entertainment at that time. She was very talented, as was her mother before her. She married Dave Stafford, a professional baseball player.

Herbert Greene married Dovie E. Wellborn, daughter of Elisha Wellborn from Randolph County, N.C. and who, at one time, was owner and operator of the old Wilkes Hotel, where dances and social gatherings were held in 1898. Herbert and Dovie were the parents of four children, all girls.

Laura Gray Greene, the eldest, now lives in Wilkesboro and has her piano studio in her home, the old home of her grandparents, Dr. and Mrs. W.C. Greene. She has taught piano for years in Wilkesboro, and also taught piano at the Presbyterian Orphanage at Baruim Springs, N.C. for many years before coming back to Wilkesboro.

Margaret Louise Greene was married to Stace Alexander, now deceased, and now lives in Wilkesboro. She taught school and also worked in the post office in Wilkesboro for many years.

Mary Linwood Green married William Munsey Alexander, now deceased, in June 1922. They had four children, two girls and two boys. She continues to live in their home on the Yadkin River.

Ida Maie Greene, youngest of the Greene family, attended old Trinity College in Durham N.C., married M. Teague Hipps, who studied for the ministry, a graduate of Trinity College also.

The great-grandchildren of the W.C. Greenes are: (1) Mary Charles, married to Dr. Robert H. Griffin of Asheville. They have three children: Susanne now married to Michael Bowman of Charlotte; Joan Alexander Griffin, not yet married; Mary Charles (Molly) married to Peter Bockmann of California; (2) Elizabeth Wellborn (Libby) married to C. Jack Caudill, minister in the Methodist church and government counselor, Marion, N.C. They have three daughters: Betsy, with a master's degree in German; Mary Lynn, married to Dave Melton, Methodist minister; and Jenny, the youngest; (3) William Munsey Alexander, Jr., social service work, married to Betty Sue Haynes; (4) Robert Linwood Alexander has two daughters, Laura Louise and Leslie Dianne, both in school; (5) Carolyn Hipps Roach, married to George Roach of Greensboro, N.C. They have four children: Robert Roach, Methodist minister; James Roach, choir director and musician; Susan Roach of Greensboro, Hal Roach of Greensboro; (6) M.T. (Mike) Hipps, Jr. trumpet player with the Minneopolis Symphony, married to Carol Turperning; (7) Herbert Hipps, school principal of high school in High Point, married to Virginia (Ginger) Hines.

Sources: family knowledge.

— Mrs. Mary Greene Alexander

THE GREENWOOD FAMILY
610

James Greenwood was a son of Samuel and Sibil Street Greenwood of Surry Co., NC. On Aug. 19, 1811 he secured a marriage bond to marry Sally Spencer. Robert B. Atkins signed with him as his bondsman. Robert was a brother-in-law and was married to Caty Greenwood.

Sally Spencer was born about 1790 and is believed to be the daughter of John Spencer.

Sally and James were the parents of six known children. Susan was born about 1814 and married Gideon McMickle. John was born Dec. 9, 1815. (This line will be continued below). Meredith was born about 1817. James G. was born about 1819. Samuel whose birthdate is unknown. Joseph was born about 1823 and married Elizabeth Ann Scritchfield in 1844. He died in 1900. Thomas whose birthdate is unknown.

James died about 1840. He left land on the Yadkin River that was divided among his children. His wife Sarah (or Sallie) was left the 280 tract where the homeplace was located. She was living with her daughter Susan McMickle in 1850.

John, son of James and Sallie, was born in Surry County. His first wife was Jeanette Thompson. They were the parents of the following children: William, born about 1840; James, born about 1843; Caroline, born about 1845; Sophia, born about 1847; John, born about 1849; Martha Ann, born about 1854; And Sarah J. born about 1855. Records indicate that Jeanette was hospitalized with a mental condition and that she and John were divorced.

John chose Sarah Money for his second wife. She was born April 29, 1827 and is believed to be the daughter of William and Catherine Money. John and Sarah were the parents of sour children. Mari Naomi, born July 21, 1866, married Calvin Triplett. Susannah, born Sept. 15, 1867, married Michael Columbus Williams in 1882. Margaret, born Jan. 29, 1870, married Joel Triplett in 1886. Thomas Jackson, born Jan. 19, 1872, married Martha Jane Williams.

John owned a considerable amount of land in Wilkes, Surry and Yadkin Counties. He was concerned with the education opportunities available and hired a private tutor to ensure his children would receive a good education. His last years were spent in the home of his daughter in Wilkes County.

On Dec. 30, 1895, John Greenwood died. His wife, Sarah died on April 25, 1904. They are buried in the Williams Family Cemetery in Goshen.

The ancestor of these Greenwoods in believed to have come to America from London in 1635. There were two boys, John 16 years of age, and followed nine months later by Thomas, 15 years of age. It is thought they were descendants of John Greenwood, graduate of Cambridge University and a minister. This John, along with William Barrow, was hanged at Tyburn Prison in London in 1593 for his nonconformity to the teachings to the Church of England. This is substantiated by history in that these boys were examined on this before sailing to Jamestown. The family here in North Carolina may have descended from John, the older one.

Samuel Greenwood came to Surry County from Middlesex Co., Virginia. He fought in the Revolutionary War. He sold his property in Virginia in Nov. 1783 and came to Surry in 1784. He was married to Sebell Street, who was the daughter of Henry and Catherine Carlton Street of Essex County, Virginia. There marriage date is not known but they were married prior to the death of father in 1784. This death date has been used as a marriage date, by mistake, in some accounts.

Samuel was probably born before 1755 and died about 1809. Sebell is believed to have been born about 1750 to 1755 and died about 1832.

The following children were legatees when Samuel died: Bartlett who may have married Nancy Cody in 1806. Thomas who married Lydia Moore in 1806. John, born about 1784 married Polly Hurst. This family moved to Buncombe County. Mary, who married Ayres Hudspeth. Catherine, born about 1780 and married Robert B. Atkins in 1808, later married John York. Elizabeth (Betsy) married William Mickle in 1813. Anna married James Kid in 1816. James, born about 1780-90, married Sally Spencer in 1811. Patsy, born about 1792 married Jesse Johnson. Sebell born about 1790-1800 married Thomas Johnson in 1813

They moved to Warren County, Tennessee. Leah born about 1796, married Thomas Reece in 1818. Nancy born about 1798 married Joel Reece.

The descendants of Samuel were farmers, bankers, stock brokers, business and medical people. Dr. Bart Greenwood, a son of John, was on the staff of John Hopkins Hospital in Baltimore.

Sources: *Old Buncombe County Heritage,* wills, estate records, deeds, marriage bonds and family history.

— Mrs. J. Arnold Simpson

JESSIE EVELYN BROYHILL GREER

611

Jessie Evelyn Broyhill was born to Ada Carlton Broyhill and Isaac Jefferson Broyhill on November 12, 1924, in Wilkes County, North Carolina. She graduated from Wilkesboro High School and Appalachian State University. She has taught school 34 years in Lenoir, Caldwell County. She is a member of Alpha Delta Kappa, International Honorary Sorority for women educators.

Evelyn was married to Thomas Greer, born in Caldwell County, North Carolina May 2, 1916 Evelyn and Thomas were married December 16, 1945 in Little Rock Baptist Church of Wilkes County. Thomas served in the United States Naval Reserve during World War II. He is retired from Broyhill Industries. To this union two children were born. Larry Frank Greer was born January 21, 1947. He graduated from Western Carolina University.

Larry married Judith Steadman, graduate of the University of Florida. They were married July 22, 1972 in Purity Presbyterian Church in Chester, South Carolina. They have two children; Jennifer Ann Greer born May 21, 1976 and Robert Thomas Greer born April 3, 1981. Larry is Merchandising Manager for A.V. Wray of Shelby, North Carolina.

Their second child, Frances Annette Greer was born January 20, 1952. She graduated from Converse College, Spartanburg, South Carolina. She married James Thomas Malcolm III, graduate of International Aviation Academy. They were married August 17, 1974 in the First Baptist Church of Lenoir, North Carolina. Frances teaches at Caldwell Community College.

Sources: personal knowledge.

— Evelyn Broyhill Greer

JOHN GREER FAMILY

612

The first record of John Greer in Wilkes County was when the county was formed in 1778 at which time he was a member of the county court along with Benjamin Cleveland and several others. On March 3, 1779, he was granted 200 acres of land along the main fork of Cub Creek next to Francis Hardgraves' corner and along Jacob Hampton's line. Born in Maryland about 1714, he was a son of John Greer (1688-post 1748) and Sarah Day of Baltimore County, Maryland. John, the father, was the son of James Greer (of Scotch origin) who was transported into Maryland on November 2, 1675. Scottish histories relate that the surname Grier/Grear/Greer, and other names like Gregor, Gregorson, Greig, and Grierson, are septs generally associated with the MacGregor clan that traces back to Griogar, son of King Alpin, in the eighth century.

The pattern of migration of the Greers from Maryland to Wilkes County, North Carolina, was through Goochland, Lunenberg, Bedford, Pittsylvania and other adjacent counties in Virginia. From John (born ca. 1714) and his brothers James, William, Moses, Aquilla, Benjamin, and Joseph, it is believed that most of the Greers of southwest Virginia, western North Carolina, and eastern Tennessee descend. Of course, descendants migrated westward into Tennessee and Kentucky, and southward into the other southern states.

John Greer of Wilkes probably married before he left Maryland. All that is known of her name is Nancy. Perhaps she was a Lowe. John and Nancy settled in what was known as the Moravian and Warrior Creek District of Wilkes County. John died around April or May of 1782, judging from his will which was probated in June of that year. Two sons, Jesse and Benjamin, fought in the American Revolution. Perhaps sons Aquilla, Joshua, and John also served. Jesse lived in Wilkes County until his death. It is believed that Aquilla moved into South Carolina before moving westward to Warren County, Kentucky. It is uncertain exactly where the daughters settled, but apparently they remained in Wilkes County with their husbands. Ann married a Mitchell. Hannah married Lewis Demoss who served for awhile as sheriff of Wilkes County, and Sarah married Francis Hardgraves. After John's death in 1782, Nancy was remarried on September 12, 1790, at the age of 82, to Thomas Demoss.

Captain Jesse Greer (ca. 1757-1788), son of John, is the progenitor of my own line. He married Judith Hampton (possibly a daughter of Jacob Hampton) on August 14, 1779, in Wilkes County. Their children were Delilah, born in 1780; John, born in 1782; Sarah, born in 1784; Nancy, born in 1786; and Jesse, Jr., born on December 30, 1788. After the death of Captain Jesse, Judith married William Mitchell and they moved to Warren County, Kentucky, joining numerous other Greer relatives there. Jesse, Jr., was placed under the guardianship of William Johnson until the estate was settled in 1799, and afterward under the guardianship of Turner Hampton (probably an uncle). After a few years Jesse, Jr., followed his mother to Kentucky where he married Polly (Nancy) Puckett, daughter of Ephriam Puckett. To her and two subsequent wives, a total of nineteen children were born — all except one were born in Pike County, Mississippi, to which place Jesse and Polly migrated about 1814. One of these children (by his second marriage to a German woman, Jennie Bladesinger) was my own great-grandfather, Amos Greer, who married Dolly Jones, and in whose home my grandfather and my mother were born, and where I spent many happy times as a child.

Amos and Dolly Jones Greer had three children: Vincent Jones, Andrew (my grandfather), and Abi. I knew Grandpa Andy very well as he lived to be almost ninety years of age. When I was a young lad I asked him about the Greer history. He would tell about his grandfather, Jesse, Jr., being born in North Carolina and migrating to Mississippi before Mississippi became a state. He would also tell of his grandfather (after the death of Polly Puckett) meeting a German girl in New Orleans on one of his trips there to sell tobacco. She became his second wife. Jesse's third wife was Betcy Davis. My mother, Carrie Greer Moak, now in her 90th year, is probably the oldest living descendant of Jesse, Jr.

Sources: Family records, court records, and census reports; Printed Genealogies.

— Franklin E. Moak

THE FAMILY OF WILLIAM FRANKLIN GREGORY

613

One of the men who contributed substantially to the heritage of Wilkes County was William Franklin Gregory. Born 5 April 1855 to John Gregory and his wife, Sarah Emily Waddell, he was John's first child, although John had previously been married at least once prior to his marriage to Sarah Emily Waddell 29 September 1849. William Franklin Gregory, called Billy by his friends, arrived on this earth at a very difficult period of time — just five years before the out-break of the Civil War. Thus, since most schools were closed during the Civil War and for at least three years after the war ended, Billy probably started to school when he was thirteen years old. Like many who were born during this period of time, Billy had very limited educational opportunities. In spite of these difficulties, he was able to obtain for himself a good education as proven by a number of writings he left behind. This certainly speaks well for his father and mother, as surely he was encouraged by them. Indeed, Billy grew up to be one of the leaders of his community.

On the 19 September 1874, Billy Gregory decided to establish his own home. It was on this date that he was married to Celia Ann Adams, daughter of William Rufus Adams, and his wife, Elizabeth Holbrook Adams. They established their first home in Walnut Grove Township, possibly on Shumate Mountain. Billy was an ambitious man, and believing that his opportunities were limited in Walnut Grove Township, he began looking for "greener pastures." By 1880, or shortly thereafter, Billy purchased a large farm on Maple Branch in Roch Creek Township, and he proceeded to move his young family to the "flat lands." Here Billy established his home and it was here that the rest of his children were born.

Billy Gregory exerted much influence on the people of this and adjoining areas especially in the field of religion. Like his father (who helped to organize Rachael Baptist Church) Billy also helped to organize churches through-out the remote areas of Wilkes County. He and ten other members were released by New Cove-

William Franklin Gregory, 1855-1930.

nant Church in 1885 to organize Round Mountain Church. He was also the chairman of a presbytery that constituted several churches in Wilkes County, notably Fairview, Cane Creek, Welcome Home, and perhaps others.

In 1893, Round Mountain Church, on motion "liberated William Franklin Gregory to exercise a public gift, using text. This was the beginning of a great preaching career for this man of the mountains. On the first Saturday in November, 1893, Billy was ordained to preach the Gospel. Immediately thereafter, he was elected pastor of Round Mountain Church and he remained pastor of this church until 1902. During this period of time, his influence permeated the hills valleys, and coves of this area. Many people joined the church and the church became very active. Billy's fame as a big preacher spread to surrounding counties and he was in considerable demand as a religious speaker on many occasions and by many organizations.

In 1902, Billy Gregory moved to Surry County. He continued teaching, preaching, and organizing churches there. He also continued to serve as associational officer in Wilkes, Surry, and Ashe Counties, and he was in demand as a religious speaker through-out the above counties.

Billy and Celia Ann Adams Gregory had seven children who carried on the traditions of the Gregory family. A short survey of the children and grandchildren of Billy and Celia Ann Gregory follows:

John Andrew Gregory, born 25 July 1875, married Mary Lou Shepherd, (daughter of Jordan and Susannah Hall Shepherd), and they made their home on Maple Branch in Rock Creek Township. Their children were: James Lester Gregory, who married Belva Blevins, (daughter of Andrew and Rhoda Blevins) was a life-time school teacher in Wilkes County, as was his wife. Their two children, Sherrill and Don, were highly successful business men.

Belva, the second child, married Romie Byrd and moved to West Virginia. Their five children are all successful business people, one of whom is a well-known attorney.

Ruth, the third child, was a teacher until she married Roy Key. Two of her daughters are professional people, and the others are business people. Her youngest child, Denver, was

a P.O.W. in North Viet Nam for nearly six years. He is now a Commander in the Navy.

Ennice, the fourth child, married Lawson Wood and had two sons, Eugene and Tony. The fifth Child, Vergie, married Dewey Johnson and they had four daughters.

Ina, the sixth child, married Milo Handy. They had two sons and two daughters. Elma, the seventh child, married Coy Adams and they had two sons, Rex and Fleet.

Paul married Ruth Proffit, daughter of William A. Proffit and his wife, Mary Lou Walsh Proffit. Both Paul and Ruth were professional educators. Paul was a high school principal for thirty-one years, while his wife, Ruth, was a career teacher. Their only son, Dr. Richard Brent Gregory, is a community college specialist in Charlotte.

Oma Jean, the last child, was born to John Andrew Gregory and his third wife, Ethel Hall, daughter of John Solomon and Emma Arlene Shumate Hall. Oma Jean is also a professional educator. She and her husband, Jack Martin, both teach in Virginia. Their only child, Stacy, is a talented student in junior high school.

Martha Ellen Gregory, the second child of Billy and Celia Ann, married John Byrd. They had only one child, Beatrice, who lived to maturity. She married the Reverend Roy Franklin. They had no children.

Lavadia Gregory was the third child in the Billy Gregory family. She married John Smoot and moved to Surry County. They had six children.

Bertha Gregory was the fourth child. She married Bee York and moved to Surry County. Bertha and Bee had four children.

Major Columbus Gregory was the fifth child. He died in infancy.

The sixth child of Billy and Celia Ann was James Elmer Gregory. He was a veteran of World War I. He also established his home in Surry County. Married to Mary Ann Atkins, this family was blessed with six healthy, intelligent children. Two of them are teachers.

The last child born to Billy and Celia Ann Gregory was Arkie Gregory. She was married to Ray Whitaker and lived in Virginia. They had four children.

There was considerable musical talent through out the Gregory generations. Preacher Billy, himself, played the organ and sang in a very creditable manner. His son John, and grandsons Lester and Paul, were quite musical and each possessed a beautiful bass voice. Billy's great-grandson, Richard Brent Gregory, studied organ, piano and voice at both Appalachian State and University of North Carolina at Chapel Hill. Many other sons and grandsons sang as needed but failed to develop their voices to the maximum.

During World War I, Billy moved his family to Virginia and lived there the rest of his life. Death came to this talented man 5 December 1930; and his wife, Celia Ann, died 29 November 1933. Both bodies were returned to Wilkes County and buried in the Round Mountain Church Cemetery.

Sources: William Franklin Gregory family *Bible*; Round Mountain Church minutes; interviews with two sons and John Franklin and James Elmer Gregory.

— Paul W. Gregory

AUBREY ROBERT GRESHAM, JR.

614

Aubrey Robert Gresham was born in 1927 to Aubrey R. and Grace Brown Gresham of Mooresville, North Carolina. He attended elementary and high school in Mooresville, graduated from Oak Ridge Military Institute of Greensboro in 1945, and attended North Carolina State University. After serving in the United States Navy for three years, he attended and graduated from Catawba College in 1951.

Robert Gresham married Margaret Ann (Marge) Newton in January of 1951, and they are the parents of three children and three grandchildren.

Through Mr. Gresham's association with Lowe's Companies, Inc., the family made their home in Sparta, and Greensboro, N.C., and Oak Hill, West Virginia. Then in 1964 they returned to North Wilkesboro where Robert joined the Lowe's Central Office staff until his retirement in 1976.

Robert Gresham was retained for three years (1977-1980) as a consultant to W.H. Smith and Sons, Ltd. of London, England. He taught in the School of Business at Appalachian University as a resident executive in 1979. Mr. Gresham and his wife remain active in civic and local affairs.

Sources: Personal knowledge.

— Jan Gresham Hagaman

THE W.C. GRIERS

615

Mr. and Mrs. Grier, long-time residents of North Wilkesboro, have contributed much to the religious, business and civic life of Wilkes.

William Crawford Grier, son of William Alexander Grier and Rachel Isabel Crawford, was born on August 30, 1892. At the age of three months he moved from Gaston County to Mecklenberg. He received his A.B. degree from Erskine College in 1916. A veteran of WWI, he served overseas with the Air Corps. From 1919 to 1937 he was office manager of the old Grier Cotton Mill in North Wilkesboro, from 1937 to his retirement in 1964 he was an official of the Forest Furniture Company. He is a trustee and life member of the Session of the North Wilkesboro Presbyterian Church, and was active in the American Legion. In 1978 Bill Grier was awarded honorary life membership in the Kiwanis Club. He was married to Bess Gordon Finley who died in 1948. In 1952 he was married to Rebecca Olivia Moseley.

Rebecca Moseley Grier, daughter of Gideon Constantine Moseley and Wilhelmina Courtney, was born in Aiken, S.C. January 11, 1900 and received her A.B. degree from Winthrop College. She was a teacher in Wilson, Fayetteville and North Wilkesboro schools. During WWII she served two and half years in the Woman's Army Corps; later for five years was Executive Secretary of the Wilkes County Red Cross. She has been active in the Presbyterian Church, the American Legion and Auxiliary, Daughters of the American Revolution, Wilkes Art Guild, and Community College Orchestra

Guild.

Sources: personal knowledge.

— Gordon Reins Smoak

GRIMES FAMILY

616

There were four mulatto Grimes families living in Ashe County, N.C. in 1850. Edmond Grimes, born 1798; Luis Grimes, born 1808; Alford Talton Grimes, born 1811 and John Wesley Grimes, born 1817 at Todd, North Carolina.

From records found concerning a town lot in Jefferson that Luis Grimes owned, and at his death, became the joint property of the other three, it may be assumed that these four were brothers, all born in North Carolina. No record of a father and mother has been found.

Edmond and Alford Talton had left Ashe County by 1860, but John Wesley Grimes remained and died in Ashe County. His wife was Rebecca Rena Ferguson, born about 1822 at Todd in Ashe County, and she died before 1870.

John Wesley bought a farm in the Oldfield township of Ashe and apparently lived out his days there. Wesley and Rena had eight children: Hugh, Henry, John W., Wiley W. who married 6 December 1873, Martha J. Harless, Mary J., Martha E., Teressa J., born March 1859, who married on 1 January 1891, her cousin, Rufus Grimes, and died 12 January 1924 in Ashe County, and George Columbus Grimes.

George Columbus Grimes was born 15 March 1862 at Todd, Ashe County, and died 5 Septmeber 1934 at Todd, Ashe County. He married about 1895, Charity Rosetta Redd, who was born 3 June 1876 in Watauga County, died 21 February 1954 in Ashe County and is buried at Bethany Cemetery with her husband, George Columbus. She was the daughter of Wesley and Irena Harless Redd.

George Columbus was a farmer. He and Charity Rosetta were the parents of eleven children: Fred V., born 6 November 1896, married 21 September 1922, Ethel Barber. He died in Wilkes County. Spencer Adam, born 16 October 1900, married Addie Belle Malone; Dewey Lee, born 20 February 1903, died 9 December 1975, married Mae Pearl Anderson. He is buried at Bethany in Ashe County; Bina Belle, born 30 June 1905, married 8 March 1937, Thomas Redding. She lives in Wilkesboro; Alberta who died young in Ashe County; Edd A. born 18 September 1907 married 23 December 1937 Linnie Watkins and lives in North Wilkesboro; Stewart, born 9 July 1910, married Marzel McMillian and lives in Ashe County; Harmon Clyde, born 25 March 1912, died 25 December 1930 in Ashe County, unmarried; Ina Lee, born 28 March 1915, married 16 September 1936 John Hamilton and died in the state of Pennsylvania; Rebecca Irene, born 2 September 1917, died 9 February 1982, married Delmore McMillian 8 March 1937. She is buried at Pleasant Hill Churchyard, Wilkes County; Ola Mae, born 4 July 1919, married 14 September 1942 Ray Burkett, and lives in Wilkes County.

Spencer Adam Grimes came to Wilkes County in 1926 from Ashe County. He was born in Ashe County 16 October 1900, and died in Wilkes County 7 December 1951 and is buried in the family cemetery on his land in the Fairplains community. He married 4 September 1923 in Shawn, Johnson County, Tennessee, Addie Bell Malone who was born 2 November 1906 in Johnson County, Tennessee, daughter of Tom and Fannie Malone.

Spencer worked with the Tannery in North Wilkesboro for thirteen years, went to Jenkins Jones, West Virginia and worked for U.S. Steel for fifteen years, returning to Wilkes not too long before he died. Addie Belle worked for the Wilkes Hospital for Dr. Fred C. Hubbard and after the Wilkes General Hospital was built, she worked there, until her retirement. She served the hospitals for twenty-seven and one half years. She lives in her home in Fairplains community.

Spencer and Addie Belle had three children:Frances Rosetta, born 12 December 1923, married 6 April 1947 George Dodson, who is deceased. She and George had four children. Freddie Dodson, born 13 January 1949, married Shelia Dowell; Jerry Dodson, born 4 January 1952, married Wanda; Jacquelin (Jackie) Dodson, born 4 October 1954, married Donald Gilreath; Rickie Dodson, born 24 January 1969.

Arlene Susan Grimes, daughter of Spencer and Addie Belle, was born 30 November 1927, married 30 December 1950, Warren Harding Brown of Arawalt, West Virginia, son of James and Catherine Brown. Arlene graduated from Lincoln Heights High school and lived in Wilkes County until her marriage. She and her husband lived in West Virginia until Warren's retirement, when they built a home and now live near her mother in Fairplains community, where she and Warren are active members in the Pleasant Hill Baptist Church.

Roy Herbert Grimes, son of Spencer and Addie Belle, was born 11 December 1932, and lives near his mother in Fairplains community.

Sources: Ashe County records, personal knowledge.

— Arlene Grimes Brown

ELIZA GWYN FAMILY

617

Prior to 1865, Eliza Gwyn was a slave of the James Gwyn family at Green Hill Plantation. Green Hill was located on a scenic hillside in Ronda, N.C. The eastbound Yadkin flows along the border of the estate. Eliza was obviously a woman of great humility and endurance. We base our assumptions on the results of our research findings. Although she was afflicted with an arthritic condition and eventually became crippled, she endured hard work, hardships and mental and physical abuse.

Although slavery was abolished in 1865, the census of 1870 indicates that Eliza was still living at "Green Hill", but in separate housing. She is listed as the head of the household (age 29) having two children ages 6 and 2 years and working as a day laborer. The 1880 census list Eliza as 38-39 years of age. She had been promoted to a servant whose specialty was cooking.

Her oldest daughter, Catherine (Katy) age 17, was also a servant. Anderson, age 14 was an errand boy. She continued as head of the household, now having five children, Katie 17, Anderson 14, Lucy 8, Walter 4, and Arthur 2 years. In December, 1883 she bore her last child, Roy Clyde Gwyn. She was approximately 36-37 years old. The years following are void of fact, except through interviews until 1900, since the census of 1890 was not accessible.

According to personal interviews and confirmations by the census of 1900, we find that her affliction was now taking it's toll. She was now living with her daughter, Katie, and her son-in-law, John Hunt. They remained on the plantation while John and Katie's home was being built. Once completed, they all moved to John's home which still stands in Ronda, N.C. just east of the present East Wilkes High School. Eliza was now 50 years old. Her sons, Arthur 22 and Roy 16, also moved in with John and Katie. At this time all of Eliza's six children were still living. John and Katie were both 37 years old and were farmers. They had nine children. At this time, seven were living and two deceased. Their ages ranged from 5 months to 16 years. At least 2 other children were born in the 1900's. Through Eliza's children, we form a link with the present generations of Gwyns who are presently living in Wilkes County or who at least spent several years in this area.

As forestated, Katie (1863) was married to John. Two of their nine children expired at an early age. Mason and Joseph had no known offsprings. Ada had one daughter, Mrs. Ruby H. Ingram, who resides in Wilkesboro, N.C. She was married to the late Rev. Milton Ingram, Sr. They had three children, James Milton, Jr., Annette, and Denise. Lillie (1891) was married to Ben Covington. They had five sons. John Will Hunt married Pearl Hawkins and had six children, Cozene, Joe Will, Argyle, Ray, Paul, and Opal who died at an early age. Mary married Sidney Gatbery. Their children were David and Cora. Hugh married Bessie Hawkins. They had three children. Kate married Jack Hardison, who resides in Wilkesboro, N.C. Their children were Elizabeth, Frankie, Jackie, and William. Walter was married to Hazel Boles. Their children were Josephine, Walter, Leroy, Bobby, Sara Elaine, Kathy and one child died as an infant in an auto accident. Anderson Gwyn (1866), Eliza's oldest son, left home at an early age. We have no record of him since 1880.

Lucy Gwyn (1872) was married to a Roberts (first name unknown to us). They had five children, Gwyn, Roy, Weaver, Odell, and Mamie Lee. Lucy died at an early age. Her children were reared by different families. We have no record of Walter (1876) other than the census of 1880 which listed him as being 4 years old. Arthur (1878) was married to Cora Wade. To this union nine children were born. Ernest Gwyn was married to Hazel Boles. Turner was married to Lizzie Sales Martin. Carlton married Helen Hawkins who resides in Wilkesboro, N.C. They had one daughter, Betty.

Wesley was never married. Mora is married to Rev. John Williams, having no children. Balton was first married to Juanita Bowers. Juanita died giving birth to their son, Balton, Jr., who is now married and lives in Germany with wife and three children. Balton, Sr. later married Louise Barker, who resides in Elkin, N.C. Ollie was married to Floyd Eller who is now deceased. Ollie has three children, Roger, Kenneth, and Brenda. Myrtle first married Ralph Dowell. They had one son, William. She later remarried. Rosa the youngest, moved to New England as a teenager. She has since married and has two children. Arthur's sons, Carlton, Wesley, and Balton are now deceased.

Roy, the youngest son of Eliza, was married to Mamie Ella Hickerson. To this union, six children were born. Beatrice, the oldest, was married to Gwyn Martin of Roaring River, N.C. Their children were Rosetta, Richard, Charles Bennett and Shirley. Gwyn, Beatrice, Rosette and Shirley are now deceased. Lillie married James Davis. She resides at the Roy Gwyn homeplace, located just above the late John and Katie Hunt home in Ronda, N.C. Lollie married Clyde Hunt of Roaring River, N.C. Their children are Oliver, Loyal, Edith, Ellis, Norma, Leon and Sara. Clyde, Edith, and Loyal are deceased. Lollie resides in Roaring River, N.C. Susie was married to Richard White. She had one son, Fred. Paul married Magaline Becknell. They had three children, Paula, Robert, and Janice. Walter Clinton, Roy's youngest son, died at an early age.

Sources: Interviews, personal knowledge, memories, gravestones, and census records.

— Peggy Alexander Hunt,
Ruby Hunt Ingram
and Sara Hunt Whittington

RICHARD NATHANIEL HACKETT

618

Richard N. Hackett, called Dick by friends, was born in Wilkesboro in 1866, the younger son of Dr. Robert F. and Caroline Gordon Hackett. His father studied at Jefferson Medical College in Phildelphia, and was a well known physician in Wilkesboro. His mother was a sister of Brigadier-General James B. Gordon. He was a brother to Geneva (Eva) Hackett Stokes; Florence, unmarried; and J. Gordon Hackett who married Mrs. Mary Grimes Smith of Pitt County, and then built a home on E Street in North Wilkesboro.

Dick Hackett studied law at Chapel Hill and was known for his eloquent speeches.

He served in the 60th Congress as a Democrat for one term, and was state Grandmaster of the Masonic Order in 1910-1911.

He married Lois Long, born 1884, the daughter of Judge Ben F. Long of Statesville, but after a few years the marriage ended in separation. One daughter, Mary Mayo, was born to them, but she did not reside in Wilkes.

R.N. Hackett died at age 57 on November 22, 1923, and was buried in St. Paul's Episcopal Cemetery in Wilkesboro.

Sources: Gravestone, family papers, family tradition and personal knowledge.

— Elizabeth C. Finley

THE HAGLER FAMILY

619

In 1971, I compiled a history of the Hagler Family from data secured from the Archives No. Seg. 163,970, London, England. It comprises some fifty typewritten pages and has to do with the family, history, original map documentary records, and personalities mostly as applied to the Haglers of North Carolina.

Hagler is an ancient surname which was first recorded in Germany and Switzerland. German military lists show Wilhelm Hagler as Garrison commander in the Palatinate in 1697 A.D.

An examination of ships' lists show that an approximate total of 30 Hagler branches sailed from German and Dutch ports to the U.S.A. and Canada between 1750 to 1840. The Hagler we know in North Carolina and adjoining states is John Hagler. John was born in Westphalia, Switzerland about 1730. He emigrated to New York about 1755. Here, he married Elizabeth Van Hoose, a native of Holland. After marriage they moved to the Great Peedee River in South Carolina. Due to a malaria epidemic there, they moved on up the river into the Yadkin Valley, Wilkes County, (Later Caldwell County) and built a log house on a promontory overlooking the Yadkin near the mouth of Kings' Creek. This old house stood up to about 1920.

The couple reared six sons but had no daughters.

John Hagler owned several hundred acres of land on and near the Yadkin. He and his sons were contemporaries of the great pioneer Daniel Boone who had cabins some six miles down the river near the present village of Ferguson.

Five of the sons married and moved to Tennessee, Alabama, and Georgia, where many of their descendents live today. The prominent member is Evelyn Hagler of Augusta, Georgia, who lives there and frequently visits the old homestead of John Hagler and her great, great grandfather, Abraham Hagler. (History of the five sons is included in my original history of 1971).

William Hagler, the youngest of the 6 sons, was the only one who remained in North Carolina and he resided in Caldwell County. In early youth, William married Elizabeth Mullens, daughter of John William Mullens, whose wife was Sarah Triplett. It is interesting to note that Sarah was the daughter of Daniel Triplett, brother of the original William Triplett who came to Wilkes County about the same time that John Hagler came from Switzerland. It will be observed that the Tripletts and the Haglers frequently intermarried.

William Hagler and Elizabeth Mullens Hagler reared ten sons and three daughters. They have hundreds of descendents in Wilkes and Caldwell Counties as well as many in Tennessee and other adjoining states. In 1838 William built a large brick house near the old log house of his father. It is still standing and has recently been remodelled and restored by William's great, great, great granddaughter, Margaret Carter Minton and her husband, Monty. They reside there today. The old building, beautifully designed, is of great historic interest and has been so recognized by the North Carolina Department of Archives and History.

About all of the ten sons of William and Elizabeth moved away to other states. Some were married and had large families. Some served in the Confederate Army. (Please note that William Hagler was a veteran of the War of 1812). Shelton and Elbert married and lived in Lenoir where they have many descendants living today. Some moved to Cherokee County, North Carolina. Delphia Hagler, the oldest daughter and oldest child, married Cornelius Howard, son of the original Benjamin Howard who built the old Howard House now owned and occupied by Clyde Wheeling who also restored it. Polly Hagler married John Tucker and moved to Tennessee where they have descendants. The third and youngest daughter, Sarah Hagler married William Kendall in 1845. (Grandparents of this writer)

From the union of William Kendall and Sarah Hagler came six daughters and no sons. (1) Elizabeth first married Henry Coffey and they had one daughter, Laura. Coffey died in the Civil War and later Elizabeth married Clingman Powell. They had two daughters, Alice and Grace. (2) Sarah married Lindsay C. Ferguson, and they had three daughters and four sons, Blanche, Beulah, Jessie (Mrs. James R. Hix), John Lindsay, William Hagler, Thomas W. and Clyde. The boys all married and have several children and grandchildren. (3) Mary Kendall married John L. Laxton, and they had sons Jesse and Wade and one daughter, who married Edgar German. Wade first married Effie Beach and they had two daughters and two sons. (4) Mattie, (5) Carolyn and (6) Etta married and moved to the West. (It is impossible here to give an account of the numerous descendants of the Kendalls but since they are all related to the Haglers, they often join in a Hagler — Ferguson Reunion held each year in July.)

Paradoxically, while there is unity in variety, this great Hagler Clan reapresents various Creeds, and political opinions. They all share in a common ambition in the good of our great country. We are proud of our great heritage of 200 years, and we are sure we will do what we can to uphold that noble and enviable record for another two hundred years and throughout eternity. Most of the descendants of Sarah Hagler Kendall live in Caldwell and Wilkes Counties and in Virginia.

The family names included in this short history are Ferguson, Coffey, Powell, Steele, Hartley, Carlton, Laxton, German, Faulkner, Frost, Hix, Brame, Marlow, Story, Dalton, Dean, Lyle, Wilson, Hoag, Ekholm, Mackintosh, Underwood, Carter, Finley, Kyle, Freeman, Tucker, Henry, Stokes and Pruett.

Sources: Research done by Mr. Tom W. Ferguson.

— Mr. Tom W. Ferguson

THE JOHN HAGLER FAMILY
620

John Hagler was born in Basil Canton, Dietgen Parish, Switzerland (German speaking), about 1730 and came to York State (New York) in 1750. He met and married Elizabeth Van Hoose or Van Huesen, or the same state. Her family was from Holland. It is said she was related to Peter Styvasent, founder of New York.

They settled on the Peedee River, but because of malaria sold their farm and moved to the Yadkin section of North Carolina in Wilkes County, now Caldwell. The lived and died there near Ferguson, North Carolina.

The original house was a log cabin. It was replaced by a hand-made brick house and is still in the William Hagler family, their son's branch of the family. They are buried on this property.

There were nine children. Two of the sons moved to eastern Tennessee. The second son, Abraham Hagler, married Esther (Ester) Neatherly 16 March 1787 and moved to eastern Tennessee. Three of their sons married three Peak sisters. Such a lot of double first cousins. Their fourth child, Benjamin, married Vilotte Peak.

The third child of Benjamin and Vilotte Peak Hagler was John Carroll Hagler. He went to Illinois with an uncle, West Peak, when a teenager. He was born in Clinton, Tennessee 28 February 1819 and is interred in Pana, Illinois. He was married twice. His first wife, Elizabeth Ethel died and he married Catharine Stevenson.

John Carroll Hagler served one year in the Illinois Legislature. He was there when Abraham Lincoln was a young politican starting out. John Carroll was a Southerner and a died-in-the-wool Democrat, however he thought Lincoln was a smart man and would go places.

The youngest child of John Carroll and Catharine Stevenson Hagler was William Kenneth Hagler. He came South to Augusta, Georgia in 1894, and married Mattie Beall Wienges. These were my parents.

My father and his brother, John Carroll Hagler, the second, started the Georgia-Car Brick and Tile Company, Augusta, Georgia.

In Basil, Switzerland, Hagler is spelled Hagler or Haegler, but not Haigler.

Sources: Family *Bible,* Family traditions of several branches of this family.

— Miss Evelyn J. Hagler

JOHN HALL FAMILY
621

My great-great grandfather, John Hall, and my great-great grandmother, Polly Powers, came to Wilkes County about 1861. He was born in Rockingham County near Mayodan, N.C. on June 11, 1822 and she, February 20, 1820. There are several families living in the Mayodan community now but there is no proof of relationship with the Halls in this genealogy.

About two miles west of the town is a cemetery where a James Hall is buried. He was born October 13, 1816, died December 11, 1911. His wife was Sarah Ann Hall, born March 27,

1815, died August 23, 1887. Some of their children were Tom, Martha, Bob, John and Joe. A Hall family living near by said he was a cabinet maker by trade and he built the first house in Mayodan. He and his sons served in the confederate army. There is a possibility that he was a brother to my Great-Great Grandfather, John Hall.

Elizabeth Hall (Reins) said she was a young girl when her parents moved to Wilkes County, but she did remember traveling in a covered wagon and that the wagon became stuck in the mud fording a creek.

In coming to Wilkes my great-great grandparents, John and Polly Hall, lived in the Boomer community for a year, then purchased about sixty acres of land for $600.00 about four miles from Wilkesboro and lived there the remainder of their lives. They are both buried at Cub Creek Baptist Church. John died January 7, 1904 and Polly died June 7, 1906. They had six children, five boys and one girl.

The oldest child was James H. Hall, born April 26, 1848 and died December 27, 1913. He married Ann Hubbard and farmed for a living. He was known as "Bay." He and his wife are buried at Moravian Falls cemetery in Moravian Falls, N.C.

The second son was Thomas T. Hall. He was born in September 1846 and died December 9, 1920. He married Lydia E. Leach and she was born June 25, 1846, and died March 4, 1911. He operated a store and was postmaster at Summitt, N.C. They are both buried at Cub Creek Baptist Church.

Elizabeth Hall was born March 18, 1851 and died July 18, 1932. She married William Franklin Reins. He was born September 18, 1848, and died May 18, 1929. They are buried at Cub Creek Baptist Church.

W. Samuel Hall was born 1852 and died January 22, 1924. He was never married. At one time he was a candidate for the N.C. Legislature. He was a well known politician. He is buried at Cub Creek Baptist Church.

Joseph F. Hall was born April 17, 1860 and died November 30, 1898. He lived in Burke County and operated a store and was Postmaster there. He never married and he too, is buried at Cub Creek Baptist Church.

Their last child was my great-grandfather, John Bethel Hall. He was born May 3, 1859 and died December 28, 1933. He married Jennie Elizabeth Davidson. She was born in Alexander County June 12, 1869 and she died February 17, 1946. She was the daughter of Mary Jane Kilby and John Davidson. All are buried at Cub Creek Baptist Church. My great-grandfather, John Hall, operated and owned a tobacco factory and store at his home near Wilkesboro. They had eight children:

The oldest child was a daughter, Bessie Florence Hall, born November 23, 1889 and died September 6, 1981. She is buried in Sharon Memorial Park in Charlotte, N.C. She was married to Earnest Keeter of Charlotte. She was a school teacher.

Next came John Davidson Hall. He was born April 19, 1891 and died February 1, 1962. He served in World War I. He married Mable Rolison of Elmira, N.Y. He retired from R.J. Reynolds Tobacco as a salesman. He is buried at Cub Creek Baptist Church.

Richard Glenn Hall was born September 8, 1892 and died December 3, 1892. He is buried at Cub Creek Baptist Church.

Selma Pearl Hall was born January 6, 1895 and died August 29, 1977. She married Claude L. Robertson of Knightdale, N.C. and she was a school teacher. She is buried in Knightdale Baptist Church cemetery in Knightdale, N.C.

Sammie Faye Hall was born December 19, 1898 and died December 20, 1928. She was a registered nurse and never married. She too is buried at Cub Creek Church.

Alton Fred Hall was born July 30, 1904 and died June 27, 1980. He married Helen Feltyberger of Pittsburg, Pennsylvania. He retired from Security Life and Trust Company. He is also buried at Cub Creek Church.

Mary Ray Hall was born January 23, 1906 and lives in Morganton, N.C. She married Thomas N. Clontz of Morganton, N.C. She was an LPN and is now active in politics in the Democratic party.

Their eighth child was a daughter, Edith Margaret Hall. She was born November 18, 1912. She owned and operated the Wilkes Beauty Shop in Wilkesboro for thirty-three years. She married James Whiteford Lowe. He was born December 22, 1907 and died October 20, 1973. He was the son of Velona Blanch Stamey and Carl Arthur Lowe, these being my grandparents.

I can remember well with my grandmother still living. Out of this union came one child, a daughter Ann Hall Lowe. She was born June 11, 1937. She married Richard Paul Absher. He was born August 20, 1933, he is the son of Della L. Rhodes and O.O. Absher of McGrady, N.C. Out of this union came four children, my mother having said she wanted a house full of children, she never liked being an only child.

The first child born was James Richard Absher, April 7, 1957, who died September 25, 1977. He was a graduate of West Wilkes High School at Millers Creek, N.C. He also is buried at Cub Creek Baptist Church cemetery, along with my great grandparents and my grandfather Lowe.

Next I was born, and since there were no Halls left by name, they named me John Hall Absher. I was born July 23, 1961 and am a rising senior at Appalachian State University in Boone, N.C.

The next year my sister, Edith Ann Absher arrived. She was born August 16, 1962. She is a freshman at Wilkes Community College here in Wilkesboro.

Next came Alton Lowe Absher. He was born March 29, 1966. He is a sophomore at Wilkes Central High School.

So far I'm the last one in the family with the name John Hall and I felt it necessary to write something about the Halls since I am to carry on that name.

Sources: Family records and personal knowledge.

— John Hall Absher

John Solomon Hall and Emma Arlena Shumate Hall.

JOHN SOLOMAN and EMMA SHUMATE HALL

622

John and Emma Hall, my grandparents, were born in Wilkes County and were lifelong residents imparting a great Christian influence on those whose lives they touched. As a grandchild growing up after their death, I was never privileged to know them, but I have a great appreciation for the kind of people they were, and I would like to record a glimpse of their lives for posterity.

John Soloman Hall was born in the Mulberry community September 30, 1874 to Reubin and Susanna Owens Hall. He was schooled at Sulphur Springs Academy from 1886 to 1889 and was a student of Professor Robert E. Lee Plummer. Following the Civil War, conditions in Wilkes County were harsh, making it necessary for many children to work to help support the family. Having attended school for only three years, and, being one of only two boys in a family of seven, John probably spent time working to help his family. He had a very good education for his day and worked at many different jobs, always making a good living for his family. He was an industrious man, well known and liked throughout Wilkes County.

Emma Arlena Shumate Hall was born in Walnut Grove Township May 12, 1879 to Henry and Emmaline Holbrook Shumate. Her father died in 1884 when Emma was only five years old, leaving her mother with two small children. Emma's mother later married Wilson Walker, who proved to be a good step-father for Emma and her sister, Dora. Emma got her education in a one-room school, attending until she was fourteen. She then quit to help her mother, enabling her younger sister, Dora, to attend and finish elementary school.

Emma worked hard as a child and probably had few pleasures. She did, however have her own horse and he was one of her prized possessions. They fell out of favor, temporarily, when he threw her and she fell in the river, ruining her pretty white dress. Emma's mother gave her a sewing machine for a wedding present and she made all her children's clothes, curtains and many things for the house. With leftover scraps of material and dyed feed sacks, she made beautiful quilts, some of which are still in existence today. She was a gentle, soft-spoken lady who never spoke ill of anyone. Her motto was, "If you can't say something good, don't say anything". She loved her milk cow and enjoyed gardening. She was a meticulous housekeeper, sometimes evoking her husband to say admiringly, "Emmie, if you wipe that tablecloth anymore, you're going to wear it out!"

John and Emma were married October 17, 1897 at the home of Wilson Walker, Emma's step-father. Being a Justice of the Peace, Wilson Walker performed the ceremony, with witnesses: P.E. Dancy, Johnny Walker and H.S. Smoot in attendance. Their early life together was spent moving from place to place, sometimes sharecropping with Emma's step-father and with neighbors. John and Emma spent about a year in West Virginia, but returned to North Carolina to find better doctors for their sick child. John was a clerk in the Farmer's Implement Store in North Wilkesboro in 1903. He worked as a salesman in Moxley, North Carolina for three years. Most of John and Emma's early life was spent in the Hays community, near North Wilkes High School. It was here that all their children were born: 1. Major Lee, born August, 1989, died 1901; 2. Estelle, born 15 May 1901, married Nansen Johnson and had children: Jarvey, Goldie, Opal, Ola Mae, Lizzie Dean, Jerry and Margie; 3. Ethel, born 14 May, 1905, married John Gregory and had one child, Oma Jean. Ethel died 19 October 1977; 4. Verna, born 12 November 1908, married Clifton Byrd and had children: Frances, Hayden and Betty; 5. Metta, born 18 May 1911, married Paul Hudler and had one child, Raydell; 6. Angie, born 22 June 1913, married Haggie Faw and had one child, Johnny.

When the children were growing up, the Halls lived near Oak Ridge Church and the children attended Oak Ridge School. In 1928, the Halls moved to Fairplains. After their Fairplains home burned, they moved to Mulberry where they lived until Emma's death.

Because he disliked being confined to inside work, John Hall spent most of his life as a traveling salesman, working for many different companies. He sometimes traveled by train to Winston-Salem to pick up samples and he sold goods in a horse drawn surrey before he had a car. When he did get a car, sometime before 1919, it was one of the first ones in the Hays community. One of his jobs that pleased his relatives was with Transou Hat Company. Many times he would give his relatives samples of his hats. The memory of this is so great, some of his nieces can describe these hats, in detail, even today. "Sol Hall" as he was sometimes known, traveled widely and made many friends in Wilkes County. John Soloman Hall was a stately man who was very generous. He once owned his own store, but went broke when he extended too much credit and gave unselfishly to those in need and unable to pay.

John loved children and delighted in "trotting" them on his knee and singing old songs to them. He loved to tell ghost stories and stories of his boyhood. John was also very kind and understanding. His children always confided in him and asked for advice and help in solving problems. He always said: "If you have a problem and there is no way you can change it, face it with everything you've got."

John and Emma were devoted to each other. Emma's health was never good and she died 16 November 1940 at her Mulberry home. John was never happy after her death. He sold thier home to Everette Cleary and bought land from John R. Jones and built another house. He and his daughter, Ethel, lived in this house until she was married in 1945. John sold this house in 1946 and lived short periods of time with each of his daughters the remainder of his life. Wherever he visited, he insisted on paying rent in the amount of five dollars per week.

Many of his last days were spent with his daughter, Ethel and her husband, John Gregory. John and Ethel's baby, Oma Jean, was born just six months before the death of John Hall. The baby was a joy to him and he enjoyed carrying her around as his failing health permitted.

John Hall met with death August 28, 1947 at the home of his daughter, Ethel. He was buried beside his wife in the cemetery of the church of which they were both memebers, Center Baptist Church in the Mulberry community.

John and Emma Hall were kind and gracious people and lived good lives, providing lovingly for their children. Neither performed outstanding deeds, but both contributed to the heritage of Wilkes County in their own quiet way. Perhaps their greatest contributions were their lives themselves, which were wonderful examples of Christian hope and faith.

Sources: Interviews with family members, 1900 Federal Census of Wilkes County, Church records, personal journal of J.S. Hall, Wilkes County marriage records, *Lest We Forget: Education in Wilkes*.

— Oma Jean Gregory Martin

THE SAMUEL HALL FAMILY
623

Just prior to the Revolutionary War, Samuel and Millain Webb Hall moved from Henry County (formerly Pittsylvania Co.), Virginia to the Elk Creek section of Wilkes County. Millian was the daugher of Merry and Elizabeth Webb of Henry Co. She was born Aug. 30, 1723.

Ten children were born to this couple. Thomas is believed to be the oldest son and was born about 1755 in Halifax or Pittsylvania Co. Thomas married Judith Dula about 1779. Judith was a sister to William and Bennett Dula who came to Wilkes at a later date.

Merry was named for his Grandfather Webb. His wife was named Mary and they were living in the Greenville Dist. of S.C. at the time of Merry's death about 1828. They had nine children.

Martin married Chloe Hendrix about 1784. They moved to Morgan Co., Tenn. He died about 1831. They are believed to have had eight children.

One son was named John, but at this time it has not definitely been identified as to who he married and where he lived.

Twin boys were born on March 25, 1760 in Henry Co., Va. They were named David and Samuel, Jr. David married Obedience Brazeal in 1784. He died in 1842 in Anderson, Tenn. David and Obedience had twelve children. Samuel married Letitia Hendrix in the fall of 1785 and was married by Esq. Brown. Samuel died in 1819 in Morgan Co., Tenn. Both men served in the Revolutionary War from Wilkes County.

Elizabeth was born about 1766. She married Darby Hendrix. They are believed to be the parents of ten children.

Mary married Julius Dugger and this family lived in Carter Co. (now Johnson Co.), Tenn. They had nine children.

Nancy married James Brazeal about 1784. They have five known children and lived in Knox Co. by 1795. She was a widow and living in Morgan Co., Tenn by 1811.

Millian, called Milly, married David Lansdown. She is believed to have moved to Greenville Co., SC. She died at an early age leaving three small children who were reared by her brothers and sisters.

The time of Samuel's death is uncertain. An inventory of his esate was taken in 1792 so he died sometime prior to this date. Millian left a will in Wilkes County naming her children. This will was probated in the May term 1803.

Sources: Will, Census records, Estate records, Deeds and Marriage Bonds.

— Mrs. J. Arnold Simpson

THOMAS D. and ELIZABETH HALL
624

Thomas David Hall is believed to be the youngest son of Thomas and Judith Dula Hall. He was born about 1806 in the Elk Creek area of Wilkes County.

In 1826 his father gave him a 100 acre tract of land situated on Elk Creek. A short time later he married a neighboring sweetheart, Elizabeth Hampton. Elizabeth was the daugher of Jeremiah and Mollie Waters Hampton. The marriage bond of Thomas D. and Elizabeth was dated Oct. 24, 1827 with Jesse Triplett as his bondsman.

Thomas and Elizabeth had five children. Oliver was the oldest child and was born Oct. 3, 1828. He married Elizabeth Grindstaff and lived in Hampton, Tenn. He died May 3, 1890.

A daughter named Allie was born to them. Her birthday is unknown at this time.

Orilla was born about 1830/32. She married Elisha Cox on Sept. 12, 1848. She is buried at Lewis Fork Baptist Church.

Not a great deal is known about their son, Samuel. He is reported to have been a tall, physical man and one of the few who served in the Confederate Navy.

Thomas David, the youngest son was born April 13, 1838. He served in the Confederate Army where he was wounded. On Feb. 22, 1867, he married Mrs. Frances Miller Eller. They resided in Wilkes County and reared their children here. He died March 9, 1914.

Elizabeth, wife of Thomas D., died quite young, probably before or around 1850. The children were still young and the husband was left a bereaved man. He is found living alone at the age of 44 on the 1850 census. The children are believed to have been reared by relatives. His death date is unknown at this time. It was after 1880.

Sources: Marriage bonds, estate records, deeds, census records, family history.

— Mrs. J. Arnold Simpson

THOMAS and JUDITH HALL
625

Thomas Hall was the oldest son of Samuel and Millian Webb Hall. He was born about 1755 in Halifax or Pittsylvania Co., Va. Along with other members of his family he moved to Wilkes County just prior or about the time of the Revolutionary War. The War Service Records indicate he and his brothers joined and served in the war from Wilkes County.

Thomas married Judith Dula about 1779. She was from Virginia and it is unknown whether he knew her in Virginia and went there to marry her or whether he married her in NC. She appears to have come to Wilkes County before her brothers and sisters. (others members in her family appear to be William, Bennett, Polly, Jean, Thomas and John Dula).

Thomas purchased land in the Elk Creek area of Wilkes County near his father. This is where they lived and reared their children.

Their children are believed to include the following: John, born about 1785; Jane, born about 1786; Milly, who married Philip Noland in 1806; Elizabeth, who married Philip Walsh in 1810; Judith, born about 1797 and who married David Green; Frances, who married Andrew Walsh Jr. in 1814; Mary Winifred, born about 1802 and married Martin Triplett in 1822; and Thomas David, born about 1806 and married Elizabeth Hampton in 1827.

Thomas died prior to 1830. Judith is believed to have died at a later date.

Sources: Deeds, census records, marriage bonds, N.C. Pensioneers: Return of Aid Volunteers and Drafts from Wilkes Co. 12 Jan 1779.

— Mrs. J. Arnold Simpson

THE THOMAS DAVID HALL FAMILY
626

Thomas David Hall was born April 13, 1838 to Thomas David and Elizabeth Hampton Hall. His mother died while he was a young boy and he lived part of his early years with relatives.

The T.D. Hall Family.

Thomas David Hall.

Frances Miller Hall.

He served in the Civil War and after the war he returned home to Wilkes County. He married Frances (Frankie) Miller on Feb. 22, 1867. Frankie was a widow. She had first married Mathis Watson prior to the Civil War and he died during the war. Mathis and Frankie had three children. Sarah Anne (1856-1942) who married J. Martin Watson. Allis Caroline (1858-1862). John Mathis (1861-1865). Frankie had lost a husband and two of her children by the time she married T.D. Hall.

Dave (as he was called) and Frankie bought property from her father, John B. Miller and lived in the Lewis Fork area near her parents.

Mary Elizabeth, their first child, was born March 9, 1868. She married Robert M. Jones and they lived and reared their family in Wilkes.

Albert Brisco (Jan 7, 1870 — Jan 27, 1910) never married and also remained in Wilkes.

Next were twins, born on Nov. 19, 1872. They were named William Gaither and Arthur Philo. Gaither married Margaret Grier and lived in Statesville. Philo married Mattie Lou (Lucy) Hall and lived in Moultrie, Georgia.

Zora Laura, their baby, was born Nov. 3, 1875 and died Oct. 6, 1886.

Dave was a rather quiet man who farmed. He enjoyed reading and always took a daily paper, The Atlanta Constitution. He never seemed to be in a hurry and loved children.

As his granddaughter, one of my favorite memories is accompanying him to pick up chestnuts in the autumn. It was better to go in the morning before the squirrels stored them away. It was no problem to quickly get a bucket full from the many chestnut trees on the mountain behind his home. When we returned, he would "cap" and roast the chestnuts for us.

I do not ever remember him being upset or raising his voice. He was always ready to help out a neighbor by loaning money, tools to work with or helping the sick.

He was a member of Lewis Fork Baptist Church and always went to "Meeting" as long as he was able. His home always seemed to be the lodging place for the preachers. Meeting was held on the first Saturday and Sunday of each month. He sat on the front bench in church and after his death, members of the church had an enlarged picture of him hanging in the church, near where he sat. He was remembered for the love and trust he had for others.

One other thing he loved to do was to go on the mountain and look for ginsing. This was hard to find and sold for a high price for medicinal purposes. He loved the birds and knew and taught us the names of the ones in the area.

Grandma Hall was a small woman, weighing about 110 pounds. She was very erect in posture and enjoyed wearing a touch of lace or ruffles on her dresses. She was energetic and always working. After she did the dinner dishes, she would always lie down and rest for thirty minutes.

You could hear her voice in the early evening, calling the cows to the barn to be milked. They knew her voice and you could see them come around the hill, one by one.

A short distance from their home was a beautiful spring with ferns on each side and a big smooth rock at the back. The spring house was built just below and jars of milk and crocks of butter were kept there, as well as any other food that needed to be kept cold.

She dried apples, berries, beans and pumpkin. The fruit was put on scaffolds that were made, while the beans and pumpkin were threaded on a string to hang and dry.

They had a cider press and always had hogs, chickens, and cattle. Sharecroppers raised the corn and the workers were called to dinner by a large oxen horn that hung on the back porch.

She was a wonderful cook and was noted for her home made yeast breads, gingerbread, and pear preserves. The preserves were always brought out for company. Tea was made from Mahogany bark.

She had a riding horse and side saddle and loved to ride. Her home was always neat and orderly. The washing was done at a branch that ran near the home. Home made soap was used and a "paddle" was also used to help clean the clothes.

She made her thread on a spinning wheel. This thread was hand woven into cloth.

Their home was a great place to visit and no one was turned away if they needed a place to spend the night.

Grandpa Hall died March 9, 1914. Grandma lived until Feb 26, 1924. They are buried at Lewis Fork.

Sources: Personal knowledge.

— Mrs. C. Glenn Williams

THE CHARLES HAM FAMILY
627

Charles Austin Ham was born September 24, 1924 in Iredell County to James Robert and Oleta Mae Arthurs Ham. He graduated from Mooresville High School and had a passion for flying airplanes. He joined the Air Force and was trained to be a fighter pilot in World War II, but the war ended before he got to see fighting action. After the war he attended North Carolina State University on the G.I. Bill. He returned to Mooresville to join his father and brother in the plumbing, heating, and air-conditioning contracting business. In 1950 he took a book to be rebound to the high school librarian, Gozelle Andrews, and in October 27, 1951, they were married.

Mary Gozelle Andrews was born to Nelson Coles and Ollie Earp Andrews of Little Rock Community in Wilkes County on November 26, 1926. She grew up on a beautiful farm at the base of the south Brushy Mountains. In the spring of 1954 when Charlie and Gozelle were expecting their first child, they decided the mountains and the family farm was where they wanted to establish their home. They built their home on Gozelle's maternal grandparent's homeplace (John and Nancy Earp) and had to clear the log cabin that stood at the site of the present Ham House. Charlie commuted via airplane to his business in Mooresville. Nelson Andrews' grass field served as an air strip until Charlie moved his business to Wilkesboro. He later became president of CHACO Realty Company in North Wilkesboro. Gozelle was a full time mother of four active children for sixteen years before returning to work in 1969 as Librarian at Wilkes Central High School. She is presently Librarian at Wilkes Central Senior High School.

Martha Louise was born December 21, 1954. She graduated from Wilkes Central High School in 1973 and from the University of North Carolina at Chapel Hill with a BS Degree in Dental Hygiene in 1977. She was employed as a Dental Hygienist in Greensboro, Chapel Hill, and Winston-Salem for five years. She completed a Master of Education in Health Education from the University of North Carolina at Greensboro in 1982. Martha married Frederick William Townes, IV, of Danville, Virginia, on a snowy day, February 27, 1982. They live in Little Rock.

Karl Andrew was born May 11, 1957. He graduated from Wilkes Central High in 1975 and from Appalachian State University with a BS Degree in Business Administration in 1979. During the summers as a college student, Karl was an outstanding book salesman for Southwestern Book Company. His excellent sales record with Southestern was the foundation for his present job in sales with the Tom James Custom Tailoring Company in Charlotte.

Margaret Ollie was born September 19, 1961. She was named after Gozelle's Mother and was an early birthday present to Charlie that year. She graduated from Wilkes Central High School in 1979 and is in Nursing School at the University of North Carolina at Chapel Hill.

Rose Marie was born June 25, 1966. She was so named because of Gozelle's beautiful rose garden and the enjoyment she received from the roses. Rose Marie is a super achiever in 4-H, school, and church. She is an honor student at Wilkes Central Senior High School. She has always loved horses and said she didn't like "Ho-Ho" one year at Christmas when Santa Clause failed to bring her one. She has since owned various rocking horses, a cow pony named Nancy, and at present has a horse named Beauty.

All of the Ham children were taught the importance of the work ethic, moral values, and education. Their Mother would say, "Education is like a good insurance policy," and their Father would challenge them with the dream that, "everything was possible if you worked hard and dealt honestly with people." Growing up in the Ham House on the family farm was filled with love and laughter as well as sorrow. On September 12, 1974, Charles Austin Ham died. He left a heart broken wife and four children ages 9 to 19. The Ham Family struggled with the loss, but with the help of friends, family, and each other, they continue to pursue their life goals and they hope their loving father and husband would be proud of them.

Sources: Personal knowledge and the Family *Bible*.

— Martha Ham Townes

JOHN HAMMON, REVOLUTIONARY WAR HERO
628

In 868 the Danish Viking "Hamond" crossed the North Sea and landed at Holkham in what later became known as Norfolk (North Folk). The family lives there to this day. About 1550, what later became the American branch moved to Clerkenwell just outside the walls of London. John Hammons of that family married Mary Allen at St. Gregory by St. Paul's in London 1636, and their son Ambrose was baptised at St. James Parish, Clerkenwell, 28 Feb. 1647. At age 19 he arrived in Old Rappahannock County, Va. on 26 March 1666.

Ambrose had a son known as John Hammon, Sr. who left a will in Cumberland County, Va., 13 Nov. 1758 naming Joseph as the son of his second family. The sons of the first family were John Jr., Ambrose, William, and James. The family was wealthy, with Ambrose owning 50 slaves and William 20. James Hammon married Mary Hargis, the daughter of Thomas Hargis who mentioned her in his will in Frederick County, Maryland, 2 April 1754. The famous "Douglass Register" of the Dover Church in St. James Northam Parish in Goochland County, Va. has this entry, "James Hammond and Mary Hargiss a Son named John born Jan: 29, 1760, Baptised 1760 Jun: 8."

James died in 1763 and Mary Hargis Hammon then married John Holbrook, the son of Randolph, in Goochland County and had several children, among them Hargis, Randolph, and Colby Holbrook. About this time the Hargis, Holbrook, and Hammon clans were leaving the Church of England and trying to worship as Baptists but were having trouble doing so. About 1774 William Hammon, the lay minister, led the entire group to Wilkes Co., N.C.

William Hammon became the first minister of the South Fork of Roaring River Baptist Chruch. John Hammon, son of James, later had this to say in the Veterans Administration File S-9-559:

Entered the service of the United States, as a militia man, in the year 1777 at the age of sixteen years, under the Command of Captain Benjamin Cleveland in Wilkes County, on Roaring River in North Carolina . . . On the return of said Cleveland he was promoted to a Colonel's commission, and his brother Larkin took his place as Captain . . . during this time in a skirmish with the Tories the said Captain Cleveland had his thigh broken by a ball, and being unable to perform his duty, Martin Gambrel was chosen in his stead. The deponent under the orders of the same Colonel Cleveland and said Captain Gambrel marched to King's Mountain, in which battle the deponent fought. After being three times driven down the side of the mountain, the British and Tories were finally defeated, and their army taken prisoner. He served as such five years . . . during which time he was actively engaged as a militia man. He was several times a volunteer, was once drafted, and never served as a substitute.

The Rev. William Hammon left a will in Wilkes 1793 naming four children and his brother Ambrose left a will there in 1794, also naming four children. Mary Hargis Hammon Holbrook died in Wilkes 1782 after which her son John Hammon left for Kentucky in what was called "The Year of Blood." Within weeks John was one of 44 riflemen who held off some 300 Indians, renegades, and Canadian Rangers in the Siege of Bryan's Station. A short time later he was in the Battle of Blue Licks in which Daniel Boone lost a son. This was the last battle of the Revolutionary War, fought after the surrender at Yorktown.

On 1 Nov. 1782 John Hammon marched under General George Rogers Clark against Indian towns in Ohio. In 1794 he fought the Indians as a Captain under "Mad" Anthony Wayne at the battle of Fallen Timbers in northwest Ohio. John married twice, his first wife is unknown. His second wife was Mildred Ann Morgan, daughter of Major Charles Morgan who fought in the Revolutionary War out of Wilkes County, N.C., and later became the first magistrate of Lexington, Ky. John Hammon had 22 children and lived to be 108 years old, the second oldest Revolutionary War veteran alive.

He settled in Owen County, Ky. and was a charter member of the Mussel Shoals Baptist Church, many members of which had come over from Wilkes Co., N.C. In addition to his farm, he operated a business in Cincinnati building the superstructures of steamboats, in an effort to provide work for his many children. He was an acquaintance of William Henry Harrison, president of the United States, and a friend of Richard Mentor Johnson, Senator and Vice-President when Van Buren was voted into the White House. John Hammon had helped save Johnson's life when a flaming Indian arrow was shot into the bedclothing of his cradle at the Siege of Bryan's Station. Kentucky has erected a roadside marker at his grave.

His last child was Jesse Franklin Hammon, named for the hero of the Battle of King's Mountain, who became an attorney and judge in Louisville, Ky.

Sources: Rev. War file, Court House Records.

— Stratton Hammon

THE AMBROSE HAMMONS FAMILY
629

Born into an independent, courageous family, young Ambrose, son of William Hammons, learned to think for himself and to value freedom. At the time of his birth in Caroline County, Va. (for he was 60 or more in 1787), the colonists in Virginia proudly considered themselves free Englishmen, with all rights and privileges thereof. When in the early 1740's Caroline County men began to leave the established Church of England, preferring to study the Bible themselves and to worship God in a less formal way, the Hammons family joined the new Baptist Church. It was a decision of heart and mind which would shape their future, and in the mid-1770's move them to North Carolina where there was no "Established Church."

Before that time there was growing up to do: skills and farming methods to learn, as well as some schooling (for he signed his will). Brothers Joseph, James and Benjamin, and sisters Drusilla and Sarah (perhaps others) joined together (certainly with cousins) in work and play.

As a young man Ambrose courted and married Ann (?). Their daughter Mary was born in 1761, followed by sons Robert, ca. 1762/3 and John, ca. 1764/5. Finally about 1768/70 a second daughter, Elizabeth, was born. There may have been others but only those four survived to be named in their father's will.

When in 1774/5 the long move to the area now in Wilkes Co., N.C., began, Ambrose and Ann Hammons had four children with Mary, the eldest, about 13. Imagine the work of such a re-location and the courage required to start! With their possessions in wagons, herding and leading livestock, they were one unit of a large group including Ambrose's parents, his brothers, the Morgan and the Halbrook families. They moved slowly, gathering at night to cook, study the bible and pray together. Perhaps they stopped long enough to plant and harvest a crop. Sundays must have been a welcome relief — a day of rest and worship.

In Wilkes County there were homes to build, land to clear and plant, and other necessary

activities; Ambrose and Ann's responsibilities were many. They joined an existing Baptist Church, and when old Roaring River Church was organized in 1779, they became members. Ambrose served as an Elder and in Sept. 1785 was one of four delegates from the church to a conference at Brier Creek Church. In October of that same year, he was appointed a Justice of the Peace. The Hammons were all involved in some way with the War for Independence — establishing local government, building roads and mills and, of course, farming.

Ambrose died soon after his father, in 1794. Ann was dead before 1830. Their children's lives followed the innovative, pioneering example of their forebears.

Mary Hammons married Capt. Samuel Johnson, son of Jeffrey and Rachel Walker Johnson. A romantic story related in the family tells the circumstances of their meeting. Sam'l. received a severe abdominal wound in the Battle of King's Mtn. As he was assisted from the battlefield by John Parks, Sam'l. met his brother William, who was then detailed to assist Sam'l. home. He was carried up to Wilkes Co. on a horse litter drawn by Parks' father's horse, and by the time the group reached the Hammons' farm Sam'l. was too near death's door to travel farther. The Hammons family welcomed him into their home where their care enabled him to make a speedy recovery. Mary assumed most of the nursing duties, and before he was well enough to rejoin his Regiment they were "bespoken." They married on 25 Jan. 1782, with Samuel's brother John signing the marriage bond as security. They lived most of their lives in Wilkes County (although their daughter Chloe was born in Henry Co., Va.), and raised nine children. (See the Samuel Johnson Family Story.)

John Hammons served with the N.C. Continental Line at White Plains and Valley Forge. He married Polly Denny in Wilkes Co., N.C., on 3 Sept. 1782 and they had at least eight children.

Robert Hammons married and by 1787 had three daughters.

Elizabeth Hammons married John Amburgey on 3 July 1787. Their children: Nancy (18 March 1790), Ambrose (24 Feb. 1792), John (20 Jan. 1794), Rose (11 Nov. 1795), Robin (27 March 1798), Umphrey (16 Feb. 1800), Jess (26 April 1802), Wilborn (10 Feb. 1804), Betsy (7 June 1806), and Polly (27 July 1808). The entire John Amburgey family moved to Kentucky about 1814.

Sources: *The Land Of Wilkes*, Johnson J. Hayes; Wilkes County, N.C. Wills, Deeds, Marriage & Census Records; Wilkes County Land Entry Book; Abst'd., Mrs. W.O. Abshire; Pension Records, Nat'l. Archives; The Draper Collection; King's Mountain & Its Heroes, Draper.

— Mrs. John M. Richards, Jr.

WILLIAM HAMMONS
630

In 1771 a radical young Virginia lawyer, Patrick Henry, saddled his horse and rode to Bowling Green in Caroline County to defend three men in gaol there: Baptist ministers who

dared teach and preach the Gospel without "Episcopal Ordination or a license from the General Court."

By Statute, the Established Church of England was the Estab. Church of Virginia; contributions and attendance required. Gov. Alexander Spottswood's General Assembly had exempted from parish levies and attendance the German Protestant settlers he brought into the Rappahannock Valley. Later (1732) Gov. William Gooch allowed Quakers from PA into VA and later still he licensed Presbyterians to preach, but when a rapid increase in the new Baptist Church membership occurred, stern measures were taken against its leaders.

William Hammons also went to Bowling Green to comfort and support the three imprisoned preachers, for the Hammons family had joined the new denomination and William too was a Baptist preacher. In 1774 he went with others to Fauquier Co., to petition the Court for "liberty to meet together for the worship of God in our way." Months passed without reply, and the move to North Carolina (where there was no State Church) began. Joining in the relocation were the Hammons, Halbrook and Morgan families, who settled in the section of Surry Co., N.C., which became Wilkes in 1777.

As a matter of interest, the earliest Hammons recorded in VA was Matthew Hamon, from England to James City in the "Southampton" in 1622. However, Stratton O. Hammon, writing for the Filson Club History Quarterly, Vol. 23, 1949, stated that William Hammon (born ca. 1700 in Caroline County, VA) was the son of John Hammon (b. ca. 1679) and grandson of Ambrose Hamond, who immigrated from England in 1666.

The Restoration of the Stuarts in 1660 had slowed the first wave of "Cavaliers" to VA, but 1665 was the year of the Great Plague in England and the New World doubtless seemed attractive. Ambrose settled in the area of Rappahannock Co. which became Essex in 1692 and (part of) Caroline Co. in 1727. Records show other Hamon/Hammon/Hammond immigrants including, to the same area, Alice, by Nov. 1666; Isaac and John in 1772; relationship, if any, unknown. By immigration and marriage the family increased and spread into other counties.

By 1774/5, among those moving to N.C. with William and Sarah Hammons were their children, grandchildren and cousins. One son, James (Deed Records in Goochland Co. mention "his brother Ambrose Hammons of St. Margaret's Parish, Caroline Co."), had married Mary Hargis and moved to Goochland Co. where he died when his son John (b. 1760) "was three." James probably had other children. (His widow married John Halbrook and had at least five children. This family and other Halbrooks joined the Carolina move.) Also along were Wm.'s four children named in his will (Ambrose, Benjamin, Drusilla and Sarah — probably most were grown and married), Joseph (probably older, who signed with his siblings in 1800 to sell land left by Wm.), Martin and Thomas Hammon. They settled in the Roaring River area, with "improvements" made on their properties when the Wilkes Co.

Land Entry Book opened March 4, 1778.

They led a busy life; clearing and planting fields, building cabins or houses, furniture, fences and roads, with simple hand tools. Intelligence, self-reliance and industry were demanded and the Wilkes settlers had those attributes in abundance.

The war with England involved everyone; the younger Hammons men enlisted. William's son Benjamin enlisted first in the Va. Continental Line, then served with Benj. Cleveland and Wm. Nall; grandson John (son of Amborse) enlisted in the N.C. Line and fought at White Plains and Valley Forge; grandson John (son of James) enlisted at 16 in 1777 under (then Capt.) Benj. Cleveland and by 1778 he and Martin Hammon (who served under Capt. John Nucholls) had gone with other families from Wilkes to Bryan Station, Ky. There they continued battling the British, Tories and Indians! Both were back in N.C. by 1790. In 1796 John and his wife Mary were granted letters of dismission from Roaring River Church. John recorded a Ky. land grant in Knox Co. in 1811. Martin did the same in Montgomery Co., Ky., in 1797. John was in Hamilton Co, Ohio, by 1832.

Life was difficult, but in N.C. the Hammons found the freedom they sought. Several Baptist churches were flourishing when the family reached Wilkes; when the Roaring River Baptist Church was organized in 1779, many became members. William and Ambrose were among the early Elders (pastors), and in April 1786 the church voted to constitute a new church in Gambill's Hollow with William as pastor.

William spent his remaining years in Wilkes Co. and died in 1793. His son Joseph married Sarah (maiden name unknown) and had sons William, Ephriam and Benjamin. That family moved on to Russel Co., Va., then to Ky. Ambrose, born before 1727, died in Wilkes Co. in 1794. Benjamin, b. 1753, who married Sarah May (one child, Mariah), died in Wilkes Co. 7 March 1835. Drusilla married James Persons in Wilkes Co. 5 July 1805. Those sturdy, faithful Hammons have descendants in all the United States and several foreign countries.

Sources: Cavaliers & Pioneers, Nugent, Vols. I & II; Wingfield's History of Caroline Co., Va.; Colonial Caroline by T.E. Campbell; The Land of Wilkes, Johnson J. Hayes; Stratton O. Hammon's article in the Filson History Club Quarterly, Vol. 23, 1949; N.C., Wilkes Co. and Virginia.

— Mrs. John M. Richards, Jr.

HAMPTON ANCESTRY

631

One of my earliest recollections includes my Grandparents Jordan and Rachel (Coffey) Hampton of Watauga County, N.C. It was an exciting event for which our Daddy took my sister and me to Grandpa's to spend the night. We were restless and fretful until Grandpa said maybe he would give us some "Hickory tea!" Learning he did not mean to give us something good to drink, we fell asleep and next morning our Dad came for us with information of a new baby sister. It was with joy we skipped homeward, pumping Daddy with questions about the little baby.

Grandpa Jordan was born 10 Sep 1856 in Watauga Co. On 15 Nov 1875 he married Rachel Lorinda Coffey, daughter born 10 Nov 1856 to Jesse Carlton and Nancy (Raines) Coffey, married in 1840; granddaughter of Reuben and Rachel (Hayes) Coffey, married 1820. Grandpa was in the lumbering business as well as farming, and he was considered a valuable asset to the community and county. His children: Martha L., Harley D., E. Arkie, Wm. Spencer, Sara E., J. Amos and Eliza J. (twins), Walter, Lindley F., Connie G., Birdie, Oliver E., Elize C., J. Russell, and T. Augustus. Thirteen of these lived to adulthood and had families of their own.

Jeremiah Russell, my Daddy, was born 6 May 1902. He married Fannie L. Herman, daughter of Carroll M. and Essie L. (Coffey) Herman; granddaughter of Elisha L. and Violet (White) Herman, married 8 Nov 1874. My parents were married 25 Dec 1921 on my Mother's parents' 21st Wedding Anniversary. Dad's children were Dawn, Mabel, Beulah, J.R., Wendell and Verdola. We three older sisters with a cousin, Ivadene Hampton, used to sing gospel music.

The 62 grandchildren of Grandpa Jordan have been engaged in a wide variety of professions, skill trades and occupations.

Emmanuel and Orilla (Moreland) Hampton were married 4 Oct 1856. She was a daughter of John W. and Rose Anna (Curtis) Moreland of Caldwell Co. Emmanuel's children: Jordan, John J., Jesse Aaron, Amos Avery, Eliza Caroline, Wm. David, Noah Sylvester, and Mary Rosanna. Great Grandpa Emmanuel was a farmer, and was a deacon in the same church as was Grandpa Jordan. Emmanuel had injured a leg in his youth, and his use of a self-made wheelchair permitted him to be locally ambulatory.

Grandparents of Jordan were Aaron, Sr., and Mary E. (Cook) Hampton; she was the daughter of Michael and Catherine (Huffman) Cook; granddaughter of Adam Cook of Ashe Co. Children of Aaron and Mary were Annie, Emmanuel, Mary and Martha (twins), Elizabeth, Eliza H., Abraham, and Jeremiah. Aaron, born ca. 1804, was a farmer in Watauga Co., where he died in 1870.

Jeremiah and Molly (Waters) Hampton of Wilkes Co. were married 1 Feb 1803. Children of this union were Aaron and Betsy (twins), Eliza, Frankie, Martha, Hiley, Kizzie, Alex and Becky. Molly was a daughter of Moses and ? (Keys) Waters. Moses was a Revolutionary War veteran who was born in Baltimore, Maryland, and went to Wilkes Co. ca. 1771.

Thomas and Abigail (Laws ?) Hampton were parents of Welcome, Jeremiah, Livingston, Jacob, Turner, James, Nancy, Judy and Polly. Tax lists indicate that Thomas Hampton was in Wilkes Co. by 1782. He is believed to be a son of James and Rachel (?) Hampton, and to have come from Virginia, perhaps with brothers and sisters after whom he named some of his own children.

Grandpa and Grandma Hampton first lived in a small house which he built near the foot of Buck's Ridge. After four years the family moved into a larger house constructed by Grandpa, and the original home became his workshop. This building and Grandma's kitchen with its fireplace and chimney made of common face bricks are still standing. Other well remembered buildings are gone. A cousin lives on the old homeplace in a house of her own located where the sawmill stood. She is visited frequently by relatives who enjoy reminiscing about such events as the time a cow with horns chased them over a fence, Grandma with her cane striking "a smark-aleck kid" for pulling her apron strings, the turkeys picking out of the ground corn grains that Grandpa had just planted, eating too many apples or chestnuts, sleeping on Grandma's feather beds when rain was falling on the roof. Pleasant, too, are memories of apple orchards with springtime blossom fragrance that could be enjoyed for so great a distance as the top of the hill between their house and ours. These grandparents died in 1934-35, one just three months after the other. Grandpa was "a citizen of sterling worth, industrious and honorable," attributes with which I agree, even though he taught me the real meaning of "Hickory tea"!

Sources: Family memories, Watauga and Wilkes County Courthouses, and personal knowledge.

— Dawn Hampton Shepherd

JEREMIAH and MARY WATERS HAMPTON

632

Jeremiah Hampton was born about 1780 to 1784 in Wilkes County where he lived his entire life. He was the son of Thomas and Abigail Laws Hampton.

On the first day of February in 1803, Jeremiah married Mary (Molly) Waters. She was the daughter of Moses Waters and was born about 1780 to 1784 also.

The complete list of their children is not known. We do know the following: (1) Elizabeth, who married Thomas David Hall on Oct. 24, 1827 (the son of Thomas and Judith Dula Hall), (2) Martha (Patsy), who married Luke Triplett, (3) William B., who is believed to be the youngest son, and (4) Lucinda, who was the youngest daughter. William B. and Lucinda were enrolled in school in the 1840's School Census.

A possible son was Jeremiah Hampton, Jr. who was born about 1810. He married Sela Laws on Jan. 1, 1829 in Wilkes County. This family is found in Wilkes County on the 1830, 1840 Federal Census records and on the 1840's School Census. By 1850 they had moved to Washington County, Tennessee with eight children listed.

Aaron Hampton, who was born about 1804 is another possible son. He is living in Watauga County at the time of the 1850 and 1860 Census with his family. He had named a son, Jeremiah, and a daughter, Mary which indicates a close relationship.

Census records show several other daughters. The others are unknown at this time.

Deed records show that Jermiah owned several tracts of land. Neighboring tracts were owned by Benjamin Hendrix, Martin Hall and Joseph Hagerman from deed descriptions. He lived on an eighty acre tract known as Middle Cove. He deeded this tract with several others tracts, totaling 234 acres to his son, William B. in April 1838 with the consideration that William would "maintain and support" his mother, Mary Hampton. Jeremiah must have been ill at that time and died shortly thereafter as his estate was sold on July 26, 1838.

William B. Hampton and his mother Mary Hampton appear to have moved from Wilkes about 1846.

Sources: Census Records, School Census Records, Tax List, Deed Records, Estate Records, Marriage Bonds.

— Mrs. J. Arnold Simpson

THOMAS and ABIGAIL LAWS HAMPTON
633

Thomas Hampton appears to have been a well respected citizen of early Wilkes County. He is mentioned frequently as serving as a juror in court from March 4, 1782 for the next number of years. His name also appears as an overseer of road duty, serving from Deep Gap down Stony Fork to Lewis Fork Creek. In 1797, he was appointed Constable with Moses Waters, Esq. as security. He and Moses Waters were probably good friends and his son Jeremiah Hampton later married Mary Waters in 1803. Mary was the daughter of Moses Waters.

In the year 1782, we find Thomas Hampton with 100 acres of land in Captain Abraham Demoss' District. A couple of years later he is shown as owning 350 acres of land in District Eight. By 1787, his name is in the third tax district with 300 acres. The records indicate he lived near Stony Fork.

His wife was Abigail (Abbey) Laws, the daugher of William Laws. The marriage date is unknown but was probably before 1765. She is mentioned in the will of Wm. Laws as Abbey Hampton. This will was probated in 1781.

According to Thomas Hampton's will, which was probated in August 1817, there were nine children mentioned. (1) Turner, probably born before 1765, died about 1834, married Sarah. (2) Welcombe W., (3) Jeremiah, born about 1780/84, died about 1838, married 1 February 1803 in Wilkes County, Mary (Molly) Waters, (4) Livingston, born about 1784, married 15 January 1806 Feby Boman. (5) Jacob, married 20 June 1806, Catey Laws., (6) James, (7) Nancy. (8) Judy. (9) Mary (Polly), who had a son named Jesse mentioned in the will.

Soucres: Tax Lists, Court Mintues, Census Records and Marriage Bonds.

— Mrs. J. Arnold Simpson

HANDY-ABSHER-WYATT
634

Great-grandpa Coy Absher was born on January 6, 1880, and he married Cora Shumate, who was born on Decembsr 8, 1881. They had seven children: Della, born February 18, 1902; Lester, born April 10, 1905; Clemie, born September 28, 1907; Gencie, born Octo-

ber 10, 1910; John, born April 11, 1913; Hubert, born March 17, 1916, and my grandma Hessie, who was born on March 13, 1919.

After Hessie grew up to be a nice young lady, she met Vance Handy, the son of Tabis and Mary Ann Handy. Tabis and Mary Ann had nine children: Maryon, born October 25, 1874; Brady, born Mary 14, 1899; Muncy, born January 12, 1902; Belva, born April 23, 1904; Floyd, born February 14, 1906; Oscar, born June 5, 1908; Clarence, born December 24, 1910, Minnie, born February 10, 1912, and my Grandpa Vance, who was born on August 12, 1913.

After a few years of courtship, Vance Elmore Handy and Hessie Marie Absher were married on December 18, 1937. They had seven children: Lemon, born October 7, 1938; Edella, born September 30, 1941; Peggy, born August 31, 1943; Ivan, born July 21, 1945; Alonzo, born December 16, 1948; Dwight, born August 26, 1951; and Junior, born April 21, 1955.

After Edella became a young lady, she met Alvin, the son of Alfred and Annie Bell Wyatt. Alfred William Wyatt was born on April 22, 1906, and Annie Bell Brown was born on January 29, 1911. They were married on April 15, 1930. They had eight children: Everette William, born November 4, 1931; Katherine Goldie, born December 17, 1933; Ellagrene, born March 17, 1936; Alvin Elce, born May 4, 1938; Talmadge, born September 6, 1940; Lorene, born September 22, 1942, Ada Sue, born April 15, 1945; and Billy Wayne, born April 3, 1953.

After a few years of dating, Alvin Elce Wyatt and Edella Marie Handy were married on September 2, 1961. They had four children: Brenda Jean, born July 11, 1964; Randy Alvin, born July 14, 1966; Ronnie David, born August 12, 1967; and Betty Marie, born December 1, 1971.

Sources: Family *Bible*, personal knowledge, interviews with family members.

— Brenda Jean Wyatt

JOHN HANDY and DESCENDANTS
635

According to U.S. Census Records, the Handy name appeared first in Wilkes County, North Carolina in 1820. These were two brothers, Thomas and John Handy. According to War 1812 Pension Record Information, these brothers were born in Kershaw County, South Carolina — Thomas, b. 1795 and John, b. 1796. They enlisted in the army in Wilkesboro, N.C. on 9 July 1814. After being discharged in 1816, they settled in Wilkes County.

Family tradition stories say Thomas and John were sons of James Handy and Betty Edwards. Other children mentioned were: Elizabeth, James, Tabitha, Sally and Samuel. The father, James Handy was believed to have gone to South Carolina from Maryland about the time of the Revolutionary War.

John Handy married Margaret Stamper 23 December 1818 and settled in the Cane Creek

Ivan Winton Handy (1917).

area. They were parents of the following children: Thomas, Richard, Rachel, John II, Nancy and Elizabeth. After his first wife's death, John Handy married Frances Adams in 1836. They were parents of eleven children: Phelia, Francis Marion, Samuel B., William Harrison, Amy, Louis, Pharabe, Huldah, James Calloway, Andrew Jackson and Ellison D. John Handy died 7 April 1860 and is buried in the Old Cane Creek Cemetery near McGrady, N.C. Six of his sons served in the Civil War.

John Handy II, born in Wilkes Co. in 1826, married Gracie Ann Duval in Ashe Co. in 1846. They were parents of Thomas Reed, Ivan Winton, Julia and Troy. According to army records, John Handy II enlisted in the army on 27 March 1862. He died in a hospital in Kinston, N.C. on 5 June 1862 of measles. Family tradition tells us the army attempted to return his body to Ashe Co. At Wilkesboro, they found the Yadkin River flooded and were unable to cross. They buried him near the river in Wilkesboro.

John Handy II's son, Thomas Reed Handy, born in Wilkes Co. in 1849, became a well-known Methodist minister and served in the Holston Methodist Conference for seventy-one years. Thomas Reed and his wife, Caroline Sophia Hall, had six children. One son was Thomas Troy Handy. He was a graduate of V.M.I. During World War I he rose to the rank of major and won the Distinguished Service Cross and the Croix de Guerre with Gilt Star. During World War II Thomas Handy rose to general and was Deputy Chief of Staff to General George C. Marshall, Army Chief of Staff. His service during this conflict won him the Distinguised Service Medal with Oak Leaf Cluster and Legion of Merit. According to War Department Records, on 25 July 1945 as Acting Chief of Staff, he issued the order for the atomic bomb to be dropped on Japan. In 1949, he went to Germany as America's Commander in Chief in Europe in charge of all U.S.

Troy Curtis Handy, Carrie Belle Phipps Handy, Georgia and Jesse (standing) Russel (in mothers lap).

troops stationed there. General Handy retired with the rank of four-star General and now resides in Texas.

Ivan Winton Handy born 1854 was second son of John Handy II and Gracie Ann Duval. He spent his adult life in Ashe County. Ivan was a farmer, traveling salesman, and, sometimes, Methodist minister. He married Julia Akers and they were parents of nine children. Two sons, Sam and Whitt, spent their adult lives in Oregon. The other two sons, Troy Curtis and Earl Hix, remained in Ashe County. Ivan Handy died 5 March 1930.

Troy Curtis Handy was born in Ashe County on 31 December 1879 and died there 15 December 1962. He was a farmer and lived in the Grassy Creek area. He married Carrie Belle Phipps in 1911. They had eight children — three sons and five daughters. Two sons, twins Carl and Clay, have lived most of their lives in Virginia.

Russell Phipps Handy, born 13 August 1917, was the eldest son. He graduated from North Carolina State University. On 12 April 1941, he and Virginia Parlier of Montgomery, Alabama were married. His career was spent as an official with the United States Department of Agriculture. His last position was that of Statistician in Charge of the North Carolina Crop Reporting Service. He retired in 1974 and contines to reside in Raleigh, North Carolina.

The two children of Russell Handy and Virginia Parlier are William Russell Handy and Barbara Lynn Handy. Bill was born on 14 June 1950 in Trenton, New Jersey. He graduated from the University of North Carolina and is in the field of journalism in Tampa, Florida. He was married to Barbara Houghton of New Bern, North Carolina on 24 August 1974.

Barbara Handy was born 27 August 1954 in Charleston, West Virginia. She is a graduate of Western Carolina University and is in the computor field in the Research Triangle Park, N.C.

Sources: Family Records, Family Tradition, Grave Markers, Census Records, Pension Records, Army Records, Wilkes County Marriage Bonds, Personal Knowledge.

— Virginia Parleir Handy

MOLLY HARRIS

636

My great-great-great grandmother Molly Harris and husband John left Culpepper County, Virginia, most likely in search of a more prosperous life, and possibly to acquire some of the land grants that could be purchased very cheaply from the state, and arrived in Wilkes County by covered wagon sometime during the late 1790s. During the westward migration, one could acquire land grants by merely becoming homesteaders in this or any other undeveloped area.

It is believed that Molly made several stops before reaching the beautiful Land of Wilkes. Her son Jehue told the census taker that he was born in Randloph County in 1787, according to the 1850 census. Her son Isaac was born in Rockingham County and her daughters Lucy and Ibby claimed Wilkes as their birthplace.

About the same time that the Harrises arrived in Wilkes, another man arrived with his family, possibly from Wake County. This family was destined to become closely associated with Mollie and her family — to become neighbors and to inter-marry with members of her family. His name was Jordan Chavers (or Chavis, as it has sometimes been recorded). Jordan married Molly's daughter Lucy and Jordan's sister Clarissy married Molly's son Jehue.

Jordan Chavers was a man of means. He could not read or write but was highly intelligent and used great skill in business transactions. Money was not a problem and he utilized it well. On March 27, 1813, Jordan Chavers bought 300 acres on Mulberry Creek, north of the Yadkin River, from John and Philadelphia Gordon. On February 21, 1814, he bought 100 acres on Mulberry Creek from a Wesley Reynolds. On January 1, 1829, Jordan Chavers sold 85 acres to Molly (Harris) Mitchell. Molly's husband John had died before reaching Wilkes County and was buried in Rowan County. She later married a Mr. Mitch-

ell. This same plantation was willed to Molly's daughter Ibby, upon Milly's death in 1834. Later on during that year Ibby married young John Anderson. On October 31, 1849, Ibby and John sold the plantation to William P. Waugh, who was a wealthy merchant in Wilkes at that time. This plantation was located in the Fairplains section of Wilkes County.

By this time the Harrises were multiplying in number and becoming leading citizens and landowners. The earlier Harrises inter-married with the Chavers, the Baileys, the Grintons, the Fergusons and the Andersons. These families were free and were never slaves. From these unions came many beautiful ladies and handsome men.

My family evolved from the union of Jehue Harris and Clarissy Chavers. She was better known as "Classy." Jehue helped survey Wilkes County when it was cut off from Surry County. They left the Fairplains Community, went across the Yadkin River and bought numerous acres of land, built a cabin, cleared and tended the land and started raising a family. They had thirteen children: Jordan, Richard, Jim, Hugh, Andrew, Wesley, Lee, Nancy, Roxanna, Lucy, Dillie, Adaline and Polly. Most of the present generation of Harrises are descendants of these thirteen.

This family was the fiery tempered, energetic set of Harrises. Almost all of them would fly off the handle at the bat of an eyelash. Yet, they were kind, helpful and responsible people. Their energy never seemed to wane. Far into old age they continued to work and grunt.

Jordan was the eldest of the thirteen. He was born on January 1, 1820 and became a farmer, a mail carrier and a shoe cobbler, a profession in which he excelled. He made shoes for the Confederate soldiers during the Civil War. On October 16, 1846, he married Rachel Grinton, a half-White and half-Indian maiden who had beautiful straight long hair that reached the floor when she sat down, and who was gifted along all lines of homemaking. She was known as "Granny Rachel". They raised three sons: Lewis, Andrew and John (better known as Devil John). At the age of 96, Jordan fell into an open fireplace and was burned to death.

Another son of Jehue and Classy was my grandfather Jim Harris. Date of birth and death is not known. He was a mysterious type of person who did very little talking but was an outstanding painter and decorator for that day. He and wife Martha Ann Bass lived in a cabin on a hill overlooking Cub Creek, south of Wilkesboro, known as Harris Hill.

Two of Jim's sons: William (Will) and James Calloway (Jink) who is my father, continued to carry on the painting trade. It is still being carried on today by their sons and grandsons.

The early generation of Harrises in this County did not go in for much education, yet Jordan sent his son Andrew to Biddle University in Charlotte. In the fourth generation more attention was paid to public education and Harrises started sending their children to school. As a result, in the fifth generation, many teachers and leaders were filling places of high learning and leadership such as school principals, scientists, nurses, carpenters, painters, radio technicians, engineers, farm demonstrators, athletes, pilots, singers and some have achieved fame in the entertainment world.

Molly would be proud of a great-great-great-great granddaughter, Lady Sara Lou Harris Carter who became a professional model and was a national poster girl and model of the year, had her own radio show and appeared on television and in short movies, voted one of the ten most beautiful Negro women in America and is the wife of Sir John Carter, the Ambassador of Guyana, South America. They have lived in Georgetown, Washington, London, Peking and currently in Kingston, Jamaica.

The Harrises in general were not a very religious people, yet later generations have produced preachers and Bishops. A bright thread of aggressiveness and high purpose runs through the Harris families of Wilkes County. Jordan Harris set aside a piece of his land on a beautiful knoll above his cabin to be used as a burial place for any Harris who desired to be buried there. His brother Andrew was the first to be buried there. It is still being used today and is known as the Old Harris Cemetery.

Molly Harris Mitchell, the grand old lady who was responsible for the early beginning of the Harris family in Wilkes County lived a gallant, courageous and exemplary live. She was a smart, hard working woman who owned a plantation, raised a fine family and was able to secure the legal services of a great lawyer, John Finlay. After all is said and done, the Harrises as a whole are well liked, admired (in some cases envied), and respected by their fellow citizens.

As a born free descendant of Molly Harris and after having contributed to the development and growth of the County, the State, and the Nation, I am proud to be a citizen of these United States of America.

Sources: Notes by Eddie Harris Ralls Ledbetter and Leonard Tabor, Court House records, personal knowledge.

— Leander Harris

Rev. and Mrs. Charles C. Harris.

REV. and MRS. CHARLES C. HARRIS FAMILY
637

I am fortunate to have been born to parents who were both public school teachers and also natives of "The Great State of Wilkes." They were the late Rev. and Mrs. Charles C. Harris, who lived between the years of 1886-1956 and 1889-1966, respectively. They were the proud parents of nine children, eight of whom grew to maturity. They were blessed to see these eight children and one grandson graduate from the now "phased out" Lincoln Heights High School. My parents also lived to see each of their children happily married and taking their places in the world. The four girls are college graduates and the sons have done Civil Service work.

A daughter, Mrs. Louise Harris Spencer, is now doing home nursing in Baltimore, Maryland. A son, James C., now deceased (1971) worked in the Navy yards in Baltimore during World War II. After the close of the war, he worked successfully for many years in the Carver Foundation, Tuskegee Institute, Alabama. James C. was their youngest son.

The middle boy, Calvin Russell, was very aggressive. After graduating from Lincoln Heights, he entered A.S.T. College, Greensboro, North Carolina. Calvin was in their very first aviation class and shortly after "Pearl Harbor" in 1941, was inducted into the U.S. Air Force. He received his training at Morton Air Base, Tuskegee, Alabama. Calvin qualified as an instructor and helped to encourage and train many air force pilots. He remained in Tuskegee until Morton Air Base closed in 1945. He later moved to Pensacola, Florida and was employed at the Pensacola Air Base until his death in 1967. Calvin owned his own plane and flew private passengers as well.

Their oldest son was George Talmadge, who served in both the Atlantic and Pacific Theaters of war. Soon after the end of World War II, George was employed by the Chemistry Department at Tuskegee Institute. He has built a new home there and is still working in the Chemistry Department.

The writer, Loree H. Anderson is the eldest daughter of Rev. and Mrs. Charles C. Harris. I finished Lincoln Heights at 17 ages of age, and was validictorian of my class in 1931. I won a one year scholarship to Knoxville College, Knoxville, Tennessee. After that year, I transfered to Winston-Salem Teacher's College and finished Normal School there in 1933, with the equivalent of three years college.

I began teaching in the fall of 1933 in Taylorsville, N.C. After two years there, I was hired by the Wilkes County Board of Education and taught there for thirty-three years, which made a grand total of thirty-five years in the two schools.

I was employed by Wilkes Community College for the next four years, (1968-1971), in Adult Basic Education. I did some further training at Moorehead University, Moorehead, Kentucky, during the summer of 1970. I was rehired by the Wilkes County Board of Education as Resource Teacher from 1972 to 1976. I am now enjoying my retirement.

My sister, Mrs. Lillie Harris Gibson began teaching in Taylorsivlle, N.C. in 1935 and taught until 1937. She has taught in Wilkes County, Rock Creek Township, North Wilkesboro, N.C., Davidson High School, Cleveland County, Kings Mountain, N.C. and in Robeson County, Rowland, N.C. She is looking forward to retiring in the near future.

My two younger sisters, Mrs. Theophra Harris Silver and Mrs. Mildred Harris Little are graduates of Shaw University, Raleigh, N.C. and Bennett College, in Greensboro, N.C., respectively. Theophra has taught in the public schools of Taylorsville, Woodlawn Elementary, North Wilkesboro, Raleigh and Baltimore, Maryland. She is a trained and gifted musician. She is now a great help to her husband in the field of music and missionary work. They reside in Baltimore, Maryland where her husband is pastor of Concord Baptist Church.

My youngest sister, Mrs. Mildred Harris Little has taught in Pensacola, Florida and in High Point, North Carolina. She graduated with honors, from Lincoln Heights at age fourteen and from Bennett College, with an "A" average in Home Economics at age nineteen.

I hope that by giving this brief history of "one man's Family", to pay tribute to the memory of my beloved parents, who are now deceased, and also to inspire other girls and boys to seek out and get a good education. To realize that it can be done and to aspire to high goals in life. To apply yourselves, to give attention to instruction; to try to realize that "life can be worth living" and that "life can be beautiful." Let us all join hands and help to make the world a better place in which to live.

Sources: Personal knowledge.

— Loree Harris Anderson

JOHN P. HARROLD
638

John P. Harrold was born in 1856. He married Matilda Whitley in 1863. They lived two miles east of Hayes on a farm. He was the son of Alexander and Mary Johnson Harrold. Alexander was a son of John and Mary Harrold.

Matilda smoked a pipe and kept it lying in a crack in the rock chimney. A local merchant named Charles Sebastian hid her pipe from her and she never smoked anymore. She was a strong willed person and after her husband's sudden death, she plowed her land and made crops without the help of any man.

John P. is buried on the Harrold Mountain that bears his family name and Matilda is buried at Round Mountain Baptist Church. They had two sons. Emanuel was born in 1875 and died in 1943. He married Mary Ann Ballard, born 30 August 1873 and died 20 August 1959. She was the daughter of William and Nancy Walker Ballard. The second son,

Doctor, was born in 1883 and died in 1923. He married Rhoda Johnson and had two children, Ray and Beatrice.

Emanuel and Mary Ann had five children: Charlie, married Freda Chipman and had Mary, Lura and Bill; Doshia married Dock Blackburn and had Wilma, Dorothy and Bufford; Nettie married Carlow Brown and had Marie, Hoyle and Jessie; Essie married Claude Caudill and had, Edwin Joe, Grady, Von, Betty Ann, Jerry, Lucy, Harrold, Lynn and Nancy; Cicero married Bernice Chipman and had Jack, Elane, Dorene and Wayne.

Sources: County records and family knowledge.

— Edwin Joe Caudill

MY HARTLEY GRANDPARENTS
639

My grandparents, James and Julia Coffey Hartley, were a strong, well adjusted couple who knew what they wanted and worked toward that end.

Before moving to Wilkes County, Grandma Julia joined the Tabernacle Advent Christian Church in Caldwell County. In fact she was a charter member. Grandma's father, Charles Coffey, joined Tabernacle Church with Grandma, and bought a melodeon for his daughter, Jane, to play for services. The melodeon was taken to and from church each Sunday. Later, members bought an organ. In Mr. W.W. Scott's book, "Annals of Caldwell County", he described grandfather Charles Coffey as a staunch old Puritan type. Grandma Julia was somewhat like her father in that respect. She never referred to the community but as "The Settlement". She never shrank from responsibility, was strong willed — a very strong character, and was deeply religious.

Grandfather James Hartley was also a man of deep conviction and believed in the Adventist doctrine. He never loved or courted any other girl but Julia Coffey. The Bernhardt farm joined the Lewis Hartley farm and the Bernhardt boys nicknamed grandpa "Julia Jim Hartley".

The Col. Horton farm in Ferguson, Wilkes County, "Daingerfield" was for sale and my grandparents, James and Julia, bought the farm partially because there was a strong Advent Christian Church at Beaver Creek, and they liked the Spicers, Fergusons and Fosters, who were representatives of the good community and church. They built a spacious two story house in front of the old log house that was Col. Horton's home. He built large outbuildings, grainery, carriage house and barn, the largest in the community. He brought with him the first turning plow sold in Caldwell County, and the neighbors came to see the new plow at work. It has been told that he was one of the best farmers of his day. They believed in good schools, good churches and community improvements and gave freely of their substance and work.

As little girls, we loved the Adventist Conferences for it meant seeing visitors from other churches and having a lot of visitors in our home. Grandma delighted in fixing baskets of

food and was noted for her salt rising light bread, fried chicken and apple pies. Grandpa usually killed a young beef for the occasion.

The ruffles and lace on our white lawn dresses were ironed to perfection by our grandmother for the Conference. She would not allow anyone else to iron our dresses for this big event. It was a labor of love and she loved every minute of it. Ruth, Mayme and I were proud of the fact that we had one of the nicest, velvet lined top surry and sleek horses in the hitching lot at church.

Grandma was Sunday School Supt. from the first time I can remember until I was in my teens and my parents moved to Virginia. She was an excellent reader and some times was very pointed in her remarks when the occasion arose, especially if we girls had attended a square dance in the community. While reading the Sunday School lesson, she would look straight at us, making us feel guilty of having strayed far from the fold.

Grandpa was a man of few words, but when he spoke, his three sons listened and usually followed his advise. If there was anything he was skilled in besides farming, it was his accuracy in predicting the weather, and his memory of dates and happenings was unequalled. He kept a diary from his wedding day until his last sickness. What zeal, what work, for a couple to have bought three of the best farms on the Yadkin river for their three sons. Grandpa read the Bible twice a day in his later years and believed he would wake up any morning to see the Lord coming in the east with his holy angels.

The Spicer family was a family set apart from any people I have ever known. They were a pious, kind family and hospitable in their home. "Miss Edie", daughter of John and Eleander Ferguson, and her two daughters lived in a large brick house with tall shade trees and running ivy. I have always associated the brick house with the brick house in the story of "Sunny Brook farm". I loved the parlor with its high ceilings, tall, deep set windows, a large library and many curios that filled the room. When I heard that the Spicer home had burned, I felt a part of my youth had gone as well as a cherished landmark.

The one thing that sticks out im my memory is the gentle, sweet way Miss Betty Spicer would ask the visitors or strangers in church to go home with her for dinner. My mother said she was the only angelic person she had ever known. Her death was a great misfortune to the church as well as the community. Miss Janie Spicer was a devout Christian too. She said Miss Betty always reproved her if she said anything unkind about anyone. Her motto was not to repeat gossip. That was being charitable toward one's neighbors. I remember stopping by the Spicer home after attending a baptising at the Yadkin River and seeing long wooden bowls filled with biscuits and dishes of good food on the back porch. So many people were in the yard and I wondered if they were all staying for dinner. The lettered and unlettered were always welcomed in that home.

Sources: Personal knowledge.

— Margaret Hartley Carter

THE HARTLEY FAMILY

640

Waightsel Hartley came to America from Shropshire, England, and settled in Maryland, near Fredricksburg. The name of his wife is not known but he raised three children: John, Mahala and Nancy. John married Elizabeth Becket, who was a waitress in the home of the Jeffersons and nursed Thomas Jefferson in his infant days. John H. was a weaver by trade using the old fashioned hand loom, and it is said he could weave 40 yards per day. Their seven children were: Finley, George, James, Reuben, Nancy, Elizabeth, and Ava. This sketch will trace the family of George Hartley.

George, Senior, married Elizabeth Davis and settled in Caldwell County. He raised six children: Clinton, Larkin, George, Jr., Alford, Waightsel and Mahala Celia.

Celia Hartley married Jesse Hartley, who was not related to the other Hartley's except by marriage. Their sons were: Lewis, John, George, and Levie (Lee). Lewis Hartley married Clarissa Smith, daughter of George Smith, Sr., and they lived at the foot of the Hibriten Mountain near Lower Creek Baptist Church. Their children were: Thomas, James, Joseph, Bingham, and William.

Thomas went to Missouri and died when a young man. James married Julia Coffey, daughter of Charles L. Coffey of Lower Creek. They had three sons: Charles, Henry, and Frank. This family moved to Ferguson in Wilkes County. Charles married Margaret (Maggie) Cowles, and they had six children: Ruth, Margaret, Mayme, Cowles, James and Julia. They later moved to Louisa County, Virginia.

Henry married Ida Harris and they had three children: Sycho, Emzie, and Dixie. They all live in Ferguson.

Frank married Lizzie Steele and had five children: Ann, Harold, Jay, Edith and Ruby. Frank and Lizzie lived in North Wilkesboro. Joseph, son of Lewis Hartley, went to Oregon in 1890. Bingham, son of Lewis, married Kate Sherrill, and had two children. The daughter, Maude, still lives in Lenoir.

William, fourth son of Lewis, married a Miss Saterwhite of Dudley Shoals and then moved to Mo. The daughters of Lewis Hartley were: Laura, Lou and Clara. Laura married Frank Moore and lived near Dudley Shoals. Lou, married P.H. German and they were the parents of a son, Lewis, who died in his teens. The mother died shortly afterwards. Clara, the youngest daughter, married John M. Downs. They raised seven children: four sons and three daughters. The sons were John, Joseph, Robert Bingham, and William. The daughters were Mary, Annie Lou, and Ruth. Annie Lou and Ruth married and lived in Asheville, N.C. Mary was the wife of Prof. T.E. Story of Wilkesboro, N.C.

John Downs, Jr., married Vesta Kerley and lived at Douglas, Wyoming. Joseph died in France in the World War I. Robert Bingham married Elizabeth Crooks and lives in New York City. He was for a number of years Librarian of the University of N.C. and also at the University of New York City. William married Mable Hudson and lived at Little Rock, Ark.

Lewis Hartley was a high-toned Christian gentleman. He was at one time sheriff of Caldwell County.

Sources: J.R. Swanson, Lenoir, N.C. Aug 9, 1940.

— Edith Ferguson Carter

CHARLES and MARGARET COWLES HARTLEY

641

Charles L. Hartley was a son of James and Julia Hartley, who had moved from Cladwell County in about 1884 to a farm on the Yadkin River in the Ferguson Community. James and Julia Hartley had three sons: Charles, Frank and Henry.

Charles married Margaret (Maggie) Cowles, daughter of Arthur J. Cowles and Amelia Horton Cowles, of Caldwell County, and they had six children: Ruth, Margaret, Mayme, Julia, Cowles, and James. Later Charles and Maggie moved to Buckner, Virginia and only two of the children remained in N.C. This account will trace the families of Ruth and Margaret.

Ruth, the oldest child, married Henry Wheeling and they lived in the old Howard House at Elkville. They had five children: Maurice, Joan, Carolyn, Clyde and Stanley. Maurice married Joyce Burke of North Wilkesboro and they had one daughter, Karen. Karen married Dick Sloop and they have a son, Ben. Joan married Harold Dean, a judge, and they live in Darien, Conn. They have two sons, Harold, and Cowles. Carolyn married Ronald Young and they live in Florida. They have two daughters, Caroline and Robin. Clyde and his wife, the former Eloise Glandon, live in the old homeplace at Elkville, and they have three children, Ruth, David and Michael. Stanley married Carol Bowers and they have a son, James. They live at Kings Creek in Caldwell County.

Margaret married Randolph Carter of the Grandin Community of Caldwell County and they had three children: George Hill, Margaret, Nancy and Martha. They lived for a while at Elkville and then lived at Grandin. Hill married Edith Ferguson and they live in the old Lindsay C. Ferguson homeplace at Ferguson. They have two daughters, Margaret, who married Monty Minton of North Wilkesboro, and Sharon. Margaret (Peggy) married Clifton Broyhill and they had five children: Radford, Alan, Jane, Susan and Randolph. Randolph (Randy) married Gerri Kastin.

Nancy married William Parlier of Charlotte and they have three children: Harry, William, and Deborah. Harry married Kay Barbre and they have two children. William married Teresa Aycoth and they also have two children. Deborah married Doug Hill.

Martha married Dr. J. Ray Kirby of Warsaw, N.C. They have three sons: Mark, Alex and Paul. They live in Durham.

Margaret Hartley Carter's husband, Randolph J. Carter was the son of Dr. and Mrs. Hill Carter, and grandson of Dr. and Mrs. Nicholas Hill Carter of Caldwell County. Both doctors were life long country doctors in Caldwell County. Dr. Nicholas Hill Carter came from Virginia and settled in Caldwell County where he married Juliette Jones. He was a descendant of the "Shirley" Plantation Carters, outside of Richmond, Va. on the James River.

Sources: Family knowledge.

— Edith F. Carter

DR. HENRY and IDA HARRIS HARTLEY

642

Dr. Henry Hartley was the son of James and Julia Coffey Hartley and they lived at "Daingerfield" on the Yadkin River at Ferguson. He married Ida Harris and they had three children: Sycho, Emzie, and Dixie. Sycho married Hazel Triplett and they had four children: Harold, who married Shirley Pearson; Lucille, who married Jerry Walsh; Gail who married Larry Ferguson; and Clyde who married Debbie Bowman. Harold and Shirley have three children: Harper, Quenton, and Shanna. Lucille and Jerry have one daughter, Melissa. Gail and Larry have two sons, Brinkley and Lewis. Clyde and Debbie have a daughter, Tammy.

Emzie married Elmo Eller of the Ferguson community. They have three children: Jane, David and Ernest. Jane married Rev. Gordon Noble and they have two children, Kimberly and Mark. Ernest married Barbara Murray and they have four children, Holly, Ernie, Michael and Nicholas.

Dixie married Vaden Eller, a brother to Elmo Eller. They had two children, Dianne and Gary. Gary died in 1975.

Source: Personal knowledge.

— Edith F. Carter

FRANK JAMES HARTLEY FAMILY

643

Frank James, son of James H. and Julya Ann Coffey Hartley, was born in 1882, died 1951. He married Elizabeth Steele, daughter of John Calvin and Laura Powell Steel, who was born in 1884 and died in 1974. They lived in Wilkes County.

Their children were 1) Jay Stanley born 1906, died 1966, married Mable Hardy. They had James Spencer who married Rebecca Ann Triplett who had children Rebecca Ann and Christopher James, and Betsy Victoria who married Wm. T. McPherson and had Michael Thomas and Amy Melissa.

(2) Ruby Steele Hartley, born 1907, married Ray Hobbs and had Ann Elizabeth and Kathy Celeste. Kathy Celeste married All Hester.

(3) Harold Howard married Agnes Powell and had Frank Powell, who married Carol Ann Perrell and had Ann Carol and Janace Lynn; Mary Agnes who married Stanley Clark and had Glenn Owen, Jeffrey Hartley and Clayton Eric Clark.

(4) Edith Celeste born 1913, died 1978, married Eddit Anderson.

(5) Ann Coffey born 1916, married Isaac Duncan and had Malinda who married Jason Mori and have Jennifer Ann and Daniel Walker Mori; Anette who married John Battle and had

Frank James and Elizabeth Steele Hartley.

John Isaac, Brian Christopher and Jeffrey David Battle; Nancye Laurice who married Joseph Johnston; and Susie Jana.

Sources: Personal knowledge.

— James S. Hartley

MAMIE McNIEL HARTLEY
644

The immortal Rosaland Russell made "Auntie Mame" famous on the broadway stage and in the movies. Similarly, Mamie McNiel Hartley is making herself immortal by the full life she has given and continues to live.

Giving is her philosophy; first, to her parents, Thornton and Eda McNiel; then to her brother, Alonzo McNiel; to her neices, Sue Colvard and Annie Gray; to her first husband, Fred Emerson; and now to her second husband, R.C. Hartley. For each of them she has provided a loving and fun-filled home.

At an early age she became matriach of the Thornton McNiel family, directly descended from the Reverend George McNiel (1720-1805) who was born in Scotland. In this feature the original spelling of the McNiel surname is used for continuity.

Each of her brothers looked to her for strength and fortitude. She has succeeded three of them, Alonzo, Tip, and Claude McNiel, as president of the corporation their father founded, the North Wilkesboro Coca-Cola Bottling Company. Her other brothers, Chal, secretary-treasurer of the plant for more than thirty years, and Osco, who died early, joined their family in learning soon in life not to attempt to be overly protective of their sister, for she was destined to lead, as she continues to do as the last survivor.

After the death of her sister, Ruth McNiel Vannoy, she made a home for her nieces. With their father's remarriage, Sue Colvard eventually moved with him to Ashe County. Annie Gray continued to live with her aunt until going away to Meredith College and later her marriage to A.R. Gray, Jr.

Much has been said about Mamie Hartley's ability as a teller of the good story, which entertains all those whom she encounters. She is a member of the First Baptist Church of North Wilkesboro, as well as numerous civic and social clubs.

She was born 29 October 1903 in the Purlear community. Her first marriage was to Fred Oscar Emerson, the son of Philo and Lillie (Ballard) Emerson of the Knotville community. He was born 2 November 1905 and died 28 April 1957.

Her second marriage 18 November 1965 was to R.C. Hartley of Charlotte. His birthdate is a well-kept secret. He is the son of George Haywood and Alice (Stallings) Hartley of Caldwell County.

Mamie Hartley was the youngest of seven children.

(1) William Alonzo McNiel was born 17 September 1888 and died 7 August 1948. He was unmarried and nicknamed "Benny."

(2) Ella Ruth McNiel, whose biography is found elsewhere in this book, was born 2 November 1890 and died 11 January 1919. She was married 10 May 1914 to H. Roscoe Vannoy, son of James Newton and Cornelia (Bumgarner) Vannoy. Their three children were: (1) Ella Sue Vannoy born 17 February 1915 and married 6 October 1934 to Carl Franklin Colvard who died 28 May 1962. They had one son. (2) Annie Louise Vannoy was born 17 May 1917 and died 4 July 1977. On 31 March 1941 she married Alexander Russell Gray, Jr., who was born 1 June 1929. There are three children and two grandchildren. (3) H. Roscoe Vannoy, Jr., called "Johnny," was born 9 January 1919 and died 27 July 1924.

(3) Claude Ackle McNiel, nicknamed "Major," was born 20 March 1893 and died 26 September 1968. He was married to Daisy Ann Hayes 15 August 1915. She was the daughter of John Lee and Sarah Julia (McNiel) Hayes. Their four children were: (1) Minnie Ruth McNiel, born 24 September 1916 and married

10 July 1948 to Joseph Samuel Gentry. There are two children and no grandchildren. (2) Dr. Claude A. McNiel, Jr. was born 11 August 1919 and married Barbara Bennett Hawkins 23 December 1943. There are two children and two grandchildren. (3) Sarah Elizabeth McNiel was born 25 January 1924 and married Richard Fuller Callaway 16 September 1944. There are three sons and no grandchildren. (4) Robert Hayes McNiel was born 12 September 1926 and died 12 February 1972. He was married 13 July 1945 to Nan Lacy Harris. There are two children and two grandchildren.

(4) Challie Odell McNiel, nicknamed Emmet, was born 24 June 1894 and died 30 May 1955, two weeks before his brother, Tip. He was married 14 March 1920 to Mrs. Luella (Tuttle) Chilton. They had no children.

(5) Richard Tipton McNiel was nicknamed "Kaley." He was born 16 September 1897 and died 13 June 1955. His marriage to Gladys Eller was 29 May 1925. Their children are (1) Patricia Ruth McNiel, born 24 June 1927 and married 9 October 1948 to Bob Frank Day. (2) Richard Tipton McNiel, Jr. was born 10 October 1930 and was married to Nannie Morguenya Roope 1 July 1956. There are four grandchildren.

(6) Osco McNiel was born 16 January 1900 and died 28 January 1919. He was nicknamed "Dooney" and was unmarried.

(7) Mamie Gertrude McNiel was the climax to the family.

Judge Johnson J. Hayes wrote, "They (the McNiels) were a neighborly type of people who were ever eager to help and to divide with each other." Certainly this has always been an apt description of Mamie McNiel Hartley. Likewise, her good deeds and sharp wit could have made her the pattern for the character, "Auntie Mame."

Sources: Absher, *The Thornton McNiel Family;* Hook, *George Michael Eller, Descendants of His in America;* Hayes, *Genealogy of the McNiel Clan;* and family memories.

— C. Frank Colvard

HAWKINS
645

The parents of Jesse D. Hawkins moved from Mountain City, Tenn. to the Buffalo Cove section of Wilkes County (which later become Caldwell County), when he was a small child. Jesse D. Hawkins married Sophia Hartley April 9, 1852 in Wilkes County. They had 9 children: (1) Sarah, (2) Jasper (3) Martha Emily (4) Kelly (5) Greene A. (6) Mary A. (7) Annie (8) Thomas M. and (9) Ninnie.

Jesse D. Hawkins served during the Civil War and was taken a prisoner during a battle in Tenn. He was taken to the Union Prison at Rock Island, Ill. A grandson has some letters which were written from Jesse to his wife during the time he was in the war and during the time spent in the Union Prison. On his return home, he lived at Buffalo Cove for a number of years.

He then purchased 234 acres of property in 1895 in the Darby section of Wilkes County on the waters of Elk Creek.

Sarah Hawkins was married three times.

The first husband was Thomas Pipes, second husband was a Ferguson and the third husband was Will Walters. She died in 1957 and did not have any children.

Jasper Hawkins died as a small child.

Martha Emily Hawkins was born 1867 and married George Franklin Hendrix, son of Wilson Hendrix, April 11, 1886 in Wilkes County. They later moved to Murphy (Cherokee County), N.C. They had a least eight children: (1) Clarence born 1896 (2) Glenn Dewey born 1898 (3) Lloyd Wilson born 1905 (4) Ethel Sophia born 1900 (5) Geneva (6) Maude (7) Nellie and (8) Carl.

Kelly Hawkins, born 1868, married Oma Triplett. They had seven children: (1) Laura, (2) Ben (3) James Calvin born, 1900 married Millie Keller (4) Marcus Dow born 1903 married Dora Hendrix (5) Bloom born 1906 — married Cora Hendrix (6) Lilly born 1910 — married Fred Hodges (7) Angeline born 1913 — married Willie Minton and (8) James Hade born Dec. 21, 1915 and married Ella Hamby.

Greene A. Hawkins was born Sept. 26, 1869, died March 10, 1951 in Wilkes County and was buried in the Hawkins family cemetery on Elk Creek. He was married to Lizzie Hendrix March 13, 1898 in Wilkes County. He had seven children; (1) Jessie born 1900 (2) Thomas Carl born May 10, 1902 — died April 3, 1966 in Wilkes County and was buried in the Hawkins family cemetery on Elk Creek (3) Mattie born 1904 (4) Sallie born 1906 (5) Hugh H. born Feb. 4, 1908, died April 2, 1941 in Wilkes County and was buried in the Hawkins family cemetery on Elk Creek (6) Kermit born 1910 and married Cordia Hamby and (7) Katy born 1913.

Mary A. Hawkins was born 1873 and married Sidney J. Barnett on Jan. 21, 1892 in Wilkes County. She had one son I.T. Barnett born in Wilkes County and later moved to Boone, N.C.

Annie Hawkins was born 1876 and married Dickson Hendrix, son of Wilson Hendrix, February 27, 1897 in Wilkes County. She had one child, which died an infant.

Thomas M. Hawkins was born December 3, 1879 and died March 14, 1958 in Iredell County. He is buried at Mount Zion Baptist Church Cemetery on Stony Fork. He married Ila Welborn, daughter of Geroge W. Welborn and Mary J. Hendrix Welborn, on January 21, 1903 in Wilkes County. He lived at Darby until 1919 and moved to the Mount Zion Community on Stony Fork Creek and lived there until his death. He had eight children: (1) Vergil, who died an infant (2) Ottie Viola, born March 13, 1905 in Wilkes County and died December 17, 1961 in Forsyth County. She is buried at Mount Zion Baptist Church Cemetery on Stony Fork. (3) Leona Mae was born May 24, 1907 in Wilkes County and married Walter Bryan. (4) Nevada was born September 16, 1909 in Wilkes County. She married R.L. Berrier and has two children, Becky and Steve. (5) Gladys Mary was born September 16, 1912 in Wilkes County. She married Edgar McNeil and has eight children: Violet, Gwyn H., John, Clark, Pat, Stanley, Muriel and Earl. (6) Myrtle was born November 15, 1914 in Wilkes County and died as an infant. (7) Thomas Casper was born

July 26, 1916 in Wilkes County. He married Annie Anderson and has two daughters; Etta Lee and Bobbie. (8) Jewel Texie was born April 23, 1919 in Wilkes County. She married Arvis Hamby and has five children: Clarence Everett, Cassie, Jewel, Caroline and Clinton.

Ninnie Hawkins was born 1885 in Wilkes County and died July 28, 1963 in Wilkes County and is buried in the Hall Cemetery on Elk Creek. She married Luther Sanford Triplett, son of Had Triplett, August 27, 1903 in Wilkes County and had three children: (1) Jasper Lawrence born 1094 and now deceased (2) Dan Rome born March 22, 1906 in Wilkes County, died May 30, 1972 in Wilkes County and buried in the Hawkins-Triplett Family Cemetery on Elk Creek. (3) Nelia Paralee was born May 29, 1909, in Wilkes County, died November 22, 1981 in Wilkes County and is buried in the Elk Baptist Church Cemetery. She married George Franklin McNeil.

Sources: Wilkes County marriage and birth records, grave stones, the family *Bible*, personal knowledge and memories.

— Bobbie Hawkins

A.B. (ASHUR) HAYES
646

The Reverend A.B. Hayes was both teacher and preacher. He began his teaching career as early as 1913, at which time he became one of the first teachers in the newly organized Mountain View Institute. Mr. Hayes taught many years. In a recent article concerning the life of Mr. Hayes, it is stated:

"In 1917, Mr. Hayes was principal of the Baptist Home School, a two-teacher school located in the Mulberry community. Miss Flossie Henren was the other teacher. There was only one room; therefore, both teachers and all the students worked in the same room. The next year a new building was completed and each teacher had his own room.

"In 1920-21 the Reverend A.B. Hayes was my teacher. He was no stranger in the community as he was currently serving as pastor of Baptist Home Church. Mr. Hayes was one of Wilkes Counties leading teachers in the rural schools. He taught school for more than forty years and he was a missionary Baptist minister for fifty years.

"On the first day of school, Mr. Hayes emphasized the importance of good behavior. I distinctly remember his saying, 'Friends made in school will last as long as you live . . . a thousand friends have not one to spare . . . make the best use of your time for you have no time to lose.' He was real good in penmanship and every day he would write on the blackboard some sentences. His good penmanship inspired many students to improve their handwriting.

"Mr. Hayes took an active role in helping organize Mountain View Institute and Junior College. According to my information, he sold some land and gave the money to the school. At the time of his death he had many friends in Wilkes County. My life, and no doubt the lives of many others, has been enriched by knowing him."

Ashur B. Hayes was born in Wilkes County

A.B. Hayes.

to Pressley and Docie Hayes on July 7, 1877 and died October 4, 1955. He was married to Molly Harrold and this union was blessed with several children, some of whom are living in 1977. He received his teacher training at Fairview College, Traphill, North Carolina.

Sources: "Life of A.B. Hayes," an article by Wake Tinsley.

— Wake Tinsley

CHARLES CLAYTON HAYES
647

Charles Clayton Hayes was born on October 9, 1881 before midnight, and Ida Huffman was born after midnight and before dawn on October 10, 1881. They were born on adjoining farms and were married when they were nineteen. The first year of their marriage, my mother went barefooted and they lived on a small place about one-half mile south of where Purlear Post Office is now located.

My father, Charlie Hayes, as he was called, worked for Jim Huffman, his father-in-law, on the farm for awhile and then moved to the old Purlear Post Office. The house that we lived in was about three hundred yards west of the existing Post Office where there were approximately three stores. The place was named Loafersville, because the young people gathered there on rainy days and when the ground was too wet to work in order to pass the time and for entertainment.

The house where C.C. Hayes and his wife, Ida Huffman Hayes, lived was on the bank of the much-traveled road and it was in the days of the horse-drawn vehicles. A camp lot, as it was called, was just beyond the barn and people would spend the night at the Hayes house and were given breakfast and a bed for twenty-five cents a night. At this location nine children were born, as follows: Nettie H. Hayes who

Charles Hayes Family First row: L to R: Mrs. D.C. (Nettie Whittington, C.C. Hayes, Ida Huffman Hayes, Burl Hayes. Second Row: L to R: Mrs. Wayne (Aline) Yates, Dr. Wm. C. Hayes, Clyde C. Hayes, Tom W. Hayes, Kyle Hayes, Mrs. Archie Lee (Lucille) Osborne.

married Duel Whittington and taught school for forty years in Wilkes County, along with her husband, Duel; Burl Hayes who married Maggie Dancy and after her death, Mabel York (Burl was in the hardward business most of his life, and he and two of his brothers operated the Hayes Hardward for approximately thirty-seven years); Kyle Hayes, who married Margaret Smithey (Kyle has practiced law for more than fifty years and is engaged in various businesses); Tom Wake Hayes, who married Bonnie Mast and taught school and was in the hardware business with his brothers; Clyde Hayes who married Ella Mae McGlamery, and practiced law in the firm of Hayes & Hayes for approximately forty-five years; Thelma who died at age of six months; Lucille, married Archie Lee Osborne and who before marriage worked in the health office in Wilkes County (she has owned and managed real estate since the death of Archie Lee); Aline H. Hayes, married Wayne Yates (Aline worked in the Wilkes County Clerk's office for more than thirty years during the time her father was Clerk of Court, during the time Miss Cora Caudill was Clerk and with her husband during the years he was Clerk of Court); Dr. William C. Hayes, the youngest in the family, married Lois Cannoy and has been engaged in the general practice of medicine for more than thirty years with his office in Wilkesboro.

C.C. and Ida lived at Ida's old homeplace from 1920 until her death on February 22, 1956. C.C. died on May 6, 1970. After the death of Ida Hayes, C.C. Hayes was married the second time to Jenny Reeves.

Until 1925, my father ran a store at various places and my mother stayed at home and raised the family. However, we farmed rather extensively for that time, or at least the writer thought so, because they would have some-thing for us to do on the farm regardless of the weather.

About 1923, C.C. Hayes went to work in North Wilkesboro, managing a hardware store on Tenth Street for C.E. Jenkins and continued there until 1927. When he was a candidate for Sheriff in 1926 against W.B. Somers, the candidate was chosen by convention. After an all-night convention, W.B. Somers was the nominee and was elected, although C.C. Hayes had more delegates pledged to him than anyone else when he came into the convention.

He served as Superintendent of the Roads in Wilkes County until the state took them over in 1931. Charles then went back to Jenkins to work and served on the Board of County Commissioners for two or more terms. He was elected Clerk of Superior Court in 1934 and served 16 years, retiring in 1950. During those years he went back and forth to town to work and Ida managed the farm and kept the family going.

At this writing all of the children of Charlie C. and Ida Huffman Hayes are living except Thelma.

Sources: Personal knowledge.

— Kyle Hayes

THE CHILDREN OF DUFF and BESSIE HAYES

648

The children of this couple, Helen, Robert and Arlie loved and respected their parents and are grateful for their guidance, love and attention. They grew up in the Purlear community and are graduates of Millers Creek High School.

(1) Helen Bernice, born 18 April 1919, married R.W. (Bill) Nichols 10 Dec. 1939. She is a talented seamstress and homemaker and assisted her husband in operating a small chicken and cattle farm. During 1960-70 she was employed as a substitute teacher. While working for Lovette & Welborn, Bill established a route in Ashe County where he made many customers and friends. He continued as route salesman for Lovette Egg Company and Holly Farms until a blood clot forced the amputation of a leg, at which time he retired. They are faithful members of Arbor Grove Methodist Church and have held many positions in the church. Helen and Bill have three daughters:

(a) Jane Marie attended ASU and is a retired office employee of Lowe's Hardware. Jane, her husband Dean Hincher, and their two sons, Richard and Bradley live in the Hays community. (b) Sharon Anne, a graduate of ASU, has taught at C.C. Wright School for 14 years. She is married to Kenneth Severt and they have one son, Nicholas Duff. (c) Joyce Lynn, a licensed realtor, attended UNC at Greensboro. She is married to Clint Marsh and they live with their daughter, Kristina Lynn, at Reidsville, N.C.

(2) Robert Kenneth Hayes, born 23 Sept. 1921, and Berta Mae Rhodes of Elizabeth City, N.C. married 30 May 1945. They came to Wilkes to live after Robert was discharged from the Navy in November, 1945. Robert has operated Serve-U-Grocery for 37 years. They both held offices in the school PTA and Robert was a Boy Scout leader for several years. They have been active in the functions of their church, Millers Creek Methodist. Robert was on the building committee when the present building was constructed and is currently serving as trustee and adult coordinator. Mae was employed five years by the Wilkes County Welfare Department. She is a charter member of the Wilkes Genealogical Society and edited the Society's Bulletin nine years. Robert and Mae have three sons:

Left to right: Arlie G. Hayes, Helen H. Nichols, Robert K. Hayes.

(a) Robert Kenneth, Jr. (Kenny) earned an AB degree in Psychology from Davidson College, MPA and PhD in Early Childhood Development from UNC at Chapel Hill. He attended the University of South Florida and is currently teaching at Venable School in Buncombe County. Kenny and Mary Lance, who are divorced, have one son, Christopher Eugene.

(b) Carl Steven received an AB degree in Economics from Davidson, MBA from Wake Forest and has earned the designation of Fellow of the Life Management Institute and Chartered Life Underwriters. He is vice-president of J.M.I.C. Insurance Company in Raleigh, N.C. His wife, Barbara, daughter of Dr. and Mrs. Albert Edwards of Raleigh, taught at Wilkesboro before they moved to Raleigh in 1981. They have three children, William, Martha, and Allison. (c) Neil Vance received a BA degree in Education, and M.Ed. from UNC at Chapel Hill. He is employed by the Burlington City Schools where he teaches physical science and is computer coordinator. He is married to Karen Knox, daughter of Dr. and Mrs. James Knox of Ravenwood near Millers Creek. Karen is a pharmacist at the Alamance General Hospital in Burlington.

(3) Arlie Gilbert, born 21 Nov. 1923, and Nina Christine Byrd, daughter of Mr. and Mrs. E. Frank Byrd of the Fairplains community, were married 12 July 1942. After his service in the Navy, Arlie attended Clevenger Business School and has managed ''R.D. Hayes & Sons'' since 1946. They are active supporters of their church (Arbor Grove) and community. Arlie is a director of the Millers Creek Branch of the Northwestern Bank and is assistant postmaster. Christine attended ASU and is employed on the administrative staff of Wilkes General Hospital. They have three children: (a) Gary Kent holds a BA degree in Psychology from UNC at Chapel Hill. He is Personnel Manager of Stouffer's Foods. His wife, Jerrye Fredrick Hayes, a registered nurse, is the daughter of Mrs. John Nichols of Millers Creek. They live in Aurora, Ohio with their two sons, Mark and Greg. (b) Arlie Gilbert, Jr. (AG) graduated from NCSU in Raleigh with a degree in Psychology. He was an Air Force pilot for six years and is presently a pilot for Republic Airlines. His wife, Susie Pardue Hayes, is a graduate of ASU. She is the daughter of Mrs. Paul Pardue of North Wilkesboro. A.G. and Susie live in Los Vegas, Nev. and have two children, Drew and Amanda. (c) Libby is married to Lewis Avery; they have one son, Michael, and live in Mooresville, N.C. Libby attended UNC at Greensboro and is a supervisor of microfilming for Duke Power Company in Charlotte, N.C. Lewis is from Hickory, N.C. and is a salesman for Luden Candy Company.

Sources: Family knowledge.

— Mae R. Hayes

son Robert Wayne Hayes born September 1, 1933 who married Ruby Campbell; and a daughter, Mary Reena, born September 18, 1936, who married William Grady Millsaps.

(2) Charles Edmond, born September 23, 1910, married Lillie Belle Johnson April 14, 1933. They had two daughters, Betty Jane, born March 18, 1935, who married Manuel Robert Lackey; and Jetty Louise, born May 15, 1938, who married Mack Wiles.

(3) Vertie Mae, born October 13, 1915, married James Fred Barnette, February 13, 1934. They had four children: Roy Claude born July 20, 1935, married Nadine Brown; Charles Clifford born December 13, 1936, married Bertha Jean Lutz; William Franklin born June 13, 1940, married Judy Donnely; and Vertie Marie born August 29, 1950, married Carl Edwin Moser.

(4) Robert Sanford, born October 8, 1914?, married Ocie Mae Barnette. They had Mary Ann, born December 2, 1940, married Daniel Kerley; Robert Gary born January 15, 1948, married Mima Jean Fox. Robert Gary was killed in Vietnam 10 January 1969.

(5) Brady Lee born February 5, 1917, married Willia Mae Tevepaugh. They had Dexter Lee born January 3, 1947, married Margaret Hagerman; and Willie Maudine born May 2, 1948, married Roy Ray Miles.

(6) Rayford Lenz born December 23, 1918, married Dorothy Matilda Barnette March 1, 1946. They had James Lynn born December 5, 1946, married Charles Michael Williams; Alvin Rayford born March 14, 1948, married Judy Coral Hiatt; Judy Ann born March 19, 1950, married Earnest Donald Varner, Jr.; Marcia Ellen born March 7, 1954, married Richard Wayne Varner; Timothy George born January 10, 1959.

(7) Stella Ree born July 2, 1920, married John Dickson (Junior) Costner, December 27, 1939. They had Martha Sue born September 27, 1941, married Kenneth Marlow Anderson; Helen Marie, born June 7, 1946, married Rex Lee Church; Phil Dickson, born June 19, 1951.

(8) Roy Parks, born December 23, 1925, married Hilda Ruth Mitchell, April 12, 1952. They have two children: Roy Michael, born May 25, 1954 and Cynthia Darlene born December 15, 1957, married David Greggery Livingood.

Sources: Personal knowledge, family members, *Bible* records, gravestones.

— Martha Anderson

Harold Hayes.

Justices of Peace held important positions in early days of our County. They appointed county officers such as County Commissioners, Sheriff, etc., and held court, which was about the equivalent to our County Court today.

Uncle Harold was elected by first popular vote of Wilkes County for County Commissioners; he was secretary to County Republican Party and Township Chairman for many years, and held many other civic positions. Harold Hayes pledged his allegiance to the Governor of North Carolina as a Justice of Peace during the Civil War, and after those tragic years, he also pledged his loyalty to the new Union.

Harold Hayes was a Baptist by faith and was a deacon and Church Clerk of Liberty Baptist Church for many years. He also gave land on which the church now stands. It has been told many times by several of his children, grandchildren, and great-grandchildren that Harold Hayes boasted of his record as a Justice of the Peace for more than 50 years of not having the high court reverse any verdict that he had already made on a case. This record shows what sound judgment he must have had, and why he was so well respected by his neighbors and friends.

Harold Hayes was married twice, first to a daughter of Jacob Estep, who died shortly after their child Isabel (Lizzie) was born. Lizzie died after she was grown, from an epidemic of typhoid. He later married Genetta Marlow January 14, 1858, and raised three children: Edward B., born July 12, 1859; Melver Loyd, born Sept. 10, 1862; and Ida Louellen, born Feb. 10, 1872.

Harold Hayes died April 18, 1914 at the age of 87 years, and he is buried at Liberty Baptist Church Cemetery on a hill which overlooks his old homeplace and a community he loved so much.

Sources: .Personal research.

— Don Hayes

FERTLE LEE ROY HAYES
649

Fertle Lee Roy Hayes, son of Edward, married Effie Campbell November 11, 1906. They lived in the Brushy Mountain community where he was a farmer. Roy died May 22, 1950. He is buried at the old Bethany Church cemetery, where he was a life-long member and a deacon. Effie died February 5, 1974 and is buried beside her husband.

They had the following children: (1) William Clyde, born March 30, 1909, married Eula Onita Milsaps November 14, 1930. They had a

HAROLD HAYES
650

Harold Hayes was born in Wilkes County, North Carolina, December 31, 1827, son of Henry Horne Hayes II, and wife, Frances Johnson Hayes. He was the fourth child of a family of thirteen children. Harold, or Uncle Harold, as he was commonly called by friends and kinsmen alike, was well educated for this era, and his education was self-taught.

Harold Hayes was appointed Justice of the Peace for Wilkes County about 1860, early in his life, and held this position for many years.

HENRY H. HAYES
651

Henry Horne Hayes was born near Hunting Creek in Wilkes County, North Carolina November 15, 1796, son of Henry Hayes I and Keziah Hayes, who were one of the first Hayes families to settle in Wilkes County. Henry Hayes I is thought to have been born around 1750 somewhere in Virginia or Granville County, N.C., and settled in Wilkes County about 1779. Henry H. Hayes II was one of the younger children of a large family, of which almost all could read or write. For this period of history, it was rare to have over one or two in a family that could read or write, and in most families not any member could. His father, Henry I, was a County Justice, which was an important position in the early days of our county, and they elected county officials, passed on roads and other matters that County Commissioners now do. Henry I also was a farmer and owned a considerable amount of land. He died when Henry II was only nine years old, thus making a hardship on his mother and the younger children who had to run the farm.

Henry Hayes II grew to be a rather good looking young man and was well respected in his church and community, and at the age of 22 he married Frances (Franky) Johnson on December 19, 1818 in Wilkes County. Frances was the daughter of William Johnson and Mary Parks. William Johnson was born in Fauquier County, Virginia, and served in the Revolutionary War from Wilkes County, N.C. Henry and Frances Hayes lived on Hunting Creek near the old Peter Moore Mill place and later on Brushy Mountains near what is now known as the Dr. Newton farm. On this land he engaged in farming and commerce, and raised a large family of 12 children as follows: (1) William Parks, born Jan. 20, 1820, married Mary Puggy Moore; (2) James Harrison, born Jan. 23, 1823, married Elizabeth Estep; (3) Mary or (Polly), born Dec. 26, 1825, married Wilson Moore; (4) A. Harold Hayes, born Dec. 31, 1827, married 1st — Estep, 2nd wife, Genetta Marlow; (5) Keziah, born Jan. 11, 1829, married James Moore; (6) Sarah or (Sac), born 1831, married Alexander Parker; (7) Martin, born 1833, died 1854, buried Estep Cemetery, single; (8) Henry H. III, born Oct. 1836, married Emaline Cook; (9) Francis R., born 1839, married George Thornburg, Sr.; (10) Elizabeth, born 1838, married Quiller Williams; (11) Levica or (Lucy), born 1844, married 1st Ephriam Cook, 2nd husband George Thornburg, Jr. (12) Martha Evelyn, born 1848, married Presley A. Mullis.

Francis (or Franky as she was called) Hayes, wife of Henry II, died in Wilkes County December 14, 1857, and she is buried beside her son, Martin, in the shade of a big spruce pine on green hill-top, overlooking Dr. Newton's farm. This cemetery is known as the Estep Cemetery now, and is believed that Martin Hayes, son of Henry and Frances Hayes, to be the first buried there.

After the death of his wife, Henry II was left with one small child of six, and several teenage children. With this burden on his mind, he sought and felt the need of a companion. In the matter of a few months he met and married Elizabeth Holland with whom he lived for the remainder of his life. There was no issue to this marriage.

Henry Hayes lived to a ripe old age of over 86, when he died in the Brushy Mountain Community of Wilkes County, a place he loved so much, and where he left many descendants. He is buried at Liberty Baptist Church Cemetery.

Sources: Personal research; Family Records.

— Don Hayes

HENRY H. HAYES
652

Henry Horne Hayes was born near Hunting Creek in Wilkes County, N.C. on November 15, 1796. He was the son of Henry and Keziah Hayes, who was one of the first Hayes families to settle in Wilkes County. Henry Hayes I is thought to have been born around 1750, either in Virginia or Granville County, N.C., and to have settled in Wilkes about 1779. Henry H. Hayes Jr. was one of a large family. Henry I was a county Justice and a farmer. He owned a considerable amount of land. He died when Henry II was only nine years old.

Henry H. Hayes II married Frances Johnson on December 18, 1818. They lived on Hunting Creek and later moved to Brushy Mountain. On his land in Brushy Mountain, Henry was engaged in farming and commerce. He also raised a large family of thirteen children here. Frances Hayes, wife of Henry II, died on December 14, 1857, and was buried beside her son in the Estep Cemetery. After the death of his wife, Henry II was left with one small child of six and several teenage children. He met and married Elizabeth Holland, with whom he lived for the rest of his life. Henry H. Hayes lived to be eighty-six. He is buried at Liberty Baptist Church Cemetery, where he was a member.

Harold Hayes was the fourth child of Henry Horne Hayes and Francis Johnson Hayes. He was born on December 31, 1827. He was appointed Justice of the Peace in Wilkes County about 1860. He held this position for many years. Harold Hayes was married twice — first to a daughter of Jacob Estep, who died shortly after the birth of their first child, Isabel (Lizzie). He later married Genetta Marlow on January 14, 1858, and raised three children. They were: (1) Edward B. born on July 12, 1859, (2) Melvin Loyd, born on September 10, 1862, and (3) Ida Louellen, born on February 10, 1872. Harold Hayes died on April 18, 1914, at the age of eighty-seven and is buried at Liberty Baptist Church.

Edward B. Hayes, first son of Harold Hayes, was a farmer, a deacon of his church and a respected member of his community. At age twenty he married Mary E. Hendren, daughter of Ambrose E. and Charlotte Hendren. To this union these six children were born. (1) Gordon, born on November 9, 1881. (2) Cora, born on December 17, 1883. (3) Fertle LeRoy, born on April 3, 1885. (4) William Noah, born March 2, 1887. (5) Bertha, born on October 30, 1888. and (6) Philo Jones, born November 5, 1894. Edward died at an early age of forty-nine. Mary, his wife, survived him for twenty-seven years. They are both buried in the Old Bethany Baptist Church Cemetery.

Sources: Personal knowledge, interviews with family members, family *Bibles*, and gravestones.

— Martha Anderson

JAMES HENRY HAYES FAMILY
653

James Henry Hayes was born July 9, 1894 and died June 6, 1979. He was the son of William Parks Hayes (1853-1904) and Barthena Barnette Hayes (1853-1930) of the Hunting Creek community. He was the grandson of George Washington Hayes and Mary (Polly) Riddle Hayes.

James Henry Hayes married Esther Felts on December 29, 1928. She was born February 19, 1902, the daughter of Newton M. Felts (1869-1936) and Ida Jarvis Felts (1870-1947). To the Hayes union was born three daughters: Aline M. Hayes, born September 25, 1929, married Rex W. Whittington. They have the following children: Sandra Jean, Susan Diane, Richard David, and Janie Lynn; Beulah M. Hayes, born April 12, 1931, married Carl Wood. They have the following children: Glenn, Ronnie, and Janet; Rowena B. Hayes, born June 3, 1939, married Ray McNeil. They have two children: David and Vickie.

James Henry grew up on the Little Brushies and attended Hunting Creek School. He joined the United States Army in 1911 when he was seventeen years old. He remained in the army through World War I, and he trained recruits in Texas during the war. After two four-year hitches in the army he joined the Merchant Marine for about eight years.

In 1927 he took a job in Winston-Salem in the lumber business. He met Esther Felts from the Mt. Pisgah community of Wilkes County. They were united in marriage and returned to Wilkes County to live in the Oakwoods Community. They later moved to the Fairplains Community.

James Henry joined Forest Furniture Company as a finishing room foreman in 1929 where he worked until World War II.

He joined the Merchant Marine again and served on many different ships during the war and until his retirement in 1960. He traveled around the world visiting many foreign countries after the war. He made numerous pictures of points of interest and shared many experiences with his children, grandchildren, and friends.

James Henry Hayes and his wife and children were faithful members of Fairplains Baptist Church. He also served as a deacon.

From his retirement in 1960 until his death in a Veterans Hospital in 1979, James Henry and Esther Hayes traveled a great deal. They visited their children annually in Delaware and Nevada. They also visited relatives and friends in California, Tennessee, Maryland, and Virginia as often as possible. He was always ready for a trip to the mountains or down to the Little Brushies and Hunting Creek. He loved people very much and never saw a stranger. He was a great conversationlist and story tell-

Seated: L. to R: James Henry and Esther Felts Hayes. Standing. L. to R: Beulah Wood, Rowena McNeil, Aline Whittington.

er. He could talk for hours about his travels all over the world.

He spent a great deal of time in later years in the Veterans Hospital where he underwent surgery many times.

Esther Felts Hayes grew up on a small farm in eastern Wilkes County. She attended school in eastern Wilkes and after finishing school, she taught school for some time. She later moved to Winston-Salem and took a job with Hanes Hosiery. After her marriage, she became a homemaker and raised three beautiful girls. She had to assume the major responsibility for their early development while James Henry served his country.

Esther Felts Hayes still lives in Fairplains where she attends church regulary. She has also found time to visit in Hawaii twice in recent years. Once with her daughter, Aline, and once with her daughter Rowena. She visits her daughter, Beulah, in Delaware regulary. In her spare time she visits friends in the church community and with relatives in eastern Wilkes County.

It has been said many times that James Henry Hayes loved to travel. This love has spread to his wife and children. If Esther Hayes

loves to do anything better than visiting relatives and friends, it must be working with flowers. She grows and maintains beautiful plants, flowers, and shrubs around her home in Fairplains. She also has a nice garden each year where she grows her vegetables for fresh consumption and freezing.

Sources: Family *Bible,* Interviews with family members, Personal knowledge.

— Rex W. Whittington

THE JOHNSON JAY HAYES FAMILY

654

The Johnson Jay Hayes family are descendants of Joseph Washington Hays who settled with his wife, Ann Grant and two sons in the Purlear community after 1850. John Lee Hayes was born there and upon his marriage to Sarah Julia McNiel, established his own home in the same area. The spelling of the name was changed about 1905. Julia was the daughter of Franklin and Rebecca McNiel, the latter a granddaughter of the Rev. George McNiel who was a chaplain in Cleveland's Regiment in the

American Revolution. They had nine children: Minnie (Mrs. J.P. Phillips), R.D., Charles Clayton, Thomas Norman, Johnson Jay, Joseph Franklin, James Madison, Daisy (Mrs. Claude McNiel).

Johnson Jay was born Jan. 23, 1886. The father of these children had no formal education but mastered reading and writing. His wife was qualified to teach so education was important in the household though there were no funds. At 17, Johnson borrowed $15.00 to go to Whitsett Institute near Greensboro where he could receive an education preparatory for college. Dr. W. T. Whitsett founder of the Institute, secured employment for the youth so that he might complete the two year course. Later Dr. Whitsett's daughter, Carrie Brewer, would marry Hayes' eldest son, Hadley. The certificate of graduation enabled Johnson to teach and he was employed in the Mendenhall community south of High Point. This six-month job coupled with low pay would not support him and led to his resignation.

In 1907, at the insistence of his brother, Tom, Johnson entered Wake Forest Law School where he was graduated in two years. He began practicing law in North Wilkesboro and served as solicitor for 12 years riding the circuit on horse, buggy and train. In 1927 he joined Brooks, Parker and Smith, a prominent law firm in Greensboro where he moved his family. Four months later he was appointed judge of the Middle District of the Federal Courts. He served thirty years and then held partial retirement status until his death in 1970.

The interest in education did not diminish, and he served as a trustee of Wake Forest College for many years. He worked diligently for the removal of his Alma Mater to Winston Salem and took pride in watching it grow from a small regional college to a nationally recognized university.

In the 1960's his interest turned to the community college movement as he was ever mindful of the cost and struggle of his own college years. His efforts with the state legislature and the citizens of Wilkes County were the moving force that saw the establishment of Wilkes Community College. He believed every student who had the desire should have the opportunity to to to college.

Johnson was married in 1911 to Willa Virginia Harless. She was the daughter of Dora Britts and David Anthony Harless of Ripplemead, Virginia. Mrs. Hayes has been active in the North Wilkesboro Woman's Club, Garden Club and the Wilkesboro Baptist Church. She gave birth to six children: J. Hadley, Johnson J. Jr., Hayden B., Willa Jean (Mrs. J. Thor Wanless), Carol (Mrs. Marion Elliott) and Rebecca (Mrs. Robert C. Hubbard).

Throughout their marriage, they have been staunch Christians and supporters of their church. Judge Hayes taught the Men's Bible Class in the First Baptist Church of Greensboro and in the Wilkesboro Baptist Church where it was broadcast until his death.

In his later years, Judge Hayes compiled a history of Wilkes County entitled *The Land of Wilkes.* He also authored an Autobigraphy and a *Genealogy of the McNiel Clan.* The efforts

Johnson J. Hayes.

were expended so that future generations might share his never-ending pride in family and community which are our heritage.

Sources: Personal knowledge.

— Willa Jean Wanless

JOSEPH ALLIE HAYES
655

Joseph Allie Hayes was born June 9, 1910 at Purlear, N.C. to J.N.H. and Carrie Belle Eller Hayes and was one of a set of twins, the other twin being a girl, Annie Belle, now Mrs. J.G. Church, living at Purlear.

J. Allie started school at Bells' View Elementary School at Purlear and after finishing there went to Millers Creek High School for two years and on to Wilkesboro where he received his diploma in May 1930.

He was active in sports, being an all-star basketball player and star track man as well as taking part in chorus and other school activities. In the fall of 1930, he entered Wake Forest College where he was in school for the next five years, finishing with a degree in Law (LLB) in 1935. During his years there he played football and was on the track team. He was also active in a debating society, worked many long hours to help pay for tuition, room and board, besides all the hours in the classroom and at study. J. Allie was the first Demon Deacon to wear the long scissor-tail coat and top hat to lead the Wake Forest College band and could he ever step high! He really put on a half-time show when the Deacons played football.

After graduation in 1935 at Wake Forest and passing the State Bar Examination, he opened a law office in North Wilkesboro, N.C.

J. Allie was married to Doris Elizabeth Bum-

garner, daughter of Rev. J.L.A. and Margaret Patton Bumgarner, in July 1934. They became the parents of four children: E. Caroline Hayes (Bentley), John Alan, Joseph Allie II, and Hamilton Hale Hayes. They lived at Millers Creek, N.C. until 1945 when they purchased a home on the Brushy Mountains where they still reside.

In 1950 J. Allie Hayes ran on the Republican ticket and was elected to the office of State Solicitor in the 17th Solicitorial District of North Carolina and started serving in that job on Jan. 1, 1951. He started prosecuting the Criminal Dockets of the Superior Courts in five counties, Wilkes, Yadkin, Davie, Mitchell and Avery. Later when the district was changed (1970), he had four counties which were Wilkes, Yadkin, Ashe and Alleghany, comprising the 23rd District. He ran for office seven consecutive terms and was elected each time, the term of office being four years. He retired from office in 1975 soon after his re-election for the seventh term.

During his years of campaigning for the Solicitor's position, he had great support from his party and from many, many others as well. One of his staunchest Republican supporters was our youngest son, Hale (though too young to vote) who never missed an opportunity to come to the aid of the GOP, and particularly his Dad. On one Sunday morning during the Sunday School hour, when Hale was only 6 or 7 years old, the teacher, Mrs. Annie J. Brookshire was teaching the lesson on how Jesus came to save the Gentile peoples of the world as well as the Jews. Turning to the class she asked "Since we are not Jewish people, what are we?" Hale jumped to his feet immediately and said, "Mrs. Brookshire, I don't know what you are, but I am a Republican!!" Needless to say, this story made the rounds of quite a number of Republican get-togethers.

Hale was stricken with polio in August 1953 when he was 12 years old. He spent four years in hospitals, completely paralyzed and dependent upon the iron-lung, rocking bed, and chest respirator and dependent upon other people for all of his other needs, as he could never recover from paralysis. His mind was sharp and he studied until he finished high school and received his diploma with his class. Later he studied for the ministry and was licensed by the Baptist Church. Before his death he spoke at several churches in the county and at First Baptist in North Wilkesboro where he was a member.

J. Allie has been associated with the Baptist Church most of his life, having been a member

J. Allie and Doris B. Hayes.

of New Hope at Purlear in his earlier years and until after his marriage. He taught the Men's Bible Class at New Hope from about 1937 until 1945. After moving to the Brushies, he and family moved their membership to First Baptist, in North Wilkesboro where he taught one of the Men's Classes. Since Mr. J.H. Whicker's death, he has taught his class of senior adult men.

Caroline was married in 1959 to Dr. Ralph L. Bentley. They have three children and live in Statesville, N.C. Joseph Allie II married Shirlene Church and they have two children. They live in Winston-Salem. John Alan remains a bachelor and lives at home on the Brushies.

J. Allie has always been an avid sports fan and for many years has played golf for recreation. Since his retirement in 1975, he has played on almost every occasion that has presented itself to him.

He says "The Lord has been good to me and for that I am most thankful."

Sources: First-hand knowledge and information from J. Allie Hayes.

— Doris B. Hayes

JOSEPH NEWTON HAMILTON and CARRIE BELLE ELLER HAYES

656

Joseph Newton Hamilton Hayes, known as "JNH" or "Toon" for short, was born at Purlear, N.C. on August 12, 1869, to William Jasper (Bill) and Mary Caroline Roberson Hayes. Bill was a hardworking and honest citizen in his community and thrived in all his endeavors. In later life he lost one of his legs, but that didn't slow him down too much. "Toon" lived with his parents until he was 17 or 18 years old, being the oldest of eleven children. While living with his father, he worked on the farm and in the family businesses.

In 1891, my father, J.N.H. Hayes, was married to Carrie Belle Eller, the daughter of Cleve and Amanda Elizabeth McNeil Eller who were residents of the Purlear community. Sometime after their marriage they went to live in Virginia where my father worked in the mercantile business. After a year or two there he moved the family back to North Carolina to a home on Cole's Creek near Purlear which he had purchased from his brother, Floyd Obediah (Obe) Hayes. He often worked away from home to provide for his family while they lived and farmed in Purlear.

Six boys and two girls were born to this union: Walter W., Edgar E., Mable Hayes Walsh, Richard R., Cecil C., Thomas Truman, and last of all twins, Joseph Allie and Annie Belle. Walter W. Hayes worked in Winston-Salem for the Southern Railway for a long period of years; Edgar E. Hayes was with Forester Beverage in North Wilkesboro until retirement; Mable H. Walsh now resides in Winston-Salem; Richard R. Hayes, deceased, operated a country store at Purlear — this store is still kept by his widow, Edna Lovette Hayes and son Dale; Cecil C. Hayes, deceased, was a carpenter and cabinet maker; Thomas

Truman, retired service station operator, lives in Purlear; Annie Belle (Mrs. J.G. Church), homemaker, lives in Purlear; J. Allie Hayes, retired lawyer and long time North Carolina Solicitor (D.A.), lives on the Brushy Mountains, Route 1, Moravian Falls, N.C.

Joseph Newton Hamilton Hayes, my father, died April 4, 1912, at the young age of 43, and Carrie Belle Eller Hayes, my mother, died Oct. 1, 1957, at the age of 82. They are buried in the beautiful cemetery at Arbor Grove United Methodist Church near Purlear, N.C.

Sources: Family records and personal knowledge.

— J. Allie Hayes

JOSEPH WASHINGTON HAYES

657

Joseph Washington Hayes (Wash) was born in Iredell Co., N.C. 27 Feb. 1825, the son of William and Matilda Current Hayes. His paternal grandparents were Soloman and Mary Hayes.

William, Matilda, and all of their children except Wash left Iredell County about 1942. William may have died before 1850 because Matilda and the children show in the records of Hawkins Co., Tenn. and he is not listed with them. In 1860 they are in Overton Co., Tenn. where they remained.

Wash married Ann Howard Grant 23 Jan. 1845 at the home of her father, Robert Grant, in Iredell County. They lived in Union Grove until shortly after 1850 when Wash purchased about 500 acres of land on Coles Creek in the Purlear community of Wilkes County from the heirs of Simeon Eller.

The years before the war were probably quiet and uneventful. Like his friends and neighbors, Wash was busy developing and farming the land. He also operated a government distillery — apple brandy seemed to be their specialty. Apparently he was a good manager and provided well for his family.

And then came the Civil War. Wash did not believe in slavery, was against secession and had the courage to stand by his convictions. There are many letters and records attesting to his "trials and tribulations" during the war. He tells about a Union Meeting at the "Revis Muster Grounds now Millers Creek when a company was organized to protect ourselves against the conscription laws ... and to keep the home guards from arresting men and sending them off to the army ... Gov. Vance sent a regiment of soldiers in on us ... they killed several and captured nearly all the rest ... they kept us under guard at Wilkesboro 'til they got about 200 men and marched us to Raleigh ... some of us were sent to the Army at Missionary Ridge ... they kept us in what was called Bull Pen Prison (those who would not join the Confederate Army) about four months 'til the battle came on and they had to give back to the Yankees ... they turned us loose and carried us back with them ... I got a chance to run away (as they called it) to come home to see what had became of my family and property ... the home guard run in on me and I would not surrender and in trying to get away, they shot me and put me in a wagon and hauled me to Dr. Calaway then the Examining Doctor and he told them it would not do to carry me on and I give him a deed to my land to give me a furlough for 60 days with the understanding that he was to attend to me and keep my furlough prolonged 'til I got able to be sent off ... in the fall of 1864 before the last furlough was out they sent three home guards to take me to camp. As I was not able to walk they let me ride my mule and as we was goin on I whirled my mule in the road and left them ... I went to Irdell into a naborhood of union people and stayed 'til February 1865 when I went through the lines to Knoxville, Tenn ..."

Copies of the medical statement signed by

Joseph Washington Hayes.

physicians, R.F. Hackett and James Calloway, and a letter signed by George H. Brown, then a banker in Statesville, N.C., formerly clerk of court in Wilkes County, who was at the Revis Muster grounds meeting verify some of the above testimony. There are numerous affidavits, etc. which relate more of his experiences during the war and his service to the Union Army.

In 1868, Joseph Washington Hayes was elected sheriff of Wilkes County. When his two years expired, he declined to run for another term and returned to farming, etc.

In 1870 Hays Arbor (now Arbor Grove Methodist Church) was established by Mrs. J.W. Hayes, assisted by a circuit rider from Iredell County, Benny Weisner. It was located about one-half mile from the present church on land owned by J.W. Hayes. Many of his descendants are buried in the beautiful cemetery there. However, Wash who died 5 Oct. 1912 and his wife who died 10 June 1899, are buried in the cemetery at Millers Creek Methodist Church (formerly Friendship) because a cemetery had not been started at their church. A son, Isaac Newton and a daughter, Cassie, are also buried at Millers Creek.

J.W. and Ann Grant Hayes were the parents of five children: (1) Isaac Newton, a Union Army soldier, married Frances Jane Crowson and they had 8 children: John Numa who was born in the old Wilkes County Jail while his father was deputy sheriff and the family were living in the jail at that time, Charles Clossie Hayes, Lual, Jettie, Myrtle, Ninnie, William Roby, and Margaret Neutie. (2) William Jasper married Mary Caroline Roberson (see his sketch). (3) John Lee married Sarah Julia McNiel and they were the parents of Minnie Magnonnie, Robert Dixon, Charlie Clayton, Thomas Norman, Johnson J., Joseph Franklin, James Madison, Daisy Ann, and Dewey who died in infancy. (4) Cassandra Jane (Cassie) married Millard Grant and they had one daughter, Dorcas. (5) Laura Ann Regina (Lottie) married J. Miles Stout. Their children were Rachel Annie, William Charlie, James Richard, Louisa H., Addie Virginia, Isaac Newton who died in infancy, Cassie Leona, Evelyn Gertrude, Ina Naomi, Carlie Johnson, Bessie Jane, Harley Thompson, and Della May Stout.

Sources: Wilkes County Wills & Marriages, family records, etc.

— Mae R. Hayes

MELVER LOYD HAYES
658

Melver Loyd Hayes was born on September 10, 1862, during the struggle of the War Between the States. He told that as a boy he saw Stoneman and his men ride through ransacking and destroying. M. Loyd Hayes was the son of Harold Hayes and Genetta Marlow Hayes of the Brushy Mountain Community in Wilkes County, North Carolina. Their home still stands near Liberty Church, where he was a deacon and faithful member.

Loyd Hayes was active in civic life, doing what he could for his neighbors and community. He was also a Justice of the Peace, like his father and great-grandfather before him, a farmer and a orchardist.

Melver Loyd Hayes.

M. Loyd Hayes was married November 30, 1884 to Martha Jane Johnson, his second cousin. She died at an early age of 39 years on July 10, 1902, leaving seven children with the oldest being only 17 years and the youngest 2 years. M. Loyd Hayes, along with the help of his older children, raised a family that anyone could be proud of. Loyd Hayes, although a young man, never remarried. He often said that he loved his wife and was dedicated to her memory. He died in a peaceful sleep during the night of December 15, 1943.

Children born to Melver Loyd Hayes and Martha Johnson Hayes were the following: (1) Getty, born Sept. 14, 1885, died May 18, 1887; (2) Pedia Catherine, born June 10, 1887, died March 7, 1969, married Joel P. Tedder; (3) Lela, born Oct. 16, 1888, died Sept. 1909, married Jim Davis; (4) Jeter

Pritchard, born Nov. 25, 1890, died Nov. 10, 1960, married Dora Mae Hendren; (5) Goldie Magile, born April 27, 1893, died Nov. 1973, married John Parks Robinson; (6) Clarence, born March 20, 1895, died Nov. 1974, married Emma Lenora Walker; (7) Infant, born April 14, 1897, died April 27, 1897; (8) Grace Jenetta, born March 10, 1898, married Dewey Fletcher; (9) Theodore Roosevelt, born Aug. 24, 1900, married Dale Kathleen Redman.

Sources: Personal research

— Don Hayes

R.D. and BESSIE HAYES
659

Robert Duff Hayes was born near Purlear 18 August 1893, the youngest child of William Jasper and Mary Caroline Roberson Hayes. As a young man, he worked for his father on the farm, in lumber, government distillery, grocery store and grist mill.

Duff married Bessie Rebecca Nichols, the daughter of David Vance and Sarah Julia Bumgarner Nichols, on 25 June 1918. Before her marriage, Bessie taught at one of the early schools, Bell's View, which was located between Purlear and Millers Creek on Bell's Knob. This land is owned today by Joe Wilson. Although she was a life-long member of New Hope Baptist Church she was an active supporter of Arbor Grove Methodist Church and taught Sunday School there for many years. She loved the outdoors and gardening was her hobby. She was noted for having the earliest and best garden in the community every year. She was an excellent cook and always had an abundant supply of canned and frozen food from her garden on hand.

Duff was quite industrious and with a very helpful mate, he was a successful farmer and merchant. He founded "R.D. Hayes and Sons" a grocery store and service station at Millers Creek in 1940. His oldest son, Robert, opened the store and operated it the first two years. He recalls that a neighbor who ran a garage, Rell Caudill, was his first customer at the store. Robert left Wilkes to work at Edgewood Arsenal, Edgewood, Md. and after a few months, enlisted in the Navy. His brother, Arlie, managed the store until he entered the Navye in 1944. Duff and Bessie kept the store going until they returned.

Duff was an agent for Durham Life Insurance Company for thirty-two years and won several awards for salesmanship. During 1928-29, Duff, Burl Hayes and Bill McNeil had the local dealership for one of the early automobiles, the Whippet.

He played an active role in the building of the first gymnasium at the old Millers Creek School which was dedicated to Wilhelmina Triplett, the daughter of his good friend, Dr. W.R. Triplett.

Duff was a devoted member of Arbor Grove Methodist Church, the church which evolved from Hays Arbor originated by his grandmother, Ann Howard Grant Hayes, in 1870. He started the building fund for the present church building, served on the building committee, and held many offices in the church

R.D. and Bessie Hayes.

through the years. He took great pride in the beautiful cemetery at Arbor Grove where so many of his friends and relatives are buried.

Bessie and Duff are remembered by many neighbors and relatives who were the recipients of their bountiful kindness and assistance during times of illness and stress.

Duff died April 30, 1978 and Bessie January 3, 1981. They are buried in the cemetery at Arbor Grove United Methodist in the same area where they were born and spent their lives.

Duff and Bessie Hayes were survived by three children, Helen, Robert and Arlie, all residents of Wilkes County.

Sources: Family Bible, family memories and knowledge.

— Mrs. Helen H. Nichols

RACHEL L. HAYES
660

Rachel L. Hayes, wife of William Lewis Carroll, was the daughter of Charles and Aley Lewis Hayes. She was the great-granddaughter of Richard Lewis of Virginia and Moses Waters of Wilkes County. According to a will written Oct. 7, 1835, Moses Waters was a Wilkes County resident, having seven daughters and three sons. His daughter, Hannah born 1791, married Jacob Lewis born 1783, son of Richard Lewis. Their daughter, Aley was born in 1821 and was married July 31, 1841 to Charles Hayes, born 1818, of Caldwell County. He was the son of John and Millie Medaris Hayes. They lived near Lenoir and had seven children: Rachel, Sally, George, Charles, Rice (moved to Buncombe Co., N.C.), Ransom, and Alfon, Ransom Hayes gave the land where Boone is located. He and his wife, Sallie Greene, had ten children and he died there in 1868.

The Wilkes County 1850 census records Charles Hayes and Aley Lewis Hayes' children as follows: Rachel, Jacob and Joel. Rebecca was not listed on this census. In his will of July 2, 1868, Charles appointed Rachel as executrix of his estate and apportioned $500 for her sister Rebecca's education, also a colt, weaned; and a cow and calf. He requested that Rebecca get common good learning.

Rachel L. Hayes Carroll's grand-daughter, Eula Carroll Cowles, remembers her as being a large woman. She would sit in the kitchen and drink her coffee with lots of cream — said she liked a little coffee in her cream. She had three strokes and one day she had a stroke and threw her coffee out over the floor. Neighbors remember that she carried feed for the mules in her apron and they followed after her.

This Rachel Hayes Carroll was the mother of P.Gasaway Carroll and is referred to in the ancestry of his daughter, Norma Carroll Collins.

Sources: Wilkes County Wills and census schedules, and family knowledge.

— Norma C. Collins

Walter Alphonso and Doss N. Hayes.

WALTER ALPHONSO HAYES
661

Walter Alphonso (Fon) Hayes, son of William Jasper and Mary Caroline Roberson Hayes, was born 9 July 1878 at Purlear. He was married to Arvey Ladosky Nichols (Doss), daughter of Abraham Anderson and Nancy Bishop Nichols. Doss was born 9 July 1882. To this union were born ten children: (1) Dessie Emily was born 1 Dec. 1899 and died unmarried 29 Nov. 1945. (2) Lessie Mae, born 3 May 1901, married Grady Albert Canter and they were the parents of Edwin Jones, William Grady (Pete), Wilma Ruth, Mildred Yvonne, Reginald Hayes and Jay Canter. (3) Avery Anderson was born 24 Dec. 1903 and died in June 1946. He had one daughter, Peggie Choate. (4) Rhuel Roosevelt, born 22 Oct. 1904, died 13 Dec. 1981, was married to Sallie Lovette and their children are Wanda, Archie, Gwenda, Shelby and Bill. (5) William Gazie died at birth. (6) Jettie Elma born 14 Sept. 1909 married William Lester Eller. No issue. (7) Muncy Russell was born 10 May 1912 and is married Florence Reavis. They had John Walter, Shirley Claudine and Susie. (8) Troy Balmer, born 16 Jan. 1916, married Dora Caudill. They have one daughter, Linda Jean. (9) Massie Dare, born 6 May 1918, married Edward McNiel and they had two children, Gary Wade and Pamela Ann McNiel. (10) Lawrence B., born 1 Aug. 1921, died 31 Dec. 1979, married Ethel Parker and they had one son, Larry Bradford Hayes.

Shortly after Fon and Doss were married in 1899, they moved to Crandull, Tenn. where they lived until 1910. During that time Fon worked at the band mill. In 1903 Fon's left leg which had been injured when he was young, became infected and he returned to Wilkesboro and entered the hospital run by Dr. White and his leg was amputated. While recovering from the operation, Fon carried the mail at Purlear until he was able to return to his family in Tennessee. He continued working at the band mill there until it closed.

In the fall of 1910, Fon, Doss and children along with her brother, Arthur Nichols and his family started their journey in covered wagons back to Wilkes County. They camped along the way and the trip took about three days. Back at Purlear Fon and Doss started building their home on the land that was given to Fon by his father and grandfather. He started farming, did carpenter work, and worked on the railroad which was being contructed at that time. Later he was appointed postmaster of the Purlear postoffice and served about thirteen years in that capacity.

Doss took care of the home, looked after the farm with the help of the children, milked cows, made and sold butter to supply the needs of the family. Her greatest contribution to the community was giving aid to the sick. The night was never too dark, too cold or bad for her to answer a sick call. She assisted the doctors in many of the births in the community, often staying away from her family two or three days at a time.

Fon was a strong politician and an active supporter of the Republican party. He and his wife were interested in education and were both life long members of Arbor Grove Methodist Church.

Although Fon suffered continuously from the amputation of his leg and a persistent and severe allergy condition, he never lost his great sense of humor. Their home was a gathering place for relatives and friends, especially on Sunday afternoons when the house would be full to overflowing. Several members of the family played musical instruments and everyone joined in singing for hours on end. When the weather permitted, children and adults alike (Fon included) played outdoor games, kick the can, hide and seek, etc. In the summer there was a swimming hole to enjoy. Doss was a wonderful cook and some of the visitors always stayed for supper. Occasionally Fon would bring out a special treat, his homemade apple cider.

Walter Alphonso Hayes died 29 April 1957 and his wife died 16 April 1962. They are buried in the cemetery at Arbor Grove United Methodist Church.

Sources: Family *Bible* and memory of family members.

— Mrs. Dare H. McNiel

WASHINGTON MUMFORD (BABE) HAYES
662

"Babe" Hayes was born in Wilkes County on March 25, 1886, to William Jasper and Mary Caroline Roberson Hayes. He died October 15, 1941. He was killed in an accident while cutting timber near his home. He and his wife, their son and two of their sons-in-law are buried in the Arbor Grove Methodist Church cemetery in the Purlear Community. The Church was established around 1870, by "Babe's" grandmother, Annie Grant Hayes with the help of Circuit Rider, Benny Weisner.

"Babe" met his wife, Essie Viola Holcomb, while working in a factory in Elkin, N.C. They were married June 6, 1918. She was one of ten children born to William McKinley Holcomb and Rosie Belle Fender Holcomb on March 6, 1897, in Thurmond Community of Wilkes County.

Most of their married life was spent on their farm in the Purlear Community which was part of the original W.J. Hayes Property. There they worked, farmed and made a living for their family of five children. In addition to farming, Babe did other part-time work including the WPA during the depression years.

He was an honest, kind and good natured person that held his family close in good times and difficult ones. He left his family values and principles that were priceless.

Essie had the upbringing of the younger children all on her shoulders when "Babe" died. She saw many trying times but she had great faith, deep courage and inner strength which she drew on. She was a fine and wonderful mother, a gentle, kind person. She was very talented. She could sketch and draw almost anything or anyone and was very skilled in handicrafts of all kinds. She did much of her own pattern designing for clothes she sewed for her family and others. Her sewing brought in extra needed income for her family when the children were growing up. She died

Washington Mumford and Essie Holcomb Hayes.

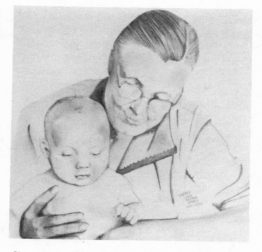

Sherry Foster Dancy (baby) and Essie Holcomb Hayes.

on March 10, 1970, four days after her 73rd birthday.

"Babe" and Essie were proud of their offspring and the children, grandchildren and great grandchildren are indeed proud of their heritage. Many of the skills and traits of "Babe" and Essie are carried on in the family.

One granddaughter, Sherry Dancy, insists that it was through her grandmother that her own artistic ability came and it was this that influenced her career in Art and Media. She graduated from A.S.U. with a B.S. in Art and M.A. in Educational Media. One of the pictures included with this article is one that Sherry sketched from a photograph of her and her grandmother when Sherry was a baby.

The children of "Babe" and Essie: (1) William Jasper Hayes, December 5, 1920 — April 8, 1959. Never Married.

(2) Mary Belle Hayes, married Lester Jones Johnson, son of Pinkney M. and Elzora Church Johnson. They live at Millers Creek, N.C. Their five children are: (a) Washington Matthew Johnson, Distribution Mgr. Lowe's Food Inc., married first to Barbara Ann Love; two sons: Kelly Matthew and Kevin Leslie; second marriage to Rebecca Ann Jarvis; one son: James Walter. (b) Lester Jones Johnson Jr., Mgr. Lowe's Hardware, Huntsville, Ala., married Gloria Ann Whittington; one son: Rickey Dale. (c) Gary Benjamin Johnson, Receiving Clerk, Lowe's Food, Inc., married to Brenda Joyce Hanks; one son:Derrick Mark. (d) Katherine Yvonne Johnson, graduated from W.C.C., married Joe S. Church; two children: Crystal Dawn and Amanda Rene. (d) Timothy Jasper Johnson, self employed in lumber business, married Rene Edminston; no children.

(3) Dicie Mae Hayes married Thomas Walter George who is deceased. Dicie is an inspector for R.J. Reynolds Co. and lives in Winston-Salem, N.C.

(4) Arvie Lou Hayes married Max Aldean Hamby who is deceased, son of Robert and Belle Andrews Hamby. They have four children: (a) Niki Aldean Hamby, works for Burke's Jewelry. (b) Kimi Max Hamby, Fork Lift opr. for Lowe's Foods, Inc., married Kathy McGuire; no children. (c) William Kipi Hamby, Night Receiving Clerk, Lowe's Food, Inc. (d) Kini Hal Hamby, Asst. Mgr. Holly Farms Fried Chicken.

(5) Dorothy Viola Hayes married James Curtis Foster, son of Albert Kelcie and Vivian Mae Watson Foster. They reside in the Purlear Community. Curt and Dot have one child; Sherry Lynn Foster. Sherry is a Media Specialist at W.C.C. and teaches Art. She is working toward her Doctorate in Education. She is married to George Perry Dancy Jr. They have one son, Jeremiah Ross Dancy, born October 5, 1981. At present this is the youngest descendant of "Babe" and Essie Hayes.

Sources: Family records, gravestones, personal knowledge, and family *Bibles*.

— Dorothy H. Foster

WILLIAM JASPER HAYES
663

William Jasper Hayes (Bill), son of Joseph Washington and Ann Howard Grant Hayes, was born 11 July 1849 in Iredell County, near Union Grove. His family moved to the Purlear community in Wilkes County shortly after 1850.

Bill worked with his father and brothers on the farm and in the government which his father operated. He suffered from what was called "White swelling" in his right leg while still a young boy. Despite this handicap, he became a large man, about six feet tall and weighing 200 pounds of more. He had blue eyes and black hair and possessed a good sense of humor, a trait which was handed down to several of his descendants. Bill was an avid reader and subscribed to all the newspapers of the day, including the *Union Republican*. He was a staunch party member and always exercised his right to vote.

According to family records, Bill's family was harassed frequently by members of the Home Guard because his father, Wash Hayes, was a strong supporter of the Union. On one occasion Wash had escaped from the Home Guard and was hiding out near his home when the Guard members came looking for him. Bill, who was only about 15 years old, was threatened when he wouldn't tell them where his father was hiding. They told him to start walking and when they counted to ten, if he still would not reveal his father's hiding place, they would shoot him in the back. They also threatened to hang him.

Bill Hayes and Mary Caroline Roberson, daughter of Walter Roberson and Nancy McGlamery Roberson, were married by the Rev. Richard Jackes in Wilkes County, bond issued 11 Oct. 1868. Mary Caroline was known to her friends as "Pood" — when she had such a pretty name, one wonders how she acquired that nickname!

This couple first lived on a farm on the north side of Lewis Fork Creek. The story is told that Bill Hayes loaned his friend and neighbor, Adney Foster, money for his marriage license and Adney promised to name his first son for him. This promise was fulfilled.

After a year or so, Bill and Pood moved from Lewis Fork to Purlear and remained there the rest of their lives. They lived in what is believed to be the old Roberson homeplace which was probably built by Walter Roberson about 1850-1860. The original part of this house was built of hand hewn logs and is one of the few of its kind still standing in the county today. Through the years, additions and improvements were made and it became known as the Bill Hayes homeplace. After Bill died, the place belonged jointly to his children. His daughter, Lucretia (Cret) bought out her brothers and sisters and she and her husband, Jeff Matherly, spent the rest of their lives there. Cret willed the place to her brother, Duff Hayes, the youngest son of Bill and Pood, and in 1981 it passed on to Duff's youngest son, Arlie Hayes.

Bill continued to suffer with his leg and about 1903 it had to be amputated just below the knee. The family rented a house near Dr. White's hospital, and remained there while he recuperated.

Bill Hayes was a very independent and industrious man. Although times were hard and he was partially disabled, he always managed to provide well for his large family. In addition to farming and operating the distillery, he sold mail order eye glasses, operated a cannery, a gasoline powered mill for grinding corn meal, ran a general store, and cut and sawed lengths of lumber which was sold to make chair legs.

Bill and Pood were the parents of 11 children. Since sketches on some of them appear in this book, comments are being made here only on those who may not be mentioned elsewhere. (1) Joseph Newton Hamilton (Toon) Hayes married Carrie Eller. (2) Floyd Obidiah (Obe) married Ennis Eller. They lived several years in Virginia and Ennis died there. Obe and his two daughters, Mimmie and Grace, returned to Wilkes around 1950 and built a home near Millers Creek. Grace taught school and worked for the Welfare Department several years. They are all deceased and buried at Arbor Grove Methodist Church, Purlear, N.C. (3) Cassie Ann Roxada (Roxie) married Walter F. Pierce. (4) Walter Alphonso (Fon) married Arvey (Doss) Nichols (6) Nancy Gary Jessica (Jess) married John William Doss and they had seven children: triplets, Pearl, Paul and Percy; twins, Forest and Frances; Ray, and Gay. This family lived in Yadkin County and Forest was the only one to make his home in Wilkes. (7) Mary Lovey Lucretia (Cret) married Jeff Matherly — no issue. They lived in Brookford near Hickory, N.C. before returning to Wilkes. (8) Washington Mumford (Babe) married Essie Holcomb. (9) Florence Lenora (DA) married first Cleve Eller — no issue; she married second James T. McNeil and they moved to the state of Washington. They had one son who died young. (10) William Blaine married Dora Miller and they had three children: (a) Pauline married Bill Bryant (deceased) and they had two sons, Jimmy and Jerry. Pauline, a talented artist, lives in the homeplace on the Boone Trail. (b) Brice and his wife, Sarah live at Little Rock Ark. and have four children, Virginia, Billy, Blaine, and Michael. (c) James married Pearl Eller and they have three daughters, Joan, Hester and Jean. They live in Bel Air, Md. (11) R. Duff Hayes married Bessie Rebecca Nichols.

Sources: Wilkes County Wills, Marriages, Deaths, etc.

— Mae R. Hayes

WILLIAM PARKS HAYES
664

William Parks Hayes was born in Wilkes County January 20, 1820, being the oldest son of Henry Horne Hayes and Frances Johnson Hayes. "Billy," as he was called by his close friends, married Mary "Puggy" Moore (1842), daughter of Elizabeth "Big Betty" Moore. She also was the sister of James and Wilson Moore, who married Keziah Hayes and Mary Hayes, sisters of William P. Hayes. William and his wife were both charter members of Liberty Baptist, which was constituted in 1843 by William Goforth and S.P. Smith. He was an active member in this Church, being a deacon and representing his church on several occasions at Associational Conventions.

The following are known children born to William and Mary Moore Hayes:

Elizabeth Louise, May 14, 1843 — Jan. 18, 1911. Married Purvis Pinnix, April 2, 1867. Children: Mary, Martha, Bertha, Delie, Rebecca. Mary was the second wife of Jeff Tedder, and mother of Joel, Silas and Mandy Parker.

Matilda Keziah, Jan. 13, 1847 — Aug. 31, 1892. Married Thos. Jefferson Tedder, Dec. 7, 1876. Children: Carley, Iredell, Thomas, Mary Elizabeth, Christy and Rellie.

William Chappel, May 14, 1854 — Nov. 20, 1938. Married Susannah (Susie) Adams. Children: Tommy, Enie, Realie, Danny, Edward and Minda.

Mary Irene, Jan. 1, 1859 — July 3, 1936. Married Wilborn (Webb) Turner. Children: Pearlie, Dinah, Parris, Dewey and Simion.

The following is copied from an affidavit by George W. Hayes (first cousin and close friend of William Hayes) sworn by him to Clerk of Court for a Pension Application in 1835 by William's wife, Mary Hayes:

North Carolina, Wilkes County, Application No. 1305 —

William Hayes' family life was cut short by the War Between the States. Although he was a middle aged man of 43 years, he entered the War October 1, 1863, and served in Company 'C' 56th N.C. State Troops. He served in this Company as a private until May 20, 1864 when he bravely met his death in a charge on Picket Lines of Union Army at Drury's Bluff, Virginia (which lies between Petersburg and Richmond).

G.W. Hayes, a resident of Hunting Creek Postoffice in said County and State, a person well known to the undersigned Clerk of the Superior Court to be respectable and entitled to credit, whose age is 62 years. Makieth as follows: "I was well acquainted with the said Wm. P. Hayes of said Company and Regiment. I was conscripted at the same time, on or about the 11th day of October, 1863, that the said Wm. P. Hayes was, and was with him placed in Company 'C' 56th Regiment. We came back to this County, (Wilkes) two or three days before Christmas 1863. And stayed here with said Company. Captain White being in command, until on or about between 15th and 25 of January, 1864. When we left with our Company and joined the Regiment at High Point, this State. From High Point we went to New Bern, and thence to Weldon, where we wintered. We were together all the time and messed (ate) together in said Company and Regiment from the time we went out from the County until the said Wm. P. Hayes was killed. He was killed in a picket fight near Drury's Bluff while charging the rifle pits on the 20th of May, 1864. I saw him as we came out from the charge lying dead. I never saw him fall, but I was within a few steps of him and knew that it was him. I passed out. And further that the said Mary Hayes is the identical person she represents hereself to be. And that he has not interest either direct of indirect in the prosecution of this claim. His reason for knowing the fact of the said widows identity is that he lives a neighbor to her and has known her all his life." Signed: G.W. Hayes. August 28, 1885.

Sources: Personal research

— Don Hayes

ISAAC N. HAYNES SR. and DESCENDANTS
665

Isaac N. Haynes, Sr. was born in 1832. The first record we have of him living in Wilkes County is the 1860 census. It is family tradition that he was raised in an orphanage. In 1857 he married Nancy E. Madison of Yadkin County, born August 31, 1839, daughter of John and Rebecca Felts Madison. They were given two negro slaves as a wedding gift from her parents. To this marriage were born twelve children: John, born 1860; James W., born 1862, died 1899; William Augustus, born 1864, died 1937; Charles, born 1867, died 1937; Mary E., born 1868; Cora J., born 1871, died young; Cleo, born 1873; Ida, born 1875; Isaac N. Jr., born 1877, died 1948; Neeley, Vance, and Wiley. He was a Baptist minister and teacher. Rock Creek Baptist Church records show that he preached there occasionally from 1861-1878. In December 1886 he helped establish

Liberty Grove Baptist Church. There is also the possibility that he taught at Liberty Grove School. He died in 1889 and his wife Nancy died January 6, 1923. They are buried at Liberty Grove Baptist Church.

James W. Haynes married Cornelia Jane Pardue, born November 24, 1858, daughter of William and Susan Adams Pardue. They made their home with her parents at Hays. He was a revenue agent and farmer. He died of pneumonia March 1, 1899 leaving my grandmother with five young children to raise. Robert, the eldest, died in 1960 and is buried in West Virginia. John Luther, born March 13, 1889, died November 19, 1955 and is buried at Bethel Baptist Church at Hays. Stella, born August 11, 1891 died July 12, 1973 and is buried at Liberty Grove Baptist Church. Isaac Spurgeon born July 10, 1893, died July 8, 1963 and is buried at The Church of Christ. James S., born November 7, 1898, died March 19, 1899 and is buried at Liberty Grove Baptist Church. My grandmother died July 6, 1934 and is buried beside my grandfather at Liberty Grove Baptist Church.

Isaac Spurgeon Haynes was a veteran of World War I 1918-1919, serving part of his duty in France. He hauled rations on a wagon to the front lines. December 23, 1926 he married Annie Mae Campbell born July 11, 1902, daughter of Carl and Leathia Dowell Campbell. The wedding took place at the home of the Rev. Jimmy Owens of Hays. He too brought his bride to the old Pardue homeplace and there they made their home with his mother. Their children are William Lee born May 7, 1928, Jimmy Carl born July 1, 1933. My father was a farmer and also worked at the American Furniture Co. and Home Chair Co. There are many pleasant memories of two such loving parents.

When I graduated from Mountain View High School in June 1947 I worked for a short time for R.J. Reynolds Tobacco Co. in Winston-Salem. I then moved to Detroit, Michigan, where I remained until 1963. I worked for National Life and Accident Insurance Co. On June 6, 1964 I married Mary Lucy Luffman of North Wilkesboro, daughter of the late Rev. William Bradford and Dollie Richardson Luffman. After moving back to North Carolina I continued my work in the insurance business being associated with Charlotte Liberty Mutual Co. until I retired in 1969 due to health reasons. Mary and I reside at Rt. 1, Hays, and attend Oak Ridge Baptist Church.

Sources: Census records, cemetery markers, family tradition and church records.

— William Lee Haynes

WILLIAM AUGUSTUS HAYNES
666

William Augustus Haynes born August 5, 1864, died April 22, 1937, was the third son of Issac N. Haynes and Nancy Madison Haynes. He was reared on a farm below Liberty Grove Baptist Church.

He married Cornelia Sebastian, born in Wilkes Co., to Zachary Sebastian and Carolyn Hall. Most of the family called her Neeley.

They set up housekeeping in the Rock Creek community just above Rock Creek Baptist Church. He operated a small country store for several years, and then for a few years ran a sawmill. And of course as most everyone else did in those days, farmed and raised the majority of what they ate.

Their children were:

(1) Beulah Grace, September 28, 1900 — October 10, 1969, married Howard Maury; (2) Lola Mae, born June, 1903, married Ambrose Clifton Brewer on April 19, 1924; (3) Paul Homer Haynes, born June 26, 1906, married Clara Wiles; (4) There was a baby boy named Wintie who was less than a year old when he died; (5) Then on January 7, 1909, a baby girl was still-born and a few days later Neeley developed what old folks called "milk-leg" and she also died. That left Will with three small children, ages 9, 7, and 3.

Approximately a year and one half later he married Sarah Liza Molan Redding born March 4, 1877, died December 15, 1955. She was the daughter of Allen and Rachel Vanzant Redding. They were from Newcastle Township.

To this union were born five children: (1) Oma Argile, April 27, 1911, married Ralph Marlow; (2) Lizzie Estelle, December 24, 1912, married Charles Wood on April 9, 1930. He died February 20, 1955. Nine and one half years later on August 21, 1964, she married John T. Kerbaugh; (3) Floyd Preston, August 7, 1914, married Dorothy Caudle; (4) Issac Hoyt, January 16, 1917, married Nellie Blackburn; (5) Walter Ray, September 23, 1919 — April 29, 1972, married Clella Mae Jones.

Lola Haynes and Ambrose Clifton Brewer are my grandparents. (See John Brewer's family heritage)

My husband and I were able to acquire the land from Great Grandfather Haynes' heirs, which contain 13 acres. In 1978 we cleared some of the land and built a house about 100 feet behind where the original house stood.

Sources: Interviews with family members, grave stones, and personal knowledge.

— Tresa Brewer Splawn

KATE McEWEN HEMPHILL
667

Sarah Catherine (Kate) McEwen Hemphill was the daughter of Nannie C. Bledsoe and John Elam McEwen. She was born on December 25, 1874. Kate attended Miss Mamie Barber's Academy, which was a boarding school in Wilkesboro.

On January 23, 1912, she married James Lafayette Hemphill. J.L. Hemphill was a etailer at Vaughn-Hemphill Dry Goods Store, which was located near the present Belk Department Store building on B Street in North Wilkesboro. Kate Hemphill was, for a number of years, secretary for the Board of Education when C.C. Wright was Superintendent of Schools.

To the union of Kate and J.L. Hemphill, one child was born — Hazel Kathryne, on May 24, 1914. Kate was also a devoted stepmother to four other children: Lee Hemphill, Ray Hemphill, Mattie Hemphill Pardue, and Frederick Hemphill.

Hazel Hemphill was married to Hubert Mathis on October 27, 1931. They resided at Route 3, North Wilkesboro in the Windy Gap community. Hazel and Hubert adopted a daughter, Kathy Jannette, who was born on August 4, 1951. Kathy has been married twice, and she is now Mrs. Daniel Morgan. She has three children, Johnny Laws, Jr., Linda Dawn Laws, and Danny Morgan.

Kate McEwen Hemphill passed away on November 27, 1937, and is buried in Mountain Park Cemetery in Wilkesboro. She was a member of Wilkesboro Baptist Church. J.L. Hemphill passed away on November 18, 1949, and is also buried in Mountain Park. He was a member of Cub Creek Baptist Church. Both Kate and J.L. Attended Wilkesboro Baptist Church.

Hubert Mathis passed away on December 29, 1980, and was buried at Cranberry Cemetery.

Sources: Personal Knowledge.

— Hazel Mathis

THE A. GRANT HENDREN FAMILY
668

A. Grant Hendren was born in Wilkes County in 1868 and lived in Wilkes until his death in 1937. He was married to Eugenia Hellard, who was born in 1874 and died in 1920.

Eugenia and Grant had eleven children: Mrs. Effie Bumgarner (1892-1978), Luther (1893-1950), Naomi Smithey (1895-1974), Russell (1897), Della Blevins (1899-1957), Freda Moore (1902), Ruby Benfield (1904-1924), Pearl Johnson (1906), Bradford (1911-1968), Mable (1914), and Clyde (1918-1922).

Grant Hendren, in his earlier years was a blacksmith in the Edgewood community. He also made furniture, cutting timber to make the lumber for the furniture.

For over twenty-five years Grant served as the first County Farm Agent. During his administration he took a great interest in the various clubs for boys and girls. This interest produced winning prizes at county, state and national fairs. He was, as county agent, particularly concerned with apple production and with terracing.

As a result of his many years given to the discharge of his duties as farm agent, he probably knew more people in the county than any other person in Wilkes.

Not only was Grant interested in his special task, but he had great interest in the building up of the communities. He allied himself with such societies and organizations as the Grange (which was first introduced in this state in 1929). He was the first member of the Wilkes Pomona Grange.

He was a member of the Liberty Masonic Lodge #45, and for several years he was its secretary. He was an active member of the Brushy Mountain Fruit Growers Association. Grant was a faithful member of Edgewood Baptist Church where he led the singing. As an active member of the Brushy Mountain Baptist Association, he was an untiring worker in Sunday School. As a Kiwanian and a member of

other similar organizations, he gave unsparingly of his time and money. He left an inheritance to the county of a richer productivity and knowledge of home and farm life. Grant Hendren was a self-educated man.

From a Resolution by the Wilkes County Board of Commissioners for the life and service of Mr. Hendren:

"He made life more livable to all those with whom he came in contact. He literally lived and thought always in terms of better agricultural opportunities for Wilkes. In his passing we have lost a noble and faithful worker whose place will be hard to fill. His energetic and diligent efforts have wrought wonders in Wilkes and will live long after him and be a monument to his memory far better than any of stone or granite. Above all, he was a noble, gentle, sympathetic Christian man whose life was so lived that his reward in the world beyond is assured."

Grant's wife, Eugenia, was a loving and kind homemaker who gave her family a warm and welcome open home to all friends. On Sundays the Hendrens often had many "table settings" as Mr. Grant was famous for inviting folks home for dinner.

After Eugenia's death in 1920, Grant married Mamie Smith Vannoy in 1923. From 1927 until 1939 Mamie was post mistress of the Gilreath Post Office; in 1980 she was the grand marshall for the Apple Festival.

Sources: Journal-Patriot, personal knowledge from Freda Moore, Grant's daughter.

— Jeanne Moore

DANIEL RILEY HENDREN
669

Daniel Riley Hendren, son of Wyatt and Sarah Call Hendren, was born 17th October 1841 in Wilkes County, died 30 March 1926 in Wilkes County, but it buried at Pleasant Hill Baptist Cemetery in Clinton, Anderson County, Tennessee.

He was a farmer, was six feet tall, and had fair complexion and blue eyes. He was twice married.

His first marriage was to Barbara C. Shinliver on the 17 October 1866 in Clinton, Tennessee. They were the parents of five children: John Frank, born 10 October 1867, died 12 November 1871, Charles J., born 1 July 1869, died 29 May 1898, David Knox, born 13 June 1873, Martha Elizabeth, born 4th June 1878, and Mary Catharine, born 6 October 1880, died 17 March 1884.

Daniel R. Hendren served in the Civil War as a Private in Company C, 2nd. Regiment, Tennessee Infantry, as a volunteer. He enlisted 7 August 1861 at Clington, Tennessee for three years. He was captured at Rogersville, Tenn. 6 November 1863, sent from Richmond, Virginia to Andersonville, Georgia, in February 1864, paroled at Charleston, S.C., December 1864, and reported at Camp Parole, Maryland 22 December 1864 and honorably discharged at Knoxville, Tennessee 8 February 1865. He applied for and received a pension for his service.

Daniel's first wife died in 1906. Sometime afterward he came back to Wilkes County,

N.C. and on the 9 March 1919, married Emily Nancy Jane (Staley) Torrence, born 17 April 1877, died 10 April 1945, a daughter of Jacob C. and Mary Ann (Call) Staley. She is buried in an unmarked grave at Fishing Creek Arbor Church, southeast of Wilkesboro, N.C.

Daniel and Emily lived at Call Post Office, where he died. As before stated his body was taken back to Tennessee for burial.

After Daniel died, Emily appeared before a justice on 6 May 1926 and made her declaration as his widow in order to receive a pension for her husband's service in the Civil War.

Daniel and Emily had only one child, Fay Lucille Hendren, born 13th March 1920, Call Postoffice, Wilkes County, N.C., married 12 August 1943, Larence Edward (Edd) Andrews, born 15 December 1919, Boomer township. They still live in the Boomer section of the county. They have three children:

Emily Goldene Andrews, born 18 August 1945, married James Harry Williams, born 15 April 1929, died 3 July 1979. They had a son, Michael Wayne Williams, born 28 March 1975. She and her child live in Caldwell County.

Patricia Diane Andrews, born 22 August 1947, married 9 November 1968 Richard Shelton Poteat, born 4 August 1943. They have a daughter, Christy Diane Poteat, born 7 October 1969.

Nellie Mae Andrews, born 5 February 1953, married Robert Clint Hefner, born 31 October 1951. They have two children: Angela Michelle Hefner, born 3 July 1976 and Gracy Nichole Hefner, born 1 March 1981.

Sources: Personal knowledge, *Bible* records.

— Pat Andrews Poteat

FRANK BYNUM HENDREN
670

Mr. Hendren was born on a farm in the Brushy Mountain Township of Wilkes County, N.C. His first American ancestor was William Hendren who was born in the Province of Ulster in Ireland of Scotch Ancestry. Coming to America as a young man, he joined the pioneers of Wilkes County and soon afterward entered heartily into the struggle for independence.

He was a member of Captain Gilreath's Company in the great battle of Kings Mountain. For his estate he secured a tract of land, heavily timbered, in which is now Brushy Mountain Township and there hewed a farm from the wilderness. From this sturdy ancestry many distinct branches of the family have sprung. The second wife of William Hendren, a Miss Taylor, was the great grandmother of Mr. Frank B. Hendren.

Stephen Hendren, a grandfather of Mr. Hendren, was born in the Brushy Mountain Township in 1897. He spent his life as a planter. The maiden name of his wife was Mary Cook. Her father owned and occupied a plantation in Iredell County and he had numerous slaves.

To this marriage eight children were born and of these children, the father of Frank Bynum Hendren was Ephriam Elbert Hendren,

who also was born in the Brushy Mountain Township in 1836. He located on lands given to him by his father near the old homestead. His success enabled him to acquire adjoining land and he finally bought the old homestead to which he returned and where he spent the rest of his life. He married Rufina Hendren, a daughter of John and Mary Davis Hendren. To this union there were four children born, Frank Bynum being the oldest.

During his early life on the farm, Frank Bynum Hendren attended the district schools. He was also a student at Cedar Run Academy in Alexander Count and at Moravian Falls Academy. In 1888 he graduated in the Literary Course from Wake Forest College and subsequently took up the study of law in the offices of R.F. and C.H. Armfield at Statesville. He was qualified and admitted to the bar in 1895 and was for the next two years in practice at Morganton with J.F. Spainhour. Dissolving that partnership, he moved to Wilkesboro, spending the remainder of his life there and enjoying a constantly increasing practice and prestige. He was associated with the Honorable T.B. Finley until the elevation of Mr. Finley to a Judgeship.

In 1893 Mr. Hendren married Emily Kathryn Campbell. She was born in Vashti in Alexander County, a daughter of William and Adeline (Deal) Campbell. Mr. and Mrs. Hendren were the parents of eight children.

Mabel Hendren (deceased) was a respected and revered teacher in the Wilkesboro and North Wilkesboro schools, teaching first and second generation students. When she was growing up, she wanted very much to become a trained nurse but Mr. Hendren persuaded her to become a teacher. In forty years many students and their parents were very glad she did.

Frances Armfield (deceased) married Ryburn B. Underwood (deceased), an accountant. They were the parents of one son, Frank Dixon Underwood, who served for many years with the U.S. State Department with assignments in Japan, Indonesia and New Guinea. He is now Editor of The Journal-Patriot.

Adeline married William A. Ellis, an engineer with the North Carolina Department of Transportation. They had two sons, William A. Ellis (deceased) and Blair Campbell Ellis, an engineer with Texaco Oil Company and living in Atlanta, Georgia.

Frank Campbell Hendren, the only son, was never married and he continued living at the old homeplace until his death of forty-eight years of age.

Gwendolyn married Aubrey C. Payne (deceased) a merchant in Rural Hall, having met him while teaching in the Rural Hall school. They were the parents of three children — Anthony Hendren Payne, with Shenandoah Life Insurance Co. in Roanoke, Virginia; Clifton G. Payne, a physician in Reidsville, N.C.; and Emily Lyndall Payne, a teacher in Columbus, Georgia.

Mary Hope (deceased) married Gordon Forester (deceased) of North Wilkesboro who was connected with Holly Farms for a number of years. They were the parents of four children — Gordon, Jr. a lawyer practicing in Washington, D.C.; Kay Myers, a teacher in

Kindergarten and pre-school in the North Wilkesboro Presbyterian Church; Susan (deceased) a former nurse living in Washington, D.C.; and Jane Joyce of Sumter, S.C., a teacher in the city schools. Hope was a highly respected and capable teacher in the Wilkesboro school system. At her death a memorial fountain was erected and dedicated in her honor.

Irene married Richard O. Rex, a physician living in Philadelphia, Pa. She trained as a nurse at Bryn Mawr Hospital in Philadelphia. They have two children — Sandra Thornton who has a gift shop in a Philadelphia suburb and Richard O., Jr. who is engaged in the sale and distribution of T.V. commercial cameras in Atlanta, Ga.

Kathryn married Henry Schulz (deceased), a former chemist with Liggett and Myers Tobacco Company, and she lives in Durham, N.C.

Mr. Hendren was greatly admired and respected by his children as well as the general public. At his death he was greatly eulogized by the news media in western and piedmont North Carolina. He was one of the county's most active citizens, serving in many capacities in his church and community. He was a champion of good roads and of every cause that he thought was to the advantage and best interest of his fellow citizens. He died in 1928 at the age of sixty-eight years.

Emily Kathryn Campbell Hendren was a member of a well-known family, a wonderful mother and a valued and beloved wife. She died in 1939 at the age of sixty-seven years.

Sources: Quotes from N.C. Biographies, 1917, obituaries and personal knowledge.

— Gwendolyn H. Payne

JEHUE JONES HENDREN
671

Jehue Jones Hendren was born September 23, 1869 to Enzer and Matilda Hendren in the Bethany Church area of the Brushy Mountains. He married a former pupil, Gertrude Robinson, daughter of John and Delia Robinson in 1899. She was born in 1879 and died in 1977, two months short of age 98. Their children were Ronda, T.J. and Addie, all deceased, Edd and Flossie of Moravian Falls, Nell (Mrs. Charlie German of Boomer), and Ray Hendren of Winston-Salem.

There was little opportunity for Jones to get the education he desired near his home. He was needed for family farm work and the school terms were short. Yet his parents were anxious to help him. In order to do so, they sent him to Vashtie Academy in Alexander County for a few terms. He took along enough food to batch one term at a time. He was a fine student and the instruction provided was excellent; for later when Supt. C.C. Wright offered a county-wide state examination for prospective teachers, Jones passed with high grades.

Jones taught sixteen terms in the Brushy Mountain area. Some names of his little one-teacher schools were Lewis (his first), Parker, Roberson, and others forgotten. Because of health problems and a growing family, he quit teaching and became a surveyor with work

Jehu Jones and Gertrude Robinson Hendren.

that took him over the county. By this time, Jones was becoming known as an outstanding citizen.

Capable, loyal, trustworthy — his word was said to be as good as his bond. Another personal asset was his fine sense of humor that endeared him to many friends. Soon he was granted other responsibilities. He served as Justice of Peace in his township. But his most important work was being for several years a member of the County Road Commission. That unit of service was dissolved when the state took over the roads. Along with the above duties he managed a good farm that provided the needs of his family. About this time apple production was becoming recognized as a valuable crop for the Brushies and he set out two orchards. These were said to be the first in that area.

Jones and his family were faithful members of Bethany Baptist Church. He died May 1,

1952, at the age of 83 and was buried at old Bethany Cemetery.

His children: Ronda Clyde, born 1900, died when he was 19 years old during flu epidemic in 1919.

Flossie Lee Hendren, born May 26, 1902, graduated Mt. View Academy becoming a teacher and taught for 8 years in Wilkes County. She never married and lives on the Brushy Mountain where she is well known by everyone.

Ray Erwin Hendren, born June 27, 1904, had two years college training in Engineering and Surveying, became a surveyor in Shelby and Winston-Salem. He carried the mail in the Brushy Mountain area for eight years before becoming a registered surveyor in Winston-Salem where he now resides. He married and divorced Ruby Beshears of the Wilkes County Area.

Edmond Bryan Hendren, born September

1907, did refinishing of antique furniture then started an apple orchard for which he is now famous. He married Zenna Beshears and they have one child, Carroll Gray Hendren. Carroll was born in 1937, married former Betty Blevins of N. Wilkesboro, and has four children of the home, Greg, Justin, Misty and Chad. They reside on the Brushy Mountains.

Nell Ree Hendren, born May 3, 1910, graduated Wilkesboro High School, became a beautician and worked for four years before marrying Charles Hamilton German, son of James Monroe German of Boomer, North Carolina. They live in Boomer, N.C. and had a dairy farm (Montview Dairy) for years which now is a chicken farm run by their first child, James Monroe German II. He was born February 17, 1939. He was never married and still lives at home. Daughter of Nell and Charlie, Kay Hendren German, born December 20, 1940, married and divorced, working at B & R Sheet Metal, Inc. for 17 years as secretary, now married to Marshall Edward Brooks who works for Northwestern Bank and lives in North Wilkesboro, N.C.

Addie May Hendren, born June 22, 1914, died August 3, 1958. She was a registered nurse in the Methodist Hospital in Dallas, Texas where she lived until she died.

Theodore Jones Hendren, born September 16, 1917, fought in World War II for four years and then came home on Brushy Mountain where he had an apple orchard. He died in a car accident in 1965.

Sources: *Lest We Forget*, 1778-1978 Wilkes County Retired School Personnel. Family *Bible*, newspaper clippings and personal knowledge.

— Kay German Brooks

SARAH HENDREN
672

Sarah (called Sally) Hendren, daughter of William, Sr. and Sarah Mullis Hendren, was born 25 July 1798 in . Wilkes County, died 27 February 1898 and is buried in Bethel Baptist Churchyard in Alexander County, N.C.

Sally fell victim in a love affair with a Henry Hayes and she had a child and named him Oliver. Later she had a child by David Inscore and named him Wyatt Hendren. Both of her sons were reared by her father to be very nice young men. They wanted their mother to live with them so they could take care of her, but before she was middle aged, her mind went blank at times. She would then roam around from one house to another. Sometimes she would lose first her shoes or a bonnet. She was a large, very dark "raw-boned" old woman. She had some education and a brilliant mind.

It is said that Sally's brother, Stephen Hendren once took her to Dr. Calloway, an eminent physician of Wilkesboro. The doctor, after carefully examining her, asked Stephen if she had ever had a severe blow on the head. He said, "Yes, once a limb fell on her head and since that time she has been queer." Sally, after hearing this story said, "It must have been a might d--- long limb, for it hit the whole Hendren family." In her old age she became normal and for many years lived a pious, chris-

261

tian life.

Sally was a stubborn and contrary old woman. She used to sit with her feet soaking in the coldest creek water in the dead of winter, trying to get sick so she could say no one cared for her. Once in her old age she went to a neighbors house with an apron full of puppies and demanded that the children give her their place at the fire, for she and her puppies were cold, it being in the bitter cold of winter. The mother of the children picked up the fire poker and said, "Now, Sally, looka here, this fire is for my children, you just get your pups and git." She went away mumbling and grumbling for her feelings were hurt.

On another occasion, she was at a meetin' at night. The preacher preached and ranted up and down the aisle. The men folk wore mustaches and whiskers. Sally was sitting at the end of the pew. She reached over, got a lighted candle and said to the preacher, "Looka here, God knows and I know you've preached long enough." As she made this statement, she put the candle under his whiskers and singed him good and he quit preaching.

One other time she was at the home of a neighbor. The "revonuers" came while she was there. They went walking off down toward the woods past the barn, poking around behind bushes and looking here and there. She knew where she had seen a small keg of whiskey, so she immediately walked on in front of them a ways, placed her long dress over the keg so the "revonuers" would not find the whiskey.

Oliver and Wyatt Hendren, sons of Sally Hendren, married daughters of Daniel Call, Sr. Oliver married Ann Call and they had children, Solomon, Emily, Irene, Linville, Eli, Oliver, John N., James, Mary, Daniel and Nelina.

Wyatt Hendren, born 30 August 1819 in Wilkes County, died 22 June 1896 in Anderson County, Tennessee. He married 1 December 1841 in Wilkes County Sarah Call, born 15 September 1822 Wilkes County, died 30 January 1888 in Anderson County, Tennessee, Daughter of Daniel and Anna Ellis Call.

Wyatt Hendren moved to Clinton, Anderson County, Tennessee sometime after 1850. He and his wife had six children, the first five having been born before they left Wilkes: (1) Daniel Riley, born 17 October 1841 and whose history will be found elsewhere in this book, (2) Anna C., born 8 July 1843, died 27 May 1855 in a brush fire, (3) Sarah E., born 12 July 1845, died 7 August 1926, (4) James Jefferson, born 28 January 1849, died 20 July 1932, (5) William Pool, born 22 April 1845, died 15 March 1921, (6) Robert Carter, born 30 August 1863, died 24 February 1931.

Sources: Research of Reba Hendren Brice, *Bible* records.

— Pat Andrews Poteat

WILLIAM HENDREN FAMILY
673

William Hendren I, of Ireland settled in Rowan County with his three brothers some time before the Revolutionary War. He was a short stocky Scotch Irishman. We do not know

where his three brothers located, but due to fever in Rowan County, William I moved to the old John Parker farm, Brushy Mountain township, in Wilkes County. He fought in the Revolutionary War and became a staff officer and was honorably discharged at the close of the war. He first married a Miss Taylor from Virginia (our line) and to this union was born nine sons. After their mother died they all left N.C. and went to Kentucky. Only the youngest, William II, came back and settled in Wilkes County.

William Hendren II went to Kentucky when a young man, but returned to N.C. and married Charlotte Ellis. Their children were Jabez, Elsie, Annie, Elbert, Jehu, John, Josiah, William III, and Jessie.

Jabez Hendren was born in Wilkes County, August 4, 1805 and married Nancy Combs. Their children were Rebecca, Charlotte, Edward B., Hix, and Thenia. He died August 27, 1888 and is buried in the Hendren family cemetery near the old home place and near the headwaters of Rocky Creek, Brushy Mountain township, Wilkes County.

Edward Bunyon Hendren was born in Wilkes County, March 22, 1836. He was a successful miller, carpenter, and farmer. He served in the Civil War and was wounded in the Battle of Gettysburg. He served as a Representative from Wilkes in the State Legislature in 1899. He first married Mary E.A.E.M. Queen on March 14, 1861. She was born Sept. 29, 1843. Their children were Vance, Jesse Hix, Lula Mae, William, Lillie, Dora, and Grace. After his first wife died he married Miss Dora V. Roberson. She was born Feb. 16, 1878. They were married on July 2, 1906 and their children were Lunda and Mattie. He died Nov. 5, 1909 and is buried in the Hendren family cemetery.

Grace Hendren was born October 13, 1884 in Wilkes County. She married William Andrew Jennings on June 13, 1906. Their children were Vaughn Edward, Sallie Grace, and Madge Marie. She died Jan. 20, 1959 and is buried in Walnut Grove Baptist Church Cemetery in the Pores Knob Community, Moravian Falls, N.C.

Sallie Grace Jennings was born February 4, 1915, Pores Knob Community, Moravian Falls, N.C. On August 3, 1935 she married John Greene Shepherd and they have three children: John Andrew, Carol Madge, and Robert Neil.

The following is a quote from the book *The School of the Prophets* by the late Rev. W.E. Linney of Wilkesboro. "The Hendrens were noted for their honesty and intergrity and for religious inclinations. Wherever a Hendren of this stock is found today there will be a path leading from his house to the nearest church. They are a sturdy stock, morally speaking, and as dependable and trustworthy a people as live on the earth."

Sources: Family *Bible;* family tradition; grave markers.

— Carol Shepherd

WILLIAM HENDREN, SR.
674

Sometime before the Revolutionary War, a

short stocky young Scotch-Irishman, by the name of William Hendren, came to this country. He first settled in Rowan County. He married Letty Taylor from Virginia, who was a cultured and educated lady. Due to the prevelance of fever in Rowan County, they moved to the Rocky Creek section in the Brushy Mountain township in Wilkes County either just before or just after the Revolutionary War, for William fought in the war with the American Army. He became a staff officer and was honorably discharged at the close of the war.

The farm upon which they lived was adjoined by land of an Oliver Hendren. Oliver may have been a brother or kinsman of William Hendren, but he did not remain in Wilkes County.

William Hendren must have liked the mountains for he lived out his life in them. He taught the women how to weave fine figured coverlets and other fancy cloth.

Sometime near the close of the 18th century his wife died and was buried on a hill near the old homeplace. She left nine sons. It is said they soon became unruly and disobedient and shot holes in fine coverlets and shot the eyes out of pictures on the walls. William, therefore, employed a Miss Sarah Mullis as housekeeper. She was industrious and saving and had plenty of grit. William married her. This did not suit his sons, and as fast as they grew up, they left home and went to Kentucky. The youngest, William, Jr. came back to Wilkes County where he lived and died.

William Hendren, Sr. was a quiet, unassuming man, well educated for his day. He was a loyal Baptist and generally a fine citizen. His marriage to Sarah Mullis seemed to be a happy one. Sarah was tall, dark and very robust, both physically and mentally. She was a devout church member and always attended regularly. She lived to be a very old lady. William died at the age of ninety-two.

The names and births of their children are from the Family Bible owned by their daughter Sarah (Sally) Hendren, as follows:

George Hendren, born 4 January 1790, married Sally Mullis, his first cousin. They had children, William, Nancy Campbell, Rena and Babe.

Peggy Hendren, born 16 February 1792, Elijah Hendren, born 16 February 1794, Ambrose Hendren, born 23 May 1796, married 29 January 1824 Nancy Mitchell, three of whom no further record has been found.

Sarah (Sally) Hendren, born 25 July 1798, whose record will be found elsewhere in this book.

Cynthia Hendren, born 16 September 1802. Cynthia had a son born out of wedlock, whom she named Joel Hendren. The old grandfather and grandmother reared him to be a good citizen. Joel tenderly cared for his mother until she died 2 March 1879. He also cared for his Aunt Sarah for a good many years before she died. Joel married Patty Mitchell and they had children Nancy, Media, Eli, Clem, Crick and Teeler Hendren.

Richard Hendren, born 4 August 1805, was witty and droll. He married Esther Brotherton 21 February 1835 and moved to Iredell County, reared a family and lived to a ripe old age.

Stephen Hendren, born 12 September 1807, married Mary Cook 14 August 1834. They had children, Enzer, Elbert, Jane, Amelia, Alcy, Elliot, Oliver and Vina. Stephen died 4 March 1876.

Solomon Hendren, born 12 September 1807, was a twin to Stephen and they were very much alike. He married Drusilla Williams 7 January 1854, lived and died in Alexander County. They had no children.

Eli Hendren, born 27 November 1811, married Elizabeth Gilreath 31st December 1834 and removed to Tennessee.

Sources: Family *Bible,* Revolutionary records, research by Reba Hendren Brice.

— Pat Andrews Poteat

THE HENDRIX FAMILY
675

Tradition is that the Hendrix families first settled in Delaware when arriving in America, but there is no proof of this statement.

Garrett and Banjamin Hendrix were among the names of the early Hendrix families who settled in Wilkes County, and its parent, Surry County.

On September 9, 1778, Garrett Hendrix, owned 150 acres of land on Stony Fork, and Benjamin owned 100 acres. Their names are listed in the 1782 "Taxables of Wilkes County," the earliest tax list that has been preserved for Wilkes County formed in 1778 from Surry County. Many Hendrix families settled and lived in this area.

Elijah Hendrix was my great-great grandfather, and was born 1792 in Wilkes County. In the year of 1815, he married Drucilla Day, born in Burke County and the daughter of Thomas Day.

Elijah purchased land in the Stony Fork area in 1838, and the deed states "for the sum of five dollars for every hundred acres hereby granted and paid into our treasury by Elijah Hendrix, have granted a tract of land lying on the waters of Stony Fork."

His name appears as a voter in School District #51 in Elk and Stony Fork in the year of 1845. The names of his children who were attending school at that time were: Lindsay, Vincent, Franklin, and Wilson. Later, on the 1850 Census of Wilkes County, the name of a daughter, Nancy, is listed in the household. Elijah may have had other children, as the 1850 Census is the first that lists all members of the household. Isham was given a land grant that borders Elijah Hendrix in the year of 1848 on the waters of Stony Fork in Wilkes County.

Sources: Census film, Wilkes County Court House Records, Land Entry Book Wilkes County 1771-1790, Wilkes County Genealogical Bulletin.

— Irene Hendrix Basey

LENZY FRANKLIN HENDRIX
676

There are many stories that my heart wants to tell of the many happy memories of our Grandpa and Grandma Hendrix, but space does not allow, so I will give the facts and hereafter use the spelling of his name as "LENZY", as this is the way it has been spelled in our family. The name was also given to my brother and then to his son.

Lenzy Franklin Hendrix (1862-1946) was born in the Stony Fork area of Wilkes County, the first child of Vincent H. and Martha Mary Walsh Hendrix.

Lenzy married Julia Ann West, (1859-1937), the daughter of Franklin and Cynthia Holder West. This marriage took place on January 1883 in the home of Franklin West. W.F. Hendrix, as the A.M. and T.B. Walsh and W.S. Hendrix were witnesses.

Hendrix Post Office was named for one or more of the Hendrix families who lived in this area of Wilkes County.

Lenzy lived on top of the mountain which separates the communities of Denny on Elk Creek and Mt. Zion on Stoney Fork Creek. It was here that he had his first country store; located midway between two communitues. He had an orchard that contained many fruit trees. Here, he made a living for his family, although this store was in an isolated area, accessible only by horse or wagon. He was ambitious, and not satisfied with his way of life, and he sought to do something about making a better life for the community. Thus, he convinced the government to establish a post office on Stoney Fork Creek. He moved his store to the property now owned by James Wooten on Stoney Fork Creek, and put the post office there, and it was named for the first postmaster, Hendrix.

Some years later, Lenzy sold this property and moved to the head waters of Stoney Fork, and established another country store, just across from Stoney Fork Baptist Church. This was a fine store. Roots, herbs, furs, leather, dry goods, and foods were among the merchandise he bought and sold. He also, was a craftsman and had a fix-it shop. His work was praised, as very fine, by many people.

In 1904, Lenzy sold his store and moved his family to Clay County. Traveling by wagon to the railroad station and then taking the train to Murphy; from Murphy to Clay County by wagon to their future home. He had purchased land from J.H. Cassanda and his wife, Minnie. The deed states that for Three Hundred and Twenty Five Dollars, he purchased 100 acres of land, more or less.

Here, too, Grandpa had a general store and a mechanically operated mill. The store was built on the curve of the road on a steep embankment. Under the store were "coops" for the chickens and pens built for the various animals that he took in trade for items such as flour, sugar, and clothing that he had in the store.

It was a special treat to visit their home. There were many wonders that existed in the eyes of a child. Grandpa would often operate the mill for my younger brother and me to watch while the corn was being ground. We would stand at the bin and watch the freshly ground cornmeal spill into it — sometimes, putting our hands out to let the cornmeal filter through our fingers.

Family meals at Grandpa's home were special, too, as we all gathered around the beauti- ful hand crafted table that he had made. A large lazy susan covered the top of the table, leaving just enough space for the plates on the lower surface of the table. The food was placed on the lazy susan and we could help ourselves to the various foods that had been placed there by our granny and mother who had helped to prepare it. I would often sneak a look under the table just to watch the cogs as they worked to turn the lazy susan. All of this work was skillfully crafted to make a piece of furniture that was admired by all who had the opportunity to bow their head in prayer of thanksgiving for the food on this table. The children would sit on specially made benches, while the adults had chairs which were made by grandpa, too.

Lenzy Franklin and Julia Ann West Hendrix were the parents of:

(1) Roxie Alice, b. Dec. 27, 1882 — died Jan. 29, 1889 and buried at the Old Mt. Zion cemetery in Wilkes County; (2) Martha Ann Hendrix (1886-1947) married Sam Adkins; (3) Omer Franklin (1889) married Addie Derreberry; (4) John Philo (1891-1938) married Carrie Lee Carter; (5) Leonard Orvil (1894-1949) married Mamie Carter; (6) Mamie Elmira (named for her Grandmother, Elmira Walsh), b. 1900, died 1915 and is buried in Clay County.

Julia Ann West Hendrix died June 7, 1937. Lenzy Franklin Hendrix died December 1, 1946. Both are buried in Clay County.

Sources: Wilkes County court house records, family Bible, family members, Clay County court house records.

— Irene Hendrix Basey

JOHN PHILO HENDRIX
677

John Philo Hendrix (1891-1938) was born in Wilkes County, the son of Lenzy Franklin and Julia Ann West Hendrix, married Carrie Lee Carter, born 1897, the daughter of William Thomas Carter and Margaret B. Greenwood Carter, of Clay County, North Carolina.

From the marriage register, R.J. Coffey, a Baptist minister, performed the marriage in his home, January 17, 1915. R.O. Smith, T.L. Lodin, and L.A. Turner were the witnesses present at the marriage.

When first married, Philo and Carrie lived on Sweetwater, Clay County, where other Carter families were living. After the birth of their first daughter, Martha Inez (named for the wife of Dr. Sullivan), they moved to the Downings Creek area, near the parents of Philo. Here Philo built their home at the foothills of the mountains where the "Double Knobbs" were in view of their farm lands. Philo was a carpenter as well as a farmer, and buildings were added for their various needs. Constructed first was a barn, (that eventually was the storage place for a Model T Ford that Philo bought); then there was the spring house, smoke house and not very far from the barn was the black smith shop where it was fun to work the bellows to make the fire hot enough to soften the steel so he could form it into various shapes that were needed. Many questions would come to my mind as I watched him work, and sometimes I would get "run off" for asking them.

There was a peach orchard in the mountains above our home, and an apple orchard at the foothills of the mountains. Plum trees grew wild, as did the strawberries and many other fruits. Philo like to experiment with the fruit trees and as a result, an apple tree bore one kind of fruit on the bottom branches, and another variety on the top branches. He had learned the art of grafting from other family members. These orchards provided fruit for the family. Mother was always busy and in the fall of the year there would be sliced apples drying on the roof of the buildings. She had a barrel that she used for burning sulphur and would hang a cloth sack containing apples over the burning sulphur. The smell was terrible, but the apples were delicious, and if you ate too many, a stomach ache would result.

In the year of 1933, Philo had the opportunity to come to Indiana. He was an ambitious man and having heard of the rich soil and the opportunities that existed, he came to see. Later in the fall of the same year, Carrie and the family loaded their belongings in a truck that had been hired to move them to Indiana, and joined Philo.

Philo worked hard and enjoyed watching the work of the newly invented mechanical corn picker. He died 5 years after moving to Indiana and is buried in Clay County, North Carolina. A family member described Philo as a hard working, honest Christian man with a high integrity.

John Philo and Carrie Lee Carter Hendrix were the parents of:

(1) James, b. April 13, 1916 — died April 17, 1916; (2) Martha Inez, b. 1917, moved to California and married James Morris Washburn. Their only child died at birth; (3) Willis — died at the age of 3 years; (4) Jarvis Ray, b. 1919 married 1st Martha Cramer and had one son, John Raymond. 2nd he married Ruth and they have one daughter, Connie. They live in Chicago; (5) Margaret Irene, born 1924, married Carl Wilbur Basey and they are the parents of three daughters: (1) Carolyn Sue — married Wayne Allford; (2) Joanna Lynn — Married Kerry Kellermeyer; (3) Linda Jean — married David William Hockett; (6) George Lenzy, born 1927, married Nov. 10, 1946, to Bonnie Ann Kroeckel, his high school sweetheart.

George served in the U.S. Navy from March 1945 to August 1946. A few years later, he joined the Prudential Insurance sales staff, and was promoted to Sales Manager and received outstanding "Manager's Award" for the State of Indiana, the "President's Award", and other high ranking awards from the Company.

George and Bonnie Ann are the parents of one son, George Lenzy Hendrix Jr., born Dec. 1952. He is an architectural designer for WED Enterprisers. The design and engineering unit of Walt Disney Productions.

Lenzy entered Ball State University in the fall of 1971, majoring in Architecture. During the summer of 1972, he worked at Walt Disney World in the Emporium, and after three weeks, he received his draft notice from the U.S. Army, and served as Military Policeman in Barbaria. In 1974, he returned to Ball State to complete the five year course.

He has been involved in many different phases of WED and has most recently worked on the planning of the Mexican and Japanese Pavillions, a part of EPCOT. He lives in Glendale, California.

Sources: Clay County court house records, family members, *Bible* Records.

— Irene Hendrix Basey

VINCENT H. HENDRIX FAMILY
678

Vincent H. Hendrix, son of Elijah and Drucilla Day Hendrix was born 1837 in the Stony Fork District of Wilkes County.

On September 28, 1861, he married Martha Mary Walsh (1843-1880), the daughter of Elberton Kelly and Elmira Walsh. A.B. West and J.W. Boone witnessed the marriage and bondsman was L. Land.

They were the parents of six children: (1) Lenzy (Lindsey) Franklin — married — Julia Ann West; (2) John Wilson; (3) Juliet E., married a Saunders; (4) Nancy L. married a Bishop; (5) Sallie L.; (6) Thomas E. married a Triplett.

When a young man, Thomas E. Hendrix moved to Union County, S.C. and became a supervisor in the textile mills.

Martha Mary Hendrix died at the age of 39 years, 2 weeks, 10 days, and is buried at the Beaver Creek Advent Christian Church Cemetery.

In 1881, Vincent H. married Sarah and they were the parents of the following children: (1) Henry; (2) Mollie; (3) M.B. and (4) Belva.

It is believed that Vincent continued to live in this area of Beaver Creek, and that his children attended the old Whipoorwill Academy. He died in 1915 and is buried at the Beaver Creek Advent Christian Church Cemetery.

Sources: Census film, Wilkes County court house records, family *Bible*.

— Irene Hendrix Basey

W.A. HENDRIX
679

William Arthur Hendrix (3/16/1871 — 12/22/1926) was the first born son of Albert Leondas Hendrix (1/12/1843 — 10/21/1903) and Celia Ann Woodruff (10/14/1848 — 9/20/1920).

His paternal grandparents were Jerome Hendrix (9/13/1818 — 12/27/1869) and Alice Jackson Hendrix (4/20/1821 — 7/26/1914). They were married September 28, 1838, and eight children were born to this union: Emily Hendrix McBride, Albert Leondas Hendrix, William Jasper Hendrix, Alphus Newton Hendrix, James Milton Hendrix, Sarah Jane Hendrix Collins, Mary Plutina Hendrix Ray, and John Derwood Hendrix.

His maternal grandparents were John Woodruff of Surry County and Elizabeth Carter (1822-1913) of Yadkin County. Nine children were born to John and Elizabeth Woodruff: A. Woodruff, Celia A. Hendrix, Charity Caroline Mosely, Sarah Cockerham, A.P. Woodruff, Elizabeth Woodruff, Burch Woodruff, William Horton Woodruff, and Henry Dallas Woodruff.

His maternal great-grandparents were

Albert L. Hendrix.

Moses Woodruff (1800-1855) and Charity Jane Cockerham (1800-1884). Five children were born to this marriage. John T. Woodruff, Rev. Aaron C. Woodruff, Moses C. Woodruff, William W. Woodruff, and Elizabeth C. Woodruff.

W.A. Hendrix and his 10 brothers and sisters: Betty Alice Roughton, John Walter Hendrix, Etta Virginia Neal, Luther Leondas Hendrix, Jettie Petterson, James Decatur Hendrix, Lillie Luelma Woodruff, Charles Woodruff Hendrix, Ila Mae Lewis, and Nellie Bernice Brown, were born at Ronda in a home that he later purchased and lived in until his death. The home is located on the south bank of the Yadkin River on the Ronda-Clingman Road. Originally the home was a two-story log house

Celia Woodruff Hendrix.

W.A. Hendrix Family Front Row: L. to R.: Carrie, W.A., baby Eva, Agnes, Grace. Back Row: L. to r.: Ola, Carl, Worth.

that was built in the 1840s. In 1870, Albert L. Hendrix purchased the home and adjoining land and expanded the log house to include ten rooms, two halls, eight fireplaces, five porches, and a full-size attic. The home is presently owned by Dr. William Henry Davis, Jr., a grandson of W.A. Hendrix and son of Willie Agnes Hendrix Davis Lindsay.

In 1903, A.L. Hendrix sold his home at Ronda to N.W. Fowler and moved to Elkin where he owned a large farm and worked as a merchant.

W.A. Hendrix married Eva Jane Hampton (6/18/1871 — 4/24/1965), the daughter of Dr. Leroy Hampton and Rebecca Madison Hampton of Hamptonville, North Carolina, on December 28, 1892. Following their marriage, they lived in Boonville for a short period of time prior to moving to Wilkes County. In 1909, they bought W.A. Hendrix's birthplace, "Claymont Hill," from A.J. Russell and lived there the rest of their lives.

There were six children born to W.A. Hendrix and Eva Jane Hampton Hendrix who are as follows: Arthur Carl Hendrix, Walter Worth Hendrix, Ola Blanche Edwards, Eva Grace Ashburn, Carrie Cowles Dunlap, and Willie Agnes Davis Lindsay.

There are eight grandchildren: Walter Worth's sons, Dr. William Gay Hendrix, and Walter Worth Hendrix, Jr. Eva Grace had two children: Peggy Jane Hart Parker and an infant son who died shortly after birth. Carrie Cowles had two children: an infant son who died shortly after birth and Mary Cowles Dunlap. Ola Blanche had twin boys: Billy Smith and Jimmy Hendrix Edwards. Willie Agnes had one son: Dr. William Henry Davis, Jr.

The twelve great-grandchildren of W.A. Hendrix and Eva Jane Hampton are as follows: Jane Gray Parker Jones, Lorrie Lynn Parker, Sandra Faith Parker (died at birth), Robin Tamantha Parker Daniel, John Thomas Parker, III, Tracy Rene Parker, Tammy Jane Edwards, James Douglas Edwards, Anna Victoria Hendrix, Eva Jane Davis Felts, William Bryan Davis, and Sandra Lynn Davis.

William A. Hendrix was one of the county's best known citizens. He was a prominent farmer, served as Postmaster of Ronda in early 1900s, and worked as a law enforcement officer for a number of years. He was greatly interested in the advancement of Wilkes County and the expansion of the Republican Party, with which he was affiliated. He was much interested in several fraternal organizations, being a Shriner, a member of the Junior Order, and a member of the K.K.K.

W.A. Hendrix served a number of years in the revenue service and for five years as United States Deputy Marshall, which position he held at the time of his death. When the first good roads commission was appointed, Mr. Hendrix was one of its members, and he served on this board for two years.

Farming was a big business to W.A. Hendrix even though his law enforcement work required his being away from home much of the time. Tenants did much of the work and lived in tenant homes on the 700 acre farm. His oldest son, Carl Hendrix, worked on the farm and served as foreman for his father. The tenants were paid money or food and clothing in exchange for work. Mr. Hendrix did much of the purchasing for his family and also the tenant families. This included clothes for the girls, Mrs. Hendrix, tenant children and families, as well as the staple goods and hardware needed for the home and farm.

Mr. W.A. Hendrix died when he was fifty-five years old; his widow, Eva Jane Hendrix, lived at the home until her death, on April 24, 1965, at the age of nearly 94 years. He and his wife are buried in the Ronda Cemetery.

Sources: Family *Bible,* and family records (newspaper articles, obituaries, photographs, deeds, etc.) of Willie Agnes H. Davis Lindsay and William H. Davis, Jr.

— William H. Davis, Jr.

JOHN E. HINCHER
680

John E. Hincher was born in Wilkes County April 15, 1908 eldest son of James Richard and Sarrah Brown Hincher. He was married February 6, 1937 to Ina Mae Johnson daughter of Ambrose S. and Ora Pendry Johnson. John worked for Home Chair Company for over fifty years prior to his retirement in 1975. He is an active member of Union Lodge NO. 331 of the Independent Order of the Oddfellows. Ina has worked at Wilkes Hosiery and Peerless Hosiery Mills.

Their only child, Loyd Dean, was born June 22, 1938. He graduated from Mountain View High School in 1956. He was a member of the Mountain View Volunteer Fire Department for over 20 years. He has been employed by the Wilkes County Board of Education, Maintenance Department for 21 years. He was promoted to Supervisor of the department in 1979.

Dean married Jane Marie Nichols, daughter of Bill and Helen H. Nichols of Millers Creek, N.C. on October 30, 1961. Jane graduated with honors from West Wilkes High School in 1961 and attended Appalachian State University. She worked for Lowe's Companies for 15 years prior to her retirement in 1977.

Dean and Jane have two sons, Richard Dean born October 7, 1964 and Bradley Scott born November 11, 1968. Richard is a 1982 graduate of North Wilkes High School and plans to attend Wilkes Community College. Bradley is a student at Mountain View Elementary School.

The Hincher's are residents of the Hays area of Wilkes County, where they have lived most of their lives.

Sources: Family knowledge.

— Jane N. Hincher

GROVER CLEVELAND HIX
681

My father, Grover Cleveland Hix, was born September 21, 1888. He was the son of Thomas Cicero and Martha Howell Hix; Martha was Thomas Cicero's second wife. The house where he was born is gone but it was in sight of the grist mill at the Moravian Falls, operated by his grandfather, R.L. Hix and his father Thomas Cicero Hix. In 1890, T.C. built a house one mile east of the falls on highway 18 and moved

Grover and Carrie Hix.

T.C. HIX FAMILY (1907) Standing L to R: Grover Cleveland, James Richard, Joseph White, wife Ida Hix White and baby Elizabeth White; Charles Davis, Walter Renn. Seated L to R: Mary Lizzie, Thomas Cicero, wife Martha Howell Hix, Bettie Belle, Thomas Cicero, Jr. In front: Children of Joseph White, Thomas Lee and Kathleen.

his family there.

I know little of Daddy's early years. He attended Moravian Falls Academy and, for a short time, Trinity College. In 1908, his name was struck from the Methodist Sunday School roster since he had gone to Pocahontas, Va. to seek employment. During World War I, he worked in the shipyards at Portsmouth, Va. and his roommate was Everette Thomas. On December 17, 1922, he married Everette's sister, Carrie Belle Thomas of Jonesboro, N.C.

Daddy and his bride moved to Akron, Ohio where he was employed by the Firestone Rubber Company. I was born there in 1924. The Ford touring car was in vogue and Daddy bought one. He liked to sing and the hit song then was Walter Donaldson's "My Blue Heaven." In later years, Daddy told me that he drove us around in the Ford singing: "Just Carrie and Me, and Gena makes three, We're happy in My Blue Heaven!"

In 1932, when our country was going into the third year of economic depression, Daddy moved us to the T.C. Hix homestead in Moravian Falls. Roosevelt's New Deal was salvation for us and countless other families throughout the land. In 1945, Raymer Oil Co. opened a service station in Moravian which Daddy operated until he retired in 1964. Mother was Postmaster for twenty-five years, retiring in 1968.

Daddy was proud of his family, his religion, his name and his politics. He regularly attended the Methodist Church, taking my brother, my sister and me with him. He continued to go even when he could no longer hear the sermon or the singing. Born during President Cleveland's first administration and named for the President, he proudly proclaimed he was a DEMOCRAT and never missed an opportunity to praise Franklin Delano Roosevelt!

Suffering from congestive heart failure, he died November 12, 1972, about a month before his fiftieth wedding anniversary, and was accorded Masonic Rites at the Moravian Falls

Methodist Church. The little church could not seat all those who came to pay their respects.

Mother is 83 years old. In spite of waning health, she attends WSCS, Woman's Club and garden club meetings. She continues to live in the homestead, the favorite gathering place of the Hix family. They are as follows:

(1) Gena Howell Hix, born July 1, 1924, attended Asheville Normal and Teacher's College and Wake Forest University, married June 12, 1942 Lewis Weimar Elias, Jr. of Asheville. Gena is on the staff of Historic Bethabara in Forsyth County. Lewis is a retired engineer from Western Electric. They have four children: Elizabeth Tim, born September 2, 1943, married June 13, 1964 Larry Morgan Gish, M.D. of Idaho. They have Teresa Ann, born January 20, 1967 and Ellen Elizabeth, born December 19, 1968; Sandra Hix born December 23, 1952, married December 18, 1971 James Edwin Hawley. Jim is vice-president — First Citizens Bank. They have a son James Brian, born August 26, 1976; Frances Carter born January 11, 1954. Frannie is a sales representative for a dental supply company; Lewis Weimar III, born August 3, 1959, married March 21, 1980 Sandra Ellen Zarembo of N.Y. They have a daughter Liane Elizabeth, born July 5, 1981.

(2) William Thomas Hix, born July 16, 1933, attended U.N.C., married August 20, 1960 Martha Jon Blackwelder. Bill is Utilities Supervisor for the City of Winston-Salem and Martha teaches. They have Martha Jon, born January 14, 1968.

(3) Lana Jon, born August 30, 1937, graduated from Woman's College, Greensboro, married July 9, 1961 James Clinton Reavis, Jr. Jim holds an EE degree from N.C. State and is an engineer with a carbon company in Morganton. Lana taught in Moravian Falls and Burke County for a number of years.

Sources: Personal knowledge and family recollections; "Land of Wilkes" by Hayes; Variety Music Calvacade, J. Mattfield; M. Falls church records.

— Gena Hix Elias

J.R. HIX

682

In every community there are leaders who greatly affect progress and growth. J.R. Hix was such a leader. His achievements directly affected all Wilkes County and northwest North Carolina. His career included the things which make a community grow and which benefit its people.

J.R. Hix's career began as an employee of the C.C. Smoot Tannery. Entering business for himself, he became a partner in a wholesale grocery firm.

While in that capacity he became president of the Bank of North Wilkesboro, heading that institution through a long period of growth until he retired in 1960. However, he remained active in banking as Chairman of the Board of Directors until his death.

Mr. Hix was not just a banker; he was also a pioneer in industry. He was interested in increasing the productive power of the area and in providing jobs for the people of Wilkes County. He was a stockholder and official in a number of corporations which have provided many jobs and have added to the general well-being of the area. These included American Furniture Company, of which he was secretary from its organization in 1927 until his death. It has become one of the largest industries in the area and is now known as American Drew, Inc. He was also secretary of Grier Mills and Gordon Mills and was a director in Turner-White Casket Company. All of these firms were assets in the growth of the County.

In his church, Mr. Hix served as Sunday School superintendent, steward, trustee, and Finance Committee Chairman.

In civic life few have equalled or will equal the record of service by Mr. Hix. Probably his most important activity was in the promotion of Wilkes General Hospital, which would serve the hospitalization needs of the people. He took advantage of medical funds to help provide the community with a 100-bed hospital. He was chairman of the hospital's governing board until his death.

J.R. Hix was a man of integrity. He lived by Christian principles in business, civic, church, and social life. He refused to grow old and worked until his final illness. He radiated cheer and was truly an example of a long and useful life. I only wish I could have known J.R. Hix. I know I would have loved my great-grandfather with all my heart.

Sources: Interviews, family records.

— Kathryn Hix

JAMES RICHARD HIX

683

My father, James Richard Hix (1878-1966), was one of the early settlers of North Wilkesboro and his life in a remarkable way parallels the growth of the town, contributing much to the business, civic, and religious life of the community. He was born October 7, 1878 at Moravian Falls, son of Thomas Cicero and Elizabeth Porter Hix. Thomas Cicero was young at the time of the family's removal from Davidson County to Moravian Falls in 1850,

James Richard Hix.

Jessie Ferguson Hix, wife of James Richard Hix.

and his father, Richard Loflin Hix acquired property at Moravian Falls and became a pioneer in the manufacturing industry in Wilkes County where he operated a carding mill and a mill for the manufacture of flaxseed oil and a mill for grinding corn and wheat. His property included the brick house at the crossroads and the mill at the Moravian Falls.

Thomas Cicero Hix was born Feb. 29, 1848 and died Aug. 16, 1922. Elizabeth Harris Porter was born Sept. 12, 1851 in Cabarras County and died Mar. 25, 1880. These two were married May 21, 1873. Their children were: Ida who married Joseph White of North Wilkesboro, Mary Lizzie, and James Richard, subject of this article. Thomas Cicero succeeded his father in the mill business until he sold it to the Moravian Falls Milling Co., after which he engaged in farming his extensive property. After the death of his first wife he married Martha Howell of Davie County. There were five children of this marriage: Charles, Walter, Grover, Thomas, and Betty Bell.

James Richard spent his early years in Moravian Falls and attended the old Moravian Falls Academy. This institution of learning could boast that many of its students became outstanding doctors, lawyers, teachers, ministers, editors, and bankers. His first association with the business world was as a youthful employee of R.A. Spainhour's store then located at Moravian Falls. Later employment was with Absher Hardware Co. at North Wilkesboro and bookkeeper for F.D. Forester and Co. In 1901 he worked for R.C. Vaughan Wholesale Co. in Winston-Salem and remained there for three years. Returning to Wilkes he was employed for some time at the C.C. Smoot & Sons Tannery in North Wilkesboro.

On June 29, 1904 James Richard Hix and Jessie Marvin Ferguson were married at her home in Ferguson and thereafter established a home in North Wilkesboro, living in one of the houses in the residential section of the Tannery property, called "Tanners' Rest". This house was totally washed away in the 1940 flood.

My mother was born Nov. 23, 1879 and

died Sept. 20, 1979 just two months short of her one hundredth birthday. She was also educated at Moravian Falls Academy as well as attending North Carolina College for Women at Greensboro.

My father's first experience in business for himself was in the Vaughn-Hemphill Wholesale Co. in North Wilkesboro, in which he was a partner with R.W. Gwyn and continued there for 23 years. In 1923, James Richard Hix, still an official at Vaughn-Hemphill, was elected president of the Bank of North Wilkesboro, following the death of J.E. Finley. From 1923 until 1960 he served as president of the bank and in 1960 became chairman of the board of directors which office he held through the bank's merger with the North Carolina National Bank in 1962 and until his death. The following words are from the Resolutions adopted by the Board of Directors of the North Wilkesboro unit of the North Carolina National Bank in memory of James Richard Hix:

"Mr. Hix, as he was known throughout his long career, was one of the farmers, designers and builders of the Town of North Wilkesboro and the Wilkes County community. He devoted a very keen mind, a very energetic body, and a charming personality toward the welfare of his town and community. He occupied more positions of trust in his town and community than any other individual in the history of the town. All his activities were directed toward the welfare of his fellow man".

Other business interests of James Richard Hix included being stockholder and director of Turner-White Casket Co. which operated a plant in North Wilkesboro for several decades; secretary of Grier Mills at North Wilkesboro and Gordon Spinning Co. at Roaring River; one of the organizers and served on the board of directors of the corporation which constructed and operated Hotel Wilkes; and in 1927 he was one of the organizers of American Furniture Co. and continued as secretary of that company from that date until his death.

Among his contributions to the civic life of his community: he was one of the founders together with Dr. Fred C. Hubbard of the Wilkes Hospital; chairman of the Board of Trustees of Wilkes General Hospital from the

time of its origination until his death and one of those responsible for the erection and operation of the hospital; served as Mayor and on the Town Board and Board of Education at various times; president of Kiwanis Club and member for 43 years; served a term as trustee of Appalachian State University; served as Food Administrator in the First World War 1917-1918 under President Herbert Hoover; served on the Draft Board in the Second World War under President Franklin D. Roosevelt.

In church life, James Richard Hix held top positions of leadership in the First Methodist Church of North Wilkesboro, having served as Church School Superintendent and as steward and trustee. He was chairman of the church's Finance Committee during the building program, when the new church plant was constructed.

He was a member of the Oakwoods Country Club and was one of the pioneer golfers in Wilkes County. In advanced age, he continued to play the game with exceptional skill.

Through the years three homes were built by my father and mother. Around 1908 a small frame house was constructed on Eighth St. In 1921 a second home was built and a move was made from Eighth St. to D St. In 1966 a retirement home was built in Finlay Park. My mother and father celebrated their Golden Wedding in 1954 and in 1964 had been married for 60 years.

Three children were born to James Richard and Jessie Ferguson Hix: a son, James Richard, Jr. who died in 1929, and two daughters, Virginia Porter and Mary Ferguson. James, Jr. married Mary Virginia Moore, daughter of Mr. and Mrs. James Dudley Moore of North Wilkesboro. Their children are: James Richard Hix, III who married Nona Eutha Spencer, daughter of Mr. and Mrs. J. Ross Spencer of High Point. They have three daughters: Jennifer Elizabeth, Melanie Leigh, Katherine Ann. Daughter of James and Mary is Mary Moore Hix who married James Franklin Dalton, son of Mr. and Mrs. John Baxter Dalton of Asheville. They have two sons, James Franklin, Jr. and Richard Jeffrey.

Virginia Porter married John Thomas Brame, son of Mr. and Mrs. Peter Joyner Brame of North Wilkesboro. Their children are: Virginia Hix Brame who married William Robert Story, son of Mr. and Mrs. T.E. Story of Wilkesboro, Marticia Folger Brame (died 1942), John Thomas Brame, Jr., and Peter Joyner Brame. There are two great-grandchildren: William Robert Story, Jr. and Dorothy Cassandra Story.

Mary Ferguson married William Cameron Marlow, son of Mr. and Mrs. James Richard Marlow of North Wilkesboro and their children are: Mary Jessica, William Jr. (died in 1945), Katherine Kendall married Charles Allen Sheppard, son of Mr. and Mrs. Edward Allen Sheppard of New York, James Richard married Mary Ann Henkle, daughter of Mr. and Mrs. Harold Henkle of Stanley. There are two great-grandchildren: Scott Allen Sheppard and Katherine Lindsay Sheppard.

Sources: *North Carolina Biography, Vol. IV, Wilkes County Sketches,* by J. Jay Anderson, family *Bibles,* family records, personal knowledge.

— Virginia Hix Brame

BERTHA REVIS HODGES
684

I was the last born of eleven children on July 26, 1897, near the village of Moravian Falls. My parents were Joseph Martin and Delilah Clementine Ray Revis.

I married Kelly Hodges of Elkin March 21, 1931, at Pores Knob. Kelly lived only thirteen months after we were married. I have one adopted daughter, Mrs. Louise Carpenter, who taught school for 30 years until sickness forced her retirement in 1981.

Bertha Revis Hodges.

One of my earlier recollections is standing beside the table where my two teacher-brothers were doing their school work. The dreams and wishes of a small girl to become a teacher engulfed me completely. The opportunities for schooling were very limited. My education consisted of two days in school before the age of eleven. At age sixteen, under the tutledge of an inspiring and knowledgeable teacher, Mr. Henry Hubbard, my desire to become an instructor was furthered. In the interim of ages eleven to eighteen, I amassed around 400 days in both elementary and high school curriculum. Good fortune came to me as I obtained a county first grade teacher's certificate, which in turn, entitled me to an elementary Grade B Certificate. These certificates opened the doors of college to me. I spent summers commuting to Appalachian State Teachers College at Boone, North Carolina. I used any extra time for extension work in the winters until I earned a Grammar Grade A Certificate.

My first employment in the educational system was in an ancient building called "The Brocktown School" in 1915. The windows were wooden shutters that were closed by hand each day as class was dismissed. My 44 years of teaching included two years at a school between Forsyth and Guilford Counties known as "The County Line School" and one year in Alexander County's Mayberry School. My efforts in instruction also include Congo, Gordon, Mt. Carmel, Gilreath, Oakwoods, Lewis, Spurgeon, Shady Grove, and last of all, Moravian Falls School, where my career was completed with retirement in 1959.

My chosen profession has given me many happy experiences despite some disappointments. My instructional life was dedicated to the pursuit of learning, and gaining knowledge as I taught. Looking back over 44 years, I have the feeling of satisfaction in becoming a teacher. This is enhanced by the many true and life-long friends I have acquired along the way.

I have continued to be very active in both public and private life after my retirement. I served two terms as president of the Pores Knob Homemakers Extension Club, over ten years as secretary of the Wilkesboro Senior Citizens Club; also I have been Sunday School teacher and librarian at Walnut Grove Baptist Church. I have been very interested in real estate; I have had six rental houses constructed.

Sources: Personal knowledge.

— Bertha Revis Hodges

EZEKIEL HOLBROOK FAMILY
685

Ezekiel Holbrook, son of Hargis Holbrook and Catherine Groce, was born in the Greenstreet Mountains north of what is now the James Oscar Billings old homeplace in Dockery around 1798/1802. Ezekiel obtained a State grant of 100 acres, paying $5.00 for it all, on Big Camp Branch of Roaring River near Caleb Holbrooks. This land he later deeded to his grandchildren, Dora and Frances Holbrook, daughters of Ralph Holbrook and Ezekiel's daughter Sarah Ann, with whom he lived his last years. He married first on March 1, 1820, Susannah Crouse (Cross or Croft?) and they had at least 3 children: Hargis, Elizabeth and Martin. Susannah is believed to have died sometime between 1830 and 1840, and Ezekiel married second Elizabeth Adams, born around 1815. To them were born 10 children: Catherine, John M., Susan, Phoebe, William, Amelia, Nancy J., Sarah A., Matilda G. and Delphia L. Ezekiel and Elizabeth were both alive in 1880 but were gone by 1900, so the exact dates of their deaths are not known.

1) Hargis Holbrook, oldest of the children of Ezekiel and Susannah, was born around 1821. He married Susan Roberts, born 1829, daughter of Thomas Roberts and Susan Gambill, and they had 6 children: Thomas, born 1843, married Mary Blackburn, daughter of John Blackburn and Charlotte Hendrix, and moved to Virginia to rear their family in the Speedwell and Comers Rock areas. Rebecca Susan, born Feb. 1848, married first Gabriel H. Smoot, son of Granville Smoot and Clarissa Hutchinson. They had one child, Martha Jane Smoot on Oct. 25, 1870. She married Alexander Blevins, son of Alvis Blevins and Celia Richardson, and they had 13 children. Rebecca Susan married second on Oct. 29, 1876, Thomas Shadrack Wiles. From this marriage, one daughter Elzina Wiles was born in Aug. 1882. Sylvania

Hulday, born around 1849, died in 1895 and is buried at Piney Grove Baptist Church. Martha Caroline, born May 5, 1853 did not marry. James Calloway, born 1856 married Alsie Cleary, daughter of William Cleary and Martha Combs. Brownlow, born May 2, 1862 married Sally Ann Combs, daughter of Zadock Combs and Nancy Ann Edwards. Sally Ann Combs was born Nov. 5, 1865, was a midwife for many years, remembered by neighbors for knitting as she walked to the homes of expectant mothers or on her way to church. In summer she wore a long print dress and a large white bonnet. She died April 18, 1849. Descendants of Brownlow and Sally Ann Holbrook include Spicers, Huies, Kennedys and Clearys. A grandson, Paul Holbrook, is an officer of Northwestern Bank in North Wilkesboro.

2) Elizabeth Holbrook, born Feb. 1827 married on April 2, 1850, William Rufus Adams, born May 15, 1827, son of Chapman Adams and Sarah Higgins. They had 11 children. One of their descendants is Paul W. Gregory, prominent school official and leader in the Mt. View community. (See Elizabeth Holbrook Adams.)

3) Martin Holbrook, born about 1829 married Mary Lyon, daughter of Alexander Lyon and Sarah Sparks born Sept. 27, 1821. They had 5 children. (See Martin Holbrook)

Two of the Holbrook daughters, Susan and Catherine, married Billings brothers, sons of William M. Billings and Sarah Childers. 4) Catherine Holbrook, born about 1832 married William Wilburn Billings, born around 1836, and they had 5 children. (See William M. Billings).

5) John M. Holbrook, born 1835, married on Feb. 12, 1858, Malinda Jane Phillips, born 1839. Malinda Jane was the daughter of Lindsey and Martha Phillips, and she and John had 11 children. She died on April 6, 1907. John is believed to be buried in a plot near the old Columbus Ford place on the road leading to the L.G. Billings home. America E., the oldest child of John & Malinda Jane Holbrook, was born Dec. 8, 1858, and married William D. Gambill, son of Nathan Hardin Gambill and Sadilla M. Kennedy. One of their 7 children, Walter W. Gambill, served as Deputy-Sheriff of Wilkes County for many years. Columbus F., born Aug. 29, 1860, married first Martha Caroline Bauguess, born Sept. 25, 1862, daughter of Jonas Bauguess and Matilda Holbrook. He married second Juliana Yale. Martha Caroline, born Sept. 4, 1862, married William M. Bauguess, son of Jonas Bauguess and his first wife, Martha J. Walker. Mary Jane born June 23, 1865, married in 1887 John Ander Richardson, son of Moses Franklin Richardson and Louisa J. Blevins. She married second W. Tom Johnson on Sept. 9, 1904. Nancy Ann, born 1868, married first Lewis Prevette, son of Alexander Prevette and Martha Mahaffey and married second Mr. Simmons. Alice L.. born 1870, married Columbus Casey. Frances F. was born 1871. Dossie G., born June 30, 1874, married in June 1896 Richard Calvin Sidden, son of Frederick Dewey Sidden and Huldah Sparks. Descendants include Hutchinsons, Warrens, Ken-

nedys and Johnsons. William Alfred, born Sept. 22, 1877, married Carrie Jane Holbrook, daughter of Joshua Holbrook and Nancy Sparks. They had 14 children.

6) Susan Holbrook, born 1838, married on March 12, 1854, Addison Billings, born about 1834. They had 6 children. (See Addison Billings.)

7) Phoebe Holbrook, born 1839, married April 29, 1858, Abraham Waddell, son of Claiborne Waddell and Sarah Pruitt. Abraham was born July 26, 1831, and died April 1922, shortly after Phoebe's death on Jan. 1, 1922. They had 4 children: William Cornelius, born Aug. 4, 1861, married Rose Ann Smoot; Nancy Ann, born 1864, married William Spicer; Marcus Monroe, born 1868, was killed accidentally; Matthew A., born Sept. 1863, married first Aug. 13, 1884 Narcissa C. Gambill, daughter of John Gambill and Mahala E. Smoot. He married second Charity Adams Rhodes. Matthew A. served as a country dentist for many years.

Little is known of 8) William Holbrook, born 1841, who married Jane Esque on June 28, 1858 and 9) Amelia Holbrook, born 1843, who married Dec. 26, 1860, William Eller.

10) Nancy J. Holbrook, born March 1845, married as second wife of William Bowers, born about 1803, on Jan. 7, 1876. They had 3 children: Colonel Young, born May 15, 1877, married on Sept. 3, 1908, Carrie Caudill, daughter of Samuel Caudill and Frances Gambill. His sister Jane married Carrie's brother, Cicero Columbus Caudill, born Oct. 16, 1877. Andrew Patrick, born May 15, 1878, married Clementine Miles.

11) Sarah Ann Holbrook, born June 1847, married Ralph W. Holbrook, son of William J. Holbrook and Malinda Walker. Their 3 children were: Dora E., born Dec. 29, 1874, married Will Waddell; Lula, born Dec. 1882, married John Ford, son of Columbus Ford and Sarah Jane Blevins; and Frances, born Aug. 20, 1886, married first N. Verl Alexander, son of Colby and Susannah Gambill Alexander, m. second Hardin Bowers, son of Finley Bowers and Mary Ann Cook. 12) Matilda G. Holbrook, born 1849, married Sept. 5, 1866, Jonas Bauguess, son of Emanuel Bauguess and Milly Sparks. They had 7 children: Robert M., born June 15, 1867, married Nancy Pruitt; Andrew Patterson, born Dec. 5, 1869, married Lula Pruitt; Neelie J., born Feb. 21, 1872, married Dec. 20, 1888 Rev. Grant Cothren, a Baptist minister and outstanding religious leader of his time, son of W.R. & Sarah Bauguess Cothren; Arthur, born June 1877, married Esther Cheek; Newton, born Dec. 8, 1879, married Nannie Richardson; Trealey, born March 13, 1883, married Effie Lyon; and Lettie Ann, born Oct. 1884, married first Grover Holloway, son of J.W. Holloway and Cora A. Wiles, and second Morgan Hawkins.

13) Delphia L. Holbrook was born 1851.

Sources: Wilkes Co. Records, cemetery records.

— Naomi B. Gordon

HARDIN SPICER HOLBROOK
686

Hardin Spicer Holbrook was the oldest son of Ralph and Nancy (Spicer) Holbrook, born January 14, 1835, and was buried on his hundredth birthday in the Old Roaring River Baptist Church cemetery.

He married on December 30, 1856, Nancy Dawson, called Dawsy, Bryan, a second cousin, daughter of J.Q.A. and Martha Bryan, founders of the Trap Hill Methodist Church in 1870. Dawsy was a steward, and they gave land for the parsonage.

In 1857 Hardin bought part of the Joseph Spicer, Sr., plantation containing the log dwelling on the hill above the scenic waterfall, and the Trap Hill mill.

Hardin as operator of the mill was exempt from military service in the Civil War.

When Trap Hill Seminary, Trap Hill Academy and Trap Hill Normal Institutte were flourishing, Hardin and Dawsy were strong supporters and furnished board to many students.

The Hardin S. Holbrook family at their home in 1904; Back row — Hardin S., R.T., DeWitt, Nannie H. McCann, Eudru (Spicer) (Mrs. C.D. Holbrook); Front row — Pearl (Sullivan) (Mrs. R.T. Holbrook), Nancy Dawson (Bryan) (Mrs. H.S. Holbrook), Verna McCann, C.D. Holbrook with daughter, Pearl.

Hardin and Dawsy had one daughter, Nancy, called Nannie, who married C.C. McCann, and lived at the homeplace, and three sons: Ralph Tyre, a successful businessman in Winston-Salem, who married first Pearl (Sullivan) and second Jennie Cranford; James C., who married Mattie (McNeill) Holbrook, widow of Attorney John A. Holbrook; and Clarence DeLoss, artist-photographer, teacher, merchant and postmaster at Trap Hill forty years, a leader in the Methodist church, Masonic lodge and school.

Sources: Wilkes records, personal knowledge.

— Mrs. DeLoss Holbrook

JAMES MONROE HOLBROOK
687

James Monroe Holbrook was born October 4, 1836. He married Elizabeth (Bettie) Spicer March 16, 1861. They had six children; Lula married J.S. Kilby, Mattie married J.O. Jarvis, Loyd Hardin married Emma L. Sparks, Luther R. was never married, Mary F. married Monroe Handy, James J. married Ella Roberts.

He was Postmaster at Traphill, N.C. from 1860 to 1866, which kept him from having to go to the Civil War.

He and his wife Bettie gave one-half acre of land ($4.00) for a colored school. The school was District #5, the committee of Benjamin & Jessie Holbrook, Yong Parks, H.J. Joines and R.B. Bryan wittnessed the deed.

He was a deacon at Old Roaring River Baptist Church about three miles West of Traphill, and also a member of the Masonic Lodge in Traphill.

Loyd Holbrook took his wife and three children, Betty, Olin and Edward out West, his brother Luther was unmarried went with them. They worked in the states of Idaho, Oregon, Washington, Montana and perhaps Colorado.

Loyd Holbrook took his family from Montana to Alberta, Canada about 300 miles from Calgary, Alberta and 20 miles West of Olds, Alberta to Eagle Valley. There were just three families living there, the nearest neighbor three miles away. Loyd H. and Luther R. Holbrook took out a homestead, joining each other. Luther lived with his brother and family. They were located in Township #34, South half of Section 4, range 4, West 5.

Earl T. was born in the valley August 20, 1904; W. Paul was born August 11, 1906.

Mother received a telegram stating that J.C. Sparks was in serious condition and to come at once. They left us children with our Uncle, intending to go to Alberta, but decided to stay in N.C. Olin, Paul and Earl came to North Carolina May, 1915. Betty and Edward stayed with Uncle Luther, Father went to Alberta to bring Betty and Edward back with him. Edward came with him but Betty married George Brown where she still lives; they had four children; Doris, Earl, Bettie Jean, and Loyd. Bettie Jean died at the age of 10 years.

Olin married Viola Gant and had 2 children: Loyd D. and Grace Iris Holbrook. They were born in Red Bank, New Jersey.

Edward married Veral Baker in Detroit, had one child David Holbrook. Earl married Pauline Smith of Benham, North Carolina. They had three girls; Bettie Jean married A.N. Balabous of Orentico, Virginia, they had two boys Nick and Mike. Angelene (Angie) married M. Dean Baskins of Watonga, Oklahoma, Emmalee married Clyde Cheek of State Road, N.C., had one adopted son Robert. Luther R. Holbrook died in a Olds, Alberta Hospital, December 1928. Buried at Traphill. Loyd H. Holbrook died May 30, 1952. Emma S. Holbrook died April 28, 1952. Paul died March 13, 1966.

Sources: Personal knowledge.

— James Holbrook

FAMILY OF JOHN HOLBROOK, SR.

688

John Holbrook, Sr., along with his brother, Randolph Holbrook, came to Wilkes County sometime before the county was formed, possibly as early as 1775. The ancestry of John has not been definitely established, although many genealogist believe that he was a son of Randolph Holbrook, Sr. of Goochland County, Virginia. There is documentary evidence to prove that John and Randolph lived in Goochland County during the period of 1750-1770. One Randolph Holbrook died there in 1778. This was the only Holbrook family known to have lived in that county during this time.

On 18 June 1778, John Holbrook, Sr. entered 175 acres of land in Wilkes County, described as being "on the south side of the mountain near Camp Branch, including the plantation where I now live." This is the area now known as Dockery, and many descendants of John still live there.

John Holbrook, Sr. was married to Mary Hargis Hammon in Goochland County, Va. in 1763. She was the widow of James Hammon who died in 1760. Mary had only one child by her first husband, namely John Hammon. John Holbrook, Sr. and his wife Mary, had several children, but only three boys have been definitely identified. It is likely that there were some girls in this family as suggested by the Federal Census. Since John was critized in 1787 by the Old Roaring River Church for "suffering dancing in the home", it seems likely that this social amenity suggests female involvement.

The 1787 State Census indicates that John Holbrook was born during or before 1727. The fact that he was exempt from paying poll-tax in 1786 seems to confirm the above date of birth. His death is unknown, for he was last enumerated in the 1810 Federal Census of Wilkes County. His wife, Mary Hargis Hammon Holbrook, died in 1782 in Wilkes County.

Known children of John, Sr. and Mary Hargis Hammon Holbrook include: (1) John Holbrook, Jr. who was born during or before 1766 as shown by the 1787 State Census of N.C. By this date, he was married with a small family. He remained in Wilkes until about 1798, at which time he moved his wife, Mollie Cooksey, and family to Russell County, Virginia, settling on a farm on Clinch River. Since most of his descendants grew up and lived in the Virginia-Kentucky area, they will not be discussed further. However, there is one exception, William Holbrook.

William Holbrook, a son of John Holbrook and wife, Martha Collier, and grandson of John Holbrook, Jr. and wife, Mollie Cooksey, was born 15 May 1815 in Russell County, Virginia, just seven months before his father was killed in an accidental explosion. His young widowed mother, married Jonas Jordan in 1817 and removed to Louisa, Kentucky, taking her two small boys, Robert and William, with her. William remained with his mother until 1840, at which time he visited his relatives in Wilkes County, arriving at Dockery 4

November 1840. Shortly thereafter, William accidentally broke his hip, and being unable to get it properly set, had to use a cane the rest of his life. He remained with his cousin, Johnny Holbrook, until he was married on 2 January 1844 to Sally Sparks, daughter of John, Jr. and Polly Fields Sparks.

William and Sally Sparks Holbrook had issue: (a) Martha Louisa Holbrook, born 3 May 1845, died in 1935. She was married to J. Alfred Brooks and had two children John Arlington and William C. Brooks. (b) John Preston Holbrook, born 30 May 1847, died 19 September 1935. He married Nancy Elizabeth Bryan, the youngest daughter of Francis Bryan and his first wife, Charlotte Atkins Bryan. They had Emma A. Holbrook, who married a relative, John Tyra Holbrook; Francis Milton Holbrook, born 11 July 1877, died 4 December 1878; Carrie Jane Holbrook who married Pedro Myers of Hays, N.C.; and Ida Anna Holbrook, who married Wiley Reid Jones of Winston-Salem. (c) Ralph Milton Holbrook, born 6 April 1849, married Nancy Smoot and lived at Traphill until 1890 when they moved to Gallatin, Missouri. (d) Sarah Ann Holbrook, born 23 August 1851, married a relative, Ralph C. Holbrook. Issue: Joseph Preston, Theodosia, Lenora Leota, Sallie Belle, Nancy Jane and William (Billy). (e) Mary Jane Holbrook, born 23 February 1854, died 22 December 1858. (f) Nancy Dawson Holbrook, born 1 November 1856, died 24 November 1860. (g) Betty Marsella Holbrook, born 12 September 1859, married J.M. Pruitt. Issue: Alice, Florence, Fannie, Emma, and Carl.

(2) Randolph Holbrook, a confirmed child of John and Mary Hargis Hammon Holbrook, was born about 1775 and was married to Elizabeth Adams during the 1790's. Elizabeth was a daughter of Benjamin and Henretta Adams who migrated to Eastern Kentucky about 1802. Since Randolph also went to Kentucky during the early 1800's it seems likely that they all went together. All of the descendants grew up and remained in Kentucky, they will not be detailed in this Wilkes County Heritage. Only John Henry Holbrook, the oldest child was born in Wilkes County and married Susannah Back somewhere in Kentucky. They have many descendants in eastern Kentucky.

(3) Hargis Holbrook, probably the last son of John and Mary Hargis Hammon Holbrook, was born about 1775 and was married to Katherine Gross about 1798. Having inherited a large farm from his father in 1805, Hargis and his wife lived out their lives in the Dockery area of Wilkes County where their farm was located. The children of Hargis and his wife, Katherine, as shown in the deed of conveyance which was made after the death of their parents, were: (1) Elizabeth, born about 1799, who married Hanry Gambill in 1816, moved to Lawrence County, Kentucky, had evelen children, and died 25 July 1855; (2) Ezekiel, born about 1800, who married Susannah Crouse and reared a large family; (3) John H. Holbrook, born about 1802, who married Nancy Absher 3 May 1822 and had four children: Caleb who married Phoebe Absher, William J. who married Malinda Walker, Katherine who married Edmond Absher, and Polly who was

unmarried in 1860; (4) A fourth child, name unknown, who married William Brooks; (5) Mary, born about 1805, who married John Collier and moved to Kentucky where they reared eight children; (6) Phoebe, who married William Baker 20 April 1828.

Sources: Wilkes County Taxables, State and Federal census, land records, wills estate records of Wilkes County, Stratton Hammon papers, Ida Holbrook Jones papers, Naomi Billings Gordan papers.

— Paul W. Gregory

JOHN ALEXANDER HOLBROOK FAMILY

689

The first John Alexander Holbrook, known as John A., was born April 28, 1878 at Trap Hill, Wilkes County, to Joseph Samuel and Frances, called Fannie, (Alexander) Holbrook, with Dr. Tyre York attending.

In early childhood his favorite make-believe was standing on a watermelon hill in his mother's garden speaking to an imaginary audience. No doubt he had attended political rallies with his father and heard campaign speeches.

He began school in 1884 at Trap Hill Normal Institute, not as a "normal" student but as a first grader. In 1888 he transferred to the Baptist school, Trap Hill Institute, where he excelled in oratory, winning the orator's gold medal at commencement, 1895, and becoming valedictorian in 1896.

In his early years he spoke at Sunday School conventions and at a county teachers' meeting in 1895, and at Rocky Ford Lodge Masonic picnic in 1899.

The fact that as a freshman at Wake Forest he was allowed to take junior English and junior Latin and made grades of 85 and 93 on the courses indicated that the Trap Hill school was equivalent to a junior college.

He passed the state bar in 1900.

On February 15, 1901, he married Mattye Elizabeth Smith, of Sparta, daughter of Dr. John Lacy and Elizabeth (Hawthorne) Smith, at her home. She had been a schoolmate at Trap Hill and the poetic Valentine and leap year messages they had exchanged had not been forgotten while she was at college in Greensboro and he, at Wake Forest.

Openings for attorneys were scarce in 1901; so to "make a stake," he heeded the Horace Greeley call to go West in May 1902, working a year in Idaho, Montana and Oregon. In the meantime his "little Beatrice" had arrived back in North Carolina.

On his return, he began campaigning for the House of Representatives, and won. Soon a son was born, Samuel Herbert Holbrook. But Mattye's health failed, and by May, 1905, she passed away, leaving "Beattie" and Sam with the Holbrook grandparents.

In 1906 John A. opened a law office in Wilkesboro in a little house now called the Law and Bride Cottage. In 1909 he moved to North Wilkesboro and took a partner, as reported in the local paper: "Mr. Johnson J. Hayes, of Parlear, a bright young man and young attorney of promise has associated himself with

John Alexander Holbrook.

Mr. John A. Holbrook for the practice of law. The style of the new firm is Holbrook and Hayes and they will occupy Mr. Holbrook's present office in North Wilkesboro.''

John A. was in demand as a public speaker. An item from The Charlotte Observer was quoted locally: "Mr. John A. Holbrook . . . delivered a Fourth of July oration . . . at Bessemer City and held the vast assembly spellbound. His deliverances were patriotic, chaste and with a little tinge of politics, just enough to make it spicy. It was talked on all sides . . . that it was one of the finest addresses ever delivered in Gaston County.'' This was his last speech.

Only four years from the opening of his office John A. died on April 26, 1910, and was buried on his 32nd birthday, in the Trap Hill Baptist Church cemetery.

In 1907 John A. had married Mattie Charlotte McNeill, daughter of the Rev. Milton and Martha (Barlow) McNeill, a music teacher in the Wilkesboro school. To that union were born two sons, James Boyd, who died October 5, 1910 the same hour John A. Jr., was born posthumously on October 5, 1910. Mattie and infant son moved to the Holbrook home at Traphill, where she continued to teach music.

The resolutions in memory of John A. presented at the August term of court, 1910, contained this appraisal: "While young in years, . . . he was rich in the fruition of his ambitious hopes . . . having gained prominence in his short practice at the bar . . . his sparkling wit and splendid humor making him the center of all crowds.'' . .

And among the many condolences was a tribute from Frank A. Linney: " . . . this state has not produced a more brilliant intellect in this generation or a more eloquent speaker.''

John A. Holbrook, II, a Wake Forest graduate, born October 5, 1910, was married January 13, 1934, to Ruth Moon, of High Point, where they live now, except for summers in Traphill. He has been a merchant, a teacher

and a salesman.

Their son, John A. Holbrook III, born March 11, 1935, with a M. Ed., U.N.C. Chapel Hill, teaches in the Greensboro city schools and conducts Holbrook Teen Tours through the West in summers. He married Marian Daileyon August 20, 1955. They live in High Point and have two sons, John A. IV, a student at North Carolina University, and Timothy, who specializes in creative production of radio commercials.

This completes our line of Holbrooks, except for the author of these sketches, B. Beatrice Holbrook, daughter of John A. Holbrook, educated at UNC-G and Peabody, a former teacher at Traphill and Dobson and a librarian in Albemarle and Raleigh, retiring from the North Carolina Museum of Art in 1973. She is now writing local history of the Traphill area.

Sources: family papers, county newspapers, personal knowledge, and interviews with family members.

— B. Beatrice Holbrook

JOHN WINFREY HOLBROOK
690

John Winfrey Holbrook, son of Ralph and Nancy (Spicer) Holbrook, was born April 10, 1849.

He had the advantage of attending school several years before the war caused the closing. He was able to teach one or more terms. On March 25, 1870, he received a voucher of $25.00.

On December 18, 1870 he was married to Sarah Jane Caudill, (1851-1931), a woman of refinement and skill with the needle, the only child of William and Frances, called Fannie, (McGrady). She inherited the whole plantation of several hundred acres, including a grist mill, but of course the ten slaves had been set free.

Between 1871 and 1886 six children were born to them: Fernando C. (1875-1892) who was married to Lula Caudill, postmistress at Abshers 39 years; Leyula (1875-1892), to Cleveland, called Cleve, Alexander, and was postmistress 13 years at Leyula, on Basin Creek, but later moved to Ashe County; Alonzo M. (1880-1971), to Viola Lyon and was merchant at Double Creek many years; William M. (1884-1964), to Maude Johnson; Dennis (1882-1952) to Carrie Kennedy and was song

John Winfrey Holbrook Family. (front row) L to R: John W., Crommie, China, Sarah Jane (Caudill), Fannie McGrady Caudill, (back row) L to R: Leyula, Fernando, Alonzo, William, Dennis.

leader at church for years; Crommie V. (1866-1973), to Fannie Johnson.

The whole family was active in the Double Creek Baptist Church, and especially John, who was church clerk for a number of years.

He died August 28, 1938 and was buried in the church cemetery, as were many other members of the family.

Sources: Family *Bibles;* tombstones; Baptist associational minutes; Wilkes County Board of Education records; interviews.

— Georgia Lue Holbrook

JOSEPH SAMUEL HOLBROOK
691

The first Joseph Samuel Holbrook, known as J.S. or Joe, was the fourth of ten children of the second Ralph and Nancy Spicer Holbrook, born in 1842, five years after the opening of Trap Hill post office, an opportune time in the development of the area.

Among his earliest playmates were children of the Siamese Twins, who lived on an adjoining farm. Once when his mother took him to visit them, a wife of a Twin remarked, "What I would give if my child were as fair as yours!''

In a log house about a mile away to which Joe walked to school with his brothers Harden and James and sister Jane, in 1848 the teacher was Robert B. Bryan, son of Thomas, who held school three months in the year for a salary of $8.00 a month. That year geography and grammar were added to the three R's.

Joe's family had strong convictions regarding the preservation of the Union, as did the Bryans. Having no grounds for exemption as his older brothers, Harden, a miller, and James, a postmaster, Joe hired a substitute, who was killed. Then in an attempt to pass through the lines to the Union army in Tennessee, he was caught and imprisoned a while. Later he was appointed captain of the home guard.

In 1865 he took the oath of allegiance, and on March 18, 1866, he took an oath of another kind of allegiance — matrimonial — to Frances Caroline Alexander, called Fannie, who was born December 30, 1839, daughter of John and Mary. Up that state road, laid off in 1858 from Elkin by Trap Hill and Longbottom, he drove with horse and buggy to bring Fannie and her trunk to a house built in 1826 on a farm then owned by the heirs.

To pay for that farm, Joe, leaving a young schoolboy, Bob Stiller with Fannie, struck out in the spring of 1869 by train from Salisbury, keeping a diary along the way, to Denver and the Fairplay gold mines; he was too late for gold, but a year's work on a ranch accomplished the mission.

In 1871, the year after his return, J.S. became a trustee, with J.Q.A. Bryan and Dr. T.W. Smith, of an interdenominational school sponsored by the Methodist church which had been organized the previous year. He remained trustee as the name changed from Seminary to Academy to Normal Institute until financial troubles forced a sale to the Methodist church, which controlled Fair View College. In a short time afterwards he became secre-

J.S. Holbrook household, mid — 1890s. Left: Jane Byrd, cook; Bob Spicer, a ward. Center: Mother and wife of J.S. Holbrook (standing); daughter of family slaves in rear. Right: son John A.; nephew F.C. Holbrook.

tary of the board, with J.S. Kilby president, of a Baptist preparatory school, Trap Hill Institute.

He was active in fraternal organizations, charter member and secretary of the first Masonic lodge #346 in 1876 and later of #483 and in 1892 of the Odd Fellows.

The only son of Joe and Fanny, the first John Alexander Holbrook, called John A. was born April 28, 1878.

A land grant for 640 acres on Greenstreet Mountain, which adjoined Joe's farm, raised his holdings to 1,000 acres in 1884. From 1884 to 1895 Holbrook Brothers, H.S. and J.S. were listed as co-operators of Trap Hill Mill.

Beginning in 1886, J.S. served three terms as county commissioner and as chairman in 1895 when the present courthouse was built, with his name on the cornerstone. He represented Wilkes in 1893 in the North Carolina Legislature.

From 1897 until his death in 1920, the chief interest of J.S. Holbrook was the attempted development of the resources of the Stone Mountain area. Under the president, G.W. Hinshaw, of Winston-Salem, he served as local agent of Stone Mountain Granite and Timber Company, Stone Mountain Railway Company and the Wolf Rock Granite Company, as well as the Payne and Deemer timber lands. A red-letter day for the area was October 16, 1917, when a lunch of country fare was served under the direction of J.S. Holbrook at the foot of Stone Mountain to 50 or 60 members of the National Granite Association, principally from New England, which was holding the annual meeting in the south for the first time.

The old farm gate at the Holbrook drive that had swung open wide to welcome two new-made brides and had closed on the funeral train of one, Mattye Smith, closed on three in 1910; Nancy Spicer Holbrook's, age 95; John A's on April 28, his 32nd birthday, and James Boyd's, his infant son, on October 5; both of the latter were buried in Traphill Baptist cemetery.

Joe and Fanny celebrated their golden wedding in 1916. Four years later in 1920, he died in a buggy accident. Although frail physically, Fanny stayed mentally alert and managed the farm 17 years longer, past her 98th birthday in 1937. Both were buried in Traphill Baptist cemetery.

At the death of Joseph S. Holbrook, his

grandson, originally named Samuel Herbert Holbrook, born Aug. 11, 1904, decided to take his grandfather's name but to write it J. Sam instead of Joseph S.

After graduation from Wake Forest and the University of Pennsylvania Medical School followed by internship at the Marine Hospital and a stint in public health work, he joined the staff at Davis Hospital in Statesville and succeeded Dr. James L. Davis as medical director. He was in 82nd Airborne Division of W.W.II to the end. Dr. Holbrook was elected as Potentate of Oasis Shrine, 1968.

He married first, Nancy Cox of Raleigh and named his first son, born May 31, 194- J.S. Holbrook, Jr., shifting back to Joseph S. Joe is an industrial real estate agent in Greensboro. Sam's daughter, Nancy, is counselor with the Downtown Church center in Winston-Salem, and his second son, Dr. Robert, is a recent graduate of Bowman Gray School of Medicine.

Dr. J. Sam was married May 9, 1970 to Frances Foley Butler.

Sources: Personal knowledge.

— Beatrice Holbrook

Wilkes was set off from Surry by the North Carolina General Assembly in late 1777. It was created for better convenience of the upper Yadkin settlements. Across this county in a northeasterly direction the beautiful Yadkin, once the Sapons, flows between the Blue Ridge and the Brushy Mountains. The valleys of the Yadkin and its tributaries are fertile, the upland in some parts of the country is good, in some poor, the mountains are rugged and well timbered.

MARTIN HOLBROOK
692

Martin Holbrook was born around 1829 son of Ezekiel Holbrook and Susannah Crouse and married Mary Lyon, daughter of Alexander Lyon and Sarah Sparks. Mary was born on Sept. 27, 1821 and died Oct. 15, 1891. Martin was buried at his old homeplace near the present home of Hubert McMenamin in Dockery, and Mary was buried with her Lyon family at Old Roaring River Church in Traphill. They had 5 children: Thirza, Emeline, Ellen R., Winfrey and Millison.

Two of the Holbrook girls, Thirza and Ellen R., married Miles brothers, sons of John Miles and Mary Jane Adams. Thirza born June 23, 1851 married Willis Miles, born April 7, 1847. They had 12 children, some of whom died early. James Franklin born 1868 married a Blackburn; he was accidentally shot and died in 1895. Laura Elvira married Bruce Eller. Rebecca E. born Oct. 13, 1872 did not marry. Lodemia born 1875 married Melvin Holbrook. John M. born 1879 married Sarah Jane Waddell. W. Roscoe married Maggie Porter, daughter of James Porter and Susan Higgins. Lura Ann married Thomas Morgan Lyons, son of Thomas M. Lyons and Ruth Wood. Martha Luell born May 28, 1886 married Thomas Welborn Shumate, son of Toliver Shumate. Trealey A. born Oct. 26, 1890 married Ava Caroline Pendry, daughter of James L. Pendry and Hannah Hinshaw.

Mary Ann Caudill and Winfrey Holbrook.

Emeline Holbrook was born Feb. 14, 1854 and married 1. in 1877 to Avery Henry Shumate by whom she had 3 children: One child died young; Emma Arlene born May 12, 1879 married John S. Hall; and Dora born Oct. 1, 1882 married Elbert C. Jennings. Emeline married 2. Wilson Walker, born Sept. 30, 1879. She died Jan. 16, 1947.

Ellen R. Holbrook was born March 17, 1856 and married on March 6, 1874 Alfred Miles. They had 4 daughters: Lou Emma born Dec. 1874 married 1. Frank Myers, son of William Augustus Myers and Eliza Jane Madison, married 2. Columbus Huie and 3. John Quincy Adams, son of William Rufus Adams and Elizabeth Holbrook. Clementine J. born Oct. 1879 married Andrew Patrick Bowers, son of William Bowers and Nancy J. Holbrook. Lettie Ann born Dec. 16, 1883 married Major Hardin Brown, son of Joshua Brown and Mary Elizabeth Hayes and they had 10 children. Nancy J. was born July 1884.

Winfrey Holbrook was born May 10, 1859 and married Mary Ann Caudill, who was the daughter of Rev. Jackson J. Caudill, skilled carpenter and minister and his first wife Mary Lafoon. Mary Ann was born May 25, 1865 and died Oct. 27, 1958. She was the aunt of Paul Caudill, well-known Baptist minister who spent most of his religious career pastoring churches in Atlanta, Ga. and Memphis, Tenn. Winfrey had a deep, rich voice and loved to sing; he conducted singing schools at neighborhood churches. He and Mary Ann had 7 children: Minnie, Dinah, Alonzo M., Mersey, Mattie, Bertha and Nona. He died Sept. 13, 1929 and is buried with his wife at Mt. Pisgah Baptist Church.

Minnie Emma, oldest of children of Winfrey and Mary Ann Holbrook, was born May 19, 1885 and married 1. Aquilla A. Freeman, born Jan. 29, 1876, by whom she had 2 children: Nona B. who married Homer Monroe Waddell, son of W.C. Waddell and Rose Ann Smoot, and Garneous who died young on July 3, 1918. Minnie married 2. on July 28, 1910

Vance Taylor. They had 2 children: Thelma Mae who married Oscar Moxley and Faith who is presently married to Wilfred Elza Loomis. Minnie married 3. in 1919 to Hubert Francis McMenamin, a young Irishman born Sept. 5, 1881, son of Hubert and Mary McMenamin.

Hubert F. remembered coming to this country from Ireland as a boy of 14 tagged for identification and help in reaching his St. Louis destination. He worked as steam shovel operator on the Traphill road when it was being built around 1918 and met his future wife, Minnie, during the time his work crew were camped in the Dockery area. He and Minnie had 3 children: Teresa married 1. Dennis Woody by whom she had four children, married 2. Norman Warren. Hubert F., Jr. married Daphne Sidden, daughter of Dewey Sidden and Elizabeth Hutchinson. Kathleen married Reid Miles, son of Trealey A. Miles and Ava C. Pendry, who is owner of a trucking business. Their son Michael Reid is a graduate of UNC Chapel Hill and District Manager of Automatic Data Processing Co. in Winston-Salem; twins Jesse Larry and James Garry became ministers, following the tradition of their Caudill ancestors; and Johnny is in charge of mechanics at Hammrey Trucking after his training at Forsyth Tech in Winston-Salem. Hubert Sr. died May 14, 1944 and Minnie died on April 26, 1975.

Dinah born Dec. 1886 married John Marlow. Alonzo Martin born Sept. 5, 1887 married 1. Verta Mae Brown, daughter of George Brown and Myrtle Elizabeth Holbrook and they moved to Maryland. He married 2. Leaford Blackburn. Mersey Nevada born Sept. 1890 married John Morris Childress, and Mattie Olive born July 1892 married J. Walter Brewer, son of Ambrose Brewer and Alice Emerson. Bertha born Sept. 1894 married 1. James Sebastian by whom she had 6 children. She married 2. Mr. Steelman.

Millison Holbrook born 1862, last child of Martin Holbrook and Mary Lyon, married Callie Eller Durham, son of John Durham and Sarah Sparks. He was born June 17, 1857 and died Oct. 26, 1917. They had 5 children: Mary A. born May 1882, Ola born 1887 who married Dock Higgins, son of Silas and Susie Higgins, Walter A. born Oct. 1890, John Marshall born March 12, 1895 who married Bertha Combs, and Rosa Lee born May 16, 1899 who married R.V. Garris.

Sources: Census Records, Cemetery Records, Family Recollections.

— Naomi B. Gordon

RALPH HOLBROOK
693

The first Ralph Holbrook must have been on the east prong of Roaring River by the time Wilkes County was formed, for it was only two years later, 1780, that he signed a deed of a neighbor, Thomas Walsh. In 1782 he had married Jane, called Jennie, Winfrey, of Surry County, and was listed as head of a household.

According to family traditions, Ralph's brothers were John S. who remained in Virginia and William B., called Buck, who married Rachel Winfrey, a sister to Ralph's wife Jennie, and acquired land east of Elk Spur. Of the three sisters, Elizabeth married first a Wheeler and second Israel Walters in 1798. They acquired a land grant but sold to William Caudle in 1801 and heeded the call to eastern Kentucky. The second sister married Joseph (?) Pruitt, a veteran of the Cherokee expedition and the Revolution. The third married a Caudle.

In 1793 Ralph served as administrator of the estate of William Hargas, acquired his home and lived in a house beside the road — the first road to the county courthouse, which passed from Elk Spur, "crossing the east prong of Roaring River above William Hargas."

On the 340-acre plantation Ralph worked as a cooper with one slave in 1800 and three by 1809.

He and Jennie had five sons: Lewis, who died young; Caleb; Ambrose; Winfrey; and John. In 1809 when Ralph wrote his will they were expecting another. Ralph provided for it: "If it be a daughter . . . I will my Negro Tamer Girl. If it be a son I will that it share equal with the other four sons." (Lewis had already died).

And so it was — another son, and another Ralph, born six months after the first Ralph died and was buried in an unmarked grave on the plantation.

In this inventory of 1808 there were a Bible, a Testament, a hymn book and two spelling books; feather beds, a looking glass, smoothing irons, besides all the paraphenalia for spinning and weaving; ten imported Delft plates, plenty of pewter (15 plates, 20 spoons, "basons" and dishes; glass tumblers, earthen porringers, Dutch ovens and a set of tea ware; two horses, four "slays" (sleighs) and harness and more and better tools than Randolph: a broad axe, cutting and drawing knives, sickels, weeding hoe, ½ bushel measure, a "lanthorne" and a still with four mash tubs.

Two of Ralph and Jane's sons, Ambrose and Winfrey, migrated to eastern Kentucky and married there, Ambrose to Nancy (Elam) and Winfrey to Betty (Walters), a first cousin, daughter of Elizabeth and Israel. Ambrose and Nancy were parents of Dr. Campbell Holbrook, who returned to Wilkes to marry Fannie, his cousin.

Caleb married Mary (Winfrey) and lived at the homeplace. He died in 1839. Their daughter Elizabeth married Austin Yates, a brother of the wives of the Twins. One son Pattison was married to Wadie Pruitt and the other, Winfrey, to Malissa Bauguess.

John married Jennie Bauguess, daughter of Robert and Mary (Sparks) Bauguess. He was a hatter, and made hats from beavers he trapped. Their daughter Sallie was married to Henderson McGrady. She was at the Hugh Stokes school in 1850 when census was taken. Lewis married Letitia Johnson and Elizabeth to Leander Johnson, Jr.

Sources: Hayes, Johnson J. *The Land of Wilkes:* Surry and Wilkes records, interviews, family papers.

— B. Beatrice Holbrook

THE SECOND RALPH HOLBROOK
694

The second Ralph Holbrook, born October 3, 1808, on the east prong of Roaring River, never knew his father, the first Ralph Holbrook of Wilkes, for he had died six months earlier. But his mother, Jennie, lived until 1854.

In 1815, when Ralph was seven years old, school was held at Elk Spur by Washington Walsh, the son of a neighbor, Thomas Walsh.

When Ralph married on February 13, 1834, Nancy (Spicer), born October 13, 1815, to Joseph and Jane (Bauguess) Spicer, their address was Wilkesborough. Their settlement was a "place called Trap Hill," but the post office was not opened until three years later, when a weekly mail service was available as the carrier on foot spent a night in their home on his way from the county seat to Mouth of Wilson, Virginia.

Ralph was one of the first school committeemen, with Jonathan Gentry and Joel Pruitt, in 1841.

His agricultural report for the 1840 census included four slaves, three horses, fifteen cattle, nine sheep, thirty-seven swine but only five poultry; his crop production ranged from 370 bushels of corn, 40 of potatoes, 25 of wheat to small amounts of oats, rye, flax and hemp.

About this time he sold a few acres to the Siamese Twins, who had chosen Trap Hill as their home. They asked Nancy to supervise their slaves as they prepared the "infare" and to welcome the brides.

Ralph and Nancy were consistent, loyal members of the Old Roaring River Baptist Church from the time they joined, he in 1829 and she in 1839. He officiated as a deacon 54 years and served frequently as a messenger to the annual association. On August 26, 1882, he was a trustee of the church when he, his son J.S. and Leander Johnson, contracted with the public school committee of district #25 for the school to use the church house and two acres "as long as needed for school purposes."

Between 1835 and 1860 Ralph and Nancy Holbrook had 10 children and eventually 62 grandchildren and 56 great-grandchildren. Their children were Hardin Spicer (1835-1935), who was married to Nancy Dawson Bryan, daughter of J.Q.A. and Martha (Bryan); James Monroe (1836-1887), who married Elizabeth Spicer, daughter of Hardin and Martha (Johnson); Martha Jane (1839-1932), who married Joshua Spicer, son of Hardin and Martha (Johnson); Joseph Samuel (1842-1920), who married Frances Alexander, daughter of John and Mary (Thompson); Ralph Calloway (1846-1938), who married Sarah Ann Holbrook, daughter of William and Sarah (Sparks); John Winfrey (1849-1938), who married Sarah Jane Caudill, daughter of William and Frances (McGrady; Joshua N. (1851-1892), who married Alice Bryan, daughter of Abraham and Margaret (Carson); Nancy Frances (1854-1948), who married Dr. Campbell Holbrook, son of Ambrose and Nancy (Elam); Elizabeth (1856-1940), who mar-

Ralph Holbrook II family (sitting L to R): Ralph, Nancy, Jane, Fannie, Bettie (standing L to R): Hardin, James, Joseph, Ralph, Jr. John, Joshua, Alice. Circa 1880s.

ried Jacob Matthew Pruitt, Augusta Alice (1860-1953), who married Millard F. Brown, son of John M. and Pheroby (Joines).

The second Ralph Holbrook died April 30, 1883, and was buried in the Old Roaring River Church Cemetery.

On September 21, 1898 Nancy (Spicer) Holbrook dictated her ancestry in America to her son, J.S. Holbrook, who entered it in the family Bible: Richard Bauguess and his first wife, Nancy (McCarty) (whose grave was the first one in the Old Roaring River Church cemetery, marked with a boxwood and a pine knot) were the parents of Jane (Bauguess), who married Joseph Spicer, son of William and Jemima (Haines) Spicer, daughter of Samuel and Abiah (Woodruff) Haines, son of Joseph and Molly (Nall) Haines.

Nancy, at the age of 95, died in January 9, 1910, at the home of her son J.S. Holbrook, and was buried beside Ralph in the Old Roaring River Church cemetery.

Sources: Wilkes County wills and deeds; church records; family *Bible;* personal knowledge; local traditions.

— B. Beatrice Holbrook

RANDOLPH HOLBROOK
695

Before there was a Wilkes County, when it was still Surry, the Parish of Saint Jude, there were Holbrooks beside the east prong of Roaring River on Holbrook Mountain, a scenic spur off the Blue Ridge between the east and middle prongs of the river.

Randolph (or Randol) Holbrook, his wife and family, accompanied by William Hargas, evidently a close relative, from Goochland County, Virginia, were among the early settlers, early enough for Surry's 1774 list.

Soon after Wilkes was formed and the land grant office opened in 1778, Randolph filed an entry for 250 acres near his brother John's (See Family of John Holbrook, Senior) on which he had made "improvements" on the east fork of Roaring River, on the south side of a mountain.

Other entries included: John Fugit for land "near the Gap of Holdbrooks Mountain"; George Brewer, "at the foot of a mountain called Holdbrooks Mountain"; and William Hargas, "on top of Holdbrooks Mountain."

Peter Greenstreet's entries, had established the name as Greenstreet Mountain.

By 1785 Randolph's acreage had increased to 410, and in 1787 the number in his household seemed to indicate that in addition to his and Mary's children, Sukey, Robert, Colby, Randall and Larkin, others, of perhaps a previous marriage probably to a Hargas, were living there.

On May 1, 1789 Randolph's daughter Susan, called Sukey, was married to Willis Alexander, son of Angus and Woenifred (Fugate) Alexander, early settlers on Longbottom. The fact that Ralph Holbrook was bondsman indicated a close relationship.

Just thirteen years after the date of his grant, Randolph died without a will very early in 1793 and was buried in an unmarked grave on his plantation. His coffin made locally of walnut lumber cost ten shillings. The sale of his estate brought 169 pounds, 11 shillings and 9 pence. The 28 hogsheads and three tight casks indicated that he was a cooper, a maker of barrels and casks. In Virginia he used hogsheads to transport tobacco to market. Here he could send hides and skins to Salem or Salisbury.

Items brought by his family included: the Bible, the razor, one saddle, the grubbing hoe and "basons" by Colby; 18 hogsheads and one horse by Robert; the loom, the table, a cow and a calf and "met" (meat) by Mary; a saddle by a nephew.

Some valuables went to neighbors: the "slay" (sleigh) and harness to Jasper Billings; the woman's saddle (side saddle) to John Hammons, Jr.; a bed, flax wheel, pair of cards and grindstone to William Alexander; the "chist" and oven to Spencer Adams; the "reep" (reap) hook and a piggin to Stephen Caudle; and the churn to Charles Cate.

Of the five children of Randolph and Mary, only Sukey and Colbert (Colbey) were living in Wilkes in 1850. Willis and Sukey Alexander had five sons, and Colbert had three sons and two daughters.

Robert had moved to Surry County and had married Frances Cook in 1803. Randall had migrated to eastern Kentucky.

Larkin, born about 1780, had an early grant near Poll Bridge on the northern end of Greenstreet Mountain soon moved to Ashe (later Alleghany) County. He married Sarah (called Sallie) Sheckles, born about 1782. He had died before 1860, but Sallie was living in Sparta near a son David, born about 1828, who married Margaret Crouse and was county commissioner for three terms, from 1872 to 1877. He moved to Oregon 1885. Another son, Washington K., born about 1813, married Mirah Wagoneer and had a general store and harness and saddle shop in Sparta in the '80's. Larkin and Sallie's other children were: Elizabeth, who married John Passmore; Jesse C., born September 20, 1809, who married Jane Elrod; William T., born April 1, 1813, who married Catherine Setzer; and Mary, called Polly, who married Hardin Phipps.

Sources: Records of Alleghany, Surry and Wilkes counties; Wilkes Genealogical Society bulletins.

— B. Beatrice Holbrook

WILLIAM and SARAN MALINDA SPARKS HOLBROOK
696

William Holbrook was born May 15, 1815, near Wheeler's Ford on the banks of the Clinch River, Russell County, Virginia, the son of John and Martha Collier Holbrook Jr. He died July 27, 1891 and is buried in the Traphill Baptist Church Cemetery, Wilkes County, North Carolina. He was married in Traphill on January 2, 1844 to Sarah Malinda (Sallie) Sparks, born October 8, 1817 (in northern Wilkes to what was later to become the township of Traphill) the daughter of John and Mary (Polly) Fields Sparks. Sallie died on May 13, 1902, and is buried at the Traphill Baptist Church. Her father John was a veteran of the Revolutionary War and is buried in the Sparks Family Cemetery on the old Sparks homeplace on Sparks Creek, Traphill. A marker commemorating his Revolutionary War service was placed on his grave by the Daughters of the American Revolution several years ago.

The following is from the papers of Ida Anne Holbrook (Mrs. Wiley Reid Jones), 1880-1970, granddaughter of William and Sarah Malinda Sparks Holbrook. Ida spent over seventy years of her ninety years doing research of the Holbrook family of Traphill. The account of William Holbrook from these papers has been condensed.

John Holbrook Jr., father of William Holbrook, was accidentally killed about 1815, in an explosion of a brandy still on the banks of the Clinch River near Wheeler's Ford in Russell

County, Virginia, leaving wife Martha Collier Holbrook and two sons, Robert and William. Both were less than two years of age. About 1817, Martha married Jonas Jordan and moved with him and her two Holbrook sons to Louisa, Lawrence County, Kentucky. Here William lived until 1838, age 23, when he, his brother Robert, Alex Goins, and Thomas Bell and family, started westward to Buford, Ohio County, Kentucky. About half way to Buford, William and Alex Goins, a horse and mule trader, left the others and went to South Carolina with a drove of mules. The rest of the party proceeded to Buford and settled there. Robert married Elizabeth Bell, daughter of Thomas. William's duties during the trip to South Carolina were to take care of the stock as Goins did his own trading along the way, much of it at night. One night while in South Carolina, Goins sent William to "buy" without money or price, a certain fine mule he had spied along the way. William went but just kept going instead of going back to Goins with the mule he was sent to get. He decided to return to Kentucky via North Carolina and visit relatives in Wilkes County. He arrived in Traphill on November 4, 1840, the day William Henry Harrison was elected President. Here he found his father's cousin, Johnny Holbrook, who lived on the east side of the east prong of the Roaring River about two and a half miles west of the present village of Traphill. He told Johnny, in whose home he was staying, of his connection and desertion of Alex Goins, adding "I am not a horse thief, I am not going to be a horse thief, and I am not going to work for a man I now know to be a horse thief, but if I go back to Kentucky, when he comes back there, he will think I am going to tell him and will see to it that I come up missing. My life is even in danger here if he should learn that I have come here." Whereupon, his Holbrook kinsmen, (calling him Cousin Billy), told him he was welcome to remain in their home and the other Holbrooks would give him the best protection they could. A few weeks later a horse ran away with him through "new ground," dragging him for some distance, bruising and mangling, breaking one hip, which was probably not properly set, causing him to use a cane the rest of his life. He made his home with cousin Johnny Holbrook until his marriage on January 2, 1844, to Sallie Sparks. They settled on the east side of the east prong of the Roaring River about two miles west of the present village of Traphill at the foot of Greenstreet Mountain.

William Holbrook was a very industrious farmer, a consecrated christian and splendid citizen in every way. His Bible was his constant companion while not at work, and he delighted in reading it aloud. He and Sallie were members of the old Roaring River Baptist Church until the constitution of the Traphill Baptist Church in 1887, where they moved their membership. Both are buried at this church. Just a few days before his death, William asked his daughter-in-law and granddaughter to sing his favorite song, "The Way-Worn Traveller," and became extremely happy as he listened to the touching words which he applied to his own life. Sallie was kind, a good mother and neighbor, and although she lived to the age of 85

years, she was never healthy and strong. She was quite a philosopher and was quite interesting when she grew nostalgic about the old days. She loved to quote scriptures, and would always begin by saying, "the book says." William and Sallie were cared for in their old age by their son, John Preston (Pea) and wife, Nancy Elizabeth (Betty) Bryan Holbrook.

William and Sallie were the parents of seven children, all born in Traphill, as follows: 1. Martha Louise Holbrook — born May 3, 1845, died August 2, 1934, buried in Traphill, was married on February 3, 1871, to James Alfred Brooks, born July 8, 1846 in Traphill, son of Larkin and Mary Brown Brooks, died February 23, 1923, buried in Traphill, children — John Arlington (Arlie) 1876-1957 and William Cleveland (Will) 1881-1951.

2. John Preston (Pea) Holbrook — born May 30, 1847, died September 19, 1935, buried Roaring Gap Baptist Church, Thurmond, married on March 31, 1873, to Nancy Elizabeth (Betty) Bryan, born November 12, 1857, in Traphill, daughter of Francis and Charlotte Hale Atkins Bryan, died December 1, 1933, buried Roaring Gap Baptist Church, children — Emma Arlena (Mrs. John Tyre Holbrook) 1873-1953, Francis Milton 1877-1878, Carrie Jane (Mrs. Noah Pedro Myers) 1879-1955, Ida Anne (Mrs. Wiley Reid Jones) 1880-1970 and Etta Floss (Mrs. Charles Alexander Sebastian) 1885-1971.

3. Ralph Milton Holbrook — born April 6, 1849, died and buried in Missouri, married in Wilkes County to Nancy Ann Smoot, born May 9, 1848, in Wilkes County, daughter of Granville and Clarissa Hutchinson Smoot, died and buried in Missouri, children — John Granville, Sarah Nancy Dawson (Mrs. Charles Swisher), Cora Elma (Mrs. Willard Youtsey), Juanita Frances (Mrs. John Shaw), Hardin Milton, Charles Wilson, and Orrie Claude. Ralph and Nancy Holbrook moved to Gallatin, Daviess County, Missouri about 1890.

4. Sarah Ann Holbrook — born August 23, 1851, died October 15, 1921, buried Traphill Baptist Church, married in Traphill on October 7, 1869 to Ralph Calloway Holbrook, born June 4, 1846, in Traphill, son of Ralph and Nancy Spicer Holbrook Jr., died November 19, 1938, buried Traphill Baptist Church, children — Joseph Preston 1870-1952, Theodosia 1875-1959, Sallie Belle (Mrs. John Claude Brinegar) 1880-1975, Nancy Jane (Mrs. Vincent Casey) 1882-1935, Lenora Leota (Mrs. Hardin Gaither Pruitt) 1877-1967, and William Ralph 1885-1958.

5. Mary Jane Holbrook — born February 23, 1854, died December 22, 1858, buried Old Roaring River Baptist Church, Traphill. 6. Nancy Dawson Holbrook — born November 1, 1859, died November 24, 1860, buried Old Roaring River Baptist Church, Traphill. 7. Elizabeth Marsella (Bettie) Holbrook — born September 19, 1859, died March 2, 1950, buried Traphill Baptist Church, married in Traphill to James Matthew Pruitt, born August 2, 1856 in Wilkes County, son of Major and Caroline Pardue Pruitt, died July 10, 1925, buried Traphill Baptist Church, children — Alice Ida (Mrs. James Monroe Shouse) 1880-1950, Sarah

Florence (Mrs. Charles Hardin Spicer) 1882-1969, Frances Ella (Mrs. John Frank Gambill) 1884-1903, Emma Leota (Mrs. Charles William Shouse) 1890-1980, Carl Milton 1893-1896, and William Major 1897-1897.

Sources: Ida Holbrook Jones papers, Wilkes County Courthouse records, family *Bible* records, interviews with family members, and personal knowledge.

— William Clinton Castevens

JAMES L. HOLDER

697

James Lafayette Holder was born May 14, 1885, died April 18, 1982, son of James Wesley Nichols and Martha J. Holder.

He married Rachel Luliza Minton December 25, 1904. They could not have children, so they adopted Ella Mae when she was three months old. She was born August 29, 1925.

J.L. Holder was a sawmill man, a carpenter, also laid rocks for the chimneys and houses. He built over 300 houses in Wilkes. He ran a grismill on Fish Dam Creek, where he ground corn and wheat.

He loved his church. His father built a Methodist Church and he and Luliza lived in it for a while after it was turned into a house. There was several families raised in the old church.

He loved a garden, and flowers, and always made me a flower garden when I was growing up.

One of the things he always told me was that it makes no difference what a man's color, religion or politics is. Never let it interfere with my belief in mankind or not to judge a person by either one of them. He was a Democrat.

Sources: Personal knowledge.

— Ella Mae Holder Faw

James L. Holder.

HENRY HOLDWAY (HOLDAWAY)

698

Henry Holdaway was born 15 September,

1753, in Virginia. He enlisted on 17 Aug., 1776, in Culpepper County, Va., in the Regiment of Riflemen under the command of Captain Gabriel Long. He also served under Col. Daniel Margaro. He was in the Battles of Trenton and Princeton, in two battles on the Hudson, and in the Battle of Monmouth, together with thirteen skirmishes. He received an honorable discharge after three years service at Rumpton Plains, New Jersey.

On 25 Jan., 1779, before his discharge, Henry was married to Eleanor Andisson Crystal, daughter of William and Mary Bruce Crystal. The Crystal (Crysel) and Holdaway families migrated to Wilkes County, N.C., probably about the same time.

A daughter of Henry and Eleanor, Elizabeth, became the wife of William Nichols. William and Elizabeth had a daughter Rebecca, who married Stephen Bumgarner.

Sources: National Archives Pension Record File; DAR Magazine, Family *Bible*.

— Flora B. Friend

THOMAS and SUSANNAH HOLEMAN
699

Thomas moved from Virginia to North Carolina 1752 with his father and mother and three brothers. The oldest brothers, Isaac, William and James settled in Rowan County, later to be Davie County. The aged parents died soon after they settled in Rowan and were buried on Isaac's farm. They did not record the names of the older Holmans, who were said to be from England.

Thomas Holman settled in Rowan County in what was to be Surry and later to be Wilkes County. He was responsible for Holman's Ford where Daniel Boone started his expedition into what is now Kentucky. We have land grant number 514 in Wilkes County on Stoney fork, dated 1764 which he was granted.

Thomas and Susannah had fourteen children. They are Absolom, Ruben, Susannah, Rachel, Joseph, Daniel, Rebecca, Isaac, Thomas, Grace, Elizabeth, Jacob, Margaret, James, Thomas Sr. died April 1798 in Wilkes County, N.C.

Thomas Holeman, Jr. was born 4 February 1756, died 3 April 1833, in Wilkes County, N.C. His first wife was a Hawkins and his second wife was Elsa, born 1766, died 1873. They had thirteen children. The children are: Joseph, Nancy, Molly, William, Daniel, Rachel, Margaret, Diannah, Rebeccah, Thomas, James, Didmama and Betty.

Rachel married David Stanberry 6 September 1806 in Wilkes County, N.C. She was born 4 May 1789, died 6 August 1856 in Whitley County, Kentucky. Rachel and David had at least six children, as follows: Malinda, born 1807; Margaret born 1812; Frances born 1814; John and Ira, twins, born 1820.

Rachel and David moved to Wayne County, Indiana in 1817 and to Whitley and Laurel Counties in Kentucky by 1825.

Sources: Wilkes County land records, wills, census. Kentucky records, Whitley County records.

— Dan Stanberry

ILA SPAINHOUR HOLMAN
700

Ila Mary Spainhour Holman, my grandmother, was born in the Dellaplane section of Wilkes County, August 25, 1870. Her father was Rufus Adkins Spainhour of Burke County and her mother was Mary ("Mollie") Ginnings of Yadkin County.

Rufus Adkins Spainhour, born October 5, 1839, was the son of Michael Spainhour and Lettie Estes. Michael and Lettie Spainhour lived at Quaker Meadows, north of Morganton. Michael was the son of Peter Spainhour and Elizabeth Rider. Peter was the 4th son of Warner (Wernhardt) and Elizabeth Spainhour. They came over from Switzerland in 1740. They first settled in Philadelphia. In 1753 they moved to New River, Va., but were driven from there by the Indians and in 1755 sought protection with the Moravians at Bethabara. So Warner was the great-grandfather of Rufus.

Rufus Spainhour escaped injury during the Civil War even though he was with General Lee in several bitter battles including Sharpesburg, Gettysburg, and Appomattox. Rufus and Mollie Ginnings were married September 5, 1866, and began their married life in the Dellaplane section. They had four children: Lelia, Ila, Bertha, and James Edgar. Lelia died at 18 years of age. Bertha was an artist. She never married and died in her forties. James Edgar married Ruby Sydnor and began and operated the Spainhour Stores.

Ila Spainhour grew up in Moravian Falls where her father operated a store after 1872. On June 6, 1889, Ila was graduated from Oxford Female Seminary with a degree in English. She loved music, played the piano, and sang well. The family said that since she could not make music her career she encouraged her daughter Bertha to get a musical education. After college, she returned to Moravian Falls and taught private piano lessons in her father's home.

On March 1, 1893, in Moravian Falls, Ila Spainhour married Floyd Gay Holman of Cool Springs (Iredell County). They lived in Moravian Falls for a few years, later moving to Wilkesboro where Floyd was in business. They built a home in Wilkesboro.

My grandmother was very active in church and civic organizations in Wilkesboro. For years, she taught a Sunday School class at the Wilkesboro Baptist Church, led the Sunbeams and served as President of the Woman's Missionary Society. She was a lady of almost unlimited energy. She served as President of the Wilkesboro Woman's Club and contributed liberally in time, energy, and means to the growth of the organization. She took a great interest in the building of a Community House, and she and my grandfather donated the building site. She served as President of the Wilkes Valley Guard Chapter of the United Daughters of the Confederacy and as chairman of the Doris Wright Scholarship Memorial Fund. Many Wilkes County girls used the fund to continue their education in college. As her pastor, Rev. Avery Church, said at her funeral, "Mrs. Holman did much work and did it well."

Ila and Floyd had five children. They were:

Ila Spainhour Holman.

(1) Mary Gay (my mother), born January 31, 1894. She married Walter Henry Spivey in February 1918. She died November 3, 1979. They had 4 children: Ila Celeste who married Byron Bell Sawyer, January 14, 1945. Their children are Charles Byron Sawyer and Ann Elizabeth Sawyer. Charles married Mary Jean Snider and they have one daughter, Amanda Clair Sawyer. Ann married James Stevens Rushing and they have one son, James Byron Rushing. Anne Bryand Spivey married Conrad Alexander Wimbish, August 1945. They had two daughters, Laura Gay and Cheryl Lee. Lee has one son, Trey Alexander. John Holman, the third child, died at four years of age. Walter Henry Spivey, Jr., married Nell Olson, June 1959. They have two children, Jill and Thomas. (2) John Rufus, born March 13, 1896. He never married and died August 30, 1921. (3) Edwin Floyd, born June 17, 1898. He married Mildred Pennington of Thomasville, November 22, 1926. They had two sons: John Edwin and Pennington Gay. John is not married. "Penn" married Mary Ramsey, April 1966. Their children are William Edwin, Robert Penn, Alan Ramsey and Mary Beth. After Mildred's death, Edwin Holman married Margery Nelson Egy. Edwin died March 1974. (4) Bertha Cornelia was born February 14, 1901. She married Herman Autenrieth. There are no children. Bertha lives in Phoenix, Arizona. (5) Ila Spainhour was born April 18, 1906, and married John William Miller. There are no children. Ila died July, 1978.

Grandmother was a marvelous cook and homemaker. Her home seemed always to have family and friends present, and there was always another place for a guest at her dinner table. I spent a part of many summers at the big house on the hill in Wilkesboro and loved every minute of the time. I could hardly wait for school to be out so that my parents would take me from Rich Square to Wilkesboro and leave me for a visit.

Grandmother died June 20, 1936, in Davis Hospital in Statesville. She is buried in the Mountain Park Cemetery in Wilkesboro.

I loved her dearly and am so fortunate to have so many happy memories of her, my grandfather, and the big house on top of the hill.

Sources: Certificates of Marriage, Certificates of Death, college diploma, grave markers, old news clippings, records of Joseph Spainhour, James Edgar Spainhour and Ruby Spainhour Bason.

— Ila Celeste Spivey Sawyer

JOHN HOPPER, SR.
701

My fourth great-grandfather, John Hopper, Sr., a native of Virginia, was born ca 1790. His father may have been the old Mr. Thomas Hopper who had a land entry in 1778 of "100 acres on Readdies River, mouth of Branch that makes into the River below his house, including his improvement." This branch was referred to as Hopper's Branch in other land entries of Wilkes County. In Wilkes land entry no. 1923, no date, John Hopper entered 100 acres Naked Creek of New River which included the Black Walnut Cove. Apparently he sold it, for John Hopper was marked out and Rowland Judd written in.

Having enlisted at Mulberry Fields in March of 1781, John Hopper, Sr., served one year in the North Carolina line of the Continental Army and was in the battles of Ninety-six and Eutaw Springs.

He and Anna Wilson were married 22 March 1785 in Wilkes County.

John, Sr. and Anna arrived with their family in Kentucky around 1800. Their children were: (1) David, b. ca 1790 NC, m. Anna Miller, daughter of John and Jane Miller, 20 January 1811, d. 1855 Orange County, Indiana; (2) Elizabeth, b. ca 1795-97 NC, m. John Turpin 7 April 1810; (3) Susannah, m. Elisha Hobb 17 February 1808; (4) Joel, b. ca 1795 Ky. m. Margaret Alford 2 July 1821, d. 31 January 1851, bur. Baxter Cemetery, Martin County, Indiana; (5) John, Jr., b. ca 1800 Ky., m. 1. August 28, 1822 to Margaret Baker, daughter of Charles Baker, d. 1880-1900, bur. Bethel cemetery 6 miles west of Orleans on Vincennes Road, Orange County, Indiana; (6) James ? (7) Samuel ? and (8) William ?. All these marriages occurred in Madison County, Kentucky.

John Hopper, Sr., age 69, personally appeared before the Madison County, Kentucky Circuit Court on September 21st to make a declaration concerning his pension. A schedule was submitted showing that he owned 2 cows and calves, T Pot, 1 kittle, 6 knives and forks. He owed about $40 and had no debts owing him. He further stated that he no longer was able to work at his occupation as a farmer. No children were living with him and no wife was mentioned.

In 1829 John Sr. requested a transfer of his pension to Orange County, Indiana as his children were living there. The 1830 census of Northwest Township, Orange County listed in this order: John Hooper, Jr., David Hooper, and John Hooper, Sr. (Note spelling) They

lived on land owned by David, for he was the only one who had any property at that time.

John, Sr.'s home was in Martin County, Indiana in the 1840 census with the family of John Hopper, age 20-30, his relationship to the elder John unknown.

On March 19, 1842 John Sr. married Catherine Piles in Martin County. He was in his nineties and she was ca sixty-three, and it is said that some members of his family were not pleased with the marriage, for they believed she married him for his pension. The truth of this belief can't be determined, but he did live for almost ten years after their marriage.

Forty acres in Owen County, Indiana were purchased by John, Sr. in 1848 from Peter Huffman for $250. He and Catherine were living in Marion Township, Owen County in 1850. (Name spelled Harper in 1850 Census.) Living with them were Leanna, age 44 b. Va., Catherine, age 15, b. Mo; and Amanda, age 7, b. Arkansas.

The heading "PATRIOT GONE" was used in an Orange County, Indiana newspaper that noted his death on 11/12 March, 1852 in Owen County. He was buried with military honors in the old Zenor cemetery, a pioneer cemetery south of Bowling Green, Clay County, Indiana. The cemetery, now on private property and neglected for many years, has been cleaned up, but the location of this Revolutionary veteran's grave is unknown. His wife, Catherine, inherited everything in the simple will he left.

The descendants of John Hopper, Sr., Wilkes County pioneer, are scattered across the nation, but many are still living in the Indiana counties of Orange, Martin, and Lawrence.

Sources: Land Entry Book — Wilkes Co. NC; 1787 Wilkes Co. Tax List; John Hopper Pension Papers #7785; Bounty Land Warrant #31273-160-55; Marriage Bond, NC Archives; Madison Co. Ky. Marriage Records; Orange Co. Probate Records, Paoli, Ind.; Orange Co. Ind. Census 1850; Madison Co. Ky. Census 1850; Martin Co. Ind. 1850 census; MARTIN COUNTY, INDIANA CEMETERY INSCRIPTIONS, Indiana State Library; DAR Papers Anna Edwards Triplett and Kathleen B.J. James; 1830 Census Orange County, Ind; 1840 Census Martin County, Indiana; Orange County Deeds, Courthouse Paoli, Ind.; 1850 Census Owen Co. Indiana; "The American Eagle;" 23 Apr. 1852 published Paoli, Ind.; Owen Co. Ind. Deeds, Spencer, Ind.; Owen Co. Probate Records, Spencer, Ind.; Family information on John Jr's burial location.

— Mrs. Jack Toliver

DR. W.P. HORTON FAMILY
702

The first of the Horton family to come to America from Leicester County, England were Thomas, Jeremy and Barnabas between 1633 and 1638. Thus, the William Phineas Horton family of North Wilkesboro are descendants of the line of Barnabas who settled in New England and from Col. Nathan who came South and settled in western North Carolina.

William Phineas, son of Hon. William Horton and Nancy Rebecca Blair, was born in 1867 near Boone in Watauga County. He grew up wanting to study medicine and obtained his goal by graduating from Baltimore Medical College.

He married Emma Wynne of Warren County. From this union there were five children:

Archie Wynne Horton who married Bernice Franklin of Carpinteria, California; Mary Louise Horton who married Phillip Robbins of Durham, N.C.' William Andrew who died very young; Jonathan Palmer Horton who married Elizabeth Lumpkin of Durham, N.C.; Annie Emma Horton who married Walter Newton of Fountain, N.C.

Dr. and Mrs. Horton moved to Wilkes County in 1890. In 1891 the town of North Wilkesboro was incorporated. During these early years Dr. Horton became one of the leading physicans; traveling by horse and buggy, never refusing to call on the sick.

I came to North Wilkesboro in 1924, two years after Dr. Horton's death. I was told over and over by various persons that there was never a night too cold, too wintery, wet or dark for him to answer a call for help.

The W.P. Hortons took an active part in all things religious, educational, civic and social thereby giving the young town a head start in the right direction.

Dr. Horton was a charter member of the First Baptist Church. His two oldest children, Arch and Louise, later, went with him. Mrs. Horton was a charter member of the First Methodist Church. The two younger children, Palmer and Annie, went with her. It was rather unusual; the two Baptist Hortons married Methodists; the two Methodist Hortons married a Baptist and a Presbyterian.

Dr. Horton was one of the first trustees of Appalachian State Teacher's College at Boone. He was connected with the Southern Railroad Company. He helped build up Main street, and he was an active member of the N.C. Medical Society.

In the meantime the four surviving Horton boys and girls were beginning and finishing their educations at various schools. Arch graduated from Wake Forest and held an office in the Bank of North Wilkesboro for several years. He and Bernice had one son, William Franklin. They both were active in local affairs while they resided in North Wilkesboro. They later moved to Carpenteria, California, where they died.

Louise graduated from Peace Institute, Raleigh, N.C. She married Phillip Robbins, and they first lived in Greensboro, N.C. Later, they moved to Durham, N.C. where Phillip was manager of Ellis-Stone Company. They had three children; one son and two daughters.

Annie graduated from Greensboro College, Greensboro, N.C. She married Walter Newton of Fountain, N.C. and much later they moved to North Wilkesboro. They had three children; two daughters and one son, who died in infancy. One daugher, Margaret, who married Robert Gresham of Mooresville, N.C. moved back to North Wilkesboro. They have three children; Rob and Scot and Jan. Robert or Bob as he is better known, is retired from Lowe's Company. They have made valuable contributions to the growth of North Wilkesboro.

Palmer graduated from North Wilkesboro High School and from The School of Pharmacy at Chapel Hill, N.C. He returned home and in 1922 opened Horton Drug Store in one of the Horton buildings on Main Street. In 1925 he married Elizabeth (Lib) Lumpkin from

Durham, N.C. who had come to North Wilkesboro as a teacher in the high school in 1924. They had two sons: Jonathan Palmer (Poddy) Horton, Jr. and William Donald (Bucky) Horton.

Palmer was a member of the Kiwanis Club, a member of the North Wilkesboro Chamber of Commerce which was organized in 1946, supported the State Association of Pharmacy, and was a charter member of the Elks Club.

He opened a Frigidair Appliance Store which he later sold. In a few years he started a propane gas plant which he operated until his death in 1961. All of these businesses were in operation at the same time as the Horton Drug Company, and each had its own work force.

It is rather interesting that Durham, N.C. played a big part in the lives of some of the W.P. Horton family. Phillips Robbins who married Louise Horton had a sister who had married Mrs. W.P. Horton's brother, Palmer Wynne. Palmer Wynne died on their honeymoon. Mrs. Wynne and her sister operated The Durham School of music where I studied piano during my high school years. She was an excellent teacher and a lovely person. I never missed going to see her every summer. After my first year in North Wilkesboro on my summer visit, we were talking and out of the clear blue she asked me, "Elizabeth, are you and Palmer going to make it?" I was speechlees, never dreaming that she had any connection with North Wilkesboro. Then she told me she had known the Horton family for years.

Back to the Palmer Horton family, each one of the four made contributions to our town. Elizabeth (Lib) Horton became the first woman ever elected to the North Wilkesboro School Board where she served twelve years. She served on many other boards in town.

Pamler, Jr. (Poddy) was educated in the North Wilkesboro schools as was Donald (Bucky) Bucky graduated from Woodberry Forest School in Orange, Virginia. Both continued their college education in Chapel Hill and graduated from the school of pharmacy.

Palmer, Jr. served in the U.S. Army during World War II and was stationed in Italy. Upon returning to the States he completed his education and returned to North Wilkesboro where he took charge of the Peoples Drug Store in Wilkesboro. In 1952 he married Ruth Carter of Kannapolis, N.C. They have three children: Elizabeth, Jonathan Palmer III and Donald Richard. Elizabeth (Libby) helps her father in the drug store.

Donald served in the Army during the Korean War. Upon completion of his duty he returned home and went into Horton Drug Store. He operated this business until it was closed in 1981 due to his health. In 1969, he was married to Delores Foster of Millers Creek, N.C. They have one son, William Donald (Bill) Jr. and two daughters, Donna and Diane.

Both boys and their families are still supportive of all the best in life and in the growth of their communities.

Sources: *The Hortons of Western North Carolina* by Texie Horton Barlow; personal records.

— Elizabeth L. Horton

HOWARD

703

William David (Will) Howard was born in Yadkin County October 25, 1861, the son of Alfred and Martha Jane (Matt) Mayberry Howard. On December 22, 1897 he married Lizzie Elizabeth Lucretia Myers. She was the daughter of Rev. (Billie) William Almon and Lemirah Jennings Myers who lived in southeast Wilkes County. Lizzie was born July 28, 1869. Will and Lizzie lived in Yadkin County for about three years then moved to Wilkes where they resided until their deaths.

W.D. Howard was appointed postmaster of New Castle Post Office January 5, 1901. In a short time the Post Office Department began establishing Rural Free Delivery service. He resigned as postmaster and organized the New Castle route. He began service as the first carrier on November 1, 1904 and continued serving the route until November 22, 1924. In the 1920s or early 1930s New Castle Post Office was discontinued and consolidated with Cycle Post Office. In January 1972 Cycle was discontinued and consolidated with Hamptonville Post Office.

Will Howard died October 13, 1925. Lizzie Howard died November 19, 1942. They were buried in Union Church cemetery about one-half mile from where they lived.

They had three sons and one daughter: William Blaine, Hugh Gwyn, Spencer Blackburn and Martha Synola (Nola).

Blaine was born March 2, 1899. He attended Mt. View Institute and Mars Hill. He taught school in Wilkes and Yadkin Counties for a short time, then accepted employment with Duke Power Company in Winston-Salem as appliance salesman. After a few years he was transferred to Madison, N.C. as office manager where he remained until his retirement. He was married twice: first to Janie Adams of Danville, Va. and second to Minnie Dodson of Martinsville, Va. He had two daughters by his first marriage: Kathleen, who married Richard Powell of Philadelphia. They live at Hilton Head S.C. and have three children. Blaine's second daughter, Mymalee, taught school for several years. She was married to Carroll Garrison of Morganton, N.C. They have two daughters. Blaine died in Martinsville, Va. June 30, 1979 and was buried there.

Hugh was born March 8, 1901. He spent most of his life on the farm and in the furniture business in Elkin. He was twice married: first to Ann Lee Van Hoy of Yadkin County, and second to Dorothy Swaim of Wilkes. He had two daughters by his first marriage: Eloise Persinger Clements of Roanoke, Va. and Faye Burton of Vinton, Va. Faye has two sons. Hugh died May 25, 1970 and was buried at Union Baptist Church Cemetery.

Spencer was born May 17, 1905. He attended Mt. View Institute and later served in the United States Naval Reserves in the South Pacific during World War II. He was with the Post office in Greensboro for seventeen years.

Nola was born November 3, 1908. She taught in the Wilkes County schools for forty-two years.

Spencer and Nola are now retired and live at the old homeplace at Route 3, Hamptonville where Nola has always made her home. Neither of them has ever married.

Sources: Personal knowledge.

— Nola Howard

HOWARDS

704

Phillip Howard, Sr. was born in 1704, came to Surry County, N.C. from Anne Arundel County, Maryland. He died in 1785. His wife was Mary. They had children Phillip, Jr., John, Benjamin, Cornelius, Christopher, Henry and perhaps others. His son John Howard was born 1742 in Maryland, died in Wilkes County in 1811. It is believed John was married twice. The name of his second wife was Nancy. He was the father of at least eight children by his two wives. (1) Sally, married Thomas Witherspoon, (2) Joshua, (3) John, Jr. married 11 April 1806 Anna Grant, (4) Phillip, married 16 January 1801, Frances Sales, (5) Christopher, born 1787, married 5 December 1809 Hannah Johnson, (6) Barbara, (7) Mary, (8) Rachael, married 2 October 1805, Joshua Horton.

Christopher Howard, son of John Howard, married Hannah Johnson, born 1786 in Pennsylvania, daughter of Charles and Hannah Johnson. They lived in the Hunting Creek area of Wilkes County. Christopher was a farmer. They had eight children: (1) Clara, born 1811, married 26 September 1938 John Myers, (2) Israel, (3) Dianah, born 1814, married Richard Walker as his second wife, (4) Larkin, born 1816, married 13 January 1836 Sarah Warren, (5) Nancy, born 1820, married 21 November 1839, John Byrd, (6) Sarah, married 13 June 1850 Sires Dacons, (7) Alice, born 1825, (8) Finley, born 10 January, died 16 January 1914, married Mary Brown.

Finley Howard married 31 January 1850, Mary A. Brown, born 1830, daughter of John and Mary (Welborn) Brown. Finley was a farmer and lived on Hunting Creek. He and Mary had five children: (1) Nancy M., born 1851, married 30 January 1868, Ephraim Holler, (2) John Martin, born 12 September 1852, died 1 March 1927, married Mary Jane Jarvis, (3) Sarah, born 1854, (4) Alice L. born 31 March 1858, died 22 April 1918, married W.F. Comer, (5) Mary C. born 1859.

John Martin Howard, son of Finley and Mary A. (Brown) Howard, married Mary Jane Jarvis, born 31 December 1853, died 25 November 1916, daughter of Lindsey and Sarah (Brown) Jarvis. John Martin was a farmer in the Hunting Creek area of the county. He and Mary Jane had six children: Wilson, Grover, Noah, Joanna, Flossie and Wade Jarvis Howard.

Wade Jarvis Howard was born 5 May 1892, died 24 August 1953, married 12 July 1918, Mary Eugenia Lewis, born 15 December ?, in Asheville, Buncombe County, N.C., died 8 November 1973 in Wilkes County. They lived on Route 3, North Wilkesboro, N.C. where Wade Jarvis was a farmer. Mary Eugenia Lewis was the daughter of William Henry and Alice E. (Campbell) Lewis. When she was three days old her mother died and she was reared by an Aunt in Gastonia, N.C. She graduated from Greensboro College, and as a registered nurse, worked at Wilkes General Hosital for twenty years. Both Wade Jarvis and Mary Eugenia are buried at Mt. Pisgah Baptist Church. They had children: (1) Mary Margaret, born 3 September 1919, died 20 May 1921, buried at home place, (2) Wade Jarvis, Jr., born 6 December 1921, Wilkes County, married Mary Margaret White, (3) William Lewis, born 25 April 1923, married Bettie Jean Tuttle, (4) Joseph Finley, born 4 December 1925, died 12 November 1939, buried Mt. Pisgah Baptist Church.

Mary Lewis Howard.

Wade Jarvis Howard, Jr. married 25 May 1946 Mary Margaret White, born 19 September 1927, daughter of Dana Flake and Ethel (Robertson) White. Wade served for two and one-half years in the U.S. Army and has been employed by the North Wilkesboro Coca-Cola Bottling Company for thirty years. Margaret is from Iredell County. They have four children: (1) Dana Wade born 25 March 1948, married 28 July 1973 Janice Lynn Souther, daughter of Calvin and Beulah Souther. Dana is employed by Coca-Cola Bottling Company and has served in the armed services. Janice is a registered nurse. (2) Robert Allen, born 24 August 1951, married 26 February 1972 Frieda Coleen Privette, born 28 December 1952, daughter of Stoy and Ruth (Johnson) Privette. Bobby is with the Coca-Cola Company and Frieda is a secretary. They have children: Chad Eric, born 26 December 1972 and Lee Allen born 30 May 1975. (3) Sharon Jill born 31 December 1956, graduated from E.C. University and U.N.C.G. and is an Audiologist in Statesville, N.C. (4) Kelly Finley Howard, born 2 February 1967.

William Lewis Howard married 20 October 1956 in Greensboro, N.C. Bettie Jean Tuttle, born 7 November 1928, Forsyth County, N.C. daughter of Charlie Edward Lee and Ruby (Brown) Tuttle of Stokes and Rockingham Counties. William has been employed by the Coca-Cola Bottling Company for twenty-nine years, was in the army in 1946-47, is a member of Mt. Pisgah Baptist Church. Bettie is

employed by the Northwestern Bank. They have a daughter, Peggie Jo Howard, born 22 September 1957 at Wilkes General Hospital, graduated from Lenoir-Rhyne College in Hickory, N.C. with a degree in Early Childhood and Deaf Education. She teaches Hearing Impaired Classes in the Wilkes County school system.

Sources: Personal knowledge, census records, marriage records, wills, tombstone inscriptions.

— Peggie Jo Howard

HISTORY OF THE HOWARD FAMILY

705

Benjamin Howard, who first appeared in the records of Wilkes County in 1778, was born February 17, 1742, in Maryland, the same year that Henry Sater, a prominent man of Baltimore County, founded the first Baptist Church in Maryland at Lutherville. Later, Benjamin Howard was employed by Henry Sater as a weaver and fell in love with Henry's daughter, Prudence. Because the family opposed this marriage, they were forced to elope and were married September 21, 1762, in Baltimore. They decided it was best to leave Maryland so they went to Rowan County, North Carolina, where they purchased 137 acres on Elsworth Creek October 15, 1763. They later removed to present day Elkville, Wilkes County, and on September 8, 1778, purchased 350 acres on the north side of Yadkin River at Elk Creek. Benjamin Howard raised cattle and farmed but in order to provide adequate pasture land for his livestock, purchased land near Boone (Watauga County) and built a Daniel Boone type cabin to serve as shelter for himself and his herders. His cabin stood on the present site of the Boys Dormitory of the Appalachian Training School in Boone. In 1845, one of Howard's herders, a slave named Burrell, who

was well over 100 years old, related to a grandson of Howard's that he had piloted Daniel Boone across the Blue Ridge to the Howard cabin the first trip Boone ever took across the mountains.

During the American Revolution, Benjamin Howard found himself living among many peopled who were opposed to the separation from Great Britain, and he too sympathized with these Tories, or Loyalists. While some Loyalists took up arms, others just refused to bear arms, including Benjamin Howard. During much of the conflict, Howard spent a great deal of time in his cabin in the Boone Valley. While he was able to keep away from trouble and patriots for awhile, he was finally forced to hide out on a mountain top to the north of Boone. The mountain since that time has been known as Howard's Knob. Finally, Benjamin Howard, in 1778, age 36, took the Oath of Allegiance and endeavored to support the American cause.

Benjamin Howard was a prominent land owner and respected civic-minded citizen. William Cook, who was an itinerant minister of the Flat Rock Church, was authorized in June, 1800, to carry his evangelical work "in the upper and in the lower end of the bounds of the church, on Dutchman's Creek, Beaver Creek, Bear Creek, and hold meetings and hear experiences at Benjamin Howard's home on Elk Creek." Benjamin Howard passed the remainder of his days on Elk Creek and died June, 1828. His wife, Prudence Howard, had died there previously on September 22, 1822. Both are buried in the small cemetery in a pasture about one mile above the Ferguson Post Office on Highway No. 268. Benjamin and Prudence Howard had the following children: Discretion, born 1764, married 1781 to Thomas Isbell, died 1848, Wilkes County; Philip, born 1766, died before 1828, Wilkes County; Mary, born 1768, unmarried, died 1836, Wilkes County;

Cornelius Howard Home — Elkville (built ca 1822).

George, born 1770, married 1799 to Mary Elizabeth Jones, Wilkes County, removed to Blout County, Tennessee; Sarah, born 1771, married Jordan Council, removed to Watauga County; Elizabeth, born 1774, died before 1828, Wilkes County; Rachel, born 1776, married Mr. Council, removed to Knox County, Tennessee; Rebecca, born 1778, married to Caleb Dyer, removed to Monroe County, Tennessee; Benjamin, born 1780, married Elizabeth Walker in 1804, died 1825, Wilkes County; widow removed to Perry County, Tennessee; Cornelius, born 1783, married 1822, Philadelphia Hagler, died 1860, Bradley County, Tennessee; Nancy Frances, born 1784, married 1807 to Joseph Calloway, removed to Monroe County, Tennessee; and Prudence, born 1787, died 1788, Wilkes County.

Cornelius Howard, the youngest son of Benjamin Howard, was born December 21, 1783, Wilkes County, and married Philadelphia Hagler on April 7, 1822, Wilkes County. She was a daughter of William Hagler and his wife, Elizabeth Mullens. Shortly after their marriage, Cornelius Howard engaged the renowned brick mason by the name of Hopkins to construct the two story brick house which currently stands at Elkville, North Carolina. Hopkins had just completed a similar residence for Jacky Ferguson, about one mile below Ferguson. After the completion of the Howard residence, Hopkins built the same house for Howard's in-laws, William and Elizabeth Hagler, which currently stands in Caldwell County on the south side of the Yadkin. Cornelius and Delphia Howard had the following children, all born in Wilkes County: William H., born 1823; Benjamin S., born 1824; G. Walter, born 1825; Elizabeth Lee, born May 2, 1826, married May 20, 1840, Bradley County, Tennessee to John Harrison Perry, died March 7, 1900, Commerce, Texas; Lindsey, born 1834; Prudence, born 1827; and John Cornelius, born 1831. Philadelphia Howard died April 13, 1834, and is buried in the Howard Cemetery. Shortly thereafter, Cornelius Howard removed to Bradley County, Tennessee where he died February 14, 1860. Their daughter, Elizabeth Lee (Howard) Perry, is the great-grandmother of G. Randle Pace, author of this article.

Sources: *Henry Sater*, by I.W. Maclay; Rowan County Recrods; HISTORY OF THE WATAUGA; Wilkes County Records; HISTORY OF WESTERN NORTH CAROLINA; Colonial Records; HISTORY OF NORTH CAROLINA BAPTIST; WORLD OF MY CHILDHOOD

— G. Randle Pace

ERIC RAYMOND HOWARD
706

My daddy, Eric Raymond Howard, born October 27, 1933 — died February 20, 1968, was the son of June Cornelius Howard born July 28, 1897 — died September 1, 1959 and Sallie Byrd born June 23, 1894.

His brothers and sisters are: Clyde, Norman, Agnes, June Cornelius, Jr., Carl, Edith, Bob, a baby girl who died as an infant.

Their family made their home near Shepherd's Crossroads on a large farm. His dad worked at a factory in North Wilkesboro and also farmed. They attended Rachel Baptist Church.

Daddy was active in sports in school, and he was valedictorian of the class of 1952 at Roaring River High School. He served in the Air Force and was stationed in Japan.

On April 15, 1956, Eric Raymond Howard and Patsy Anne Wiles, daughter of James Burette Wiles and Selma Kathleen Campbell, (see Joseph Alexander Lafayette Campbell's family heritage) were united in marriage. They lived in a little house in Winston-Salem on Ferndale Avenue. Daddy was employed with Mutual of Omaha Insurance Company, and Mother worked in the office at McLeans Trucking. On January 11, 1957 I was born and three years later on October 18, 1960, Michael Warren was born. Then we all moved back to Wilkes County and lived just off Highway 268 about six miles east of North Wilkesboro.

Daddy worked for Call's Insurance and later went to work for the insurance department at the Northwestern Bank.

They bought a farm in Hays in 1963 and eventually acquired a few head of cattle along with chickens and hogs. For a few years they raised burley tobacco.

I attended Mountain View Elementary School and graduated from North High in 1975. On June 27, 1976, I married Danny M. Wiles, born April 14, 1950, son of Grant Wiles and Faye Harrell of the Hays Community.

We built our house on part of the Grant Wiles homeplace in 1977, located on Wiles Ridge. Danny is employed with the Wilkes County Ambulance Service, and I was employed by Lowe's Companies until our daughter, Stephanie Anne, was born. Her birthday is June 4, 1981.

Sources: Grave stones, interviews with family members, personal knowledge.

— Scarlette Howard Wiles

HOWELL FAMILY
707

Joseph Howell, Sr. came to Surry County from Kent County, Delaware. He was married to Mary Furches. Their son, Joseph Howell, Jr. was born 19 July 1779 and died 13 August 1861. He was married to Jane Creson (1786-1862) 10 January 1802. Both are buried in Davie County at Eaton's Baptist Church.

Jane Creson's grandfather, Abraham Creson, was a Regulator prior to the Revolutionary War. He was imprisoned in Salem in 1769.

Joshua Howell (1806-1886) was one of the fourteen children of Joseph Howell, Jr. and Jane Creson and was born in Davie County. He married three times. His first wife was Amanda Shelton, whom he married 28 February 1837, ceremony performed by Davie County Register of Deeds. His second wife was Eliza, and his third wife was Sarah (Sally) Ann Harville. Joshua is buried in Davie County in the Harville family cemetery near Huntsville, N.C. Sarah Ann is buried in Yadkin County near Huntsville at Legion Memorial Park, Coolemee, N.C.

Joshua is remembered as being a land owner of many acres. He was interested in the community and gave land for a much needed school.

William Lewis Howell (1865-1942) was a son of Joshua and Sally Ann. He came to Wilkes County as a young man to work on the farm of his cousins, the Cisero Hixs'. Besides farming, he was an accomplished carpenter. He soon met Lelia Isadore Pearson (1870-1954) and about a year later they were married on the 9 January 1890. To this union, nine children were born:

(1) George Ransom, born 20 October 1890, died 15 March 1964, married Laura Martin; (2) Herbert Franklin, born 4 February 1892, died 3 July 1943, married Lula Lewis; (3) Mattie Joyce, born 13 March 1894, died 13 February 1939, married L.C. Dula; (4) Charles Herman, born 4 October 1896, died 4 November 1922 unmarried; (5) William Clyde, born 20 December 1899, died 21 January 1974, married Gladys Corker; (6) Lytle Blaylock, born 7 January 1903, died 9 November 1944, married Frances Laws; (7) James Cecil, born 3 January 1906, married first Janie Humphries and second, Ruth Norman, is living; (8) Lelia Bell born 8 January 1909, died 3 December 1954, married R. Don Laws, Jr.; (9) Harvel Pearson, born 7 April 1913, married Dare Eller, is living.

Harvel Pearson Howell was the seventh son of William Lewis and Lelia Pearson Howell. His parents lived in Wilkesboro and Moravian Falls. He has spent most of his life in North Wilkesboro as a salesman for Penny's and Belk's stores. He married Vetra Dare Eller 18 July 1937. They are avid gardners and trout fishermen. They are active members of the North Wilkesboro First Methodist Church. They have two daughters:

Linda Dare, born 14 October 1940, married Daniel Wellborn Edmiston 5 August 1962. They have one son, John Howell Edmiston, born 20 January 1964. Linda is a secretary in the insurance department of Ithaca. Dan designs saw mill equipment, and John is a spring 1982 graduate of Wilkes Central and talented in fine line drawing.

Ella Virginia Howell, born 8 March 1943, married William Zack Rhodes 17 October 1963. They have a son, William Andrew Rhodes, born 8 April 1965. Ella is a good homemaker and seamstress. Bill works for the State of North Carolina Highway Department. Andy is a junior at Wilkes Central and an

Joshua Howell.

accomplished guitar player.

Sources: Davie County records; Family Bible; Personal knowledge.

— Dare Eller Howell

WILLIAM HOWELL, CONFEDERATE VETERAN
708

William Howell was born October 29, 1843 at the old Howell plantation in what was later known as the Fleetwood community in Ashe County. He was the son of David Howell, one of the early settlers of Ashe County.

William entered the services of the Confederate Army in the Sixty-Fifth Calvary Regiment-Company L. Family tradition has it that he ran away to enlist a short time before his nineteenth birthday and that his father had a servant take his horse to him because he did not want him in the infantry. He was in many battles and skirmishes, including Chickamauga, New Bern, Perryville, and Richmond. He was taken prisoner on December 3, 1863 at Philadelphia, Tennessee but escaped. He was never wounded, but his clothing was torn by bullets of the enemy. He was a valiant soldier fighting bravely for a cause that he believed right.

On September 12, 1867 William Howell married Elizabeth Jane Garvey, a daughter of James J. and Rachel Johnson Garvey. They moved their family to Wilkes County in approximately 1903, buying a farm in what later became the Cricket community.

Four of the Howell daughters lived in Wilkes County: Eudora Melinda Howell (Mrs. W.H. Waugh), 1870-1927; Julia Ione Howell (Mrs. N.H. Waugh, Jr.), 1875-1953; Ella Mae Howell (Mrs. J.H. Pennell), 1879-1971; Mary Adelaide Howell (Mrs. Walter Jones), 1886-1958.

Both Mr. and Mrs. Howell were active in church and community affairs. Mr. Howell served as a deacon and Sunday School Superintendent in the Baptist Church. Mrs. Howell was postmistress of the community, keeping the post office in a room of her home. Both were known for their hospitality and willingness to help others.

William Howell died in 1926 at the age of 83. Mrs. Howell died in 1930 at the age of 82.

Sources: Family Bible, obituaries, family tradition, and the Roster of North Carolina Troops in the War Between the States.

— Billie Johnson Stringfield

THE HUBBARD FAMILY
709

The first Hubbard in Wilkes County was Benjamin II, whose marriage to Rosanna (Rosannah) Dier was recorded in the Marriage Bonds Asbtracts Book at the Wilkes courthouse in 1784. Benjamin II came to Wilkes County from Halifax County, Va. Benjamin I and his wife Hannah had eight children, including Benjamin II, who built a log home near Moravian Creek about 1785. "The Old Place," with later additions, still stands just north of Highway 18 South and is the site of the annual Hubbard reunion. It is owned by Dr. Fred C. Hubbard of Wilkesboro.

Benjamin II and his wife has seven children, including Joel, born in 1801. Joel married Sarah (or Sallie) Gilreath in 1823. She was born in 1805 to Henry and Levina Parks Gilreath. Her grandfather, William Gilreath, was a captain under Col. Benjamin Cleveland at the Battle of King's Mountain and served in other campaigns. Joel and Sarah's only son, William Henry, was born in 1824. It is believed Joel died the night of his son's birth.

William Henry Hubbard married Jane Elizabeth Saner in 1846. William Henry was a Methodist and served on the Board of Stewards at Sharon and Beulah churches in Moravian Falls. He was the first farmer in his section of the country to terrace land and build up soil, and was an early advocate of livestock laws. He was a county commissioner for years and served as a magistrate. Before the Civil War he was the Democratic member of the court in the days of Whig rule. The force of former Confederates under Maj. Harvey Bingham of Boone camped in his yard and was fed before their successful assault on Fort Hamby, a stronghold of Union deserter-out-laws which terrorized Northwest North Carolina shortly after the Civil War.

Jane Saner Hubbard was born in 1830 to Peter Saner III and Anne Smith Saner, who built a home in Boomer on Warrior Creek about 1820. Her great-grandfather, Peter Saner (Sehnert) Sr., was born in Germany in 1713 and joined the Moravian Church shortly after coming to Pennsylvania in 1740. Her grandfather, Peter Saner, was born in 1749 and came with the first company of boys to the Moravian settlement of Bethabara in present-day Forsyth County about 1764. He was one of the first to live in the single brothers' house in Salem. He left Salem about 1777 to enlist in the Continental Army for three years. He married Catharina Schafer in 1780 and died in 1822 in Hope, N.C.

William Henry Hubbard died in 1897 and Jane Elizabeth Saner Hubbard in 1901. The couple had 11 children, including Julius Cicero Hubbard, who was born in 1859 and died in 1910. He married Lula Cornelius Williams in 1883 and they lived in Wilkesboro. They had four children: Jesse Ferguson, born and died in 1884; Robert Williams, born and died in 1886; Mary Vestal, born 1890 and Julius Cicero, born 1898 and who died in 1972.

The first Julius Hubbard has been described by a sister as "the sunshine of our family." He possessed a cheerful disposition that made others happy to be with him. He operated a store with J.T. Ferguson in Wilkesboro for a number of years and later was a traveling salesman. He was an active member of the Wilkesboro Methodist Church and was Sunday school superintendant for many years. Although left a widow at a relatively young age, and with few resources, Lula Hubbard maintained her home and reared her family, always keeping her independence. She died in 1948.

Mary Hubbard married Edgar Lee Hemphill in 1914 and they had one son, James Edgar. Lee Hemphill died in 1945 and since that time Mrs. Hemphill have lived in her parents' old homeplace in Wilkesboro. James Hemphill married Phyliss Frazier of Greensboro and they live in Charlotte. Their three children are James Lee, Melissa Frazier and Frederick Raymond.

The second Julius C. Hubbard was 12 years old when his father died. He began work on *The Wilkes Patriot* in Wilkesboro at that age and through the years learned all phases of the newspaper business. He was attending Guilford College when World War I began, and he entered the army. He was publisher of *The Wilkes Journal* until its merger with *The Patriot* in 1932, when he became co-publisher of *The Journal-Patriot*. In 1963 he acquired full ownership. He had an optimistic and tenacious nature which helped him be successful in many undertakings. Like his forebears, he was a Methodist, and held positions of leadership in the Wilkesboro Methodist Church. He married Nellie Katherine White, the daughter of Dr. and Mrs. J.W. White of Wilkesboro. Their children are: Nell White, Julius Cicero III and John White. Nell married Corneal L. Domeck Jr., Louisville, Ky. They have four children, Corneal III, Anne Winifred, Amanda Katherine and Julia Hubbard. Corneal III married Nancy Lindahl of Louisville, and Anne married James Burke. They live in Galveston, Texas. Corneal and Nancy have two sons, Corneal IV and Robert Craig. Julius III married Dorothy Shiver of Charlotte. Their children are Frances Shiver, Julius Cicero IV and Ellen (Nellie) White. John married Rebecca Shiver, sister of Dorothy. They have three children: John White, Jr., Caroline Elizabeth and Charles Noble.

Sources: Personal Knowledge and Family Records.

— Julius C. Hubbard III
and Julius C. Hubbard IV

HISTORY OF HUBBARD FAMILY
710

The history of the Hubbard Family extends from the year 868 at which time Hubbards from northern Europe landed on the coast of east Anglia. In the year 1600 several families came from England and settled in the Virginia colonies.

The history of the Hubbard Family began with Benjamin Hubbard I who settled in Halifax County, Virginia in 1770. Benjamin Hubbard II came to Wilkes County, N.C. in 1785, changing land with John Dyer of Halifax County, Va. In July, 1789 Elisha Dyer transferred to Benjamin Hubbard 200 acres on Warrior Creek. A few years later, Benjamin Hubbard acquired 245 acres of land on Moravian Creek from Nathaniel Hubbard, his brother.

Benjamin Hubbard I and his wife Hannah, of Halifax Co., V.A., had eight children: Benjamin II, Hannah, Rebecca, Nathaniel, Joel, Judith, Sarah, and Druscilla.

Benjamin II married Rosanna Dier January 26, 1784 in Wilkes County. They had seven children: Nathaniel, Elizabeth, Elisha, Nancy B., Lewis, Joel, b. 11-23-1801 and Cynthia. Benjamin II was the first Hubbard who lived on the Hubbard Farm at Moravian Creek. More will be said about this later.

Joel Hubbard, son of Benjamin II, married Sally Gilreath, 2-20-1823. She was born 2-22-1805 and died October, 1841. There is no date of Joel's death. However, it was approximately 1824 or 1825. Joel is buried in Gilreath graveyard at Moravian Falls. It has been said that Joel's only son, William Henry b. 4-6-1824 and d. 12-27-1897, was born the same night that his father died. More will be said about William Henry and his family later. On 10-3-1826, Sally Hubbard married Benjamin Hubbard Brown.

William Henry Hubbard who raised the third family at the old place married Mary Jane Elizabeth Saner on 12-22-1846. Jane was the daughter of Peter and Anna Smith Saner who lived at Boomer, N.C. Jane was b. 3-23-1830 and d. 9-9-1901. Both are buried in Moravian Falls Cemetery. They lived their entire married life and raised a large family at the old Hubbard Home Place. The old place which is now in its 200th year, was further developed by William Henry Hubbard into an 800 acre estate. He was not only a progressive farmer, but for years was county commissioner and a squire who tried many cases at the old home place.

The old Hubbard Home Place is about one-half mile beyond the Moravian Creek Bridge on Hwy. 18. The old highway upon which the home place was, is about 200 ft. north of Hwy. 18.

The children of William Henry and his wife Jane were as follows: the first, Sally Ann b. 7-5-1848, d. 2-28-1920, married James Harrison Hall, 1-17-1878, lived at the old Saner place at Boomer. She had three children: Marvin, Mamie Jane and Annie Lou. Marvin died as a baby, Mamie Jane married Thomas Howell and Annie Lou married Martin Gibbs.

The second child Henrietta Mathilda b. 1850, d. 1905, married Roland Lloyd Scorggs, 1-22-1879. They have five children: Harriet Jane, b. 1880, married Bartlett Alphonoso Ferguson. William Clegg, b. 1881, married Judie Mae Sloop 1907; Robert Keener, b. 1883, married Fannie Cooper, George Stacy, b. 1885 married Monroe Sloop; Charles David, b. 1888 married Eva Bouchelle.

The third child Benjamin Saner b. 1852, d. 1871. He did not marry and is buried in the Edgewood Cemetery.

The fourth child Joel Thomas, b. 8-11-1855, d. 11-18-1933, married Annie Yeakle Calloway, daughter of Dr. James Calloway, 4-18-1882. They had six children: James Calloway, b. 1883, married Margaret Wright, 1904; William Eugene, b. 1886, married Hattie Alexander, 1905; Thomas Saner, b. 1887, never married; Annie Elizabeth, b. 1891, d. 1942, married Guy Welborn 1914; Frederick Cecil, M.D., F.A.C.S., b. 1893, married Ann Somers 1917; Alice Yeakle, b. 1895, married Arthur Samuel Cassel 1915.

The fifth child Julius Cicero Clingman, b. 1859, d. 1910, married Lula Cornelius Williams 1883. They had four children: Jessie Ferguson, b. 1884, d. 1884; Robert William, b. 1886, d. 1886; Mary Vestal, b. 1890, married Edgar Lee Hemphill, 1914; Julius Cicero, Jr., b. 1898, married Nellie White, 1923.

Julius was editor of the *JOURNAL PATRIOT* in North Wilkesboro for years.

The sixth child Nancy Virginia, b. 1860, d. 1861.

The seventh child Robert Edward Lee, b. 1862, d. 1931, married Mamie Roth, 1893, they had three children: Mary Elizabeth, b. 1894, d. 1897; Catherine, b. 1896, married Oscar K. Merritt who was a prominent businessman in Mt. Airy; Emily Elizabeth, b. 1900, married Raymond Harris, 1924. He was a businessman in Elkin, N.C.; Robert Edward Lee was a prominent businessman and manufacturer in Elkin, N.C.

The eight child John Summerfield, b. 1864, d. 1867.

The ninth child Charles Calvin, b. 1868, d. 1944, married Frances Porter 1893, had three children: Hope b. 1894, never married; Faith died in infancy; Dorothy, b. 1897, married Elbert Kearns, 1921. Charles Calvin graduated in medicine at Jefferson Medical College and practiced for many years in Randolph County, N.C.

The tenth child William Rufus Jackson, b. 1871, d. 1955, was the fifth generation who rasied a family at the old Hubbard homestead. He married Ella Joann Chatham 1890. They had ten children; Henry Chatham, b. 1891 married Esther Pardue 1914; Robert Bidwell, b. 1893, d. 1895; Ruth, b. 1896, d. 1967; James Owen, b. 1897, married Lois Stevens 1940; Paul Mesley, b. 1899, married Gladys Switzer 1935; Frances Elizabeth, b. 1901, d. 1901; John Dwight, b. 1902, d. infancy, Minnie Gertrude, b. 1904, d. 1942, married Harvey Bruce Pearson 1926; Ralph, b. 1908, d. 1964, married Jean Dickson 1931.

The eleventh child Mary Lella Jane, b. 1874, d. 1956, married William Sherman Surratt 1897, had two children: Wilhelmina Badgett, b. 1898, d. 1981, married William Walter Greer 1921; Agnes Elizabeth, b. 1906, married Griffin Welt Humphries 1930.

Sources: Records of Lucy Hubbard Critcher; Wilkes County Register of Deeds; *1,000 Years of Hubbard History,* by Day.

— Fred C. Hubbard, M.D. F.A.C.S.

WILLIAM HUBBARD

711

William Hubbard owned and ran Hubbards Mill on Lewis Fork Creek. The mill became one of the centers of action in the Lewis Fork township. Elections were held at the mill in a far different manner than in the case today. In those days the men of the township, and possibly some of the non-voting women, would begin to gather early on the day of election. Much powerful political persuasion would ensue until the appointed hour of the election. It is said that Will Hubbard would utilize a touch of apple brandy from time to time as an agent of such persuasion, and it is further said that the brandy could be far more effective than the glibbest of arguments. At the appointed hour the election holder would ask those who so desired to stand and be counted for their party or their candidate. It is, of course, possible that some of those influenced by the brandy

persuasion might have stood a little less straight than others, but the mountain men stood then as now by that in which they believed.

Martha Ann Hubbard, daughter of William and Susan Hubbard was married to Adney Foster, and they raised their family in a home along the creek.

Sources: Personal knowledge.

— Roy Foster, Jr.

THE CHARLES HENRY HULCHER FAMILY

712

My dad, C.H. Hulcher, and mother, Inez Butler Hulcher, moved to Wilkesboro with their four children in 1922. They were married in 1914 and had lived in Mountain City, Tenn., for eight years where their children were born. He built a brick home on 404 South Cherry St. in Wilkesboro around 1924 where we all lived until we finished school or college and married. This was their home for the remainder of their lives and is still owned by the family. Dad was a life long Democrat and mother, a Republican.

My mother, Inez Butler Hulcher, was born Oct. 29, 1884. She was a graduate of Sullins College in Bristol, Va., with a degree in music and a major in piano. She devoted her life to the care and rearing of her family. However, she enjoyed and made use of her musical talents. She was a member of the Music Club and often entertained the Club in her home. She was a dedicated member and faithful worker of the Wilkesboro Methodist Church. She was a member and was President of the Wilkesboro Womans Club and a member of the Eastern Star. She died Sept. 29, 1964.

C.H. Hulcher started in the feed business as the manager of Miller-Pharr & Co. He was the first to manufacture poultry feeds on a commercial basis in Wilkes County. In the early twenties he manufactured and encouraged the use of laying mash instead of farm grains for increased growth and egg production in poultry. This feed store which was located on Cherry St. N. Wilkesboro, was damaged when the water from a flood of the Yadkin River completely covered and destroyed the contents of the store. He then moved the business to 10th St. where he became sole owner. He later moved to a rock building on the corner of Forester Ave. and 10th St. Afterwards he purchased a building and installed storage and modern grinding and milling facilities at 100 South 6th St. in North Wilkesboro. It is now owned and operated by the Hulcher family as Hulcher Brothers & Co.

Around 1900 my father and his brother, C.A. Hulcher, operated a store and a root and herb business in Mountain City, Tenn., under the name of Hulcher Brothers. They also, as Hulcher Brothers owned property near the corner of 10th and C. St. in North Wilkesboro. It contained 8500 sq. feet and was sold to W.L. Hendrix in 1903 for $500.00.

From 1913 to 1921, my dad worked as a salesman for E.W. King Co., Bristol, Tenn. He drove a hack, a covered four wheel buggy,

Charles H. and Inez Butler Hulcher.

which was filled with trunks of samples and was pulled by two fine horses. He sold to large country stores from Mountain City, Tenn., through Wilkes County. After eight years with E.W. King he resigned and moved to Wilkesboro, where earlier he had attended Moravian Falls Acadamy.

The first Hulcher to come to Wilkes County was my grandfather, W.C. Hulcher. He was born in Richmond, Va. Dec. 22, 1851. He was the youngest soldier to enlist in the Confederate Army at 10½ years of age. When the Civil War ended he came to Wilkes County and lived for sometime with Charles N. Hunt and wife, Minnie Stokes Hunt, relatives of Monford Sidney Stokes. In 1876 he married Laura M. Dobbins, daughter of Hugh A. Dobbins of Watauga County. My grandfather's home still stands in Todd, N.C. in good condition. He was a merchant and government whisky tester and also a Mason. These grandparents had six children. Three died very young. The others were: my father, Charles Henry Hulcher, born Dec. 18, 1876, died July 15, 1957; Clinton A. Hulcher, Mar. 29, 1878-Apr. 23, 1918; Margaret Hulcher Baird, Apr. 21, 1885-Nov. 26, 1978.

I was born in Johnson County, Tenn., publicized a number of years ago as being the most Republican county in the U.S. Mother's family, the Butlers, were all very prominent in Republican politics. Mother's father, Richard H. Butler married Nancy Ann Ingram. He was a member of the Johnson County Court for 34 years and chairman for 28 years, and also a Mason. My great-grandfather, Roderick R. Butler, was elected in 1867 and served 10 years as a member of the U.S. Congress, and 24 years in Tenn. State Legislature. He was a Lieutenant Colonel in the Union Army during the Civil War, where my grandfather, Richard H. Butler also served. Records of the Butler family are preserved in the Roderick Butler House in Mountain City, Tenn., built in 1870, and entered in the National Register of Historic Places by the U.S. Dept. of Interior Jan. 25, 1974.

The children of Charles H. and Inez B. Hulcher were: Charles Butler Hulcher, born Jan. 17, 1915, married Adelene Graham Jones. Their children are Charles B. Hulcher, Jr., and William Franklin Hulcher; Anna Laura Hulcher married Albert S. Garwood. Their children are Albert S. Garwood, Jr., Marilyn Garwood Hayes and Robert Garwood; Margaret Ruth Hulcher married Thomas E. Story, Jr., Wilkesboro. Their children are, Rebecca Story Wilson, Ed. Story, and Clarissa Story.

Clinton Lucas Hulcher was born April 30, 1921, died June 28, 1964. He married Dorothy Divan. They had two children, Marie Hulcher and Anne Hulcher of Mt. Vernon, Ohio.

Charles Henry Hulcher, Inez B. Hulcher and Clinton L. Hulcher are buried in Mount Lawn Cemetery, near North Wilkesboro, N.C.

Margaret H. Baird and Thomas J. Baird are also buried in Mount Lawn Cemetery.

Sources: Family Bibles, Family records Watauga Democrat — July 7, 1898 Personal Knowledge.

— Charles B. Hulcher

CHARLIE HUNT'S FAMILY
713

Charlie Hunt was born in Wilkes County January 12, 1869, to Perry and Levine Carmichael Hunt. He was a brother of John, Lee, Robert, Ulyses, Effie, Sue, Lucy, Cora and Clara. Perry, the father of Charlie, was a slave in Wilkes County and his mother, Levine, was a slave in Ashe County.

Charlies had no formal education and could only read and write his name. He was a shrewd and brilliant businessman and trader, worked on the railroad and helped to build some of the first roads in the Ronda and Roaring River areas. He was also the owner of more than four hundred (400) acres of land surrounding his homeplace.

The wedding of Charlie and Virginia (Jenny) Dowell took place when she was fourteen (14) years old and he was sixteen (16). Their chil-

dren were Paul, Weaver, Raymond, Isadora, Carl, Ralph, Lee, Travis, Clyde, Norman, Minnie (Mrs. Jesse) Bowers, Bessie (Mrs. Will) Hampton, Effie (Mrs. Thurman) Martin, and Susie (Mrs. Owens) Dobbins.

Charlie was an outstanding and powerful leader in the Poplar Springs Baptist Church near Roaring River, and a co-founder of the Mt. Pleasant Baptist Church in Jonesville, North Carolina. He and several of his children are buried in the Poplar Spring Baptist Church Cemetery.

When Charlie worked on public jobs, he also farmed, growing tobacco, wheat, and corn. I can remember the threshing machine coming to Grandpa Charlie's farm to thresh his wheat. Aunt Minnie, the oldest daughter, would cook a feast for the workers. I remember the cakes she made and called sweet bread, and just how delicious they were, also the huge apple and blackberry pies.

Grandpa Charlie had a pair of beautiful mules he used for plowing. One was a big, beautiful, reddish-brown, and the other one was big and black. My father had a small white mule, and sometimes my brother and I would race him with another mule that we used to haul corn. Grandpa saw us racing and threatened to tell on us, but he never did.

Charlie lost his wife in 1908 and had a hard time rearing his family. My father (Ralph) told me how he, his brothers, and sisters took turns wearing the less than adequate shoes they had to share. He said sometimes some of them would have to stay at home because they didn't have adequate clothing for all of them to attend school.

All of Charlie's children lived in West Virginia sometime during their young adult life except Travis, Paul and Lee. Charlie lived there several years in the early 1920's, but moved back to Wilkes County, North Carolina to start farming again.

Although Charlie had no education, he stressed education to his children and had three (3) to attend college. Weaver and Effie attended A. & M. College in Greensboro (Now A & T University) and Travis attended Winston-Salem Teachers College (now Winston-Salem State University).

All of Charlie and Jenny's children are deceased except Weaver, Effie, and Carl. Weaver is ninety (90) years old, living near Roaring River, attends Poplar Springs Baptist Church and is a very active person. Effie lives near Roaring River and is very active in Poplar Springs Baptist Church. Carl lives near Roaring River and has a little country story that keeps him very busy. On cold winter days he sits around his wood stove visiting with his customers giving away drinks and candy to anyone who will accept them.

My father (Ralph) was a cold miner in West Virginia for twenty-one years. He then moved to North Carolina to work in a textile mill and farm along with raising chickens to sell. I am one of seven (7) children, having five (5) brothers and one (1) sister. They are Ralph, Jr., Chester, Wavely, Billie and Bobby (twins), and Freddie.

In 1970 we had our first "Hunt" family reunion and we only had a very small group of relatives. In the past eleven (11) years the crowd has increased to close to two hundred relatives, coming from as far away as California and several states across the country.

Our relatives have become doctors, nurses, lawyers, engineers, mechanics, secretaries, teachers, and held many other prominent positions.

Sources: Interviews with old family members, Wilkes County records, and personal knowledge.

— Dorothy Hunt Mitchell

THE JOHN HUNT FAMILY
714

The Hunts of eastern Wilkes County were hard-working, proud descendants of slaves who spent at least a part of their lives in that area.

According to Census records, Perry Hunt was born between 1842 and 1845. He remained a slave on a plantation east of Wilkesboro until probably the early 1860's when he escaped from his master and married Levine (Vina) Carmical of Ashe County. Perry was well-known for his bravery and horsemanship. He later owned land in the Edwards Township area of Wilkes County. At one time he and his family lived in a small house on the land that is now owned by his great-granddaughter and her husband, Ronald and Sara Hunt Whittington.

John Hunt Family, c. 1912: Sons Mason and Joseph, Father John C. Hunt and son Will.

Of the ten children born to Perry and Levine Hunt, John Charles was the oldest (born 1863).

John married Katie Gwyn, daughter of Eliza Gwyn, a former slave on Green Hill Plantation at Ronda. In the early years of their marriage, they lived in a small house near Green Hill. Some time later they built a large, beautiful house on land that he owned, just off of what is now Highway 268 in Ronda. Though structural changes have been made, the house still stands at this spot. For most of John's life he and his family farmed this land as well as other

land that he rented along the Yadkin River.

To Katie and John were born these children: Mason, who married Lillie Martin of Surry County; Mary, who married Sid Gadberry of Yadkin County; Ada, who for approximately thirty years worked as the cook for the Presley Brown family in Wilkesboro, and had one daughter Ruby, wife of Milton James Ingram; Lillie, who married Benjamin Covington of Hamlet, and had five sons. Two of their sons are deceased, one lives in California, and Benjamin and the other two sons live on Long Island, N.Y. Will married Pearl Hawkins of Wilkes County. They had six children. One is deceased, one lives in Ronda, and four live in New York. Hugh married Bessie Hawkins of Wilkes County and had three children. Kate married Jack Hardison (who still lives in Wilkesboro) and had four children who now live in Virginia and North Carolina. Walter married Hazel Boles of Surry County. They had seven children. One is deceased and the others live in Detroit, New York and North Carolina. Joe worked for most of his adult life in the mines of West Virginia.

After Katie's death, John married Cora Hickerson. Their children were Gordon, Gwyn, Charles and a daughter who died as an infant. Gwyn was killed during the Korean War. Gordon is married and lives in New Jersey. Charles married Vici Hash of Virginia. They have one son and live in Maryland.

Throughout John's adult life he was a deacon and ardent supporter of Poplar Springs Baptist Church in Roaring River and a member of the Yadkin Valley Baptist Association.

John was highly respected in the farming and business communities of the area. He is remembered by his family and friends as an industrious farmer and a devout Christian.

Sources: U.S. Census Records, personal knowledge and family memories.

— Ruby Hunt Ingram

JAMES T. HUTCHENS FAMILY
715

James Thomas Hutchens I (1 May 1860 —

20 Oct 1923) was born in Yadkin County the son of Catherine Hutchens. He had two brothers: William (@ 1850-3 Apr 1937) who married Mary Goff; and Edward Hauser (15 Jun 1857 — 21 Feb 1930) who married Janie Williams Warren. James Thomas had four sisters: Letty Hutchens Whitaker, Sarah Hutchens Mathison, Alsey Hutchens Aldrid and Nancy.

James came to Wilkes County about 1880. He met and married his wife Polly Mitchell (21 Apr 1856 — 14 Apr 1926) on 13 Aug 1881, the daughter of Joseph William and Susanna King Mitchell. For several years he worked for Turner White Casket Company. At one time he owned and operated a general store in Wilkesboro. After his store burned, they moved to the Buck Community of Wilkes where he was a farmer until his death.

James and Polly had a large family: Commadore (27 July 1885 — 20 Oct 1949) who married Meg Adams; Freeland (10 May 1887 17 Mar. 1937) who married Bessie Shumate; Mary Ann (2 Jun 1890) who married Walter Parsons; Ellen (28 Aug 1892 — 11 Mar 1957) who married Jessie Nichols; P.C. "Doc" Hutchens (31 Jan 1895 — 2 Mar 1982) who married Bessie Frith; John (30 Mar 1897 — 21 May 1975) who married Dottie Smith; Ada Bertha (16 Apr 1901 — died infant); Bradshaw (6 July 1902 — 19 Apr 1981) who married Nona Whittington; Eugene (27 June 1906 — 10 Apr 1954) who married Roberta Tuttle; and William (15 Jan 1911), the daughter of Mack and Rosa Church Bishop. John, William, P.C. and Bradshaw all celebrated fifty years of marraige with their wives.

William and Nellie Hutchens had seven children: Agnes (13 Mar 1932) married Griffen Wilcox; James Thomas (J.T.) (20 Sept 1933) married Shirley Foster; Conrad (6 Feb 1935 — 10 Mar 1935); Billy E. (17 Sept. 1936) married Colena Lambert daughter of Wiley and Mary Church Lambert; Bernice (13 Aug 1943) married first Lloyd Byers and second Buddy Rhodes; Johnny (2 Aug 1945) married Joyce Smithey daughter of W.O. and Clara Johnson Smithey; and Tony (26 Mary 1947) married

James T. Hutchens Family. Front: l. to r. — John, James I, Polly, Gene, Bradshaw. Back: l. to r. — P.C. (Doc), Commodore, Freeland, Ann, Ellen.

Ann Kilby daughter of Roy and Dorothy Anderson Kilby.

James Thomas (J.T.) Hutchens graduated from Millers Creek School in 1952. He served in the United States Army from July 1955 until May 1957. He was stationed at Fort Knox, Kentucky in Company A 7th Tank Battalion 3rd Armored Division, where he had basic training. Later he was stationed in Germany.

J.T. married Shirley Foster (2 Dec 1935) daughter of Walter M. and Florence Parsons Foster on 24 Nov 1953. To this union were born two children: Teresa Carol (15 Aug 1954) married first Terry S. Kilby, son of Sylvan and Maie Faw Kilby, on 1 July 1972. They had one son Terry Stephen, Jr. (19 Oct 1974). Teresa's second marriage was to George "Butch" Woodie, son of George Doughton Woodie Sr. and Virginia Dare Neely Woodie. They have a son Joshua Derick Woodie (30 May 1980).

Will and Nellie Bishop Hutchens.

James Thomas Hutchens, Jr. (18 Aug 1956) married first Marie Wyatt, daughter of Herman and Mary Brown Wyatt. A son Christopher (7 Feb 1977) and daughter Jennifer Lynn (10 Feb 1979) was born to this union. James' second marriage was to Lisa Kay Call, daughter of Hubert and Margaret Stone Call. They have a son Joey Thomas Hutchens (8 Oct 1981).

This line of Hutchens are descendants of Strangeman Hutchens (1907-10 Feb 1792) and Elizabeth Cox (25 Feb 1713 -ca 1800). Strangeman was born in Henrico County, Virginia and moved to Surry County in 1786 (in the part which became Yadkin County in 1850), when he was seventy-nine years old. The first Hutchens family in Surry County can be located approximately N.E. of Yadkinville on the branches of Forbush Creek and Deep Creek in what is now Yadkin County.

Sources: *Descendants of Strangeman Hutchens*, by Rita Hineman Townsend, courthouse records, and personal knowledge of family members.

— Shirley Hutchens

THE MILTON INGRAM FAMILY
716

Milton James Ingram, Sr., was a man of "many hats". He was just as happy in the classroom as he was in his church, in the out-of-doors, in school or civic club meetings; at sports events, or just at home watching a game with his family, where he was both "armchair coach and referee". Of all the "hats" that Milton wore, those of father and husband were most important to him.

Milton was born on May 4, 1920, at Lancaster, South Carolina, the son of Milton and Roxie Beckham Ingram. His father was a presiding elder in the A.M.E. Zion Church, and his mother was a school teacher. The father died when Milton James (as he was called in Lancaster) was very young, but his mother and other family members were Christians and Milton grew up with a strong snese of devotion to the church. His aunts, Mamie Beckham Cunningham, Mattie Beckham Parker, and Carrie Beckham Parker, were also school teachers, so the importance of education was stressed in the home.

Milton was educated in the public schools of Lancaster County. After graduating from high school, he enrolled in Friendship Junior College at Rock Hill, S.C. where he graduated in 1941. He also graduated from Winston-Salem Teachers College in 1946, and A. & T. College Graduate School in 1955.

From 1942-1945, Milton was a soldier in the U.S. Army and saw duty in Europe and North Africa. After his discharge from the army, he re-entered WSTC.

It was there that he met his future wife, Ruby Hunt of Wilkesboro. They graduated in May, 1946, and were married on June 28, 1947, in Wilkesboro.

Milton taught school in Lancaster for one year. Then in 1947, he was appointed to teach at Woodlawn Elementary School in North Wilkesboro. In 1951, he was appointed principal, but continued his teaching and coaching duties. After the black and white schools were merged in 1967, Milton was assigned to North Wilkesboro Elementary School as a classroom teacher. There, from 1967-1971, he was teacher and coach. From 1971, until his heart attack in September 1976 and his death in January 1977, Milton was assistant principal, teacher and coach.

Milton's religion was his life. He lived on faith and strongly believed that God would see us through all our trials. After moving to Wilkesboro, he joined Denny's Grove A.M.E. Zion Church where he later served as Sunday School teacher and superintendent, steward, trustee and pastor. He was ordained by the A.M.E. Zion Church and also pastored churches in Davie, Alexander, and Iredell Counties.

But sports, education and religion did not consume all of Milton's time. Gradually he became involved in other affairs of the community. He was a charter member of the Board of Trustees of Wilkes Community College, a member of the Boy Scouts of America, the Board of Directors of Wilkes Boys Town, the N. Wilkesboro Optimist Club, and the N.C. Parks and Recreation Commission. It was through these organizations that he worked for the youth of Wilkes County.

The desire to become a viable part of one's community seemed to be an inherent characteristic in the Ingram Family. The children were also very much a part af their school and church communities. They were christened at Denny's Grove A.M.E. Zion Church. Later on they joined the church and became active in yough activities.

Milton James Ingram, Jr., was born May 16, 1948, in Wilkesboro. He graduated from Lincoln Heights School in 1966. He attended A & T College in Greensboro where he was a member of the Air Force ROTC and the Arnold Air Society. Jim is now employed by Lowe's of Orangeburg, S.C.

Carol Annette was born on December 22, 1953, in North Wilkesboro. She attended Lincoln Heights School and graduated from Wilkes Central High School in 1972 and Appalachian State University in 1976. On January 3, 1976, she married Zaphon Robert Wilson, the son of Zaphon and Dorothy Denny Wilson and the grandson of Robert and Kathryn Denny of North Wilkesboro. They have one son, Kevin Anson Wilson, born July 9, 1978 at Elizabeth City. Annette is currently employed by the Morehouse School of Medicine while Zaphon is on leave of absence from the faculty of Appalachian State Univ. and studying at Atlanta Univ.

Carrie Denise Ingram was born January 27, 1957, in N. Wilkesboro. She attended Lincoln Heights and North Wilkesboro Elementary Schools and graduated from Wilkes Central High School in 1975, and N.C. State Univ. in 1980. She is now completing a two-year program as a forest agent with the Peace Corps in Senegal, West Africa.

By precept and example, Milton taught his children the importance of honest work, love and service to others. Though one of his faults might have been that of becoming too involved in the world around him, Milton's life was one of service.

Sources: School and family records; personal knowledge.

— Ruby Hunt Ingram

THE JARVIS FAMILY
717

Rev. Richard F. Jarvis was the last Confederate Veteran to die in Wilkes. He died in 1942 at the age of 99. He was the son of William and Lucinda Kemp Jarvis, a grandson of John J. and Sally Chambers Jarvis. (They both lived to be over one hundred years old. One was 103, the other was 106.) They had fifteen children, the last was born when she was 53.

William's family lived on the Wilkes-Iredell county line. They owned slaves and each child was to inherit slaves and land, but the Civil War freed the slaves.

Their children were Ransome Lee (who built the first brick store in North Wilkesboro), Joseph, John, Alonzo, Tom, Lodemie, Sarah Ann, Minda and Ida. After his first wife died he married Nancy Roberts and they had Sidney, Lindsay, and Conrad.

Richard and Martha Ann Pardue Jarvis were the parents of Lodemie who married James E.C. Gilreath, William Felix who married Martha Ann Barlowe, Clara Eva who married Thomas McNeil, James R. Jarvis who married Margaret McKellar from Utah. They lost a son, Hugh in World War II. Their son Howard ran against his father for Senator and lost. He then went to California. He remained in politics. In

1979 he led the fight to lower taxes with Proposition 13 in California. He has traveled all over the United States and several foreign countries to help with lowering taxes.

Lodemie Jarvis Gilreath's uncle was Rev. Ancil Pardue. He was a well known Baptist minister in Wilkes County. Her other uncle was Dan Pardue of Moravian Falls.

Sources: Personal research and knowledge.

— Cornelia Gilreath Bumgarner

JAMES McBRIDE and JULIA ANN GRAY (GARNER) JARVIS
718

When James McBride and Julia Ann Gray Garner Jarvis, widow of Hillary T., moved into the Constant Gray homeplace, they had a few family of five sons and five daughters, the oldest being Marcue LaFayett, born in 1866. He operated the Jarvice, N.C., post office with his wife, Sally Armstrong Jarvis. The building also served as a general store. One end of the counter next to the door had iron rods from floor to ceiling and pigeon holes behind where Uncle Mack would put the mail for the community. There was a big grist mill just below the post office run by water power piped from Brier Creek and sent pouring over a big wheel. He would give me banana candy every time I went to the store with Daddy. The building still stands near Cranberry Church on 421 to where it was moved when the road was built. It is now known as the A.H. Robert's place. Uncle Mack had one son, Lee, who lived in Winston-Salem, and one granddaughter, Ethel.

James Oliver Jarvis (born 1867) went to California after finishing his school work and marrying Mattie Holbrook of Traphill. They had two children, Vena Leah and Tirra. He did well in real estate and died in his car while returning home from a fishing trip. He is buried in Turlock, California.

Noah Thomas Jarvis (born 1870) like his brother was not satisfied with the short school years at home so he went to Traphill Institute to acquire more education. He later married Nellie Mastin and they had Leona (Mathis), Lois (Roberts), Dwight married Bonnie Martin, James married Vickie Billings, Nell (Walker), Minnie Sue (Church) and Noah, Jr., married Reba Staley.

Uncle Noah was known as a good preacher and man and was loved by all who knew him. He was pastor of Brier Creek Church for thirty-six years, at Ronda many years and also at Cranberry, Fishing Creek and others. He baptized the writer in Brier Creek which runs through the Jarvis farm. We always had good swimming ponds in the creek and legend is that when Eula, my sister, was baptized in the creek, the preacher did not get her completely under. Daddy said, "Reverend, I like to see the water cover her," and he baptized her again. While she was under, the preacher looked up to see if Daddy were satisfied. Eula says that they drowned her sins instead of washing them away.

The baptizing service was held sometimes in Brier Creek between Uncle Noah's and the

James McBride Jarvis.

Mansfield home in the swimming pool. The cold water came from the side of Little Brushy Mountain into a green pasture land. It was said Vena's baptism would have looked natural had she entered the water from the diving board.

Columbus Franklin, (born 1876) visited friends in California. He liked it so well he lived there and had one daughter, Anita Ballard, now of San Francisco. Anita came east to visit her many cousins a few years ago. Her father had grape and orange groves in California.

Uncle Frank was the only one of the Jarvis or Garner boys who could not be trusted to haul barrels of government liquor on a two-horse wagon to Statesville. It seems he had a way of removing the government label and getting a hose in the opening. This was an overnight trip. It was a good business when the seven boys were on the farm and in school. Several men were employed to keep the wood cut, fires going under the boilers, buildings in repair, liquor stored to age, and waterpipes operating. A government agent was there much of the time and Grandma said she made bigger profit from boarding the government agents than the boys did from the sale of the liquor. Most of the mountain was fenced with split rails to keep in the pigs to fatten on the distillery mash. It was piped across the branch into long troughs. They say it all worked together for a good income.

Lydia Jane was the first of the family to die. She was born in 1869 and died at the age of three. While she was playing in the garden with her mother, she ate a little Irish potato while it was green. It is believed this killed her. She is buried in the Jarvis cemetary on the farm.

Julia Mathis, born 1872, wife of M.M. Mathis, died in Sheridan, Wyoming. Samantha Ever, born 1879, wife of Marcus Mathis, died in Wyoming. Jetty Embesetta, born 1877, wife of Edward H. Glass, contractor, died in Bluefield, West Virginia. They had six children. Minnie Adiline Glass died in West Virginia.

Sources: Family records, grave stones, personal knowledge.

— Pauline Jarvis Clark

LINDSEY MANSFIELD and EULORA HENDERSON JARVIS
719

Lindsey Mansfield Jarvis was born in 1874 in Wilkes County, died in 1955, and was buried at Cranberry Baptist Church. He was the son of James McBride, born 1841, and Julia Ann Gray Garner Jarvis, born 1840 in Wilkes, and was a descendant of John and Lydia Nicholson Jarvis and of John, born 1758, and Sally Chambers Jarvis.

The legend is that Sally received permission from her parents to ride her horse to the Canadian border to marry John Jarvis, who was serving in the Revolutionary War. She spent most of the summer on horseback; they were married in 1779 and returned to Yadkinville where they had fifteen children; eleven known to be James McBride, John, Nelson, Wiley, Levi, Noah, William of Kings Creek, Lydia, Mary and Nancy.

Mansfiled's parents, James McBride and Julia Ann, gave the land and were instrumental in founding Cranberry Baptist Church. He started to church in the log building and served as a deacon fifty-one years, was a teacher and choir director. Mansfield attended Jonesville Academy.

He went west and worked for the railroad while waiting for Eulora to reach age sixteen so they could be married. She was ten years younger, and he called her "Tadpole" because of her big dark brown eyes.

Eulora May Henderson Jarvis, born 1884, died 1980, is buried at Cranberry also. She was the daughter of John Eli and Margaret Wood Roberts Henderson, granddaughter of Caroline Somers and Eli Henderson.

Floyd and William Roberts were sons of her mother's first marriage. Her sister was Vera White and brother, James Garfield. Following her mother's death, her father married Jane E. Blackburn and they had Pearl, Johnson, Bertha Culler, Besta Bowers, Grace Hill, Esta Henderson, and John Eli.

Legend is that Abram Henderson great grandfather of Eulora Jarvis was a man of wealth who had bought property in Iredell County. While bringing his wife and two children by wagon from Kentucky, he went ahead scouting the road. It is believed he was robbed and killed. Only his hat was found in New River. The family came on to Iredell and started a new life.

Eulora attended schools at Dellaplane and Shady Grove. She was a Bible scholar and taught Sunday School; she was talented in arts and crafts; and was a convert in the log church called the Meeting House.

Eulor and Mansfield were married in 1900 at her home by Rev. Daniel Honeycutt. She wore a white silk lace-trimmed wedding dress she had made from material sent to her by Floyd Roberts from England. For her honeymoon trip to Roaring River by buggy, she had made a pink cashmere dress and wore a black cape given to her by her husband for a wedding gift.

Eulora's father owned a gristmill, saw mill, straight chair and coffin business on Brier Creek where she helped her father keep records. It was located a mile below the Jarvis,

Lindsey Mansfield and Eulora Henderson Jarvis.

In 1972 she married Lewis E. Correll who died in 1981. Eula resides in Clemmons.

Jay Franklin, born 1916, died in 1946 in a highway accident; leaving his widow, Dorothy DeHart Jarvis, and two daughters, Linda Jean Pullen of Washington, D.C. and Juanita Faye Hutchins of Farmington.

Vena Leah, born 1918, married William Shephard John, owner of Lefkowitz Tailor Shop, now retired. They were married on the farm by her uncle, the Rev. Noat T. Jarvis, and the house was beautifully decorated with home-grown flowers. Their children are Wanda Leah Priddy of Clemmons, William Shepard, Jr., of Charlotte, and Lora Lynn of Winston-Salem.

Dorothea Mozelle "Zelle", born 1920 died 1973, attended college in Salisbury, Md. She was Miss Winston-Salem in 1941 and worked as an accountant for twenty years in Wilmington. She and John Robert Pegg were married in 1942.

Lindsey Mansfield, Jr., born in 1924, married Jeraldine Brown in 1953. Their son is Lindsey Robert and they live on the Jarvis farm which was originally purchased by James Gray in 1799. L.M., Jr., in management with Carolina Mirror Corporation, was previously married to Mary Gilreath and their daughter is Nina Marie Anderson.

Sources: Family scrapbooks, Bible records, and memories.

— Pauline Jarvis Clark

THE JENNINGS FAMILY
720

In 1785 John Jennings and several of his children with their families came to Wilkes Co. and settled on Mulberry Creek on a tract of land purchased from Owen Hall. The old Jennings Graveyard is on this property with the graves of John and his son Luke. John died in 1811 at the age of 104.

John's son, Luke was born in 1748. He moved with his father to Wilkes in 1785. His children were Caleb, Elizah, Lettie, Daniel, Rebecca, Mary, Luke II, Phoeba, John, and Elizabeth. These were by two marriages: first to Lettie Townsend and second to Sarah Matilda Townsend. Luke died Nov. 1837.

Luke and Sarah's son, Daniel, was born July 1802. He married Rebecca Powell (1803-1875) in Feb. 1822 and they had eight children: Henry, William, Presley, Senter, Jane, Susan, Melinda, and Mary Polly. After Rebecca's death, he married Lucinda Wells in 1876 and then died Sept. 17, 1882 or 1889 and is buried at Mt. Zion Church.

Daniel and Rebecca's son, Henry (June 16, 1828 — Jan. 3, 1904 or 1934) married his first cousin Susannah McGrady on Sept. 21, 1851. They had three children: James, Leander, and Samuel Smith and are buried at Center Baptist.

Samuel Smith Jennings was born May 5, 1856 and married Rhoda Elledge on Nov. 14, 1872. Rhoda was born Dec. 9, 1853 to Joseph Elledge and Betty Hawkins. Samuel became a minister for Center Baptist of which Rhoda was a charter member for over 50 years. Samuel died Feb. 1, 1897 of pneumonia at the age of 40. Rhoda lived until Feb. 25, 1936 and the

N.C. post office.

While living on the farm, she was a member of the Book Library in Raleigh, and she read "Little Orphan Annie" to us from the newspaper. She spent most of her life on the farm except for the few years after they built a house in Wilkesboto so the children would be closer to a good school.

Each week Daddy and Mother gave the devotional in the home. The Bible was read; we all prayed, and a song was sung; Daddy would often play his violin. We cherish these memories still. Mother boarded the teachers who taught at Cranberry's one-room school, and they could not smoke, drink or play cards in the home.

Mansfield loved to sing and this was the alarm clock for the family each morning. He was buried with a hymn book of his favorite songs in his hand.

Mansfield's and Eulora's children were: Annie Marie, born 1902, a schoolteacher, who married Harrison L. Greene in 1920, also a teacher but now deceased. In 1972 she married Preston E. Inscore.

Ruby Ethel, born 1904, married Monroe M. Mathis. Their twin daughters, Doris Marie Baugham and Dorothy Lee Hamrick reside in Shelby, and each has two sons.

James Shadrick, born 1908, married Evaline Poetker and resides in Ohio where he is in real estate and jewelry business. Their daughters are Carol Ann Walton and Donna Jean Dautel.

Letita Pauline, born 1911, was outstanding in sports in high school and married James Blaine Henderson, Jr., in 1933, a bakery supervisor (deceased). While attending school in Washington, D.C., she met and married Col. H.H.H. Clark, U.S.A.F. Retired. He was an active and life member of the Masonic order of India. He is a 32nd degree Mason and a member of the Scottish Rite. They have travelled extensively, and Pauline is active in church and community affairs in Clemmons, N.C. and is an artist.

Eula May, born 1913, attended business college, married A. Dick Sale (deceased) and had two sons, Donald Jarvis (deceased) and Linville Mack and also a stepson, A. Dick, Jr.

age of 82. My father remembers seeing her only once. She was sitting in a rocker on her front porch and was already forgetful. She asked everyone who came by if they had seen Milard today. Milard was someone who had died years before. Samuel and Rhoda had six children: Henry Calvin, Sarah Elizabeth, Alice Eugenia, Elbert Clinton, C. Leazier, and Maggie Marie.

Henry Calvin Jennings (my grandfather) was born Jan. 12, 1874 or 1876. He married Mary Jane Blackburn on Jan. 14, 1894. She was born Sept. 25, 1875 to Columbus Franklin Blackburn and Sarah Jane Crouse. Henry was a farmer on his share of the Jennings' land. He then started working for the Norfolk and Western Railroad. During this time the first three of eight children were born. Ethel Virginia was born Feb. 11, 1895, Pearl Emmergene later in 1895, and Evert Theodore on Sept. 15, 1900. Evert died in Oct. of 1901 of some childhood disease. The family then moved from Wilkes Co. (where their ancestors had lived since 1785) to settle in Yards or Flattop, Va. because had started working for the Singer Sewing Machine Company. Here two more children were born; Grace on July 28, 1902 and Samuel Smith (my father) on Feb. 25, 1906. Henry left Singer and worked as a machinist for a coal company, then on to a powder company in Nemours, West Va. Here, Ina was born Mar. 1909, Vernon was born Sept. 9, 1911, and Irene was born on June 3, 1913. This same year, their oldest daughter, Ethel married Robert Clinton Spraker on Sept. 13. World War I came and went and their second daughter, Pearl, married Henry Goosby and had a son. In 1919, she died during the influenza epidemic. Shortly after, the family left for Ferndale, Fla. There Henry farmed and was Ferndale's first postmaster, as well as becoming a minister. After a while they brought Mary Jane's mother to Fla. to live with them. She died of colitis in 1922. Mary Jane was killed in 1939 at the age of 65 in a hit and run accident. Henry remarried in 1940 to a woman named Mattie. Henry died in 1947 of diabetes at age 73. All three are buried at Ferndale Cemetery. Following is a brief account of each of their children.

Ethel had one son by Clinton Spraker, divorced in 1921 in Fla., then married Julian Hunter Aug. 20, 1921 and had two daughters. She died May 7, 1974.

Grace married Clifton Crawley Oct. 16, 1921 in Ferndale, Fla. They had eight children and still live in Ferndale, Fla.

Ina Mae married Delmar Huchingson Apr. 8, 1927 in Bushnell, Fla. They had four children and still live in Tavares, Fla.

Vernon married Eula Walker Aug. 16, 1930 in Independence Va. They had 12 children most of whom live in N.C. Eula died in 1973. Vernon remarried and is a minister presently living in Va.

Irene married Quince Brown Sept. 19, 1930 in W. Jefferson, N.C. They had 10 children, most of whom still live in Wilkes Co.

Samuel Smith (my father) is now 76. He worked for the railroad in Fla., was in the Navy for over 20 years, serving in W.W. II, Korean War, and Viet Nam, and worked in Civil Service. He was married 6 times, had four daughters, and has lived on both the east and west coast. He presently lives in Chula Vista, Ca.

Sources: personal knowledge, interviews with family members, Census records, grave stones.

— Retha Jennings Cutler

JENNINGS FAMILY

721

The Jennings legend circulated among many Jennings descendants of Wilkes County and elsewhere, is contradictory and very seldom corresponds with any records found. John Jennings, Sr. who came to Wilkes County and settled on Mulberry Creek about 1785, came from Orange County, Virginia. It is possible he was the son of a John and Mary Jennings of Orange County.

John Jennings, Sr., whose wife is uncertain, died in Wilkes County in 1811 and is buried on his farm. Six of his children have been identified: (1) Ludewick (called Luke), born 24 February 1755 in Virginia, died 22 November 1837, Mulberry, buried on his farm. He first married Letes Townsen, and 2nd. Sarah Matilda Townson. (2) Frances, born 1766 in Virginia, died 29 January 1829, Mt. City, Tennessee, married first, in Orange County, Va. 1 March 1786 Silence (Silas) Atkins, 2nd. 17 August 1807, Wilkes County, Robert Donnelly. (3) Daniel, (4) Nancy, born about 1769 in Virginia, died 1818, married 1789 William Absher (5) Pressley, born about 1764, Virginia, removed to Grayson County Virginia, (6) Elijah, married Sarah Shepherd and removed to Kentucky.

Luke Jennings, Sr. rendered patriotic service during the Revolutionary War while living in Orange County, Virginia. He is on the DAR roster. He and his first wife, Letes Townsen, who died about 1800 in Wilkes County, had seven children, six of whom have been identified: (1) Sarah Agnes, born 1781, Va., died after 1850 in Wilkes, married 23 November 1802 John Rhodes, Jr., (2) William M. born 1784, Va. died after 1850 in Alleghany County, married Martha Joines, (3) John left Wilkes County (4) Elijah F. born 1790, died 7 February 1874, married 25 July 1812, Elizabeth Absher, (5) Elizabeth, married John Hall, (6) Letes (Lettie) born 1799, married Wesley Brown.

On the 7 July 1801, Luke Jennings, Sr. married as his second wife, Sarah Matilda Townsen, born 1766 in Va. died 6 February 1859 Wilkes County. They had eight children, six of whom have been identified: (7) Daniel, born 7 July 1802, died 17 September 1889, married Rebecca M. Powell, (8) Luke, Jr., born 1804, died 11 February 1893 following a fall from a horse, married Elizabeth Bullis, (9) Mary, born 6 May 1806, died 30 June 1887, married 27 March 1826 George Wyatt (10) Caleb (11) Rebecca, born 1812, married 22 February 1828, Lewis Shepherd, (12) Phebe, born 14 June 1814, died 7 March 1890, married 9 February 1828, Andrew McGrady.

Letes Jennings, daughter of Luke, Sr. and Letes (Townsen) Jennings, married 30 January 1816, Wesley Brown, son of Aaron and Sarah Brown. Wesley was a miller and farmer, lived between Mulberry and Reddies River. He and Letes were members of the Old Reddies River Primitive Baptist Church. They had ten children, eight of whom have been identified (1) Susannah, born 1823 (2) Emily, born 1825, (3) Aaron H., born 26 February 1829, married 27 March 1852 Mary Shumate (4) Wesley W. born 1833, married 27 March 1852 Sarah Stamper, (5) Letes Jane (Jeanette) born 15 October 1835, died 25 June 1891, married 30 July 1851 Adam Absher as her first husband, and married second John A. Brown. (6) George Jackson, born 17 March 1838, died 8 April 1926, married 26 December 1858, Sarah Wilcoxson, (7) Rebecca born 1840, (8) Elizabeth, born 1842.

Daniel Jennings, son of Luke, Sr. and Sarah Matilda (Townsen) Jennings, married 12 February 1822 Rebecca M. Powell, born 23 April 1803, died 2 April 1875. They lived in the Mulberry community. They had eight children (1) Malinda, born 4 February 1822, died 13 February 1876, married Elijah F. Jennings, Jr., her cousin. (2) William M., born 11 July 1824, died 4 March 1911, married 17 December 1852, Mary Ann Dancy (3) Henry, born 16 June 1828, died 3 Jan 1904, married Susannah McGrady (4) Jane, born 1830, married 3 February 1841 James Kilby, (5) Susannah born 17 March 1835, died 7 November 1930, married 29 March 1855, Alexander B. Dancy. (6) Mary, born 1837, married 1st, 20 October 1850 William H. Absher, 2nd. 2 December 1865 William H. Brown (7) Drury Senter born 1839, married 5 October 1861 Amanda Malvina Brown, (8) Pressley, born 1842, was killed in Civil War.

Henry Jennings, son of Daniel and Rebecca M.(Powell) Jennings, married 21 September 1851, Susannah McGrady, born 22 March 1829, died 1 September 1902, daughter of Andrew of Phebe (Jennings) McGrady. They lived in Mulberry township. They had three children: (1) Jame Kilby, born 18 March 1853, died 20 May 1944, married 19 December 1872, Tennessee Owens (2) Leander C. born 20 August 1854, died 18 January 1906, married 8 October 1874 Sallie M. Brown, (3) Rev. Samuel S. born 5th May 1856, died 2 February 1897, married 14 November 1872, Rhoda Elledge, born 9 December 1853, died 22 February 1936, daughter of Joseph and Elizabeth (Hawkins) Elledge. Their youngest daughter, Maggie Jennings married Wiley Matthew Brooks.

Luke Jennings, Jr., son of Luke Sr. and Sarah Matilda (Townsen) Jennings, married 21 December 1822 Elizabeth Bullis, born 1806, daughter of Benjamin and Elizabeth (Adams) Bullis. Eight of their children have been identified: (1) Sarah born 1829, married 13 December 1844, Vickery Wyatt (2) Levi, born 1833, married 8 October 1855, Martha Dancy (3) John (4) Myra, born 1838, married 14 October 1858 Thomas Jefferson Brown, (5) Reuben born 1842, (6) Elizabeth born 1844, died 11 March 1895, married Benjamin F. Elledge (6) Susannah, born 1848, married 27 December 1866 Rev. John N. Brooks (7) Phebe Amanda, born 24 April 1850, died 2 April 1939, married 26 January 1869 Nelson P. Rhodes.

Sources: Wilkes County deeds, marriage bonds, Federal Census, School Census, Family Bible Records, Church Minutes, *Chronicle* Newspaper, Tax lists, Public Service Claims, Orange County, Va.

— Mrs. W. O. Absher

THE FAMILY OF ETHEL V. JENNINGS

722

The Jennings family originally from England, moved to Wilkes Cty, NC from Virginia in 1785.

My Grandmother, Ethel Virginia Jennings was born in Mulberry, Wilkes County on 2/11/1895. She was the eldest of 8 children born to Henry "Calvin" & Mary Jane Blackburn Jennings. Calvin was the son of Rev. Samuel Smith & Rhoda Elledge Jennings. Mary Jane was the daughter of Columbus "Franklin" & Sarah Jane Crouse Blackburn. Calvin & Mary Jane's 2nd child was Pearl Emmergene, born 9/30/1897. Evert Theodore was 3rd & was called Theo, born 9/15/1900. When Ethel was 6 yrs. old, the family moved to Yards-Flattop, Tazewell County, VA. Theo died there of a childhood disease on 10/21/1901, he is buried in Wilkes County at Center Baptist Churchyard. Their 4th & 5th children were born in Yards-Flattop. Grace Beattrice was born 7/28/1902 & Samuel "Smith" was born 9/25/1906.

Around 1908 the family moved to Nemours, Mercer County WV. where Calvin went to work for the E.I. Dupont Powder Co. The last 3 children were born there. Ina May was born 3/3/1909, Vernon Elvies was born 9/9/1911 & Irene Elizabeth was born 6/3/1913.

Ethel married Robert Clinton Spraker in Tazewell, VA on 9/13/1913. Their son Irwin Lindsey was born in Cooper, Mercer County WV. Ethel & Robert were divorced in 1921. Robert died in 1923 in Cooper, WV.

Pearl Jennings married Henry Goosby in Bristol VA, they had 1 child & lived in Nemours. Pearl died at the age of 22 on 2/28/1921 of infulenza & is buried in Nemours Cemetery.

After World War I in 1919, Calvin & family came by train to Ferndale, Lake County, Fl. Ethel & her son Irwin joined the family later that year. Calvin primarily farmed; however he became the 1st postmaster of Ferndale & later became an ordained minister of the Baptist Church. Mary Jane, who was born 9/25/1874 in Roaring River, Wilkes County was married to Calvin on 1/14/1894 in Wilkes County by Rev. Grant Corthen. She died after being hit be a car as she was crossing the road on 5/27/1939 & is buried in Ferndale Cemetery. Calvin, who was born 1/12/1874 in Wilkes County died of diabetes on 3/7/1949, & is buried in Ferndale Cemetery.

Ethel went to work for Fl Telephone Co., in Tavares, Fl as a operator at the salary of $30.00 monthly in 1919. She retired in 1963 after working there for 44 years. On 8/30/1921 she married Julian Douglas Hunter in Orange County, Fl. Julian was the eldest child of Thomas Elliott & Ellen Louise Hardman Hunter. He was born 6/6/1893 in Orange Home, Sumter County, Fl. Julian was a watchmaker & jeweler. Ethel's son Irwin L Spraker, was later

Ethel Jennings Hunter (1940).

adopted by Julian. Irwin married Aldelphia Starbird on 4/2/1938 in Kissimmee, Fl. They have 3 children. Aldelphia died 9/2/1958. Irwin now resides in Winter Haven, Fl. Ethel & Julian had 2 children. First Ethel "Virginia" born 1/14/1926 in Leesburg, Lake Cty. Fl. She married Sam Dominic Caccamise on 6/5/1944 in Leesburg, Fl. They have 3 children & reside in Leesburg, Fl. Second, Mary Louise born 6/1/1931 in Leesburg, Fl. She married Robert John Hohman on 9/17/1949. They have 7 children & reside in Eustis, Fl. Julian Hunter died 3/23/1960 & is buried in Leesburg, in Lone Oak Cemetery. Ethel Jennings Hunter died 5/7/1974 & is buried in Lone Oak Cemetery also.

Grace Jennings married Clifton Crawley on 10/16/1921 in Ferndale, Fl. They have 8 children & reside in Ferndale. Smith Jennings married 6 times, He & his wife Carol Stover married in 1963 resides in Chula Vista, CA. Smith has 4 daughters. Ina Jennings married Delma Hucherson on 4/8/1927 in Bushnell, Fl. They have 4 children — reside in Bassville Park, Fl. Vernon Jennings became a minister like his father Calvin — his grandfather Samuel. Vernon married Eula Walker on 8/16/1930 in Independence, VA. They lived in North Wilkesboro until Eula died on 10/6/1973. She is buried in Wilkes County. Vernon remarried & now lives in Bruceton Mills, WV, with his wife Dora. Irene Jennings married Quincy Brown on 9/19/1930 in West Jefferson, NC. They have 10 children. Quincy died 10/2/1976 & is buried in Wilkes County. Irene resided in Millers Creek, NC.

Other related families to the Jennings in Wilkes County are the Wiley Brooks family, Abshers, McGradys, Dancys, Shepherds, Sebastains, Browns, Hays, Vannoys, Etc.

Sources: Family Bible (Jennings-Blackburn), birth records, marriage records, death records, obituaries, Census, Wilkes County, Will books, School census, newspaper articles, family memories & personal knowledge.

— Jo Ellen Caccamise Gilbert

ROMULUS CALL JENNINGS, SR.

723

R.C. Jennings, Sr., was a resident of the Pores Knob community. A lawyer by profession, he was also a dealer in timber and real estate as well as being a postmaster of the Pores Knob Post Office. In his earlier days, he had served as rural route carrier from the Pores Knob post office, carrying the mail on horseback.

R.C. was born in Pores Knob, Wilkes County, October 14, 1889, to Leander C. and Sarah Matilda (Sally) Brown Jennings, being their eighth child. R.C. was a descendant in the sixth generation from John Jennings (1) the immigrant ancestor, the line of descent being through Luke (2), Daniel (3), Henry (4), Leander (5), and R.C. (6).

John Jennings (1) was born in England December 8, 1706, to John and Mary Green Jennings. John married Ann Burton on October 19, 1742. He came to America in 1754, first lived in Orange County, Virginia. Later, he moved to Wilkes County around 1785, settled in Mulberry section (McGrady). John died in 1811 and is buried in the old Jennings family cemetary in McGrady.

Luke Jennings (2) was born in Birmingham, England February 24, 1748. He came to America with his father. Luke married Sarah Matilda Townsend (born in Virginia — died February 6, 1859). Luke died on November 22, 1837, and is buried in the old Jennings family cemetary.

Daniel Jennings (3) was born on July 7, 1802, being the son of Luke. Daniel married Rebecca M. Powell on February 12, 1822. He died September 17, 1882 and is buried in Mt. Zion Baptist Church cemetary.

Henry (4) the son of Daniel Jennings, was born June 16, 1828. He married a cousin, Susannah McGrady (the daughter of Andrew and Phoebe Jennings McGrady) on September 21, 1851. He died on January 3, 1904. Both Henry and Susannah are buried in Center Baptist Church cemetary.

Leander (5), son of Henry, was born August 20, 1854, in the Mulberry section. He was married on October 8, 1874, to Sarah Matilda (Sally) Brown, daughter of Mary Lucinde Lane Brown and Thornton Asbury Brown. Leander was a farmer and resided in the Pores Knob community. He died on January 18, 1906, and is buried in Walnut Grove Baptist Church Cemetary in Pores Knob, N.C.

The other children of Leander and Sally Brown Jennings are: (1) Son — stillborn (September 27, 1876); (2) Eugene Buel (January 6, 1878 — May 27, 1880); (3) Minnie (October 4, 1878 — November 4, 1961); (4) James Garfield (October 14, 1881 — October 22, 1910); (5) William Andrew (December 2, 1883 — October 22, 1951); (6) Samuel Carl (December 20, 1886 — July 18, 1899); (7) Henry Olin (August 2, 1888 — March 15, 1934); (8) Romulus Call; (9) Susannah (Annie) (May 30, 1891 — February 16, 1905); (10) John Senter; and (11) Floyd McKinley (twins) (April 1, 1895 — John died November 21, 1934) Floyd is still living In the Pores Knob community; (12) Lula

(May 3, 1898 — April 3, 1971); and (13) Maud (November 10, 1899 — resides in Greensboro, N.C.)

R.C. attended the short school terms of the local neighborhood schools. One time (it was told by his famly) he climbed a tree between his home and the school to avoid going that day. R.C. was an avid reader and would read anything for hours. Later in life he took an interest in the law. He studied at night and when he stood the North Carolina Bar exams, he passed with honor, having made higher grades than the students who had attended the regular law schools.

On June 18, 1911, R.C. was married to Annie Verniece Meadows, daughter of W.G. and Grace McCrary Meadows and the granddaughter of W.C. and Mary Elizabeth Price Meadows. Annie was born on May 23, 1893, and died October 28, 1975.

To this union were born six children: (1) Annie Beatrice (June 21, 1912 — September 6, 1960 — buried in Walnut Grove Baptist Church cemetary) married Karl H. Hemmerich. Three children — Anne Elizabeth, Frederick Karl, Hugo; (2) Romulus Call, Jr. (born March 4, 1914) married Margaret Parlier. Three children: Eric Lee, R.C., 111, James Floyd; (3) Grace Elizabeth (born February 7, 1918) married Melvin Guy Stahl. Two children: John Melvin and Martha Jennings; (4) Dorothy Meadows (born August 28, 1923) married Guy Owen, Jr. Two children: William James and John Leslie; (5) Willie Virginia (born July 14, 1927); (6) Betty Jo (born November 30, 1931 — died December 3, 1931 — buried Walnut Grove Baptist Church cemetary).

R.C. died in Davis Hopital due to a stroke on September 18, 1956. He and his wife are buried in Walnut Grove Baptist Church cemetary.

Sources: Family Bible, personal knowledge.

— Virginia Jennings

JOHNSON FAMILIES
724

Jeffery Johnson, Sr., was born in England in 1697. He was the son of John and Ann Gooche, also of England. Jeffery was first married to a lady named Sara, and his second wife was named Margaret. Our research doesn't show if she came to America with him or if they were married in Prince William County Virginia. We found they had five children, there were: Jeffery Jr., William, Charles, Moses, and Thomas.

As we follow Jeffery Jr., we found he was born in 1722 in Prince William County, Virginia. He was married to Rachel Walker and they had twelve children: Winneford, George , William, John, Rachel, Chloe, Martha (or Mary), Jeffery III, Benjamin, Samuel, Barbara and Lewis. The family moved around a lot, some of the children were born in Fauquier, Virginia, some in Surry County, North Carolina. Jeffery II died August 1788 in Wilkes County. Rachel also died in Wilkes County in 1816.

William was born, April 6, 1751 in Fauquier, Virginia. During his life he lived in Surry County, Ashe County and then Wilkes County. He was married to Mary Parks and they had twelve children. It seems the Johnsons thought they were cheaper by the dozen. Their children were: George, Moses, Aaron, Samuel, John, Ambrose, Nancy, Elizabeth Jane, Sarah, Rachel, Chloe and Frances.

We will continue with the son Ambrose, who was born 1786 and died 1859 in Wilkes County. He was married first to Elizabeth Dowell, they had two children: William P. and Nancy. Our line stayed with his first family. The son William P. was born 1810 died 1872 in Wilkes County. He fought in the Revolutionary War at Kings Mountain. His first wife was Lettie Armstrong. They had seven children: Ambrose, Elizabeth, John, James, Richard, William Riley, and Moses. He married his second wife Nancy Elizabeth Curry, around 1850 or 1851. She was the daughter of George and Elizabeth Curry. Their children were: Margaret, Peter, George Dallas, Samuel, Martha Jane, Cling, Parks and Nancy.

Going back to John in the first family, he was born in 1840 in Wilkes County. He was married to Fannie Inscore October 6, 1857. Fannie was born September 23, 1838. They moved from the Windy Gap area on the Little Brushies in 1860. The house they built and raised their nine children in still stands today. Several other families have been raised there. The fruit trees that John planted are still standing and bearing fruit. His G-granddaughter and her husband, Bell and Albert Mathis live there now. John and Fannie's children were: Lettie, Carolina, Elizabeth, Fannie Ann, Andrew, Ruben, Peter, Mitchel, Jim and Jane.

Jane Johnson was born December 19, 1870, and was married to John Call August 18, 1888. They only had two children: Aaron Conley and Daniel. John died while still a young man. Jane, with no means of support, took the two boys back to her parent's home on the Brushies. They were both raised in the house where Mr. and Mrs. Mathis lives. My husband, Jay Call, remembers when he was a small boy going to to visit his grandmother and on Sunday they would go to the barn yard catch a chicken, wring its neck, and soon they would have fried chicken for lunch. I have visited there with him several times; I love it on the mountain. You can feel the warmth and love that so many families have shared over the years.

Sources: Wills, Estate records, marriage records, revolutionary war records, census and Bible records.

— Gracie F. Call

BASIL LEROY JOHNSON
725

My Johnson ancestors trace back to Jeffrey Johnson I, who was born in England. He was in King George Co., Va. by 1712 and owned land there at that time. His will dated in 1725 was proved in King George County in 1726. His son, Jeffrey II, died in Prince William Co., Va. about 1750.

Jeffrey Johnson III was born in Fauquire Co., Va. (Prince William Co.). His wife, Rachel Walker, was the daughter of George and Winifred Walker. Jeffrey III was in Wilkes County, N.C. before the county was officially created in 1778. He died in Wilkes 1788-89: His son, William, was born 6 April 1751 in Fauquier County and died in Wilkes about 1835. His wife was Mary Parks, daughter of Thomas and Priscilla Parks.

Moses Johnson, son of William and Mary, was born in Wilkes in 1778 and died there in Jan. 1855. His wife, Elizabeth, was the daughter of George Johnson, Sr. (known as "old Eli").

Eli (II), son of Moses and Elizabeth, was born 3 Nov. 1799. His wife, Sarah, was the daughter of George and Mary Turner Curry Wheatley. She was born 4 Aug. 1803 and died 3 May 1878. Their son, George Washington Johnson, born 10 May 1829, married Elizabeth Elvira Martin Curry, daughter of Simon Curry. They lived in the Dellaplane community of Wilkes County. He died 31 Mar. 1880.

Eli (III), son of George Washington Johnson, was born 29 June 1858 and died 23 Aug. 1927. He operated a government distillery in Wilkes at one time. His wife, Cornelia Chappell, was born 17 July 1861, and died 18 Nov. 1949. Her parents were Silas and Amanda Parker Chappell.

My paternal grandfather, Basil Leory Johnson, was born to Eli and Cornelia on 1 Aug. 1880. He was married to Pearl Viola Hall, born 12 June 1888, died in Oct. 1981. She was the daughter of Huston and Mary Jane Patterson Hall. Leroy attended the Moravian Falls Academy and an academy in Virginia. During the 1930's he invented a bee gum and had it patented. He operated a bee gum factory in Ronda which also made chicken coops, baby cribs, etc. Stockholders in the company included Rich Finley, Sherman Anderson, and Branson Benton. He was depot agent and telegraph operator in Roaring River, Ronda, and Elkin for a number of years and also operated a silent movie theatre in Elkin. He was a bookkeeper for the government when the Blue Ridge Parkway was being constructed. Basil Leroy Johnson died 16 Nov. 1956.

My father, Julius Jackson (Jude) Johnson, was born to Leroy and Viola on 9 Feb. 1907. He married Hazel Ethel Holland, daughter of George and Dora Henderson Holland. He is a veteran of World War II and has been in the lumber business most of his adult life. Jude and Hazel have six children: Julius J., Jr. (Ike), Carolyn, Shirley, Archie, Loretta, and Hayden.

Shirley married James Dwight (Jake) Johnson, son of Spurgeon and Letha Prevette Johnson. They own and operate the American Artcraft Ceramics located in the Broadway community of Wilkes County. Their children are as follows: Gary who married Madeline Parsons — no issue; Debbie who married Arthur Kerley — they have two children, Jessica and Jeremiah; Chris married Rebecca Shew and they have a son, Brian; and Jerome who is unmarried and living at home.

Sources: Genealogical research and personal knowledge.

— Shirley J. Johnson

CALVIN FLETCHER JOHNSON
726

Lewis Johnson was born October 22, 1827, in Walnut Grove Township, Wilkes County to Robert and Celia Johnson. Lewis married Nancy Wheatley. They had thirteen children. Ten lived to maturity. The family lived near the head waters of Roaring River where Lewis was a blacksmith and farmer. Lewis died in 1827 and was buried in the family cemetery.

One of Lewis and Nancy's sons was Calvin Fletcher Johnson, born May 29, 1858, married Belle Miller on January 1, 1886, who was born on July 17, 1865 and died in 1960. Belle was reared in Alleghany County, so Fletcher and Belle reared their family in Alleghany, where Fletcher was a farmer. Fletcher went to Blackfoot, Idaho to visit some members of his family, became ill and died there in February, 1920. His body was sent home by train.

The oldest child of Fletcher and Belle was Charles Robert Johnson, called Charlie by family and friends. As a young man Charlie had a stutter in his speech. In 1904 his parents sent him to St. Louis to attend a school to help him improve his speech. While in St. Louis, he attended the 1904 St. Louis World's Fair. This was quite an experience for a young man from North Carolina.

Charlie was a rural mail carrier in Alleghany County. While carrying the mail, he met Dema Lou Reeves. Dema told this story, "I tried not to be near the mail box when Charlie came, because his stuttering speech made it hard to talk with him." Evidently he was a persistant man in seeing Dema, because they were married in 1911.

A quote from their marriage write-up was in Alleghany County paper "Laurel Springs was the scene of a pretty wedding December 23, 1911, when Mr. Charles Johnson led to the altar Miss Dema Reeves. The music was beautifully rendered by Mrs. W.F. Doughton. First came the ushers, then the attendants, followed by Mr. Frank Taylor, after which came the groom with the best man, Mr. Albert Wingate. Then came the bride leaning on the arm of Miss Blanche Reeves, maid of honor. Rev. George M. Reeves performed the ceremony."

Dema became Charlie's mail carrier assistant. She had always ridden side-saddle. Charlie would not let her ride side-saddle on his horses, because it rubbed his harness raw. So Dema rode astride.

One day when Dema was carrying the mail a small boy on the mail route happened to see her. He returned to his house and told his mother that the new mail carrier was a funny looking little man. Next day his mother wanted to see the new mailman, so what she saw was Dema in her riding habit, which these people were unaccustomed to seeing.

The Johnsons were not permitted to pick up passengers in their buggy when on the mail route. They could carry packages or groceries their neighbors might be taking home from the country store.

Many people on the mail route could not read nor write, so the Johnsons often helped make orders from the catalogue.

Once a lady from Peach Mountain Area asked Charlie to help her make out an order. Not quite understanding the measures of ladies' garments, he used a string to measure her waist and hips, tied knots to show the size, took the string home and asked Dema to order the lady a corset.

Charlie and Dema had one child, Virginia, born January 16, 1916. When she was four years of age, the family bought a farm in Wilkes, and moved on the land which was near the orginal farm where Charlie's father had been raised.

On arriving in Wilkes at the farm, four-year-old Virginia took one look at the unpainted farm house and refused to get out of the wagon and move into a "black" house.

Mr. Johnson was a farmer in the Dehart Community until his death on April 19, 1934.

Mrs. Dema Johnson later married Mr. Claude McGee, and they lived in the Mulberry Community until their deaths.

The Johnson daughter, Virginia Kilby, has two daughters, Mrs. George Lou Sprinkle Reins and Mrs. Virginia Ann Kilby Dorsett, one granddaughter, Vickie Susan Reins Murphy, two grandsons, William Franklin Reins, Jr. and Robert Rex Dorsett, one great grandson, Drew Douglas Murphy.

Sources: Personal knowledge, family records.

— Mrs. Bill Reins

ISAAC CALLOWAY and LAURA ANN HANDY JOHNSON
727

Isaac Calloway Johnson, my father, was born to Sidney Lewis and Elizabeth Jane (Betty) Adams Johnson in what is now the Walnut Grove section of Wilkes County on May 3, 1886, and was named for two Baptist preachers, Isaac Landreth and Calloway "Uncle Callie" Blevins. Six sisters: Mary, Martha, Nannie, Fannie, Dona and Bessie; a half-brother, Wiley, and a half-sister, Ellen, lived to adulthood.

On June 15, 1821 Jesse and Nancy Johnson Gambill sold their home place on the west prong of Roaring River (now the Walnut Grove community) to her brother, Robert Johnson (eldest son of Captain Samuel Johnson, Revolutionary soldier, who came to Wilkes County from Virginia). Robert Johnson and wife, Celia Bourne, his son, Samuel, and wife, Elizabeth (Betty) Brown, his son, Sidney Lewis and wife, Elizabeth (Betty) Adams, lived on this land for their lifetimes and are all buried in the family graveyard there.

Sidney Lewis Johsnon's son, Isaac Calloway and wife, Laura Handy, owned and lived on this same land and their two children, Ray Vaughn and Butrice Irene Johnson Luffman (Mrs. Winfrey) grew up there and owned the land jointly until his death in 1961. In 1974 Butrice sold the land to Jessie Alexander Smith (a great-granddaughter of Sidney Lewis Johnson) and her husband.

My parents were married September 23, 1906. Butrice was born January 3, 1911, and Vaughn was born December 1, 1913.

Vaughn's vision was very poor due to con-

Isaac C. and Laura Handy Johnson on their wedding day.

genital cataracts. When he was eight, my father took him to the Johns Hopkins Hospital in Baltimore, hoping for help through surgery, but was advised it was too great a risk.

Vaughn entered school at eight years old and later earned a medal for seven years perfect attendance. In his twenties he had eye surgery and his vision was much improved though still far below normal. He worked for the State Highway Department for a number of years. Vaughn married Mae Adams Faw on August 6, 1944, and they were divorced in 1959. He was crushed by an overturning tractor on May 25, 1961. He was the last to bear the name Johnson in this particular branch of the family.

Vaughn was very kind and helpful, especially to the sick and the elderly. He had a good sense of humor and laughed just as heartily when the joke was on him. When he was a little boy, he found a half-filled bottle of whiskey that someone had hidden beside a path. When he went to feed the pigs, he poured the whiskey into their bucket of feed. They were a happy bunch of pigs, squealing and running all over the lot to the concern of the family, until Vaughn confessed what he had done.

My mother was the third daughter of Jacob Israel and Polly Brown Handy. Four sisters and four brothers grew to adulthood: Frances, Samantha, Elmore, Lura, Quincy, Mary, Ira, and Charlie. Jacob Israel was the youngest son of Thomas and Margaret Peggy Richardson Handy and inherited the home place. Thomas' father was Irish and his mother, Sally, was English. (Father's first name unknown.)

Polly was the daughter of Aaron and Frankie Irene Brown. Aaron was the son of Wesley and Lettie Jennings Brown.

Aaron Brown served as clerk of the Mount Zion Church which was organized in February, 1848 and, according to available records, the first church in this community. Other ancestors of both my parents were listed as members: Thomas and Margaret Handy; Francis (Frankie) Brown; Robert and Celia Johnson; and various other relatives known from family records. There was no church building and meetings were held in the homes. The last date appearing in the church book is March, 1873.

My father was a Baptist deacon for more than sixty-six years and both my grandfathers were Baptist deacons.

My parents worked hard and knew of necessity how to stretch a dollar. Both were skilled above the ordinary. My father designed and built our house as well as many other things for use and enjoyment. My mother was a good cook, sewed beautifully, could crochet,

Johnson family Seated: l to r: Sidney Lewis, Betty, Adams Johnson, Isaac C., Laura, Butrice. Standing l to r: Fannie, Martha, Bessie, Dona, Wertt and Nannie Johnson Walker (1911).

L to R: Laura Handy, Isaac C. and Vaughn Johnson (1931).

knit, and make perfect buttonholes by hand. Both set high moral standards and Christianity and the church was an integral part of our home. They were both interested in community affairs. My father was instrumental in getting an independent telephone line for the community about 1920 and served as secretary and treasurer. My father "led" the singing in our church and in many other churches where he visited. Our family enjoyed singing together and my brother, Vaughn, developed a rich bass voice and later sang in church quartets.

When my father was ten years old, Grandpa Sidney had typhoid and he and Grandma Betty plowed to make the crop.

Grandma Betty was the daughter of Henry and Nancy Adams in the Mulberry area which she always called "the Flatwoods." Her mother died when whe was a little girl and she lived with an older sister. She met the handsome young widower who was my grandfather at a church service and they were married October 21, 1880. Her white wedding dress is still in the family. Grandpa had a cupboard made for her as a wedding present and it is still in use. She brought her clothes and linens in a chest, which she called a "chist", that was

painted brown with black coin dots. She said during the Civil war when it was rumored the Yankees were coming, whatever was considered of most value would be put in the "chist" and hidden in the leaves in the woods. This "chist" is still in the family as is a copper lustreware pitcher inherited from her mother and passed to the youngest daughter in each generation.

My mother died December 31, 1936, and in 1937 my father married Flora Absher Felts. She died in 1971 and my father died September 15, 1974. My father, mother and brother are buried in Mount Lawn at North Wilkesboro.

My story is under the title "Virgil Winfrey and Butrice Johnson Luffman."

Sources: Family Records, family traditions, personal knowledge.

— Butrice Johnson Luffman

JAY HUGH JOHNSON
728

Jay Hugh Johnson was born in Iredell County, North Carolina, on August 7, 1891, the son of Elijah Allison Johnson and Barthenia Catherine Myers Johnson. His father was killed in a buggy accident when Jay was six months old. His mother raised him and his four brothers on a large farm near Union Grove, North Carolina.

Catherine, a strong mother, kept her farm producing while teaching her sons to work by going into the fields with them. While Catherine and her three eldest sons worked in the fields, the two youngest Johnson boys, Floyd and Jay, played on a quilt under the nearest tree.

Jay utilized the limited educational resources in his community and even taught for a few years in the one-room schoolhouse in order to raise money to further his education. He attended Mars Hill College to get the neces-

sary credits for pharmacy school.

In 1914 Jay came to North Wilkesboro where he went to work for R.M. Brame and Sons, again, saving his money to attend Atlanta College of Pharmacy.

While in North Wilkesboro, Jay married Mayme Elizabeth Waugh, daughter of William Hicks Waugh and Eudora Howell Waugh. Mayme was born in Ashe County, North Carolina on May 13, 1898. Her family moved to North Wilkesboro in 1908. Mayme finished high school and received her teaching certificate from Appalachain State Teachers' College (now Appalachain State University).

Jay graduated from Atlanta College of Pharmacy and became a registered pharmacist on June 6, 1917. He continued to work for Mr. Brame for a few years but later moved his family to Elkin where he and three of his brothers started the Johnson Oil Company.

Around 1925 Jay returned to North Wilkesboro to go into business with Tal Barnes at the North Wilkesboro Drug Company, established in 1908 and locally known as the Rexall Store. In 1930 Jay bought out all other interests in this store, operating it until his death in 1949. His daughter, Billie Johnson Stringfield, also a pharmacist, and his son, Jay, Jr., continued to operate the store until its closing in 1959.

Both Jay and Mayme were active members of the First Baptist Church of North Wilkesboro. Jay was a deacon for many years and Mayme was active as a circle leader and as a member of the Woman's Missionary Society.

Jay and Mayme Johnson had three children: Elizabeth Johnson Bingham of Southern Pines, North Carolina, Billie Johnson Stringfield of North Wilkesboro, and Jay Johnson, Jr., who died in 1960. Mayme died in 1967.

Grandchildren are James Hugh Bingham, Jayne Bingham Rhodes, William Frank Bingham, Preston Calvin Stringfield, III, Jay Johnson Stringfield, William Waugh Stringfield, and Ann Elizabeth Stringfield.

Sources: Deeds, diplomas, obituaries, and family tradition.

— Billie Johnson Stringfield
and Ann Elizabeth Stringfield

JEFFERY JOHNSON FAMILY
729

Jeffery Johnson and his wife, Rachel Walker, settled in Rowan County, now Wilkes County, in about 1769, on the north side of the Yadkin River. They moved from Fauquier County, Virginia in about 1767, to Loudoun County, Virginia. They lived in Loudoun County two years, selling property which had been inherited from Rachel's father, George Walker (Rachel's mother was believed to have been Frances Hardwick, 1st wife of George Walker.) Jeffery was the son of Jeffery and Margaret Johnson of Fauquier County, Virginia.

Jeffery Johnson is listed in 1771 and 1772 tax list of Surry County with four polls, probably himself, son, William, son, John and Negro Lett. (The oldest son, George, did not come to N.C. till 1781.)

The 8th of December 1775, Jeffery Johnson of Surry County, gave Power of Attorney to his son, George, in Fauquier County to sell his

Jay Hugh Johnson.

estate in Virginia. John Johnson and Samuel Johnson were witnesses. Jeffery and his brother, Moses, of Fauquier County, sons of Jeffery and Margaret Johnson, sold 513 acres of land in Fauquier County, 26th Feb. 1776.

Jeffery purchased several parcels of land (the first on 7th Sept. 1778) on the north side of the Yadkin River, at the mouth of Roaring River. In 1782, Jeffery is listed with 800 acres, 4 slaves, 6 horses, and 9 head of cattle.

Jeffery Johnson died in Wilkes County prior to January 1789, leaving a will dated 23 March 1788 — probated 27 January 1789 — in Wilkes County Court. In the will he names, wife, Rachel (she died in 1816), children George, William, John, Samuel, Jeffery, Lewis, and Benjamin; and Barbara, the last five under age or not married. Grandchildren; James, Rachel, and Winnifred Dodson. In other probate records, daughters: Chloe and Rachael are named.

Jeffery and Rachel Walker Johnson are known to have had the following children, all born in the Fauquier County Area of Virginia. There may have been other children:

(1.) Winnifred Johnson, born about 1747, died before 1788. She married, 30th June 1762, William Dodson. They had three children: James, Rachel, and Winnifred.

(2.) George Johnson, born, 25 Nov. 1749. He served as a Private in the Rev. War from Fauquier County, Virginia. He moved to Wilkes County in about 1781. It is unknown who he married or who his children were. It is believed he had at least two daughters: Sarah Ann, born about 1785, married her cousin, George Johnson (Wilkes Bond, 19 Nov. 1800/1); Elizabeth, born about 1780, died 1864/5. She, also, married her cousin, Moses Johnson, brother of George, sons of William.

(3.) William Johnson, born, 6 April 1751. He served as a Private in the Rev. War, under Col. Cleveland in Capt. Herndon's Company. He married, Mary Parks, daughter of Thomas

and Priscilla Parks. William and Mary were the parents of fifteen known children: Moses, Winnie, George, Aaron, John or Saddler, Barbara, Sally, Ambrose, Elizabeth, Frankie, William Parks, Chole, Rachel, Nancy, and Samuel.

(4.) John, born about 1753. (5.) Benjamin, born about 1755;

(6.) Capt. Samuel Johnson, born 1757, died, 15 Sept. 1834. He served as a Private, Lieutenant, and Captain in the Rev. War, under Col. Cleveland. He was seriously wounded at the Battle of Kings Mountain. Capt. Samuel married, 24 June 1782, Mary Hamon, daughter of Ambrose and Ann Hamon. They were the parents of nine known children: Robert, Nancy, Chloe, Samuel Brumfield, Ambrose, Mary or Polly, Lewis, Col. John Simpson, and Rachel W.

(7.) Chloe Johnson, born about 1760. She married, 3 April 1782, Williaam Rutledge.

(8.) Lewis Johnson, born about 1761. He married, (bond) 20 Dec. 1879, Susanna Chandler.

(9.) Rachael Johnson, born about 1763. She married John Parks.

(10.) Barbara Johnson, born about 1765. She married Richard York. (He may have been a 2nd husband. Her first, possibly being, John Shumate, who she married in 1786.)

(11.) Jeffery Johnson, born 3 April 1768. He married, Rebecca Chandler. Jeffery and Rachel Walker Johnson family were among the first Johnsons in the Wilkes County Area.

Sources: County records of Fauquier County, Virginia; Loudoun County, Virginia; Rowan, Surry, and Wilkes Counties, North Carolina. Rev. War Pension files.

— Verl F. Weight

JOHN and LILLIE McCARTER JOHNSON

730

John Johnson's parents were Moses and Susanah Catherine Glass Johnson, who were married on January 8, 1852. Moses was the son of John and Edney Gray Johnson. Catherine was the daughter of John and Hesse Shew Glass. Catherine could count to 100 in the Dutch language, being taught by her grandmother who was said to be "full-blooded" Dutch.

Moses and Catherine lived in the Windy Gap community where they farmed their land. Their children were as follows: (1) Rufus (1854-1927). (2) William was born January 12, 1853 and died at a young age. (3) Hessie was born September 16, 1856 and married Francis Gray. They lived in Tennessee for several years, but moved back to Wilkes County. (4) Mary (1859-1931) married Ambrose Chapel Moore. Mary and Chap are buried at Lewis Baptist Church. (5) Catherine, born in 1861, was listed as age 19 in the 1880 census. She died at a young age. (6) Amelia (1862-1932) remained single and was known as Aunt Millie. (7) John Johnson, named for both his grandfathers, was born May 10, 1865. (8) Edna (1868-1932) remained single. (9) Peggy (1872-1954) married Eli Johnston and (10) Eliza (1874-1941) also remained single and

John and Lillie McCarter Johnson.

was known as Aunt Lizzie. Rufus, Millie, Edna and Lizzie are buried at Antioch Baptist Church near their sister Peggy and her husband Eli Johnston.

John R. (?) Johnson's first wife's name was Renie. After her death, John went to Park City, Utah where he was a foreman on the railroad. After four years he returned to Wilkes and married Lillie McCarter, a daughter of John and Almeda Jane Foster McCarter. John and Lillie returned to Park City where he worked in the gold silver and copper mines in the canyon. While in Utah they had two daughters. Hope was born and died in 1904. She was buried on the knoll at the City Cemetery. Minnie Belle was born on January 26, 1906.

Late in the year 1906 John, Lillie and the baby Minnie moved back to Wilkes, by traveling on the railroad. John's mother had been sick and was very concerned that she would not live to see her son again. She had written to him pleading for their return. However, very shortly after their arrival Lillie's mother died suddenly. John's mother lived until November 1907.

John and Lillie bought a farm that had been part of the estate of the Gov. Monfred Stokes, West of Wilkesboro. There was a small two-roomed house on the land where they lived. John also bought horses and wagons to haul lumber from the sawmills. Two other children were born: Gertrude Mae, on November 14, 1907 and Roby Wilson, on September 2, 1912. John was especially happy now that he had a son. They began to cut lumber and make plans to build a new house. This happiness was short lived, because John became sick of pneumonia and died on January 25, 1913. Lillie continued his plans to build the house.

Times were difficult for the widow lady rearing three small children on the land. They kept cows, pigs and chickens on the farm and most of their food came from the garden. There seemed to be continuous chores of feeding the animals, carrying water from the spring, chopping and bringing in the wood. The house was heated by a fireplace and the wood cook stove. The children walked over a mile to the Adley School, sometimes wading snow up over their knees since school was not closed for bad weather.

The rare shopping trips to Wilkesboro were made by walking the railroad tracks or with neighbors who had a wagon. A picnic lunch on the way back home was a special treat.

Minnie dropped out of school to stay home with their ailing mother. Gertrude went to Wilkesboro High School by riding on a truck used as a school bus. In winter the roads sometimes became too bad for bus travel so she boarded in town. She finished high school in 1927, attended Appalachian College and is a graduated of Lenoir Rhyne College. Roby also graduated from high school.

Minnie Belle (1906-1976) was married on September 2, 1933 to Wilborn Guy Eller (1907-1981) Their daughter Vella Faye married Charles Stanley Minton and is a teacher.

Gertrude Mae was married on July 11, 1932 to Willard Rayyaughn Eller (1909-1978). Their daughter Jewell Christine is married to William Glenn Walker and has a son Glenn Rayvaughn Walker. She is a teacher in Wilkes County.

Roby Wilson married Vera Gladys Huffman and has six children: Treva Irene J. Frasier, Harold Edward, Bobby Dean, John David, Anganette, and Bryce Eugene Johnson.

Sources: Census of 1850 and 1880 for Wilkes; family records, tombstones and personal knowledge.

— Gertrude J. Eller
and Christine E. Walker

LEWIS and NANCY WHEATLEY JOHNSON FAMILY

731

Lewis Johnson, born 22 Oct. 1827, on the old home place on the Roaring River in Walnut Grove Township, was the son of Robert and Celia Bourne Johnson. He married 1 Nov. 1849, in Wilkes County, Nancy Wheatley, born 15 Aug. 1830, daughter of Martin H. and Polly or Maryann Johnson Wheatley, also, of the Walnut Grove Township Area. Lewis acquired part of his fathers' farm and was a farmer.

Lewis died, 20 Nov. 1880, leaving his wife, Nancy, with four young children, the youngest three years old. The older children were always available to give their help and assistance. Members of the family have always gone to the aid of others in the family and a closeness has prevailed.

Nancy died 24 Aug. 1906. Lewis and Nancy are buried on the old home place in the family cemetery.

Lewis and Nancy were the parents of thirteen children:

(1) Celia Ann, born 27 Aug. 1850, and died 4 July 1927. She married 6 Jan. 1867, Thomas Bee Handy, son of Thomas and Peggy Richardson Handy. They were the parents of seven children: Walter Empton married Rebecca Jane Brown; Mary Ann married Franklin Joines; Martin Monroe married Mary Fannie Holbrook; Thomas Freeland married 1st, Mary Jane Myers, 2nd Ellen Cockerham; Carolyn or Carrie married Marcus Thornton; Martha Ellen married Chy Opher Pruitt; and Cora Ester married Joshua Talmadge Pruitt.

(2) Mary Jane or Polly, born, 23 Feb. 1852, died, 27 April 1932. She married, 1873, Rev. William Waters Myers, son of John Napolin and Mary Caroline Holland Myers. They had ten children: Lewis Napolean; Noah Pedro married Carrie Jane Holbrook; Celia Emeretta; Iredell Ivy Martin married Nannie or Nancy Fanny Spicer; Nancy Caroline or Carrie married Doctor Gordon Wilkes; Mattie or Martha Jane married James Avery Burcham; Evy Vance married Maie Alexander; McCager Guy married Dora Whittington; Nettie Ann married Clint Alexander; and Hessie Levena married Pigram S. Alexander.

(3) Matilda Caroline, born 20 May 1854, and died 10 June 1937. She married 17 April 1873, William Frankling Absher, son of Alfred J. and Martha or Patsy Johnson Absher. They were the parents of two children, sons: Bob or Martin Felix married Mary Eugenia Higgins; and Sam or Alfred Samuel, married Myrtle Brown.

(4) William Martin, born 23 Feb. 1856, died 12 Sept. 1934. He married 5 Jan. 1878, Francis Janie Long, daughter of Levi and Martha Handy Long. They had seven children; William Edgar married Cora Ellen Hanks; Levi Gilmore married Celia Jane Hanks; Martha Victora married Chromodore Absher; Lewis Oscar married Zula Arvada Kessinger; Nancy Ina married James E. Caudill; Della Jane married Marchus G. Steelman; and Mary Ada Emiline married Conrad Tharpe.

(5) Calvin Fletcher, born 29 May 1858, died 20 Feb. 1920. He married 1 Jan. 1886, Isabelle or Bell Miller, daughter of John S. and Biddie Long Miller of Alleghany County. They lived in Alleghany County and were the parents of ten children: Charles Robert married Dema Reeves; John Frank married Ollie Maie Waddell; Fannie married Hardin Alfred Whittington; Monroe V.; Fielden E. married Arta Ola Cox; Roby Louis married Ildria Lucile McReynolds; Jesse Martin married Eva Mae Tilley; Octavia

or Nancy Biddie; Georgia Belle married Cary Wagoner; and Ivery Letcher married Mabel Taylor.

(6) Samuel Freeland, born 10 Feb. 1860, died 20 Oct. 1937. He married 18 Nov. 1888, Mary Long, daughter of Levi and Martha Handy Long. They moved to Mound, Alberta, Canada with their four children: Martha Leora Alverda married John George Niddrie; Isaac Morgan; Arthur Fletcher married Grace Evelyn House; and Ira Martin married Sophie Pauline Boychuk.

Sons of Lewis and Nancy W. Johnson. Front row: L to R: Joshua Vance; Lewis Franklin; Isaac Robert; Daniel Christopher. Back Row: L to R: William Martin; Calvin Fletcher; Samuel Freeland.

(7) Joshua Vance, born 21 Jan. 1862, died 18 April 1927. He married 1901, Catherine or Katie Bare, daughter of Henry H. and Margaret Cox Bare of Ashe County. They lived in Idaho and were the parents of seven children: Margaret Mary married Edward Joseph Goodwin; Nancy Alvira married Robert L. Maddox; Martin Joshua married Clara Casperi; Esther Hadessa married William A. McCloud; Eugene Patrick married Jessie Watt; Dorethia Estora married Elmer Carrier; and Lillian Lenora.

(8) Ludd or Lewis Franklin, born 4 Feb. 1865, died 30 Jan. 1894. He married 5 Sept. 1886, Fredonia Long, daughter of Mary Jane Long. They were the parents of three children: Freeland Christopher married Carrie V. Miller; Ernest Washington married Verna Miller; and Hallie Jane married Hilery Jones Joines.

(9) Martha Elizabeth, born 18 Oct. 1867, died 22 Jan. 1940. She had a son, Guy, who never married.

(10) Bob or Isaac Robert, born 21 Mar. 1870, died 17 Nov. 1913. He married, 20 Dec. 1890, Lillie Frances Bare, daughter of Henry H. and Margaret Cox Bare of Ashe County. They moved with their oldest child to Idaho. They were the parents of five children: Hattie Lenore married George Fredrick Weight; Gladys Susie married Nels Nelson; Ira Martin; Garney Vessie married Wilhelmina Marie Neerings; and Roah Robert married Marie Allen.

(11) Little Doc, born 12 Aug. 1872 and died as a child, 6 Dec. 1873.

(12) Nancy Ferbie, born 3 April 1875, and died as a child 29 Jan. 1876.

(13) Bud or Daniel Christopher born, 27 June 1877, and died 24 Dec. 1961. He married 6 Oct. 1906, Bessie DeBoard, daughter of Jonathan W. and Lair Lucinda Sarilda West BeBoard of Ashe County. They lived in Canada for several years and then settled in Idaho. They were the parents of five children: Lewis Earl married Lenore Deeds; Ilena Mae married, Olen Decker; Hazel Irene married Robert Holmes; Edna Nancy married Haskell Reeder; and Georgia Violet married Frank V. Hills.

Sources: Family Bible of Lewis and Nancy Johnson; Family Bibles of the children; grave stones; family records; personal knowledge of living family members.

— Verl F. Weight

MAE and AVERY JOHNSON
732

Annie Mae Church was born Feb. 22, 1911 to Annie Bumgarner and Commodore Welborn Church, on Sawmill Road, Millers Creek, N.C. The family earned a living on a hilly thirty-five acre farm, as their ancestors had done before them. They were devoted Methodists and Mae joined the church at the age of twelve. When she was very young, Mae was ambitious to go on to school and become a teacher. After her graduation from Millers Creek High School in 1929, with the help of her brother Tam (who had graduated from UNC at Chapel Hill that year) she was accepted at Lincoln Memorial University, Harrogate, Tn. She paid her entire expenses by doing hand-weaving at the Arts and Crafts Department operated by the University, desk duty in the girls dormitory, etc. She graduated June 6, 1934 but stayed at the college an extra year and taught weaving to finish paying her debts.

Mae began teaching in 1935 (English) at Millers Creek and continued there until Mount Pleasant and Millers Creek were consolidated into West Wilkes High School in 1957. She remained at West Wilkes until her retirement in 1972. After her retirement, she wrote an autobiography "My Place in the Sun" which was published in 1978.

James Avery Johnson was born July 18, 1915 in North Wilkesboro to Thomas Calvin and Hattie Hayes Johnson. After graduating from North Wilkesboro High School in 1934, he helped his father on the family farm for several years. There he learned the skill of growing things in the earth and a great love of the land. He worked at a local furniture factory briefly but left that for salesmanship. In 1940 Avery became a representative for the Durham Life Insurance Company and remained in that position until he took early retirement in 1977. During those 37 years he earned many convention trips, awards, and the love and trust of a multitude of friends and policyholders.

His work was interrupted when he went into the U.S. Navy for two and a half years of military service during World War II. Twenty two months of that time were spent overseas in Australia, Iwo Jima and other Pacific Islands.

James Avery Johnson was married to Annie Mae Church July 27, 1940 in a twilight garden wedding at her sister Neta's home. They were married for thirty-nine years. He had been a member of the Fishing Creek Baptist Church from the age of fourteen until his marriage, at which time he joined Friendship Methodist Church where Mae was a member. He was a very active and faithful member until his death of a heart attack Dec. 11, 1979. He held many offices in the church including membership on the building committee, the trustees, elected delegate to annual conference, and was a member of the administrative board. He was Sunday School Superintendant at several different times including the very difficult and trying time of consolidation in 1952 of the two churches, the Friendship Methodist Episcopal Church and the Millers Creek Southern Methodist Church which formed the present Millers Creek United Methodist Church.

After returning from military service, Avery became a life member of the Veterans of Foreign Wars Post 1142. A VFW Auxiliary was soon organized and Mae became its charter president, and she has been a continuous member for the thirty-seven years of its exist-

Avery and Mae Johnson.

ence.

Mae and Avery have three children, two daughters and a son, who have brought them much happiness and joy: (1) Holly Sue was born in North Wilkesboro Dec. 6, 1942. She was married to James Ray Triplett June 11, 1961 and they have made their home in Dalton, Ga. since that time. They have a daughter and a son, Amanda Joy, and Thomas Johnson. (2) Joyce Ina was born in North Wilkesboro January 15, 1944. She and James Edward Ledoux were married July 27, 1974. They live in Fort Walton Beach, Fla. Their children are Jamie Leta, named for both her parents, and Charles Avery, named for both his grandfathers. (3) James Lee is Mae's and Avery's youngest child and only son. He was born July 19, 1949. He was married to Carol Jean Nichols, June 15, 1969 and they now live in Salem, Virginia. They have two fine children Lisa Nicole and James Lee, Jr.

After their retirement, Mae and Avery did some travelling, mainly to visit their children and their families in Virginia, Georgia, and Florida. They spent two wonderful weeks in Hawaii in April 1978.

Sources: Personal knowledge and family Bible.

— Mae Church Johnson

CELIA BOURNE and ROBERT JOHNSON

733

Robert Johnson, first child of Capt. Samuel and Mary Hammons Johnson, was born 25 Oct. 1783 on Roaring River in Wilkes Co., NC. He was part of a large, close family which included grandparents Jeffrey and Rachel Walker Johnson, and Ambrose and Ann Hammons. His Aunt Mary and Uncle William Johnson had 15 children, so Robert and his eight younger sisters and brothers (Nancy, b. 1785, Chloe — 1788, Samuel B. — 1790, Ambrose — 1792, Mary J. "Polly" — 1796, Lewis — 1800, John Simpson — 1803, and Rachel — 1806) had many first cousins to play with.

On Sundays Bobby, as he was called, was taken to church where he sometimes heard his great-grandfather William Hammons preach. No one rushed home after church then; it was an opportunity to be with friends and relatives. Children scampered about playing while their elders visited. Often there was dinner "on the grounds" or at a nearby home, followed by an evening or twilight worship service.

Without doubt the children heard many stories of the war for independence, for most men in the family (indeed, in the county) had been part of the fighting. Robert's favorite tale described how Col. Benjamin Cleveland presented his Battle Sword with silver mounted guard and buck horn handle to Robert's father, Capt. Samuel Johnson, after the Battle of King's Mountain. Capt. Sam'l. treasured the sword; when it was borken accidently he drew a shank on the broken edge and fitted it into the handle and continued to use the sword, "now about one half its original length and otherwise in a good state of preservation."

Possibly Robert's parents lived in Henry Co., VA, for a while, for his sister Chloe was born there 3 Sept. 1788, according to Gambill family records. It may have been only a visit, for the family was in Wilkes in the 1787 census and the 1790 census (with two sons, two daughters, and five slaves). There was a considerable amount of traveling between counties, surprising in view of the difficulty. Some trips were for pleasure and some for more practical reasons: markets, mills where corn and wheat could be ground, a tanner who sold leather for shoes, etc.

In any event, before 1813 Bobby Johnson had wooed and won the hand of Celia Bourne, daughter of William and Rosamond Jones Bourne who had come from Hanover Co., VA, to the Knob Fork area in Wythe Co., soon to be Grayson. Celia Bourne was born on Christmas Day, 1790. By Dec. 1792 her father and his neighbors succeeded in getting the southern portion of Wythe Co., VA, taken to form Grayson Co. so the county seat would not be so far removed from the settlers along New River. The First Court, in 1793, was held in Wm. Bourne's barn, it being the largest building in the county. Wm. Bourne was appointed Clerk of Court.

Celia's siblings were: Patience Bourne, b. 18 Nov. 1770, m. Jonathan Thomas; Milly Bourne — 7 March 1773, m. Jesse McKinney; Charity Bourne — 7 Nov. 1775, m. John Blair; Stephen Bourne — 26 Feb. 1779, m. Patsy Mays; Mary Bourne — 5 Jan. 1782, m. Martin Dickinson; Elizabeth Bourne — 20 March 1785, m. Capt. Lewis Hale; Frances Bourne — 5 Jan. 1788, m. Stephen Hale, Sr.; and William Bourne, Jr. — 4 May 1794, who married Mary Johnson, sister of Bobby Johnson who married Celia Bourne.

Rob't. and Celia B. Johnson lived in Wilkes Co. On 15 June 1821 he bought his brother-in-law Jesse Gambill's "homeplace" on Roaring River. By that time they had three children with four more to arrive. Their children were: Nancy "Polly" Johnson, b. 19 Sept. 1813, m. 5 Mar. 1833 John Richardson of Surry Co., NC; Rachel Johnson, b. 1815, m. 1 Jan. 1836 Joseph Porter. One of their daughters, Rachel Porter, m. James Warren and had a daughter Josephine who m. Charles Hunter. William Bourne Johnson, b. 22 May 1817, d. 1 April 1856, m. 29 Oct. 1838 Frances Ellinor Foster, daughter of John and Ann Vannoy Foster; Frankey, b. 1824; Samuel J., b. 1822, m. Elizabeth Brown, daughter of Eli Brown; Lewis, b. 22 Oct. 1827, d. 20 Nov. 1880, m. 1 Nov. 1849 Nancy Wheatley; and Caroline, b. 27 March 1832, d. 12 Aug. 1910, m. 25 Oct. 1855 William Carson, son of Matthew & Jane McCullough Carson.

Robert "Bobby" Johnson was named in his mother's pension application in 1840; he died before his mother's estate settlement in 1854. Celia Bourne Johnson and her two sisters were widows "at the same time" and in "Pioneer Settlers of Grayson Co., VA" Nucholls reports that all three managed their estates efficiently. Celia died in Wilkes Co., NC 19 Jan. 1863.

Sources: Johnson Family Bible; family knowledge; "Pioneer Settlers of Grayson County, Va." by Nucholls; Grayson Co., VA Wills The Draper Collection; Wilkes Co. Records.

— Mary J. Richards

ROBERT and CELIA BOURNE JOHNSON

734

Robert Johnson, first child of Capt. Samuel and Mary Hamon Johnson, was born 25 Oct. 1783, near Traphill on the head of Roaring River. He married Celia Bourne, born 25 Dec. 1790, in Grayson County, Virginia, the daughter of William and Rosamond Jones Bourne.

Robert Johnson, 15 June 1821, bought the Jesse Gambill place on Roaring River in Walnut Grove Township, where he and Celia lived the rest of their lives and raised their family. (Jesse Gambill was a brother-in-law of Robert, husband of his sister, Nancy.)

Robert is listed in the 1850 Federal Census as a farmer. Celia, his wife was a mid-wife.

Robert died before Feb. 1834 (date of the administration of his fathers estate) and is buried in the Johnson family cemetery on his old home place. Celia, his wife, died 19 Jan. 1863, and is, also, buried in the cemetery on their home place. There are no markers at their burial places.

Robert and Celia Bourne Johnson were the parents of seven known children: (1) Mary or Polly, born 19 Sept. 1813. She married 5 March 1833, John Richardson, of Surry County. They were the parents of seven children: Susannah, Celia, William or Billy, Franky, Merdia, Mary or Polly, and John Calvin. The Richardsons lived in the Ashe County Area.

(2) Rachael, born 1815, died at the age of 100 years, 20 May 1915. She married (bond) 1 Jan. 1836, Joseph Porter. They lived in Warrensville, Ashe County. They were the parents of seven children: William, Elisha, Marion, Joseph, Celia, Andrew, and John.

(3) William Bourne, born 22 May 1817, and died April 1856. He married Frances Ellinor Foster. They were the parents of eight children: Mary Ann, Samuel, John, Celia Jane, Lewis Franklin, Robert Thomas, Edmund Foster, and Caroline or Carrie. They resided in the Ashe County Area.

(4) Samuel, born about 1822. He married Elizabeth Brown, daughter of Eli Brown. They lived on part of his parents' old home place. They had six children: William, Sidney Lewis, Harvey, Nancy Carolyn, and Samuel.

(5) Frankie, born about 1824. She married, 1st Joseph Chote; after his death she married 2nd Martin H. Wheatley. They went to Johnson County, Missouri. Martin H. Wheatley died there and Frankie returned to Wilkes County, and lived with her brother, Lewis, and her sister-in-law and step daughter, Nancy. Frankie had no children. She was buried on the mountain above the Lewis Johnson home.

(6) Lewis, born 22 Oct. 1827, and died 20 Nov. 1880. He married 25 Oct. 1849, Nancy Wheatley, daughter of Martin H. and Polly or Maryann Johnson Wheatley. Lewis and Nancy lived on part of the Robert Johnson old home place. Lewis's great grandson, John Robert Johnson, lives on the property today. Lewis and Nancy were the parents of thirteen children: Celia Ann, Mary Jane or Polly, Matilda Caroline, William Martin, Calvin Fletcher, Samuel Freeland, Joshua Vance, Lewis Franklin, Martha Elizabeth, Isaac Robert, Little Doc,

Nancy Ferbie, and Bud or Daniel Christopher.

(7) Nancy Caroline, born 27 March 1832, and died 12 Aug. 1910. She married 25 Oct. 1855, William or Bill Carson, and they resided in the Ashe County Area. They were the parents of eight children: Celia Jane, Francis E., Mary Ann, Martha Ellen, Chloe Caroline, Matthew, Emma, and John.

Sources: Bible, cemetery and public records, family knowledge.

— Verl F. Weight

CAPTAIN SAMUEL JOHNSON
735

Samuel Johnson, born, 1757, probably in Prince William County (now Fauquier County) Virginia, the son of Jeffery and Rachel Walker Johnson. Samuel came to Surry County (now Wilkes County) with his parents and family in the early 1770's. They lived on the left bank of the Yadkin River, where the Abitibi plant now stands, in Roaring River.

Samuel married, 25 June 1782, in Wilkes County, Mary Hamon, daughter of Ambrose and Ann Hamon. Mary was born about 1762, believed in Caroline County, Virginia.

Samuel and Mary, very soon after their marriage, settled near the head of the Roaring River (Traphill Area) not far from the Blue Ridge. They lived out their lives here and are buried on the old home place, in what is called the Old Newt Johnson Cemetery. Samuel died, 15 Sept. 1834, and Mary, his wife, died, 27 Jan. 1853.

Samuel and Mary Hamon Johnson were the parents of nine known children: (1) Robert, born, 25 Oct. 1783, and died before Feb. 1854, married Celia Bourne; (2) Nancy, born, 2 Oct. 1785, married Jesse Gambill, and moved to Ashe Co; (3) Chloe, born, 3 Sept. 1788, died, 9 Jan. 1877, married William Gambill; (4) Samuel Brumfield, born, 18 May 1790, died, 1852, married, 25 Nov. 1816, Susana Alexander; (5) Ambrose, born, 15 May 1796, married, Lucinda Franklin; (6) Mary or Polly, born, 7 June 1796, married 9 July 1817, William Bourne of Grayson County, Virginia, son of William and Rosamond Jones Bourne; (7) Lewis, born, 1800, married, 22 Jan. 1829, Nancy Lamirah Martin. They lived on part of his father's home place; (8) Col. John Simpson, born, 20 Feb. 1802, died, 11 Oct. 1872, married, 1849, Nancy Adelia Holbrook. They lived on his parents' home place; (9) Rachel W., born, 19 June 1806, and died, 1872, married, 1833, William M. Forrister, and they lived in Rock Creek.

Samuel, in the summer of 1776, served as a Private in the Company of Capt. Benjamin Cleveland in a campaign against the Cherokee Indians.

In the fall of 1778 or 79, he was in command of a Company of Cavalry on a three month expedition to Little or Deep River against the Tories.

In 1780, with the rank of Captain, he led a Company of Cavalry to Kings Mountain. Capt. Samuel Johnson was a Lieutenant in the battle. He was wounded in battle.

Shortly after his marriage, Samuel and his wife were attending Sabbath Services at the Roaring River Meeting House, when a messenger arrived from the west side of the Blue Ridge with information that Tories were committing depredation upon the settlements. Capt. Johnson, leaving his bride to return home by herself, immediately summoned his men that were at hand and hastened with them across the mountains — where they met the invaders in battle and defeated them.

He was highly esteemed by the county.

Samuel Johnson was an invalid pensioner for the wound received at the Battle of Kings Mountain — after his death his widow received pension until her death.

Sources: Personal Research.

— Verl F. Weight

THE FAMILY OF THOMAS JOHNSON SR.
736

From early childhood I had heard about our family that was "twice Johnsons." Many times my father, Samuel Gideon Johnson Sr., had explained our history back to Thomas Johnson, B. 28 June 1729, probably in Va. Sometimes he would take the old copy book from the safe and tell me and my brother about how the book was home-made and how old it was. The book has heavy pages, sewn with linen thread, into a cover made of deerskin. We were told that the ink had been made from "ink balls" from oak trees, the pen a quill.

The research of Dr. Lorand Johnson has shown our Johnston (original spelling) family came from Caskieben, near Aberdeen in Scotland. The Johnston/Johnson Clan Tartan is predominately blue and green, with yellow and black pivots. The Clan Badge bears a motto which means "Aye Ready". There are Johnstons from the border at Annandale. The first of our Johnstons in America was Edward (who married Elizabeth Walker in 1677) who had been excommunicated for being a Quaker and had come to New Kent Co., Va. ca. 1677.

No one has learned the maiden name of Thomas Johnson's wife, Rachel, B. 30 May 1737. They were married ca. 1753 and had a family of 8 sons, 3 daughters, and twins, who died soon after birth. The oldest, B. 28 July 1754, was William, my third great-grandfather, who testified in his application for a Revolutionary War Pension that he was born in Amelia Co., Va., moved with his family to Johnston Co., N.C. in 1759, then to Rowan (now Surry) Co., where he lived until he volunteered for service in Feb. 1776. In another Claim Document dated 25 June 1833, William stated that he had lived "for 68 years in Wilkes Co., N.C. and before that in Loudon Co., Va.", so now I have found another puzzle.

Thomas Johnson had received a grant for 480 acres in Rowan Co. in 1759, and in 1771 the land fell into the newly formed Surry Co. Then in 1777, when Wilkes Co. was created, much of the Johnson land was included in the new county, and Wilkes became Thomas' home. The Johnsons were there from the beginning of Wilkes County. Thru grants and purchases Thomas Johnson acquired over 2,000 acres of land which were in areas on "the south side of the Yadkin River", on "Panther Creek", "Dropping Off Branch", near Round Top Mountain, and in the middle fork of Roaring River.

Thomas Johnson died before July, 1786. Rachel died after 1800 and both are believed buried in the William Johnson Cemetery.

This family lived in Wilkes thru the terrible times of the Revolution. Thomas Johnson Sr. was a member of the Safety Committee in Surry Co. in 1775. Their oldest son William served as Ensign and Private in many campaigns. Their second son, Thomas Jr. (B 1757), served as a soldier and on his march back from N.Y. under General Hogan his enlistment expired, and he was to report to Halifax, N.C. He was detained in Greensville, Va., did not receive his discharge, was accused of desertion. Thru his testimony he was cleared of all charges. I believe their third son, Philip (B 1761), is listed with his brother William on the Abstract of William Lenoir's Payroll for the Expedition to King's Mtn., Sept. 7, 1780.

Their seventh child was Richard Henry Johnson (B 1768) who was my second great-grandfather. So being descended from two sons of Thomas and Rachel Johnson I am "twice a Johnson".

I am proud of my strong pioneer ancestors who with their strength and stamina built their homes, churches and schools, and all things needed for their subsistance and well being. They met the threat to their freedom with their own courage and patriotism, and they won.

Sources: Family papers; Cemetery records; National Archives; Wilkes County Records; Records from Ayla Dean Irwin.

— Esther Johnson Wirt (Mrs. D.E.)

JOHNSTON FAMILY
737

In the mid to late 1700's in old Granville County, North Carolina, Noel Johnston and Catherine Hayes became man and wife. Times were hard, but they came from hearty stock and they persevered.

Noel and Catherine's son Joshua felt the need to search out a new frontier. He moved westward into Wilkes County, North Carolina about 1800 with his wife Sara Glass. Wilkes County had many early settlers and by the time Joshua and Sara moved here the wilderness was pushed still further to the west. However, the land was good, the air was fresh, and the people were friendly so the young Johnstons decided to make Wilkes County their home.

Joshua and Sara had a son and named him after Joshua's father, Noel. The younger Noel Johnston, born April 5, 1808 in Wilkes County, was married on December 15, 1829 to Lettuce Marlow, who was born September 18, 1811. During their lifetime they lived in the present day Fishing Creek Arbor Road section of Wilkes County. Noel and Letty had the largest recorded family of the Johnston clan. Eighteen children in thirty years were born to the couple. Although several children died young, quite a few families in Wilkes can trace their roots to Noel and Letty. The children and their birthdates were: (1) David — January 28, 1831; (2) Matilda — September 13, 1832; (3)

Joshua — December 17, 1833; (4) James — December 4, 1835; (5) Sammuel — May 8, 1837; (6) Martha — January 7, 1839; (7) Randolph — February 29, 1840; (8) Noel, Jr. — May 2, 1842; (9) Mary Ann — May 12, 1844; (10) Joseph — October 24, 1846; (11) Frances — April 17, 1848; (12) Parks — June 4, 1849; (13) John — November 21, 1850; (14) Lettie — November 17, 1851; (15) Levine — February 23, 1853; (16) William — June 11, 1855; (17) Elizabeth — September 13, 1858; and (18) Adam — October 18, 1860. Sustaining such a large family was a tremendous undertaking. Food was always a problem as there were no corner stores at which to shop. The children were put to work in the fields at an early age. Everyone had to share and the younger children were lucky if the clothes of the older children were still usable.

The oldest of the eighteen children of Noel and Letty was David. David left home at an early age and probably traveled for a short time before he settled in Wilkes County not far from his mother and father. On September 24, 1852 he married Margaret Juletty Johnson. Their four children were: Letty E., John A., Edna, and Noel.

John A. Johnston was born August 26, 1854 in Wilkes County. He died of a cerebral hemorrhage on April 13, 1924 in Wilkes County. He is buried at Edgewood Baptist Church. He was married to Sarah Staley probably about 1875. (Sarah Staley was a daughter of Joseph and Nancy Buttrey Staley.) Born from this marriage were: Claude, Millard B., Lonnie, Beula May, Bertha, John Iredell, Avery, and a daughter whose name is unknown and married a Harris.

John Iredell Johnston was twice married. The name of the first wife is Edie Triplette and this marriage produced one son, Lindsey. The second wife of John Iredell was Ida Lodema Moore, a descendant of Starling (Sterling) Moore who came to Wilkes County from Rowan County in 1816. From this marriage came: Donald E., William H., Elamay, Barney, Louise, Bessie, Richard, Robert, Julius Jay, Howard, and John Iredell, Jr.

John Iredell Johnston lived out most of his life in the Brushy Mountain area as did his antecedents. Johnny Iredell, as he was often known, was an itenerate farmer with a talent and fondness for apple and other fruit trees. Into late life he continued to bud new trees and prune the mature ones, working at the request of orchard owners who knew of his exceptional knowledge. John Iredell Johnston died on December 29, 1966.

Julius Jay Johnston, one of John Iredell's younger sons, was born in Wilkes County on February 11, 1923. Julius Jay worked in the Civilian Conservation Corp created under "The New Deal" in company 3420 at Laurel Springs, North Carolina from May 20, 1941 to July 18, 1942 at which time the Corp was being disbanded due to the military draft. On January 22, 1943 he entered military service in the U.S. Army. After basic training he was shipped to England aboard the "Mt. Vernon." After England, Jay served in France, Belgium, Holland, and Germany. In 1946, after not see-ing home for three years, he returned to the United States aboard the "Rock Hill" and was discharged on March 6, 1946 having attained the rank of Staff Seargeant.

Julius Jay Johnston was employed by Wilkes Hosiery for twelve years, Granite Hosiery of Mt. Airy, North Carolina for two years, and was employed by Peerless Hosiery Company on October 10, 1959 where he remains employed to date. He is a past member and Sunday School Superintendant at Mt. Zion Baptist Church and is presently a member of Haymeadow Baptist Church.

Julius Jay Johnston and Ruby Faye Faw were married on April 19, 1946. Faye Faw is a daughter of Jacob Heggie Faw and a grand-daughter of Henry Judson Faw (see "A Brief History of the Faw Family in Wilkes County" in this book) of Ashe County, North Carolina. She was born in Wilkes County on July 28, 1927 to Jacob Heggie and Mamie Louise Wyatt Faw. Julius Jay Johnston and Ruby Faye Faw have two children: James Vernon (m. Nila Elledge on March 2, 1973) and Janet Lynn (m. Alton Dennis Church). Jay and Faye's grandchildren are Jarrett Alan Johnston (August 4, 1980 — August 6, 1980), Jeremy Scott Johnston (b. August 7, 1981), and Anthony Benjamin Church (b. June 14, 1974).

Sources: Family Bible, census, marriage bonds, and Mrs. W.O. Absher's records.

— James Vernon Johnston

ANDREW BLAINE (DICK) JOHNSTON

738

Andrew Blaine (Dick) Johnston, fourth son of John Andrew and Frances Bell Johnston was born June 3, 1886, in a log cabin 3 miles east of Wilkesboro. He attended a one-room school nearby until he was 13 years old. He quit school, and his first job was carrying drinking water to employees at the Turner-White Coffin Company — later the Turner-White Casket Company. He walked 4 miles each way and earned 15 cents a day. By the early 1920's Dick (a nickname given him by his uncle) had worked his way up to general manager while learning every facit of the business.

In 1913 he married Gertrude Hunt, daughter of Charles S. and Minnie Stokes Hunt. Gertrude was a Great Granddaughter of Montford Sydney Stokes, Wilkes's only Governor and U.S. Senator. Two children were born to this union. A son, Richard Blaine, was born May 20, 1915 and a daughter, Gertrude Elizabeth, was born August 26, 1917 and died of pneumonia December 25, 1917.

In 1927 Dick Johnston, joined financially by J.R. Hix, W.B. Carlton, and W.B. Gwyn, started American Furniture Company with about 25 employees. From this small beginning the company had grown to 500 employees manufactureing 700 pieces of bed-

Andrew Blaine Johnston.

room furniture per day by 1936.

In 1936 his son Richard graduated from the University of North Carolina and joined the U.S. Air Corp and served with distinction as a Fighter Pilot in the Guadalcanal Campaign in the South Pacific, receiving the Silver Star and Distinguished Flying Cross, and as a test Pilot at Wright Field in Dayton, Ohio, during the last two years of World War II. On July 8, 1944 Richard married Elicia Howland Caroon originally from New Bern, N.C. and to this marriage 4 sons were born: (1) Richard Blaine, Jr. married Patricia Lewis and they have 3 children: Andrew Lewis, Mary Lewis and Blaine Patrick. (2) William Charles married Jennifer Jones, and they have 3 children: Elicia Fair, Joseph Richard and William Tate. (3) Joseph Andrew married Nancye Duncan. (4) Keith Wythes is engaged to Amanda Vannoy. On October 11, 1945 Gertrude Hunt, Dick's first wife died. In May 1947 Dick married Ruby Pearson.

American Furniture Company continued to grow. In 1955 Dick Johnston, joined by his management team of his son Richard, Tom Story, Jr. and Wayne Coffey organized and started Drew Furniture Co. on the former site of the Oak Furniture Company, which had been destroyed by fire. This company was to manufacture a step higher priced bedroom furniture than American Furniture. Just two years after Drew was organized and going well Andrew Blaine (Dick) Johnston died on August 11, 1957 at the age of 71. The two companies, American Furniture Co. and Drew Furniture Company continued to grow under the management team Dick had put together, with his son Richard as President and chief executive officer. In 1970 both companies were sold to the Sperry and Hutchinson Co. of New York City. They continue today as a part of Ladd Furniture Co.

The furniture industry in Wilkes County stands as a monument to the dreams and foresight of a self-made man who was born, grew up and lived in Wilkes County.

Sources: Personal knowledge.

— R.B. Johnston

CLAUDE EDMOND JOHNSTON
739

Claude Edmond Johnston was born Feb. 7, 1890, died Nov. 20, 1961, son of John A. and Sara Staley Johnston. He married Bessie Roland, daughter of Bill and Elizabeth Gryder Roland, on Dec. 24, 1907. Eleven children were born to this union: Elbert, married Dora McCarter — their children are Gertrude, Mildred, and Charles; Lillie, married Ivy Waddell — their children are Alton, Sue, Jolene, Edna (dec.), Albert, and Shirley; Sally, married Harmon Wyatt — their children are Raymond (dec.), Marie, and Maggie Mae; Everette, married Ella Mae Pendergrass, their children, Everette, Jr. (dec.), Jean, Judy, and Mary Lee Etta; Bryce, married Virginia Anderson — their children, Tom and Timothy (Timothy died in early childhood); Mary, married Garland Reeves — their children, Brent, Velda, and Michael; Gordon, married Bernice Owens — their children, Dean, Ann, and Kay; Lonnie,

married Sidney Brooks — their child, Wm. E.; Arlie, married Jeannie Brown — their child, Loretta; Claude, Jr., married JoAnn Richardson, their children, Sherry, Lynn, Gwyn (twins), Claudene, and David; Clifton, married Evelyn Bauguess — their children, Eugene, Cathy, Charlie, and Jody.

Probably the best way to describe this family is to say, "Claude and Bess were honest, hard working, God fearing people." This had to be true or they would never have been able to raise eleven children on the earnings of one man during the days of the "Great Depression." Grandma Johnston never went outside the home to work, while Grandpa worked seven days a week at a local manufacturing company.

Four of their eight sons served their country during two wars, Bryce and Gordon was in the U.S. Army during the World War II. Bryce was injuried in North Africa, for which he received the Purple Heart. Lonnie and Claude, Jr., both served in the army during the Korean War.

It could well be said that Claude Johnston did a good job bringing up his family.

Source: The Bible, gravestones, family knowledge.

— Sidney Johnston

JOHN A. JOHNSTON
740

John A. Johnston, son of David and Margaret Gelettie Johnston was born August 26, 1854 and died April 13, 1924. He married Sarah Staley, daughter of Joseph and Nancy Buttery Staley. This union had eight children: Lonnie, first married Elvira Harris, second marriage, Lottie Glass; Avery, first married Rebecca Roberts, second marriage was to Alice Marshall; Johnny Iredell, first married Edie Triplette, second marriage, Ida Moore; Beaulah Mae married Samuel Long; Claude E. married Bessie Roland; Millard, married Sally Beach; Bertha married Marshall Anderson; and Cornelia married James Henry Harris.

Cornelia died in young womanhood, leaving two small children. Beaulah Mae moved to Concord, N.C. The remaining children lived out their lives in Wilkes County.

Source: Public records, grave stones, knowledge obtained upon inquiry.

— Sidney Johnston

JOINES DESCENDANTS
741

In a letter written, in 1920, by Wesley Joines Sr. he states that his Great grandfather, Ezekiel Joines, emigrated from Scotland. He entered one hundred acres of land on the waters of Double Creek, known as Joines Creek, in Wilkes County. He was twice married and raised two sets of children. Of the first set he had Thomas and Major. Major was killed in the battle of Eutaw Springs in 1781. Of the second set there was Edmond and Jack who settled in the Brushy Mountains. He had two daughters, Sayer, who married a Roberts and Piety, who married James Parsons.

Thomas Joines, Revolutionary War soldier, married Mary, daughter of Benjamin Caudill.

They had ten children. Sarah, Lydia, Lear, Martha, Rachel, Sela, Moses, Major (born 24 April 1793, died 6 May 1889), Ezekiel (born 2 June 1800, died 8 May 1893), Thomas (born 15 Jan. 1802, died 26 April 1860).

Ezekiel Joines (1800-1893), married Pheroby Caudill, born 1800, died 1870, daughter of Jeremiah Caudill. They had the following children: Willian Henry (born 17 Oct. 1828, died 25 Nov. 1910), married Candis Andrews (born 7 Jan. 1830, died 20 Sept. 1918); Mary, born 1830; Major Finley (born 1 May 1833, died 23 Dec. 1917) married Molly Edwards (born 7 May 1850, died 22 Nov. 1918); Sarah Jane (born 29 Sept. 1835, died 24 March 1893) married Ashley Johnson 18 Feb. 1843; Martha Matilda (born 18 Sept. 1838, died 11 April 1922) married Thomas B. Caudill (born 30 Aug. 1838, died 4 Nov. 1928); Shadrach Franklin (born 17 Oct. 1840, died 24 Aug. 1915) married Nancy McGrady (born 1 April 1843, died 27 July 1903); Cynthia (born 3 April 1843, died 14 Oct. 1891) married Aaron R. Truitt (born 2 June 1851, died 1 April 1914); and Hardin Joines, born 1845.

Shadrach Franklin (Shade) and Nancy McGrady Joines, married 9 July 1864. Their children were: Alice, born 24 March 1865, died 9 July 1938, married George Winfield Absher, born 12 Sept. 1853, died 28 June 1891; James Hardin, born 12 Dec. 1866, died 18 June 1953, married Carrie Belle Buttrey, born 25 July 1866, died 24 Jan. 1918; John Avery Joines, born 21 July 1868, died 24 Nov. 1931, married first Mary Alexander, born 29 Jan. 1869, died 23 May 1921, married a second time to Cora Long Holbrook, born 13 May 1881, died 8 May 1963; Shadrach Franklin Jr. born 22 March 1870, died 16 Feb. 1927, married Mary Ann Handy, born 5 Jan. 1870, died 18 June 1945; William Henry, born 1 April 1872, died 25 Feb. 1907, married Eula Kennedy, born 17 May 1875, died 17 Dec. 1942; Pheroby, born 20 June 1874, died 9 March 1938, married Johnson Brown; Aurora, 3 May 1876, died 16 May 1975, married Daniel Shumate, born 30 March 1866, died 2 Feb. 1963; Major Finley, born 28 April 1878, died 17 May 1949, married Alice Miller, born 6 July 1873, died 18 Feb. 1945; Ezekiel (1880 Census shows as David), born 30 March 1880; Carrie Belle, born 9 June 1881, died 18 Feb. 1947, married Robbins Miller; Charlie, born 27 June 1883; Tyra York, born 12 May 1885, died 8 June 1931, married Minnie Smoot; Hilary Jones, born 11 May 1888, died October 1961, married Hallie Johnson.

James Hardin Joines and Carrie Belle Buttrey, daughter of John Timothy and Winnie Matilda Wiles Buttrey, were married 3 Feb. 1886, at Dockery, Wilkes County, N.C., by and in the home of W.M. Absher, a Justice of the Peace. They had nine children: (1) Mac, born 18 Feb. 1887, died 22 July 1918 at Camp Hancock, Augusta, Ga. was a 1st Lt. in U.S. Infantry; (2) Metta, born 25 July 1888, married Robert Vance Thompson, born 26 March 1882, died 28 August 1958. They had three children, Metta Ruth, Robert Mac (Jack), and Daniel T;

(3) Maude, born 14 Jan. 1890, died 22 Sept. 1981, married 20 May 1911, Grover

James Hardin Joines Family. Front Row: L to R: Hardin, Vance, Carrie, Ruth. Back Row: Myrtle, Metta, Maude, Dean, Paul.

Mac Joines.

Cromwell Owens, born 19 Oct. 1888, died 21 April 1959. They had eight children. Robert Cromwell, Clara Estelle, John Carl, Carrie Pauline, William Hardin, Annie Ruth, James Oliver and Vance Joines Owens; (4) Dean, born 29 July 1892, first married Verga Waddell 23 Aug. 1911. They had six children: Velma Beatrice, William Clint, Mac, Paul Clayton, Metta and Franklin Delano. They were divorced and Dean was married again to Zena Douglas Taylor; (5) Paul, born 24 Feb. 1895, died 31 Aug. 1972, married Lois Monday, they were divorced and he married Ethel Harrison Rittenburg; (6) Myrtle, born 7 July 1898, married Walter Clay Joines, 12 Jan. 1916. They had three children Doris Edna, Carrie Beatrice and Patsy Kathryn;

(7) Vance, born 14 Oct. 1900, married Gladys Lorraine Blevins, born 16 May 1913. Gladys was born at Toms Creek, Wise County, Va. She was the daughter of Charles Franklin and Martha Ellen Roberts Blevins. Vance and Gladys were married March 22, 1932, at Lebanon, Va. by Rev. A.L. Young, a Baptist Minister. They were married in the Baptist Parsonage. Mrs. Young being the only witness to this ceremony. They had three children. Carrie Ellen, born 20 Jan. 1933, married Donald Blaine Moore, born 5 Dec. 1930, married 29 Aug. 1953. They have three children, Tim Alan, Tracy Ann and Ted Arlan and live in Monaca. Pa.; Ethel Lorraine, born 25 Sept. 1934, lives in Sewickley Pa. and James Franklin, born 7 May 1938, married Joyce Ann Baker, 18 Dec. 1960. They have two sons, James Bryan and Scott Alan and live in Wilmington Delaware;

(8) Ruth, born 19 May 1903, married 31 July 1925, Samuel Patrick Morrah Jr. born 2 Oct. 1893, died 2 Sept. 1947. They have two sons, Samuel Patrick III and James Edward; (9) Ethel, born 6 Aug. 1907, died 20 March 1908.

Most of these people were farmers. James Hardin Joines, was not only a farmer, but also a country storekeeper. He was Postmaster at Abshers (discontinued) and for many years a Justice of the Peace. Mac Joines was a railway locomotive engineer prior to his voluntary enlistment in the Army. Paul Joines was a Private in Co. F 51st Pioneer Infantry, during World War 1 and served several months with the army of occupation, in Germany, after the armistice was signed. In his earlier years he was a traveling salesman. In later years he was in the real estate and insurance business, in Winston Salem. His hobbies were picking the banjo and playing checkers.

The writer, Vance Joines, retired from Koppers Company Inc., Engineering and Construction Division, Construction Department, Pittsburgh, Pa., July 31, 1966. Was first employed by them as millwright helper, Feb. 9, 1940. Most of this time was at various locations in the States but had been on assignment to jobs in Canada, Mexico, Brazil and Spain. At time of retirement was Mechanical Supervisor. Carrie Ellen Moore is associated with her mother in telephone answering and Radio Communications, Beaver Falls Pa. Ethel is an Executive Secretary for Alcoa, Pittsburgh, Pa. and James Franklin is in real estate, in Wilmington, Del.

Sources: Family records; letter of Wesley Joines, Sr.

— Vance Joines

EZEKIAL JOINES DESCENDANTS

742

William Thomas Joines was born to Robert Frank Joines and Martha Byers on April 1888 in a small house near the Wilkes County Courthouse. William's grandfather, Poindexter Joines, was a member of the Ezekiel Joines family. They were some of the first settlers of Wilkes County.

William had a sister, Ethel Joines, who was born in 1889 and whose death date is unknown. William Thomas was a mail carrier in Wilkesboro for a period of time. He also was responsible for turning the city lights on every evening after dark and off the following morning. This, of course, was when electricity was first installed in the city. The switch for the lights was located behind the jail.

In 1928 William Thomas and his family left Wilkesboro for High Point, NC. Upon his arrival there he worked for the High Point Yarn Mills and several furniture companies. On April 1, 1938, William Thomas died at his home. Elizabeth (Lishie) Minton had married William Thomas on November 13, 1909. They had seven children:

(1) The oldest son of William Thomas Joines was Charles Addison, who was born January 29, 1912. He spent the first 15 years of his life in Wilkesboro. The family home was located where the Connie's Day School now stands, at the intersection of Woodland, Henderson and West Streets. In High Point Charles Addison spent many hours at the YMCA, and it was there that he met his sweetheart of today, L.C. Plampin. They were married August 31, 1934. Shortly thereafter on September 1, 1935 Charles Kenneth was born.

Three years later on September 28, 1938 in Jacksonville, FL, Emma Lou was born. After serving in World War II, Addison returned to his family and lived in various areas of the country. After living in California for over twenty years, Addison and L.C. retired and returned to High Point where they presently reside. Charles Kenneth, their older child, married Jutta Grundmann on July 20, 1960, in Berlin, Germany, where he was a member of the armed forces. They have three children: Charles, Karen, and Jessica. Emma Lou married Norbert Alvin Kemp on August 1, 1958 in Denver, Co. July 13, 1959 Deborah Charlene was born. After Norb's graduation from the University of Denver, the family moved to Kansas City. It was there that the other two children were born: Bryan Scott, on December 1

1962; Gregory Allen, on August 28, 1964. Emma's family still resides in Kansas City where Norb is a project manager for Northland Park and Emma, a reading specialist for a local school district. Debbie is a service secretary; Bryan, a full time missionary in Japan for The Church of Jesus Christ of Latter Day Saints; and Greg, a recent graduate of S.M. Northwest High School.

(2) The second child of William Thomas Joines and Lishie Minton was Ethel Juanita, who was born on February 1, 1916. After moving with the family to High Point in 1928, she married William Robert Gurley on May 5, 1934. They have two children: Velina Elizabeth, born on July 12, 1937 and Thomas Michael, born on February 10, 1940. Tommy now lives in Greensboro with his wife Ann and daughter Cynthia.

(3) The third child was Dorothy C. Bagwell, who was born on April 9, 1920. After high school, Dorothy worked with the USO during World War II before marrying Marshall E. Bagwell of Atlanta, GA on June 3, 1944. They have one daughter, Marsha Lynn Bagwell, born on July 12, 1946. Marsha is now an actress on Broadway and has several commercials currently showing on national television. Dorothy and Marshall now reside in High Point, NC.

(4) The fourth child of William Thomas Joines and Lishie Minton Joines was Agnes Elizabeth, who was born on November 30, 1922. She married Warren Howard Bowers on April 19, 1941. Howard Bowers passed away on January 24, 1954. They have two sons: Paul Warren, born on May 23, 1942 and Charles Ray, born on June 4, 1947. Paul lives with his wife Martha Morris, and two daughters Pagie Elizabeth and Marcie Jane in Warrenton, VA. Charles Ray lives with his wife, Teresa Pardue and their two daughters Heather Elizabeth and Holly Ann in High Point, NC.

(5) The fifth child of the family was Mary Orlean (Marilyn) Potts, who was born August 31, 1925. Marilyn married George W. Potts on September 10, 1950. They live in Charlotte, NC, where Marilyn works for Wachovia Bank. They have one son George Michael Potts, who is a Presbyterian minister in Tampa, FL.

(6) Betty Jean Joines was born on September 9, 1930, after the family moved from Wilkes County. She attended High Point schools and now has a position as bookkeeper with Dutch Laundry in High Point, NC.

(7) The Seventh child of William Thomas Joines and Lishie Minton Joines was Robert Clayton Joines, who was born on September, 5, 1934. Bob served in the Navy and lived in California a few years. He married Loretta J. Way on January 1, 1958 and now works as a produce manager for a supermarket in Poolsville, MD. They have one son David Allen, born on April 21, 1962.

Sources: Census information and records in the Wilkes County Genealogical Library, family records, memories and personal knowledge.

— Deborah C. Kemp
and Emma Joines Kemp

THE EXEKIEL JOINES FAMILY

743

Legends say that brothers Ezekiel, Thomas, and Moses Joines journeyed from Edinburgh, Scotland to England then to America via Holland ca 1750. Supposedly Thomas and Moses died before they married. Other legends say that the three brothers came down from Pennsylvania with Daniel Boone, but I have found no documentation of this either. Closer to fact is that Ezekiel Joines, born around 1730, married twice-once to a red-haired Scotch woman whose maiden name may have been Pruitt and then to Sarah, whose maiden name may have been Gunter.

By the first wife Ezekiel fathered two sons, Thomas and Major and by his second wife, Edmond and Jack. Ezekiel also had two daughters, Sayer (Leah), who married a Roberts, and Piety, who married James Parson on 1 February 1792. The eldest son Thomas married Mary Caudill and fathered ten children: (1) Sarah, (2) Lydia, (3) Leah, (4) Martha, (5) Celia, (6) Rachel, (7) Moses, (8) Major, (9) Ezekiel, (10) Thomas, Jr. Both Thomas and Major served in the Revolutionary War, and Major was killed in the Battle of Eutaw Springs.

Ezekiel Joines's second set of boys was Edmond and Jack. Jack died young with no issue. From Thomas Joines and Edmond Joines came the Joineses in Wilkes County and most of the United States. Edmond, born

in 1776, married Elizabeth Laws, died April 1850, and had three children: (1) Larkin, born in 1802, married Franky Church, (2) John Wesley (Jackie), born around 1805, married Elvira Broyhill who was born in 1834, daughter of Norman Broyhill and Polly Davis (3) Rebecca, born in 1809, married William John Laws on 12 January 1826.

Larkin Joines and Franky Church had eight children: (1) John W., born in 1826, married Margaret L. Wilcoxen on 15 June 1854; (2) Elizabeth L., born in 1827, married Hugh Minton 26 January 1849; (3) Catherine, born in 1829; (4) Ann, born in 1831, married Hamilton B. Church 3 August 1847; (5) Hugh, born in 1833, married Susannah Barker 3 October 1851; (6) Hamilton, born in 1835, married Mary Jane Clanton 4 January 1859; (7) Poindexter, born in 1837, married Susan M. Edmiston 20 December 1859; (8) Martha M., born in 1840.

John Wesley, Edmond and Elizabeth (Laws) Joines's second son, married Elvira Broyhill and had ten children: (1) Jesse Frank, born 1835, married Nancy Duncan first and then Sarah Clanton, died 4 April 1903; (2) Rebecca Irene, born 14 March 1846, married John Bebber, 3 January 1855, died 25 January 1903; (3) Mary M., born 4 May 1843, married Caleb Lowe; (4) Edmond, born 1839, married Elizabeth Church; (5) Elizabeth, born 1840, married James W. Duncan 11 January 1876; (6) James, born in 1842; (7) Willis Wesley, born 27 May 1847, married Nancy Lou Meredith 20 August 1867, died June 1898; (8) John, born

George Wesley and Allie Carrigan Joines.

ca 1848; (9) Peter, born 10 July 1851, married Lorina Meredith 7 November 1874, died 21 October 1925; (10) Martha, married Nick Meredith.

Willis Wesley Joines and Nancy Lou Meredith (1851-1944), daughter of James Meredith and Susannah Moreland of Carter County, TN, had eleven children: (1) Susan Elvira, born 6 September 1868 married Johnny Davis, died 19 February 1961; (2) Mary Clementine, born 6 October 1870, married Joe Long, died 5 July 1953; (3) Julia, born 17 November 1872, died 15 May 1907; (4) William Thomas, born 15 June 1875, married Dovie Jane Brock (See Reiney Brock), 18 April 1909, died 12 April 1952; (5) John Jr., born 10 November 1876, died September 1885; (6) Larkin Poindexter, born 12 December 1879, married Vena Murray 9 September 1901, died 19 January 1958; (7) Josephine Genena, born 23 August 1882, married Coffey Smith, died October 1970; (8) Jerdon Calaway, born 17 February 1885, married Lou Lowe, December 1910, died in 1961; (9) Lelia Lorraine, born 22 January 1888, married John Braxton Laws 6 July 1910, died 6 July 1975; (10) Rachel Victoria, born in 1891, married Barney Sparks, died 23 September 1964; (11) Bertha Rowena, born 18 September 1893, married Everette Gambill 3 March 1920, died 14 August 1979.

William Thomas and Dovie Jane Brock Joines had four children: (1) George Wesley, born 20 April 1910, married Allie Pearl Carrigan 21 December 1929; (2) Thomas Mack, married Hessie (Coffey) Sparks; (3) Bertha Grace, born 21 December 1919, married first Jesse Dial 10 December 1944 and second Fred Childers 12 August 1960; (4) Joseph, died in a car accident in 1938.

George Wesley and Allie Pearl Carrigan Joines are my parents and have four children: William Thomas, born 20 November 1931, married first Elizabeth Baird Vance and second Shirley Ford. Bill teaches in the Electrical Engineering department at Duke University in Durham, NC; (2) Joyce Aileen, born 9 May 1936, married Keith L. Bentley, a local dentist, 2 August 1958. Aileen taught school until her family needed her at home; (3) Peggy Jo, born 25 November 1938, married Edwin Hugh Martin 6 March 1959. I have worked in public education as an English teacher and as the Director of Instruction at Wilkes Central Senior High; (4) Marion Max, born 13 May 1941, married Lovina Harvell 28 November 1963 and is employed as an Industrial Engineer in Statesville, NC.

Sources: Family interviews, records in Wilkes County Courthouse and Wilkes Genealogical Society Library.

— Peggy J. Martin

THE ARTHUR BELL JONES FAMILY

744

Arthur Bell Jones was born in the Beaver Creek section of Wilkes county on March 29, 1885 to Jackson and Rebecca Foster Jones. He was educated at the Whippoorwill Academy and his church affiliation was Advent Christian. He died May 20, 1966.

He married Ollie Mae Ferguson, who was also born in Wilkes county, in April, 1911. To this marriage were born seven children:

Topsy Lee was born October 12, 1912. She married William J. Earp in October 1933 and he died in November, 1980. They were the parents of three children: Linda Ann, born in February, 1935, married Worth Bentley in 1959 and they have a son, Alan, born in May, 1964. William Arthur, born July 21, 1937; married Dianne Price of Charleston, S.C. and they have two children, William Arthur, Jr. (Artie), born March 14, 1968 and Caroline, born September, 1978. Elizabeth Jones, born October 3, 1942. She married Charles Edd Billings and they have two children, Charles Edd, Jr., born August, 1964 and Sarah Elizabeth, born September, 1968.

Thurmond Bell was born May 11, 1914. He married Mae Wellborn in December, 1936. They had six children: Ina Mae, born February, 1938 married J.V. Reins in 1961. They had one son, J.V., Jr. Dorothy Jean was born August 1942 and has three children, Jacquelyn, Jolanda and Gerald. She married Clyde Rogers. James McArthur, born August, 1945, married Patricia Shew and they have three children, James McArthur, Jr., born October 1969, Yvonne Nicole, born May, 1971 and twin sons, Matthew and Christopher, born February, 1976.

Glenn Thomas, born April, 1948 and married Bobbie Tevepaugh. Joan, born January 1952, married Ira Myers and has no children. Mary Alice, born November, 1957, is not married.

Wilna Mae was born August 22, 1916. She married Earle Thomas German in December, 1939 and they had two children: Sylvia Jones, born October 1939. She married Glenn Wellborn and they have two children, Sylvia Lynn, born December, 1960 and David Anthony, born May, 1962. John Thomas born, August, 1943 married Wilma Sue Curry and they have six children, John Dana, born January, 1965, Andrea Sue, born July, 1966, Lara Michelle, born June, 1968, Brandon Thomas, born November, 1969, Kendall Rebekah, born December, 1974 and Kristen Adele, born April, 1978.

Thomas William was born December 8, 1919. Thomas married Catherine Quilici of France while in the Navy during World War II. No children were born to this marriage. Catherine had a son, Augustine who cmae to America at age 13. He married Suzanne Somers and has two children, Marc and Suzanne Catherine.

Harless Hope was born June 4, 1921. She married Dewey Prevette and they are the parents of three sons: Dewey Steven, born March 1949, married Jeannie Wiles and has three sons, Michael, Keith and John Paul. Thomas Lee, born May, 1952 married Rebecca Warren. Douglas Kent, born June 1957, married Patricia Staley, June, 1981.

Arthur Harold was born July 14, 1923, married Ella Mae Smith and has no children. He was in the Army during World War II.

Hill Eugene was born September 2, 1925, married Veoria Elledge and had one son, Ronald, who married Maxine Brock. Hill was in the Navy during World War II and was awarded citation for action beyond the call of duty at Hiroshima.

Arthur Bell Jones was a "sawmill man". He began sawmilling at age seventeen. He had one accident in which he lost the fingers of his right hand, leaving stubs. This loss did not stop him from pulling the lever that ran the saw and many people considered him to be the best "sawyer" of his day. The boys followed his trade for several years but are now engaged in chicken farming and one is a store operator.

Ollie is living and will be 90 years old on June 19, 1982. She is able to care for herself and lives with a daughter, Topsy Earp. She has a good memory, reads quite well and is in reasonably good health.

Sources: Personal knowledge.

— Wilna Jones German

DANIEL and SARAH CRAVEN JONES

745

Daniel Jones was born about 1834 in the Mill Creek section of Randolph County. He was a farmer by profession and records indicate that he was 5' 9" tall. He married Sarah Craven in Randolph County. She was born about 1833, daughter of Joshua and Sarah Lambert Craven of the Moffett's Mill community in Randolph County.

The first son, Leander L. was born on Oct. 24, 1860 or 1861 in Randolph Co. Lee, as he was called, moved to Wilkes at a very early age and grew up here. On March 9, 1882, Lee married Martha Jane Simmons. He died on July 31, 1942.

His younger brother, Robert M. Jones was born on May 13, 1867 in Randolph County. He also grew up in Wilkes. On March 6, 1890, he married Mary Elizabeth Hall, daughter of Thomas David and Frances Miller Hall. He became ill with pneumonia and died on Jan. 28, 1908.

Daniel enered the Confederate Army at the age of 26 in March of 1862, when his son was still an infant. He died at an early age as a result of being in the service. Sarah found herself as a widow with two young sons to rear at a time when conditions must have been very difficult.

Some of Sarah's brothers and sisters had moved to Wilkes and Ashe Counties, so about 1870 Sarah brought her two sons to live in that area.

Mr. Coot Shepherd, who was a neighbor and remembered Sallie quite well, said Sallie had worked for Mr. and Mrs. Wyatt Rose to support her family. She was excellent in helping those who were sick and "could draw fire out of burns by rubbing the place". People came from miles around for her soothing aid and treatment. She was an industrious woman and "quite a worker". She is reported to have carried her knitting as she went to the barn to milk the cows — never wasting a moment! From a dress that is still carefully preserved in the family, we can judge that she was a tall, slender woman.

She was "mighty even-tempered, quiet and never gave a short word to her children". She loved children and was an excellent mother.

Daniel Jones.

She was well-liked and a highly reguarded and respected person in the Lewis Fork Community.

Her later years were spent with her son Lee and his wife. She died on Dec. 5, 1887 of pneumonia when she was about fifty-four years old. Her grave is located in the Miller Family Cemetery near Lewis Fork Baptist Church.

Sources: Family Bible, Census Records, Civil War Records, Personal Interview with Mr. Coot Shepherd and Mrs. Conrad Jones.

— Mrs. J. Arnold Simpson

GEORGE JONES

746

Accounts of the Jones Family of Wilkes Co., state Hugh Jones came from Carmarthanshire, Wales, to settle in Orange Co., Virginia. His name does appear on a list of tithables there in 1752. His Will, dated 5 Oct. 1788, pro. 24 Oct. 1791, names his second wife Catey and seven of his eight children. One son, Joseph, left a Will in Orange Co. having "died a soldier in the Continental Army" in which he named his parents, Hugh and Elizabeth Jones, sisters, Elizabeth Jones and Frances Foster and brother Morton.

Children of Hugh and Elizabeth Jones were: (1) Hugh, Jr. b. c. 1740, d. 1797 Jasper Co., Ga., m. Lydia White. (2) George b. 13 June 1743, d. 1830 Wilkes Co., N.C., m. 10 Jan. 1769 Phebe Foster. (4) Morton b. 10 Aug. 1747, d. 8 Nov. 1841, Coffee Co., Tn., m. Frances Foster. (4) Catlett b. 15 June 1749, d. 1829 Columbiana Co., Ohio, m. first Ann Douglas Barksdale, second Sarah Crow. (5) Benjamin b. c. 1750, d. 27 Dec. 1820 Wilkes Co., N.C., m. Elizabeth Foster. (6) Frances m. 25 Feb. 1777, Thomas Foster (lived Wilkes Co.). (7) Elizabeth m. a Jones.

All the sons of Hugh Jones, Sr. served in the Revolution and with the exception of Joseph were at the Surrender of Cornwallis. In 1789 George and Phebe Jones sold 200 acres in Orange Co., Va., and moved to Cub Creek near Moravian Falls, Wilkes Co., N.C. Three children predeceased their father, and when his wife died in Dec. 1828, he being "85 years old" wrote his Will naming his ten surviving children: (1) Philadelphia Garnett b. 11 Jan. 1770 d. 24 Aug. 1857, m. 4 Jan. 1791, Andrew Bryan Jr. (2) Edmund b. 1 Sept. 1771, d. 17 Mar. 1841, m. Anne Lenoir. (3) George b. 28 Jan. 1773, m. Elizabeth Mills. (4) Larkin b. 20 Nov. 1774, d. c. 1804 unm. (5) Catlett b. 9 Oct. 1776, Orange Co., Va., d. 1 May 1856, Caldwell Co., N.C., m. 8 Sept. 1801 Wilkes Co., Ann Dula. (6) John b. 28 July 1778, d. 1813. (7) Ann Foster b. 16 Sept. 1780, m. Ambrose Mills. (8) Phebe b. 28 Sept. 1782, m. Benjamin Jones, Jr. (9) Hugh b. 4 Nov. 1784 unm. (10) Elizabeth b. 5 Dec. 1787, m. Samuel Downs of S.C. (11) Lucy b. 17 Dec. 1788, m. Hilary A. Gilreath. (12) Thomas Foster b. 24 Dec. 1791, d. 4 June 1873, m. 1. Julia Lenoir Pickens, 2. Emily Thompson. (13) Matilda b. 15 April 1794, died young.

Ann, daughter of William and Theodosia Beasley Dula, was born 1785, died 21 May 1846. About 1804 she and her husband, Catlett Jones, Esq., built a home in the Yadkin Valley in present Caldwell County where most of their fourteen children were born. Catlett served in the War of 1812, was commissioned a Justice of Wilkes Co. by the General Assembly in 1820, and when he died in 1856 he left 1300 acres and nineteen slaves to eight of his children. The children of Catlett and Ann Dula Jones were: (1) Elizabeth Eveline b. 17 Nov. 1803, m. David Ernest. (2) Larkin Garnett b. 9 Feb. 1806, d. Charlotte, m. Martha Mira Jones. (3) William Bartlett b. 10 July 1807. (4) George Oliver b. 16 July 1809, m. Martha Bowman. (5) Mary Louisa b. 21 Jan. 1811, m. first John Cunningham, second Joel Berry of S.C. (6) Calvin Catlett b. 7 Jan. 1813, d. 2 Nov. 1896, m. Sarah Louisa Kendall Russell. (7) Harriett Newell b. 14 Jan. 1815, m. Rev. Bailey of W. Tn. (8) Sarah Orilla b. 8 Dec. 1816, d. 11 Aug. 1856. (9) Martha Caroline b. 26 Jan. 1819, "Gables Inn", Wilkes Co., N.C., d. 5 Oct. 1905, Ashe Co., N.C., m. 16 May 1843, John Freeland Greer Sr. (10) Edmund Haines b. 18 Feb. 1821, m. Harriett N. Dunlap. (11) John Langdon b. 18 Nov. 1823, d. 6 Sept. 1867, m. Sarah Llwelyn. (12) Thomas Dula M.D. and Capt. Co. A. 22nd N.C. Reg., b. 8 April 1825, d. 1862 in the Battle of 7 Pines, unm. (13) Juliet Josephine b. 12 Mar. 1827, m. Dr. Geo. N. Carter. (14) Charles Pinckney b. 12 Mar. 1830, d. 21 July 1901, m. Mildred Adelaide Horton.

Martha Jones Greer carefully kept many letters from her relatives below the mountain as did her son, William Calvin Greer, as evidenced by one written to him from Cilley, Caldwell Co., N.C. May 11, 1889 by his uncle, Calvin Catlett Jones: "My dear Nephew your welcome and interesting letter . . . just received and I hasten to reply to it but I fear it may not reach "Grassy Creek" before you leave home . . . brother Pinckney and Mariah Ernest are often unwell . . . I fear brother John's widow and daughters Carrie and Ida are unhappy in Kansas . . . Dr. Carter's death was like an electric shock to us all . . . Your affect Uncle C.C. Jones."

Sources: Orange Co., Va., Wills, Deeds, Marriages; Rev. Pension Applications of Morton and Benj. Jones; Jones-Bryan Bible; Eilkes and Caldwell Cos., N.C., Wills, Deeds, Marriages, Cemetery Records; Jno. F. Greer Sr. Bible Record; Greer-Jones Family Letters.

— Myrtle Greer Johnson

THE FAMILY OF LEANDER L. JONES

747

Leander L. Jones was born in Randolph County on Oct. 24, 1860 or 1861. He was the son of Daniel and Sarah (Sallie) Craven Jones. His father served in the Civil War and died when Lee was quite young.

About 1870, Sallie brought Lee and his younger brother, Robert, to Ashe County where some of her family were living. She remained in this area and moved to Wilkes County where she worked to support her family. This period of time was just following the Civil War.

Lee grew to be a rather tall, large man. He had 'sandy' red hair and blue eyes. He fell in love with Martha Jane Simmons, daughter of Edmond and Jennie Nelson Simmons of Lewis Fork, and they were married on March 9, 1882.

In December of 1882, their first son, Albert C. was born. A daughter, Alice A. was born in August of 1885. In 1886 there was a diptheria epedemic that took the lives of both children within a week. Albert died Nov. 15, 1886 and Alice died Nov. 22, 1886. Their mother, Martha Jane almost died at this time also. She did recover and on Sept. 5, 1887, another daughter Emma L. brightened their lives.

Sadness again struck this family with the death of Lee's mother, Sarah Jones. She was stricken with pneumonia and died Dec. 5, 1887. She had been living with her son. This family lost two children and a mother in about one year's time.

Another son, Samuel L. was born Dec. 4, 1889. He moved to Livingston, Montana in 1912. He served in France in World War I. His wife was Minta McDonald. He died on Feb. 5, 1981.

Conrad Hill Jones was born to Lee and Martha Jane on Dec. 17, 1891 at Ready Branch, N.C. He taught school and was a farmer in the Lewis Fork Community. He married Ola Ruth Welch Nov. 27, 1924. She is the daughter of Wm. G.W. and Ida St. Clair Luther Welch. She was born May 29, 1903 at Mt. Zion in Wilkes Co.

Conrad and Ruth have two children. (1) Gwyn Welch Jones, born September 5, 1925, married Virginia Dare Jarvis on February 16, 1946. They have one daughter, Yvonne Gwynne, who married Michael Pardue. The Pardues live in Fairfield, Virginia with their two daughters Angela Dee and Shanna Yvette; (2) Fred Charles Jones, born March 7, 1931 at Purlear in Wilkes County, married November 4, 1955 Phyllis Elaine Roseman. They have two children — Charles (Chuck) Scott Jones born March 14, 1958, presently a student at U.N.C. at Charlotte and Stephanie Ann Jones, born June 21, 1961, presently a student at U.N.C.

at Chapel Hill.

Other children of Lee and Martha Jane Jones are: Robert Lee, born March 26, 1894, served in World War I, died December 28, 1954; Stella, born September 19, 1896, married Willard Welch in 1914; Matoka, born September 24, 1899, married Sam Triplett October 29, 1930. Sam Triplett was the son of Dr. Bynum and Annie Cooper Triplett. They had one daughter, Annie Garnet Triplett, born November 7, 1931 — died five days later.

Lee was a hard worker and a good family man. He was a member of Lewis Fork Baptist Church which he helped to build. He died July 31, 1942 and is buried at Lewis Fork.

Sources: Bible records and personal knowledge.

— Mrs. Conrad Jones

PRESTON C. JONES
748

My great-grandfather, Preston Cadwallader Jones, was born 2 March 1840 in Davidson County to Jesse Spurgeon Jones, born 7 September 1798, died 24 February 1879 and Aletha Kennedy, born 14 April 1804, died 21 February 1891. Both Jesse Spurgeon and Aletha Jones are buried in the Abbotts Creek Baptist Cemetery near High Point in an area where their ancestors first settled.

The first North Carolina Jones ancestor, Cadwallader Jones, came to Rowan County, now Davidson, in the 1700's from Pennsylvania. The name Cadwallader, from a Welsh ancestor, was used prolifically throughout Jones families. Preston C., though proud of his ancestry, would never willingly acknowledge that the C in his name stood for the tongue-twisting Cadwallader.

Preston Jones married Martha Ellen Hauser on 25 December 1867 in Salem, N.C. She was born 26 July 1852 to Emanuel Hauser, born 4 June 1815, died 1 December 1868, married 4 April 1842, and his wife, Ruth Carmichael, born 18 July 1820, died 17 May 1890. Emanuel Hauser was a descendant of Martin Hauser and his wife, Maria Margaretha Schaefer, who came from Reicheneueir, Alsace to Pennsylvania and then settled near Bethania, North Carolina in 1753. Ruth Carmichael descended from Duncan Carmichael, a Revolutionary War soldier, who, by tradition, came to Stokes County from Scotland.

When Preston Jones married Martha Hauser, she was only fifteen years old. He always said that since she was reputed to be one of the prettiest girls in the county he was afraid someone else would marry her before he could, hence the early marriage. They had affectionate nick-names for each other, his being "Pet" and hers being "Biddie."

They lived for a time on a farm in Yadkin County off the present Shallowford Road. Two children were born to them: Lelia Augusta Jones, born 27 February 1820, who married Charles Augustus Sink; Jesse Walter Jones, born 1 January 1872, died 30 November 1962, who married on 27 April 1904, Mary Poe Clingman, daughter of Dr. John J. and Cora Hackett Clingman. J.W. and Mary Jones were the parents of two children, Mary Louise and Jesse Walter, Jr.

Preston Jones first came to Wilkes County in the early 1890's and was associated with his son-in-law, Charles A. Sink in the lumber business. For a time he maintained his farm in Yadkin, but later moved to North Wilkesboro where he built several homes including one on C Street and another one on Trogdon Street. He became a merchant, and one prominent North Wilkesboro native recently related how he gathered white oak acorns to exchange for peppermint candy at Mr. Jones' small store on Trogdon Street.

In later years the Jones family lived on a small farm a mile north of town where the writer of this sketch now resides. Twelve years before her death, Martha Ellen Jones suffered a disabling stroke and she and her husband went to live with her daughter, Lelia Jones Sink. Here he died on 11 January 1919 and she on 21 December 1931.

Sources: Family Bible records, cemetery records, Revolutionary War pension files, the genealogy Alsatian-American Family Hauser and personal knowledge.

— Mary Sink Smithey

ROBERT M. JONES FAMILY
749

Papa was born May 15, 1867 in the Moffett's Mill Community of Randolph Co. At a very early age he accompanied his mother, Sallie Craven Jones and an older brother, Lee, to Ashe Co. and on to Wilkes County (See Daniel Jones story).

Papa courted and married Mary Elizabeth Hall on March 6, 1890. They started their married life in Ready Branch. Their first daughter, Ethel Beatrice was born on Dec. 20, 1890.

They moved to Johnson City, Tenn. for a short period of time and their second daughter, Bessie was born Jan. 15, 1893 there. She died before she was two, on Dec. 27, 1894.

By the time Coite Hall was born on Oct. 11, 1894, they had returned to Wilkes County where they were to remain.

Other children born in Wilkes Co. were: William Clyde, born May 31, 1897; Arlee Marie, born March 27, 1899; Howard Philo, born Dec. 11, 1900; Frances Agnes, born April 8, 1902 and Pearl Elizabeth, born Feb. 1, 1907.

Papa bought property in Mount Pleasant and built a home that is still standing today, next door to the present Mt. Pleasant Baptist Church. He also built a large country store with a large room to take care of the roots and herbs that the people from all over the area brought to exchange for what they needed. The "drummers" would come in buggies to take the orders that were made from the store.

I was quite young but I remember the barrels of sugar, coffee and different kinds of candy. My favorite kind was the sticks of candy that had little rings around them. My father would bring home to my mother some of the best china and items from the store. Some of the china dishes are still cherished by family members.

The revival meeting was held in the Baptist Church once a year with two sermons during the day and one at night. There was a well house built in our back yard, and the people

Robert M. Jones.

Coite, Clyde, Arlee, Howard, Frankie and Pearl Jones.

from the church would come to get water. The spring for the church was a good distance away and down a long hill.

Papa was a member of the Mt. Pleasant Baptist Church. He was also a Mason. He loved children and would give them things from his store. He was a thoughtful and caring man who was always helping people in need.

On one occasion at Christmas, I was going to be in a program saying a speech. There was a beautiful doll in the store that I particularly liked. He was so proud of me that he gave me that doll.

The Champion Post Office was also located in the store. Papa enjoyed seeing the people as they came to the store and post-office.

He was always good to help out when there was sickness in the home or at a neighbors. He had been sitting up with a neighbor who had pneumonia just before he became ill. He died with pneumonia on a cold January day. My mother and I also had pneumonia and were quite ill at this time. I remember him with a great deal of love.

After Papa died, mama was left with six children to rear. Disaster struck again when the country store burned. She returned to Lewis Fork to take care of her mother and to look after the two farms that they owned there. She boarded teachers in her home and made knotted (French knots known as candlewicking now) bedspreads to help with the family income. The oldest sons as well as a daughter

Mary Elizabeth Hall Jones.

was sent to Mars Hill College. Some of the other children received their education at Mountain View Institute. The family believed strongly in education and many of the children entered the teaching profession.

Mama enjoyed people and loved to have company. Our home was a favorite place for relatives and friends to visit. She also loved to travel and in her later years, visited her various children in their different homes. She was a tall lady and very pretty. She had an even temper and I never remember her raising her voice. She was quite adaptable and was a cheerful, happy person. She was a faithful member of the Baptist Church and took her family to church with her. She also did crocheting and embroidery and taught several of her grandchildren these skills.

She was dealt a rather severe financial loss when she entrusted her savings with a prominent North Wilkesboro business man for investment. He soon declared bankruptcy and never repaid her money to her. She remained an "unsinkable Mollie Jones". Certainly she was not the wealthiest person with money, but perhaps she had a greater wealth that she bestowed upon her children. She gave them love, peace and happiness in the home.

Robert M. Jones died January 28, 1908. Mary Elizabeth (Mollie) died July 15, 1943. They are buried in the community they loved so well at Mt. Pleasant Baptist Church Cemetery.

Sources: Personal knowledge.

— Mrs. C. Glenn Williams

THE WALTER ELMER JONES FAMILY
750

My father, Elmer Jones and mother, Lila Jones moved to North Wilkesboro from Elkin, N.C. in 1932. He was a native of Clemmons, N.C. in Forsyth County, and my mother was a native of Davie County. He came here as a freight agent for the Southern Railway.

Elmer Jones was the son of Franklin Arlindo Jones and Mary Bradford Jones. My grandfather, "Daddy Frank", as we called him, was the son of Howard Jones and Jane Harper Jones from Forsyth County. "Daddy Frank"

owned a general merchandise store in Clemmons just across from the depot at Clemmons. Therefore, as a young boy, my father became interested in the railroad business. In 1905 at the age of 17, he became a station agent's helper in Clemmons, and that same year he accepted a job as freight agent at Cooleemee in Davie County. In 1914, while still in Cooleemee, he married my mother, the former Lila Kurfees of Davie County. While living in Cooleemee, in 1916, a daughter Adelene Graham Jones was born. In 1917 he was transferred to Elkin, N.C. where he was freight agent until 1932.

During his residence in Elkin, both my father and mother were prominent civic leaders. He was a member of the Masons there, and my brother tells me that he was Master of the Masonic Order in Elkin. He also was a Steward in the Methodist Church, a director in the Elkin Bank, and a director and Charter member of the Elkin Kiwanis Club. He was a member of the Knights of Pythias and was on the board of the Bilt-Rite Furniture Company of Elkin.

My mother was also an active leader in Elkin. She often worked with her "Missionary Meeting", or her Garden Club, or Book Club or whatever. The entertaining was done in the homes in those days, and I can remember all the waxing of floors and the arranging of flowers for one of these numerous occasions. Mother was an avid gardener and would often send me to a friends home or to the Church with a large bunch of dahlias, her specialty. We lived in Elkin during the worst of the depression years, and my parents helped others, but it was a great secret. My father saw to it that anything he did for others was kept quiet. He did not want anyone to be embarrassed and his reward was the feeling it gave him. During their Elkin residency my brother, Walter E. Jones, Jr. and my sister, Margaret Louise Jones were born.

In Davie County, my mother was born just outside of Cooleemee on an eighty-seven acre tract of land which her mother had inherited from her father, Thomas Maxwell. My mother's mother was Louzene Maxwell Kurfees, a daughter of Thomas L. Maxwell and Zelpha Graham Maxwell. He was a son of Dr. David Maxwell and Jane Allison Maxwell. My great-grandmother, Zelpha Hamilton Graham Maxwell kept a diary from around 1838 when she was a pupil at Mrs. Hutchinson's school at Salisbury, N.C. I have all of these diaries, which she called journals. They are fading now and hard to read. However they extend from the time she was a young girl until after 1893 when my mother was born. Zelpha was a descendant of John Knox who came to America from Scotland about 1730. Her grandfather was a brother to the mother of James Knox Polk, President of the U.S.

My mother's father was Rufus Walter Kurfees, a son of Chalmers Kurfees and Marich Leach Kurfees. He was the son of Caleb Kurfees and Emily Keller Kurfees. He was the son of John W. Kurfees and Mary L. Kurfees, who came to America from Germany in 1781.

In 1932 my parents, Elmer and Lila Jones, moved to North Wilkesboro where he still held the position as Freight Agent with Southern

Walter E. Jones (father), Lila K. Jones (mother), Adelene (middle), Margaret, Walter, Jr.

Railway. He was a member of the Board of Stewards of the First Methodist Church and the Methodist men. He was a member of the North Wilkesboro Board of Education, and past President of the Kiwanis Club. He enjoyed his close men friends and enjoyed his nights with his "Set-Back Club". They were his special friends and he admired them all.

My sister Margaret says she remembers going out with Dad in snow storms and at Christmas with the car loaded down with canned goods and cover. They would drive to isolated, snowed in places to take supplies to people in need. It was his own feelings of doing good quietly that were foremost, even at times when it was a sacrifice.

After 54 years of railroading, dad retired and enjoyed visiting and talking in his yard to his good neighbor Cleve Kilby, Mrs. Ney Tomlinson, and Mrs. Emma McNeil. My favorite little sayings of his is this:

Mr. Jones: "I have joined a new club since I retired." Friend: "What new club is that?" Mr. Jones: "Honey Do." Friend: "I haven't heard of that one." Mr. Jones: "Lila says, Honey do this, and Honey do that."

Mr. and Mrs. Jones had three children. Adelene Garham Jones married Charles Butler Hulcher of Wilkesboro. They now live in Wilkesboro. They have two children Charles B. Hulcher Jr. and William Franklin Hulcher. Walter Elmer Jones, Jr., married Anne MaGuire of Elkin. They live in Elkin and have two children, Stephen Jones and Patricia Jones Hooper, and two grand children. Margaret Louise Jones married Frank Dresser of Appomatox, Va. and now live in Laurel, Md. They have three children, Charles Dresser, Thomas Dresser, and James Dresser and one grandchild.

Elmer Jones passed away in 1964, and Lila Jones passed away in 1971. They are buried in Mt. Lawn Memorial Park in North Wilkesboro, N.C.

Sources: Family records, personal knowledge, Family Bible, personal records and diaries, "Knox Family Records." by Hattie Goodman — Page 34 — Book 2 Public Act, Revolutionary Records, Dept. State Auditor.

— Mrs. Adelene Jones Hulcher

WILLIAM CLYDE and NESTER IRENE ELLIS JONES
751

My Father, William Clyde Jones, was born May 31, 1897, in the Champion community. He was the third child of Robert M. and Mary E. (Mollie) Hall Jones. The house in which he was born, is next door to Mount Pleasant Baptist Church, and was later bought by my Mother's baby sister and her husband, Lennis Triplett. They have lived there most of their married life. Daddy lived in this house most of his youth. He attended school at Mount Pleasant, Mountain View and Mars Hill College.

My Mother, Nester Ellis Jones, was born March 15, 1899, in the home place of Franklin Ellis near Naked Creek. She was the seventh child of James Columbus and Julia Stout Ellis. When she was a small child her father built a new house on the crest of the hill overlooking the old home place, and this house is still occupied today. She attended school at Mount Pleasant. My Daddy told me that Mother was a beautiful young woman with an outgoing personality and very talented in many things.

My Daddy and Mother were childhood sweethearts. They grew up in the same church and school and enjoyed going to the community socials together.

Daddy and Mother were married on December 27, 1917. They were together for fifty one and one-half years before my Mother's death May 27, 1969. They celebrated their Golden Wedding Anniversary and many friends and relatives came for this celebration and made this a very eventful day of their lives. Daddy said "She was a wonderful wife", and I say, "She was a wonderful loving, caring Mother."

The first home of Clyde and Nester Jones was in Lewis Fork, N.C., where their first child, Melverine Elizabeth was born, March 6, 1919. When Melverine was just six weeks old they traveled by train and moved West to Livingston, Montana. Later they moved to Delcano, Washington and then back to Deer Lodge, Montana. At the end of the summer of 1920 they moved back to North Carolina to the Grandpa Hall place at Lewis Fork, N.C. Irene Marie, was born there January 20, 1921, they then moved to the Grandpa Miller house at Lewis Fork, N.C. and lived there until June 19, 1924.

Daddy went to work for Alcoa Aluminum Co., in Badin, N.C. with the police division, and moved his family there. Identical twin sons, William Bain and Clyde Wayne, were born on November 5, 1924; Doris Nester, was born November 13, 1926; Ethel Janette, was born February 10, 1929.

My Father worked for Alcoa for thirty eight years, and was Chief of Police for many years before his retirement. He was well known, and was called "Chief" by every one who knew him. His death came on November 21, 1979. He was survived by one sister, Frankie J. Williams, Wilkesboro, N.C., by his six children and their spouses, thirteen grandchildren, and five great grandchildren.

Melverine, married Edward Fant Young and they live in Charlotte, where four children

The Clyde Jones family.

were born: (1) Eleanor Irene married Jay B. Dixon, Jr., they live in Raleigh, N.C. and have two daughters Julia Ellen and Charlotte Leah. (2) Angela Sue married Jon Rash and they live in Banner Elk, N.C. and have one child, Angela Sue. (3) Martha Elizabeth married to Darryl P. Gilland. They live at Myrtle Beach, S.C. and have Michael and Melissa. (4) Edward Ovid Young, lives in Charlotte, and is single.

Irene, married Luther G. Burgess and they live in Springfield, Va. They had one son, John Andrew, who is deceased.

Wayne, married Gretchen Philbeck and they live in Memphis, Tenn. They have one daughter Debra married to Jack R. Owen and has Wayne, Jr. and Keith.

Bain, married Marie Herlocker and live in Albemarle. They have Bain, Jr. married to Betsy Lindley; and Stuart.

Doris, married Robert J. Redwine, and they live in Columbia, S.C. They had Jim, Tom and Neil. Jim and Neil are deceased.

Janette, married Ovid G. Watson and they live in Badin, They have David and Don. Don married Marcia Turner.

My Parents, Clyde and Nester, were wonderful Christian people. They loved their children, their spouses, grandchildren and great grandchildren. Mother really enjoyed cooking a big meal, Sundays and Holidays, and having her children and grandchildren home, plus all the relatives and friends. We grew up in a happy home and were a very close-knit family and we are still close.

Sources: Family Memories from my Daddy, some research, and personal knowledge.

— Melverine Jones Young

THE JAMES FLOYD JORDAN FAMILY
752

James Floyd Jordan was born in Wilkes County May 24, 1891, the son of Mr. Charlie Thomas and Malinda Jane Burcham Jordan. He attended public school in Wilkes County, graduated from Yancey Collegiate Institute, Burnsville, N.C. and received his LLB Degree from Wake Forest College in 1922. He passed the State Bar Exam in 1922.

He served with the Army during World War I, achieving a rank of corporal, in his two years of service. He served overseas in France and Germany.

Mr. Jordan was married to Mrs. Kate McLain Erickson Jordan Oct. 29, 1932. He has two step daughters, Mrs. Goldie Erickson Michael, who has a son Jerry L. Michael.

Goldie married R.J. Michael Feb. 28, 1943. The other step-daughter is Mrs. Violet Erickson Deviney, she married Edward R. Deviney on Jan. 15, 1939; they had six children: Raymond Deviney, Clinton Deviney, Enola Nicholson, Kathryn Williams, Linda Williams and Edwina Staley.

Mr. Jordan was a Mason, holding membership in the Wilkesboro Lodge as a Past Master. In 1981, he was presented his fifty year award in ceremonies at Liberty Lodge 45 located in Wilkesboro, N.C. by Attorney Kyle Hayes of Wilkesboro, N.C.

Mr. Jordan was a faithful member of the Wilkesboro Baptist Church, where he was an Adult Sunday School teacher for 35 years. He also worked in the Brotherhood and Training Union of the church. He served as Clerk of the Brushy Mountain Baptist Association for sixteen years, and was Association Sunday School Superintendent for two years. He was elected to the Board of Trustees in 1955, and held that position until his death.

For several years Mr. Jordan was Town Clerk for the Town of Wilkesboro, and then was elected Mayor of the Town of Wilkesboro, at which time the Town installed their own Water system, bought the First Fire Truck for the Town, and built a new building to be called "The City Hall." He was also instrumental in getting mail delivery started in our town.

Mr. Jordan practiced Law in Wilkesboro from 1922 until his death on April 30, 1981. In fact, he went to his office the day before he died. His office was in a little white two-room building across from the "Old Tory Oak", and the Wilkes County Court House. This building still stands, is owned by the Smithey heirs, and is going to be left as it is, as a Memorial "Law Office".

He was wonderful Step-Dad.

Sources: Brushy Mountain Baptist Association Minutes, 1964, Paper Clipping — 1981, personal knowledge.

— Mrs. Goldie E. Michael

KANADAY
753

The 1787 state census of North Carolina listed four families of the Kanaday (Kennedy, Canady, Cannaday) Families; William, Andrew, Mark, and Samuel.

The Kanadays were early settlers of Wilkes and Surry Counties. Land records indicate they purchased land on the Big Elkin, Mitchells and Christian Rivers and Bugaboo Creek between 1778 and 1785.

Aaron Kennaday Sr. born about 1760, is listed on the 1790 census in Wilkes County. He purchased 100 acres on Mitchells River in Surry County, February 26, 1805. He lived until 1845. Aaron Sr. had four sons, William, John, Aaron, Jr., and Larkin and at least four daughters. It is believed Aaron, Sr., was a son of the William Canady listed on the first census.

My great-great grandfather was Aaron H. Kanaday, Jr., born December 8, 1798, Wilkes County. Aaron Jr. married Mary Caudle November 7, 1821 in Wilkes County. They made their home in Wilkes County for seventeen years. All but one of their children were born in

Wilkes County: (1) Shadrack H., born May 17, 1824, died June 2, 1909, Lumpkin Co. Ga., (2) Elizabeth L., born March 31, 1828, died April 16, 1909, Lumpkin Co. Ga., (3) Eliza, born October 2, 1829, died September 30, 1925, Ga; (4) Myra B. born December 8, 1831, died date unknown, Ga. (5) William C., born 1834, died May 15, 1863, Vicksburg, Mississippi and (6). Aaron ''Gold'', born March 2, 1838, White Co. Ga., died date unknown, Ga.

Aaron, Jr., and Mary moved from Wilkes County about 1837, settled on Shoal Creek in White County Georgia. Aaron died August 20, 1882 and Mary died March 25, 1888. They are both buried in Shoal Creek Cemetery.

Shadrack and Martha (Collins) Kanaday were my great-grandparents. They married Februray 22, 1848, in Lumpkin County Georgia. My grandparents were Aaron Harvey and Rebecca Jane (Abercrombie) Kanaday, married December 17, 1874, Lumpkin County, Georgia. Joseph Edward and Annie Emily (Gunter) Kanaday were my parents. They married August 26, 1916, Blount County, Alabama.

Sources: Land records — Secretary of State, Raleigh, N.C. Marriage Bonds, N.C. Archives, N.C. Census, Ga. Census

— Bill and Betty Kanaday

THURMAN SCOTT KENERLY FAMILY

754

Thurman Scott Kenerly and Bessie Eulalia Thompson were married April 4, 1907, in Woodleaf, North Carolina. He was born January 18, 1890, in Davidson County to George and Ellen Walton Kenerly. She was born in Rowan County on October 16, 1889, to Locke and Jenny Provience Thompson. Their children:

(1) John Thurman, born February 16, 1908, married Cleo May Harrison. Their Children: Agnes, Betty Lou, and Margie (2) Arnold Grimes, born May 30, 1910, died 1971, married Daphine Spainhour. Their Child: Arnold, Jr. (3) James Melvin, born September 10, 1914, died 1954, married Treva Spainhour. Their Child: Sylvia (4) Thomas Locke, born August 22, 1922, married Evelyn Faw. Their Child: Rebecca (5) Jessie Ward, born April 4, 1925, married Mildred Williams. Their Children: Lynn and Scott.

Thurman Scott Kenerly, better known as Scott, owned a farm in Woodleaf, North Carolina, where he and his wife worked until 1924. At that time, they gave up farming, and the family moved to Salisbury, North Carolina, where Scott went to work as a car salesman for McCanless Motor Company. It was in this same company that John Thurman, the oldest son, worked for a short time and began his career in the auto parts business. He later opened and continues to operate two auto parts stores in Wilkes County.

In 1926 Scott bought an interest in a Dodge dealership in Wilkes County and moved his family to North Wilkesboro. In 1930 he sold this interest and joined the North Wilkesboro Police Force where he served until 1933. He then bought another Dodge and Plymouth dealership and went back into the business of selling cars.

After having some health problems in 1941, Scott Kenerly was told by his physician to get his personal and business affairs in order. He was also advised that by retiring and taking good care of himself, he could possibly live another five years. Scott again sold his car dealership and began his retirement.

During his so-called ''retirement'' years, Scott Kenerly ran a tire recapping shop; worked as a builder, who managed to oversee the construction of his sons' houses; did defense work at Norfolk, Virginia, during World War II, specifically constructing an airstrip at Chincoteague Island; and was Public Works Superintendent for the Town of North Wilkesboro. He was always interested in politics and this interest culminated in his serving as Mayor of North Wilkesboro in 1948-49. Also, he was a member of the Board of Commissioners for several years. Scott's extended and extremely active retirement became the subject of many family jokes.

Bessie Thompson Kenerly worked diligently as a housewife and mother and was a constant source of comfort and encouragement to her family. She and Scott had a long, happy life together and their deaths came four months apart. Scott died on April 2, 1979, at the age of 89, and Bessie died on August 4, 1979, at the age of 90. They are buried in a family plot at Mount Lawn Cemetery in Wilkes County.

Sources: Court Records of Rowan County; family traditions, family records, and grave stones.

— Margie Kenerly Hughes

THE KILBYS

755

John Kilby left a will in Brumfield Parish, Culpepper Co., Va., dated 8 Dec. 1770, pro. 18 May 1772 in which he left his ''plantation I now live on'' to his wife Elizabeth. He also provided for his sons, Henry, Michael, John, William and Adam, as well as his daughters, Ann, Catherine, Elizabeth, Nancy and Susannah and stated he ''gave to other sons at their settlement and marriage.'' On Feb. 19, 1776 William Kilby (b. c. 1745/50) and his wife Frances sold 72 acres in Culpepper Co. to Thomas Gains. The land ''was willed to the said William Kilby by his father John Kilby.''

William Kilby Sr. was granted from 1779-1799 over 1200 acres on Reddies River, Tumbling Shoal Creek, Mulberry Creek, Maiden Cane Branch and Meadow Branch in Wilkes Co., N.C. The homeplace of William Kilby Sr. was on Main Reddies River below the mouth of Meadow Branch within the bounds of present Reddies River Township. He had become a fairly prosperous man before his death in 1815, acting as banker for his neighborhood.

The children of William Kilby Sr. and wife, Frances, were: (1) James b. c. 1765 Va., d. 1817 Wilkes Co., m. Margaret Robbins. (2) Humphrey b. c. 1765/70 Va., d. May 1850 Wilkes Co., m. Nancy. (3) Reuben b. c. 1770/74 Va., d. 1810/16 Wilkes Co., m. 1793 Elizabeth James. At least some of their children moved to Hurricane, Wis. (4) Elizabeth b. 12 Jan. 1777, d. prob. Monitou Co., Mo., m. John Vannoy. (5) Abraham b. c. 1778, d. 1816 Wilkes Co., m. Elizabeth Rash. (6) Sarah b. 20 Oct. 1780, Wilkes Co., d. after 1850, m. Leonard Whittington. (7) William Jr. b. 1782/83, d. 1816 Wilkes Co., m. Elizabeth Hubbard. (8) Mary b. 19 Sept. 1785 N.C., d. 14 Feb. 1864, Wilkes Co., m. 1st John Sheppard, 2nd Jesse Vannoy. (9) Frances b. c. 1787, d. 1860/70, Wilkes Co., m. Thomas Rash. (10) John b. c. 1790/91, d. after 1850, m. Nancy. Elizabeth Rash Kilby m. 2nd William Fletcher and Elizabeth Hubbard Kilby m. 2nd Benjamin Grayson and 3rd Isham Hubbard.

Humphrey and Nancy Kilby lived near the present rural community of Whittington in Union Township. Eventually, a nephew, Allen A. Whittington, Esq., acquired most of their plantation. Squire Whittington was a successful merchant and planter. It is noted his fortunes increased as those of his Kilby cousins decreased. Humphrey and Nancy Kilby were the parents of at least seven children but only six are known: (1) Elizabeth, m. William Wheatley and lived in Grayson Co., Va. (2) Thornton m. 1st Lucy Shepherd, 2nd Elizabeth Colvard, 3rd Sarah Yeates. (3) James Welborn m. 1828 1st Rachel Colver, 2nd Mary Gambill and moved to Grayson Co., Va. (4) Reuben b. 21 Aug. 1805, Wilkes Co., N.C., d. 26 Oct. 1895 Grayson Co., Va., m. Anna Jones, daughter of John and Leah Long Jones of Alleghany Co. (5) Frances m. Jeremiah Judd. (6) Elsey or Alsey m. Noah Dancy.

Abraham Kilby, 4th son of William Sr. lived next to his brother, Humphrey, on Reddies River. After Abraham's death in 1816, some or all of his children were reared by their Uncle Humphrey who was their Guardian. Although he could not write, Humphrey was able to keep very exact accounts of his wards' estate, written no douby by some member of his family.

Reuben, son of Humphrey and Nancy Kilby, was licensed to preach by Old Piney Creek Primitive Baptist Church on the first Saturday in April 1840. He served as pastor for 55 years at Big Helton Primitive Baptist Church in Ashe Co., until his death Oct. 26, 1895.

Following a careful study of the records, Allan L. Poe, Caldwell Co. Historian, expressed his impression of the early Kilby family by saying William Kilby Sr. and his sons were prosperous yeoman farmers who usually had plenty of good land and occasionally a slave or two; neither vastly wealthy nor very poor. Most of them were literate in a day when nearly half of the population of North Carolina was illiterate. Some held county offices and all seem to have been respectable citizens.

Sources: Culpepper Co., Va. Wills and Deeds; Wilkes Co., N.C. Records; Kilby Family Bible; Senter District Primitive Baptist Association Minutes.

— Myrtle Greer Johnson

ANDREW FRANKLIN KILBY

756

At about the age of 17 Andrew (Drew) left the farm of John Jackson and went to work in the commissary for Giant Lumber Company

Mr. and Mrs. Andrew F. Kilby.

which cut timber on the Reddies River and transported it by flume to North Wilkesboro. Later he was a store keeper in Ronda. Here he met Grace Lomax. He drove one of the few 1916 Model T. Fords in the area. In 1917 he enlisted in the Army Corp of Engineers and served in the French Alps during World War I. After his discharge in 1919 he returned to Wilkes. He was employed by Yadkin Valley Motor Company as General Manager at the branch agency in West Jefferson. After two years he returned to the agency in North Wilkesboro. In 1930 he purchased stock in the Company.

On September 5, 1922 he married Grace Lomax. The progeny of this marriage were Grace Frank and Andrew Lomax, affectionally known as "Bud". "Drew" and Grace were very sociable and enjoyed good times in local, and state functions whether they were of a business, civic, or social nature. They had a strong sense of family which they instilled in their survivors.

His activities during his lifetime were varied. He was always interested in construction and took an active role in the actual building of the YMCA, Wilkes General Hospital, and business additions. He was Chairman YMCA Building Committee and a YMCA Director, member and Chairman of Wilkes General Hospital Board of Directors, member and officer of the local American Legion Post, deacon and trustee of the First Baptist Church, member of N.W. Board of Commissioners, charter member of the N.C. Automobile Dealers, Association, Director of N.W. Savings and Loan.

Drew was a healthy and robust individual always intent on improving whatever conditions he might find be they social, civic, business, or family. For many years he enjoyed hunting game. Before he took up golf he would scoff and say "there is nothing to hitting a little white ball around the golf course." This is probably why he became an avid golfer.

In 1970 he was stricken with Cancer. He survived. He remained active until about a year before his death, the 22 June 1977. His mind was always alert, but time had taken its' toll on his body.

After a tour of duty in the Air Force in World War II and student at Bowling Green Business

University, Bowling Green, Kentucky, Andrew Lomay (Bud) joined Yadkin Valley Motor Company. He married Betty Summers (daughter of Harry and Emma Lee Summers) on 25 December 1949. They have three childen — Andrew Lomax, Jr., John A. (third generation with stock in Yadkin Valley Motor Company), Betty Ann. John married Phyliss Wilson and they have a daughter, Elisha. Andrew, Jr. married Mary Foster Blackwell of Columbia, S.C. They have a daughter, Sarah Elizabeth. Betty Ann married Stephen Foster (son of Zane and Gladys Foster). They have two children — Jennifer and Stephen, Jr.

Grace Frank attended Salem College and had a dancing school before her marriage to Lott Mayberry (Jonesville) 17 December, 1949. They have four children — Andrew (Drew) McNeely, Janice Kilby, Franklin Lott, and John Samuel. Drew married Pamela J. Priester in 1975 and they have three children — Andrew M., Jr., James Quinn, and Lauren Kilby.

Sources: Personal knowledge.

— Grace Frank Mayberry

ELI COLUMBUS KILBY
757

Eli Columbus Kilby was born May 10, 1862. He was the son of John Wesley and Delilah Bumgarner Kilby. Delilah was the second wife of John Wesley. His first marriage was to Martha Wilcoxson.

Eli was married to Fannie Rash, daughter of William and Margaret Kilby Rash. They had two boys James Wilforn and William F., and one daughter, Mary. James Wilborn was married to Nancy Caroline (Callie) Bumgarner. They had one daughter, Nancy Lillian. William F. was married to Docia Brown. They had four sons; Alvin, Sylvan, James, and Clark. Mary was married to Ambrose Whittington and their children were two daughters, Stella and Ella, and one son, Alfred.

Schooling was hard to come by in those days and Eli had very little formal education, but read quite a bit, especially the Bible, wrote a neat hand and was good with numbers. He owned and worked a small farm, was a beekeeper, and did woodcutting for himself and other people.

He was a member of Pleasant Home Baptist Church. He was 81 years old when he died. He and his wife are buried in the cemetery of Pleasant Home Church.

Sources: Family knowledge and records.

— Lillian K. Walker

JAMES REUBEN KILBY
758

James Reuben Kilby was born August 30, 1880, in the Mountain Valley section of Wilkes County. He was the son of James and Caroline Kilby Kilby. He made his living on the small farm he owned on the banks of Kilby Branch.

He was married to Emma Church Higgins, daughter of Harrison and Mary McGlamery Church. They had four children: Cranor, Car-

lie, Edith and Mae. Cranor married Mae Dowell; Edith married Turner Nichols; and Mae married Spencer Wyatt. Carlie died when he was a small child.

Emma was previously married to William Higgins, who died as a young man. The children of this marriage were; Edward, John, Calvin (Shad), Mattie, Eulala and Hobert. Edward married Marie Love, John married Effie Brown, Calvin married Rachel Kilby, and Eulala married Avery Brown. Mattie died in childhood. Hobert was never married.

Reuben died January 7, 1946. He is buried in the Mt. Zion Church Cemetery, in the Mulberry section of Wilkes County.

Sources: Personal knowledge.

— Grace N. York

JAMES WILBORN KILBY
759

My father, James Wilborn Kilby (1887-1918), was the son of Eli Columbus and Fannie Rash Kilby. He had one brother, William and one sister, Mary.

He was married in 1914 to Nancy Caroline (Callie) Bumgarner (1881-1961), who was the daughter of William Amos and Nancy Cooper Bumgarner. I, Nancy Lillian, am an only child of that marriage and I am married to Ernest Walker.

Father had a small farm, was in the sawmill and lumber business with his brother, William. He also worked in a blacksmith shop. I still have some of the tools he used to shoe horses.

My father was killed in an electric storm when he was only 31 years old. I was two years old at that time so I cannot remember him, but I cherish the things that my mother and others have told me about him. He and my mother were members of Millers Creek, (Old Friendship) Methodist Church and are buried in the church cemetery.

Sources: Family memories and records.

— Lillian K. Walker

JOHN KILBY
760

On 18 May 1772, the will of John Kilby, Brumfield Parish, Culpepper County, Virginia was proven. He was survived by his wife, Elizabeth, six sons, Henry, Michael, William, John, Adam, James; four daughters, Ann Catherine, Elizabeth, Nancy, and Susannah. To his wife, Elizabeth "I lend the use of the plantation whereon I now live with all the stock of every kind and household furniture I shall die possessed of and the use of the stil and all its utensils and after my wife's decease I give the plantation to my son, Henry and his heirs." It can be assumed that John and Elizabeth were being cared for by their son, Henry, in their old age. From the will it seems that he had already made settlements with his other sons when they were married.

After Elizabeth's demise the stock and furniture were to be divided equally between Michael and Henry. The remainder of his holdings were to be divided between his four daughters. He bequethed to William and John the plantations on which they lived. To Adam, James, and Michael he left sixty acres to each. On his wife's decease the "stil" and all its utensils was to be appraised. Henry was to keep the "stil" but he must pay his brother Adam the "sum of nine pounds current money which he formerly lent me. "The remainder of the vaulation of the "stil" was to be equally divided among the daughters. This will was signed, sealed, and published in 1770.

Sources: Personal Research, Culpepper Co. Va.

— Grace Frank Mayberry

QUINCY O. and FANNY N. KILBY
761

Fanny N. Kilby descends from John McKee who was born in Ireland in 1766 and fought with Wellington in the Battle of Waterloo in Belguim in 1815. His daughter, Mary, born in Ireland 23 Sept. 1803, married John Wright in the Cathedral of Armaugh in North Ireland on 10 August 1831. Their first three children were born in Ireland: Ann, born May 3, 1832; Mary Jane, November 20, 1834; and Joseph, May 3, 1836.

The Wright family with John McKee left Peny Coose, Ireland May 10, 1839 and landed in Philadelphia on July 6, 1839. They travelled to Wilmington, N.C., thence through Fayetteville to Wilkes County on the last of August or first of September 1839. They settled on a 640 acre farm at Millers Creek running from Wilkesboro to Jefferson in Ashe County. Their fourth child, Fanny Wright Owings, was born after the family left Ireland.

Ann Wright married Alexander G. Gaither and their children were: Mary Ann, born 1860; John W. 1862; Joseph M. 1865; and William Edward 1871. Mary Ann Wright married James Wesley Nichols and they had six children: John Milton married Nell McLean; James C. married Maggie Adams; Elizabeth Ann married Milton Gaither; Alexander G. married Betty Thompson; Fanny Mae married Quincy O. Kilby; and Eula married Jim B. Gaither.

Quincy Kilby was the son of W.T. (Billy) Kilby and Sarah Jane Brown. He grew up on the family farm in Milers Creek. Dad had a brother Cyrus who married Viola Pierce, a sister Isabelle who married Spainhour Whittington, a sister Etta who married Roby Vannoy and another brother, Carl who went to Chicago when he was 19 years old. Carl was killed; we never knew why or by whom.

Quincy Kilby and Fanny Nichols were married Sept. 27, 1914 and to this union was born six children.

Edith Jane born July 28, 1915, married Ruff Dockery, and they had two daughters, Patsy Ann who married Ronnie Bumgarner and Fanny Kaye who married Roger Davis. Fanny Kaye and Roger have one daughter, Danielle.

Mary Bernice, born Oct. 1, 1917, married Allen O. Phillips. They owned and operated Phillips Electric in North Wilkesboro for 22 years. They have three children: (a) Mary Ellen married Bill S. Clark and they have two chil-

dren, Leslie Ellen and Kevin S. Clark. (b) Ray O. Phillips married Gail Miller and they have three daughters, Shannon Laray, Tarran, and Melinda. Ray and Gail live in Yarba Linda, Calif. (c) Barbara Jane married John W. Marsh. They live in Jefferson, N.C. with their son, Eric.

James William Hugh Kilby, born July 4, 1919, married Ruth Caudill. He is an Army veteran of World War II. They have five children: (a) James married Elizabeth Miller. Their children are James Jr., Darlene and Billy. (b) Carl married and divorced, has three children: Carl Jr., Hugh and Angela. (c) Jennifer Mae married Larry Brown and their children are Barry, David and Cindy. (d) Audrey married Ken Souther and they had one son, Kenny. Audrey married second John Anderson and they have a daughter, Crystal. (e) Elizabeth married Clarence Hammond and their children are Daniel and Kristian.

Pearl Marie, born Dec. 19, 1921, married Thomas L. Wellborn and they have two children: (a) Thomas L., Jr. married Nancy Evans and they have Thomas L. III, Michael and Scott E. Nancy Marie married John Keever and they had one son, John Wesley. Nancy and John divorced and she married second Bob Parlier. They are living in Charlotte, N.C. My sister, Pearl Marie, was killed in an automobile accident in 1946.

Mabel Francis, born June 11, 1926, was married to Alvin Pearson who was killed on Iwo Jima in 1945. She is now married to Roger G. Wellborn and they have three children: (a) Gary married Myrna Stultz and they have a son, James. (b) Constance Marie married John Buecker and they have a daughter, Erin. (c) Judith is single and lives in Macon, Ga. Mabel and Roger live in Orlando, Fla.

I, Betty Jean, was born April 15, 1928 and married Gene R. Phillips. He is a watchmaker at Burke's Jewelry in North Wilkesboro. We live in the Mulberry community and attend the Baptist Home Baptist Church. We have three sons, all graduates of Wilkes Central High School. (a) Bobby Gene married Janie Jennings. He works in the offices of Carolina Mirror in North Wilkesboro. (b) William Ray (Bill) married Mary Beth West of Fayetteville, N.C. He is a salesman for Carolina Dealers Warehouse of North Wilkesboro. They make their home in Greensboro. (C) Terry Lee is single, lives at home and works for Burke's Pawn Shop.

My Mom and Dad both went to school at Cross Roads in Millers Creek. Dad was a farmer, raising many crops. We also raised chickens and always had a big garden. Dad was tax lister in Reddies River Township for many years. He was very active in the Republican Party in Wilkes County.

Mom was a homemaker, always doing for others. She was active in church and very proud that her greatgrandmother gave the land that Millers Creek Methodist Church is built on. Mom, Dad, my grandparents, and my greatgrandparents are all buried in the cemetery at this church.

Sources: Family records, tombstone inscriptions, members of the Wilkes Genealogical Society, and the Genealogical Library in North Wilkesboro.

— Betty Kilby Phillips

WILLIAM KILBY, SR.
762

From existing records it seems that the sons of John Kilby sold their holdings in Virginia and migrated to Wilkes County. The land in Northwestern North Carolina had been closed for settlement by Lord Granville's Land Office, so no one was able to secure legal title. Evidentally, these Virginians settled in the Reddies River and Millers Creek area anyway. In other words they were "squatters". After the Revolution North Carolina began to issue land grants. Williams first grant was issued in August, 1779 though he had actually been in occupation and possession of the place for several years. From extant records he ammassed a considerable estate buying and selling land. Down through the generations these properties were sold and divided by his inheritors.

William was married to Frances Eddins (daughter of Abraham Eddins) in Virginia and his first three sons were born there — James (1765-1817), Humphrey (1767 ca-1849 ca), Rubin (1770-1815 ca). After moving to North Carolina there were seven more children — Elizabeth (12 January 1777 - ?), Abraham (1778 ca - 1810-16), Sarah (20 October 1780- 1850 ca), William Jr. (1783 ca - 1814-16), Mary (19 September 1785 — 14 February 1864), Frances (1787 - 1860-70), John (1790 - 1860 ca). It is interesting to note that he listed the births of all his children only giving the exact birthdates of the three eldest daughters. Otherwise, he gives no dates at all and gives no information about his sons except their names.

William died in 1815 and Frances (Fanny), his wife, in about 1833. William and his sons were prosperous yeoman farmers who usually had plenty of good land and occasionally a slave or two — neither vastly wealthy nor very poor. Most of them were literate in a day when nearly half of the population of North Carolina was illiterate. Some held county offices and seem to have been respectable citizens. There was some variation in the fortunes of the later generations — some went up and others went down.

James married Margaret Robins 24 March 1792; Humphrey married Nancy ?; Rubin married Elizabeth James; Elizabeth married John Vannoy in 1796; Abraham married Elizabeth Rash in 1802; Sarah married Leonard Whittington; William, Jr. married Elizabeth Hubbard 12 April 1802 and settled in what is now Moravian Falls; Mary (Polly) married John Sheppard 12 October 1802 and then Jesse Vannoy 12 January 1804; Frances (Fanny) married Thomas Rash in 1812; and John married Nancy A. Wall (daughter of Jonathan Wall) All of these children lived and died in Wilkes with the exception of Elizabeth and John Vannoy who migrated to Missouri.

The home place of William Kilby, Sr. descended to his youngest son, John (1790-1860 ca) through his mother Frances (Fanny). The deed states his inheritance — "Fanny Kilby to sone, John, his heirs and assigns personal property and debts consisting of one sorrel horse, the increase of one cow and calf, one bed and its furniture, all kitchen furniture,

John Jackson Kilby.

one trunk, one table, one arm chair, two joggs, spinning wheel, weaving apparel, and some — spun cloth, one bed stead.'' This deed was dated 21 September 1827 and registered 28 March 1833.

John married Nancy A. Wall (believed to be the daughter of Jonathan Wall who, also, migrated from Virginia.). They had three children — John Wesley (1816 ca), Mary, and Sarah (1822 ca). According to the 1839 property tax list for Wilkes he had horses, cattle, sheep, swine, poultry, acreage in wheat, corn, potatoes, cotton, an orchard, and one distillary, 100 gallons made in 1839, and 50 capital. John Wesley married Martha Wilcoxson on 20 November 1829. They had five children — William (1840), John Jackson (28 April 1842), James (1846), Elizabeth (1848), and Sarah (1853). Martha died after 1860 and John Wesley married Deliah A. (nee Bumgarner) who had children by a precious marriage. From this union there were two more sons — Eli C. and Henry. They both died around the turn of the century. At a conference for the Wilkes Circuit of Methodist Episcopal Churches on November 7, 1840, John Kilby represented Charity Church. He reported the church ''in good repair with a debt of $40.00 hanging over it. The Trustees were Joseph E. Kilby, John Kilby, Thomas Rash, Humphrey Kilby, Stephen Bingham, William Wheatly, and Griffin Summerlin.''

In 1877 John Wesley was appointed by the Wilkes County Board of Commissioners to the Reddies River School District 50 for a two-year term along with W.E. Bumgarner and W.A. McNeil.

On April 5, 1862 John Jackson, second son of John Wesley, enlisted in the Confederate Army. He Was twenty years old. He was wounded in the battle at Gettysburg on 3 July 1863 and was hospitalized in Baltimore as a prisoner of war. He was later transferred to City Point, Virginia and then to Hart's Island, New York Harbor where he took the oath of allegiance and was released June 17, 1865.

In 1871 ca he married Martha Jane McNeil (7 September 1847, daughter of James Harvey and Susanna McNeil). They lived in Ashe County briefly where their first son was born — Henry Cleve (31 May 1872 — 26 Nov. 1945). After returning to Wilkes there were seven additional children — Thomas G. (Au-

gust, 1873), Granville J. (June, 1875-1903), Emma F. (Dec. 1882), Elmore (13 Nov., 1884), Andrew F. (10 September 1886), James H. (Nov. 1888), Etta E. (Feb. 1, 1891. He continued to farm throughout his lifetime. John died 23 November 1925 and Martha died 7 March 1931. They are both buried in the Mt. Pleasant Baptist Church Cemetary in Millers Creek.

Sources: Personal research.

— Grace Frank Mayberry

THE KLINKOSUM FAMILY
763

Nithi Klinkosum, a native of Bangkok, Thailand, and his wife, the former Elizabeth Hopkins of Raleigh, NC adopted Wilkes County for their permanent home in 1967 when they both assumed teaching positions with Wilkes Community College. This unusual couple from diverse backgrounds brought a flavor of internationalism to Wilkes County; and, in turn, both individuals found a genuine friendship and acceptance common only to Wilkes County and her people.

Nithi Klinkosum was born June 26, 1938, in Bangkok, Tahiland. His early education was in Thailand. At the young age of thirteen, he left his homeland and his native language to travel to England to further his education. He arrived in the United States in 1956 to continue his education by attending Wilbraham Academy in Wilbraham, Massachusetts. His college education was begun at Babson Institute, Babson Park, Massachusetts; after completing a year there, he transferred to Wake Forest University, Winston-Salem, NC in 1959 and completed his undergraduate studies in 1962 with a B.A. degree. Still not satisfied with his accomplishments, he continued to study at Wake Forest and received a North Carolina Teacher's Certificate. Later, he entered Appalachian State University in Boone, NC and completed his Master's degree in 1965. After successfully completing these educational opportunities, he taught at Lees-McRae College, Banner Elk, NC and at South Carolina State College, Orangeburg, SC. In 1967, he accepted a teaching position with Wilkes Community College in Wilkesboro.

Elizabeth (Betsy) his wife, is the daughter of the late Rev. Julian and Mrs. Elizabeth Hopkins, formerly of Raleigh, NC. Nithi and Betsy met each other in 1962 during their senior year together at Wake Forest University. Betsy attended and graduated from Wake Forest with a B.S. degree in Medical Technology. She was employed after her graduation at Bowman Gray School of Medicine and N.C. Baptist Hospital as chief technologist and instructor in the Blood Bank, a part of the Department of Pathology. Eager to seek further education, in 1966 she enrolled at Appalachian State University and graduated in 1967 with a Master's degree in Biology. It was after this that she accepted employment with Wilkes Community College as instructor of biology and related sciences. Surprisingly enough, Betsy's paternal grandmother was Mary Colvard of Deep Gap, NC. So even though it seems that this

family should be totally strange to Wilkes County, there are roots already established with the many Colvards in the area.

Nithi and Betsy were married in December of 1967 by Betsy's father who was an outstanding Baptist minister during his lifetime; the pinnacle of his career was serving as Secretary of Evangelism for the N.C. Baptist State Convention in Raleigh. He served ably in this office for seventeen years and laid much of the groundwork necessary for establishing the Chair of Evangelism at Southeastern Seminary in Wake Forest, NC. The two Klinkosums established a home in Westwood Hills of Wilkesboro where they still live. In March of 1970, a son, Maitri, was born to Nick and Betsy. Maitri is their only child and is more commonly known around the area as "Boot".

Nick and Betsy have continued to teach at Wilkes Community College and will, at this writing, complete their fifteenth year of service to the College and to the community. In addition, they have owned a retail gift business in Wilkesboro since 1973.

Sources: Personal knowledge.

— Nithi Klinkosum

JAMES M. and LOLA S. KNOX
764

James Mitchell and Lola Spencer Knox and their three children moved to Wilkes County in June of 1974. James and Lola were married in Monticello, Arkansas, on June 8, 1956. Their children are Karen Elizabeth (born September 6, 1957 at Fort Benning, Ga.), Sara Kathryn (born July 5, 1961 in Charlotte, N.C.), and James Spencer (born February 24, 1963 in Charlotte, N.C.) Karen is a registered pharmacist and resides in Burlington, N.C. She married Neil Vancy Hayes, son of Robert Kenneth and Mae Rhoades Hayes of North Wilkesboro, on August 6, 1977. Sara is a senior in the School of Nursing at the U.N.C. at Chapel Hill, and James Spencer (Jamie) is a sophomore in the School of Engineering at N.C. State Univ. in Raleigh.

James Mitchell Knox was born April 6, 1933, in Gastonia, N.C. His parents are the Reverend Law Pierce and Clara Mitchell Knox, who now reside in Charlotte, N.C. He has one brother, John Law, who is a high school teacher in Redisville, N.C. After being educated in the public schools of Brighton, Tenn. Monticello, Ark., Charlotte, N.C. and Gastonia, N.C. He received a B.S. in Biology from Davidson College, an M. Ed. in Science Teaching from the U.N.C. at Chapel Hill, and an Ed. D. in Higher Education from Highalnd Univ. His teaching career began at Victory School in Gastonia, N.C. where he taught eighth grade science and mathematics. A year later he entered military service as an officer in the United States Army, serving two years at Fort Benning, Ga. The next twelve years were spent as a biology teacher at East Mecklenburg High School in Charlotte, N.C. where he also served as chairman of the biology department for several years. From 1970-1974, he was an Assistant Professor of Biology at Piedmont College in Demorest, Ga., and since then has been associated with Wilkes Community College. He is a memaber of the North Wilkesboro Kiwanis Club and Assistant Scoutmaster of the North Wilkesboro Presbyterian Church Troop 336.

Clara Mitchell was born October 8, 1903, in Red Level, Ala. the third child of six for William Thomas Mitchell and Kate Brantley Mitchell. The parents of Kate Brantley Mitchell were Ed and Mary Thomas Brantley, and the parents of William Thomas Mitchell were David and Patty Saunders Mitchell. Clara married Law Pierce Knox on May 23, 1930, in Red Level, Ala.

Law Pierce Knox was born September 24, 1902, in Mecklenburg County, N.C., to Anna Lavinia Caldwell and James Francis Marion Knox (named after South Carolina patriot, the Swamp Fox). Anna Lavinia Caldwell (1873-1965), daughter of John Smiley Pharr Caldwell (1837-1897) and Margaret Elizabeth Rea (1841-1924), married James Francis Marion Knox, son of Samuel W. and Sara McAuley Knox on April 30, 1893.

Lola Spencer Knox was born to Adlai Perry and Bertie Jones Spencer in Drew County, Ark. on August 21, 1934. She attended schools in Drew County, graduating from Monticello High School in 1951 and obtaining a B.S. degree from Arkansas A. & M. College (now the Univ. of Ark. at Monticello) in 1955. She has one sister, Betty Brown Guzal, of Memphis, Tenn. While the family lived in Georgia, she attended Piedmont College and later taught business courses in the public schools of Habersham and Stephens Counties. Now, she is Executive Secretary for the Department of Arts and Sciences at Wilkes Community College.

Bertie Louise Jones, oldest child of eight for Fletcher Ernest and Hattie Cowan Jones, was born on November 24 1904, in Drew County, Ark. Hattie Cowan Jones (1884-1964), daughter of William Jackson and Sara Knowles Cowan, married Fletcher Ernest Jones (1878-1947), son of Nathaniel and Mary Binns Jones. Bertie married Adlai Perry Spencer, son of George Perry and Vennie Downey Spencer, on December 3, 1922. Adlai Perry (known as Ladd to his family and friends), was born on November 14, 1892. Vennie Downey, daughter of John Cook and Dorcas Calloway Downey, married George Perry Spencer, son of Calvin and Emily Waddell Spencer.

The name Knox has had many spellings — Cnoc, DeCnok, Knoc, Knox. The word "Cnoc" comes from the Celtic language and means "a small hill." The Knox ancestors came to America from Scotland. Many of the Knoxes have followed the Reformed and Presbyterian tradition.

Sources: Family Bibles, the Caldwell Family History by Grace Bradford McDowell, and from oral history passed from generation to generation.

— Lola S. Knox

AMOS LADD

765

Amos Ladd was born in Virginia in about 1797. The names of his parents are not known; however it is suspected that they were William and Doskea Ladd.

On the 4th day of December, 1829 Amos Ladd married Nancy Felts, daughter of William Felts and Susannah Oliver. Two children were Aaron and Patterson Elijah Ladd. Nancy died sometime between 1850 and 1859, then Amos married Sarah Sparks in Wilkes County.

In 1860, Amos and Sarah were living in Newcastle Township, Wilkes County. Amos was a farmer. The value of his real estate was $1000 and his personal property value at $2000. Aaron, his 28 year old son was living with them; Elijah had already moved to his own home.

In 1870, Amos was 70 years old, a farmer living at Briar Creek, Newcastle Twsp. His second wife, Sarah Sparks had died and his son Aaron, a clerk, 40 years old, with his 20 year old wife Julia as a housekeeper were living with him. There were two blacks listed with them, Bowers and George. The value of Amos property $150 real estate and $100 personal property. Aaron had real estate value at $1000 and personal property valued at $200. They were now living next door to Elijah and his family. In 1880, Amos was living with Aaron and his wife Emily. They had a 18-year-old daughter Sarah, a 12-year-old son, Leander.

Amos passed away on the 18th of April 1881 in Wilkes County. His son, Patterson Elijah Ladd had died the day before. There was no connection in the cause of death of father and son. They were buried in the same cemetery where Nancy Felts was buried. The cemetery is on the John Casey farm in Hamptonville, North Carolina. A marker has been placed by Mrs. Clyde P. Trotter. William Felts, Susannah Felts, Amos and Nancy and several infants as well as the slave George are buried there. Elijah's family moved to Oklahoma Territory after the death of his father and Elijah.

The family home is still standing and is now the property of Minnie Bell Shore of Hamptonville, North Carolina. Her family live on this same land where Amos made his home.

Sources: Personal research, Wilkes Census.

— Patricia Leone Wall

PATTERSON ELIJAH LADD

766

Patterson Elijah Ladd was born 23 September, 1835, in the Newcastle Township, Wilkes Co. He was the eldest son of Amos and Nancy Felts Ladd. He married Eliza Jane Couch, daughter of Jesse Couch and Elizabeth Moffett, on April 7, 1859 in Yadkinville, Yadkin Co. They had eight children: Jesse LaFayette Ladd, Aaron Patterson Ladd, Charles Ladd, Vera Elizabeth Ladd, Walter Raleigh Ladd and Wm. Franklin Ladd. All of their children were born in N.C.

Elijah served in the Civil War in Capt. Allen's Company, as a Sergeant in the Confederate Infantry. After the war was over, Elijah would not talk about his experiences. He said they were too terrible to relate. Like most other people who lived in this area, he hated the Yankees, particularly the Yankee soldiers.

During the Civil War, Elijah and Eliza Jane lost a son, Charles when he was about two years old. On July 12, 1870 they lost another child, Delsey, when she was only 15 months old.

According to the 1860, 1870 and 1880 Federal Census, Elijah and Eliza Jane Ladd lived in Newcastle Township, Wilkes County, N.C. In 1860 Elijah is shown to be a farmer with real esate valued at $500 and personal property valued at $300. In 1870 he is shown as a merchant with real estate valued at $3000 and personal property at $2000. In 1880 Elijah is again shown as a farmer.

Elijah and his family lived in a log cabin. The cabin no longer stands but the location is on County road 2408, just off the Somers Road in Hamptonville. On the same plot of land is a large house which was owned by Amos Ladd, and in now owned by Minnie Bell Shore, daughter of Aaron Patterson Ladd. There is an old tobacco drying shed to the South. The house is well cared for and sits firmly on its foundation.

Elijah took the 1880 Federal Census and wrote in a beautiful hand. He was considered to be a successful merchant and had a license to deliver liquor. A renewal license dated 27th Apr. 1881 was issued to E. Ladd, U.S. Storekeeper and Guager of Statesville. The rate of compensation under assignment to the distillery warehouse was three dollars a day to take effect, May 2, 1881.

Elijah died the 17th of April, 1881, just one day before his father, Amos Ladd died. Amos was said to have died of old age. Elijah, along with his father Amos, was buried in the same cemetery as his mother, Nancy Felts Ladd, William & Susannah Felts, some infants and slaves in the Ladd-Felts cemetery on the Casey Farm in Hamptonville, N.C.

Upon Elijah's death, Eliza Jane, took her children, Vera Elizabeth, Walter Raleigh and William Franklin and moved to Lawrence, Kan. Two of her children were dead, and her eldest son, Jesse LaFayette Ladd, his wife Martha Jane Myers Ladd remained in N.C. Her son, Aaron Patterson Ladd, married Mary Jane Green, daughter of Thomas Green and Elizabeth Victoris Sale and they too stayed in North Carolina. Later, sometime after their daughter, Laura Leona who was born August 4, 1884, Jesse and Martha Jane moved to Lawrence, Kan. Thomas Clinton Ladd had already gone to Oklahoma Territory with some Couch relatives to try to get land opened to settlement and he made the run of 1889 to open the Terriroty. The Couch men, were among a group of men called the Sooners, these were persons who tried to get land before the Opening.

In December 1892 Eliza Jane and family moved to Oklahoma Territory. Many of her Couch relatives had already settled in Oklahoma City and nearby vicinity.

Eliza was living in Oklahoma in 1900, age 60, a widow. Her daughter Vera and son Walter Raleigh were still single and living with her.

Eliza Jane passed away in Oklahoma City on the 18th of June, 1906 at the age of 66 and 9 months old., she is buried in Fairlawn Cemetery in Oklahoma City, Ok.

Sources: Personal research; census records.

— Patricia Leone Wall

JESSE LAFAYETTE LADD
767

Jesse LaFayette Ladd, eldest son of Elijah Ladd and Liza Jane Couch, was born February 9, 1860, in Wilkes County, N.C. He died in Oklahoma City, Oklahoma on the 11th of December, 1928 at the age of 68 years and 10 months. He was buried next to his wife, Martha Jane Myers in the same cemetery as his mother, Eliza Jane Couch Ladd, Fairlawn Cemetery, Oklahoma City, Oklahoma.

He was married to Martha Jane Myers, daughter of William Almon Myers on December 18, 1881. They had one child, Laura Leona Ladd, born at Osbornville, Wilkes County, N.C. Laura Leona married Anthony J. Stoll who was born in Dyersville, Iowa. They had three children, Gladys Antonia Stoll who married Robert William Beaty; Patricia Leone Stoll who married Windle Wall and Daisy LaRue Stoll.

Jesse LaFayette Ladd owned a meat market in downtown Oklahoma City (Territorial Days) and in later days became a successful stock broker.

Sources: Personal research.

— Patricia Leone Wall

THOMAS LAND FAMILY
768

Little is known of the early migration of the Thomas Land family into Wilkes County. It is assumed they came from Ireland in the 1700's and had settled in Georgia or South Carolina, thence moving northward to Wilkes County, N.C.

Thomas Land, of Mount Zion, married Jane Carlton of Wilkes 16 November 1814. They were the parents of nine children, all born at Mount Zion. (1) Wilson Land, married 22 October 1836 Rebecca Miller and had Mary L., born 1838. (2) Narcissa Land, married 10 October 1837 Henry Harrison Miller and had Wm. J. Miller, born 1838, Thomas Miller, born 1840 and Henry H. Miller, born 1842. (3) Mary Land, married 9 January 1859, William Hall. (4) Thomas C. Land was born 1830 and married in 1878 Jane Dula. He died after 1905. Thomas C. attended Beaver Creek Academy while Hugh Stokes was principal. He was a school teacher in Wilkes County and in Tennessee. He was also a poet. He wrote many verses about his extensive travels throughout the south and west. He farmed in Georgia, mined silver in the mountains of Nevada, worked on the railroad in Tennessee and Kentucky. He also wrote verses about Wilkes County and the "fair maidens thereof". (5) Linvill Land, married 4 August 1849 Rhoda Proffit. They had Mary J., Wilson, William and Calvin.

(6) James Calvin Land was born in Wilkes County, N.C. at Mount Zion 14 July 1837, and was in his 88th year at the time of his death in 1925. He served in the war between the States, and shortly after its close married on 4 November 1866, Nancy Wagoner of Tennessee. She was the daughter of David and Catherine Arnold Wagoner, and one of their thirteen chil-

dren, viz: Jacob, David, Joseph, Daniel, Mathias, John, Sarah, Susan, Rebecca, Elizabeth, Nancy, Catherine and Martha. After their marriage, James Calvin and Nancy lived at Mount Zion on his father's farm. He was the youngest and took care of his father and mother. His brother, Thomas C. Land lived with them. They sold their property and made their home in Mount Pleasant, Tennessee at the home of their son, David Land. James Calvin and Nancy had four children.

Jane Catharine "Jennie" Land, daughter of James Calvin and Nancy, was born 6 June 1868, Mount Zion, Wilkes County, died 29 October 1943 at Boone, N.C., married 23 September 1891, Charles Calvin Wright (1862-1933). Jennie is buried in the family plot in Edgewood Baptist Church cemetery, Wilkes County. They had children Mary Dorris, David Ralph, James Thomas Carr, Clyde Robert and Charles Calvin, Jr.

William Thomas Land, the Poet.

Thomas David Land, son of James Calvin and Nancy, was born 18 May 1870 at Mount Zion, died 19 June 1948 Mt. Pleasant, Tennessee, married Annie Robinett who died in 1879. Both are buried in Tennessee. They had children: Calvin, Thomas, Dudley, Charles and Mary Frances.

Sallie Caroline Land, daughter of James Calvin and Nancy, was born 25 December 1876, Mount Zion, died 28 July 1960 at Parsonsville, Wilkes County, married 15 November 1905 James Cicero Parsons, born 10 January 1871, died 1 December 1948. Both are buried at New Hope Baptist Churchyard, Wilkes County. They had children Mary Dorris, Nannie Elizabeth, Jennie Lucille, Mattie Land and Jesse Catherine.

Mary Elizabeth (Mollie) Land, daughter of James Calvin and Nancy, was born 10 March 1879 in Wilkes County, died 20 May 1912, Mt. Zion, Wilkes County, married R.C. Robinett. They had two children, Guerney and Vera. R.C. Robinett married Bertha Spainhour after Mollie died and moved to Georgetown, South Carolina.

"Nannie" Wagoner Land was a consisten member of Mount Zion Baptist Church and was well loved by all that knew her. She died in 1918, shortley after the move to Moun Pleasant, Tennessee and is buried there along with her husband, James Calvin.

(7) Martha Land, seventh child of Thomas and Jane Carlton Land, was born 3 September 1840, married 25 October 1865 L.J. Hendrix. (8) Nancy Land, eighth child of Thomas and Jane Carlton Land, was born in Wilkes County, died 6 December 1918, married 4 February 1951, A.B. West. (9) Betsy (Lizzie) Land ninth child of Thomas and Jane Carlton Land, married 9 September 1866 Charles C. Miller.

Sources: Family records, personal knowledge, family Bible of Thomas Land.

— Jessie Parsons Rhyne

THE HENRY CLAYTON LANDON FAMILY
769

Nathaniel Landon of England arrived i America in 1643 settling in Westfield, Mas sachusetts. His great grandson married Re becca Sloan, daughter of General Samue Sloan of the Revolutionary War. Their home is now the president's home of Williams Colleg in Williamstown, Massachusetts. Through the Sloans, the Landons are collateral decendent of Oliver Hazard Perry.

Seven generations later in 1911, Henr Clayton Landon and his wife Inez Allwood ar rived in North Wilkesboro, North Carolina with their six children. Mr. Landon, a graduate i civil engineering from Lehigh University wa General Manager and Chief Engineer of the Watauga Railway.

The Landons became very involved in com munity and church activities. A family stor goes that The Reverend Charles P. Robinson minister of the Presbyterian Church preache two sermons on the Landons ... one fo unloading train equipment on Sunday, and th second for playing bridge.

Mr. Landon became the unofficial Chambe of Commerce for Wilkes County. Mr. J.E Spainhour, owner of Spainhour's Departmen Store, often told that while on a buying trip t New York, he received a telegram from Colone Landon which instructed him to go as the Wilkes delegate to the U.S. Chamber of Com merce national meeting in New York. Aske what he did, Mr. Spainhour said, "I stoppe buying and went to the meeting."

The railroad progressed to Grandin wa slowed by the necessity of building a tunnel 20 trestles and local opposition. The flood o 1916 washed away track, trestles and the tun nel and it was decided not to rebuild. Th Landons remained in North Wilkesboro. Mr Landon had become more southern than mos born southerners. He and Mrs. Landon wer extremely active. He was president of the American Red Cross and she a most activ helper during World War I. He was a founding member of the North Wilkesboro Kiwani Club.

After his death in 1931, Mrs. Landon an five of the children returned north. His son an namesake, Henry Clayton Landon, Jr., had his feet firmly planted in North Wilkesboro. He married Sue Ennis, a schoolteacher, from Milledgeville, Georgia, daughter of Elias Nathaniel and Beatrice Boyer Ennis. He attended the University of North Carolina, leaving school to join the army during World War I and also served as an officer in World War II. Active with veterans groups following service, he was commander of the American Legion and instrumental in setting up housing for veterans on Legion Drive. He followed in his father's footsteps in the Kiwanis Club. Both Henry and Sue Landon devoted themselves to their children, Henry Clayton III and Sue Ennis and to their community.

Henry C. Landon III was the first graduate of North Wilkesboro High School to become a medical doctor. After graduating from the University of Virginia and the University of Virginia Medical School, he returned to North Wilkesboro to set up a general practice. Dr. Landon served in the U.S. Army and U.S. Air Force in Korea. He married Helen Barbara Sisk, daughter of Albert Fletcher and Helen Marvel Sisk of Preston, Maryland. Their two children are Henry Clayton Landon IV and Helen Sisk Landon. Clay Landon graduated from Avon Old School, Avon, Connecticut, in 1980 and now attends North Carolina State University. Helen Landon is a junior at St. Catherine's School, Richmond Virginia. The Landons are nationally known as collectors of American antiques and art. The Landon Collection of American Art was exhibited in ten museums in Eastern United States (1979-1981), and individual paintings have been exhibited in major museums across the country.

Dr. Landon has served as a trustee of North Carolina Museum of History Associates and The North Carolina Bicentennial Foundation, member of North Carolina Executive Mansion Fine Arts Committee, board of directors of Stagville Preservation Center, and The Historical Preservation Society of North Carolina and was recipient of the Ruth Coltrane Cannon Award in 1973 for contribution to historic preservation in North Carolina.

Locally he was president of the Kiwanis Club, first Chairman of Old Wilkes, Inc., Chief of Staff of Wilkes General Hospital and Vice Chairman of the North Wilkesboro School Board.

Sue Ennis Landon married Richard Jeffrey Alfriend III of Norfolk, Virginia. A daughter, Sue Landon Alfriend, was born in North Wilkesboro. Mrs. Alfriend graduated from Randolph-Macon Woman's College, Lynchburg, Virginia, and received a M.S. Degree from the University of North Carolina. She returned to North Wilkesboro to become head of Marketing for Northwestern Bank. Mrs. Alfriend is a speaker at regional and national banking events and is active in community affairs. She served as co-chairperson of Old Wilkes, Inc., and chairperson of the North Wilkesboro Retail Merchants. Her daughter Landon also graduated from Randolph-Macon Woman's College and Mercer University Law School and now practices law in Wilkesboro.

The Landons who settled in Wilkes County have loved the area and wanted to contribute to the well-being of their fellow citizens. Four generations have already declared this love.

Sources: Family letters, books, clippings and personal knowledge.

— Mrs. Sue L. Alfriend

THE LAWS FAMILY
770

The Laws family in the Pores Knob-Brushy Mountain area of Wilkes County sprang from the six sons of John Laws Sr., who lived originally in Halifax County in Virginia, near Staunton. These six brothers were Berry, Joseph, Abednigo, Shadrack Sr., David, and Meshak. Although information about the six is limited, everything points to their having been small landholders in Wilkes as they had been in Virginia.

Berry Laws is mentioned in J.J. Hayes' *State of Wilkes* as "living on Berry's Mountain" (about 3 miles from the present village of Moravian Falls). Doubtless, the residential development of Berry Mountain Estates derived it's name erroniously from this reference. David married Martha Mitchel and Meshak married Elizabeth (?). Both left descendants who still live in the Brushy Mountains. Shadrack Sr., who married Mary Tribble in 1779, was my great, great, grandfather. His children: Elijah, Joshua, Jesse, John, David, Shadrack Jr., Timothy, and Rosanna. By marrying James Laws, a distant cousin, Rosanna kept the Laws name, but she had no descendants. One notes at this point the prevalance of Biblical given names, despite the limited references to their church activities. Elijah, John, Shadrack Jr., Jesse, David, and Timothy all married and have numerous descendants. Joshua, my great grandfather, born November 27, 1791, either came from Virginia by way of Kentucky or else was in Wilkes prior to going to Kentucky and returning to North Carolina in 1818. After marriage to Caroline Lane, a neighbor girl, on January 1, 1819, he settled in the Cove Gap near Pores Knob mountain. It is said that he brought scions of limbertwig apple trees from Kentucky and set out a large orchard in the Gap. Remnants of this orchard are still evident. There, he and Caroline raised apples and also seven sons and one daughter: Wesley, Lindsey, Finley, Bentley, Hilley, Berkley, Coffey, and Mary Adeline. Wesley had a grandson John Crouch, who, after working on local newspapers, made his way to New York and became an editor of the *New York Times;* Lindsey went to California, married and had several children. One son, whom he named Joshua, became a lawyer and later the editor of the *Nevada State Journal;* another son, Leonard, became a doctor in Cabool, Mo., and had a daughter who worked in the U.S. Census Bureau. My brother, Shafter, met and visited with her while he worked in the Government Printing Office. Finley moved to Yancy County and has descendants who live there and in Bristol Virginia; Bentley is listed in the 1860 Wilkes County census as a farmer with four children; Hilley had no descendants; Berkley married Sarah Hubbard and lived on Joshua's Cove Gap homeplace for years; Coffey, who was my grandfather, married Amanda Roberson in 1868 after his return from the Civil War. He spent the last year of the War as a prisoner, was exchanged and then furloughed home near the end; Adeline, Joshua's only daughter, married Hartwell Queen of Alexander Co. They had a grandson, Larry Queen, who has been on the editorial staff of the *Winston Salem Journal* for years. Coffey and Amanda had seven children: R. Don, Mattie, Leonard, Alice, Bynum, Curtis, and Jones.

My father, R. Don Laws, was born August 22, 1868 and married Dora Wallace, a distant cousin. He was first a teacher; then in 1895 he began publishing *The Yellow Jacket* that eventually attained a circulation of over 200,000 copies. He moved into the village of Moravian Falls and continued the unique business for 51 years. His wife shared his work throughout the years until her death in 1943.

R. Don and Dora had seven children, three boys and four girls: Barney Weaver, mechanical engineer in Clearwater, Florida; Shafter Robert worked with his father in the printing business before going to Washington, D.C. to work in the Governemtn Printing Office and the printing department of the CIA; Thelma Margaret, high school teacher; Frances Amanda Howell, housewife; Rose Elizabeth Jennings, high school teacher and co-ordinator; R. Don Jr., building contractor; Virginia Hairston, secretary and bookkeeper.

Thus we see Lawses coming out of the Brushy's and into the World.

Sources: Conversations with my father, mother, and grandparents, court records, grave stones, letters, notes left by my father and grandfather; U.S. Census.

— Thelma Laws

FAMILY of MARTHA LAWS
771

Martha Laws, a native of Wilkes County, has left many descendants in Tennessee. It appears that she was a daughter of Joseph Laws, having been born in October, 1814. In 1830 she married Sherrod Segraves who was a native of Wake County, N.C. Sherrod's parents had died when he was a young boy and he was bound out to James Jones.

Sherrod and Martha only had one child, Moses Segraves (born 1833; died 1910). When Moses was yet a young boy, his father Sherrod deserted the family, went to Tennessee, and married Margaret Neely. He settled in Dyer County, Tennessee by 1840, where he raised a large family.

Martha and her son Moses continued to live in Wilkes County. They lived near William P. Waugh. The Laws family had been close friends with William Pitt Waugh ever since 1805 when Mr. Waugh first came to Wilkes County. William P. Waugh was born about 1785 in York County, Pennsylvania (at Carrol's Delight in the section which later became Adams County), a son of William Waugh (1739-1823). William P. Waugh was a merchant and senior member of the firm of Waugh, Poe and Murchison. During the War of 1812, William P. Waugh was captain of a troop fo Light Dragoons attached to the 7th Regiment, North Carolina Detached Militia, in the United States service.

William P. Waugh died in 1852 in Wilkes County. In his will he left everything to his brothers and friends, nieces and nephews. No marriage record has been found and it is believed that he was a bachelor. But according to family tradition and circumstantial evidence he fathered a son by Martha Laws Segraves. This son was born in 1844 in Wilkes County and took the name William Segraves.

The next year, 1845, Martha (Laws) Segraves and her two sons, Moses and William, left Wilkes County and moved to Henderson County, Tennessee. She exchanged her mountain home for a place in the gentle hills of the old "Southwest" as this section of the nation was known at the time. Here she married Benjamin Philips, by whom she had two more sons, Charles and Joseph Philips. After Benjamin Philips died, Martha married once again to Mr. S. Thomason shortly before 1860.

Martha's son, William, served in the Civil War on the Union side. Family tradition says that he and his step-father could not get along. Mr. Thomason, according to the tradition, mistreated his step-children William, Charles and Joseph. Moses had already left the household, having married Miss Susan P. Crabb on August 22, 1852 in Benton County, Tennessee. She was the daughter of Hilliard Crabb and Mary (Hogg) Crabb of Benton County. One day, William, in self-defense, was forced to shoot and kill his own step-father. William left Tennessee and went to Massac County, Illinois, where he was married on July 20, 1865 to Miss Cyrena Elizabeth Stacy. She was the daughter of James Stacy and Mary L. (Harrington) Stacy. At this time he changed his name from William Segraves to the name of his natural father, William P. Waugh. From Illinois, the family moved to Coahoma County, Mississippi. By 1867 they had moved back to Henderson County, Tennessee. William P. Waugh was a farmer and part-time schoolteacher.

Martha (Laws) Thomason died in 1879 and was buried in a family plot in Henderson County, Tenn. The following winter, in February, 1880, her son William P. Waugh caught pneumonia and followed her in death. Both of Martha's sons, Moses Segraves and William P. Waugh, left children in Henderson County and many of their descendants still live there. Descendants are also to be found in Texas, Oklahoma, Kansas, Colorado, and perhaps other western states.

Moses Segraves and his wife, Susan P. (Crabb) were the parents of six children: M.E. (born 1854), William Thomas (1855-1880), Mary Hannah (1859-1932), John Henry (1865-1953), Nancy Camilia (1867-1946) married May 30, 1886 to Lemuel Anderson Smith, and Sidney J. (1871-1942).

William P. Waugh and his wife, Cyrena E. (Stacy) had eight children: William Lee (1866-1893), James Monroe (1867-1937), Mary Eliza (1869-1943) married February 23, 1890 to Irvin Columbus Gibson, Joseph Edward (1871-1932), Martha Elizabeth (1872-1959), Joanna (1876-1889), Martin Louis (1877-1880), and William Rupert (1880-1946).

Sources: Census, Henderson County, Tenn.; Goodspeed History of Henderson Co., Tenn.; Adams Co., Pa. and Wilkes Co., N.C. courthouse records; family records, family traditions.

— Johnny D. Walker

R. DON LAWS
772

The Yellow Jacket, established in Wilkes County in 1895 by R. Don Laws, was one of the most unique perodicals ever issued in the U.S. He started it from scratch and built up a nation-wide subscription list by sheer originality and determination." This tribute was expressed by Red Buck Bryant, a *Charlotte Observer* columnist on March 28, 1948.

R. Don Laws, son of Coffey and Amanda Roberson Laws, was born on August 22, 1868, in the Cove Gap of the Brushy Mountains. His paternal ancestors were from England and his maternal ancestors from Scotland and Ireland.

Having obtained his early education in what were called "Old Field Schools", and under his father who was a county teacher, he continued his studies at Moravian Falls Academy for a total of eighteen months. As a schoolboy he exhibited a great love for books — particularly in literature and history, and was fortunate to have had two of the early Academy principals who encouraged him to develop his talents and interests. Some of his notebooks kept at that time point out samples of his writing: stories, essays, poems, etc. Supporting that

R. Don Laws.

activity were diaries of the period. One of the entries quotes Wendell Phillips: "Let me make the newspaper." This could have been Don Laws' slogan.

At age 10, instead of playing ball with the other boys, he was developing a printshop. He carved type from hardwood, made ink from walnut tree root bark, and then putting his native talents to use, he manufactured from his own design the first printing press he ever saw. With this equipment, at age thirteen, he was printing some of his own compositions. (The family still has a poem which he com-

posed and printed at that time).

Although his educational advantages were limited, he acquired a broad knowledge of books through home reading and study all his life. He acquired the reputation of being one of the best historians in the state. His store of literary and historic knowledge was amazing to those who listened to him talk. His lecture, *"High Spots of History,* from Adam and Eve to Amos and Andy", drew large audiences as he delivered it in Tennessee, Virginia, and Kentucky, as well as in different places in North Carolina. The chart which he used in delivering the lecture had been worked out when he was fifteen. He also delivered lectures and wrote articles on astronomy. He had invested in a powerful telescope and welcomed neighbors and friends who were eager to look at Saturn's rings, or other astronomical wonders.

From 1888 to 1897 he continued teaching, but his determination to be a newspaper man never abated. In the spring of 1895 he bought a second hand printing press and some type which he installed in the basement of his home. In June 1895, he put out the first edition of *The Yellow Jacket,* 50 copies, which he carried to the Moravian Falls Post Office in his coat pockets.

By 1897 the fledgling publication seemed to be headed for success; so the editor quit teaching and devoted his time and attention to his newspaper. In 1901 he moved his family, consisting of his wife, Dora Wallace Laws, who was his helpmeet in every respect, and two sons, into the village of Moravian Falls. With the birth of a daughter in December 1901, the family began entering the life and activities of the community. Don became the chairman of the school board, joined the Good Roads promoters, and was made a director of the Deposit and Savings Bank in North Wilkesboro.

While devoting time to civic activities and finding himself more involved in his growing business affairs, he found time to buy the first automobile in the county, build a lake, survey and build a road to the top of Fores Knob Mountain, and deliver his "High Spots" lecture.

Though The Yellow Jacket was strongly Republican, the editor did his "Swatting Liars and Leeches and Hypocrits and Humbugs" wherever he found them, whether Republican or Democrat.

Ruth Linney in *The Wilkes Journal,* April 16, 1949 gives an excellent characterization: "R. Don Laws, "The Sage of Moravian Falls", editor of *The Yellow Jacket* is known nationally because of the stupendous circulation (200,000) of his stinging combination of humor and common sense, as well as for his talent and intellectual brilliance. Mr. Laws, an authority on local history and astronomy, is a striking and refreshing contrast to the bitter invective of some of his articles."

Another Wilkes County newspaperman, Buddy Hubbard, in a recent Viewpoints column in *The Journal Patriot,* has this to say: "R. Don Laws and his *Yellow Jacket* made an impact on Moravian Falls and Wilkes County which is still felt today. He was truly one of the most remarkable men this county has produced." R.

Don Laws died on November 11, 1951.

Sources: Personal knowledge.

— Thelma Laws

THOMAS WESLEY LAWS
773

My father, Thomas Wesley Laws, was born January 13, 1892 in Surry County. The family moved to Wilkes when he was 16 years old and lived here the rest of their lives. His parents were Lawson and Sarah Laws Laws. Two daughters and three sons were born to this union.

My daddy married Rosettie Elizabeth Williams in February 1916. They had four daughters and one son. At this writing my mother is in good health at age 94.

Dad never attended school, never learned to read or write, but he certainly had a head for arithmetic. He could add, subtract, multiply and divide with amazing speed. It sure was surprising to many people how he could count and figure in his head and get the right answers.

In my dad's youth times were hard. He often told us what a hard time they had to get enough to eat and enough clothes to wear to keep warm in the long cold winter.

My dad worked at many jobs. He made a vow that his children would never have the hard life he had. We were raised on the farm, and we grew what we ate. We were taught how to work when we were little, and that's something we never forgot.

Daddy sure did work hard. He would arise at 4:30 every morning, rain or shine, and everyone else had to get out of bed too. Long before daylight he was on his way to the sawmill or to cut timber. I think cutting timber was his favorite job; he cut it with a cross cut saw and a pole axe. He would work long after dark, and would light the kerosene lantern to do his chores.

My grandfather, Lawson Laws, was a little man. He never weighed over one hundred pounds in his entire life. No one knew his exact age. The birth records were destroyed in a house fire, but folks say he lived to be well over one hundred years old. He was always laughing and friendly with everyone he met. Folks said he was a man of exceedingly great strength. His trade was cutting millstones. He could carry five bushels of wheat upstairs to the grainery.

My daddy was a man that didn't believe in trivial, foolish stuff. He didn't have time for frills. He worked like a slave from early morning until late at night, as long as he was able.

We always had flour for biscuits — he loved biscuits. Even during the depression, when times were very bad, my dad believed in hard work. I remember him coming home late at night drenched in sweat and staggering, he was so tired, but he was happy when he worked hard, and it made him angry if everyone else didn't work. He helped many young people get started. He loaned them money to build houses and chicken houses.

Daddy was an excellent animal doctor. He would go in all kinds of weather, often walking several miles, and he never set a fee. He just took whatever anyone would give him. He didn't learn his knowledge from books; it was a God-given talent.

Daddy passed away March 28, 1972.

Sources: Personal knowledge.

— Royster Laws Wolfe

MALCOMB LEITCH
774

Malcomb Leitch, born in 1755, died in 1920, the progenitor of a large and representative family in North Carolina, was a native of Argyllshire county, Scotland, lying in the southwestern part. He came to America in 1804, landing at Wilmington.

On February 8, 1780, he married Katrine Lamony, whose family was to become closely entwined with the Leach and Blue families. To Malcomb and Katrine was born six children: Daniel, born 1781, died 1804; Mary, born 1782, died 1850; Alexander born 1784, died 1886; Angus, born 1788; died 1846; Archibal born 1792, died 1890; Christian born 1796, died 1875.

Alexander Leach, son of Malcomb was born May 13, 1784, died November 26, 1886. In 1912, he married his first cousin Christian Blue, born November 15, 1792, died June 16, 1882, daughter of Daniel Blue, with whom his parents had lived briefly. Alexander and Christian had nine children. Their names with dates insofar as possible to obatin are: Archibal, born April 13, 1813, died 1862; Margaret Leach Wright, born March 15, 1815, died 1875; Daniel born December 23, 1817, died May 15, 1907; Edwin born December 30, 1818; Malcomb born April 11, 1821, died 1898; Mary Leach Owen born June 30, 1825; Angus born February 23, 1830, died 1864; Alexander born April 1, 1833, died 1881; and Jane born December 5, 1839.

Daniel was the progenitor of the Wilkes Leaches. He married a cousin, Rebecca Lytch, daughter of John Lytch, no known kin. He came to Wilkes from Montgomery County. Daniel and Rebecca began life in Wilkes with seven children: Calvin, born July 3, 1842, died May 30, 1864; Margaret born August 11, 1844, died August 29, 1927; Lydia born June 23, 1864, died March 11, 1911; Louisa born February 6, 1849, died December 2, 1898; Enos born November 17, 1850, died February 13, 1926; Catherine born June 3, 1857, died July 16, 1876; and John born June 3, 1857, died September 11, 1920. After the birth of the twins, Catherine and John, Angus was born September 6, 1869, died June 10, 1945.

John Leach, son of Daniel and Rebecca, married Julia Lackey who was born February 17, 1867 and died April 12, 1954. They were married June 15, 1893. They had issue: Winnie Davis Leach, born October 31, 1894, married Dr. H.G. Duncan August 19, 1925. They had a son, Eric Gerald Duncan, born January 16, 1936. Eric married Betty Staley who was born June 30, 1938. They have three children: (1) Richard Gerald Duncan born August 1, 1957, married Wanna Johnson who was born September 30, 1957. They have a son, Daniel Gerald who was born June 29, 1981. (2) Cathy Lynn Duncan was born March 28, 1962, and (3) Eric Gerald Duncan was born June 13, 1964.

Angus Alexander Leach, son of Daniel and Rebecca, was born September 6, 1869, died June 10, 1945. He married May 31, 1899, Julia Walden, born October 16, 1872, died December 14, 1946. They had two children: (1) Fred Daniel Leach, born May 24, 1900, died April 28, 1980, married December 25, 1923, Rebecca Parlier, born May 2, 1901. They had two children: Paul Alexander, born November 19, 1926, married Barbara Handy and has a son, Tim Richard born March 30, 1962. (2) Mary Virginia Leach born June 23, 1929. She married John Harley Thompson. They had two children. Fred Leach divorced Rebecca and married Virginia Beatrice McGee June 29, 1952.

The second son of Angus and Julia was Thomas Calvin Leach, born June 29, 1906. He married Adelle Campbell, born November 2, 1908, on the 15 November 1927. They had two sons (1) Hal Thomas Leach, born August 13, 1928, married Virginia Ellen Rickert who was born November 18, 1930. They were married February 1, 1953. They had four children: John Thomas, born April 23, 1954; Malema Ruth, born May 23, 1957; Barbara Ellen born December 16, 1958, and Judity Gail born November 12, 1960. (2) John Robert Leach born February 1934, married Nancy Ann Kirby, born March 12, 1937. They were married January 23, 1960. They have two daughters, Phyliss Ann, born November 1, 1964, and Suzanne Marie born October 20, 1966.

Sources: Personal knowledge, personal research.

— Winnie Leach Duncan

WILLIAM LENOIR
775

William Lenoir was born on the 20th day of May, 1751, in Brunswick County, Virginia, the youngest of the ten children of Thomas and Mourning Crawley Lenoir. At about the age of eight, he moved with his family to near Tarboro, N.C. where he lived until adulthood. In March 1775, he and his wife, Ann Ballard Lenoir, of Halifax County, moved to the rich valley of the Yadkin River, locating near the Mulberry Field Meeting House, which later became the town of Wilkesboro.

William Lenoir, almost immediately after locating in his new home, became active in the defense of that area against the Cherokees, and later fought with distinction in the Revolutionary War as a Captain under Colonel Benjamin Cleveland. In the battle of King's Mountain, Lenoir with his company officers, volunteered as privates and proceeded to help to bring Ferguson's forces down to defeat. After the war he continued to serve in the military affairs of the state as Major-General of the Militia for 18 years.

In 1800 William Lenoir drew the plans for the town of Wilkesboro and lots were sold starting around May 22nd, 1800. During this time he had build a home, which he called Fort Defiance, in the Happy Valley area of the Yadkin in what was then Wilkes County and now

Caldwell County. That home has been restored and is now open to the public as a historically significant structure of that era. In a civil capacity, Lenoir's record of service was no less distinguished than his military record. He was appointed a justice of the peace by the convention that framed the state constitution and continued as such for 62 years. He also served at different periods in the office of register, surveyor, chairman of the County Court and Clerk of the Superior Court for the county of Wilkes. He served many years in both branches of the State legislature and for five years as speaker of the Seante. He was one of the original trustees of the University of North Carolina, and for two years President of the Board, being the first citizen to hold that position.

From all accounts passed down by the members of his family and associates, William Lenoir, in spite of his busy schedule in military and civic affiars, had time to be a loving and kind husband and father, a steadfast friend and a generous and hospitable gentleman to all with whom he came in contact throughout his life.

Many descendens of William Lenoir are still living in our area today and can be rightfully proud of their heritage as members of the family of this remarkable man.

Sources: Family records, *Happy Valley*, Hickerson.

— George Forester Jr.

DR. ROBERT EDWARD LEWIS
and FAMILY
776

Dr. Lewis (Bob) was born September 19, 1920 in Lumberton, N.C., the only child of Robert and Mary Margaret McArthur Lewis. His father was sheriff of Roberson County for many years. Bob was educated in the public schools of Lumberton. After two years at Davidson College, he transferred to UNC-CH where he completed his undergraduate studies and his first two years of medicine. He entered Jefferson Medical College for his last two years of medicine. Being in the Navy V-12 program during medical school, he chose to intern in the Philadelphia Naval Hospital, after which he was assigned as chief medical officer to the destroyer USS Irwin in the Pacific during World War II. At the close of the war he was stationed at the Charleston Naval Separation Center until his release from service.

In April 1946, we came to North Wilkesboro. Bob's mother, who had been widowed in 1930, also moved here and lived with us until her death in 1954. Bob worked with Dr. Fred Hubbard in the old Wilkes Hospital, assisting with surgery and doing much of the obstetrics. In 1949 he entered a three year surgical residency program at Watts Hospital in Durham. At the end of that time we returned to North Wilkesboro where he established a private practice of surgery. In 1955 he became a Fellow of the American College of Surgeons; and that same year he completed requirements for, and became a Diplomate of athe American Board of Surgery.

In 1943 we were married. I was formerly Dorothy Plonk of Kings Mountain, the third child in a family of four girls and a boy. My parents were John O. and Elvira Foust Plonk. I am a sister of Douglas Plonk McElwee who lives here and who, with her husband Bill, was instrumental. in our coming to North Wilkesboro. I graduated from Greensboro College, majoring in chemistry. After teaching in the Franklin, N.C. high school for a year, I entered graduate school at Chapel Hill and received an MS degree in biochemistry. I worked as a chemist for DuPont in Philadelphia for a year and a half.

We have four children. Mary Suzanne (Suzie) was born in 1945. She received a BS degree in nursing from UNC-CH and is married to Dr. Ernest R. Tonski of Weirton, W. Va. Their son, Jacob Edward, was born in 1977. They are presently living in Charleston, W. Va. where Suzie is teaching in the school of nursing of the University of Charleston. Patricia Foust (Pat) was born in 1946. She attended UNC-G and graduated from UNC-CH with a degree in English Education. Pat is married to Richard Blaine Johnston, Jr. who is manager of Johnston Lumber Co. in North Wilkesboro. They have three children-Andrew Lewis born in 1972, Mary Lewis born in 1975, and Blaine Patrick born in 1978. The Johnstons are members of North Wilkesboro United Methodist Church. Robert E., Jr. (Robby), born in 1950, attended Lenoir Rhyne College and graduated from Florida Institute of Technology in Melbourne, Florida with a BS degree in air transportation. He is a corporate pilot for Lowes of North Wilkesboro and is a member of the Wilkesboro Baptist Church. Margaret Elvira (Margi) was born in 1952. After two years at Wake Forest, she transferred to UNC-G and received a BS degree in nursing. She is married to Charles Douglas Turner of Ripon, Wisc. He is assistant personnel manager at Modern Globe. Margi and Chuck have one son, Robert Charles, born in 1980. They are membersof North Wilkesboro Presbyterian Church.

We have been active members of the North Wilkesboro Presbyterian church since coming here in 1946. Bob also often spoke in various churches in this and nearby communities. He was a devoted follower of Jesus Christ and took every opportunity to witness for Him.

Bob died May 9, 1978 at the age of 57, with a coronary attack. The medical library at Wilkes General Hospital is named for him, a tribute to the fact that he valued books very highly and enjoyed sharing his library with others. He was interested in education and helped make it possible for a number of young people to have a college education. For several years he served on the North Wilkesboro school board. He had a special interest in the young doctors coming into the community and was eager to help them in any way he could as they began their practice of medicine.

Bob enjoyed his work and was dedicated to it. He especially enjoyed orthopedic surgery. Seeing injured hands and bones functioning normally again gave him particular satisfaction. Many who knew him recall his sense of humor, his ability as a story teller, his knowledge of and love for nature, his avid interest in photography, camping, music, and other hobbies, and — what became almost a hallmark for him — his cheerful whistling. His patients appreciated his availability and his willingness to listen and talk with them.

Coming to Wilkes County fulfilled his often expressed wish to live in the mountains. He loved and appreciated this part of the state — not only the beautiful terrain, but also the people to whom he felt a deep debt of gratitude.

Sources: Personal knowledge, memories, and family records.

— Dorothy Plonk Lewis

THE LINNEY FAMILY
777

William Coplin Linney was born in Manchester, England October 7, 1739. It is not known exactly when he came to America, but a list of tithes for the year 1777 recorded in Louisa County, Virginia, shows William Linney paying on four (4). Another record for the years 1782-1787 in Louisa County, Virginia, lists William Linney paying poll on one (1) and eleven (11) slaves. Records in Bedworth, England, dated 1820, state that the Linney family was one of the oldest families in the parish, Bedsworth not having been without a William Linney for over 200 years.

William Coplin Linney lived in the state of Virginia until about 1817 when he came to Snow Creek, North Carolina. Here he purchased over 1000 acres of land from Richard H. King, February 10, 1817, and J.H. Allen, August 1, 1817. (Records in county clerk's office, Iredell County, Statesville.) These tracts of land touched the South Yadkin River and Snow Creek. Some descendants of Zachariah Linney still own 900 acres of the original land purchase.

William Coplin Linney was a silversmith and at his death had accumulated a large estate. He was married three times. First to Ann Bell, Orange County, Virginia, on September 2, 1773. They had three children: Margaret, George and Elizabeth. Ann Henderson Burrus, widow, was his second wife. They were married in Orange County, Virginia, November 20, 1780. Children born to them were Zachariah Linney, June 30, 1782, in Virginia, and Henderson Linney who later settled in Kentucky. He and his third wife, Nancy White, had no children.

Zachariah Linney, son of William Coplin Linney and Ann H. Burrus Linney, was born in Louisa County, Virginia, June 30, 1782. He served in the War of 1812 under the command of General John Thomas, detached Kentucky Militia, commanded by Major John Andrew Jackson.

Zachariah Linney married Lucy White August 20, 1818. She was the daughter of John White of Virginia. To them were born William Coplin Linney II, August 11, 1819, Iredell County, Julus Linney, Anelem Linney, John M. Linney, and Gates Linney. Zachariah was a soldier in the War of 1812 and was severly wounded in the battle of New Orleans.

William Coplin Linney II was born August 17, 1819, in Iredell County, North Carolina. He married Martha Baxter of Rutherford County, N.C., February 11, 1841. William Coplin Linney II was a physician and received part of his educational training at Davidson College. His wife, Martha Baxter, was a college graduate. Their children were Romulous Zachariah Linney (state senator, three term member of the United States Congress, and spent a decade as prosecuting attorney of Alexander County), Joseph Wellington Linney, born March 16, 1844, William Coplin Linney III, Virgil Linney, James K. Polk Linney, Cleopatria Linney, Lillian Linney, and twins who died in infancy.

Joseph Wellington Linney was born March 16, 1844, in Alexander County, N.C. He married Sue A. Smith of Taylorsville, N.C. February 2, 1865. She was the daughter of Sheriff John Smith og Alexander County, and was a graduate of Mitchell College, Statesville, N.C. To them were born Cora Lee Linney, James Clayborn Linney, Joseph T. Linney, Emma Linney, Grace Linney, William Ernest Linney, Margaret (Maggie) Linney, and Clyde Linney.

Entered in the diary of William Ernest Linney at the death of his mother, Sue Smith Linney, are these words dated November 26, 1914: "Mama died this morning at 1:30 o'clock. She professed faith in Christ when a girl; she loved her church and its services; she loved her Bible and read it often; she loved her fellowman; she rejoiced to see others living Christian lives; she prayed much; she spoke evil of no one, living or dead; she strove to grow more like Him whom she served; she was as absolutely unselfish as a human can be; her standards of virtue and piety were the very highest; she was as gentle as a mortal can be; she never claimed to be perfect.

William Ernest Linney wrote in his diary March 9, 1922 following the death of his father, Joseph Wellington Linney: "Father died today from heart failure, following pnuemonia. He was laid to rest at Linney's Grove Baptist Church beside the grave of our mother. The only man on this earth upon whom I would depend at all times and under every condition is gone! He was a men of jovial, cheerful disposition. He had such a magnetic personality that little children, neighbors, and strangers alike would follow him wherever he desired. He professed religion fifteen years before his death and lived a wonderfully sweet Christian life all the way, missing Sunday School and preaching service only three times in all those years."

William Ernest Linney was the third son of Joseph Wellington and Sue Smith Linney. He was born in Alexander County, N.C. December 3, 1880. He married Florence Catherine Poole, daughter of Reverend and Mrs. Daniel Wilson Poole of Alexander County, December 26, 1906. To them were born twelve (12) children. (See The Reverend William Ernest Linney)

Sources: Public records in England, Iredell County, Orange County, Virginia, Louisa County, Virginia, family Bible, family records and letters, "The Linney Family" by James Earle Linney of Kentucky.

— Lillian Linney Foster

REV. WILLIAM ERNEST LINNEY

778

William Ernest ("Bub") Linney, son of Joseph Wellington and Sue Smith Linney, was born in Alexander County December 3, 1880.

He received his formal education in the schools of Alexander County, Concord, and Wake Forest College. He remained a dilligent student all his life. He was widely read and was conversant on any subject of Biblical, social, economical, national, or international interest.

He married Florence Catherine Poole, daughter of Rev. and Mrs. Daniel Wilson Poole, December 26, 1906. Mrs. Linney was a woman of great inner strength and beauty. She gave the kind of support important to his career and maintained stability in the home from which he was often absent.

Mr. Linney was licensed to preach in August 1906 by Linney's Grove Baptist Church. His ordination took place in December 1907, and for 33 years he served churches in Alexander, Wilkes, Yadkin and Surry Counties. He was in his 22 year as pastor of Pilot Mountain Baptist when he died.

His colleagues had this to say: "Mr. Linney was a very forceful speaker, had the best natural modulation of voice of any speaker ever heard. He could take an oratorical flight that would lift his hearers to the heights of heaven and in an easy flow of the English language and natural tone of voice could bring them back to earth without a jar of shock. When he selected a text, thought it through, analyzed and delivered it, it was so complete that there remained nothing more to be said.

He was endowed with superior powers of thought, logical reasoning, quickness of conception and personal magnetism."

He was called to pastor Wilkesboro Baptist Church in December 1914 and served this church until 1921, living in the parsonage. Mr. Linney wished to give his family a sense of security and permanence, and so bought a house and twelve acres of land on Woodland Blvd. Most of this property remains in the family.

Mr. Linney served as Wilkesboro Postmaster from January 5, 1922 until September 20, 1934. During the later years of his life he devoted much time to writing and his book, The School of the Prophets, was widely distributed in the state.

Twelve children were born to William Ernest and Florence Poole Linney: Jennie Pauline, born November 18, 1907, married Herbert C. Wall August 14, 1935. Their daughter, Nancy Carol, born December 23, 1940, died December 18, 1969. Herbert C. Wall, Jr. born December 8, 1947, married Nancy LaVern Harper in 1981.

Madge Elizabeth Linney, born April 7, 1910, married William Kent Sturdivant August 25, 1932. (see Sturdivant).

Helen Fred Linney, born February 26, 1912, died July 29, 1977, married John A. Cashion and had two children: Molly Anna, married Jack Gallion and had three children: Frank, Jackie and Laurel: John Fred Cashion married Georgia Burgess and has a son, Matthew.

Twin sons, William Ernest, Jr., and Edgar Wellington were born January 31, 1916. Edgar died December 31, 1939. Ernest died July 1958.

Lillian Catherine born June 22, 1918, married Robert Lee Foster July 16, 1941 (see Foster family).

A second set of twin boys was born October 1, 1920. Douglas Miller married Inez Triplett. He died January 20, 1979. Donald Poole married Molly Wilkins. Donald lives at the home place.

Carolyn Sue Linney, born March 22, 1923, married Stokes Pearson. They have three children: Rebecca Sue, born June 28, 1946, married Michael Lane; Ronald Stokes born August 17, 1950; Robyn Sherry born August 13, 1961.

Joseph Baxter Linney, born January 13, 1925, married Adelaide Wright of Lockport New York in 1945.

Betty Jean Linney, born January 17, 1927, married Henry Waugh June 23, 1951. Children are: Henry B. Jr. born August 13, 1952; Ann Linney born July 11, 1954, married Ernie Page; William Joseph born January 19, 1956, married Marsha Jobe. Richard Daniel, born June 30, 1960 is single.

Daniel Armfield, born April 13, 1930, married Geraldine Perkins June 4, 1960. Their three children are: Elizabeth born July 1, 1963; Daniel A. Jr. born April 21, 1968; and William Ernest Linney III, born November 25, 1972.

Sources: Family Bible; personal, public, and church records; diary of Wm. E. Linney; interviews with family and friends.

— Lillian Linney Foster

LOMAX

779

Elijah Lomax was born in Rowan County in 1812. About 1850 he married Nancy Darnell Norman (1820 — 10 January, 1885). She had three children by a previous marriage to William Norman, William, Elizabeth, and Wade. Nancy was also born in Rowan, but sometime after her first child was born the family migrated to Wilkes as had Elijah. The progeny of this marriage were Dennis Lomax and Pinkney Asbury (14 October 1851 — 28 March 1929). Elijah died around 1855. Nancy then married William P. Darnall 20 May 1856. Evidentally he did not live long because she is listed as the head of the household in the 1860 and 1870 censuses.

In his youth "Berry" was a schoolteacher, merchant, and postmaster. On 27 January 1886 he married Sarah Elizabeth Carpenter (20 December 1862 — 1 July 1939), daughter of William and Henrietta (Smith) Carpenter of Traphill. There were seven children born to this union. Three girls died in infancy or childhood from Diptheria. The surviving children were Chauncy Bret (1 June 1891 — 19 April 1953), Bessie Conrad (24 September 1893), Bernice Grace (7 February 1898 — 22 January 1978), Gladys Virginia (22 July 1901).

The family resided in the Lomax community (no longer has a post office). Berry was a storekeeper, postmaster, and farmer. His grandson, Phillip, remembers his father, Bret, telling him about the trips he and Berry would take to Salisbury in the wagon to buy merchandise for the store. They would have to camp out under the stars.

In 1896 he was elected Chairman, Wilkes

County Commissioners, and in 1897, Chairman, Wilkes County Board of Education. He was involved in the founding of Mountain View Institute which was a boarding school. All the children attended this Institute. From a journal Grace kept while in school there one can find out what a typical Sunday might have been — "January 21, '17. Went to S.S. Joined Christain Endeavor. Came home and wrote letters. Dinner at 12:30, then to Bible Class. During quiet hours I wrote a letter to Gladys, then at 4:00 went to band concert. Then after supper talked to Mrs. Turner for a long time. Went to church and then came home and feasted on 'lassy' bread."

About 1915 Berry sold all his property in Wilkes and moved his family to Maryland to farm. After one year of homesickness and failure, the Lomaxs returned to Wilkes and settled in North Wilkesboro. He became a stockholder in Oak Furniture Company.

Bret Lomax attended Mars Hill College and Bliss Electrical School, Washington, D.C. Berry and Bret were in the Coca-Cola Bottling business in Newland (where he met Marian English Phillips). In 1930 he joined Yadkin Valley Motor Company as a stock holder where he remained until his death. On 29 November 1928 he married Marian E. Phillips in Abington, Virginia. For many years he was Treasurer for the First Baptist Church, and she was a dedicated schoolteacher.

Bret and Marian had three children — Phillip A., Mary, and Martha (twins). Phillip was born October, 1935. He finished school at Duke University in 1957 and spent three years in the Navy. In 1957 he married Sarah Shatley. Their daughter, Elizabeth was born in October, 1960 and they moved to Pensacola in December where he went to work as an accountant with Monsanto Company. Their son, Bret, was born in March, 1962. Phil pays tribute to his parents by saying, "Mother and Dad were great parents, gave us a lot of love and good times — the numerous maple tree limbs notwithstanding."

"Con" became a nurse — in fact, she was the first operating Room nurse when Dr. Fred C. Hubbard opened his Wilkes Hospital in 1923. On 22 April 1926 she married John Michael Quinn (Jack), who was a traveling furniture salesman. They had one son John Michael, Jr. (Mike). His occupation required that they live throughout the South — N.C., Tennessee, Texas. After his retirement they returned to North Wilkesboro for nine years.

Mike attended the McCallie School in Chattanooga, University of Texas in Austin, did a tour of duty in Korea, and graduated from the University after his discharge. He has been a Washington correspondent for a newspaper in Dallas, Director of Public Relations at the University, and at present is a professor of Journalism at the University in Austin. He married a Texas girl, and they have three children. "Con" and "Jack" moved to Austin in 1973 and at this writing reside in a nursing home there.

Grace graduated from the Shenandoah Conservatory of Music in Dayton, Virginia. On 5 September 1922, she married Andrew Franklin Kilby. They had two children — Grace Frank

and Andrew Lomax. She was a voice and piano teacher from 1936 until her death. One of her greatest desires was to try and stimulate interest in good music in the town and county. She was, also, involved in many community affairs — Musical Arts Club, Choir Director at First Baptist Church, State Federation of Music Clubs, Wilkes General Hospital Auxiliary. She was stricken with cancer in 1965 and survived. While driving in town in January, 1978 she experienced a heart attack and died in a short while.

Gladys became a business secretary and for many years was private secretary to Edd F. Gardner, Carolina Mirror Corporation. At this writing she resides at Vespers Nursing Home.

Sources: Personal knowledge, personal research.

— Grace Frank Mayberry

Betsy Longbottom Allison.

THE LONGBOTTOM FAMILY
780

Joseph Longbottom families were early settlers and land owners of Wilkes County. The 1779 court term ordered a bridle way to be opened from New River to Longbottom on Roaring River. In 1799 Joseph Longbottom helped lay out the road at the lower end of the county up Hunting Creek to John Howards. On June 8, 1799, Joseph Longbottom received a N.C. land grant for fifty acres for 50 Shillings. Joseph had acquired approximately five hundred acres on Hunting Creek by 1840.

All of his children were born on this farm. The name of his wife is unknown. Joseph was born in 1760s and died July 1846 in Wilkes. The known children of Joseph are: (1) Joseph Jr. born 1787, married Rebecca Wiseman 1820 in Harrison Co., Ind. Served in War 1812, 8th Regt. 4th Co. (2) Elizabeth, married Isaac Lovelace May 15, 1809. (3) Nancy married William Mize June 24, 1817. (4) William married Polly Mize April 19, 1820. (5) Luckey married Ann Jarvis February 27, 1822. (6) Elisha married Hannah Jarvis October 23, 1823. (7) James married Leah Lakey May 24,

1825. Joseph Longbottom's estate was settled in 1848, with Luckey Longbottom, administrator.

Luckey Longbottom and family moved to Surry County, N.C. and from there to Lawrence Co., Ark. in 1860. Luckey and Ann had five children, all born in Wilkes: (1) Elijah born 1823, married Rachell Money 1847 of Surry Co. N.C. While crossing Tenn. to Ark. this couple had two children, John b. 1854 and a daughter b. 1856. (2) Elizabeth "Betsy" born Dec. 16, 1825, died Aug. 11, 1911 in Llano, Tx., buried Oxford cemetery, married James L. Allison, Lawrence Co., Ark. (3) Hannah born April 30, 1831, died April 11, 1861 in Ark, married Wiley Smith. (4) John born 1833, died June 26, 1923 in Austin, Tx., buried in Confederate section, Texas State cemetery. He

John Longbottom.

married June 16, 1861 in Lawrence Co., Ark.Celisia Jane Baldridge. Served in Civil War Co. C, 38th Infantry.

John and Celisia Jane had the following children: Andrew C. (Lum), Wiley, Elijah, John, Mary. In 1880 John's wife died and he, with his children, moved to Llano Texas to be near his sister Elizabeth, who was a mother to his children. She was called "Aunt Betsey" to all children. John Longbottom was called to help clear Llano County of the Indians in 1880. There were lots of Indian raids of cattle, stock, and many homes of the white people. John retired and went to the Confederate Home in Austin, Texas and died there June 26, 1923, aged 90.

Sources: Wilkes County records; war records.

— Ethel Longbottom White

THE AUSTIN H. LOVETTE FAMILY
781

Austin Henry Lovette was the first born son of James L. and Fannie Belle Brown Lovette.

Austin was born June 16, 1905, and died June 30, 1950 in Wilkes County, North Carolina. He married Minda E. Higgins, daughter of Calvin Clayton and Rachel H. Kilby Higgins on October 28, 1908. To their union were born Gladys, Madge, Fern, Joyce, James and Dawn. Austin and family spent most of their lives in North Wilkesboro.

When he finished school at Millers Creek High, he became a furniture finisher at Forest Furniture Company in North Wilkesboro and was there for seventeen years. Then, he went into business for himself, after spending two years as a city policeman. He owned and operated a service station. After selling the station, he went into partnership in City Sales Company with Odell Whittington, Jr. He sold interest in this to Paul Billings in exchange for Piedmont Mountain Freight Lines. The frieght lines was a failure that cost him his entire life savings and cost him his health.

He was involved in making a comeback in operating Wayside Grocery and Service Station in Wilkes County when a fatal heart attack ended his life. His widow and six children all survive at this time in Wilkes County.

Sources: Personal knowledge.

— Mrs. A.H. Lovette

Charlie O. and Ruth B. Lovette.

CHARLIE ODELL LOVETTE
782

Charlie Odell Lovette was born July 20, 1900 in a cabin on the bank of the Yadkin River in the Ferguson Community to Nelson and Lilly Riggs Lovette. When he was about four months old, his father bought a small farm in the upper Reddies River area and moved there where he grew up.

He began helping his father with the farm work as soon as he could hold up the plow handles and attended school at Cross Roads when in session. In those days education did not seem very important, and Charlie quit school in the fifth grade to work on the farm and drive a mule team for his father. At that time there was much wood and lumber to be hauled from the mountains to North Wilkesboro by wagon. He also worked for Mr. W.J. Palmer planting what was once known as the Boone Trail Orchards. He then went to Winston-Salem and worked in the R.J. Reynolds tobacco plant for a period. He did not like the city life, came back home, and hired out to do farm work again. This, of course, did not pay so well; and he went to West Virginia and worked in the coal mines for awhile.

He never liked working by a whistle or for the other man. He had a dream of starting his own business, that of gathering country produce and hauling to city markets; but he felt he did not have enough education in the three R's. He swallowed his pride and at the age of 21 years he went back to school in the lower grades at Cross Roads where he mastered the knowledge of figures.

In 1924 he bought a Model T truck Chassis, had a wooden cab and bed built on it and went out into the country contacting the country stores for their barnyard fowl, eggs, butter, country hams and what have you. The merchants were more than glad to have a ready market at their door. In February 1924 Charlie went into Charlotte with his first load of country products, found a market in the hotels and boarding houses; this began his career in the poultry business.

On May 18, 1924 he was married to Ruth Bumgarner of the Pleasant Home Church community. They began housekeeping in a log cabin near this church where they stayed for a few months. Then they moved further out the road to a rented house where their first son was born, Charles Fred Lovette, who has pioneered in the poultry business. In May 1925 they bought their first home still near Pleasant Home Church where one daughter and six more sons were born. One died in infancy; the other seven are involved in the poultry business. C.O. never moved from the original home bought in 1925, kept changing, remodeling and adding to the house until it was adequate for his large family.

He loved the church and was interested in all phases of the church activities. He loved farming, and kept some going on the side when he could hire good help. He increased his little farm of 18 acres to 50.

As his sons finished school and began to take over the poultry business as his health failed, he was unable to be on the road with the trucks as much. He became interested in raising Hereford cattle. He could feed them and watch them grow, and he enjoyed being a bit of a cow trader. When he retired from work, his hobby was visiting the sick and shut-ins. He was not so much on reading newspapers and other books but took much pleasure reading the Bible, one of his daily pastimes. He was director of the first bank in Millers Creek and was always interested in community improvement. His policy in dealing with people was strict honesty. He loved people, enjoyed doing favors for them, and having them take meals with him. He especially loved having ministers in his home for a meal. He never asked an employee to do a job he would not do himself.

Although the poultry business grew far beyond his expectations, he would not take much credit for it. He was just happy that his sons and daughter and many others could carry it on and go far with it.

At his passing, June 22, 1978, he was survived by his wife, 7 children, 15 grandchildren, 2 great-grandchildren. The hosts of friends and business associates that attended his funeral service at Pleasant Home Church attested to the esteem in which he was held.

Sources: Personal knowledge.

— Ruth B. Lovette

THE LOWE FAMILY
782A

David Lowe was born in 1787 in the area near Moravian Falls, Wilkes County. He married 30 October 1807 to Elizabeth Vickas, the daughter of Elias and Lucy (Hopkins) Vickas, in Wilkes County. Elias and Lucy married 23 October 1778 in Wilkes County. The father of David Lowe is believed to be Caleb Lowe; his mother's name is unknown. Elizabeth (Vickas) Lowe was born 1790 in Wilkes County.

Land entries in Wilkes County show Lowes living on land bordering waters of Moravian Creek as early as 1779 — Thomas; Isaac; Samuel; William; and Caleb. A 1799 land entry — #912 of Richard Price states he owned 50 acres on Moravian Creek branch that runs through Caleb Low's plantation; another 1799 land entry — #915 shows Caleb Low with 30 acres on Falling Fork Moravian Falls, running up mountain creek and adjacent his own line.

The land surrounding the falls at Moravian Falls was a part of two land grants made to the Moravian Brethren who settled at Salem, North Carolina. These grants were made in 1752 by Lord Granville, one of the eight Lords Proprietors appointed by Charles II of England. This section was transversed by a creek named "Moravian" by the surveyors sent out by the Moravian Brethren. Hence the beautiful cascade on Moravian Creek became known as Moravian Falls. (In 1874 the little village, ½ mile from the Falls, was officially named Moravian Falls at which time the post office was established.)

Wilkes County Will Book One (1778-1799), on page 44 lists the Will of William Low, written 12 January 1780, proven in Court during June term 1780, which names wife, Mary, and sons, Isaac, John, David — his children "begotten by body last wife" and refers to a grandson, Stephen, son of Samuel who is given 109½ acres of land in Bedford County, Virginia "on Fich Creek adjoining place I myself lived on." It is believed William Low had a first wife and Caleb Low (Lowe) is possibly a son of William and his first wife, name unknown.

The 1800 Wilkes County federal census shows these Lowe families: John, William, Samuel, all aged 26-45 years and Isaac, Sr., Caleb, Thomas, Sr. all aged over 45 years. These Lowe families moved to Warren County, Kentucky, and first appear on tax lists there in 1804. By 1809, David, Caleb, William, Isaac, Joseph and James Lowe are on tax lists in Warren County. Caleb Lowe is on 1810 federal census for Warren County, aged over 45 years, but is not listed on 1820 census; he last appears on 1815 tax list.

David Lowe owned land located on Doughty's Sinking Creek in Warren County, Kentucky, in eastern part of the County, near Barren County Line. He is listed in Warren County tax lists through 1833; he then moved to Barren County where he lived until his death in 1861. He is listed as a farmer on 1850 Barren County census; he was quite likely a tobacco farmer. His wife, Elizabeth, died 11 October 1852 in Barren County, Kentucky.

The children of David and Elizabeth (Vickas) Lowe include the following: (1) Elizabeth, born 1812, married Alexander Crabtree 1833 Barren County, Kentucky. Children: James born 1834; John born 1836; Phebe born 1839; Martha born 1844; Thomas born 1846; Joseph H. born 1849. (2.) Caleb, born 1814, married Mary Ann. Children: Angeline born 1836; Martha J. born 1839; Mary F. born 1841; Nancy V. born 1844; Louisa born 1847; Pryor born 1846.

(3.) Jason W., born 1815, married Rachel Reed in Edmonson County, Kentucky on 8 October 1839. Children: I. Dillard born 1840; Paradine (or Paschal) born 1842 married Jane Lewis; Mary R. born 1844 married James Roller 1863; Elizabeth H. born 1848 married 1) S.R. Totty 1897, 2) A. Huff, died at age 102 in 1950; Samuel H. born 1848 (twin of Elizabeth) married Elizabeth Wheeler 1869; Sarah A. born 1853 married Andrew Hawkins 1871; Louisanna born August 1854 married 13 July 1876 Barren County, Kentucky to William S. Simpson, died 27 September 1933 (William S. and Louisanna Lowe Simpson are my maternal great-grandparents).

(4) Vincent, born 1816, married Nancy Christy, daughter of Andrew Christy, 20 September 1838. Children: Lydia A. born 1839; Permelia Jane b. 1841 married Thomas Ashley 1860 Warren County, Kentucky; William D. born 1842, married Margaret Fulks 1868; Franklin born 1846, married Eliza Ann Mar-

shall 1871; James Marshall born 1849, married Margaret Fehler 1884; Frances Elizabeth born 1854, married Charles Atkinson 1882; Woodford born 1857, married Mary C.; Edmonia born 1857, married Tandy Shackelford 1878.

(5.) Maria, born 1820, married Thomas Ragsdell 1836. Children: William born 1838; Elizabeth E. born 1840; Martha born 1842; Gabriel born 1845. (6.) Joseph, born 1823, married Hannah. Child: Artimesia born 1843, married 1) John Fulks, 2) Pleasant Beckham 1879 Warren County, Kentucky. (7.) Vachiel, born 1824, married Sarah Ann Gibson 1846. (8.) George Washington, born 1827, married Frances Lindsay 1850. (9.) Cynthia Ann, born 1829, married 1852 Andrew Jackson Hood, died 1904. Children: John, married Eliza Johns; "Ody" Lora, married Rose Ella Johnson; David; Tandy; Buckhanan; Perlina, married David Hendrick; Sarah M., married a Monroe.

The children of David and Elizabeth (Vickas) Lowe were all born in Warren County Kentucky; some married in Barren County, some in Warren County and my great-great-grandparents married in Edmonson County (Jason and Rachel (Reed) Lowe). The area where the Lowe families lived is near County lines of all three Counties. It is near Mammoth Caves, Kentucky, and the town now named Park City one of the entrances to the Caves. My mother was born a few miles outside Park City on the family farm, in 1914. The town was named Glasgow Junction until 1936. My mother's parents are William Jason Simpson (1880-1959) and Sarah Florence (Wilson) Simpson (1880-1957). William's father, William S. Simpson (1850-1930) and mother, Louisanna (Lowe) Simpson (1854-1933) lived nearby. They were farmers, with their main crop being tobacco. Family tradition is that the Lowe family was of German heritage. Glasgow Junction was located on the Louisville-Nashville stagecoach route, and due to the popularity of the Mammoth Caves, was an established town early in the 1800's, first called Three Corners because of transportation routes converging at that point (the main north-south route of travel in the County crossing the Louisville-Nashville stagecoach route, later the L&N railroad was built along this route). Later the name of the town was changed to Bell's Tavern when this famous eating place and hotel for travelers to Mammoth Caves was in use. It was destroyed by fire shortly before the Civil War; the ruins of the foundation are still in existence and Bell's Tavern is on the designated list of historical monuments by the State of Kentucky.

Sources: Barren County Heritage, by Barren County Historical Society, Glasgow, Kentucky; Courthouse records in Barren County, Warren County, Edmonson County, Kentucky; Courthouse records in Wilkes County, North Carolina; Census records 1790-1880 of North Carolina and Kentucky; Wilkes Genealogical Society February 1974 Bulletin, Volume 6, Number 1; and family records.

— Mrs. Mary Greathouse

THE CALEB ANDERSON LOWE FAMILY
783

Caleb Anderson Lowe was the son of

Joshua and Lucy Lowe, born on June 21, 1820 in Wilkes County. Like his father, he took up the farming trade. He first married Lydia Brown, a seamstress from Yancy County, N.C., who was born in 1830. On December 8, 1842, Caleb bought 60 acres along Moravian Creek from the state for only $3. He and Lydia had at least seven children, all born in the Moravian Falls area: Fenia Elizabeth (b. 1848), John Anton (1850), Vilot L. (1853), Thomas M. (1855), Mary Ann (1858), Lydia Margaret (1861), and Barbara (1864). Just before the birth of Thomas, Caleb purchased an additional 29 acres at 5¢ an acre on June 5, 1854. Then, sometime between 1865 and 1870, Lydia died.

However, Caleb remarried soon after to Mary M., who was born May 4, 1843. Together, they produced at least five more offspring: Frances (b. in 1872), Vina (1874), Almedia (1876), Peden V. (1878) and Hettie (Dec. 1879). Mary died on August 26, 1884 and Caleb outlived her by 18 years, before he finally expired on April 29, 1902. Active members of the Walnut Grove Baptist Church, both Caleb and Mary are buried there in the churchyard.

In 1860, Caleb declared that he had real estate valued at $150 and personal property worth $200. These amounts became $150 and $150 respectively in 1870. Caleb and both of his wives could read and write.

Sources: Wilkes Co. records.

— Ben Lowe

CANEY and NANCY SMITH LOWE
784

Elkannah Partee Lowe (Uncle Caney) (1866-1945) son of W. Tilford and Sopheronie Tritt Lowe. He had three brothers; Bill, Ves and Jim, one sister Mary Jane (James). He was born in the area of Wilkes and Alexander County line on the Taylorsville road. At the age of 25, in May 1892, he took for his bride a young girl of 16, Nancy Smith.

Nancy Smith (1875-1953) dau. of John A. and Frances Kilby Smith. She had six bros.; Coffey, Thomas, Parks, Richard, Henry and Will, two sisters Margaret (Kerley) and Anne (Shook).

Caney and Nancy lived on a farm, had apple orchards (the 3rd generation of apple growers in the area) and as the years passed were very successful in their efforts. He had his own Delco plant to furnish electricity, having among the first lights, refrigerator, and radio. They had running water, piped from a spring about a quarter of a mile into a large water tank on the hill beside the house. This furnished water for washing machine, bathroom and kitchen. They had one of the first phones which was always available for the community. Many nights there would be many people sitting around the radio and on the big front porch listening to the news, and the Grand Ole Opry.

To this union seven children were born; Mack (wife Elizabeth Davis), Grace (husband

Caney and Nancy Smith Lowe.

Frank Freeze, Ethel (husband Burtle Broyhill, Perry (wife Mary Reavis), Gay (husband Monroe Blevins). Glenn (wife Edith Williamston), Clayton (having had infantile paralysis as a child did not marry).

I remember my grandparents as living with a strict code of ethics. Their word was their bond. He made an appointment to go to a man's house to do a task for him about six miles away. On that day the car would not start; the truck was away with a load of apples. He simply hired one of his workmen to ride a horse to tell the man he was sorry he would not be able to come that day.

Corn shucking and wheat harvest time was always a joyous occasion for everyone, nearly everyone in the community was present, as grown-ups worked and shared time talking, laughing and sometimes singing. Children were running and playing everywhere. Then as the night came to a close there was always a party atmosphere as refreshments were shared, food and fellowship in abundance.

Apple harvest time was also a time of sharing; on week-ends cars would be parked everywhere, as they came from far and near to see the mountains, buy apples and visit with Uncle Caney. Everyone that knew him thought of him just that way.

In the summer time as they took the big yellow Ford truck with all the workmen to the farm at Moravian Falls. They took me along for what they teasingly called "Water Boy" and my Grandfather's pet name "Dink." I am sure in those early years of life money was not plentiful, but I never knew that, as we returned home in the evening, he always had my Dad to stop the truck at Scrogg's General Store in Moravian Falls. When he returned he always placed a little bag of candies in my hand.

My grandfather was a hard worker, planner and doer, and was always thinking how he might help someone else. He gave generously to the Walnut Grove Church building, also donated the land for the Apple Growers Research Station.

My grandmother was the neatest person I have ever known. She worked from morning to late at night, in the house and garden, but she was never without a clean dress and apron. She was very quiet, choosing her words carefully. Never in all the years did I hear her belittle, or criticize anyone. She was always an example for each of us.

They were faithful to God in all their doings. Their lives were centered around the Walnut Grove Baptist Church, supporting it in every way they could. Their home was always open for all visiting preachers and anyone passing by, as their home was about half way between the Taylorsville and North Wilkesboro Railroad Station. He was a Mason for 55 years.

He created jobs for people that would come to him asking for work. There was always a creek bank that needed to be mowed, an apple tree that needed to be dug under. This way they never knew that he was just giving them a helping hand.

They never tired of seeing their 21 grandchildren come. They delighted in making lemonade, hiding orange slice candy, peppermint sticks and oranges in a closet to distribute as they came. There was always pies, ham and biscuits and other delectables on the dining room table, covered with a white table cloth, for each of us to partake as our appetites insisted. Nothing was ever said, unless we in our hurry dripped molasses or honey from our biscuits as we made our fast exits.

He always sent the big yellow truck to North Wilkesboro each Saturday afternoon. He always had my Dad drive the truck so all the workmen or anyone else along the way that needed to go to town would have transportation. By the time it got to its parking space on Tenth Street hill it had many passengers. In about three hours everyone knew to be back with their supplies for the return trip home.

They loved and appreciate God's beautiful handiwork. Many times after the days work was done, and the clouds looked just a certain way, Grandad would say lets all ride up to the Pores Knob Tower to see the sunset. Their lives even today leave a beautiful glow.

— Zelma Broyhill Helton

THE JOHN ANTON LOWE FAMILY

785

John Anton Lowe was the second child and first son of Caleb and Lydia (Brown) Lowe. He was born March 10, 1850 in Moravian Falls. While growing up he received a common school education and learned farming from his father. At the age of 20 he married Marinda ("Minda") Dowell, also of Wilkes Co. Together their personal peoperty amounted to only $100. She was the daughter of Joshua and Dicey (Watkins) Dowell. Minda was born on June 19, 1852 and was bereft of a formal education, although she could read some.

The year after they were married, on February 12, 1871, Minda gave birth to her first child, Christopher Columbus. Thereafter, Calvin was born in 1873, Crotina in 1875, William G. in 1877, and Lucisous in 1879. All of the children were born in Moravian Falls and attended school there. During these family building years, the Lowes were active members of the Walnut Grove Baptist Church. Organized in 1845, the "first Church building was built of hewed logs, heated by means of chimney built of rough rock and banked with red clay, with a huge fireplace. The seats were made from split logs into which pegs were fastened for legs."

Beginning in 1884, John had reached the point where he was able to financially purchase additional tracts of farm land. In that year he bought 200 acres along the middle prong of Moravian Creek, for $600, from W.A. Broyhill Sr., and 25 acres more from the state for 12½¢/acre. Minda's parents granted them 57 acres in the same area on May 29, 1886.

After his children had grown and his land wealth had become greater, John assumed a more important role in the community. On July 10, 1889, he was appointed one of three school board committeeman from Moravian Falls. But it was also around this time that he began experiencing health problems. In 1902 one of his kidneys started to cause him pain, and he continued to have trouble with it until he died on August 7, 1915, at the age of 65.

Minda outlived her husband by 14 years. Her death on September 19, 1929, at age 77, was explained as a failed heart. She missed the Great Depression by one month. She was buried beside John in Moravian Falls Cemetery.

Sources: Wilkes Co. records.

— Ben Lowe

THE JOSHUA LOWE FAMILY
786

Joshua and Isiah Lowe, who founded strong Lowe lines in Wilkes County, were probably the sons of Caleb Lowe, but documentation has remained elusive. The older of the two brothers, Joshua, was born around 1774, married first Mary Teague 1 October 1805 and then Lucinda Hubbard 9 June 1818. Isiah, the younger brother was born 17 September 1778 and married Nancy Jane Pearson 29 June 1834.

Joshua and Mary Teague Lowe had two daughters: (1) Rosanna H., born ca 1807, married John McLeod Frazier, (2) Elizabeth, who married John McKay (McCoy). By his second wife Lucinda Hubbard, daughter of Isham Hubbard, Joshua had eleven other children: (1) Caleb Anderson, born 1822, married Lydia Brown first then Mary Joines, died 29 April 1902, (2) Joshua, Jr., born 1822, left the country and was never heard from, (3) Jesse, also left the county and disappeared, (4) Rebecca, born 1824, (5) Mary, born 1825, married Lewis H. Smith, (6) Eliza Rinda, born 1827, married William Clanton, (7) Jane C., born 25 June 1830, married Edmund C. Edsel, died 22 December 1916, (8) James Martin, born 26 May 1832, married Clarinda Laws 19 November 1860 and then Matilda Kilby, died 21 November 1914, (9) Serena, born 1834, married a Phillips, (10) Betsy, married David Smith, (11) Annie.

The daughter of Jane Lowe Edsel and son of Mary Lowe Smith married as first cousins and were my great grandparents: Mary Alice Edsel and Lewis Francis Marion Smith. Marrying first cousins is unusual, but Mary Alice's background has a particular interesting story. Jane C. Lowe had married Edmund C. Edsel in 1830 and they had one child, Richard. Then according to the local stories, Edmund went out to feed the stock and disappeared. Whether he left the country or was killed is not known. After his disappearance Jane had three other children, one of whom was my great grandmother Mary Alice. According to local interviews, her father was Fred Welborn.

Joshua Lowe's brother Isaiah Lowe, married Nancy Jane Pearson and they had eight children: (1) W. Tilford, born 18 April 1836, married Sophona Tritt, died 11 May 1905, (2) Robert Bryant, married Susan Davidson 16 February 1869 and then Mary Woodrine, (3) Benjamin, married Nancy Matney 25 July 1873, (4) John, (5) Elizabeth, married Benny Davis, (6) Caroline, (7) Mary, married Bartley Davis, (8) Rachel, married Jimmy Parsons.

From these two brothers come many of the Lowes of Wilkes County.

Sources: Courthouse records, interviews with family members, Census records, "The Lowe Family of Wilkes County."

— Peggy Joines Martin

JOSHUA LOWE FAMILY
787

The Lowe family lived in Surry county for many years before becoming part of the new Wilkes county formed in 1777. The earliest Lowe mentioned in the old county tax lists is William Lowe, who had one poll taxable while residing in Rowan county in 1771. The following year mentions William, Isaac, Calep, Thomas, and John Lowe. Surry county was formed in 1771 and from Rowan and a William Loo is found on the 1771 and 1772 tax lists. In 1775, Calob Loe, Isaac Low, Aquila Low and Thomas Loe are all listed. In the Will Abstracts of 1774, one John Lowe is listed.

After Wilkes county was organized, the Lowes settled into the Moravian Falls area, where to some extent they have continued to live ever since. The Land Entries indicate that William, Caleb, Isaac and Thomas Lowe each owned several hundred acres of land all around Moravian Creek in 1778. By the end of the century, the state of North Carolina continued to grant literally thousands of acres to various members of the Lowe family, in the Moravian Creek area. The names Caleb, William, Isaac and Thomas Lowe continue to recur on the county tax lists from 1782 to 1805. The 1790 Census lists William, Rachel, Caleb, Isaac, Mary, Thomas and Sam Lowe as residents of the Morgan District. In 1800 we find John, Isaac, William, Samuel, Ezekiel, Caleb and Thomas.

While there is some indication that the Caleb Lowe listed is one of my direct ancestors, I can only identify the subsequent generation's head of household as a positive relation. Joshua Low, my great-great-great-great grandfather was born sometime between 1770 and 1775. On October 1, 1805 he married Polly Teague in Wilkes county and after her death, Lucinda (Lucy) Hubbard in 1818.

Joshua is first found in the 1810 Census as between 35 and 40 years of age, with two girls under 10 and a wife between 16 and 26 (Polly). In 1820 he had two boys under 10, one girl under 10, two girls between 10 and 16, and wife between 16 and 26 (Lucy). He was a farmer. By 1830, Joshua had six family members employed in agriculture but only one who could read or write. And in 1840 there were a total of 11 household members. It is likely that Joshua died sometime between 1840 and the next census of 1850. (Although a Lucinda Lowe was sold 100 acres at 5¢/acre along the last prong of Moravian Creek from the state of North Carolina on May 17, 1854).

Sources: Wilkes Co. Records.

— Ben Lowe

PERRY ROOSEVELT and MARY REVIS LOWE
788

Perry Roosevelt Lowe was born in Wilkes County, May 29, 1901. His parents were E.P. and Nancy Smith Lowe. He spent his childhood in Mooresville and the Pores Knob Community of Wilkes.

Mary Revis Lowe was born in the village of Moravian Falls, February 1, 1900. Her parents were Leonard Monroe and Martha Ida Pearson Revis.

Mother grew up in an atmosphere that stressed that the importance of obtaining an education. She was always a very studious and obedient child in school. After completing her studies at Moravian Falls, she attended Mt. View Institute. She completed the necessary work required to become an elementary teacher. Her teaching career began at Mt. Crest on the Brushy Mountains and continued at Cherry Grove, Ferguson, Moravian Falls, and last of all Pores Knob.

Teachers, during those times, would usually board in a home near the school they were teaching. The young bachelors of the community would want to "court" the new school teacher. However, Mother's heart felt for only one, Perry R. Lowe. She met him at Walnut Grove Baptist Church. Although Mother was a Methodist, young people then visited different churches in the area.

On November 29, 1922, Mother and Daddy were united in marriage by the Rev. E.E. Yates at the Moravian Falls Methodist Parsonage. They were given a very loud sernade on their wedding night by many young men of the area. A well remembered wedding present was one from Prof. C.C. Wright, a six month subscription to the Winston-Salem Journal.

In 1927, their first child, Clyde Revis Lowe, was born. Daddy asked Mother, "Had you rather see his sweet smile everyday or be away from home teaching?" It was not a hard decision for her to make; thus, ending her eight years of teaching. Their children to follow were Perry Roosevelt Lowe, Jr., Caney Lee Lowe, and their long awaited daughter, Mary Jo. All of the children are presently living in the Moravian Falls area.

Daddy was a fourth generation apple orchadist in northwestern N.C. He was also well known throughout the state. Many years, when they made their home at Pores Knob, they were hosts for the Brushy Mountain Fruit Growers Association. People came from many area of western North Carolina to attend this event.

Mother was very active in the Alexander Home Demonstration Club. She served as county council president and held other positions of leadership with this group. They were very active members of Walnut Grove Baptist Church. Mother was a Sunday school teacher for several years. Daddy served as church clerk and aided greatly in the financial support of the building of the present structure.

In 1948, they moved to their new home on the Country Club Road in Moravian Falls. They wanted to be nearer the school for their daughter, Mary Jo.

Mother became very active in the community life of Moravian Falls. One of her first undertakings, was to help organize a P.T.A. at Moravian Falls School. Their main goal was to establish a lunchroom at the school. She was a charter member of the Moravian Falls Woman's Club and also of the Rainbow Garden Club. They were active members of the Moravian Falls Baptist Church, especially in the fiscal affairs when the new church was built

Perry Lowe, Sr. Family L. to R: Caney Len, Mary Jo, Mother, Daddy, Clyde, Perry, Jr.

in 1949. Mother also served as church treasurer for many years.

Daddy assisted in many apple experiments in Wilkes. He aided in establishment of the N.C. Apple Research Laboratory at Kilby's Gap. He served on many agricultural committees and helped establish the Wilkes Agricultural Center. He was instrumental in organization of the Carolina Refrigeration Co-operative here, in 1946, which made possible storage of apples for the fruit growers. During his last year of life, he saw a dream come true, the completion of the Brushy Mountain Apple Co-op in Moravian Falls.

In addition to his orchard interest, he was also active in the lumber business. He was also a staunch Republican.

He was past president of the Pores Knob Baseball Team, past president and one of the organizers of the North Wilkesboro Flashers professional baseball team, and past president of the National League and one of the organizers of the Wilkes County Little League Baseball.

During their latter years, Mother and Daddy spent the last 17 winters of his life at Flagler Beach, Florida. Daddy enjoyed fishing and playing shuffleboard with his many friends from the Midwest and Eastern United States. Daddy's passing in 1964 was a traumatic happening for Mother. She continued to be active with her clubs, needlework, cards, and many friends during the remainder of her life. She passed away February 13, 1976, at Moore Memorial Hospital, Pinehurst, N.C. Their death left a void that can never be filled for their many friends and loved ones that knew them.

Sources: Family memories, the family Bible, and personal knowledge.

— Mary Jo Lowe Lovette

VIRGIL WINFREY and BUTRICE JOHNSON LUFFMAN

789

Virgil Winfrey Luffman was born on Easter Monday, April 4, 1904, in what is now the Pleasant Ridge Church community in the eastern edge of Wilkes County. The first born son of Caleb Luther and Pheroby Alice Harris Luffman, he was given the name of his two grandfathers. His parents were married in Wilkes County in February, 1902.

Winfrey's paternal grandparents were Caleb Winfrey and Sarah Sallie Ann Luffman. Caleb enlisted in the Confederate Army October 4, 1861, and his brother, Joshua, enlisted the following March. Calsb was wounded on August 17, 1864, at Fayzel's Mill and his brother was killed in the same battle. He was under the command of General "Stonewall" Jackson and was in the battle at Chancellorsville in May, 1863. He was scheduled for guard duty on a certain night, but was sick so a replacement was assigned. His replacement was the soldier who shot General Jackson, mistaking him and his escort in the dusk for a detachment of Federal cavalry. General Jackson died eight days later. Grandpa Caleb said if he had been the guard that night, he believed he would have recognized the General.

His maternal grandparents were James Virgil (Verdal) and Lucy Jane Young Harris. Verdal's parents were Henderson and Pheroby Harris. Lucy Jane's parents were Solomon and Phebe Young. Solomon Young came over from Holland around 1830 and acquired the extensive acreage of land that is now Klondike Farm.

Winfrey had three sisters and five brothers, all of whom lived to adulthood: Curtis, Walker, Sarah Jane (named for her two grandmothers), Clyde Verlie, Flora, Lester and Ivan.

From a little child Winfrey loved shop and carpenter tools. His father made him a set of

tools and a box to carry them in. As he grew older, his father taught him the skills of carpentry and shop work.

At nineteen, Winfrey became principal of Cool Springs public school in Wilkes and the next two years taught at a public school in Surry County.

In March, 1926, he was appointed Rural Letter Carrier for the State Road route consisting of mileage in both Wilkes and Surry. This post he was to hold for thirty-eight years.

He was married March 30, 1930, to Butrice Johnson. (For Butrice's family background see "Isaac Calloway and Laura Handy Johnson" in this book.)

My parents, Isaac and Laura Johnson spent the winter of 1910-1911 in North Wilkesboro awaiting my birth so that my mother would be near a doctor. I was born January 3, 1911, at seven o'clock in the morning, just as the Tannery whistle blew. The first time they took me back home to Grandpa Sidney Johnson's they put me in my great-grandmother's lap. She passed her hand all over my face and told them I was a pretty baby. This was Grandpa Sidney's mother, Betty Brown Johnson, and she had been blind for more than forty years. She lived at Grandpa Sidney's and was always called "Blind Granny" by the family. The front porch had a railing all around and a second one about shoulder high at the place where "Blind Granny" always sat. She could knit stockings and socks which she did by the hour. She could tell when she had dropped a stitch and would ask someone to pick it up for her.

Grandpa Sidney was too young to go into the Confederate Army, but was planning to leave with some other boys to join the Home Guard. The young folks had a party at which they played kissing games. He kissed my great-aunt Cassy Handy who was taking mumps, so when the other boys left for Home Guard, Grandpa was nursing a case of mumps.

Front Row: Winnie, Jean, Lucy Back Row: Winfrey and Butrice G. Luffman in 1940.

Winfrey and Butrice J. Luffman (1980).

Ninette Humber.

My maternal great-grandfather, Aaron Brown, was a Corporal in the Confederate Army.

Butrice was a 1927 graduate of Mountain View Institute, doing the four years high school work in three years. She was secretary to the president of Mountain Park Institute and Junior College, taught Business Education and French there during the war years, served as Director of Missions in the Stone Mountain Baptist Association for seven years and in the Elkin Baptist Association for nine years.

During World War II, Winfrey worked eight hours a day as a machinist in addition to carrying his mail route. After his retirement they both worked at Old Salem for five and one-half years; he as a host-craftsman, and she interpreting the period rooms in the Museum of Early Southern Decorative Arts (MESDA).

Winfrey became choir leader in Pleasant Ridge Baptist Church at the age of sixteen and continued more than 40 years until his voice failed. He was elected deacon in June 1930. For six years he served as clerk in the Stone Mountain Baptist Association. Both have been Sunday School teachers for more than fifty years and have served their church in various other capacities.

Winfrey has a well-equipped hobby shop where he made tinware, cut and polished gem stones, made jewlery, made leather belts, pewter spoons and many other craft wares.

Winfrey and Butrice have three daughters: Winnie, who teaches Home Economics at the University of Georgia in Athens; Jean (Mrs. John L. Humber), who lives in Chapel Hill and was Carrboro school librarian for a number of years; Lucy (Mrs. John P. Dearing) who, with her husband, teaches in the Phelps School in Malvern, Pennsylvania.

They have six grandchildren: Ninette and Michael Humber and Lucie Humber Swanson; Laura Ann, Rachel and Briana Dearing; and two great-grandsons, Jeremy and Brian Swanson. Ninette is wearing the wedding dress of her great, great grandmother, Betty Adams Johnson (1880) in the photo.

Sources: Family Records, family traditions, memories, personal knowledge.

— Butrice Johnson Luffman (Mrs. Winfrey)

WILLIAM BRADFORD LUFFMAN
790

Wilson Luffman married Alice Vicie Carter. I have no record of any children except John, born June 6, 1827. He married Lucinda Simmons born November 26, 1841. They are buried at Cool Springs Baptist Church.

Joseph Newton Luffman was born November 8, 1869 the son of John and Lucinda Simmons Luffman. He married Kizzy Morrison born January 11, 1873, daughter of Wesley and Tobitha Harris Morrison. They lived in the Lomax Community. Their children were: Lou born 1892; William Bradford born May 10, 1894; Worick born 1896; Walter born 1898. Kizzy died December 16, 1904, and is buried at Macedonia Baptist Church. Joseph later married Eula Gentry of Laurel Bloomery, Tennessee. They didn't have any children. He was a sawmill operator and lived for several years in Chase City, Virginia and in Laurel Bloomery, Tennessee. After the death of his second wife about 1944 he moved to Ronda, North Carolina where he lived until his death November 26, 1946, and is buried at Macedonia Baptist Church.

My father, William Bradford Luffman better known as Will — born May 10, 1894 was the son of Joseph Newton and Kizzy Morrison Luffman. His mother died when he was 10 years old and he lived a short time in the home of Mrs. Lula Bauguess of the Lomax Community of whom I remember him speaking so fondly. On April 11, 1914 he and Dollie Richardson, born December 3, 1894, daughter of Arthur Calloway and Rhoda Jane Prevette Richardson, eloped and were married sitting in their buggy. Magistrate Ambrose Wiles performed the ceremony. Both of them attended a one room school in the Lomax Community. They had the following children: Paul Newton born January 7, 1917; Edna Alice born April 12, 1920; Curtis Claude born March 14, 1925; John David born September 10, 1928 died December 22, 1932; Mary Lucy born February 20, 1931.

He worked for John Myers who owned a general store in the Dockery Community hauling supplies by wagon to and from North Wil-

kesboro, spending the night on the camp ground where the Wilkes County Public Library is now located. They also lived in Chase City, Virginia where she worked at his fathers sawmill. In 1922 they bought a home in the Rock Creek Community. They became active members of Rock Creek Baptist Church; both of them sang in the choir and he was a deacon and Superintendent of the Sunday School. He did some farming and worked at factories in Roaring River and North Wilkesboro.

May 9, 1942 Papa was ordained as a Baptist minister and devoted the remainder of his life to Christian service. His pastoral work was in Surry County and the following churches in Wilkes County: Little Elkin, Benham, Mountain Valley, Davis Memorial and Bethel at Hays three different times. In 1963 he retired from pastoral work due to health reasons but continued doing evangelistic work. My father died November 28, 1971 and Mama died November 19, 1979. They are buried at Mountlawn Memorial Park. Our home was filled with lots of love and haipiness.

I graduated from Mountain View High School June 2, 1949 and from the North Wilkesboro School of Beauty Culture 1951. I am employed at the Artistic Beauty Salon. On June 6, 1964 I married William Lee Haynes son of Annie Mae Campbell and the late Isaac Spurgeon Haynes. Bill and I reside at Route 1, Hays and attend Oak Ridge Baptist Church.

Sources: Family memories, cemetery markers and death certificates.

— Mary Luffman Haynes

ALEXANDER LYON FAMILY
791

Born about 1785 to William Lyon and Magdilla Corbin/Brown, Alexander Lyon was the only member of his family who stayed in N.C. when his parents, brothers and sisters and their families left for Kentucky in the early 1820s. He and his first wife, Sarah Sparks born around 1792, a sister of Reubin Sparks who is believed to be the son of John Sparks and Sarah Fields, had 3 children: Rhesa, Matilda and Mary. On Sept. 27, 1827 Alexander married as his second wife Mary Blackburn, born about 1794 daughter of William and Sarah Blackburn and a sister of John Blackburn. They had no children. In 1839 he is listed as raising wheat, oats, rye, corn and tobacco and he also had a distillery. Alexander died May 8, 1879 and his wife Mary died March 1, 1881.

Rhesa Lyon, oldest child of Alexander Lyon and Sarah Sparks, was born Aug. 15, 1816 in the area later known as the old York place near Traphill, and in his last years went back to the old home place to sample water from the spring. He was married on March 13, 1854 to Martha N. Brinegar, born 1834, but the marriage was soon dissolved, and he went to Kentucky to join his relatives, living there with the William Holbrook family. While in Kentucky, he taught school and a letter to his parents, dated July 26, 1856 states: "I have taken a school for 3 months. I commenced it the 21st of July at the Blain Meeting House.

Elizabeth Blackburn Lyon.

have the promise of $40.00 teaching it, clear of boarding when it comes due to the district, which will be next spring. I have a good house to teach in. I have taught one week but I have a powerful large school." He travelled by horseback late in November of that year, returning to N.C. to stay near his aging parents.

A teacher in subscription and public schools of Wilkes County for most of his life, Rhesa also was much sought after by his neighbors to read and write letters, help in counting stitches and constructing their weaving designs. He bought and sold land, including the plot in the Dockery community on which he lived and died, purchased from Siler Brewer, property once possessed by Jasper Billings; and he served as a lender of money.

Times were hard and the Civil War disrupted homes in the area, with many of his neighbors and friends split in their loyalties. Armies from both sides, as well as scalawags and scoundrels, raided their farm for food and provisions. Families hid their cattle in the woods, buried many of their prized possessions, and yet lost much of their goods. Elizabeth Blackburn, who later became the wife of Rhesa Lyon, had this poignant memory of the war: "They took my best tablecloth and my favorite dress." After the turmoil of the conflict ended and reconstruction progressed, Rhesa married on May 1874 for the second time to Elizabeth Blackburn, daughter of John Blackburn and Charlotte Hendrix and niece of his father's second wife, Mary Blackburn. Elizabeth, born on April 15, 1845, had come to live with Alexander and Mary Blackburn Lyon after John Blackburn died and her mother Charlotte remarried on Sept. 9, 1868 in Surry Co. to Thomas Norman, son of Henry Norman.

Rhesa was instrumental in founding Mt. Pisgah Baptist Church in Dockery and gave the property on which the church now stands in the area where Mt. Airy Church formerly was located. He and his wife Elizabeth were charter members and strong supporters of the church. Elizabeth died Nov. 18, 1938 and she and Rhesa are buried with his parents and other members of his family group at Old Roaring River Baptist Church at Traphill.

Four daughters were born to Rhesa and Elizabeth: Mersey, Edith, Maud and Cynthia. Mersey Lyon, born April 10, 1875, lived only

to adulthood and died on Oct. 24, 1896. Edith, the second child, was born on June 19, 1880, married briefly on July 7, 1899 to Joseph M. Hamby, who was born Nov. 1879 son of Commodore L. Hamby and Emeline E. Darnell. She spent the remainder of her life living with her sister Maud and her family, being a second mother to their children and active in church and community affairs. She lived to be over 100 years of age, dying on Aug. 11, 1980, and lies buried by her younger sister Cynthia at Mt. Pisgah Baptist Church. Maud was born Feb. 26, 1884 and after her father Rhesa's death on Oct. 11, 1899, became a school teacher. In a career covering over 10 years, she taught at the Holbrook School, Mt. Pisgah, Oak Ridge No. 2 (Scourge-out), Piney Grove and Stoney Ridge. She served as Postmaster of Dockery from 1919 to 1924. On April 11, 1918, she married Bruce Billings, son of James Oscar Billings and Phoebe Cansadie Smoot. Bruce was born March 12, 1894 and died Oct. 24, 1965. They reared 3 daughters and worked together to improve their farm by using progressive agricultural practices. Maud died on March 26, 1971. The last child, Cynthia, was born April 24, 1890 and on July 17, 1908 married Avery A. Holbrook, son of Columbus F. Holbrook and Martha Bauguess. A child was born and died on Sept. 9, 1911 and Cynthia died about a year later on Sept. 30, 1912.

Matilda Lyon, the second child of Alexander Lyon and Sarah Sparks, was born on June 22, 1819 and married John Bauguess, born May 23, 1827 son of William Bauguess and Sarah Waddell. They had 4 children: Irving Matthew, Lodemia, Sarah Jane and Franklin. Matilda died Aug. 29, 1903. Most of their descendants lived in the Stoney Ridge area and are buried at Round Hill Baptist Church.

Irving Matthew Bauguess, born 1850, had 5 children: Cling, John, Hort, Dock and Charlie. His sister, Lodemia Bauguess born Nov. 10, 1851 married Joel Ander Pruitt, son of Hardin Pruitt and Lucinda Brooks on March 14, 1876. Joel Ander was born March 5, 1855 and died July 20, 1934. Lodemia died Aug. 20, 1899. They had 2 children: Charlie Walter and Lula. Charlie Walter Pruitt, born March 22, 1877, became the magistrate of his district and was the Postmaster of Chuckle, N.C. He married on May 3, 1896 Martha Clementine Wiles, daughter of Robert Wiles and Angeline Wheatley. Lula Pruitt, born Dec. 7, 1882 married Andrew Patterson Bauguess, son of Jonas Bauguess and Matilda Holbrook. Their daughter Edith recently retired from the position of Postmaster of Traphill and is married to Robert C. Pruitt, who was a rural mail carrier for many years. Sarah Jane Bauguess was born around 1854 and married Lewis Newton Durham, son of John Durham and Sarah Sparks. They had 5 children: Nettie married Andrew Hutton, Luzette married Kelly Hutton, Shober did not marry, Bertie married Edd Hutton, and Julia married Will Royal. Franklin, the last child of John and Matilda Lyon Bauguess was born around 1858.

Mary Lyon, the third child of Alexander Lyon and Sarah Sparks, was born Sept. 27, 1821. She married Martin Holbrook, born 1827 son of Ezekiel Holbrook and Susannah Crouse, and

they had 5 children: Emeline, Thurza, Ellen R., Winfrey and Millison. Mary died Oct. 15, 1891. (See Martin Holbrook.)

Sources: Family records, Cemetery & Census Records.
— Naomi B. Gordon

COMMIE LYON FAMILY
792

Commodore Schelley Lyon, known as Commie, was born in Austin community in Wilkes County on June 7, 1898. He was the son of Meredith A. and Mary Pruitt Lyon, who were farmers.

I have often heard my father tell of the days when he was growing up. He used to plow with a steer doing the pulling. He used to walk ten miles to Elkin and back in one day. He remembered when the mountains were abundant with chestnuts. He would go up there and bring back a bushel of chestnuts at a time, on the back of a mule or horse. He liked to tell the story of when he saw his first automobile, how it scared the horses and some people.

In 1916, my father helped to clear the railroad between Elkin and North Wilkesboro after the flood.

He married Luray Hawkins December 27, 1918. She was the daughter of Luther M. and Emma Smoot Hawkins. She was born December 28, 1898. Dad and Mother were the parents of five children: Dorothy Mae, born October 12, 1919; Kermit Luther, born November 9, 1920; Harold William, born August 3, 1922; Rosa Lee, born May 22, 1924; Willard Amos, born August 3, 1926. All five of us were born in a span of less that seven years, so Mama had a hard job caring for us, but she did a good job even though her health was bad. In those days she had none of the modern conveniences we take for granted today, not even running water or electricity.

Life was hard during the Great Depression years, but Mama and Dad always managed to have food on the table and clothes on our backs. Dad worked for Brookfall Dairy near Elkin and we lived there for more than two years. In 1929, he took a job with Elkin Furniture Company and moved into a company house near the plant.

In 1930, Dad was only working one or two days a week at the furniture factory, so we moved back to our little house on the farm at Austin. There we did not have to pay rent and we could grow most of our food.

In those days we had time to visit our neighbors and we didn't mind walking for miles to their homes. Our neighbor, Guy Cox, lived about a mile from us. He bought the first battery powered radio in the community. We would walk to his house early Saturday night and listen to the Grand Ole Oprey.

My sister, Dorothy married Raymond Harris. They had four children: James, Wayne, Carol and Lorene. James married Arlene Hincher. They had three children, Donna, Kimberly and James Earl, Jr. Wayne married Linda McArthur. Carol married John D. Collins. They had two children, Anthony Tate and Kelly Ann. Lorene married Roger Luffman. They had two children, Melissa and Jason.

The Commie Lyon Family — golden anniversary Commie and Luray. Left ro right: Harold Lyon, Dorothy Harris, Commie Lyon, Luray Lyon, Rosa Lee Collins, Kermit Lyon, Amos Lyon.

I, Kermit, married Justine Cheek. We had two children, Gary Wallace and Sheridane Lura (Sheri). Gary married Karen Pardue. They had two children, Michael Gary and Suzanne Pardue. Sheri married William D. Reese. They had a daughter, Wendy Allison.

Harold William married Maxine Sparks. They had three children: Allen Ray, who was killed in a boating accident near Oregon Inlet in 1972, David and Gay. Allen married Elizabeth Holbrook. They had a daughter, Ramona. David married Nancy Cacey. They had three children, Christopher David, Jonathan Allen and Kella Cacey.

My sister, Rosa Lee married Albert Collins. They had two children, Frances and Anthony (Tony). Frances married Denny Morrison. They had two children, Daniel Mark and David Matthew. Tony married Mary Finney. They had two children, Denise Michelle and Mitchell James.

My brother, Amos, married Lois Byrd. They had two children, Nancy and Kenneth. Nancy married Glenn Fasanella and they had a child, Timothy. Kenneth married Donna Caudill. They had a child, Michael David.

Commie Lyon, my father, died March 4, 1982. My mother, Luray Hawkins Lyon died November 3, 1978.

My grandfather, Meredith A. Lyon was born June 19, 1862, died October 7, 1945. My grandmother, Mary Pruitt Lyon was born November 3, 1866, died June 4, 1926. My grandfather married Phoebe Wyatt after the death of my grandmother. Phoebe was born May 8, 1862, and died April 4, 1943.

The children of Meredith A. and Mary Pruitt Lyon were: Joshua M., Jesse H., Commodore S., Bertha, and Charlie. Joshua married Nellie Hayes. They had three children, Marvin, Conrad and Delos. Jesse H. married Fannie Hayes. They had eight children, Myrtle, who died at birth, Stella, Posie, Worth, Marie, Jesse, Jr., Mary, and Martha. Bertha married first Horace Buttrey. They had three chiildren, John Waymoth, Josephine and Ruth. Bertha married second Bryant Taylor. They had two children, Mary and Alan Bryant. Charlie married Fay Durham. They had nine children, Howard, Bobby, Betty Mae, Dorix, Judy, Jack, Caroline, Ruth and Kathy.

Meredith A. Lyon wqs the son of Jacob J.

Lyon, born October 5, 1829, died 10 February 1904, and Susanna Thornton, born March 19, 1822, died December 16, 1904. They had five children, Meredith A., Sarah and the triplets, Martha, Mary and an un-named son who died at birth.

Jacob L. Lyon fought with the confederate army in the Civil War. Some of the letters he wrote home to his wife mentioned that he was sending her money to use to plant a crop. He told her to use the money for the crop and not to use any of money they had saved. He had a good idea that the Confederate Money would be worthless. He was stationed at Camp Saltville, Virginia, guarding the precious salt works there; one of the few sources of salt the southerners had. Once he sent his letter by some fellow soldier who was coming to Wilkes to "hunt the boys who have not come up." He added a note to his brother, Austin Lyon, who had the first postoffice at Austin, that he could get his saddle at James Weaver's.

Jacob J. Lyon was the son of Solomon Lyon, born April 18, 1807, died January 12, 1870 and his wife Susanna, born 1808. They had children, Jacob J., Almira, Mary, Nancy, Austin and Susanna. Solomon Lyon was a son of Jacob Lyon, Revolutionary War soldier who came to Wilkes County after the war.

Sources: Family cemeteries, family Bibles, Jerry Q. Gentry's research and personal memory.

— Kermit L. Lyon

JACOB LYON

793

Jacob Lyon was born in Culpeper County, Virginia in 1763, son of Alexander Lyon. His mother's name is unknown. He is believed to have had two brothers, William, who came to Wilkes County and moved to Kentucky in the 1820's and John, who settled in Caswell County, North Carolina.

Alexander Lyon was the son of William and Elizabeth Lyon of Culpeper County, Virginia. He had two brothers, James and Thomas.

On January 10, 1779, Jacob Lyon enlisted in the Virginia Militia and went with Col. George Rogers Clark to the Northwest territory to fight against British General Hamilton, who was known as the "hair buying General" be-

cause he paid a bounty to the Indians for white scalps. On February 16, 1779, they reached the flooded plains of the Wabash River, made the crossing within nine days and captured the "hair buying General" and he was taken back to Williamsburg and placed in chains until the end of the war.

Jacob Lyon was discharged from the Militia on May 28, 1780, and in September of the same year he enlisted in the Virginia Continential army. He marched to Cheraw in South Carolina to join General Nathaniel Greene. They marched back into N.C. where they fought Lord Cornwallis, Jacob being in the third line. On April 26, 1781, Jacob fought with General Greene at Hobkirks Hill near Camden, S.C., and was in the Seige of Ninety-Six, after which he was transferred to the Cavalry under Ligh Horse Harry Lee, the father of General Robert E. Lee. After serving with other noted Generals and Colonels, Jacob Lyon was discharged at Salisbury, North Carolina February 1982.

Jacob Lyon's first deed of land in Wilkes County was a grant for 100 acres, entered October 1, 1789. It was witnessed by William Lyon, believed to be a brother of Jacob. The land was in the are between Austin and Traphill.

Jacob Lyon and his wife, Jane had ten children: Frances, Rachael, Valentine, James, Elizabeth, Soloman, Meredith, Jacob, Jr., and Ruth.

Frances Lyon never married. Rachael married Atha Gentry. Valentine was married, but his wife's name is unknown. He had six children: Polly, Suze, Aliza, Oicen, William and John.

James Lyon and his wife, Polly, had five children: Jonathan, Jane, Jacob, Walt and Calvin. Elizabeth Lyon married John Gentry. They had ten children: Malinda, who married William Jolly; Lucinda born about 1825; Iredell married Elizabeth Bauguess; Stanley married Jane Alice Burcham; Ruth married Haywood Crouse of Alleghany County; Martin who died in the Civil War; Elizabeth who married Levi Dobbins Burcham; Daniel who died of pnuemonia while in the Civil War and married Sally Hanks; Matilda who married Augustus Pruitt, and Marinda who married William Counts Walker.

Austin Lyon married but his wife's name is unknown. He had six children: Jordan, Addison, who fought for the North in the Civil War, was shot and killed by rebel sympathizers in Alleghany County as he was returning home after the war was over; Thomas, Mary and Stephen.

Solomon Lyon will be found elsewhere in this book.

Meredith Lyon and wife Nancy had seven children: Emaly, Hanson, Mary, Thomas, Nancy John and Joshua.

Jacob Lyon, Jr. married Malinda Sparks. They had four children living with them in 1860: Nancy L., Gabriel M., Hiram, and Ira W.

Sources: Wilkes Genealogical Society quarterly; State Library, Richmond, Va.; Jonathan Hunt Chapter DAR, Elkin; National Archives; The Gentry Family by Jerry Q. Gentry; Culpeper County courthouse records.

— Kermit L. Lyon

James Major Lyon.

Samantha Ann Walls Lyon.

JAMES MAJOR LYON

794

James Major Lyon (10/5/1868 — 8/29/1941) was the son of Calvin Lyon (4/27/1836 — 12/8/1914) and Nancy Waddell Lyon (1847-1918). He had four sisters and one brother as follows: Jane Lyon married Richard Cothren and had three known children; Minnie Lyon married Arthur Lafayette Gant and had four children; Mead Lyon married Will Harpe and had two children; Mary Elizabeth Lyon married T. Hilton Settle and had seven children; and Toliver Dolphus Lyon (4/4/1875 — 1/10/1924) married Emma Darnell and had two children. Emma died and he married Nancy Norman and they had six children.

His paternal Grandfather was James Lyon (6/10/1796 — unknown), born near Traphill. His wife Polly Gentry (6/14/1800 — unknown). There were six known children born to this marriage. Reverend Jonathan Lyon (1/27/1822 — unknown); Sally (3/24/1823 — unknown); Jacob (1/11/1826); Bryson (4/5/1828 — unknown); Wiley (1/15/1830 — unknown); and Calvin (4/27/1826 — 12/8/1914).

His paternal great grandfather was Jacob Lyon who married Sarah Jane Cook and fought in the Revolutionary War.

James Major Lyon married Samantha Walls Lyon on December 24, 1891. His father, Calvin, lived in the Little Elkin Community. He was known to be a millwright, skilled carpenter, and farmer. He was also a member and deacon of Macadonia Baptist Church. During World War I, he worked as a civilian and built army barricks in Petersburg, Virginia.

He had seven children by Samantha Walls Lyon: (1) Hessie M. Lyon (12/23/1894 — _____) married Luther G. Settle. They moved to Colora, Maryland and had four children: Iva Wyatt, LeRoy Settle, Elwood Settle, and Eugene Settle; (2) Lexie Levada Lyon (8/25/1897 — 12/18/1919) married James C. Durham. They had one son, Hollis M. Durham, who lives in Florida and is married to June Gruneau; (3) Pearl Beatrice Lyon (1/30/1899 — 7/19/1936) married Lester Boyd. They had two sons, Ray and Alton Boyd. Alton

married Elsie W. Nixon; (4) Viola Vesta Lyon (6/2/1901 — _____) C.D. Beacham. She worked a number of years as a nurse for the Wake County Health Department. She is now retired and resides in Raleigh; (5) Theodore Walter Lyon (6/15/1903 — 9/3/1957) married Verlie Olivia Smith (10/18/1903 — _____), daughter of Eli Smith and Samantha Settle Smith, in November, 1930. Ted was a school teacher at Benham and Barker Town in the early 1930's. He was a salesman for Moseley & Reece Wholesale Company. They had two children: 1. Baxter Franklin Lyon (8/23/1931 — _____), a Ronda Rural Mail Carrier, who married Betty Marie Dimmette (11/5/1930 — _____). They have two children: Perry Franklin Lyon (10/22/1957 — _____) who married Donna Lawrence (8/5/1959 — _____), and Penny Lee Lyon (3/17/1964 — _____). Baxter lives in the Little Elkin Community; 2. Linda Ann Lyon Davis (6/29/1939 — _____). She married Dr. William H. Davis, Jr. of Ronda. They have three children: Eva Jane Davis (9/10/1960 — _____) who married George Steven Felts; William Bryan Davis (4/24/1963 — _____); and Sandra Lynn Davis (3/10/1965 — _____). Linda Davis is a Wilkes County school teacher and William Davis, Jr. is an administrator at Wilkes Community College; (6) Ina Lizzie Lyon (4/6/1906 — 10/4/1906); (7) Sue Ella Lyon (11/9/1907 — _____), living in Wilkesboro and worked as Deputy Clerk of the Federal Court, married Charlie Grant Bumgarner (10/29/1907 — _____), Mayor of Wilkesboro for 20 years and Wilkes County Tax Collector. Two children were born to this marriage: 1. Charles Ryan Bumgarner (5/17/1943 — _____), a commercial pilot who married Mary Alice Kennedy and lives in Atlanta; 2. Janet Sue Bumgarner (10/6/1947 — _____) married David Whitney Dail and had two children, Rebecca Whitney Dail (2/19/1977 — _____) and Jennifer Suzanne Dail (8/28/1974 — _____) and reside in Atlanta.

Sources: Family Records of Linda Lyon Davis, Mrs. Sue Bumgarner, and Verlie Lyon. Photo, obituaries, Bible, etc.

— Linda Lyon Davis

WILLIAM HENRY HARRISON LYON

795

William Henry Harrison Lyon was born in Traphill February 2, 1841, died January 20, 1922. He joined Northern Army in 1861, as did his brother Addison. After the war he married Sarah Fanny Woodruff and they had two children, Margaret Josephine 1870 and John Gideon 1872. For the remainder of his days he was an excellent farmer, Master Mason and according to my father, "a good christian man."

John Gideon was my grandfather. He married Martha C. Lyon. They had three sons; William McKinley, Thomas E. and Charlie Quincy. My first memory of my grandparents is a September day in 1929. My father, William McKinley Lyon along with Mother and I moved into the dear old log cabin in which my father was reared. Gideon had moved his family into the W.H.H. Lyon house to look after his widowed mother and manage the farm. Gideon was a merchant, mail carrier and a federal whiskey gauger.

William McKinley went west as a young man and worked with his uncle in the lumber business. He lived in Elk River, Idaho and in Spokane, Wash. During World War 1 he served 3 years in the U.S. Army. He married Nova Combs in 1923. I, Emma Lyon Billings was their first child. I was born in Granville County, N.C. My sisters, Wilma and Bonnie and our brother John G. were born in Traphill.

In these beautiful foothills of Wilkes County I learned of my family heritage, back to William Henry Harrison's great grandfather Jacob Lyon, a Rev. War Soldier.

Meredith was born in Traphill in 1815. His first wife was Melinda Sparks, daughter of Joel and Nancy Blackburn Sparks. They had 4 children: William Henry Harrison, Addison, Emily and Mary. Their dwelling had a separate cook house. After Melinda's death Meredith married her sister Nancy. According to family memories Aunt Emily didn't fancy the idea of Meredith's new wife moving into their house. Determined to live peacefully and keep his family close together, he built a new dwelling and a new cookhouse for Nancy practically by the side of the originals.

Here Meredith and Nancy had 4 children: Their names were Washington, Fanny, John (who was said to have drowned as a very young man) and Tom. Tom was brutally killed by a runaway horse pulling a load of corn down a steep incline. This left his grieving widow Nan with 4 children to finish rearing alone.

This makes a total of three family tragedies I heard while growing up. Addison Lyon, Civil War soldier was gunned down by an armed robber while returning home from the war. One of my uncles told me Addison was within 5 miles of home when he was shot.

From the Meredith and Nancy Lyon family came some descendants which are very precious to me. Tom and Nan Lyon's family lived in a snug log cabin only a few yards from the William H.H. Lyon home. I never knew them, but do remember their sons Worth and Albert. Worth's 4 children are, Stewart, Reason, Mar-

William Henry Harrison Lyon and wife, Sarah Fanny Woodruff Lyon.

Flora Billngs.

William McKinley Lyon.

vin and Joyce Lyon Naylor.

Just a quick rundown on my family. My name is Emma Lyon Billings. On Sept. 11, 1943 I married Claude Billings, son of John and Flora Billings. Claude's sisters: Cannie, Lala, Pearl, Lessie, Maude and Ruby. His brothers; Garland and Marvin.

Claude and I have 4 children: Brenda Carole, Daniel Claude, Philip Ray and Vivian Lynn. I do not know much of my husband's family history. I do know that he had a great uncle who was a Civil War soldier. His name was Daniel (Dank) Billings and he is buried at Billings Hill Church. He has a military grave stone. According to family history, he is a brother of Claude's grandfather Harrison (Hack) Billings.

Sources: Personal knowledge, family and Bible records.

— Emma Lyon Billings

WILLIAM S. LYON
796

William S. Lyon was born Feb. 17, 1752 in Roanoke, Va. According to family tradition, he was a brother of Jacob Lyon, who in the Archives report gave his father as Alexander Lyon, son of William and Elizabeth Lyon of Culpepper Co., Va. William S. Lyon fought in the Revolutionary War, entering service in Wilkesboro, N.C. on 29 March 1781 in skirmishes against the Tories, who he declared were more troublesome than the British Army. He served under Col. Branham, Capt. James Henderson, Lt. William Reynolds and Ensign Aaron Parks. After 4 months service, he was discharged, but again on Sept. 5, 1781 he engaged for 9 months service under Col. William Nalls, Capt. Larkin Cleveland, Lt. Martin Gamble and Ensign James Bumgarner (a Frenchman by birth), serving in Surry, Iredell and Mecklenburg counties. On one occasion when going down the Catawba River, an engagement ensued and Capt. Larkin Cleveland was shot in the thigh, disabling him for future service. William was discharged in June 1782. In his application for pension, he gave references as William Holbrook, Mathias Kelly, Samuel Kelly, William Walters, Randall Holbrook, Druery Ewals, Miles Perry, Rev. Elias Kazee and Rev. James Wheeler.

He married Magdilla Corbin/Brown of Culpepper Co., Va., daughter of John and Frances Corbin and they had 9 children. Early in the 1820s, the Lyon families sold their land and many of their possessions and started on their westward trek to Kentucky, settling for the most part in eastern Kentucky in Lawrence County. Their children were: John, James,

William, Sarah, Frances, Mary, Alexander, Jesse and Lewis. Three of their children, John, Mary and Jesse, and also William the Redhead, married children of William Holbrook and Agnes Collier, friends and neighbors who had gone west to Kentucky about the same time as did the Lyons.

1) John, born Feb. 10, 1774 married Mary Holbrook, born Sept. 12, 1783, on Jan. 2, 1812. John died Sept. 11, 1862 and his wife died soon after on Sept. 21, 1864. 2) James was born in 1776 and died July 12, 1864. 3) A possible son William born around 1777 is believed by some to be the father of William the Redhead and Jesse but his wife is unidentified. William the Redhead was born May 21, 1799 and died on Feb. 24, 1886. He married on Aug. 2, 1819 to Sarah Holbrook, by whom he had 8 children. She died Aug. 20, 1866. 4) Sarah born around 1781 married Levi Sparks as his second wife. He was the son of John Sparks and Sarah Shores, born Oct. 2, 1778 and died Oct. 21, 1851. 5) Frances born in 1782 did not marry but lived mainly with her brother Jesse and his family. She often told the story of carrying a favorite pitcher in front of her as she rode horseback on her trip from N.C. to Kentucky. 6) Mary born Sept. 12, 1783, married Jan. 2, 1812 to John Holbrook, born Feb. 10, 1786. They had 11 children and John died Sept. 17, 1862. 7) Alexander born in 1785 stayed behind in N.C. when all the others in his family moved to Kentucky. He married 1. Sarah Sparks, born 1792 m. 2. Mary Blackburn. (See Alexander Lyon.) 8) Jesse was born April 12, 1789 and died April 2, 1879. He married Frances Holbrook born 1793 on July 17, 1815. Jesse farmed, hunted and trapped in Kentucky, and built his cabin near Keaton Fork of Blaine Creek. He was also a blacksmith, making farm and home equipment for his friends and neighbors. 9) Lewis, the last of the children, was born 1797 and married on Sept. 16, 1823 in Lawrence Co., Ky. to Sina Grizzle.

William S. Lyon died April 15, 1847 and he and his wife Magdilla Corbin Lyon are buried on a forested hillside on what was once the Rice Farm in Martha, Kentucky along with most of their children.

Sources: Cemetery Records, family information.

— Naomi B. Gordon

JOSEPH TYRE McBRIDE

797

Our father, Joseph Tyre McBride, born August 23, 1870, at Traphill, Wilkes County, North Carolina, was the son of Martin Green and Sarah Jane (Harris) McBride, who were married in 1866. Joe had two sisters, Frances Victoria (Mrs. John Q. Brown), Mary Ann (Mrs. John T. Miles) and five brothers, John Robins, Robert William, James Walter, Martin Edgar, and Charles Quincy.

Martin Green McBride, born in 1844, was the son of John and Elizabeth (Gray) McBride, who were married in 1831. He and his family lived on a farm on Big Sandy Creek near the east prong of Roaring River, where with planning and hard work, he gained a good living.

In an article in memory of our grandfather, his pastor, Elder G.W. Miles, gave some distinctive qualities of our grandparents' way of life: "Martin Green McBride procured an honest living for himself and those who were dependent upon him, by toil and well laid plans of council of his own good judgment. The courtesy and exceptional hospitality shown by him to the humble Christian soldiers, and especially the ministry, made his home a lodging place for these people."

The "drummers" (salesmen) who traveled by horse and buggy, were always welcome as they came concerning merchandise for the McBride Brothers store. Our uncles, John Robins and James Walter were joint owners of the store until John moved to another community and it then became McBrides store and was kept open by the family members for more than fifty years.

Our great grandfather, Charles Harris, who was born in Dublin, Ireland, in 1801, came to America as agent of the Siamese Twins, and married Frances Bauguess in 1839. He was appointed third postmaster at Traphill in 1843. Their daughter, Sarah Jane, was born October 19, 1848, at Traphill. Charles died in 1849 and was buried in St. Pauls Episcopal Church cemetery. Frances died in 1891 and was buried in old Roaring River cemetery.

Our mother, Margaret Ann, born May 22, 1871, was the daughter of Jesse Tyre and Frances (Spicer) Yale of the Joynes community of Wilkes. Jesse was the son of Vallet Yale of Wallingford, Connecticut, and Susan Pennill of Burke County, South Carolina, who were married in 1829. Jesse was born April 28, 1839. Frances, born 1845, was the daughter of Harvey and Nancy (Brooks) Spicer.

Joseph Tyre and Margaret (Yale) McBride were married in February, 1893. They lived first in Ashe County, but in 1895, they purchased 65 acres of scenic land on top of the northern end of Greenstreet Mountain, where we grew up and learned what love and rewarding work is like. The priceless values we were taught cannot be numbered.

Union Grove Methodist Church near our home and Holly Grove school (later Double Creek) had a great impact on our lives, as did Traphill High School which some of us were privileged to attend.

The waterfalls on the west side of Greenstreet Mountain, which thrilled hearts in its beauty, was a site visitors enjoyed with our family.

Three boys and three girls in the Joe McBride family were: Barney, born June 30, 1894, married Maggie Brooks. Their son Paul Fredrick married Frances Parsons.

Clyde, born September 9, 1896, died July 22, 1898, and was buried in Old Roaring River Cemetery ar Traphill.

Joseph Walter, born December 2, 1911, married Myrtle Ruby Brown. Their children were: Janice, who was married to Elmer Billings; Tyre, to Reo Billings; Betty Jo, to Donald Cothren; Margaret Elizabeth to Paul Staley; David to Annie Ruth Sidden.

Eddie Mae, born February 12, 1900, married Claude Franklin Brown. Their children were: Margaret Elizabeth who was married to Harvey Holbrook; Walter Franklin first to Opal Goforth and second to Annie Lou Foster; Glenn Washington to Audrey Hoots; Clyde Mac first to Marva Dove and second to Elaine (?); Fred Green to Lolieta Jordan.

Sarah Frances (Fannie), born February 1, 1906, married Phinas Ama Bauguss. Their son Harold Jerome married Delores Smith and their daughter Anna Ruth married Otis W. Mobley.

Ruth, born February 17, 1908, married Roy Franklin Billings and had two sons. James Edward married first Jeanette Bauguess and second Dorothy Shephard; and Chy Franklin first married Lila Tate Duncan and second to Margie Scott.

Sources: Family Bible records, memories and personal knowledge.

— Frances Bauguss
and Walter McBride

McCANN

798

Part of the history of Wilkes County includes the descendants of the McCann family, who have been a part of the Roaring River area for several generations.

The Rev. Levi McCann, a son of James and Polly Richardson McCann, born in 1871, was a Baptist minister to several of the churches in the county until his death in 1953.

Joe McCann and his wife, Gail, have made their home in Wilkes, as have many of the McCann descendants. They and their two sons, Chris and William, live in Roaring River, where he operates a service station in the business area of the community. He is a son of J.B. and Evelyn Cothren McCann. His wife, Gail, is the daughter of the late Rev. John A. Johnson and Mae Wood Johnson, also of that area.

— Gail J. McCann

McCARTER FAMILY

799

According to Iredell County census in 1850, Thomas McCarter, age 34, was born about 1816 in Virginia and was married to Annie Eliza Cummings, age 26. She was born about 1824 in North Carolina. The 1860 census lists this family living in Wilkes County. The old family was very near the Wilkes-Iredell county line and could account for the difference in the census listings.

On June 26, 1880 Thomas and Eliza McCarter and members of their family — Emma, William, Rebecca, and Naoma A. — were among the charter members of the Mt. Pisgah Baptist Church. Many of their descendants have remained faithful members serving the church in many offices.

Although there are many descendants of Thomas and Eliza living in Wilkes, several heard the call "Go West" and now there are more with the McCarter family name living in Kansas and Missouri area of our country. Thomas and Eliza had ten children as follows:

Jacob was born about 1844 in N.C. He married Nancy A. and lived in the Summers Township of Wilkes. They had five children: Georgia, Charles, Audy E.E., Minnie, and Thomas Walter before the family moved to Kansas. Thomas Walter (1878-1885) is buried at Lewis Baptist Church in Wilkes County.

John was born January, 1843, and married Almeda Jane Foster, daughter of Anthony and Rachael Curry Foster. Their nine children were Rachael, John Wesley who moved to Kansas, Lillie who married John Johnson, Thomas Anthony who married Mattie Benton and moved to Kansas, Briant, Barthenia and Minnie who died young, Delia who married Silas Johnson and Florence Rebecca who moved West, married Arthur Post and lived in St. Joseph, Missouri. John and his second wife Della Honeycutt had two sons — Jesse M. and Granville McCarter.

Mary McCarter the third child of Thomas and Eliza was born about 1847.

Rebecca was born 1853 and died 1909, remained single and was buried in the Mt. Pisgah Church cemetery.

Thomas Wesley McCarter was born May 30, 1855 and died March 14, 1933. Wesley and Dicie Clembine had five children: Florence M. Byrd, Ella M. Higgins, William Lee, Rosco C., Ezetta M. Ellis, and Charlie McCarter. Several members of this family are buried in the Liberty Grove Baptist Church Cemetery, East of North Wilkesboro.

John McCarter.

Rachel E. was born about 1856 and died June 12, 1924. She married James Souther.

William Henry "Uncle Billy" McCarter was born January 6, 1858 and died August 23, 1943. He was married on February 28, 1886 to Amilia Glass. Their children were: Naoma M. Davis (1887-1923), Eva M. Templeton, E. Hobert (1896-1970), William Ernest (1899-1962), Lester Carl (1903-1962) who married Eva Sloan. Carl and Eva are the parents of Dr. George Sloan McCarter.

Emma Nancy (1861-1938) remained single.

James Pascal McCarter (1863-1942) married Dicy E. Goforth. Their children are: Ruth E. who died an infant, May, Edgar T. (1904-1905), Lacy, and Edith McCarter. James and his second wife had a daughter Blanche, who married Thomas Hendren.

Eliza Jane McCarter (1868-1928) remained single.

Sources: Census of Iredell and Wilkes Co. family Bibles; Church records; family memories and tombstones.

— Christine Eller Walker

BARBARA FORSYTH MacDONALD

800

Barbara Forsyth was born 1845 in Lossiemouth, Scotland, to George and Jane Reid Forsyth. She was the second wife of James MacDonald who went from Cawdor, Scotland to Chicago, where he was in business. He later lived in Highland Park, Ill. His first wife, Ellen Reid was Barbara's aunt.

Barbara's niece, Nellie Ogilvie (Mrs. Edward Hamilton Squire), came from Dundee when a small child to live with her. Jane Phillips Read (Mrs. James) Barbara's grandmother born 1788 died 1881, came to Lake Forest Ill. in 1859 from Duffus, Scot. She lived with her son, Simon, a wholesale grocer.

After the death of James, Barbara and Nellie made several visits to Oakwoods in 1909 and 1910 and built the large white one story house near the Baptist Church at Oakwoods near her Ogilvie relatives to which they moved. At present, Mrs. Robert S. Ogilvie lives in this house.

Barbara died at Oakwoods, Aug. 1916 and was buried with her husband in Highland Park, Ill.

Sources: Family records.

— Jeanie Forsyth Ogilvie

WILLIAM HENRY McELWEE, JR. and FAMILY

801

William Henry McElwee, Jr. was born October 13, 1907 in Statesville, North Carolina to William Henry and Elizabeth Cranor (Bess) McElwee. He was the oldest of three children. The two younger children were Sarah Cranor and Elizabeth Frances McElwee. He attended the Statesville city schools and McCallie Military Institute in Chattanooga, Tennessee, graduating from Statesville High School in 1925.

There were strong family ties in the McEl-wee family, both paternal and maternal. The family home, on Water Street in Statesville, was a part of a compound of the homes of aunts, uncles, cousins and grandparents. Well worn sidewalks connected each home with the others. All families were expected to be present at the grandparents' home for Sunday dinner each week. This was the McElwee tradition. Bill's mother was reared in Wilkes County and these family ties to Wilkes were held dear all her life. She brought each of her three children to Wilkes County to be baptized by the Reverend Charles W. Robinson, beloved minister of the Wilkesboro Presbyterian Church, where she had been a former member.

Bill graduated from Davidson College with a degree in Political Science and came to Wilkes County where he taught in the Millers Creek school for one year, then went to the Ferguson community as principal of the school there. He has valued memories of his life in that fine community of Wilkes County.

Having determined earlier that he would study law, he left the teaching profession and attended Wake Forest Law School. In 1933 he opened his law office in North Wilkesboro after passing the Bar exam and earning his North Carolina law license. He practiced law in North Wilkesboro until 1942 at which time he volunteered for military duty with the United States Army in World War II. He served for eight months in an ordnance battalion in San Francisco, California but was transferred to the Judge Advocate General Department in 1943. He attended the Judge Advocate General School at the University of Michigan, Ann Arbor, Michigan and went on to graduate from the school in Advanced Foreign Claims at Cumberland University, Lebanon, Tennessee. He was then sent to the European theater of war where he served as a Major from August 1944 until November 1945. He received a commendation ribbon and the Bronze Star as a result of his work in foreign claims.

Bill returned to North Wilkesboro early in 1946 where he has practiced law until the present time. Recently he has been presented with a citation for his fifty years service to the North Carolina Bar.

In March 1943 he married Douglas Regina Plonk who is the writer of this article. I was an English teacher in the North Wilkesboro High School. I am a native of Kings Mountain, North Carolina, the second daughter in a family of four daughters and one son. My parents were John Oates and Elvira Foust Plonk. I graduated from the Woman's College of U.N.C. at Greensboro, North Carolina in 1938 and taught in the Cabarrus County school system for three years before coming to North Wilkesboro in 1941. During the war years our two oldest children and I lived in Kings Mountain with my parents.

Our five children are: (1) Douglas Marian who was born in 1944. She died in an automobile accident in 1961 at the age of seventeen years. (2) William Henry III (Billy) was born in 1945 and was married to Catherine Parks of Wilkesboro, North Carolina in 1968. Billy graduated from Wake Forest University and Wake Forest Law School. He is a partner in the law firm, McElwee, McElwee, Cannon and Warden. The children of Billy and Cathy are William Henry IV, born in 1971, and Mary Catherine, born in 1974. (3) Elizabeth Elvira (Bit) was born in 1947 and married Bedford Cannon of Asheboro, North Carolina in 1970, who is an attorney in Statesville, North Carolina where they live. Elizabeth graduated from the University of North Carolina at Greensboro and then earned a Master's degree in Library Science from the University of North Carolina in Chapel Hill. Their children are Ashley Elizabeth, born in 1973, and Jean McElwee, born in 1977. (4) Dorothy Plonk (Dotty) was born in 1949 and married Gary Shartzer of Miami, Florida in 1977. He is a Nuclear Engineer with Westinghouse Corporation, and they live in Columbia, South Carolina. Dotty graduated from Greensboro College and went on to earn her Master's degree in counseling and guidance from Appalachian University. Presently she is attending the University of South Carolina as a student in the Nurse's Training Program. Their children are Douglas Truman, born in 1978, and Samuel Bryan, born in 1981. (5) John Plonk was born in 1954. He is unmarried. He graduated from Lenoir Rhyne College and then went to Wake Forest University Law School where he learned his Juris Doctor degree. He is a practicing attorney in the office of McElwee, McElwee, Cannon and Warden.

We have been members of the North Wilkesboro Presbyterian Church since March 1946 where we have served on the Diaconate and Sessional Boards and Bill is a church trustee.

Bill has been general counsel for Lowe's Hardward since its beginning in 1946 and then for Lowe's Companies, Inc. and a member of the Board of Directors of the corporation since 1961. He is a former County Attorney and former President of the Wilkes County Bar. He has served on the Wilkes County School Board, is a fifty year member of the Masonic Order, former trustee of Wilkes General Hospital, and former President of Kiwanis Club. He is a trustee of Davis Hospital in Statesville and is a member of the Board of Directors of North Carolina National Bank. He has been Vice President and President of the North Carolina State Bar, a member of the North Carolina Board of Law Examiners for twelve years, a member of the North Carolina Bar Association. He is a Fellow in the American College of Trial Lawyers, a member of the Board of Legal Advisers of the Southeastern Legal Foundation. He is a former member of the North Carolina Board of Correction and is now Chairman of the Governor's Highway Safety Commission and a member of the Governor's Task Force on Drunken Drivers. He is a member of the Executive Committee of Wake Forest Law School Alumni Association. He was a delegate to the Democratic National Convention in 1940 and also in 1972.

Sources: Family records, personal knowledge and memories.

— Douglas P. McElwee

JOHN ELAM McEWEN

802

John Elam McEwen was born October 28, 1842, in Iredell County, the son of Rachel Phoebe and Ebenezer Erskin McEwen. The McEwens had come to the U.S. in the early 1800's from Scotland. John Elam's maternal grandparents were Polly Stevenson and Major John Morrison; his paternal grandparents were Elizabeth Murdock and William McEwen.

While Mr. McEwen was still living in Iredell County and not quite 20 years old, he volunteered his services to the Confederate Army in March, 1862, and was made a member of the Second N.C. Cavalry. He was assigned to the outfit of the great Virginia cavalier, General J.E.B. Stewart — "That Great Cavalry Outfit That was the Eyes and Ears of General Lee" Stewart's men were the pick of the South for their horsemanship and courage. By October, his regiment was in Virginia, under the command of General J.B. Gordon of Wilkes County. These regiments fought with Lee at Gettysburg and other famous battles. McEwen's regiment was in northern Virginia when Lee surrendered. In his journal (which he wrote in 1927 at the age of 85) McEwen states that he made his way home after the war on his faithful horse, Calhoun, as best he could.

In August of 1866, Mr. McEwen married Sallie S. Kimball. In December of that same year, he and his new bride moved to Wilkes County and settled along the Yadkin River about 4 miles west of Wilkesboro.

In 1885, Mr. McEwen was appointed U.S. Gauger and Deputy Collector of Internal Revenue, and in that year with 303 bonded fruit distillers in Wilkes County, this position brought him in contact with a large proportion of the County's population. He remained in charge until November 1886, when he was elected to the office of Sheriff of Wilkes County. When he was nominated on the democratic ticket for sheriff, Republicans and Democrats alike supported him, and he won over his republican opponent despite the fact that the county went, as usual, overwhelmingly Republican.

Quoting from a newspaper article, "There has been only one democratic sheriff in Wilkes County since McEwen, whose term was served more than 40 years ago. His service as Sheriff is remembered for another reason; however, for in 1887 James Byers was condemned to hang in Wilkes County for murder, and the Sheriff, by his oath, was executioner. Byers was the last man to pay the death penalty in Wilkes.

It was the sheriff's business to guard the prisoner in the Statesville jail, to tear him from the arms of his wife and family, and bring him to Wilkesboro for execution. McEwen took Byers to a pond to be baptized at his own request. 'It was my sworn duty. Friends said I couldn't do it. I knew I would do it,' said McEwen."

The hanging took place. 'If the law retained some of the grimness that sent Byers to the scaffold, there would be more respect for it today,' said McEwen."

After his term as Sheriff, McEwen was reappointed Deputy Collector of Internal Revenue in 1889. He held this position until 1893. The remaining years of his life were spent serving the community in various capacities until his death on March 10, 1931. He is buried in the St. Paul's Episcopal Church Cemetery in Wilkesboro.

Mr. McEwen was married three times. In 1866, he married Sallie S. Kimball. From this union were born three children: Arthur M., William W. (Bud), and Mollie L.

In 1875, he was married to Nannie C. Bledsoe. To this couple were born five children: Sarah C. (Kate), Jesse E., Minnie S., Johnnie L., and Maude S.

In 1901, he was married to Bettie Reeves. They were blessed with one child, Rachel.

Sources: The 1900 Wilkes County Census, Family Bible, 1888 and 1928 newspaper articles, grave markers, John Elam McEwen's Biographical Journal.

— June Bishop Gambill
Jean Bishop Bullis,
Bill Bishop Griffin
and Morguenya Roope McNeil

McGEE FAMILY

803

McGee is of Celtic origin and originally meant "Son of Gee or Ge". The name is found on ancient British and early American records in various forms of which the most common form of spelling is MaGee or McGee.

Families of this name were first found in Scotland, then later in Ireland and England. The earliest recorded name in Scotland was Michael McGee who was a wealthy land-owner in the County of Gallaway as early as the year 1339.

There were many lines of McGees in the British Isles. They were owners of large tracts of land and were aristocrats who held high positions in their country. They were also among the first settlers to come to America. According to records, our particular line of McGees came from Ireland on the Mayflower in the year 1620. Three brothers came at this time. They were George, Ralph (Raff), and Hensley and as far as known we are descendants of Ralph, who supposedly was a minister, and the son of John Calvin McGee of Ireland. Therefore John Calvin McGee is the first of our ancestors of which we have record.

The majority of McGees in our state are Baptist and are known for their loyalty to their church. McGees have spread all over the United States and have contributed both intellectually and materially to the advancement of American Civilization. They have always been known as a sturdy and reserved race, possessed of literary ability, intellectual capacity, and courage. They are known for their musical talents as well as their wit and humor, not to mention the fact that they have been known for their Irish temper.

My mother Margaret McGee Church was born on December 16, 1921 to Claude Watson and Octavia Fairchilds McGee, who also had another daughter Evelyn.

My grandfather, Claude, was born March 13, 1897 to Jesse Franklin McGee and Mary Alice Watson McGee in Wilkes County. I remember my grandfather as being a happy-go-lucky man, who, with his typical McGee red hair, loved to tell jokes. He also enjoyed fishing with his buddies and I remember hearing him from time to time share his latest recipe for fish "bait", such as a plug of chewing tobacco. "Pappy," as he was lovingly known, was a jack-of-all-trades. He was a good carpenter and barber as well as a school teacher.

There were five other brothers and sisters in Pappy's family. His younger brother Albert became a farmer and helped with the family corn mill. He was a World War I veteran and

The McGee Family Front: L. to R: Claude; Jesse Franklin; Albert; Matilda; Esther. Back: L to R: Bertha; Lula; Nora.

was choir director for 35 to 40 years at Mt. Pleasant Church before his death.

My Great Aunt Esther is the only one still living and she resides in Windsor, N.C. where she moved with her husband, the late Dr. J.B. Nicholls, early in their marriage.

I have fond memories of my Great Aunt Lula and her husband Dr. W.R. Triplett who lived in a large country home in Purlear. She served as an assistant to his family practice in his office next to their house. The many medicine bottles and instruments that lined the walls truly amazed me.

Another sister, Nora, was a very dear person. She became a widow at a very early age and was left to support two daughters. She was a talented seamstress and earned money for her family by making "knotted" bedspreads that sold in several states.

The oldest sister, Bertha, died at the early age of eighteen of pneumonia.

My grandfather's grandfather, F.M. McGee enlisted in Wilkes County on October 1, 1862 to join the Confederate States Army with the Company I, 32nd Regiment, North Carolina Troops and died on July 10, 1863 of wounds received at Gettysburg, Pa. Our family is so fortunate to have the letters that he wrote to his wife and children during this time. They are so touching and so descriptive of the sadness and horror of war.

Sources: family Bibles, family tradition and information received from the Confederate Service Record of Franklin M. McGee.

— Nancy Church Canter

THE FAMILY OF GERALD and ESTELLE CHURCH McGEE
804

Gerald McGee married Estelle Church in 1928. Gerald worked as a mechanic at the Wilkes Hosiery Mill for twenty-eight years, working until the plant closed in North Wilkesboro in the 1950s.

Estelle Church McGee was the first daughter born to Zolley Coffer and Rececca Eller Church of Ready Branch, N.C. Estelle graduated from Mountain View Institute, Hays, N.C., and attended North Carolina College for Women (now UNC-G) in Greensboro, N.C. Estelle taught school for ten years (1927-1937) in Wilkes County; teaching at Ferguson, New Hope, Maple Springs and Mount Pleasant.

Gerald and Estelle purchased the former L.L. Church and Dr. A.J. Eller country store in 1945. They operated the store for approximately thirteen years, closing it in 1958. They still own the store building which is a community landmark. Gerald is a retired farmer at the present time and he and Estelle both live near the homeplace at Route 1, Ferguson, N.C. Gerald and Estelle have three sons: Edwin Harold, David Franklin and Clyde Eugene. All live at Route 1, Ferguson, N.C.

Edwin H. McGee was born December 2, 1929. He attended Mount Pleasant Elementary and High School. He was the N.C. State 4-H Club forestry winner in 1947 and 1948. He graduated from North Carolina State University in 1953 with a B.S. degree in Forestry. He served in the United States Army in Korea and was discharged in 1956.

Edwin started working as a forester with the North Carolina Forest Service in 1956 and was stationed in Asheboro until 1960. At this time he was transferred to Wilkes County as County Forester. He has held the job as County Forester in Wilkes from 1960 to the present date.

Edwin married Ivo Dean Eller, daughter of Mr. and Mrs. Taft Eller of Purlear, August 10, 1952. They have three children: Karen Edwina, November 26, 1956; Nathan Dean, September 16, 1958; and Sherwin Harold, April 25, 1962. Edwin and his family are members of Trinity Fellowship Church.

Karen married Donald McNeil, son of Mr. and Mrs. Hoke McNeil, Route 1, Wilkesboro, February 20, 1977. Donald is a surveyor and a forestry graduate of N.C. State University. They have two children: Joshua, November 20, 1979 and Jennifer, March 5, 1982. Nathan is a senior at N.C. State majoring in Aerospace Engineering. Sherwin finished Wilkes Community College, is a professional saxophonist, and is now working at Holly Farms Industries in Wilkesboro, N.C.

David Franklin McGee, Gerald and Estelle's second son, was born January 24, 1938. He finished Mount Pleasant High School, attended Mars Hill College and N.C. State University. He married Martha Hardin, daughter of Blain and Ruth Hardin of West Jefferson, on August 10, 1966. They have two sons: Albert, September 5, 1969 and Marty, June 6, 1971, who are both attending Mount Pleasant Elementary School. Martha was a teacher's aide for several years, and is now babysitting for neighbors. David is employed as a mechanic at Holly Farms in Wilkesboro, N.C. They are all members of Trinity Fellowship Church.

Clyde Eugene McGee, Gerald and Estelle's youngest son, was born on Pearl Harbor Day, December 7, 1941. He attended Mount Pleasant Elementary School, and West Wilkes High School. He married Mary Lou Church, daughter of Lattie and Ester Church, on June 4, 1965. They have a daughter, Renee, March 1, 1966, who is now attending West Wilkes High School. Clyde, Mary Lou and Renee are members of Mount Pleasant Baptist Church. Clyde is a group leader at Holly Farms Foods. Mary Lou also works at Holly Farms in Wilkesboro, N.C.

Sources: Family memories and personal knowledge.

— Edwin H. McGee

WILLIAM McGILL
805

Early census records indicate that William McGill was born about 1755. Very little information is known about his private life; however, the records of the county and state reveal he led the typical and poignant life of an early settler in the county, and his story deserves to be told.

He had already built himself a cabin with improvements when the first land entry was made in his name, October 1778. Other land entries were listed for him in 1778 and 1779, in the areas of Moravian and Warrior Creeks, off the Yadkin River. The Benjamin Elledge family was frequently mentioned as adjoining his land. A land grant of 200 acres "on Branch of Warrior Creek" was recorded 23 October 1782. He lost some property in court action when sued by Reuben White and James Potts. He acquired some property, or proceeds from the sale of, when he brought suit against John Elledge. He sold some acreage, and he bought some acreage, but never had title to much property at a time.

Court minutes of the county reveal the following: 1779, "William McGill be allowed 10 pounds for wintering four head of cattle." At the "December Term of the County Court of Pleas and Quarter Sessions, 1779, the Jurors for the State of North Carolina upon their Oath present that William McGill late of the County of Wilkes aforesaid, labourer, being a person of evil Mind and Disposition and of wicked Life and Conversation, on the tenth Day of October in the Year of Our Lord one thousand seven hundred and seventy nine, with Force and Arms in the County aforesaid, did on the tenth Day of October (which day being the Lord's Day commonly called Sunday) play a Game commonly called Hufslecap to the common Nusance of the good people of this State to the great Displeasure of Almighty God, to the evil Example of all Persons in like Case offending and against the Peace and Dignity of the State."

William McGill sued Philip Jacob Christy. He served as a member of a jury during trials in 1780, 1782, and 1787. Reuben White sued him in 1788. At the "July Term, 1787, the State attached John Moore, William McGill, and William Crai? to answer the State of a Plea on a Presentment for Habitual Profane Swearing etc. at a Court fourth Monday of April 1787." A previous order dated 1778 was "resinded (requiring the) viewing (of) the road up river just above widow Pattersons across into 'Birk' (Burke) road," which order listed William McGill and others. (This order probably has to do with marking off, clearing, or maintaining the road).

In February 1806, William McGill took into his home an orphan, Elizabeth Saunders, about 6 years of age, apprenticed "to learn the occupation of a Spinster" and "servant until the age of 18," by court order signed by "William Lenoir, Esquire, Chairman of the County Court." On 30 October 1810, the Constable was "ordered to proceed immediately to William McGill's and bring orphan child bound to said McGill by name of Sanders to appear in court." Probably, this action was taken because 15 days earlier William McGill sold all his land, 279 acres in two tracts, on the "waters of Warrior Creek" to James Broyhill. The surname of McGill then disappears from the county.

The census records reveal that William McGill had a large family, about 5 boys and 4 girls. Marey McGill married Amos Landtrip 13 March 1802. Nancy McGill married Joseph Elledge 3 December 1799. Two sons were in the military service of the country, one of whom died after being taken prisoner.

William McGill was reported to be a Wilkes County revolutionary war soldier by William

Lenoir, as found in the William Lenoir Papers at the University of North Carolina. One William McGill "furnished 1 pr. breeches" to the Militia, voucher No. 985, specie 1:10:0 as allowed by auditors of Salisbury District in January 1782, State Archives, N.C. Also recorded in the State Archives is Voucher No. 1371, listing William McGill as receiving 7:2:0 "for services performd. against the Chicamaga Indians."

As a pioneer in the county, the life of William McGill was probably typical. The land was his livelihood. He was involved in matters concerning others in the county; witnessing wills and deeds (he signed with his mark); serving on juries; helping maintain roads; but, occasionally, he was in trouble with the law. He and his family gave to the country's military efforts whenever possible in whatever way they could. He spent the entire prime of his life in Wilkes County, N.C. Further research is needed to ascertain where he lived out the remainder of his life.

Sources: Census records, Wilkes County records, N.C. Archives records.

— Idalyn McGill Stinson

McGLAMERY

806

The name McGlamery originated in Ulster, Northern Ireland and was very rare there. It is still fairly rare according to research based on census reports in 1972. It was found that there were only 300 families that showed the head of household as McGlamery.

According to earliest family records, three brothers came to America from Ireland. Two came to Wilkes County; it is not known where the third one went. The name does show up in Virginia and Tennessee. The name Captain John McGlamery and elsewhere John E. McGlamery is found in the "Historical Register of Virginia in the Revolution" by John H. Gauthy.

It is believed that the McGlamery families in Wilkes descend from the two above mentioned brothers, one of whom was named George. His descendants include Martin, Martha, Jesse, Andrew and Jacob. Martin's children were: Rebecca born Nov. 2, 1851; George H. born July 31, 1853; Jacob C. born July 6, 1855; Sallie C. born June 4, 1857; Mary E. born Sept. 9, 1859; John M. born Feb. 23, 1862; Jesse Ishom born June 18, 1865. Martin died Nov. 11, 1910. He was 89 years old. (This information was copied from a paper in a Bible in the Ishom McGlamery home, where his daughters Katrina and Ella J. now live in the Purlear community.) Two other daughters, Nettie Y. and Mary V. are deceased. None of the daughters ever married.

The Andrew McGlamery line is as follows. No birth or marriage certificates have ever been located. Andrew is believed to have been a brother to Martin's father; Andrew's son, David, married Susanna Eller Oct. 30, 1823. Their children were: Frank, James married America Eller, John married Joan Byers, Morrison married Delphia Eller, Mary married Harrison Church, Nancy married Walter Roberson, Carolina married Enoch Cooper, Murphy

Augustus married Laura Ann McNeill. The children of Murphy and Laura Ann were Allen born Dec. 1876, Richard E. born 1879, Andrew born 1882, Charlie N. born 1884, Grover Clayton born Oct. 27, 1886, Finley Eugene born Feb. 6, 1889, Nancy Mattie born Aug. 21, 1891, William Vance born 1894, Talmadge born 1896; of these children four died in infancy and two in early adulthood and were never married.

The three remaining sons were Charlie who married Lola Whittington. He died during the 1918 flu epidemic. Their children were (1) George married Ruby Landreth and moved to Alabama. They had three sons, Charles, Clinton, and Gerald. George died January 1975. Charles and Gerald live in Alabama and Clinton lives in Texas. (2) Carrie Mae married Dewey Myers, (3) Ruby married Newland Campbell and they live in Salisbury, N.C. (4) Glenn married Rachael Foster and had two children, Carol and Bill.

The other two sons of Murphy and Laura Ann were Clayton and Eugene both of whom became well known citizens of the Millers Creek and surrounding communities. Eugene married Lizzie Taylor and had three children, Ella Mae married Clyde Hayes, Minnie Fay married Gwyn Nichols, and Vernon died in infancy. Eugene was a skilled road construction worker and travelled throughout the southeastern states with the Nello Teer Construction Company. He married second Mrs. Blanche Lovette, widow of Eugene Lovette. There were no children. Eugene died Feb. 6, 1953 on his 64th birthday.

Clayton McGlamery married Virginia Rash Oct. 16, 1910. Their children: (1) William Howard born Nov. 5, 1911 died Feb. 17, 1929. (2) Annie L. born Feb. 13, 1917 married Sidney Carter — no issue. (3) Mary Louise born Sept. 9, 1920 married Wade H. Houck and they have one daughter, Mary Wade who married Larry Sluder. Mary Wade and Larry have two children, Amanda and Daniel. (4) Grover C., Jr. born Dec. 3, 1922 married Jeanette Raper. They live in Kansas City, Mo. and have two adopted daughters, Susan and Lisa.

Clayton McGlamery early in adult life developed many skills in various occupations including carpenter work. He was known to have made several coffins by special requests from neighbors. He was a talented blacksmith, a trade which is well known in the early generations of McGlamerys. His blacksmith tools are housed in a shop he built for that purpose at the home of his daughter on the old house site in the Millers Creek area. He became one of the first automobile mechanics in Wilkes County. He followed this occupation until his retirement as foreman at the Gaddy Motor Company in North Wilkesboro in 1952.

Clayton was best known for his tireless efforts and devotion to his church. Upon his father's death in 1920, he became Sunday School Superintendent at Charity Methodist Church and served in that capacity for 50 years. He also taught a class and served as church lay leader for many years. It was through his support and dedication that the church survived, and is still active today. He died Feb. 27, 1975.

Sources: Census records, the book "Historical Register of Virginia in the Revolution," family papers and memory.

— Anne McGlamery Carter

JOHN McGRADY

807

John McGrady was born April 17, 1875, and died April 25, 1962. He was a great choir leader of sacred songs.

Mr. McGrady became a public school teacher in early life. He taught in the Wilkes County for about forty years. Those who knew him in school days as a young boy noticed that he took such a great interest in singing and music. By the time he had reached the age of 17 he was widely known in the community as a good singer and with a strong will to go forward. This attracted the attention of many preachers because of the great interest he took in singing at the church.

In 1917 at a Fourth of July singing at the courthouse in Wilkesboro, he won the prize as an outstanding singer and choir leader. He was a leader in Sunday School.

Mr. McGrady is buried at Mt. Lawn Memorial Park cemetery.

— Wake Tinsley

JOHN ALFRED and EDITH STEELE McGRADY

808

John Alfred McGrady was born October 13, 1894 in Wilkes County. He was the son of Frank and Alice Tidline McGrady. He lived most of his life in Wilkes with some short periods of time spent working in the coal mines in eastern West Virginia.

John was married to Edith Victoria Steele on November 23, 1918. Edith was born October 24, 1904, in Wilkes County. She is the daughter of Andy and Laura Smith Steele. To this union were born seven children: Edna Louise, Virginia, Frances, James, Cornethe, and two unnamed children who died at birth.

Louise was born January 24, 1919 and was the only child who lived beyond six months of age. She attended Woodlawn Elementary School and Lincoln Heights High School. She married before finishing High School, Marvin Greer on November 16, 1935. Mr. Greer was from Ashe County. They had one daughter Edith Geraldine, who was born October 18, 1937. After Marvin's death Louise married Arzolia Rice. Louise, in later years, went back and finised her high school education at Wilkes Community College. She is now finishing her associate degree at Wilkes. She is a very ambitious lady, with lots of courage to get her college education after all these years. Louise has 4 grandchildren and two great-grand children.

Louise's daughter, Geraldine, attended Wilkes County Schools and boarding school in Cheney and Downing Town, Pennsylvania. She was married to Benjamin Vannoy of Wilkes County. Their children are Benjamin Vannoy, Jr., born December 11, 1954; Vernette, born September 13, 1956; Alfreda, born

March 6, 1960; and Arlene, born September 25, 1962. All of the children attended North Wilkesboro City Schools. Benjamin and Vernette graduated from North Wilkes High School.

Benny graduated from Appalachian State University with a Bachelor of Arts degree in Radio and Television. He is the first member of the McGrady family to attend college. He is now employed with Channel 8 TV, of High Point, in the Sports Department. Benny is married to Frances Cocherham.

Vernette attended Wilkes Community College and is employed with Wilkes County Board of Education as a secretary to John Tugman, in the Exceptional Children's Dept. Vernette is married to Larry Levon Harris, and they have two children. Their names are Abigail Maretta, and Larry Levon, Jr.

Alfreda Virginia and Varonica Arlene finished high school in Wildflicken, Germany, June 1978 and 1979, respectively. Alfreda is married to Roderic Simpkins, and they have one daughter, Celecia Rochelle, born December 31, 1981. Alfreda and Roderic live in Fort Polk, Louisiana. Arlene will be graduating from Modeling School on June 23, 1982 at Fort Polk, LA. She has a son, Maurice, born December 27, 1979.

The McGrady family now has five generations living of which they are very proud. John McGrady would have been a very grateful man to see his offspring reach such accomplishments in the educational field. John and his wife, Edith, only went to the fifth grade in school. They learned many things from their ancestors that has stayed with them. John loved flowers and was an excellent gardener. He loved to work in someone else's garden where he always did his best. He was a member of Pleasant Hill Baptist Church which he attended until his death on April 28, 1972. He was buried in the Cemetery close to the church.

Edith, is a very good housekeeper and cook. She worked at Wilkes General Hospital for ten years in the Diet Department. She is also a member of Pleasant Hill Baptist Church, and now resides near her daughter, Louise Rice, in the Fairplains Community.

Source: Birth and Bible records and personal knowledge.

— Louise Rice

McNEIL-RASH-TAYLOR
809

Most records indicate that George McNiel was born in Glasgow, Scotland, in 1720. In 1780, he owned land on the Reddies River near Deep Ford Hill. It is not known exactly when he reached America, or the extent of his travels before settling in Wilkes County. He had married Mary Coats prior to arriving in Wilkes, and it is believed that her family lived in Virginia.

He was a Baptist minister, organizing a number of churches in western North Carolina and Virginia. He was also often moderator of various associational meetings of Baptist churches, and served as Register of Deeds of Wilkes County from 1787 until his death on 7 Jun 1805. His grave is near Parsonville.

James, the third child of Rev. George and Mary Coats McNiel, was born ca. 1763. He married Mary Shepherd, daughter of Robert and Sarah Rash Shepherd. Robert owned land on Reddies River near Deep Ford Hill as early as 24 Apr 1778, and was a neighbor of the George McNiel family.

The fourth child of James and Mary was named George. He was born 17 May 1802, and lived on Reddies River for a time. He married Susan Vannoy 21 Nov 1822. Later, they moved to the area not far from the present Charity Methodist Church. He died 21 Apr 1878.

Jesse A (Tess) McNiel was the second child of George and Susan. He was born 4 May 1825, and worked with his father to pay for the land they had bought in the Charity Church area. After the land was paid for, Tess married Susan Taylor on 6 Mar 1860. She was the daughter of John and Catherine Osborne Taylor, and the granddaughter of George and Unity Wyatt Taylor who came to Wilkes County in 1791.

Tess and Susan's children are: Cornely (m. Smith Norris from Watauga County); Robert (Bob) Johnson (m. Ida McCrary and lived on the headwaters of Maiden Cane Creek); George Franklin (b. 14 Jun 1866); John Bunker (Bunk) (b. 12 Dec 1867, m. Nornie Bumgarner and lived on the opposite side of the creek from Bob, near the present residence of Ernest A. Eller); William (Bill) Coats (b. 21 Jun 1871 m. Bettie Huey and lived in Charlotte); James (Jim) Powell (m. Florence Hayes, daughter of William J. Hayes, and lived in Washington state); Carrie (m. Toon Church, son of James Church and lived near Ronda); Annie (m. Mitch Church, son of James Church and lived on Brier Creek).

Tess died on 3 Sep 1891, and was the first person buried at Pleasant Home Baptist Church. His grave was on the oppostie side of the church from where the cemetery was later established. The grave was moved to the present cemetery.

Family recollections indicated that Tess lost his right hand during the Civil War. The loss was confirmed when the grave was moved and a complete skeleton, minus the right forearm and hand, was found.

Susan died 5 Jan 1898 and was buried beside her husband. Her grave was also moved when the new church was built.

George Franklin (Frank), son of Jesse A and Susan Taylor McNiel, married Elma Rash of 8 Mar 1891, daughter of John Clark and Mary Elizabeth McNiel Rash.

John Clark was the son of Rev. John Warren and Valisha Bullis Rash. John Warren was the son of Thomas and Frances Kilby Rash. Thomas was the grandson of William and Elizabeth Warren Rash who settled on Beaver Creek in 1779. Thomas' wife, Frances, was the daughter of William Kilby, who owned land on Maiden Cane Creek in 1778.

Frank and Elma lived on Millers Creek near the present Green Acres development. Their children are: Alda (b. 18 Jan 1892, d. 8 Dec 1965, m. Clay Shepherd. They lived at Ferguson for many years, then returned to the old Rash place at Millers Creek. They had no chil-

dren.); Bertie (b. 14 Apr 1894, d. 30 Oct 1981, m. David McLean and lived near Upton. They had several children.); Blanche (b. 5 Feb 1896, d. 7 Jan 1968, m. 1st Fred Arnold, 2nd a Haynes. They had no children.); Commodore Christa (b. 21 Jul 1898, m. Eva Green Clary); Jessie Pardue (b. 3 May 1900, m. 1st Eugenia White, 2nd Ruth. He lived at Roanoke Rapids for many years, and now lives at Norfolk, Va. They had no children.); John Milton (b. 18 Apr 1902, d. 13 Jun 1948, m. Pearl Pendergrass. They lived at Washington, D.C., and had one son, John, Jr.); Nealie Pearl (b. 17 May 1906, m. an English and lived at Charlotte. They had no children.); Daisy E. (b. 6 Apr 1908, m. Fred Coffey but were soon divorced. They had no children. She lives at Millers Creek.)

Elma died 13 Apr 1908 and is buried in the old Millers Creek Methodist Church cemetery. After her death, Frank married Launa Walsh, daughter of Calvin Walsh. They lived at Boomer. Their children are: James Wilson (b. 10 Oct 1915, m. Sadie Earp); Calvin McAdo (b. 2 Jan 1919, d. 25 Apr 1919); Ruth (b. 30 May 1920); George Franklin (Frank) died 5 Nov 1935, and is buried at Pleasant Home Baptist Church cemetery.

Commodore Christa, son of George Franklin and Elma Rash McNeil, lived at several places after his mother's death. He wound up at Roanoke Rapids, N.C. While working there, he met Eva Green Clary, daughter of George and Ella Clary. They were married 2 Jun 1924 and for the next sixteen years made their home most of the time in Brunswick County, Va. They had two sons: Commodore Clary, b. 3 May 1925, m. Keiko Yoshimura. He served in the U.S. Marine Corps, participating in the battles for Siapan, Tinian and Iwo Jima during World War II. He was twice wounded in those actions. During the Korean conflict, he was again wounded in battle. He met his wife while in Japan while recouperating from those wounds. His military decorations include the Bronze Star and the Silver Star. He and Katie have two daughters, Susan and Alice. They live in southern California, where he is a computer engineer for Burroughs Corporation.

George Franklin, b. 5 May 1934, m. Joyce Dancy, daughter of Ira Gilbert and Ella Phillips Dancy. Joyce's ancestors, both paternal and maternal, lived in Wilkes County more than two centuries ago. George Franklin retired as Captain, NCARNG, and will complete 30 years employment at Northwestern Bank in 1982. They have a son, Kevin Lee, b. 25 Nov 1964, a rising senior at West Wilkes High School, and live on Dancy Road west of Wilkesboro.

Sources: Wilkes County census records, family Bibles, family records, family memories.

— Mrs. Joyce D. McNeil

C.O. and LUELLA (TUTTLE) McNIEL
810

Challie Odell McNiel was born on Cole Creek in the Purlear community of Wilkes County the 24th of June 1894. He died 30 May 1955 in the Wilkes General Hospital of heart disease. He was a son of Thornton Sylvester and Eda Eliza-

C. O. McNiel.

Luella Tuttle McNiel.

beth (McNiel) McNiel. On the 14th March 1920, Chal married Mrs. Mary Luella (Tuttle) Chilton, who was born 18 November 1899 in Stokes County, a daughter of John Gray and Luretta (Ward) Tuttle. They were married in the parlor of the home of her parents in Rockingham County, N.C.

At the age of sixteen, Luella had married Roscoe James Chilton of Stokes County. They were living in Richmond, Virginia where he was a medical student, when the flu epidemic struck that city. Her husband died of the disease, leaving a young widow to return to the home of her parents in Rockingham County.

When the town of North Wilkesboro began to build up around the railroad in 1891, an aunt of Luella's, Mrs. E.L. Hart and her husband, came here and he established the E.L. Hart Hardward Company. Irene, one of the Hart daughters and Luella were the closest of first cousins and the young widow Chilton visited in the Hart home often. Irene, a natural born matchmaker, thought that one of the McNiel brothers would be a good catch for her young widowed cousin. One of the brothers was, but not the one Irene Hart had selected!

Chal brought Luella to North Wilkesboro where they started housekeeping in an apartment, but soon bought a house on the northwest corner of D and fourth streets, where they lived until 1936, when they moved into a white brick house they had built on the site of the "old stalls" in the middle of the same block on D Street. When Chal died in 1955, Luella continued to live alone and lived there until six weeks prior to her death on the 21st of October 1981. They are both buried in the North Wilkesboro Cemetery on Sixth Street.

Chal McNiel was Secretary-Treasurer of the North Wilkesboro Coca-Cola Bottling Company, a company founded in 1906 by his father, an active Democrat, Chairman of the Wilkes County Board of Education for many years, a Deacon and active member of the First Baptist Church, a Director of the Northwestern Bank and a Kiwanian.

Luella McNiel was a member and past president of the North Wilkesboro Womans Club, a member of the Idlewise Bridge Club, the Current Topic Club and several other social clubs. She was a Methodist when she married Chal and joined the first Methodist Church in North

Wilkesboro, but soon joined the First Baptist with Chal. Her greatest pleasure was entertaining in her home. She was an excellent cook and lived in a ten room house which was close to the school. North Wilkesboro "imported" their teachers before there were "local teachers" to be found. Many of these teachers lived and ate in the McNiel home over the years. When she no longer "kept teachers", Luella had a special group of friends and relatives who very often were invited to "eat with her". Many fond memories spin around in my head of those ten or twelve or more people sitting at her table partaking of the good food with three kinds of dessert she always prepared herself. Especially remembered is the enjoyment of the tall tales that were told by some of the guests!

I grew up in the McNiel home, for they were my sister and brother-in-law. I came to live with them in 1923 at the age of eight, a year after my mother died in Rockingham County. They had no children born to them, but were the closest people to parents that I knew. They were loving grand-parents to our two children and she was an adoring great-grandmother to our four grandchildren.

Source: Personal knowledge.

— Ruby Tuttle Absher

REVEREND GEORGE McNIEL
811

Rev. George McNiel married Mary Coats of Virginia and soon after the marriage, they moved to the Deep Ford Hill section of Reddies River where he acquired a great deal of land and buildings. Rev. McNiel was a Baptist Minister, having arrived in the U.S. from Scotland around 1750, landing in Maryland and making his way southward. After marching with the armies of Col. Ben Cleveland it was natural that he marry and settle in this valley. He later purchased a large tract of over 400 acres of land on the Lewis Fork Creek in the western part of the county where he and his family lived and died. George and Mary had nine children: John married Fanny Cleveland, niece of Col. Ben Cleveland; William married Elizabeth Shepherd from whom he had purchased the first land in Reddies River; James born 1763

and died 1834, married Mary Shepherd sister to Elizabeth, and this couple are the ancestors of the great host of McNiel's in the region of New Hope Church; Joseph born 1772 died 1855; Elizabeth married Robert Bingham of Watauga County; Mary (Polly) married Henry Miller in 1803; Benjamin married in August 1805; Thomas born 1782 and died 1865.

It was interesting to read the will of James McNiel, husband of Mary, and the direct ancestors of my family. This couple lived on the Reddies River and lastly in Ashe County, on the North Fork of the New River. In his will he left to his daughter Fannie, wife of Simeon Eller, the sum of $325.00 (as he had to the several older children). Some of the younger children received a good saddle and bridle, or a cow and a calf worth $10, or a horse worth $75, a tract of land . . . each child received items totaling $325.00, so that everything would be equal.

There were nine children born to James and Mary: Larkin; John, born January 30, 1796, and died January 21, 1877 — was married August 22, 1820, to Rachel Eller; Fanny, born January 12, 1799, died January 21, 1877, and married Simeon Eller (appearing later on the maternal side of our family); George, born 1803, married November 21, 1822 to Susan Vannoy; William S. (Squire Billy), born 1805, married Polly Wilcoxen on December 23, 1833; Rebecca, born 1806, married in 1833 to Rev. John H. Vannoy; Oliver, born 1808 and married on August 4, 1828, to Delilah Eller; Nancy married Edward J. Dancy; Eli, born 1812, married Fanny Eller on February 8, 1839.

John, the second son, married Rachel Eller, and they lived on Cole's Creek at the foot of the Rendevous Mountain as did several of their children. The children, all born in Wilkes County, were: William (Big Bill or Billy), born May 15, 1821, and died April 18, 1865, married on March 10, 1843 to Sarah Kilby who was born in Wilkes in 1825; Clarinda, born 1822; Alfred, born January 19, 1823, married on November 6, 1844, to Frances Vannoy and died March 23, 1891; Susannah, born April 15, 1825, married James H. (Jimmie Dee McNeil) on February 4, 1845; Peter born August 26, 1827 died February 14, 1909, married Mary Ann Phillips; George Franklin, born January 13, 1830, died September 21, 1880, and married Rebecca McNeil; Mary born May 17, 1832, and died September 26, 1901, married David Eller on February 1, 1854; Nancy Caroline, (Aunt Nan) born October 8, 1834, died July 13, 1913, unmarried and buried at New Hope Baptist Churchyard; Frances Emaline, (Aunt Em) born May 13, 1838, and died November 8, 1912, was unmarried and buried in New Hope Churchyard; Jesse, born January 1841, married Nancy McNeil; Laura Ann born November 2, 1845, died February 12, 1926, married John Canter (this is Annie Laura Canter Wilson's mother and father).

Sources: Hook, *George Michael Eller, His Family in America* Hayes, *Genalogy of the McNeil Clan* Personal knowledge

— Pat McNeil Day

J.C. and BESSIE FAIRCHILD McNEIL
812

J.C. McNeil, better known as "Uncle Jimmy", was the 12th child born to James Oliver and Sarah Ann Stout McNeil on September 16, 1889. James Cary McNeil and Bessie Fairchild were married October 8, 1911.

A long productive and enjoyable life has been his, being an active father in caring for his family. He visited and shared with those less fortunate through his active 89 years, driving his own car up to that age. Now, nearing 93, he is somewhat of an invalid, but still nurtures an alert mind.

Mother contributed much to the life of Mt. Pleasant community, boarding teachers for several years. During this time teachers were compelled to board due to transportation difficulties. Twenty dollars per month was her fee, setting a bountiful lazy-susan table for both breakfast and dinner. She was a great artist in housekeeping, cooking, growing flowers and vegetables, and sewing, making most of her own patterns from pictures. She also did a good job keeping all of us busy on the farm, as daddy went about his tasks away from home.

J.C. McNeil taught school in several early Wilkes schools: Mt. Pleasant, Champion, Dix Hollar, Congo and Maple Springs. He received his teaching "Life Time Certificate" by taking a written test furnished by the State of North Carolina and given by Wilkes Superintendent, C.C. Wright. He attended a summer session at Asheville Normal School, took a six week course in Wilkesboro and a short term at A.S.T.C. in Boone.

In teaching, emphasis was placed on learning the alphabet, spelling with the Blue Back Speller, and lessons held at the "recitation bench" at the front of the room. Discipline was no problem, because parents and children were cooperative.

J.C. McNeil supplemented the family income by selling American Tobacco Products. This required traveling and he often had to stay with families over night, one in which were twin girls named Reba Dew and Rena Ruth. Mother had been told she would have twins, for she was expecting her fourth child. Daddy remembered the names and when twin girls were born, they were given these names.

He resigned his teaching and tobacco sales to become a shipping clerk at the Wilkes Tannery. He worked there until the 1940 flood destroyed the Tannery.

During the years mother and daddy were faithful to the church and community with the entire family participating in activities. Daddy's priorities were the church, his family, the Masonic Lodge, the people of the community and his work.

He held all offices in the Mt. Pleasant Lodge, being Master of the Lodge at least six years. He received both the 50 and 60 year membership emblems, life membership in the York Rite in October 1970 and was recognized with an engraved gold plaque for services in Masonary and the Easter Star in 1974. He holds honorary membership in the Ashler Lodge of Deep Gap and the Wilkesboro and North Wilkesboro

J.C. and Bessie Fairchild McNeil.

Lodges in Wilkes County.

Four girls and two boys were born to J.C. and Bessie McNeil. All six either attended college or went into their chosen profession. The children are: Marie Hendrix of Murphy; Opal McLain of Winston-Salem; Hoke and Hoyle, of Wilkesboro; Reba Smith of Asheboro and Rena Spicer of Millers Creek. There are 12 grandchildren, and 21 great-grandchildren. All of mother's and daddy's children were born at home.

Mother and daddy celebrated their golden wedding anniversary October 8, 1961, with a reception given by their children at the Mt. Pleasant Lodge reception room. Mother died November 28, 1970. Daddy now lives at the home place with Hoyle, the youngest son, his wife, Alda and their two sons. To "Uncle Jimmy" home is the place to be.

The children grew up knowing how to do everything there was to do, educated by school and experience, and are now finding joy in being able to do it. They owe all the praise to their daddy, "Uncle Jimmy" and Mother, "Aunt Bessie". They had a rich christian family life with parents who provided an outstanding example of honesty, dignity, and dedication, with which to guide their own lives.

Sources: Personal knowledge.

— Rena McNeil Spicer

RICHARD TIPTON McNEIL, SR.
813

My Father, Richard Tipton, "Tip" McNeil, was born in the Purlear Community of Wilkes County on September 16, 1897. His Scottish roots go back a long way. The emigrant ancestor of the McNiel clan in Wilkes was Rev. George McNiel who was born in Glasgow, Scotland.

Mother and Daddy met at the Roaring River Baptist Church at a B.Y.P.U. party. In the crowd that Sunday evening were Dr. Paul Caudill of Traphill and W.K. Sturdivant, Sr.

Their courting was done at the socials of 1924 and 1925 at the church in North Wilkesboro and with both families, and they married in 1925 at the First Baptist Parsonage in North Wilkesboro. Charlie Day and Annie Catherine Moore Carrington, as young children will do, stood out front that day in May and watched Mama and Daddy leave in his Buick Roadster, with cans tied to the bumpers!

Their children were: Patsy Ruth, born June 24, 1927, married October 9, 1948 at First Baptist Church in North Wilkesboro Bobby Frank Day, son of Charles Gray and DeEtte Hampton Day. She graduated from Meredith College in Raleigh in 1948.

Three children were born to Pat and Bob: (1) Laura Kathryn, named for her maternal great-grandmother, born February 2, 1950, married May 29, 1972 James Edward Robinson of Winston-Salem, son of Bascom and Alice Robinson. Laura graduated from A.S.U. in 1972 with Special Ed. degree. Laura and James Edward have: David Hamilton, born October 29, 1976, and Kathryn Gray born Au-

R.J. McNeil, Sr. with 1925 Buick Roadster.

R.J. McNeil, Sr. and Jr. 1946.

gust 24, 1978 both in Forsyth County. (2) Richard Franklin, born October 10, 1951, married Sandra Gail Oakley September 6, 1974, daughter of Frank and Pauline Oakley. Frank attended A.S.U. and is now associated with the North Wilkesboro Coca-Cola Bottling Company as the fourth generation of McNeil's in the family business. Their children are Richard McNeil (Neil) born September 22, 1975 and Ellen Rebecca, born October 1977, both in Wilkes County. (3) William Daniel, born August 20, 1958, is single, graduated from Garner-Webb College December 1981 with a degree in Business and Marketing.

Richard Tipton McNeil, Jr. "Dick" was born October 10, 1930, married Morguenya "Butch" Roope July 1, 1956. He graduated from Fork Union Military Academy, Fork Union, Virginia and Roanoke Business College. Their daughter, Jacqueline Elizabeth, born February 19, 1962 is a rising junior at N.C. State University. Dick is Secretary-Treasurer of the North Wilkesboro CocaCoal Bottling Company, the third generation active in the family business.

Daddy followed his father and brother in the Coca-Cola business after a stint at the Newport News Shipbuilding Yard during World War I. I have heard that the brothers worked in all areas of the plant business; all week they helped with the bottling and also driving the one pickup over to Ashe County to deliver drinks (a two day trip over the Blue Ridge Mountains). The three brothers Alonzo, Chal, and Tip continued to operate the company and at the death of Alonzo in 1948, Tip became president of the company. His untimely death occurred in June 1955. Daddy and Uncle Chal (C.O.) died, as had their father and brother and sister, within a two-week period, both of heart problems.

Daddy was a member of the First Baptist Church in North Wilkesboro, a former deacon, and a Kiwanian. He served the Town of North Wilkesboro as its Mayor for six terms from 1934 to 1947 and for two terms beginning in 1949 until 1953 and was never defeated in any town election. He was on the original committee to plan for and initiate the building of the Kerr Scott Reservoir.

Daddy was always a "home-body." His hobby was being at home and being a real companion. He was a good son, I'm told, too. When he got paid at the end of his week's work, before he was married and still living with his mother and sister, he always bought his mother snuff which she used and liked! He

was also the one who got up early on winter mornings and built the fire in the stove so the house would be warm for the others when they got up. Very thoughtful he was in all things. Daddy was a real tease too; all the brothers were. He used to drive a 1935 2-door Chevrolet and he would take Dick and me to ride, putting one of us in the back seat, jumping the car in low gear and telling us they used to punish the prisoners by jerking them that way! Daddy's names for Dick and me were "George" and "Polly" and we were always called that as children.

He loved to take us "to ride" on Sunday afternoons. One of the many excursions I remember was going to the old airport (now West Park Shopping Center) and there would be two or three airplane to give rides to paying customers. He liked to do that; maybe the seeds for Dick's love of flying were planted then!

Mama and Daddy's marriage in the early depression years meant hard work for all and a great dependence on their own abilities. We had much time at home together; listening to the radio "little Jimmie" singing, H.V. Kaltenborn and Gabriel Heater for news, Amos and Andy; how drab it seems today!

Tip McNeil led a good and simple life, but what a great heritage he left for his family.

Sources: Hayes, *Genealogy of the McNiel Clan;* Hood, *George Michael Eller, Etc.* Personal knowledge.

— Pat Day McNeil Day

WILLIAM H. McNIEL
814

My Great-grandfather, "Billy" William H. McNiel born 1821, died 1865 and Sarah Kilby married in 1843 and always lived in Wilkes County near New Hope Church.

Billy was a member of the Home Guard that traveled on horseback to protect homes, farms and families during and after the Civil War.

He was considered a "well-off" man at that time, known to be a very good carpenter and wealthy in land as well as in his avocation. In his spare time he made furniture, a few pieces of which his granddaughter and my aunt, Mamie McNeil Hartley, have. There is a beautiful solid oak cupboard, chest of drawers, table and a chair made by William H. There would have been more items, but on one occasion the "bushwackers" broke in on this home when the men in the Home Guard were off on tour of duty and took whatever they could; broke up furniture and destroyed crops.

Billy and Sarah had the following children, all born in Wilkes County: Mary born 1844, died young; Nancy Caroline (Aunt Cap) born March 5, 1846 died Feb 3, 1926, married James Addison Vannoy; John H. born 1848, married Sophrone Eller; Benjamin F. born October 3, 1850, died Aug 8, 1889, married Frances Matilda Bishop; Pinkney Marshall (Uncle Marsh) born Feb 14, 1852, died Nov 17, 1935, married Julia Ann Vannoy (Aunt Julie); Rachel Camilla (Aunt Miller) born Nov 28, 1855, died Nov 28, 1924, married James Rufus McNiel (Bud); Richard Ellison born 1856; Thomas A. McNiel called Sam, born

1858, died 1920, married Dec 18, 1886 to Jane Riggs; Thornton Sylvester, born Dec 25, 1860, died Jan 13, 1919 in North Wilkesboro, married Eda Elizabeth McNeil, May 7, 1886, daughter of James Calvin and Mary (Dancy) McNiel of Ashe and Wilkes Counties.

My grandfather and grandmother McNiel lived on Cowles Creek in the Purlear Community until 1919 at his death. Thornton was the founder of the North Wilkesboro Coca-Cola Bottling Company, known as its inception in 1906 as the Red Top Bottling Company. During the week he stayed with his daughter Ruth Vannoy and her family, and returned home on weekends. During the terrible influenza epidemic in the winter of 1918-1919, three members of this family died within a fifteen day period. When Thorton McNiel and his daughter's family became ill, the other children and Eda, my grandmother, came from the country to take care of them. After his death Eda moved to North Wilkesboro to make her home.

The children born to them were: William Alonzo (nicknamed "Benny") born Sept 17, 1888, died Aug 7, 1948, of coronary thrombosis. He did not marry. He was associated with the North Wilkesboro Coca Cola Bottling Co. and was president at the time of his death.

Ella Ruth, born November 2, 1890, died Jan 11, 1919 of influenza and pneumonia, married Hannibal Roscoe Vannoy. Their children were Ella Sue who married Carl F. Colvard of Ashe County; Annie who married Russell Gray, Jr. of Wilkesboro; and Hannibal, Jr. who died young.

Claude Ackle (nicknamed "Major") born March 20, 1893, died Sept 26, 1968, married Daisy Hayes, daughter of John Lee and Sarah Julia McNeil Hayes of Wilkes County. Their children were: Claude A., Jr.; Minnie Ruth (Mrs. Sam Gentry); Elizabeth, (Mrs. Richard Callaway); Robert Hayes, who died Feb 12, 1972.

Challie Odell (nicknamed "Emmet") born June 24, 1894, died May 30, 1955 married Luella Tuttle Chilton, March 14, 1920. No issue.

Richard Tipton (nicknamed "Kaley"), born Sept 16, 1897 died June 13, 1955, married May 29, 1925 to Gladys Graybeal Eller of Ashe County, daughter of Edwin Cicero and Laura Catherine Graybeal Eller.

Osco, born Jan 16, 1900, died Jan 28, 1919 of acute bronchitis and Spanish influenza, He was unmarried.

Mamie Gertrude, whose history is elsewhere in this book. She is the family historian and story-teller. Aunt Mamie and Aunt Ruth were the only ones in the family who were not nicknamed by their brothers.

Sources: Hayes, *Genealogy of the McNiel Clan* Personal knowledge Hook, *George Michael Eller.*

— Pat McNeil Day

HATTIE McNEILL
815

Hattie McNeill, "Miss Hattie", as she was most affectionately called, was born July 21, 1885, in Wilkes County to Thomas Jefferson and Clarissa Louisa Kilby McNeill. She re-

Miss Hattie McNeil.

ceived her early education at Crossroads school and Miss Mamie Barber's School. For a short time, she taught school, as did most of the young ladies of her day after finishing their own schooling. In the early 1900s, Hattie moved to Gastonia, North Carolina, to begin training for a nursing career at City Hospital. After her graduation, she was selected Superientendent of Nurses there and served in that capacity until she resigned to join the staff of Wilkes Hospital when it opened in 1923.

The nurses life was not an easy one in those days. Shifts were long, many times ten hours or more with extra duty the rule rather than the exception. I'm sure, however, that Hattie took joy in her job, under whatever conditions prevailed. I remembered when I was in her home while she was preparing to go to work, she always hurried about enthusiastically, dressed in her strached white uniform and cap, always humming or whistling softly.

For many years, Miss Hattie worked with maternity patients and their little offsprings. She took a great deal of satisfaction in being involved in so many exciting and happy experiences. She kept up with many of her former patients and their families and often received letters and pictures at Christmas or birthdays from them.

I've had so many people tell me that in the early days, Miss Hattie accompanied them home after their release from the hospital — sometimes with a new baby or following surgery or other serious illness. I'm certain she enjoyed those special duties and must have brought a prevading sense of calm and order to all the homes in which she ministered.

Although Miss Hattie never married and had a family of her own, she touched the lives of many people in our area. She was my aunt, and a very special person to me.

Sources: Family records, newspaper records, Dr. Hubbard's book

— Elizabeth McNeill Forester

JEFF McNEILL FAMILY
816

Our father Thomas Jefferson was born in Wilkes County, April 20, 1878 to James Oliver and Sarah Ann Stout McNeill.

He was a brother to John, Hilda Jane (Eller), Zera Elmer (Church), Harvey Clay, Lily Geneva (Foster), Martha Alverta (Proffit), Sarah Lou (Proffit), Judson, Albert S., Elizabeth Ann (Shoemaker), James Creary, and Jessie Mathis. Their homeplace is owned by James C., the youngest son. He and Elizabeth Ann are still living.

Both grandparents were charter members of Mt. Pleasant Baptist Church and nearly all of the deceased are buried in the church cemetery.

Dad was a descendant of George McNeill who was born in Scotland. My grandfather was the son of William, and his father was Joseph, and his father was George. Dad's education consisted of one room schools and the Academy at Moravian Falls, but he was an avid reader so to a degree was self educated.

Dad moved to Roaring River in the early 1900's to measure lumber for Roaring River Box Company. He met and married Lela Jane Felts in 1905. To this union nine daughters were born. In that same year he purchased the homeplace where I now live. In 1909 he and others organized the Parks Lumber Company and a few years later bought the Elkin Table Company in Elkin which he operated until the great depression claimed it.

All the years he worked in Elkin he rode the train, the "Shoo Fly". When there was shopping to be done or a doctor or dentist to be seen, Mama took any of us that needed to go and we rode the noon train. It was fun and the train men became familiar figures.

A hired man did the heavy farming and we girls donned our overalls and straw hats to help out since we had no brothers. The farm produced most of what we ate. There were cows, chickens and hogs for milk, eggs, and meat. Canning, pickling and preserving took care of food for winter. Mama sewed nearly all of our clothes with the help of her sister. We picked the styles from the Sears Catalogue, and they could make them like the picture.

Our social life would seem dull to many today, but we had fun. The neighborhood children came to see us or we to see them, and we played hour after hour. We were never bored for lack of something to do. Families gathered for homemade ice cream on Saturday night and there was horse shoe pitching and baseball. We had picnics, swimming in Roaring River, plays at school and other activities such as church socials, pie suppers and church Christmas programs with caroling afterwards. Later on there were movies.

Church life was very important to us. In 1906 eighteen persons met and organized Roaring River Baptist Church. Among the charter members were Dad, Mama, Grandpa, Grandma, two aunts and one uncle. All nine of us girls, eight grandchildren, one great granddaughter and three sons-in-laws joined the church and all were baptized in Roaring River. Several of us have our membership there and most of our dead are buried there.

With the loss of Dad's business and the home place in the depression many long hard hours were spent to survive and regain the farm. In 1940 Dad began to produce seed corn. He grew three kinds but was especially proud of "McNeill's Golden Early", a no-cob corn he developed by crossbreeding the other two. He built a good business and kept it until his death. We still grow "Gold Early" in our garden.

Dad was a great believer in progress especially for the farmer. He helped bring the Wilkes Farm Bureau and the F.C.X. to Wilkes County serving as Chariman and on the advisory boards of these organizations. He helped organize the Yadkin Valley Dairy. He was a Mason and Shriner. He saw that each of us had an education.

Mama became ill in 1932 and was an invalid several years before her death July 1, 1945. Dad lived until September 1, 1960. When Mama died he made a most unusual request. He said since Mama was sick so long and we all cared for her he wanted eight of us girls to be the pall bearers at her funeral. This we did and Carol, the youngest walked with him. Nine daughters survived: Jessie (Grimes), Lillian (Miner), Evelyn (Hackman), Juanita (Huggins), Hazel (Patterson), Mamiana (Sears), Inez (Boles), Tommye (Chatham), and Carol (Evans). To date there are 19 grandchildren, 32 great grandchildren and 7 great-great grandchildren. Our lives have been filled with happiness and love, thanks to devoted christian parents.

Sources: Memoirs and personal knowledge, Genealogy of the McNeill Clan by Johnson J. Hayes, and family records.

— Inez M. Boles

DESCENDANTS OF PETER GAITHER McNIEL
817

Peter G. McNiel was born on Cole's Creek, near the foot of Rendezvous Mountain, August 26, 1827, son of John and Rachel Eller McNiel. He left Wilkes at an early age, migrated to the Beaver Creek section of Ashe County and taught in the public schools there where he met and married one of his students, Maryann B. Phillips, (2-4-1855) daughter of C.W. and Margaret Phillips of Old Fields township.

Before, during and after the Civil War in which he was a CSA soldier, Peter and Maryann had 14 children: (1) Phinais Gaither McNeil born Nov. 20, 1855, died Dec. 31, 1918, married Cynthia Alice McMillian, daughter of Capt. Andrew and Cynthia Reeves McMillian. Their children were: John Reeves; Jennie McNiel Koontz; Andrew Benjamin; Dora McNiel Duval; Charity Lorena; Fora Della

P.T. McNeill.

Mrs. P.T. McNeil.

McNiel Speaks; Roger Lester; State Senator Peter Thurman McNiel, later Clerk of Superior Court of Ashe County. (2) Julia Emaline born Nov. 6, 1850, married Mack Absher of Wilkes County. Their children were: Dr. Darius Absher; Nora; Mabel; Agnes; and Claude. (3) Orlando H. McNiel born Sept. 19, 1861, died at Hastings, Nebr. July 31, 1887. (4) Peter Rufus born May 24, 1864, married Fina Faw. Their children were: Charles S. born Feb 12, 1894, died April 25, 1945 married Lillie Rose McGuire; and Jones McNiel married Edna Walters. (5) Laura B. McNiel born April 18, 1866, died March 27, 1938, married Joseph Black. Their daughter Mary married J.O. Benfield. She had a son Jack B. Lawson. (6) John Franklin McNiel born April 11, 1868, died at Hastings, Nebr. November 21, 1887. (7) Joseph Walter born June 21, 1870, died Jan. 31, 1895, went out west.

(8) John Quincy born Sept. 18, 1871, died Dec. 31, 1956, married Ida Bell born June 18, 1869, died Oct. 3, 1955. Their children were: John Allan, Annie Alice and Ralph. (9) Elihu Alexander born June 18, 1872, married July 18, 1872 to Mary Jean Davis. Their children were: Robert Davis and Elihu. (10) Rachel born Sept. 26, 1874, died August 26, 1894, unmarried. (11) Lizzie Rebecca born April 2, 1879, died May 5, 1956. She married Edward Everett Eller July 30, 1896 who was born Feb. 12, 1870, died Oct. 18, 1955. He was a merchant in North Wilkesboro for many years. Their children were, Mary Elizabeth born Sept. 10, 1897, married William M. McCulley; Ernest born Jan. 23, 1903, Rear Admiral U.S. Navy, Retired. He married Agnes Pfohl May 27, 1926.

(12) William Heggie McNiel, born April 12, 1879, died Jan. 15, 1925, married Mollie Evelyn Eller, born May 11, 1881. Their children were: Frank and Frances (twins) Margaret, Robert who died young, and Edward. (13) Benjamin Avery McNiel born July 10, 1881, died July 4, 1939 at Los Angeles, Ca. He married Maude Catherine Phipps. They had one child, Ruth McNiel, who never married.

She lives at the old Phipps homeplace at the foot of Mount Jefferson. (14) Wiley Emmett McNiel born Apr. 13, 1885 died June 26, 1949, married Astoria McConnell. Their children were Willard; Mary Lillian Sturdivant; Catherine Goswick; Wiley Emmertt, Jr. who married Carrie Taylor, public health nurse for Ashe County; and Laura Ann Jacks.

Peter G. McNiel's eldest son, Caither McNeill, was one of the first Democrats to be elected sheriff of Ashe County (around 1904).

Peter Thurman McNeill, born Aug. 18, 1896, died March 23, 1960, married Martha Ellen Fletcher of Somerset, Ky. She and her identical twin, Mary Belle, were the only children of G.W. and Amanda Clark Fletcher. Thurman and Martha bore ten children: (1) Mary Theresa Scott, (2) Robert Fletcher (3) Amanda Evangeline (Ann) Garwood (4) Peter Thurman, Jr. (5) Marshall Gaither. (6) Martha Alice who died in infancy, (7) Cynthia Alice who died age 4, (8) Martha Eleanor Scott (9) George William, (10) Joseph Franklin.

P.T. McNeill, Sr. served in the N.C. Senate in 1927 and again in 1933. He was a member of the N.C. Legislature in 1929 and served as Senate clerk in 1931. He was a Deputy Collector with the Internal Revenue Service from 1933 until 1937 when he resigned to serve as State Probation Officer. He was a life-long Democrat. When the news of his death reached Raleigh on March 24, 1960, the Legislature adjourned out of respect to him and order a resolution written into the Journal. Following is an excerpt from the Skyland Post of March 30, 1960: "Hundreds of friends filled the church to overflowing and many more stood in the yard at the Beaver Creek Primitive Baptist Church Sunday afternoon to pay final tribute to Peter Thurman McNeill, 64, one of Ashe County's most popular men, who died suddenly last Thursday morning at the Ashe Memorial Hospital. There were lawyers, judges, and other officials from Raleigh and other distant points who had known and worked with Mr. McNeill, who was serving his second term as Clerk of Court of Ashe County.

And there were neighbors and friends from all sections of Ashe, gathered at the church, which Mr. McNeill, an ordained minister, had helped to build. Conducting the service was Elder Edd Davis and Elder Dewey Roten and burial followed in the McNeill family cemetery, bringing to an end a long career of public service."

Ann McNeill Garwood was born in West Jefferson Aug. 2, 1924 and graduated from West Jefferson High School in 1941. She attended WCUNC, Greensboro, and graduated from the Secretarial School in 1942. Her first position was with the Extension Service. She resigned that position to become secretary in the law firm of Bowie & Bowie. She resigned in 1944, left Ashe to work as a secretary in the office of the Wilkes County Board of Education. Later she accepted a Civil Service job in the Farmer's Home Administration office.

In 1947 she married Charles E. Garwood, son of J.L. and Annie Carrigan Garwood. She resigned her job to become a homemaker. She then accepted work with the Sentinel Insurance Agency in 1954.

Charles E. Garwood, Sr. has been with Lineberry Foundry & Machine Co., following his graduation from Wilkesboro High School in 1941, with the exception of his service with the Seabees of the U.S. Navy during World War II, from which he was honorably discharged in 1945. Their children are Mary Ellen, born Oct. 8, 1947 and Charles Edward, Jr. born March 24, 1953. Mary Ellen married James Thomas Mikell, an attorney in Beaufort, S.C. where they reside on Distant Island. She teaches first grade in Beaufort Academy. Edward is employed with DML, McCrary Div., Lenoir, out of Lexington, Ky., Vermont-American Corp. He lives in Alexander County.

Ann and Charles live in Ken Acres with their little poodle, "Tinker".

Sources: *Land of Wilkes* by J.J. Hayes; *McNiel Clan* by J.J. Hayes; *Skyland Post*, newspaper.

— Ann McNeill Garwood

THOMAS JEFFERSON McNEILL
818

Thomas Jefferson McNeill was born April 24, 1851, the son of James Harvey (Jimmy D.) and his wife Susannah McNeil McNeill. He was the great, great, grandson of the Reverend George McNeil, Chaplain of the Revolutionary forces from Wilkes County, on both his father and mother's lines.

In keeping with his thrifty Scotch-Irish heritage, my grandfather, who was a woodworker and farmer, spent the year preceding his marriage building the furniture he and his bride-to-be needed for their home. Much of this original primitive furniture is in the possession of his descendents today. On March 1, 1874, he married Clarissa Louisa Kilby, daughter of Lovel Dogan Kilby, Jr. and Rachel Tinsley Kilby.

To Jeff and Lou were born five children: Sinai Delilah, born December 23, 1874, and died June 5, 1876. Cora Elizabeth, born May 16, 1878, and died March 27, 1970, at the age of 91. Minnie Ellen, born April 7, 1882, and died September 4, 1969, at the age of 87. Twins — Charles Poole and Hattie Belle, born July 21, 1885. Charlie died June 3, 1956, at the age of 70. Hattie died February 27, 1957, at the age of 71.

Cora McNeill taught school in Wilkes County as a young woman and later moved to a teaching position in Lowell, N.C., where she remained until shortly before her retirement.

Minnie McNeill also taught in the Wilkes County school system for several years, but retired early in order to care for her invalid mother.

Hattie, after teaching briefly, entered nurses training at City Hospital in Gastonia, N.C. She returned to Wilkes County in 1923 to work in the Wilkes Hospital when it opened on April 2nd, to assist in general surgical nursing, and continued her nursing career until retirement shortly before her death.

Charlie McNeill spent his early life working on the family farms in the Purlear and Millers Creek areas. He later worked for Cleve Kilby in his general store at Crossroads. For 27 years, until his retirement in 1954, he was wholesale grocery buyer for S.V. Tomlinson Wholesale Company in North Wilkesboro. On September 21, 1929, he married Hattie Simpson Gambill, daughter of William Bourn and Elizabeth Jane Brown Gambill, who had come from Walnut Grove to teach school in the Millers Creek community.

To Hattie Gambill and Charles Poole McNeill one child, Elizabeth Louisa, was born December 1, 1930. In 1935 Charlie moved his family to the Mulberry community where Hattie taught in the Mulberry Elementary School from its opening in 1936 until her retirement in 1965.

Elizabeth McNeill was married on August 28, 1949 to George Stewart Forester, Jr., son of George, Sr., and Harriet Augusta Lenoir Forester. Their children are Charles Stewart, Isaac Gambill and Elizabeth Lenoir Forester.

Sources: Family records, personal knowledge.

— Elizabeth McNeill Forester

WILLIAM B. McNEILL
819

William B. McNeill, born 11 February 1876, was the son of Thomas Winslow and Jane Nichols McNeill. Thomas Winslow McNeill was the son of George and Susanna Vannoy McNeill. George was the son of James and Mary Shepherd McNeill and James was the son of the Rev. George McNeill (the immigrant from Scotland, according to family tradition) and his wife, Mary Coats McNeill who was from Virginia.

Jane Nichols McNeill was the daughter of Elijah Nichols and his wife Susanna Minton Nichols. Elijah was the son of John Nichols, Sr., the first Nichols in this line to come to Wilkes County.

These families were among the early settlers of Wilkes and lived near Deep Ford Hill and Lewis Fork. Most of them were devout Baptists and are mentioned frequently in the early church records.

William B. McNeill married Louisa H. Stout, daughter of J. Miles and Laura Ann Regina (Lottie) Hayes Stout. Several years ago, a friend who was researching the Hayes family, found a record Joseph Washington Hayes had written which listed the names and birthdates of his children. The friend called Mrs. Anne Staley, a descendant, and asked if her grandmother was Laura Anne Regina Hayes Stout. Her quick reply was, "Lord, No! My grandmother was Lottie Hayes Stout!" Laura Anne Regina Hayes, daughter of J.W. and Anne Grant Hayes, was always called "Lottie" and that is the name engraved on her tombstone.

William B. McNeill and his wife were the parents of ten children: (1) Grace born April 1, 1901, died Aug. 24, 1926 — did not marry. (2) Marbrit, born June 9, 1903, died Nov. 4, 1976, married Blanche Parsons. They had two children, Elizabeth and Richard Eugene (Gene) McNeill. Marbrit owned the Pontiac dealership in North Wilkesboro for many years. (3) Thomas W. McNeill was born Feb. 24, 1905 and died March 4, 1905. (4) Mollie V., born March 5, 1906, married Wade E. Phelps and they live in Winston-Salem. They have two children, James Clifton and Jean. (5) Charles C., born Oct. 21, 1908, married Ruby Wagoner of Millers Creek and they made their home in Wilkesboro. They have two daughters, Christine and Elaine. Charles was superintendant of Wilkes County Department of Public Welfare (Social Services now) for many years and is an officer of Wilkesboro Savings and Loan.

(6) Rachel Anne, born July 4, 1911, married W. Thornton Staley and they live in Millers Creek. They have one son, William McNeill Staley who is in the United States Air Force. (See sketch entitled Adam Staley). (7) William Woodrow McNeill, born Feb. 11, 1913, married Frances Smith and they live in Greensboro, N.C. They have one daughter, Gail. (8) Sallie Fay born March 5, 1915, died June 28, 1978, married Roy McCollum and they resided in Winston-Salem. They had two daughters, Mary Lou McChuson and Jo Anne McCollum. (9) John Mark, born 24 July 1917, married Virginia (Fanny) Vickers, and they live on his father's old homeplace in Purlear. John and Fanny own and operate The Ice Cream Parlor in North Wilkesboro and the Ponderosa restaurant in Millers Creek. They had three daughters, Linda, Joan and Frances. (10) Sue Grace, born June 3, 1921, married George O. Livingood who died Dec. 4, 1975. Sue lives in Baltimore, Md., and has one daughter, Brenda.

Sources: Record kept by William B. McNeill, Genealogy of the McNeill family by Judge Johnson J. Hayes, Hayes and Nichols family research by Mae R. Hayes and personal knowledge.

— Anne M. Staley

McSHANE REMINISCENCES
820

My childhood memories begin when my father, Patrick McShane, had a store on the Yadkin. We lived just behind the store. I had a sister Margaret Virginia who was two years younger than I. We used to go visit our grandparents on my mothers side of the family in a buggy. My mother was Minerva Josephine Kendall, a daughter of Larkin Leroy and Leah Waters Kendall who lived on Kendall Mountain. It had been said that the Kendall Valley had been a land grant from the State of North Carolina to the ancient forebears of my Grandfather Kendall. I do know that the huge mountain that was situated on one side of the valley was called "Kendall Mountain" and Kendall Branch flowed through the valley.

The area where we lived was to be considered modern, as compared to where my mother was reared. To get there you had fairly good roads, depending upon the weather, until you reached the point where Elk Creek intersected with the Yadkin River. This point was within shooting distance of Ferguson, NC, a wide place in the road.

When we started up Elk Creek, I seriously doubt that the trail we took was any better than when Daniel Boone took the same trail up the Elk to Darby and points beyond. The trail was rocky, rutted and ran around the edge of a bluff that was so high above the onrushing waters of Elk Creek several hundred feet below, that everyone alighted from the conveyance and with one member of the party leading the horse, the rest of us walked until the land leveled off quite some distance past the bluff. It was not far from here to my grandparent's house across Elk Creek.

My grandparents house, that is the main part of it, was made of logs chinked with mud. It was two stories high, the upstairs was called "the loft" and it had two double beds. The shingles on the house were called "shakes"; handmade with an adze. You could see moonlight through the shingles and I always wondered why it never rained in through them. There was no heat in the loft. You got up into it by climbing a very steep set of stairs. The big room downstairs was furnished as the living room but it still had two double beds in the far corners. The kitchen apparently had been built later since it was built of lumber from a saw mill. It had, like the living room, a very large fireplace and there hung a rod out from between the stones upon which to suspend a pot. There was a small cook stove that sat up on four legs, but most of the cooking, except for biscuits, was done in the fireplace. The dining table was long and built out of smooth lumber. You sat in straight backed cane bottomed chairs to eat. There was a huge corner cupboard. You washed your hands and face on a shelf on the back porch because that's where the water bucket and wash pan sat. There were only girls in my mothers family so besides my grandfather they were all females.

There was a boom in the lumber business in that part of the state at that time and at one time they used prison labor to build a railroad all the way up to Darby so they could haul flatcar loads of lumber out to the flatlands. But it didn't last. The old residents in that area told the railroad promoters that the first flash flood that came would wash all the railroad trestles out and sure enough it did. But not before a lumber train killed my grandfather as he walked down the middle of the railroad tracks. He was taking a shortcut by walking the tracks while he was on a mission to the store in Ferguson to purchase nails. He was both senile and hard of hearing. The engineer and fireman saw him on the tracks, blew the train whistle, and applied the brakes. The train was pulling a heavy load and could not stop. The good man never knew what hit him, as it killed him instantly. The train crew came bringing his body back to the house wrapped in a blanket.

As it was customary in that area, in those days, the menfolk of the neighborhood came and washed and dressed his remains. Lastly they put the cape he had worn in the Civil War around his shoulders. The railroad people obtained him a store bought coffin in Wilkesboro and he was placed in that. The coffin rested on two cane bottomed chairs which faced each other and supported the coffin at each end. The men of the community sat up with the corpse. They had his funeral the next day, hauling his coffin in a two horse wagon up to the family graveyard on top of the ridge across the valley from the mountain. There he was laid to rest. A Civil War Monument was obtained for the head of his grave. This same family graveyard contains the graves of early members of our family who were buried there long before the Civil War.

Sources: An excerpt from an unpublished autobiography by my uncle, Daniel Edward McShane, Sr. (1905-1968).

Nina Joan Cobb

NORMAN MARION
821

Norman Marion was born in Surry County on Nov. 25, 1911, son of Henry Frank and Ella Hardy Marion. He was the youngest of a family of 14.

At 17 Norm joined the U.S. Army. After serving at various posts in the States and in Panama, he was discharged in April, 1934. Upon being discharged he came to Wilkes County to visit a sister, Mrs. W.O. (Mae) Elliott. It was during this visit that he met Lucy Rash, daughter of Stephen and Elvira McNeil Rash. They were married Dec. 9, 1935, in Independence, Va.

This couple have three children, Tony, married Helen Anderson (their children are Cathy Lynn and Tony, Jr.), Francis, married Charles G. Huffman, one child, Darien, Katherine, married James Weinstein, one child, Cassandra, (Sandee).

During World War II, Norm was employed in Baltimore, Md. at the Glenn L. Martin Aircraft Plant. Upon his return to North Wilkesboro he was engaged in the carpet business for many years. In Sept. 1954, he became employed at Carolina Mirror Corp. where he retired in 1976.

No one could ask for a better neighbor than Norman Marion. He is always ready and willing to do a good deed for anyone in need.

Norm and Lucy reside at the old Rash homeplace where they raised their family.

Source: Family knowledge.

— Sidney Johnston
and Lucy Marion

BEN F. and ROBERTA MILLER MARSH
822

Ben Marsh was born in Union County, December 20, 1912 to Frank Benson and Eula Marsh. He was educated in Marshville, N.C. and Kings Business College in Charlotte, N.C. He served active duty in World War II with U.S. Marine Corps. He came to Wilkes County in 1947 and he and his brother-in-law, E. Hight Helms, operated the Wilkes Farm Center & Hatchery for many years between the Wilkesboros. This business was dissolved and Ben became manager of the Essco Poultry Equipment Company, leaving them to join his brother in his Kentucky Fried Chicken franchises in several N.C. cities. Before his retirement in 1981, he was the manager of the N. Wilkesboro Kentucky Fried Chicken for several years.

Roberta Miller Marsh was born in Charlotte, N.C. to Fannie Faulkner and Dr. Julian Sydney Miller on December 18, 1917. Her father was in newspaper business all his life and at the time of his death had been Editor of the Charlotte Observer for 25 years. She attended Queens College, Charlotte, N.C. and was graduated from Erskine College, Due West, S.C. in 1938. She held an important position with Ralston Purina Company for 10 years, was married on June 12, 1948, and moved to Wilkes County. Roberta has been a housewife since marriage with an occasional part time job.

Both have been active in church and community affairs, members of N. Wilkesboro Presbyterian Church, where they have both served as officers of the church, and Roberta has held many offices of the Women of the Church. She has also written the history of the church and of the local YMCA.

Frank Benson was born to them on August 25, 1950. He was educated in local schools, and was graduated from N.C. State Univ. He also has his MBA from Duke University. He was married to Barbara Morton from Greensboro on October 11, 1975. She is a graduate of Meredith College and they have a son, Bradley Benson, born September 26, 1980. Benson has been with IBM in Raleigh for several years where they now reside.

Wayne Miller Marsh was born June 24, 1953, attended the local schools and was graduated from UNC at Chapel Hill. He is with Carolina Dealers as a sales representative. He resides in Myrtle Beach, S.C.

Rosemary Roberta was born on November 8, 1956, attended local schools and U.N.C. at Chapel Hill, Wilkes Community College, and U.N.C. at Charlotte. She was married June 14, 1980 to David John Skridulis from Charlotte, N.C., a civil engineer in Pipe Designing, and they now reside in Tampa, Fla.

Sources: personal knowledge

— Roberta Miller Marsh

MARTIN
823

The family of Benjamin Martin, born 1746, moved from Fluvanna County, Virginia, to Wilkes in the winter of 1782 and established their home on a plantation along the south side of the Yadkin about two miles west of Ronda. This Benjamin Martin, ensign and Revolutionary soldier in Virginia, was the son of Henry Martin and Sarah Bryan, daughter of John Bryan of Pennsylvania, a relative, probably, of Col. John Bryan who came to Wilkes. Henry Martin was the son of Peter Martin and Mary Anthony Rapine Martin of Goochland County, Virginia, whose Huguenot ancestors came to America in 1700.

Ensign Benjamin Martin married in 1766, Diana Harrison, daughter of Benjamin Harrison of Pittsylvania County, Virginia. Their ten children were: (1) Dr. Robert, born 1767, married Amelia Wright; (2) Patsy, born 1769, married Benjamin Parks, parents of Col. Lyndolph and Col Marcus Parks; (3) Benjamin married Frances Martin; (4) Sarah Meredith, born 1776, married Hiram Rousseau of Wilkes County; (5) James born 1777, died 1846, married in 1806 Elvira Bryan; (6) Anne, married Edmund Bagby; (7) John, married Mildred Jones; (8) Elizabeth, married John Martin, son of William Martin; (9) Amelia, born 1786, died 1874, married John Harrison Cleveland, grandson of Ben Cleveland of King's Mountain fame; (10) Diana, born 1788, died 1858, married John Martin.

The children of Col. James Martin (1777-1846) and his wife, Elvira Bryan Martin (1790-1863) were : (1) John born 1808, moved to Georgia; (2) Diana Adelaide born 1810, died 1886; (3) James; (4) Benjamin who was twice married, and had three sons killed in the Civil War, and a daughter named Alvira; (6) Emaline who died 1861; (7) Felix, died 1852 in Macon, Georgia; (8) Mary, married J. Carsler, moved to Indian territory; (9) Leland, married Laura Corpening of Morganton; (10) Rufus, marrist first Jane Hickerson, second Ann Hickerson, moved to Little Rock, Ark; (11) Oscar; (12) Augustus Harrison, born 1833, married Susan Virginia Corpening.

The children of Leland Martin and Laura Corpening Martin were: (1) Mary, married Dr. Barker of Jonesville; (2) Ella, died 1923 unmarried; (3) James D., bachelor, lived in Arco, Idaho; (4) Harry C., died 1939; (5) Clara, married John Sale, parents of Fred L. Sale, a lawyer of Asheville, N.C; (6) Philetees (Fleet) (1866-1937), a lawyer in Texas.

The children of Capt. Augustus Harrison Martin, born 1833, C.S.A. and Susan Virginia Corpening Martin were: (1) Dr. James Everett, M.D., died 1924; (2) Julius, a lawyer in Asheville, later Director of Bureau of War Risk Litigation in Washington, D.C.; (3) Laura Adelaide, married first Frank McCulloch, and second, James Linney, parent of Ruth Linney of Roaring River, N.C. now deceased.

Col. James Martin acquired a large body of land on the south side of the Yadkin River between Ronda and Roaring River. His home built in 1806 near Brier Creek stood until 1975, when vandals burned it.

Sources: Excerpts from *Happy Valley* by Felix Hickerson.

— Eleanor Parks Elam

MARTIN FAMILY

824

The Wilkes County August 1870 Federal census lists Isaiah Martin, age 60, as a farm laborer; Fannie, his wife, age and three children, Stephen, age ten, Clementine age fifteen and William Walter, age twenty-one. William Walter was my great grandfather so his line is the one I know the most about.

He was born October 2, 1848 in Wilkes County. He was a cobbler and made shoes on two lathes; one for men and one for women and children. He married Fannie Rebecca Rash, daughter of Joe and Matilda Bumgarner Rash (12-11-1841 — 4-30-1824) on January 25, 1877. They lived in a three room house in Millers Creek. The homeplace is now owned by Clate and Alpina Martin Bumgarner.

When Fannie's brother's daughter died in the late 1800s, she and William gave land for the infants burial. This was the beginning of the Martin Family Cemetery on Hensley Eller Lumber Yard Road in Millers Creek. William died on January 16, 1902 of "white swelling" or diabetes and he is buried in the cemetery. Granny Becky lived until a bowel blockage killed her on December 9, 1938. She was found by a neighbor, was dressed at home in a black cotton dress she had made and stored for herself, a black bonnet and black stockings. She was carried from her home to the cemetery in a wooden coffin.

Granny Becky must have been a religious lady, for I was told she would take eggs to the Methodist preacher to pay her tithes because she had very little or no money.

William and "Granny Becky" had ten children. The oldest was Annie. She was born February 6, 1878 and died September 17, 1906. She had gone to Statesville to get a picture enlarged and caught pneumonia; Martha Almedia born August 1879, died August 1962, married Pearl Pinkney Cleary and had five children; James Washington (2-27-1882) — (12-9-1967) was a farmer in Wilkes County. He married Bessie Alice Brown (11-10-1888) on October 1, 1905 and had nine children, several of whom still live in the county with their families. Two males were born dead.

The next child of William and "Granny Becky" was Walter Filmore (2-1-1887) (February 1974), moved to West Virginia and married Ella Rose on December 18, 1912. They had eight children; Sherman Steven (5-10-1890) — (12-19-1978) was a farmer, married Eva Laura Isenhour on September 13, 1914 and had fourteen children; Joseph Edmond (2-20-1893) — (9-4-1970) married Rosa Lee Harrison October 20, 1916 and had six children; Stacey Doughton, my grandfather (5-20-1895) — (9-15-1952) served in the army in World War I. He met my grandmother in September 1924 at Friendship Methodist Church and married her on March 4, 1925. She is Manda Vada "Ada" Marsh, daughter of William Judson Marsh (3-10-1880) — (4-29-1971) of Ashe County and Ida Mertie Ann Powell (11-26-1882) — (10-4-1962) of Wilkes County. The had three children:

(1) Josephine Mary Martin Gray (12-9-1925) — (7-20-1973) who had three children: (2) Eugene Briton (11-24-1929), my father who married Shirley Mae Braswell on May 10, 1949. They have three children all of which live in Millers Creek. (3) James Dewey Martin (11-26-1932) who lives in Alaska with his wife and two children. J.D. works at the airport in Anchorage.

Grandpa Martin became ill in 1934 and went to the V.A. Hospital in Salem, Va. where he stayed until a stroke took his life. Granny Martin lives alone in the Fairplains Community of Wilkes County.

The last of the clan, child of William and "Granny Becky" was George Dewey (1899) — (12-8-1964), who married Clarice Grey and had three children. He worked for many years in the Greensboro Post Office. When he retired, he and his wife moved to Florida. Dewey wasn't satisfied there, so they came back to Greensboro and built a home which took two years to build. Right after it was finished, he entered the hospital and died there.

Sources: Relatives, Family Bibles, Wilkes County records.

— Linda Martin Milam

BILLY THOMAS MARTIN FAMILY

825

My Daddy Billy Thomas Martin was born on May 12, 1932 to William Harvey Martin (born September 9, 1909) and Verlie Marie Pruitt (born Janurary 15, 1912). He is the oldest of five children. Billy Thomas was born in 1932; Mary Lafayette was born June 26, 1934; James Harvey was born September 17, 1936; Jacob B. was born April 30, 1941 — died May 7, 1941; Joseph W. was born April 27, 1942 — died April 28, 1943.

Daddy met Shelby Jean Weatherman (now my mama) and they married on November 20, 1953. They raised tobacco and farmed. Many times they have told me about an old house in Surry County they first lived in. They said you could lie in bed at night and see the stars shinning through the cracks in the roof and walls.

My older sister Sandra Gail was born on May 12, 1955. When she was two years old she kept jumping off the front porch. It was a high porch and Daddy had told her many times not to jump off it but she kept doing it and Daddy spanked her. To my knowledge that is the only time he ever spanked any of us four kids. I'm not saying he didn't want to or that we didn't need it, he just left the whoopings up to Mama.

They moved from this house to Wilkes County in 1959. Daddy bought twelve acres of land from Thurmond Carter. Daddy and my grandpa T.O. Weatherman (Thurmond Odell), Garner Martin, and Roy Chipman built a small four-room house.

I (Sarah Frances) was born on February 2, 1959. People say my daddy and me are the most alike of all of us kids. I'm the only one who has his red hair and temper.

Daddy still farmed and he also hauled junk radiators, copper, brass and batteries. He quit farming in 1965 to haul junk full time.

My younger brother Steven Thomas (named after Daddy) was born on May 6, 1964. I was supposed to have been a boy, so when Steve was born they were very glad.

In 1969 Daddy and Mama remodeled their house. They built on two rooms, a basement, and carport, and finally a bathroom. I was ten years old but I had never missed having a bathroom because I had never had one. I'm glad I didn't have a lot of luxuries when I was younger because it made me a stronger and more independent person.

My youngest brother William Scott was born on April 5, 1970. He was named after my Grandpa. Now there were two girls and two boys so I reckon they decided to stop there.

My sister Sandra Gail graduated from East Wilkes High School in 1973, and married Timothy Dale Whitaker on June 30, 1973. Their first child Olivia Dawn was born on Feburary 4, 1974. Their second Andrea Daile was born on August 24, 1981. They now live in the Popular Springs Community in Surry County.

I graduated from East Wilkes High School in 1976 and married Jerry Dwayne Byrd on June 18, 1976. He was from Roaring River in Wilkes County. We have one little girl, Wendy Rae born April 24, 1979. Jerry has been working with my daddy for about four years now in the junk business. We live in Surry County now right on the edge of Wilkes County. I hope to move back to Wilkes County very soon, and spend the rest of my life there.

My brother Steve is a Senior at East Wilkes High School, and helps daddy and Jerry in the junk business. He plays ball and hunts all the time. He still lives at home.

My youngest brother Scott is in the sixth grade at C.B. Eller Elementary School.

Daddy has always made sure his bills were paid and we always had plenty to eat, no matter what. You really have to know Daddy to understand him. He can give the impression that he is an old meany, but he's really a very loveable person.

Well to end my story, I'll tell you the old story on Wilkes County: you have to either had to have made, sold, or drank moonshine to be a true Wilkes-countian, and I'm sure most of my family has done all three so I guess we're all true Wilkes-countians for sure.

Sources: Family knowledge, gravemarkers.

— Sarah Martin Byrd

WILLIAM HARVEY MARTIN FAMILY

826

My grandpa was born on September 9, 1909 to William J. (January 15, 1870 to February 14, 1912) and Pheobe Jane Carter Martin (April 26, 1872 to March 20, 1960). He was one of five sons. The oldest, James Manley, was born in 1899; Conley Ford was born in 1902; Garner Franklin was born in 1905; William Harvey in 1909; and John Marven born 1911.

Grandpa was born in Surry County and has always lived there, except when he was first married; then he and grandma lived with her parents in Wilkes County.

Grandpa has always been a farmer. He has also done some painting and hauled scrap metals. Mostly he has farmed though, always raising a large garden and tobacco crop.

Grandpa met my grandma and they were married in Galax, Virginia on August 16, 1931 by the Reverend McCarthy. They then moved in with grandma's parents for a while. They built their first house on a piece of grandma's daddy's land. The house was a small log cabin. I've heard grandma say she could keep that house cleaner than any house she's ever lived in.

My daddy, Billy Thomas Martin, was born to them on May 12, 1932. My aunt, Mary Lafayette, was born June 26, 1934. Then my uncle James Harvey was born on September 17, 1936. Two more sons were born to them; both died as infants: Jacob B. Martin (April 30, 1941 to May 7, 1941) and Joseph W. Martin (April 27, 1943 to April 28, 1943).

In 1939 grandpa bought approximately 30 acres of land from Brady Felts and Charlie Carter, seventeen of which was in Wilkes County. Then the following year they built another house, a little frame one. In the early 1960s they built the house they now live in. It is right up the road from their old one.

On November 20, 1953 their first child, Billy Thomas, married the former Shelby Jean Weatherman. They live in Wilkes County and have four children. Sandra Gail was born May 12, 1955, on Daddy's birthday. She married Timothy Dale Whitaker on June 30, 1973 and the following year their first child was born, Olivia Dawn on February 4, 1974. On August 24, 1981 their second child Andrea Daile was born. They live in Elkin, in the Poplar Springs Community.

Then on February 2, 1959 I was born. They named me after two of my great-grandmothers; Sarah Frances. I married Jerry Dwayne Byrd on June 18, 1976. We now have one little girl, Wendy Rae, born April 24, 1979. We live in Elkin.

Finally Daddy's third child was a boy, Steven Thomas (named after my daddy) born on May 6, 1964. He is now a Senior at East Wilkes High School and lives at home.

Last born to my parents was William Scott (named after my grandpa) who was born on April 5, 1970. He is in the sixth grade at C.B. Eller Elementary School.

Grandpa's next child, Mary Lafayette, married John Billy Lawrence on February 19, 1951. They live in Elkin, and have one child, Billie Kaye, born on September 12, 1955. Kaye married Michael Simon Avara on May 10, 1975. They now live in North Bergen, New Jersey.

Grandpa's last living child, James Harvey, married Jo Ann McCann on April 19, 1957, They live in Elkin, and have two sons. The first, Larry Dean was born on April 6, 1958. He married Diane Quellette on May 3, 1980. They live in Winston-Salem.

Their last child, Timothy Allen, was born on September 28, 1963. He married Brenda Louise Andrews on March 15, 1982. Brenda has one child, Danielle Nicole. They now live in Jonesville.

Grandpa and Grandma celebrated their 50th wedding anniversary on August 16, 1981. They may be old enough to have been married 50 years but you wouldn't know it by looking at them. They both look much younger than their age. I guess it's hard work and love that keep them so young. They still raise a large garden and sell produce. I know they have more pep and youthfulness than some 20-year-olds, and if I know my grandpa and grandma they always will.

Sources; Family knowledge, and grave markers.

— Sarah Martin Byrd

THE MASTIN FAMILY
827

The Mastin family in Wilkes County originated with the immigration of the Reverend Thomas Mastin to Wilkes from Spotsylvania County, Virginia about 1802. Thomas was born in 1749 in Caroline County, Virginia which was the birthplace of the Baptist religion. Although his family left Caroline County for Spotsylvania when he was 11, the influence of these first Baptists apparently infected the young boy, and he was ordained a Baptist minister. Virginia records indicate that he was an active minister in Spotsylvania County during the 1790's.

The origins of the Mastin family date back to the early Virginia settlements in the 17th century. Originally the name was probably spelled Marston. The Mastin's of Wilkes County probably derive from Marston or Mastin settlers of Glouchester County in the Tidewater areas of Virginia. The first certain ancestor was John Marston (Mastin) of Caroline County. His son, John Mastin, Jr. was born about 1720 and was the father of the Reverend Thomas Mastin.

After coming to Wilkes County, the Reverend Thomas became pastor of Brier Creek Baptist Church. He served as pastor for 26 years until his death in 1828. He was the first moderator of the Brier Creek Association which was organized in 1822.

Thomas settled on a part of the Roundabout plantation at the mouth of Bugaboo Creek at Ronda, with his second wife, Mary. His first wife, Priscilla, had died a few years after marriage and prior to his coming to Wilkes. Thomas Mastin, Jr. was born of this first marriage. Descended from the second marriage of Thomas, Sr. was five children, John, Dolly, Jefferson, Flower, and William. The Mastin's and related families now living in Wilkes County are descendants of these six people.

Sources: Personal research.

— Mrs. Eileen Mastin Nisewanger

EDGAR JONES MASTIN
828

Edgar Jones Mastin was born in Wilkes County March 28, 1914 to James Franklin Mastin and Elizabeth Agnes Fowler Mastin.

Edgar entered the Army in World War II on November 21, 1941, receiving his training at Fort Bragg, North Carolina and was assigned to coast artillery. He went overseas in September, 1942, and was killed in action in North Africa on March 28, 1943. He was awarded the Purple Heart, decorated for wounds received in action; the award was made posthumously. The award was presented to his parents of Route two, Wilkesboro, North Carolina in the Antioch township.

Sources: Family records, World War II records.

— Irene Mastin Whittington

EDWARD OLIN MASTIN
829

Edward Olin Mastin, only surviving son of William(s) Mastin and Rebecca Amanda St. Clair Mastin, was born 14 August 1863 at the Yeargin Old Place. He was born when his father was fifty-seven and his mother forty-eight. In 1876, at the age of thirteen, he inherited the family estate upon the death of Judge Williams, his father. Under the supervision of his mother, Rebecca, he lived on the farm and halped her until her death in 1889. During his early years, he was also a revenue officer for the county of Wilkes.

Edward Olin was a very intelligent, self-educated man, prone rather to read his law books than work on the land. He was not a very successful farmer and soon the land was heavily mortgaged.

Before the death of his father Judge Mastin, the county of Wilkes had gone Democratic, Edward Olin was a staunch Republican, and had many political enemies during his career. At the age of thirty-three he became representative for the Legislature in Raleigh. He served as Speaker of the House about 1896.

Shortly before World War I, when the country was in a depression, Edward Olin became a salesman for several companies and traveled throughout the South. He was so determined that his children receive a good education, he rented his home, and moved his family to Guilford so his children could attend Guilford College.

He returned to Wilkes in 1911/12 and served on the Draft Board of Wilkes during the war.

About 1917, Edward Olin sold the Yeargin place and removed with his family to Quakertown, Pennsylvania, where he bought a large farm. He died in Quakertown 21 August 1920, and is buried there. The farm passed to his youngest son, Edward Olin Mastin, Jr. Edward Olin married Elizabeth Johnson, commonly called Neely, of Taylorsville (now Mountain City), Tennessee. She was born in 1860 and died in Quakertown 26 December 1931.

Edward Olin and "Neely" had three sons and five daughters, all born at the Yeargin old place near Wilkesboro. After the death of her husband, Neely kept a foster child, Lillie May Reeves, who married Walter Bergey. Edward Olin and Neely had children as follows: Martha Amanda, called "Mattie", was born 17 March 1887. In 1920, at age of thirty-three, after a broken engagement, she journied to California to meet a man she had never seen, a friend of a friend. She met and married Constant Lamont, born in Belgium, died 1969. They had three daughters: Alma, born 1921, married Russell Mathias and had four children; Constance, born 1923, married Raymond Bradshaw and had two daughters; Frances, born 1927, married Donald Burgar and had a daughter. Mattie is now 97 years old and living at the home of her daughter, Constance in Carmel, California.

Mary Alma was born 28 December 1888, married John Henry Hogg in 1911 and moved to Buffton, Indiana. During the 1917 Spanish Flu epidemic, she and her husband returned to the home of her parents in Quakertown, to remain during this terrible time. There Alma caught the flu she had so hopefully tried to avoid, and died. She is buried at Quakertown. Her sister Carrie returned with Mr. Hogg to Indiana to care for these small young children. Later Carrie and John Hogg married. Mary Alma and John Hogg had two sons, and a daughter: Bruce Lee, born 1913, married Willmina Monier in 1946; Gertrude, born 1915, married first, Paul Sharpe in 1940. He was killed in the Philippine Islands in 1945. There were two children born of this marriage, Constance Jean (1941) and Jane Ann (1942). Gertrude married second Harvy Milton Luce in 1948 and he was killed in 1977. There were two children of this marriage: Carolyn (1950), and Donald Milton (1952). Max Olin born 1918, married Dorothy Johnson and had John 1949, and Rebecca 1954.

Edward Bruce was born in 1890. He married Gertrude Smith of Danville, Virginia. Bruce lived in Greensboro and worked for the South Atlantic railroad. He died in 1961. Two children were born of this marriage, Harry Bruce (1919-1920), Edward Bruce, Jr. born 1921, married Virginia Todd and had four sons, Edward in 1944, Phillip in 1948, David in 1949 and Todd in 1963.

Philip Olin Mastin, born 1893, married first Ethel Smith, issue 1 son. He married second Grace Alta Hayward, and had three children: Robert in 1921; Dorcas died in infancy; Patricia in 1931. Philip Olin died in 1969 and is buried in Berkley, Michigan. His widow, Grace, later married a childhood sweetheart in Michigan, moved to Leesburg, Florida, became a widow again and married Philip Olin's brother, Edward Olin Mastin.

Roxie Sinesca Mastin, known as Sinie was born 1895, married James Thomas Carr Wright of Hunting Creek. Dr. Wright taught for thirty-four years at Appalachian University in Boone, and died in 1963. Sinie is now living near her daughter in Winter Park, Florida. Three children were born of this marriage: Charles Olin, born 1919, married 1943 Helen White and had issue: Gail in 1945; Stephen Charles in 1948; Frances Carolyn in 1951; and Gregg Clifford in 1954. The second son, Thomas Carr, born 1921, married Billie Gordon Smith in 1946. They had three children: Rebecca Leigh in 1948; Thomas Carr, Jr. in 1951; Elizabeth Ann in 1961. A daughter, Mary Doris, born 1923, married William Devin Gooch and had three sons: Michael Devin in 1950; Steven Carr in 1958; and Richard in 1960.

Carrie May, born 1898, at age 19 returned with the husband of her deceased sister Alma to Indiana, where she lived and raised her sister's children. She later married John Hogg. Carrie is now living with Gertrude, a

child of John and Alma Hogg, in Clearwater, Florida and Indiana.

Edwin Olin Mastin, Jr. born 1910, inherited his father's estate in Quakertown, Pennsylvania. He married first Marian Landenberger and had issue: twins, Joan and Jean born 1931; Joan died in 1935. Jean married Gilbert Welsh and had issue, Joan in 1961, Doris in 1962. Edward Olin Mastin was born in 1938, married Marjorie Bower and had Sharon in 1966, Christine in 1968. Jay Mastin born 1946 married Margaret Gander and had Jason in 1971.

Duella Augusta Mastin, called Ella, was born 25 June 1903. She married Paul Zweir of Pennsylvania in 1926. They had three children: Bruce, born 1927, married Jane Ann Bush and had Susan in 1953, Carolyn in 1956, Eric in 1958. Katharine born 1933, married Walter Eaton, Jr. and they had Derek in 1963, Scott. Pauline, born 1936, married Robert Iantoni and had Janice in 1959, Jill in 1961, Nina in 1964 and Carey in 1969. Paul Zweier died in Pennsylvania in 1980. Ella still lives at their home in Kingston, Pennsylvania.

Sources: Wilkes County will books, court records; Virginia Quit Rent Rolls, Church records of Spotsylvania County, Va.

— Sinesca Mastin Wright

JOHN L. MASTIN

830

John L. Mastin was born in Wilkes County to James Franklin Mastin and Elizabeth Agnes Fowler Mastin on January 14, 1911.

John married Minnie Pearl Richardson, daughter of James Franklin Lloyd Cornealius Richardson and Manda Jeanettie Higgins Richardson on July 6, 1935. They were married at a country store located on Old Highway 60, by C.G. Glass, Sr., who was the owner of the store.

There were five children born to this marriage; Irene Mae, Hazel Marie, Johnny Junior, James Phillip (Phil), and Jeanettie Gevenia Mastin who is deceased. They have nine grandchildren.

They were married during the depression years, and very little work was available, so in able to support his family he started making moonshine and was caught and brought to trial before Judge Johnson J. Hayes.

Judge Hayes, asked him if he had a job would he quit making moonshine, and John's answer was yes. Judge Hayes gave John a job working at a sawmill.

In 1945, John bought Dave Mink Lumber Company located on Old Highway 60, and changed the name to Mastin Lumber Company. Later he started H.M.S. Refrigerated Service, a trucking company.

John was one of the founders and charter members of the Broadway Volunteer Fire Department located three miles east of Wilkesboro, North Carolina; the department was organized in 1968.

John was an active member of Fishing Creek Baptist Church and was elected to the board of deacons (1956-1975) on which he served for eighteen years. He had twenty-one years of perfect attendance in Sunday School. His wife Minnie has seven years, Irene six years, John-

ny twenty-five years, Phil twenty-six years. Grandchildren Claude Curtis has fourteen years, and Mrs. Johnny Wayne (Claudia Mae) Cleary has twenty-one years. Children of Claude Allen and Irene Mastin Whittington; Leslie Marie had eleven years, and Eric John has ten years, children of Johnny J. Mastin and Betty Sue Bell Mastin, B. Sue has ten years; Phillip Todd has eleven years, Christopher Scott (Chris) has five years, and Kimberly Michelle has one year, children of James Phillip and Nancy Carolyn Brown Mastin, N. Carolyn has three years. There are one-hundred-seventy-one years of perfect attendance in Sunday School in his family.

John and Minnie's home was always open to anyone who needed a place to live. Over the years, they took in a lot of people, giving them a home as long as they wished to stay.

John lived a Christian life before his family and friends. John was a fair, honest man. When he gave his word it was like a written contract. He brought a many boundary of timber on a hand shake, and didn't go back on his word.

John has left his children and grandchildren with good morals to follow, pricless memories, and a name to be proud of for generations to come. His family and friends furnished the Nursery II Department, in the educational building at Fishing Creek Baptist Church in his memory.

On July 7, 1975, John wrote a thank you note to his friends, which read as follows: ''I would like to thank the many friends I have at Fishing Creek for the prayers, love offering, visits, and especially for every act of kindness you have shown to me and my family during my illness. I trust you will continue to pray for me that God's will be done in my life, and to give me and my family the spiritual strength we need for one day at a time.'' He died on Friday July 11, 1975 of lung cancer. The above was read by the Rev. Vaughn Brown at church on Sunday morning the day of his burial.

Sources: Family records, personal knowledge and memories.

— Irene Mastin Whittington

LESLIE MARIE MASTIN

831

Leslie Marie Mastin was born at Wilkes General Hospital in North Wilkesboro, N.C. to Johnny Junior Mastin and Betty Sue Bell Mastin on February 17, 1964. She was fatally injured after the vehicle she was driving skidded on ice and overturned at 3:15 p.m. on Shew Ridge Road four miles east of Wilkesboro, North Carolina on Wednesday, February 4, 1981. She was a junior at Wilkes Central Senior High School. Leslie is survived by her parents, one brother Eric John Mastin. She was the granddaughter of Minnie Pearl Richardson Mastin and the late John L. Mastin and of Marie Illa Staley Bell Miller and the late Claude Marvin Bell. Marie Staley Bell Miller was married to Leslie Gavin Miller, who was killed in an automobile accident in August, 1954.

Leslie was an active member of Fishing

Creek Baptist Church where she had eleven years perfect attendance in Sunday School. She was the organist and pianist for the Youth Choir. She was instrumental in her Sunday School visiting Vesper's Nursing Home. On Sunday afternoons, Leslie would visit the elderly at Vesper's trying to bring a little sunshine into their lives.

Leslie attended C.C. Wright Elementary School where she had four years perfect attendance. Leslie was a cheerleader for two years. For the school year 1977-1978, she was presented an award for "Most Talented in Cheerleading." In 1977, Leslie placed second in the school talent show. During the eighth grade graduation ceremony, Principal Alexander Erwin presented Leslie the award for "Most Outstanding Eighth Grade Student."

Leslie excelled in piano and organ. She performed before the National Federation of Music Clubs and in many other competitions. She received superior ratings.

In June, 1980, she was invited to attend the School for Gifted Students in the Arts at Brevard College, Brevard, N.C. She attended this special session for two weeks at which time she studied piano, choral music, and ballet.

Leslie had completed six years of dance instruction at Canipe School of Dance. She had competed in Dance Masters of America competitions. Her group received a superior rating. Leslie had performed before many civic organizations in Wilkes County. In 1977, Leslie was presented with the Senior Cup in Ballet by Margie Canipe. Leslie took tap, jazz, and ballet lessons. She auditioned at Wilkes Community College for a part in "Coppelia." She earned a dancing part as a Czarda. The performance was given in March of 1980. She also had a dancing and singing part in "May Fest" in May, 1980 at Wilkes Community College.

Leslie was nominated to attend the Governor's School of North Carolina, which is a special session for gifted and talented high school students, for choral music. Her death came just two weeks before she was to audition for the Governor's School. Leslie also was listed in the 1981 edition of "Who's Who Among American High School Students."

Leslie was a varsity cheerleader, a member of the Highlighters Choral Group, a member of the American Field Service Club, a member of the French Club, and was acitve in the Wilkes Central Drama Club. She was in the classes for the gifted and talented. Leslie was an honor roll student.

The morning after her death a memorial service was held for Leslie at Wilkes Central Senior High. She was the third member of her class to die in an automobile accident. Leslie was described in the memorial service as an "Eagle we will miss."

The Class of 1982 at Wilkes Central Senior High School had a special tree planting ceremony to honor the former classmates: Teresa Porter, Kathy Green, and Leslie Mastin. In the benediction, Andrea Childress, Class Vice-President, spoke of the appropriateness of the memorial. "We thank Thee now for beautiful and everlasting memories of Teresa, Kathy, and Leslie. Help us to prepetuate their memory by resolving today that our lives shall be forever growing, radiating goodness, love, and mercy."

In addition to the tree memorial, the junior class has established a scholarship fund, which will be awarded in the spring to a member of the Class of 1982.

A youth section was established on April 26, 1981 in the library of Fishing Creek Baptist Church in memory of Leslie by her aunt, Irene Mastin Whittington. Many memorials were made to Fishing Creek Baptist Church in memory of Leslie. These monies have been used to purchase books to be placed in the youth library. This special section was established so that the youth of today and future generations can have the opportunity to read good books. In this way, Leslie can always live on in the lives of future generations.

Leslie was a fine Christian, beautiful and talented sixteen year old girl, who has been greatly missed by her family and friends. She achieved so much in her short life and touched so many people with her kindness and smile. Knowing her has made this a better world.

Sources: Family records, personal knowledge and memories, and interviews with family members.

— Irene Mastin Whittington

REV. THOMAS MASTIN
832

The name Mastin/Marston seems to have been originally Marston, and was so spelled by many members of the family well down into the 19th century. The Rev. Thomas Mastin, founder of the family in Wilkes County, North Carolina, at one period in his life signed himself Marston, and at least two of his sons used Marstin during their earlier years.

The Marston family came to the colony of Virginia from England sometime in the 17th century, and they first appear in the old Tidewater counties of James City (around Williamsburg) and Gloucester. The 1704 Quit Rent Rolls for a sort of census of landowners in the colony of Virginia, and they include the following names: James City county: Thomas Marston 1,000 acres, William Marston 150 acres. Gloucester county, Petsworth parish: Elizabeth Mastin 360 acres.

Petsworth is the westernmost parish of Gloucester county, and it is probably from the Marstons or Mastins of Petsworth that the Wilkes county family descends. Many settlers from Petsworth moved up the Mattaponi River in the 18th century to the newer counties of Caroline and Spotsylvania.

The first generation, John Marston or Mastin of Caroline county, is the first certain ancestor of the North Carolina family. He was born in the late 17th century, listed in 1704 Quit Rent Rolls. It is most probable that he was a son of the widow Elizabeth Mastin of Petsworth parish. Nothing further is known of John Mastin, as the colonial records of Caroline county have been almost totally destroyed.

The second generation, John Mastin, Jr., was probably born about 1720 and reared in Caroline county, where he married Elizabeth., and where their elder children were born including the Rev. Thomas Mastin. They moved to Spotsylvania county by 1761, where John Mastin, Jr., bought a 275 acre plantation in St. George's parish, not far from Fredericksburg. In 1770 they moved to Berkeley parish, in the southern part of Spotsylvania county, and bought a plantation of 332 acres, where they continued to reside thereafter. They had sons William, Benjamin, Thomas, Mordacai, and probably others.

Rev. Thomas Mastin (or Marston), third son of John Mastin, Jr. and wife, Elizabeth, was born in 1749 in Caroline county, Virginia, and died 10 December 1828 in Wilkes County, aged 79 years. When he was about eleven years old his parents removed to Spotsylvania county, just west of Caroline, but the county of his birth had a profound influence on Thomas Mastin's later life. Caroline county was the birthplace on the Baptist denomination in Virginia, and it was in the Caroline Gaol that a group of pioneer Baptist ministers were imprisoned in 1771, for preaching without licenses. Under the influence of these zealots young Thomas Mastin became an ardent Baptist and was subsequently ordained to the ministry of that faith.

He was first married to Priscilla, and in 1784 received a Deed of Gift from his parents for 100 acres of their home plantation in Berkeley parish, Spotsylvania county. In 1786, he removed to St. George's parish, in the more populous northern part of the county, near Fredericksburg, where he purchased lands totalling 289 acres. His first wife having died after a few years of marriage, he married secondly Mary Trible, born 1763/64, died after 1850, probably about 1854.

During the 1790's Thomas Mastin was very active in the Baptist ministry around Fredericksburg, and the Spotsylvania, county records contain a list of fourteen marriages performed by him between 1795 and 1799. About 1802 he sold out in Spotsylvania, and migrated to Wilkes County, North Carolina, to become pastor of Brier Creek Baptist Church, a position which he held until his death twenty-six years later. Many of his former neighbors and friends in Spotsylvania had preceded him to Wilkes county, including the Darnells, Sheppars, Stubblefields, Gordons, Herndons and others, and it was probably through the influence of some of these that he was induced to come to Brier Creek Church. He was many times a delegate from Brier Creek to the meetings of the Yadkin Association in the period 1803-1822, and on 23 November 1822, he became first Moderator of the Brier Creek Association at its organization.

Shortly after his arrival in Wilkes he settled his family on a part of Roundabout plantation, which then belonged to Col. James Sheppard, who had married Elder Mastin's niece, Phebe Mastin. In 1806 Col. Sheppard gave him a deed for this land, a tract of 80 acres at the mouth of Bugaboo Creek, near the village of Ronda. He added to this by other purchases, and spent the remainder of his life at this place. He made his will on 3 September 1828 (Wilkes County Will Book 4, p. 125) and died three months and 8 days later, on 14 December 1828 and is buried at the Brier Creek Baptist Cemetery, Wilkes County.

By his first wife, Priscilla, Elder Thomas Mastin is known to have had one son, Thomas Mastin, Jr., (about 1780-1830), who is the ancestor of most of the Mastins now living in Wilkes County. Thomas Mastin, Jr. was married to Olive Rose, born 1781, daughter of Sterling Rose of Wilkes County, and resided on Brier Creek. They had issue twelve children, seven sons and five daughters, as follows: (1) Nancy Mastin married 1836 Thomas Pardue; (2) William Mastin married Sarah., and must be carefully distinguished in the Wilkes records form his half-uncle, Judge William(s) Mastin, as the two were almost exactly the same age; (3) Benjamin Mastin (1810-1888), married Malinda McDonald in 1829; (4) Lucy Mastin married Nathan Redding; (5) John Elliott Mastin, sometime deputy clerk of the Wilkes County court under his half-uncle, Judge William(S) Mastin; (6) Thomas Trible Mastin, born about 1815, for many years a bachelor who lived with his widowed mother at the homeplace on Brier Creek, but married in middle life; (7) James Maston born about 1819, married 1840 Harriet Joyner/Joiner; (8) Alexander Mastin, born about 1823, married 1849 Martha Curry; a daughter married Isaac S. Call, Jr. and a granddaughter married David E. Call, both of whom were nephews of Isaac Slater Call; (9) Joseph Harrison Mastin married 1844 Martha Joyner/Joiner; (10) Amelia Wright Mastin married 1843 Thomas Nelson Foster and died shortly afterwards, leaving one daughter, Lemira Foster; (11) Mary Mastin married 1848 William Childers; (12) Susannah Mastin married 1847 Willis Dimmett/Dutson/Dueson.

The Reverend Thomas Mastin, by his second wife Mary, had issue five children, three sons and two daughters: (1) John Mastin married 1822 Elizabeth Head; (2) Dolly Mastin married 1815 Stephen Gentle and lived near Wilkesboro. She died in 1860 and had Sarah, born 1818, Rebecca, William, Thomas, Martha, Louisa who married William Scarlett 2 December 1860; (3) Jefferson Mastin, unmarried, born 22 October 1838, died 28 September 1853, buried at Yeargin place, Wilkes County; (4) Flower Mastin married 22 December 1823 John Joyner/Joiner, born about 1797. They had issue Leah who married Leander Cothren, Susannah who married Edmund Boas and Lucy born 1832. (5) William(s) Mastin (1806-1876).

Sources: Spotsylvania County, Virginia records, Wilkes County records and personal knowledge.

— Sinesca Mastin Wright

WILLIAM(S) MASTIN

833

William(s) Mastin, youngest child of Elder Thomas Mastin and his second wife, Mary, was born 14 January 1806 in Wilkes County, at his father's plantation near the mouth of Bugaboo Creek, and died 15 October 1876 at his residence, the Yeargin place, near Wilkesboro, aged 70 years, 9 months and 1 day. He was given the first name Williams, and is so called in his father's will and other papges, but for practical purposes he later dropped the final "s" since the general public assumed that his given name was simply William.

Williams Mastin was reared at his birthplace, now a part of the village of Ronda, and received a fairly good country education for the time and place. At the age of twenty-two he became executor of his father's will and the principal beneficiary of the estate. Early in life he showed a marked talent for business; he learned the mercantile trade under Col. William P. Waugh of Wilkesboro, the leading merchant of the county, and the two men became close friends, though young Mastin soon went into business for himself. With Mr. David Gray as his partner, under the firm name of Mastin & Gray, he established stores at Wilkesboro and Traphill, and in a few years had increased his patrimonial inheritance into a small fortune.

Though not born to wealth, for clergymen in that era were notoriously underpaid, Williams Mastin grew up with certain unusual advantages as the youngest and favorite son of the pastor of Brier Creek Church. Unlike many rural Baptist churches, Brier Creek was an established congregation of considerable prestige, due to the fact that many of its members were river planters of wealth and education. Consequently young Mastin was reared in society of a higher type than that ordinarily enjoyed by the sons of country preachers. His own natural abilities, backed by the friendship of these river families and the influence of his friend and patron Colonel Waugh, soon brought the young man into public life.

In 1832 he had removed permanently to a plantation on Cub Creek, near Wilkesboro in order to be nearer to the center of his business enterprises and of the political life of the county. This was during the presidency of Andrew Jackson, and it was about this time that a new, conservative political party began to take form, the Whigs, who were basically opposed to Jackson's policies. Wilkes County had always tended toward conservatism, and the new party made rapid strides in the county; young Mastin's friends and associates were active Whig leaders, and he soon found himself drawn into politics. In 1833, at the age of 27, Williams Mastin was elected Clerk of the County Court and Judge of the Probate Court of Wilkes County, which offices he held for a period of twenty-eight years (1833-1861). Thus during the last half of the ante-bellum period Judge Mastin was one of the political powers in Wilkes County. A sort of Whig dynasty controlled the county throughout this period, composed of Judge Mastin and his close personal and political friends — Colonel Joel Vannoy (his brother-in-law), Colonel Waugh, Major John Finley, Dr. James Calloway, Judge Anderson Mitchell, the Martins, Carmichaels, and other families of wealth and influence. The Whigs were generally opposed to the principle of secession, and at the outbreak of the Civil War their influence in Wilkes underwent a temporary eclipse; Judge Mastin lost his office to a young Democrat, Capt. Nelson Anderson Foster, and thereafter retired from public life.

Though opposed to the war in principle, Judge Mastin was loyal to the Confederacy, and like so many other wealthy planters was completely ruined by the outcome of the war. He went into bankruptcy, and his considerable property was sold at public auction, inlcuding his beautiful manor house at Ronda. However, the principal part of his home plantation was saved for him through the loyalty of his son-in-law, Isaac Slater Call and his faithful friends, Dr. James Calloway and Judge George Hamilton Brown. He was to retain the plantation known as the Yeargin old place, called Cedar Grove.

Though born and reared in the Baptist faith, Judge Mastin married into a Methodist family and afterwards associated himself with that communion. He was one of the original trustees of the First Methodist Church in Wilkesboro.

Judge Williams Mastin married Rebecca Amanda St. Clair (1814-1889), formerly wife of William S. Falls of Iredell county, and a daughter of John St. Clair, Esq., of Wilkesboro, who represented Wilkes County eight times in the House of Commons and was for many years a Justice of the County Court and Deputy Clerk.

Judge Williams and Rebecca had fifteen children: (1) Louisa Mariah Mastin (1830-1860) unmarried, a dwarf, but highly intelligent, and much beloved by her family. (2) Laura Jane Mastin (1832-1916) married in 1863 Basil A. Hackney (1839-1880/86) of Chatham County and lived at Yeargin place. No issue. She is buried nearby in an unmarked grave at Eschol Methodist Church. (3) Mary Ann Mastin (1834-1916) commonly called Molly, married 1865 Henry Turner (1815-1881) of Turner's Mill, Iredell County. They had six children: Charles, Joseph, Henry C., Annie A., Eva M., Lucy. (4) "Mattie" Martha Caroline (1836-1920), married 1854 Judge Isaac Slater Call (1825-1893). (5) William J. Mastin (1839-1853) died in his 14th year, and is buried at Yeargin place. (6) Elizabeth E. "Betty" born about 1841, married 1868 Walter A. Bouchelle, issue two children Charles A., and Margaret A. (7) Henry Clay Mastin (1843-1843) buried at Yeargin place; (8) Margaret born 1844, married William Ensor Bouchelle born 1832, removed to Texas in the 1870s, settling in Killeen, Bell County, where they died. (9) Sinesca Adelaide (1847-1908) commonly called Sinie, married in 1869 Sidney Montfort Transou (1847-1932) son of James W. and Mary A. (Rousseau) Transou of Wilkes; settled near Laurel Springs in Ashe County, where they died and are buried at Transou Methodist Church. Issue: Eugene, William M., Charles S., Bertha May, Carrie, Bessie, Ella R., and Frank. (10) Duella "Ella", (1849-1920) married 1897 John H. Carson, no issue. (11) Georgiana born 1852, removed to Texas and died there. She married John M. Bouchelle. (12) Charles C. (1854-1868) is buried at Yeargin place. (13) Rosanna E. born 1856, married Zachary Taylor Bagby (1849-1918), removed to Sioux City, Iowa and died there. (14) Ida May (1860-1924) married 1884, George Hartzog McGlamery (1853-1930). (15) Edward Olin Mastin (1863-1920, married 1886 Mary Elizabeth Elizabeth Johnson.

Though Judge Williams Mastin was one of the dominating figures in Wilkes County history for more than a generation, his descendants in the male line have completely disappeared from the county. The female line, however, is still preserved in Wilkes in the persons of descendants of Mrs. Call, Mrs. Augustus Bouchelle, Mrs. Transou through the children and grandchildren of Mrs. I.T. Prevette, Clarence Call, Buel S. Call, Charles A. Bouchelle and Mrs. J.W. Fletcher.

Over a thirty year period, Judge Mastin purchased either independently or in partnership, well over 2,000 acres of land in Wilkes County, principally around Wilkesboro, including a house and two lots on West Main Street in Wilkesboro, which he gave to his son-in-law Isaac Slater Call, the site occupied in 1957 by Norman Smoak. His own residence was first on Cub Creek near Wilkesboro, afterwards the Martin Chatham place, but in 1839 he purchased from Dr. Robert Martin the plantation known as the Yeargin old place on Yeargin Creek, a tributary of Fishing Creek, several miles east of Wilkesboro on the Statesville road and made his residence there for the remainder of his life. His dwelling house was still standing in 1957, but in a much altered and modernized condition; a large brick chimney was the only remaining evidence of the antiquity of the building, which was once a log cabin.

A small family cemetery was located near the house, containing the graves of Judge Mastin, his wife and four of their children. In the 1840s these graves were moved to Eschol Methodist Church. The original head stones were taken, by request, and placed in the front yard of a relative and only small markers are used at the Eschol Methodist Church.

Sources: Wilkes County records, gravestones, personal knowledge.

— Sinesca Mastin Wright

T. HAROLD MAYES
834

T. Harold Mayes was born 3 October 1926 in Alexander County, N.C., the son of Troy and Ida Little Mayes. He died 22 October 1978 in Wilkes County, N.C.

Harold had one sister, Rose Ellen and three brothers, Don, Wayne and Steve, all of Alexander County. He came to Wilkes County when he married Hazel Parsons. He worked with Forester Beverage Company for some time, then went into business for himself opening the Artistic Beauty School. Later he was one of the founders of Empire Cadillac-Olds and also College Park Cinema. He served for two years in the U.S. Navy near the end of World War II.

Harold married on the 28 June 1952 at the First Baptist Church in North Wilkesboro, Hazel Marie Parsons, born 10 July 1929, daughter of James Walter and Mary Ann Hutchens Parsons. They had one daughter Sabrina Ann who was born 13 February 1956 in Wilkes County.

Sabrina Ann married 10 June 1978 Daniel Bowles Franklin who was born 12 March 1955 in Greensboro, Guilford County, N.C., son of Billy Joe and Tina Bowles Franklin. Sabrina

T. Harold Mayes.

and Dan have a daughter Tamara Ann who was born 9 April 1981.

Hazel is owner and operator of the Artistic Beauty Parlor and she and Sabrina own and operate the Artistic Beauty School, both businesses in North Wilkesboro.

Sources: Personal knowledge.

— Sabrina Mayes Franklin

REV. WILLIAM CALLOWAY MEADOWS
835

W.C. Meadows resided in the Pores Knob Community in Wilkes County. He was well known as an earnest worker in religious and charitable undertakings as well as being a man of integrity. He was born in Sugar Loaf Township, Alexander County, N.C., February 11, 1845, of English ancestry, being a descendant in the fifth generation from Daniel Meadows (1), the immigrant ancestor, the line of descent being through Daniel (2), Gilham (3), Harvey (4) and W.C. (5).

Daniel Meadows (1) was born and bred in England. He was married to Elizabeth Jennings of London, England. As a soldier in the British Army, he came to America during the Revolutionary War. He evidently sympathized with the colonists, as he never returned to his native land. He sent for his wife to join him and they settled in Virginia at the end of the war and remained there until death.

Daniel Meadows (2) migrated from Virginia, the place of his birth, to North Carolina when young, becoming one of the earlier settlers of that part of Wilkes County that is now included within the limits of Alexander County. He purchased a tract of wild land and began its improvement and was there engaged in tilling the soil for the remainder of his life.

Gilham Meadows (3) was born and reared on the home farm in Alexander County. He was a farmer by choice and was married to Sally Laws.

Harvey Meadows (4) was born November 14, 1806 in Alexander County and was a lifelong resident and farmer. He married Jane

Grayson, who was born in Wilkes County in 1814, of Virginian ancestry. They had six children: Elizabeth, Martha, William Calloway, John G., Serena and Clementine. Harvey's second wife was Mary Blair.

William C. attended the short terms of the Sugar Loaf township school and also assisted his father with the farm. In November, 1863, he enlisted in Company F, Second Regiment, North Carolina Troops and participated in many battles. William C. was severely wounded (being shot in his neck) in October 1864 during the battle at Winchester, Virginia. Two months later, after recovering from his injury, he rejoined his company and was again at the front in several battles. On April 3, 1865, he was captured by the enemy and being taken to New York was held as a prisoner of war until June 20, 1865 when he was paroled.

After returning to his home, he helped his father farm. On April 3, 1867, William married Mary Elizabeth Price (born October 23, 1846 — died November 7, 1895) daughter of James W. and Rosannah Kilby Price. They settled on the farm given them by James W. Price. To this union were born the following children: (1) William Gilsen (March 20, 1868 — December 19, 1930). (2) Franklin Dean (March 14, 1870 — November 18, 1932) (3) Jane Gertrude (December 17, 1872 — October 25, 1878) (4) Daughter — stillborn — April, 1874. (5) Robert Carl (January 18, 1876 — January 6, 1965) (6) Clarence Edgar (January 14, 1878 — December 11, 1878) (7) James Harvey (November 6, 1879 — August 11, 1880) (8) Annie Viola (November 3, 1881 — July 21, 1927) (9) Mack Arthur (November, 1884 — January 2, 1888) (10) Pansy Alma (November 20, 1887 — May 30, 1967) (11) Felix Green (April 14, 1892 — November 14, 1895).

Soon after settling on the farm which was located on Moravian Creek, William C. built a grist mill and a saw mill, building up to the millwright's trade successfully for several years erecting mills in various sections of Virginia, Tennessee and North Carolina. In 1901 he invented the Meadows Mill, a portable mill for grinding corn and in 1907 took out a patent for the mill. He and his son Franklin Dean began to manufacture these mills on the home farm. At the Jamestown Exposition, they were awarded the gold medal for the best mill.

William C. joined the Baptist Church in 1857 and from that time was deeply interested in religious matters. In 1871 he was licensed to preach and in 1879 was ordained as a minister of the gospel. Among the churches he served were: Pilgrim Church in Alexander County, Pleasant Home Church, Little Rock, Mt. Carmel, Mt. Pleasant, Pleasant Hill and New Hope (all in Wilkes County). He also led in the organization of Oakwoods Baptist Church. He devoted much time and financial support to Walnut Grove Baptist Church in his home community of Pores Knob.

William Calloway Meadows died on December 18, 1933. His funeral was held at Walnut Grove Baptist Church and he was buried in the church cemetery.

Sources: Family tradition, Bible records, Wilkes County Records.

— Virginia Jennings

WILLIAM G. MEADOWS
836

William Gilsen Meadows was a resident of Pores Knob. He was the owner and operator of the store in the community of Pores Knob. This store was located across the road from the Meadows Mill Company, and the building is still standing on the property once owned by Will Meadows with the house he built right beside the store. This property is now owned by Mrs. Edith F. Davis.

Will (as everyone called him) was the eldest child of W.C. and Mary Elizabeth Price Meadows. He was born March 20, 1868. He attended the short terms of school located in this community. He was noted as being a good student who loved to read. He had dreams of going to medical school and becoming a doctor. However, he did not attain this dream. But he continued reading in the available medical books and people in the community would come and ask for his advice on their medical problems.

Will married Grace Creola McCrary on October 14, 1886. His wife was the daughter of Ahiram and Ellen G. Watts McCrary of the Millers Creek community. Grace was born December 31, 1869 and died October 23, 1937. They had three children: (1) Pansy Vetra (born January 6, 1889) married Arthur Deal and had two daughters, Lucille and Wanda. (2) William Mack (born October 14, 1891 — died February 26, 1976 and buried in Forest Lawn Memorial Park in Richmond, Va. He married Margaret Louisa Pennell and had one child, Pauline. (3) Annie Verniece (born May 23, 1893 — died October 28, 1975 and buried in Walnut Grove Baptist Church cemetary, Pores Knob community. She married R.C. Jennings, Sr. and had five children: Beatrice, R.C. Jr., Elizabeth, Dorothy and Virginia.

Will died on December 19, 1930. Both Will and his wife are buried in Walnut Grove Baptist Church cemetary not far from his father's final resting place.

Sources: Family Bible, Wilkes Records, and Tradition.

— Virginia Jennings

GEORGE McT. MILLER
837

Mr. George McT. Miller was born March 10, 1883, in Ashe County, N.C. No one today has ever known what the McT. stood for unless it was McThomas, which has been the most popular guess. After he completed his schooling, "Mr. Mack", as he was fondly called, moved to Wilkes County where he met and married Minnie Gibbs McEwen, born March 2, 1890. "Mr. Mack" was employed by the postal service until his retirement.

The children born to this union were Arthur Dwight Miller, born November 18, 1921, and Mack T. Miller, born December 1, 1923, both of whom served in World War II as commissioned officers in the United States Air Force. Dwight served in the Pacific theatre of war and Mack, in the European.

After service and schooling at Brevard and Appalachian, Dwight married Nancy Lenoir Forester, born August 15, 1927, the daughter of the late Harriet Augusta Lenoir and George Stewart Forester, Sr., of North Wilkesboro. The children of this marriage are: Judith (Judy) Forester Miller, born December 27, 1947; Carolyn (Callie) Lenoir Miller, born January 19, 1951; and Arthur Dwight Miller, Jr., born March 25, 1956.

Judy is married to William Edward McMichael and has one child, Lenoir Dorsey McMichael, born August 20, 1975. Edward was born in Homestead, Florida, and graduated from Fork Union Military Academy and Appalachian State University. Judy graduated from Appalachian and has her masters' degree in Education from UNC-G.

Callie married Thomas McMurray, who graduated from the Cleveland Institute of Art. He is now director of the Cleveland Art Museum and is himself a successful artist. Callie and Tom have one child, Glennis Forester McMurray, born April 12, 1979.

Mack Miller, after graduating from N.C. State as a construction engineer, married Geneva Godwin of Tampa, Florida, where they now reside.

Source: Personal knowledge.

— Mrs. A. Dwight Miller, Sr.

JOHN and JANE MILLER
838

I do not know the number of years my g.g.g.g. grandparents, John and Jane Miller resided in Wilkes County, but I do know they were there during the Revolutionary period for they signed affadivits for John Hopper, Revolutionary soldier from Wilkes, when he applied for a pension in 1819.

In a land entry dated 28 July 1779 John Smith entered 150 acres at John Miller's old path where it crosses Reddies River road above George Gordon's toward Thomas Hopper.

Jane's mother may have been the Mary Hickerson, who in a will dated 5 December 1793, left her daughter, Jane Miller a Chest and Tea Ware.

The family moved to Madison County, Kentucky in the early 1800's, for a son, William, married there in 1804.

On March 5, 1844, a deed was produced in Madison County Circuit Court in a dispute over the sale of a tract of land that had belonged to John Miller, then deceased. This parcel of land was situated on the dividing ridge between Muddy Creek and Otter Creek.

The children of John and Jane Miller were: (1) Thomas, b. ca 1788 NC, m. 20 February 1812 to Patience West; (2) Michael, b. 1783 NC, m. 20 October 1807 to Polly Jones; (3) William, m. 19 June 1804 to Hannah Lockey; (4) Samuel (5) Susan; (6) Rebecca, m. David Owens; (7) Charity, m. March or May 8, 1817 to Elias Gulley; (8) Anna, m. 20 January 1811 to David Hopper d. 1853-55 Orange County, Indiana; (9) Elizabeth (10) Jane, m. 17 February 1814 to Thomas Land. All these marriages were in Madison County, Kentucky.

David and Anna Miller Hopper migrated with their family to Orange County, Indiana in 1829.

Sources: John Hopper Pension Papers #7785; Land Entry Book Wilkes County, NC; WILKES COUNTY, NORTH CAROLINA WILL ABSTRACTS BOOK ONE; Madison County, Kentucky Marriage Records; Madison County, Kentucky Deeds, Orange County Indiana Probate Records Paoli, Ind.; Orange County Deeds, Paoli, Ind.

— Mrs. Jack Toliver

THE JOHN B. MILLER FAMILY
839

On Dec. 5, 1812, John B. Miller was born to Joseph and Nancy Bingham Miller of the Lewis Fork Community. He courted and married Mary (Polly) Triplett who was born Feb. 14, 1813 in Wilkes Co. to Jesse and Dicie Gray Triplett.

John B. and Polly were married Oct. 2, 1833 with Enoch McNeil as his bondsman. A daughter Frances (also known as Fannie and Frankie) was born Aug. 4, 1834. Frankie first married Mathis Eller who was killed in the Civil War. Her second husband was Thomas David Hall.

Nancy Ann, the second child was born Jan 12, 1840. She married Harvey Bingham. Sarah, the third child, was born July 12, 1844. She married Noah Brookshire. Mary E., the fourth child, was born June 28, 1851. She married William Daniel Wagoner. According to a family letter in 1878, they were living in Taylorsville, Tenn. The fifth child was a son and was named John for his father. He was born Dec. 6, 1854. He grew to be a rather tall man, farmed with his father and remained unmarried. In 1883 he had pneumonia and died on Dec. 12, at the age of 29.

John B. Miller and his family were faithful members of the Baptist Church of Christ at Lewis Fork. He was ordained a Deacon of this church in April of 1855 and was a deeply religious man.

In 1856, Polly Miller died, leaving John B. with small children to rear. About this time he was trading horses and cattle and traveling some to Tennessee with his business. There he met and married Susie Wagoner. She died, leaving him a bereaved widower. Family legend says John B. had gone to Tennessee to visit her people and was bemoaning what he would do. Susie's sister Sally is quoted as saying "Aw, Mr. Miller, Good God Almighty, I'll take her place" and she did.

Sally was much loved by the family and was a good mother for John B's children. She was called 'Granny' Miller and is well remembered by my mother. She enjoyed watching lightning during thunder storms and would sit in an open doorway to watch the brilliant flashes in the sky. She also enjoyed teasing the girls as they walked by her home returning from attending church. She is remembered as asking "Gals, did you catch you a feller today?" She had beautiful clothes — silk dresses, black silk slippers, a lace cape, silk gloves as well as beautiful jewelry. She kept these in a special chest and what a treat it was to be shown these items!

She was of strong character with definite beliefs and was quite outspoken. When a neighbor came by who had been imbibing in the spirits, she would quickly send him on his way.

John B. Miller

Sallie Wagoner Miller.

Family legend says that during the Civil War, some Yankees came riding by and raised a gun to shoot her dog. She had a small black hearth shovel that she raised to protect her dog. They apparently reconsidered the matter and allowed the dog to live. The shovel is still preserved in the family.

She was an excellent cook and was ready and happy to feed a bountiful meal to anyone who stopped by — always preferring to feed someone who had a good appetite.

They lived in a log house near the present day Lewis Fork Baptist Church. John B. died Feb. 2, 1904 and is buried in the Miller Family Cemetery.

Sources: Family Legend, Marriage Bonds, Deeds, Census Records, Bible Records.

— Mrs. J. Arnold Simpson

JOSEPH and NANCY BINGHAM MILLER

840

Joseph Miller is believed to be a son of William and Mary Eldridge Miller and was probably born between 1775 to 1780. He married Nancy Bingham on July 6, 1807 in Wilkes County. Nancy was born about 1790, the daughter of Robert and Elizabeth McNeil Bingham. They lived in the Lewis Fork area of Wilkes County near his parents and other brothers and sisters.

His brother Henry Miller signed his marriage bond with Joseph in 1807. This family belonged to the Baptist Church. Nancy's maternal grandfather was the Reverend George McNeil a Baptist Minister. The minutes of the Lewis Fork Baptist Church show they were members of that church.

A complete record of their children is not known at this time. The oldest known son is John B. Miller who was born December 5, 1812 (over five years after their marriage.) Census records indicate earlier children in the household. Other known children include Betsy, born about 1822, showing ten years difference between John B. and Betsy. Census records show additional children. Betsy married Enoch McNeil and they had nine children: Harriet S., Jesse, Nancy Permiller, William E., Mauli, Columbus M., Mary, Larkin and Parilee. (I would like to add that this family is

erroneously written up in Judge Johnson J. Hayes' book. He indicates Enoch married Elizabeth Vannoy. Records clearly indicate she was Elizabeth "Betsy" Miller.)

Another child of Joseph and Nancy was Jesse, who was born in January of 1824 and who married Elizabeth Proffit. The 1860 Census shows eight children in their household. These children were Julia Ann, Nancy Minerva, Mary, Martha J., America, Isadora, Jesse Calvin, and William. Jesse lived in Wilkes in Lewis Fork but by 1880 was in Watauga County.

Nancy Miller was left a widow by the time of the 1840 census. School Census records indicate her other children were: William, born about 1828; George N., born about 1831, and Mary, born about 1834 as well as her son Jesse. All were attending school in the 1841 and 1843 School Census.

The death dates of Joseph and Nancy are not known. Joseph is believed to have died about 1840. In the court records, Alfred Miller is appointed Administrator of Joseph Miller's estate in 1841. Nancy was deceased by 1879 — how much earlier is uncertain.

Sources: Census records, school census records, marriage bonds, estate records, church minutes and deed records.

— Mrs. J. Arnold Simpson

MICHAEL MILLER and DESCENDANTS

841

As far as we can ascertain, my great-grandfather, Michael Miller, known as "Mike," born in 1820 and died about 1887, migrated with his brother, Josiah ("Jose"), from Germany to the Dutch area of Pottstown, Penn. at an early age. They came South to the head-waters of the Reddies River in western Wilkes County and traded a cow and a calf even for a farm. Michael Miller met and married Millie Bare (born 1819) and bought a 150-acre farm for $350.00. Millie Miller was of German "Dutch" descent. My grandfather, "Preacher Lee" Miller, told me when I was a young girl of how his mother would "fly into talking Dutch" when she would discipline the children. They didn't know the language, but they understood the message.

Michael and Millie Bare Miller had ten children: Troy (1840); Isom (1842); Louisa (11-15-1846 — 9-25-1921); Nathan (1848); Delphia (1851-1929); Rufus and Alvus, twins (11-24-1854); Juline (1856); Leander Michael (7-12-1859 — 1-27-1951) and David Clemens (1864-1961).

Troy Miller was a musician in Co. "A," 34th N.C. Infantry, in the Civil War, and lived to return home.

Isom Miller was in Co. "A," 26th N.C. Infantry, during the Civil War. He was captured in the Wilderness at Mine Run, Va. and was taken prisoner May 5, 1864 near Harper's Ferry, Va. He was transferred to Elmira, N.Y. July 31, 1864 and died at U.S. General Hospital there on July 16, 1865.

During the Civil War, the Homeguards came to the home of my great-grandfather, Michael Miller, and tried to confiscate his horses. He got out his Ward rifle and told them that the first man who tried to take a horse would die, and they left.

My grandfather, Leander Michael Miller, married Rachel Clementine Phillips, daughter of Robert Franklin Phillips and Rebecca Powell Phillips. Grandmother Clementine died at age 48. To this union was born six children, Lucretia (1-28-1882 — 1953), who married Hege H. Beshears; Orpha (born 8-17-1891 and married C. Andrew Keys); Lora (who married Mac Church and is deceased); Sheridan Franklin (born 12-13-1894 and married to Lizzie Mae Funkhouser, of Virginia); my father, Ordan Rayvaughn (born 12-9-1897 and married Marado Voria Nichols); and Lillian, who died as an infant. Leander ("Preacher Lee") Miller pastored many churches, such as Poplar Cove, Oak Grove, Big Ivy, Stony Hill, Yellow Hill, Piney Ridge, White Oak, Union Baptist and Blue Ridge Baptist.

My father, Ordan Rayvaughn Miller, married Marado Voria Nichols (born 5-21-1904), daughter of McClellan ("Mack") Nichols and Adinah Spears Nichols on 3-22-1922. Their children are: Athel Dustin (born 9-14-23 and married to Katherine Parsons); Maynard Lee (born 7-2-25 and married to Clara Bowman, of Virginia); Joyce Edell (born 5-2-30 and widow of Ralph Tillman Chewning, of Atlanta, Geor-

Rev. Leander Michael Miller (7-12-1859 — 1-27-1951) and a grandson, Vonley Church, son of Lora Miller Church (photo made at home of Lee Miller, Purlear, N.C. about 1940).

gia); and Toyce Cleo (born 5-3-36 and married to Bobby Lee Davis, of Winston-Salem.) Athel Miller has two daughters, Brenda Kaye (Mrs. James McGlamery) and Deborah Lynn (Mrs. Jerry Miller). He has two grandsons, James Darren McGlamery and Rodney Allen Miller. Toyce Miller Davis has two children, Angela and Christopher.

As could be said of most of the pioneer settlers of Wilkes, my ancestors were tough, honest and self-reliant Christian men and women and they struggled and worked against great odds to survive in a very hard environment. It is a privilege and an honor to pay tribute to all of them.

Sources: Wilkes County Courthouse Records, 1850 and 1860 Census, family Bible records, family memories and personal knowledge.

— Joyce Miller Chewning

MONT MILLER FAMILY
842

My Dad, Mont E. Miller, was born on April 13, 1886 in Ashe County, the oldest son of John Alvius and Jane Burgess Miller. Dad had four sisters and two brothers: Lelia, born 1877, died 1954; Belle, born 1879, died 1921; Maude, born 1883, died 1970; Clyde, born 1897, who at this time lives in Idaho; Lynn, born 1889, died 1954; and Lonford, born 1893, died 1972. Dad grew up in the Idlewild community of Ashe County and as a farm boy, he learned early in life the meaning of hard, honest work and an independent spirit that molded his life.

On October 13, 1907 he was married to Carrie Mae Phillips, daughter of James and Sarah Ann Winebarger Phillips. During the next twenty years, seven children were born to them and after moving to North Wilkesboro, two other children were born: (1) Jean, born February 1909, married O.R. Bell, Sr., of Gastonia, N.C. (now deceased). They had four children — Virginia, Shirley, O.R., Jr., and Joe, who was killed in action in Vietnam in May 1968. Jean is now married to Lee Letting and lives in Orlando, Fla. (2) Claude, born December 1910, who resides in North Wilkesboro, married Leora Milam, who died in February 1979. (3) Ralph, born December 1912, is a Baptist minister and married Ruby Osborne, who died in May 1977, lives in Wilkes County. Their children are Shirley, who died in infancy, Jane, Brayn, Gail, Lanny, Diane, Keith and Pamela. (4) Rudd, born April 1915, married Evelyn Keye, deceased October 1970. Their children are Phillip, Dean and Sharon. Rudd lives in Wilkes County and is now married to the former Vanie Beshears. (5) Ruth, born 1918, married Roy Reep, resides in New Orleans, La., and their children are William S., Kenneth, and Rex, who died as an infant. (6) Bruce, born 1921, married Wilma Baker and lives in Winter Park, Florida. They have two children — Judy Ann and Raymond Bruce, Jr. (7) Grace, born January 1925, married Vester C. Dancy, who died October 1975. She also resides in North Wilkesboro. (8) Clate, born January 1928, is married to the former Nancy Grace Hayes. (9) Joyce, born 1929, married Kiffin C. Caudle of Mt. Airy, N.C. who died

February 1980.

Dad and Mama had to work hard to support their growing family, and during the early years of their marriage, Dad made many trips between Idlewild and North Wilkesboro in a horse-drawn wagon, hauling various items. I have heard him tell of the night in 1916, (the time of the big flood) he was going up the mountain returning home from North Wilkesboro, when the flood waters came rushing down the mountain, he had to abandon the wagon and take refuge in a barn. His wagon was lost in the water and he had to continue the journey home the next day on horseback.

At one time Mama carried the mail on horseback in Ashe County, and one of the things I remember her telling about those days was how, at time during the harsh winter months when she finished a day's mail delivery, her feet in the stirrups would be encased in ice as a result of fording icy creeks.

Dad moved his family to North Wilkesboro in 1927 and for the next several years he worked for Adrian Phillips' Root and Herb Co. and also for a time was a policeman in North Wilkesboro under Chief John A. Walker. In the early 1940's he became self employed in trucking, dealing in coal and produce, such as watermelons and peaches.

During World War II, three of their sons served in the Army — Claude in Italy, Rudd and Bruce in France. During the 1950's, another son, Clate, served four years in the Air Force. Claude retired in December 1978 from thirty years service with Kerns Bakeries.

Mama passed away in June 1972 and Dad continued to live alone in the house he had built in 1945, but on Christmas Eve 1973, he went to rejoin Mama. Their last resting place is in Gordon Baptist Church cemetary, north of North Wilkesboro.

At this writing, the larger number of Mont and Carrie Miller's descendants live in Wilkes County. Grace has been with J.C. Penny Co. for forty years and Clate is a City Mail Carrier in North Wilkesboro. Mama and Dad left behind a large number of descendants the total living today consisting of nine children, twenty grandchildren, twenty-eight great-grandchildren, and eight great-great-grandchildren.

Sources: Family records, personal knowledge and memories, and interviews with family members.

— Clate Miller

THOMAS S. MILLER, SR.
843

My grandfather, Thomas Samuel Miller, Sr., was born July 22, 1852 in Davie County to Luther and Cynthia Miller. As a young man he came to Wilkesboro where he met and married Clara Blanch Rousseau born September 6, 1867. They were married October 27, 1885. My grandfather was a traveling salesman and covered the State of North Carolina for the Herb Medicine Co. of Springfield, Ohio. He told me many times that he traveled from "Manteo to Murphy" and it was while he was in Western North Carolina on one of his regular trips that he was stricken and a few days later,

October 29, 1937, died in Sylva. He was a man who gave the impression of being younger than he actually was. He wanted to think and act young to the extent that he promised me a suit of clothes if I would call him "Uncle Tom" rather than "Grandpa".

He and my grandmother became the parents of eleven children, three boys and eight girls. They were William Warner, Thomas S., John, Minnie Miller Pugh, Ella Mae Miller Shields, Helena Miller Clark, Louise Miller Davis, Lily Miller Parker, Eula Miller Clement, Dolly Miller Underwood and Lucille Miller Gallimore.

My father, William Warner Miller, Sr., was born in Wilkes County, January 21, 1889 and married Kate E. Forester April 23, 1913. My father was a grocer most of his life and prided himself in being a good one. My mother was the daughter of James A. and Mary Jane Crowder Forester. She was born September 21, 1889. My father used to walk from Wilkesboro to North Wilkesboro in the early morning hours, work all day in a grocery store, and walk home late in the evening. During World War I, being too old for service in the Armed Forces, he went to W. Va. where he worked in the Commissary by day and dug coal at night. There were four children in my family — three boys and one girl. They were William Warner born May 9, 1914 in Wilkesboro, James Thomas born January 12, 1918 in Twin Branch W. Va., Frederick Clifton born March 6, 1920 in Twin Branch, W. Va. and Marjorie Elma (Mrs. Tommy Crysel) born June 11, 1925 in Wilkesboro. Clifton Miller has one daughter, Nanelle, and Marjorie Crysel has one daughter, Kathy Crysel Sebastian.

I married Edith G. Crater, daughter of R. Roy and Gertrude Gray Crater April 20, 1941. My wife was born June 14, 1918 in Yadkin County. After our first child was born March 5, 1943, I was inducted into the Army Air Force on April 8, 1943 and served some thirty-two months.

Our children are Ann Crater who has two daughters, Lorrie and Amy, Mary Jane who has one son, Brian and Marjorie Lorraine who has two sons, Drew and Wesley. Ann is married to Tommy Arnold, Jane was married to Barry Mims and Lorriane is married to Russell Golds.

Sources: Family Bibles, newspaper obituaries and family knowledge.

— Warner Miller, Jr.

WILLIAM and MARY MILLER
844

One of the pioneer families of Wilkes County was William Miller and his wife Mary. Research seems to indicate that William Miller was born in England about 1735. Upon reaching maturity, he became engaged to Mary (Polly) Eldridge (sometimes spelled Alderidge). William came to America first and legend says that he worked out enough money to pay Polly's transportation cost to America. She joined him in New Jersey where they were married. William probably came about 1750 to 1755.

They moved to North Carolina in the 1760's,

settling in the region of the Jersey Settlement. William Miller joined the Jersey Baptist Church by letter from Boone's Ford Church in 1775. Not much later they were living at Holman's Ford on Lewis Fork in Wilkes County. They remained there until 1783 when they moved with Elizabeth and Nathan Horton and the Ebenezer Fairchild family to Cook's Gap (now in Watauga Co.). This was approximately six miles east of Boone, N.C. They also owned land at Meat Camp in Ashe County with the Blackburns and James Jackson. About 1801 they moved to Lewis Fork and are believed to have remained there the rest of their lives.

Tradition holds that William Miller fought in the Battle of King's Mountain under Col. Benjamin Cleveland's regiment of Whigs during the Revolutionary War.

William and Mary appear on the records as charter members of Three Forks Baptist Church which was organized Nov. 6, 1790. They were very active and faithful while members of this church.

There are numerous land records pertaining to this family including land on Elk Creek, North Fork of Meat Camp Creek, New River, Coleman's Branch, Riddles Fork Camp Creek and on a path leading to Three Forks of New River.

By 1801 he had bought land on the South fork of Lewis Fork near land owned by Hugh Montgomery, James Patton, Ebenezer Fairchild and William Jackson.

The children of William and Mary Miller are believed to include the following: (1) Henry, conflicting reports show him married to Catherine Lipps in 1787 and moving to Missouri and others believe he is the Henry Miller who married Polly (Hillory) McNeil in 1803. A family letter indicates that he married Polly McNeil. (2) Mary (Polly) married John Brown in 1799. (3) Virginia (Jennie) married a McNeil. (4) David, born Feb. 5, 1775 and married June 4, 1801 to Elizabeth Norris. They had 12 children. David died March 28, 1845. (5) Joseph, who married Nancy Bingham (daughter of Robert Bingham) in 1807. (6) William, Jr. who married Rebecca . There may have been other children.

It is not known when either William or his wife Mary died, but the date appears to be between 1820 and 1830.

Sources: History of Watauga County, church minutes, census records, marriage bonds and land records.

— Mrs. J. Arnold Simpson

DR. JAMES C. MILLS
845

James Cobb Mills was born in Apex, N.C. on November 8, 1916, son of Joseph Franklin Mills and Elizabeth Claire Uzzle Mills.

He attended public schools in Henderson and received a B.S. Degree from Wake Forest College in 1937. Four years later he was graduated from the medical school of Tulane Univ. at which time he received the rank of lieutenant in the Army Medical Corps. He served a year's internship at Greenville General Hospital in S.C. before being sent to the European theater of World War II for two years.

In 1946, he entered private practice of medicine in North Wilkesboro. He served as a staff member of Wilkes Hospital and currently is on the staff of Wilkes General Hospital.

In 1939, he married Sara Brinson Griffin. Their children are James Cobb Mills, Jr., Elizabeth Claire Mills Anderson, Franklin Griffin Mills, and Caroline Smith Mills Lawry.

Sources: personal knowledge.

— Sara G. Mills

DEWEY L. and BEATRICE V. NICHOLS MINTON
846

Dewey Lincoln Minton was born March 22, 1901 in the Purlear community of Wilkes County, the only son of Alva A. Minton and grandson of Purvis Minton. It is interesting to note that while Purvis' name appears on the roster of Confederate soldiers, there are documents in the possession of the family indicating that out of moral conviction, he had indeed crossed the mountain into Tennessee and joined the 86th "Mt. Grifty" regiment of the Union Army. His widow, Minerva, received his veteran's pension from the U.S. Government until her death.

Dewey was named for President Lincoln, who was revered by the family. He spent his boyhood and young in the community in which he was born, working on the small family farm, located between old highway sixty and old U.S. 421, now the site of West Wilkes High School. The Arbor Grove Methodist Church was located nearby on land donated in part by his great uncle, Mack Minton and was Dewey's home church. As he had the opportunity, Dewey attended school in the one-room school. He also attended the newly established high school at Millers Creek.

At the age of eighteen, Dewey and several of his friends traveled to Bluefield, W. Va. to work in the yards of the Norfolk and Western Railroad. The winter of 1919 was a bitter one and the exposure to the elements took its toll on young Dewey so that he was forced to return to Wilkes. He sought employment in North Wilkesboro, first in furniture plants and then in Williams Manufacturing Company which soon merged with W.C. Meadows to form Meadows Mill Company. Dewey worked with that firm as shipping clerk and parts manager for over forty-five years until his retirement in 1970.

In 1928, Dewey was married in a simple ceremony performed by the Rev. Finley C. Watts to Beatrice Varina Nichols, youngest daughter of David Vance and Julya Bumgarner Nichols. Beatrice was born January 6, 1903 in the Purlear Community. Her father was a farmer, school teacher collector of Internal Revenue, County Commissioner and merchant. The family attended New Hope Baptist Church where Mr. Nichols was a deacon and Sunday School teacher. There were thirteen children in the Nichols family, Beatrice being ninth. She attended grammar school in the local one-room school, then was a member of the first class at Millers Creek High School which she helped organize. She received a number of

gold metals for scholarship and attendance. She attended one year at Mountain View Junior College and two summers at Appalachian State Normal School and was awarded a teaching certificate and became an elementary teacher.

Beatrice taught four years before she married and settled down to homemaking. Their first home was an apartment in North Wilkesboro. They then moved to a house on F Street and lived there until they built a home in the Mulberry community in 1939, where they lived until she died and where Dewey lived until shortly before he died in 1981.

Dewey and Beatrice had three sons: Dean Lincoln was born in 1928. He graduated from North Wilkesboro High School in 1946, attended Mars Hill Junior College, graduated from Wake Forest College with a B.A. in 1951 and received the M. Div. from the Southern Baptist Theological Seminary, Louisville, Ky. Dean was ordained by the First Baptist of North Wilkesboro and served as minister of several N.C. churches before entering the U.S. Air Force as a chaplain in 1961. Assignments took him and his family to several overseas locations as well as throughout the U.S. He retired in 1981 at the rank of Lieut. Colonel and is currently a student in the Physician Assistant Program of Bowman Gray School of Medicine, Wake Forest University, Winston-Salem. In 1950 Dean married Patsy Ruth Hawkins of North Wilkesboro and they have three sons: Dean L. Jr., an artist in Germany; John Wallace a U.S. Air Force instructor; and James Eric, Copy Editor for the Oklahoma City Times. John is married to Mary Susan Magnuson of Milford, Ma. and has two sons. Eric is married to Lt. Pamela Bridges of Savannah, Ga.

Blan Vance, their second son, was born in 1939. Blan graduated from Wilkes Central High School and Wake Forest College in 1962. He also was ordained by the First Baptist Church and attended Southeastern Baptist Theological Seminary in Wake Forest, N.C. He then graduated from the School of Social Work, University of N.C. Chapel Hill, with a M.S.W. degree. He served as administrator of the I.G. Greer Children's Home in Chapel Hill and is currently on the faculty of the Child Development Institute and School of Medicine of the University of N.C. He is a certified marriage and family therapist and has held several state and national positions of leadership in his field. He is married to Mae Lee Smith of Chester, Virginia and they have two children, Melanie Elizabeth and Keith Ian.

Avalon Nichols, "Nich", their third son, was born in 1941. He also graduated from Wilkes Central High School and Wake Forest College. He has done extensive graduate work at the University of Massachusetts and at Brown University. He is currently on the Political Science faculty at Lowell State University, Lowell, Ma. He is married to Cheryl Ann Renniger of Wilminston, N.C. and with their daughter, Teressa, lives in Arlington, Ma.

Dewey and Beatrice were active members of the First Baptist Church in North Wilkesboro. Dewey had been active in the First Methodist Church as a choir member and member of the Board of Stewards. After becoming a Baptist he became active in the choir, an officer in the

Sunday School, and was elected to the Board of Deacons. He was honored by the church by election as a Life Deacon. Beatrice served many years as a Sunday School teacher and officer of the WMU.

In 1950, Beatrice returned to the public school system as a temporary teacher, a term which lasted twenty years! To upgrade her skills she returned to summer schools and extension centers and in 1963, at the age of sixty, was awarded the B.S. degree by Appalachian State University. She continued teaching well past the usual retirement age, spending the last years as a first grade teacher at Mulberry Elementary School. She retired in 1971 and after an extended illness, died July 15, 1973, age 70.

As teaching had been Beatrice's life, Dewey's life was in music. His choir work has been mentioned. He was also a tenor in quartets specializing in barbershop and gospel. Quartets he helped form were aired on WHKY in Hickory and WKBC in North Wilkesboro. He frequently sang at funerals for the funeral home, and just before his death on November 15, 1981, he was leading singing in the rest home where he was convalescing.

Sources: Personal knowledge.

— Dean L. Minton

JULIUS MINTON FAMILY
847

My grandfather, Julius Edward Minton was born in Wilkes County 6 Sept. 1897 to William Thomas and Mary McGlamery Minton. He was a brother to Otto Minton who married Belva Eller, Carl Minton who married Ina Vannoy, Floeta Minton who married Ted Ferguson, Coy Minton who married Ester Faw and Viola Minton who married Jomes Frank (Doc) Vannoy. They were raised on a 360 acre farm in the Congo community. Most of the land is now a part of the W. Kerr Scott Dam.

Julius married Ester Parker, born in 1905 to Rufus and Vadia Parsons Parker, on 26 January 1925. They built their home on Pads Road near Millers Creek and continue to live there today.

"Paw" was a chicken farmer most of his life. He was one of the first men to ever have a motorcycle in Wilkes County. He and his wife raised four children: (1) Julius Edsel Minton born in 1926, married Opal Church, daughter of J.A. (Angus) and Annie Church Church. Edsel and Opal had five children: (a) Eddy, their first child, died in 1966 at age 21 from injuries received in a motorcycle accident. (b) Jean married Ray Owings and they have two sons, Jeff and Jason. (c) Judy married Gary Hamby and they have a son, Chad. (d) Larry married Sharon Deal and they have two children, Matthew and Rebecca. (e) Jill married Joe Woodie and they have a son, Joseph.

(2) Mary Katherine Minton born 1929, was married to J.C. Byers who died 3 June 1979. They were the parents of two sons, Gary and Greg. Gary married Carol Warren and they have a daughter, Kimberly. Greg lives with his mother and attends West Wilkes High School.

(3) William Thomas Minton born 1931, married Oaklen Church and they have two children, Janice and Joey. Janice married Tam Cheek and they have a son, Joseph. Joey lives at home with his mother and dad.

(4) Jimmy Clayton Minton born 1933, married Nancy Porter and they had four children. (a) Henry married Susie Spears and they have a daughter, Jane. (b) Hal married Karen Triplett. (c) Shelia married Terry Minton and they have one daughter, Heather. (d) Ginger lives with her mother and attends Roaring River School. Jimmy and Nancy are divorced and he married second Janie Wyatt.

All of the above descendants of Julius and Ester Minton reside in Wilkes County today.

Sources: Personal knowledge and interviews with family members.

— Judy M. Hamby

DR. GURNEY TALMADGE MITCHELL
848

Dr. Gurney Talmadge Mitchell was born in Iredell Co., N.C. October 12, 1897, son of Ella Magnolia Fletcher, born April 24, 1871, died July 28, 1955, and Jonah Francis Mitchell born June 24, 1871, died March 8, 1907, who were married May 1, 1895. Jonah Mitchell built a home on his father's farm. His parents were Edmond, born March 22, 1842, died June 18, 1920, and Rebecca Howard born Feb. 20, 1846, died Nov. 10, 1910.

Dr. Mitchell's sisters were, Dina Lenora b. May 31, 1899, married Commie Lee Comer Nov. 10, 1920; Flora Dell, born Feb. 12, 1903, married Ralph Dowell Oct. 1936, Amy Lou b. Sept. 20, 1904, and Eva Mae born Feb. 16, 1896, died Dec. 13, 1918.

When he was ten his father died and his mother built a home beside her parents Pinkney Claywell Fletcher, b. Sept. 12, 1842, died June 19, 1937 and Susan Catherine Parker, born Feb. 14, 1845, died May 21, 1929. Amy Lou remembers those early years. "We grew cotton and peas for money crops. Mother sold pigs, calves, dried fruit, eggs, butter, jimson leaves, and blackberries at our Uncle Jessie Templeton's store. Gurney plowed with our mules and expected us girls to keep hoeing behind him as long as he plowed. We had a wagon that we used to haul corn and fodder. When we went to revival meetings at Grassy Knob Baptist Church, we put a top on the wagon."

Dr. Mitchell attended Zion and Morgan Schools, the latter a one-room log cabin.

During an influenza epidemic, he and his mother went to the home of Dr. L.P. Somers to help take care of the sick. Dr. Somers encouraged Dr. Mitchell to become a physician.

In October 1918, at age 21, Dr. Mitchell arrived at Mars Hill College to take high school and junior college courses. While there he had the opportunity to learn about photography and helped install the first movie projector and screen in Mars Hill for the college.

It was at Mars Hill that he met his future wife, Julia Frances Phillips, born September 18, 1902 at Dalton, N.C. She made a request to have her lamp repaired. Dr. Mitchell

Dr. G.T. Mitchell.

repaired it and scratched his initials on it. They dated while on campus.

Mrs. Mitchell tells about the Sunday afternoon stroll. "Couples couldn't date two Sundays in succession. A date meant walking in a line with other couples with a chaperone in the back. If inappropriate gestures were observed, the couple might be denied the privilege of dating for several weeks. It was called the 'soup line' by the students because of the spooning that went on."

In June 1921, G.T. Mitchell and Julia Phillips were graduated from Mars Hill. Until 1925 Dr. Mitchell attended the U.N.C. at Chapel Hill. Occasionally he visited Julia who was majoring in music at Woman's College at Greensboro.

He also studied at Jefferson Medical College in Philadelphia from 1925 until his graduation in 1927. The summer after graduation he interned at Davis Hospital in Statesville, N.C.

Dr. Mitchell began his practice in a room he rented in his sister Dina's home. She tended the switchboard for him.

He continued to correspond with Julia. In a letter to his mother he explained that Julia was "that girl I was 'foolish' about at Mars Hill." Julia taught public school music in Spartanburg, S.C., Winston-Salem and Greensboro, N.C. She accepted his Acacia fraternity pin a year before they were married. Dr. Mitchell was in this fraternity because he was a Mason.

They were married in a double wedding ceremony with her sister Louise and Dr. Lee E. Kiser on the east lawn of the Phillips home at Dalton in Stokes County Sept. 3, 1929.

In January 1933, the Mitchells moved to Wilkesboro. In October 1933, they moved into the combination home and office he built across from the Old Presbyterian Church. Dr. E.N. Phillips, Julia's brother, joined Dr. Mitchell's practice in 1936.

In 1947, Dr. Mitchell had surgery several times at Duke Hospital. He returned home to stay in March 1951 and died June 21, 1951.

Dr. Mitchell was a member of the Wilkesboro Business and Professional Men's Club, the Kiwanis Club, serving as its president in 1947, was on the board of directors of the Y.M.C.A. and a loyal supporter of the Wilkesboro Baptist Church.

The Mitchells had the following children: Frances Rebecca born May 26, 1931, married Thomas O. Foster, born June 2, 1928, on September 12, 1974. They graduated from Mars Hill and attended A.S.T.C. Frances received her BA degree, cum laude. They have Marie, born April 1951, married Jack F. Steelman born Nov. 2, 1949, on Oct. 11, 1969. Marie graduated at Chapel Hill with a BS degree in Nursing. They have two children, John Scott born June 24, 1970 and David Talmadge, born July 4, 1974. Stephen Mitchell born Nov. 26, 1952, attended U.N.C. at Chapel Hill and Wilkes Community College. Thomas Alston born Jan. 21, 1963, graduated from high school in 1981.

Elizabeth Dalton Mitchell born June 24, 1935, graduated from Mars Hill and from Baptist Hospital with a Nursing degree. She worked last at Chapel Hill where she met Haroutune Dekirmenjian, born June 1, 1936 in Aleppo, Syria. They were married July 24, 1965. They have Liza born Aug. 19, 1966 and Krikor born Sept. 12, 1972.

Julia Carolyn Mitchell, born Feb. 4, 1941, married Zeb Marion Harry, Jr. July 8, 1961. They have Philip Scott born July 22, 1962 who is a student at Davidson, and Kevin Mitchell born May 15, 1966 and is in high school in Culpeper, Va.

Sources: Personal knowledge.

— Mrs. Zeb M. Harry, Jr.

ARCHIE W. MOORE
849

Richard Moore, born February 9, 1871 and died June 16, 1951. He was the son of Henry and Mary Moore. He had brothers, Nathan, born November 13, 1878, died February 21, 1968; John Wilson, born June 22, 1869, died June 26, 1965; Joe, deceased, and one sister, Mary Moore Johnston, deceased.

Richard married Maggie Parker, daughter of Leroy and Emelie Anderson Parker. She was born September 26, 1885 and died March 20, 1979. Her brothers and sisters were: Vetra Parker Combs born September 26, 1887, died July 9, 1965; Robert, born January 26, 1891, died July 16, 1976; Andrew Cleveland born January 24, 1893, died October 6, 1965; Harrison, born March 6, 1896; Cathy (brother) born April 5, 1899; Lena Woodie born May 4, 1905; and Connie Minton Frye born September 10, 1910.

Children born to Richard and Maggie were:
(1) Roy born July 13, 1906. He attended school at Edgewood and married Laura Jane Johnson, daughter of Sam and Cash Johnson. She died March 17, 1972. They had: (1) Harless born October 7, 1932. He attended school at Wilkesboro and is a farmer. (2) Dorothy born December 23, 1936, attended school at Wilkesboro, married Randy Moore, son of Richard and Ruey Moore. They had: Debbie, born October 17, 1956; Babbie, born December 23, 1958; Tabby, born August 9, 1962; and Libby Dean, born August 22, 1963. (3) Margie born May 8, 1939, attended school at Wilkesboro, and married Flake Weber, son of

Thomas and Mattie Weber. They had: Vickie, born November 16, 1955; Penny Gaye, born May 21, 1964; and Laura Mattie, born September 11, 1970. (4) Gladys (Sissy) is married to Bernice Call. They have 5 children.

(2) Luther Harrison born January 8, 1908. He attended school at Edgewood and in 1943 went to work at Carolina Mirror and worked there until his retirement. He married Ennis Baity, daughter of Zenuth and Mary Baity. She was born July 25, 1908. Luther is a patient at Vespers Nursing Home, and Ennis is retired and lives at home on Moore Ridge. They had: (1) Dean born July 16, 1935, attended school in Wilkesboro, and is a car painter. He married Janie Roberts, daughter of Carl and Cleo Roberts. She was born August 2, 1939 in Wilkes County. They had Gary born June 18, 1958, married Libby Clonch. They have two boys, Gary Shawn and Jonathan Lee; Janet born October 29, 1960 and Kevin born July 20, 1971. (2) Virginia Ennis born April 25, 1939. She went to school at Wilkesboro and Wilkes Central High School, married Sidney Albert Waddell, son of Ivy and Gilly Waddell. He was born March 20, 1939 in Wilkes County. Virginia (Ginny) is a housewife and Albert is a night watchman at the American Drew. One son was born: Dennis Wayne, born March 4, 1958. He attended school at C.C. Wright and Wilkes Central, married Karen Marie Gilley, daughter of Carl and Mary Gilley of Ashe County. One son, Dennis Shane was born December 30, 1979 in Ashe County. (3) Kent Luther Moore was born December 9, 1946. He went to school at C.C. Wright and Wilkes Central. His occupation is at Holly Farms. (4) R.B. Moore, was born September 21, 1937. He died in a car wreck on July 1, 1962.

(3) Thelma born November 1, 1909. She attended school at Edgewood, and married Luther Johnson. They moved to Winston-Salem and both were employed at R.J. Reynolds Tobacco Company. Thelma died December 20, 1970. One daughter, Doris, was born on December 25, 1934. She married Bill Tise of Forsyth County. They have one son, Jay.

(4) Sylvester was born January 12, 1921 in Wilkes County. He went to school at Edgewood and is a farmer.

(5) Marie born April 28, 1925. She went to school at Wilkesboro, and married Pete Dudley. He was born June 10, 1918. Marie works at Hanes Corp. They have two sons: Kenneth, born April 15, 1946, married Linda Grant, daughter of Stella and Thomas Grant. They have one son, Mark, born May 15, 1970; Billy was born August 11, 1949, married Joyce Lambert, and they have two sons, Larry and Byron.

(6) Lester G. (Jim) born December 12, 1927. He was a farmer. He died August 27, 1968.

(7) Cecile Alma born June 10, 1911 attended school at Wilkesboro. She died January 5, 1974, married Carey LaFayette Moore, son of Myrtle and Johnson Moore. He was born June 28, 1903. He died December 15, 1975. Two children were born: Fannie Alma Moore, born February 12, 1935, married to Robert Gene Francisco, son of Samuel and

Mr. and Mrs. Archie Moore.

Macie Francisco. They have three chiidren: Lisa Jay, born February 23, 1966; Kimberly Diane, born December 15, 1973; and Shannon Gene, born July 24, 1975; Ralph Norman Moore was born September 5, 1939. He is in the U.S. Marine Corps. He married Beulah Louise Hall. They have three daughters: Melody Lynn, born May 9, 1963; Patricia Ann, born August 12, 1965; and Susan Dawn, born August 13, 1968.

(8) Farry (Dolly) Moore was born November 23, 1918. She is deceased. (9) Herman Moore — He has 3 sons, Carl, Coy, and R.B. Moore. He is deceased. (10) Robert Moore lives in Millers Creek. Has 5 children.

(11) Archie William Moore, was born April 25, 1916 in Wilkes County. He went to school at the old C.C. Wright. He married Rosla Chambers on June 24, daughter of Rosa and Charlie Chambers. She was born December 31, 1928. She went to school at Mt. Sinai. Archie worked at Coble Dairy for 28 years. He is semi-retired and works for Mathis Brothers Construction Co. Rosla is employed at the Journal-Patriot Newspaper. They have two daughters: Helen, born February 12, 1945. She graduated from Wilkes Central (1963), and married Larry Ernest Eller on August 2, 1963, son of Ernest A. and Geneva Faw Eller; Magdaline (Maggie) born September 10, 1949. She graduated from Wilkes Central and Draughn's Business College. She married Billy Mathis on February 14, 1970. Billy is the son of Mont and Mattie Johnson Mathis. He is co-owner in Mathis Brothers Construction Co. Maggie is a homemaker. They have three children: Berry William was born March 6, 1971, died March 5, 1972; Bridgett Dawn was born July 27, 1974; and Bart Christopher was born March 27, 1976.

Sources: From Personal information obtained from individuals named.

— Helen M. Eller

ELIZABETH MOORE
850

Elizabeth Moore, also called Big Betty Moore, was born about 1799, daughter of Sterling Moore. Elizabeth Moore never married but did have four children. There is no indication that she owned land in Wilkes County, but she resided at one time on the land of her brother-in-law Jacob Estep and in her later years she lived with her elder child, Mary Moore Hayes, who owned a small farm near the Estep's. Big Betty was unusual among the early Moores in that she could both read and write, rare educational accomplishments for that period.

Her children were: Mary (Puggy) Moore, born 1821, married to William P. Hayes, son of Henry and Frances Johnson Hayes; Wilson, born 25 April 1823, married to Mary Hayes, daughter of Henry and Frances Johnson Hayes; James Moore, born 6 July 1825, married to Keziah Hayes, daughter of Henry and Frances Johnson Hayes; Sarah Moore, born 13 March, 1829, married to Enoc Anderson.

Elizabeth Moore's grave stone shows that she was born Jan. 14, 1800, and died October 17, 1888. She is buried by her daughter Mary Moore Hayes in the old Anderson Family Cemetery on the Brushy Mountains.

Sources: Personal knowledge.

— Betty Jean M. Baity

IVEY and FREDA MOORE
851

Ivey Moore was born in Collettsville, N.C. in 1902, the son of J.D. Moore, Sr. and Annie Lee Houck Moore. In 1905 the family moved to Wilkes County. Following his education, Ivey went to work for his dad at Home Chair Company in North Wilkesboro.

In 1923 Ivey married Freda Emily Hendren, a resident of Edgewood community and the daughter of A. Grant Hendren and Eugenia Hellard Hendren. Freda was born in 1902, the sixth of eleven children.

Ivey, throughout his entire lifetime, has had a keen interest in the Boy Scout movement, and he has served as Den Dad, assistant scout master, scoutmaster, as well as assistant commissioner of the Wilkes District. In 1974 he received the highest award given to adults who work in the Scout program when he was presented the Beaver Award. Prior to this, on November 25, 1972, a Certificate of Appreciation had been presented to Ivey Moore in recognition of his outstanding service to boyhood by the Old Hickory Council, Boy Scouts of America.

On July 1, 1948, Ivey and two of his sons, Jim and Dudley, received the Eagle Scout Award, a first for Boy Scouting.

In 1943 Ivey served in the Navy in the South Pacific on a destroyer, the U.S.S. Thatcher, receiving his discharge from the service following two years and eight months of duty.

Ivey, a member of the Masonic Order, has provided leadership in many areas of life in Wilkes County. He has been on the Board of Stewards of the First Methodist Church in North Wilkesboro. He has served as President of the Wildlife Club, the Wilkes County Historical Society, the Genealogical Society, the American Legion, and the Lions Club. For a time, in the interest of the libraries in the schools of Wilkes County, he performed as an amateur magician on the stages of the schools to raise money for books.

In 1942 he was an active member of the Knights of the Pythian Lodge. He was district deputy and served on the credentials and youth committees of the Grand Lodge. Ivey Moore organized and was first President of the Little League Baseball clubs.

Ivey was instrumental in the organization and leading of the Daniel Boone Wagon Train. From 1963 to 1968 he served as chief scout in its annual trek from Wilkes County to Boone, N.C. In this capacity, he appeared on C.B.S. television show "To Tell the Truth" in 1964. Ivey is the only North Carolinian to appear in John Steinbeck's "America and the Americans."

During the bicentennial clebration, July 4, 1976 was proclaimed Ivey Moore Day by the Wilkes County Board of Commissioners in appreciation for the years during which Ivey spent his time, energy, and resources in acts of civic, cultural, and historic service to the people of Wilkes.

To commemorate Daniel Boone's trek to Kentucky 200 years ago, Ivey led a group of five on a hike to Boonesborough, Kentucky. The walk, 368 miles, was begun on April 10, 1975 and ended when they reached their destination on May 10, 1975. This trek was made in Mr. Moore's interest in getting the trail marked in the National Trail System. He later appeared before Congress carrying his rifle and dressed in pioneer clothing. The rifle had been used in the Revolutionary battles of Cowpens and Guilford Court House.

Throughout his life, Mr. Moore has been constant in his promotion of the historical value of Wilkes County and his interest in his beloved valley.

Freda Moore, Ivey's wife, has been equally involved in promoting causes beneficial to Wilkes. She has been president of the American Legion Auxiliary, the Garden Path Club, and the Women's Club. A faithful member of the First Methodist Church of North Wilkesboro, she served as president of the United Methodist Women for two terms, has been a member of the Board of Stewards, and worked actively as a member of the choir, as circle chairman, and on several commissions of the Methodist Church.

For many years, Freda was active in the P.T.A. organization of the North Wilkesboro Schools. Within the work of the Women's Club, she was District President of this district and Ameridan Home Chairman in the North Carolina Federation of Women's Clubs. For fifty years she has been a member of the North Wilkesboro Women's Club.

First and foremost she is the mother of six children and has made a good home for them. Eugenia, the first child, was born in 1924. Roy Ivey, Jr., was born in 1926 and died in 1929, two days before the birth of Carolyn. In 1932 Dudley was born and eighteen months later James Marshall was born. Edward, the youngest child, was born in 1936.

Sources: *Journal Patriot*, "General Federation Club-woman," the family Bible, knowledge of Ivey and Freda Moore.

— Jeanne Moore

THE J.D. MOORE FAMILY
852

James Dudley Moore, Sr. was born December 31, 1871 in Caldwell County, the son of Newton and Mary Clark Moore.

In 1900 he married Annie Lee Houck who was born on October 15, 1879 and died on October 9, 1955. During their life together, seven children were born to the Moores — James Elliott (1901-1909), Roy Ivey (1902), Milton Edwin (1904-1905), Mary Virginia (1906-1978), Henry Lee (1907), J.D., Jr. (1912-1972), and Annie Catherine (1917.)

In the year 1905 J.D. Moore, Sr. and his family moved from Collettsville to Wilkes county where he entered the lumber and manufacturing business.

For a number of years he was actively engaged in the management of Meadows Mill Company. Later, in 1922, he sold his interest and founded the Home Chair Company where all types of chairs were made. In 1935 the firm manufactured 195,000 chairs.

Mr. Moore was a member of the First Methodist Church of North Wilkesboro and a member of the board of Stewards. He was a Kiwanian and always took an active part in church and civic affairs. He was a Mason, Shriner, and a member of the Knights of Pythias.

During the flood of 1940, the Home Chair Company was destroyed in North Wilkesboro and was reorganized in Ronda, where it was running at full capacity at the time of the death of Mr. Moore in 1943.

The Journal-Patriot editorialized: "It is with regret and a feeling of loss to this city and community that we comment on the life and accomplishments of J.D. Moore, who died Sunday.

"Too often all too few people realize the value of a life until it ends, but we believe that during the lifetime of J.D. Moore many people in Wilkes county and at distant points had some realization of the life and accomplishments of Mr. Moore.

"J.D. Moore came to North Wilkesboro when this town was only a sprawling village and went into business. In that instance it was Caldwell's county's loss and Wilkes' gain.

"Mr. Moore had faith in the future of North Wilkesboro ane he knew the people in this section of North Carolina. In 1922 he founded Home Chair company, which grew steadily and became one of the leading industrial firms in this immediate part of North Carolina.

"North Wilkesboro will of course feel the loss of Mr. Moore, but his life lives on through the good influences of his character and through the sound business enterprise which he founded and guided through the years."

Following the death of J.D. Moore, Sr., Henry Moore, a son of the founder of the Home Chair company, became president of the company.

Annie Lee, the wife of J.D. Moore, Sr., was a faithful member of the First Methodist Church and made a good home for her family. Her friends, of whom there were many, called her "Big Mama."

Sources: Family Bible, personal knowledge from Ivey Moore, the Journal-Patriot.

— Jeanne Moore

The Moore Family Front Row. L. to R: Jeannie and Ivory Ball middle Row. L. to R: Leander, Rebecca, Julia Johnson Moore, baby Sanford. Back Row: L to R: Loyd, Martin, Jesse, baby Clyde, Asa Ball, Kiziah Moore Ball.

"Papa" Moore.

MARTIN MOORE FAMILY
853

The Moores who have for nearly a century and a half resided in Wilkes County, in Brushy Mountain and Lovelace townships, are mostly descendants of Sterling Moore who came to Wilkes in 1816 from Rowan County. Sterling Moore was a resident of Rowan from 1799 until 1816. There are several deeds for land on waters of Dutchman's Creek involving him.

On 26 September 1816, Sterling Moore of Rowan bought from James Hayes of Wilkes, a plantation of 200 acres on Carne's Creek in Brushy Mountain township. A few days later on 8 October 1816, Sterling Moore of Rowan bought an additional 30 acres in Wilkes.

These combined tracts seem to have been Sterling's homeplace for ten years, until he sold them 15 October 1826 to his son-in-law, Jacob Estep. This property continued to be the Esteps for many years thereafter.

After the sale of this land, Sterling Moore took up various lands on the Brushy Mountain on the waters of Hunting Creek in Lovelace township. Here he spent the remainder of his life. This place subsequently descended to his youngest son, John Moore, who remained there until he removed from Wilkes County shortly before the Civil War.

Sterling Moore was born about 1770 in N.C. and died about 1836 in Wilkes. He was married about 1792 to an Elizabeth who was born in N.C. about 1770 and died after 1850. Sterling left a will in Wilkes which named only his youngest son, John and a Robert Moore. The executors of his will were Daniel Moore and Jesse Moore, who were clearly his sons.

The following are descendants of Sterling and Elizabeth Moore:

Elizabeth Moore (1800-1883) daughter of Sterling, often called "Big Betsy", resided in the Brushy Mountain township. Betsy was un-usual among the early Moores in that she could both read and write, rare educational accomplishments at that period. She was not married but had four illegitimate children; the first two by Shadrack Stanley and the next two by Jacob Estep, her brother-in-law. James Moore (1825-1893) third child of Elizabeth, married Kiziah Hayes (1829-1910) in 1847 and they had 14 children. Their third child Rebecca, born in 1850, married Jesse Leander Moore about 1870.

Jesse Moore (1804-1880), son of Sterling, for many years lived in Lovelace township, but sometime after 1870 he removed to Brushy Mountain township. He married Judith Price in 1824 and they had 13 children. Their last child, Jesse Leander Moore, "Pappy", (1848-1925) married Rebecca Moore (1850-1929). She was known as "Mother" by her own children and by everyone in the community. They had 8 children but only 4 lived to adulthood: Judith Kiziah (1876-1939), Jesse (1878), Loyd (1880-1972), and Martin, born March 16, 1883.

Martin Moore ("Papa") married Alice Marlow (1887-1969) August 23, 1908, and they had 8 children: Lonnie, infant (died in 1910), Virgil, Berlwyn, Roy (1919-1928), McKinley, Boyce, and Sylvia. Papa lives on Armory road in North Wilkesboro with Lonnie and Sylvia.

Virgil is married to Nellie Marlow and they have 3 children: Wayne, Kenneth, and Diane. Wayne married Joy McNeil and they have 3 children: Julie, Joey, and Nicky. Kenneth is married to Marguerite Taylor and they have Donna and Crystal.

Berlwyn married Agnes Kilby and they have Elaine and Ann. Elaine married Bill Michael and they have Greg.

McKinley married Juanita Bumgarner (deceased). They had Len who married Maggie Burchette and have Glen and Martin.

Boyce married Juanita Westmoreland and had Bryan (deceased). Boyce is now married to Fern Faw.

Sylvia (Sis) married Harrison Johnson and had Carol Jean and Steve. Carol Jean married James Clayton (Jap) Lovette and has David and Jimmy. Steve married Sarah Shaver and had Steven; he later married Susie Reeves and had Tate; he is now married to Mary Tilley.

Sources: Family knowledge.

— Ann Moore

NATHAN EDWARD MOORE
854

Nathan Edward Moore was born in Wilkes County 11-13-1878, the son of Henry Eli and Sarah Elizabeth Williams Moore, grandson of Wilson and Mary Hayes Moore. Nathan married first to Mary Treadway, daughter of Eli A. Treadway and Ruie Smith Treadway, on the 29th day of November 1899. They lived at several different places in Wilkes County.

Children of this union were: Cora Viola, born Oct. 10, 1900, married to John Monroe Moose; Bertha, married Carl Ranson Benge and still residing in Iredell County; Gertrude, married to Bud Cloaninger and residing in California; Julie, married to Edward Parker; Henry Eli, married to Gertha Money; Robert Lee, married to Lorene Money (sister of Gertha Money); Roy Edward, married to Fannie Weaner; Faye, who resided in the State of Michigan until her death in early part of 1982; Woodrow, born March 24, 1919.

Mary Treadway Moore passed away 5th day of July, 1927, and Nathan remarried August 22, 1928, to Sarah Mae Speece and he had the following children of this union:

John William, born July 16, 1929; Nathan Edward Jr., born June 14, 1939; George Richard, born March 6, 1942; Lonnie James, born May 2, 1947; Dorothy Laurn, born May 8, 1951; Polly and Minnie (their dates of birth are not known by this writer).

Nathan Edward Moore passed away 2-21-1968 in Robeson County from cancer and is buried in the cemetery in Wilkesboro on corner of Hinshaw and 6th Streets. Mary Treadway Moore is buried at Snow Creek Methodist Church in Iredell County with no marker at her grave.

Sources: personal knowledge

— Betty Jean M. Baity

STERLING (STARLING) MOORE
855

The Moores for nearly a century and half resided in Wilkes County, in Brushy Mountains and Lovelace townships and are mostly, if not entirely, descendant of Sterling Moore, who came to Wilkes County in 1816 from Rowan (now Davie) County. The earlier antecedents of this family are as yet uncertain, though some clues suggest that they may have come to Rowna from Montgomery County, N.C.

Sterling was a resident of Rowan County (now Davie) at least as early as 1799 until 1816. On 26 September, 1816, Sterling Moore of Rowan bought from James Hayes of Wilkes County, a plantation of 200 acres on Cane Creek in Wilkes, in what is now Brushy Mountain township; the witnesses were Samuel Anderson and John Mise. A few days later, on the 8th day of October, 1816, Sterling Moore of Rowan bought an additional 30 acres in Wilkes from Jeremiah Gilreath; witnesses, Jacob Estep and James Moore (son-in-law and son of Sterling). These combined tracts seem to be Sterling's homeplace for about ten years, until he conveyed them on the 15th day of November, 1826, to his son in law Jacob Estep. This property continued to be the residence of the Esteps for many years thereafter.

After the sale of the Cane Creek plantation, Sterling Moore took up various lands on the Brushy Mountains, some distance east of the previous location, on the waters of Hunting Creek, in what is now Lovelace Township; here he spent the remainder of his life. This place subsequently descended to his youngest son John Moore, who remainded there until he removed from Wilkes County shortly before the Civil War.

Sterling Moore was born probably about 1770, somewhere in North Carolina — perhaps in Anson (now Montgomery) County, and died in what is now Lovelace Township, Wilkes County in 1836/37. He was married, perhaps about 1792, to Elizabeth ?; who was born in North Carolina about 1770, and died after 1850 in Lovelcae Township.

Issue of this marriage were: William Moore, born about 1793, married in Wilkes County to Rachel Ferguson; Nancy Moore, born about 1795, married in Rowan County to Jacob Estep; James Moore, born about 1797, married to Mary Stanley in Wilkes County; Elizabeth Moore, born about 1799, never married; Robert (Robin) Moore, born 1802, married in Wilkes County to Sophia Anderson; Jesse Moore, born 1804, married in Wilkes County

to John Watson; Daniel Moore, born about 1808; John Moore, born about 1813, married in Wilkes County to Rachel Holland (presumably Holland). There was a female child born about 1813, but her name is not known.

Sources: Personal knowledge.

— Betty Jean M. Baity

WILSON MOORE
856

Wilson Moore was born 25 April 1823, the son of Elizabeth Moore, on the Brushy Mountains of Wilkes County. He was married March 19, 1844, to Mary Hayes, daughter of Henry and Frances Johnson Hayes. Mary Hayes was born 26th day of December 1825 and died the 13th day of August 1905. Wilson and Mary resided in Lovelace Township and both were very religious. Notation on Mary's grave stone — "Deaconist 64 yrs. Consistent member 58 years." Notation of Wilson's grave stone — "Consistent member 64 years and deacon for 60 years". Wilson died 21st day of October, 1911, and both he and his wife are buried at Hunting Creek Baptist Church — old abandoned cemetery upon the mountain.

Wilson and Mary had fourteen children, eight sons and six daughters. Frances, born about 1844; Sarah, born about 1846; James Oliver, born 1848; Henry Eli, born 1849; Rhoda, born about 1852; Lina K., born 1854; Wilson Jr., born 1856 and died at a very young age; William Swain, born 1857; Peter Harrold, born 8-9-1858; Ambrose Chapel, born 1860; Mary Jane, born 1862; Richard Robert, born 1865; Beulah Lavinia, born 1867; and George S., born 1869.

Frances married George Thornburg; James Oliver married first to Martha D. Marlow and then to Mary M. Johnson; Henry Eli married Sarah Elizabeth Williams; Rhoda married to William Adolphus Baity; Peter Harrold Moore married to Hesse Ann Glass; Ambrose Chapel married Mary M. Johnson, daughter of Moses and Catherine Glass Johnson; Mary Jane married her cousin James Harold Hayes; Richard Robert married Mary E. Bell, daughter of James C and Canie Marlow Bell; Beulah Lavinia married Wilborn Moore and George S. Moore married Mary Ball.

Sources: Personal knowledge.

— Betty Jean M. Baity

THE MOREHOUSES
857

Herbert Harrison Morehouse was born in Brooklyn, New York July 20, 1868, and died in his favorite hospital, Wilkes General, at the age of 96, November 24, 1964. He and his wife, Emma Margaret Lang, born in Toledo, Ohio, February 28, 1869 (she died four days earlier in the same friendly hospital, November 20, 1964) had been married 71 years on November 18, 1964.

They met at Cornell University, Ithaca, New York when 'Bert' was a junior in the new electrical engineering school, and she was a freshman at Sage, the woman's college, on the

same campus, with the same faculty.

They married in 1893 in Toldeo, and before going to Quezaltenango, Guatemala where Morehouse had established a home in the town of his employment (at the age of 21, he was managing the city's electric light plant) they had much enjoyed the delayed but remarkable Chicago World's Fair.

Both Morehouse sons were born in Quezaltenango: Andrew Richmond (1895-1953 — at the time of his death Sterling Professor of Romance Languages, Yale University) and Robert Lang (1901-).

In 1902, the eruption of Santa Maria, and the great earthquake changed many lives, and eventually Morehouse, and his partner, Grant A. Morrill, transferred their successful electrical business to Chihua, Mexico, Pancho Villa's home. Villa's revolutionary tactics were also responsible for many changes, and in 1913, Morehouse and Morrill decided to take up orchard properties they had bought in the Brushy Mountains, Wilkes County.

Later that year, the owners divided the acreage. The Morrills built the hilltop house now owned by Arthur and Rebecca Waugh Lowe. Mrs. Morrill's health, always fragile, was the main reason that family moved back to her girlhood home in New England. The two Mexico-born daughters, and the son born in the As Pearson valley place, now in their retired years living separately in Texas, New Mexico and Massachusetts, still think fondly of their early Brushy Mountain years.

The Morehouses moved further east on the ridge, nearer the old hotel site. Delighted to be home again from foreign shores, they were discovering the boundary lines when they were suddenly accosted by a native of the Brushies, known up hill and down dale as Aunt Dovie. "Be you furriners?"

Foreigners always in one sense, but they soon became established residents. H.H. who had always wanted to be a farmer spent the rest of his long and useful life improving the good earth, and lending two hands wherever he knew how to help.

Due to his efforts, piped water was supplied to the cottage colony which, before the turn of the century, had grown up around both old oaken buckets, and the Iron and Lithia Springs. And on foot, he worked out the right of way for both power and telephone lines, and talked up the development of the Rousseau cut-off, a short route to the Yadkin River bridge from Oakwoods. The Brushy Mountain Fruitgrowers organization owed much to his enthusiasm as did the Great Wilkes Fair, and Kiwanis Club during his always active memberships, and even more during his presidencies. It amused, and rather pleased him to be dubbed The Mayor of the Brushies.

St. Paul's Episcopal Church was to the Morehouses a home church. There they made many life-long friends, and without ceasing, gave of their time and strength. HH was for years church treasurer, as well as Senior Warden, and Clerk of the Vestry. Mrs. Morehouse who had taught in the Toledo schools before her marriage went on teaching, not in schoolrooms, but by quiet example to the neighborhood girls, and their mothers, She put to good use, ever so gently, her larger parish experiences.

English, Spanish, German both HH and Emma knew comfortably, and they kept up their life-long habit of reading aloud. Their interests, due to Central American life, and later to European travel, were always growing. Their hospitality to all comers, family, friends, those who became friends, was genuine and generous.

Funeral services at St. Paul's were held four days apart in late November of 1964. "St. George's Windsor," a favorite Thanksgiving hymn, was sung by the congregation. The graves in the old church yard are on the south side, nearest their long-loved Brushy Mountains.

At this writing, they are survived by their younger son, Robert; four grandchildren; Andrew's daughter in Connecticut, his son in Utah; Robert's daughter in Florida; his son in Massachusetts; nine great-grandchildren; five daughters, four sons.

Sources: Family

— Kathleen Morehouse

David Alexander Morrison family (1884), Seated, L. to R: Rachel, Clinton, David Alexander, Jane S., Sophronia, Grace. Standing L. to R: Fletcher, Nancy, Columbus, David, Jr., Joseph.

THE JAMES MORRISON, SENIOR, FAMILY

858

James Morrison, Senior, the son of David Heriman and Sarah (Bray) Morrison was born about 1772 in Old Surry County, a part of which is now Wilkes County. James married Bethlehem Collins, daughter of Obediah and Patsey Collins in about 1800. James and Bethlehem had eight sons and 4 daughters. Of these children 6 sons and 1 daughter are known: Andrew b. ca 1802, John b. ca 1806, Jesse b. 1809, Nancy b. 1812, James Jr. b. 25 Nov. 1817, David Alexander b. ca 1818, and Peter b. 1825.

Andrew Morrison married Matilda Gillie and they had 5 sons and 3 daughters: Mary b. 1835, James b. 1837, Thomas b. 1838, Alfred b. 1839, Elizabeth b. 1842, Nancy b. 1843, Charles Sinclair b. 1846, and Jesse b. 1848.
— Charles Sinclair Morrison married Carrie Newman, served in the Civil War, and a number of their grandchildren are living in Wilkes County at present (1982).

John Morrison married Rebecca and reportedly moved to Tennessee. It is legend that John and Rebecca Morrison became the owners of a large plantation and had numerous slaves. At the end of the Civil War when the slaves were set free, John gave each of his male slaves a new hat. Inscribed inside the head band of each hat was his name and address. John told each hat recipient that if he ever had trouble or needed help, to show the authorities the inscription inside the head band of their hat and have them get in touch with him.

Jesse Morrison — see The Jesse Morrison Family.

Nancy Morrison married Henry Eldridge and they did not have any children.

James Morrison, Junior — see The James Morrison, Junior, Family.

David Alexander Morrison married Jane Swim/Swaim, believed to be the daughter of Abraham and Mary (Holcomb) Swaim in about 1839. Eleven (11) children were born to David and Jane in North Carolina. In 1858, David A. and Jane (Swaim) Morrison loaded all of their possessions onto wagons drawn by oxen and horses and joined a wagon train of 25 to 30 wagons headed West. This wagon train was to join a larger wagon train at St. Louis, Missouri for a destination farther west.

A true story is told of the mountain crossing into Kentucky. Because of the rough terrain, the large family cooking kettle came loose from its lashing on the wagon. The kettle rolled over a cliff and became lodged in the brush below. It was necessary to unhitch the horses from several wagons and fasten the traces of the harnesses together; then one of the boys was lowered over the cliff to retrieve the "cooking pot". That kettle meant survival to the family of 2 adults and 11 children.

The wagon train traveled through Laurel County, Kentucky along the Wilderness Road and on to Louisville, Kentucky at the Ohio River. There, near the Ohio Falls, they crossed the river into Indiana. Following the road west, which was originally the Old Buffalo Trace from New Albany to Vincennes, Indiana, they soon were approaching Vincennes and just beyond, the Illinois border. Near Vincennes, however, some wagons in the Morrison group belonging to James, Jr. and David Alexander broke down. After some deliberation, it was decided that the two families, a total of 25 persons, would settle in Gibson County, Indiana.

In Gibson County, 2 sons were born to David Alexander and Jane (Swaim) Morrison. This made a family of 13 children: Rachel b. ca 1840, Louis M. b. ca 1841, Nancy C. b. 17 Sep. 1842, Gracy E. b. ca 1845, Columbus R. b. ca 1847, William G. b. 29 Jul. 1848, Henry S. b. 23 Oct. 1849, Fletcher b. May 1851, Jesse C. b. ca 1852, Sophronia Ann b. 8 Nov. 1854 (my grandmother), David A. Jr. b. Oct. 1856, Joseph b. 1859, and Clinton F. b. 15 Apr. 1861. Descendants of David Alexander and Jane (Swaim) Morrison are active residents of Gibson County, Indiana at present (1982). The picture of David and Jane with 9 of their children was taken in about 1884. In remembrance of our ancestors from North Carolina, a Morrison Reunion is held annually on the first Sunday in August at the Lafayette Park in Princeton, Indiana, county seat of Gibson County.

Peter Morrison, youngest of the James, Sr. and Bethlehem Morrison family did not marry. He spent most of his life working with his brothers in Wilkes County: Andrew operated a grist mill and Jesse owned a farm.

Sources: North Carolina Wills, census Gibson County, Indiana Marriage and Birth Records, Tombstone and personal sources.

— Leslie L. Dunning

THE JAMES MORRISON, JUNIOR, FAMILY

859

James Morrison, Junior, the son of James and Bethlehem (Collins) Morrison was born 25 Nov. 1817 in Old Surry County, a part of which is now Wilkes County. James, Jr. married Sarah West, daughter of William R. West on 14 Nov. 1834. James and Sarah (West) Morrison had 10 children: Nathaniel b. 28 Dec. 1836, Hetha C. b. 8 Nov. 1838, David b. 14 Mar. 1840, Benjamin H. b. 8 Jan. 1842, Nancy Ann b. 8 Mar. 1844, Willliam Thomas b. 4 May 1846, John R. b. 2 Mar. 1848, James Floyd b. 3 Aug. 1850, Sarah Jane b. 6 Aug. 1853, and Margaret Isabell b. 17 Apr. 1856. The first five children were born in North Carolina and the next four were born in Virginia. The youngest, Margaret Isabell, is believed to have been born in Virginia; however, she died at age of 4 and was buried in Gibson County, Indiana.

James, Jr. and Sarah (West) Morrison lost

their farm, crops, livestock and household furniture in the early 1840's and removed to Virginia. Later, in 1958, the family joined a wagon train from North Carolina which was headed West (see David Alexander Morrison in "The James Morrison, Senior, Family") and ended up in Gibson County, Indiana.

Of this family, Nancy Ann married Doctor Franklin Bennett, a veterinarian, on 5 Oct. 1862 and William Thomas married Isophenia Bennett on 31 Aug. 1865, in Gibson County, Indiana. Dr. Franklin Bennett and Nancy Ann (Morrison) Bennett had 3 daughters: Letta Jane b. 11 Mar. 1863, Mary Alice b. 6 Oct. 1865, and Fannie Maud b. 17 Dec. 1871. William Thomas and Isophenia (Bennett) Morrison had 11 children: Genevier b. 1868, Nancy E. b. 1869, Martha E. b. 1871, Margaret b. 1873, Joseph b. 1875, Daniel S. b. Aug. 1878, Thompson b. 1882, William b. Mar. 1884, Delia b. 21 Feb. 1886, Florence b. 20 Mar. 1888, and Roscoe b. 26 Dec. 1889. Descendants of these families live in Gibson County as of this writing (1982).

Just before the Civil War James, Jr. and Sarah (West) Morrison and the children still living at home removed to Tennessee. There, Nathaniel joined the Confederate Army and fought in the Civil War. After the war, Nathaniel went to Washington County, Virginia where he married Rebecca Mahala Ramsey, daughter of Hiram and Mary ( ) Ramsey on 21 Nov. 1865. Nathaniel and Mahala (Ramsey) Morrison had 3 children: William Samples b. 12 Jan 1867, Sallie J. b. 12 Dec. 1870, and James H. b. ca 1873.

Taking these in reverse order — James H. Morrison went to Montana as a young man and that is all that is presently known. Sallie J. married John W. Keys of Johnson County, Tennessee on 27 Mar. 1892. They had one daughter, Cettie b. 4 Mar. 1895. Cettie currently lives on the old homeplace just north of Mountain City, Tenn. William Samples Morrison married Alice Estelle Hawkins, the daughter of Landon and Emma (Keys) Hawkins on 22 Sep. 1891. William and Alice (Hawkins) Morrison had 18 children and 17 lived to reach adulthood. One daughter died as an infant.

The children are as follows: Ada Pen b. 19 Dec. 1891, Walter Clyde b. 2 Feb. 1893, DeEtte Mae b. 21 Feb. 1894, Jesse James b. 12 Mar. 1895, Frank James b. 4 Apr. 1896, John Hobert b. 4 May 1897, Dana Nathaniel b. 9 July 1898, Thomas Harrison b. 16 Sep. 1899, Robert Burley b. 26 Nov. 1900, Sarah Elizabeth b. 3 Mar. 1902, Lena Hill b. 12 Aug. 1903, Infant Daughter b. & d. 10 Feb 1905, Charles Holland b. 1 Apr. 1906, Hattie Lee b. 12 Apr. 1908, William Alfred b. 19 Sep. 1909, Carrie Lucille b. 12 Apr. 1911, Edna Pauline Dec. 1912, and Hugh Hamilton b. 18 Sep. 1914. Of these children, DeEtte May, Thomas Harrison, Charles Holland, Carrie Lucille, Edna Pauline and Hugh Hamilton live in the area of Mountain City, Tenn.

The place where James, Jr. and Sarah (West) Morrison died and were buried is presently unknown but research is continuing. Sarah is believed to have died and was buried in Tenn. However, James, Jr. was last heard of in Wilkes County and is believed to have spent his last days near the area of his childhood.

Sources: Family Bible of James, Jr. and Sarah (West) Morrison, census data, Gibson County, Ind. marriage and birth records, and personal sources.

— Leslie L. Dunning

THE JESSIE MORRISON FAMILY
860

Jessie Morrison of Surry and later Wilkes County, married first to Nancy West 19 Apr. 1837 and they had a son, Levin Morrison, who married Susan T. York on 10 Dec. 1868. Jessie married second, Mary "Polly" Money, the daughter of Thomas and Elizabeth Money on 3 Jan. 1848. Jessie and Mary had 3 sons and 1 daughter: William Wesley b. 1849, Richard Aaron b. 8 Feb. 1893, James S. b. 1856, and Barbara b. 1861

William Wealey Morrison married Tibitha Harris and they had 6 children: M.C. Morrison b. 11 Jan. 1873, James L. b. 20 March 1878, Thomas Franklin b. 19 Dec. 1884, Minnie 23 Oct. 1892, Margaret b. 1893, Tyra. Many of these descendants now live in Wilkes County.

Richard Aaron Morrison married Mary Jane Jolly, daughter of Wesley and Nancy (Cockerham) Jolly on 24 Oct. 1892. Richard and Mary Jane had 6 daughters and 4 sons, including one set of twins: Nancy Jane and Polly Ann b. 1 July 1873, Harding Asby b. 25 Apr. 1875, Charles Peter b. 23 May 1878, Sarah Texana b. 22 Oct. 1880, John Franklin b. 17 Nov. 1882, David Harriman b. 9 Apr.1885, Lealier Joice b. 25 Jun. 1887, Mamie Victoria b. 11 Nov. 1890, and Lucy Magnelia b. Dec. 1893.

Of Richard Aaron and Mary Jane (Jolly) Morrison's children, Harding Asby Morrison is probably best represented with descendants in Wilkes county as of this writing (1982). Harding Asby married Amanda Jenkins daughter of Alaxander and Annie Jenkins on 27 Aug. 1893. Their children are as follows: Walter Marion b. 20 July 1894, Mary Bell b. 17 Feb. 1897, Annie b. 12 April 1899, Richard b. ca 19801, Charles b. 5 Oct. 1903, Granville b. ca 1905, Luther b. 28 Nov. 1907 and Bretta b. 28 Oct. 1911.

Walter Marion Morrison married Hessie Estelle Chambers, daughter of John A. and Suzanna Augusta (Martin) Chambers on 20 July 1919. Walter and Hessie had five children: Violet b. 3 May 1920, Eddie Clark b. 24 Dec. 1921 and was a Depot agent for Southern Railway in North Wilkesboro for many years, Roger Cecil b. 12 Jan. 1924 and is Depot Agent for SRR at Elkin N.C. Eddie and Robert followed in their father's foot steps, as Walter was a S.R.R. agent for over thirty years at Roaring River. Ruby May and Catholin Lois (twins) b. 27 May 1928, Walter and Hessie also adopted Catholin Lois' son Dwayne L. Myers, adding another Morrison to the family.

Luther Morrison married Agnes Brewer, daughter of John and Myrtie (McCoy) Brewer on 29 Nov. 1928. Their family of 8 children were born in Wilkes County. They consisted of Roy David b. 8 Dec. 1929, Bettie Ruth b. 14 Mar. 1931, Nolan Eugene b. 5 Sept. 1933, Luther Jr. b. 5 Oct. 1935, Thomas Allen b. 11 Jan. 1939, Harrold Dean b. 29 Jul. 1940, Bobby Lewis b. 26 Mar. 1943, and Jerry Ronald b. 3 Apr. 1951.

James S. Morrison, the youngest son of Jessie and Mary (Money) Morrison married Mary E. about 1876. They had 6 children Name of the first is unknown, Julia A. b. May 1879, William (Willie) T. b. May 1880, Sarah K. b. Nov. 1883, Mary J. b. Dec. 1886 and Eliza D. b. Dec. 1892.

Sources: Census data; marriage records and personal sources.

— Leslie L. Dunning

ALARISON E. MYERS
861

Alarison E. "Allison" Myers was born in Iredell County May 9, 1925, died in Wilkes County July 19, 1906, son of William and Lillis Tharpe Myers. He married Elizabeth Mullis, born July 23, 1825, died October 1, 1904, the daughter of George and Mary Green Mullis of Iredell County. A.E. was a Baptist Minister, serving several churches in Wilkes County. He was ordained October 5, 1864 and served churches in the area for thirty years. In August, the first Sunday 1866, he helped conduct the funerals of five members of one family at Zion Baptist church near Hays, N.C. — three men who were killed in the Civil War in 1864, their mother, her grandson and her granddaughter.

A.E. lived on a 400 acre farm three miles east of Hays, N.C. There are now about fifty families living on this land. He and his wife are buried in the Rock Creek Baptist Church Cemetery east of Hays, N.C.

Their children were as follows: (1) John W., born September 5, 1847, in Iredell County, died in Virginia, married Sarah Staley, daughter of Jacob and Sernetta Buttrey Staley. He was a farmer and Baptist Minister. John W. and Sarah moved to Virginia sometime after their marriage and had several children. (2) Mary Isobell, born January 13, 1849, married

George E. Myers.

Allison E. Myers.

Elizabeth Mullis Myers.

Franklin Miles and lived in the Dehart community of Wilkes County. They had four children. (3) George E., born January 19, 1851, died 1917, married Mary Rosana Staley, born May 23, 1854, died May 17, 1934, daughter of Jacob and Sernetta Buttrey Staley. They lived at Dockery near Traphill. George E. was a farmer and worked in the construction of the railroad from Winston-Salem to North Wilkesboro. They are buried in the Mt. Pisgah Baptist Church Cemetery near Traphill.

The children of George E. and Mary Rosana Staley Myers were: (1) Elzina, born 1872, died 1960, married William M. Sebastian. They had two children; (2) Lucinda born 1875, died 1964, married Rev. C.M. Caudill and had six children. (3) Mae, born 1881, died 1966, married Pete Hollar and had one daughter. (4) John A., born 1879, died 1926, married Mae Rudy, and had five children. (5) Tyra S., born 1885, died 1950, married Maude Bryan and had four children. (6) Ellen M. born 1887, died 1970, married Eli L.S. Sebastian and had eight children. (7) Florence born 1892, married Oid Wiles and had seven children.

(4) Dolphus J. Myers, son of A.E. and Elizabeth Mullis Myers, born 1853, died 1936, married Sernetta Staley, born 1861, died 1836, daughter of Jacob and Sernetta Buttrey Staley. Dolphus and Sernetta lived in Wilkes County and West Virginia. He once had a livery stable in North Wilkesboro. Both are buried in the Rock Creek Baptist Church Cemetery east of Hays; (5) William E. Myers, born 1855, died 1929. He was married three times: first to a Kilby, second to a Shumate and third to a Bowers. He fathered five children. He is buried at Oak Ridge Baptist church Cemetery near Hays. (6) Sarah E. Myers, born 1857, died 1935, married George Poplin. They had a daughter, Mary E. Poplin. Both are buried at Macedonia Baptist Church near Roaring River. (7) Thomas A. Myers, born 1860, died 1940, married Burchette. They had three children (8) Lillis Canzady Myers, born 1862, and never married. (9) Joseph H. Myers, born 1865,

died 1939, married Alice Porter and had seven children. Alice and all the children except one, died of Typhoid. All of them are buried at Rock Creek Baptist Church Cemetery.

Sources: Family Knowledge, Bible records, Iredell County records, Wilkes County records.

— Samuel E. Sebastian

CAGER G. and DORA WHITTINGTON MYERS

862

My father was Cager Guy Myers and my mother was Dora Whittington Myers. They were married on July 12, 1912 at Mt. Pisgah Church. My mother was born May 16, 1891 in the Mulberry Community. My father was born July 24, 1891 in the Covenant Baptist Church community.

My mother's parents were Emory Mitchell Whittington and Cornelia Ann Shepherd. She was their second daughter. My mother's parents lived on a 56 acre farm which they bought when they returned to Wilkes County from W. Va. in a wagon, with young daughter, Pearl, about 1889, where my grandfather Whittington had worked as a maintenence man on the rail road tracks. My grandfather did much farming for those early days and he also had an apple orchard and brought apples to town to sell on his wagon. He would stop on the streets in the residential sections and all the women would come running to his wagon to buy his apples. My grandfather Whittington died in 1931 at the age of 84 years. My grandmother, Cornelia Shepherd Whittington was born in Reddies River Township in 1867 and died in 1956. Her father was D. Frank Shepherd, a large land owner in Reddies River Township, a Justice of the Peace, and a highly respected citizen. Her mother was America Whittington Shepherd and she died when my grandmother was only three years old, and her sister was five. The grandmother on their mother's side was Ann Whittington who was a

very intelligent lady. My grandmother and her sister would visit her quite often and they felt toward her and loved her as if she were their own mother.

My mother's father, Emory Mitchell Whittington, was born in the Tumbling Shoals section of Wilkes County in the year 1847. His parents were Jesse and Serilla Whittington.

My father's parents were the Rev. William Waters and Polly Nancy Johnson Myers, who lived in the Rock Creek Community where I can remember my grandfather operating a mill house where people came from all around in that part of the country to get their corn ground and wheat made into flour. I remember particularly the large water wheel he had in a nearby creek which gave power to his mill.

We have traced the Myers family back to Joseph Myers who was born in London, England, and came to America about 1770 as a young man. He settled in Surry County, now Wilkes County, and married a Campbell. Among their children was James Myers, and to him and his wife was born a son named William Myers, and they lived in the Dehart section of Wilkes County. William Myers was the father of Napolean Myers who was the father of William Waters Myers, who was my father's grandfather. Four of William Myers' sons walked to Greensboro to enlist in the confederate army.

My grandfather, William Waters Myers was a farmer, miller, school teacher, and was a well known Baptist Minister, having served churches in Wilkes and Surry Counties, and he had served on the Wilkes County Board of Equalization. He died in 1928.

My mother, Dora Whittington Myers, attended school at the Mulberry Academy. This building is still standing near the present Mulberry Elementary School. She received a certificate permitting her to teach school. The building which housed the Academy has been kept in repair and the only change is that the belfry has been torn off. The Oddfellows Lodge uses the building for their meeting place.

After my mother and father were married they lived with her parents until after my brother, Von, and I were born, and then they lived in a small house on land my father's parents had given my father. They then moved to North Wilkesboro in 1918

My parents joined and were active in the First Baptist Church in North Wilkesboro in 1920 by letters from Rock Creek and Mt. Zion Church respectively. They were regular attendants in Sunday School and worship services, and they took their children with them to church. My mother was a member of the TEL S.S. Class and was active in missionary circles. She was a member of the North Wilkesboro Woman's Club and The Garden Club, where she was active until her death. My father died in 1960 and my mother died in 1980. My father had read the Bible through at least four times and was a good Bible Student. He was a lumber inspector for Home Chair Co. and later Forest Furniture Co. The children of my parents are: Von Myers, born 1913, married Pauline Carrico and has 4 children. He is a member of Mt. Zion Baptist Church in the Mulberry Community where he is superinten-

Dora Whittington Myers.

dent of the Sunday School. He is now retired, having worked at C. & S Motor Express. His children are Howard, Ralph, Leonard and Vonnete.

Ina Myers, born in 1916, Secretary and Legal Assistant in Law Offices of Hayes & Hayes for over 40 years. Active in Church work, being a member of First Baptist Church. Member of North Wilkesboro Woman's Club, and is now President of the Garden Path Garden Club.

Clifford Myers, born 1918, married Elsie Rhoads, is Purchasing Agent for Key City Furniture Co. He is member of Pine View Baptist Church in the Mulberry Community and has taught the Young Adult Sunday School Class for more than 35 years.

Granville Myers, born 1920, married Barbara Barringer of Lenoir, where they live. Active Member of First Presbyterian Church in Lenoir, where he has served as an Elder. Was formerly President and Manager of Barringer Oil Co., and B & M Transp. Co. 1966-1978, and is presently manager of Smithey's Department Store in Lenoir. He has two married children.

Ethel Myers, born 1926, married Hunter S. Seabright, CP.A., and they are members of First Presbyterian Church in North Wilkesboro.

Betty Jean Myers, born 1931, married Jay C. Parker, member of Wilkesboro Baptist Church and is Assistant Clerk of the Superior Court. One daughter, Ina Jean Parker, who is Secretary to attorney Kyle Hayes.

Sources: personal knowledge; information from other members of my family.

— Ina Myers

JOSEPH MYERS
863

Legend has it that Joseph Myers was born in London, England, about 1740 and came to America before the Revolutionary War. He got a land grant for 400 acres of land on the forks of the great Buck Shoals of Hunting Creek. This was then in Surry County but now is in Yadkin County. About 1773, he married a Miss Campbell of Iredell County and to them were born three known sons: (1) James Myers, who was born about 1775, married Sarah Easley and had five sons and two daughters. Shadrick, Jeremiah, Winfred, Jason and Zedikiah, Lydia and Levica, both of the girls marrying Campbells; (2) Joseph, who was born about 1777, married Lydia Wallace, daughter of Edward Wallace, and had eight children. (3) John, who was born September 18, 1781, died March 11, 1853, married Rebecca Brown in Surry County. John is buried at Mt. Vernon Baptist Church in Iredell County beside three children of William and Lillis Tharpe Myers who died of typhoid in 1853.

All the children of John and Rebecca Myers are not known, but they had a daughter named Mahala, born 1822, died 1859 unmarried, and is buried at New Covenent Baptist Church in Wilkes County. From all the records and family legend it is indicated that William Myers, who came to Wilkes County in 1858, was also a child of John and Rebecca Myers.

Quoting from Dr. John Q. Myers of Charlotte, N.C. in 1915 who said: "I am Dr. John Q. Myers, son of Turelius C. Myers, son of John N. Myers, son of William Myers, son of John Myers, son of Joseph Myers who was born in England in 1740 and came to America as a young man."

William Myers was born August 13, 1803, died July 15, 1896, married August 11, 1824, Lillis Tharpe, born October 13, 1803, died June 18, 1893. She was a daughter of Zedic and Lurena Parker Tharpe of Iredell County. Their children were: (1) Alarison Elfonsie, born May 9, 1825, died July 28, 1906, married Elizabeth Mullis, born July 23, 1825, died October 1, 1904, daughter of George and Mary Green Mullis of Iredell County; (2) John N., born April 15, 1827, died 1908, married Mary C. Holland, born 1827, died 1898, daughter of Watters and Elmira Sharpe Holland, who had eight children, After the death of Mary C. John N. married Mary Johnson, but had no children; (3) Zedic S., born August 21, 1929, died 1905, married Caroline White, born March 9, 1832, died 1916, daughter of Fredric and Elizabeth White; (4) Mary Ann, born October 17, 1831, died 1863, married John M. Ballard. and lived in the Dehart area; (5) Thomas Lee, born 1834, died 1853, unmarried; (6) William H., born 1836, died 1853; (7) Augustus W., born July 8, 1838, died 1868, married Aliza Jane Madison, daughter of John B. and Rebecca Felts Madison; (8) Joseph H., born 1840, died young; (9) Noah F., born January 21, 1842, died 1875, married Celia J. Johnson, born 1845, died 1915; (10) Rebecca A., born March 8, 1844, married first, Willis Walker in 1858. Who had two children, and later Rebecca married Joseph Spicer and had four more children. (11) Martha L., born September 21, 1847, died 1870 unmarried; (12) Lillis C. born May 9, 1850 and died in 1853.

Four sons of William and Lillis Myers went to Guilford County and enlisted in the Confederate Army on July 28, 1862, viz: A. E., A. W., N. F., and Z. S. They all served as privates, but A. W. was a minister and served as a Chaplain. Twelve or more members of this family died of typhoid fever from 1850 to 1910. Legend says that the Myers family and others left Iredell County to get away from the disease, however, one of the older women was believed to be a 'carrier'. After she died the others in the family stopped having the fever.

Sources: Iredell County, Wilkes and Surry County records; Family history and Bible Records.

— Samuel E. Sebastian

WILLIAM ALMON MYERS FAMILY
864

William Almon Myers was the eldest son of Shadrick and Hessie Windsor Myers. He was born in the South-west corner of Yadkin county on July 15, 1833. He spent his early life in the vicinity of Zion Church.

He married Lemoriah Emaline Jennings, daughter of Susanah Felts and John Jennings, September 30, 1856. They had eleven children: (1) Martha Jane Myers, born July 3, 1858 and died June 25, 1923 in Oklahoma City, Oklahoma. She married Jesse LaFayette Ladd and had one child, Laura Leona Ladd who was born in Wilkes County. (2) Their second child, Thomas E. Myers died in infancy. (3) John E. Myers, born October 15, 1861, married Martha Jennings and died in 1907. He followed in his father's footsteps and became a Baptist preacher. (4) Delia Myers, born April 25, 1863, married James M. Crater and died in 1940; (5) Sarah Myers, born May 16, 1865, married James H. Casey and died in 1949;

(6) William Guss Myers, born September 11, 1867, a merchant and preacher, married Demie Lonsford and died in 1953; (7) Elizabeth Myers, born July 28, 1869, died in 1942, was married to Wm D. Howard; (8) Elijah M. Myers, born July 15, 1871 only lived two years; (9) Addie Myers born April 17, 1873, died in 1944, and was married to John E. Sale; (10) Hessie Myers born March 1, 1875, died in 1911, and was married to Kernal R. Lonsford; (11) Margret Myers born January 29, 1880, died in 1956, and was married to W. Fred Rash.

All of their children were successful merchants, preachers, teachers and farmers.

William Almon Myers was first listed in Wilkes County in 1870. A deed shows he purchased a tract of land between the Felts place and Norman Land, September 14, 1869. He and Lemoriah received additional land from her father, John Jennings, at a later date.

William Almon Myers was a well known and loved preacher. He was called Uncle Billie. He was a Baptist Minister and a successful farmer. He was ordained while still a young man. All of his life as a minister he served churches in Briar Creek Baptist Association. He served as many as two churches a day in the following counties: Alexander, Irdell, Surry, Yadkin and Wilkes. He was often called upon to hold revival Meetings. He was first pastor of the First Baptist Church in Elkin. He died suddenly on June 24, 1912 on the way home from preaching tour.

In the community of Hamptonville, N.C., the home he built is still standing. There are several families directly descended from William

Almon Myers living in this vicinity. They are Nola and Spencer Howard, daughter and son of Elizabeth Myers Howard; Ed Myers, son of Guss Myers; Bonnie Pardue Clayton, granddaughter of Guss Myers, as well as Sales, Cadeys, Craters and Rashs.

The Myers descendents have a reunion every two years in the Community House in Hamptonville, with Myer families coming from Georgia, South Carolina, North Carolina and Oklahoma. Two of Guss Myers' sons: Lewis Clark Myers and John Myers live at Winston Salem, N.C.; Al Rash son of Margret Myers Rash lives in Statesville, N.C. and two granddaughters of Martha Jane Myers, Patricia Leone Wall and Daisy LaRue Stoll live in Oklahoma City, Oklahoma.

Sources: Personal research

— Patricia Leone Wall

AUGUSTUS WILLIAM MYERS
865

Augustus William Myers, son of William and Lillis Tharpe Myers, was born July 8, 1838, and died September 22, 1968.

Augustus was one of four brothers who joined the Confederate army on July 18, 1862. He was captured by the Yankees at Goodsmills, Maryland July 12, 1863, and was confined at Point Lookout, Maryland until an exchange of prisoners at City Point, Virginia on March 20, 1864.

Being a Baptist preacher, Augustus used his time as a prisoner of war as an opportunity to preach not only to his fellow prisoners but to the Yankees as well. I have in my possession his Bible that he carried with him during the War. It was handed down to me by his son Jonah, who was my grandfather.

Augustus was married to Elizann Madison who bore him four children.

(1) Nancy, born December 11, 1861, married Center Brown and their union produced four children. First, Martha Ann, who became Mrs. Jessie Blackburn. Second, Minnie Jane, who became Mrs. Charlie Dancy. Third, Charlie and fourth, Lytle.

Many of the Browns and Blackburns in Wilkes are from this generation.

(2) Rebecca, who was Augustus' second daughter, first married Jim Shumate and had one son, Shober. After Jim's death she married Elias Johnson and had a daughter, Mamie (Mrs. Grady Harris).

(3) Jonah was the third child, born April 9, 1867, died February 7, 1959. This was my grandfather. We will tell you more about him after we mention the fourth child of Augustus and Elizann.

(4) Franklin, the fourth and last child, was born three months after his father's death of a lung problem — probably from the war. Franklin was married to Emma Miles and fathered a daughter, Etta. Franklin was stabbed in the thigh (at a young age) and bled to death. The man who did it was chased to Virginia by horseback but escaped and was never brought to trial.

Jonah was married to Almedia Felts who bore him 13 children. In addition to having 13 children of her own, Almedia became a midwife and delivered more than 3,600 babies in this area of the state. Three of Jonah and Almedia's children died in infancy and four more had polio or some kind of paralysis that left them invalids from their childhood days until their death. (Three died at quite an old age — one in the forties.) Thus Jonah and Almedia had a task of rearing a very large family — four of them invalids whom they had to care for until their own deaths. Yet under these trying conditions Johan and Almedia's health was amazingly good. He raised crops until he was almost 90. They both lived past 91. Their children that reached adulthood were: James Monroe, Dora, Franklin, Sanford, Hattie, Herman, Commodore, Mattie, Bessie, and Arbutus. Mattie married Lemon G. Combs. They had seven children of whom I am one. Mattie and Bessie, who became Mrs. S.E. Adams, are the only surviving children of Jonah.

He was little of stature, a man so slight, But to those that knew him, Jonah was a giant. I can see him now as he walked down the lane Oh, to be like Jonah and never complain.

— Ted Combs

JAMES YOUNG NANCE
866

James Young Nance, son of Miles Nance and Lovina Stanley, was born the 12 of December 1844 in Wilkes Co. He was the tenth child in a family of thirteen. He ran away from home before he was eighteen years old and joined the army and fought in the Civil War. His nickname was Bud.

He married Mary Clementine Ball, a girl from his own community the 16 of November 1865. He worked as a farm hand to earn a living for his family. They had eight children. Mary worked in the fields some of the time. Bud also had a still and made whiskey for the government.

James Young and Mary C. Ball Nance.

They joined the Mormon Church. Mary and her son Augustus were baptised. When an Elder went back to Utah, Augustus went with him. Augustus obtained work and saved enough money to get his parents and brothers and sisters to Utah.

In 1889 the family went by train to Utah and made their home in Kaysville, where Augustus had settled. They rented the Hyrum Stewart farm. Their life here on the farm was quite diffeent from what they were used to. They left a green wooded land for a dry, hot, barren one. It took time to get accustomed to a new climate and new surroundings. They were never sorry they went west to Utah. James Young died 16 August 1906 and is buried in Kaysville Cemetery.

A son, General Young, built Mary Clementine a little house next to another son, John and she lived there until his wife died. Mary had her home moved next to her daughter, Amanda Louise.

Mary Clementine did not like anything that wasn't good or proper. She lived her religion and loved to work in the church. She died at the home of her daughter Amanda Louise on the 30 of March 1923 and was buried in the Kaysville Cemetery.

Sources: Wilkes Co. and Church records; family history.

— Mrs. C.W. Ball

THE NEELS
867

James Wilburn Neel was born in Paintlick, Tazewell County, Va., 29 September 1890, died 2 July 1969. He married 17 June 1916 Pheroby Elizabeth (Bessie) Brown, born 14 December 1887 in Mulberry, Wilkes County, died 31 January 1976. To this union were born two children, a son who lived only a few hours, and a daughter, Elizabeth Brown Neel, 6 March 1922, in North Holston, Smyth Co., Va. She married Arthur Clyde Lowe in 1940 and to this union were born three children: Rebecca Alice, born 28 January 1941; Arthur Clyde, Jr. born 28 July 1949; and Elizabeth Neel, born 25 April 1953, died 30 July 1971. Elizabeth Neel Lowe has been secretary of Lowe Fur and Herb, Inc., North Wilkesboro, for fourteen years. This business was established in 1968 by her husband Arthur C. Lowe, Sr.

The Neels first lived in Pounding Mill, Va., where Mr. Neel was a rural mail carrier and a clerk in a general store. During World War I he was supply clerk for a government warehouse in North Holston and after the war remained there working as payroll clerk for Gypsum Mining Co., of Saltville, Va. In 1925 he moved his family to Mulberry and lived on the old Brown farm and homeplace until 1927. From there they came to Wilkesboro where he served as plant manager of P.E. Brown Lumber Co., for twelve years. During World War II he worked on defense jobs and later bought pulpwood before retiring.

Mrs. Bessie Neel graduated from North Wilkesboro High School, attended Virginia Intermont two years and then State Normal, Harrisonburg, Va., from which she received her degree in education in 1909. She taught in the Virginia public schools nine years; she was a member of the Wilkesboro Baptist Church and a teacher of the Ila Holman Bible Class.

The Neel home was always open to those seeking higher education and among those were four nieces and two nephews. One niece Augusta Rosalie Osborne Creedmore, a nurse in Statesville, made her home there from age two until her marriage. Not only was the home open to youth but to the elderly and sick including Mrs. Neel's mother, Augusta Alice Holbrook Brown, her father, Millard Filmore Brown, brothers Presley Elmer Brown and John McKinley (Mack) Brown and sister Maud Brown Osborne.

During the Neels' retirement years, Mr. Neel's hobby was growing vegetables and Mrs. Neel's growing flowers, specializing in roses and tulips. At one time she had forty varieties of roses. They often shared their vegetables and flowers with neighbors, friends and loved ones. They celebrated their Fiftieth Wedding Anniversary in 1967.

The Neel's grandchildren are (1) Rebecca Lowe Whicker of Raleigh. She was graduated from Wilkes Central High School in 1959, attended Woman's College, Greensboro, for two years and was graduated from U.N.C., Chapel Hill, in 1963, receiving a Master's Degree in 1966. She is married to James H. Whicker, M.D., who also attended U.N.C., Chapel Hill, receiving a medical degree, and he interned at Mayo Clinic, Rochester, Minn. He specialized in otorhinolaryngology. Their two children are Carmen, born 3 November 1966, and Ashley, born 23 April 1971. (2) Arthur Clyde Lowe, Jr., who attended Wilkes Central High School, and was graduated from Riverside Military Academy in 1968 also attended Lees MacRae College. He joined his father in the family business in 1969 and he was married to Rebecca Waugh, a graduate of A.S.U., on 25 July 1970. They have two daughters: Laura Beth, born 4 June 1972, and Myra Day Lowe, born 2 September 1977.

Augusta Alice Holbrook Brown, my grandma, was petite in body but strong in personality, wit and humor. Her hair was auburn and she was often accused by her husband of having the red-headed Baugess temper. Her mother was Jane Baugess Spicer who married Ralph Holbrook. Ten children were born to them, six sons and four daughters, with Alice being the youngest. She married Millard Filmore Brown and they had four children — Presley E. Brown, Maude Brown Osborne, Bessie Brown Neel and John M. Brown. Alice never ran out of energy and she could keep everyone in the household busy. Once she told her grandchildren who were sitting in the shade of a maple tree, "While you're resting, go get a bucket of water from the well." She was a mother to her twelve grandchildren. On occasion she told one of her granddaughters "everyone is beating you dressing." The child replied, "I want you to know I'm not playing beating."

When Alice's children were young, they lived in Mulberry where she was postmistress of the Mulberry post office. She always managed to have money of her own to buy beautiful material to make her daughter's dresses with leg o'mutton sleeves.

The family moved to Tazewell County, Virginia, and lived there until the children were grown. Alice's days in Virginia were spent raising her children, running a farmhouse, and rearing other children from outside the family. She was the midwife and doctor of the community. She used herbal medicines of her own making and she was a liberated woman before her time.

"Aunt Alice" as she was known by her relatives and many friends lived to be ninety-four years old. Most other family lived to be between ninety and one hundred years of age.

Sources: Bible records, family tradition and personal knowledge.

— Elizabeth Brown Neel Lowe

LEWIS M. NELSON, SR. FAMILY

868

Lewis M. Nelson, Sr. lives at 1014 G street in North Wilkesboro, N.C. He was born in Florence S.C. on May 21, 1899 and was the youngest son of James Ransom and Florence Greenwood Nelson. He graduated from the University of North Carolina at Chapel Hill in 1921 with a B.S. degree in chemical engineering. Nelson came to North Wilkesboro in 1921 as a chemical engineer for Smoots Tannery. In the spring of 1923 he resigned and went to West Jefferson as co-owner of the Coca-Cola Bottling Company and in 1924 was elected a commissioner of the city. He has been a Kiwanian for fifty years, is a former president and a former Lieutenant Governor of the Carolina's district of Kiwanis. Nelson is a W.W. I veteran, is a former commander of the local legion post, and a former district commander. Lewis has served in Boy Scouts for over 50 years and in 1961 was awarded the Silver Beaver, the highest award an adult Scouter can receive. He was elected to the planning and zoning board of the city and was the first chairman of the city and county board. Nelson has been a member of the North Wilkesboro Presbyterian Church for over fifty years and is a lifetime ruling elder on the session. He is a former moderator of the Winston-Salem presbytery and a former commissioner to the General Assembly.

Nelson married Ellen Lenoir Finley, the daughter of Judge T.B. and Mrs. Finley on June 1, 1925. In 1975 then celebrated their fiftieth golden anniversary. Ellen died November 3, 1981 of double pneumonia. Ellen graduated in 1918 from Queen's College with a post graduate degree in piano and organ, and was organist and choir director at the North Wilkesboro Presbyterian Church for over 30 years. They had two sons, Thomas Finley Nelson and Lewis Mann Nelson, Jr. Thomas graduated from N.C. State University and is an engineer with Scientific Atlanta. Lewis, Jr. graduated from Davidson College in 1953 and is a senior vice-president with the First and Merchants National Bank in Roanoke, Va. He is a member of the Roanoke City School Board and a Commander in the U.S. Naval Reserve. Tom mar-

ried Marguerite Sikes of North Augusta; they have two girls and a boy. Lewis, Jr. married Alice Albert of Shelby and they have three girls and a son. Their oldest daughter, Martha is now a freshman at Davidson College. Alice has a Master's Degree from the University of N.C. at Chapel Hill.

In 1925 Lewis, Sr. became affiliated with Exxon Corporation in sales for thirty years. He took early retirement in 1958 and took over the Exxon Bulk Pant as a distributor of Exxon products which he now operates.

Sources: Family records, church records and personal knowledge.

— Lewis M. Nelson

WALTER RICHARD NEWTON
869

Walter Richard Newton was the son of Walter Scott and Lanie Parker Newton. He was born April 16, 1902 at Fountain, N.C. and died January 23, 1949 in North Wilkesboro. Walter married Annie Emma Horton who died in 1951, a native of Wilkes, and they had three children, Mary Louise, Margaret Ann and a son who died in infancy.

Walter R. Newton was the oldest of five brothers. He received schooling at Fountain, N.C. and Red Springs Academy. He met Annie Emma Horton while working in Bolton, N.C., and they were married in 1926. Both of their daughters were born in Bolton.

In 1930 the W.R. Newton family moved to North Wilkesboro and Walter became assistant to his brother-in-law, John Palmer Horton, in Horton Drug Store. He was later assistant to the druggist in the Horton Drug Store in Wilkesboro.

Mr. Newton and his brother, Dr. William King Newton, became associates in the mercantile business in North Wilkesboro, Boone and Galax, Virginia, until his death in 1949.

Mary Louise married Henry Thales Sink of Mooresville, N.C. in 1948. They have two children, Richard Newton Sink, born in 1950, and Cathrine Louise Frye, born in 1952. Margaret Ann (Margie) married Aubrey Robert Gresham of Mooresville, N.C., in 1951. (see Robert Gresham Story).

Sources: Bible Records and relatives in Wilkes County.

— Margie Newton Gresham

WILLIAM KING NEWTON
870

William King Newton was born in 1906 and died in 1972. His parents were Walter Scott and Lanie Parker Newton, of Pitt County.

William attended elementary and high school in Fountain, N.C., had his premedical work and first two years in medicine at the University of North Carolina at Chapel Hill. This was followed by two years at the Medical College of Virginia in Richmond, from which he was graduated in 1931. He interned at the City Hospital in Winston-Salem, N.C. in 1932. Following one year of general practice in North Wilkesboro, he entered New York Polyclinic

Hospital where he specialized in eye, ear, nose and throat work. Doctor Newton then returned to North Wilkesboro and opened an office in the Wilkes Hospital building and practiced his speciality. He was also engaged in the mercantile business for many years, having stores in both North Carolina and Virginia.

Doctor Newton was one of the founders of Nancy King Textiles, which has grown continously since its beginning. His great love throughout the years was his work with the Boy Scouts. He was always ready to participate in activities which made boys grow through scouting. His efforts in the development of playground facilities for the under-privileged children, such as the "Dr. William King Newton Park" on Third Street, stand today as a monument to him. He took pride in his chairmanship of the City Recreation Board and worked hard in its behalf.

In 1933 Doctor Newton married Nancy Savannah Harris, a member of an old Wilkes County family. William and Savannah had two children — Nancy King and William King Newton, Jr. Savannah Harris Newton died in 1979.

Nancy King Newton married Turner Vann Allen Adams of Warrenton, N.C. in 1965. They have two children, William Allen, born in 1965, and Nancy Elizabeth, born in 1971.

William King Newton, Jr., was born in 1943. He married Janet Goddard and they had one daughter, Mary King Newton, born in 1966. William died in 1969.

Sources: "Doctors and Hospitals in Wilkes County" by Dr. Fred C. Hubbard and Family records.

— Nancy King Newton Adams

ABRAHAM ANDERSON NICHOLS

871

Abraham Anderson Nichols (Anse), born about 1846, was the son of Abraham Edwards and Katherine Eller Nichols. He was married to Nancy Emily Bishop, the daughter of John and Elizabeth Smith Bishop, on 12 April 1866. To this union was born the following children: (1) Margaret married Robert (Bob) Bishop and they were the parents of Monroe, Dosky, Elbert, Nora, Millard and Connley Bishop. (2) F. Hacket married first Sarah Almedia Bumgarner and they had Jennie, Della, Newton, Andrew and Carlie Nichols. Hacket married second Martha Church and their children were Stewart, Dexter, Charlie, Mollie, Onnie and Vallie Nichols. (3) David Gordon married Fannie Spears. Their children were Mary, McKinley, Mae, Arthur, Carrie, Dora, Charles and Edward Nichols. (4) Rudy Emmit married Alice Nichols and they had Vennie, Eda, Theodore (Ted), Jessie, Lundy and Genevieve Nichols. (5) Esley Obediah married Julia Asburn. Their children were Herbert, Trula, Nell, Earleigh, Burleigh, and Zollie Nichols. (6) Edward Monroe married Jane Cooper. They had Wardie, Claude, Shuler, Forest and Tina Nichols. (7) Arthur Filmore married Martha (Matt) Hamby. Their children were Viola, Monroe, Emma, Challie, Hattie, Ethel, Florence, Minnie and A.F. Nichols, Jr. (8) Arvey Ladosky (Doss) — See Walter Alphonso Hayes.

Sources: Family records and personal knowledge.

— Mrs. Dare H. McNiel
and Mrs. Jettie H. Eller

ABRAHAM EDWARDS NICHOLS

872

Abraham Edwards Nichols, the youngest child of John Nichols, Sr., married Catherine Eller on 13 Jan. 1835. She was the daughter of Peter Eller, Jr. and his wife, Mary Anne Pennington. Abraham Edwards Nichols inherited his father's homeplace and continued to live there until his death 11 Jan. 1864. The children of Abraham and Catherine are as follows:

(1) William Berry Nichols born 18 Nov. 1835 married Cynthia Roberson, daughter of David and Temperance Peasley Roberson. They had six children: David Vance Nichols married Sarah Julia Bumgarner, Merica Evaline (Tint) did not marry, Tempie Ann (Doll) married John Morgan Bishop, James Thomas married Lula Ann Eller, Minnie Victoria (Tory) did not marry, and Martha married Silas Decater Minton.

(2) I have no data on David Nichols (born 1836-37) except that he entered the Confederate Army June 12, 1861. (Twenty-Sixth Regiment-Infantry-Company C).

(3) After serving in the Confederate Army, Henry H. Nichols married Matilda Minton 31 Jan. 1866. Their children were Uriah who married Almedia M. Eller, Elvira married Bob Dick Nichols, Ray married a Hamby, McClelland married Dianah Spears — he married second Elizabeth Foster 19 July 1891.

(4) Elizabeth Caroline married John E. Pierce in 1864. (See sketch on Pierce.)

(5) Joseph E. Nichols married Maria Summerlin Church 3 Feb. 1868. They were the parents of Bob Dick and Callie Nichols. Joseph married second Adeline Bare and they had three children: Rayner, Mattie and Jenny Nichols.

(6) Abraham Anderson (Anse) Nichols married Nancy E. Bishop daughter of John and Elizabeth Smith Bishop. They were the parents of Arthur, Lodosky, Rudy Emmett, Monroe, Obediah, David Gordan, Hackett, and Margaret Nichols.

(7) I have no informtion on John Pinkney Nichols. He was listed as age 3 in the home with his parents when the 1850 census was taken and age 12 on the 1860 census.

(8) Peter H. Nichols, born 31 July 1849, married Matilda Church. Their children were James Wheeler, John, Amanda, Molly and Trona Nichols.

Sources: Wilkes County marriages, census schedules, family records, militiary records.

— Mrs. Robert K. Hayes, Sr.

ABRAHAM EDWARDS NICHOLS and DESCENDANTS

873

My great, great-grandfather was Abraham Edwards Nichols (Feb. 21, 1812 — Jan. 11, 1864). On January 13, 1835, he married Catherine Eller, who was born about 1822. They had eight (8) children: William Berry (11-18-1835 — 8-1-1905); Daniel (born 1836); Henry H., my great-grandfather, (born 1839); Elizabeth Caroline (born 1841); Joseph Nichols (7-8-1843 — 6-18-1912); Abraham Anderson, known as "Anse," (born 1845); John Pinkney (born 1848); and Peter H. (7-31-1849 — 5-19-1907).

My mother's grandfather, Henry H. Nichols, served in the Civil War in Co. "F" — 3rd N.C. Mtd. Infantry. He married his first wife, Matilda Minton (12-8-1847 — 5-22-1890) on January 31, 1866, and they are buried at Arbor Grove Methodist Church. They had four (4) children: Uriah (4-12-1875 — 7-29-31), who married Almedia Eller (11-29-1873 — 1-4-55); Elvira, married to "Bob" (Robert Richard) Nichols; Raye, a daughter, and McClellan Nichols, my mother's father (3-29-1879 — 1-26-1943); who was born at Milers Creek, N.C. He married Aley Adinah Spears (9-17-1881 — 9-17-1958), daughter of Daniel and Mary Waters Spears.

After Henry Nichols' first wife, Matilda, died, he married Elizabeth Foster, and they had two daughters (names unknown to the writer) and a son, Landon, who married someone in West Virginia.

McClellan and Adinah Spears Nichols had eight (8) children: Kiter V. (4-5-1900), married to M. Shober Phillips, deceased; Vado Lucretia (1-26-1902, deceased), married to Shafter Phillips; Marado Voria, my mother, (5-21-1904), married to Ordan R. Miller; Eulalah Elberta (11-28-1906), married to Dallas F. Phillips; Morris Leonard (9-3-1910, deceased), married to Maie Phillips, deceased; Vaughn Jones (8-27-1912); Norwood McClellan (4-15-1916), married to Nell Hartley: and Waldon R. Nichols (3-9-1922), married to Mozelle Parsons.

Marado Nichols on March 22, 1922, married Ordan R. Miller, son of Leander and Clementine Phillips Miller. Their children are: Athel Dustin (9-14-23); Maynard Lee (7-2-25); Joyce M. Chewning (5-2-30) and Toyce M. Davis (5-3-36).

Sources: Family Bible, census records and personal knowledge.

— Mrs. Joyce Miller Chewning

ANCIL TURNER NICHOLS

874

Ancil Turner Nichols was born July 28, 1896 in the Pleasant Home Church Community of Wilkes County, North Carolina, the youngest child of Gaither Alexander and Louisa McNeil Nichols. He had two sisters, Debbie and Hatavah, and a brother, Luther.

Turner was a very active boy, full of fun and mischief. When he was nine years old he and two neighbor boys were playing with guns, which they had fashioned from pieces of wood. They had procured some old-fashioned gun caps which they would burst between rocks in order to produce an explosion. A piece of a cap flew into Turner's left eye. With medical knowledge and facilities limited as they

Turner Nichols.

which he operated with speed. Many customers would bring chicken, eggs, butter, or herbs which they wished to exchange for coffee, sugar, or a piece of dress material. This was all weighed or measured as the case required.

He later added gasoline pumps and automobile accessories to his line of goods. Turner also operated a grist mill and became very handy at working on the engine.

On August 10, 1929, Turner was married to Edith Hartford Kilby, daughter of James Reuben and Emma Church Higgins Kilby, of the Mountain Valley Community.

During the Depression years he bought locust posts and home-made chairs from local people and found markets for them enabling many of his neighbors to have an income.

In the early 1930s, Turner began dealing in used cars and used car parts. He had a nephew who drove for him, as did many of the other boys in the community.

He was skilled in chair-seating and cane weaving. He also traded on horses and cattle and was one of the first in the county to own Ayrshire cattle.

Turner was always concerned for others and often made a trip to the Wilkes County Welfare office in behalf of someone. He was instrumental in helping many people find work. He spent long hours writing letters to those in authority asking for better roads, power lines, and telephone lines.

His optimistic outlook on life encouraged those he met.

Turner was interested in young people and in the school system of Wilkes County, serving at one time as a member of the school committee.

In the early 1940s he added mattress making to his line of work, a trade he learned while in school.

During World War II he corresponded regularly with many of the local young men who were in the armed forces.

He died on August 12, 1945, of a heart attack. His funeral was conducted on August 14, at Pleasant Home Baptist Church, on the day the war was officially declared "ended." He was buried in the church cemetery.

Turner and Edith had one daughter, Grace Louisa. She is married to Zack York, son of Isaac Columbus and Jettie Day York, who lived in Iredell County. They have three children, Charlene, Debbie and Timothy, and reside at the homeplace where Turner was born and reared.

Sources: Turner's own manuscripts and personal knowledge.

— Grace Nichols York

BYNUM NICHOLS FAMILY
875

I remember my great-grandfather Bynum "Bine" Nichols as a jolly man with white hair and a smile for everyone. Once he told me about the only time he was ever drunk. Someone hired him to move a whiskey barrel on a "slide" from one location to another. He decided to sit on the barrel instead of walking,

were at that time, he lost the vision in that eye.

His right eye became infected and after months of treatment, he had very limited vision. After a fall against a harness rack in the barn, he lost the sight in this eye also, becoming totally blind for the rest of his life.

On February 14, 1909 Turner left his parents' home to enter the North Carolina State School for the Blind, in Raleigh. Here he spent six and one-half sessions and completed the tenth grade, receiving a diploma in the industrial department.

Turner learned early in life to trust in God. In 1912 he joined Pleasant Home Baptist Church, where his mother was a charter member and his father a deacon.

In the spring of 1916 he left school for the last time and returned to his parents' farm home. Here he opened a small country store, after purchasing from a wholesale house in North Wilkesboro, $37.50 worth of items, to be paid for when sold.

His business grew steadily and he was able to attend to the store without assistance. He did his own bookkeeping by means of a New York Point slate and an Oliver typewriter,

Bine and Bethany Nichols.

The stopper, or "peg", fell out of the barrel and he smelled the whiskey odor until it made him drunk and he fell off the barrel.

Great grandfather Bynum's great, great grandfather was James Wesley Nichols I, who was born in Fredrick County, Maryland about 1726. Two of his several children were James Wesley II (14 Aug. 1807 — 11 Oct. 1899) who married Nancy Shepherd; and Joseph Waggner Nichols who was born 24 Oct. 1805 and married Nancy Bullis.

James Wesley II's daughter Catherine (15 Mar. 1833 — 19 Feb. 1923) married Anderson Nichols, son of Joseph and Nancy Nichols. Anderson Nichols was a Private in Company C 26th Regiment N.C. Troops of the Confederate Army from 12 June 1861 until 3 July 1863, when he lost his life at Gettysburg, Pennsylvania.

James Bynum Nichols (23 Sept. 1855 — 21 Dec. 1947) married Bethany Minton (30 Jan. 1857 — 18 July 1941), daughter of Jessie and Polly Minton, January 1874. On 10 Nov. 1874, they had twin girls named Frances Isabell (10 Nov. 1874 — 7 Apr. 1966) who married Greely Osco Parsons; and Alice Jane (10 Nov. 1874 — 11 June 1942) who married Emmet Nichols. Other children of Bynum and Bethany were James Linney (21 Apr. 1878 — 19 Apr. 1968) who married Minnie Nichols; Katie who married Mitch Holder; Wilborn (22 Mar. 1885 — 6 Sept. 1972) who married Ida Bumgarner; Roby (12 Oct. 1887 — 8 May 1972) who married Minnie Faw; and Oner Mae (10 Nov. 1892) who married Joseph "Wince" Bumgarner.

Grandpa Bynum was easy going. He said not losing his temper and worrying over needless things helped him to live a long life. He died of pneumonia at the age of ninety-two.

Sources: Family records and memories of family members.

— Shirley Hutchens

CICERO G. NICHOLS

876

Cicero Granville Nichols was born in Wilkes County July 16, 1878, the son of Elijah Samuel and Liza Bishop Nichols. He had two brothers, Coy and Cleve.

Cicero was married Sept. 22, 1904 to Mertie Leona Pierce who was born April 17, 1886. She was the daughter of James W. and Camilla Church Pierce. Cicero professed faith in Christ at the age of 16 and joined Arbor Grove Methodist Church. He was a farmer and very active in the community and Church. He was a member of the New Hope Council of the Junior Order and lived all his life in Wilkes County.

Cicero and Mertie had six children: (1) Conrad Mansfield was born July 8, 1905 and married Beth Myers. They had no children. Conrad died Jan. 27, 1970. (2) Selma Delight was born July 8, 1908 and was first married to Albert Church who was killed by lightning March 18, 1933. She later married E. Richard Eller. They have one son, William Kyle, who married Ella Jean Whittington. They have two children, Greg and Lee Ann. (3) Gladys Pearl was born July 15, 1912 and married William Glenn Eller — no issue. (4) R.W. (Bill) Nichols was born Feb. 4, 1915 and married Helen B. Hayes. (See sketch, R. Duff Hayes). (5) Hazel Glee was born July 20, 1917 and married W. Forest Doss. They have one daughter, Lois Anne. (6) Willa Fern was born Dec. 11, 1919 and has never married. She lives in the homeplace on old highway #60.

Cicero and Mertie Nichols.

Cicero died Feb. 6, 1944. Mertie died May 31, 1977. They are buried in the Arbor Grove United Methodist Church Cemetery ar Purlear.

My parents, Cicero and Mertie Nichols, were wonderful parents. Daddy, being a farmer, worked long hours trying to make a living for the family. In those early days a farm produced almost everything we ate. Mama canned, pickled, and preserved fruits and vegetables. As long as she was able, she enjoyed cooking and having the family and friends in to eat with her.

They often spoke of their love for their Master and showed no fear of coming into His presence. It was their strong faith in the good things of God that gave them patience in suffering; rejoicing in the hope of a home in Heaven.

They loved their earthly home and toiled, planned, and prayed for its betterment in the things that give bodily comfort and spiritual peace. I loved them very much and am very thankful to have had them as my parents.

Sources: Family memories, the family Bible and personal knowledge.

— Willa Nichols

DAVID VANCE NICHOLS

877

D.V. Nichols, son of William Berry and Cynthia Roberson Nichols, was born 9 Dec. 1862. He was educated in neighborhood schools and Moravian Falls Academy. On 27 Dec. 1885 he married Sarah Julia Bumgarner (See Adam Bumgarner sketch). In addition to farming, Vance taught school to make a living for his rapidly growing family. They were God-fearing people who taught their children the principles of Christianity. This training and their strong faith in God was continued throughout their lives. In 1900, Vance was ordained a deacon in New Hope Baptist Church. His brother, James T. Nichols, was ordained a minister by this church in 1902.

In the late 1890's, Vance was employed by the government as Tax Collector and "brandy gauger" and was assigned several counties in N.C. and Va. On one well-remembered occasion, he was in Virginia and looking forward to returning home. The appointed time of departure arrived, but Vance's work was not completed and he had to postpone his trip. It so happened that the train he missed was derailed — it went down in history as the "wreck of old 97." Many adults today will recall the song which was written about it.

Vance and Julie built a new home on a beautiful 90 acre tract of land. The eight room house had a fireplace in each room. The brick for the fireplaces and foundation were made in their own kiln by Eb Church. The lumber came from heavy forest pine. All the windows had shutters and there were porches upstairs and down. Another intersting but expensive feature of the home was a carbide system for lighting. In addition to the usual farm animals, they kept sheep and the wool was woven into cloth for clothing and Julie knitted their socks.

Vance bought a place from Jim Alexander and opened a general store, "D.V. Nichols & Son." Living quarters adjoined the store and Julie would frequently bring the younger children and stay at the store with Vance, leaving the older ones to take care of the home and farm. Another store was established in the Stanton community and was managed by Vance's oldest son, Edgar. Ted Nichols recalls another store in Jefferson and states that it was operated a short time by Julie's nephew, Andrew Vannoy. Vance bought out Philmore Wyatt's store at Millers Creek (on property which was later purchased by C.H.M. Tulbert). It was while working at this store that Edgar met his wife to be, Ruby Bullis.

The family operated a mill for grinding corn. They specialized in seed corn and sweet potatoes. Vance continued to be active in church and taught the card class (beginners) for many years. He served on the school committee for Reddies River township, and was a magistrate and county commissioner. His son, Dwight, has the corner stone from the old Wilkes jail with names of the commissioners who held

Mr. and Mrs. David Vance Nichols.

Dwight Vance Nichols.

office when the jail was constructed engraved on it as follows: D.C. Sebeastian, Chairman; J.F. Barlow, D.V. Nichols, and W.H. Foster, Ex Offico. The date on the stone is 1915.

Julie was a hard-working, frugal homemaker who didn't always approve of her husband's plans for expansion. She was especially opposed to borrowing money. Vance was a warm-hearted, generous man who couldn't say "no" when a friend or neighbor wanted credit, and this was greatly responsible for the loss of many of their holdings.

David Vance Nichols died 3 Nov. 1932 and his wife died 28 April 1948. They are buried at New Hope Baptist.

The thirteen children of Vance and Julie Nichols are as follows: (1) Dora Effie married Joshua Sikes and they had Vernon, Paul, Ralph, and Hester. This family moved to Lee Co., N.C. about 1929. (2) Edgar Olin married Ruby Bullis and they made their home in Lee County. Their children are Olin, Winton, and Ollie. (3) William Harrison married Ina Stout. (4) Della Bertha, a teacher, was born 10 Jan. 1891 and died 13 Dec. 1925, unmarried. (5) Rudy Milton died young. (6) Romilus Don married Mary Lovette. (7) Bessie Rebecca married R. Duff Hayes. (8) Mary Camilla died soon after birth. (9) Queen Esther married Oliver Elledge — their children are: Buford, Imagene, Oliver Jr., Treva, Anita, and Lutrelle. (10) Beatrice Verina married Dewey Minton. (11) Teddy Roosevelt married Ethel Holcomb. (12) Tyndall Paul was born 23 March 1908 and died 3 April 1910. His father was collecting taxes in Virginia at the time and became so distraught that he resigned his position with the Revenue Service in order to stay home with his family. (13) Dwight Vance married first Louise Pearson and second, Lou Brooks. Ted and Dwight are the only surviving children of Vance and Julia Nichols.

Sources: Personal knowledge.

— Dwight V. Nichols
and Mae Hayes

DWIGHT VANCE NICHOLS
878

Dwight Vance Nichols, editor and news man for over fifty years, was born in Wilkes County near Purlear March 3, 1910, son of David Vance and Sarah Julia Bumgarner Nichols.

He attended Bell's View (later Millers Creek) School. After three years at Millers Creek High School he attended Wilkesboro High School and graduated there with academic honors in 1926.

Dwight attended a business college in Winston-Salem while being employed in the evenings at R.J. Reynolds Tobacco Company. Following business college he returned to Wilkes County and began work at the Wilkes Journal newspaper. The Wilkes Journal and the Wilkes Patriot were merged in 1932 and for two years he was with the Wilkes News, which was later discontinued. Returning to The Journal-Patriot, Nichols continued there until retirement in 1982 with the title of Editor Emeritus.

Dwight, during his career, talked with and interviewed two presidents as well as several governors, U.S. Cabinet members and other widely known and respected leaders.

Twice in his career Dwight was awarded first place in the state for best editorial and he collaborated with an employee in creating the advertisement judged best in North Carolina Press Association.

Dwight was honored for his first place achievement in the nation in Veterans of Foreign Wars Auxiliary. He was awarded the Ernie Pyle Plaque which was presented to him in 1958 in Los Angeles, California.

Dwight has been recipient of many local, county and state honors.

Dwight, since age ten, has been a Baptist and for the past twenty years has been a teacher or assistant teacher at Center Baptist Church. In early life he was active in New Hope Baptist Church.

Dwight was married to Louise Pearson (divorced) and later to Lou Emma Brooks, who worked for Carter-Hubbard Publishing Company.

He is the father of three sons and two daughters. The oldest, Bonnie Louise Nichols Bauguss, was killed in an auto accident which occurred while she was on the staff of Wilkes Community College. The sons are David Vance, Daniel Grey and Dwight Ray. The youngest daughter is Nancy Julia (Nan).

Dwight has backed and supported major improvements in Wilkes County, including Wilkes Community College, Wilkes YMCA, Wilkes General Hospital; new and major industries, as well as better school, and active in civic clubs.

Sources: Family records, personal knowledge and memories.

— Lou Brooks Nichols

JAMES BYNUM NICHOLS
879

My great-grandfather, James Bynum Nichols, born 23 Sept. 1855, was the son of Anderson and Catherine Nichols. Anderson and Catherine were cousins. Anderson was the son of Joseph Wagoner Nichols and his wife Nancy Bullis Nichols and the grandson of John Nichols, Sr., the first in this line to come to Wilkes County about 1796. Catherine was the daughter of James Wesley and Nancy Shepherd Nichols and the grand-daughter of John, Sr.

According to military records, Anderson was killed at Gettysburg, Va. 3 July 1863. However, there are rumors that he was not killed but chose to stay in Virginia. In any event, he did not return to Wilkes County.

James Bynum (Bine) Nichols married 11 Jan. 1874, Bethany Minton, daughter of Jesse Minton who was born 12 Oct. 1833, and died 26 Dec. 1905. Jesse was the son of Meredith Minton who the family believes came from Ireland to Wilkes County. Jesse married Polly Gullet (or Johnson) who was born 8 Jan. 1835 in Gainsville Hall, Ga. Bethany was born 30 Jan. 1857 and died 18 July 1941. Bine died 20 Dec. 1948 at the ripe old age of 93 years, 2 months, and 27 days. They are buried at Pleasant Grove Baptist Church (formerly Buck's Arbor).

Bine and Bethany had seven children: twins, Isabel and Alice, Linny, Louie (female), Wilburn, Roby and Oner May. Oner May born 10 Nov. 1892, married Winston (Wince) Bumgarner, son of John Wesley and Frankie Emily Minton Bumgarner, and they had five children: Clora Rea (my mother), Arlin, Florine, and twin daughters, Nella Dean and Ella Jean.

As a child I spent a lot of time with Grandpa Bine. I really loved him. He was a wonderful man. I remember him as an old man, quite stooped and walking with a cane. He had a thick moustache and a full head of beautiful white hair with a scattering of black in it. He had twinkling, blue eyes. He always took time to answer my childish questions and he humored me as a doting grnadparent will.

A vivid memory of an incident that occurred when I was about four years old was my first experience with tobacco. I begged for a chew of his tobacco and finally he cut off a small bit from his plug. Needless to say, I became quite ill. Grandma became upset and admonished Grandpa Bine for giving the "Baby Doll' tobacco!

I poved all of my grandparents and ours was a close family, but this is my special tribute to Grandpa Bine. He was an honest, upright man and was highly respected in his community. He used to say that "if you couldn't say something good about someone, don't say anything." This was a creed that he lived up to all of his life. I realize now the important influence he had on my life as well as the lives of others, and I will always be grateful for Grandpa Bine.

Sources: Personal knowledge.

— Carol B. Crane

JOHN NICHOLS, SR.
880

There are approximately one hundred Nichols' families in Wilkes County today and no doubt, most, if not all of them, can trace their ancestry back to this John Nichols, Sr.

A valued record now in possession of a descendant and apparently in John's own handwriting reads as follows: "John Nichols, Senior now in his sixtieth year takes this account of his offspring's births by both his wives. Written in Wilkes County June 7, 1809. The first wife's children are the five following, all born near the Federal City, called Washington now, but Georgetown formerly. His first wife's name was Elisabeth, who deceased in 1796. 1st. John Nichols born Nov. 16, 1772. 2nd. Mary born September 27, 1774. 3rd. Thomas born August 12, 1781. 4th. William born August 24, 1784. 5th. Nancy born September 12, 1789. John Nichols, Senior and Catharine, his second wife's offspring, all born in Wilkes County, N.C. near Yadkin (River). 6th. Mercy born October 3, 1796. 7th. Elijah born February 14, 1802. 8th. Joseph Wagoner born October 24, 1805. 9th. James Wesley

born Aug. 14, 1807." (the corner is torn and the next line is indistinct: " .. sbury born January . . . " The following data appears on the back of the small, yellowed sheet of paper: "11th Abraham Edwards Nichols born February 21, 1812. James W. Nichols and Nancy his wife. John Nelson Nichols was born July 13, 1829."

According to the above record, John Nichols, Sr. was born about 1749, birthplace unknown. He is found on the Frederick Co., Md. Federal Census of 1776, age 26 with Elisabeth age 26, John age 4, and Mary Ann. age 1. James Nicholas age 50 and Ann, age 48 are also listed. They are probably the parents of John Nichols, Sr.

The record also indicates that John came to Wilkes County during the 1790's. He purchased sixty acres of land on Fishdam Creek, a tributary of the Yadkin River, in 1800 and lived there until his death in 1833. After the death of his wife, this property was inherited by his youngest son, Abraham Edwards Nichols.

I do not have any information concerning the first three of John's children. The fourth child, William, married Elisabeth Holdaway in Wilkes County, marriage bond issued 19 Dec. 1807. (5) A Nancy Nichols married Jonathan Woodie in 1810 — she may have been the fith child of John Nichols, Sr. (6) Mercy married Aden (Eddins) Kilby 25 Jan. 1840. (7) Elijah married first Margaret Bullison and second, Susana Minton. (8) Joseph Wagoner married Nancy Bullis, bond issued 17 Aug. 1824. (9) James Wesley married first Nancy (perhaps Shepherd) and second Martha Holder. (10) I have no information on Asbury Nichols. (11) Abraham Edwards Nichols married Catherine Eller, bond issued 11 January 1864.

The remaining information on the back of the paper listing the children of John Nichols, Sr., apparently refers to his ninth child, James Wesley Nichols and his wife. John Nelson Nichols was the first child born to this couple.

The will of John Nichols, Sr. is recorded in Wilkes Will Book 4, page 162.

Sources: Family records, Wilkes County deeds and wills, Wilkes County tax lists and census schedules, 1776 Frederick Co., Md. Federal Census.

— Mrs. Robert K. Hayes, Sr.

R. DON and MARY LOVETTE NICHOLS
881

Romulus Don Nichols was born 3 Aug. 1895, the son of David Vance and Sarah Julia Bumgarner Nichols. Articles about his ancestors and family appear elsewhere in this book.

Mary Lou Lovette, daughter of Wiley and Amanda Church Lovette, was born 20 Jan. 1900. Wiley was the son of James Hersey and Amanda Louise Wilcox Lovette and the grandson of Absalom Harper Lovette and his wife whose surname was Billings. Amanda Church was the daughter of Wilson and Mary Griffin Church.

Wiley and Amanda Church Lovette were the parents of ten children: Cora married Garfield Eller; Anderson married Queen Bumgarner, daughter of Daniel Bumgarner; Fidell married

Kiter Phillips; Charlie married Sadie Nichols, daughter of Coy Nichols; Elmore married Pearl Laws; Bessie married Vernon Eller; Minnie married Charles Link; Hattie married Rob Cardwell; Artie married Grover Yates; and Mary Lou married R. Don Nichols on 16 Sept. 1917. Mary recalls attending school at Cross Roads and two of her many teachers were Claude Faw and Cora McNeil. Her family lived between Pleasant Home Baptist Church and Charity Methodist Church and they attended both churches. Mary later became a member of New Hope Baptist Church.

In 1932 Don and Mary bought the Curtis place about three miles west of Millers Creek and Mary continues to live there.

Don was a well known carpenter and helped with the construction of many houses in the area. He was especially interested in growing fruit trees and became skilled in grafting. He sold fruit trees for the Stark Company for awhile. He developed a white corn which was known as the Wilkes County white corn, and received several awards for it. The seed has been kept and is still used by his brother, Ted Nichols. When the Purlear Baptist Church was organized in 1932, Don was a charter member. He served on the building committee when the new building was erected in 1949. Don died 15 Aug. 1967 and is buried in the cemetery at Purlear Baptist Church.

Don and Mary Nichols had four children: (1) Romulus Quentin born 14 July 1919 married Ola Della Rae McGlamery and they had two children: Mary Jane and James Quentin. Jane married Roby Chambers and they have a daughter, Gabrielle Kim. James married Judy Mae Poteat, no issue. Romulus Quentin is a retired mail carrier and he and his wife live near his mother. (2) Kermit Don, born 4 Feb. 1923, married Veora Rachel Huffman and they have two sons: Tim Kermit married Patricia Hamilton and they have two children: Gregory Tim and Michell Lynn (Shelly). This family lives in Norcross, Ga. Their second son, Vance Everett is unmarried. Kermit is a draftsman for an aircraft company and he and his wife live in San Diego, Calif. (3) Della Faye, born 30 Dec. 1926, married James Henry Eller and they live in Baltimore, Md. Faye has managed a Woolworth store there for many years. They have seven children: Kay married Teddy Dalecki and they had three children: David Brian, Theodore John (Teddy), and Suzanne Michelle Dalecki. Kay and Teddy Dalecki are divorced, and Kay then married Stanley Caffey. They live in Texas. James Anderson Eller is unmarried. Renee married Larry Markland and they were divorced. Renee then married Kenny Miller, and they live in Texas with their son, Jeremy Thomas Miller. Regina married Danny Lanzl; they have a son, Justin Daniel, and live in Texas. John H. married Judy McMahan — no issue. Don Garfield married Cynthia Francis — no issue. Theresa Faye, age 16, lives at home with her parents. John and Don also live in the Baltimore area.

Sources: Personal knowledge and family Bible.

— Mrs. Mary L. Nichols

The Tom Ogburn family.

THE TOM OGBURN FAMILY
882

The Ogburn family consists of Tom and Jane, and their two sons, Jack and Dan. They live in North Wilkesboro, but earlier made their home on the front ridge of the Brushies.

Tom, son of the late Thomas Chester and Lillie Wrenn Ogburn, was born on September 7, 1929, in Smithfield, N.C. He grew up in Garner and attended Wake Forest College, where he was a member of the varsity basketball team. He served in the U.S. Army during the Korean Conflict and graduated from Wake Forest in 1952. He took one year of postgraduate studies in business administration there. He first came to North Wilkesboro in 1953 as a time payment field agent of Wachovia Bank. Later he worked for Wachovia in Winston-Salem and Greensboro, before returning here in 1959 to work for Carter-Hubbard Publishing Company. In 1963 he began work for North Carolina National Bank, where he is now city executive and senior vice president.

In his civic activities he has been president of the Wilkes Chamber of Commerce, president of the Wilkes Community College Endowment Corporation, chairman of the North Wilkesboro Presbyterian Church board of deacons, president of the Wilkes United Fund, director of the Wake Forest Alumni board, trustee of Lees McRae College and director of the Mid-Piedmont Business Development Association.

On September 21, 1957 he married Jane Lewis Carter, daughter of Mrs. Daniel Jennings Carter and the late Mr. Carter. A native of North Wilkesboro, she is a graduate of Sweet Briar College and of the University of North Carolina at Chapel Hill. She has worked for Old Salem Restoration and the Winston-Salem Journal. She has been president of the Wilkes Arts Council and on the executive board of the North Carolina Association of Arts Councils.

The Ogburns have two sons, John Thomas, Jr. and Daniel Carter Ogburn. Both graduated from Wilkes Central High School and are Eagle Scouts. Jack, born July 18, 1960, is now a student at Appalachian State University and Dan, born Dec. 27, 1962, is a student at Guilford College.

Sources: Personal knowledge.

— Jane C. Ogburn

ARCHIE REID OGILVIE FAMILY
883

Archie Reid Ogilvie was born 1875 in Aberdeen, Scotland, a seaport on the North Sea, son of William (1816-1883) and Jeanie Forsyth Ogilvie (1843-1893). He was one of eight children born in the second marriage of William in 1864.

In 1890 the family moved to Dundee where William was a wood merchant. The oldest living son, George, and Archie helped him. After the death of William, George made a trip to the U.S. to find a source of lumber for British markets. He returned to Scotland excited about the forests he saw in North Carolina. He persuaded his mother, brothers and sister to visit relatives in Highland Park and Lake Forest, Ill. George and Archie would go look further into prospects in western North Carolina.

Ship reservations were paid for, when suddenly two weeks before sailing, their mother died May 12, 1893. Another crisis was the failure of an Australian bank where the family money was lost. However, the trip was made to North Carolina in 1893. George, Bessie, Archie, then 19, Robert, and Alex, an older half-brother who was mentally retarded, came to Wilkes Co. and stayed. Jane Reid, the oldest sister, a teacher, engaged to Adam Ramsey stayed in Dundee. Henry stayed with her a year. Nellie had already gone to Highland Park

to live with James and Barbara Forsyth MacDonald, her mother's sister.

George and Archie travelled over Wilkes and other counties to buy logs and lumber to ship to Britain. Old letters George wrote tell of trips he made to Liverpool, Glasgow and Dundee to get orders. In 1911 he sailed in January on the Lusitania, the largest ship afloat then. (The 1915 sinking of this great liner off the Irish coast by the Germans with 1,198 deaths is well known.) George described the grace and speed of this great liner and "many passengers from every country under the sun. In my room is a Scotsman called MacDonald from Durham, N.C. He is with a Tobacco firm there and is going home to Dingwall (on Cromerty Firth, North Sea)."

There was a market for white pine logs, hickory, poplar, oaks, but difficulties getting the wood to a sea port, and collecting the money after it reached its destination. It ceased to be profitable and was discontinued.

Archie, always interested in the out-of-doors and nature, grew plants, flowers to sell. He grew apples, peaches, quince, raspberries — red, black and yellow, goose berries, strawberries. In addition to the usual beans and potatoes, he had asparagus, okra, spinach, kohlrabi, leeks, parsley, rhubarb. Pansies, jonquils, lilies, peonies, iris, and many others were grown. English boxwoods were popular as evergreens. All of these were sold at various times. Milk was sold to a dairy.

In 1911 Archie married Ellen T. Finley, school teacher, at the old Gordon home, "Oakland" where she grew up. They were both active members of the N. Wilkesboro Pres. Church. Archie was an elder. Their children are: (1) Clara Finley, b. 1912, Chief, Div. Family & Children's Service, Rowan Co. Dept. Soc. Services at time of retirement. (2) Gordon Finley, b. 1915, married Irma Harless, presently connected with Wilkes Comm. College. Their children are Angela K. Hedgepeth (Mrs. Tommy O.) and Gordon Finley, Jr., students.

(3) Jeanie Forsyth, twin to Gordon, b. 1915, Presbyterian Dir. of Christian Ed., Charlotte, (4) Sam Reid, b. 1917, married Eugenia Luttrell; both own and manage Sam's Insurance & Finance Co. Their five children are Ellen Edmonds (Mrs. Alan), Greensboro, Kate Whitley (Mrs. R. Andrew), Charlotte, Sam R. Jr., Martha, and Margaret — all college students at present.

(5) Kate Cameron Ogilvie, b. 1919, teacher Henrico Co., Richmond, Va. (6) George McDonald (1921-1975), Presbyterian minister in Richmond at time of death, married Minta Hopkins Critzer. Both buried at Oakwoods Cemetery, Pulaski, Va. Their daughter, Sarah Aston, college student, makes her home with her Aunt Kate in Va.

The Ogilvie house, added to in 1911 and 1930's was bought earlier from the Jones family. A number of buildings on the land have been taken down — the well, stone milk house, smoke house, tool house and dairy equipment, two barns for horses, cows and hay, corn crib, chicken house, a pit for plants, storage shed for wagons, buggy, mowing machine, and later a car. Rock walls were built along the Oakwoods road and the driveway. There were many large oaks, white pines, hemlocks, dogwood, lombardy poplar, near the house and very large English boxwoods.

Archie and Ellen F. Ogilvie are buried in Evergreen Cemetery, N. Wilkesboro.

Sources: Many old family letters and records, photographs of tomb stones; and living family members; The Finleys of Wilkes (1981).

— Jeanie Forsyth Ogilvie

GEORGE FORSYTH OGILVIE
884

"George Ogilvie," to quote a column by the late Ray Ervin's *Newsweek* in 1932, was "one of Wilkes County's most interesting men." Others have said "colorful" or "different." He kept his Scottish burr all his life and it usually got people's attention. He might tell them if asked that he learned to talk that way in Aberdeen, Scotland, where he was born in 1867, the second son of William and Jeanie Forsyth Ogilvie.

George liked to read and talk. He subscribed to *The New York Times,* although it arrived a day late; he wanted world news. He went to grade school a few years in Lossiemouth where his Forsyth relatives lived. He enjoyed telling that he sat in the same seat with Ramsey MacDonald who became Prime Minister of Britain in 1924, 1929-35.

George was a letter writer. The family has letters written by George and his oldest niece, Janey Ramsey, daughter of his oldest sister who lived in Dundee, to each other. In 1903 when Janie was five she and her mother came to the U.S. to visit Nellie Ogilvie, her mother's sister who lived at Highland Park, Ill. with Barbara F. McDonald. They also spent some time at Oakwoods with the Ogilvies. This visit made it easier for Uncle George to write his niece, Janie and she to him. In one letter he wrote, "I wish you were here now. There are lots of wild flowers, I think the prettiest that grow here is the Ladies Slipper Orchid." He would describe the wild iris, the maidenhair and Cinnamon ferns. He asked Janie to look for some white heather in Scotland and send him a sprig. "It is said that it will bring good luck," he wrote.

In another letter he said he was mailing her a necklace of chinkapin nuts. He talked of walking through the woods and seeing a hornet's nest and drew a small picture. "It hung to a limb like this," he explained. Then he drew the hornet buzzing around. Janie wrote "Last time I took my humming birds nest to school the master said he wished he had one. Do you think you could send me another one?"

George went to the University of Edinburgh. He was good at reciting quotations from Shakespeare, the Bible and Robert Burns; perhaps that was where he learned to do this. At times at social gatherings in Wilkes, George would entertain the group by reciting such poems as "Little Orphan Annie" and "Raggedy Man" by James Whitcomb Riley, popular in the early part of this century. Perhaps his accent was more Scottish than the Hosier one used by Riley.

George was tall and slender all his life and stood so straight one would think he went to a military school. He was a good hiker. When cars first came to Wilkes Co. the story was told that some young man was proudly driving his car from Oakwoods to Wilkesboro. He saw George walking to town, stopped and asked "Mr. George, come get in and ride to town." George replied, "No thank you. I'm in a hurry, I'll walk on." In later years he was willing to ride.

He liked naval history and working with plants and flowers. Many would admire his borders of flowers in the garden on the Oakwoods road.

George was the first of his immediate family to come to the U.S. looking for a better life. He wanted to buy lumber to ship to Great Britain. In a letter written to his brother, Archie after the family had come to Wilkes to live and he was on a trip to England and Scotland looking for orders, he spoke of his dreams for making a profit, his trust in the honesty of his customers to pay a fair price, but things did not work out well and the business discontinued about 1911 or 12. In the Florida boom of the 1920's, George went to Florida and bought an island near Cedar Key on the Gulf of Mexico. The depression came and the island was never developed and was finally sold. For a number of years he was the bookkeeper for the Lineberry Foundry and Machine Co. with his brothers Henry and Robert. To look at the way he made his figures and addressed envelopes, one would think he had studied calligraphy. It was the way he was taught to write.

George and his brothers and sister all missed the salt water fish and salmon sold daily in the markets of Aberdeen and Dundee unavailable in Wilkes. The Brushy Mountains were not unlike those in Scotland and that was good. Then having grown up in a city where there was very little space for growing things, it was a joy to have so much space at Oakwoods. George's youngest sister, Nellie said it this way in a letter to him, "One reason I like to go to Oakwoods is because I can just waste the flowers there were so many."

George died a bachelor in 1946. He is buried at Mountain Park Cemetery, Wilkesboro.

Sources: Family letters, personal knowledge of relatives and friends who knew him.

— Jeanie Forsyth Ogilvie

GEORGE McDONALD OGILVIE FAMILY
885

George McDonald Ogilvie was born 1921 at Oakwoods, the youngest son of Archie Reid and Ellen Finley Ogilvie. He was class president, valedictorian of his class at Wilkesboro High School. He graduated at Davidson College in 1946, delayed by service in World War Ii, European Theater; Union Theological Seminary, Richmond, Va. 1945; New College, Edinburgh, Scotland 1952-1954.

George married Minta-Hopkins Critzer in 1956 in the First Pres. Church, Pulaski, Va. where he was the minister, Dr. Ben R. Lacy, Pres. of Union Theo. Seminary, performed the ceremony.

George served the following churches: Assistant at First Pres. Church, Roanoke, Va.; First Pres., Pulaski, Va.; Davis Memorial, Elkins, W. Va.; Overbrook Pres., Richmond, Va. at the time of his death in 1975, a week after an automobile accident. He was a member of the General Assembly's Board of World Missions. He was interested in travel and directed tours of young people to Mexico and Ecuador to see missionaries at work there. At other times he led tours of adults and youth to Israel, British Isles and Europe.

Another interest was music; he sang tenor, played the piano and French horn. He enjoyed sports, gardening and photography.

Minta-Hopkins was born 1931 in Charlottesville, Va. to Frank James and Mildred Lake Critzer. Her father was Supt. of Schools in Pulaski. She graduated at Longwood College, Farmville in 1951 and taught in Richmond and Charlottesville schools. She died in 1962 in Elkins, W. Va. when daughter, Sarah Ashton, was sixteen months old. George's sister, Kate Cameron, went to live with them in Elkins to help him care for Sarah. She also taught school there.

A significant person in the life of this family from 1961-1967 was Mrs. Mary Chisom, a black woman. She came to the manse next door to the church in Elkins each weekday. She helped to care for Sarah when her mother was ill and later while Kate was teaching. In addition to her other duties, at times she would efficiently take and give messages to people connected with the church.

George and Minta are buried in Oakwood Cemetery, Pulaski, Va.

Sarah, born 1960 in Roanoke, Va. graduated from Henrico High School, a member of the National Honor Society. She attended Governor's School 1979 at Mary Washington College. She is a member of Overbrook Pres. Church, Richmond. In 1976-77 a young woman from Costa Rica lived at Sarah's home and attended Henrico High School.

Sarah is a rising fourth year student at the University of Virginia. She was in the group of students recognized for academic achievements in Oct. 1981.

Sources: Finleys of Wilkes and members of the family.

— Jeanie Forsyth Ogilvie

GORDON FINLEY OGILVIE SR. FAMILY
886

Gordon Finley Ogilvie Sr. was born at Oakwoods to Archie Reid and Ellen T. Finley Ogilvie. He attended Wilkesboro High School and Presbyterian Junior College, now St. Andrews. He was in World War II three and a half years, eighteen months in the European Theater.

He married Irma K. Harless 1953 in First Baptist Church, Lenoir. He worked at Wilkes Hosiery Mill, Carolina Freezor Locker Co., Wilkes Co. Board of Ed. School Food Service and is now at Wilkes Community College. He is an active member of the North Wilkesboro Pres. Church; served as Elder, Deacon. Recently he was a member of the pulpit committee. He has been a member of the N. Wilkesboro Kiwanis Club since 1955, secretary for fifteen years. He is interested in plants and flowers.

Irma, his wife, was born 1927 in Durham to Wiley C. and Kate Grist Harless. She is a member of the N. Wilkesboro Pres. Church and sings in the choir. She was educated at Lenoir High School, Mars Hill College, and graduated at Wake Forest, Cum Laude. She has taught English and Spanish at Woodward Jr. High and at Wilkes Central.

Their children are (1) Angela Katherine, b. 1957 in N. Wilkesboro, educated at Wilkes Central, National Honor Society, Mars Hill College, UNCC 1977-80. She served as a teacher's aid at Myers Park Traditional School, Charlotte 1980-81. July 25, 1981 she married Tommy O. Hedgepeth, born 1957, Raleigh, son of Elbert Nelson and Sara Jo Bell Hedgepeth Jr. He was educated at Mars Hill College, Central Piedmont Comm. College and Appalachian State U. Angela is also at Appalachian working on a masters in psychology.

(2) Gordon Finley Jr. was born 1960, in N. Wilkesboro, is a member of the N. Wilkesboro Pres. Church, a student at East Carolina University.

Two children who died young were: James Mark, twin to Angela, buried Greenwood Cemetery, and Carolyn Mariana born 1964, buried in Greenwood Cemetery.

Sources: Excerpt from Finleys of Wilkes printed 1981 and personal knowledge.

— Jeanie Forsyth Ogilvie

HENRY JACKSON OGILVIE
887

Henry Jackson Ogilvie was born in Dundee, Scotland, in 1880 to William and Jeanie Forsyth Ogilvie. He came to Wilkes Co. in 1894. He had stayed in Dundee with his sister, Jeanie O. Ramsay (Mrs. Adam) a year after the rest of the family came to N.C.

Henry and his brother, Robert owned and operated the Lineberry Foundry and Machine Co. in North Wilkesboro. He married Nellie Winnona Jones in 1921. Their home on the Oakswood Road, where "Nona" still lives part of each year, was built in 1904 by Burrett and Bessie O. Foster.

Their children: Barbara Forsyth (Mrs. Robert M.) Bronson lives in Eustit, Fla. She was born in 1925 in Wilkesboro. She graduated in music at Flora Macdonald College (now St. Andrews). She teaches music in Eustis. In 1950 she married Bob, who has a hardware store in Eustis. He is a graduate of the University of Fla. and was in the Navy in World War II. Their children: Bonnie Gale, born 1953 in Eustis, graduate of Phiffer College, Counsellor, University of N.C. at Cullowhee; Robert M., Jr., married 1978 Sharon Lynn Doss.

Carolyne Winonna was born 1929 at Wilkesboro, graduated in home economics at Woman's College, Greensboro. In 1952 she married William Roy Wallace, Jr., in the N. Wilkesboro Pres. Church. He is now a graduate of VPI, Blacksburg, Va. and an architect in Winston-Salem with his father. Their children

are: Roy Wallace III and Betsy Wallace.

Sources: Newspaper clippings, family members.

— Jeanie F. Ogilvie

SAMUEL REID OGILVIE SR. and FAMILY
888

Sam was born 1917 at Oakwoods to Archie Reid and Ellen T. Finley Ogilvie. He graduated at Wilkesboro High School. He attended Presbyterian Junior College one year and was unable to return as he was paralyzed with polio at seventeen years.

During World War II he was clerk of the draft board. He worked at Insurance Service and Credit Corp. from 1949 to 1975. He started his own business, Sam Ins. and Finance Co. in 1975.

In 1955 he married Eugenia R. Luttrell at First Pres. Church, Boone. Eugenia was born 1932 to Edward Murphy and Pearl Robbin Luttrell at Shulls Mills. She graduated at Cove Creek High School and Appalachian State. She is a member of the N. Wilkesboro Pres. Church and sings in the choir. She was assistant home demonstration agent in Wilkes County. Now she is an insurance underwriter in business with her husband.

Sam has served as president of the Junior Chamber of Commerce, president of Lion's Club, sec. — treas. Association of Finance Co's. Ins.; member Wilkesboro School Board, Wilkes Central High School Board; Chmn. Wilkes Co. Board of Education; member and Chmn. Wilkes Co. Welfare Board; director Wilkes Co. March of Dimes; member and chmn. Wilkes Co. Chapter National Foundation for Infantile Paralysis.

Sam is an active member of the N. Wilkesboro Pres. Church, where he has served as a deacon and elder.

Sam and Eugenia have five children: Ellen Edmonds (Mrs. Alan B.), born 1956 in N. Wilkesboro, married 1980, National Honor Society at Wilkes Central, graduate at Davidson College 1979. She was selected for the Honor Society based on grades and achievements in speech. Presently she is with a brokerage firm in Greensboro. Alan, her husband, son of Edith and Marion M. Edmonds, Sr. Greensboro, is a graduate of Davidson and Law School, UNC, Chapel 1980. He is with Central Carolina Legal Services.

Kate Robbins, born 1958, graduated at Meredith College — Biology Major, Chemistry Minor, works at Biomedical Reference Laboratories, Inc. In 1982 she married Robert Andrew Whitley, son of Marvin R. and Barbara Whitley. He is a graduate of N.C. State University and employed at Catalytic, Inc., Charlotte.

Sam Reid, Jr., born 1960, is a student at Ohio State University, majoring in horticulture. Martha Campbell and Margaret Tate, twins, were born 1962; both attended Governor's School. Martha is a student at UNC-Chapel Hill and Margaret at East Carolina University.

Sources: Excerpt Finleys of Wilkes printed 1981 and personal knowledge.

— Jeanie Forsyth Ogilvie

WILLIAM OGILVIE I FAMILY
889

William Ogilvie I was born 1789 in Elgin, Scotland. He married Isabel Cook and they lived in Aberdeen where they built a three story house at Mile-End, out from the city at that time. Photographs taken in the 1950's show it still standing in good condition.

William was a flax dresser with a shop under the Wallace Tower, Netherkirk Gate. He was an Elder at Belmont St. James Presbyterian Church in Aberdeen. William and Isabel are buried in Old St. Marchar's Cathedral in Old Aberdeen. It dates back to the 11th century. The two front towers were added in the 15th century.

Their children were: (1) Alexander Ogilvie, b. 1814 in Aberdeen, cabinet maker, he married Sarah Skene Dick; (2) Agnes and (3) Ann, both engaged to be married died of consumption in their early twenties; (4) William, b. 1816, first married Bessie Dick and then Jeanie Forsyth in 1864, parents of the Ogilvies who came to Oakwoods in 1893.

Sources: Letter by Sarah Lilly Ogilvie.

— Jeanie Forsyth Ogilvie

WILLIAM OGILVIE II
890

William Ogilvie, b. 1816 in Aberdeen, called the Granite City, (Marischal and King's Colleges and many other buildings are made of granite), was the oldest son of William and Isabel Cook Ogilvie. His first marriage in 1840 was to Bessie Dick. Their children were Lily, b. 1855, d. 1932. She married George G. Harper, b. 1852, d. 1903. He was a draper in Mosgiel, New Zealand; Sam, b. 1859, d. 1922, in Johannesburg, South Africa, where he and his wife lived. He was a court recorder and she, a nurse. William, James and Charles died young. Alex, d. 1921 at Oakwoods, Wilkes Co., where he came to live with his half-brothers and sister in 1893.

William and his brother, Alexander, were cabinet makers in a shop in Aberdeen. A walnut chest, carved mahogany sideboard and dining room chairs, a grandfather clock made in the 19th century by William, were brought to Oakwoods by the Ogilvies and are used by the families today.

Jeanie Forsyth was the second wife of William. They were married in 1864 in Lossiemouth. William was 27 years older than Jeanie who was born in 1843. They were buried in Dundee where they moved in 1880.

Their children were George Forsyth (1867-1946), buried at Mountain Park Cemetery, Wilkesboro; Jeanie Reid (1869-1922) married Adam Ramsay 1895, lived in Dundee, Scot.; Bessie Dick (1872-1963) married Burett Foster 1898, built house at Oakwoods in 1904, buried at Mountain Park; Archie Reid (1874-1951) married Ellen T. Finley (see his story); Henry Jackson (1879-1949), buried at Mountain Park, married Nellie Winnona Jones 1921; Nellie (1880-1962) Eustis, Fla.; Robert Smith (1882-1967) buried Mountain Park, married 1965 Nell Smithey.

Sources: Family records, letter, gravestones.

— Jeanie Forsyth Ogilvie

KELLY PAUL OSBORNE
891

Kelly Paul Osborne was born December 15, 1905 in Tazewell County, Virginia. He was the son of Nancy Maude Brown Osborne and James Madison Osborne. There were nine other children besides Paul: Bessie Maie (Patrick), Elmer, Archie Lee, Lucille (Saunders), James, Howard, Roselie (Creedmore), Ruth (Necessary), and John M. Osborne. The first time Paul came to Wilkes was in 1911 at the age of six. He came to visit his Uncle Presley who was living at the Smithey Hotel and who at that time was Sheriff of Wilkes County. His grandmother Brown (Presley's mother) came with him to visit her relatives in the Wilkes area. They hired a man to drive them in a buggy to the New River, which was a one day trip, where they had to catch a ferry to get across the river. If the water was real choppy and rough, they had to load all their belongings into a rowboat and cross the river in that fashion. Being a young boy, Paul enjoyed the bouncing ride but his grandmother Brown, fearing the worst, prayed hard and spanked him for laughing.

Paul attended grade school at Tannersville and graduated from Saltville High School. He lived with his Aunt Bessie (Brown) Neal and Uncle Jim in order to be near the school. He had to walk to school although later on, his Uncle Bob gave him a bicycle to help him cover the long distances. Paul attended Berea College, in Kentucky, for two years and graduated from Oberlin College in 1929, working his way through with summer jobs, usually in Michigan working for car companies. He also drove a car as a tour guide and was able to travel across the country while doing this. He still has many photographs made on his cross country trip. He taught school in New London, Ohio for four years after graduating from Oberlin.

In 1936, he came to Wilkes County to work for his Uncle Presley Brown in the lumber business. On October 22, 1937, he was married to Marjorie Dula (daughter of Louis Brown and Ethel Lena Dula) of Wilkesboro. The marriage was performed in Lenoir by the Rev. Boston Lackey in St. James' Episcopal Church.

Paul and Marjorie have four children: Paul Brown, Samuel Louis, Marilyn Louise (Payne), and Ethel Susan Osborne.

Paul Brown was born in 1938. He was graduated from East Tennessee State University in 1961. He was first married to the former Brenda Byers and is now married to the former Jenny Beshears. They have two children, Michael and Jessica. Brown is engaged in the timber and real estate business.

Samuel Louis Osborne was born in 1939. He graduated from the University of North Carolina in Chapel Hill in 1961 with a B.S. in English. Afterwards, he became a navigator with the U.S. Naval Air Force. He then went back to the University and received his law

Cowles Brown home now occupied by the Paul Osbornes.

degree. He practiced law for three years and then was elected to serve as judge of the 23rd judicial district court, which covers Ashe, Wilkes, Alleghany and Yadkin counties. He was first married to Katharine Ricks and they had one son, Samuel Alan. He is now married to the former Loretta Johnson. They have two children, Melissa and Louis Kelly Osborne.

Marilyn Osborne (Payne) attended Sullins College in Bristol, Virginia. She has worked for several years for Holly Farms Poultry Industries, Inc., in Wilkesboro as an executive secretary and is now office manager in the sales department. She is married to Eric Payne and they have two daughters, Ellen Camille and Stephanie Susan.

Ethel Susan Osborne graduated from St. Mary's Junior College and attended the University of North Carolina at Chapel Hill. She graduated from Appalachian State University in 1972.

Paul Osborne has long been active in the civic and community affairs in Wilkes County. He is past president and still an active member of the N. Wilkesboro Kiwanis Club and the Wilkes Chamber of Commerce. He has served as Senior Warden on the Vestry of St. Paul's Episcopal Church in Wilkesboro for several years and has.been interested and involved in preserving the historical importance of the church. He is involved also in the preservation of the Old Jail in Wilkesboro and has long been involved with local historical associations.

During the Korean War, he served two years on the U.S. Draft Board. He also served four years as a member of the State Board of Elections. He went to Chicago in 1960 as a delegate to the Republican National Convention and has long been considered a leader in the Republican Party in our county and state.

In the earlier days, the Republican party was in the great majority in the county and there were many divisions within the party. A candidate did not have to worry about the election, he had to get through the primary. Paul has always been heavily involved in primary meetings and for many years has always gone to the court house to wait for the election returns. His advice and support is often sought by people hoping to run in the Republican primaries.

Paul and Marjorie live in Wilkesboro in what is known as the old Brown (or Cowles) home which at one time belonged to his uncle Presley and is now an historical landmark in Wilkes County.

Sources: Personal knowledge.

— Paul and Marjorie Osborne.

THE JOHN CARL OWENS FAMILY
892

John Carl Owens was born June 1, 1914 in Wilkes County, North Carolina, the third child of Grover Cromwell (October 19, 1888 — April 23, 1959) and Maude Joines Owens (January 14, 1890 — September 22, 1981). He had four brothers — Robert Cromwell (born November 30, 1911), William Hardin (born November 21, 1918), James Oliver (born March 22, 1923), and Vance Joines (June 12, 1926 — October 10, 1981) and three sisters — Clara Estelle (born December 2, 1912), Carrie Pauline (born July 30, 1916), and Annie Ruth (born February 1, 1921). He grew up on the Owens' farm in the Halls Mills Community, attending Fairview School located on the property he later bought.

In 1929 he began helping build roads. About 1933 he went to work for Hobbs and Peabody, building bridges. In 1934 he began to work with heavy equipment for Perry McGlone Construction Company from St. Louis, Missouri, hauling rock out of the "Ice Rock" and helping build the section of the Blue Ridge Parkway between NC 18 and US 21. In 1937 he went with Perry Mc Glone to Kentucky. There in 1939 he met Nettie Rhoda Becknell (born April 10, 1916) in Owsley County, Kentucky, the youngest child of Henry Lily (July 5, 1867 — July, 1949) and Martha Ellen Ball Becknell (February 22, 1882 — January 9, 1974). The men working construction were staying at a boarding house run by her cousin Andy Becknell. Nettie and John were married after his return from World War II.

July 19, 1941 John joined the Army as a Private. He was promoted to Staff Sergeant April 14, 1942, Technical Sergeant May 13, 1942 and Master Sergeant September 17, 1942. He served with the Headquarters Company 818th Engineering Batallion, helping to build air bases in England and on the European continent. He served three years overseas without furlough in England, France, Germany, and Belgium, and was involved in the Battle of Normandy. He was awarded the American Defense Service Medal, EAMET Campaign Medal with three Bronze Stars, Good Conduct Medal, and the Legion of Merit. The Legion of Merit was awarded in February, 1944 in England for leadership in keeping the runways open during the bombardment of England. Master Sergeant Owens and Lieutenant Joe Wingo of Littlefield, Texas improvised a method of cutting steel planking for use in building frontline air strips which resulted in uninterrupted construction on vital airfields. The method resulted in an increase of 600 percent in production. John was given an honorable discharge from service September 14, 1945.

On August 4, 1945 John and Nettie were married at First Baptist Church in North Wilkesboro, North Carolina. They made their home in the Halls Mill Community on land John bought from H.B. Hall in 1939. They attended Pine View Baptist Church where John served as a deacon.

They had two daughters, Patricia Ann born

June 2, 1946, and Sandra Sue born January 8, 1948. Patricia Ann graduated from UNC School of Pharmacy in 1969. She married Daniel Guy Bumgarner (born September 23, 1946) on June 7, 1969. They have a daughter Sandra Nicole, born August 14, 1976 in Raleigh, North Carolina. Sandra Sue attended Wake Forest University where she met Bruce F. Reeve (born July 11, 1946) of Toms River, N.J. They were married on June 13, 1970.

After getting out of the Army, John worked with heavy equipment in Wilkes County and surrounding areas. He worked primarily with his bulldozer, clearing land, digging basements, building roads, frequently changing the face of Wilkes County and the course of her streams. He died working on his bulldozer April 12, 1982. He is buried in Mountlawn Memorial Park in Wilkes County.

Sources: Family records, family memories and service records.

— Patricia Owens Bumgarner

MAUDE JOINES OWENS
893

"The night I heard that she was failing I sat down to write a final tribute to her. Please bear with me.

Who was this woman? She was born in the last century, when the horse and wagon and the water-wheel were still king, and she died 91 years later, after man has walked on the moon, and begun to unlock the secret of the stars. Yet who was she? She never traveled far from these mountains. She was wife to one man, mother to eight children. She was teacher; she was mid-wife; she was grandmother. But why is she so special to all of us?

My boyhood memories are full of vivid pictures; of her hands kneeding dough; of open fires, and boiling water to wash clothes; of stained fingers and more buckets of blackberries than could be imagined; of her stooped for hours in her great garden with her straw hat on, and of rattling pick-up trucks, and barking dogs as another woman sought her skilled hands to help new life into the world.

Never in my mind is she there in anger; always she is there in strength and love. Her life was dedicated to others: to her family, to her community, with never a thought of reward or compensation. She embodied the frontier spirit as surely as any woman who crossed the Great Plains or climbed the Rockies. She was the rock on which her family was built. Her simple strength and basic morality never wavered; it stood almost as a religious symbol for her family; as a goal.

So go, grandmother, to your eternal rest. Honestly, you lived and honestly, you died, and none can say they bear you any ill. In the truest spirit of our kind you bettered everyone you touched. From you we learned the truth of freedom, the freedom that accepts responsibility for self, for others less able, and for those in need and those we love.

Why was she so special? She is among the last of a vanishing breed that built this land and gave strength to all of us. To forget her would be to forget who we are. Sleep grandmother,

we won't forget. Your grandson, Robert"

Sources: A paper written and read at her funeral by Robert Cromwell Owens, Jr. her oldest grandson.

— Robert Cromwell Owens, Jr.

THE PARDUE FAMILY
894

"The patriarch of all the Pardues in Wilkes and Yadkin was the old Bevel Pardue who came up to Wilkes from Warren County, N.C. before 1910." So said genealogist Allan Poe of Lenoir.

Bevel's son John was the only one of the early Pardues to own land in Wilkes. He settled in the eastern part of the county. His first acquisition of land was on Wright's Creek near Ronda. He sold out there in 1820 and in 1829 he bought a place on the east fork of Brier Creek. Five years later he sold this and moved to the Rock Creek neighborhood where he possibly rented land, and apparently spent the rest of his life.

John and his wife Elizabeth Godfrey were parents to ten children, six of whom have been positively identified. One son, James W., lived in the Traphill District, as did his sisters Rebecca and Tabitha who were the first and second wives respectively, of Joel Watkins. Another sister, Mary, wife of Willis Watkins, lived in the Rock Creek Township near her father and two brothers, William and Mickens, in the vicinity of Roaring River. William and Mickens later became land owners.

John's seventh child, Bevel Mickens, married the 16 year old, red-headed Prudence Padgett, daughter of William Padgett who was said to have been master of a finishing school for girls. Prudence, though very young, had learned her lessons well, and she instilled in her children the refinement she had gained in her parents' home.

Mickens and Prudence were the parents of ten children, of whom nine were married and had families. The youngest, Bergin G., born 1867, died at age twenty-one, unmarried.

In order of birth, the other children were Martha Ann, 1845-1934, married Richard Jarvis; William Franklin, 1847-1903, married Libbie Shoemark of Ohio; John Oliver, 1849-1920, married Ann Hartin; Emily Loucinda, 1851-1924, married John Childers; Nancy Elizabeth, 1853-1926, married Houston Steelman; Jimmie Lewellen, 1855-1923, married Becky Boldin; Ancil Thomas, 1857-1936, married Martha Ann Joines; Peter Henry, 1860-1915, married Mary Susan Smith; and Daniel Joseph, 1865-1941, married Rosa Ferguson.

Peter Henry, grandfather of this writer, was a skilled carpenter. He was working in Caldwell County when he met the perky little lady Mary Susan Smith who became his wife in 1888. Pete and Mary lived in Caldwell until after 1900. They moved then to Ronda and bought a large farm on the south side of the Yadkin. Pete built a handsome two-story house on a knoll facing the river, and overlooking the fertile bottomlands which he farmed.

The first child and only daughter of Pete and Mary was Lilla Pansy, 1889-1959. She was a

student at Ronda High School when her principal, Millard F. Bumgarner, seven years her senior, asked her to be his wife. She had already taught school a year or two, and returned for additional study. They were married in June 1910 at her home, with her uncle, the Reverend A.T. Pardue, officiating.

Pansy moved with her husband to his home near Millers Creek, and was for the rest of her life a constant strength to him, to their church, and to the community.

Sources: Research by Allan Poe, genealogist, of Lenoir; Family records; personal knowledge.

— Flora B. Friend

PARKS
895

Benjamin Parks emigrated from Virginia to Wilkes County and married Patsy Martin, daughter of Ensign Benjamin Martin and Diana (Harrison) Martin, born in 1769. They established their home on the north side of the Yadkin, west of Roaring River. Among their children were: William who married Matilda Bryan and lived in the home of her father, Col. John Bryan; James who married Mary Bryan, sister of Matilda, lived at Roaring River.

A son of William and Matilda (Bryan) Parks was Col. Felix Parks who married Louisa Hampton (1818-1894) of Swann Pond. Their children were, William, Clarence, Lee, Bryan of Savannah, Georgia, Eddie, Ida, Louisa, the last two are still living today (1940) at the old home place.

The children of James and Mary (Bryan) Parks were: (1) Col. Lyndolph who married Lucinda Petty, lived just west of Roaring River, old home now owned by his two sons, Felix and Herbert. (2) William who moved to Virginia (3) John Andrew who moved to Mouth of Wilson, Virginia. His daughter, Mec. married John A. McMillan and Sue married Joe Spainhour of Morganton, N.C. (4) James, moved to Alleghany County where he married Cynthia Gentry, daughter of Col. Allen Gentry. Their daughter Susan Gentry, married R.A. Doughton, Esq. of Sparta, N.C. (5) Marcus A., Lieut. Col, C.S.A., married Mary Lenoir Hickerson, moved to California, then to Muskogee, Oklahoma. (6) Oliver, Capt. C.S.A., student at U.N.C. (7) Cynthia married Addison Lafayette Rousseau (8) Felix, who died while a student at Emory and Henry College. (9) Mary who married Dr. A.A. Scroggs who after her death married Julia Anne Hampton. (10) Emily who married J.M. Connelly.

The descendants of Col. Lyndolph and Mary Bryan Parks still own some of the original land in Wilkes where the village of Roaring River now stands. The owners are: Eleanor Parks Dudley Elam, David Parks, Mrs. Helen Parks Hendren, Mr. and Mrs. James Parks, Mr. and Mrs. Dan Parks; James and Dan, sons of Harold Wellborn Parks who died in 1965.

Mrs. Electa (Foote) Cooper Thomas, daughter of Major James Foote described the Col. Lyndolph and Lucinda (Petty) Parks, her cousins, and I quote. "I remember so well Col. Lyndolph Parks and his wife, Lucinda (Petty) Parks, my cousins. Cousin Lyndolph was a man of stately dignity and culture, a gentlemen of the "old school' and Cousin Lucy, a beautiful woman in her old age, and Cousin Ida and Lou Parks; Cousin Almeda (Hampton) Brown on her visits home from Georgia; Miss Add Allen of great mentality and character, presiding in their homes with the hospitality and culture which had been their inheritance from a long line of ancestry in North Carolina and Virginia. Patriotism, reverence, honor, pride of family and their good names were the key notes of their characters, and for which the early settlers of the beautiful valley of the Yadkin were far famed."

Sources: Family knowledge.

— Eleanor Parks Elam

FELIX PARKS FAMILY
896

Felix Parks, son of Col. Lyndolph Parks and Mary Bryan Parks, married Davie Wellborn Green in 1913. The former Mrs. Herbert Greene, Mrs. Parks had four daughters by her first husband: Miss Laura Gray Greene, Mrs. Stace (Louise) Alexander, Mrs. W.M. (Mary) Alexander and Mrs. M.T. (Ida) Hipps.

The children of Mr. and Mrs. Felix Parks are: (1) David L. Parks who married first, Chloe M. Michael. They had children: Cathie, who married W.H. McElwee, III and have Mary Catherine and William McElwee; Patricia, who married Charles McArver and has one child, Jocelyn McArver. David L. married as his second wife, Elizabeth Hobson. (2) Eleanor Parks Dudley Elam, first married A. Dixon Dudley of Shelby, North Carolina. She married second, Reuben Lee Elam of Shelby, N.C. She had one daughter Eleanor Ann Dudley, who married David Dixon Gold. They have two children, David Dixon Gold and Eleanor Gold Armstrong. (3) Harold W. Parks, married Naomi Broyhill. They had children: James Harold Parks who married Brenda Ritchie and have two children, Jamie and Jodi Parks. Daniel Broyhill Parks who married Carla Cox and have two children Anna Lyndolph Parks and Daniel Parks.

Sources: Family knowledge.

— Eleanor Parks Elam

HERBERT PARKS FAMILY
897

Herbert Eugene Parks, son of Col. Lyndolph and Mary Bryan Parks, was born September 19, 1874 and died May 9, 1944. He married Sallie May Boldin December 25, 1907.

They were the parents of the following children: (1) Lois Alberta; did not marry. (2) Helen Louise Parks, married Charles Bradford Hendren. They had one daughter, Lynda Josephine Hendren who married Freddie Lee Belk. They have two children, Bradley Teal Belk and Brian Lee Belk. (3) Julius Eugene Parks, married Ruby Pruitt. Their children are Barbara Ann Parks, who married Jack Sparks and have one child, Curtis Sparks; Julia Elizabeth Parks who married Roger D. Norman and have one child, Roger Norman, Jr.; and Julius

Felix Parks home, Roaring River.

Eugene Parks who first married Shirlene Hawkins and married second, Ginger Parks and they have one child, Donna Marie Parks.

Sources: Personal knowledge.

— Eleanor Parks Elam

DESCENDANTS OF WILLIAM R. PARLEIR
898

Although I was born in Montgomery, Alabama and lived there until I was married, my family roots are all in North Carolina. I am Virginia Parleir (Handy). My mother, Mabel Beaty, daughter of James Pinkney Beaty and Mary Elva Freeman, was born in Mecklenburg County, North Carolina on 20 June 1891. My father, William Walter Parleir, was born 11 October 1886 in Wilkes Co. North Carolina. He died on 5 April 1937 in Alabama. I was an only child. On 12 April 1941, I married Russell Phipps Handy who was born in Ashe County, N.C. We have spent most of our married life in Raleigh. We make our home there permanently now that my husband has retired from a career with the United States Department of Agriculture.

My grandfather was John Irwin Parleir born 14 May 1858 in Wilkes County, N.C. He was married to Almedia McLean, daughter of Rorrah McLean and Margaret Jeanette Holder. They had two sons, William Walter, mentioned above, and John R. who died at the age of eighteen. John Irwin Parleir died 16 May 1930 in Montgomery, Alabama. In his later life, he had made his home with his son, William Walter.

William R. Parleir born 14 May 1819 in Wilkes Co. was my great-grandfather. He was married to Sarah C. Ellis on 21 May 1844. They were the parents of the following children:

Leonard Lafayette, Jonathon Wesley, Nancy M., Jacob J., Benjamin F., William L., and John I. William R. Parleir's occupation was listed as a weaver in the 1850 Census. I have a small note book which belonged to him. In this he kept records of family births and deaths. He also included directions and measurements for making looms. William died in February 1858, three months before his youngest child, my grandfather, was born. The mother and two oldest sons, both in their early twenties, died in 1867. It is believed that some disease, probably diphtheria, prevalent at that time struck the family. The only daughter, Nancy M. Parleir, married Franklin S. Brown of Moravian Falls on 2 September 1875.

Jonathon Parleir was the father of William R. and was my great, great grandfather. Jonathon was born about 1785. On 2 February 1811, he married Rebecca Shin, born 1798. They were the parents of eleven children: Jacob, Sarah, William R., Jonathon W., John F., James W., George Wesley, Rebecca E., Elbert A., and Nancy C. Jonathon Parleir died 21 July 1845. His wife, Rebecca, died 27 April 1872. Sons George Wesley and James W. enlisted in the army at Camp Holmes on 23 September 1862 and served several years during the Civil War. James W. was wounded. I have in my possession a letter that he wrote 11 January 1865 from a camp near Petersburg, Virginia to his brother, Noah B. He was asking his wife, Phoebe, and his brother, Noah, to send him a box of food as he "only got half enough to eat."

Isaac Parleir, the first of the Parleir name I have found in Wilkes County, is thought to have been the father of Jonathon. In the 1830 Census, Isaac Parleir was listed as being 80-90 years old. Since he was not shown in the 1840 Census, it is likely that he died prior to 1840. Names of children believed to have been

John Irwin Parleir and William Walter Parleir (1906).

Isaac's are: John, Jonathon, Isaac, Jr., Rachel, Elizabeth, and Margaret. Court minutes of Wilkes County refer to Isaac as Constable and also Attorney. His Constable Bond dated 2 May 1793 is in the North Carolina Archives in Raleigh. He appeared to have been closely associated with the courts of Wilkes County for many years.

The birth place of Isaac Parleir is unknown. Tradition tells us the family came from France but their names and dates have not been found.

Sources: U.S. Census Records, Wilkes County marriage bonds, North Carolina archives, *N.C. Troops, 1861-1865* by Jordan, grave markers, family records, personal knowledge.

— Virginia Parleir Handy

JONATHON PARLIER DESCENDANTS

899

Jonathon Parlier was born in Wilkes County about 1785, possibly a son of Isaac. Isaac Parlier settled in Wilkes prior to 1781 and was the only Parlier in the county in 1790.

Records indicate the following were children of Issac: John, Isaac, Jr., and Jonathon. John and Jonathon were the progenitors of the Parlier descendants. Isaac, Jr., did not father any children.

John Parlier married Betsey Bullis June 27, 1800. His son James was the father of Thomas Phillips Parlier, who was one of the founders of Moravian Falls Academy in 1876. Both Thomas P. and brother, John, Jr., were active in establishing education in Wilkes.

John, Jr., was appointed a committeeman for District 14 in March 1841. The school budget was $13.31.

Jonathon married Rebecca Shinn February 12, 1811. They lived in the Pores Knob area. There were eleven children of this union according to the settlement of Jonathon January 14, 1873: Jacob, Sarah, William R., Noah B., Jonathon W., John F., James W., George Wesley, Rebecca E., Elbert A., and Nancy.

Jacob married Mary Elizabeth Watts December 29, 1838 and lived in Alexander County, N.C.

Three of Jonathon's children married Gilreaths: Sarah married Alexander, December 27, 1836; Jonathon W. married Rhoda, November 15, 1852; and John F. married Mary Ellen, March 23, 1854.

John F. Parlier was a schoolteacher during the 1860s, qualified to teach spelling, reading, writing, mathematics, grammar, and geography.

William R. Parlier married Sarah Ellis May 21, 1844. They had seven children. William was a weaver by trade. He was also a schoolteacher in the 1850s and was paid $20.85 for one month and 14 days. William was a Civil War Veteran and enlisted at Camp Mangum September 21, 1862 in 26th Regt. Co., B.

Noah B. Parlier married his cousin, Mary Elizabeth Parlier, daughter of James A. and Lucretia Phillips Parlier. Noah fathered six children: James Calloway married Susan Williams; John Thomas married Ella Shuford; William Jefferson married Jennie Smith; N. Elisha married Molly Hickerson; Rebecca Lou and Jane.

Noah was a tanner by trade. His son, James Calloway was a physican and known in the community as "Dr. Cal".

James W. Parlier married Pheobe Day. They were the parents of nine children. James was a school teacher in Walnut Grove in 1850s. He taught for 3 months and 5 days for $28.42. He was a Civil War Veteran, enlisted at Camp Holmes September 23, 1862 in 26th Regt Co. I, was wounded and hospitalized in Richmond May 16, 1864.

George Wesley Parlier married Mary Elizabeth "Polly" Cook January 15, 1856. He was a carpenter and wheelwright by trade. "Wes" and Polly were the parents of ten children. He was a Civil War Veteran and a member of 26 Regt. Co. I.

Rebecca E. Parlier married Jesse Hendren June 5, 1851; Elbert A. Parlier; and Nancy,

who married R.B. Queen December 1865.

Jonathon, Rebecca, George Wesley, Polly, James and other family members are buried in a family cemetery located on a mountain road near Pores Knob. This property is currently owned by Hubert Hawn, grandson of George Wesley.

The youngest male descendant of Jonathon Parlier, at this writing, is Cecil Franklin, two years old, grandson of Frank and son of P. Bentley and Sally Gibson Parlier.

Sources: *Lest We Forget;* Letters from family members; N.C. Troops; N.C. Archives.

— Mrs. T. Frank Parlier

PARSONS FAMILY

900

Legend has it that three brothers and one sister came over from Ireland. Their names were Jim, Pat and Mike. What became of the girl is unknown. They all settled in North Carolina. Mike settled in Wilkes County on Reddies River; Jim settled in Alleghany County, N.C. near the Virginia line; and Pat settled in Boomer, Wilkes County.

Mike Parsons married Jenny Norris. Mike and Jenny had the following sons: (1) John Parsons, who married Polly McNeil, daughter of Thomas McNeil born February 1782 and died 8 September 1865, and Hannah Parsons, daughter of Rev. James Parsons of Surry County, North Carolina. John Parsons was buried at Parsonsville in the family cemetery. (2) Peyton Parsons; (3) Billy Parsons; (4) Hamilton Parsons; (5) Martin Parsons, who married Elizabeth McNeil, sister to Polly McNeil.

John Parsons, son of Mike Parsons, and Polly McNeil had the following children: (1) Gordon, (2) Jesse Franklin; (3) a daughter who died in her teens; (4) James.

Jesse Franklin Parsons, son of John and Polly, married Elizabeth Lenderman. Elizabeth's first marriage was to Alexander Hawthorne who died in the Civil War. Alexander and Elizabeth had one child named Vestie, who married Elison Phillips. Jesse Franklin Parsons departed this life August 26, 1899. Elizabeth Parsons departed this life March 7, 1914. They are buried at Lenderman-Powell cemetery at Parsonsville. Elizabeth Lenderman's parents were Henry Lenderman and Polly Whittington. Henry Lenderman's father was Leonard Lenderman. They came from Reddies River. The Whittingtons came from Reddies River, also.

Jesse Franklin and Elizabeth Lenderman Parsons had the following children: (1) Gaither Parsons, born in 1868; (2) James Cicero Parsons, born Jan 10, 1871; (3) Henry Odell Parsons, born 6 February 1873; (4) Ron L. Parsons; (5) Andrew Parsons born August 24, 1876; (6) Gertrude Parsons, born August 4, 1882, died at the age of four or six; (7) John Parsons, died in infancy.

James Cicero Parsons, son of Jesse Franklin Parsons, married Sallie Caroline Land in November 1905 at the home of Rev. Milton McNeil in Wilkesboro, N.C. James Cicero began to teach when he was 17 years of age. He taught the first years in Ashe County for $18.00 per month. He taught school for forty-two years and retired at the age of sixty. The last two years he taught at Blue Ridge. He received 100.00 per month, which was the most he ever made. He finished his education at Trade, Tennessee, after he started teaching. He was also a farmer. He departed this life December 1, 1948. He was a good father and husband and had many friends and was loved by all that knew him.

James Cicero and Sallie Land Parsons.

Sallie Caroline Land was born December 25, 1876 and departed this life July 28, 1960. She was eighty-three years old when she died. She was a good mother and wife and was loved by all that knew her. She and Cicero were the parents of the following children: (1) Mary Dorris Parsons, born October 14, 1906, departed this life January 17, 1913; (2) Nannie Elizabeth Parsons, born August 15, 1908, departed this life March 22, 1909; (3) Jennie Lucille Parsons, born February 21, 1910; married Conrad Monroe Forester April 6, 1929. They had no children. Conrad Monroe Forester departed this life on December 6, 1962, age fifty-four, on U.S. highway 19 and 23 in Alexander, Buncombe County, due to a pickup wreck. Jennie Lucille was a teacher. She taught school for forty-three years and retired in 1972. All but a few years of her career were spent teaching in Wilkes County. (4) Mattie Land Parsons was born September 28, 1913. She married Robert L. Wiggins on June 8, 1935 by Rev. Avery Church. They had one child, Carol Jean Wiggins, who was born May 21, 1937, and departed this life on May 22, 1937 and is buried in Willow Dale Cemetery in Goldsboro, N.C. Mattie was a teacher until she married Robert. They lived at Goldsboro. Mattie departed this life January 14, 1978 and Robert died January 14, 1978. They are buried in Willow Dale cemetery. (5) Jessie Catherine Parsons was born June 22, 1917, married Charles Craig Rhyne December 23, 1937. He was born December 9, 1912. They had one child, June Carolyn Rhyne.

June Carolyn Rhyne was born May 21, 1939, married Colbert S. Eller July 2, 1961. They have one child, Melody Caroline Eller, who was born March 25, 1968.

Sources: Family records, personal knowledge, McNiel Book p. 82.

— Jessie Parsons Rhyne

JAMES GORDON PARSONS FAMILY

901

James Gordon Parsons descends from one James Parsons who was born in 1796, and married 3 February 1817 in Wilkes County, Massey Church, born 1799, daughter of John and Jane Andrews Church. To them were born the following children: Mary A. born 11 April 1823; James Nelson born 1928, married Mary Bumgarner; John born 1832, married Alpha Church; Elizabeth (Betsy) born 1834; Alfred born 1837, married Martha Roberts; Calloway born 1840; Adelaid born 1843, married Joe Nichols.

Mary A. Parsons.

Mary A. Parsons was born 11 April 1823, died 18 October 1912. Mary had the following children: America born 1845; Mary, called Babe, born 1849; Harriet, born 1851; Susan, born 1854; James Gordon, born 1855; William Calloway, born 1857; Martha Ann born 1858; George Washington, born 2 June 1859; and Fannie Clarinda, born 18 January 1863.

James Gordon Parsons was born 1855 and died 15 November 1935. He is buried at Pleasant Grove Churchyard. He married 7 November 1877 Sarah O'rilla Minton, daughter of Lovelace and Susan Summerlin Minton. Sarah O'rilla was born 28 April 1856 and died 29 April 1933. She is also buried at Pleasant Grove Churchyard.

In the early years James Gordon Parsons

James Gordon and Sarah Orilla Minton Parsons.

was a brandy gauger, a farmer and a carpenter. He was one of the founders of "Bucks Arbor", now Pleasant Grove, Baptist Church, serving as superintendent for approximately forty years. Gorde, as he was called by his many friends and associates, was postmaster of Buck Postoffice for many years. He was also a Justice of the Peace and as a child, I can remember young couples coming to his house to be married.

Gorde and Sarah O'rilla Parsons had six children: James Walter, who first married Emma Church and after her death, Mary Annie Hutchens; Dorcas who married Charles Cannon; William Edgar who married Nora Walsh (Welch); Ella Mae who died young; Mamie who married Roosevelt Summerlin; and James Everett who married Zora Adams.

James Walter Parsons was born 5 November 1880 and died 21 November 1947. He spent his life in Wilkes County. His first wife was Emma Church Nichols, daughter of Elijah F. Church. They were the parents of Rudix Earl born 18 June 1901, died 18 September 1969 unmarried; Edgar born 12 September 1903, died 29 January 1923, married Esther Call; Ocie Thomas born 13 September 1905, married Estelle Hutchins; George Clelland born 7 December 1907, married Alma Broyhill; Lavon born 19 April 1911, married Dave Summerlin.

After the death of Emma, James Walter Parsons married 4 March 1922 Mary Annie Hutchens, born 2 June 1890 on the south prong of New River in Ashe County, daughter of James Thomas and Polly Elvira Mitchell Hutchens.

In his early years, James Walter Parsons was a road contractor. He built roads in North and South Carolina. He later went into the timber and real estate business, buying acres of timber land, using horse power in those days for the building of roads and logging for the timber business. He employed a number of workers on the farm as well as in the businesses. He furnished a separate house, called a camp house, for the workers to live in. He also had a country store that was a

James Walter Parsons.

gathering place for the entire community. This was during the 1929 depression and needless to say, he was the one people called upon when they were in need or hungry. Also being a knowledgeable business man, people of the area came to him for help and advice. "Walt" as he was called by many people was known as the local "tooth puller". I can remember neighbors bringing children to have their teeth taken out. He would also pull the teeth of the adults. People in those days had very little money and dentists were few.

Our house seemed to be the gathering place for horse back riding, hay rides, corn shuckings and wheat threshings when a lot of young people got to see each other or date as we now call it.

Since there were a number of young men working for my father, having a house full of company, "mostly young neighbor girls," was a pleasure. Being too young for the company of a boy friend, I have fond memories of the many courtships of my older sisters and their friends.

James Walter and Mary Annie Parsons had five children, all born in Wilkes County. Ada Mae was born 26 July 1923, married Charles Frank Gambill; Alma Ansley was born 25 May 1925, married Warren G. Staley; James Walter, Jr. was born 7 April 1927, married Inza Bumgarner; Hazel Marie, born 10 July 1929, married 28 June 1952 T. Harold Mayes; Ina Evelyn, born 6 January 1932, married Troy Foster Jr.

Sources: Wilkes County records, family Bible and personal knowledge.

— Hazel Parsons Mayes

GREELY OSCO PARSONS FAMILY

902

Greely Parsons' mother, Harriet (18 Aug 1851 — 10 Mar 1873) granddaughter of James and Massy Church Parsons, died two weeks after Greely was born. As was the custom of the day, her funeral service was not held until two years later. Greely's grandfather carried the little two-year old boy to the funeral.

During Greely's lifetime (23 Feb 1873 — 2 Mar 1959), he often related the account of his riding on horseback with his grandfather, stopping in a creek for the horse to drink water, and being frightened that he and his grandfather would slide down the neck of the horse into the water.

On 13 June 1892, Greely was married to Frances Isabell Nichols (10 Nov 1874 — 7 Apr 1966), daughter of Bynum and Bethany Minton Nichols. Their children were: Harriet (10 July 1893 — 5 Dec 1978) who married Finley Curtis 10 June 1912; Grace (23 Aug 1899) who married first Joel Curtis on 18 Dec 1917 and after his death married Elisha W. Walker 23 Apr 1935; Pearl (7 June 1903 — 6 June 1976) who married Noah W. Adams on 1 Aug 1921; Florence (17 Jan 1906) who married Walter M. Foster on 21 Apr 1928, they had one child Shirley born 2 Dec 1935; and McKinley (14 May 1908) who married Gay Steelman on 24 May 1929.

I remember as a child when I came home from school Grandma Isabell would have gingerbread or cornbread left from lunch. She kept it in an old "cupboard" that had belonged to grandpa's grandma, Mary Ann Parsons. I can still remember how it smelled and tasted. It was much better than cake.

After supper Grandpa Greely would take a lantern and go visiting the neighbors. I loved to go with him to hear the "old folks" tell scary stories. Then there were the molasses boiling, bean stringing, and corn shucking where all the neighbors gathered together to help each other. Those were such fun times even though we had to work very hard.

During his life, Greely was a good neighbor, a good father and grandfather, and served as a deacon of Pleasant Grove Baptist Church, which he helped to build. He was a farmer all his life. We loved him and miss him very much.

Sources: Family Bible; memories; personal knowledge.

— Shirley Hutchens

JAMES PARSONS

903

James Parsons (Jim Parsons) was a son of John Parsons and a grandson of Mike Parsons. Jim Parsons was married to Amanda Powell Parsons and they had the following children: (1) Ida Parsons, who married Chris Laws; (2) Laura Parsons, who married John Hamby; (3) Grover Parsons, who married Lelia Whittington; (4) Bertha Parsons, who married Alonzo Welch; (5) Frank Parsons, who married Lille Welch; (6) Alice Parsons, who married Oscar Faw; (7) Bynum Parsosn, who married Dewie Staley; (8) Belva Parsons, who married Willie Beshears; (9) Viola Parsons, who married Bynum Johnson; (10) Arabella Parsons, who married Luther Kiser; (11) Orrin Parsons, who married Nelia Staley; (12) Turner Parsons, who married Ruby Dequosie; (13) Alton Parsons, who married Ophelia Welch. Two of his children departed this life young, names unknown. Jim and Amanda also raised Ruby Parsons, who married Walter Whittington.

Grover Cleveland Parsons (born 11-27-1884), was a son of Jim Parsons and a grandson of John Parsons. As a young man, he left Parsonsville and went West becoming a ranch foreman near Billings, Montana. After a few years, he returned to Parsonsville and bought several acres of land. He then married a young girl of 19, Lelia Lois Whittington, on July 11, 1911. They built their home and opened a country store. The Parsonsville Post Office was moved into a part of the store building, and Grover became postmaster. After a number of years serving as postmaster, he went to work for the North Carolina State Highway Commission. At that time, his wife became postmistress and operated the store in connection with the post office. He retired from the State around 1950. Lelia Parsons died November 22, 1962 and Grover died February 1, 1968.

They had two children: Cleo Patria Parsons, born on March 2, 1914 and Grover Grayson

Greeley Parsons Family. Front: Greeley, Isabell, McKinley, Pearl, Florence. Back: Harriet, Grace.

Parsons, born on February 25, 1924.

Cleo Patria Parsons is a daughter of Grover Cleveland and Lelia Parsons. She graduated from Appalachian State University and taught in Wilkes County at Union Elementary School and Millers Creek School. During this time, she married Ira B. Whittington of Winston-Salem on November 16, 1935. She left Wilkes County and resumed her teaching career in Winston-Salem/Forsyth School System. After teaching in the classroom a number of years, she became reading coordinator. She held the office for International Reading Association and then became President of the North Carolina Association. Cleo and Ira had no children.

Grover Cleveland and Lelia Parsons.

Grover Grayson Parsons, is a son of Grover Cleveland and Lelia Parsons. Grayson attended Draughon's Business College in Winston-Salem. He married Betty Louise Kilby in 1942. After serving in the Navy during World War II, he started a trucking business, later becoming known as G.G. Parsons Trucking Company which he still operates.

They had three children: Jerry Grayson Parsons, born on March 17, 1945; Julia Ann Parsons, born January 24, 1947; Jenny Sue Parsons, born on March 3, 1952.

Jerry Grayson Parsons, son of Grover Grayson Parsons and a grandson of Grover Cleveland Parsons, married Jane Johnson. They have three children: Grayson Keith Parsons, born July 13, 1963; Jerry Kevin Parsons, born November 3, 1966; Christopher Bryan Parsons, born May 19, 1970.

Julia Ann Parsons, daughter of Grover Grayson Parsons and a granddaughter of Grover Cleveland Parsons, married Duane Dancy. They have two children: Jennifer Ann Dancy, born September 21, 1966; Jason Duane Dancy, born December 23, 1968.

Jenny Sue Parsons, daughter of Grover Grayson Parsons and a granddaughter of Grover Cleveland Parsons, married Charles Church. They have two children: Monica Dawn Church, born April 16, 1973; Joseph Charles Church, born July 29, 1977.

Sources: Personal knowledge.

— Mrs. Jerry G. Parsons

JAMES EVERETTE PARSONS, SR. FAMILY

904

James Everette Parsons, Sr. was born April 19, 1893, died April 7, 1977. He was a son of James Gordon and Sarah O'Rilla Minton Parsons.

After the death of his father, James Everette, Sr. was postmaster of the Buck post office. He was postmaster until the small rural post offices were discontinued. In the same building where he had the postoffice, he ground corn for local people and people who came to the post office.

James Everette was in the Spanish American War where he served on the Border Patrol. He was a member of Zion Hill Penecostal Holiness Church where he was very active. He married Zora Adams in 1926. Zora was born December 17, 1911.

James Everette and Zora had three sons: James Everette, Jr. born June 22, 1927, died August 11, 1972; James Garfield born April 18, 1929, died October 19, 1969; and William Herman who died at age of twenty months.

James Everette, Sr., his parents, and his sons are buried in Pleasant Grove Baptist Church Cemetery. His wife Zora is still living at their home.

James Everette Parsons, Jr. resided at his home on the site of the postoffice until his death. He married Ella Mae McGlamery February 18, 1945. Ella Mae is the daughter of George and Barbara McGlamery. To this union were born four children: (1) Jerry Lane, born October 12, 1945, married Priscilla Lugunda Myers, daughter of Quincy and Lula Belle Myers. Jerry and Lugunda live in Winston-Salem. (2) Bobbie Jean, born February 5, 1947, married Thomas Grant Bumgarner, son of James Thomas and Grace Wilson Bumgarner. To this union a son, Jacob Thomas was born August 8, 1978. Bobbie, Tommy and Jacob Thomas live in Wilkesboro. (3) Lucinda Mae, born March 15, 1955, married Robert G. Davis, Jr., son of Robert G., Sr. and Marie Eller Davis. Cindy and Bobby live in Wilkesboro, N.C. (4) William Gordon, born November 21, 1962, lives with his mother at the home place at the old Buck Post Office site.

As a child I remember all the colorful people coming to the post office from all around the area. They would ride in the back of the mail truck, drive their cars or even ride horses, and some of the older ones came in their wagons pulled by horses or mules. They came to get their mail, to get their corn ground and stock up at the general store across the road from the post office. The "William Edgar Parsons General Merchandise Store" was operated by James Everette and brother William Edgar Parsons.

Buck, N.C., as it was then, was a colorful place and a gathering place for a lot of good country people, and a place of contentment and play for a child and her family.

Sources: Family records, personal knowledge and memories.

— Bobbie Jean Bumgarner

ANNIE CLINE BARNHARDT PAYNE

905

Annie Cline Barnhardt came to Wilkes Coun-

Annie Cline Barnhardt Payne.

ty in the fall of 1927 after graduating from The North Carolina College for Women in Greensboro, N.C. She was born to William Nelson Barnhardt and Mary Jane Triece March 29, 1905. Annie Cline was the eighth of nine children who worked on the family farm in Cabarrus County.

One by one her brothers and sisters were sent off to school. During Annie Cline's first year at college she wrote, a little disheartened, to her mother that school was hard and that she was coming home on the train. Her mother wrote back and said if she did come home that she would return to school on the next train. Annie Cline remained at school and graduated in 1927. That fall she accepted a teaching position in the North Wilkesboro Elementary School.

In those days, young ladies found appropiate and adequate housing in private homes located near where they taught. Annie Cline lived with Mr. and Mrs. Walter A. Fender on D Street where the sanctuary of First Baptist Church is now. Later she secured a room at the corner of D and Fourth Street in North Wilkesboro in the home of Mr. and Mrs. Chal McNiel and she took board with Mrs. Hoyle Hutchens.

During the next five years she met and was courted by Ira D. Payne, a local merchant, who owned and operated a clothing store later known as Payne Clothing Company. They were married July 10, 1932 and moved into their newly built home at 406 Fifth Street in North Wilkesboro. According to school policy at the time, Annie Cline had to resign her teaching position when she married. She then became a supportive co-worker in her husband's clothing store.

Annie Cline joined the Order of the Eastern Star Wilkes Chapter Number 42 as a charter member where she served as Worthy Matron. Later she traveled many miles to other chapters as District Deputy Grand Matron.

Annie Cline's first born lived less that 2 years dying of pneumonia April 27, 1936. March 20, 1937 Bettie Chloe Payne was born and April 23, 1940 Sarah Jane Payne was born to Annie Cline and Ira D. As the "pigtailed" girls were growing up in North Wilkesboro, Annie Cline was active as a Girl Scout Leader, P.T.A. Treasurer, and substitute teacher.

Annie Cline was a dedicated church worker beginning in the First Methodist Church in North Wilkesboro. One Sunday morning in the early 40's, Bettie Chloe asked her mother, "Which church are we going to this Sunday — Daddy's church or your church?" After that Annie Cline was baptised into the First Baptist Church and continued her enthusiastic church work. She taught Sunbeams and served as Superintendent of the Primary Sunday School Department for 33 years.

Memories of special times with Annie Cline's family are Sunday dinner at the Hotel Wilkes in downtown North Wilkesboro and country ham suppers at Shatley Springs in the middle of the summer.

February 22, 1954 Ira D. died of a heart attack. Annie Cline continued to operate the clothing store until May 1961, when the store was liquidated. During these years she put both girls through college. Bettie Chloe graduated first from Mars Hill in 1957 and then Wake Forest in 1959. Sarah Jane graduated from Woman's College in 1962.

Annie Cline returned to teaching in 1961 at the First Methodist Church Kindergarten. After having her teaching certificate updated in 1961, she taught at Traphill, Mountain View, and Mulberry Schools until she retired in November 1970.

Annie Cline's grandchildren, who call her "Payne-Payne" like to describe her simply by saying, "She's kind."

Annie Cline continues to be active. She "gets about" Wilkes in her Ford quite well . . . enjoying eating out with her friends and visiting long-time friends now in the Rest Home. On Mondays you can find her working as a Pink Lady at Wilkes General Hospital. On Wednesday evenings she is usually with the group that attends Prayer Meeting. She still attends the Eastern Star and almost every Sunday morning, if you walk down the aisle of the First Baptist Church . . . look to your right and Annie Cline will be there in her place a few pews from the front.

Sources: Personal knowledge.

— Sarah Payne Absher

GEORGE PAYNE
906

George Payne, Sr. was born in 1732, died in 1801 in Wilkes County. He married, 3 September 1779, in Wilkes County, Nancy Ann Fugit, daughter of John Fugit. He owned land in the Moravian-Warrior Creek area of the county, land he willed to his two youngest sons, as per his will in Wilkes County.

George, Sr. and Nancy Ann had four sons: (1) Henry, born 1780, left Wilkes County, (2) William, born 1781, left Wilkes County, (3) Jonas, born 1782, married 18 February 1804, Rhoda Smithey and removed to Tennessee before 1850, (4) George, Jr., born 1784, died after 1860 in Wilkes County, N.C.

George Payne, Jr.'s wife is unknown. She died before 1850. He was a farmer. Eight chil-

Ira Dewitte Payne.

dren have been identified as belonging to George, Jr. and his wife: (1) Walter W., born 1808, died after 1860, married 1st. 23 January 1833, Rebecca Tugman, 2nd. Rebecca Laws, (2) Zebulon, born 1811, married 23 July 1835, Charity Lipps, removed to Johnson County, Tennessee. (3) Lucinda born May 1812, married 14 February 1834 George W. Bradley, (4) Alfred Burton born 1815, married 27 March 1836, Martha Vannoy, (5) Uriah, born 1816, left Wilkes after 1850, (6) Narcissa, born 1826, married 6 March 1856 John Bentley (7) Rhoda, born 1828, married 29 September 1844 Joel Church (8) Amanda C. born 1832.

William R. Payne was born in 1842 in Wilkes County, a grandson of George Payne, Jr. He died before 1880 in Watauga County, married 18 March 1866 in Ashe County, Sarah Brown, born 1843, died before 1880, daughter of Jesse and Mary (Summerlin) Brown. This couple lived for a short while in Harlon County, Kentucky, but returned to then Watauga County and died there. They had three children (1) George Lafayette, born 21 September 1867 in N.C., died 8 March 1938 in Watauga County, married Chanie Adeline Welborn, (2) William Andrew Jackson, born 25 August 1871 in Harlon County, Kentucky, died 20 May 1936 in Watauga County, married Sarah Elvira Mast., (3) Mary who married a Regan of Watauga County.

George Lafayette Payne married 3 January 1894, Chanie Adeline Welborn, born 19 November 1878, died 21 March 1963 in Watauga County, daughter of James Larkin and Jane America (Blackburn) Welborn. They were the parents of five children, all born in Watauga County: (1) Ira Dewitte, born 28 November 1895, died 22 February 1954 in North Wilkesboro, married Annie Cline Barnhardt, (2) Claude Dahley, born 21 April 1897, died 8 December 1963, married Eva Greene, (3) Annie May, born 1 October 1898, married 1st. 13 December 1913, Gene P. Watson, 2nd. 19

December 1917, Mont Welborn, (4) Minnie Ethel, born 1 April 1900, died 3 March 1974, married Bynum Triplett, (5) Fred Edwards, born 4 May 1905, married Hazel Greene.

Ira Dewitte Payne came to Wilkes County as a young, single man in 1916. He was manager of the C.C. Clothing Store. He established the Payne Clothing Store in March of 1930. He was a member of the First Baptist Church and was chairman of the board of deacons when he died. He was a Kiwanian, a Mason, a Shriner, and was a member of the North Wilkesboro school board. In 1940, the Winston-Salem Journal & Sentinel newspaper featured personalities of the Northwest. In the Sunday March 17th issue the following appeared: "Ira D. Payne is one of the local boys who made good. He is a prominent clothing merchant in North Wilkesboro, where he is well known by the many people who visit that metropolis as well as home towners. His personality fairly bubbles over with courtesy and kindness and he always is apparently making efforts to spread cheer among all he meets. He is secretary of the Masonic Lodge and is active in fraternal circles. He is a staunch Baptist, a faithful church attendant and supporter, always lending his help and influence to causes promoted for the public good."

Ira D. married 10 July 1932, Annie Cline Barnhardt, born 29 March 1905 in Cabarrus County, daughter of William Nelson and Mary Jane (Triece) Barnhardt. She graduated from Woman's College in Greensboro and taught school in North Wilkesboro where she met Ira D. They had three children: (1) Ira Dewitte, Jr., born 12 July 1934, died 27 April 1936, buried in Mt. Lawn Cemetery, (2) Bettie Chloe, born 20 March 1937, married 16 October 1960 at Red Springs, N.C., Harold Powell Dew of Raeford, N.C., son of Harry C. and Vera (Powell) Dew. Bettie attended Mars Hill College and graduated from Wake Forest University. She is a librarian in the Raleigh School System. They have two children: (a) Harold Powell, Jr., born 27 January 1962. He is a student at Mars Hill College, (b) Mary Ruth, born 4 February 1967, (3) Sarah Jane, born 24 April 1940, married 24th June 1962, Henry Gray Absher, son of William Oliver and Ruby (Tuttle) Absher of North Wilkesboro. Sarah Jane graduated from U.N.C. Greensboro and taught school in the Charlotte, N.C. system before her children were born. They have two children: (1) Elizabeth Barnhardt Absher, (b) William Gray Absher. They live in Dunwoody, Georgia.

Sources: Personal knowledge, marriages of Ashe and Wilkes Counties, Wilkes wills, deeds, Federal census, court minutes, Bible records, "Personalities of the Northwest," *Winston-Salme Journal & Sentinel*.

— Sarah Jane Payne Absher and Bettie Chloe Payne Dew

THE WILLIAM ANDREW PAYNE FAMILY
907

According to all available sources of information, the Paynes of Wilkes County, especially my family, had their origin in England

Some of the earlier spellings were Paine, Payn and Paganus. All other spellings were perhaps derived from this Latin work "Paganus" meaning village or rustic.

Some of the earliest Englishmen having the name were John Pain, Hampshire 1200, and Stephen Paynes, Worcestershire 1230. Many others were mentioned but space does not permit listing.

As these sturdy people found their way first to the state of Virginia then to North Carolina, a number of them settled in Alexander County. I was told by my forebearers that they and their parents visited occasionally their Payne relatives in Alexander up to the time of the Civil War. Thereafter, all family ties seem to have been broken between the Paynes of Wilkes and Alexander.

Walten Payne lived in Wilkes near Stony Fork and owned quite a large acreage of mountain land. Since that time all his property has gotten away from his descendants. Walten was my great grandfather, born about 1818, but we do not know the date of his death. It has been stated that Walten was an industrious man who spent most of his time trading rather than farming. He was a well-liked and public-spirited man. His first marriage was to Becky Tugman. Their marriage produced seven children and Frank, one of them, was my grandfather.

Frank Payne was born November 2, 1839 and died March 21, 1908. My father, William Andrew, was one of eight children born from his marriage to Sarah (Sally) Carolyn Church. My grandfather was a quiet unassuming type of person who enjoyed working somewhat but talking on any subject, whether he was versed on it or not. This was his favorite way of passing his time with neighbors and friends.

Frank was a soldier in the Infantry in the Civil War. He came through several battles and was never wounded. Frank was once asked if he had any regrets about shooting at the enemy, the Union soldiers. Frank replied, "I was scared not to shoot in the general direction of the enemy, but I never aimed my rifle at an enemy soldier to try to kill him." He and his family lived in the Chestnut Mountain area, near Stony Fork, until the children were practically grown up. He made a modest living by farming and working for other people in the community when he found the time.

My father, William Andrew, was a large man in stature being six feet, four inches tall with a normal weight of two hundred forty pounds. He was born February 15, 1878 and died May 22, 1947. He was married to Annie Mae Blackburn, who is still living. My mother was born on May 7, 1891.

There were ten children born to this union, all of whom are living at this time. They are Dorman Thomas, born April 20, 1911, married Effie Beshears; Wake Franklin, born July 12, 1912, married to Merry Delight Foster; John Laymon, born June 17, 1914, married to Joy Belle Foster, the sister of Merry Delight; Edna Atha, born July 17, 1916, married Albert Minton; Joseph Reid, born April 14, 1919, married Grace Parsons; Calvin Baxter, born December 2, 1923, married Lucille Phillips; Paul Lemuel, born December 11, 1925, mar-

ried Stella McNeil; Sarah Irene, born December 9, 1927, married Richard Church the first time and Roy Bishop the second time; William Andrew, Jr., born March 7, 1930, married Emogene Phillips.

All of the first nine children were young and at home during the twenties, and I very well remember how difficult it was to eke out our existence on a small mountain farm and try to stay in school during the winter. Our father, Andrew, was rather industrious and had a small income at intervals as he was postmaster for several years at Summit, North Carolina. This post office is no longer in existance. I also remember his listing taxes for the people in Job's Cabin township which paid a small fee.

In the early twenties my father served as Deputy Sheriff for a few years which also provided a small amount of income. That avocation required his attending court in Wilkesboro.

Following a March term of court in 1919, my father came home ill with a bad case of influenza which was a very much dreaded disease. Every member of my family was in bed within ten days. I was the only one who did not get the disease, therefore, I had to be nurse, cook, and errand boy for two weeks. This was quite an experience for an eight year old chap. The neighbors would bring in food and place wood on our doorstep for fuel but none of them would take the chance on coming inside the house.

Somehow we made it and finally along came World War II. Four of my brothers served in the military or were drafted. Brother Baxter received the Purple Heart for injuries received in the Battle of Midway in 1944. Wake has been and still is doing ministerial work when his health permits.

Sources: Family Bible, Deeds and Grants, gravemarkers; older family members; and letters.

— Dorman T. Payne

GEORGE LAWRENCE PEARSON (1836-1900)

908

My grandfather, George Lawrence Pearson, was born March 30, 1836, at Boomer, Wilkes County, a small settlement between Moravian Falls and Lenoir, North Carolina. He was the son of Enoch and Patsy Walker Pearson and the grandson of Lawrence Pearson and his wife, Lydia. The exact year Lawrence and Lydia migrated from Pennsylvania to the Goshen community of Wilkes County is not known, but in February, 1793, he bought one hundred eighty-one acres of land lying on Little Warrior's Creek that had been put up for sale for back taxes. The price of the land was twenty-one dollars and a few cents! In 1807 Lawrence's will was probated in which he left all his property to his wife. For some reason it was necessary for Lydia to sell thirty acres of the land to William Rich for thirty dollars. There is no record that I have found as to what happened to the rest of the land, so one would assume the terms of the will were carried out.

Information concerning my great-

grandfather, Enoch Pearson, has been very ellusive. He was married to Patsy Walker March 12, 1833, and his name is listed in two censuses of the period but I have very little additional information about him. The census of 1850 records an Enoch and Patsy Pearson listing their four children: Nancy, my grandfather George, Lydia, and Sallie. During the ten years between the taking of census, George had married and had established a family of his own.

George Lawrence Pearson married Mary S. Saunder. Eventually, he bought the Satterwhite farm at Boomer, North Carolina, consisting of two hundred sixty-eight acres. In his will, probated at his death, the land was divided equally among his surviving children. George and Mary Pearson reared a family of eleven children. At this time I'd like to tell you who they were, their spouses and the children of each.

The oldest child was Cordelia Ann, born February 25, 1859, who remained single. She died February 2, 1887.

I am not sure of the order of birth of the other children so I'll just give the list. The other two girls were: Mattie E. Pearson, birthdate and deathdate unknown, married a Whitt and had two daughters; Venie M. Pearson, born 1869 — died October 18, 1946, married George Andrew Crysel. Her children are James Walter who lost his life in World War I; Zora Crysel Osborne; John T., and Jeter Crysel.

The rest of George's children were boys. Thomas Aaron Pearson, born August 27, 1861 — died July 28, 1927, was married to Kenner Alice Sharpe. His children are Leah Alice, Minerva Estella, Henry, Thomas Lester, Rosa, Piccola May, Mary Lizzie, and an unnamed infant daughter.

John Lee Pearson, born August 28, 1866 — died July 30, 1928, married Martha Ellen Brookshire. John's children are Walter Lee, Lindsay Anderson, William Howard, Joseph U.D., Jeffy G., and an unnamed infant child who lived about a month.

William Seymour Pearson, born January 1, 1871 — died March 19, 1927, did not marry. Even though he was not the oldest son, he seemed to have been the leader of his brothers. It was Seymour who bought all the tracts of land willed to his brothers by their father in order to have it back into the original farm of two hundred sixty-eight acres.

Riley Hampton Pearson, born August 10, 1872 — died March 25, 1935, married Mary Jane Morgan. His family consisted of ten children: Ethel Linda, Mildren Jane, Claude Lawrence, Twins: William Allie and Joseph Tallie, George Seymour, James Frank, Paul Hampton, William Hardon, and Marie Pearson Bumgarner.

Joseph Pomroy Pearson, born October 2, 1875 — died December 7, 1940, married Dovie Callie Laws. This couple had five boys and four girls. They are Nellie Vera Pearson, Mary Lou Beulah Pearson James, Joseph Lawrence, William Alonzo, Ollie Louise Pearson Sweet, twins, Connie and Donnie, Lonnie Hampton, and Romie Spencer.

George Edward Pearson, born September 11, 1879 — died July 10, 1929, who married

Rosa Melvina Brooks had a large family of ten children. They are Mary Lee Pearson Bumgarner, Hilton Edward, Raymond Seymour, Joseph Hampton, Eulalia Pearson Eller, Alvin Wiley, Henry Marshall, Rachel Louise Pearson Nichols, Fred Willard, and Roby Thomas. Joseph Hampton and Alvin Wiley lost their lives in World War II.

Isaac Everette Pearson, born December 23, 1878 — died May 27, 1944, married Florence Huffman. Everette's children are Mary Jo Pearson Faw, Peggy Florence Watts Faw, and William Everette.

Romie Hall Pearson, the youngest child of George Lawrence and Mary Saunders Pearson, was born April 18, 1884 — died April 9, 1956, married Maude Verona Holler. Since this is my father I'd like to record in just a little more detail the activities of this particular family.

Romie knew the furniture manufacturing business from the bottom up. Actually, that is the way he had progressed during the years. When his health failed, he was forced to retire from this line of work to something that would not be so strenuous on his heart. In comparison to modern days and times, he had very little education (two school terms of two months each) but his lack of formal education was no handicap to his ability to learn and get ahead in whatever he set his mind to. After his retirement, he went into business with two of his brothers, Hampton and Everette, in a wholesale grocery store located in North Wilkesboro, North Carolina. Realizing his own sons might wish to be in business with him, he sold his interest to his brothers in order to become an independent merchant owning his own store.

There were six children in the family, four of whom are deceased.

(1) Harry Hall is the oldest and after serving fourteen years in the Marine Corps, he returned to North Wilkesboro and married Joyce Marie Wellborn. They had two children, Harry Hall, Jr., and Loretta Joyce. Harry, Sr. lives in Birmingham, Alabama, with his present wife, the former Nell Barnett. (2) Cleo Beatrice at the time of her retirement was connected with Wilkes Central High School as the Guidance director. She remained single. (3) William Clyde married Margaret Vannoy and they had three children: William Clyde, Jr., Ruth Vannoy, and Janice. (4) Lucy Maude married Franklin Amzie Killian of Lincolnton, North Carolina. Lucy taught and served as school librarian in the Lincoln County Schools for more than thirty years and is now retired. Her husband, also retired, was the Assistant Post Master in the Lincolnton post office. They have three children: Nancy Jane Killian Conner, a teacher; James Franklin, a pharmacist, and Charles Frederick, a pharmacist also. (5) James Everette died in his youth. (6) Russell Glenn married Margaret Ann Church. They have three children: Russell Glenn, Jr., Margaret Annette Pearson Wyatt, and Martha Juliet Pearson Ray.

Sources: Personal knowledge, family memories, and legal documents.

— Lucy Pearson Killian

ALEXANDER J. PENDLEY FAMILY

909

My grandfather, Alexander J. Pendley, moved his wife and five children to Wilkes County from Watauga in 1905.

"Alec" was born in the Globe community of Caldwell County on October 8, 1860, the son of Silas Pendley and Elizabeth Filyeaux (or Philyaw). His brother, Simeon, remained in Watauga and was one time mayor of Blowing Rock. Another brother, John, lived on Howard's Knob.

My grandmother, Martha Jane Austin Pendley, was born on Christmas Eve, 1858. Her father, Hillman Austin, was a casualty of the Civil War and is buried in the Seven Pines National Cemetery near Richmond, Virginia.

Silas Pendley was wounded in that same war and received a pension for the rest of his life. From the incident of his war record, the family has passed on the story of his bravery and the stamina of the Appalachian women.

"Betsy" Pendley, on hearing of Silas' injury, took a buckboard wagon, drawn by a team of mules, and went to Richmond and brought her husband home. The half-gallon of corn whiskey she also packed among the blankets and straw-tick made the soldier's wagon ride back to Caldwell more endurable.

Alec and Martha Pendley, my grandparents, built the home located at 1101 E Street. My grandfather was foreman at Meadow's Mill Company and the bases of the columns on the front porch are made of three small millstones each. He was employed there until his death in 1923.

My grandmother lived to be eighty-seven years old. She was a kind, kind woman and an excellent seamstress. Another Appalachian woman of stamina, she took her one and only airplane flight in a single engine two-passenger plane when she was eighty-three years old.

My father, Ronda Neal Pendley, and his

Alex J. Pendley and Marcella.

brothers and sisters were all Watauga natives. Walter, the eldest, died in World War I and is buried in Arlington National cemetery; Alice became a milliner and married Thomas J. Garrett of Henderson; Woodfin, the younger daughter, also married a Henderson native, Roy Whitmore, a baker. My two aunts lived in Henderson for many years. Otto Austin moved to Greensboro where he owned and operated a sanatorium for drug addicts and alcoholics. He had also served in World War I.

Otto, Woodfin and Neal Pendley.

My father attended a business college in Roanoke, Virginia and learned the Palmer Method of handwriting and on his return to Wilkes, he opened a business. R.N. Pendley, Sign and Card Writer, (Cornet Soloist, North Wilkesboro Band). Later stationery reads, "Tell the World with signs." It also lists typewriter repairing, Kodak finishing and picture framing. He did work for the State Highway Department at one time as a sign painter. Little wonder that he didn't include "Baritone Soloist." In that talent he is best remembered by those who knew him. He was a Kiwanian.

He courted my mother, Ruby Gernell Barnes, for three years and married her on July 4, 1916. She was a beautiful girl, daughter of Stacey and Eugenia Barnes. Her diary, dated 1913, written during her seventeenth year and her letters so beautifully penned weave a love story. They were addressed to "Rube" and signed, "Pen."

My mother was an artist and did mostly oil paintings and hand-painted china. She gave art lessons in our home and years later in a studio in downtown North Wilkesboro.

In 1925 we moved to Greensboro where my father went into business with my uncle. A few years later they bitterly disolved their partnership. At that point, my parents went into business and owned and operated Penmar Sanatorium, until my father's death in 1932.

The Pendley grandchildren number five. They are Thomas J. Garrett, Jr, Charlotte, N.C., Evelyn Garret Hauser, Fayetteville, N.C.; Ada Whitmore, Lee, Nashville, Tn.; Alexander

Pendley Whitmore, Tulsa, Okla, deceased; and Marcella Pendley Church of Wilkesboro.

The Alexander Pendleys, their sons and Neal's wife, Ruby, are buried in the Greenwood Cemetery in North Wilkesboro.

Sources: Federal Census and personal knowledge.

— Marcella Pendley Church

GROVER CLEVELAND PENDRY
910

Alfred Pendry and Lucinda Farrington were married in Yadkin County. They had four sons: James, Bloom, George, and Houston. Both Alfred and Lucinda died in 1885.

James Pendry left Yadkin County and went to Ashe County to live where he married Hannah Hinshaw, and they were blessed with the following children: Grover Cleveland, Theodore, Bert, Ora, Winnie, Avie and Dessie.

After Hannah's death James moved to Wilkes County and opened a country store one mile north of Hays. This building has been converted into a dwelling and is now one of the older buildings in Wilkes County.

Grover married Fannie Ballard and four children, Eula, William Virgil, Dovie, and Willard, were born to this union.

After Fannie's death, Grover married Mary Jane Sidden. Their children are Rosalie and Edward.

Grover was interested in politics and was chairman of the Democratic Party in Rock Creek Township for many years. He was appointed Justice of the Peace, serving as such until his death. Grover was section foreman for the State Highway Commission during the late thirties and forties. He served on the Selection Service Board in the late forties. Grover was a member of the Mtn. View School Board for many years. He enjoyed his work and fellowship in the Odd Fellows Lodge.

Some of the land where Mtn. View School now stands was donated by Grover. He also supplied part of the property for the Wild Life Lake in Hays.

Three of Grover's children followed in their father's footsteps and became teachers. Eula, Rosalie, and Edward taught in the Wilkes County School System.

Edward served as rural mail carrier for thirty-three years after his return from his tour of duty with the U.S. Navy during World War II.

William Virgil was bridge foreman for the district before his retirement.

Dovie was cafeteria manager at North Wilkes High School for many years before her retirement.

Sources: Family Bible and personal knowledge.

— Rosalie Prevette

THE PENNELLS
911

John Pennell, born 1789, died 26 February 1864, was the son of Joshua Pennell. His mother was believed to be a Miss Judd. He married Susannah Curtis, born 1790, died 6 October 1882, daughter of Samuel and Susannah Cottrell Curtis. Their known children were Harvey C., born 1821; Samuel, born 1824, died in Battle of Chancellorville, 3 May 1863, married Susan Greene; William, born ca 1826, married Minerva A. Carlton; and John.

Harvey Calvin Pennell, born 14 June 1821 in Watauga County, died 10 April 1903, married in Ashe County December 3, 1841, Rachel Louise Curtis, born 5 January 1822, died 16 June 1879, daughter of Thomas and Nancy Harmon Curtis. Both Harvey and Rachel are buried in the Old Pennell Cemetary near Wilkesboro.

Harvey was an active member of Union Methodist Church, having served on the building committee from 1875 until completion of the building in 1877, and he was among the early Church school Superintendents. It is also noted that he served as executor of a number of wills during his lifetime. Judge Tam C. Bowie of West Jefferson in a speech in Wilkes County mentioned the Pennells among other families whose pioneer patriarchs laid well the foundations of the county and he further recalled that one of the Pennell girls shot and killed one of Stoneman's raiders when he came back against her command to take the last horse from the barn.

L. to R. Jessie W. Pennell, John Warren, George Murphey, Tom Pennell and George Pennell.

Harvey and Rachel had eleven children: (1) John (Jr.) born 1842, died in Battle of Chancellorville, 3 May 1863. (Note: he and his Uncle Samuel Pennell were killed the same day in the same battle.) (2) Clarissa, born 1844, died 1815, married William Harrison Witherspoon. (3) Nancy Caroline (Nannie), born 1848, married John Thomas Forester. (4) Susannah (Sue), born 1849, died 1906, married Jeremiah A. Crysel. (5) Elizabeth (Aunt Bettie) born 1851, died 1929, unmarried. (6) William Thomas, born 1854, died 1922, married Jessie Julia Warren. (7) Mattie Jane, born 1857, died 1896, married Rufus A. Eller. (8) James Holland, born 1859, died 1935 (see separate story). (9) Mary Melissa, born 1861, died 1943, married John W. Gaither (see separate story). (10) Laura Addeville, born 1863, died 1926, married Rufus Philmore Wyatt. (11) Sara Ellen (Ella), born 1864, died 1867.

William Thomas Pennell, born 18 March 1854, died 16 January 1922, in Greensboro, N.C., was married in 1883 to Jessie Julia Warren, born 7 October 1865, at Dellaplane, N.C., daughter of Peter Mason and Margaret Shoaf Warren. She died 19 April 1939, in Norfolk, Va. They are buried in Greensboro.

Tom and Jessie, my grandparents, also had eleven children, all born in Wilkes County but only one Emma Pennell Bumgarner, remained here her entire life. Their children were: (1) Ada Rosella, born 1884, died 1961, New York City, married (1) Young Royall and had one son, Worth, (b) Eddie Curry. (2) Florence Agnes, born 1885, died 1949, married (a) George Murphy and had one son, George, Jr., (b) Andrew A. Paris of French-Canadian ancestry. (3) Joseph Orin, born 1886, died 1961, married Florrie Bethune, had four sons: Joe, Jr., Sam, Frank, and Will. (4) Emma Louise, born 1888, died 1973, married James M. Bumgarner, and had one daughter Helen Louise. (5) Maud Warren, born 1890, died 1968, married Lee Johnson Bentley and had two daughters, Lucille and Mary Lee. (6) Margaret Louisa, born 1892 (still living) married William Mack Meadows and had one daughter, Pauline. (7) Bessie Mae, a nurse, born 1895, killed in automobile accident in Shreveport, La., in 1922, married a Mr. Lynch. (8) Mary Annie, born 1898, (still living), married James Dewey Strader and had one daughter, Ruth. (9) Bryan Lee, born 1899, died 1982, married Annie Harper and had four children: Mildred, Bryan, Jr., Bobby, and James Thomas (Jimmy) (10) Nellie Lee, born 1902 (still living) married Vernon Spencer Yow and had two children, Raymond M. and JoAnn. (11) George Wright, born 1905, died 1972, married (a) Florence Wilson, had a son, Donnell, and (2) Betty Bryant, had a son George Allen.

My grandparents left Wilkes County in 1918, moving to Greensboro in order to send several of their younger daughters to college. Among my fondest childhood memories are the weeks spent in Greensboro during the summers. Mother and I would travel by train from North Wilkesboro then take a "jitney" to the house. A couple of weeks later, Daddy would come in our Model T, a full day's trip, spend the night and bring us home. Those were the days! And how I enjoyed sitting on the front steps watching the streetcars "clang" by. Then when we went shopping, I got to ride by the window.

— Helen B. Bell

JAMES HOLLAND PENNELL
912

The eighth child of Harvey Calvin and Rachel Louise Curtis Pennell was James Holland Pennell, born 27 June 1859 in Wilkesboro, North Carolina. After completing all the schooling available in Wilkes County, he attended Trinity College, now Duke University, and he taught school from 1881 to 1900 in several localities.

Mr. Pennell was converted at a camp meeting and in 1875 joined Union Methodist Church where he served as steward, district steward, trustee of church property, church secretary, and was Sunday School superintendent for more than thirty years.

On 17 May 1883 he was married to Elizabeth Milliken, granddaughter of Daniel Milliken, a Quaker, born 17 March 1861 in Randolph County and died 10 May 1892. She is buried in the Pennell family cemetery near Wilkesboro. They were the parents of Cora Gertrude and Eula May Pennell, both of whom died in in-

James H. Pennel.

Elizabeth Milliken Pennell.

prevent or stop his determination to become a dedicated physician. He studied with many individual teachers: Rev. D.P. Hurley of Holston Conference; Hon. Horton Bower of Lenoir, N.C.; Judge Joseph F. Spainhour; and Dr. J.O. Wilcox of Ashe County. His preparatory work completed, he went to Baltimore, Maryland, where he entered the Baltimore Medical College (now University of Maryland Medical University) and graduated in the top ten of his class in 1891. Following his graduation, he and his family returned to his native land where he began his medical practice. Though practicing medicine, he frequently returned to his Alma Mater for seminars in new and advanced medical developments.

Dr. Perkins first married Floranza B. Shultz of Mt. Pleasant, Frederick Co., Maryland, on 2 January 1889; Florance was born 3 January 1867, and died 28 April 1909. They had five children: Ensa Lee, Stella May, Bohn Soisson Perkins, Nellie Helen, and "Baby" (born: 1907 — died: 1909). Second marriage: Sallie Ada Parks of Yadkin Valley, Wilkes County, North Carolina, b. 28 August 1889. They have two children: Annie Lee and Samuel Clayton.

Dr. Perkins had a library of over three thousand volumes, chiefly medicine, history, and travel. He travelled over the forty-eight states of the U.S.A. He was a scholar in the truest sense of the word and continued so until his death. Dr. Perkins' contribution to Wilkes, Ashe, Watauga, and Alleghany counties was quality, humane professional medical services, day or night to all of the people who so desperately needed his professional medical skills. Not only did he give of his medical skills but he gave medication regardless of the financial resourses of the patient. One must remember that during this period of our history, there were no drug stores, no welfare programs, no medicare, no medicaid and no insurance programs. Patients needed medication immediately. Dr. Perkins shared his skills and medication.

fancy; Franklin Harvey Pennell, born 10 January 1888, died 9 January 1963, and is buried in Arlington National Cemetery near Washington, D.C. Frank served thirty years in the U.S. Navy and was a veteran of World Wars I and II. Ora Rosey Pennell, born 6 March 1890, married Edward Grey Farthing of Boone, N.C., the son of John Watts and Addelaide Rivers Farthing, on 17 April 1911. They were the parents of Addie Louise Farthing who married Elmer G. Miller; Edward Grey Farthing, died at age ten; James Bruce Farthing, died 16 April 1981; Mildred Elizabeth Farthing who married Myron H. Wright; Cecil Watts Farthing who married Carolyn Hayes; and Rhea Rivers Farthing who married Florence Messick. Ora Pennell Farthing died 11 December 1951 and is buried in Boone, N.C.

James Holland Pennell was married a second time on 3 August 1893 to Ida Belle Pheiffer, born 10 November 1860 and died 20 November 1899. They had three children: Laura Estelle Pennell, born 9 July 1894 and died 18 April 1964. She was a very dedicated teacher and taught for many years in Forsyth County before returning to her native Wilkes to teach at Union Elementary School near her home. She was an active member of Union Methodist Church and is buried in the cemetery there. James Monroe Pennell, born 23 October 1896, died 9 April 1961 in Cleveland, N.C. He was married to Willie White Steele on 24 November 1926 and they were the parents of two sons, Walter and Edward. The third child was John Kilgo Pennell who died in infancy.

James H. Pennell's third wife was Ella Mae Howell to whom he was married on 3 November 1909. She was born 3 Jun 1879 in Ashe County, the daughter of William Howell and Jane Garvey Howell. They were the parents of Stuart Winston Pennell who died in infancy. Ruth Pauline Pennell, born 3 June 1912, married 25 June 1945 Roy Ernest Dunn. They live in Baton Rouge, Louisiana and have one daughter, Melissa Diane Dunn Johnson. Edward Harold Pennell, born 8 March 1914, mar-

ried Ennie Scott, born 27 June 1917. They are the parents of Mary June Pennell who first married Jimmy Benton. Their children are James Steven Benton, Michael Edward Benton and Barbara Lynn Benton Edminsten. Lynne is the mother of twin sons, Bryan Scott and Ryan Andrew. June is presently married to Jack Johnson. William Howell Pennell, born 9 July 1917, died in 1971 in Mooresville, N.C., and was married to Pauline Combs Pennell who died in June 1977.

For a number of years Mr. Pennell was a member of the Wilkes County Board of Education, an office he held with pride and esteem. He served as a Justice of the Peace for several years also.

While walking along the highway near his home in the Cricket community, Mr. Pennell was struck by an automobile driven by an intoxicated driver and he suffered multiple internal injuries and fractures. He died a few days later on 8 October 1935 as a result of this accident and is buried in the Union Methodist Church Cemetery. His last wife, Mae Howell Pennell died 11 June 1971 and is buried beside her husband.

Sources: Bible Records, newspaper articles, cemetery records and personal knowledge.

— Mildred F. Wright (Mrs. Myron H.)

DR. SAMUEL LUTHER PERKINS

913

Dr. Perkins was born 3 October 1859, Ashe Co. on Buffalo Creek, Treetop, N.C. and died 29 January 1936, in Wilkesboro, Wilkes Co., N.C.

Dr. Perkins, a fourth generation of Perkins in Wilkes County, North Carolina, and an eleventh generation of Perkins in the U.S.A. When Dr. Perkins was born, North Carolina's educational facilities were practically nil, in the vicinity where he lived. However, this did not

Bohn Soisson Perkins.

Floranza Biembrinck Shultz Perkins.

Bohn Soisson Perkins was born 11 August 1900 in Solitude, Ashe Co., North Carolina, and died 14 November 1981 in Wilkesboro, Wilkes Co., N.C. He was the son of Dr. Samuel Luther Perkins, a fifth generation of Perkins in the Wilkes area and a twelfth generation of Perkins in the U.S.A. Bohn was educated in the educational system of North Carolina and the John Hopkins University of Baltimore, Maryland. He studied engineering and became a civil engineer with the State Departments of Maryland and North Carolina, State Roads Division. He married Elizabeth Winkler, issue: one son.

Bohn was a person of high integrity, congenial personality. He practiced fairness and honesty in all his dealings with his associates. He insisted on quality materials and work on the job. He believed in safety in all roads for the benefit of the public who used these roads. Today the results of his efforts are still being enjoyed by the traveling public in North Carolina.

Sources: Bibles and records of various family members Census Reports; Church records; Cemeteries deeds and wills.

— Helen Perkins Argenbright

PERRY

914

Henry R. Perry was born 19 Sept. 1827 and died 15 July 1919. He married in 1848 Mrs. Mary Royal, maiden name unknown, who was born in 1815 and died 10 March 1895. Their children were: (1) Ebenezer B., born 19 Feb. 1850, died 12 Jan. 1929. He married Mary Malinda Wyatt, daughter of John G. and Mary Brown Wyatt who was the daughter of Ezekiel and Susan Brown. Mary Malinda was born 15 Dec. 1855 and died 9 March 1932. Their children were Jonathan, Isaac and Mariah. (2) Elizabeth was born in 1854. (3) Margaret was born in 1858. Floyd was born 9 Aug. 1860 and died 30 Oct. 1913. (5) Nancy was born in 1863.

Jonathan Perry was born 24 Nov. 1872 and

Dr. Samuel Luther Perkins.

died 15 July 1916 in the flood which swept through Wilkes County. He married Barbara Emaline Nelson, daughter of John and Mary Jane Wagoner Nelson, on 14 May 1895. Barbara Emaline was born 4 Oct. 1880 and died 21 May 1871. They were the parents of 13 children. Franklin, Viola, Holly, and Minnie all died before 1916, unmarried. The seven who lived to adulthood were: (1) Mary married Treely Royal. (2) Ebby married Laura Wyatt. (3) Linda L., born 5 Sept. 1902, married Alonza H. Porter. (4) Ada Lou, born 7 Oct. 1904 married 21 Jan. 1920 Arville Monroe Porter. (5) Lena married Joe Patrick. (6) Nettie A. married Commodore Dancy. (7) Dosky A. married Ed Fanclier (Fansler?).

Sources: Wilkes County Marriage records, Census Schedules, and grave stones.

— Arville Edward Benton

PETTY FAMILY

915

The Petty, orginally Pettey, family emigrated to America from Ireland. Some of the family came to Wilkes County about 1790. One of the early Pettys was Nancy, born 1785, who married John Hickerson and moved to Manchester, Tennessee. Eli Petty, probably a brother of Nancy, married Lucretia Wright.

Col. Benjamin F. Petty, son of Eli and Lucretia Petty, established his home on the south side of the Yadkin River about four miles east of Wilkesboro. He married first in 1829, Cynthia Bryan and second in 1852 Jane Amanda Nisbet. The children of the first marriage were: Julia, Laura, Joanna, Lucinda who married Col. Lyndolph Parks, William B., Capt. John, C.S.A., Leory, Adelia, and Felix.

The children of the second marriage were: Dorcas Virginia who married Joseph Edwards and lived about two miles north of Ronda, who were the parents of Mrs. Ada Holland and Mrs. Sue Church, Thomas Ernest, Nesbit, Millard, Mary Jane McConna Edwards.

Sources: excerpts from *Happy Valley* by Felix Hickerson.

— Eleanor Parks Elam

REV. and MRS. GEORGE WASHINGTON PETTY

916

George Washington Petty, known to many as "Uncle George", was a fine Christian gentleman. Born in Wilkes County in the early 1800's.

The writer, Loree Anderson, is the eldest daughter of the late Bessie Petty Harris, who was the oldest child of the second marriage of George and Mary Jane Petty.

This story, I find especially interesting. I have heard it from a very reliable source — Grandpa's youngest daughter, Lila Petty Bailey Parks. She related it to a group of us, since the book *Roots* has been portrayed on television. It goes like this: "Young George was actually sold, as a slave at the age of eight years. I know little about the intervening years. However, the year I was going to be five years old, my parents left me in the home of my grandparents. I thought I had heard all of the good stories firsthand, at Grandpa's knee. On with this one — At the close of the "Civil War", he was down in Texas. Some time afterward he had made his way back to his parents' home in Wilkes County. There was a companion with him. I reason, that his father must have passed on in the interim, because his mother was hesitant to invite him in. (Having lived a whole school term with my grandparents, Grandfather would not leave anyone out in the elements overnight.) Finding his mother hesitant, he asked of her, "Would you turn away your own son?" Her answer: "Is that you George?" I am reminded of the story of "Joseph" in the Bible. Joseph was sold into slavery when just a lad. My grandfather was just eight years old when sold. He was then twenty-one years of age.

I also wish to relate a few of my fondest memories of my grandfather. Especially before going to bed at night, the whole family assembled together in the room with the open fireplace. "Sweet Hour of Prayer" was sung. A scripture lesson was read and a prayer was prayed. These devotionals have left quite an imprint on my memory and have helped influence my private and public devotional life. Speaking of a good memory — Grandpa Petty used to visit the schools, and when given time to make an expression and/or encouraging remarks, I remember well his recitation of "A Psalm of Life," etc. I also remember him in the pulpit. He was a very Spiritual minister. One of his favorite songs, which I remember well, was "My Soul Looked Back and Wondered, How I Got Over."

Another of my favorites: Let us say, plantations are four or five "country miles" apart. After dinner on a Sunday afternoon, if a young man wished to visit a young woman or "girl friend" on another plantation, he had better plan and manage to be back by or before nightfall. Why? The "Patty-Rollers," patrols would be on horseback. Slaves would lie down

Rev. and Mrs. George Washington Petty.

along side a hollow log and "hold their breath" until the patrols were convinced that none were in the area. How relieved they must have felt, when and if not apprehended. The punishment was to be hung up by one's thumbs and beaten until the blood ran down — salt would then be rubbed into the open wound.

The writer happens to have been blessed to teach in the Public schools of Wilkes County for more than forty years. My mother taught for thirty odd. I count this a blessed heritage. It has, no doubt, made of me, a more compassionate human being.

While teaching in the now "phased out" Lincoln Heights High School, a patron who knew my grandfather sent me a newspaper clipping which commended my grandfather for visiting the prisoners (locally) and ministering unto them. I have always been told that he went back to school after he was forty years old. This always inspired me to keep studying and to earn my "Master's Degree" by the time I was forty. I remember my grandfather proudly. I attended his funeral. He was eighty-one years old when he died.

My grandmother, "Aunt Mary" as she was affectionately referred to by many, was a quite, humble woman. She made a superb minister's wife and mother to her children as well as to three step-children, by Grandpa's first marriage. I will give an example: In those days, there was no indoor plumbing or running water. My mother's oldest daughter told us often of how Grandma would awaken her early to go with her to bring water from a spring located some distance from the house. She would tell her (my mother), "Bessie, you come and go with me to the spring; you know how people critize stepmothers." Grandma gave us a good example of cleanliness. She loved to sweep and made sure not to sweep anything "under

the rug," to move furniture if need be to clean under beds, etc. She wore several white starched "petticoats" and always kept Grandpa's clothing and the children's spotlessly clean. She also lived in our home at various times. She lived to be ninety-three years of age. She died peacefully, and as I remember, with a smile on her face.

She was a native of Alexander County, Stony Point Community. She counted her age from the number of years she was old "at the surrender." She was blessed with good eyesight and was still threading her needle without the need for glasses for as long as she lived. Her maiden name was Reddick. Her father was Jiles Reddick.

Sources: Personal knowledge.

— Loree Anderson

PHILLIPS — VIARS — WOODIE — BESHEARS
917

Prior to his death on 3 Nov 1800, John Phillips lived in the part of Rowan County which is now Davie County. His will, recorded in Salisbury, appointed his wife, Diannah and Lewis Hicks as executors. Sons and daughters named as beneficiaries in his will are: Thomas, John, Gabriel, Ezra, Jonathan, Robert, James, Elijah, Stephen, Sarah Bayley, Ruth Spiers, Elizabeth Viny, Ann Cummins and Rebecca Williams. The Phillips land adjoined that of Col. Jonathan Hunt, a prominent figure in the early history of Rowan County.

Ezra Phillips, son of John, was born 12 Nov 1762. He married Hannah Randolph, who was born 15 Apr 1761, daughter of Samuel Randolph. Their wills seem to indicate they moved

to North Carolina from New Jersey. Their children are: Eli Payton (b. 5 Sept 1783), Nancy (b. 3 Aug 1788), Rebeckah (b. 21 Apr 1791), Hannah (b. 4 Nov 1794), Polly (b. 30 Aug 1797), Amy (b. 6 Jun 1799), Sarah (b. 2 Jun 1802), Joseph (b. 8 Apr 1805), Elizabeth (b. 12 Apr 1808), Elinda (b. 11 Jul 1811).

Eli Payton Phillips, oldest son of Ezra, is said to have married Martha from Boonesborough, Ky. They had at least two sons, Billy and Eli, and a daughter Melissa. The date of Eli Payton's death is not known to this writer, but family legends indicate that he lived to be 100 or more years old, and died from smallpox. His grave is located on the crest of a hill just south of the Blue Ridge Parkway near Calloway Gap. It is marked by a hand hewn stone from which all lettering has vanished. Five or six other graves are at the same site, but it is not known whose they are.

Eli Phillips, son of Eli Payton, was born ca. 1815. He married Nancy Matilda Viars, daughter of Robert and Elizabeth Powell Viars, and settled on the south side of the crest of the Blue Ridge Mountains. Robert Viars was the son of William and Ann Shepherd Viars. William lived on Raccoon Branch, a tributary of Reddies River, as early as February 1780. William's wife, Ann, was the daughter of John and Sarah Shepherd, who came to the Reddies River area in the fall of 1775 or early spring of 1776.

Just across the crest of the Blue Ridge from Eli's home, in Ashe County, his brother and wife Jamima reared a family of twenty two children.

Eli and Matilda had only nine children: George (b. 1839 — m. Nancy Powell); Caroline (b. 1841 — m. John Kees); William Payton (twin, b. 1844, m. Mary Ann Powell); Robert Franklin (twin, b. 1844, m. 1st Rebecca Powell, 2nd Julia Beshears); James Calvin (b. 1846 — died in Civil War); Nathan (b. 1848 — m. 1st Melissa Woodie, 2nd Ellen Canter); Amanda (b. 1850 — m. Jim Watson); Rhoda Emaline (b. 1855 — m. George Blackburn); and John Wesley (b. 7 Mar 1857 — m. Rachel Catherine Woodie).

Eli died in 1908, and is buried in a small family cemetery near the Summit community in Wilkes County.

Rachel Catherine Woodie, who married John Wesley Phillips, was born 25 Mar 1860, daughter of Jonathan P. and Martha Patsy Beshears Woodie. Jonathan was born ca. 1821 and was killed on 18 Mar 1863 in the Civil War. His wife, Martha, was born ca 1825, daughter of Catherine (Katie) Beshears, and granddaughter of Martha Beshears, who was a widow at the time of the 1810 census.

John Wesley and Rachel lived near Summit until about 1890, and then moved to the Obids community in Ashe County. Their children are: Elbert Commodore (b. 23 Mar 1877, d. 6 Sept 1971, m. Julie Phillips, daughter of Harvey Phillips); William Romulus (b. 15 Nov 1878, m. Julie Mash); Calvin McKeiver (b. 28 Mar 1880, m. Elizabeth Miller, daughter of John and Etta Mash Miller); Lillie Bell (b. 27 Feb 1882, m. Ham Miller, son of Neil Miller); Laura Ann (b. 25 Apr 1884, m. Ellis Miller, brother of Ham); Levi Nathan (b. 26 Mar 1886, m. 1st, Clydie Severt, daughter of Wiley Severt, 2nd,

Ethel Phillips, daughter of Ira Phillips), Edmond Harrison (b. 13 Mar 1889 — d. 16 Oct 1954, m. Ollie Irwin from Missouri); John Lovell (b. 10 Sept 1891, d. 22 Jul 1977, m. Annie Long, daughter of John Long); Clarence McKinley (b. 21 Mar 1894, d. 29 Dec 1981, m. 1st Estel Hart, 2nd Lena Church, daughter of Jones Church); Bessie Louvenia (b. 9 Jul 1898, d. 21 Sept 1980, m. 1st Lester Birdwell, 2nd Rufus Shepherd, 3rd Benjamin H. Wood); and Ella Nora (b. 21 Feb 1903, m. Ira Gilbert Dancy, son of Norman M. and Mary Ann Whittington Dancy. She is now a resident of a local nursing home.)

See article titled "Dancy — Shepherd — Whittington — Vannoy" for children of Ira and Ella Phillips Dancy.
Sources: Rowan County Wills, Mormon Church records at Fort Wayne, Ind., early Wilkes County records, family memories and family records.

— Mrs. Joyce D. McNeil

ADRIAN F. PHILLIPS
918

Adrian F. Phillips was born in Watauga County in 1877. He was the son of George Washington and Margaret Loretta Morphew Phillips. His family on both sides have, since before the Revolution, had roots in this area. An ancestor on his mother's side, Silas Morphew, a Tory, was hung for support of the crown but was cut down by his wife and friends; the Tory Oak losing at least one victim.

My father, George Ward Phillips, Adrian's brother, recalled that at the early age of ten Adrian developed an interest in roots and herbs. He gathered them himself and had the neighbor children working for him. He sold the herbs at Arthur Cowles' General Store in Deep Gap. At the time it was the largest store in the area and a portion of it is standing even today.

This early interest in crude drugs was the basis for his life's work. After a prospecting expedition to the Klondike at the turn of the century, during which he suffered frozen feet in an attempt to make a fortune mining gold, he returned to his section and to his early vocation of crude drugs.

In the early nineteen hundreds he formed a partnership with Ed Vannoy to deal in crude drugs. The business was located in the Ed Vannoy Building on Tenth Street. This building was one of the oldest brick structures in North Wilkesboro and has since been demolished. Some years later he built a building on Tenth Street and went into business for himself. This business was known as A.F. Phillips and Company.

From this Adrian Phillips became one of the largest independent crude drug dealers in the nation and, according to World Almanac, in the world.

As his crude drug business progressed, Adrian invested extensively in business, industrial and farm property in this area, erecting a number of buildings which are still standing and are in use today. He was instrumental in the development and growth of North Wilkesboro from a couple of muddy streets to the town that it is now.

His knowledge of crude drugs and crude drug processes was regarded by his contemporaries as being monumental. During his career he developed a market with most major manufacturers of drugs in this country and in many countries in Europe and Asia as well.

Although having a limited formal education of only a few grades of public school, he never ceased trying to educate himself. During the course of his life, he attended night school, took correspondence courses and made extensive use of self-help teaching materials.

He was a bachelor, having no children of his own, but loved little ones and kept candy in his safe to pass out to them. He would also give them movie money. My father recalled that no matter how important a client was he sometimes had to wait as much as thirty minutes while Adrian visited with his young friends.

He has a number of nieces and nephews who remember his generosity. Among them are my brothers: Adrian Bruce Phillips, Howard D. Phillips, and myself, Miriam P. Hennessee, who live in the Wilkesboros; and my sisters, Margaret P. Jenkins and Joan P. Watson, who live in West Jefferson.

Adrian died in June 1939 at the age of 62, and, according to his wishes, is buried in the family plot in Watauga County, which is less than one-half miles from where he was born.
Sources: Information from relatives and friends.

— Miriam P. Hennessee

DR. ERNEST NICHOLAS PHILLIPS
919

Ernest Nicholas Phillips was born in Dalton, Stokes County, North Carolina, on 21 October 1893, the son of Matthew Dalton Phillips, M.D. and Margaret Melissa Dalton.

He recieved his Bachelor of Science degree from Wake Forest College. When the United States entered World War I in 1917, he volunteered and served until the spring of 1919. He and his brother Matthew were stationed at Kelly Field, Texas, when their group was selected as ground crew for the air force of the Army (there was no separate Air Force then). That group later became part of the American Lafayette Escadrille.

For the sake of accuracy it should be noted that the original Lafayette Escadrille was organized in 1916 by American flyers who volunteered to the French Army (a total of 209 served). The United States declared war in 1917; the members transferred to the American Army and regrouped, and in February, 1918 took the name American Lafayette Escadrille, and more members were added. The group in which Ernest and Matthew served was the 103rd Aero Squadron, arriving in France on December 24, 1917. The squadron was "loaned" as support groups for several French divisions as needed in the major campaigns. One famous person who transferred into the A.L.E. from the British Army was James Norman Hall who wrote *The History of the Lafayette Escadrille* and with James Nordhoff wrote *Mutiny on the Bounty*. The Memorial Arch near Paris, erected by the French government in 1928, lists only the members of the original Lafayette Escadrille.

Ernest returned to the United States and civilian life in the spring of 1919. For a time he farmed and had an automobile repair shop. On November 4, 1922 he married Mary Belle Smith of Rural Hall, North Carolina, the daughter of William Allen Smith and Molly Lucinda Shouse Smith. They had a daughter, Helen Lucinda, born 4 October 1924. In 1926, he decided to study medicine at the Medical School of Wake Forest College, transferring to the Medical College of Virginia in 1928 and graduating in 1930. He interned at St. Luke's Hospital in Richmond, Virginia.

Doctor Phillips practiced medicine in Rural Hall, N.C. for three years, in Hope Mills, N.C. for two years and in 1936 located in Wilkesboro, N.C. in association with his brother-in-law, Dr. Gurney T. Mitchell. They later moved their offices to North Wilkesboro.

Doctor Phillips was a member of the Medical Staff of Wilkes General Hospital, the American Medical Association, the North Carolina Medical Society and the Wilkes Medical Society.

He was a member of the First Baptist Church of North Wilkesboro and in 1950 was president of the North Wilkesboro Kiwanis Club.

Doctor Phillips died 19 July 1963. He is survived by his wife, Mrs. E.N. Phillips of North Wilkesboro, his daughter, Mrs. William B. Cothran, Jr., and three grandchildren, Mary Lucinda Cothran, Susan Melissa Cothran and William B. Cothran III of Burlington, N.C.

Among the newspaper editorial comments were the following: *(The Journal-Patriot)* "In the passing of Dr. E.N. Phillips the community and all Wilkes County lost a valuable citizen. As a family physician he was more than a doctor, he was a friend. As a physician he had compassion for the diseased, the suffering and the unfortunate. He served where there was need, often administering medical skill to those not able to pay for services rendered. There is no yardstick for measuring the worth of a career such as that of Doctor Phillips to a community. There are many to whom he was both benefactor and friend."

From the Funeral Prayer: "Many are here today who have witnessed his quiet, frequent and unsung acts of kindness and love as he went about doing good."
Sources: Family Bible, personal knowledge, newspaper.

— Helen Lucinda Phillips Cothran

PAYTON PHILLIPS AND DESCENDANTS
920

The Phillips family came to this part of America from England around 1800. My great, great, great-grandfather was Payton Phillips. He had a son named Eli (or Elie) and Eli's son, Robert Franklin, was my great-grandfather.

Robert Franklin Phillips was born on August 7, 1844 and died June 8, 1926. He is buried at Yellow Hill Baptist Church in Wilkes County. This church was established in 1853. Franklin Phillips' tombstone indicates that he served in the Confederate Army during the Civil War in "Co. 1 — 4th N.C. SR Res., C.S.A." Frank-

Robert Franklin Phillips and wife, Rebecca Powell Phillips.

lin's twin brother, William Phillips, was also a Civil War Veteran and he is buried at Blue Ridge Baptist Church.

Robert Franklin Phillips married Rebecca Powell. They had six children: Rachel Clementine, my father's mother, who married Rev. Leander ("Lee") Miller; Dianna, who married Jim Baker; Ira, who married Josie Blackburn; Hoy, who married Nancy Church; Raynor, who married Nancy Phillips; and Della who married Fowell Beshears.

After Franklin's wife, Rebecca died, he married Julia Beshears, and they had a daughter named Avanell, who married Carlie Cornett.

William Phillips, twin brother of Franklin Phillips, married Mary Ann Powell, and they had eleven children; These were (1) Monroe married Lou-Ellen Church; (2) Osco married Florence Watson; (3) Ida married Bert Miller; (4) Bennie married Isabell Tomlinson; (5) Minnie a twin, married Smith Watson; (6) Grant a twin, married Ella Phillips; (7) Mary a twin, married Will Church; (8) Martha a twin, married Lee Walker; (9) Philo married Cora Beshears; (10) Genelia married Jake Bare and (11) Clarissa married Russell Miller.

On back in the Phillips history, there was a woman named Jemima Yates Phillips (1809-1889) who married William ("Billy") Phillips (1806-1857), and this couple had twenty-four children. When Jemima Phillips was 80 years old, she walked a distance of sixteen miles to visit a friend and walked back home that evening.

My father's brother, Sheridan Franklin Miller, born December 13, 1894, lives in the Shenandoah Valley in Woodstock, Virginia. In 1964, he wrote a manuscript entitled, "Life in the Hill-Country — A Man, A Boy, A Dog . . . . and the Black Killer." This is a true story of exciting mountain folklore handed down from Eli (or "Elie") Phillips, who was in his nineties, an invalid and totally blind when my uncle and father were small boys. The story gives descriptive passages involving the lives and customs of the inhabitants of the rugged and sparsely-settled upper Wilkes County at that time. The climax of the story centers around Eli Phillips as a young lad witnessing a ferocious battle to the death between the family guard-dog and a huge black panther.

I shall never forget the stories related to me by my parents and grandparents when I was a young girl; stories that truly depicted the courage and the bravery of those people who "blazed the trail" for us in the beautiful "State of Wilkes."

Sources: Family tradition, family memories and gravemarkers.

— Mrs. Joyce Miller Chewning

The old place was sound but despite all efforts the mountainous windy weather was hard to keep out. Many a'morning a skimmering of snow covered the ladder rungs as the boys drowsily climbed down from the loft. Mamo always saw that there were plenty of thick, warm handmade quilts on hand though so their roughly made beds were cozy and warm. Clothing was all handmade, of course, but they did get one new pair of shoes every year. We recall Papa saying, "better take care of 'em boys, that's all you're gonna get." — From Life on the Moore Farm.

PIERCE — HAYES
921

Walter Franklin Pierce married Cassie Ann Roxada Hayes, daughter of William Jasper and Mary Caroline Roberson Hayes. Roxie was born August 17, 1876. They raised their family of seven children in the Millers Creek area. Walter farmed, hunted, kept honey bees, cut timber and in the summer season he ran a cannery. They canned apples from the farm, etc. At one time, he had a peach orchard. He even tried raising tobacco.

Walter loved children and it seemed that the youth of the community loved his company. They trusted him with their secrets.

In the days before radio and television, we sat before an open fire at night during the winter season. Grandpa Bill and Granny Jane who lived next door would come, Grandpa carrying his violin and a kerosene lantern. We enjoyed music and storytelling until bedtime.

The children of Walter and Roxie are as follows: (1) Thurman Otto, born Feb. 20, 1904, lives with his wife, Myrtle May Ball in Winston-Salem, N.C. Myrtle was interested in kindergarten and specialized in preparing good food. Thurman is retired from Hanes Dye & Finishing Company. They had three children: (a) Ella Mae who has been Audit Supervisor for Sears, Roebuck & Co. for the past 35 years, lives at home with her parents. (b) Violet Page married Gerald Glenn Holcomb of Yadkin County and they own and operate The Holcomb Real Estate and Auction Company in Winston-Salem (c.) Thurman Oliver Pierce, Jr. (Top or Bud), was born in Forsyth County, died March 10, 1982. He was married to Thomasine Carter of Davie Co., N.C. and they had four children: Dexter Lee, Walter Gray who died Feb. 21, 1982, Bryan Carter and Deborah Sue. Top was married second to Dena Posey Mullis and had two stepchildren, Tod and Dedra Mullis. Top was in charge of Plant Securities at Western Electric, Guilford Center, N.C.

(2) Nena Pearl, born Aug. 16, 1906, married John Harrison Kilby who was born March 28, 1896, on May 17, 1924. They had three daughters: (a) Evelyn Pearl married Ambrose Jackson Pierce, son of John Ambrose Pierce and his second wife, Elizabeth (Lizzie) Snyder Pierce. Evelyn and Jack were married June 5, 1943 — no issue. Jack is a carpenter and raises chickens at their home near Millers Creek. (b) Dorothy married Ralph Caudill April 3, 1948 and they have two daughters, Donna Jayne married Danny Bliech. Teresa Darlene

married Gerald Thomas Pardue and they have two sons, Charles and John Christian. (c) Virginia Dare was born Sept. 20, 1929 and only lived two days.

(3) Eunella Braska Pierce, born Dec. 20, 1908, has not married and lives on the homeplace near Millers Creek.

(4) Lundy Franklin, born July 13, 1911, married Elsie Miller whose birthdate is July 24, 1919. They were married on Feb. 23, 1946 and have one son, Timothy Oid Hall Pierce. Tim married Sharon Lynn Osborne and they have three children: Timothy Mark, Tammy Renee, and Tanya Michele. Lundy Pierce operated a service station and grocery store for several years and later went into farming.

(5) Nettie Y. Pierce, born Dec. 18, 1913, died unmarried Jan. 1, 1933.

(6) Joseph Samuel Pierce, born June 22, 1916, died Nov. 14, 1974, was a well known meat cutter in Wilkes County. He married Velvaree Ellis June 15, 1940. She was born Nov. 18, 1918 and died Sept. 2, 1981. They had two sons: (a) Joseph Samuel, Jr. who married Vickie Jolene Jenkins. They have twin sons, Jeffrey Scott and Gregory Scott. Sam , Jr. is in construction business and they live in Gastonia, N.C. (b) Danny, who is employed by the state, married Sandra Jean Hamby and they live with their son, Michael Brian, near Millers Creek. (7) Ella V. Pierce, born July 22, 1919, died the same day.

A grandson, William Hayden Pierce, born Dec. 12, 1924 (mother, Hattie Lovette) was reared by the Walter Pierce family. He was married to Christine Dolores Shultz and they had two children, Michael, deceased, and Judy who married David Dick. Judy and David have two daughters, Stephanie and Michele. Bill and Dolores separated and Bill later married Gertrude Dorsey of Newport, Tenn.

Roxie Pierce died 10, April 1936 and Walter Pierce later married Lizzie Snyder Pierce, widow of John Ambrose Pierce. They did not have children.

Sources: Personal knowledge, family Bible, etc.

— Eunella B. Pierce

LEANDER BOBBIT PIERCE
922

Rev. John Ennis Pierce, of Scotch Irish descent, was born 13 October 1819, died 22 January 1892, came to New York from England. Later he landed at Charleston, S.C. before coming and settling in Wilkes County, North Carolina.

He was first married to Sarah Shepherd 1 January 1851. She was born the 19 September 1831, died 19 March 1862. Their children were: (1) Thomas Jefferson born 1853, died 12 April 1912, married 13 December 1882, Nancy Elvira Whittington. (2) Martha, born 1855. (3) Suffronia, born 1857. (4) William, born 1859. (5) James W., born 22 May 1860, died 22 October 1922. He married Camilla A. Church 17 April 1881, daughter of Jesse F. Church and Sarah Adlaide Miller.

Rev. John Ennis Pierce's second wife was Elizabeth Caroline Nichols, born 24 April 1842, whom he married 27 October 1864. Their children were: (1) John Ambros, born 1866. (2) Leander Bobbit, born 5 August 1867, died 24 June 1951, married 5 November 1885, Mary Ann (Molly) Bullis, daughter of James Elbert and Eliza Jane McNiel Bullis. (3) Sarilda C., born 1870.

Leander Bobbit Pierce and Mary Ann (Molly) Bullis Pierce had eight children: (1) Viola, born 8 October 1886, died 27 November 1951, married Cyrus C. Kilby. (2) Dora Bell, born 24 June 1888, died 3 May 1927, married Thomas McNiel. (3) Ella Vetra, born 17 May 1892, died 4 June 1958, married Zollie O. Eller. (4) Ruel Shafford, born 4 August 1897, died February 1972, married Fanny Watts. (5) Pansy Vistula, born 29 September 1900, married Paul E. Rogers. (6) Fred Marvin, born 12 August 1907, died 25 June 1972, married Faye. (7) Jennie Gwendolyn, born 20 November 1907, died 29 August 1951, married Major Smith. (8) Eliza Lucille, born 11 December 1910, died 4 July 1975 unmarried.

Sources: Bible printed in New York in 1814 "cost 37½¢" belonged to John Ennis Pierce, now in possession of Vistula Rogers; Vetra Pierce Eller Family Bible.

— Dare Eller Howell

REV. JOHN ENNIS PIERCE
923

John Ennis Pierce, a handsome man of Scotch-Irish descent, was born 13 Oct. 1819. He was married 1 Jan. 1852 to Sarah Shepherd, daughter of Larkin and Alley Irwin Shepherd. To this union was born five children:

(1) Thomas J. married Nancy Whittington and they had five children: Jesse E., Frank O., Delia, Mamie and Roby Pierce. (2) Martha Carolina married Benjamin (Billy) Azmon and they had six children: Edith, Mary C. (Dicie), Ellen, Ben, Julia and Albert Azmon. (3) Mary Saffronia married Leonard Bynum Church. Their children were Robert Leroy, Julie Elvira, Jarvis Bynum, Millard Cicero, Commodore Wellborn, A. Wiley, Jesse Monroe, Ernest Eugene, Dillard, Avery Mansfield, and Fayette Wilson Church. (4) William Lawson married Sarah Caroline Eller and they had four children: Monnie, Walter, Annie and Lola.

(5) James Wilson married Camilla A. Church on 17 April 1881 and they had ten children:

(a) Jesse Filmore, born 5 Feb. 1882, married Octavia McNiel, (b) James Jentry, born 7 Dec. 1884, married Esther Eller, (c) Mertie Leona, born 17 April, 1886 married Cicero Nichols, (d) William Arthur married Dorothy Ellis. He was born 21 June 1888. (e) Richard Eller, born 22 Oct. 1890, married Oma McNiel. (f) Sarah Elizabeth, born 1 Feb. 1892, married Hoy Phillips. (g) Ada Milo, born 21 April 1896, married Privette Phillips. (h) Newton Johnson, born 6 Jan. 1900, married Elvina Shaver. (i) Nellie Mae, born 22 Aug. 1902, married Commodore Eller. (j) Nora Belle, born 30 May 1901, married Jeter Bumgarner.

Sarah Shepherd Pierce died 19 March 1862. John E. Pierce then married Elizabeth Caroline Nichols on 27 Oct. 1864 and they had three children: (1) John Ambrose, who married Elzora Dillard and had eight children: Ransom

M., Mary Jane, Jennie Estelle, Mida Pansy, Edward Jacob, Fannie Elzora. John Ambrose married second Elizabeth Snyder and had two children: Jack Ambrose and Charlie Eugene. (2) Leander Bobbitt married Mollie Bullis and they had eight children: Viola, Dorabelle, Vetra, Rhuel, Vistula, Fred, Gwyndolyn and Lucille. (3) Serilda Catherine married John Lewis and they had seventeen children: Millard Lawson, Ila Virginia, Luna, Rosena, Jacob C., Daniel, Della Mae, Charles Leroy, Esther Elsie, Minnie Jane, John William, Constance Jeanette, Archie Clifton, Bernice Irene, Lora Alberta, Woodrow Wilson, and Nellie Ruth.

John Ennis Pierce was the first trustee listed for Arbor Grove Methodist Church. He was a local Methodist preacher in the Wilkesboro Circuit of the Statesville District, Blue Ridge Annual Conference of the Methodist Church. On August 23, 1882 he was recommended to this Conference by the members of Arbor Grove Church as a "sutiable person" to obtain license to preach. Several reports he made to Conference are recorded in the church minutes in his own beautiful handwriting. Following is a typical report he made in 1887 (words are spelled as they appear in his report): "January 15, 1887 Reporte of John E. Pierce Local preacher i have preached six times during this quarter and excorted eight times attended class meetings had good attendence good order three conversions visited the sick and hoping for better times it is my desire to do all the good I can. brethern pray for me (signed) John E. Pierce"

He died 22 January 1892 and he and his second wife, Elizabeth Caroline, are buried in the Arbor Grove United Methodist Church cemetery at Purlear, N.C.

— Willa Nichols

WALTER FRANKLIN PIERCE
924

Walter Franklin Pierce, born 16 March 1884, was known to his many friends as "the mountain man" because he liked to hunt squirrels and roam through the mountains. He specialized in hunting bees. During the summer he would meet his brother-in-law, Jack Hayes, on top of Sharper Mountain and they would plan their bee hunt for the next two or three days. They would check all the branches for bees drinking water to raise their young. When they spotted some bees, they would get a line on the way they went and the hunt was on! They scrambled up and down the mountain until they found the bee tree, and then they had to get permission to cut the tree. They would take a gum sawer, etc. to the place they would cut the tree about day break. It would take a long time to get the bees in the gum and they would have to wait two or three days for the bees to get settled. Then they would bring the gum home during the night. It got too rough for Hayes, so he pulled out.

About that time, the Rev. John Kilby married his daughter, Nena Pierce. John was a jack-of-all-trades and he joined Pierce in bee hunting and they hunted together for quite a while. After Kilby passed on, Bill Johnson

joined Pierce. They quit bee hunting and changed to ginseng hunting — business was good 'til competition began.

Walter Pierce died 6 Feb. 1950. Bill Johnson is a deer hunter now.

Sources: Personal knowledge.

— Thurman O. Pierce

WILLIAM LAWSON PIERCE
925

William Lawson Pierce, son of John Ennis and Sarah Shepherd Pierce, was born August 19, 1858. On April 18, 1880 he married Sarah Caroline Eller who was born June 2, 1854. Four children were born to this union:

(1) Money Elizabeth, born Feb. 25, 1881, did not marry, died August 29, 1913. (2) Walter Franklin, born March 16, 1884, married Cassie Ann Roxada Hayes, in February 1903. (3) Annie Bessie Mae, born Oct. 16, 1887, married John Nichols who was born March 24, 1884. John was the son of Peter H. Nichols and the grandson of Abraham Edwards and Katherine Eller Nichols. Their children were: Sears O., Charlie, Frances Nichols Saylor, Odous R., Murley Nichols Maines, and Grace Nichols Pickard. After living in Wilkes County for some time this family moved to Winston-Salem, N.C. (4) Lola Bertha, born March 29, 1891, was married to William Arthur ("Bouge") Eller who was born March 27, 1881. They were married by Rev. James T. (Jim) Nichols. They had the following children: Chessie Mae, William Lester, Edna Fay, Minnie Hazel, Freida Gay, Richard Arthur, John Walter, Jimmie Thomas, Argel Jerue, Annie Ruth, Jackie, Ramonia Dean. Lola and Bouge raised a large, well-thought-of family. Lola died April 20, 1961; Bouge died July 15, 1962; and William Lester died Dec. 27, 1978.

Sarah Caroline died January 19, 1904. William Lawson Pierce married second to Jane Church Eller about 1905 — no issue. Jane Church Eller, born Feb. 3, 1867, was the widow of Cleve Eller. They had one son, Troy, who married Bessie Rash. She was loved by all the children and grandchildren in the Pierce family and was known as "Granny Jane." William Lawson Pierce died Jan. 15, 1937 and Jane followed on Dec. 8, 1938.

Sources: Personal knowledge and tombstone inscriptions.

— Eunella B. Pierce

THE PIPES FAMILY
926

The first known Pipes in Wilkes County was Hiram Pipes, born about 1785, in Surry County. Unverified family stories persist that he was bound to the Ellison Family on Elk Creek, married a daughter of the home, which angered her parents, causing them to disown her and to move to Tennessee. If such a marriage took place, no records have been found and no children are known to have been born to the marriage.

Factual information shows that Hiram Pipes served with the Wilkes County Regiment in the

War of 1812. He married Elizabeth Morris in Wilkes County, the marriage bond dated 5 November 1816. He purchased land on Beaver Creek in 1818 which he sold to Charles German in 1820. In 1825, he received a land grant in Darby on Dugger Creek from the State of North Carolina. At the time of his death about 1854, he owned 219 acres of land in Darby.

To the marriage of Hiram Pipes and Elizabeth Morris, who was born about 1790 and died between 1833 and 1840, were born ten children. Many of the Pipeses in Western North Carolina descend from the five sons, and the four married daughters also leave a long line of descendents of other names.

Elvira Pipes, born about 1817, married William Leander Robbins and moved to Ashe County. They had at least eight children and many of their descendents can be found in both Ashe and Watauga counties.

Thomas Pipes, born about 1819, married first Julia Barlow in 1845 in Wilkes County and had three sons and three daughters. He married second Elizabeth Winkler of Caldwell County in 1858 and they had one daughter. Thomas died about 1862. Many descendents of Thomas and Julia Pipes can be found in Caldwell County including the writer of this article.

Sarah Pipes, born about 1822, did not marry. She remained with various members of the family in Darby where she died sometime after 1887.

Rachel Pipes, born 23 August 1823, married William Lewis of Caldwell County about 1859. They had one son. Rachel died 1 July 1892.

Rebecca Pipes, twin to Rachel, married Samuel Day in 1851 in Wilkes County. They moved to Watauga County about 1857. Through their two sons and three daughters, many descendants can be found in Watauga County. Rebecca died 6 May 1886 and is buried in the Day Family Cemetery in Aho, Watauga County.

Larkin Pipes, born 16 October 1825, married Elizabeth Lewis, a sister to William Lewis, in Caldwell County in 1859. Four children were born to the marriage but only two sons lived to adulthood. Larkin, a Baptist minister, pastored and aided in the organization of many churches in Watauga and Caldwell counties as well as in Wilkes County. He died 3 February 1893 and is buried in the Lewis Family Cemetery in Buffalo Cove, Caldwell County. Many of his descendents can be found around Lenoir.

William Riley Pipes, born 5 March 1828, married Emily Penley Hartley, widow of George Hartley, about 1852. They had five children and many of their descendants are in Wilkes and Caldwell counties. One son moved to Murphy, N.C., and left a long line of descendants in Western North Carolina. A family legend says Riley was wounded in the Civil War and walked with a pronounced limp for the remainder of his life until his death on 22 November 1891.

John Wiley Pipes, twin to Riley, married Matilda Brown about 1852. They had at least three daughters and one son. It is believed that Wiley died in the Civil War and Matilda soon after. The son moved to California and has

descendants there.

Susanna Pipes, born 30 April 1830, married John Day, brother of Samuel Day, on 11 October 1857. They had one son. John was killed in the Civil War. Susanna and her son moved to Caldwell County where she died on 24 May 1901. She is buried in the Bethany Baptist Church Cemetery, Caldwell County. Many of her descendants are in Caldwell County and Burke County.

Jesse Pipes, born December 1832, married Julia Triplett on 9 October 1856. He served in the Civil War. Jesse and Julia had two daughters who grew to adulthood and married. After the marriage of the first two daughters, two more children, a daughter and a son, were born to the couple. In 1887 Jesse, Julia, and the two younger children moved to Idaho where Jesse died in October 1914.

Although Hiram Pipes's occupation is not known, he was probably a farmer. A deed refers to a mill site on his land, but the type of mill is not specified.

Sources: Wilkes and Caldwell County Courthouse records; U.S. Census Records; Family Bible records, family traditions, Buffalo Cove Baptist Church records.

— John O. Hawkins

JOSEPH and FRANCIS PORTER
927

The early records of Wilkes County do not reveal any other family bearing the name "Porter" other than Joseph and some of his children. His will was written April 1820 and proved during the October term of court of the same year. This will referred to three children, namely; Joseph Jr., Molly and Francis. The will was witnessed by John Reynolds and John Rousseau whom he called his "trusty friends". No wife was mentioned which indicates that she preceeded him in death.

Joseph Porter received a land grant of 349 acres bearing date of 3 March 1779. This property was on the South Fork of the Yadkin River.

Joseph Porter was paid for various services furnished the militia during the Revolution, January 1782.

It is not known to this writer when or where Joseph was born. Joseph was probably born around 1760 and his relatives were in the joining counties of Wilkes.

Francis Porter, son of Joseph, was born before 1782 in Wilkes County, North Carolina. He met and married Malinda Johnston 27 November 1802. Her parents are unknown to me but the name "Johnston" is common both in Virginia and North Carolina.

Francis owned property that joined his fathers but by 1825 sold out and by 1828 was located in Russell County, Virginia.

Francis and Malinda had at least nine children and all were born in Wilkes County, the oldest about 1803 and the youngest about 1825. His son John married in Wilkes County before coming to Russell County. At least seven of his children were possibly married in Russell County.

Francis settled on the waters of Molls Creek on a 50 acre tract purchased from Jeremiah Elam. This was in November 1828 which indicates that he might have come to Russell

County earlier because November is much to late to prepare his family for winter.

Francis' health began to fail him for in February 1833 it was ordered that Francis Porter be exempted from payment of county levies due to his age and bodily infirmities. By 1839 Francis was dead. This is confirmed by a deed recorded in Russell County in which he died intestate thereby, in settling his estate, eight of his children sold out to their brother John Porter.

After Francis' death, Malinda became the head of household (1840) and by 1850 was living in Scott County, Va. near her son William; however; by 1860 she was back in Russell County living near her son Francis Jr. Malinda was born in North Carolina about 1785 and died sometime after 1860.

Francis & Malinda had nine known children. They were: (1) John Porter b. ca 1803, married first Sally Show and second Senath Salyer; (2) Melvin Porter b. ca 1805, moved to Tennessee; (3) William D. Porter Sr. b. ca 1807 and married first to Mary Polly and second to Catherine Burke Hartsock; (4) Elizabeth Porter b. ca 1809 married Thomas Meade; (5) Rebecca Porter b. ca 1811 married Benjamin C. Bundy; (6) Sebra Porter b. ca 1813 married William "Billie" Fyffe. This couple moved to Kentucky about 1840; (7) Francis Porter Jr. b. ca 1817 married Elizabeth; (8) Caroline Porter b. ca 1821 married Thomas P. Carty; (9) Larkin Porter b. ca 1825 married first to Catherine Vicars and second to Lucinda Salyer.

I am the Seventh generation from Joseph. Many descendants of Joseph are presently living in Southwest Virginia and of course, coast to coast.

Sources: Wilkes County Records; Russell and Scott County Records, Va.; and Census Records.

— Billy R. Porter

THE DESCENDANTS OF JOSEPH PORTER, SR.
928

Joseph Porter, Sr. married Sarah Reynolds and they had a son, Joseph, Jr. who was born 13 or 14 Feb. 1784. Joseph Porter, Jr. married Sarah Johnson. Their son, James was born in 1805 and married Melinda Bernette on 26 April 1825. Their children were: William, Sarah, Nancy, Franklin, Peter, and Elizabeth.

Franklin Porter was born 5 July 1839, died 5 June 1915, married Mary (Polly) E. Higgins 17 Jan. 1856. Mary was born 20 June 1840 and died 1 June 1918. Her death certificate states parents "unknown." Franklin and Mary had the following children: John, Will, Jim, Joe, Alice who married Frank Higgins, Martha who married David Stone, Jane who married a Stone and Carrie who married John Higgins.

John Monroe Porter son of Franklin and Mary, was born in 1879 and died in 1945. He married Lillie E. Bauguess, the daughter of John V. (Bud) and Mary Ann Dowell Bauguess. Lillie was born in 1881 and died in 1923. John V. Bauguess was the son of John K. and Martha Forrester Bauguess and his wife, Mary was the daughter of Frances and

Agnes Porter Benton and Son, Edward, age two years.

Betsy Ann Mahaffey Dowell. The children of John V. and Mary Ann Dowell Bauguess were: Robert, Molly, Charlie, Marshall, Myrtle, Verda and Lillie E.

The children of John Monroe and Lillie Bauguess Porter were: Bessie, Hessie, Stella and Lillie both moved to Richmond, Va.; Dorothy, Johnny lived in Winston-Salem; Paul, Charlie, Everette who was born in 1905 and died in 1930; and Arvil Monroe Porter who was born 11 Feb. 1900 and died 30 Jan. 1961, in a grader accident. Arvil Monroe Porter married Ada Lou Perry 21 Jan. 1920. She was born 7 Oct. 1904. Their children were: (1) Pansy Louise born 22 March 1922, married Arvil Waddell. She died 7 Oct. 1967 in King, N.C. (2) Paul Edward born 4 Nov. 1923, married Annie Alexander. (3) Lessie Mae married Royal Lee Rhoades. (4) Dessie Fae (twin to Lessie), born 4 Jan. 1925, died 27 April 1925. (5) Agnes Viola, born 20 June 1926, married Warner H. Benton who was born 30 Dec. 1926. (6) Joyce Camelon was born 27 Aug. 1929, is married to Gerald Lee Nethey and lives in Pennsylvania.

Agnes Porter had 10 children. Her oldest child, Arville Edward, was named for his grandfather, Arvil Monroe Porter and his uncle, Paul Edward Porter. Edward was born 31 Jan. 1946 and was married to Norma Gayle Collins on 15 April 1967. She is the daughter of Leander (Nick) and Norma Virginia Carroll Collins of Millers Creek.

Edward graduated from West Wilkes High School in June, 1964. He served in the Air Force and we lived at Spangdahlem, Germany for two years where we travelled through several countries. He returned to the United States in January 1969.

Edward studied aeronautics at the Quaker City School of Aeronautics in Philadelphia, Pa., after which he was employed by the Cannon Aviation and Carolina Airways in Hickory, N.C. for six years. We moved back to Millers Creek in Wilkes County in July 1978 and Edward is currently working for Holly Farms in the aviation department. Our son, Phillip Edward, was born 6 Nov. 1972. We have attended Millers Creek United Methodist for the past nine years, and live nearby in Green Acres.

Sources: Personal knowledge.

— Gayle C. Benton

HUGH VESTER and LUVELLA REID POTEAT

929

Our father, Hugh Vester Poteat, was born April 27, 1911, in Wilkes County, N.C., eldest son of Tom and Mattie Mae Johnson Poteat. He attended Osborneville School in the Somers township until it was closed. After that he attended Union Grove High School where he graduated in 1931.

Dad came from a large family, and at the time he was growing up, things were very difficult. He missed a great deal of school in order to help supplement the family income.

He enjoyed being outside and working with his hands. During his lifetime he farmed, sawmilled, drove a truck, did construction work and various other odd jobs. Once, he worked in a factory at Statesville, N.C., but that only lasted a few months.

Hugh was married December 20, 1933, to Luvella Reid. Since money and modes of travel were tight, they hitched a ride with the mailman to the Wilkesboro Courthouse where they were married. Dad had $20.00, so they began their marriage by having soup for supper and going to a movie.

One special thing Mom remembers about her wedding day was that she got her hair cut. Since this was the first time it had ever been cut, her father became very upset and it was a month before he forgave her.

Luvella was the daughter of Romas Franklin and Vicey Emaline Cass Reid. She was born August 2, 1913 in Iredell County, N.C. and she grew up there. She attended Osborneville School in the Somers township, also.

Dad and Mom moved several times in the early part of their marriage. At last, Dad built their permanent home in the Somers community.

They joined Sweet Home Baptist Church and took an active part in it. In 1960, they donated adjoining land to the Church for additional parking space, and in 1974 more land was donated for additional cemetery space.

Their first child, Hugh Vester Poteat, Jr. arrived on October 10, 1934. Junior married Shirley Garner of Flint, Michigan, and their marriage produced one son, Hugh Vester Poteat III, born March 20, 1972. Junior died on April 2, 1973.

After Junior came five girls: Vica Mae Poteat was born July 6, 1937. She married Joseph King Jordan, son of Jim and Leola Templeton Jordan of Union Grove, N.C. They have three children: Carlton Layne Jordan born March 31, 1962, Carol Jo Jordan born September 24, 1965 and Dale Alan Jordan born August 14, 1975.

Agnes Lou Poteat was born on May 12, 1940. She married Russell Neal Poole, son of Wesley Cleve and Mary Sprinkle Poole of Statesville, N.C. They have two children: Rory Neal Poole born October 4, 1958 and Kimberly Dawn Poole born December 3, 1963.

The next born on August 24, 1944 was Kathleen Poteat. Kathleen married Clyde Reese Huffman, son of Joseph and Ethel Allen Huffman of Winston Salem, N.C. They have three sons: Bradley Todd Huffman born May 27, 1968, Brian Keith Huffman born July 11, 1970 and Gregory Hugh Huffman born March 24, 1974.

The fifth child was Charlotte Carolyn Poteat born on November 2, 1946. She married Danny James Whitaker, son of Gaither Elbert and Cecil Wagoner Whitaker of Elkin, N.C. They have two children: Dana Lynn Whitaker born February 2, 1971 and James Christopher Whitaker born December 30, 1974.

The last child was Patricia Ann Poteat born on May 2, 1950. She married Perry Mitchell Welborn, son of William Edgar and Wilma Sale Welborn of Ronda, N.C. They have two sons: Jason Mitchell Welborn born November 17, 1974 and Jon William Welborn born September 14, 1980.

Our Dad was a wonderful person. He was honest, hard-working, respectable, loving and enjoyed being with people, especially his family. Dad passed away on September 17, 1974 after a long battle with cancer. The memories of things he said and did for us will last forever.

Our Mom still spends the cold winter months making some of the prettiest handmade quilts in the county. In the warm months she can be found on a creek bank waiting for the fish to take her bait. She enjoys having all her children and grandchildren to dinner and serving her latest catch of catfish.

Sources: Family Bible, personal knowledge and memories, Wilkes County Courthouse records.

— Vica Mae Jordan

TOM and MATTIE MAE JOHNSON POTEAT

930

Tom Poteat was born October 19, 1885 in Wilkes County and died January 27, 1982. He was the son of James and Martha Mathis Poteat. James and Martha were married on November 18, 1883, both were 24-years-old.

On June 19, 1909, Tom married Mattie Mae Johnson. She was born in Wilkes County April 7, 1891 and died August 3, 1978, a daughter of Eli and A.E. Cornelia Chapel. Eli and Cornelia were married October 16, 1879 in Wilkes County.

Tom and Mae's marriage produced nine sons and four daughters: Hugh V. Poteat (deceased); Coy R. Poteat; David V. Poteat; Carl S. Poteat; Glenn W. Poteat; Everette L. Poteat; Thomas (Jack) Poteat; Ralph R. Poteat (deceased); Jim E. Poteat (deceased); Ethel Poteat Hendren; Minnie Sue Poteat Shew; Mozelle Poteat Williams; and Lillian Poteat White.

Sources: Family Bible, Wilkes County records.

— Pat Welborn

ANSEL PREVETTE
931

Hile Prevette was born in 1817, possibly the son of Williford, Sr. and Susan Durham Prevette. Williford's father was John Prevette who lived in Iredell County.

Hile Prevette married Mary Sparks and they had the following children: Ansel, Creed, Alexander (Alex), Susan (Sis), and Jim. They lived above one branch of Roaring River near Welcome Home Church and farmed.

To follow the male line in our family, Ansel married Mary E. Baldwin, the daughter of John K. Baldwin who was part Indian. She was born May 9, 1844 and died December 25, 1924. They had six children: John, Matt, Daniel Hort, James, Canzadie, and Julia (Sis). They lived and farmed along the same branch of Roaring River.

Daniel Hort Prevette was born May 20, 1869, died May 22, 1941. He married Mary Elizabeth Mahaffey Prevette, widow of Ambrose Prevette (son of Williford Prevette, Jr.). At the time of their marriage she had one son, Snow Prevette. Mary and Hort had the following children: Maudie, Luther, Marcus, and Maggie.

Hort was a merchant and had his store near New Light Baptist Church, Roaring River, N.C. He was known for being a good violin player. Mary was a Mid-wife. I have no idea how many children she delivered in that area, but quite a few. They had a large farm close to New Light Church, now owned by John Grit.

Luther Prevette, my father was born April 7, 1894. He married Nannie Jane Richardson, daughter of Andrew Jackson (Jack) Richardson. They had the following children: Lora (Vickey); Eugene; Mary Geneva; Hazel (died age two); Lee (died age two); L.J. (died age two) and J.D. who was killed in an automobile accident at the age of sixteen.

Luther and his brother Mark (Marcus) had a store in Sheppard's Cross Roads until 1925 or 1926. Luther moved to the New Light Church community and farmed and became deputy sheriff for a few years. He sold his farm, moved to Hays, and lived there for twenty-eight years before his death March 25, 1972.

My brother, Eugene Prevette, married in 1946 and had four children: Barbra Carol; Kenneth Eugene; Vickey; and Joan. He lives in Clemmons, N.C. with his second wife, Mary Jones Pickett, a widow from Jacksonville, Florida. Mary has three children, David Pickett, III, Diana and Marcia Pickett.

Kenneth E. Prevette married Demetra Milner. They have one son and we hope to have another nephew or niece this fall!

You will note that Hile Prevette had a son named James (Jim). He married Matildia Byrd, daughter of George Byrd. Her grandparents, Wiley and Elizabeth C. Buttery Jones raised her as George Byrd deserted Matildia's mother.

Matildia and Jim Prevette had the following children: Hile, Creed, Sina, Rhoda and Geneva. Geneva married Jack Richardson and is my grandmother.

Sources: Census records and personal knowledge.

— Vickey Prevette Call

JOSEPH TALMAGE PREVETTE
932

Rev. Irdell T. Prevette married Alice Call; children: Royal, Talmage, Viola, Buel Dr. Isaac, Roscoe, Earl, Mattie, Pearl, Gyp, and Annie.

Talmage married Nellie Grant Benbow when he was eighteen years old. At age twenty he began a retail clothing store on Main Street in North Wilkesboro, which he operated until his death in 1943.

He was vice-president of the Deposit and Savings Bank for twenty-five years. This bank later became known as The Northwestern Bank.

For many years he served as a director of the Wilkesboro Savings and Loan.

Talmage and Nellie had five children. They are John R., Lacie, William C., Slater, and Cynthia.

John married Jessie Rice and they had one daughter, Joanne, who is married to Jim Hethcock. Jim and Joanne have one son, Don. Jessie died when Joanne was born, and John later married the former Clara Eller. They now reside in Charlotte, N.C.

Lacie married Bob Huffman. They had one daughter, Lacie, who is married to Carroll Lackey. They have three children; Randy, Denise, and Stephanie.

Slater and his wife, the former Rosalie Pendry, live in Hays. They have two children: Nellie Jane, a kindergarten teacher at Mtn. View and LCDR Henry Jr., who is stationed with the U.S. Navy in Norfolk, Va. Henry is married to Susan Thomas, and Nellie Jane to Rick Ward.

William C. helped operate Prevette's Stores until they burned in 1954. After this tragedy, he moved to Tenth Street and has operated Bill Prevette's Men's Shop until the present time. He is one of the directors of Surety in Wilkesboro.

Bill was married to Virginia Carter and they had three children: Jeannette, Joe, and Billy. Jeannette married Joe Powell and they have one daughter, Debbie. Joe married Judy Pruitt and they have two daughters; Cindy and Michelle. Joe is regional sales manager for Mortez Mills in Newton, N.C.

Virginia died in 1980 and Bill married Mrs. Blanche Taylor.

Cynthia married Chase B. Hewitt. She taught several years in the Wilkesboro Elementary School before moving to Annandale, Virginia.

Source: personal knowledge.

— Rosalie Prevette

JAMES W. PRICE
933

James Price was one of the earliest settlers of the Pores Knob section of Wilkes County, having been granted land from the state of North Carolina in the years between 1840-1854. It is generally believed he was the grandson of Thomas Price who immigrated to Iredell County from England in the eighteenth century and a son of Philip Price. Philip Price and his wife Sarah are listed in the 1860 census as being in a household between James Price and his son's household.

On September 27, 1832, James was married to Rosannah Kilby (born June 15, 1813), the daughter of William and Elizabeth Hubbard Kilby, Jr. To this union two children were born: (1) William Logan Price (born July 21, 1833 — died September 5, 1897) married Elizabeth Robinson. They had eleven children. (2) Mary Elizabeth Price (born October 23, 1846 — died November 7, 1895) married William Calloway Meadows. They also had eleven children.

James Price was probably a man who was interested in community affairs. He was one of the committeemen in the local school district. It was at his home that Walnut Grove Baptist Church of Pores Knob was organized. Harvey Meadows (future father-in-law of Mary Elizabeth Price) was present at this meeting, along with R.L. Steele and J.G. Bryant.

Rosannah Kilby Price's brother and sisters were: Benjamin C. Kilby (born January 22, 1806 — died in 1880) married Emiline Earp (born March 8, 1808 — died ca 1890) on March 20, 1826. This couple settled in the Pores Knob community on land sold to them by James Price. They had eleven children. William S. Kilby married Caroline Earp (sister to Emily Earp Kilby). This couple also lived on land sold to them by James Price. Elizabeth married Jason R. Laws. They also settled in the Pores Knob community. Frances married John B. Greer. They lived in this community also.

Rosannah Price's grandparents were Benjamin and Rosane Dyer Hubbard on her mother's side and William and Frances Eddins Kilby on her father's side. The children of William and Frances Eddins Kilby were: James Humphrey; Reuben; Elizabeth; Abraham; Sarah; William; Jr.; Mary; Frances; and John.

James Price died on August 5, 1880. Rosannah Price died on June 7, 1893. They are buried in Walnut Grove Baptist Church cemetery. Their graves are located close to their daughter's and son-in-law's (Mary Elizabeth Price Meadows and William Calloway Meadows) final resting places.

Sources: Family Bible, census records, Wilkes County records and family tradition.

— Virginia Jennings

THE EARLY PROFFIT FAMILIES
934

John Proffit, Sr., was the first with this name to come to Wilkes County, having arrived well before the county was formed. Since he and his wife were baptised into the fellowship of Mulberry Fields Church 28 November 1773, he certainly was here on this date and probably came sometime before. Born in Goochland County, Virginia, about 1734, he was a son of Sylvester Proffit, the immigrant, and his wife, Alice. John was married in Goochland County, Virginia 10 March 1757 to Susannah Arrington.

When John and his family arrived in Wilkes County, he established his home on land lying on the south side of the Yadkin River, adjoining the property of James Fletcher and James

Tanner. Later, when Wilkes County was formed, John entered his 130 acres of land, "including his improvements." This property was only a short distance down the river from the town of Wilkesboro. It was there that John and his wife lived the rest of their lives.

Apparently John was a farmer as were most of the men of that day. He was also a Baptist Minister, "having been set forth to look to the Lord for His teaching." by Old Roaring River Baptist Church on the second Saturday in April 1789. He pastored Cub Creek Baptist Church, near Wilkesboro, from 1794 to 1811. As a religious leader, his influence was wide spread on both north and south sides of the Yadkin River.

John Proffit, Sr. and his wife, Susannah, had a large family as indicated by census data. However, all the children assigned to this family have not been proven beyond the possibility of error. Since there was only one Proffit family in Wilkes County during the 1770s and 1780s, it seems reasonable to assume that those young Proffit men and women clustered in and around this home during the above time periods can safely be assigned to this family. Therefore, with the help of the Last Will and Testament of John Proffit, along with Wilkes County official documents, the following Proffit children have been assigned to this family:

Sylvester Proffit, born 18 April 1758 in Goochland County, Virginia, married Nancy Tompkins 26 August 1782 in Wilkes County, and later moved his family to Tennessee. They had a large family, all of whom lived and died in Tennessee and Kentucky.

William Proffit, Sr., a veteran of the Revolutionary War, was born 8 July 1759 in Virginia, and was married in Wilkes County to Elizabeth Elmore 10 January 1783. He is the ancestor of the Proffits who now reside in Wilkes County.

Pleasant Proffit, born about 1760 in Virginia, was with Captain Lenoir at the Battle of Kings Mountain. After the war, he moved to Kentucky, married and had a large family there and also died there.

John Proffit, Jr. born about 1762, moved to Eastern Tennessee during the 1790s. He had a large family there.

Mary Proffit, born 31 January 1764, was unmarried and without issue when her father died in 1814.

James Proffit, born 26 January 1766, was married in Wilkes County but later moved his family to Yancy County, North Carolina. He has many descendants.

David Proffit, born 31 May 1759, may have died young. Martha Proffit, born 7 August 1771, may have died young.

Nancy Proffit, born about 1780, was married to James Fletcher in Wilkes County 10 October 1799. Lydia Proffit, born about 1782, was married to Joshua Souther and lived on Hunting Creek. They had several children, all of whom have not been identified.

Samuel Proffit, born about 1784, was married in Wilkes County to Lucy Shumate 31 August 1804. He moved his family to Tennessee during the 1830s. They had issue.

Polly Proffit, born about 1788, seems to have been the last child born to this couple. She was married to Coleman Ferguson 3 No-

vember 1811, and they moved to Northern Georgia shortly after Polly's father died.

John Proffit, Sr., made his will 15 November 1813, naming some of his children. The will was probated in May 1814 in Wilkes County. The death date of Susannah his wife, has not been established.

Sources: Family Bible, State and Federal Census, Wilkes County Taxables, wills, deeds, land grants, Revolutionary War Pension Applications and family correspondence.

— Ruth Proffit Gregory

ALFRED NEWTON PROFFIT FAMILY

935

Alfred Newton Proffit, born 27 April 1842 in Wilkes County to William Proffit, Jr. and Polly Walsh Proffit, was one of four brothers who served in the Confederate Army during the Civil War. In fact, there were only four boys in this family and Alfred Newton was the sole survivor of this tragic conflict. (see family of William

Proffit). Alfred Newton was involved in several battles in northern Virginia, and received a number of injuries. However, he was back on the line and was with General Lee at Appomattox when the Confederate Army was surrendered.

One of the injuries received by Alfred Newton is worthy of note. A mini-ball pierced his skull and lodged in his sinis cavity remaining there for many years. Following his return to civilian life, he had frequent and severe headaches until, several years later, he sneezed and the mini-ball was discharged. This bullet is in the possession of one of his grandsons.

Alfred Newton Proffit was married to Sarah Ann McNeil, daughter of Captain George and LaVisa Triplett McNeil. They lived on Lewis Fork Creek and reared a large family, as follows.

Robert Lee Proffit, born 12 January 1871, died 9 February 1952. He married Martha McNeil, daughter of James Oliver and Sarah Ann Stout McNeil, 10 of October 1900, and reared his family in Wilkes County. Robert and

Sole survivor of sons William Proffit Sr., Alfred Newton Proffit (civil war).

his wife were both teachers, and Robert also was on the Wilkes County Board of Education for a number of years. Their six children were: (1) Glen Proffit, a teacher, principal, and County Superintendent of Schools, devoting his entire life to education. He married Edna Quenna, also a teacher, and their only child, Robert, is a highly skilled orthodontist. (2) Commodore Proffit died young. (3) Cline Proffit married Evelyn Satterwhite and had Joyce, Don and Carrol. This family moved to Virginia. (4) Lola Porffit, a graduate of Woman's College at Greensboro, married F.M. Davis and lives in Lumberton, N.C. (5) Oliver McNeil Profitt, a graduate of the University of North Carolina and a veteran school principal, married Ursula Blevins, daughter of Mr. and Mrs. Oliver Blevins. They had two sons, Dan and Eugene, both college graduates. Ursula is a musician. (6) Hight Moore Proffit attended Appalachian State College before he went West. He married Dorothy Marsh in Wyoming and has four children, Lola, Larry, Don and Diane, all college graduates. Hight is a state senator from Wyoming. (7) Charlee Wright Proffit, the youngest, married Irene Shore and has one son, Thomas. Charlie was employed by the Wilkes County Board of Education until his retirement in 1981.

Benjamin F. Proffit was born 15 November 1872, died 26 March 1944. He married Ella Thomas 15 February 1911. Both Ben and Ella were teachers in Wilkes County. They had no children.

Augustus Judd Proffit was born 23 September 1874, died 17 July 1937. He married Wilma McNeil 11 November 1921. They had one son, Harrold, who married Menita Wellborn. Harrold is a business man in North Wilkesboro.

Lougerta Lenora Proffit was born 23 September 1874, died 6 January 1953. She married 10 January 1893 Joel Triplett. They had no children.

Wade Hampton Proffit was born 3 November 1876, died 4 May 1915, unmarried.

George Hamilton Proffit was born 3 July 1878, died 28 December 1957. He married Lou McNeil 5 May 1909 and had two children, Blanche and Thomas. This family moved to Wyoming.

William Albert Proffit, born 6 January 1880, died 10 April 1954. He married 25 December 1904 Mary Lou Walsh, daughter of Gordon and Seline Stout Walsh. Bill and Mary Lou made their home on Elk Creek and lived there all of their lives. He was a merchant, postmaster, farmer, deacon and trustee of the Baptist Church as well as Sunday school teacher and superintendent. As a leader of the community, his services and guidance were sought by many people and several organizations and he always responded in a generous manner. Bill and Mary Lou were blessed with nine children, viz: (1) Nettie Proffit, married William Reece Miller 24 December 1926. Before moving to Alleghany County, they were both teachers in Wilkes County. (2) Wayne Thomas Proffit, married Blanche Shepherd. They lived in Lenoir and had three children, John, Gwyndoln, and Sue. (3) Ray Hamilton Proffit moved to Wyoming and married Helen Burton. They

had Bruce and Polly, both college graduates. (4) Ruth Dare Proffit married Paul W. Gregory 1 July 1937. She is an Appalachian State University Graduate, as is her husband. They both taught in Wilkes County until they retired. Their only child, Dr. Richard Brent Gregory is an educational specialist and is employed by the Central Piedmont Community College in Charlotte, N.C. (5) Seth Alfred Proffit married Marie Wooton 8 December 1940. They have children Bob, Jerry, Tommy, Patricia and Gary. (6) Jewell Proffit died in infancy. (7) James Paul Proffit married Emtraud Dishart 2 December 1951. Their children are James Rockland, Richard P., Brady S., and Rita Ann. (8) William Albert Proffit, Jr., married Katherine Taylor 19 April 1953 and moved west. His children are Donna Elaine and Sherri Lynn, both of whom are college graduates. (9) Howard Van Proffit married Julia Church 8 July 1951. Their children are Keith, Debra and Kenneth. Van is a Baptist Minister.

John Proffit, born 1883 in Wilkes County, moved to Nebraska and married Maggie Wilhelm. They had Lawerence, Howard, William and Wilbur.

Lavisa Proffit, born 6 September 1885, died 12 March 1929. She married Samuel Triplett and had one son, Homer. He taught school in Wilkes County.

Sarah Elizabeth Proffit, was born 28 November 1887. She married Robert Taylor and had Edgar, Stella, Margaret, Howard, Virginia, Harvey, Joe and Harley.

Alfred Newton Proffit died 3 August 1929 and his wife, Sarah Ann McNeil Proffit died 7 May 1921. Both are buried in the Lewis Fork Baptist Church cemetery, located a short distance from the Proffit ancestral home.

Sources: Family Bible, Grave markers, Civil War Letters of Alfred Newton Profitt, interviews with Proffit relatives.

— Ruth Proffit Gregory

WILLIAM PROFFIT, SR. FAMILY

936

William Proffit, Sr., son of John and Susannah Aarington Profitt, was the only male member of this early family to remain in Wilkes County. His home was on Lewis Fork Creek and he and his wife, Elizabeth Elmore Proffit, to whom he was married 10 January 1783, had a large family. Their children were:

Elizabeth Proffit, born 1 August 1784, married Thomas Walsh in Wilkes County 23 September 1824. This family lived on Lewis Fork and reared a large family: Susannah Proffit, born 20 November 1786, probably died young; Thomas Proffit, born 20 April 1789, married Sally Bingham 7 June 1809. He died in 1826, leaving behind his wife and small family; Mary Rhoda Proffit, born 10 September 1791, married Samuel Walsh 6 January 1823. Samuel and his wife had a large family, many of whom remained in Wilkes. Both Mary and Samuel died sometime after 1880.

Aarington Proffit, born 12 March 1794, married Jemima Bingham 21 May 1816 in Surry County. He moved his family to Tennessee on or before 1830 and was living in

McMinn County in 1850. At that time he and his wife had six boys living at home: John Proffit, born 9 May 1796, married Elizabeth Holeman 1 April 1823 in Wilkes County. He died in the Meat Camp area of Ashe County where he moved his family in 1841. Most Proffits of Watauga County descend from this couple.

Nancy E. Proffit, born 19 August 1798, married Benjamin Bingham 19 March 1818. This family probably moved to Watauga County; William Proffit, Jr. born 4 June 1803, married Polly Walsh 4 February 1829 in Wilkes County. This family lived on Lewis Fork Creek and all of their descendants remained in Wilkes County; Rebecca Proffit born about 1809, married McAlpin Walsh 30 May 1829, and died sometime after 1880. They had a large family, many of whom remained in Wilkes County.

Thornton Proffit, born 15 August 1813, married Elizabeth Brown in Wilkes County 6 November 1838. This family lived near the Watauga-Wilkes line, sometime in Wilkes and sometime in Watauga. Thornton and his wife had eight known children, seven of whom were girls. The only boy, William Chapman, joined the Army of the Confederacy 18 August 1862. Three months and one day later, Chapman died somewhere in Virginia and was buried in the Mount Jackson, Virginia cemetery. Thornton and his wife are buried in the Chestnut Mountain Church cemetery, a short distance from the Proffit home place.

William Proffit, Sr. was a Revolutionary War soldier, having served under Cleveland, Lenoir and others. The pension application of his widow reveals that William died in Wilkes County 7 June 1832. His wife, Elizabeth Elmore Proffit, died 5 November 1862.

William Proffit, Jr., also remained in Wilkes County all of his life, as did all of his seven children, except one. Most of what is known about this man was revealed by his obituary furnished this writer by Jimmy McNeil, a descendant. In part the obituary, written by J.Q. McNeil, J.M. Eller and J.M. Watson in 1888 said: "Brother William Proffit was born in Wilkes County 4 June 1803, and departed this life 21 April 1888, at the advanced age of 84 years, 10 months, and 17 days. He professed faith in Christ about the year 1832 and joined the Lewis Fork Baptist Church, and was baptised the second Sunday in May 1832. He was appointed a Deacon and remained a faithful member until 1875 at which time he and his devoted wife, along with a number of other members, were released by letter to help constitute Mount Pleasant Church. Brother Proffit was a man of sound judgement and deep thought on the Scriptures; sound in the faith and doctrine of the Baptist and all who knew him, only knew to love him."

William Proffit, Jr. and wife, Mary Walsh Proffit, has the following children: Elizabeth Proffit, born 3 November 1829, married Jesse Miller in Wilkes County 18 November 1850. This family moved to Tennessee. Some of their children remained in Wilkes County; Rhoda Proffit, born 5 September 1831, married the Reverend Linville Land and reared their family here. Both are buried in the Mount Pleasant Church cemetery; Andrew J. Proffit, born 8

January 1834, died 27 March 1865 at Richmond, Virginia, in the service of the Confederacy.

Rachel Proffit, born 19 December 1836, married George J. Ball, a Civil War Veteran, 20 December 1866. This family moved to Texas in 1871 and there are many descendants of this couple: William Harrison Proffit, born 11 June 1839, joined the Confederate Army and died at Gordonsville, Virginia 23 October 1863; Alfred Newton Proffit, born 27 April 1842, married Sarah McNeil 3 April 1870. This couple lived out their lives in Wilkes County. Alfred died 3 August 1929. Sarah, his wife died 7 May 1921. Both are buried in the Lewis Fork Church cemetery, near the home they loved so much.

Calvin L. Proffit, twin to Alfred Newton, also joined the Confederate Army and fought in Virginia. He died 23 October 1863 while in the service of the Confederacy. According to his service record, he was buried at Camp Cragg, Virginia.

All of the Proffit boys in this family fought with the Confederacy in the Civil War and only Alfred Newton returned home as the others died or were killed during this tragic conflict. Alfred was injured in the battle of Wilderness Road 9 May 1864. A rifle ball lodged in his sinus and was sneezed out many years later.

Harrison died in a hospital at Gordonsville, Virginia 25 October 1863. Andrew was captured 12 May 1864 at the battle of Bloody Angle, and he was held prisoner at Point Lookout, Maryland. He was exchanged in 1865 and died shortly thereafter in a Richmond Hospital. Calvin Luther died in 1863 and was buried in a Confederate cemetery.

These men fought in many battles. Of these men, one notable writer in Wilkes County wrote: ''The record of the Proffit boys during the Civil War has probably never been surpassed by any family in the history of this county.'' Their bravery, determination, loyalty, and patriotism inspired Miss Mary Hancock of Wilkes County to detail their exploits in a book entitled, ''Four Men in Gray'', and this book is now required reading in the Wilkes Community College.

Sources: Family *Bible*, Court House records of Wilkes and Surry Counties, N.C. and Goochland County, VA. *THE DOUGLAS REGISTER;* State and Federal Census; gravestone inscriptions; *A HISTORY OF NORTH CAROLINA BAPTIST:* Mount Pleasant and Old Roaring River Church Minutes; correspondance with relatives.

— Paul and Ruth Gregory

THE ISAAC WINTFREY PRUITT FAMILY

937

Joseph Pruitt was born July 16, 1774, in Pittsylvania County, Virginia. He moved to Wilkes County 19 years later in 1777. Pruitt entered the American Revolutionary Army under the command of Benjamin Cleveland against the Cherokees. He also served under Captain Larkin Cleveland and Captain William Waugh. Joseph Pruitt was discharged by Captain Cleveland at Wilkes Court House. He served against the Tories 3 months and against the Tories on New River 5 weeks. Pruitt was with Colonel Cleveland at Ramseur

The Isaac Winfrey Pruitt family.

Mills. William Spicer and Benja Hammon served with him. Pruitt moved to Ashe County in 1829. However, most of his family remained in Wilkes County. Joseph Pruitt died after August 1, 1833.

Joel Pruitt was the son of Joseph Pruitt. In 1853, Joel Pruitt appointed Abram Cornelius his attorney to secure pension due him as heir to Joseph Pruitt, his father, from the U.S. Government.

In 1828, Joel Pruitt and wife Polly became the parents of Hardin Pruitt. Hardin Pruitt later married Lucinda Brooks (1833-1899). This marriage resulted in children as follows: Joel Ander, Isaac Wintfrey, Julie, Mark, Preston, Joshua, John, Sally, Nancy, and Rosie.

Isaac Wintfrey Pruitt (1869-1942) married Mary Ann Wiles (1878-1953). This union resulted in children as follows: Bertha A. (1894-1977), m. B. Harrison Barker (parents of Glenn Rex Barker); Della (1896-1960), m. Mart Whitaker; Lura, b. 1905, m. Cortez Wiles; Myrtle, b. 1909, m. Dewey Billings; Devoe, b. 1920, m. Virginia Crouse; Arvel (1906-1981), m. Johnnie Mae Holbrook and Ruth Sparks; Pansy, b. 1915, m. Freel Johnson; Manley, b. 1900, m. Trustie Crabb; Tessie, b. 1902, m. McKinley Billings; Robert (1898-1898); and Carmel (1912-1914).

Memories of visiting my Grandma Pruitt many years ago remain firmly imbedded in my mind. The water bucket, which traveled a cable drawn by a large windlass to the spring at the bottom of the hill below Grandma's house, was a special attraction to me. It was a thrill to unwind the rope and listen to the bell jingle as the bucket made its way toward the spring. One could tell when the bucket made contact with the spring water as the pressure on the rope relaxed and the bell stopped ringing. Winding the windlass up was an equally enjoyable experience. The greatest reward was a cold drink of spring water as the water bucket came to rest on its return trip.

My mother, Bertha Angeline Pruitt Barker, was the eldest child of Isaac Wintfrey and Mary

Ann Wiles Pruitt. On May 15, 1910, Bertha Angeline married B. Harrison Barker. This marriage was truly blessed with thirteen children as follows: Cecil, Ethel, Grace, Pansy, Ermal, Luther, James, Flora, Mary Lee, Hazel, Kenneth, Benny, and Rex.

Bertha A. Pruitt Barker was an avid Bible scholar. She read the Old Testament a total of 13 times and the New Testament a total of 60 times. My mother was a strong woman both physically and spiritually. Her love and care for our father and her children never ceased. Our mother's life was an example of the way life should be lived. Her influence in the lives of her children, grandchildren, and many others will never be forgotton. Sweet memories of Bertha A. Pruitt Barker will remain with us forever.

Sources: Wilkes County Will Book, Personal knowledge and interviews with family members.

— G. Rex Barker

RASH

938

The earliest records in my family show that William Rash married Elizabeth Warren and came from Spotsylvania County, Virginia to Beaver Creek, N.C. in 1789. We have no record of the number of children in this family. There is a record showing a son, Joseph born 1755 in Spotsylvania Co. This Joseph died in 1829 at Reddies River in Wilkes Co., N.C. He married someone named Millie and had a son named Thomas who married Fannie Kilby and lived at Beaver Creek, died circa 1850. The family of Thomas Rash and Fannie K. Rash is as follows: (1) John Warren, born 1813, in Wilkes County, died Nov. 16, 1889. He married Valisha Bullis who died Sept. 20, 1895. John Warren became a Methodist minister and was the first pastor of the Millers Creek Methodist Episcopal Church. This little church was built around the time of the Civil War. (2) Billie. (3) Betsy who married a Crysel. (4) Frances (Frankie) married a Nichols. (5) Polly. (6) Sarah (Sally).

The family of Rev. John Warren and Valisha Bullis Rash were: (1) Joseph S., born 1838. (2) Zeno Melvin born April 16, 1840, served in the Civil War and never returned. (3) Levi (Lee) born Feb. 4, 1842, died of illness contracted while serving in the Civil War. (4) Ziliah Caroline born Nov. 12, 1844, married Cleveland McNeill. Their daughter, Clora McNeill Faust was the author of the publication, "Horse and Buggy Days in the State of Wilkes." (5) John Clark born Feb. 10, 1847, died March 27, 1935. (6) Sarah Ann born Jan. 6, 1849. (7) Frances (Fanny) married John Andrew Faw. (8) Mary Elizabeth (Betty) born February 1853, married Thomas Faw. The Faw gentlemen were brothers. (9) Thomas Benjaman born March 4, 1855, died Nov. 27, 1891. His descendants live in Caldwell County, N.C. (10) Nancy V. (Nan) born Dec. 23, 1857, married Chap Minton.

The family of John Clark and Mary E. McNeill Rash are as follows: (1) Julia Elmer born May 28, 1871, married Frank McNeill. (2) Lillie Joan born Sept. 21, 1872, died May 1942, was never married. She lived in the old home with her father and helped to raise several of her older sister's children. At the death of her sister, Elmer, she took her infant daughter, Daisy, and raised and educated her. Daisy McNeill still lives on the old home property in Millers Creek. Miss Lillie as she was known, was loved and respected by all who knew her. She was an avid reader and had at her command a vast knowledge of many subjects. She was one of the first women in her community to become active in church and school programs. (3) Carrie died in infancy. (4) Robert Levi born Aug. 30, 1875. (5) Ira Melvin born April 27, 1878, married Mattie Cooper and their children were: (a) Ada married Monroe Miller and lived in Charlotte. (b) Minnie married Roe Wyatt. (c) John married Thelma McNeill and they are the parents of five children: Paul who married Julene McGlamery — one son, Andy. Billie married Jerry Crable and they have two sons, Bryan and Graylon. Violet married Dennis Francis. Robert married Pauline B. Gambill — no children. Evans. (6) Richard Cristy born Sept. 6, 1881, never married. (7) Laura died in infancy. (8) Frances Virginia, my mother, was born Mar. 5, 1885, died Aug. 6, 1968, married Clayton McGlamery (See McGlamery sketch). She was a remarkable woman in many ways. She possessed a never ending interest in books, poetry, and all things beautiful. She also possessed a wealth of knowledge concerning the flower and fauna of Wilkes County. Aside from being a good mother in all the usual ways she had the rare gift of instilling within her children the same desire to pursue their interests, and the comforting knowledge that some of our most treasured possessions are the gifts of nature. She died Aug. 6, 1968. (9) Bessie Irene born July 7, 1888, married Troy Eller. (10) J. Bynum born Feb. 18, 1891, married Bessie Rash. They had five children: (a) Ralph married Blanche Hamby — both deceased. (b) Ruth married Charlie Cain. (c) Nora married Cecil Bishop. (d) James married Ruth Wyatt. (e) Madeline married Durant Foster. Bynum is now 91 years old. His wife is deceased.

John C. Rash lived to be 89 years old. He led an exemplary life not only in his church activities but also in his daily life, which became an example in self discipline to his children and grandchildren. He was an active leader in the Methodist church which was within walking distance of his farm. He continued to walk to each service as long as he lived. He was recognized as a Bible scholar and a singing master. He not only used these talents in serving his church but instilled the love of music and reading in his children and grandchildren. When he died his casket was carried the short distance from his home to the church, along the path he had walked so many times.

Sources: Personal knowledge and information from family members.

— Anne McGlamery Carter

STEPHEN RASH

939

Stephen A. Rash was born May 29, 1869, and died July 25, 1946. He was the only son of Joseph (Joe) E. and Matilda Bumgarner Rash. Stephen had three sisters: Rebecca (Becky) who married Bill Martin; Martha, who married Wesley Rhoades; and Sarah, who died in infancy.

Stephen and Amanda Elvira McNeil Rash.

He married Amanda Elvira (Vira) McNeil, daughter of Alfred and Mariah Bullis McNeil, on March 6, 1891. This union was blessed with 10 children: Bessie Eveline married Bynum Rash; Maudie Matilda married Vincent Bumgarner; Joseph Orrin died in infancy; Nora Della married Clyde Jones; Ida Bell, died in early childhood; Beatrice Mariah married D.G. Church; Anna Elvira married G.C. Lemmons the first time, her second marriage was

to James Chittye; Pansy Ellen, first married Fred Dancy, second marriage was to Joseph Wornimenh; Lucy Mae married Norman Marion; Virginia Dare married Marshall Lemmons.

Although Stephen's formal education was limited, he was quite well learned in many fields. When he was 17 years old he began the building of a log house which was to serve as a home for his family until 1961. By trade he was a farmer, a timberman, and he made hand hewn crossties for the railroads.

He was Justice of Peace for many years. Stephen probably performed more weddings than any other Justice of Peace in his time. Couples would travel for miles around to get the knot tied. He had no office or designated place to perform marriages, anywhere that Stephen could be found became a wedding chapel let it be a wheat field, corn field, or the middle of a muddy road.

From 1926 to 1932, Stephen was County Coroner. During this time he had many unique experiences. As far as the writers have been able to determine, he was (is) the only coroner in Wilkes County that was ever faced with the untimely task, by virtue of his office, to preside at an inquest hearing involving the High Sheriff of the County. This incident occurred when Sheriff W.B. Somers was forced to kill the notorious outlaw, Ed Atwood.

Steven was a devout Christian. He served his church faithfully in just about every official capacity at some time during his lifetime. He was a good neighbor and a friend to many.

Sources: Family records and personal knowledge.

— Lucy Marion and Sidney Johnston

GRADY and DOROTHY REAGAN

940

Henry Grady Reagan was born in Asheville, N.C. on September 5, 1920, the son of the late Henry Grady Reagan and Grace Lee Reagan. He was educated in the Asheville City Schools, Asheville-Biltmore College, and graduated from the University of North Carolina at Chapel Hill with a degree in journalism. He was married on May 19, 1946 to Dorothy Rose Payne.

Grady has been employed by the North Carolina Employment Security Commission since 1946, being stationed in Asheville and Charlotte before moving to North Wilkesboro in 1950 as a Claims Deputy.

He served in the U.S. Army for 3 years as a member of the 83rd Infantry Division. He was a part of 5 campaigns in Europe, including the Normandy Invasion, Battle of the Bulge, and Rhine River. He was awarded the Combat Infantry Badge and Bronze Medal.

For 31 years Grady has served as Choir Director at the First United Methodist Church, where he also teaches Sunday School. He is also Director of the Wilkes Choral Society. Grady is active in community affairs, especially where music and art are concerned, and is well-known as a bass soloist. For many years he has reviewed cultural events for the Journal-Patriot, and has participated actively in events such as the N..C. Symphony Orchestra, the North Carolina Opera Association, and the Wilkes Community Symphony.

Dot is the daughter of the late Collie Lautice and Ethel Turnbull Payne. She was born in Asheville, N.C. on June 19, 1919, and was educated in the Asheville City Schools. Her work life has been spent as an executive secretary, and since coming to North Wilkesboro she has been secretary to the City Director of North Carolina National Bank, the treasurer of American Drew Furniture Company, the principal of North Wilkesboro Elementary School, and the president of North Wilkesboro Candy Company, from which she retired in 1981.

Dot is a member of First United Methodist Church, where she sings in the choir and teaches Sunday School. She is active in the work of the United Methodist Women, the Wilkes Art Guild, and the Homemakers Extension Club.

Gail Reagan Brock was born on September 20, 1952, and was educated in the North Wilkesboro City Schools and graduated from Pfeiffer College. She is a resident of Spencer, N.C., and is married to Joe Douglas Brock. She is Office Manager and buyer for Dave Carter Associates in Spencer, a company which provides building materials for mobile homes. Like her mother and father, she is a musician, pianist and dramatic soprano.

James Miles Reagan was born on January 1, 1956. He was educated in the North Wilkesboro City Schools and Wilkes Community College. He is married to the former Kathy Enola Wyatt of Millers Creek, and is employed as computer operator at Northwestern Security Life.

Sources: Personal knowledge.

— H. Grady Reagan

EDWARD REAVIS

941

Edward Reavis, an Englishman, was born about 1680, arrived in America about 1685. He was a colony planter of Henrico County, Va. on the James River. He first married Hannah Alley and they had five sons and one daughter. His second marriage was to Sarah Gilliam, of Norman origin. They had three sons and one daughter, all born in Va.

In 1745, the Reavis families moved over the line into Northampton County, North Carolina from their home in Henrico County, Virginia. Schools there were few or lacking, churches weak and scattered, transportation chiefly by waterways or over what had been Indian trails. Virginia lands had already been cropped for a century without the application of fertilizers, and profitable tobacco growing called for virgin soil, wherefore frontier Carolina had its allure.

Edward and his family located on contiguous farms and apparently lived happily.

Edward died in 1751. More than twenty years passed before any family dispersion began. Reavis men and women kept pace with their country's receeding frontier until now they are distributed from the Atlantic to Pacific.

As a people they have been pioneers.

Farming and the mechanic arts have been their most usual occupation. However, they have also made their mark in business and various professions. As a people, they are peaceable and law abiding. Politically they differ as do other large families. They are Protestant.

Edward Reavis, founder of the family, was of course a colonial; he died a quarter of a century before the establishment of our United States. Some of his sons outlived the colonial period, and his descendents from the third to the present generation of the family have had their part in the gradual growth and development of our great country — loyal Americans all.

It is hoped that this family, in the generations to come, retain the virile characteristics of its founder.

Sources: The Reavis family history.

— Mary Jo Lowe Lovette

JAMES REAVIS

942

James, second son of Edward by his first wife, Hannah Alley, was born near the James River in Henrico County, Virginia, in the year 1719.

About 1744, James married a woman named Elizabeth. Two of their children were born in Virginia. In 1747, James moved the beginning of his family to Northampton Co. N.C. It was in this county his third son, Joseph, was born in 1755. James became a "planter as were his father and brothers. Their money crop was tobacco, and tobacco meant slave owning. Two of James' brothers were large plantation owners.

James farmed in Northampton County until he was fifty. Then came the Revolutionary War, accompanied by economic depression that was severe and general. It was hard on planters. James' half-brothers, and sister, and step mother and his own two married sons migrated to Surry County, N.C. about 1770. James, himself, did not long delay, but gathering about him the younger members of his family and selling his property in Northampton County, and obtaining church "letters" for himself and wife, he moved to Surry County, and affiliated by letter with the Dutchman's Creek Baptist Church on June 5, 1773.

James was living in Surry when the first U.S. Census was taken in 1790. Already his children had become established in homes of their own, and the census lists James and wife, Elizabeth, with four slaves. Elizabeth died in Surry County. James sold out and followed three of his sons and a son-in-law to Rutherford County, N.C. Only his son Joseph remained in Surry where he reared his family and where he died.

A strong bond of friendship apparently existed between James and his youngest son, James, whose large family of children was still quite young when the older James went to live with them in Rutherford County. The younger James died early in the year 1803, wherefore his father James immediately provided that all he owned should go to these orphaned grandchildren upon his death, which occured the

following year at the age of eighty-five.

Sources: The Reavis Family History.

— Mary Jo Lowe Lovette

JOSEPH REAVIS

943

Joseph Reavis was born in 1755 in Northampton Co., N.C., son of James and Mary Reavis. He was in his late teens, but already married, when his father moved to Surry County, N.C. on the watershed of the Yadkin River.

Joseph was a farmer, was married to a Mary, and died in 1805, leaving a will in Surry County.

Joseph Reavis is on the list of Sundries furnished the Militia as being paid for services in the Revolutionary War, which proves that he was a Patriot.

He owned land on Harmon's Creek and it was not until the year 1828 that the descendants of Joseph Revis, namely, William Reeves, Charles Steelman, Joseph Reeves, Asa Reeves and David Reeves, all of Surry County, deeded away the land on Harmon's Creek which their father had left in his will.

The exact location of his grave has not been found. At present one will find Reavises buried at South Oak Ridge and Courtney Baptist Churches in Yadkin County, N.C.

Sources: The Reavis family history.

— Mary Jo Lowe Lovette

JOSEPH REAVIS, JR.

944

Joseph Jr., son of Joseph and Mary Reavis, was born in Surry County, N.C., about 1799. However, there is a deed record in Surry County, dated in 1816 which discloses the purchase of 240 acres on Dutchman's Creek by William Reavis, with Joseph Reves as a witness on the deed. If these two were brothers, as seems possible, Joseph must have been born as early as 1795, which date would make him of what age in 1816.

He married Elizabeth Axom, daughter of Joseph and Nancy (May) Axom. She was born in 1810 and died in 1894. Suffering the misfortune of losing his home in a fire, and being threatened with the loss of his land through forecloseure by his brother-in-law, Charles Steelman, Joseph undertook to move his family into Georgia. On the way one of the children became so ill that the family got no further than Wilkes County, N.C. There Joseph settled as a farmer and reared his family, and there he died in February 1877. He and his wife are buried in a small cemetery on the farm of Odell Wyatt, Boomer Highway, Moravian Falls. He was active in the Walnut Grove Baptist Church, its clerk from 1856 to 1865, when he was ordained a deacon. His sons adopted the simplified spelling of the family name, Revis.

He and Elizabeth had the following children: Caswell unmarried; Monroe, unmarried; Andrew married Elizabeth Lowe; William unmarried; Joseph Martin born November 23,

1845; Samuel Smith Revis, born May 23, 1849; and Mary Revis.

Sources: The Reavis family history.

— Mary Jo Lowe Lovette

JOSEPH MARTIN REVIS
945

Joseph Martin Revis was born November 23, 1845, in Yadkin County, N.C. His parents were Joseph and Elizabeth Reavis. He was of English and Irish descent.

Joseph Martin Revis, for some unknown reason, simplified the spelling of the family name for his own use, and his descendants use the form Revis.

On February 6, 1867, Joseph Martin Revis married Delilah Clementine Ray, daughter of Elizabeth St. Clair. Her Mother had remarried after her father passed away. Samuel Smith Revis and Andrew Revis, his brothers, were witnesses. Delilah Clementine was born October 29, 1850, and died April 11, 1922, at Moravian Falls. She was of Dutch descent.

To this union were born the following: (1) John Smith born January 3, 1868, died March 7, 1896, unmarried; (2) Lenard Monroe born March 8, 1869 and died December 12, 1935, married Martha Ida Pearson July 18, 1894; (3) Almedia Elizabeth born December 17, 1870 and died October 4, 1960, married March 11, 1888, Henry Clay Adams; (4) Mary Clementine (Molly) born February 27, 1873 and died August 1963, married John Marshall Duncan December 21, 1892.

(5) Dora Lucinda born June 14, 1875, died January 1953, married Jones Estep June 7, 1893; (6) Joseph Andrew, called Andy, born August 30, 1877 and died June 14, 1903, unmarried; (7) Hattie Arabella born January 17, 1880 and died October 31, 1946, married Jeff Brock on August 30, 1896; (9) Sylvestie M. born May 2, 1882, died May 16, 1884; (10) William Samuel born April 29, 1884, died March 1961, married Grace Bentley on April 29, 1908. He uses the spelling Reavis; (11) Max Caswell born July 9, 1887, died July 11, 1911, unmarried; (12) Bertha Viola born July 26, 1897, married Kelly Hodges March 21, 1931, she is still living at the Revis homeplace in Moravian Falls.

Joseph Martin Revis grew up in the pre-Civil War days. He was not quite old enough to go to war. As times were hard, he learned the trade of making cabinets, tables, and shoes. In order for his children to have a better opportunity for schooling, Joseph Martin moved nearer the village of Moravian Falls in 1884. He wanted to be close to Moravian Falls Academy.

Joseph Martin lived an exemplary life being honest, truthful, and helpful to his neighbors. For a living he farmed, worked some in the Internal Revenue Department of the government. He believed in education.

His politics was Democratic. He belonged to the Moravian Falls Baptist Church. His wife belonged to the Walnut Grove Baptist Church. Joseph died December 22, 1914, at the age of sixty-nine. He and his wife and the following children Amedia, John, Sylvestie, Hattie, Mac and Will, are buried at Walnut Grove.

Sources: The Reavis family history and Bertha Revis Hodges.

— Mary Jo Lowe Lovette

THE REINS FAMILY
946

The Reins family resided near Wilkesboro. Originally the name was spelled Rains, but the spelling was changed over 100 years ago.

All the Reins in Wilkes County are descended from Jesse Reins (circa 1822) and Dorcas Baity Reins. They were married in January 4, 1838, and had six children. Jesse was a harness maker. They are buried in the Cub Creek Cementery.

Jesse's father is thought to be John Rains, who married Elizabeth Laine, January 19, 1814, but this cannot be verified at this writing. A John Rains from Wilkes County fought in the War of 1812.

One of the children of Jesse and Dorcas Reins was William Franklin (September 1848 — died May 1929). He was a carpenter by trade and his obituary stated that he built many of the houses around the Wilkesboros.

In January 1878, he married Elizabeth Hall, the daughter of John and Polly Powers Hall. She was born in Rockingham County (March 1851 — died July 1932) and had come to Wilkes County as a young girl. She told her children she remembered traveling in a covered wagon, and the wagon became stuck in the mud while fording a creek.

William and Elizabeth had five boys and three girls. They were William Edward; James Calvin; Rosa Belle; Robert Franklin; Charles; Lora Mae; Maude; and Ralph Randolph.

Most of them were of rather large stature, and possessed a dry wit.

William Edward, a farmer, was born December 1878 and died November 1956. He married Lizzie Stewart. They lived near Wilkesboro. They had three children: Roy Stewart; William Fred; and Sibyl Elizabeth. Roy died in 1970 and Sibyl is also deceased.

James Calvin was born February 1880 and died August 1961. He married Virginia Netherland. He was a North Wilkesboro businessman. They had two daughters: Elizabeth Gordon, and Rebecca Montague.

Rosa Belle ("Dink") was born January 1883, and died February 1975. She married Thomas M. Foster, and they had one daughter, Edith. She died in 1944.

Robert Franklin was born February, 1885 and died August 1951. He married Emma Elizabeth Seehorn. They had three daughters: Frances Irene, Elizabeth Teckla, and Emma Roberta. Bob was in the monument business, and he spent most of his married life in Lenoir. Elizabeth or "Lizzie" died in 1960, and Robert, or "Bobbie" in 1973.

Lora Mae was born November 1886 and died August, 1971. She married Charles T. Foster, a railroad engineer. They had three sons: Charles, Howard, and Norman. The Fosters lived in Kernersville. Charles and Howard are deceased.

Charles C. was born January 1889, and died January, 1954. He married Ella Armstrong of

Elizabeth and William Franklin Reins.

Belmont, and they had three children: Charles, Joseph, and Irene. "Charlie" was a druggist, and lived most of his married life in Winston-Salem. Ella Reins survives and is living in the Methodist Home in Charlotte; Charles Jr. died at an early age.

Maude was born May 1892 and died November 1973. She was first married to a Mr. Watts, and later to William Minton. At one time, she and William Minton were both mail carriers. They had no children.

Ralph Randolph Reins was born March 1894, and died October 1962. He was married first to Maizie Vannoy, and they had two sons: Ralph Richard, and William Franklin. After her death, he married Mildren Hinton, who survives. Ralph was a colonel in the U.S. Army.

Sources: Grave stones and family records.

— Gordon Reins Smoak

JAMES SIDNEY REINS FAMILY
947

James Sidney Reins was a son of Jesse O. and Dorcus Baity Reins who lived in Wilkesboro. His grandparents were probably John and Elizabeth Laine Reins. John was age 59 and Elizabeth 63 in 1850. They were both born in Virginia, and married on January 19, 1814 in Wilkes County, N.C.

Jesse O. Reins, age 28 in 1850, was born in Wilkes County. His wife Dorcus, age 22 that year, was born in Mecklenburg County, N.C. They had eight children: (1) Myra, who was age 9 in 1850; (2) Mary, age 7 in 1850; (3) William Franklin "Dick" Reins was born September 18, 1848; died May 18, 1929. He married Mary Elizabeth Hall; (4) Martha was listed as age 8 in 1860; (5) James Sidney Reins was born April 26, 1856, died March 20, 1946; (6) Nancy Reins married R.F. Joines on June 4, 1893; (7) Lizzie married Will Anderson; (8) Emeline Reins married a Mr. Lane. She was buried at Cub Creek Baptist Church where her mother and sisters Lizzie, Myra, and Nancy were buried.

James S. and Martha A. Reins.

James Sidney, known to many as "Buck Reins" married Martha Jane Adams. They lived and farmed in the West end of Wilkesboro. At that time the house was not in the city limits. The house was torn down when the new 421 highway was built.

"Buck" and Martha Reins had six children: Alice Hilder was born January 15, 1895, died January 5, 1959. She married Paul Dockery Walker on November 28, 1924. Their four children are: Virginia Lucille W. Spears; William Glenn Walker; Martha Irene W. Wyatt; Alice Elizabeth W. Jarvis.

Eunice, the second daughter, was born August 8, 1889 and died January 3, 1954. She married Adam Staley. Her daughter Maude married Bill Higgins.

Myrtle Reins was born March 8, 1900 and died February 16, 1959. She married Wade Gilbert and had six children: Myrtle Zell; Mildred G. Minton; Jimmy W.; J.V.; Bob; Allie Gilbert.

Alma Reins was born March 10, 1903 and died September 30, 1974. She married Edgar Staley. Their children are Bud; Lake, Margaret (1931-1934); Patricia S. Whittington; Jewel S. Bullis; Betty S. Duncan; Edgar S. "Cookie" Staley, Jr.

William Chester Reins was born August 6, 1897 and died at the age of three years. He was buried in a cemetery near the Smithey Hotel building.

Jesse Vance Reins was born November 15, 1891 and died on December 29, 1960. He married Vera Adams. Jesse served his country during World War I. Their children are: James Sidney; Ray Clanton "Shane"; Mary R. Church; Emma R. Byrd; Annie R. Craven; Joyce R. Phillips; J.V. Reins, Jr.

Beatrice Reins was born November 5, 1908 and married Richard Higgins. Beatrice is the only child of "Buck" and Martha Reins that is living at this time. She has three children: Margie Elma; Helen Jenette and Billie Richard Higgins.

"Buck" Reins was a small man who seemed to walk so very slow, but if you got behind, you had to run to catch up with him.

The three grandsons and four great-grandsons continue to carry on the James Sidney Reins line of the family name. There are other Reins in the county who are decendants of Jesse O. Reins.

Sources: Personal Knowledge.

— William G. and Christine E. Walker

JAMES and VIRGINIA REINS
948

James Calvin Reins was born near Wilkesboro February 9, 1879, and spent all his life in the Wilkesboros. He was the son of William Franklin and Elizabeth Hall Reins.

He went to work at an early age, and never retired. In his later years, he enjoyed going to the monument business and having friends drop by to visit and talk and hear him relate some of his many colorful yarns.

In 1894, he had established a monument business in Wilkesboro, which was later moved to North Wilkesboro. He entered the undertaking business in 1917, establishing the funeral home which was the forerunner of Reins Sturdivant Funeral Home. He later sold his interest in that firm.

In September 1924, he married Virginia Netherland, who had come to North Wilkesboro to teach school. She was born December 19, 1889 to William Ball and Caroline Gordon Netherland of Powhatan County, Virginia.

The Reinses had two daughters, Elizabeth Gordon, born December 12, 1928, and Rebecca Montague, born August 29, 1934.

Gordon married Robert Smoak, and they reside in Wilkesboro. They have four children: James Norman (1948) married Lucille Mary O'melia, and they have two children, Benjamin Ryan (1977) and Katherine Page (1979). William Samuel (1950) married Mary Martha Vickery. They have one son, William Samuel Jr. (1980) They reside in Spruce Pine, N.C. Robert Smoak Jr. (1956) married Marjorie Lynne Bradburn. They have one daughter, Lyndsay Elizabeth (1982). Their home is in Richmond, Virginia. At this writing, Caroline Gordon (1962) is a rising senior at Vanderbilt University in Tennessee.

Rebecca Montague Reins married Rufus Max Turner, and they live in Atlanta, Georgia. They have three children: Virginia Lenora (1955), George Gregory (1956), and Carol Elaine (1959).

Jim or J.C. Reins, served as postmaster in North Wilkesboro for 15 years. He was president of the North Wilkesboro Savings and Loan for 38 years. In the Baptist Church he served as a deacon and trustee. He was a member of the North Wilkesboro Board of Commissioners for a number of years, and served as Democratic Executive Committee chairman.

Mrs. Reins was also active in many phases of community life. She helped organize the first library in Wilkes County and served as secretary for many years. She was a faithful member of the United Methodist Church, where she held many positions of leadership. She was a charter member of the Woman's Club, and was also active in Garden Club work and beautification of the town. Her family and friends remember what an excellent cook she was.

Mr. Reins died August 7, 1961, and she died two years later, August 17, 1963. They are buried at Mount Lawn.

Sources: Family and newspaper records.

— Gordon Reins Smoak

RALPH RANDOLPH REINS
949

Ralph Randolph Reins was the youngest child of William and Elizabeth Hall Reins. He was born near Wilkesboro, March 29, 1894.

Virginia Netherland Reins.

James Calvin Reins.

Ralph R. Reins.

Ralph served with the Wilkes County National Guard and the United States Army during World War I and World War II, until the end of both wars.

He became a major in 1940, a lieutenant colonel in 1943, and was made a full colonel after retiring from active duty.

He married Maizie Susan Vannoy, who was born December 17, 1900. Two sons were born to this union, Ralph Richard, May 17, 1927, and William Franklin, July 9, 1932. Maizie died December 8, 1955.

Ralph later married Mildred Jones Hinton who was born April 7, 1907.

William Franklin married George Lou Sprinkle, who was born September 10, 1933. They had two children: Vickie Susan, born April 27, 1954, and William Franklin Jr., born April 7, 1961.

Vickie married James D. Murphy, and they have one son, Drew Douglas Murphy, born October 7, 1981.

Ralph died October 28, 1962 and is buried at Mount Lawn.

Sources: Personal records.

— George Lou Reins

LENARD MONROE and MARTHA IDA PEARSON REVIS
950

Lenard Monroe Revis, born March 8, 1869, died December 17, 1935. His parents were Joseph Martin and Delilah Clementine Ray Revis.

Martha Ida Pearson, born March 28, 1878, died October 3, 1940. Her parents were William Asa "Acie" Pearson and Elizabeth Smithey Pearson. She was a Methodist.

Grandpa was mainly a farmer. He also kept bees and worked as a lathman. He was a Baptist, Democrat, member of the Masonic Order; he served in the U.S. Army (calvalry) at Fort Leavenworth, Kansas.

On July 18, 1894, he married Martha Ida Pearson at Moravian Falls. To this union were born the following children:

Ray Martin Revis born September 24, 1896, died March 1937 in Virginia. He married first Gertrude Minnie Smith July 18, 1922 at Chicago, Ill. and second Agnes Forehand in June 1933 at South Mills, N.C. They had no children. He served 18 years in the U.S. Navy, retired as Chief Quartermaster, he was a Methodist and member of the Masonic Order.

Maude Sylvestia Revis born June 3, 1898, died December 28, 1977 at Elkin, N.C. She married Marvin B. Clark July 1918 at Pores Knob. She was a Methodist and a Democrat. They had two daughters: Margaret Lucille born May 1, 1921, died January 7, 1980, at Elkin, N.C. and Dorothy Elizabeth born February 12, 1924.

Mary Clementine Revis born February 1, 1900, died February 13, 1976 in Pinehurst, N.C. She was first a Methodist and a Democrat; later a Baptist and a Republican. She was also a school teacher. She married Perry R. Lowe November 29, 1922, at Moravian Falls. They had Clyde Revis Lowe born January 2, 1927; Perry R. Lowe, Jr. born February 19, 1930; Caney Len Lowe born June 8, 1932; Mary Jo Lowe born August 25, 1941.

Dorothy Louise Revis was born December 15, 1901 and died January 28, 1969 in Charlotte. She was a Methodist, Democrat, and school teacher. On January 31, 1921, she married Walter Smith Revis. They had two daughters: Blodwin Fay born December 23, 1921; died in infancy and Mildred Irene born November 3, 1923.

Joseph Monroe Revis was born April 5, 1907 and died July 7, 1953. He was a Methodist, Democrat, farmer, and bee-keeper. He married Georgia Lee Short in April 1929. They had one child, Joe Lenard Revis, born June 1930 at Dany, W. Va.

Blanch Elizabeth Revis was born January 14, 1912 and died March 6, 1969, in Charlotte. She was a Methodist and a Democrat. She made her home with her sister, Dorothy, for many years.

There was always something going on in the household. As a little girl, Aunt Maude had a vivid imagination. She had been watching birds fly; paying close attention to the movement of their wings. One day, she decided she would try to fly. She worked building wings suitable for her arms. She climbed upon the buggy shed and worked her arms until she thought she had the movement just so. She went to the edge of the roof and leaned forward — instead of flying out into the air like she thought she would, she hit the ground with quite a bang. She almost had the breath knocked out of her. Needless to say, she never tried this stunt again. She has told this story many times. It always became funnier each time she would tell it.

Sources: The Reavis Family History, family memories, and personal knowledge.

— Mary Jo Lowe Lovette

REYNOLDS
951

The pioneer John Reynolds, who settled on the Yadkin River and Mulberry Creek when this area of North Carolina was still Bladen County, was descended from one Christopher Reynolds, who was born 1530 in Kent County, England. John Reynolds was born 5 October 1710 in Norfolk County, Virginia, married Sarah Rebecca Jenkins and died in 1756 in then Rowan County (later Wilkes). He was the son of Robert and Grace (Clark) Reynolds of Norfolk County. Eight children were born to John and Rebecca: (1) John Francis who married Anne Blackburn, (2) Eliza who married a Sidden, (3) Sarah who married Joseph Porter, Sr. and lived in Wilkes County, (4) Elisha born April 1755, died 13 Dec. 1836 on Mulberry Creek, married 5 August 1786 Judith Eddins. Elisha was a Revolutionalry War soldier, (5) James who died 1809 on Fishing Creek, married 1st Mary Baker, 2nd. 20 Feb. 1806 Mrs. Jane (Hickerson) Miller, (6) William who married 4 April 1781 Martha Cook. (7) Jenkins born 1753, died Sept. 1779, married Martha Sale, (8) Charles.

John Francis Reynolds, referred to as Francis, was the administrator of the estate of his father, John, in 1756 in Rowan County. Francis was born 1734 in Bladen County, N.C., died 12 October 1804 on the Yadkin River in Wilkes County, married 1770 Anne Blackburn, who was born 28 April 1750, died 16 February 1827 in Georgia and is buried in the Decatur City Cemetery, Dekalb County. She was a daughter of Ambrose and Hannah (Ashley) Blackburn of Rowan County.

Francis Reynolds was a planter and large land owner, kept an Ordinary in his dwelling house and is listed as a member of Old Roaring River Baptist Church at Traphill in 1792. His wife and some of his children are listed as members of Brier Creek Baptist Church in 1790. Francis Reynolds' will is recorded in Wilkes County. He and Anne had thirteen children: (1) Hannah married 11 November 1788 Reuben Parks, Esq., (2) John Ashley born 1774, married 1st. Nancy Cleveland, daughter of Capt. Robert Cleveland, and 2nd. Elizabeth Brooks, (3) Ann born 1775 married 1794 James Patton and removed to Buncombe County, (4) Lois Elizabeth was born 1777, married 5 July 1799 Isaac H. Robinette and removed to Mississippi, (5) Nancy married 1 March 1813 Samuel Sale, (6) William Elisha married 8 February 1802 Elizabeth Greer and removed to Warren County, Tennessee, (7) Jenkins married 1st. 22 May 1802 Mary Vannoy, 2nd. 5 November 1804 Margaret Greer, removed to Warren County, Tennessee, (8) Mary married 12 March 1804 John McCord and left Wilkes County, (9) Sarah Evoline married Geroge Tomlinson and removed to Buncombe County, (10) Silas born 13 February 1784, married 1st. 27 March 1817 Parmelia Bartlett, 2nd. 11 Sept. 1827 Nancy Bartlett, died in Coweata County, Georgia, (11) Martha married James Galbraith, (12) Elzy Baker born 4 April 1792, married 1st. 13 September 1824 Susan P. Welborn, 2nd. Rowena C. Evans, died 26 August 1863 in Dekalb County, Georgia, (13) Harden married 9 January 1822 Elizabeth Talbor, died in Wilkes County, Georgia.

John Ashely Reynolds, Sr., eldest son of John Francis and Anne (Blackburn) Reynolds, was born 1774 in Surry County, died 20 November 1859 of heart dropsy after an illness of thirty days. He is buried in an unmarked grave on his homeplace where Mulberry Creek enters the Yadkin River. He married about 1795, Nancy Cleveland, who was born 9 May 1779, died 1 February 1846 and is buried on the homeplace in an unmarked grave. She was a daughter of Capt. Robert and Alice (Alley) (Mathis) Cleveland of Lewis Fork in Wilkes County.

John Ashley Reynolds was a farmer and slave owner. After the death of his wife, Nancy, he married Elizabeth Brooks on 15 October 1846. His will names his wife, Elizabeth and some of his children. His Bible shows that he and Nancy had thirteen children; (1) Harden born 6 February 1796, died 9 September 1823, (2) Alice (Alley) born 1 September 1797, died 22 August 1880, married 12 December 1815 Jacob Hutcherson who was born in Stokes County, N.C., (3) Larkin C. born 10 August 1799 and removed to South Carolina, (4) Clarissa born 25 October 1801, married 1 January 1822 Stokes H. Brooks, (5) Nancy Blackburn born 3 May 1803, married David Cautheran and removed to Cherokee, Alabama, (6) Sarah born 16 Februray 1805, died 3 June 1875, married 3 January 1824 Absalom Eller of Lewis Fork, (7) John Ashley, Jr. born 2 December 1806, left Wilkes County, (8) Mary born 22 December 1808, married 1st. 11 June 1828 Jeffrey Johnson, 2nd. Joshua Waites and died in Phelps, Missouri, (9) Francis born 5 March 1811, died 1863 unmarried, in Sullivan County, Indiana, (10) Jeremiah born 14 December 1813, died in Hardiman County, Tennessee, (11) Micah (Mickey) born 6 September 1815, died 27 June 1871, married Owen Hall, Sr. of Traphill, (12) William Elisha born 17 November 1817, married Susannah Adams, (13) Elzy B. born 14 January 1821, died March 1895 in the poor house in Wilkes County, married April 1843, Susannah Jennings. They were divorced.

William Elisha Reynolds, son of John Ashley and Nancy (Cleveland) Reynolds, was born 17 November 1817, died 7 January 1870, married 11 January 1849 Susannah Adams, born 13 March 1828, died 4 July 1878, daughter of Charles and Nancy Adams. They are buried in unmarked graves on his homeplace in Haymeadow Township. He is consistently on record as Wm E. Reynolds. He was a farmer and county surveyor for many years, earning the reputation of being one of the best surveyors the county ever had. He joined Zion Primitive Baptist Church August 1864. He and Susannah had seven children: (1) Nancy Jane born 12 July 1849, died 26 May 1916, married September 1871 William Matthew Absher, (2) Francis Asbury born 27 January 1851, died 8 November 1896, married 16 March 1871 Jane Rhodes, (3) John Cleveland born 7 April 1852, died 1881 in Johnson County, Tennessee, married 22 August 1868 Martha Ann Brown, (4) Henry Harrison born 24 July 1853, died 1 December 1930, married 1st. 21 May 1876,

Sarah E. Absher, 2nd. 10 December 1883 Nancy E. Salmons, (5) Larkin C. born 21 September 1855, died 7 May 1937, married 1st. 5 December 1875 Mary Jane Dillard, 2nd. 3 January 1888 Martha Hincher, 3rd. 21 January 1904 Sarah E. Roberts, (6) Sarah Ann born 12 May 1859, died 11 April 1937, married 25 April 1875 John G. Rhodes, (7) Clarissa Elizabeth born 26 March 1864, married 17 August 1881 Thomas F. Wadkins.

Sources: Rowan County estate records, deeds; Wilkes County deeds, wills, marriage bonds, court minutes, church minutes, Bible Records, *Reynolds* Genealogy by S.F. Tillman in Duke University Library, *Cleveland* Genealogy by E.J. Cleveland (1899).

— Mrs. W. O. Absher

RHOADES (RHODES)
952

Victory Adams married Charity Rhoades and four known children were born to them: Charity Luiza, Nancy, Sally and John. Nancy is believed to be the mother of twelve children.

Charity Luiza born 9 March 1864, died November 1937, married William W. Rhoades, born 14 September 1842, died 10 March 1911, and their children were: Henry Harrison born 21 July 1880, died 19 October 1958, married a girl named Evia who had Angie, Joshua and an unnamed child. The next child was Charity L. Rhoades born 31 August 1883, died in Virginia, married L.D. Hayes and lived in Danville, Virginia. A daughter of theirs who was killed in Winston-Salem in a car accident 9 September 1943 was survived by five brothers and three sisters.

The third child born of this union was Freeland Franklin Rhoades born 31 July 1886, died 13 January 1953, who married Nora Catherine Buinn, born 12 November 1904. She now lives in a nursing home. Their children were: two children who died in infancy; Geneva Catherine born 17 July 1927 married James E. Boggs and lives in Hillsville, Virginia and have two children, Toni and Eddie.

The fourth child, William Jack born 26 August 1934, married Ella Virginia Howell 17 October 1963, daughter of Harvel Pearson and Dare Eller Howell. They have one son, William Andrew Rhoades born 8 August 1965. Andy attends Wilkes Central High school from which he will graduate next spring. He is an accomplished guitarist and loves all music. His mother is a talented seamstress, cook and homemaker. She shares his love of music. His father, Bill, has been with the N.C. State Highway department for seventeen years. During this time he attended night classes at college for nine years. They are members of First United Methodist Church in North Wilkesboro, N.C.

Sources: Rhoades Family Bible and personal knowledge.

— Ella Howell Rhodes

OSCAR CICERO RHOADES
953

Oscar C. Rhoades was born in Wilkes County 21 January 1896 in the Dehart Community,

the son of Willis J. Rhoades and Sarah Frances Absher Rhoades. He spent his early life on his father's farm helping with the farm work and helping at this father's saw mill and grist mill which were run by water power.

The lumber and farm products were hauled by wagon and mule team to North Wilkesboro. They would have to camp overnight in town at the camp ground which was located about where the present library is.

The Mill Dam was washed out in the 1916 Flood and was never rebuilt. Steam engines began to replace water power.

Oscar attended elementary school at Dehart and Mt. View Institute, Hays, North Carolina.

He was drafted in the Army in World War I and was sent to France and Germany and served in the 81st Wildcat Division. He was assigned to an ammunition train, hauling supplies.

He married Cordia Alice Wyatt 18 November 1921, a school teacher, daughter of Jesse M. Wyatt and Nannie Handy Wyatt in the Dehart Community.

About January 1922, he started a country store and farmed for a living. He ran the store and farm for about 45 years in the Dehart Community. In the early years in the country store he bought dried fruit, hams, herbs, chickens and eggs which were hauled to North Wilkesboro and sold at the markets.

Sometimes the sacks of herbs were too bulky to be hauled by car, and the mule team and wagon was used to haul them to town. I remember telling him about the mule team getting scared on the town hill and running away. Frank Tomlinson caught them on Cherry Street at the blacksmith shop.

Country store prices Year 1922: Coffee — 15¢/lb.; Soap — 5¢/cake; . . sugar — 8¢/lb.; Kerosene Oil — 10¢/gallon; Pair of Overalls — $1.25; Cloth — 20¢/yd.

Oscar C. Rhoades joined Dehart Baptist Church in August, 1925 and always tried to help build a better church and was active in civic affairs.

He is a member of the North Wilkesboro Masonic Lodge #407 AF & AM and has a fifty year membership award.

Cordia Alice Rhoades, first wife of Oscar C. Rhoades and mother of all his children, died in 1936. Their children include the following:

Ira Dean Rhoades lives in Wilkesboro, N.C. He was in World War II, served in the Army Postal Service in New York for fourteen months, remainder of time served as Transport Clerk on a Navy Troop Transport in the Pacific area. After the War, attended Clevenger College and studied Business Administration. He married Dorothy Blackburn. He has been Town Clerk-Treasurer for the Town of Wilkesboro since 1971. They are members of Wilkesboro Baptist Church and active in civic affairs.

Vera E. Rhoades, married Chall Hayes. They operated truck stops several years in Virginia, Ohio and Maryland, and now are retired, living in Kernersville, N.C. They have two daughters, Sandra and Karen Hayes.

Veva Marie Rhoades, died at age two.

Dewitt E. Rhoades, married Mary Naylor, lives in Kernersville, N.C. He attended High Point College, was in the Air Force for four

Oscar Cicero Rhoades.

J. ELIJAH RHOADES, JR.
954

Elijah Rhoades, Jr. was born February 9, 1841 in Wilkes County in the Dehart Church Community, died 5 November 1925 and married Caroline Whitley in 1872. She was born in 1851 and died 17 February 1910. Both are buried in the Dehart Baptist Church Cemetery.

He was a farmer and ran a corn mill and saw mill which was run by water power. I have heard it said that he hauled a corn mill from Salisbury, North Carolina by wagon.

He had the following children:

(1) Willis J. Rhoades, born 8 November 1874, died 28 July 1947, married Sarah Frances Absher 12 April 1895. She was born 15 September 1876 and died 11 June 1950. They are both buried in Dehart Baptist Church Cemetery. (2) Elijah A. (Babe) Rhoades, born 12 March 1876, married Carrie Porter. (3) Ellen Rhoades, born 14 November 1878, died 15 May 1904 and was buried in the Dehart Baptist Church Cemetery. She married Tipton Wood. (4) Sina Rhoades, born 20 February 1981. She was buried in the Dehart Baptist Church Cemetery.

(5) Susan Rhoades, born 6 April 1883, married Arthur E. Shumate. Both are buried in the Dehart Baptist Church Cemetery. (6) Alice Rhoades, born 26 August 1886, died 9 May 1970, married Hardin Shumate.

(7) Wiley P. Rhoades, born 8 August 1887 and died 14 September 1952, married Donia Bell. Both are buried in the Dehart Baptist Church Cemetery. (8) Sarah Jane Rhoades, born 5 August 1890, died 29 May 1973, married Joseph P. Hayes 3 February 1907. She was buried in the Haymeadow Baptist Church Cemetery. (9) Minnie Rhoades, born 16 April 1893, died 21 April 1899, was buried in the Dehart Baptist Church Cemetery.

J. Elijah Rhoades was my great-grandfather.

Sources: Family Bibles and grave monuments.

— Ira Dean Rhoades

WILLIS J. RHOADES
955

Willis J. Rhoades was born 8 November, 1874 in the Dehart Church Community in Wilkes County. He died 28 July, 1947. His father was J. Elijah Rhoades, Jr., born 9 February, 1841 and died 5 November, 1925. His mother was Caroline Whitley, born 1851 and died 17 February, 1910.

He married Sarah Frances Absher 12 April, 1895. She was born 15 September, 1876 and died 11 June, 1950. She was the daughter of Levi Absher who served in the Civil War.

Willis J. Rhoades was a farmer and operated a saw mill and corn mill that was run by water power in his younger days. In 1916 the Mill Dam was washed out by the Flood and was never rebuilt. He later used a steam engine to grind corn and saw lumber.

He was a man of good character and it could be said his word was his bond. I have heard my father tell about them cutting a tree on the farm that was so big they couldn't move it, They had to use dynamite to burst the log before it could be dragged to the saw mill.

years in the Korean War and served as a gunner on the B-50 Bombers over North Korea. He is now president of Facts, Inc., Office Machine Business in Winston-Salem, N.C. They have three children, Mary Lynn, Gregory and Neal Rhoades. They attend the Baptist Church.

Vade G. Rhoades, M.D. in Dermatology, married Sarah Williams. He went to UNC-Chapel Hill, N.C. for pre-medical schooling. He got his M.D. Degree at Bowman Gray School of Medicine at Wake Forest University. He went in the Navy for three years and was stationed in Pearl Harbor, Hawaii. After leaving the Navy he went to Duke University and recieved his Degree in Dermatology. He is now practicing in Winston-Salem, N.C. He married Lila Hayes in 1963 and they have two children, Mark and David Rhoades. They attend the Episcopal Church.

Sources: Family memoirs, family records and personal knowledge.

— Dean Rhoades

He was a member of Dehart Baptist Church and was on the committee appointed in 1917 to build a new church.

He had the following children:

(1) Oscar C. Rhoades, born 21 January, 1896 and still living. He married Cordia Alice Wyatt 18 November, 1921. She was born 6 June, 1896 and died February 4, 1936. She is buried in the Dehart Baptist Church Cemetery. In 1963 he married Lila Hayes, his second wife.

(2) Cora L. Rhoades, born 8 March, 1900 and died 13 June, 1978. She married Charles M. Robertson 5 January, 1926. Both buried in Winston-Salem, North Carolina. (3) Archie C. Rhoades, born 29 October 1902, died 29 July, 1934 and buried in the Dehart Baptist Church Cemetery. She married Carl Gambill 12 March, 1922. (4) Estel E. Rhoades, born 29 April, 1905 and died 22 May, 1981. He was buried in the Dehart Baptist Church Cemetery. He married Maie Barlow 5 January, 1931. (5) Della L. Rhoades, born 8 November, 1907 and still living. She married Ochis O. Absher 5 January, 1927. (6) Fred H. Rhoades, born 5 June 1910 and still living. He married Lillie Shumate 18 September, 1937. (7) Ina E. Rhoades, born 14 April, 1913 and still living. She married James Arthur Handy.

(8) Ruth B. Rhoades, born 19, February, 1916 and died 28 September 1966. She was buried in the Pine View Baptist Church. She married R. Don Bumgarner. (9) Infant son, born and died 12 April, 1912. He was buried in the Dehart Baptist Church Cemetery. (10) Minnie Rhoades, born 14 April, 1913 and died 10 September, 1913. She was buried in the Dehart Baptist Church Cemetery. (11) Infant daughter, born and died 6 February, 1899. She was buried in the Dehart Baptist Church Cemetery. (12) Lillie Rhoades, born 1 October, 1897 and died 27 May, 1898. She was buried in the Dehart Baptist Church Cemetery.

Sources: Family Bibles and cemetery monuments.

— Dean Rhoades

ELIJAH L. RHODES, SR.
956

Elijah L. Rhodes, Sr. was born 12 October 1805 and died 18 April 1877 in Wilkes County. He was buried in the old Rhodes Cemetery on a hill near Cane Creek in the Dehart Community where his father, John R. Rhodes, Jr., divided 990 acres of land in 1857 among his children. Elijah married Susanah Hall 18 December 1935. In his will dated April 18, 1877, he willed his personal and real property to his wife and children after paying any debts he owed. He was a farmer and blacksmith by trade and owned sheep, cattle, hogs and horses and kept bees on his farm. He had the following children:

(1) Elizabeth Rhodes, born 17 July 1831, and died 18 April 1877. She married Alfred Elledge. (2) Benjamin A. Rhodes, born 10 February 1833 and died March 1875. He married someone named Elizabeth; (3) Martha Rhodes, born 17 October, 1835; (4) Sarah Lucinda Rhodes, born 4 December 1837. She married Elijah Walker. (5) J. Elijah Rhodes,

Jr., born 9 Feburary. 1841, and died 5 November 1925. He married Caroline Whitley in 1872. She was born 1851, and died 17 February 1910. Both were buried in Dehart Baptist Church Cemetery. (6) Caroline Rhodes, born 1842; (7) Biddy Rhodes, born 1845; (8) Susan Rhodes, born 1847; (9) James Rhodes, born 1851; (10) John G. Rhodes, born 4 July 1853. He married Sarah Ann Reynolds; (11) Louise Rhodes, born 1 August 1854, married a Shumate.

Elijah Rhodes, Sr. was a great-great-grandfather of mine.

Sources: Family Bibles and census records.

— Dean Rhoades

JOHN RHODES, SR. and JR.
957

John Rhodes, Sr. was born in Virginia, died in Wilkes County in 1790. In his will he named his wife, Sarah, son, John, Jr. and daughter Nancy and Elizabeth. According to old family papers, Sarah Absher, daughter of the widow Absher who "managed" to marry a Hall, married John Rhodes, Esq. It is assumed this is the wife, Sarah, named in the will.

John Rhodes, Jr. was born 16 September 1780 in Virginia, died in April 1857 in Wilkes County, married 2 November 1802, Sarah Agnes (Aggy) Jennings, daughter of Luke, Sr. and Letes (Townsen) Jennings.

John Rhodes, Jr. was a miller and farmer. At the time of his death he owned eight hundred and twenty six acres of land on Mulberry, Lousey, Haymeadow Creeks, Reddies River and Beetree branch, which was allotted to his children. He and Aggy had twelve children, all born in the Haymeadow community: (1) Elizabeth, born 20 September 1803, died 23 September 1899, married 30 November 1826 Willis Walker, (2) Elijah, born 12 October 1805, died 22 April 1877, married 18 December 1830, Susan Hall, (3) Hiram, born 31 March 1808, died 2 February 1877, married 20 October 1838, Sarah Pardue (4) John W., born 25 September 1809, married 28 August 1833, Sarah Adams (5) Nancy, born 27 February 1812, died prior 1857, married 18 March 1826 William Ellis (6) William, born 3 May 1814, possibly died young. (7) Solomon, born 12 June 1817, married 11 September 1838, Frances Adams (8) Sarah, born 21 April 1819, died 19 August 1910, married 12 December 1840 James D. Tinsley (9) Wesley Washington, born 26 October 1822, died 8 April 1909, married first, 30 April 1840, Margaret Adams, second 15 August 1864, J. Elizabeth Havener (10) Rebecca born 11 March 1824, possibly died young (11) Benjamin Franklin born 24 August 1827 died 20 April 1895, married 1st 2 February 1849 Mary Elledge, 2nd. 14 October 1878 Alice M. Walker, (12) Agnes Caroline born 1830, possibly died young.

Elizabeth Rhodes, daughter of John and Agnes (Jennings) Rhodes married Willis Walker, born 23 September 1804, died 22 January 1870. Both are buried at New Covenant Baptist Church at Dockery. Willis was the son of Josiah Walker, who is believed to have come to Wilkes County from Maryland. Elizabeth and

Willis had six children: (1) John F. born 16 September 1826, died 27 April 1894, married 19 August 1852, Nancy Matilda Absher (2) Sarah Lucinda, born 14 November 1830, died 7 December 1897, married 1850 Wiley Patterson Absher (3) William Hamilton, born 2 September 1834, died 15 June 1913 in Alleghany County, married Mary Ann Johnson (4) Willis Milton, born 11 September 1836, died 16 May 1871, married Rebecca A. Myers (5) James Dolphus, born 25 May 1840, died 22 February 1911, married in August 1877 Samantha Caroline Buttery (6) Josiah, born 28 July 1845, died 4th March 1925, married 17 February 1867, Lodemia Buttery.

Sources: Wilkes County deeds, marriage bonds, death certificates, wills, family Bibles, gravestone inscriptions.

— Mrs. W. O. Absher

CHARLES CRAIG RHYNE FAMILY
958

The first Rhyne to come to America was Jacob Rhyne, who came from the Palatine section of Germany on the upper Rhine River. Jacob came to Philadelphia, via England. He lived for a short time in York, Pennsylvania before coming to North Carolina and settling in Gaston County on upper Hoyle's Creek.

Peter Rhyne, son of Jacob, was born in 1754 and died in 1828. He married Magdeline Wills, who survived her husband by many years to run the farm and rear their family of ten children, the sixth of whom was Solomon Rhyne, who married Elizabeth Hoffman.

Solomon and Elizabeth Hoffman Rhyne are buried in Christ's Luthern Churchyard at Stanley in Gaston County. Solomon was born 15 January 1793 and died 1 April 1865. Elizabeth was born 10 June 1794 and died 17 September 1882. Their children were: Simon, Jonas Labon, David, Perry, Jacob, Daniel W., Eli, John, Miles A., Henry Malachi, Margaret, Louisa and Andrew.

Howard and Mattie Patton Rhyne.

Henry Malachi Rhyne, son of Solomon and Elizabeth, was born 27 July 1838 in Gaston County, died 1 July 1907 in Burke County. He first married Elizabeth Jenkins and after her death, he married Synthia Hoyle Clemmer 23 July 1863. She was born 24 July 1840 and died 5 May 1934, daughter of George, Jr. and Mary Withers Clemmer.

Henry Malachi was in the Civil War, was shot in the arm through the elbow and was permanently disabled for duty. In 1886 he and his family moved to Burke County, N.C. and settled on Canoe Creek on the old Wilkesboro road. He and Synthia were the parents of eleven children, all born in Gaston County: John Larkin C., Mary A.E., Thomas Edgar L., Samuel Wadsworth, Henry Mortimore, Lloyd Wills, Otis Otega, Dorcas I., Ferriby Morris, Ural Allan and Howard Wilmot.

Howard Wilmot Rhyne was born 4 April 1882, died 28 April 1954. He married Mattie Patton, daughter of William and Sarah Cannon Patton. Mattie was a school teacher. William Patton, her father, was a brother to Robert Logan Patton, who was a professor of Moravian Falls Academy in the 1890s and also pastor of Moravian Falls Church and North Wilkesboro Church in the 1890's.

Howard Wilmot Rhyne was a farmer and worked for a number of years for the N.C. State Highway Department. He and his wife reared five girls and four boys on the home place of his father on Canoe Creek in Linville community on the old Wilkesboro road. The house was a six room frame building, with a tin roof and huge chimneys, and the first house in the community to be painted. A two-room house was built later below the driveway, called the "Boys House" where the boys of the family slept. Both original houses still stand, occupied by Howard Wilmot's daughter, Ethel and her husband, Paul Little.

The children of Howard Wilmot and Mattie Patton Rhyne were (1) Vera who married Ivey Bumgarner and had Howard, Ivey, Herman, Sue and Doris. (2) Harry Henry married Gertrude Parks, and had no children; (3) William Bennett married Velse Craig. They had one child Richard. William Bennett married Neil Cubertson and had one son, Benny. (4) Robert Howard married Myra Ledbetter and had no children. (5) Charles Cra_ married Jessie Parsons and had one child. (6) Ethel Patton married Paul Little and had one daughter Dorothy Elizabeth, who died at age of three. (7) Mattie Amadeline married Sonny Rhodes and had one daughter, Patsy. Mattie moved to Napa, California. She married as her second husband, Homer Conant. They had one daughter, Marcia. (8) Dorothy who never married. (9) Edna who died at the age of six with pneumonia.

Charles Craig Rhyne, son of Howard Wilmot and Mattie Patton Rhyne, came to Wilkes County in 1936 and worked for the State Forestry Service at the C.C. Camp in Purlear. His uncle, Will Patton, was superintendent of the State Forestry Service at that time. Charles worked for Lovette Egg Company for thirty-six years before his retirement.

Charles Craig married Jessie Catharine Parsons 23 December 1937 at the home of Rev. A.W. Eller in Purlear. Jessie Parsons was the fifth daughter of James Cicero and Sallie Land Parsons of Parsonsville, N.C. Charles and Jessie lived in Parsonsville until 1971 when they moved to Route 4, North Wilkesboro.

Charles and Jessie had one child, June Carolyn Rhyne, born 21 May 1939. She married Colbert S. Eller 2 July 1961. They have a daughter Melody Caroline Eller, born 25 March 1968 at Wilkes General Hospital. June Rhyne Eller works for the Wilkes County Board of Education. Colbert owns and operates Eller's Exterminating Company and they live on Route 4, North Wilkesboro.

It is of interest to note that Daniel E. Rhyne, a cousin of Howard Wilmot Rhyne, was a good friend of Mr. Lenoir and donated money to Lenoir College in Hickory, thusly having Rhyne added to the name of the college.

Sources: *Burke County Heritage;* the Rhyne family book; Linville Methodist Church 1874-1974 in Burke County; personal knowledge.

— Jessie Parsons Rhyne

TOMMY RICHARDSON FAMILY
959

Tommy Richardson came from Ireland and settled in the Walnut Grove Community. Tommy had a son Burl, born February 20, 1820 — died May 2, 1907. Burl married Matidla Louisa Adams. She was born July 7, 1827 and died August 15, 1895. They are buried at Walnut Grove Baptist Church.

Burl and Matidla had a son name Moses Franklin, born June 4, 1845 and died October 21, 1922. Moses Franklin married Lousia Blevins. She was born May 13, 1843 and died April 1919. They are buried at Round Hill Baptist Church in Traphill. Moses Franklin and Lousia had six sons: Authur, Jack, Hamp, Oliver, Trillie and John Ander, and one daughter, Nanny who married Newton Bauguess.

Authur was born May 31, 1869 and died December 12, 1947. Authur married Rhoada Jane Prevette and they moved from Traphill to the Rock Creek section to raise their family. Rhoada was born September 17, 1870 and died September 7, 1934. Authur and Rhoada had eight sons: Lyod, Charlie, Brack, Bruce, Lonnie, Paul, Curtis and Roy, and two daughters, Dolly Luffman and Alice Spicer.

Brack has two sons, Brack Jr. and James Authur (Jim). Charlie has three sons: Tam, Dean, and Charlie, Jr. Lyod had one son, Woodrow. Charlie Jr. has two sons, Bennie and Jeff. And Tam has one son named Darryl.

Tommy and his son Burl were grain farmers. Moses Franklin was also a farmer and fought in the Civil War.

Jack was a blacksmith and had a shop on the Cut Throat Ridge road in Traphill. He was also clubfooted and made his own shoes from wood. Jack had a son named Ike who had a son named Jackie who is a minister. Jackie is now the pastor at Flint Hill Baptist Church.

To the best of my memory grandfather Authur was gifted with a lively way of stating things. He was a carpenter, made coffins, and was also a constable. Mrs. Roy Richardson has the book that he kept records of the trials and so forth.

All of the clan of Richardsons seem to be the sanguine type, cheerful, optimistic, and very friendly. And most of the Richardsons have the Irish temper.

Bruce and Charlie, children of Authur are still living. Bruce has been a successful poultry and cattle farmer. Charlie is a minister and has pastored many churches in Wilkes. They are retired.

Sources: Personal knowledge.

— Linda Richardson Parker

JOHN and CELIA ROBERSON FAMILY
960

The earliest Roberson my family knows much about is John Roberson, who came to Wilkes County from the Charleston, S.C. area after his marriage. He was a well-to-do man according to his daughter Anne who stated to my mother that he owned much land and had "swarms of slaves." He married Celia O'Sullivan, who came from Ireland with her parents.

John and Celia came from S.C. to Wilkes County and settled on the Brushy Mountains on the southeastern side of Pores Knob. It was near Sugar Loaf Mountain to which they probably gave its name after Sugar Loaf Mountain in Ireland. The O'Sullivans were said to have retained their Irish brogue throughout their lives and also their Irish pride.

John and Celia had four daughters and four sons: (1) Anne, who married Martin Wallace, was my mother's grandmother, who reared her after her mother's death. Anne and Martin built their home near the top of Pores Knob Mountain near a spring which has always been known as the Martin Wallace Spring; (2) James married a Miss Davis and went to Illinois; (3) William went to Illinois also, but did not keep in touch with his family; (4) Thomas migrated to Missouri; (5) Lydia married Enoch Ellis and had several children; (6) Nancy died unmarried; (7) Polly married Hugh Smith but had no offspring; (8) John married Almeda Williams and had three sons and four daughters.

Their daughter Amanda Roberson (born March 5, 1841) married Coffey Laws and was my grandmother. She died on her ninety-eight birthday and was buried in the Laws family cemetery near Shady Grove Church near the Kerr Scott Dam.

There was much intermarriage within the Wallace, Roberson, Broyhill, and Laws families who were close neighbors.

Several members of these families are buried in the Bethel Church cemetery in Alexander County, with imposing stones. John's stone reveals that he "died on November 10, 1855, aged seventy years," while Celia lived on for twenty-two years and "died November 9, 1877, aged ninety-one years."

One loses track of some of the descendants who changed their name to Robinson, for what reason I have never learned.

Sources: Bethel Church Cemetery marker, family knowledge.

— Thelma Laws

THE REVEREND C.W. ROBINSON

961

Charles Wilson Robinson was born near Holly Springs, Miss., of North Carolina parents, Col. Thomas H. and Catherine Hope Robinson. He spent his childhood in Oxford, Miss. The town of Oxford was burned by Union Troops during the War between the States and the Robinson house was lost in the flames. After this, young Charles, his mother and sisters refugeed to the old family home near Concord, N.C., as his father and four older brothers were in the Confederate Army. This was a dangerous trip — made on an ammunitions train which was the only transportation available due to the war.

Mr. Robinson attended private schools, and was graduated from Davidson College and Columbia Theological Seminary. His first pastorate was in Glasgow, Kentucky, where he met and married Miss Nellie Rogers. Mrs. Robinson was a lovely, gracious lady and a wonderful minister's wife. She gave unstintingly of her time and talent in her work in the church which she loved. She died in 1906.

There were three children of the marriage: Kate, (deceased) who married James C. McDiarmid of Fayetteville and lived there all of her married life. Edmund, a veteran of World Wars One and Two (now deceased), and Ellen, now a retired music teacher who lives in Wilkes County in the Brushy Mountain Community.

In 1884, Mr. Robinson returned to North Carolina, and was pastor of Historic Sugar Creek Presbyterian Church near Charlotte for several years. He was also pastor of Churches in Monroe, Gastonia and Winston-Salem before coming to North Wilkesboro with his family.

Although the North Wilkesboro Church had been organized, its first building erected and dedicated, before Mr. Robinson became its pastor, the membership was small and it was grouped with the Wilkesboro and Elkin Churches. Mr. Robinson was pastor of all three churches until the North Wilkesboro Church became large enough to support a full time pastor, at which time he resigned from the other two churches, and devoted all his time to the work in North Wilkesboro.

He was always deeply interested in both Home and Foreign Missions, and did Home Mission work in his early ministry, as well as in Wilkes and Ashe Counties, after coming to North Wilkesboro.

Mr. Robinson had a well-balanced, logical, finely trained mind and was an able preacher. His sermons revealed his knowledge of the Bible, his depth of thought and deep spirituality. They gave spiritual food to his learners, as well as practical help for everyday living. He was a teaching preacher and felt deeply the responsibility of interpreting God's Word. His greatest desire was to win souls for Christ and many were led to accept Christ by his prayers, his sermons and his influence. He was truly a man of God, and his whole life was dedicated to service to God and his fellow man.

When he celebrated his 50th anniversary in the ministry, he preached from the same text he used for his first sermon: "I Corinthians 2:2 — For I determined not to know anything among you, save Jesus Christ and Him Crucified."

Mr. Robinson was an unusually good pastor and his pastoral visits were a vital part of his ministry. He entered into the joys and sorrows of the people of the community, and was ever ready to respond to any call for help and to sympathize with and comfort those in sorrow. He was greatly beloved by people in all walks of life. Children were devoted to him and he to them.

In addition to his ministerial work, Mr. Robinson was active in civic affairs, giving generously of his time and efforts to many worthy causes, and was very patriotic. He helped organize the first Y.M.C.A. in Wilkes in the 1890's, and was county chairman of the Red Cross during World War I. He was a Pythian, a Mason and a member of the Kiwanis Club.

Mr. Robinson preached for 59 of his 89½ years. During his 43 years in North Wilkesboro, under his leadership, the church grew from 21 members in 1895 to 170 when his pastorate ended with his death in 1938.

After his death, the congregation placed a beautiful bronze tablet in the Church in his memory, the inscription on which is a summary of his characteristics. Part of this inscription is copied from a memorial tablet to his grandfather, the Reverend John Robinson, D.D., in the First Presbyterian Church of Fayetteville, N.C.

The following is the inscription on the tablet in the North Wilkesboro Church: 1848-1938.

The organ chimes and this tablet are given as a memorial to the Reverend Charles Wilson Robinson, beloved pastor of this church for 43 years, 1895-1938, as a tribute to his life and work and an expression of love by his devoted people.

"He was a polished gentleman, a finished scholar, an able instructor of youth, a genuine Christian, and a faithful and affectionate pastor. In him were beautifully blended and happily united, all those qualities of the mind and heart which are naturally adapted to attract attention, to command respect, to conciliate esteem, and to beget pure and lasting affection: He Walked With God."

Sources: Church records and personal knowledge.

— Miss Ellen Robinson

FREELIN FILMORE ROOPE

962

The Roope name is Scotch-Irish in origin, and was at one time O'Roop. Five O'Roop brothers came over to the U.S.; two settled in North Carolina, two in Virginia, and one in Tennessee.

Freelin Filmore Roope was born in Wilkes County on August 12, 1883, son of Andrew and Mary Ann Richardson Roope. F.F. married Mary Belle Absher, daughter of Abram and Lucinda Belle Absher. They had 13 children: Genie; Alverda; Delpha; Morgan; Elmina; John; Warren; Marvin; Vada; Victoria; Maxine; Clifton; and Garley. Belle was born on August 6, 1887 and died on December 20, 1935. F.F. died on January 15, 1969. Both are buried at Mountlawn Cemetery.

Genie Roope married Rell Parsons; they had one daughter, Shirley Jean. Shirley, who married Gurney Davis, works for the Veterans Service in Wilkesboro. Gurney is employed at Beacon Ins. Co. They have three children: Kenneth, Brian, and Diane. Kenneth is an assistant coach at Georgia Tech in Atlanta; Brian is employed at The Northwestern Bank; Diane is a student at Woodward Junior High.

Alverda Roope married Clarence A. Jones who was a supervisor for the N.C. Dept. of Transportation. They had two children: (1) Maxie Lou and Jerry Ray. Maxie Lou married Richard Elledge, who is Controller for Lowe's Companies, Inc. They have four children: Donna; Debbie; Todd; Derek. Donna and Debbie are students at Western Carolina University, Todd is a student at North Wilkes High School, and Derek is a student at Mountain View Elementary. (2) Jerry Ray Jones married Virginia Martin. They have one son, Joseph Ray, who is the youngest descendant of F.F. Roope. Jerry is a partner in Jones and Staley Logging Company.

Delpha Roope married William M. (Bill) Watkins. Bill was employed at Turner-White Casket Co. and later at Wilkes Furniture Exchange; Delpha worked at Peerless Hosiery. Thay have no children.

Morgan Roope married Kathleen Bishop. Morgan was a furniture retailer for 40 years. They have one daughter, Morguenya ("Butch"), who married Richard (Dick) Tipton McNeil, Jr. Dick is Secretary-Treasurer and Manager of the N.W. Coca-Cola Bottling Company. Dick and "Butch" have one daughter, Jackie, who is a rising junior at N.C. State University.

Elmina Roope married Layafette (Fate) Eller, and they live in Lenoir. They ran Cherry Hill Office Equip. Co. Thay have one son, Kenneth, who works for Remington Rand. Kenneth married Judy Goode who is a librarian in the Catawba County School System.

John Roope married the former Prudie Hawkins. John was employed by Mark-Down Furn. Co. He and Prudie have two children: Larry and Peggy. Larry is a graduate of ASU in Boone and is employed by Lowe's Companies as General Ledger Auditor. Peggy is married to Ray Redmon, who is employed by Holly Farms as a welder. They have one daughter, Heather Leigh.

Warren Roope married Beatrice Sloop. Warren lost his life in World War II on September 18, 1944 and is buried in Mountlawn Cemetery.

Marvin Roope was single and a painter by profession. He was a veteran of World War II. He passed away on September 22, 1976 and is also buried in Mountlawn Cemetery.

Vada Roope married Harvey Bullis, and they reside in Burlington. Harvey owns Bullis Hosiery Mill. They have two sons: Gary and Donald. Gary is a graduate of N.C. State and is employed by the Dept. of the Navy. He married Linda Buchheim from Scranton, Kansas, and they have three children: Bryan, Brandon, and

Sonya. Donald Bullis was graduated from Cincinnatti College of Embalming and Mortuary and is employed by Rich and Thompson Funeral Service.

Victoria Roope married Clyde Bumgarner who is a Security Officer for the Northwestern Bank. They have two daughters, Patricia and Sandra. Pat Bumgarner married William Hamby who is a dispatcher for Lowe's Companies. They have two children: Jody and Derek. Jody is a student at Woodward Junior High and Derek is a student at Moravian Falls School. Sandy Bumgarner married Harry J. Warren, Jr. who is a purchasing agent for Lowe's Companies. Sandy is a secretary at Wilkes Community College.

Maxine Roope married James Dyer. She is employed as a supervisor at Modern Globe, Inc., and James works at Mulcher Bros. Maxine and James have one son, Jerry Michael who is married to Linda Cannon; Jerry is employed by Simon Poultry Equip. Co. in St. Louis, Missouri.

Clifton (Click) Roope married Elizabeth (Lib) Pickard. They live in Burlington, where Click is employed by G.K.M. Automotive Component, Inc. Lib is employed by General Electric. They have two sons: Ronnie and Timothy. Ronnie is married to Patricia Harmon who is employed at UNC-Chapel Hill as a secretary. Ronnie works for General Electric. Timothy is a student at ASU in Boone.

The youngest son of F.F. and Belle Roope is Garley Roope. He and his wife, Ann, have one son, Randy. They live in Burlington where Garr is Department Manager at Anna-Dean Hosiery. Randy is a student hairstylist.

Sources: Personal knowledge and grave markers.

— Morguenya Roope McNeil

ROUSSEAU
963

After the repeal of the Edict of Nantes in 1685, members of the Rousseau family left France to come to the colonies. These Rousseaus were Huguenots and they came to Charleston with the first Franch settlers. Later several family members settled in Virginia.

In 1770 two brothers, Hiram and Hillaire Rousseau, came to Wilkes. Hiram was a surveyor and married Sarah Meredith Martin.

Hillaire (1743-1829) purchased 199 acres of land in Mulberry in 1779. He married Sarah Rogers (1748-1799) and had eight children. This family had a home five miles east of Wilkesboro on the south side of the Yadkin River.

Their son John (1786-1880) married Sarah Gordon, daughter of Nathaniel Charles Gordon and great-granddaughter of Charles Gordon, Sr. They had thirteen children. Among these was Addison Lafayette (1812-1895).

Addison Lafayette married Cynthia Anne Parks dond had eleven children. This family built a home on a hill overlooking Wilkesboro where family members continued to live until 1980.

Their son James Parks (1852-1905) married Lila Gilbert of Atlanta, Georgia, and they had six children. The children were: Nellie

Claire (1884-1939), who taught school in Wilkes County for many years; Cynthia Anne; James Rogan (1887-1956); Julius Addison; William Archibald; Malcomb Andrew (1894-1930); and James Parks Jr. (1896-1966), who was a doctor of radiology in Winston-Salem.

Cynthia Ann (1885-1969) married S.V. Tomlinson of North Wilkesboro and had six children. They were: James Rousseau; William Seebohm; Sara Virginia; Annie Ruth, who married Carlyle Ingle of Lenoir and had three children: Anndora, William Carlyle and Archibald Tomlinson; Worth Evan, who married Nan Davis of Winston-Salem and had three children: Worth Evan, Jr., Neal Rousseau, and James Davis; and Archibald Benbow, who was killed in action during World War II.

Julius Addison (1889-1958) was Judge of the North Carolina Superior Court, 1935-1958. He married Gertrude Hall of Yadkinville and had four children: Nelle Gertrude, Frances Hall, Nancy Hart, and Julius Addison, Jr. His son married Gary Maxwell of New Bern and now lives in Wilkes. He is Judge of the North Carolina Superior Court (1972-   ) and has one son, Julius Addison, III.

William Archibald (1891-1954) married Timoxena Crawford of Franklin and had two daughters: Margaret Diane and Cynthia Anne. Mrs. Rousseau, a retired educator, lives in Wilkesboro.

Sources: *Happy Valley* by Thomas Felix Hickerson, pages 31-32; family notes; and tombstones.

— Mrs. J.A. Rousseau, Jr.

LORA ISABELLA ROUSSEAU
964

Lora Isabella Rousseau, or Belle as she is

L. to R: Lora Isabella Rousseau; Delsie Rousseau Barber.

affectionately known, was born March 1, 1889, one of nine children of Samuel and Cora Rousseau. Of those, Henry Rousseau, Delsie Barber, and Belle remain. Their ages are 91, 83, and 93 respectively. Their grandparents were Joe and Delsie Greer.

The Rousseaus had a farm; were lifelong residents of Wilkes, and their homeplace is near what is now the Edgewood Church. Belle's father, in addition to farming, held public jobs including working at the tannery. Her mother was cook and housekeeper for Judge Rousseau's mother.

Belle was educated in Winston-Salem at Slater College and taught school in Wilkes and Iredell Counties in one-room schools. Later, Belle worked in the homes of Mrs. Dan Carter, Dr. William Newton, and Dr. W.L. Bundy.

Lora Isabella Rousseau is a God-fearing woman and a member of Rickards Chapel in North Wilkesboro where she serves as "Mother of the Church," and for many years was a member of the church choir. Belle has a deep respect for nature and can identify every flower, tree, and bush and has an uncanny knack for spotting a four-leaf clover almost on demand.

Bell has a great mastery of the English language which is very evident in her speech, spelling and poetry. A very wise woman about people and things, she seems to have a sixth sense. It has been said that she doesn't dream unless it comes true.

Belle has a genuine love for children, and no one knows that better than I. Her namesake is Lora Jordan Welborn, daughter of Kenneth Philip and Julia Bundy Welborn, who were married on Belle's birthday.

Belle is an accomplished cook as anyone who has tasted her pies can attest. Her hobbies include tatting.

Lora Isabella Rousseau is a truly remarkable woman that Wilkes County can be proud of.

Source: Personal knowledge and an interview with Miss Rousseau.

— Julia Bundy Welborn

JOSEPH ROYALL

965

Joseph Royall, born in Virginia before 1775 and died before 1830, was the son of John and Mary Royall of Virginia and Surry County, North Carolina. A fifth generation descendant of Joseph Royall (1600-1658) who came to Jamestown in 1622, he first is listed in 1810 in Surry County and then in the Wilkes County Census of 1820, with his widow, Elizabeth, being listed in 1830 in the Ashe County Census.

According to Wilkes County records, Joel Vannoy, high sheriff of Wilkes County, sold to the highest bidder 50 acres of land "not far from Dark Hollow near Fish Dam Creek" belonging to Joseph Royal in order to satisfy a debt of $18.20 to Amos Church. Michael Bumgarner paid $4 for this land 3 November 1818.

Though five sons and six daughters have been listed in census records, only the following have been positively identified.

(1) Thomas was born in 1795 in Virginia and died in 1877. His Bible is extant.

(2) John was born before 1810 and died before 1850, killed by a falling tree in the vicinity of Sparta, according to family information. He married Mary Wagoner, and their five children included Franklin (1833-1915); William (1838); Elizabeth Royal Perry (1838-1927); Thomas (1840), a private in Co. A, 9th Reg NCSY (1st Reg N.C. Cav.) who enlisted 3 June 1861; and John (1842). Many of their descendants still reside in Wilkes County.

(3) William (1812-1896) enlisted 4 October 1861 in Co. D, 33rd North Carolina Infantry, C.S.A. and was discharged in August, 1862. He married Sarah Sanders, and their twelve children include Janetta Royall Crouse (1840-186?); Wiley (1841-186?), a branch of whose family moved to Indiana; Sarah Ann Royall Brooks (1844-1914); John W. (1846-1923), many of whose descendants live in Wilkes County; Nancy Royall Sanders (1848-1911); Thomas (1850), who moved to Floyd County, Virginia; Rosannah Royall Brooks (1852-1935), many of whose descendants live in Wilkes County; William Franklin (1855-1936), some of whose descendants live in Wilkes County; Elizabeth Royall Johnson (1857); James Wesley (1859); Joseph M. (Bud) (1860-1932); and Martha Royall Smith (1861-1930).

(4) Mary (Polly) Royall McCann was born in 1816 and died in Alleghany County.

Sources: Census records, family Bibles, personal interviews, tombstone dates, and Royall, *Log Cabin Families of Stone Mountain, North Carolina.*

— Hardin J. Royall

WILLIAM FRANKLIN ROYALL

966

My grandfather, William Franklin Royall (1855-1936), son of William and Sarah Sanders Royall, married Mary Frances Brown (1860-1929), daughter of George W. and Elizabeth Roberts Brown on October 25, 1878. They were the parents of ten children: John Andrew Royall (1879-1951), Thomas Wilson Royall (1881-1962) of Montana, James Franklin Royall (1882-1958), Sarah Elizabeth Royall Hayes (1885-1968), William Harrison Royall (1887-1962), George M. Royall (1889-1972), Morgan M. Royall (1892-1964) of Wyoming, Frances Jane Royall Lyon (1895-1955), Martha Rosannah Royall Smith (1897-1976), and Margaret Tennessee May Royall (1905-1907).

William Franklin Royall was a merchant, who operated a general store near Stone Mountain, located half a mile north of Elk Spur Church at the fork of the old road. The north fork, now discontinued, led to Liberty Knob School — Church and on to Cherry Lane, while the southwest fork led to Stone Mountain. The store was some three miles from his home at the old William Royall homeplace, from which he commuted daily on horseback.

In the early 1900s Doughton, North Carolina, became a booming town with several thriving businesses. The E. and A. Railroad form Elkin ended here at the foot of the Blue Ridge Mountains, where there was a depot. The mountains were covered with virgin timber, and to Doughton the mountaineers hauled their timber products by mules, horses, and oxen from their steam-driven sawmills to be sold and shipped to other parts of the country.

Leaving the homeplace to his son, George, he moved to Doughton, where he opened another store. William F. Royall's General Store was near the depot, and farmers and sawmill workers could pick up their supplies when they brought their products to town. After the death of his wife his son, James F. Royall, moved in with him and cared for him, assisting in the operating of the store.

In his older years although he was crippled and moved about the store by holding to the counter, he always had a sunny disposition, and it was a joy to be around him. I recall that he always had candy and a beguiling tale for a small boy.

He is buried beside his wife in the cemetery at Roaring Gap Baptist Church about a mile and a half from his home and store.

Sources: Royall, *Log Cabin Families of Stone Mountain, North Carolina,* and personal memories.

— Hardin J. Royall

THE JOHN J. RUSSELL FAMILY

967

The Russell family made its first known appearance in Wilkes county when Daniel Russell came from Virginia and bought 100 acres of land near Moravian Creek on August 4, 1806. More land of various amounts were acquired through 1826. Russell's Gap between Taylorsville and Boomer was named for this family.

One of Daniel's sons, A.B., which seems to have stood for Abednego though often referred to as Ben or even Benjamin, was born in Virginia in either 1800 or 1801. He married Sarah Hubbard who was born in North Carolina around 1806. Their third son, John J. was born on April 3, 1832.

John J. Russell grew up in Moravian Falls. As a child he attended school and worked on the family farm. Just after his thirtieth birthday, he enlisted in the Confederate Army of Northern Virginia on April 12, 1862. As a member of the 37th N.C. Regiment Infantry, he fought under General A.P. Hill and quickly was promoted to sergeant. After recuperating from an undisclosed illness at Wayside Hospital in Richmond and at home, he returned to action during the Chancellorsville campaign. While fighting at Gettysburg he was wounded and captured during Pickett's Charge (July 3, 1863). Union General Schenck confined him to the federal prison at Point Lookout, Maryland on October 15, 1863. There he stayed until released during a prisoner exchange at Ft. Lee (near Richmond) on February 23, 1865.

Soon after returning to the stillness of civilian life, John J. married Dosea M. Pearson of Wilkes county on February 17, 1866 in Moravian Falls, where they took up residence. Dosea was the daughter of Thomas and Agnes Pearson.

John J. resumed farming and Dosea kept house and raised their children: Thomas B. (b.

in 1867); William L. (1869); Sallie Agnes (1870); R.J. (1873); Elizabeth (1875); Mattie A. (1877); H.J. (1880); Ila (1880). All of the children were born in Moravian Falls and attended school.

Both John J. and Dosea lived to a ripe age, and eventually succumbed to natural causes. She died at age 89 on September 3, 1927 and he on July 24, 1925 at the age of 93. They are buried in Boomer where they had spent their last years.

Sources: Wilkes Gen. Bulletins; death certificates, Confederate war records and census records.

— Ben Lowe

BENJAMIN SEBASTIAN
968

Benjamin Sebastian was born in Virginia 1740-50 and died in Wilkes County 1819. The name of his wife is unknown. He was possibly the son of Stephen Sebastian, born 1733 in Virginia, died Wilkes County 1784. Stephen was a chain carrier for Washington and Fairfax in Fredrick County, Va. in 1748. He also served seven years in the Revolutionary War. Benjamin possibly was a brother to Isaac, William, Lewis, Elisha, Ailse and others.

Benjamin came to Wilkes County with his family and brother, Lewis, in 1774. Lewis was born 1762. Benjamin got a land patent from the State of North Carolina for 150 acres of land on Haymeadow and Sebastian Branch on the waters of Mulberry in 1779. He built his house on a knoll near Hays, N.C. now owned by Lena Alexander, a descendant of Benjamin's. In the 1790's he bought 241 acres of land from Phillip Johnson, which he later gave to his son, John. In 1782 he leased a farm from William Lenoir located on the waters of Fishing Creek. He was to give fifteen barrels of corn, repair the fances and give four gallons of brandy if the orchard did good.

Benjamin is listed on the payroll of the Morgan District receiving pay for services in the Revolutionary War.

In his will, probated in 1819, he mentions only one son, William, and Susanna Barker, who appears to be his daughter.

Lewis Sebastian went to Scott County, Ky.; William went to Madison County, Ky.; Isaac died in Orange County, N.C.; and Elisha went to north Georgia.

Benjamin's children were: (1) William, born in Virginia 1770, died Wilkes County after 1840, married 1794 Elizabeth Carter, born 1775, died 1866, daughter of Henry and Millender Carter. Henry Carter was a Revolutionary soldier, fought at Ramseur's Mill. Henry and Milly lived at the mouth of Rock Creek on the Yadkin River below North Wilkesboro. Elizabeth was an early member of Mulberry Church, a charter member of Cross Roads Church and a charter member of Zion Baptist Church near Hays, N.C. where she remained a member until her death. William was a prominent farmer of the Haymeadow community. He served on juries, signed bonds and was a constable and an officer of the court in 1800. He got permission to build two gates across the road on his farm where the road crossed going form Traphill to Wilkesboro. He and

Elizabeth were the parents of eight children. (2) Elijah Sebastian, son of Benjamin, was born 1772 in Virginia, died in St. Francois County, Missouri in 10 October 1853, married 1st. Phebe Brown in 1801, she was the daughter of Walter Brown and died in Missouri in 1812. They were the parents of five children, one of whom was adopted. Elijah married 2nd. Sarah Kelly Dennis in 1813 in Missouri. Five children were born to this union.

Elijah first went to Kentucky where he served in the war of 1812, and then moved to Missouri. He is buried on the old homeplace near Libertyville, Mo.

(3) Nancy Sebastian, daughter of Benjamin, was born in 1780 in Wilkes County, died in Kentucky in 1822, married Jesse Stamper, son of Jacob and Susannah Stamper.

(4) Mary Sebastian, daughter of Benjamin, was born 1783, died in Kentucky. She married Jonathan Stamper, son of Jacob and Susannah Stamper. They lived in Kentucky and had several children.

(5) John Sebastian, son of Benjamin, was born 1784, died in Kentucky, married Sarah Turner, daughter of the Revolutionary War soldier, Roger Turner of North Carolina. They had five or more children.

(6) Susannah Sebastian, daughter of Benjamin, was born 1771, died in Kentucky, married in Wilkes County, Hezekiah Barker, a Revolutionary War soldier, who died in Wilkes County in 1816. They had several children. Susannah and five of her sons went to Carter County, Ky., about 1826.

The children of William Sebastian, son of Benjamin, and his wife, Elizabeth Carter were: (1) Benjamin, born 1806, died in Grayson County, Virginia in 1872, married Elizabeth Adams, daughter of William H. and Nancy (Adams) Adams of Wilkes County. They moved to Grayson County about 1860. They had eight children. Both are buried in Anderson Cemetery near Volney, Virginia. (2) Lewis, born 1806, died 1864 in Civil War. He married Rachel Adams, daughter of Charles and Nancy (Stamper?) Adams. They were the parents of nine children; (3) Wesley, born 1895, married Nancy Pennington in Kentucky. They had several children (4) Henry, born 1803, married Nancy, and was last found in Johnson County, Missiour in 1850 with several children. (5) Ellen, born 1797, married a Turner and removed to Kentucky. (6) Sallie, born 1817, married William F. Brown, lived in Wilkes County and had several children. (7) Nancy, born 1804, married David Call, lived near Hays, N.C. They had two daughters. (8) William, Jr., born 1814, died 1864 in Civil War, married Eliza Grimes, daughter of Adam Grimes. Lived in Haymeadown township and is buried in the family cemetery. They had eight children.

Sources: Old Church records, Wilkes County records, Kentucky records, family information by word of mouth.

— Samuel E. Sebastian

THE ELI SEBASTIAN FAMILY
969

Eli Lewis Spencer Sebastian was born Janu-

Eli L. and Ellen Myers Sebastian.

ary 23, 1887; died November 12, 1971. He was the son of Samuel and Mary Blackburn Sebastian. On April 1, 1908 he married Ellen M. Myers, born January 7, 1887; died February 25, 1970. She was the daughter of George Elihue and Mary R. Staley Myers.

Eli and Ellen lived on the old Samuel Sebastian farm, three miles east of Hays, N.C. Eli was a lumberman and farmer. He raised cattle and was an early poultry producer in Wilkes County. He was a devout Christian, a deacon in the Baptist church and was known for his honesty, truthfulness and fairness by all who knew him. At his funeral, the Rev. B.C. Owenby said, "There was a man in the land of Wilkes whose name was Eli Sebastian, and this man was a man of mature faith, moral rectitude, reverenced God and was against evil."

After Eli and Ellen's death the farm was sold to a distant cousin, O.F. Sebastian and his wife, Grace. This farm is now the Rock Creek Country Club, a beautiful golf course. In early life Ellen was a teacher in the county schools, but quit after her marriage in order to devote her time to her family. Eli and Ellen were members of Mountain View Baptist Church and are buried at Mount Lawn Cemetery north of North Wilkesboro. Their children were:

1. Alma Pearl, married to Ross Withers and lives in Mobile, Alabama. Ross is retired from the U.S. Army and Pearl is a retired accountant. They have no children.

2. Clarence O. married Dorris Parker and they live near Rock Creek Church. Clarence is a retired furniture manufacturer. Their children are Charles Douglas and Nancy. Charles Douglas married Nancy Norman of Surry County. They have three children: Tammy, Susan and Chris. Nancy married Eugene Jones, Jr. and they have one daughter, Michelle.

3. Samuel E. married Hettie Woodall, daughter of Millard M. and Hettie Davis Woodall of Smithfield, North Carolina. Samuel

Hettie and Sam Sebastian.

L. to R: Samuel E. Jr. and Gary Sebastian.

is a poultry producer and Hettie is a secretary in the Agricultural Extension office in Wilkesboro. They are members of Mountain View Baptist Church and live 3 miles east of Hays, N.C. Their children are Samuel E., Jr. and Gary Michael. Samuel E., Jr. is unmarried. He is a parttime ABE instructor for Wilkes Community College. Gary Michael married Loretta Mendenhall and lives in Elkin, N.C. Gary is Employment Manager for Wayne Poultry Company in Dobson, N.C. Gary and Loretta have no children.

4. Mary Clair was kicked by a mule colt when very young which left her severly handicapped and an invalid. She died in 1968.

5. Alta Mae married Richard W. Jones of Wilkesbarre, Pennsylvania. They lived in Wilkesboro, N.C. Their children: Katherine and Richard W., Jr. Richard W., Sr. died in January, 1981. Alta still lives in Wilkesboro.

6. Arvona married Paul Cleary. They had one daughter, Jeanne, who is an executive with Bell telephone Company. She is married to Donald Gore. They have no children. Paul is deceased and Arvona now lives in Alabama.

7. William Clay is married to Hwaja Yuk, born in South Korea. They live east of Hays, N.C. on the Rock Creek Road. Clay is a disabled veteran of World War II. He has two children by a former marriage, Debbie and Eric, who live in California.

8. Johnnie Mae married Archie F. McNeil and lived on Shady Lane in Wilkesboro, N.C. until her death in September, 1965. She suffered an aneurysm and lived only two days afterward, never regaining consciousness. She is buried in Mount Lawn Cemetery beside Highway #18 North of North Wilkesboro, N.C. They had two adopted children, Michael and Patricia. Michael was killed in an automobile accident in August of 1979. Archie and Patricia still live on Shady Lane in Wilkesboro.

Sources: Family Bibles and family Members.

— Samuel E. Sebastian

LEWIS SEBASTIAN

970

Lewis Sebastian, born 1808, died 1864 in the Civil War, was the son of William and Elizabeth Carter Sebastian. He married in 1833, Rachel Adams, born 1809, died 1893, the daughter of Charles and Nancy Stamper Adams.

Lewis and Rachel lived in the Haymeadow community of Wilkes County near Zion Baptist Church. They were both members of this church and are buried in the family cemetery nearby. The land for Zion church was given by the Sebastian family.

Lewis owned several hundred acres of land which supplied lumber, corn and wheat for flour and meal and feed for his livestock. Lewis was a teacher in the public schools. He was a land surveyor and was sworn in as a deputy surveyor in 1849. In 1862 he was sworn in as a justice of the court and swore his allegiance to the Confederacy. He was a deacon in the Zion Church and was clerk of the Roaring River Association in 1857 and until his death in 1864.

Rachel Sebastian was postmistress of Haymeadow Postoffice in 1866.

Lewis and Rachel had the following children: (1) Elizabeth Emily, born 1835, died March 12, 1915, married Francis Hutchison, born 1831, died 1862 in the hospital in Goldsboro during the Civil War. He was the son of Jacob H. Hutchison. After his death, Emily lived in Alleghany County and is buried at Woodruff Baptist Church. (2) Henry C., born 1839, died 1921, married Maro Hall, born 1850, died 1895, daughter of John Hall. Henry C. served in the Confederate Army as a sergant. He served as a Justice of the Peace and was Register of Deeds of Wilkes County from 1882 to 1888. He was called "Doc" by his relatives and friends. He is buried at Zion Baptist Church and Maro is buried behind his parents old homeplace in Haymeadow. They had a son, Robert. (3) William Gray, born 1839, died 1916, married 1866, Franky Shumate, born 1851, died 1925. William Gray served in the Confederate Army during the Civil War. He and Franky lived in the Mulberry community. They had ten children. (4) Martin H., born 1841, served in the Confederate Army. After the war he went west and was never heard from again. (5) Susan, born 1842, died 1900, married 1858, John W. Harrold and lived at Haymeadow. They had children, Billy and Wadie. (6) Charles F. born 1845, died 1864 in the Civil War, married 1864 Louisa

Harrold, a sister to John M. He was killed one week after his marriage. He is buried in the family cemetery. (7) Alexander P., born 1847, died 1854, buried in the family cemetery. (8) Samuel, born 1852, died June 13, 1901, married February 1872 Mary Blackburn, born December 5, 1853, died March 4, 1913, a daughter of Spencer and Elvira Wiles Blackburn. Samuel and Mary lived at the foot of Round Mountain three miles east of Hays, N.C. on Round Mountain Branch. They had twelve children. Both are buried at Rock Creek Baptist Church cemetery.

Sources: Bible Records, family members, church records and Wilkes County records.

— Samuel E. Sebastian

SAMUEL SEBASTIAN

971

Samuel Sebastian was born at Haymeadow, Wilkes County in 1852, died June 13, 1901, married February, 1872 to Mary Blackburn, born December 5, 1853, died March 4, 1913. Mary was the daughter of Spencer and Elvira Wiles Blackburn. Samuel and Mary lived in the Rock Creek area at the foot of Round Mountain, three miles east of Hays, N.C. On their 354 acres of land they grew wheat, corn, rye and oats. He grew a lot of wheat which he had milled into flour. He hauled the flour to Alleghany County and sold it for 90 cents per barrel. His house became too small for his growing family. In 1891-92 he build a two-story house on a hill above their present one. The new house had 8 rooms, a large back porch and a large portico on the front. The bricks were made in the bottom on the farm, now the No. 1 fairway of the Rock Creek County Club golf course. Carpenters were paid 25 cents per day and the foreman was paid 50 cents per day. Total cost of the house was $1,400. It was moderately remodeled in 1943 by their son, Eli, who raised his family there and lived there until his death. The house is now occupied by Lisa Sebastian Cheek and her husband, Michael. Lisa is the daughter of Fred Sebastian, present owner of the place (Rock Creek Country Club Golf Course).

Samuel and Mary were members of Round Mountain Baptist Church. They were very religious and were active in Christian work. In 1901 Samuel died in a tragic accident. He was kicked by a mule he was working and died shortly afterward. Mary died of the measles at her home in 1913. Both are buried at Rock Creek Baptist Church east of Hays, N.C. Their children were:

(1) Janie, born December 23, 1872; died 1964, married Morgan Gentry and lived in Surry County. Morgan was a brickmason and farmer. Their children were: Ike, Charlie, Hessie, Gertha and Annie Pearl.

(2) Mary Ann, born December 22, 1874, died February 24, 1973, married Charlie Haynes in 1923. They lived at Welcome, N.C. Mary worked before her marriage at the P.H. Haynes Knitting Company in Winston-Salem. Charlie was a maintenance superintendent for the Southern Railway. No children.

(3) Charles A., born September 11, 1876,

Samuel L. Sebastian.

Mary Blackburn Sebastian.

died January 10, 1966, married 1906 to Etta Holbrook, daughter of J.P. Holbrook of Traphill. Charles was a merchant and salesman. He had a store at Burch, below Elkin, N.C. and later a furniture store in High Point, N.C. They were members of the First Baptist Church in High Point. Their children were: Vern, Nellie, Nannie Bee, Hazel, Byerly, Lorraine, Ronda and Bettie Sue.

(4) Matilda was born March 8, 1878, died September 9, 1949 in Waco, Texas, married James Greenwood in 1903. They lived at Roaring River where James ran a roller mill, made flour and corn meal. After James' death Matilda moved with her children to Texas. Their children were: Lottie, Moneta, Mary Nell, Lenna, Clifford and Dorothy.

(5) Nancy Naoma was born February 26, 1880, died in 1951. She married William F. Alexander in 1912. Their children were: Alda, Lenna, and Edgar. William F. and Nancy Naoma are buried at Haymeadow Baptist Church.

(6) Aldoria, born October 15, 1881, died in 1945 in Washington, D.C. She married Clay Darnell in 1901. They had a general store at State Road, N.C. They later moved to Washington, D.C. Their children were: Mable, Beulah, Hugh, Glenn, Paul, Bessie, Basil, Edgar and Emoline.

(7) Stella Eva was born September 10, 1883, died in 1975. She married James A. Gilliam, son of Paten and Sarah Wiles Gilliam. James taught school and later was a rural mail carrier until his retirement. They lived near Hays, N.C. James (Jim) was active in the Baptist Churches. James and Eva are buried at Mount Lawn Cemetery north of North Wilkesboro. Their children were: Erie, Roy, Gwyn, Harlan, Pansy, Arlie, Jessie, Mildred and Ruby.

(8) James C., was born May 26, 1885, died in 1934. He married Bertha Holbrook in 1912. Bertha was born in 1895, died 1978 and was the daughter of Winfrey and Mary Ann Caudill. James and Bertha lived in Winston-Salem, N.C. James is buried at Rock Creek Baptist Church east of Hays, N.C. Their children were: John, Nell, Beatrice, Claude, James, Jr., and Archie.

(9) Eli Lewis was born January 23, 1887,

died November 12, 1971; married Ellen Myers in 1908. Ellen was born January 7, 1887, died February 25, 1970. She was the daughter of George E. and Mary Staley Myers. Eli and Ellen lived on the old Samuel Sebastian farm, three miles east of Hays, N.C. Their children were: Pearl, Clarence, Samuel E., Mary Clair, Alta, Arvona, William Clay and Johnnie Mae. Eli and Ellen are buried in Mount Lawn cemetery north of North Wilkesboro.

(10) U.S. Grant was born in 1889 and died in 1890. (11) Martin Luther was born April 4, died October 4, 1977. He married a Phillips first and second, Dee Mae Bowman. They lived in Phoenix, Arizona. (12) Vallie, born May 5, 1898 married B.T. Long and later divorced him. She retired from P.H. Hanes Knitting Company and lives in Winston-Salem. She had no children.

Sources: Family members, Bible records, Wilkes County records.

— Samuel E. Sebastian

DOCTOR FRANKLIN SHEPHERD

972

Doctor Franklin Shepherd, the second son of Issac and Amanda Stikeleather Shepherd, was born May 1, 1869, in Ashe County.

When Doctor (Dock) was about three years of age, the Shepherd family moved to the Lewis Fork Community in Wilkes County.

He grew up working on the family owned farm. At an early age he walked from Wilkes County to Huntington, West Virginia, to work in the coal mines. With the earnings from his labor, he purchased a farm in the Lewis Fork community.

On December 19, 1897, Doctor Franklin Shepherd married Lou Phenia Triplett. In 1900 to this union was born a son Coy Lee, who died at 18 years of age in 1918.

After the death of his son, he and his wife moved to the state of Washington, where he worked in the lumber industry. Some years later he returned to his Lewis Fork home where he was engaged in lumber business.

Dock was active in community church, po-

litical and civic activities. He served as a deacon, Sunday School superintendent, Sunday School teacher, and as a lay counselor for those who needed a friend.

He served as the Master of Mt. Pleasant Masonic Lodge #573 A.F. and A.M. He was active in Masonry and church affairs until death.

In 1929, he was appointed to the Wilkes County Board of Education. At the time of his appointment there were approximately 120 schools in the county. Due to his influence, leadership, and support of education; consolidation was begun and continued throughout his entire tenure as a member of the board. He voluntarily relinquished his seat as a member of the board in 1951. As a member of the board, his intentions were to provide better education for every child in Wilkes County. He thought in terms of the overall school system. His intense desire was to leave Wilkes County educationally better than he found it.

Having no children of his own and by having an interest in children, he adopted a niece, Etta Lee Triplett. Through his influence and support Etta Lee was educated at W.C., U.N.C., and A.S.U. and became a teacher in the Wilkes County school system. She married John V. Idol, also a teacher, who became principal of Millers Creek High School, District Principal of Millers Creek Schools, District Principal of West Wilkes Schools, Assitant County Superintendent, Vice President For Student Affairs at Wilkes Community College. John was elected by the citizens of Wilkes County to the Wilkes County Board of Education and is serving in that capacity at the present time. Together Etta Lee and John have contributed 72 years to education.

John and Etta Lee are the parents of two children, John Franklin Idol and Sharon Idol Oxford. John Franklin Idol earned a B.S. degree from E.T.U. and an M.A. from U.N.C. at Greensboro and works as a vocational rehabilatin counselor in Rockingham County. Sharon Oxford earned a B.S. from U.T. at Knoxville and an M.A. from Utah University at Salt Lake. She now works as an associate Home Extension agent in Wilkes County, working chiefly with 4-H boys and girls.

Dock Shepherd's influence on the Idols as well as the lives of others he touched, will continue in Wilkes County and far beyond throughout the ages.

— Etta Lee Idol

THOMAS SHEPHERD, SR.

973

Samuel C. Shepherd, Sr., was born 29 Jul 1918, in Haywood County, N.C., to Calvin Greenberry and Cora M. (Evans) Shepherd of Macon County. They were married 5 Dec, 1915.

Calvin Greenberry was killed by a state highway accident on 21 Sept, 1925, in Macon Co., leaving a wife and three small children. Although he had been a farmer, at the time of his untimely death, Calvin was working for the North Carolina Highway Department. He was buried in the Cowee Baptist Church Cemetery near the church where he had been an active participant. His widow reared their children, Samuel, Edna, and Dora, during the Great Depression and is now 94 years of age. For years she lived in Alexandria, Virginia, with her son and his family. She now resides with a daughter, Mrs. Frank Dirr, in Cincinnati, Ohio.

Cora M. (Evans) Shepherd is a daughter of William R. and Louisa (Roper) Evans of Macon Co., who were married 10 Mar, 1889, granddaughter of Jackson and Amanda (Rowland) Evans, married 24 Nov, 1853, and great granddaughter of Zachriah and Mary (?) Evans, all of Macon County.

Calvin Greenberry Shepherd was born 5 Feb, 1878, son of Josuah and Mary (Payne) Shepherd, who were married in Macon Co. in Sep, 1870. His brother and sister were Samuel, who married Jossie Galloway, and Julie, who married Jossie's brother, William. Josuah was a farmer and a member of the Liberty Baptist Church.

Parents of Josuah were Calvin Grandison and Pheraby (Ammons) Shepherd who were married 9 Aug, 1849, in Macon Co. Their other children were John R., Gracey E., Martha, Henry B., Nancy, Adaline, Sallie, Mary, Martha, and Legia. Calvin Grandison was first married to Sarah Bryson, being married on 12 Jan, 1847. They had one son, James Thomas.

In 1868, Calvin Grandison Shepherd was a member of a committee appointed by the Cowee Baptist Church to supervise financing and constructing a new church building, the original structure having been builg ca. 1830.

Thomas E. Shepherd, Jr., of Buncombe County and Narcissa Welch, daughter of Doc and ? Welch of Rutherford County, were married in 1824. Thomas and his Dad purchased land together in Buncombe County in 1810-1823, and both were farmers in that county. Children of Thomas and Narcissa were: Calvin Grandison; Emiline who married James Bryson; Nancy; Martha Ann, who married Martin Dehart; Arzela, who married Riley D. Rickman; Tyrica, who married ? Raby; and Henry C.

This Shepherd family was one of the original families to settle in the Cowee Valley of Macon County, N.C.

Thomas Shepherd, Sr., was born 3 Oct, 1761, and it is believed that he was in Wilkes County in 1790, being listed in the U.S. Federal Census as head of a household in the Morgan District, 13th Company. Between 1790 and 1800, he migrated to Buncombe Co. and later to Macon Co. where he became a successful farmer. It must be assumed his wife was deceased at the time he wrote his Last Will and Testament, 22 Apr, 1841, in which the following children were listed: Joseph; Elijah; Thomas E., Jr.' William; Nancy; John; and Elizabeth.

There is an old family Bible in the Cowee Valley which indicates it belonged to a Scotsman named Thomas Shepherd who arrived in this country in 1767. It is not now known where he landed.

Thomas Shepherd, Sr., died 1 Aug, 1842, in Macon County, North Carolina, and is buried in the Shepherd Memorial Cemetery as are many of his descendants.

Sources: Macon County Courthouse records, 1790 U.S. Census, N.C. Archives, Raleigh, N.C., and family memories.

— Dawn Hampton Shepherd

SARAH MARTHA VANNOY NOOE SHIELDS

974

Born on July 18, 1835 in Wilkes County, Sarah Martha Vannoy was the daughter of Joel and Lemira Sudderth Vannoy. She was married in 1857 to John Nooe, also of Wilkes. He died in 1873, leaving five children who were:

Julia Texanna Nooe (1863-1934) married Junius T. Gardner of Shelby, N.C. Their children were Margaret Pearl Gardner (1885-?) who married Joseph Graham Morrison of near Lincolnton; Junius T. Gardner (1886-1946); Louis Williams Gardner (1892-1965); John Nooe Gardner (1896-1967); and Helen Gardner (?-?) who married T. Bright Carrick of Shelby.

Robert Edward Nooe (1865) resided in Statesville, N.C., wife's name unknown, and his children were Sarah McKee Nooe, a former biology professor at Queens College in Charlotte; Katherine Vannoy Nooe, who married W. Bonner Knox and taught at Mitchell College in Statesville; and Robert Sharpe Nooe who married Evelyn Little.

Sarah M. Nooe (1867-1919) was married to Johnston Davis McCall, an attorney and former mayor of Charlotte. They were the parents of five children: Prentiss Horace McCall of Charlotte; Fred Bayes McCall of Chapel Hill; Johnston Vannoy McCall of Chevy Chase, M.D.; Robert Nooe McCall of Charlotte; and Isabelle McCall who married C.J. Christianson of Charlotte.

Martha Allie Nooe (1869-1951), a teacher in the Charlotte school system for many years. John Francis Nooe (1871) a physician in Texas.

Sometime between 1873 and 1975, place unknown but probably Burke County, Sarah Martha Vannoy Nooe married Joseph Preston Shields, a native of Virginia. They lived in Rutherford College (Burke County), N.C. and were the parents of two children. The were:

Josie E. Shields (1875-1957) married Edward G. Wiseman of Ingalls, N.C. and they were the parents of twelve children. Those who lived to be grown were: Earle Vannoy Wiseman (1895-1982), a surgeon in Greencastle, Indiana who married Helen Townsend and had one child; Carl James Wiseman (1897-1967) married Rebecca Louise Harmon; Ruth Wilma Wiseman (1899-?) married Wood Hall, lived in Chicago, and had four children; Scott Greene Wiseman (1909-1981) married Myrtle (Lula Belle) Cooper and they were the parents of two children (Lula Belle and Scotty were nationally-known country music stars in Chicago); Linda Inez Wiseman (1910-?) married John F. Leonard, parents of three children and lived in Chicago; Howard Knox Wiseman (1914-1967) was married to Buena I. (Susie) Wiseman; Glenn Wiseman (1917-?) who married Frances Murphy; and Fred Louis Wiseman (1910-1960). Many of the Wiseman descendants still live in Avery and Mitchell counties.

David R. Shields (1880-1947) was married to Carrie Lee Crowell of Rowan County. He traveled for a metalworking firm in Richmond, Virginia for many years before his death. Three of their five children reached adulthood and are: Carmine Shields (1902-living) was married to J.R. Satterfield, lives in Clayton, N.C. and had four children. David R. Shields, Jr. (1903-1938) married Grace Freeman and had one daughter. Rebekah Lee Shields (1908-living) married Cecil E. Bell and they were the parents of two children. Mrs. Shields and Mrs. Bell live in Raleigh.

Sarah M. Nooe Shields died in Charlotte on February 12, 1905 at the age of 70 and is buried at Elmwood Cemetery in Charlotte.

Sources: Bible records, grave markers, census records, family records, Wilkes County records.

— Virginia Lee Satterfield

HARRISON ILTER and ELIZABETH ANN McNEILL SHOEMAKER

975

My father, Harrison Ilter Shoemaker, was born July 13, 1879 in the Stony Fork Community of Wilkes County. His parents were John Abner Shoemaker and Mary Walker Shoemaker. The family lived in the area until Dad was a young. man, at which time they moved to the Lewis Fork Community where grandpa was a merchant in the general merchandise business. Dad worked for him until 1905 when he moved to the Congo Community and started a business for himself. He was well educated for the time in which he grew up, having taken advantage of all the schooling available. He was also a surveyor and magistrate. I can remember well how he would hear cases in our home.

At the age of 28, Dad met my mother, Elizabeth Ann McNeill, daughter of James Oliver and Sarah Ann Stout McNeil, who lived in the Mount Pleasant Community. They were married December 22, 1907.

Mamma was born October 17, 1885. She attended school at the Hubbard Mill School. Her first teacher was Bob Proffit, who later became her brother-in-law. Her second teacher was Grant Foster and third and fourth was Roan Billings and Philo Hall. She later went ot Dix's Hollar School where her teacher was Hayes Foster and Florence Vannoy. The Mt. Pleasant Academy was built around 1905. Dr. Romillis Triplette and Alice Hamby were the first teachers. Mama finished the 7th grade at the academy which was as high as they taught. My grandfather, Oliver, was one of the organizers of Mount Pleasant Baptist Church in 1879. My parents were members of this church and attended regularly.

After their marriage they continued to live in the Congo section. Dad built a new home with a store connected and Mamma helped him both in the store and with the farm. While living there they became parents to nine children: Fred, Novella, James Ray, Tam Lee, Charles Hugh, Ralph Dennis, Lutrelle, Clyde Warren and Ursulla (Sue). Economic conditions were very hard after the third child, so Dad decided to go west for work on the railroad where he could earn enough to pay for their home and any debts they had. He stayed in Wyoming for 2 years. While he was away, Mamma looked after the family by sewing, housekeeping, farming and store-keeping. Martha Hall stayed in the home for awhile to help and, after her, Mary Shoemaker Parsons. Millard Eller would do the plowing with a team of mules and sometimes Mamma would hire someone to help with the heavy field work. Often, she would do the harrowing with the team herself, rather than get someone.

After Dad returned home things were still not easy but there weren't any debts and we always had plenty of food to eat. We were always blessed with guests. Mamma never seemed to mind as she grew up in a home that was like a hotel and where people were always welcome. She never cooked less than a peck of potatoes, a peck of beans, and several cakes of cornbread. Also, we consumed about 2 pounds of butter and 2 gallons of milk at each meal.

Dad's health became bad about 1942 and he could no longer care for the farm. He died in 1947. Mamma continued to live in the Congo Community until 1951, at which time she moved back to Mount Pleasant near her old home place. She is now 96 years of age. There is only one other member of her family living, a brother, J.C. McNeil, who lives near by at the old home place.

Mamma is no longer able to attend church but stays interested and listens every Sunday to Kyle Hayes teach the Sunday School lesson on radio. Her church also tapes each Sunday worship service and brings it to her. She reads the Bible daily, having read it through 12 times. A good friend and neighbor, Melba Eller, began bringing books to her from the church library and later from the public library, not to mention books given to her by family members. In 1980 Melba thought it would be interesting to keep a record of title, authors, etc. of the books she read. To date she has read over 300 books. She reads with the aid of an electric magnifying glass as she has very poor sight. She has only one good eye and the sight in the other is very poor. She also passes time by listening to records and tapes supplied by the North Carolina National Library Service for the Blind.

Our mother is a remakralbe person. She loves people and is an inspiration to talk with. Her love of God and her fellow men is evident now as it has been throughout her life.

Remaining at this time to love and honor her are 7 children, 8 in-laws, 11 grandchildren and 16 great grandchildren. We are grateful for her long life and the example she has set for us.

Sources: Personal knowledge given to me by my mother.

— Ursula (Sue) Shoemaker Eller

THE C.C. SIDDEN FAMILY
976

Chauncey Columbus Sidden, respected North Wilkesboro businessman, industrialist,

and county official, was born in Wilkes County June 4, 1896 and died at his home in N. Wilkesboro Sept. 19, 1971. He is survived by his wife, Mabel Joyce Holbrook (born 4-12-1900 in Wilkes Co.), daughter of John Tyre Holbrook (1867-1902) and Emma Arlena Holbrook (1873-1953). Both Mr. and Mrs. Holbrook were of old Wilkes County lineage — the former being the great-great-grandson of Randolph Holbrook, Jr. (died 1793 Wilkes Co.) and the latter the great-great-granddaughter of John Holbrook, Sr. (died ca. 1805). Mr. and Mrs. Sidden's children include: Nancy A., who married George J. Earp (their children: Charles J., Mary Joyce, Judy, Audrey A.); Blanche M., who married Claude H. Triplett (their children: Elizabeth M., Philip C.); Mabelle I., who married Johnny Higgins (their children: Ann H., Joelle); Tyre A., who married Audrey Whittington (their children: Tonya L.; Neil; Terrie, deceased); Emma Nelle, who married Harold V. Lloyd (their children: Harold A., Perry A.); Doris Sue, who married Rex Shumate (their children: Kimberly D., Cynthia S., Mark); Ruth E., deceased, had married Glenn Winters (one child: Donald); and Carl C., deceased in childhood.

Mr. Sidden commenced his career as a Wilkes County schoolteacher, but later entered the business world, where his interests proved extensive. He became a large landowner in the Traphill area, with some of his holdings now part of Stone Mt. State Park. He also began the Blue Eagle Bus Company of Winston-Salem which he owned and operated in the 1940s. He later founded the Model Chair Co. in North Wilkesboro, Sidden Furniture Company at another plant (at the sight now occupied in North Wilkesboro by the Wilkes Vocational Center), and was the owner of a lumber manufacturing business at another facility he constructed in North Wilkesboro. He also engaged in an array of smaller ventures and was a Mason at the Traphill Masonic Lodge and a life deacon at Traphill's Old Roaring River Baptist Church, as well as a Wilkes County Commissioner from 1938-1940 and from 1944-1950 and Wilkes Co. Register of Deeds for eight years.

Mr. Sidden ("C.C." to his friends) possessed a keen intellect, a large moral sense, an equally sense of humor, and the unswerving disposition to work long and hard toward the goals he set for himself. He presented an impressive figure to all those who knew him.

Mr. Sidden's father, Abraham Sidden (1864-1947), a farmer in Wilkes Co., was the son of Richard Sidden (1828-1925) who appeared in Wilkes County in the 1850s. Mr. Sidden's mother, Nancy Susanna Yale, possessed a colorful and impressive heritage. Her mother, Frances Spicer (1843-1900) was an eighth generation American whose first American ancestor, William Spicer (born ca. 1615 in England) settled in Northumberland County, Va., ca. 1650. Nancy's great-grandfather, Wm. Spicer, Sr. (1754-184-), fought in the Indian Wars of the 1770s and also at the Battle of the Kings Mt. Nancy's grandfather, Valet Tyre Yale (1806-1892), came to Wilkes Co. as a farmer and school teacher from Wallingford, Conn., the son of Joseph Yale (1770-1841)

and Lois Hitchcock. Valet was a seventh generation American, whose first American Ancestor was Capt. Thomas Yale (born 1600s at Chester, England) who settled at New Haven, Conn. in the 1630s.

Thomas was an uncle of the immensely-wealthy Gov. Elihu Yale of Madras, India, the namesake of Yale University and is mentioned in Gov. Yale's will. Thomas Yale was also the stepson of the first governor of New Haven, Theophilus Eaton. Thomas wife, Mary, was the daughter of the interesting Capt. Nathaniel Turner, an explorer of the Connecticut region, who was lost at sea in 1646, and Thomas' mother, Anne Lloyd Yale Eaton (born 1500s in England and married the future Gov. Eaton after the death of Thomas's father, Thomas, Sr., in 1619 at Chester, England) was the daughter of George Lloyd (1560-1615), the Anglican Bishop of Chester. Thomas Yale of New Haven's grandfather, Dr. David Yale (died ca. 1626), the Chancellor of Chester, was also a prominent and wealthy man in that city.

Sources: Family Material; U.S. Census Data; *The Yale Family*, 1850, by Elihu Yale; Bulletin of the Stanford Genealogical Society, April 1961; *Hobbies Magazine*, Feb. 1956; The biography of Elihu Yale; The Spicer Family History and Ida Holbrook Jones papers.

— Harold Anthony Lloyd

THE J. ARNOLD SIMPSON FAMILY
977

My dad, Judge Arnold Simpson was born Sept. 26, 1928 in Union Co., NC to Judge Ellis and Rena Ann Little Simpson. He attended New Salem High School and graduated from N.C. State College in Raleigh in 1951. After graduation, he entered the United States Army where he was assigned to the Counter Intelligence Corp. After training in Maryland, he served in Germany for two yeras.

While stationed in Germany, he traveled to many different countries and attended the Queen's Coronation in England. He returned to Union County after service where he purchased a farm.

On Dec. 26, 1954, he married my mother, Nancy Ruth Williams. She is the daughter of Glenn and Frankie Jones Williams. She was born July 13, 1931.

She attended Wilkesboro High School and graduated from Woman's College of the Univ. of NC in Greensboro where she majored in home economics. Following graduation she taught home economics, then worked as a Home Service Advisor for Duke Power Co. in Charlotte.

My brother, Glenn, was born May 8, 1959. He attended Wilkes Central High School where he was active in the band. He was also a member of our church choir and active in the youth group at church. In the scouting program he earned the Eagle Scout Award. While at Davidson College, he was active in the Wind Ensemble and Pep Band, was director of the latter his senior year and was a member of the Kappa Alpha Fraternity. He graduated in May of 1981 and entered the MBA program at UNC at Chapel Hill. He will graduate from this program in 1983.

The Arnold Simpson family.

Nancy Rebecca was born on May 8, 1961 in Charlotte Memorial Hospital. I also attended Wilkes Central and was active in the band. My senior year, I was one of the Drum Major's for this band. I, too, was active in our youth group at church and enjoyed being a member of the Interact Club. After graduation, I entered Queen's College as one of their Presidential Scholars. This has been a very rewarding and challenging experience for me. Last year I was exceptionally fortunate, and was the recepient of the Saint Andrews Scholarship Award for a year's study in Scotland. I have spent my Junior year at the Univ. of Aberdeen in Aberdeen, Scotland.

This has been a most exciting and interesting year and one that I have loved every minute of. I have been able to travel a great deal in Great Britain, Israel and in Europe. I am looking forward to returning to Queen's College and my friends there for my senior year.

We moved from our farm in Union Co. to Asheville, NC where my dad was President of the Federal Land Bank Association of Asheville. We moved from Asheville to Wilkes County in 1971 when Dad opened his own real estate business.

We live on the Kerr Scott Reservoir and especially enjoy boating, skiing and picnicing on the lake. The lake is beautiful with its wooded shore line as it nestles in the valley on the Yadkin River above Wilkesboro. However, I'm sure my mother misses the beautiful farm land that she loved so much in her childhood.

My family has been active in church, civic and community affairs. Activities include being president of the Lion's Club, Board of Realtors, Home builders and Band Boosters. Dad is also a Shriner. My mother is busy also and is a member of the Home Economics Club, a book club, Symphony Guild, Art Guild, American Association of Univ. Women and Wilkes Genealogy Society. She is the editor of the WGS Bulletin.

We enjoy doing many family activities together and are a close family group. We are members of the North Wilkesboro Presbyterian Church where Dad has served as Deacon.

We all agree Wilkes County is an especially great place to live!!

Sources: Personal knowledge.

— Rebecca Simpson

CHAS. A. and LELIA J. SINK
978

Sink is the anglicized form of the German name Zink. The Zinks of Europe tended to cluster in an area around the upper reaches of the Danube River. The heaviest concentration of them centered in the states of Baden-Wintembury and Bavaria, now lying in the West German Republic.

Coming from Europe two Zink or Sink brothers and "Big John," settled on the Brushy Fork and Rich Fork branches of Abbotts Creek which was then in Rowan, now Davidson, County. Jacob acquired 300 acres of land there on 27 June 1763.

A great-great-great grandson of Jacob, Charles Augustus Sink was born in Waughtown, now part of Winston-Salem on 12 August 1865 to William Lafayette Sink, born 5 October 1834, died 25 February 1925 and married on 14 June 1859 Susan A. Glasscock, born 15 December 1835 and died 23 July 1903.

On 27 December 1888 at Panther Creek, N.C., Charles A. Sink married Lelia Augusta Jones who was born on 27 February 1870 to Preston C. and Martha Ellen Hauser Jones. A son, Charles Shelton, was born to them on 18 November 1889.

In April 1891, C.A. Sink moved his family to North Wilkesboro where he had previously been engaged in the lumber business with other family members including his father and father-in-law. The Cleveland Panic of 1893 caused this business to be unprofitable.

On 15 May 1893, he received a government appointment in the postal railway service. For two years he worked in the Salisbury-Norwood

Chas. A. and Lelia J. Sink.

Railway Post Office. He then transferred to the Greensboro-North Wilkesboro run. During this time the family lived in Norwood, Winston and Salem. They then moved again to North Wilkesboro. In 1906 they moved into the large house at the top of Sixth Street, a house which no longer stands.

In August 1927, C.A. Sink retired from the postal mail service where his North Wilkesboro to Greensboro run had lasted for thirty-two years. On this run he traveled many, many miles.

Formal schooling at the time he grew up was quite unlike graded schools of today, but he was an inveterate reader and an excellent speller. Shortly before his death he was able to repeat line after line of Shakespeare from memory.

He knew by name and loved an endless number of flowers, shrubs and trees, and liked nothing better than to work in his yard after retirement.

He was a member of the First Baptist Church of North Wilkesboro where he served on the Board of Deacons, and was an honorary deacon at the time of his death. He taught the Men's Bible Class and sang in the choir for years. When he sang in the choir, he embarrassed the family by appearing to be asleep during the service, but when accused of this, he never failed to tell the details of the minister's sermon.

Today, Lelia J. Sink, his wife, would qualify as a crafts person for she liked to sew, make quilts, bedspreads and to crochet.

She liked persons, young and old. It has been told that long before the days of "trick or treat" she treated Halloween pranksters to pumpkin pie so that her premises were left intact.

She enjoyed parties and loved to square dance. Having "company" in their home was a great pleasure to her, and as a small child, I remember an endless number of visitors who included aunts, uncles, cousins and friends. It seemed to me at that time that she must have been related to everyone!

She also helped a number of young persons to further their education and reared in their home a foster daughter who is now Mrs. E.S. Cooper.

She died on 26 March 1935. C.A. Sink died on 16 April 1953, leaving as his descendants, a son, two grandchildren and two great-grandchildren. Since that time two other great-grandchildren have been added to the family.

Sources: Papers of John E. Sink, Wilkes Journal, Bible records, Rowan County Deed Books, the Chronicle, personal knowledge.

— Mary Sink Smithey

The C. A. Sink home.

DR. and MRS. C.S. SINK
979

One of the last of Wilkes County's "Horse and buggy doctors," Charles Shelton Sink was not born here, but came to live here early in his life.

Born in Yadkin County on 18 November 1899 to Charles A. and Lelia Jones Sink, "Shelly," as he was known to family and friends, was educated in private schools, including Salem Boys School. He graduated from N.C. Medical College in 1912. Since internship was not required by law at that time, he began the general practice of medicine in North Wilkesboro soon after passing the State Board of Examiners.

He traveled by horse-back and buggy in the early years. Perhaps he was never as proud of any automobile he owned as he was of his Kentucky Horse, "Polly," who carried him many miles in all kinds of weather to visit the sick. After he purchased a car, travel was still difficult because country roads left much to be desired.

Early in practice, he and Dr. W.P. Horton were doctors for the workers on the Watauga and Yadkin River Railroad being built in Grandin. His experiences in the railroad camp gave rise to some of the "tall tales" he later told.

It may be difficult to believe, but during the first years he practiced, he was paid fifty cents for an office visit, one dollar for a house visit, and the princely sum of ten dollars for delivering a baby. This he did not always receive in cash for payment was often made in firewood, apples, potatoes, chickens, ducks, canned goods and an occasional ham. Once he received a black and white cow with horns!

On 15 May 1915, he married Agnes Mae Walter, daughter of Charles Preston and Carrie Hovermale Walter. Two children were born to them: Mary Lelia, writer of this article, born 1 May 1916, and Charles Shelton, Jr., born 13 April 1920.

As children we were quite accustomed to our father's irregular hours for the telephone and door-bell at our home rang with little regard for the time, day or night.

In order to see more of him, we accompanied him on calls to the country as often as we could. Many times, our Mother would accompany us, and we would have fun singing together all the way to our destination and back.

When Dr. F.C. Hubbard opened his hospital in North Wilkesboro in 1923, he had the full support of my father who realized the need for a local hospital.

Having served as anesthetist for Dr. J.W. White at times, Dr. Sink became anesthetist for the Wilkes Hospital in addition to his general practice.

He served on the staff of the hospital until it closed and then on the staff of Wilkes General Hospital after it opened. He delivered the last baby to be born at Wilkes Hospital and the first to be born at Wilkes General Hospital.

He held offices in the Wilkes-Alleghany Medical Society and was a member of the N.C. Medical Society from which he received a fifty-year practice award in 1962. He was an early

Dr. C. S. Sink.

Mrs. C. S. Sink.

Dr. Sink on "Polly."

member of the then American Academy of General Practitioners.

He served on the Medical examining boards in both World Wars I and II. He also served in the Volunteer Medical Service Corps during the influenza epidemic of 1918.

He was an active member of the Masonic Order. He served as commissioner of the Town Board of North Wilkesboro. He was a member, and one-time deacon, of the First Baptist Church.

A stroke disabled him in February 1957, but with therapy he recovered enough to do limited office practice until the summer of 1966. He died 13 February 1968.

Agnes Sink, coming to North Wilkesboro at the age of five, attended local schools including Miss Mamie Barber's. She attended Salem College for a year as a day student and then Greensboro College as a "special student." In both colleges she studied voice, piano and organ. For a short time she gave music lessons, but after marriage, devoted her life to her family.

However, she found time for her musical interests. She sang in the Methodist and Baptist Church choirs; directed the First Baptist Choir for years; served for awhile as pianist for the Kiwanis Club and participated in musical events.

She was also active in the P.T.A. and belonged to several social clubs.

Out home was always open to our young friends, and she delighted to give parties for us.

Mary Lelia Sink married Charles Darwin Smithey on 10 June 1937. He died 8 April 1957. They had two children: Martha Walter, born 16 January 1948, who married Bobby Nichols on 20 June 1970, and Charles Herbert II, born 15 January 1955 who married Belinda Wassum on 19 March 1978. Martha Smithey and Bobby Nichols have two children: James Darwin born 27 May 1975 and Jonathan Shelton born 14 February 1980.

Charles Shelton Sink, Jr., married Corinne Faw on 25 March 1950 and they had two children: Charles Shelton III, born 6 May 1952 who married Janet Johnson 12 June 1976; David Preston born 30 March 1956 who married Anne Fulcher 19 July 1980. Charles Shelton Sink, Jr. died 12 May 1975.

Fortunately, the grand-children remember their grand-parents well, and they enjoy reminiscing about the good times they, too, had in their home.

The great grand-children have enjoyed the songs their great-grandmother, who died 26 September 1969, taught her own children.

Sources: Bible records and personal knowledge.

— Mary Sink Smithey

DAVID B. SMITH
980

David B. Smith, son of Robert Martin Smith and his first wife, Chariety E. Edwards was born May 24, 1856, in Wilkes County. He died in California, but was living in Hawaii.

David B. Smith was well educated and became very wealthy as a sugar planter. He was living with his father, R.M. Smith, and his stepmother in 1870. He was 14 years of age.

After receiving his education at home, David B. attended New York Medical College where he graduated and began practice in Texas. After several years spent there, he moved with his wife to Indian Territory, where he engaged in mercantile pursuits. There his wife died shortly after the birth of their daughter May or Mamie. She was eighteen years old at the time of her father's death, and attending school in California.

From the Indian Territory, David B. came west and lived in California for sometime for the benefit of his health. While in San Francisco, he determined whether he would go to Panama or Honolulu by flipping a coin. The coin chose Honolulu.

He established a toboggan railway in Honolulu, which was in its day one of the popular sports of the town. He was then engaged in the electric lighting business and finally established the Manufacturer's Shoe Company.

He died suddenly at the Occidental Hotel in California December 25, 1899. He was seated in a chair in his apartments, chatting with his daughter, when he died.

He was a wealthy retired merchant of Honolulu and a resident of the Hawaiian Islands for seventeen years.

He visited his half-brother, George M. Smith in N.C. on April 19, 1899. He was the grandson of Rev. Samuel P. Smith and the son of Robert Martin Smith of Wilkes County.

Sources: *The Pacific Commercial Advertiser,* Honolulu, Hawaii; Wilkes records.

— Jean Nichols Smith

JAMES PHILANDERS SMITH
981

James P. Smith was born June 13, 1904, son of James Robert and Hattie Elizabeth Morrison Smith of Wilkes County, N.C. He was born in Knoxville, Tennessee.

James P. joined the U.S. Navy seeking a new way of life. When he returned to Knoxville he married 25 February 1928, Nellie M. Goforth, daughter of George W. and Beulah E. Atchley Goforth. They lived with their parents for a year or so, then after the birth of their first child, James A., they moved to Dayton, Ohio. The young couple decided to move back to Tennessee and tried their luck with farming on numerous farms throughout Blount County by sharecropping.

James P. tried carpentry and became a very reputable contractor in the construction of homes. It was only natural for him to train his four eldest sons in this business.

James P. and Nellie had fourteen children, four of whom died in childhood: James Allen;

James P. and Nellie Goforth Smith.

Beulah Geneva Rowland; Raymond Charles; Kenneth Wayne; Gerald Davis; Rebecca Carolyn Green; Edward Lynn; Donald Richard; Patricia Faye Kanatzar; and Larry Dale Smith.

The children were born with a natural ability to sing and the three daughters played the piano by ear or sound, and specialized in gospel music. The two eldest daughters were at one time regular church pianists in their home churches and the three eldest sons were choir directors.

Sources: Personal knowledge.

— Jean Nichols Smith

JAMES ROBERT SMITH
982

James Robert Smith, son of Robert Martin and Mary J. Lyndon Smith, was born in Wilkes

James Robert and Hattie Morrison Smith.

County in 1878. His father died 6 July, 1882, and is buried in the Martin Family cemetery. After Robert M.'s death, Mary J. Lyndon Smith removed from Wilkes with her children to Knoxville, Tennessee. The children were: Charles; Henry L. who married Lorena B. Weaver 1 November, 1888; Samuel, born 1869; John, born 1872; Mary, born 1873, George, born 1876; and James Robert Smith, born 1878.

James Robert Smith married Hattie Elizabeth Morrison, daughter of Jesse and Melvina Fortner Morrison, October 21, 1899. James Robert died in 1904 of smallpox. He and Hattie had children: Pearl, born 1901, married Ed Mathis; Ruby, born 1902, married Ed Wallace; and James Pilander, born June 13, 1904, married Nellie Mae Goforth.

Hattie worked in Knoxville Woolen Mill as a weaver, while her sister cared for her three children. She soon married Dave Goodman and had a son, Emory Wilson Goodman. Dave Goodman then abandoned his family and Hattie died when Emory was only a few weeks old. Emory Wilson Goodman died when he was six. Hattie is buried in Knotts cemetery.

James Philander Smith, son of James Robert and Hattie, carried the Smith family names on in the family: Kenneth W., James Allen, Donald Richard, Larry Dale and Edward Lynn.

Sources: Library in Knoxville; census.

— Mrs. Kenneth Smith

JOHN ALEXANDER SMITH
983

John Smith (1849-1935) was the son of Louis Smith I and Mary Lowe Smith. He had three brothers and one sister: Dave (wife Betty Edsel); Louis II (wife Alice Edsel); Bill (wife Clementine Smith); Betty (husband Dolphus St. Clair).

He married Frances C. Kilby (1852-1922) in 1870, dau. of William and Frances Eddins Kilby. She had six brothers and three sisters: William Jr.; James; Humphrey; Reuben; Abraham; John; Elizabeth; Sarah and Mary.

John and Frances had nine children: Margaret (husband Cal Kerley, Alexander County); Coffey (wife Josie Joines, Pores Knob); Nancy (husband Caney Lowe, Pores Knob); Thomas (died young in a mine); Parks (wife Della, Johnston City, Tenn.); Richard (Lunda Shook, Banners Elk, NC); Henry (killed in mail train accident as young man); Anne (husband Joe Shook, Banners Elk, NC), Will (Ernestine Green, Johnson City).

After the death of his wife in the Banners Elk area, he made his home with his daughter Nancy and husband Caney Lowe in Pores Knob area. Hard work was his tonic. Mowing creek banks at the age of 86 was fun.

He could not hear if you talked normally, but if you whispered something to someone he would hear every word. He enjoyed sitting in the rocker and singing the old time favorite hymns. His favorite "There Is A Balm In Gilead."

A teasing and tenderhearted man, he never went to town without bringing back something

John Alexander Smith.

Jean and Ken Smith.

special (the same, but different shape or color) to his three great-granddaughters that lived next door; Nola, Grace and Zelma Broyhill. Some of these things today are treasures in our homes.

— Zelma Broyhill Helton

KENNETH WAYNE SMITH
984

Kenneth W. Smith, son of James P. and Nellie Goforth Smith, and descendant of Rev. Samuel P. Smith, Sr., of Wilkes County, N.C., was born April 10, 1938, in Blount County, Tennessee. He was an athlete and with family members, sang in gospel quartets. His was a close-knit family and he is still associated with a brother in business.

On May 4, 1957, Kenneth married Elizabeth Jean Nichols, daughter of James Rufus and Elizabeth Jean Morrison Nichols. They eloped to Lafayette, Georgia . . . They moved to California where Ken started working as a machinist in Long Beach. He was in ceramic tile and marble business. His brother was president of a development company and Ken sold out his shop and started to work for his brother. In 1979, the brothers formed Saddleback Associates, Inc.

Ken and Jean and their children are members of Capistrano Valley Baptist Church, with the exception of Jennifer.

Their children are: Ronald Craig, born 27 January, 1961; Steven Wayne was born 18 June, 1963, and will marry Kerri Lynn Jones in November 1982; Jennifer Lynn born 19 April, 1973.

After attending Saddleback College, Craig and Steven went to work for Saddleback Associates, Inc. Craig married Wendy Eliza-

beth Hall.

Sources: Personal knowledge.

— Mrs. Kenneth Smith

ROBERT MARTIN SMITH
985

Robert Martin Smith, the son of Samuel P. and Amelia Matilda Martin Smith, was born in Wilkes County April 14, 1831. He married Charity E. Edwards on October 21, 1852, and they had three children: Montgomery, born 1854, died April 26, 1856; David B., born May 24, 1856, died 1899 in California; Charity E., born December 1858. Charity E., wife of Robert, died January 20, 1859, and he married as his second wife, Mary J. Lyndon October 30, 1861. She was born in N.C. in 1842. They had children: Charles C., who married Annie Roberts in Knoxville, Tenn. December 1886, died in Ca.; Henry L., married Lorene B. Weaver in 1888, died in Tenn.; Samuel F., married Hilia Whittle and moved to the state of Washington; Mary E., lived in Knoxville with her mother and brother Henry and worked in the woolen mills there; George B. was an invalid; James Robert, born 1878, married Hattie E. Morrison.

Robert Martin Smith held many county offices and was the sheriff of Wilkes in 1861-1864. He was then clerk of Court 1866-1868. Robert Martin Smith died July 6, 1882, and is buried in the Martin Family cemetery. There are many land transactions for the Smiths in Wilkes, but too numerous to mention here.

Sources: Wilkes County records; research of Mrs. Marilyn Childress, Knoxville.

— Jean Nichols Smith

SAMUEL P. SMITH, SR.
986

Samuel P. Smith, Sr. was the son of Samuel Smith of Rowan County, N.C. where he was born in 1804. He married Amelia Matilda Mar-

tin, daughter of Robert, Esq., and Amelia Wright Martin, January 4, 1825. Robert Martin was a doctor in Wilkes and Clerk of Court in 1828. Amelia M. was born 1801. They had ten children: Amelia E., born 1827, who first married a Weber and second, a Jones; Diannah Lucinda Harrison who married W.S. Edwards; Sarah M., born 1830, who married Uriah Douthit; Robert Martin, born 1831, died 1882, who first married Charity E. Edwards and second Mary J. Lyndon. He had three children by Charity and seven by Mary, who moved to Knoxville with her children after the death of Robert Martin Smith; Susannah J.; Samuel P. Jr., born 1833; Mary D., born 1836; John Kerr, born 1838, died 1862; William H., born 1840; Olivia A., born 1843, married George H. Brown. Her husband removed to Iredell County where he was active in politics there.

Fishing Creek church, four miles east of Wilkesboro, was constituted as an arm of Brier Creek. It was "set off" to meet at Robert Martin's, Esq. The meetings were held for sometime in the Robert Martin home. Robert Martin was generous with the Smith family in the distribution of his property.

Rev. S.P. Smith was the pastor of Fishing Creek Church for 48 years. The church house stood as of 1960 near the old Robert Martin house. The Martin and Smith families are buried in the graveyard near the house.

Samuel P. Smith, Sr., was active in the Brier Creek Association, but left this Association during the excitement upon the mission and temperance question and formed the Taylorsville Association and became its moderator. He was the first missionary officially appointed to ride and preach in the Brier Creek Association.

In 1861 he was elected a member of the State Convention in opposition to secession. At the close of the war in 1865, he was chosen a member of the State convention to restore the State to the Union. He was elected to the Senate for the 39th District in 1868. On 5 March, 1873, he was appointed to fill the unexpired term of A.L. Marley who resigned as register of deeds and relected register of deeds in 1880. At Smithville High Academy, he deeded the academy building as a church, but it was used as a school until 1914.

It was written about him on 18 October, 1882, "It was also pleasant to witness the zeal of Brother S.P. Smith, now feeble with age, having spent nearly half a century in the ministry." Rev. Samuel P. Smith died in 1883.

Sources: N.C. Baptist Archives; Elkin's Assoc'n. Biblical Recorder; History of Brier Creek Association; *Land of Wilkes* by J.J. Hayes; Wilkes County records.

— Jean Nichols Smith

THE SMITHEY FAMILY
987

Robert Franklin Smithey and Bessie Eller were married December 21, 1904. To this couple was born ten boys: Otto, Roscoe, Alfonzo, Plato, Tedro, Briscoe, Wacoe, Genio, Leo, Essco and one daughter, Cleo.

My grandfather and grandmother were

wonderful people. They lived back in the reared four sons and six daughters. Clyde to support their children.

When I was a little girl, I loved to stay with my grandparents. I guess it was because my Aunt Cleo and I were close to the same age. I remember my grandmother's big wood stove in the kitchen and the big pans of biscuits she used to make. They were delicious.

My father, Walter Otto Smithey, the oldest child in the Smithey family, was born August 18, 1906. He died October 6, 1969. Otto Smithey and Clara Lavilla Johnson were married January 16, 1925. Clara is the daughter of John I. and Mamie Moore Johnson, also of the Brushy Mountain.

To Otto and Clara was born eleven children: Gladys, Ralph, Ruth, who is deceased, Worth, Willa Mae, Lucille, Wayne, Joyce, Clayton, Geraldine and Debra.

My Dad was a proud man, not because he had lots of money but because of his love for his family and because of our love for him. He taught us to be God-fearing, honest and trustworthy.

I remember how Daddy worked long hours just to get us the little extra things we wanted. And how Mama stood and washed cloths by hand on the wash board so we could go to school clean and neat as pins.

I remember the long table with the bench behind it so all of us could gather around the table at one time for our meals. The hugh wood stove in the kitchen and the large vessels of food she would prepare.

Even now we like to gather around the table in Mama's dining room to eat, and talk to each other about all the things that has been happening to us. About our dreams, hopes and even share our sorrows.

Before my Daddy died we were a very close family and still are. We meet every August to celebrate Daddy and Mama's birthdays which are close together — August 18 and August 14. Also we always have a family Christmas party. This has been a tradition that my father started long before he died. Besides that we always have a Smithey — Eller family reunion every year for the entire families.

Gladys has five children, nine grandchildren and one great grandson; Ralph has five children, seven grandchildren; Ruth (deceased) has one daughter, two grandchildren; Willa Mae has three children, one grandchild; Lucille has two children, four grandchildren; Wayne has three children; Joyce has two children Clayton has two children; Geraldine has no children at this time but she is a school teacher and teaches many children; Debra has two children.

There is five generations living now in the family: Clara Smithey, great-great grandmother; Gladys Anderson, great-grandmother; Angela Mastin Reavill, grandmother; Donald Mastin, father; and Christopher Mastin son.

For this family we are proud and ever so thankful.

Sources: family records, personal knowledge, memories.

— Gladys Anderson

Isaac and Sarah McLean Smithey.

ISAAC and SARAH ELIZABETH McLEAN SMITHEY
988

Isaac Smithey and his two brothers came from Ashe County to Wilkes county. Isaac first settled in the Cricket community near Millers Creek, N.C. where he met and married Sarah Elizabeth McLean. They then came to Wilkesboro, bought a farm and built a two story house on the Taylorsville road about a mile from Wilkesboro.

They had the following children . . .

Mack C. Smithey; Myrtle Freeland; Nickard B. Smithey; Jeanette Sherrill; Waney Shoaf; Britton; Vecie Smithey Call Poindexter; Ney Smithey Tomlinson.

Isaac Smithey sold his farm near Holly Farms and the Blue Ridge Shoe company, and he and his son N.B. Smithey bought the Wilkesboro Hotel, later named SMITHEY HOTEL.

Isaac Smithey operated one of the first meat, beef and produce stores in North Wilkesboro, N.C. He and his son N.B. had one of the first five and ten cents stores in this section of the state, located on "A" street, in North Wilkesboro.

Isaac died February 1914 and Sarah died May 1933.

Sources: Family records.

— Ney Tomlinson

NIKEARD BRUCE SMITHEY
989

Nikeard Bruce Smithey was born August 11, 1880 in Wilkesboro, North Carolina to Isaac and Elizabeth McLean Smithey. He had five sisters and two brothers. His sisters were Jeanette S. Sherill, Myrtle S. Freeland, Wanie Shoaf, Vecie Call Poindexter and Ney S. Tomlinson. His brothers were Mack and Brit Smithey. What schooling Mr. Smithey had was in a school located in the south edge of Wilkesboro, not far from his home.

His first venture in merchandising was selling fresh beef from a one-horse wagon with Parks Lenderman as his partner. He and his father opened a store in a frame building in Wilkesboro around 1908. The hotel across from the courthouse was built around 1890 by a group of citizens, but had encountered financial difficulties in operating so a receiver had been appointed for the hotel property. The receiver was trying to dispose of it when he was approached by a long and lanky young man (Mr. Smithey), who asked him what he wanted for the hotel. Mr. Welborn, the receiver, thinking him an unlikely prospect, asked "What difference does it make Nike, you could not buy it anyway." Mr. Smithey replied that he might buy it. Mr. Smithey bought the hotel in 1906 and took his bride there the same year.

Superior Court sessions were occasions for a gathering of people throughout the county. Mr. Smithey learned early that these courts were a good place to sell anything you had to sell.

Mr. Smithey and Welborn Minton were on their way to Catawba County County Court one Sunday, and had to cross the Catawba River on a ferry. They ended up at noon at the home of Cephas Little in Catawba County. As they approached the home, two of his daughters saw them coming and Hattie Little said to her sister, "There comes my sweetheart." The sister asked "Which one?" and Hattie said, "The tall one." After lunch the girls played the organ and Mr. Smithey and Mr. Minton spent the night there. They went on to court the next morning.

Nike and Hattie corresponded, resulting in their marriage in June 1906. Mr. Smithey took his bride to the hotel and they continued to live there until his death. He ran his merchandising business and Mrs. Smithey ran the hotel. They had two daughters born to their marriage. The first, Marie Smithey, married G.M. Kirkpatrick. The Kirkpatricks have one daughter, Elizabeth Kirkpatrick Arndt, who married George Arndt. The Arndt's have two children, Karen Arndt who married Daniel McClure and Tamra Arndt, unmarried at this time. On August 11, 1911 the second daughter, Margaret Smithey was born to Mr. and Mrs. Smithey on Mr. Smithey's thirty-first birthday. Margaret is married to Kyle Hayes and they do not have any children. The two girls are the only persons to have been born at the Smithey Hotel.

About 1925, Mr. Smithey started expanding his business, while Mrs. Smithey continued to operate the hotel. He was successful and so impressed the business school at Harvard, that they sent someone down to interview him. He had a little pamphlet printed on his method of doing business, which was to buy for cash and sell for cash. At his death on September 3, he had seventeen stores in operation. Many of his buildings he helped build with his own hands and many of them stand today as a monument to his building ability.

Many stories are told and most of them are true about his modesty. The only luxury he ever permitted himself, if it could be called a luxury, was to buy a new plain Ford automobile every year. When he bought a new one, it has been told that if it were not a rainy day, he would smear some mud on it himself or have someone else to do it so that the fact that he had a new car would not be noticed.

Another story told on him was about the salesman who came to Smithey Hotel on a Sunday night, registered, and asked for the bellboy to come and pick up his baggage. Mr. Smithey was the bellboy who went down and picked up his luggage. The man tipped the

Old Smithey hotel.

bellboy a quarter which Mr. Smithey took. The next morning the same salesman went to Smithey's Store to sell merchandise and found the bellboy to be the man who had taken his bags.

Another story is told of the salesman who came to the store wanting to see Mr. Smithey and was told that Mr. Smithey was not there, but was down at a new building site. The salesman went down and came back and said he did not find Mr. Smithey, that there was only one man down there laying rocks and had a boy waiting on him. The salesman was told that the man who was laying the rocks was Mr. Smithey.

He never took anything from his own stores for personal use, including Cokes, unless he put the money in the cash register for it.

He brought up his daughters to be good merchandisers. Marie managed the Taylorsville store and has continued to manage it. Margaret was her father's secretary and still is the secretary-treasurer of the corporations. It was his ambition that his stores continue to operate after he was gone. The girls, with the help of the employees and personnel, have continued to operate eleven of those stores.

Mrs. Smithey is still living and was 100 years old on the 5th of April, 1982. She devoted her life to running the hotel and entertaining the guests until she left the hotel for a home she built in North Wilkesboro, where she lived for approximately twenty years. She suffered a stroke and for the last seven years has been a patient at Wesley Nursing Home in Charlotte, North Carolina.

It has been said that behind every successful man is a great woman. This can truly be said of Mr. and Mrs. Smithey.

Sources: Personal knowledge.

— Kyle Hayes

DANIEL ELLIOTT SMOAK, SR.
990

D.E. Smoak was born in Orangeburg, South Carolina, on January 15, 1853. He was a direct descendant of Johann George Rauch who came to America from Germany in 1740. The name Rauch, which meant smoke in German, was changed first to Smoke and later to Smoak. D.E. Smoak's father was William Fredrick Smoak, born in 1830 and died in Charlottesville, Virginia, in June of 1864 as a

results of wounds suffered in a battle at Trevilian Station, Virginia, on June 12, 1864.

D.E. Smoak married Agnes R. Rickenbaker, also of Orangeburg, South Carolina, on February 15, 1977. The 1880 census for the Orangeburg District of South Carolina listed him as a merchant. He shortly thereafter moved to Winston-Salem, North Carolina, where he dealt in real estate. His interest in real estate brought him to Wilkes County in 1888.

He purchased many tracts of land on the south side of the Yadkin River in speculation that the Southern railroad would be built on that side of the river to Wilkesboro. Unfortunately for him, the Railroad Company, which had contracted to come within one mile of the Wilkes County Courthouse in Wilkesboro, brought the track up the north side of the river, stopping one mile from the Courthouse where North Wilkesboro is today.

His later years were spent as a merchant in North Wilkesboro, selling stoves, furniture, buggies and automobiles.

D.E. and Agnes Smoak had thirteen children, three of which died in infancy. The ten who lived are: Herbert Smoak (1877-1967) spent most of life in California; Alice Smoak Thompson (1879-1958) also lived in California; Norman O. Smoak (1885-1967) lived in Greensboro and Wilkesboro; Jessie Smoak Pharr (1887-1965) lived in Wilkesboro; Ethel Smoak Gainer (1889-1940) lived in Statesville, North Carolina; Nettie Smoak Dula (1891-1928) lived in Wilkesboro; Emma Smoak Greene (1892-1962) lived in Indiana; Edith Smoak Hemphill (1894-1972) lived in Wilkesboro and later in Franklin, North Carolina; Agnes Smoak Hart (1896-1973) lived in Wilkesboro; and Daniel E. Smoak, Jr. (1899-1948) lived in Wilkes County.

After bearing thirteen children, Agnes R. Smoak died on May 10, 1900. She is buried in the Wilkesboro Presbyterian Cemetery. On March 4, 1904, D.E. Smoak married Minnie Howell, a resident of the Boomer community in Wilkesboro. From this union two children were born, Minnie Smoak Vestal, a resident of Wilkesboro, and Eleanor Smoak Senarius of Toledo, Ohio.

D.E. Smoak died on April 10, 1934 and is buried in the Wilkesboro Cemetery.

Sources: Smoak Family Bible, Smoak Book by George A. Lefbendahl, 1880 Orangeburg, S.C. Census, and family records.

— Robert R. Smoak

NORMAN OSCAR SMOAK
991

Norman O. Smoak was born to Daniel E. Smoak and Agnes R. Smoak on September 2, 1885 in Winston-Salem, North Carolina. His parents moved to Wilkesboro, North Carolina in 1888, where he spent most of his life.

Norman Smoak was educated in the Public Schools of Wilkes County and received a business course at the Oak Ridge Academy in Guilford County. He worked, at an early age, at the Forest Furniture Company in North Wilkesboro, where his first position of responsibility was lumber inspector. He later was Postmaster at Wilkesboro, and for four years was general manager of the Keely Institute in Greensboro, North Carolina. In 1921 he returned to Wilkesboro to work again at the Forest Furniture Company. He later became president of that company, a position he held for thirty years until his retirement in 1955.

He held a number of positions of leadership in the community. These included membership on the Wilkesboro Town Board of Commissioners, Chairman of the Wilkesboro School Board, and many different positions in the Wilkesboro Methodist Church.

On May 10, 1916 Norman Smoak was married to Savannah Blevins, a lifelong resident of Wilkesboro and Wilkes County. From this marriage three sons and one daughter were born. They are: George Herbert Smoak is retired from the United States Air Force and a resident of Surfside Beach, South Carolina. He is married to the former Ruth Bumgarner and they have two sons. Sam Smoak, a Sergeant in the United States Army Air Force, was killed in action over Yugoslavia June 14, 1944. Norma Blevins Smoak is now married to A.R. Gray, Jr. and a resident of Wilkesboro. She has one daughter by a previous marriage. Robert Riggs Smoak is a resident of Wilkesboro and a vice president of Bernhardt Industries, Inc., Lenoir, North Carolina. He is married to the former Gordon Reins and they have three sons and one daughter.

Norman O. Smoak died on March 20, 1967 and is buried in the Wilkesboro Cemetery.

Sources: Smoak Family Bible, family records, and personal knowledge and memories.

Robert R. Smoak

JAMES CLINTON SMOOT
992

James Clinton Smoot was born in Alexandria, Virginia on September 29, 1857, son of Charles Calvert and Susan Anne Smoot. In 1895, he moved with his family to North Wilkesboro, N.C. to establish a branch of the C.C. Smoot & Sons Company Tannery which he operated until his death in 1922.

He was a direct descendant of an old Dutch family, which so far, has been traced back to 1500. The surname Smoot is derived from the old Holland name of Smoudt or Smout. The latter found numbered among the strong families of England. William Smoot, born in 1596, later moved to England, married, and then emigrated to America in 1645 where he settled in Maryland.

Early life of J. Clinton Smoot was spent in Alexandria, Virginia. The old family home still stands at 301 South St. Asaph Street and is sometimes referred to as the Lafayette House since the French General was entertained there at one time during Revolution.

In 1880, he became associated with C.C. Smoot & Sons, partnership, a tanning business which had been established in 1820 by Charles Calvert Smoot. The Company owned not only the Alexandria Tannery, but also one in Sperryville, Virginia, as well as other properties in Alexandria. On May 30, 1889, the Alexandria Tannery burned and the business suffered a great loss. On July 1, 1894, the business was incorporated under the name C.C. Smoot and Sons Company and in 1895, land was purchased in North Wilkesboro, N.C., where a complete tanning operation including an extract plant was to be built.

On October 5, 1881, J. Clinton Smoot married Frank Elizabeth Wood, daughter of Robert Lewis and Melissa Ann Hussey Wood, and granddaughter of Samuel Bancroft Hussey, a New England Sea Captain, Skipper of the Clipper Ship, "Westward Ho." (Alexandria was at one time one of the three largest seaports in America.) Her home, 617 South Washington Street, has since been razed. Children: Charles C. Smoot III; Sibyl (Mrs. Edward G. Finley); Frances (Mrs. Ralston M. Pound); and James Clinton Smoot, Jr. Mrs. Smoot died July 1, 1952 at the age of 92 in North Wilkesboro, where she had lived since the death of Mr. Smoot with her companion Miss Elizabeth (Lizzie) Hisle.

On moving to North Wilkesboro, he built a home along with other company officials in a residential area known as "Tanners Rest," now Smoot Park. The Tannery opened in North Wilkesboro March 4, 1897, and his daughter, Sibyl (Mrs. E.G. Finley) blew the whistle which announced the beginning of the operation. Her brother, Charles C. Smoot III, started the fire under the boiler. The Tannery at that time was a major industry in Wilkes County providing employment for many hundreds of people. Its whistle could be heard for miles around notifying the beginning and end of each work day. It also was used for fire warnings. The flood of 1916 caused a great amount of damage, but the Tannery was rebuilt and continued operating under the Smoot name until it was sold in 1925 to the International Shoe Company.

James Clinton Smoot was not only active in business, but also in civic life. He was the first President of the North Wilkesboro Building and Loan Association, a director of an insurance Company, and was a member of the First Methodist Church of North Wilkesboro. He died in Charlotte, N.C. December 6, 1922 and is buried in Alexandria, Virginia.

Sources: Family Records, The Wilkes Record, Sept. 8, 1964, and UVB Report March 1982, "Old Town Alexandria."

— Edward S. Finley

GEORGE WHITFIELD SMOOT FAMILY

993

George Whitfield Smoot was born May 10, 1792 in Henry Co., Va., named for the famous Methodist minister, George Whitfield. He is believed to be a descendant of William Smoot, born in 1596 who came to America in 1633 from Holland via England and settled in York Co., Va. George W. was married in Henry Co., Va. to Frances Shumate on Nov. 23, 1813. Frances, born April 30, 1793, was the daughter of Samuel and Ann Peppers Shumate.

George W. and his family were in Wilkes by 1840. He was a farmer and an associate of Joshua Spicer in the tannery business. He lived on the middle prong of Roaring River and served as Justice of Peace in 1850.

George W. and Frances had eleven children: (1) Mahala E. born Dec, 30, 1814 married 1st John Gambill and 2nd Randolph Alexander. She and John Gambill had two children: Joseph J. and Narcissa. Joseph J. Gambill born 1856 married Rousie E. Cornette Carrico, widow of Aaron K. Carrico and they had 7 children, most of whom moved to the midwest and western Canada. Narcissa Gambill born 1857 married Matthew Waddell, son of Abraham and Phoebe Holbrook Waddell and had 7 children. (2) Delia S. born Sept. 1, 1816 married 1st Huston Brown and 2nd Cook and moved to Polk Co., Tenn. (3) Gabriel born June 22, 1818 married in 1844 to Rena Hail and moved to Wyoming Co., West Virginia.

(4) Granville born June 7, 1820 married Clarissa Hutchinson, born Nov. 22, 1818 and died June 27, 1859, who was the daughter of Jacob Hutchinson and Alice Reynolds. He married 2nd Susan Phillips, daughter of Lindsey Phillips and Martha . . . . . He was ambushed and killed in Jan. 1865 during the Civil War while recruiting for the Union.

Eleven children were born to Granville and his wives: John Wesley; Frances Elizabeth; Elisha L; Gabriel William; Nancy Ann; Robert by his first wife; and Mary Caroline; Joseph W.; Ellen; Phoebe Cansadie; Andrew J. by his second wife. Elisha married Ellen Staley, daughter of Jacob Staley and Nettie Buttrey and owned a mill on the east prong of Roaring River. Gabriel W. was first married to Susanne Holbrook. He left N.C. and lived and married in the mid-west. Later, he returned to N.C. and married Mattie Waddell. Nancy Ann married Ralph Milton Holbrook, son of William Holbrook and Sarah Sparks. This family moved to Gallatin, Mo. about 1890. Robert married Frances Gambill and they had two children. He died in Newton Co., Mo. Mary Caroline married William C.A. Cornette. She and brothers Joseph W. and Andrew J. moved to the midwest and have many descendants there. Ellen married William W. Ballard. Mr. Bill Pendry is a descendant. P. Cansadie married James Oscar Billings and raised a large family in the Dockery area. (See Addison Billings Story)

(5) Gideon S. Smoot, born Dec. 1826, was married on Oct. 1, 1844 to Elizabeth Rachel Gambill. They lived in the Austin area and had at least 5 children: William Verlin; George Washington; Elizabeth Frances; Mary Emma and John B. Gideon S. and son, William Verlin, both served in the Union Army during the Civil War. According to family tradition, Gideon S. reached the rank of colonel. W. Verlin born May 17, 1846 married Elizabeth Hanks.

Mr. Kermit Lyon and Rev. Amos Lyon are descendants. George Washington born Dec. 27, 1848 married Caroline Hanks. Elizabeth Frances born May 31, 1852 married Hiram Lyon, son of Jacob and Malinda Sparks Lyon. Mr. Claude Billings of Traphill, who served as County Commissioner for a number of years, is a descendant. Mary Emma born May 1856 married Joshua Parton Hanks. John B. born May 20, 1858 married Sally E. Hanks.

(6) Frances Millicent Smoot, born Oct. 13, 1834, married A. Jackson Blevins, son of John and Caroline Carter Blevins. They had nine children. many of their descendants live in the North Wilkesboro area. Earl Leonard Caudill, who was County Surveyor for many years and Dr. George Vincent Blevins of Washington, D.C. are descendants of this couple.

(7) Leonard Gameliel "Loam" Smoot born June 28, 1838 married Nancy Clementine Walker, daughter of Robert Walker and Diane Shepherd. They had a large family and lived in the Piney Grove Church area. Dossa born Jan. 17, 1861 married A. Jackson Billings. Ex-Sheriff Claude Billings is a grandson. Rose Ann born March 25, 1862 married W. Cornelius Waddell. William Granville born July 31, 1864 married Elizabeth Taylor Browning. Elisha Grant, born Feb. 8, 1867 married 1st Martha A. Joines, 2nd Callie Yale and 3rd Caroline Sarah Truitt. George W., born March 29, 1868 married Rosa Slaybaugh. Frances E., born April 28, 1870, William S. Brewer. Nancy C., who was born Nov. 29, 1874 and lived to be 100 years old, married James Huie. John W., born April 5, 1877, married Mary Hannah Browning. His daughter, Elizabeth Clementine wife of Francis Schmoyer, lives in Longview, Washington. Lura, born Oct. 13, 1884, married Oliver H. Dillard. Mrs. Minnie Reynolds, wife of Austin Reynolds is one of her descendants. Charles L. was born Oct. 22, 1880, married first Betty Spicer and second Mae Bauguess. Ella Mae born Jan. 20, 1883, married Charlie Brown.

(8) Gilson S., was born Aug. 1, 1829 and (9) George B. on May 1, 1832. Two other children were born in 1823 and 1824, but there is no further record of them.

Sources: George Whitfield Smoot Family Bible; The Smoots of Maryland and Virginia by Harry Wright Newman; Court House Records; Family Recollections.

— Alice Billings

THE JOHN A. SOMERS FAMILY

994

John A. Somers was born to James and Mary Somers in 1806 in Patrick Co., Va.

As a young man, John moved to Davie County in North Carolina, where he married Frances Studevant, also of Virginia, who bore him fourteen children. Their children were: James F.; Hamilton C. father of Dr. L.P. Somers; William Howard; Lee Augustus; Calvin; Winfield; Adolphus; Nathan Asbury; Newton; Caroline; Louisa; Betsy; Salina; and Jane.

In 1851, John decided to move this large family west. He traveled as far as Wilkes County where he found a 700 acre farm for sale. The owner refused the offer of $1,000.00, but agreed to accept $1,001.00. This township was later named Somers in appreciation of his community service.

James F. Somers (1834-1907) married Sara Felts (1833-1897), and their children were as follows: (1) Ruth (1862-1927) who married Harrison Lewis, (2) Ida (1863) who married Wiley C. Lewis, (3) Mary Jane (1864-1910) who never married, (4) Charles Hamilton (1866-1925) who married Lunda Louisa Bingham, (5) James Winton (1870-1824), and Martin Luther (1873-1895).

Public service and a love of politics seemed to be an inherent trait in this branch of the family. James served as Justice of the Peace in 1863, as County Commissioner in 1864, as County Surveyor and Coroner in 1872, and was elected Sheriff in 1874. When he ran for re-election in 1878, he and T.J. Alexander received the same number of votes, and the tie was broken in favor of Alexander by polling the Justices of the Peace of the county. Later he served as Clerk of the Court in 1886 and as Mayor of Wilkesboro in 1896.

Although Jame's two younger sons died in their twenties, his oldest son, Charles, survived to carry on the family tradition of public service.

Sources: History of Somers Family (1851) by Arthur and Graham W. Somers.

— Margaret Somers Story

ALBERT BINGHAM SOMERS
995

Albert Somers (1904-1953), son of Chas. H. and Lunda Bingham Somers, better known as "Ab," was born and grew up in Wilkesboro. As a young man, he was very interested in aviation and was one of Wilkes County's first pilots. The old air strip, located in the West Park Shopping area, was the scene of much activity in the twenties and early thirties when crowds would gather on week-end afternoons hoping for free rides over the Yadkin Valley and surrounding areas.

Albert worked for the Yadkin Valley Motor Company and later ran the Ford Motor Company in Elkin, N.C. He came back to Wilkesboro and went into the insurance business. He was Mayor of Wilkesboro at the time of his death.

He married Margaret Pritchard of Chapel Hill, daughter of Isaac W. Pritchard and Emily A. Atwater Pritchard, both natives of Chapel Hill. Margaret graduated from the University of North Carolina and entered the teaching profession. She taught in several North Carolina towns, ending her career in the Wilkesboro Elementary School after she was married.

Margaret and Albert were the parents of two children, Albert B. Somers, Jr., and Emily Lou Somers. They are both graduates of the University of North Carolina and became teachers. Emily taught several years in Heidelburg, Germany, and in Alexandria, Virginia, where she met and married Lt. Col., George B. Lowery. Since his retirement from the army, they have lived in Atlanta, Georgia.

Albert Jr., received his Masters degree from the University School of Education and his Doctorate from Florida State University at Tallahassee. He is now Chairman of the Education Department at Furman University, Greenville, S.C. Albert Jr., married Cynthia Heard of Greenville. They are the parents of Susannah H. Somers.

Sources: Personal knowledge.

— Margaret Pritchard Somers

CHARLES HAMILTON and LUNDA BINGHAM SOMERS
996

In 1893, Charles H. Somers (1866-1925) married Lunda Louisa Bingham (1868-1937), daughter of Major Harvey Bingham (1839-1895) and Nancy Miller Bingham (1840-1914) of Watauga County. Their pride in the Bingham name is obvious from the names given to their ten children: Annie Bingham; Sadie Bingham; William Bingham; Hallie Bingham; Nellie Bingham; Frances Bingham; Albert Bingham; Eugene Bingham; Louisa Bingham; and James Harvey.

This large family lived first on East Main Street in Wilkesboro and later moved to a farm on the southern edge of town. The lovely old farm house and most of the land itself were removed in 1966 to accomodate new highway 421.

Charles was elected to the N.C. House of Representatives in 1896, serving two years, and was elected Clerk of Court in 1898, serving sixteen years in that office. Later he was appointed Deputy Collector of Internal Revenue for North Carolina, and he served in that capacity until his death.

The following letter is proof that Lunda's work was never done while her husband worked in Raleigh: Sunday evening — 10-4-25 — Dear Luna. Your letter just rec'd. If the ground is wet enough have "Jack" to sow the rye below the hog pen.

Don't have beans & peas cut until you think it is going to frost unless the beans are ripe and need to be cut now.

I am not feeling very well, haven't improved much. Unless I improve in a few days I expect I will come home until I feel better. Tell Bill to write me at once. Love, Papa

In addition to overseeing the farm, Lunda reared her ten children and an orphaned Negro girl, Florence Howell, who was taken into the Somers home when she was eight years old. Her older grandchildren remember a house full of love and laughter, and "The Farm" was the center of their good times until the death of their grandmother in 1937. There were periods of great sadness also, "Papa's" death, the death of their son Gene following an appendectomy, the death of grandson Joe Bingham from polio, and the accidental fatal shooting of grandson G.P. Dockery, Jr., occurred within a few years time.

It is unusual that this couple chose to educate their daughters, but not their sons. Long before the day of "Woman's Liberation", each of these girls was prepared to earn her living, and each one worked in schools or offices or hospitals.

Annie (1893-1978) was educated at Greensboro College for Women, worked as her father's assistant in the Clerk of Court's office, and married Dr. F.C. Hubbard. Her family story will be included in the Hubbard history.

Sadie (1895-1980) also went to Greensboro College, taught school, and married Dr. Letcher R. Bingham of Watauga County. Upon her marriage, her name became Sadie Bingham Somers Bingham. She and Dr. Bingham moved to Knoxville, Tennessee, and their descendents continue to live in that area. Their children are Anna; Joe who died in childhood; Charles; Betty; Margaret, and Reeves.

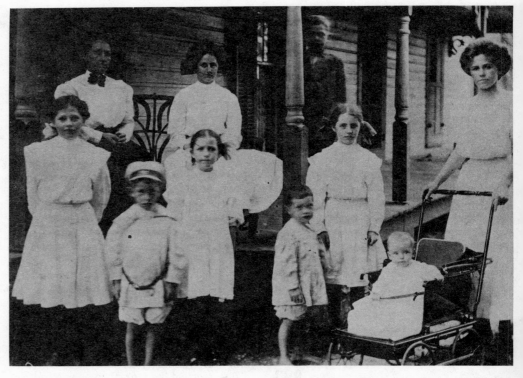

Charles H. Somers Family — front, L to R: Hallie, Albert, Nellie, Eugene, Frances, Pattie, Annie. Back: Lunda Bingham Somers, Sadie, Bill.

Hallie (1898-1975) was educated at Greensboro College, worked for F.D. Forester & Co. in North Wilkesboro, and married Garland P. Dockery of Surry County. Their first child, G.P. Jr., (1922-1935) died in a tragic accident while the family lived in Elkin, N.C. Charles Samuel (1926-) and Betty Bingham (1937-) were also born in Elkin. The family later lived for many years in Winston-Salem. Betty still lives there while Charles, his wife, Jane Spengler of Vicksburg, Miss., and their son Charles S. Jr., live in Statesville, N.C. Charles is the owner of Piedmont Knitting Mills.

Nellie (1899-1974) was educated at Greensboro College, taught school, and married Joseph Richard Barber of Wilkesboro. Her family will be included in the history of the Barbers.

Frances (1901-1977) was educated at Elon College, taught school in Farmington, Norwood, and Wilkesboro. For many years she worked as legal secretary for Attorney Charles G. Gilreath, but is probably best remembered as "Miss Frank", Deputy Clerk of Court.

Louisa (1908-) has always been called Pattie. She attended Davenport College in Lenoir where her Mother had been a student and received her nurse's training at Gaston Memorial Hospital in Gastonia. Pattie nursed at the old Wilkes Hospital and at Wilkes General until her retirement.

Sources: *Land of Wilkes*, Johnson J. Hayes Family Bible, family records and scrapbooks.

— Margaret Somers Story

JAMES HARVEY SOMERS
997

James Harvey (1911-), son of Chas. H. and Lunda Bingham Somers, was named after his grandfathers, James F. Somers and Harvey Bingham. James, better known as Jim, spent many years in both the automobile business and insurance business.

Following the family tradition, he, too, has always been interested and active in politics. Upon the death of his brother, W.B. Somers in 1959, he was appointed U.S. Marshall of the Middle District of North Carolina and served from 1959 to 1961.

Jim is a charter member of the Wilkesboro Business and Professional Men's Club and the Wilkesboro Lion's Club. He is a lifelong member of the Wilkesboro United Methodist Church and currently holds the second longest male membership in the church.

Jim married Margaret Hemphill Wilkins, (1913-), daughter of Dr. William Robert and Carrie Neisler Wilkins. Dr Wilkins was a pharmacist in North Wilkesboro for twenty-five years. He and Mrs. Wilkins were members of the North Wilkesboro Presbyterian Church and active in church and civic affairs.

Jim and Margaret were the parents of four daughters: Eugenia Neisler (1932-), married James Dewey (Bill) Byrd, Jr., (1930-). She graduated from Clevenger Business College and is employed at the Northwest Regional Education Center in North Wilkesboro, N.C. To this union were born one son, James Somers, (1950-), and two daughters, Melodie Ann (1953-), and Frances Louisa

(1961-). Melodie Ann married Brian Christopher Moran and had two sons, James Christopher (1974-), and Brian Sean (1977-).

Margaret (Mickey) Wilkins, (1934-) married James Anthony Emerson and lives in Asheville, N.C. Their marriage produced five children; James A. Jr. (1952-); Phyllis Karen (1954-) who is married to Edward Lane Taylor, II; Margaret Jewel (1957-); Rebecca Lynn (1960-); and William Eric, (1966-).

Susanne (1942-) married Dr. Augustin Francois Laurent Quilici (1940-) of Toulon, France, currently Professor of French at Lenoir-Rhyne College, Hickory, N.C. Susanne graduated from the University of North Carolina at Greensboro, where her mother also attended. She is currently Director of Social Services at Catawba Memorial Hospital in Hickory. They had two children, William Marcel Laurent (1969-) and Susanne Catherine (1971-).

Jane Harvey (1948-) married Dr. Ross Harleston Daniel of Lake City, S.C. She graduated from the University of North Carolina at Greensboro and is presently employed with the North Carolina Employment Security Commission. One son was born to this union, John Arthur (1978-).

Source: Personal knowledge.

— Eugenia Somers Byrd

DR. LEE PRESTON SOMERS, SR.
998

Dr. L.P. Somers, Sr. was born in Wilkes County on September 12, 1864; the son of Hamilton C. and Tabitha Campbell Somers. His parents died when he was less than twelve years of age. However, he remained at home where he farmed in the summer and attended local subscription schools in the winter.

When he was sixteen he gathered up some provisions and walked a distance of twenty five miles to Moravian Falls Academy to start his academic education. At the academy he swept classrooms and rang the bell to pay his tuition. During his years of study there he lived alone in a log cabin and did his own cooking.

After graduating at Moravian Falls Academy in 1884, he walked to Jefferson, North Carolina where he read medicine under Dr. J.C. Wilcox who was a very popular, graduate doctor practicing in Ashe County at that time. With some financial help from his uncle, Howard Somers, he was able to attend lectures at the University of Maryland in Baltimore. There he entered medical school under the "pauper plan," which required him to pay only half the regular fees. By soliciting boarders at a boarding house he obtained room and board in Baltimore for $3.50 per week.

After graduating from medical school, Dr. Somers returned to his home community in Southwest Wilkes County served the medical needs of people in Wilkes, Yadkin, Iredell and Alexander counties.

His over 40 years of service in the medical profession were marked by frequent trips, first by horseback, then by horse and buggy and later by T Model Fords, over poor roads and

Dr. Lee Preston Somers, Sr.

under adverse conditions.

He was very energetic, intelligent, and active in his profession. He had a kind and compassionate nature along with a sense of humor and a great bedside manner. He never lost a mother in childbirth. He was a doctor's doctor and was widely recognized among his colleagues as an expert diagnostician.

This country doctor's struggle to obtain his own education led him to assist others to attend college. He gave financial assistance to a number of young country boys who could not otherwise have obtained an education. Ten of these become physicians and dentists, five lawyers, one an agricultural graduate, and one young lady completed a literary course in college.

He found time for community affairs and financed the building of roads and bridges in the area. He had an active interest in business and politics. In 1906 he accepted the nomination to represent his district comprised of Wilkes, Yadkin, and Davie counties in the State Senate. He received the largest vote majority that any candidate had ever received. The day after the election the one person who voted for the opposing candidate came and apologized saying he was drunk and did not realize what he was doing.

President William McKinley appointed him United States Examining Surgeon. He served as president of the United States Pension Board at Wilkesboro for sixteen years. He was instrumental in seeing that all widows of both the confederate and union army soldiers received pensions and all deceased soldiers of both armies had grave markers.

He was a 32d-degree Mason, a Shriner, and he was responsible for many deserving children being placed in the Oxford Orphanage. Likewise, he saw that all blind babies that he delivered attended the school for the blind. The same was true for the deaf.

Dr. Somers and Minnie Dell Couch of Yadkin county were married on January 28, 1892. To this union five sons and one daughter were born: Infant; Couch; Hal; George; L.P., Jr; Clara Dell. Only L.P., Jr. survives.

Mrs. Somers gave her utmost support to her husband in his professional and all other activities.

On April 16, 1932 this respected and beloved country doctor passed. The day of his funeral some five thousand people came to pay their respects to the one who had so unselfishly given his life to the service of humanity.

Sources: *Doctors and Hospitals in Wilkes County* by Dr. Fred C. Hubbard family records, personal knowledge and memories.

— Mr. L.P. Somers, Jr.

WILLIAM BINGHAM SOMERS
999

William B. Somers was born December 12, 1896, son of Chas. H. and Lunda Bingham Somers, and received his education in the Wilkesboro schools and, he always added, in France. In January 1918, he enlisted in the U.S. Army and was assigned to Company B, 103rd. Regiment of Engineers, 28th Division. This division went immediately to France, and for seventy-two days, from June 28 until September 2, they were never out of sight and sound of firing. Bill participated in battles from Chateau Thiery to Meuse Argonne and was twice the victim of poison gas attacks. He was back on the battle line when the Armistice was signed and wrote the following in a letter home.

"I know you had some celebration when the news reached you, and you might know we did, too. This company was attached to our infantry at the time, so we were right on the line when it was over. I bet I did something you wouldn't do, and that was shaking hands with those Dutchmen just after it stopped. They came over with their hands up yelling "Komerad", and we just forgot it all. We traded souvenirs and got along pretty well. Some of them could speak quite a little English".

Upon his return home, he married Margery Allen Somers (1898-1981) of Taylorsville, daughter of William Jeptha Allen and Margaret Thompson Allen. Their marriage produced one daughter, Margaret Louisa (Peggy) born in 1924.

In his business life, Bill was involved in automobile dealerships in Wilkes and in Georgetown, S.C., in local bus companies in Georgetown and in Hickory, N.C., and in the poultry business.

However, his principal interest was politics and the Republican Party. He was elected Sheriff in 1928 and again in 1932. Those were not quiet times in Wilkes as proven by his scrapbooks. (It is interesting to note that he clipped and saved every published word of criticism as well as of praise.) In 1944, he was elected to the N.C. Senate, one of three Republicans serving in that body, and was able to accomplish much that benefitted his county. In 1952 he was a delegate to the Republican National Convention and was appointed U.S. Marshal of the Middle District of North Carolina in 1953. He held that office with distinction until his death in 1959. His respect for law was always tempered with compassion, and many

William Bingham Somers.

wives and children were helped by him while fathers served prison terms.

In his book, *People, Politics, Religion,* Sim A. DeLapp wrote the following about Bill Somers:

"He loved people everywhere . . . Maybe most of all he loved the gentle, frail and sometimes sinful and erring mountain folks of Wilkes and surrounding counties. He never took a man to prison without leaving a small part of himself inside the prison walls."

Margery Allen Somers survived her husband by twenty-two years. A life-long collector of antiques, she became a successful antique dealer after his death until failing health made it necessary to give up her business, but never her interest in all things old and beautiful.

They are survived by their daughter Margaret L. (Peggy), who married Donald Downs Story, (1922-   ), son of Mr. and Mrs. T.E. Story, Sr., of Wilkesboro. Their daughter, Martha Lynn (1946-   ), had both grandfathers serving in the N.C. Legislature at the time of her birth. She was first married to Michael Forester Absher (1940-1976) by whom she had the following children: Pamela Lynn, Julia Ann, and Michael, Jr. She is presently married to Jerry Douglas Moore, local attorney, son of Mr. and Mrs. S.B. Moore. Donald D. Story, Jr., (1952-   ) is a professional musician, and his wife, Beverly Bowling Story, is a teacher at North Wilkesboro Elementary School. She is a native of La Plata, Maryland.

Sources: *People, Politics, Religion,* Sim A. DeLapp *Land of Wilkes,* Johnson J. Hayes Letters, scrapbooks, memories

— Margaret Somers Story

THE JOEL NEWTON SOUTHER FAMILY
1000

My grandfather, Joel Newton Souther was

born August 26, 1874, and died February 11, 1952, in Wilkes County. He was a son of Joseph and Annie Dishman Souther. On February 19, 1899, he married Lillie Henderson, daughter of Billy and Adeline Lewis Henderson. Grandma was born October 21, 1879, and died September 16, 1965, in Wilkes County. Both Grandpa and Grandma are buried at Mt. Pisgah Baptist Church Cemetary located on Highway 115 south of North Wilkesboro.

Grandpa owned a farm in the southeastern part of Wilkes County in what is known as the Somers township. There they had fifteen children: Edward Olin, born December 3, 1899, died December 29, 1981, married Foda Mayberry and had one son; Vesta, born August 24, 1901, married Dewey Porter and had 13 children; Clesta, born October 1, 1903, married Arlie Myers and had two sons; Pheloy, born March 18, 1905, died June 9, 1977, married Glenn Mitchell who died and later married Raymond Clark and had one son; Mallie, born January 22, 1907, died February 4, 1981, married Otto Somers and had three children; Kermit Wakefield, born October 22, 1908, married Lucille Hayes and had three children; Flavil, born November 25, 1910, married Erniest Shumate and had two daughters; Ronda Rowe, born October 26, 1913, married Violet Robbins and had five children; Alta, born October 6, 1915, married Quils Roberts and had one son, divorced him and later married Johnny French and they had three children; Wenton Belo, born November 16, 1917, married Ora Nichols and had two sons; Zeb, born January 31, 1920, married Martha York and had eight children; Graydon Yale, born May 16, 1922, married Vennie Wells and had three children; Warren Nathaniel, born April 30, 1924, married Mary Ruth Mayberry and have no children; Calvin Newton, born April 30, 1924, married Beulah Canter and had two children, (Warren and Calvin are indentical twins); Ulysses Grant, born December 28, 1927, married Margaret Davis and had three children.

My father, Graydon Yale was the twelfth child of Joel Newton and Lillie Henderson Souther. He married Vennie Edna Wells May 16, 1945, in Wilkes County. Mother is the daughter of Hiram M., Sr. and Vallie Anderson Wells, and was born February 17, 1926, in Wilkes County.

After they were married, they moved to South Carolina where Daddy drove a bus for Grayhound. Then they moved to Greensboro, where Daddy worked for the Pespi Cola plant and Cones Mills. In 1960, they moved to Winston-Salem where Daddy was the manager of LA Reynolds Garden Store. In 1961, Daddy decided to move back to Wilkes County. They bought a store in the Somers township and moved in back of the store to live and run the store. After running the store for about three years, they sold the stock out and converted the store into living quarters where they live now.

Daddy and Mother raised three children: Joe Yale, born September 19, 1949, in Guilford County. He married Rosie Lee Gregory December 12, 1970 and they have two daughters, Cynthia Diane and Cheryl Renee. Joe is an ordained Baptist Minister.

Jane Edna, born December 21, 1952, in Guilford County. She married Jerry Allen Moxley September 17, 1977 and have no children.

Marie Vennie, born August 23, 1960, in Forsyth County. She married Jerry Michael Elliott August 26, 1978. They have no children. Michael is also a Baptist minister.

Daddy was ordained a Baptist minister in 1960 by Gospel Baptist Church in Greensboro. He has pastored churches in Wilkes and Iredell Counties. Due to his health, he is not able to pastor now.

The family also sung as the Souther Family Gospel Group. We had many wonderful times together. Joe played the guitar and sung lead, Marie and I sung alto and Daddy sung bass. I later played the piano for us. We do not sing much any more and we all miss it very much, but each has their own activities at church now.

Sources: family records, personal knowledge and memories and Wilkes County Courthouse records.

— Jane Souther Moxley

JAMES SOUTHWELL FAMILY
1001

James Southwell was born in Port Penryn Bangor, North Wales in the year 1896; the son of Frank Southwell, Harbor Master of Port Penryn, a sea going port.

Lord Penryn, who in those days owned a 25 mile square estate, complete with a castle, manicured gardens, roaming deer and peacocks, etc.

As the eldest son of my father, James Southwell, my sister and I would visit our grandparents and as Port Penryn was a part of Lord Penryn's estate, we were privileged to be allowed to roam freely in the parks adjoining Lord Penryn's castle.

Both our Grandfather and Grandmother Southwell were of English descent, having moved to Wales from the East coast in the mid 1800's. A part of the Southwell family remained in the East of England, settling in towns such as Norfolk and Wisbeech. My grandfather's brother became Lord Mayor of Wisbeech in 1901.

Although the Southwell family can be traced to the early 1500,s (one Robert Southwell, a Jusuit martyr was beheaded during the reign of Henry VIII) brevity of the family history will not allow the accounting.

Having served in the Royal Navy in World War II, I must admit that more enemy action was encountered on the home front than at sea.

Our eldest son was born during an air raid in Rugby, England. Three years later our second son, Paul was born in Manchester.

In 1951, my wife, Muriel and our two young sons, Malcolm and Paul, emigrated to the United States. The family settled in Columbia, S.C. and lived there for nine years.

While in Columbia, a third son, Michael was born.

In 1959, we moved to Statesville, N.C. and eventually, after a short period, we moved to Wilkesboro.

The fourth son Andrew was born to Muriel and Wyndham Southwell in 1962.

The family now resides at the Bandits Roost area of Kerr Scott Resevoir in Wilkesboro.

Sources: Personal knowledge.

— Wyndham F. Southwell

THE SPAINHOUR FAMILY
1002

Rufus Atkin Spainhour, son of Michael and Lettie Estes, was born in Burke County, October 5, 1839 and died March 27, 1928. He married Mary Ann Ginnings, September 5, 1866, who was born Oct. 7, 1840 and died July 4, 1921.

In 1870, R.A. Spainhour opened the first Spainhour Store in Dellaplane, later moving to Moravian Falls. Besides being a first-rate merchant and a school teacher, he was very interested in his church and community. He was a member of the Board of Directors of Baptist Childrens Home in Thomasville. The music department there is named in his honor. He was one of the founders of the Mountain Park Cemetery in Wilkesboro where most of his family is buried. He also gave the land for the Baptist Church in Wilkesboro where the present church now stands.

His simple frame store in Dellaplane has grown to seven stores in Wilkes and neighboring counties, and they are still owned and operated by the third and fourth generations.

From this union of R.A. and Lettie Spainhour, five children were born: John Edwin and Lelia Elizabeth died within a year and are buried in the Moravian Falls Cemetary. Ila Mary, born August 25, 1908, and died July 20, 1936. She married Floyd Gay Holman on March 1, 1892. They lived in Wilkesboro where they were very active in the church and community affairs. Ila gave the land for the present site of the Womans Club House in Wilkesboro. Bertha Ann was born February 5, 1872 and died March 27, 1923.

James Edgar Spainhour was born September 10, 1874, and died on November 1, 1965. He married Ruby Onyx Sydnor on September 29, 1896 in the First Baptist Church in North Wilkesboro. She and her twin sister, Pearl White of Wilkesboro, were born on the same day and the same year as J.E. Spainhour. Ruby died May 9, 1963. All of the above mentioned people, except two infants, were buried in the Mountin Park Cemetery.

Ruby and Edgar Spainhour started housekeeping in Moravian Falls, later moving to Wilkesboro and on to North Wilkesboro where they lived until their death. Mr. Edgar, as he is better known, was an excellant merchant, and a faithful and generous member of the First Baptist Church in North Wilkesboro, which he loved very much. He was an inspiration to both the old and the young during his active years.

To Ruby and Edgar Spainhour were born seven children: James E. Spainhour was born December 29, 1897 and died October 16, 1898.

William Rufus Spainhour was born August 6, 1899, died December 22, 1945. He married Elizabeth Harding on December 31, 1921; she died August 1, 1980. William and Elizabeth had one daughter, Elizabeth Harding Spainhour, born September 16, 1923. She married Cliff Olsen on January 11, 1946. Cliff and Betty, as she was better known, had three children: Barbara Elizabeth, born September

James Edgar and Ruby Sydnor Spainhour.

16, 1946, married to Howard D. Kirby on June 16, 1976. William Spainhour, born December 17, 1950. Amanda Jane, born December 12, 1956, married Belton Scott Shuford on May 5, 1979.

Ruby Sydnor Spainhour was born December 28, 1901, and died April 30, 1972. She married William Jennings Bason on December 28, 1926. Their children were, an infant son born November 2, 1928, died same day. William Spainhour Bason, born December 2, 1930.

Eugene Sydnor Spainhour was born March 10, 1903, married to Elizabeth Brame on October 26, 1926.

Lincoln Sydnor Spainhour, born February 19, 1908, married to Mozelle Cochran on April 19, 1934. She was born March 3, 1913. Their children are: Mary Cochran Spainhour born June 28, 1937, married to Dr. John Henry Giles on October 25, 1958. They had three children, Mary Ellen, born August 2, 1959; Stephen Bierce born December 18, 1961; and John Keith born June 4, 1963. Mary and John divorced and she has since married Dennis Brockland. James Edgar III, born November 18, 1940, married Eloise Alvis on July 15, 1963. They have two children: Michael Sean, born November 18, 1966, and Mary Shannon, born February 27, 1969. Lincoln Sydnor, Jr., born November 11, 1947, married to Virginia Dare Raymer on June 6, 1970. They have three children: Kristina Angelique, born February 25, 1974; Wesley Johanan, born November 30, 1977; and Julian Sydnor born July 27, 1979.

Roy Alfred Spainhour, born August 12, 1909, married Hazel Taylor on April 3, 1947. They have two sons: Roy Alfred, born July 27, 1948, married to Victoria Lee Cuthbertson on August 9, 1969, and Eugene Sydnor born February 18, 1950.

John Edward Spainhour born April 17, 1914, married Mary King Mallonee June 3, 1940. She died November 5, 1975. They had two sons: John Edward Jr., born March 18, 1951, married to Elise' Givhan on August 15, 1976. They have one son, John Christian, born July 29, 1980. David Sevier born September 7, 1954, married Stephanie Harris on July 2, 1977.

Sources: family members, tradition, grave markers and earlier family histories.

— Mrs. Mozelle C. Spainhour

THE AARON ELIJAH SPARKS FAMILY

1003

My Dad, Aaron Elijah (Babe) Sparks was the youngest in a family of four sons, born July 27, 1874, in Wilkes County, to Elijah and Millie Louiza (Combs) Sparks. He was the brother of Henry Sherman Sparks born February 11, 1868; Wiley Marshall (Bud) Sparks born October 15, 1870; and Willie R. Sparks born August 7, 1872. Dad often spoke of his two brothers, Sherm and Will who died young. Sherm died May 21, 1889, at the age of 21. Will died May 23, 1890 at the age of 18. One of the brothers died with typhoid fever, the other

with penumonia. They were never married.

Dad and Uncle Bud married sisters in the early 1890's. When Wiley Marshall (Uncle Bud) Sparks was 21 and Lillie Cora Harris was 18, they were married at the home of Aunt Cora's parents, James Henry and Mary Lucinda Byrd Harris. This union was blessed with 11 children.

When Dad was 18, and my Mom, Sarah Emma Harris, was 15 (she always said almost 16) they too, were married at the home of Grandpa and Grandma Harris. Dad said he and Mom married so young they grew up with their 9 children. Today there are a lot of Sparks who are double first cousins.

Dad and Mom attended a one room school in Wilkes County. They were taught from the Blue Back Speller. Dad often talked of the school he attended in Traphill. He and a friend walked a distance of 14 miles to the school, boarded for a week, then walked back home for the weekend.

In those days traveling was difficult, the roads were muddy and rough. Dad taught school for a short time, but his first love was farming. It must have been hard making a living from the old hillside farm Dad called his rock pile. Dad and Mom always had a large garden, they loved to plant and watch it grow. Mom, the girls in the family and Aunt Clem did a lot of canning, putting up pickles, and drying green beans which we called ''leather-britches.'' They were delicious cooked and eaten in the winter as was the kraut Dad always helped make in a 50 gallon wooden barrel.

Mom loved to piece quilts and I still treasure one she appliqued red on white background in 1907 which she called the World's Wonder.

Oil lamps were used in our home for light. Water was carried a short distance up a trail from a spring for drinking, cooking and washing dishes. Mom with the help of the children did the washing for the family at the spring. She would fill an old black iron pot with water, then build a fire on the ground around it. When the water was hot, she would mix it in a wash tub with cold water from the spring and using homemade lye soap, scrub the clothes on a washboard until when hung on the line to dry, they would sparkle in the sun.

There was ironing to be done, using an old flat iron that was heated on a wood burning kitchen stove. And, oh yes! milking the cows and churning the milk for butter, also the chickens to be fed. Dad and the boys would feed the mules, Old Alice and Old Joe. They were used for plowing the fields, garden and hauling wood for the kitchen wood burning stove and fireplace. Dad and Grandpa Sparks kept the home fires burning in the fireplace in winter.

My earliest memories are centered around the old fireplace, where the family and often neighbors gathered on cold winter nights, with the wind whistling around the corners of our home. It was fun listening to the ghost stories they sometimes told, but frightening to walk across a large kitchen before entering my bedroom. Those nights, the kitchen seemed twice as large as it really was, but after I jumped into bed everything was fine.

Dad was a large man. How comfortable it

was sitting on one of his knees with my brother Clate sitting on the other while he talked, read the Bible or the newspaper. We must have been little pests although he never seemed to mind. I remember Mom sitting on the porch in summer time, especially Sunday afternoons reading the Bible.

When the work was finished for the day, the Sparks family spent many happy moments in the warm early evening hours, sitting on the porch. The older ones talking; the children listening to the whip-poor-wills, the frogs on the creek banks, a cow bell tinkling in the night and other country sounds.

The old seven room house was home for my Dad and Mom, nine children: Shelton; Hillyard; Wayne; Clate; Ora; Callie; Alma; Ila and Genevieve.

Grandpa Elijah Sparks, a Civil War Veteran, came to live with Dad and Mom after Grandma Millie Sparks death (2-6-1917) at the age of 71. He lived there until his death (2-9-1930) at the age of 88. Aunt Clementine Byrd, the sister of Grandma Mary Harris lived with Dad and Mom for years. She was born 9-27-1843, died 2-8-1942. She was never married. Mom's Dad, Grandpa Henry Harris, lived his last remaining years at the home of Dad and Mom. He died 3-18-1939, age 90. Dad died 10-18-1937, age 63. Mom lived until 1-3-1966, died at the age of 88.

They are all buried in the cemetery at White Plains Baptist Church, Roaring River; the church they all loved so much, where they had gone for so many years.

Sources: Wilkes County Courthouse records, Personal knowledge and memories and gravestones.

— Genevieve Blackburn

REUBEN and CASSA (BUTTERY) SPARKS

1004

Reuben Sparks was born in Rowan Co., N.C., probably in 1755. His father, Solomon Sparks, was born in Maryland during the 1720s and was probably the son of the Joseph Sparks, who died intestate in Frederick Co., Md. in 1749. Solomon Sparks married Sarah prior to 1750. They settled near Salisbury, Rowan Co., N.C. in 1753 and in Wilkes Co., N.C. in 1772. When the dividing line between Wilkes and Surry Counties was surveyed in 1778, it was found that the line cut through Solomon Sparks' plantation, but according to the court minutes, his house was on the Surry side. Thus, the Sparks family lived just south of the present village of Swan Creek in the western part of what is now Yadkin Co., N.C. Both Solomon and Sarah Sparks died prior to 1800. Their children were: John Sparks, born Feb. 25, 1753; Reuben Sparks, born ca. 1755; Solomon Sparks Jr., born ca. 1757; Mary Sparks, born ca. 1759; Hannah Sparks, born ca. 1761; Susannah Sparks, born ca. 1763; Joseph Sparks, born ca. 1765; and Abel Sparks, born Jan. 8, 1767.

Reuben Sparks married Cassa Buttery about 1783. She was born about 1765 and was probably the daughter of John and Ann (Allen) Buttery. Reuben Sparks, like his father, owned land in both Wilkes and Surry Counties. However, Reuben Sparks seems to have been more oriented to Wilkes County and was frequently mentioned in the land and court records of that county. He served on juries, helped to lay out roads and was an active member of the South Fork of Roaring River Baptist Church. He served as a delegate to the Baptist Association in 1829, 1830, 1832, and 1834. On March 5, 1835, he sold a tract of 100 acres on the Roaring River in Wilkes County to his son, William R. Sparks. On the same day, he sold an adjoining tract of 70 acres to his son, Jonas Sparks. According to the records of the Old Roaring River Baptist Church in Wilkes County, Reuben Sparks died at 2:00 a.m. on July 13, 1840. Cassa (Buttery) Sparks died on June 7, 1842.

Reuben and Cassa (Buttery) Sparks had at least eleven children: Benjamin, born 1783; Lydia, born 1785; daughter, born 1787; John, born 1786 or 1790; Solomon, born 1792 or 1793; Jonas, born 1794 or 1800; William Russell, born Jan. 3, 1797 or 1803; Amelia, born 1799; Matilda, born March 1805 or 1807; Reuben Jr., born 1808; and a daughter, born 1810.

Benjamin Sparks married Sarah Jeffreys about 1802. He died in Yadkin Co., N.C. in 1876. His children were: Elizabeth, William Russell, John, Joseph, Mary, Hannah, Lydia, Solomon, Martha C., Sarah, and Benjamin Franklin Sparks.

Lydia Sparks married Henry Bauguess prior to 1810. More information can be found in the section on the Henry Bauguess family.

John Sparks married Elizabeth about 1806. They died in Alleghany Co., N.C. before 1870. They had six children, two of whom were: Emanuel and Reuben Sparks.

Jonas Sparks married Mary Brown in 1817. He died in Tazewell Co., Va. in 1875. His children were: John Henry, Rueben R., a daughter, Malinda, Timothy, Shadrach, Joshua William, Jonas J., and Joseph Sparks.

William Russell Sparks married Sally Wilcoxson in 1821 and Permela Gentry before 1839. By Permela, his children were: Hugh, Lotty, Martha, and Whitfield.

Amelia Sparks married Emanuel Bauguess. Their children were: Elizabeth, Sarah, Richard, Cassie, Reubin, Jonas, and Liddia F. Bauguess.

Matilda Sparks married Wiley Gentry in 1825. She died on Aug. 18, 1878 in Surry Co., N.C. Her children were: Tinison, Reuben, Jonathan, Cassy, Levi, Jonas, William, Sally, John, Wiley, and Allen Gentry.

Sources: *The Sparks Quarterly*, Vol. XV No. 3, Sep. 1967; ''Sparks Summation'', by Orella Chadwick.

— Timothy E. Peterman

SOLOMON SPARKS FAMILY
1005

My great grandfather, Solomon Sparks, and my great-grandmother, Mary (Sallie) Day were married January 30, 1838 in Wilkes County.

Six children was born to this union. One of the children was Elijah Sparks who became my granpa. He was a carpenter, miller and farmer and married Millie Louiza Combs.

The Sparks family was very much saddened when two brothers, Wiley and Solomon never returned from the Civil War. One died from pneumonia and the other was never heard from.

A son Jacob was a farmer and miller and married Millie Billings. A daughter Mary married William Frank Combs. The other sister, Amanda, married John Crabb.

The Sparks family saw their share of grief and sorrow as all families do. They continued to be blessed and to multiply until they grew into a large clan.

Sources: Personal knowledge, Wilkes records.

— Genevieve Blackburn

DANIEL SPEARS and DESCENDANTS
1006

My great-grandfather, Daniel Spears, of Wilkes County, was the son of Odum and Jane Dillard Spears. The Spears' are of English ancestry.

Daniel Spears married Mary Waters, daughter of Joseph and Melinda Beshears Waters.

Daniel and Mary Waters Spears had eleven (11) children: Jane; Aley Adinah (9-17-1881 — 9-17-1958), my maternal grandmother; Lillie; Sam; John; Romillus; Clausie; Ida and three other daughters, whose names are not known to the writer.

Sources: Family Bible, Census Records and personal knowledge.

— Mrs. Joyce Miller Chewning

JOSHUA SPICER and DESCENDANTS
1007

Joshua Spicer was born October 24, 1843, died February 7, 1930, son of Hardin and Martha Johnson Spicer.

Hardin Spicer was the son of Joseph Spicer who was the son of William Spicer, a Revolutionary War soldier, born in Culpeper Virginia in 1754. William came to Wilkes County in 1775 and is believed to have fought at Kings Mountain and later against the Cherokee Indians. William married Jemima Haines or Hinds. He died in 1833 and is buried in the Round Hill Church cemetery south of Traphill.

Joshua Spicer married Martha Jane Holbrook in 1866. She was born January 22, 1839, died May 5, 1932. They lived on the middle prong of Roaring River in a large two story Victorian house. He farmed, owned a tannery and for a time manufactured plug tobacco. His principal income was from the tannery where he received a ''toll'' from the farmers and cattlemen who brought their hides to be tanned. He in turn sold the hides to neighbor merchants who needed them, and I am sure much of this ''selling'' was barter and exchange.

When the leather had accumulated he would load it into his wagon or wagons and go into surrounding areas to sell and trade for other

Adinah Spears Nichols, daughter of Daniel and Mary Waters Spears, and wife of McClellan Nichols (9-17-1881 — 9-17-1958).

useful commodities along the way. I have heard him talk of these wagon trips to as far away as Fayetteville, N.C., sometimes in the dead of winter when the team and wagon could cross the streams on ice without breaking through.

My grand parents and family were devoted to their church, contributing not only money and land but much time to the furthering of Christianity. Their church was the Piney Grove Baptist where they remained members until death and are buried in the cemetery there.

Their children were: (1) John Henry, born 1867, died 1903, married Nancy Bryan in 1894. Their children were Clay who married a girl by the name of Tina from Pa., Bessie who married Clyde Reeves and Mattie Jane who married Sherman Bauguss. (2) Joseph Charlie, born 1870, died 1871; (3) Nancy Fannie, born 1872, died 1954, married Iredell M. Myers. Their sons were: Walter who married Dixie Sheridan; Willie who died in childhood; and Presley who married Toyce Nichols (4) Martha Alice, born 1875, died 1913, married William D. Woodruff in 1898. Their children are: Ina who married Clyde Gentry; Vernon who married Bertha Holder; Grace who married Glenn Gollier; and Wilmer who first married Verna McLean and after her death, married Charley Lou Brookshire; and a fifth child who died when about two. (5) Joshua Thomas was born in 1882 and died in 1883.

Sources: Family Bibles, memories and personal knowledge.

— Eldon Woodruff

VINCENT SPICER FAMILY
1008

Vincent Spicer was born 6/10/1857 and was the seventh child of Harvey Spicer by his first wife, Nancy Brooks. On December 28, 1879, he married Martha Caroline Hall. Both Vincent and Zachariah Spicer married sisters, Martha Caroline and Micah Pauline who were daughters of Owen Hall. The Vincent Spicer farm in Traphill was given to the family by Owen Hall. This home is now the home of Verna Spicer Joines (7th child of Vincent) and her family.

Vincent and Martha had seven children and raised six of them on the Spicer farm in Traphill, N.C.

I. Caroline (Carrie), 10/23/1880, married M. Wesley Joines II and from this union were seven children: (a) Guy V., 1/20/02, married Vaudie B. Blackburn (died 1966.) Retired farmer, East Bend, NC, two children. Remarried Mae Jester. (b) Ima, 8/14/05, married William Raymond DeJournette, 9/14/02, Ima — retired teacher of 35 years, Raymond — retired Traphill highway employee. Home is beautiful with restored antique mountain furniture. No children. (c) Ruby Jane, 9/8/08 — 9/26/39, married M. John Smith, Alleghany Co. Three children. (d) Verna Caroline, 10/8/11, married Ira Rown Truitt, 5/10/10, Sparta, NC, six children, Retired carpenter and building inspector. (e) Carrie Spicer, 7/10/14, married Quentin Hawkins, 3/23/09, four children, retired farmer. (f) Mary Ruth, 9/29/19 — 8/1/1934. Died, ruptured appendix. (g) John Wesley, 3/19/22 — 6/3/46, married Hazel Baugess. Died of heart attack aboard LST 1153, Norfold, VA, 11/19/51, two children.

II. John W. Spicer, 1/17/83 — 5/10/42, married Clara Brown. As a young man he came west but returned to Atlanta and Daytona Beach. Died from a heart attack while wading in ocean. Clara died several months later. No children.

III. Martha Bell (Mattie) Spicer, 4/27/85 — 2/21/76, married Wm. T. Brinegar. Aunt Mattie and Uncle Bill were the first of the V. Spicer family to go west. They settled on a ranch on the Green River, south of Green River, WY. This ranch is now covered by Flaming Gorge Reservoir. Two sons, Walter and Lester, were born in WY but died from diptheria brought to the ranch by the infant son of Maude Spicer McBride who with Ed McBride, her husband, were traveling to WY for the first time. The infant, Ernest Oscar McBride, died a month later. This left both families childless until Vaughn Brinegar was born in 1910. (a) Walter Earl, 1/14/1906 — 12/29/1909. (b) Lester, 2/19/1908 — 12/31/1909. (c)Vaughn, 5/20/1910 — 8/2/1972, and his wife Charlotte were both teachers in Wyoming and California, two children. (d) Beatrice, died from tomaine poisoning while very young. (e) Ernest Vernon Brinegar, 6/25/1917, and his wife, Mary, live in California. Banker. Two sons. (f) LeeRoy Brinegar, 10/30/1920, and his wife, Dorothe, live in Rock Springs, WY. Ex-rancher, real estate, one daughter.

IV. William H., Mattie's twin, died seventeen days after birth. Buried in Traphill, N.C.

V. Marvin Ernest Spicer, 8/25/88 — 3/17/61, came west to Wyoming in 1906. Worked as a herder for various sheep reaches in SW Wyoming and then bought one-third interest in the Brinegar Ranch. He married Ruth Stevens, 6/25/17, and that Fall was inducted into the Army; shipped out to France on Thanksgiving,

1917. Was a signalman, 1st Division, was at St. Hehill, Swasson and Argonne, where he was gassed. Upon returning he sold his interest back to the Brinegars, worked for a local bank as livestock examiner and in 1927 bought a ranch north of Rock Springs which remained in the family until it was sold in 1965. Ernest and Ruth had six children: (a) Eldon Marvin, 11/16/20, married Beverly Morian, Rock Springs, a rancher and presently beverage wholesaler. Have five children. (b) Nedra Marie, died in infancy. (c) Carol, 5/2/24, married Harol Luntey, lives at Kehei, Maui, Hawaii, both are educators, have two daughters. (d) Kathleen Ruth, 11/16/26, married Chester A. Allen, both educators in Pamona, CA, have three children. (e) John Austin, 9/25/30, married Erika Gruendig, divorced. PhD, works for Gov't in Dayton, OH. Three children. (f) David Vincent, 8/ /32 — 12/17/37, died in a sleighriding accident.

VI. Maude L. Spicer, 9/6/91 — 4/19/76, married Martin Ed McBride in Traphill and came to WY in 1909. Their first child Ernest Oscar died in infancy. Uncle Ed ranched and then worked for the Union Pacific, the first to become a railroader. Both had green thumbs and their Green River home had beautiful flowers and a prolific garden. Their children were: (a) Mabel Ernie, 2/10/1911, married John Lewis, John was a railroader, retired, died in 1982. One daughter. (b) Virginia Fay (Virgie), 11/23/1914, married Francis Mengel, also retired railroader and live in North Platte, NB. Two children. (c) Stella, 3/28/1917, died in fire at McBride home in 1929. (d) Mary Clydia, 5/6/1921, married George Burke, now live in Brownsville, CA after working in Wyoming and Alaska. Mary is a nurse. Four children.

VII. Verna Spicer, 11/10/1894, married Johnson S. Joines. Johnson was a jack-of-all-trades. They had three children: (a) Vivian Marie, 12/18/1920, married first, William R. Connell, divorced. One daughter — Kim. Married William R. Gent. Reno, Nevada. (b) William Lynn, married Beatrice Cleary, Traphill, NC. 5 children. (c) Vernon Shafter, 10/24/1935, married Arleigh (Shorty), Roden, N.C.

— Eldon M. Spicer

WILLIAM SPICER, SENIOR
1009

William Spicer was born around 1614 in England and emigrated to Northumberland County, Virginia around 1650. His sons: Benjamin Spicer was born around 1660 in Northumberland County, Virginia. His son: William Spicer was born around 1682 and married Elizabeth   . They settled first in Hanover County, Virginia and later in that part of Orange County, which became Culpeper County. Their son: Joseph Spicer was born around 1720 and married, September 14, 1741, Margaret Sullivan. They lived in Culpeper County, Virginia and were the parents of my great-great-grandfather, William Spicer, hereafter referred to as William Spicer, Sr.

William Spicer, Sr., Revolutionary War soldier, was born in Culpeper County, Virginia, January 11, 1754. Early in life he displayed his

adventurous and patriotic spirit when, at the age of 21, he participated in the famous Battle of Point Pleasant which was fought October 10, 1774. It is said that the victory of this battle was significant in that it was won by the Colonial troops without the support of regulars. Moreover, it saved the West from the savagery of Indian warfare during the first years of the American Revolution. Having distinguished himself in battle, he was discharged in Staunton, Virginia and returned to his home in Culpeper County.

After a brief respite, William Spicer, Sr., in the year 1775, moved to a location on the waters of Roaring River, then Surry, now Wilkes County. He acquired land there and later added to his holdings either by purchase, gift or grant.

His efforts in support of the freedom of his country did not cease upon his arrival in Wilkes. His war record indicates that he participated in the Battle of King's Mountain and engaged in many skirmishes against the Indians and engagements against the Tories throughout the western part of North Carolina and surrounding areas, "whenever the circumstances or exigencies of the Country required it."

Upon his first marriage to Jemima Haines (Hinds-Hines) about 1780, William Spicer, Sr. became the patriarch of the Spicer family of Wilkes County as we know it. By this union there were four children: Joseph Spicer (5/7/1782 — 12/29/1845) m. 4/3/1805 Jane Bauguess (10/20/1783 — 2/2/1855); Samuel Spicer (1784-1849) m. Sallie Jane Turner, and moved to Kentucky about 1815-1817; Mary Spicer b. 1790 m. Ransom Cooper and moved to Tennessee; Benjamin Spicer (1794-9/12/1877) m. Nancy Bauguess and moved to Kentucky with most of his family between 1841 and 1850.

Soon after the death of his first wife, William Spicer, Sr. remarried. There is some difference of opinion as to whom he married. First source indicates he married Sarah Jane Watts November 16, 1796. Second source claims he married Mary   . Nevertheless, there were two children by the second marriage: Sarah Spicer m. 7/17/1814 to William Holbrook and moved to the state of Washington; William Spicer, Jr. b. 1799 m. 1st 2/22/1817 Jennie (Jane) Bauguess, m. 2nd 5/19/1853 Permelia Hoots.

The date of death of our Revolutionary War ancestor is unknown; however, it is known that he was living in Wilkes County with his son William Spicer, Jr. when the 1840 U.S. Census was taken. He is buried in Round Hill Church Cemetery. At last count he had living descendants in all fifty states of the Union.

Sources: Culpeper County, Virginia Records, Breathitt County Kentucky Records, St. Pauls Parish Register, St. Thomas Parish Register, U.S. Census Records, Wilkes County Records, The Beatrice Holbrook Papers, *The Spicer Family of Breathitt County, Kentucky*, by Griffith.

— Bernard F. Spicer

JOHN ST. CLAIR FAMILY
1010

This is an ancient Scottish family of Norman-French origins, taking their name from the chateau and village of Saint-Clair in the old duchy of Normandy near the extreme northern tip of Scotland. From this section various branches of the family migrated to the American colonies during the 18th century.

The Scots rendered the original French form of this name into variations of spelling, of which the most common forms are Saintclari. Sinclair, and Sinkler. The form last mentioned approximates the pronunciation of the name used in Scotland and in America until recent years. In Wilkes County, older people still refer to the St Clairs as Sinklers.

Th founder of the Wilkes County family was John Saintclair, Esq. who in early life signed himself, John Sinkler, but later adopted the more ancient spelling. Most of his descendants, especially those of his second marriage, subsequently took up the shortened form, St. Clair.

When the original fifty acres of the town of Wilkesboro were purchased in the year 1800 from Rebecca Welborn and Rachel Stokes, heirs of Hugh Montgomery, one of the first purchasers of town lots was John Thomas St. Clair. Having been born in Scotland about the year 1774, John St. Clair came to America with his father, shortly after the Revolutionary War. After a short stop-over in Virginia where he had already taken a wife, he appeared in Wilkes County in the fall of 1796 as a witness to a land transaction on the Yadkin River.

John St. Clair purchased lot number 31 in the town of Wilkesboro, which at that time was the last lot to the west and on the south side of main street. Here he built his home and resided for almost forty years. On this same lot the Wilkesboro High School was later built, now the Federal Building.

Very little is known of the early life of John St. Clair, but from the records of his later life, it is certain that he had an unusually good education for that time and place, wrote a fine hand and had an excellent command of the English language. Very shortly after moving to Wilkesboro, he became active in business and political life of the town and county. For several years he owned and operated a tannery near Wilkesboro in partnership with Francis Barbard, Esq., another early and prominent citizen of the town, and at the same time conducted a smithey on his home lot in the village.

During the War of 1812, he entered public life as an active leader of the conservative political party which bore, in his lifetime, the successive labels of Federalist, National Republican, and Whig. In 1814, John St. Clair was elected one of Wilkes County's representatives to the General Assembly, which office he held successively for five terms *1814-1818, and afterwards again in 1826, 1828 and 1832. These years which his family spent in the State Capital enabled them to acquire an extensive circle of friends among the best people of the state, and gave to the Saintclair children a broader social and cultural education than would have been possible in the small village of Wilkesboro.

During this period John Saintclair also held various county offices. He was long a justice of the County Court, and for some years deputy

clerk. As he advanced in years he gradually retired from public life, bequeathing his considerable political influence to his son-in-law, Col. Joel Vannoy, a longtime sheriff of Wilkes, and Judge Williams Mastin, probate judge and county clerk for almost thirty years, both of whom became political powers in Wilkes County during the latter part of the antebellum period.

Though equipped with ability and education, John Saintclair suffered from an erratic temperament and faults of character which prevented him from reaching the rank in public life which he might otherwise have attained. He was not a competent business manager, and several times in his life was brought to the verge of financial ruin.

His first wife died about 1803, leaving two sons and two daughters: Hirum, James A., Elizabeth and Mahala. Later John married Mrs. Nancy Holman Johnston, widow of Daniel Johnston and daughter of Thomas Holman of Wilkes. By this marriage there were two sons and two daughters, Thomas H., John E., Rebecca Amanda, and Harriett.

His daughter Elizabeth, married Col. Joel Vannoy, who operated one of the first cabinet-making businesses in western North Carolina and operated, among his varied business interests, the Mansion Hotel in Wilkesboro, one of the two principal Inns of the town.

His other daughter by his first marriage, Mahala, married Joseph James of Stokes County, another cabinet maker. They lived first in Wilkesboro then later moved a few miles from town to the Edgewood community.

The two sons of his first marriage left Wilkes County for the western frontier before 1830 and both became quite prominent in Texas. The other two sons remained in Wilkes and played an important part in public life here. The eldest of the two, Thomas Holman St. Clair, was a county justice for several years, Register of Deeds for thirteen years until his death in 1865. Another son, John Elbert St. Clair was commissioned Colonel Commandant of the 75th Regiment, N.C. Militia in 1844, and elected chairman of the county commissioners in 1865 and helped reorganize the county government after the Civil War. His papers, in the manuscript collection of Duke University Library, indicates that he was county political boss and party chairman of that period.

Rebecca Amanda married Williams Mastin, whose story is elsewhere in this work. Harriet married Wiley Howard of Wilkes and left descendants in Hunting Creek area.

After the death of his second wife, John broken in health and fortune, went to live with his daughter Rebecca Amanda and died there a few years later. John and both his wives, along with his daughter, Elizabeth Vannoy, are buried in the old Wilkesboro Cemetery in Wilkesboro. Although he left many descendants in Wilkes the name St. Clair is practically non-existent here now. The only members of the family that carry his name are largely residents of northern Alexander County and the part of Wilkes that adjoins Alexander between Moravian Falls and Taylorsville.

Sources: Article in Wilkes Genealogical Bulletin (May 1968)

— Sinesca Mastin Wright

STALEY

My best known ancestors lived in Union Township on the three branches of Reddies River. My parents were Noah Jacob Staley and Laura Mae Whittington Staley. When I was born, November 2, 1909, they lived in an old-fashioned two-story log house on the Harvey Vannoy farm on the middle prong of Reddies River.

Living in an adjoining log house was my great-aunt, Mariah E. Whittington Vannoy (April 9, 1831 — January 10, 1922), widow of my great-uncle, James Harvey Vannoy (March 9, 1826 — February 24, 1898). Aunt Mariah was the daughter of Allen Whittington (born 1801) and Elizabeth Lenderman who were married December 18, 1826. Harvey was the son of Rev. James and Sarah Shepherd Vannoy, married December 13, 1813.

Mariah had a keen intelligence, a good memory, and was a good story-teller. As a little girl I was her "sitter" and was an avid listener to her stories of relatives, and especially of the War Between the States.

She was the half-sister of my maternal great-grandmother, Emily C. Whittington (October 4, 1841 — June 14, 1910), who married Neil C. Vannoy (December 17, 1838 — December 2, 1862). Neil and James Harvey were brothers. Neil was a Confederate soldier who died from wounds and fever at Powell Valley, Virginia. Emily later married Alexander Faw, a Confederate soldier, son of Absalom Faw. Emily's mother was Mary (Polly) Eller, second wife of Allen Whittington and the daughter of the Rev. George Simeon Eller and his wife Fannie McNeil Eller.

Fannie McNeil (Dec. 11, 1794-Oct. 4, 1856), daughter of James McNeil, was the granddaughter of the Rev. George McNeil, a chaplain with Col. Benjamin Cleveland. Whether or not George helped Ben toot the horn on Rendez-vous Mountain to call the Revolutionary soldiers together, I like to think he did. Anyway, I have kept the trees growing tall and strong in his memory on the acres I own on the Reddies River side of the mountain.

My grandmother, Sarah Jane Vannoy (Oct. 25, 1860-Jan. 29, 1942) married her double first cousin, James Vance Whittington (July 5, 1860-Jan. 29, 1942). Vance was the son of Col. Alexander G. Whittington, son of Allen, and Susanna Vannoy, daughter of the Rev. James and Sarah Shepherd Vannoy. Alexander G. Whittington was a member of the Home Guards Militia.

The children of Vance and Sarah Jane were: Cleveland married Annie Johnson; Elizabeth and Laura Mae, recorded later; Maggie married Monroe Joines; and Lalar married Roby Staley.

The 1790 Census, Hillsborough District, Randolph County, lists Coonrod, Christopher, Martin, and Adam Jacob Staley. Coonrod is probably a misspelling for Conrad, as a legal title to property in Virginia is made to Conrad of Randolph County, N.C.

Adam Jacob (1740-1824), came to Wilkes County in the early 1800's. Wilkes records indicate he was drowned at the age of 84, attempting to cross the Yadkin River by boat, about eight miles east of Wilkesboro. His wife was listed as Eve Paster. One of his children was Jacob (1785-1865), who married Ben Cleveland's daughter, Martha; a son, Alfred who married Cleveland's daughter, Dianah; and my forefather Adam, who married Nancy Kilby, April 17, 1843.

Adam was the first Staley to live on Reddies River, on land inherited by his wife, Nancy, who was the granddaughter of John Shepherd born 1760, in Spottsylvania, Virginia, and died on Reddies River in 1812. His daughter, Lucy Shepherd, married Thornton Kilby, on October 10, 1822, and Nancy was their daughter. Thornton's father was Humphrey Kilby. Thornton later married Betsy Colvert in 1829, and Sarah Yeats in 1847.

The oldest child of Adam (1817-Oct. 16, 1888) and Nancy Staley (April 24, 1824 — April 20, 1914) was my grandfather, Thornton Staley, (March 14, 1844 — Jan. 2, 1918). He once told me he was too young to enter the Confederate Army, but carried the mail between Jefferson and Statesville riding mule back. He married Susan Dancy (Dec. 17, 1847 — April 11, 1934) on December 24, 1867.

Susan Dancy, was the daughter of Abraham J. Dance, Sr. the son of Edward Dancy, born March 1769, in Rowan County and his second wife Amelia Vannoy, whom he married July 8, 1802. Abraham J. was twice married. Susan's mother was his second wife, Sarah Ann Brown, whom he married October 14, 1845. My grandmother told me that each of Abraham's two wives had ten children, but I can find only 18. She also said two brothers died at Gettysburg, but I found only one. Abraham was a Primitive Baptist minister.

As a child two of my grandmother's brothers, Obediah and Edward Taylor Dancy, were my favorite relatives. Uncle "Obe" and Uncle Taylor were both tall, handsome men. Uncle Obe entertained me with his Confederate Army experiences. Uncle Taylor had a very straight figure and a long snow-white beard. We called him General Lee when he rode horseback because he looked like the pictures in our history books of General Lee. Uncle Taylor's first wife was Diana Staley, sister of my grandfather, Thornton Staley and his second wife was Martha Kilby, related to my grandmother Susan. Susan helped raise her youngest brother, Jim, who left his family in Wilkes and went to Bondtown, Virginia. He came back occasionally driving the biggest cars I saw during my early years.

Thornton and Susan Staley's ten children lived to maturity. They were: (1) Benjamin Franklin (Oct. 31, 1869-Sept. 6, 1957) married Mary Roberts and had 16 children; (2) Ollie (Oct. 10, 1872-Oct. 15, 1945) married Todd Whittington; (3) Cora (Dec. 10, 1874-May 23, 1969) married Allen H. Whittington who died young and Cora took her children, Ransom and Callie, back to her father's home; (4) Adam (April 22, 1876— July 19, 1955) married Elizabeth Whittington (Sept. 18, 1882-June 14, 1921); (5) Noah Jacob (June 14, 1878-Feb. 14, 1961) married Laura Mae Whittington (May 19, 1888 — April 13, 1974); (6) Mary Jane (Molly) married T.B. Jarvis; (7)

John (July 2, 1883-Feb. 25, 1965) married Dollie Whittington (Dec. 12, 1887-Sept. 11, 1979); (8) Nancy married Monroe Barlowe; (9) Hamilton D. (Mar. 20, 1877-April 1, 1951) married Nora Dancy; (10) Cromwell B. (April 6, 1896-Oct. 6, 1960) a veteran of World War I, married Ennis Shepherd, now living.

I have an older sister, Nellie Susan Billings, a retired teacher and widow of Everette Billings. My brother Joseph Taylor Staley, married Nancy Edna Johnson. They have two children, Laura Mae and Donald Joseph. Laura Mae married James Richard York, and they have two sons, Randall Eugene and Brian Keith. Donald married Ann Elizabeth Mathis (March) 26, 1956 — October 7, 1979), who died on the first birthday of their daughter, Crystal LeAnne.

I am Edna Staley Bivens, widow of Haskell Marsh Bivens (Hap), whose parents, Alice Marsh and Ellison H. Bivens were from two old Union County families. I am retired after 45 years in the teaching profession.

Sources: my memories of yesteryears, research in all available public records, gravestones, church records, family records.

— Edna S. Bivens

JACOB STALEY
1012

Jacob Staley was born in Guilford County, North Carolina in 1785, and died in Wilkes County about 1865. He was the son of Adam Jacob Staley who was born in Germany in 1740 and had settled in Guilford County, North Carolina by 1760.

Jacob came to Wilkes County with his father about 1800. In February 17, 1801, Adam Jacob Staley bought 150 acres of land on the waters of Brier Creek. The deed states that he was of Chatham County. Adam Jacob Staley was drowned while crossing the Yadkin River about seven miles below now North Wilkesboro in May of 1812. The wife of Adam Jacob Staley was Eve. The estate of Eve Staley was settled in 1834.

Jacob Staley married in September 1815, Ellender (called Nelley) Childers. They lived near the present Anitoch Baptist Church. The old Dutch Church was across the road from Antioch in the woods near a spring. It was built of logs with a balcony for the slaves to sit in. Below the old church site was the cemetery. There are about 125 graves there marked with field stones and have some dates on them, but are almost extinct. Some of the old Staleys are buried there.

Jacob and Ellender were received by Brier Creek Church by experience and baptism November 28, 1834. They reared a large family, as follows: (1) Esley, born 1815, died 1885, married Martha A. Cleveland 15 August 1843, daughter of John Harrison and Amelia Eliza Martin Cleveland. Esley was sheriff of Wilkes County from 1852 to 1860. He was also register of deeds for three years. He is buried in the old Presbyterian cemetery in Wilkesboro. (2) Adam, born 1817, married Nancy Kilby 17 April 1843, daughter of Thornton Kilby. Adam was also sheriff of Wilkes County in 1865. He is buried in the Staley cemetery on Reddies

Jacob and Sernetta Buttrey Staley.

River. (3) Jacob, born March 18, 1826, died April 25, 1903, married Sernetta Buttrey, daughter of Abraham and Sarah Barker Buttrey. They lived in the Dockery community near Traphill. Jacob had a mill on Camp Branch where he ground grain for meal and flour. He never locked his mill. He said that someone might come along hungry and need some bread. He also wove cloth and made clothes. Once at an election, a man killed another man with a knife. Jacob made a citizens arrest and held the man by his thumbs until the law came for him. (4) Alfred, born 1822, died 1898, married Dianah E. Cleaveland 2 December 1846, daughter of John Harrison and Amelia Eliza Martin Cleaveland. (5) Andrew Jackson, born 1836, died 1896, married Sarah E. Miller 11 February 1858. (6) Joseph, born 1830, married Nancy Buttrey, daughter of Abraham and Sarah Barker Buttrey. (7) Enoch, born 1832, died 1912, married Sarah Whittington in 1861. Both are buried in a family cemetery near Antioch Church. (8) Martha

Jacob and Sernetta Buttrey Staley had four children: (1) Sarah A. married John W. Myers September 11, 1867, the son of Allison and Elizabeth Mullis Myers. They lived and died in Virginia. (2) Ellen, born June 4, 1850, died October 11, 1933, married J.O. Brewer, son of Phelix Brewer. They lived near Traphill, where they had a store and a mill. (3) Sernetta, born 1861, died 1936, married Dolphus J. Myers, son of A.E. and Elizabeth Mullis Myers. (4) Mary R., born May 23, 1854, died May 17, 1934, married George E. Myers, son of A.E. and Elizabeth Mullis Myers. They lived at Dockery, N.C. They were members of Mt. Pisgah Baptist Church and are buried there.

Sources: Family members, records, Wilkes County Records.

— Samuel E. Sebastian

WILLIAM THORNTON STALEY
1013

Adam Staley, son of Jacob and Nellie Childress Staley, was born 19 Jan. 1817. Jacob was the son of Jacob and Eve Staley, the first of the line to come to Wilkes County, N.C. from Randolph County, N.C. This first Jacob drowned while crossing the Yadkin River in 1812.

Adam married Nancy Kilby, daughter of Thornton and Lucy Shepherd Kilby, on 17 April 1843. Thornton Kilby was the son of Humphrey who was born 1765-70 probably in Culpepper Co., Va. Humphrey was the son of William and Frances Eddins Kilby. William died in 1815 in the Reddies River area of Wilkes County. Lucy Shepherd, born about 1798, was the daughter of John Shepherd who was born about 1760 in Spotsylvania Co., Va. John died in Wilkes in 1812.

Adam and Nancy Kilby Staley were the parents of twelve children: (1) Thornton, born 14 Feb. 1844, married Susan Dancy, born 17 Dec. 1847, the daughter of a Baptist minister, Abraham J. Dancy, Sr. and his second wife, Sarah Ann Brown Dancy. Abraham was the son of Edward Dancy who was born about 1769 in Rowan Co., N.C. Edward married 8 July 1802 Amelia (Milly) Vannoy in Wilkes County. Edward's parents were John and Ann Morgan Dancy. Milly was the daughter of Francis Vannoy who was the son of John and Susannah Anderson Vannoy. Sarah Ann Brown is believed to be the daughter of Joseph and Fanny Brown. (2) Diana born about 1845 married Edward Taylor Dancy. (3) Sarah Ann was born about 1847. (4) Jacob, born about 1850, married Ellen Edminston 18 July 1888;

(5) Samuel E. Staley, born about 1852, died 26 Jan. 1942, married Julia Houck; (6) Martha Jane (White) born 25 Sept. 1853, married Adam Snyder; (7) Ellen born about 1855; (8) Franklin Oustin (F.O.) born 10 Oct. 1856, died 20 Feb. 1945, married to Diana Eller; (9) Elsie born about 1859; (10) Mollie, born about 1862, married W.H. Joines. (11) Shadrach H., born about 1865, married first Molly Eller 26 Feb. 1888 and married second Jennie Bumgarner 5 Oct. 1918. He died 1 July 1938. (12) John W. was born 13 Nov. 1868, married Martha Johnson 7 Aug. 1892, died 7 Nov. 1938.

Thornton and Susan Dancy Staley had ten children: Benjamin Franklin; Ollie; Cora; Adam; Noah Jacob; Mollie; John M.; Nancy; Hamilton D. and Crom B. Staley. More data on this family will be given in another sketch in this book.

Benjamin Franklin Staley, born 31 Oct. 1869, died 6 Sept. 1951, was married to Mary Elizabeth Roberts 11 Feb. 1893. She was born 22 June 1874, the daughter of William M. and Susan Adams Roberts. William was the son of Zachariah and Nancy Absher Roberts. Zachariah was the son of Joseph and Margaret Roberts Elledge and Nancy's parents were Ezekiel Absher and Jane Brown. Susan Adams was the daughter of Henry A. and Nancy Adams. Henry's parents were William H. and Nancy Adams Adams (daughter of an older Henry Adams). Henry A. Adams married first in 1835 Nancy Wyatt, daughter of Vickory Wyatt, Sr. and his wife, Mary Robbins. Henry married second, Nancy Brown, perhaps the daughter of Lindsay Brown who came to

Wilkes from Rockingham Co., N.C.

Benjamin F. and Mary Elizabeth Roberts Staley were the parents of sixteen children: Clarence (C.C.); Sallie Lou Ann; Nettie Bell; Annie Dewie; Nelia Cora; Sarah Belva; Ola Nancy; William Thornton; Richard Martin; Freddie Moore; Robert Doughton; Howard Taft; Thomas (Tam) Calloway; Jesse Willard; Mary Jane who drowned in Reddies River; and Willie Frances.

William Thornton Staley was born at Wilbar 28 Jan. 1906. He was inducted into the Army in 1942 while he was principal of Union Elementary School at Cricket in Wilkes County. He was captured by the Germans in Tunisia 14 Feb. 1943 and was a prisoner for twenty-eight months. After his release, he completed a retired teacher's term at Miller Creek school and again became principal of Union where he served until his retirement in 1972.

Thornton married Anne McNiel 6 June 1949. She was the daughter of William B. and Louisa H. Stout McNiel. Thornton and Anne were both teachers, having received their master's degrees from Appalachian State University in 1952. Anne taught at Maple Springs, Roaring River, Millers Creek and Union Elementary for a total of 34 years before retiring in 1969 due to arthritis. Thornton stays busy on his farm near Wilbar and Anne enjoys reading and sewing. She teaches an adult Sunday School class at Millers Creek United Methodist Church.

Their only child, William McNiel Staley, graduated from West Wilkes High School and was in his third year at UNC at Chapel Hill when he was drafted in 1973. He has served in the U.S. Air Force since then and is presently a technical sergeant stationed at International Airport in Los Angeles, Calif.

Sources: Personal knowledge and research by Mrs. Robert K. Hayes, Sr.

— W.T. Staley

DESCENDANTS OF JONATHAN STAMPER

1014

Jonathan Stamper, of English descent, was born in Middlesex County, Virginia April 24, 1719, died in Wilkes County in 1799, the son of Powell and Mary Brooks Stamper. He was named for his grandfather, Jonathan Brooks. The name Jonathan has been used by this family dozens of times since.

Before coming to North Carolina, he and his wife, Rachel, lived in Amherst County, Virginia where most of their children were born. He came to Rowan County (later Surry, now Wilkes) bought land on Bugaboo Creek adjoining the lands of Richard Allen, Revolutionary War soldier and first sheriff of Wilkes County. This land was about two miles from the present town of Ronda, N.C.

In 1772, Jonathan Stamper was a constable in the King's service in Surry Co., the Parish of St. Jude. In 1778, he was granted a license to keep an Ordinary (Tavern) in his now dwelling house with Richard Allen and Benjamin Cleveland as securities. Jonathan was a Patriot in the Revolutionary War, furnishing horses and

provisions for the army. In 1783, he sold his land on Bugaboo Creek and moved to upper Roaring River where he lived until his death.

An inventory and sale of his estate indicated that he was a man of means. His descendants intermarried with the families of Brown, Handy, Sebastian, Toliver, Davis, Burton, Moore, Carter, Adams, Turner and others. His children were: (1) James, born 1750, married Sarah Moore and went to Morgan County, Kentucky with his children and their families. His known children were William and Thomas Moore. (2) Joshua, born 1753, married Jane Woodward, lived in Clark County, Kentucky. His children were: John, Jonathan, Rachel, Richard, Susan, Polly and Nancy. (3) Joel, born 1755, married Nancy Cannaday, lived in Wilkes County. Their children were: Joel, Jr., Nancy, Asa, Richard, Nathaniel, James and possibly Margaret and Mary. (4) Jonathan, Jr. born 1757, married Mary Davis, lived in Ashe County. Children were: William, Jobe, Joshua, John, Solomon, Susan, Frances and one unknown. (5) Jacob, born 1762, married Susan, went to Owen County, Kentucky. Children were: Jesse, Jonathan, Elizabeth and Nancy. (6) Frances, born 1760's married Jesse Tolliver. Children were: Jane, Susan, John, Martha, Jacob, Allen, Solomon, Starling and Hirum. (7) Jesse, born 1760's married Barbara, lived in Wilkes County. They had children Jacob, Susannah, Sarah Ann Harissee, Rachel, Delphia, Frances, and Rinda. (8) Susannah, born 1767, married John P. Burton, lived in Ashe County, later moved to Lawrence County, Indiana. Children were: Richard, Martha, Allen Burton, John, Mary, David, William, Hutchings, Hardin and Zachariah.

Joel, Jacob, and Joshua Stamper and the son-in-laws, John P. Burton and Jesse Tolliver served in the Revolutionary War. Jacob Stamper was a man of small stature, served as a mounted scout, he not being able to walk long trips. Jesse Stamper was a dwarf, as were two of his daughters, Rachel and Delphia. Jacob and his sons, Jesse and Jonathan went to Cincinnati, Ohio, where they made brick and built houses. They later came back to Owen County, Kentucky and spent their last days there.

Jesse married Nancy Sebastian and his brother Jonathan, married Mary Sebastian her sister, daughters of Benjamin Sebastian of Wilkes County, N.C.

Jesse and Nacy's grandson, F.M. Stamper founded the Stamper Food Company in Missouri, a multi-million dollar company, which is now the Banquet Foods. Other descendants of Jonathan and Rachel Stamper became teachers, lawyers, doctors, politicans, and successful business people in North Carolina, Kentucky, Missouri and Virginia.

The Stamper families now living in Wilkes County are descendants of Jonathan, Jr. and Polly Davis Stamper, who lived in Ashe County, N.C. until their deaths in the 1830's.

Sources: Christ Church Parish records, N.C., Ky., Mo. and early Va. records.

— Samuel E. Sebastian

NATHAN and JULIE STANBERRY

1015

There is very little information that has been located about their early years. Some records indicate that Nathan was born about 1755 and could be tied in with the Stanberrys of Elizabeth and Woodbridge, New Jersey; but there is no proof.

The first record we have of them is the 1787 Census of Wilkes County, even though two of their children indicated in later records that they were born in North Carolina prior to that date. They obtained Land Grants for 100 acres and 25 acres in 1788 and 1789. The land was located just east of the present town of Darby on Elk Creek. They farmed the same land for about 30 years and raised a large family.

In 1818, both tracts of land were sold to Darby Hendrix. Apparently, the lure of new land in Indiana swept through Wilkes County at this time, because Nathan and some of his neighbors moved to Wayne County. Nathan's will is recorded in the Wayne County records in 1819. It lists the distribution of his worldly goods to his children David, Moses, and Elizabeth. We must assume that Julie, his wife, died sometime prior to the death of Nathan. In fact, Julie, is mentioned only once in all the records located to date. Nathan and Julie Stanberry are listed as the parents of David in the Whitley County, Kentucky, death records of 1855.

Of their large number of children, six have been identified as follows:

John Harrison, born about 1780 and died prior to 1850 in Ashe County N.C. He married Ann Ernest on 11-28-1811 in Wilkes County and did not move to Indiana with the rest of the family. They had ten children: Mary, Eda, David N., Jesse, Harriet, John H., Anna H., Nathan W., Joshua Sentor, and Margaret.

David, born 2-1-1784 in N.C. and died 2-12-1855 in Whitley Co., Kentucky. He married Rachel Holman (daughter of Thomas) on 9-6-1806. Moved to Indiana with his father and remained until about 1825 and then to Kentucky where they lived in Laurel and Whitley Counties. They had five children: Malinda, Margaret, Francis, John, and Ira.

Prudence, born after 1784 in N.C. and died about 1869 in Henry County, Indiana. She married Daniel Jackson on 8-11-1807 in Wilkes County. They moved to Indiana and finally settled in Henry County. Daniel Jackson's will in 1823 was witnessed by his brother-in-law Moses Stanberry. They had a large family, but we only know the names of Daniel C. and Martha E.

Nathan, born after 1790 and died prior to 1850 in Owen County, Indiana. He married Polly Allen on 4-20-1817 in Wilkes County. They moved to Indiana and had four children: Malinda, David, John, Betsy.

Moses, born about 1800 and died in 1862 in Whitley County, Kentucky. He moved with his father to Indiana. After his father's death, he lived with his sister Prudence or brother David until about 1825, when he moved to Whitley County, Kentucky. He married Mary Elizabeth Snyder on 5-11-1827. They had ten children:

William I, Justin A., Ollie J., John M., Nathan J., Letha E., Henry C., Sarah A., Martha E., and Moses.

Elizabeth, born about 1802 and died in 1881 in Laurel County, Kentucky. She married William McHargue. They had seven children: Nancy, James, John, Jane, Barbara, Malinda, and Mary. A.

Sources: Census, Tax, Court, and Land Records of North Carolina, Indiana, and Kentucky; family records.

— R.W. Stanberry

JOHN H. STANSBURY

1016

John H. Stansbury and his wife, Ann Earnest, were my great-great grandparents. He was born in Wilkes County about 1780. She was born about 1790. They were married in Wilkes County on November 28, 1811. Although John's father, Nathan Stansberry, and his brothers and sisters moved to Wayne County, Indiana in 1818, he chose to remain in Wilkes County with his wife and young family.

In 1818, John H. Stansbury bought 99 acres of land from William Lenoir located on both sides of the Yadkin River. In 1826 the State of North Carolina granted him 100 acres of land on the Waters of the South Fork of New River in Ashe County. This land would now be in Watauga County.

John and Ann Stansbury were members of the historic "Three Forks Baptist Church" near Boone, North Carolina. According to the records of the church he was an active and consistent member. He died before 1850. She died before 1870.

The children of John H. and Ann (Earnest) Stansbury were:

Mary Matilda born in 1814. Married David Cook about 1835. Their children: Emiline married (1) Harrison Taylor (2) Jackson Lewis; Elizabeth married Franklin Dolinger; Edith married (1) John Taylor (2) Harrison Baker Miller; John Henry married Evaline Miller; Harrison married Mary Ann Tucker (my grandparents) and Jesse married Matilda Phipps.

Jesse married Martha Hodge. Their children: Smith; Thomas; Mary; Louisa; Adolphus married Polly Wheeler; Martha; McDuffy; Nancy; and Melinda.

David Nelson married Mary Lawrence. Their children: John Senter married Martha Alverta McNeil; William Henry married (1) Caroline Graybill (2) Julia Toliver; Mary; George and Sebastian.

Joshua Senter married Mary Brown September 6, 1859. Their children: Nancy; William; David H.; Virginia; Harrison; Arthur; Emit; John; Sarah; and Cordie.

Nathan William born February 10, 1828. Died September 13, 1914. Married Olive Howell on January 15, 1858. Their children: Amos married (1) Mary Ann Tatum (2) Rosa Norris; John never married; Melinda married a Davis; and Sara married Westley Phillips.

Anna Harriet never married, but had a son John Stansbury.

John H. Stansbury, Jr. born November 29, 1829. Died August 16, 1923. Married Cynthia Goss. Their children: William Jehu married (1)

Ellen Graybill (2) Lena Cox; Emit married Susan Tucker; Jane married David Graybill; and Joseph Orrin married Millie Ann Snow.

Edith (Eda) married Hugh Phipps on January 20, 1842. Lived in Alleghany County, North Carolina. Their children: Ruth Ann married a Dixon; Matilda married Jesse Cook; Melinda married James Landreth; Alex; Zana; John Andrew married Martha Landreth; and Rhoda married Alex Hash.

Margaret married Harvey McGuire on January 29, 1847. No further information on this family.

Elizabeth is believed to have married a man by the name of Parsons of Grassy Creek, North Carolina.

Most of the children of John H. Stansbury and his wife Ann (Earnest) Stansbury changed the name back to the original spelling Stansberry and Stanberry.

Sources: Wilkes and Ashe County Records; family recollections.

— Violet (Cook) Bohnert

NATHAN STANSBERRY

1017

Among the early settlers of Wilkes County was Nathan Stansberry. He is first listed in the 1787 Wilkes County State Census. In 1789 the State of North Carolina granted him 100 acres and in 1798 another 55 acres of land on Elk Creek.

Nathan Stansberry is included in the Wilkes County Taxables from 1787 to 1797. He is also listed on jury duty in the 1794 Court Minutes and in 1792 and 1796 on road maintenance.

The 1800 Wilkes County Census list him with ten children. The known children were: David, John H., Nathan, Jr., Moses, Prudence and Elizabeth. Nathan, Jr. married Polly Allen on April 20, 1817. John H. married Ann Earnest on November 28, 1811. Prudence married Daniel Jackson on August 11, 1807. Prudence and her husband moved to Wayne County, Indiana in 1812. Daniel used the Mississippi River to haul meat and other farm produce to New Orleans. On one trip he contacted malaria and died in 1823 before his last child was born.

In 1817, after the death of his beloved wife, Julia, Nathan Stansberry sold 125 acres of land on Elk Creek to Darby Hendrix. This land on Elk Creek is now known as Darby. After selling his land, Nathan Stansberry moved to Wayne County, Indiana with his children Nathan, Jr., David, Moses, and Elizabeth. My great-great grandfather, John H. Stansberry, chose to remain in Wilkes County with his wife and young family.

In 1819 Nathan Stansberry died in Wayne County, Indiana. His will was dated February 13, 1819. Nathan, Jr. moved to Owen County, Indiana with his family and died before 1850. David, who married Rachael Holman, Moses who married Elizabeth Snider, and Elizabeth who married William McHargue III, moved to Kentucky.

Sources: Wilkes Co. Records, Wayne Co., Ind. Will Book, Family Research.

— Violet (Cook) Bohnert

MISS NORMA STEVENSON
1018

Though not a native of Wilkes County by birth, Norma Stevenson has been a valued citizen of the county for sixty years.

Interestingly enough, and perhaps unknown to many, her maternal grandfather, Alexander H. Matheson, had a mercantile store at Boomer in Wilkes County when her mother was a small child.

Miss Stevenson traces her Scotch-Irish ancestry to William Stevenson who migrated to the United States from Ulster, Ireland in 1745. She was born 9 July 1901 in Taylorsville, North Carolina to Dr. Thomas Franklin Stevenson and his wife who was Sophia Jane Matheson before their marriage on 4 November 1896.

Dr. Stevenson, a native of Iredell County, born 18 May 1868, died 31 January 1928 was the son of James Harvey Stevenson, a one time member of the North Carolina State Legislature, and his wife, Elizabeth McFarland Stevenson. Mrs. Stevenson, a native of Alexander County, born 3 February 1877, died 7 April 1959, was the daughter of Alexander Hall Matheson and his wife Harriet Bolick Matheson.

Dr. Stevenson received his medical education at the University of Louisville in Kentucky. He practiced medicine in Taylorsville, Huntersville and Hickory, North Carolina.

To Dr. and Mrs. Stevenson were born three children: Charles Louis, who married Josephine Bartlett; Norma; and Mary Esther who married Joseph Robert Barrett, Jr. The Barretts were the parnets of one son, Joseph Robert Barrett III.

Norma Stevenson, better known as "Steve", received her nurse's training at Richard Baker Hospital in Hickory, N.C. She was employed for a short time at Davis Hospital in Statesville before coming on 1 April 1923 to Dr. F.C. Hubbard's newly established, Wilkes Hospital.

Here she was chosen to assist in the operating room, help in the doctor's office, and later to assist in X-ray and laboratory procedures. In short, to do whatever needed to be done. There were no "eight-hour shifts" at that time, so she with other hospital personnel served long hours whenever patients needed attention. Many of the conveniences of today were unobtainable at that time, making their tasks even harder. On occasion she accompanied Dr. Hubbard to assist him in surgery on patients who could not come to the hospital for lack of ambulance service.

After the establishment of Wilkes General Hospital she has continued to assist Dr. Hubbard in his office.

She has been a faithful member of the First Presbyterian Church, having served as president of the Women of the Church, circle chairman, and on various committees. The members of her Sunday School class, of which she has been president for many years, look forward to the special flowers she brings each Sunday.

In addition to church work, she has been very active in the American Legion Auxiliary

Miss Norma Stevenson.

and has done volunteer work in other civic organizations.

Forthright in speech, firm in her convictions, compassionate beyond the call of duty, Norma Stevenson has been a comforting presence in time of trouble to patients, friends and acquaintances.

Distinctive in appearance and with a refreshing attitude toward life, she enjoys a wide circle of friends of varied ages, contributing socially as well as professionally to the community.

Sources: The Stevenson Genealogy; *Doctors and Hospitals in Wilkes County, 1830 to 1975* by Dr. F.C. Hubbard; personal knowledge.

— Mary S. Smithey

STOKES FAMILY OF "MOURNE ROUGE"
1019

David Stokes was a citizen of wealth and influence in Lunenburg county, Va. His fortune had been greatly aided by his marriage to Sarah Montfort, whose family was wealthy. Two of the sons of this union came to North Carolina, John and Montfort.

Montfort Stokes was born in Lunenburg county, Va. in 1762 and apparently had an excellent education. In 1776 at age fourteen, he volunteered in the new American Navy, was captured by the British near Norfolk and spent seven months as a prisoner on a British warship. He had a tendency to the free use of profanity and a passionate love of gambling.

After the War, Montfort came to N.C. Montfort studied law in his brother John's law office in Salisbury. In 1790, at age 28, he became Clerk of Superior Court of Rowan County and a captain in the State Militia. In the next two decades he rose rapidly to become the principal political leader of western N.C. In 1799 he became Clerk of the State Senate, a position which he held continuously for 17 years.

After his retirement from the Senate, Gen.

Stokes spent several years quietly at Morne Rouge, representing Wilkes county twice in the General Assembly. In 1830 his public career was crowned by his election as governor of North Carolina, and in the following year he was re-elected. During his second term, he resigned to accept from President Jackson an appointment as Indian Agent in Arkansas, and immediately moved to Fort Gibson, where he spent the last ten years of his life, dying there in 1842 at age eighty.

In 1790, Montfort Stokes married Mary Irwin, daughter of Gen. Henry Irwin. The following year, shortly after the birth of their only child, Mary Adelaide, Mary died. In January 1796, Montfort Stokes married at "Fort Definace", Wilkes county, Rachel Montgomery, daughter of Hugh Montgomery. He was 34 and she was 16.

The marriage of Montfort and Rachel did not prove to be a happy one. From the disparity of their ages and the differences in their backgrounds, their marriage was doomed from the beginning. Their married life covered a period of 46 years and the birth of 10 children, but they were never congenial. With the passing of the years they grew further apart.

Stokes' lifelong habits of swearing, drinking and gambling, were repugnant to the strictly reared Rachel. As a reaction she turned to religion, was "converted" to Methodism, and became so devoutly pious as to border on the fanatical. When Stokes resigned the governorship to become Indian Agent, he went west alone. Rachel remained behind at Morne Rouge, and they lived apart for the remaining ten years of his life.

His first seven children were born in Salisbury, but in 1813 the family removed to a large plantation on the Yadkin River in Wilkes which Rachel had inherited from her father. Gen. Stokes named this place Morne Route, French for "red hill". There he built a large, square frame mansion.

His eleven children were: (1) Mary Adelaide, married at Morne Rouge her first husband, Henry Chambers. After his death she returned to live at Morne Rouge where in 1822 she married Maj. Wm. B. Lewis. She died the year following her marriage. (2) Hugh Montgomery, born 1796 and graduated from the University of N.C. at age 18. He moved to Morganton, but because his drinking became steadily worse, he was obliged to give up his law practice. He returned to Wilkes to live with his mother and became an itinerant school teacher in Wilkes. He died unmarried in 1869 and was buried at Morne Rouge.

(3) David Montfort, born 1799, was in the Navy and Revenue Marine Service. In 1833 married Eliza Mimmo. He died five years later, at the age of 39. (4) Rebecca Camilla, born 1800, at age 19 married at Morne Rouge, Maj. William C. Emmit. Emmit fell into such severe financial straits that they were obliged to return to Morne Rouge to live. Camilla, embittered like her mother, sought solace in religion and became even more fanatically devout than Rachel. She died childless at Morne Rouge and is buried there. (5) Thomas Jefferson, born 1800, married a young woman his parents bitterly disapproved and became the fami-

Governor Montford Stokes.

children. He was educated at the old Appalachian Training School in Boone, Trinity College, and Chapel Hill, from which he received a master's degree in 1920. He received his law degree from Wake Forest College School of Law and his law license in 1933.

Mr. Story served nine terms in the General Assembly from Wilkes County and was minority leader of the legislature for four years. He was state Republican Chairman in 1953.

The early part of his life was dedicated to education. He came to Wilkesboro in 1924 and headed the district high school as principal for 15 years. He took up the practice of law in 1939 when he was 51 years old.

He was a leader and faithful member of the Wilkesboro Baptist Church. He served a term as moderator of the Brushy Mountain Baptist Association.

He was a member of the Masonic Lodge, Knights of Pythias, and served as secretary of the North Wilkesboro Kiwanis Club for many years.

Mr. Story married Mary Clarissa Downs. She was born in Caldwell County June 19, 1895. She died in 1951.

Three sons were born to this union: Thomas E. Story, Jr. married Ruth Hulcher. They have three children, Rebecca Story Wilson, Thomas E. III, and Clarissa.

Donald D. Story married Margaret (Peggy) Somers. They have two children, Martha Lynne Moore and Donald D. Jr.

Robert Story married Virginia Brame. Their children are William Robert Story, Jr. and Sandra Story. They reside in Charlotte.

Mr. Story died June 20, 1972, and he and Mrs. Story are buried at Mount Lawn.

Sources: Newspaper articles and grave stones.

— Thomas E. Story, Jr.

STURDIVANT FAMILY
1021

John C. Downing made a contribution to the Atlanta Journal on the Sturdivant name, October 5, 1975. Sturdivant was a name given to an attendant who preceeded the Herald through the streets and on the highways. It was the "Sterten-avaunt" (goer before) who would call out "Make way for the Kings Herald" and also make arrangements at the various Inns along the road for the Hearlds lodging. Usually only Kings and Nobles employed Herolds.

In England William Stircivant and Robertus Stircyvant were on the 1379 Yorkshire Poll Tax Rolls. John Richard Thomas and Alan Sterevant lived in Yorkshore between 1404-1445. John Sturdivant is listed in the register of St. Dionis Backchurch, London in 1570. Elizabeth, wife of Thomas Sturdivant was buried in the St. Mary Aldermary Church Yard in 1685.

Burkes General Armory describes the Sturdivant Arms. Samuel Sturtevant or Sturdevant was noted in Massachusetts in 1641 and William was noted in Connecticut in 1676. Three Sturtivants, all from Mass. were officers in the American Revolutionary Army. In Virginia John Sturdevant shared a 600 acre land grant in Henrico County in 1652.

ly "black sheep". He died in Tennessee in 1852, aged 49 years.

(6) Sarah Montfort, born 1806, married in 1833 her cousin, Capt. Joseph W. Hackett and took up residence on the south side of the Yadkin, directly opposite Morne Rouge. Eight years later she was dead, leaving five orphans. The only surviving child of this family was the youngest, Sallie Hackett, who married Capt. Thomas S. Bouchelle.

(7) Algernon Sydney, born 1810, on attaining the years of discretion replaced his first name with his father's and is known in history as Montfort Sydney Stokes. His management of Morne Rouge was highly successful, and the people of Wilkes held him in such high esteem they elected him to the office of Chairman of the County Court. At the age of 47, he married Sarah Eliza Triplett, age 20, daughter of a neighboring planter. Three years later Sydney was appointed Lieut-Col. of the 1st N.C. Regt. CSA. His wife died May 10, 1862, and on June 26, 1862 he was mortally wounded in the Seven Days Battle around Richmond and died July 3rd. His body was brought back

to Wilkes and buried at Morne Rouge. They left children: Laurence Crain and Rebecca Camilla. "Larry" grew up to become a physician but died young and childless. Camilla called "Minnie", married Charles N. Hunt of Maizefield. Gertrude, daughter of Minnie and Charles N. Hunt married Andrew Blaine Johnston.

(8) Henry Irwin born 1813, died young. (9) Catherine Jane born 1815, married age 38, Dr. Abram Franklin Alexander, and died a year after her marriage. (10) Anne Neville born 1818, married Judge Roland Jones. (11) Rachel Adelaide born 1827, married Laurence P. Crain.

Sources: Excerpts from a paper on "The Stokes Family of Morne Rouge".

— R.B. Johnston

THOMAS EDGAR STORY
1020

Thomas Edgar Story was born in Watauga County March 11, 1888 to Joshua Clingman and Martha Ann Day Story. He was one of 14

Thomas Edgar Story.

The Reins Sturdivant Burial Association was organized in 1933 by W.K., A.A. and Madge Sturdivant and C.A. Canter. It has remained one of the largest and strongest in the state. Since the death of A.A. Sturdivant in 1971, the officers of the association are W.K. Sturdivant, Sec'y., Madge L. Sturdivant, president and Thomas Lenderman, assistant secretary and manager.

W.K. Sturdivant helped acquire and organize six Reins Sturdivant Funeral Homes in western N.C. and Virginia. In 1956, he was instrumental in the organization of Sturdivant Life Insurance Company and served as the first president.

In 1961, Reins Sturdivant Funeral home was re-located in a new building with spacious grounds on Armory Road. Reid Sturdivant, Jr. was a stockholder and manager from 1960 until 1968.

Mount Lawn Memorial Park was started in 1942 in a north-west area beyond North Wilkesboro. Beside being located on beautifully rolling hills, the Blue Ridge Mountains are viewed from west and north and the Brushy Mountains from the south. Later, the Sturdivant Memorial Mausoleum was established.

W.K. Sturdivant has also been involved in church, community and state affairs.

William Kent Sturdivant and Madge Elizabeth Linney were married August 25, 1932 and to this union were born: William Kent, Jr., March 16, 1934 and Nancy Kathryn, March 31, 1936.

William Kent Sturdivant, Jr. married Linda Sue Walker and to this union were born: Lisa Lynn, born September 1961; Leslie LeAnn born March 6, 1963; and William Kent, III, born January 31, 1964. Lisa Lynn married June 1981, Randall Blake Jarvis and they have Laura Kathryn Jarvis, born May 5, 1982.

Nancy Kathryn Sturdivant married Gilbert A. Martinez. To this union was born Heather Amelda Martinez, born September 18, 1970.

Sources: Personal research and knowledge.

— Madge Linney Sturdivant

WINBURN SUMMERLIN
1022

The spelling of the Summerlin family name has taken many forms in early American records. Can you picture a County Clerk, probably English, listening to a Scotchman pronounce his name and then write it on a document? Is it any wonder the name might be spelled differently each time it was written? One document alone has spelled Summerlin three different ways.

This family goes back to James Somervaill of Gladstaines, Scotland, born about 1620-25. A John Somervell of Edinborough came to the Isle of Wight county, Virginia in the 1687. At this point our Summerlin family began to grow.

Winburn Summerlin was born in Bertie County, NC in November, 1762 son of Lazarus and Susanne Bunch Summerlin, daughter of Henry Bunch of Bertie Co. Lazarus owned land as early as 1757. The family farm of 450

John Wesley Sturdivant was born in Wilkes County in 1834, married Gemima Mayberry September 20, 1857. To this union were born: Mary Sturdivant Bedwell in 1859; James Franklin Sturdivant May 24, 1862; Eliza Sturdivant 1864. Gemima died in 1870. The family then moved to Grayson County, Va. in 1874. Eliza died in 1896 and was buried in Pleasant Grove Baptist Church cemetery, east of Independence, Va. John Wesley Sturdivant died in 1906 and was buried in the Pleasant Grove cemetery.

James Franklin Sturdivant, son of John Wesley and Gemima, married Bessie Alverta Watson in 1878. To this union were born: Robert M. who married Pearl Donalson and moved to Hoquiam, Washington; Gemima who married M.E.H. Wingate; Everette Reid who married Myrtle Draper; Lynn Watson who married Allie Rose Wingate; Fieldon Lundy

who married Geneva Wingate; Mattie Eliza who married T. Kelly Morton; Alma Jane who married T.C. McKnight; Dewey Franklin who married Marie Wingate; William Kent who married Madge Elizabeth Linney and Alvin Alexander who married Rosalyn Caldwell.

William Kent Sturdivant, Sr. arrived in North Wilkesboro from Richmond, Va. on April 22, 1926 to assist J.C. Reins with Ready Undertakers. He had just completed eight years of service with Pruden Hutcheson General Store and Funeral Home in Chase City, Va. After assisting Mr. Reins for awhile, he aquired a financial interest in the business.

In 1930, the remainder of the funeral home was purchased from Mr. Reins by W.K. Sturdivant, A.A. Sturdivant and C.A. Canter, and became Reins Sturdivant Funeral Home, on Main Street. Also this funeral home offered ambulance service.

acres located at the mouth of the Muddy Branch and bounded by Cushy and Guyshall Swamp. "Lazarus, Susanna, and their son, Winburn of Orange Co., NC." sold part of this land in 1774.

The family moved westward to Wilkes County, NC by 1782.

Winburn enlisted in Washington Co., Tennessee, in the North Carolina Volunteers in August, 1781 at age 18. After serving 8 months he returned to the family farm located on the Lewis Fork.

He married Milly Davis Pearson, a widow, in February, 1786. Milly's first husband, Abel, had been killed by the Tories after the Battle of King's Mountain. Winburn and Milly's seven children were born and raised on their farm. Their dates of birth are: Griffin, 8 Oct. 1787; Susanna, 1 Sept 1789; Miles, 16 May 1790; Lazarus (Jr.), 26 Dec 1792; Hannah, 17 Dec 1794; Thomas Davis, 7 May 1797; and Sarah, 27 Nov 1799. These children married the following: Griffin married Patsy Cleveland 4 Dec 1813; Susanna married Abner Trible 17 June 1815; Miles married Sarah Proffitt 10 March 1814; Lazarus (Jr) married Tempy Cross, daughter of Asel Cross, 24 May 1815; Hannah married William Minton; Thomas Davis married Bathsheba Robards 1 Dec 1824, and Sarah married John Hamby 28 Mar 1842.

Thomas and Lazarus Jr. left Wilkes around 1830. Thomas, Bathsheba, son Rufus, daughters Edith, Hannah, and Lorena left in 1833, finally settled in Scotland Co., Missouri. Life on the farm was harsh, and the family was split between the North and the South. Thomas died prior to 1859 and Bathsheba prior to March, 1864.

Lazarus (Jr) with Tempy and his daughter, Milly, left Wilkes Co. before 1830 for White County, Illinois where he was listed on the 1830 Census. Milly was married in Hamilton Co. on 22 Aug 1839 to William Bradford. The other Winburn children remained in North Carolina.

Winburn is listed occasionally in the Wilkes Co. Court of P & Qs for various activities. He helped build roads in May of 1801. On 4 May 1814 William Gwynn was bound over to Winburn by the Court. On 1 May 1820 Jonathan Yates, age 13, was bound over to Winburn to learn the blacksmith trade. But Winburn was a farmer and that was his trade. Winburn appeared before the Court of Pleas at age 70 on 14 Nov 1832 to qualify for his American Revolutionary War Pension. He was placed on the rolls on 7 Oct 1833. He died on 24 April 1842 on his farm.

His wife, Milly, at age 89 years applied on 2 June 1843 for her benefits under the pension. She was in ill health and could not personally appear, but her daughter, Susannah Tribell, did appear as did a long time friend, Emily Alspaugh. Emily stated she had witnessed the marriage of Winburn and Milly back in February, 1786. Milly lived only a few more years.

Sources: Family Bibles; Personal Letters; Wilkes Co. N.C. records; Nat'l. Archives; *Families of Summerlin, Etc. by J.H. Hines;* Bertie Co. N.C. records.

— Robert Summerlin Monson

HARRY SUMMERS FAMILY
1023

Jacob Summers, the original Summers immigrant to North Carolina, was born in 1710 near Ober Bexbach in Germany, and died in 1790 at home in Guilford County. His burial is marked on a massive granite rock in Friedens Cemetery near Gibsonville, N.C. The inscription on the marker reads: Jacob Summers, aged 80 years, Margaret Summers died 1810 age 90 years.

Jacob married Margaret Faust in 1751, and they sailed soon after for America, on the ship "Neptune". Landing in Philadelphia on September 24, 1751, they spent their first winter in Pennsylvania, and in the spring of 1752, traveled by wagon to North Carolina. They settled in Guilford County near where the Reedy Fork Creek empties into the Haw River.

Jacob was one of the founders of Friedens Lutheran Church in 1771. He and Margaret were survived by 2 daughters and 1 son, Peter.

Captain Peter Summers was a member of the First North Carolina Battalion in the Revolutionary War. He was with President Washington during his visit to the grounds of the Battle of Guilford Court House in 1791.

Peter erected the first brick house in Guilford County in 1785. According to an article published in *The Greensboro Patriot,* dated August 2, 1928, "this is a handsome structure and is still standing in an excellent state of preservation".

Being a faithful and devoted member of the church which his father helped establish, Peter was seldom absent from services. According to old records kept at Friedens Lutheran, his name always appeared first on the communion lists.

Peter married 4 times and had 9 children.

The Summers lineage can be traced to the present through Peter's son Abel; Abel's son, Nathan Iley (about 1842-1877); and his son Oscar (1873-1936).

Oscar was a contractor in Raleigh and married Jennie Powell. They had 6 children.

Among them was Harry Lee Summers, born in Wake County, January 16, 1904. He attended schools in Raleigh, and in 1926, came to North Wilkesboro as a cashier for the Southern Railway. Harry was later employed in the office of the International Shoe Company Tannery. After the Tannery in North Wilkesboro was destroyed in the 1940 flood, he was transferred to Morganton for 2 years. Upon his return to North Wilkesboro, Harry was appointed a Deputy Collector for the North Wilkesboro Office of the North Carolina Department of Revenue. He served this position well until his retirement in 1970.

Harry was instrumental in the organization of the Wilkes Rescue Squad and was an active member for 11 years. He was a lifetime charter member of the North Carolina Association of Rescue Squads. For over 25 years, he was a member of the North Wilkesboro Fire Department, and served as secretary. He was a member of the First Presbyterian Church, and was a Mason and a Shriner.

Harry married Emma Lee Gentry in 1926,

Harry Summers.

and their marriage announcement, published in *The Wilkes Journal,* read as follows:

A wedding of much interest was solemnized last Saturday night when Mr. Harry Summers and Miss Emma Lee Gentry were united in marriage, Reverend George G. Reeves officiating.

The bride is the attractive daughter of Mrs. C.B. Gentry of D Street and has many friends throughout this section who will wish her much happiness. She has been employed for some time by Dr. Casey.

The groom is a popular young man and holds a position with the Southern Railway.

Harry died in January, 1972. He was survived by 7 children: Mrs. A. Lee (Dorothy) Deal; Mrs. A.L. (Betty) Kilby; Charles Summers; Mrs. J.W. (Jean) Beasley; Harry L. Summers, Jr., Mrs. Alan (Rita) Foster, and William D. Summers.

His wife Emma Lee, in addition to their children, has 17 grandchildren and 9 greatgrandchildren.

Sources: Family records, and personal knowledge.

— Betty Kilby Foster

MRS. HARRY SUMMERS
1024

At the turn of the nineteenth century, Willie Daniel Lee and Cornelius Bonaparte Gentry came to North Wilkesboro from Guilford County, North Carolina, bringing with them their household belongings and seven children. Their ninth child was to be born several years later, their first having died in infancy.

My grandmother, Mama Gentry, had a brother, John Robert Alonza Caffey, who had journeyed to North Wilkesboro earlier, on the first scheduled passenger train to go to the western termius of the railroad. John went into the furniture business and built a house near the bridge in Wilkesboro. In 1901, he was one of the organizers of the Forest Furniture Company. Cornelius Bonaparte, affectionately known as Boney, sought employment with the Forest Furniture Company and worked with them until he suffered a stroke and was paralized.

John Caffey became very interested in the town of North Wilkesboro and was one of the "founding fathers" there, building the third house in the town, which is known as the Rector home on E Street. He also built for his sister, Maggie Hayes, a home, which was later to become the Presbyterian Manse on E Street. He twice served the town of North Wilkesboro as mayor, but resigned during his second term, so he could sell land to the town for a new waterworks. In 1911, John and his family moved to Guilford County where he became a U.S. Commissioner.

The ninth child of Willie and Boney was born in North Wilkesboro. Her name was Emma Lee. She attended the North Wilkesboro school. Since my grandfather was paralyzed and bedridden, my Mother spent her afternoons with him. She has such fond memories of these times together. My grandfather passed away when my Mother was only ten years old.

My grandmother and her son, Claude started a bakery in North Wilkesboro, on Sixth Street. This bakery, known as City Bakery, rapidly grew, and a new bakery was built near the school on D Street. Mother has told me of the many times she had gone to the bakery at night with her mother to prepare the dough for the following day.

Emma Lee Summers (Mrs. Harry).

In 1926, Harry L. Summers came to North Wilkesboro, from Raleigh, with the Southern Railway. He met and married Emma Lee, November 20, 1926. They had seven children; Dorothy Deal; Betty Kilby; Jean Beasley; Charles Summers; Harry Summers, Jr.; Rita Foster and William Summers.

At the time of this writing, they have eighteen grandchildren, and nine great grandchildren.

Sources: Caffeys, Iseleys & Irelands Genealogies and family Bible.

— Mrs. Jean Beasley

JOSEPH RALPH and VENNIE LEE CARLTON SWANSON
1025

Joseph Ralph Swanson was born September 16, 1895 at Boomer N.C. the son of Sidney and Julia Sherrill Swanson. He was a Veteran of World War I. He attended Appalachian College at Boone and was the only male student in music at that time. He taught three years in the Wilkes County Schools.

He was married to Vennie Lee Carlton October 16, 1920. They had one son Sidney Carlton Swanson born November 22, 1935. Carlton Swanson was a graduate of Lees-McCrae College and N.C. State College. He served three years in the U.S. Army.

Carlton Swanson and Sue Ferguson were married January 16, 1958. They have one daughter, Karen. She was a graduate of ASU. Karen Swanson married Mike Coffey December 14, 1980.

Ralph Swanson was a farmer and had a dairy. He was also a land surveyor. He died August 19, 1956.

Vennie Carlton was born in Caldwell County to Daniel Milton Carlton and Julia Elizabeth Brookshire. She helped with the farm; sold on the curb market; was Postmaster at Boomer from 1953 through 1972. She does volunteer work at the Cancer Clinic, Bloodmobile and has worked as a Pink Lady at Wilkes Hospital.

Carlton and Sue Swanson live at Boone where he works for Southern Bell Telephone Co and Sue works for ASU in the Alumni department.

Mike and Karen Coffey moved from Boone to Boomer N.C. in May 1982. Mike and Karen Coffey drive a transfer truck and are planning a Christmas tree farm. Mike and Karen Coffey were students at ASU.

Sources: personal knowledge.

— Vennie L. Swanson

Ernest A. Tedder.

ERNEST ATWELL TEDDER
1026

Ernest Tedder was born July 18, 1931, on the Brushy Mtns. He is the youngest of seven children born to Rellie Jefferson and Pearlie Louvenia Treadaway Tedder. His brothers and sisters are Lona Belle, Eli, Dean, Edna, Daniel and Rouie Mae.

On July 5, 1951 Ernest married Esther Ruth Hayes. His children are Ernestine Holland, Ernest Arthur; Kathy Louis Crysel; Steven Douglas; Kimberly Carol; John StClair; Charles Ray and Richard Treadaway.

Ernest graduated from Wilkesboro High School in 1948. He was a salesman for Frank H. Crow Co. for about seventeen years. In 1970 Ernest was appointed as Wilkes County's first full time magistrate, and served as judge for most of the small claims cases. He held this position until June of 1981 when he had a stroke and retired on disability.

His greatest interest was in genealogy, and he spent most of his spare time for about thirty years searching old records and obtaining information on his and other's families in Wilkes and other counties. He discovered that a lot of the older rural churches kept their very old church records and that they often contained family data that could not be obtained from other sources. His favorite "Find" was records about one church member, who frequently got excluded from the church's membership for having children out of wed-lock. He thought she finaly had it made when the church records read that she had gotten married and had been taken back into the church. However, a short time later, the records read that it had became obvious to the deacons of the church that she was with child before her marriage, so out she went again. No further mention was made of her, so she must have given up on that church.

Ernest was amoung the group that organized the Genealogy Society Of The "Original" Wilkes County, and was a charter member of the society. He was elected as the first "Keeper of Records" of this society, and later held other offices.

Over the years, Ernest collected priceless information, old photographs and letters, some of which were written in Wilkes County during the civil war. He had hoped to someday write a book containing his collection. Hopefully, someday his health will improve enough for him to fulfill his dream.

— Esther Hayes Tedder

PHILLIP TEVEPAUGH FAMILY
1027

Phillip Tevepaugh, our great-great grandfather (5-10-1815 — 1893) was born and died in Mecklenburg county. He was buried in the old Steel Creek Presbyterian church cemetery. He married Dorothy (Dolly) Herron (7-4-1819) on (1-18-1837). Phillip had a sister, Elizabeth who married Robert N. Walker on (10-19-1835). Phillip and Dolly had 5 children: John L.; Sara Ann, married Henry Allison Walker on (12-30-1857); Cathey; Easter; Henrietha married Issac Reid on (6-25-1853).

John L. Tevepaugh (5-15-1844) — (12-19-1932) was a veteran of the Confederate Army, married Sara R. Wingate (10-10-1845) from Mecklenburg county on (10-7-1863) John was a very good fiddler and took part in the conventions held at the county Court House and most always won the first prize. He and Sara had 3 children: Charles Martin; Thomas Canceler; and Anna. Sara later died and John married Nancy Jane (Granny) Hoagland, born (11-21-1855), died (3-28-1936). To this union were born 4 sons — and 4 daughters: Henry; Dave; Harve; Ellie; Hallie (10-17-1880) — (1-20-1975), married Bunk Parker; Mollie; Beatrice (1-1-1893) — (2-19-1978); Thena. Most of these children settled in Iredell and Alexander counties. John L. moved from Mecklenburg County to Wilkes County when the older set of children were very young. John and Nancy Jane were buried in the old Parker Cemetery on the Brushies.

Charles (Charlie) Martin Tevepaugh (4-11-1867) — (10-16-1952) married Thena Hendren, daughter of Jabus Hendren. Charlie was a business man in North Wilkesboro. Charlie and Thena had one son, John Jabez (6-6-1888) — (12-9-1941) who married Grace Foster, born (4-6-1891) — (3-21-1942). They had no children. John worked for the town of North Wilkesboro for a number of years. After Charlie's first wife, Thena died; he married Stella Miller (3-13-1880) — (5-3-1955) daughter of Rance Miller, Edgewood community. Charles Martin, Stella, John and Grace are buried in the Mountain Park Cemetery, Wilkesboro. Charles and Stella have a son, Charles living in North Wilkesboro, who is not married.

Thomas Canceler Tevepaugh (5-5-1869) — (3-19-1960) married Sallie Jane Herron (5-2-1859) — (3-1-1923), daughter of John and Sarah Jane Todd Herron. Sallie came from Mecklenburg County. Their 5 children were: Lulie Jane; William (Bill) Herron; Thomas Earl; Austin Young; Zella. After the death of Sallie Jane, Thomas married Clete Barnette, daughter of Mart Barnette. She died (6-18-1971) To this union were born 2 children: (1) Maggie Lee (3-1-1929) married James Leo Hayes, son of Jeter and Dora Mae Hendren Hayes — their children: Wanda married Ricky Dean Simms; Marie; Gary. (2) Howard Tevepaugh (3-14-1931) married Shirley Dula — children: Shelia married a Carson — child Angel; Phyllis; Cynthia; James. Thomas owned and operated a mill, had his own blacksmith's shop. In later years he become one of the leading orchardist of the Brushy Mountain community. He did a lot of hard work and continued to work until near his death. Thomas was the first to be buried in the new cemetery at the new Bethany church.

Lulie Jane Tevepaugh (10-19-1893) married Maurice Hendren, son of Edward and Martha (Matt) Baker Hendren. Their 2 children are: (1) Thomas Edward (11-25-1923) married Peggy Troutman — children: Diane married Wesley Stuart — child Heather; Phil; Mark. (2) James Dwight (6-21-1932) married Janet Martin — children: Renee married Terry Deal — child Joshua; Kevin.

William (Bill) Herron Tevepaugh (3-14-1897) — (3-11-1969) married Allie Mae Walker Tevepaugh. They had 4 children. More will be written about Bill in another story.

Thomas Earl Tevepaugh (7-3-1899) — (6-11-1977) married Earlie Baker from Pineville, N.C. He retired from the Southern Bakery Co. after several years of work. Thomas Earl was buried in the Forest Lawn cemetery, Charlotte. They had one child: Thomas Earl II (1-3-1941) married Patty Martine — children: Kelly; Thomas Earl III.

Austin Young Tevepaugh (9-13-1901) was the fourth child of Thomas Canceler Tevepaugh; his wife's name was Ethel from Oklahoma. They had no children. Austin retired from a produce business and lives in Texas.

Zella Tevepaugh (7-5-1904) married Clarence Hendren, son of Edward and Martha (Matt) Baker Hendren. To this union were born

L. to R.: Thomas C. Tevepaugh, Harvey C. Walker, Anna Tevepaugh Gwaltney, Charles M. Tevepaugh

14 children: (1) Gladys married Belt Campbell — children: Susan; Dona. (2) James (Jim) married Margaret Brittain — child: Steven. (3) Donald married Rhoda Ann Welborn — children: Donna married Jimmy Church; Debbie married Ervin Stephen Pruitt; Becky. (4) Max married Elrea Marlow — children: Karen married Roy Harrold; Janice married Mike Lentz — child Beth; Kathy married Randy Huffman — child Tracy. (5) John married Thelma Reavis — children: Herron married Judy — children: Jason; Jessica; Reavis. (6) Libby married Mack Oliver — children: Elaine; Paula; Ina Lee; Mack. (7) Betty first married Bill Burleson — children: Gary; Myra; Lisa; twins — Leslie; Lori. Betty's second husband Bill Rufty. (8) Lowell married Sue — children: Barry; Kim; Joel. (9) Joann married Tony Powers — child: Jason. (10) Sally married Tommy Moore — children: Sandra married a Adams — child son; Jeffrey. (11) Janie died (9-79) age 38, married Clay Reid — children: Laura; Sarah. (12) William married Diane — child: Cindy. (13) Martha married James Billings — children: Richard; Marsha; Missy. (14) Roger married Donna (divorced) child: Scott.

Anna Tevepaugh died at the age of 89 and was buried in the Linney Grove Baptist church cemetery. She was a charter member of that church. Anna married the Rev. J.P. Gwaltney. She was his third wife. He was a prominent Baptist minister of Alexander County. To this union were born 7 children: J.P. (Jay); Jeff; Otha; Laura married Jack Ford, parents of the Rev. Howard J. Ford, well known Baptist minister, who has had several assignments with the Baptist State Convention. He was president of the Convention (1964-1965), later was on the staff as director of the Division of Missions, before retiring; Lola married Allie Patterson; Elsie married Clyde Alexander; Minnie died when an infant.

Sources: Family records, personal knowledge, grave stones, and interviews with family members.

— Willie Mae Hayes

WILLIAM (BILL) HERRON TEVEPAUGH FAMILY
1028

William (Bill) Herron Tevepaugh (3-14-1897) — (3-11-1969) son of Thomas Canceler and Sallie Jane Herron Tevepaugh, World War I veteran married Allie Mae Walker Tevepaugh (11-1-1896) — (6-4-1975) on December 6, 1919. She was the daughter of Harvey C. (12-21-1867) — (1-27-1954) and Nolie Hendren Walker (3-3-1876) — (11-21-1937). Bill purchased 100 acres of land on top of the Brushies, which was part of the Mitch Vannoy property. In the early years he grew tobacco and sold to help pay for the farm. Later he set out apple trees and became involved in the orchard work instead of the tobacco. He worked at several feed mills and did a lot of hauling for others with his truck. His wife, Allie Mae was involved in Home Extension work and community affairs. She was very dedicated to her home and family. As one said, she was surpassed by no one in her civic interest, unselfishness and willingness to help others. She

had great courage, character, culture and citizenship; and was known for her good cooking and enjoyed doing it. They had 4 children: Willie Mae; William Harve; Joe Dean; Robert (Bob) Owen.

Willie Mae Tevepaugh (9-17-1920) and Brady Lee Hayes (2-5-1917), son of Roy F. and Effie Campbell Hayes were married (8-1-1945). Brady was a World War II veteran — served five years in the U.S. Army. He has done auto mechanic work in North Wilkesboro for 38 years. Their children are: Dexter Lee (1-3-1947) four years in the U.S. Navy, graduate of A.S.U. Boone, and Virginia Polytechnic Institute, (V.P.I.) at present is county planning Director of New Hanover county. He married Peggy Hagerman on (8-30-1975). Peggy is from Wilmington, Delaware and is also a graduate of V.P.I. Children are: Christina (10-15-79); Meredith (3'10'82) Willie Maudeen Hayes (5-2-1948) married Ray Miles (6-4-1972). Ray was born (6-12-1946), son of Albert Miles, veteran of the U.S. Army and works with the N.C. State Highway Department. Children are: Kendrick (4-14-1976) and Carmen (10-17-1981) They live in North Wilkesboro.

William Harve Tevepaugh (2-27-1925), World War II veteran, married Velma Johnson. They have 4 daughters: Susan (5-10-1952) married Tyler Warren of Robersonville. She is a teacher and Tyler an attorney; Lisa married Phillip Mobley and live in Rocky Mount. Lisa is a nurse and Phillip Recreation park director; Kelly (10-14-1963); Allison (4-5-1965) live with parents in Cary.

Joe Dean Tevepaugh (9-17-1930) — (6-13-1976) U.S. Army veteran, married Marion Hayes, daughter of Jeter and Dora Mae Hendren Hayes. Joe died at the age of 45 with a very rare liver disease. To this union were born 3 children: (1) Coleen (1-12-1953) married Kenneth Taylor, son of Ray Taylor. Coleen's children are: Christopher, Jennifer. (2) Armit (7-12-1954) married Tammi Walsh, daughter of Bob Walsh. They built a nice home in the apple orchard and are now carrying on the orchard work which was started by his grandfather, Bill and later operated by his father Joe until his death; (3) Ronald (10-24-1959) They all live on the land and home-place of William (Bill) Tevepaugh.

Robert (Bob) Owen Tevepaugh (5-31-1933) veteran of the U.S. Army (Korean) War, married Nadine Anderson, daughter of Cicero and Drusie Soots Anderson. They were later divorced. To this union were born 9 children: Vernell (8-25-54) married Gerald Durham — child: Melisa; Bobby Lynn (9-20-55) married Phil Caudill; Phyllis (6-14-58) married Michael Richardson — children: Christy, Jennifer; Robert C. (4-25-59); Terri (4-16-60) married Ricky Minton — child: Richard Chad; Julie (10-2-63); Branda (4-3-66); Scott (3-9-68); Elizabeth (Beth) (7-20-69). Bob does construction work (Supervisor) locally and, in and our of state. He is now married to Mary Lou Moore Queen, daughter of Herman and Byrd Barnette Moore. They live on the old Lane road, near the old Bethany Church Cemetery on the Brushies.

Sources: Family records, personal knowledge.

— Willie Mae Hayes

THE BOB and BETTY ROBERTS THOMPSON FAMILY
1029

Bob Camp Thompson was born September 23, 1931, son of Donald Mead and Nellie Phillips Thompson of Pinecola and Othello, N.C. He has three brothers and two sisters Donald Maynard, Beatrice Nell, Everette Dale, Barbara Joan and Phillip Dellano. After graduation from Crossnore High School he attended Lincoln Memorial University, Harrogate Tennessee, where he graduated in 1954, with a BA Degree.

In January, 1955 he entered the Naval Aviation Flight Training Program in Pensacola Florida as a NavCad. He received his Commission as Ensign in the Navy and Navy Wings in Pensacola and following advanced training in Corpus Christi, Texas, reported for duty to H.S.-5 in Key West, Florida. After four and one half years on active duty as a Naval Aviator he joined the Naval Reserve. In 1980 he was promoted to Captain and now he is affiliated with VTU-706 Triad Armed Forces Reserve Center in Greensboro, N.C.

Bob received his Master's Degree at A.S.U. in 1960, and his Doctor of Education Degree at Nova University, Fort Lauderdale, Florida, in 1976. He has done additional graduate work at the University of Georgia, N.C. and at Cal State at Los Angeles.

He was employed as teacher-counselor at Kernersville High School, guidance director at East Forsyth Senior High School, and director of student personnel at Forsyth Technical Institute in Winston-Salem. He joined the staff of Wilkes Community College in 1970 where he is now serving as Dean of Student Services. He and his family moved to Wilkesboro in 1970.

He is a member of the North Wilkesboro Presbyterian Church and serves as Ruling Elder and Receiving Treasurer. As a member of the North Wilkesboro Lions Club, he serves on the Board of Directors and is past president. He is a Director of the Wilkes Chamber of Commerce. He is immediate past president of the Wilkes Chapter of the North Carolina Symphony. He serves as a member of the Advisory Board for the New River Mental Health Center. He is a member of Phi Delta Kappa, a National Professional Fraternity, and is listed in the 1972 edition of the Outstanding Educators of America.

In 1959 Bob C. Thompson married Betty Roberts in Key West, Florida.

Betty is the daughter of Anna Monin Roberts (Glendale, Kentucky) and the late Charles Eugene Roberts (Key West, Florida). She was born on September 21, 1932 in Louisville, Kentucky. She attended public school grades in Key West and graduated from College Heights High School in Bowling Green, Kentucky in 1950. She attended the University of Chattanooga and graduated in their Secretarial Science Certificate Program in 1952. She participated in the Westminster Study Abroad Program in 1953. In 1972-74 she attended the Survey and Management Seminar in Oberlin, Ohio. Her professional record includes the following: Owner and operator of Betty Ann Stationers, Secretary to Mirawall, Inc., Kinder-

Bob C. Thompson Family in 1977.

garten Instructor, Manager Wilkes Community College Bookstore.

She is a member of Alpha Delta Pi Sorority, a member and past president of Beta Sigma Phi Sorority, president of Kernersville Womans Club, elected member of the Steering Committee Kernersville Presbyterian Church, secretary of Wilkes Central Band Booster Club, president North Carolina Symphony, president North Wilkesboro Musical Arts Club, immediate past Chairman Board of Deacons Presbyterian Church 1976-82, Senior High Youth Advisor chairman of the youth committee 1982 and Ruling Elder of the Presbyterian Church.

On June 22, 1960 their first child, Phyllis Ann was born in Winston Salem, N.C. Phyllis attended Kernersville Elementary and Wilkesboro Elementary School, and graduated from Wilkes Central High School in 1979. In girl scouts she attained the rank of First Class; in Rainbow girls she was Worthy Advisor and a Charter member in Wilkesboro, she studied ballet for twelve years and she was chosen Wilkes County Junior Miss 1979. Phyllis was Captain of the Color Guard — Wilkes Central High School band and very active in the North Wilkesboro Presbyterian Church. Phyllis is a rising Senior at the U.N.C. in Greensboro.

On December 14, 1961 Barbara Charlene was born in Winston Salem, N.C. Barbara attended Kernersville Elementary, Wilkesboro Elementary and graduated from Wilkes Central High School in 1982. Barbara was active in Girl Scouts, Wilkes Central High School Band, Student Government, Varsity basketball and track and the North Wilkesboro Presbyterian Church. She won the trophy for Most Dependable in girls track and also a trophy for placing first in her age group in the Wilkes County 10 K Run.

The Bob C. Thompson Family hobbies include, hiking, camping, boating, trout fishing, water skiing and snow skiing.

Source: Personal knowledge.

— Bob C. Thompson

THE FAMILY OF DICK and FLORENCE CHURCH THOMPSON
1030

John Harley (Dick) Thompson was born March 12, 1901 to Moses Elkanah and Minnie Etta Yates Thompson of the Harley Community in Wilkes County. He was one of nine children in his family. On March 24, 1933 Dick married Florence Mae Church. They moved to their new home in the Cricket Community where Florence still resides. Dick died March 17, 1979.

On June 4, 1906 Florence Mae Church was born to Zolley Coffer and Rebecca Eller Church who lived in the Ready Branch Community of Wilkes County. Florence graduated from Mountain View Institute, in 1923. She attended North Carolina College for Women where she received her Primary A Teacher's Certificate in 1931. After teaching for forty years Florence retired in 1971.

Florence was an active member of the North Carolina Education Association, the National Education Association and the Classroom Teachers Association. Presently she is a member of the National Retired Teachers Association.

As a young girl Florence became a member of Lewis Fork Baptist Church where she was a primary Sunday School teacher and was active in the Baptist Young People's Union. After her marriage she joined Welcome Home Baptist Church in the Cricket community. For many years she worked in the Junior Department as a Sunday School teacher and superintendent. She was a teacher in the Baptist Training Union, a member of the Woman's Missionary Union, a leader of the Young Woman's Auxiliary and a teacher in Bible Schools. Presently she attends Trinity Fellowship Church where her husband was a member.

As a young man Dick worked with the state bridge construction crew who erected most of the early bridges in the state of North Carolina particularly those in the eastern and coastal sections of our state. He attended Greensboro Barber College in Greensboro, N.C. where he received his barber's license. For fifty years he was operator and owner of Tenth Street Barber Shop in North Wilkesboro before retiring in 1976. Dick's hobby after his marriage was farming and raising livestock.

Dick and Florence had two children, Kay Rebecca and Clayton Harley.

Kay Rebecca was born October 7, 1939. After graduating from Wilkes Central High School, she entered Woman's College, Greensboro, N.C. In 1962 she graduated with a B.S. degree in interior design.

In August, 1962 Kay married Ronald Hubert Carpenter. Ronald was born February 27, 1939 to Theodore Roosevelt and Norma H. Carpenter. After their marriage Ronald served four years in the Air Force and they lived in Amarillo, Texas and Sumter, S.C. Their daughter, Kara Lisa, was born in Sumter, S.C. May 16, 1963.

Kay and her family moved to Asheville, N.C. in 1966. While Ronald, who had finished Mars

Hill Junior College before their marriage, entered Mars Hill College and received a B.S. degree in math in 1968. He became a licensed land surveyor in 1972. During this time Kay was a designer for Talman Office Supplies, Inc. Kara attended Little Beaver Nursery School and Kindergarten and the city schools in Asheville.

In 1973 they returned to Wilkes County where they reside with Kay's mother. Ronald is president of Northwestern Surveying and Mapping, Inc. He has served two terms as president of the Northwest Chapter of the North Carolina Society of Surveyors, Inc. and is active in the State Society. While Kay has been the homemaker for her family, she has developed a great interest in the cultural heritage and many crafts of the Appalachian Mountains, such as basketry, knotting and tying fringe for bedspreads.

After Kara graduated from West Wilkes High School in 1981, she enrolled in the American Business and Fashion Institute, Charlotte, N.C. majoring in fashion and merchandising. She will graduate in September, 1982.

Clayton Harley Thompson was born February 19, 1944. He graduated from Wilkes Central High School in 1962 and from N.C. State at Raleigh, in 1967 with a B.S. degree in aerospace engineering. For the past fourteen years he has lived in the state of California. He has held positions with McDonald-Douglas Aircraft in Los Angeles and with Toledo Scales in Oakland. Presently Clayton is president of Polk Street Tiffany, Inc. in San Francisco where he currently resides. During the last several years he has traveled extensively to Tokyo, Hong Kong, Bangkok and Australia on business as well as pleasure trips.

Sources: Family Bible, family memories and personal knowledge.

— Kay Thompson Carpenter

VIRGINIA FOSTER THURSTON
1031

Virginia (Gin) Lee Foster was daughter of Roy G. Foster and Lula Lee Stokes Foster, having been born in Wilkesboro 1924 and having lived there for several years when family travels following highway construction commenced. She then lived throughout the Southeast with her family. She had one brother, Roy G. Foster, Jr., and one sister, Elizabeth (Betty) Stokes Foster, who was the only child of Roy and Lula Lee born in Georgia.

Gin was educated in Wadley, Georgia through high school, and went on to Wesleyan College of Macon, Georgia, from which she also graduated. She remained active throughout her life as a loyal supporter of Wesleyan and later sent her daughters, Lee Stokes Thurston and Jenna Foster Thurston to Wesleyan for a part of their education. Gin married Dr. M. Stevenson Thurston, son of Dr. Asa and Jenna Echard Thurston of Taylorsville, North Carolina. This marriage took place after Steve's return home from World War II during which he was an Army pilot flying vitally needed supplies over the Burma hump in Asia.

As an example of Gin's love and appreciation of Wesleyan, she encouraged her father to build a very beautiful lake on the Wesleyan campus in honor of Lula Lee Stokes Foster. This lake remains as a place of serene beauty on the Wesleyan campus.

Gin and Steve lived in Salisbury, North Carolina, and in addition to the daughters mentioned above, had one son, Asa Stevenson Thurston, who lives in Salisbury with his wife and father while completing his education. Gin was involved in Salisbury art and literary groups and she was the moving force behind the founding of the Friendship House of Salisbury that was of inestimable benefit to area veterans of need. Steve serves in many capacities of community endeavor, having been honored with the Boy Scout Silver Beaver Award and as Deacon and Sunday School Superintendent of the Salisbury Presbyterian Church.

Virginia Foster Thurston was a loving and talented wife — mother — daughter — sister — aunt and friend, and her memory will live long amongst those who knew and loved her — and we will tell others about her because we care.

Sources: Personal knowledge.

— Roy Foster Jr.

TINSLEY
1032

Rev. David Luther Tinsley was born January 5, 1793. He married Nancy Kilby October 28, 1818. Nancy Kilby was born September 17, 1798.

Isaac Tinsley married Elizabeth Perlier May 16, 1811.

Rev. James D. Tinsley was born November 20, 1817. He married Sarah Rhodes December 12, 1840. She was born April 21, 1819.

Rev. James D. Tinsley had a large family. Many of his children died of diptheria in infancy. He lived in the Reddies River section, was a farmer and owned 1800 acres of land. He operated a corn and flour mill. He gave two acres of land in Mulberry township to build Baptist Home Church upon. He was its first pastor. He helped found the Wilkesboro Baptist and Cane Creek Baptist Churches.

He was a strong believer in freeing the slaves during the Civil War. He supported the North and was a supporter of President Lincoln. He was a great friend to young preachers.

He took an active part in education. In 1877 he was appointed on the school committee in District 32. He had a fine library in his home containing the best religious and history books.

Rev. James D. Tinsley died December 12, 1885. His wife, Sarah, died August 19, 1910. They are buried in a home graveyard on the old turnpike road in Mulberry township.

Sources: family records.

— Wake Tinsley

NAT K. TOLBERT
1033

Nat K. Tolbert, son of Jack and Janie Tol-

bert, was born August 14, 1905 in Stokes County. His mother died when he was six years old. As a young man he started work at High Point in the furniture industry. It was here he met Belva Dean Eller, daughter of John W. and Cora Kilby Eller, from Wilkes County and they were married May 8, 1927.

On April 2, 1928 their first son, Jimmy Jason was born. Their second son, Max Dean was born November 24, 1935.

Nat moved his family to North Wilkesboro late in 1935. In 1936 he built a home at Millers Creek. He continued working in the furniture industry and was working at the Home Chair Company in 1940 when it was destroyed by the flood. At this time he started work for the Wilkes Hosiery Mill, and continued to work there until it closed. He worked for Peerless until he retired in 1970.

Nat and Belva's third son, William Ray was born December 6, 1942 and their fourth son, Gary Allen was born February 22, 1945.

Nat and Belva joined the old Millers Creek Methodist Church in 1942 and were active in the merger with Friendship Methodist Church in 1953. Nat was a reliable family man who enjoyed working in his garden or handyman jobs around home. He was an active member of his church until his death August 31, 1971. Belva still resides at the home place and enjoys the visits of her children and grandchildren.

Jimmy Jason was married April 2, 1949 to Jamie Ethel Clark, daughter of Arthur and Pansy Clark. Their only child David Clark was born October 7, 1956 and died December 23, 1959.

Max Dean was married July 2, 1955 to Linda Jean Hayes, daughter of Balmer and Dora Hayes. They have one daughter, Sheila Dean born March 24, 1957. Sheila married Harold Lloyd "Butch" McWhirter, Jr. on February 19, 1977 and they have one son, Joseph Rhett, born July 6, 1978.

William Ray is married to the former Alan Bumgarner Chamberlain, daughter of Archie and Mintie Bumgarner. They were married July 1, 1972 and have one child of this marriage, Christopher Lee, born November 10, 1974.

Gary Allen left Wilkes County in 1967 to work in Charlotte. It was here that he met Deborah Anne Miller and married June 20, 1968. They have two children Susan Denise, born April 24, 1971 and Sarah Anne born September 4, 1974.

Sources: Family and personal knowledge.

— Jimmy Tolbert

FRANK CLAUDIUS and NEY SMITHEY TOMLINSON
1034

Frank C. Tomlinson was born in Yadkin County, son of W.C. and Sarah Benbow Tomlinson, Feb. 9, 1889. He came to North Wilkesboro N.C. early in life. He worked with the firm of Tomlinsons and sold all the items the firm handled, which was about everything. He married Ney Smithey. After the death of S.V. Tomlinson, Frank went in business for himself on Cherry Street. He handled farm machinery

and Nissen Wagons. He sold real estate and had farms and did a lot of farming and raising and selling cattle.

Frank Tomlinson was a Director in the North Wilkesboro Savings and Loan, for ten years. His greatest desire was to see everyone have a home. He died March 1956, and at the regular meeting of the Directors of the Savings & Loan, they went on record as paying a tribute of love and esteem to his memory. Mr. Tomlinson was instictively a lover of simplicity and truth, a loyal friend and ever ready to give his best to promote the welfare of this association. He was always a Building & Loan man. He wanted to see the community grow. He was interested in bringing in new industry; working and helping make Wilkes County a better place to live.

Ney S. Tomlinson.

Frank C. Tomlinson.

437

His finest achievement was the cultivation of a nature so thoughtful for others, whatever their station, that none who came within its radiance failed to be warmed and inspired by it. He was a man of strong character and charming personality.

Sources: Personal knowledge.

— Ney Tomlinson

NEY SMITHEY TOMLINSON
1035

Ney Smithey Tomlinson was the youngest daughter of Isaac and Sarah McLean Smithey. She was born in Wilkesboro. Her parents owned a farm about a mile out on the old Taylorsville road. Later, this farm was sold and Isaac Smithey and his son Nikard bought the Smithey Hotel and the family moved there. Ney graduated from Wilkesboro School, and attended A.S.T.C. at Boone, N.C. She married Frank C. Tomlinson and was with the firm of TOMLINSONS for some time in the bookkeeping department.

Ney was quite active in the Baptist Church, garden clubs, and woman's clubs. She served as finance chairman when the Woman's Club house was built. She served on the Board of Trustees of the Daniel Boone Native Garden for twelve years on the Garden Club State level. She held many positions on the State level of the Garden Clubs of North Carolina.

When her husband Frank C. Tomlinson died, she went to Chapel Hill to the Real Estate Institute, and was the first Realtor in the county for a number of years, and is a Charter Member of the Real Estate Board in Wilkes County. She has handled a lot of property in this county as she and Frank Tomlinson had a lot of property to sell. She sold one place to the American Drew and they built a nice plant there that gives a lot of people employment.

Ney has owned and operated NEY'S GIFTS, a very nice gift shop with fine porcelain, crystal, and brass. The gift shop is her pride and joy.

Sources: Personal knowledge.

— Ney Tomlinson

EDWIN LAFAYETTE TRANSOU
1036

Edwin Lafayette Transou was born on the 16th of May 1835 in Wilkes County, the eldest son of James W. Transou and Mary Rousseau. He served in the Confederate Army in 1861 to 1865 as drummer in Company "C"; Regiment "The Sharpshooters". He was standing in rank when General Lee surrendered. His only injury was to the fingers of one hand. He walked home to Wilkesboro by a devious route around the foot of the Blue Ridge, fearing to travel any main roads on account of meeting Yankee soldiers going home.

Edwin married Nancy Gertrude Flynt on Monday morning at 6 a.m. 28 January 1867. After their marriage they lived in Little Abe Reece house near Boonville. While living there, Mary Elizabeth was born, 8 November 1867. Edwin was running and working in the

tan yard, just below what is now known as Jones property on the east side of the branch. Then they moved to Iowa, lived in Dr. Olvis Est place.

They lived there two years or more and came back to Boonville and lived near Vet Spear place where son John Bryon was born 27 March 1870. At birth this son only weighed one and half pounds. He was given the nickname of Tom. Jennie Spear nursed him with her own baby until he was almost a year old, due to his mother's health. Little Tom grew and at nine months he walked and talked.

The little family moved to Brendle Mill and Edwin ran a tanyard. Clarence Rufus was born 28 February 1872. Later Fannie Leola was born on the 31 July 1876. Edwin bought a house and 80 acres of land in Boonville, north of Main Street from the post office, where he ran a tanyard.

Edwin Lafayette Transou died in Yadkin County November 1919.

Sources: Family letters and records.

— Sandra Ball

THE TRANSOU FAMILY
1037

Abraham Transou was married 4 February 1721 in the German Reform Church at Mutterstadt, Pfaltz, Germany, to Elizabeth Munster. He came to America, landing at the port of Philadelphia, Pennsylvania, 29 August 1730, on the ship "Thistle of Glasgow". He took the oath of allegiance the day of his arrival. He brought with him, his wife, Elizabeth, and two children who were both born in Germany. They settled near Emmanus, Pa. They were members of the Protestant Reform Church. Later their children joined the United Brethren Church or Moravians.

Abraham was born about 1700 and died before 1772. Elizabeth Munster died about 1733. Their children were: Anna Catharina, Johann Philip, Johann Abraham, Johann Jacob and Elizabeth.

Johann Philip Transou was born 2 October 1724 in Germany, married 16 February 1755 in Bethlehem, Pa. Maria Magdalena Gander, born 18 February 1729 in Germany died 12 November 1803 in Salem, N.C.

Philip and Magdalena Transou and their three children, who were born in Pennsylvania came to North Carolina with several other families, leaving Bethlehem 20 April 1762. They came by sloop to Wilmington, N.C. arriving 8 June 1762. Philip moved his family into his home in Bethania 26 July 1762.

Johann Philip and Maria Magdalene had the following children: Abraham, Maria Magdalena, Philip, Jr., Anna Rosina, Johannes, Elizabeth, and Catharine. These children married Shobers, Voglers, Freys, Leinbachs and Reiches in Salem.

Abraham Transou, son of Philip and Magdalena, was a wagoner. He was born 15th March 1756 in Friedenthal, Pa. He was twice married, first to Anna Maria Pfaff and to this union seven children were born: Johann Philip, Abraham, born 5 November 1785 in Bethania, Stokes County, married Lucinda Bryan

from Virginia and removed to Wilkes County, Maria Elizabeth, Salome, Solomon, Maria Magdalena and Catherine. His second wife was Eva Schulz and they had a daughter Philippina.

Abraham Transou, son of Abraham, Sr. and Anna Maria, was born 5 November 1785 in Bethania, Stokes County, N.C., married Lucinda (Lucy) Bryan from Virginia, who was born 1790. They left Stokes County and settled in Wilkes County. Abraham was a farmer, wheelwright and wagon maker. He died before 1880 and Lucy died before 1870. They had children:

Nancy, born 30 July 1808 in Va. died 27 September 1893; James W., born 1811 in Va. died 3 December 1893, married Mary A. Rousseau; William B., born 1813, Stokes County, married Mary; Harriet born 1816, married 6 May 1835 Nathaniel Garland Lane, left Wilkes; Mary born 1818, married 1 January 1840, William Perkins; Sarah Blum born 1823 Stokes Co., married 13 February 1837 George Jones.

James W. Transou, son of Abraham and Lucinda, was a tanner and farmer. During the Civil War, he had several horses that he hid in the woods to keep them from being stolen by the soldiers. He married 16 August 1834 Mary A. Rousseau and died 3 December 1893 at Straw postoffice, Wilkes County. James W. and Mary A. were the parents of eleven children:

(1) Edwin Lafayette, born 16 May 1835, died 4 November 1919 in Yadkin County, married Nancy Gertrude Flynt (Flint); (2) Rufus, born 12 January 1838, died 20th January 1919, married first 26 February 1860 Jerusha Matilda Wright, and second 4th April 1867 Irene Elizabeth Hendren; (3) Frances Almeda born 19 June 1839, died 18 May 1907, married 18 July 1861 James W. Wright; (4) Clinton born 1841 died in infancy; (5) James A. born 1843 married Sarah Annette Colbert; (6) Lucy born 1845 married a Greene; (7) Montford Sidney, born 1847 married a Mastin and lived in Ashe Co., (8) Mary Ellen born 29 September 1849 died 19 July 1920 unmarried; (9) David born about 1851 died in infancy; (10) Ann Janette born 1853 married Franklin Sleetman; (11) Magdalena (Maggie) born 1856 married Tillman Howell.

Rufus Transou, son of James W. and Mary Rousseau Transou, served in the Civil War, was wounded in the head and had a metal piece put there. He was a famer and tanner, lived in the Hunting Creek area of the county. He was the father of ten children by his two wives:

(1) James Robert born 15 December 1860, died 18 August 1927, married Mary Combs, daughter of Hix and Nancy Jarvis Combs. (2) Rufus Beauregard born 2 November 1862, died 15 January 1937 in Utah, married Ary Alvina Nance (3) Mary Ann (Molly), born 1 February 1868, died 19 January 1917 in Utah, married John Wesley Nance, (4) Sidney Oliver, born 20 May 1870, died 21 December 1929, married Della Victoria Parker; (5) Edwin Lafayette, married Rebecca Coleman; (6) Nancy Gertude, born 20 October 1874, died 12 May 1960, married Floyd Estep; (7) Clara Louna, born 6 May 1879, died 12 May 1960,

Rufus Transou House and Family, 1900. Front row, L. to R. — Susan, Clara, Irene (Rufus's wife), Rufus, Grover, Minnie Anderson (visitor). Back row, l. to r. — Edwin and daughter Lucille, and wife Rebecca, Nancy Transou Estep and son. Rufus Transou's grandson (Rufus Transou) and his family in this house today, located on Hwy. 115 south, Route 3, North Wilkesboro.

(8) Lena Lucy, born 1 March 1881, died 12 August 1893, unmarried; (9) Grover Cleveland, born 10 March 1887, died 20 December 1946, married Martha Louise Nance; (10) Amelia Susanna Alta, born 9 May 1892, died 16 April 1967 in Surry County, married Mayshack Couch.

Edwin Lafayette Transou, son of Rufus and Irene Hendren Transou, was born 30 October 1872, died 11 June 1945, married 25 December 1897 Rebecca Coleman, born 6th June 1870, died 22 June 1957, daughter of Emmet Coleman and Lucy Walker. He was a farmer. He and Rebecca had the following children:

(1) Lucille Irene, born 16 October 1898, died 15 May 1979, married Charles Taylor; (2) Hester Ludemia born 10 August 1899, died 22 April 1969, married Richard Bouchell; (3) Jeanettie Mary Ann born 29 April 1903, died 25 February 1948, married Cesero Hall; (4) Fannie born 2 August 1905, died 14 April 1907; (5) Ada Emily born 3 August 1908, married Rom Hayes; (6) Wilson Woodrow born 3 August 1912, married Ruby Triplette; (7) Ann Madonna born 1 October 1914, married Hansford Durant Ball 15 November 1936; (8) A daughter died at birth 4 December 1917.

Sources: Transou Family Genealogy by Mrs. C.W. Ball, personal knowledge. Chronicle Newspaper, Wilkes Marriages, census.

— Ann Madonna Transou Ball

ADAM DAVID TREADWAY
1038

Adam David Treadway was the great, great, great grandson of Richard and Elizabeth Coles Treadway of Cumberland County, North Carolina.

He was born May 18, 1870 in Swain County,

to Eli Asco and Rebecca Beaulah Smith Treadway. He died Jan 9, 1952 and buried in Walnut Grove Baptist Church Cemetery, Moravian Falls.

Adam David married Aug 23, 1891 to Rispie Clementine Childers, daughter of John Wilson and Martha Bentley Childers.

Their children, all born in Wilkes County, are: Jesse R (born May 15, 1895, died Dec 11, 1960); William Rufus (born Sept 18, 1897, died Dec 5 1967); Lara Ellen (born Dec 8, 1899); Emmer (born 1902); Johnny (born 1904); Coleman (born Sept 20, 1914).

William Rufus Treadway was born in Pores Knob community to Adam David and Rispie Clementine Childers Treadway.

He married Alma Catherine Kerly, daughter of Zeno Parmemus and Allia Adlaide Laws Kerley. They were married at Alma's home on Sunday 24 Dec, 1922, by The Rev John McAlpin.

Rufus was an apple orchardist most of his life. In the late 1920s with a two horse drawn wagon, he took apples to sell in Kannapolis and Concord, N.C. This round trip took almost a week. In 1929 he bought an A-Model Ford pick-up truck in which to transport his apples. The last fifteen years of his life he was a poultry farmer.

Rufus died due to lung canser and is buried in Walnut Grove Baptist Church cemetery, Moravian Falls.

Rufus and Alma's children were all born in Pores Knob Community. (1) Graceteen (born Sept 18, 1923), married Mack Lydon Johnson, May 4, 1945. They have three children: Linda Sue, William Bruce and Grady Wayne. (2) William Gaither "Jack" married Betty Sue Blankenship. (3) Mack (born June 26, 1928), married Sandra Gail Smart, May 26, 1965.

They have two children: David Mack and Nancy Ellen. (4) Pauline Elizabeth (born Aug 3, 1930), married Lewis Charles Parker, July 5, 1952. They have two sons: Lewis Charles Jr and Tim.

William Gaither Treadway "Jack" son of William Rufus and Alma Catherine Kerly Treadway was born Feb 21, 1925. He got the nickname "Jack" when he was a teenager and is still called "Jack" by friends and acquaintance. He has been a truck driver most of his adult life, except for ten years he was a cattle and poultry farmer.

William Gaither "Jack" married Sept 2, 1945 Betty Sue Blankenship, daughter of William Walter and Letha Stewart Blankenship. Jack and Betty had two sons: William Gaither "Jackie" Jr was born May 3, 1947 and died June 16, 1964 due to injuries resulting from a car accident, and Gary Vinson Treadway. Both sons attended Moravian Falls Elementary and Wilkes Central High School. Gary served in the National Guard from 1969 to 1974.

Gary Vinson Treadway born Dec 2, 1950, son of William Gaither "Jack" and Betty Sue Blankenship Treadway, married Aug 29, 1971 Kathy Suzanna Johnson, daughter of Robert Clegg and Grace Holder Johnson. They have one son, Chad Johnson Treadway, born April 10, 1979.

Sources: family records, personal knowledge and interviews with family members.

— William Gaither Treadway

DANIEL TREADWAY and DESCENDANTS
1039

Daniel Treadway was born 1752 in Baltimore County, Maryland to Richard and Elizabeth Coles Treadway. In 1775, he moved with his parents to Washington County, Virgina. After serving in the Revolutionary War, he established a permanent home in Anson County, N.C. He was the only Treadway of his period to settle in that county.

Daniel married Mary Jones of Cumberland County, N.C. Aug 8, 1776. Mary was born 1755 in Cumberland County, and died Aug 20, 1844 in Anson County.

Daniel and Mary's children were: Richard (born 13 Sept, 1777, died 1851), John (born 16 Jan, 1779), Eliza (born 1781), Anne (born 21 March, 1783), Daniel Jr (born 10 March, 1786, died 1859), Mary (born 29 April, 1788), Pleasant (born 1 March, 1791), Sarah (born 2 July, 1793), Arthur (born 7 Feb, 1798).

Daniel Treadway Jr, son of Daniel and Mary Jones Treadway was born in Anson County and died about 1859-60 in Wilkes County, N.C.

Daniel Jr. married 1811 Elizabeth Steagall. They had twelve children: Moses (born 12 May, 1812, died 7 Nov 1890), Thomas (born 1814), Mahalee (born 1816), Daniel (born 1818), Anne (born 1820-22), George Washington (born 1824), William B. (born 3 May 1827), Edna (born 1829), Jackson (born 1831), Wade H (born 1833), Martin V (born 1935), Jane E (born 1838, died 7 May. 1900).

Eli Asco Treadway was born Oct 23, 1840 in

Anson County, N.C. son of Moses and Mary Ragsdale Treadway.

He was the grandson of Daniel Jr and Elizabeth Steagall Treadway. His great grandparents were Daniel and Mary Jones of Anson County, N.C. and his great, great grandparents were Richard and Elizabeth Coles Treadway of Cumberland County, N.C.

He married Rebecca Beaulah Smith, Feb 10, 1861. She was born Nov 1, 1844 and died June 27, 1938.

Eli Asco was a Civil War Veteran from Wilkes County, N.C. 26th Regiment — Company D.

Eli and Rebecca's children were: Margaret (born June 10, 1862, died 1912), Infant unnamed (born May 12, 1865, died May 14, 1865), Ollie (born Oct 22, 1867, died Aug 12, 1869), Infant unnamed (born Aug 4, 1869, died Sept 3 1869), Adam David (born May 18, 1870, died Jan 9, 1952), Allie Theophilus (born July 13, 1872, died Jan 14, 1948), Eliza Kizell (born Feb 2, 1874, died 1964), Wiley (born Sept 16, 1875, died Dec 3 1876), Mary Rebecca (born April 10, 1878, died July 15, 1927), Jane (born Jan 5 1880, died May 3, 1883), Betsy Ann (born March 12, 1882, died June 8, 1882), Jennie (born Aug 7, 1884, died Aug 5, 1886), Moses Eli Daniel (born Dec 5, 1886, died March 27, 1966), Pearly Luvenie (born May 6, 1888, died June 15, 1955).

Sources: Census, grave stones, deed books and interviews with family members.

— William Gaither Treadway

MY TRIPLETT ANCESTORS
1040

William Triplett was a great grandson of Francis Triplett who came to Virginia from London before 1668. He was born in Prince William County, Va. His parents and family moved to Loudoun Co., Va. in 1741. His father died there and in his will, left 305 acres of land to be divided between William and his brother, Daniel.

William married Eleanor Harbin. They had several children born in Loudoun Co. by 1769 when they moved to Orange County, N.C. where he bought 100 acres of land 1 June 1779. The records of Wilkes County show that he bought (25 December 1778) 150 acres of land on the big branch of Beaver Creek in Wilkes County, N.C.

There were eleven children born to William and Eleanor. William and two of his sons lost their lives during the Revolutionary War. Eleanor signed an Administratrix Bond of his estate in 1784. Her descendants say that she lived to be 109 years old. She was over 100 in 1830. The children are as follows:

(1) Micajah born in Va. died in N.C. about 1789; (2) Nimrod; (3) Mason born 1762 in Va. married Mary Mullins his cousin 28 March 1785 in Wilkes. She was a daughter of Daniel Triplett, a brother of William who also came to Wilkes County. (4) William, born 15 November 1763, married Nancy Ferguson 17 March 1785. In 1803 he sold his land in Wilkes and moved to Adair County, Ky. He was in the Revolutionary War. (5) Thomas born 1765, married Jane Ferguson 25 February 1788. (6)

Frances born 1767, married Jeremiah Ferguson 17 March 1787. (7) John born 1779, married Linda Ferguson 25 February 1795. (8) Virlinda born 1775, married Richard Ferguson (9) Nancy born 1776, married Jno. Sander (10) Jesse born 1777 married Dicie Gray. (11) Priscilla born 1780, married John Ferguson.

These hardy pioneers faced dangers and hardships and built homes, tamed the wilderness and made it possible for their descendants to enjoy the freedoms and blessing that are ours today.

Sources: Personal research.

— Hortense E. Abbott

ARLON A. and EDITH FOSTER TRIPLETT
1041

My grandfather, Arlon Artemus Triplett, was born December 17, 1900, to William Cicero and Susan Jane Foster Triplett, in the Mount Pleasant community. As he has related to me on many occasions, he decided at an early age that the farming life wasn't for him, so he broke all family tradition and left home at the age of 16 to find a job elsewhere. He worked, among other places, in Winston-Salem; Bluefield, West Virginia; and Jacksonville, Florida, before returning to Wilkesboro in the early 1920's.

Once back in Wilkesboro, my grandfather (whom I shall refer to as Daddy Trip, since that's what all of us in the family call him) began "courting" my grandmother, Edith Foster. Edith (whom we all call Mama Trip) was born March 28, 1909, to Rutherford (Rell) and Ina Elledge Foster, also in the Mount Pleasant community. She and Daddy Trip were married on September 7, 1925, and it was at about the same time that he opened the old Wilkes Texaco station beside the Courthouse in Wilkesboro, which he ran for many years. Around the start of World War II he began his own business, Triplett Electric and Plumbing Company, which he operated until his retirement in 1973. Daddy Trip was active in both civic and political affiars, occupying a prominent position in the Wilkes County Republican Party and serving as a Wilkesboro Town Commissioner for five straight terms, from 1947 to 1957.

Four children were born to Mama Trip and Daddy Trip. The first was Robert Arlon, born November 26, 1928. Robert graduated from Wilkesboro High School in 1947 and attended U.N.C. at Chapel Hill before graduating from A.S.T.C. in 1951. In both high school and college he was an excellent student and athlete, and he later coached baseball and basketball at Ronda High School before being appointed a Federal Probation Officer 1955. Robert has also been very active in civic and church affairs. On September 28, 1951, he was married to Mary Steelman, and they have four children: Mary Catherine, born August 17, 1952; Steven Robert, born October 17; 1953; Terry Charles, born February 21, 1961; and Timothy Neal, born July 27, 1968. Mary, a Registered Nurse, also pursued a career during this period, working for many years with Dr. Robert Lewis, as well as being very active

in church affairs at the Wilkesboro Baptist Church.

The second of Mama Trip and Daddy Trip's children was my father, Ray Spencer, born November 4, 1830. In 1949 Dad became the first football player from Wilkes County to make the North Carolina All-State and Shrine Bowl teams, and he later played football for and graduated from A.S.T.C. He was the head football coach and also coached baseball and basketball at West Wilkes High School from 1955-56 to 1964-65. He joined Lineberry Foundry & Machine Company in 1966 as purchasing agent and personnel manager. Dad has been active in civic and church affairs, too, and has served as a Wilkesboro Town Commissioner since 1977. On January 27, 1951, he married my mother, Nancy Garwood, and they have three children: Anthony Ray, born October 22, 1955; Nancy Lynn, born January 22, 1957; and Elizabeth Ann, born April 13, 1962. My mother has pursued a career as well, having worked at the Northwest Regional Education Center as a child nutritionist before joining the faculty at Wilkes Community College in 1971 as an instructor in food service management. She, too, has been active in civic and church affairs.

The third of Mama Trip and Daddy Trip's children, Rebecca Ann, was born on October 6, 1939. Ann graduated from Wilkes Central High School in 1957 and from A.S.T.C. in 1961, after which she taught at Wilkesboro Elementary School. On December 6, 1958, she married James S. Hartley, a 1961 graduate of Appalachian State. Jim accepted a position with the Northwestern Bank in 1969 and has been with the Bank since that time; he is a 1982 graduate of the School of B.A. at the U.N.C. at Chapel Hill, and is currently Executive Vice-President of the North Wilkesboro branch of the Northwestern Bank. Ann is still an occasional substitute teacher at Wilkesboro Elementary School, and she and Jim are both active members of the Wilkesboro Baptist Church. They have two children: Rebecca Ann, born April 19, 1962; and Christopher James, born October 10, 1966.

The youngest of Mama Trip and Daddy Trip's children, Martha Janey, was born on July 16, 1946. Janey graduated from Wilkes Central High School in 1964, and on June 11 of the same year she married Jerry R. Lackey. Jerry, a 1962 graduate of Wilkes Central, obtained his Associate of Applied Science Degree in Civil Engineering Technology from Gaston College in 1967, and subsequently worked for the N.C. Department of Transportation as a licensed surveyor. Today he operates his own surveying business, and is a real estate broker. Jerry has also been a member of the Wilkes County Planning Board since 1976 and the Wilkesboro Town Planning Board since 1977. Janey, after completing a year at Lenoir Rhyne College, has pursued a career as well, having been with the Northwest Regional Education Center since 1974. They have one child, Jennifer Lynne, born September 13, 1970.

The ten grandchildren of Mama Trip and Daddy Trip's family have an age difference spanning 18 years and have followed differing paths, but we are all still very close. Mary Catherine (Cathy) graduated from Wilkes Central High School in 1970 and from the U.N.C. at Greensboro in 1974. On July 4, 1976, she married Roger Neil DePriest. She and Roger live in Bristol, Tennessee, and have a son, Jacob Andrew, born August 16, 1981.

Steven Robert (Steve) graduated from Wilkes Central High School in 1971 and from Gaston College in 1977 with an Associate of Applied Science Degree in Civil Engineering Technology. On August 7, 1977, he married Kathryn Jean Clifton. Steve in a Quality Assurance Examiner with Duke Power Company, and Kathy is a Registered Nurse. They have a daughter, Emily Anne, born June 13, 1980.

Arlon A. and Edith F. Triplett.

Anthony Ray (Tony) graduated from Wilkes Central High School in 1974, from UNC at Chapel Hill in 1978, and from the UNC at Chapel Hill School of Law in 1981. He is currently an associate with the law firm of Vannoy, Moore & Colvard.

Nancy Lynn (Lynn) graduated from Wilkes Central High School in 1975 and from A.S.U. in 1979. She married David William Brooks II on August 3, 1980. Lynn teaches at Millers Creek Elementary School, and David is with the Northwestern Bank.

Terry Charles (Terry) graduated from Wilkes Central High School in 1979 and attended Gardner-Webb College before transferring to U.N.C. at Chapel Hill in 1981.

Elizabeth Ann (Beth) graduated from Wilkes Central High School in 1980. She is currently attending UNC at Chapel Hill.

Rebecca Ann (Rebecca) is also a 1980 graduate of Wilkes Central High School and currently attends U.N.C. at Chapel Hill. She and Beth are roommates at Chapel Hill.

Christopher James (Chris) is currently a student at Wilkes Central High School.

Timothy Neal (Neal) is currently a student at Woodward Junior High School.

And Jennifer Lynne (Jennifer) is also cur- rently a student at Woodward Junior High School.

Sources: Family records and rememberances, Wilkesboro Town Minutes and personal diary.

— Tony Triplett

JESSE and DICIE GRAY TRIPLETT

1042

Jesse Triplett was born in Wilkes County during the Revolutionary War in 1777. He was the youngest son of William and Elonar Harbin Triplett. Times were very difficult and sad for his mother during those long hard years. He lost his father and his two oldest brothers in the war.

Jesse married Dicie Gray, daughter of John and Ann Gray. Dicie was about ten years youn- ger than her husband according to census records. She married at a very early age. They reared a large family of eleven children includ- ing one set of twins.

Jesse owned land in the Mt. Zion area of Wilkes County and both he and Dicie are buried in the Old Mt. Zion Cemetary. Dicie died in 1875, at about the age of 68, while Jesse lived until about 1876, which made him about 98 years old. Dicie's sister, Mary, had remained unmarried and was living with them in her later years also.

Their children were: (1) John (1892-1846) named for his maternal grandfather, married Sarah Ferguson in 1829. (2) Eleanor, named for her paternal grandmother, was born about 1804 and married John Foster Ferguson. (3) Elizabeth (1808-1909) married Wilson Fair- child in 1829. (4) Lindsay, born about 1809, married Fanny Foster in 1833. (5) Frances, born about 1810, married Wyatt Rose in 1846. (6) Mary (Polly), (1813-1856), married John B. Miller in 1833. (7) Thomas, born about 1818, married Susannah Triplett in 1849. (8) Annie, born about 1822, married Thomas McGuire Dula in 1844. (9) William (a twin), born April 18, 1824, married Annie Emeline Waters (daughter of Joel Waters) in 1850. (10) Joel (a twin), born April 18, 1824, married Mary Adeline Gray. (11) Nancy, born about 1826, married William Hodges in 1848.

Jesse was living with his son, Joel, and his family at the time of the 1860 Census. At that time he was listed as 84 years old. His sister-in-law, Mary Gray, is also living in the house- hold. She was listed as being 70 years old.

Sources: *Triplett* by Hortense E. Abbott, marriage bonds and census records.

— Mrs. J. Arnold Simpson

NAOMI BROYHILL PARKS TRIPLETT

1043

Naomi was the second daughter of Isaac Jefferson and Ada Carlton Broyhill. She was born November 10, 1922 in Wilkes County.

She graduated from Wilkesboro High School and received a B.S. degree in Grammar Grade Education from A.S.T.C. Naomi taught school at Wilkesboro Elementary School and Roaring River Elementary School for a total of 26 years.

She married Harold Welborn Parks, son of Felix L. and Davie Welborn Greene Parks, July 15, 1950. They resided in Roaring River.

Harold attended Lees-McRae College. He served in the U.S. Naval Reserve in World War II and was employed at Chatham Manufactur- ing Co. in Elkin.

Naomi and Harold had two sons: James Harold born September 5, 1951 and Daniel Broyhill born July 16, 1953.

James graduated from North Carolina State University with a degree in Furniture Manufac- turing and Management. On September 17, 1971 he married Brenda Ritchie, daughter of John and Delores Elledge Ritchie. They have two children Jamie Michelle and Jodi Lynn and reside at Roaring River. James is employed at American Drew Furniture Company and Bren- da works at the Family Medical Clinic in North Wilkesboro.

Daniel graduated from North Carolina State University with a degree in Recreation and Park Administration. Daniel married Carla Cox, daughter of Lee and Nancy O'Brien Cox, December 29, 1973. Carla and Dan have two children, Daniel Broyhill Parks, Jr. and Anna Lyndolph Parks and live in Hays. They own and operated the Key City Bakery in North Wilkes- boro.

Harold died September 21, 1965 and is buried in the Roaring River United Methodist Church Cemetery.

Naomi married Thomas Lowell Triplett, Sr. June 30, 1973. He is the son of Elbert and Minnie Storie Triplett of Lenoir, N.C. and was in the U.S. Naval Reserve during Wolrd War II. They reside in Conover, N.C.

Source: Personal knowledge.

— Naomi Broyhill Parks Triplett

WILLIAM and ELONAR HARBIN TRIPLETT

1044

William Triplett was born about 1732 in Prince William Co., Va. (later to become Fair- fax Co. and then Loudoun Co.) He was the son of Francis and Elizabeth Triplett, one of their nine children. William and his brother Daniel were to divide 305 acres of land left to them by their father in his will of 1758.

Just before his fathers death, William had married Elonar Harbin. Their first six children were born in Loudoun County before his mother died in 1769. After her death, we find them in Orange Co., N.C. where he purchased 100 acres of land June 1, 1770 from Daniel Adams for 50 pounds. Since Orange County was much larger at that time, we aren't sure exactly where this land was located.

Next, he is found in Wilkes County, where he purchased land on Dec. 25, 1778. He selected 150 acres located on the big branch of Beaver Creek.

The Revolutionary War, with it's difficult times, brought a great deal of sadness and heartbreak to this family. A family legend tells us that William an his two eldest sons, Micajah

441

and Nimrod, died in an army camp at Hanging Rock in what is now Watauga Co. They died during an epidemic of measles.

The exact dated of William's death is unknown. His son William states in his Rev. War Application that he entered service in 1780 under Capt. Wm. Sloan. He further states that since his mother was a widow and needed his assistance that he was induced from maternal feelings to hire a substitute by the name of Jeremiah Ferguson, who served faithfully for him until he returned as a volunteer for three more months. William, Jr. states that he was born Nov. 15, 1763 in Loudoun Co., Va. He signed his name on his pension.

William, Jr. would have been only sixteen or seventeen when he entered service in 1780. With a mother who had lost her husband and two sons and who had seven small children at home at care for including a baby born in 1780, it had to be a difficult time for this family.

Elonar must have been unusually strong of spirit and character. She apparently was educated as she signed her name on the bond as Administratrix of her husband's estate on Jan. 28, 1784. Her brother Thomas Harbin signed this bond with her. She was listed on the 1830 Census as over 100 years old. This would make her birthdate before 1730.

Their children were: (1) Micajah, born about 1758, died in the Rev. War. (2) Nimrod, born about 1760, died in Rev. War. (3) Mason, born about 1762, married Mary Mullins (a cousin and daughter of William and Sarah Triplett Mullins) in 1785. They moved to Kentucky in 1803. (5) Thomas (1765-1851) married Jane Ferguson in 1788. (6) Frances, born about 1767, married Jeremiah Ferguson in 1787. (7) John, born about 1770, married Linda Ferguson in 1795 and later moved to Kentucky. (8) Verlinda, born about 1775, married Richard Ferguson (son of John). (9) Nancy, born about 1776, married John Sanders in 1797 in Wilkes. This family moved to Kentucky. (10) Jesse (1777-1875) married Dicie Gray. (11) Priscilla, born about 1780, married John Ferguson in 1804.

The earliest ancestor of William Triplett to remain in America was Francis Triplett (son of John Triplett who came to America but returned to England). Francis came from London, England about 1660 to Rapphannock Co., Va. His will was proven in 1701 in Richmond Co., Va.

Sources: *Triplett* by Hortense E. Abbott, Rev. pension records, marriage bonds, deeds, wills and estate records.

— Mrs. J. Arnold Simpson

WILLIAM CICERO
and
SUSAN JANE FOSTER
TRIPLETT
1045

William Cicero Triplett was the oldest son of Larkin and Mary Etta Dyer Triplett. Larkin Hodge Triplett, born 21 June 1848 in Wilkes County, died 5 November 1916, married Mary Etta Dyer, 25 August 1870. She was born 16

October 1852 and died 27 September 1927. Both are buried in the cemetary at Lewis Fork Church.

William Cicero was born 4 July 1871 and married Susan Jane Foster, 24 December 1893. She was the first child of Absolem (Adney) Mathis and Martha Hubbard Foster and was born 10 June 1877. Mr. Triplett was a highly respected citizen of Lewis Fork Township where he lived all of his life. He was an active member of Lewis Fork Baptist Church for many years but later moved his membership to Mr. Pleasant Baptist Church. He died 5 March 1954 and Susan Jane died 15 April 1971, two months before her ninety-fourth birthday. They had celebrated their "fiftieth" wedding anniversary in 1943 but had had their sixtieth prior to his death. He was a member of Mt. Pleasant Masonic Lodge 573 and had been presented his fifty-year membership pin in 1950.

William Cicero and Susan Jane F. Triplett.

Cicero and Susan Jane were the parents of nine children whose lives reflect the fine upbringing they had received during their early years. (1) Belva Lou, born 8 November 1894 and who is still living. She married William Percy Bumgarner, born 4 July 1890, died 27 December 1977, on 25 December 1920. Their children are Howard, Rex (deceased), Jene and Billy (deceased). (2) Veoria Elzora, born 14 September 1896, died 22 July 1933, married Hill Gorden Walsh 8 January 1916. They reared a large family of children in Bluefield, West Virginia. (3) Cartas Hubbard, born 25 October 1898, died 30 November 1955. (4) Arlon Artemas, born 17 December 1900, married in September 1925 Edith Foster, born 28 March 1909. They are the parents of Robert, Ray, Ann T. Hartley and Janie T. Lackey. (5) Alta Bradford, born 7 February 1903, died 24 March 1952, married 14 June 1934 Cleo Hamby, born 20 April 1910, died in June 1962. Their children are Lloyd, Jewel Dean T. Myers, Clara Jane and Jerry Lane. (6) Zera Veona, born 24 March 1905, married 15 September 1926, Elster H. Greene, born 1898, now deceased. They had Elster Hal, Jr., Mary Sue Greene Watkins, and William Elbert (deceased). (7) Lennis Guy, born 29 March 1907, married 21 December 1935, Vera Ellis, born 17 November 1910. There were three children: Hazel T. Triplett, Bobby Lennis, and Betty Lou T. Curley. (8) Vada Mae, born 10 May 1909, married John William Foster, born 7 May 1913, died 9 December 1966. They had Dr. John Thomas Foster and Kay Neil Foster

Mann. (9) Raeford Lonnie, born 1 December 1910, married 16 June 1940 Ruth Eller Mikeal, born 12 June 1912. They had Roy Clinton, Linda Ruth T. Morrison, William Clay and Johnny (deceased). (10) Hazel Laverne, born 1 December 1913, died 24 September 1915.

Sources: Triplett Book, personal recollection.

— Belva Triplett Bumgarner

GLENN MONROE TUCKER
1046

Glenn Monroe Tucker was born in Wilkes County, N.C., June 9, 1909., in a one room log cabin, son of the late J. W. Tucker and Elmah I. Settle Tucker. He attended Benham Elementary and Ronda High School. After two and one-half years at Ronda, where he played football and baseball, he transfered to the Traphill High School for the spring semester of 1927-1928.

When E. R. Settle returned to Mountain View Institute for 1928-29 as principal of the Baptist School, Glenn moved with uncle, Mr. Settle and graduated in 1929.

He attended Wake Forest College at Wake Forest, N.C. graduating with a BS in Science and Math, in 1933.

In 1933, he accepted a teaching and coaching position at Roaring River High School. While at Roaring River Glenn met and married the English and French teacher, Blanche Silver of Horse Shoe, N.C. They are the parents of four sons and one daughter. Kenneth M., deceased; Elton G., is an Attorney; J. Hiram and Thomas O., are Realtors; Sylvia Lynn a Registered Nurse.

Glenn taught at New Hanover High School in Wilmington, N.C. where he served as faculty manager of Athletics. During this time David Brinkley was one of his students. While still at Hanover High School, Glenn moved to Carolina Beach and went into Real Estate and operated a store on the midway.

In the fall of 1938, Glenn began a seven year term as principal of Bolivia High School in Brunswick County, returning each summer to Carolina Beach and the Real Estate business.

In 1945-46, Glenn was principal of LeLand High School and commuted from Carolina Beach. He resigned from the public school system to devote full time to real estate.

He served on the Carolina Beach School Board, the Town Board, a member of The First Baptist Church, S.S. Supt., Deacon, Trustee, Teacher, Chm. Pulpit Committee, and in the choir.

He served on the Cape Fear Area Council of the Boy Scouts of America, helped organize Southeastern N.C. Beach Association, All Seashore Highway Association; Travel Council of N.C.; served on Board of Directors for the Bank of Carolina Beach; and Chamber of Commerce; N.C. Confederate Centennial Commission.

He organized the first Carolina Beach Lion's Club and was President for two years. His sons Hiram and Tommy have also been President of this club. He initiated and organized the Bank of Carolina Beach and served on its Board until

Glenn Monroe Tucker.

the merger with First National Bank of Eastern North Carolina, now Bank of N.C., Inc.

In the Real Estate World, Glenn has over forty years. He became a Realtor, in the Wilmington Board 1945. Later organized the Carolina-Kure Beach Board of Realtors, Inc., and President for ten years. Glenn was State President of the North Carolina Board of Realtors in 1962.

In 1970 he sold his interest in the Carolina Beach Real Estate and moved to a farm near Raleigh where he operates a Real Estate business, and raises beef cattle.

Sources: Personal Knowledge.

— Glenn M. Tucker

C. H. M. and SENA A. TULBERT
1047

Jesse and Louisa Sparks Tulbert were the parents of four children. (1) A son who died young. (2) Laura, who did not marry, was superintendent of Salem Female Academy in Salem (now Winston-Salem, N.C.) until her health failed. (3) Eva married Virgil Forrester and lived in North Wilkesboro. They had one daughter, Grace Dean who married Harold Burke. (4) Charles Henry Martin Tulbert, the subject of this sketch.

Henry, father of Jesse Tulbert, chose his homesite in Buck Shoals Township in Yadkin County, N.C. because of an excellent water supply on the property. This place was inherited by Jesse who raised his family there. After his death, C. H. M. Tulbert bought his sisters' shares. The land including the family graveyard is now owned by Guy Tulbert, son of C. H. M. Tulbert.

C. H. M. Tulbert was educated at the academy at Boonville and the original Draughn's Business College in Nashville, Tenn. He began his career as a schoolteacher in Yadkin and lower Wilkes Counties. About 1900

he moved to Wilkes and built a store in the Spurgeon community. A post office was established there and it was housed in his store building. It is believed that Mr. Tulbert was the first postmaster at Spurgeon. He was succeeded by P. M. Reid who was his partner in the store, Reid and Tulbert.

While operating the store at Spurgeon which was located about a mile from Hunting Creek Baptist Church, Mr. Tulbert met and married Sena Gertrude Anderson, daughter of William (Little Will) and Mary Somers Anderson. Mary was the daughter of Howard and Rebecca Somers. Leaving Mr. Reid to run the store at Spurgeon, the Tulberts moved to Wilkesboro sometime during the early 1900s. Mr. Tulbert was associated with Turner-White Casket and Forest Furniture Companies of which he was a director and stockholder.

In 1913 the family moved to Millers Creek and bought the R. Filmore Wyatt farm. They renovated the house and store and operated the store there until about 1926 when Mr. Tulbert became active vice-president of the Deposit and Savings Bank in North Wilkesboro. Mr. Reid, also a partner in the Millers Creek store, and Mr. Tulbert agreed on a settlement which left the store at Spurgeon to Mr. Reid and the one at Millers Creek to Mr. Tulbert. Mr. Tulbert was postmaster at Millers Creek for several years. Mr. Claude Faw, Mr. C. H. M. Tulbert and other interested citizens were responsible for establishing the first high school at Millers Creek about 1920.

Mr. Tulbert died 23 November 1932. His wife and family continued to live at Millers Creek. Mrs. Tulbert was an excellent cook and gardener. She assisted in the store and the post office during the years. She enjoyed visiting friends and neighbors, especially those who were sick. The family completed their new, brick home at Millers Creek in 1951. Mrs. Tulbert died in 1974 and is buried with her husband in sight of their home in the cemetery where the old Millers Creek Methodist Church once stood. They had long attended and supported this church.

C. H. M. and Sena A. Tulbert had six children. (1) Guy succeeded his father as postmaster and served 15 years. He owned and operated a service station at Millers Creek for many years, and has been engaged in farming. Guy has not married and continues to live at the homeplace. (2) Reno (deceased) married first Rachael Johnson and they had two children: (a) Norma Jean married Jim Foster and they live in Fayetteville, N.C. (b) Ray married Bobbie Ann Walsh and they live in Purlear. They had three children, Julia, Tony, and Pamela. Reno's second marriage was to Alfretta McGlammery (deceased) and they had one son, Michael, who lives in Ohio.

(3) Violet married Ralph Wooten and they live in Fairfax, Va. They had two children. (a) Julia married Blake Lovette and they are living in Russellville, Ark. (b) Charles Richard and his wife, JoAnn Wingler Wooten, are teachers at North High School. They purchased his parents' home at Millers Creek and live there with their children, Jody and Derik. (4) Hester and her husband, James Booker, live in Cherryville, N.C. (5) Vivian lives with her husband,

William Cole, in Silver Springs, Md. (6) Doris and her husband, David Robinson, reside in Greensboro, N.C.

Sources: Article in *Greensboro Daily News*, 23 Nov. 1932 and personal knowledge.

— Guy Tulbert

DEWEY EDGAR TURNER, SR.
1048

Dewey Edgar Turner, Sr., was born May 2, 1898 in the Gilreath community near the site of New Hope Baptist Church. He attended the Parker School at Gilreath for what little formal education that he had. Times were hard and taxes to support the schools often ran out after 3 or 4 months' term. Also, due to the need for all the family to work, most young people had to leave off school to help at home full-time.

He was the son of Wilburn and Mary Hayes Turner. His brothers were Wiley E., Simeon Purvis and Paris Vaughn. His sisters were Verdie and Arvie. He had two half-sisters, Adina Mae who never married and Pearlie, who married Paul Baity. A brother, Winston McKinley and a sister, Texie, died in infancy.

His mother was the daughter of William Hayes, who died at Lowery's Bluff in the Civil War and Peggy Moore. His father was the son of Mary Benge Turner whose husband, James E. Turner, died at the Battle of the Wilderness in Virginia during the Civil War, also. The remains of the Mary Turner cabin stands near the McDiarmid home on the Brushy Mountains.

Dewey E. Turner moved with his family to the New Hope Township in Iredell County near Grassy Knob Church in early youth. It was so difficult to farm in the hilly, rocky soil of the Brushies that it was easier to provide a growing family as tenants on the larger farms in the flatlands of Iredell County.

Dewey Turner married Ruby Forester on December 24, 1921, and returned to live in Wilkes County permanently in the Cricket community. He opened the first rural service station between North Wilkesboro and Boone. Cricket post office was in a corner of the store and his wife was post mistress many years.

In the early days, the service station served as a way station for the wagoneers from Ashe and Watauga Counties as much as for the automobile trade. Having installed one of the first telephones in the area, the wagoneers from the isolated communities often stopped to make calls to check on markets for their goods and produce.

Hub Parsons, a notorious outlaw, once robbed the station-post office at gunpoint. The Turner daughters, little girls at the time, cried and begged him not to shoot mamma and daddy in the terror-filled time that their parents were held at gunpoint. Feeling ran high after the robbery and a massive manhunt was undertaken. Paris Turner, a deputy at the time and brother of Dewey, and Clarence Staley, who was specially deputized for the manhunt, captured Hub Parsons in the White Oak community near Parsonsville.

Dewey and his brother, Paris, were always close throughout their lives and one of their favorite stories of their young days was an episode about cake baking. The two youngsters found themselves alone at home one day and never having had all the cake that they wanted to eat, they decided to remedy the situation by baking one. Neither knew the first thing about baking, but they decided the more sugar they used the better it would be. The cake was a diaster, of course, and the worst part was when their mother discovered the waste of the precious sugar — she never whipped the boys but left that up to her husband. The boys were very contrite and begged her not to tell on them, but she told them she was going to tell their father and she wouldn't back down on her word. However, the good behavior and contriteness of the two little fellows tugged at her tender feelings until she compromised as best she could without giving in to their pleas. Just before their father returned she gave each of them an extra pair of pants to provide some padding in the area where the blows would be felt.

Dewey Turner engaged in the lumber business on a rather extensive basis during the forties and founded the D. E. Turner Oil Company in 1945, which he operated until his death and which his family carries on today.

He was interested in fishing and sports and was a familiar figure at ball games with his Boxer, Patsy at his side. He encouraged young people in sports and education and many young men who strayed afoul of the law knew that they could get a helping hand from him. Many people who found it hard to make ends meet at times were carried on the books at the store for long periods of time. Some never paid these aaccounts, but from time to time, even after many years, people repaid him. After his death in 1972, his family received many testimonials from people he had helped and for kindnesses he had done that his family never knew about.

His zest for life was manifested in his singing and for many years he was a familiar figure in church choirs at regular services and in the 5th Sunday singings which were widely attended. These choirs used the shaped note, sacred harpe's type hymnals.

His family consists of: D. E. Turner, Jr. (Tommy) and his wife Adeline Messic Turner, Mozelle Shumaker and husband Clyde W. Shumaker, Marie Snider and husband Clate Snider. His wife Ruby is now retired. There are 5 grandchildren: Mark Shumaker, Gena Shumaker Pries, Michael Turner, Alex Turner and Timothy Snider.

Sources: Family records and personal knowledge.

— Mozelle Turner Shumaker

THE VANNOY FAMILY
1049

The genealogy "James Hook and Virginia Eller" published in 1925 contains about all that is yet known about the first generation of the Vannoy family in the United States. That source states that the Vannoy family is of Huguenot extraction, the early family having fled from France to Holland and later to England during the reign of Charles I. The name in France was spelled Vannoise or Venois. The later were names of distinguished families in France during the 16th and 17th centuries.

The emigrant to America, John Vannoy settled on Statler Island, New York. The best records indicate his children to be: John, Francis, Abram, Rachel, Catherine, and Sarah. The second generation traced is through Francis Vannoy. The children of Francis Vannoy were John, Hannah, Cornelius, and Andrew. The third generation traced is through John Vannoy. The children of John Vannoy were Rachel, Andrew Vannoy who married Susannah Shepherd October 18, 1779, Abraham, Francis, Nathaniel who married Elizabeth Ray of Ashe County, Hannah, Daniel, Susannah, and Katherine.

The fourth generation is traced through Andrew Vannoy and Nathaniel Vannoy. Andrew was a captain in the N.C. Regiment, Revolutionary War, and Nathaniel was a sergeant major on the staff of Col. Ben Cleveland. Both Andrew and Nathaniel participated in the Battle of Kings Mountain. Nathaniel Vannoy was granted 100 acres of land on December 15, 1798 on a branch of Lewis Fork Creek. On December 10, 1802 and November 28, 1812, two additional tracts containing 20 acres and 50 acres respectively both on the waters of Lewis Fork Creek were granted to him. Nathaniel Vannoy and his wife were founding members of the New Hope Baptist Church. The church was constituted June 26, 1830 to serve the people of Lewis Fork Creek. The children of Nathaniel Vannoy and wife, Elizabeth, were John, Joel, Sarah, Jesse, Andrew, Elizabeth, Jane, Ann, and Susannah.

The fifth generation is traced through Jesse Vannoy. The children of Jesse Vannoy were Elizabeth Ray, Joel Eden, Sarah Jane, John Humphrey, Katherine Ann, William Kilby, Jesse Whitfield, James Nathaniel, Abraham Wesley, Frances Susannah, Andrew Jackson, Mary Caroline, Franky Matilda, and Anderson.

The sixth generation is traced through Anderson Vannoy. Anderson Vannoy died in 1862 at Winchester, VA, from wounds received at the Battle of South Mountain in the War between the States. The children of Anderson and Martha Wheeler Vannoy were Richard Leroy, Catherine (Eliza), James Newton, Mary C., Doane, and Hester.

The seventh generation is traced through James Newton Vannoy born July 6, 1857; died March 17, 1926; married Cornelia Bumgarner October 1881. Cornelia, born September 28, 1865, died April 9, 1936, was the daughter of Adam and Polly (Brown) Bumgarner. They had a family of sixteen children as follows: George Everett, Hannibal Roscoe, Mary Ethel, Robert Glenn, John Thomas, William Andrew, Jesse Albert, Mattie Mae, Virginia Dare, William Raynor, Mintie Hester, Benedict Arnold, Richard Newton, Joseph Conrad, Carl Johnson, and Clyde Smith.

Source: *James Hook and Virginia Eller* published in 1925.

— Thomas G. Vannoy

THE VANNOYS and RAYS
1050

John Vannoy, grandson of John Vannoy and his wife Susannah Anderson went from New Jersey to S.C. about 1735-6, and after several years moved to the "Jersey Settlement" in Rowan Co., N.C. There John sympathized with the "Regulators" in their opposition to unjust taxes and the service fee policy. After the Battle of Almance in 1771 many homes along the Yadkin River were destroyed, including the Vannoy home, and they went up-river to the Wilkes area.

Children were Rachel, b. 1741; Andrew, b. 12 Aug. 1742, m. 18 Oct. 1779 to Susannah Shepherd, d. 9 Oct. 1809; Abraham b. 15 Jan. 1745; Francis, b. 13 Aug. 1746, d. 26 July 1822 in Knox Co., KY; Nathaniel, b. 16 Feb. 1749, d. 26 July 1835, married Elizabeth, daughter of William and Elizabeth Ray. Hannah, b. 26 Mar. 1751; Daniel, b. 22 Feb. 1752, m. 2 Oct. 1779 Sarah Hickerson; Susannah, b. 6 July 1754; and Katherine, b. 26 Dec. 1755.

Nathaniel Vannoy lived most of his life in Wilkes Co. He served as Sgt. Major to Col. Benj. Cleveland at the Battle of King's Mtn. and in skirmishes with British, Tories and Indians. He became a planter, Register of Deeds for Wilkes Co. 1814-15 and, finally, a Baptist evangelist. He died at the home of his daughter Sarah Cleveland in Greenville, SC. Nathaniel married Elizabeth Ray ca. 1773 in Surry Co. They were "founder members" of New Hope Baptist Church in 1830. After a full life she predeceased him and was buried, in a Yates family cemetery on Lewis Fork. Her parents, William and Elizabeth Ray, came from Amherst Co., VA, ca. 1772.

On 1 June 1778, Nathaniel, Daniel and Andrew Vannoy were among those appointed "jurors" to "lay out" roads in the county. In the 1782 tax list and the 1790 census Elizabeth Ray appears as head of family; apparently William died between 1778 & 1782.

Their son Col. Jesse Ray (b. 1760, Amherst Co. VA) married Elener Baker 8 Jan. 1782. He was active in the organization of Ashe Co. from Wilkes in 1799.

Daughter Ann Ray and her husband Nathaniel Vannoy had nine children: John Vannoy, b. 22 May 1775, m. 1st Elizabeth Kilby, and died ca. 1796 in Missouri. Joel Vannoy, b. 22 Feb. 1777, moved to Pike Co. KY; Sarah Vannoy, b. 16 Jan. 1779, d. 23 July 1856 in SC, m. 31 Aug. 1801 to Jerimiah Cleveland, son of Robert Cleveland; Jesse Vannoy, b. 2 July 1781, d. 26 Nov. 1875, m. 12 Jan. 1804 Mary "Polly" Kilby Shepherd, widow of John Shepherd; Andrew Vannoy, b. 4 Nov. 1783, d. 22 Jan. 1869, m. 1st Elizabeth Degan in NC and 2nd Jane McMichales in TN. He was a soldier, school teacher, Baptist minister and Clerk of Court in Bedford Co. TN. Elizabeth Vannoy, b. 4 March 1786, m. 1806 Neil Patton. Jane Vannoy, b. 20 Aug. 1788, m. a Thurston. They moved to Arkansas. Ann Vannoy, b. 4 May 1790, d. 21 May 1873, m. 3 Jan. 1809 to John Foster, son of Thomas and Elizabeth Jones Foster. Ann and John lived on a plantation on the Yadkin, some nine miles east of Wilkesboro and had 15 children.

Susannah Vannoy, b. 4 Nov. 1790, a twin to Ann, m. a Parks.

Sources: "Geo. Michal Eller" by Hooks; Hunterdon Co. N.J., Rowan, Wilkes and Ashe Co. records; "King's Mtn. & It's Heroes" by Draper.

— Mrs. John M. Richards, Jr.

HANNIBAL ROSCOE VANNOY
1051

H. Ross Vannoy was born 9 April 1884 and died 3 September 1974. During his ninety years, he left a significant influence for descendants, friends, and community.

He was the son of James Newton and Cornelia (Bumgarner) Vannoy of the Purlear community. He left his father's farm at an early age and began selling insurance in North Wilkesboro. New Hope Baptist was his church. He was married to Ruth Ella McNeil, daughter of Thornton Sylvester and Eda Elizabeth (McNeil) McNiel 10 May 1914.

After his marriage his father-in-law, Thornton McNiel, brought Ross Vannoy into his business, the North Wilkesboro Coca-Cola Bottling Company. He worked there until after Ruth Vannoy's death 11 January 1919.

Their three children were (1) Ella Sue Vannoy Colvard, (2) Annie Louise Vannoy Gray, and (3) H.R. Vannoy, Jr., called "Johnny." Information about them may be found in their mother's biography, located elsewhere in this book.

The Vannoy lineage is rich in history. Ross Vannoy's grandfather, Anderson, the youngest of fourteen children, died in Winchester, Virginia, after being wounded at South Mountain as a Confederate soldier. His great-grandfather, Jesse, was a soldier in the Revolutionary War, serving in the regiment of Col. Benjamin Cleveland. He was granted land for his military services. Jesse Vannoy was a founding member of the New Hope Baptist Church in 1830.

The Vannoy family is of Huguenot extraction, having fled from France to Holland. Later they went to England during the reign of King Charles I. The emigrant to America, who settled on Staten Island, was John Vannoy, who had fought under Oliver Cromwell and was related to him by marriage. He was the great, great-grandfather of Jesse Vannoy.

After the death of his wife, Ross Vannoy moved to Ashe County in 1923 where he had a sub-franchise for Coca-Cola, a distributorship for Gulf Oil, and he founded the Dr Pepper Bottling Company of West Jefferson in 1934.

He returned to Wilkes County to court and marry Lena Florence Poplin, eldest child of Leet and Kushat (Harris) Poplin of Ronda. Lena Vannoy was born 19 July 1901, and she and Ross Vannoy were married 13 September 1925. Her father was a member of the Wilkes County Board of Commissioners.

Ross Vannoy's daughter, Ella Sue, moved with him to Ashe County, while his other daughter, Annie, remained living with her aunt, Mamie McNiel, in North Wilkesboro. Johnny had died in 1924.

Lena and Ross Vannoy had two sons, (4) James Leet Vannoy, who was born 4 October 1926, and (5) Raymond Kyle Vannoy, who

was born 9 May 1928. Leet Vannoy resides in Austinville, Virginia, and is married to Mildred Dean Phipps. They are the parents of (1) Patricia Vannoy Inge, (2) Edith Vannoy, and (3) Neil Vannoy. Kyle Vannoy lives in West Jefferson and is married to Shirley Hartzog. His children from former marriages are (2) Teressa Vannoy, (3) Phyllis Vannoy, (4) Michael Vannoy, and (5) Susan Vannoy. His oldest son, (1) James Kyle Vannoy died in 1978.

Ross Vannoy was the second eldest of sixteen children, all of whom were born at Purlear.

(1) George Everette Vannoy was born 21 July 1882 and died 18 July 1945. He was married 18 March 1916 to Julia Florence Maxwell. They had two children and two grandchildren. (2) H. Roscoe came next and his lineage is found above. (3) Mary E. Vannoy was born 1 March 1886 and died 9 May 1960. She was married to James Harrison Davis 29 April 1906. Their children number ten and their grandchildren, twenty-six. (4) Robert Glenn Vannoy was born 16 May 1888 and died 1 August 1974. He was married 8 August 1915 to Lessie Phillips. They were the parents of six children and seven grandchildren.

(5) John Thomas Vannoy was born 23 December 1889 and died 26 February 1975. He was married 26 September 1915 to Lora Ellen Watts. They had five children and eleven grandchildren. (6) William Andrew Vannoy was born 5 November 1891 and died 5 August 1927. He married Margie Lee Dosse and had two sons and seven grandchildren. (7) Jesse Albert Vannoy was born 27 March 1893 and died 13 April 1973. He married Lilla Gilliam 6 February 1916 and they had two sons and two daughters. There were seven grandchildren.

(8) Mattie Mae Vannoy was born 26 April 1895 and died 26 January 1972. She was married to John David McLean 5 November 1921. They had a son and a daughter. Their grandchildren number four. (9) Virginia Dare Vannoy was born 24 December 1896 and died 18 February 1970. She was married 1 May 1926 to Robert Lee Reavis. They were the parents of a son and a daughter and four grandchildren. (10) William Raynor Vannoy was born 29 December 1898 and died 19 August 1947. He was married to Lacy Florence McNiel 7 January 1923. They had one daughter and no grandchildren.

(11) Mintie Hester Vannoy was born 29 December 1900. She was married to Archie Allen Bumgarner. She has one daughter and five grandchildren. (12) Arnold Vannoy was born 14 March 1903 and died 27 May 1919. He was unmarried. (13) Richard Newton Vannoy was born 28 July 1904. He was married to Dorothy Scott 5 September 1925. They had two sons and two grandchildren. (14) Joseph Conrad Vannoy was born 19 March 1906. He was married 12 February 1929 to Helen Whittington. There were four children and seven grandchildren. (15) Carl Johnson Vannoy was born 18 November 1909 and married Leida Church 1 January 1931. There are three daughters and five grandchildren. (16) Clyde Smith Vannoy was born 3 March 1911. He was married to Virginia Money 5 February 1935. There are three chil-

dren and five grandchildren.

Ross Vannoy has only one surviving sister, Mintie Vannoy Bumgarner, and four surviving brothers, Richard, Conrad, Carl and Clyde Vannoy. Forty-six nieces and nephews were born, although some are deceased.

With the large family and humble beginnings, Ross Vannoy learned early to make a contribution to mankind. His life was interesting and full. The counties of Wilkes and Ashe benefitted from his having been one of their noble citizens.

Sources: Hook, George Michael Eller, Descendants of His in America; Vannoy, The James Newton Vannoy Family; family records and memories.

— C. Frank Colvard

THE FAMILY OF JAMES NEWTON VANNOY
1052

(1) George Everette Vannoy (July 21, 1882; July 18, 1945) married March 18, 1916 Florence Maxwell (April 23, 1880; January 14, 1970). They had two daughters, Annie Laurie (January 1, 1917), married Charles Raymond Hill December 24, 1937, and Winnie Marie (March 30, 1918) married Troy Manus Church June 16, 1940.

(2) Hannibal Roscoe Vannoy (April 9, 1884; September 3, 1974) married May 1914 Ruth Ella McNiel (See Ruth Ella McNiel Vannoy story).

(3) Mary E. Vannoy (March 1, 1886; May 9, 1960) married April 29, 1906 James Harrison Davis (July 8, 1884; February 19, 1955). They had ten children; Theta Ester (February 1, 1907; October 18, 1913); Parks (March 29, 1908); Scott (April 18, 1909; married Vallie Whittington September 11, 1928 and had four children; Ralph (February 2, 1911) married September 18, 1937 Pansey Kendall and had one son; Ruth (October 24, 1919) married Van Wiles June 27, 1934 and had three children; Gladys (March 25, 1914) married Eugene Billings November 5, 1938 and had five children; Grace (September 13, 1915) married February 12, 1938 Arlie O. Foster and had three children; Warren G. (February 26, 1921, October 26, 1981) married Jurileen Nicholson February 28, 1942 and had one son; Doris (October 29, 1922) married George Eysenbach May 13, 1944 and had seven children; and Marjorie (August 22, 1925).

(4) Robert Glenn Vannoy (May 16, 1888; August 1, 1974) married August 8, 1915 to Lessie Phillips Vannoy (September 13, 1895; June 16, 1959). They had six children: Cecil Cliffton married Reba Campbell; Elenor Phillips; Inez Dora (January 20, 1920; November 15, 1934), Robert Glenn Jr.; Susie Jeanette; and Betty Jean.

(5) John Thomas Vannoy (December 23, 1889; February 26, 1975) married on September 26, 1915 to Lora Ellen Watts (May 27, 1890; February 4, 1973). They had five children: Wayne Winifred (September 1979) married Ruby Belle Baker and had two daughters; Reuben Wrenn (January 23, 1975), married Annie Belle Pardue and had two sons; Ardena Faye, married Roy Taylor Cashion (died Octo-

ber 21, 1958) and had four children, her second marriage was to Jim Spicer; John Thomas Jr. married Ada Sue Lovette and had four children; Howard Hadley married Mary Gladus Benton and had three daughters.

(6) William Andrew Vannoy (November 5, 1891; August 1927) married Margie Lee Dosse (February 11, 1896; January 23, 1972). They had two sons: Lacy French and William James (deceased).

(7) Jesse Albert Vannoy (March 27, 1893; April 13, 1973) married February 6, 1916 to Lilla Blanche Gilliam (August 9, 1892, December 22, 1972). They had five children: Sarah Cornelia (January 3, 1917), Charles Albert (April 23, 1919), Margaret Ruth (February 27, 1924; January 17, 1925), Betty Louise (April 19, 1927; December 10, 1927), Mary Elizabeth (August 19, 1928).

(8) Mattie Mae Vannoy (April 26, 1895; January 26, 1972) married November 5, 1921 to John David McLean (September 3, 1895; November 15, 1978). They had two children: Frederick Carl (August 26, 1922) and Winnie Sue (November 25, 1923).

(9) Virginia Dare Vannoy (December 24, 1896; February 18, 1970) married May 1, 1926 Robert Lee Reavis (May 9, 1897; September 26, 1972). They had two children: James Arnold and Iris Allene (Nancy).

(10) William Raynor Vannoy (December 29, 1898; August 19, 1947), married on January 7, 1923 Lacy Florence McNiel (May 29, 1902). They had one daughter: Mildred Katherine.

(11) Mintie Hester Vannoy (December 29, 1900) married Archie Allen Bumgarner (February 19, 1886; March 25, 1936). They had one daughter: Archie Alan Bumgarner (November 25, 1936).

(12) Arnold Vannoy (March 14, 1903; May 27, 1919).

(13) Richard Newton Vannoy (July 28, 1904) married September 5, 1925 to Dorothy Scott (September 11, 1906). They had two sons: Max Clinton (January 7, 1929; June 8, 1938), and Thomas Gene. (April 20, 1933). Thomas Gene married Evelyn Englebert and had two children: Sharon Ann (Sherry) (October 7, 1953) and Larry Thomas (December 3, 1956). Larry married Susan Dare Wachter September 26, 1981.

(14) James Conrad Vannoy (March 19, 1906) married Helen Whittington and had four children: Louise; Joseph Smith (March 13, 1934; November 11, 1939), Linda; and Frank Douglas (November 16, 1943).

(15) Carl Johnson Vannoy (November 18, 1909) married January 1, 1931 Leida Church (January 7, 1914). They had three daughters: Carlee, Barbara Jean, and Mary Maxine.

(16) Clyde Smith Vannoy (March 3, 1911) married February 5, 1935 Virginia (Virgie) Money (October 21, 1918; February 19, 1975). They had three children: Mildred Carolyn; Eugene Smith; and Daniel Jeffrey.

Sources: family records and personal knowledge.

— Thomas G. Vannoy

JOEL VANNOY
1053

Joel Vannoy was born in 1792, presumably in Wilkes County, N.C. It has been said, "Sheriff Vannoy was a man of great prominence in his day. He was sheriff of Wilkes County almost for a life time. I have been told that he was a very striking personality, strong mentally and physically." Offical records of Wilkes County indicate that he only served as sheriff for six years, from 1824 to 1830. He was the father of 22 children, 17 of whom grew to adulthood. Seven of his sons served in the Civil War.

So far as we know, no definite proof ever has been found as to the father of Joel Vannoy. Two sources say he probably was the son of Daniel Vannoy who married Sarah Hickerson in Wilkes in 1779. Others have stated he was the son of Nathaniel Vannoy.

Joel Vannoy served as a corporal in the Fifth Regiment of Wilkes County in the War of 1812.

A marriage bond was issued March 18, 1817 in Wilkes County to Joel Vannoy and Elizabeth Saint Clair. She was born on September 12, 1796 and died February 10, 1831. She is buried at Presbyterian Church in Wilkesboro. Seven of her children lived to maturity and were:

Joel Alfred Vannoy (1818- ?); Elizabeth Caroline Vannoy (1819-1876) married Horatio Nelson Miller and had ten children; John Hamilton Vannoy (? -1862); Rebecca Elvira Vannoy who married a Walsh; Emily Amanda Vannoy (1821-1888) married Edward Welch and had a large family; Amelia Adeline Vannoy (1827-1897) married to Willis Parker and they were parents of ten children; and Ann Marie Vannoy who married first Rodolph McCleland, married second Henry S. Swink with issue by both.

On July 6, 1832 a marriage bond was issued in Burke County, N.C. to Joel Vannoy and Lemira E. Sudderth, daughter of Abraham and Martha Sumter Sudderth. She was born in 1819 and died in 1858 at the age of 49. She also is buried in the Presbyterian churchyard in Wilkesboro. Ten of her children lived to be grown and were:

Abram McLean Vannoy (? -1862) with one known child; William Wiley Vannoy (1834-1905) had two children; Sarah Martha Vannoy (1835-1905) married first John Nooe and had five children, married second Joseph P. Shields and had two children; Alexander Washington Vannoy (1836-1862); James Vannoy (1838- ?); Harvey Sudderth Vannoy (1840-1935); Thomas Irwin Vannoy (1842- ?); Elijah Ross Vannoy (1844-1863); Catherine A. Vannoy (1849-1872) was married to Vance Taylor and had two known children; and Anderson Mitchell Vannoy (1854-1922).

In 1833 Vannoy wrote a letter to Gov. D.L. Swain in which he said that he had been to Cherokee County, N.C. He was protesting intruders from other States who were destroying the land and timber by gold mining. Sometime between 1836 and 1840 he moved his family to Cherokee. He purchased about 900 acres of land there in 1839. He and his family of eleven males and five females are listed in the 1840 Census of Cherokee County. They also appear in the 1850 Census of Cherokee.

Family tradition says that he was appointed by the Governor of North Carolina to gather up the Indians of Cherokee County for their removal to Indian Territory, or what is now the State of Oklahoma. This may be true, but if so, he only served a short time. Records from Washington, D.C. indicate that he paid a substitute to serve in his place.

It is not known when Joel Vannoy returned to Wilkes County, but he died on October 25, 1858 and is buried in Wilkesboro between his two wives. He left a will which was probated in Wilkes County.

Sources: *Land of Wilkes*, by Johnson J. Hayes; *Our Heritage, The People of Cherokee County*, by Margaret W. Freel; *Muster Rolls of the Soldiers of the War of 1812*, by Adjutent General; *Abraham Sudderth Family History*, by Alfred A. Kent, Jr.; Wilkes County records, Cherokee County Records, family correspondence, census records, grave markers.

— Virginia Lee Satterfield

JOEL VANNOY ANCESTORS AND DESCENDANTS
1054

John Vannoy was born about 1716, died about 1778 in Wilkes County. He settled in the Jersey Settlement of Rowan County with his wife, Susannah Anderson of New Jersey. He rendered public service during the Revolutionary War. He and his wife had nine children, all believed to have been born in North Carolina. (1) Rachel, born 12 April 1741, married Neil Patton, (2) Andrew, born 12 August 1742, died 9 October 1809, married 18 August 1779 in Wilkes County, Susannah Shepherd, (3) Abraham, born 15 January 1745, (4) Francis, born 13 August 1746, died 26 July 1822 in Knox County, Kentucky, (5) Nathaniel, born 16 February 1749, married Elizabeth Ray, (6) Hannah, born 26th March 1751, (7) Daniel, born 22 February 1752, married 2 October 1779, Sarah Hickerson, (8) Susannah, born 6 July 1754, (9) Katherine, born 26 December 1755.

Daniel Vannoy, son of John and Susannah (Anderson) Vannoy, and his wife Sarah had at least nine children, one of whom was Joel Vannoy, who was born in 1792, died 1858 in Wilkes County. Joel lived for awhile in Cherokee County, N.C., was a cabinet maker, a Col. in the War of 1812, and sheriff of Wilkes County from 1824 until 1830, and was married twice. He and his two wives are buried in the Old Presbyterian Cemetery in Wilkesboro.

Joel Vannoy first married on the 18 March 1817 in Wilkes County, Elizabeth St. Clair, born 12 September 1796, died 10 February 1831. There were eight children born to them, as follows: Joel, Jr., Elizabeth Caroline, Alford, John Hamilton, Rebecca, Emily Amanda, America Adeline and Ann Mariah.

Joel's second marriage was about 1832 to Emily Lemira Suddeth, born 1809, died 1858, daughter of Abraham and Martha (Sumpter) Suddeth. Joel and Emily Lemira were the parents of nine children, viz: (1) Abraham, born 1832, married Martha James, (2) William Wiley, born 22 June 1834, died 9 January 1905, married Susan Elizabeth Crowson, (3) Sarah Martha, born 18 July 1835, died February 1905 in Charlotte, N.C., married 1st 4 July 1857 in Wilkes County, John Nooe, and 2nd.

John Preston Shields, (4) Catharine, born 1836, died 1910 Laurel Springs, Alleghany County, married Vance Taylor, (5) Washington Alexander born 1839, (6) Harvey Suddeth, born 1841, died 15 January 1835 at Ronda, Wilkes County, married 19 September 1867, Catharine Welborn, (7) Thomas Erwin, born 1843, died 1864 at Gettysburg, (8) Elijah Ross, born 1844, (9) Anderson Mitchell, born 6 February 1855 died 21 March 1922, married Mamie Smith. He was sheriff of Wilkes County and is supposed to be buried in the old Presbyterian Cemetery, Wilkesboro, N.C.

William Wiley Vannoy, son of Joel and Emily Lemira (Suddeth) Vannoy married 7 July 1867 in Wilkes County, Susan Elizabeth Crowson, born 7 November 1837, died 22 April 1903, daughter of Adam and Nancy Crowson. He was a major in the Civil War. They are both buried in the old Presbyterian Cemetery, Wilkesboro, N.C. They were the parents of five children: (1) William A., born 4 April 1868, married 8 February 1898, Addie Forester, (2) James Edward, born 4 April 1868, twin to William A., died 26 January 1819, married 27 May 1899 in Stokes County, Hartie Roberta Rebecca Ward, (3) Joseph, born 1879, died young, (4) Anderson Mitchell born 1875, (5) Aurlola Belle, born 1879, married January 1904, Jesse M. McNiel. They lived at Donnaha, Forsyth County; then Winston-Salem and are buried in the Salem Cemetery there.

James Edward Vannoy, son of William W. and Susan Elizabeth (Crowson) Vannoy, married Hartie Ward, born 25 February 1876, Stokes County, died 5 August 1963 in Wilkes County, daughter of Samuel Marion David and Mary Ann Ruth (Hutcherson) Ward of Donnaha, Forsyth County, N.C. Ed was a well-to-do merchant of North Wilkesboro, dealing primarily in roots and herbs. He is buried in the North Wilkesboro Cemetery, Sixth Street. She is buried in Mt. Lawn with her second husband, L.A. Lippard. James Edward and Hartie had nine children: (1) Maisie Susan, born 17 December 1900, died 8 December 1955, married Ralph Richard Reins, (2) Lucy Roberta, born 20 November 1902, married June 1922 in Boone, N.C., Alvis M. (Jack) Hadley, (3) Ruth Inez, born 6 December 1904, died 17 April 1956, married, 1st. 11 January 1836, Kenneth D. Chilton, 2nd., Walton LeGrand Black (4) James Edward, Jr. born 20 July 1906, is unmarried, (5) William Wiley, born 1 December 1908, died 1914, (6) Harvey Suddeth, born 4 March 1910, is unmarried, (7) Mary Margaret, born 2 January 1914, married William Clyde Pearson, (8) Infant boy born and died 31 January 1916, (9) Jackson Mitchell, born 3 February 1917, is unmarried.

Mary Margaret Vannoy, daughter of James Edward and Hartie (Ward) Vannoy, married 5 August 1834, in North Wilkesboro, William Clyde Pearson, born 4 January, 1913, died 8 September 1956 in Winston-Salem hospital, son of Rom Hall and Maude (Hollar) Pearson. Clyde was a wholesale grocer, in business with his father. He is buried at Mt. Lawn Cemetery. He and Margaret were the parents of three children: (1) William Clyde, Jr., born 12 August 1935, married 14 October 1964, Catharine Ray Snell. They live in Cape Coral, Florida,

(2) Ruth Vannoy, born 22 November 1836, married 15 February 1961, James Allen Bumgarner, born 2 October 1934, died 1973. Jim and Ruth had two children (a) Rebecca Lynn, born 24 September 1965, (b) Mark Allen, born 12 March 1968. Since Jim's death, Ruth and her children have lived in North Wilkesboro, (3) Margaret Janice, born 27 December 1948. Jan is a cytologist at Wilson Memorial Hospital, Wilson, N.C. She is as yet unmarried.

Sources: *George Michael Eller* & his Descendants, etc. by Hook, Wilkes Marriage records, Bible records, tombstone inscriptions, birth certificates, Federal Census, newspaper items, personal knowledge.

— Ruth Pearson Bumgarner

RUTH MCNIEL VANNOY
1055

Twenty-eight bright and giving years were the life span of Ruth Ella McNiel Vannoy. During her relatively brief life, she gave the gift of contributing perfection to her surroundings.

She was the second child of Thornton Sylvester and Eda Elizabeth (McNiel) McNiel. Born 2 November 1890, she died during the 1918-1919 influenza epidemic in the same month as did her father and brother, Osco McNiel. Her death was 11 January 1919.

Ruth McNiel was married to Hannibal Roscoe Vannoy 10 May 1914. He was the son of James Newton and Cornelia (Bumgarner) Vannoy of the Purlear community. His birth date was 9 April 1884. Ross Vannoy's biography is found elsewhere in this publication. There were three children, all of whom were born in Wilkes County, as were their grandchildren.

(1) Ella Sue Vannoy was born 17 February 1915. She attended Appalachian State University and was married to Carl Franklin Colvard 6 October 1934. Born 22 March 1908, he was the son of Charles Hampton and Elizabeth (Vannoy) Colvard of the Wilbar community. (Their biographies may be found elsewhere in this book.) They had one son, Carl Franklin Colvard, Jr., unmarried, who was born 30 August 1939. He attended Wake Forest University and resides in West Jefferson with his mother. Both are members of the West Jefferson First Baptist Church. Carl F. Colvard, Sr. died 28 May 1962.

(2) Annie Louise Vannoy was born 17 May 1917 and died 4 July 1977. She was married 31 March 1941 to Alexander Russell Gray, Jr., born 1 June 1919, son of A.R. and Sarah (Campbell) Gray of Wilkesboro. Annie Gray graduated from Meredith College and was a member of the Wilkesboro United Methodist Church. Her three children are (1) Alexander Russell Gray, III, unmarried, born 13 June 1943, and he attended Lenoir-Rhyne and Wilkes Community Colleges. His church membership is with the Wilkesboro United Methodist Church, and he lives with his father. (2) James Robert Gray was born 12 May 1946 and was married 28 June 1969 to Mary Iva Reinhardt, born 23 February 1945, the daughter of Walter Ramseur and Gwendolyn (Parker) Reinhardt of Northampton County. They are communicants of St. Paul's Episcopal Church in Wilkesboro. Jim Gray is a graduate of the University of North Carolina. Their children are

(1) David Christopher Gray, born 26 February 1974 and (2) Martha Elizabeth Gray, born 27 January 1978. Annie Gray's only daughter was born 27 May 1950. Named for her two grandmothers, Sarah Ruth Gray, unmarried, graduated from the University of North Carolina at Greensboro. She is a communicant of St. Paul's Church. All of the Grays live in Wilkesboro.

(3) Hannibal Roscoe Vannoy, Jr., nicknamed "Johnny," only lived five years, having been born 9 January 1919 and died 27 July 1924.

Ruth Vannoy had five brothers and one sister, (6) Mamie McNiel. Her brothers were (1) William Alonzo, (2) Claude Ackle, (3) Challie Odell, (4) Richard Tipton, and (5) Osco McNiel. For a complete description of their lineages, reference should be made to the section on Mamie McNiel Hartley. The Honorable Johnson J. Hayes wrote about the McNiel clan in general: "As their name implies they were of that sturdy, thrifty Scotch-Irish stock who loved liberty and believed in and practiced earning their bread by the sweat of the face . . ."

All the McNiels were born and lived on Cowles Creek in the Purlear community. Although there are variations in the spelling of the surname wihin the immediate family, the original composition of McNiel is used for continuity.

They were a fun-loving family, and each had a great sense of humor. They, likewise took the business of citizenship and community-involvement seriously.

Eventually their father, Thornton McNiel, founded the North Wilkesboro Coco-Cola Bottling Company. He lived with Ruth Vannoy and her family in North Wilkesboro during the week to look after his business interests in town, returning home on week-ends. His death was two days after his daughter's.

Ruth Vannoy was reared in a devout Baptist home. This legacy was continued when her own home was established. Judge Hayes further wrote, "The outstanding characteristic of the (McNiel) family is its loyalty and dedicated support of the church in their community."

She was a fine homemaker and an excellent cook. Ruth McNiel Vannoy's many accomplishments during her short life continue to be remembered and to serve as an inspiration.

Sources: Absher, *The Thornton McNiel Family*; Hook, *George Michael Eller, Descendants of His in America*; Hayes, *Genealogy of the McNiel Clan*; and family memories.

— C. Frank Colvard

THE WORTH and BEATRICE CHURCH VANNOY FANILY
1056

Walter Worth Vannoy, Sr. was born in Ashe County April 7, 1907, son of Joseph L. and Lillian Colvard Vannoy. He received his education in the Ashe County schools and moved to Wilkes County in 1924. He has been self-employed in a trucking business for several years.

He married Beatrice Teresa Church on July

28, 1928. She was born January 8, 1904, at Ready Branch, being the second of three daughters born to Zolley Coffer and Rebecca Eller Church. She received her education at Mountain View Institute, Woman's College in Greensboro, and Ive's Business School in North Wilkesboro. She taught school in Wilkes County for six years, and did clerical work for an oil company in North Wilkesboro for two years.

Four children were born to this union: James Madison Vannoy, born October 29, 1929, received his education at Millers Creek High School. He married Mildred Dean Whittington on December 22, 1951. She was born March 2, 1933, daughter of Walter and Ruby Parsons Whittington. She received her education at Mount Pleasant High School.

Annie Lee Vannoy, born February 11, 1933, graduated from Millers Creek High School, and Clevenger Business College, and worked for Ralph Davis, Attorney-at-Law, for several years. She married Ivery Haynes on August 5, 1956. He was born November 26, 1932, son of Major Dewey and Mollie Brown Haynes, of the Mulberry community. He received his education at North Wilkesboro High School and Clevenger Business College. He worked several years for Lowe's Companies, Inc., retiring in 1971. He is now self-employed in investments.

Claude Elbert Vannoy was born July 5, 1935. He is a graduate of Millers Creek High School and received a Master's Degree in business administration from the University of Utah. He retired from the U.S. Army with the rank of Lieutenant Colonel in 1977. On September 25, 1956, he married Virginia Alene Brown, born December 4, 1934, daughter of Edward and Clara McDaniel Brown of Oklahoma. She is a graduate of Cambridgeshire Technical College, Cambridge, England. They have three children: David Bryant Vannoy, born January 20, 1958, graduated from the University of Baltimore. Cynthia Anne Vannoy, born June 4, 1959, is a graduate of the University of Maryland. Marie Alene Vannoy, born July 27, 1963, is a student at Catonsville Community College, Catonsville, Maryland.

Walter Worth Vannoy, Jr., who lives in the Cricket community, was born December 3, 1938. He is a graduate of West Wilkes High School and is self-employed in a trucking business. He has three daughters: Catherine Anne Vannoy, born January 11, 1967, Brenda Sue, Vannoy, born April 14, 1969, and Amanda Lynn Vannoy, born September 2, 1971. The three daughters are piano students.

Sources: Family Bible and personal knowledge.

— Mrs. Annie Lee Vannoy Haynes

WALKER FAMILY OF WILKES
1057

Samuel Walker, an early settler and landowner in Wilkes Co. entered 200 acres of land adjoining Aquila Lowe's line in 1779. Samuel was born 7 May 1749, married Martha, born 6 Aug. 1759.

This family moved to Henry Co. Ky. between 1790 and 1798. Samuel made an Indenture, 5

months and 24 days before his death, to his son Charles, in exchange for "engaging to support and maintain the said Samuel his father in good and comfortable victualing, cloathing and lodging the ballance of the said Samuel's natural life."

Their children born in N.C. except the last one in Ky. (1) Jacob (1778-1854), m. Sarah Biggers; Mary Polly Sharp; and Sarah Miller. (2) Zephaniah (1780-1852), m. Polly Butcher and Lydia Wheaton, he was living alone in Brown Co. In. in 1850. (3) Isaac b. 1782, m. Elizabeth Pritchard and moved to Johnson Co. In. (4) Ellender b. 1784, m. Jesse Baker and moved to Bartholomew Co. In. (5) Rachel b. 1787, m. Littleton Baker (half brother of Jesse), moved to Boone Co. In. (6) Betsy (Elizabeth) b. 1790, m. James Crawford. (7) Charles Montilion 1798-1843, m. Ann Thixton and Elizabeth Parks.

Jacob Walker, son of Samuel, b. 6 Aug. 1778, d. 31 Sept. 1854, buried in Walker Cemetery, Brown Co. In., m. Sarah Biggers. Children all born in Ky. (1) Samuel 1804-1872. (2) James b. 1800/10, and moved to Missouri in 1836. (3) Benjamin Franklin 1808-1890, m. Frances Long. (4) Arlanda (Landy) b. 1812/13 m. Nancy Baker and Rachel Young, daughter of John Young, moved to Illinois. (5) Zephaniah 1813-1897, bur. Hopewell Cemetery, Boone Co. In., m. Martha Baker, Mary Paxton and Mary Petro. (6) Isaac. (7) Betsy/Patsy. (8) Charles Hazard 1816/17-1890, m. Jane Rariden and Mrs. Nancy Burton, sons Samuel, John, Henry T. and Jacob C.

Samuel Walker, son of Jacob, b. 19 July 1804, died 3 June 1872 and was the first person buried in the Sprunica Church Cemetery, Brown Co. In. He m. Nancy Young, b. 20 May 1807, daughter of John Young. Children: (1) Jacob Perry 1828-1907, m. Cynthia White and Rachel Amanda Wright. (2) Franklin 1830-1922, m. Nancy Curry 1836-1892, (3) Sarah Jane 1832-1915, m. Wm. Fraker. (4) Wm. J. 1835-1898, m. Elizabeth Taggart 1839-1924. (5) Orlondo (Landy B) 1839-1914, was deaf, m. Mary E. Kennett 1842-1913. (6) Harrison 1841-1925, m. Eliza Ann Hurd. (7) Nancy 1843-1908, m. Samuel Tracy, (8) James Knox 1845-1932, m. Catherine Campbell, (9) Scott Samuel 1847-1929, m. Clarissa Duchamel 1852-1895. (10) Daniel b. 1850, d. young. Two more children died of Malaria in swampy Johnson County, so the Walker family moved to higher ground in Brown County, Indiana.

Harrison Walker, son of Samuel and Nancy, b. 26 Aug. 1841, d. 23 Nov. 1925 in Ind., m. Eliza Ann Hurd 1866, daughter of Charles Willard and Mary A. Henry Hurd. The Hurd family came from Somersetshire England to Connecticut, and finally came to Indiana. Eliza b. 2 June 1845, d. 23 Dec. 1928 in Ind. Children: (1) John Willard 1872-1936, m. Florence Etta Dine. (2) Alta Belle 1875-1958, m. James R. Brickey 1874-1956. (3) Bertha Ellen 1883-1960, (4) Lydia Evaline 1888-1973, m. Ira Weddle, and had Irwin H., Norma, Virgil and Virginia. (5) Male b & d 1878. (6) Female b. & d. 1881.

John Willard Walker, son of Harrison and Eliza, b. 19 Sept. 1872, d. 12 Jan. 1936. m. Florence Etta Dine 26 Sept. 1894. She was b.

26 Feb. 1876 in Brown Co. In. daughter of Samuel Dine and Mary Ann Pitcher. Florence Etta d. 23 Mar. 1936. Children: (1) Dettie Eressa 1895-1973, m. Ross Catt, Lloyd Holder and Rentist Shultz. Sons, Leland, Lawrence and Russell Catt. (2) Ora Ervan 1897-1918, unm. (3) Leatha Mable 1899-1972, m. John P. Elliott. (4) Herschel Oscar b. 1902, living 1982, m. Eloise Rodgers; children Helen, George, Reva and twins Tom and Jerry.

Leatha Mable Walker daughter John Willard b. 13 Sept. 1899, d. 4 March 1972, m. 19 June 1919 John Parker Elliott 1896-1973, both d. in Seminole, Florida and are buried in Glen Cove Cem., Knightstown, In. Children: (1) Lloyd Earl 1920-1942, unm. (2) Florence Louise b. 1922, m. James R. Abraham and Robert A. (Lamb) Shaw, children, Patricia (Abraham) Albers, James John Abraham and Robert A. Shaw II. (3) James Preston b. 1929, m. Jean Shertzer and had Steven; m. second Jan Shultz, and had James Lee; married third Mary Boyd, and fourth Diana Garrett.

My grandmother, Florence Walker was beautiful with auburn hair and blue eyes. I spent many a happy weekend in her home. She would find pieces of pretty cloth to make doll clothes and let me play tea party with her best china cups and saucers. Grandfather John was always ready to open his coin purse and take me to the 10¢ store to buy a doll to sew for. Grandfather had a little story he told "A small boy asked his mother, "where am I going to die?" His mother asked, "why do you want to know?" The little boy replied, "because I won't ever go there!" Whenever I fill in charts with my grandfather's death place and date, I think of him and want to say, "Grandpa, don't go to Lebanon, Indiana!"

My mother, Leatha Elliott was a wonderful person. She could make a warm inviting home anywhere, which she did many times, as we moved frequently. My father traveled, and being alone she took us fishing, wild strawberry picking and told us and the neighbor children ghost stories in the kitchen with all the lights out. Once, on my birthday, I sent her a bouquet of roses and said "Thanks Mom," I hope she knew how much I loved her.

Sources: Wilkes Co. N.C. records; Henry Co. K. Records, Family Bibles.

— Florence Elliott Shaw

CHARLES and SOPHRONIA DOCKERY WALKER
1058

Charles Spurgeon Walker was born December 29, 1880 to Isaac Jeffrey (1849-1918) and Minerva Caroline McNeil Walker (1852-1904). His grandparents were Isaac (1815-1907) and Sallie Roberts Walker (1817-1905); and Alfred and Matilda Vannoy McNeil. The Walkers lived on Morris Knob in the Boomer community. Charles, his father, and grandfather were farmers.

A family story relates that when the earlier Walkers were corssing the ocean, a child died and was buried at sea. The other children were told that this sea burial was necessary to prevent the large whales from attacking their ship.

Charles and Sophronia D. Walker.

Charles's brothers and sisters were: Will, Isaac A., Richard, Ellen W. Earp, Cora Lee W. Watts, Sophronia Matilda W. Watson and Jesse Walker.

Charles S. Walker married March 15, 1900 Sophronia Irene Dockery, daughter of Elijah H. and Emma Watson Dockery.

Charlie and Froney lived many years in a log house on the mountain. They raised pigs, cows, chickens, vegetables and fruit on their land. Their children remember their hard working parents who would take time out for a game with the children. Often Froney and the children tended the fields and garden while Charlie walked to a job building the railroad line that went along the Yadkin River from North Wilkesboro to Darby.

Nine of the twelve children of Charles and Froney were born in the log house on the mountain. Their children are: (1) Spencer Blackburn born December 15, 1900, died March 16, 1979. (2) Paul Dockery born April 21, 1902, married Hilder Alice Reins and had four children: Lucille W. Spears, William Glenn Walker, Irene W. Wyatt, and Alice W. Jarvis. (3) Noah Bernard born June 5, 1904. After his first wife May Reins died, he married Nora Pilkington. Their children are — Gladys Elizabeth W. Walker, Virginia Kaye W. Steele and Barbara Ann W. Carlton. (4) Vernon born December 16, 1906, died February 2, 1907. (5) Emma Mariah born March 8, 1908, married Howard Ferguson. They had Don Ward Ferguson and Linda Beatrice F. Rosenberg. (6) Cowles Earl born Sept. 1, 1910 and first married Carrie Barlow. His second wife was Myranell Earp. (7) Olee born September 27, 1912 married Emitt Harris. Their children are Lloyd Martin, Travis Benjamin, Carrie H. West, Mary Irene and Shirley Ann Harris. (8) Della born June 8, 1917, married Clarence Smith. They had four children: Maynard, Melvin, Marvin and Iona S. Dorsey. (9) Ray McDonald born September 7, 1919, married Velma White. (10) Reath born February 6, 1922, married Betty Sue Price. They had Brenda and Phyllis. (11) Roland born September 11, 1924, married Corinne Davis, had twins Mary Rebecca W. Cady and Martha Lynn W.

Sougher, and Sharon Ann W. Souther. (12) James born March 20, 1928, died January 6, 1929.

The family moved off the mountain, and on election day in 1920 they moved to the Sheriff Johnson farm in Wilkesboro.

Sophronia Irene Dockery Walker was born September 11, 1883 and died April 14, 1942. Charles S. Walker's second wife was Zonie Goforth. They had two children: Virginia Irene W. born February 26, 1944, married David Williams. (2) John Jefferson Walker born and died on September 27, 1945.

Charles Walker had seven sons who grew to maturity, but only one grandson who carried on the Walker name in his family, William Glenn Walker has two sons William Michael and Glenn Rayvaughn Walker.

The descendants and friends of Charlie and Froney Walker have a family reunion each year on the third Sunday in August. This reunion has continued for about fifteen years. There is always plenty of food and memories to share.

Many memories of the Walker family are highly regarded for the succees they have with their grades.

Sources: Family Bible, tombstones, interviews with family members.

— William G. and Christine E. Walker

H.C. WALKER FAMILY
1059

Harvey Columbus Walker was born in Mecklenburg County on the Catawba River, in Steele Creek Church Community. He was born December 21, 1867, son of Henry Allison Walker and Sarah Tevepaugh. His father owned a cotton gin and was an inventor of sorts. He invented a piece that improved the methods of removing seeds from the cotton.

H.C. Walker came to Wilkes County to live quite by accident. He was on a visit in the Brushy Mountain Community with his uncle and cousins, John, Tom, and Charlie Teve-

Harvey Columbus and Nolie Hendren Walker.

paugh. Here he met his wife to be, Lenora Delaney Hendren, born March 3, 1876, daughter of Ephraim Elbert and Charlotte Rufina Hendren.

After their marriage, they resided with his wife's parents, Elbert Hendren, Lenora's (Nollie) father died soon after their marriage and they lived with Mrs. Hendren and bought the farm, containing about 120 acres.

Harvey Walker was a farmer and had a workshop where he repaired clocks, spinning wheels, looms and other necessary tools of the community. He also was one of the few in the community that built homemade caskets. Burial in those days was mostly left to the relatives and friends. Neighbors would gather and prepare the grave free of charge and most of the burials were at churches where plots were free also.

A few years before his retirement, Harvey Walker and the younger children moved to North Wilkesboro, where he worked at the tannery and Mrs. Walker kept a boarding house. After his retirement he and Mrs. Walker moved back to the mountains where she died in 1937. Harvey Walker died January 27, 1954 at the age of 87. Children of Harvey and Nollie Walker are as follows:

Lester, who was a World War I Veteran and employee of the State Highway Dept. for many years. He married Della Hayes who survives.

Allie Mae, a housewife and very active in the Home Demonstration Club and church activities. She married William H. Tevepaugh. Both are deceased.

John Elliott, Chief of Police for the town of North Wilkesboro for many years, Mayor Pro Tem and employee of the State of North Carolina for many years. He married Florence Rhymer of Charlotte, N.C. They live in North Wilkesboro.

Elbert Allison, who was a farmer in Iredell County. He married Emily Crater, who taught school. His wife still lives at the old homeplace.

Emma Lenora, housewife. She married Clarence Hayes and both are deceased.

Sally Ree, died young in a drowning accident.

Pearl Etta, housewife and designer for a textile mill in Wallace, N.C. She married the late Bonnie Usher of Teachey, N.C. where she still lives.

Charles Frank, who was employed in the printing trade for several years. He also is an ordained Baptist Minister and has been pastor of several churches in Wilkes and Watauga Counties. He is married to Margie Adams. They live in the Oakwoods Community of Wilkes.

Harvey Columbus, Jr., a retired furniture worker. He married Miss Gryder and they live in North Wilkesboro.

Sources: Personal research, personal knowledge.

— Don Hayes

IRA COLUMBUS WALKER
1060

Ira Columbus Walker (1897-1978) was the son of William and Rose Ann Harrold Walker.

His brothers were Charlie, Ransom, and Norman Walker. His sisters were Eda and Minnie Walker. He had one half brother, Howard Kilby.

He was married to Flossie McNeil (1893-1963), daughter of Zeb and Octavia Whittington McNeil. Their children were Ernest, Clyde, and Fred Walker. Also a step-daughter, Thelma McNeil.

Ernest married Lillian Kilby; Clyde married Maisie Walker; Fred married Vallie Adams; and Thelma married Johnny Rash. Fred and Vallie had one daughter, Betty Walker, and one son, Sammie Walker. Johnny and Thelma had one daughter Violet Rash Frances and two sons, Paul and Bill Rash; making a total of five grandchildren.

The great-grandchildren are Kirk and Elisa Walker; Bryan, Gralyn and Andy Rash; Morgan and Ricky Frances.

Ira and his wife were members of Pleasant Home Baptist Church. He was a farmer and also worked in the lumber business. He was known for his skills as a hunter and fisherman. Many of these skills he passed on to his children and grandchildren as well as other young men in the community. He lived to be 80 years old. He, his wife, and one son, Fred, are buried in Pleasant Home Church cemetery.

At the present time (1982) all the children and grandchildren except for the one son, Fred, are still living and all reside in Wilkes County with the exception of one granddaughter, Betty Walker, who teaches school in Greensboro, N.C.

Sources: Family knowledge.

— Lillian K. Walker

JOHN WILSON WALKER FAMILY
1061

J.W. Walker born in Wilkes County August 13, 1873. He was married to Julie Alexander in 1898. They lived on a farm near Roaring River, NC, and attended Rock Creek Baptist Church.

Born to J.W. and Julie were five children; Mrs. Olen (Ina) Brewer, Lester Walker, Mrs. Cecil (Margaret) Justus, Commie Walker, and Gene Walker.

J.W. owned a new Model-T Ford, although the roads were rough and sometimes muddy, they could depend on the Model-T to get them there and back from hauling, visiting and shopping.

Julie died at the age of forty-two. J.W. remarried Fannie Mahaffey in 1921. To them were born five children, four girls and one boy. John Amous Walker, Gladys, Ella Mae, Myrtle and Juanita. J.W. and Fannie were blessed with good health until they were in their seventys.

They were good parents and always gave their children good advice, be kind and gentle to those who are old for kindness is dear and better than gold.

Sources: Personal knowledge.

— Gladys Church

THE WALLACE CONNECTIONS
1062

My great-grandfather, Matthew Wallace, came from Iredell County to Alexander County about 1800 and settled in the Brushy Mountains where he was a big land holder. He was possibly from Mecklenburg County. He and his wife, Caroline Matlock, had six sons.

Their son Matthew left home at an early age, married in Texas, and then settled in Eugene, Oregon, where he became very prominent and wealthy. He was one of the first settlers in Eugene and his cabin has been preserved as a historic landmark and museum. Newspaper clippings sent to his parents revealed that he was the second largest tax payer in the city. He visited his parents several times, and the last time he was able to make the trip he erected a stone for his father's grave which simply reads: "Matthew Wallis, Erected by his son M. Wallis of Oregon."

John migrated to Iowa or Illionois, where he married and had at least one child, names Silas; Martin married Anne Roberson (see Roberson family record); Washington, Sylvester, and Richard left home as young men and went to Georgia, Alabama, and Tennessee, and never returned to North Carolina.

Martin and Anne Wallace built their home at a spring on the southeast side and near the top of Pore's Knob Mountain. This spring is still referred to as the Martin Wallace spring. They had twelve children, nine boys and three girls: John, Goodman, Matthew, William, Elbert, James, Bryant, Hampton, Frank, Caroline, Martha, and Matilda.

John married Betty Clanton, and when the family was quite young they set out in a wagon train for parts unknown. They ended up in Minnesota, where they lived for years. They had five boys and three girls: William, Van, Clark, Ararat, Matthew, Delilah, Nellie, and Frances. Of these Delilah married a Watkins and went to Riverside, California, where she reared a large family and built up a prosperous real estate business. Among her grandchildren was Dr. Ernest Osborne, an outstanding professor at Columbia University in New York City, until his death about twenty years ago. In later life Delilah visited in my parents several times.

Caroline Wallace married Rufus Laws and had four children. After his death she married Squire William Broyhill; Goodman married Caroline Roberson; Elbert married Phoebe Collins in Tenn. and had four sons. James married a Rogers and had one son, Silas; Bryant married Mary Broyhill and had eight children, most of whom live in Wilkes County; William, Hampton, and Matthew died without offspring; Silas Franklin married Frances Lucinda Broyhill, whose daughter Dora Anne Caroline married R. Don Laws. (See Broyhill, Laws, and Roberson families). To this marriage were born seven children, all of whom are living except Barney Weaver Laws, the oldest son.

It must be evident to any one reading this history that the Broyhill, Laws, Roberson, and Wallace families were close knit. In fact, the connections are such as to make me my own fourth cousin.

Sources: Correspondence; grave stones at Bethel Church in Alexander County.

— Thelma Laws

BENNET HALL WALSH FAMILY
1063

Family records show the first Walsh in this family line to be Master Walsh, who was from Wales. He settled in the Elk Creek area of Wilkes. He married a Miss Poteat. It is possible that Master referred to title rather than a given name, he being a teacher and weaver.

Second in the family line is Phillip Walsh who married Elizabeth "bet" Hall on Dec. 10, 1810. They had a daughter named Elizabeth and a son Melvin W. Walsh who married Sally Foster. In 1860 M.W. Walsh was a farmer with a family of three sons: Thomas age 20, George age 17 and Bennet age 22.

Bennet Hall "Buck" Walsh (Mar. 15, 1837 —Dec. 11, 1928) married Mar. 6, 1866 Sarah Ann Melton (May 21, 1842 — Mar. 29, 1883). She was the daughter of Henry and Elizabeth Russell Melton. Bennet H. Walsh entered military service on June 12, 1861 and was promoted to Corp. in 1864 in the 26th Regiment Infantry. He was as a merchant's clerk in 1870. Bennet and Sarah Ann had three children: Andrew Wellington (1867-1902); Thomas Jefferson (1870-1959) and Martha Ann (1874-1959). Sarah Ann was buried in a family cemetery near Elk Creek where her sister-in-law Ann Foster Melton is also buried.

On August 24, 1884 Bennet married Mary Ann McNeil and they had four children: Mary Victoria (1886-1973); James Hamelton born 1888, moved to Colorado and was a sheep herder; Fannie Cornelia 1888 and Henry King Berguyn Walsh (1892-1945). Mary, Fannie, and Henry lived in the Elk Creek community.

The first child Andrew Wellington, whom my grandmother Martha Ann referred to as "brother Will," was killed in a logging accident. He was married to Velma McNeil and had four children: (1) Sallie Jewel born 1896, married Fred Sharpe. (2) Nina Joyce (1898-1903); (3) William Albert was born 1900, married Belva Virginia McNeil. (4) Amelia Ann (1900).

The second son, Thomas Jefferson Walsh married Feb. 27, 1897 Sophia Elmira Eller (1867-1953). "Uncle Tom" lost a hand in a sawmill accident. He used to tease the small children with his wooden peg. Tom and Sophia moved to the State Road area of Wilkes and lived on the farm of Rev. L.B. Murray. After a few years they had farm of their own. Their children are: (1) Zollie Lafayette (1897) (2) Iona Camilla (1900) married Amy Luffman and has three children: Mabel L. Turpin, Dale Wayne and James Ralph Luffman; (3) Maude Elmire (1902-1957) remained single and stayed home with her aging parents. (4) Odell Green Moore (1904) married Pauline Taylor and has a daughter Louise W. Roland; (5) Thomas Gentry (1906-1978) married Elizabeth Carter (1910-1972), and had Thomas Rainbow Walsh and Mary Sue W. Johnson; (6) Ocie Wayne (1909-1913); (7) Luther Columbus (1912) is married Ruth Taylor the sister of Odell's wife Pauline.

Bennett Hall Walsh.

The third child of Bennet and Sarah Ann Walsh was Martha Ann. She married March 20, 1898 Thomas Gaither Eller (1866-1937). Their children were: (1) Sophia Camilla (1899-1964) married Jesse A. Walsh. Their children are Warren, Ruth Hori, Wade, Grace Boyd, Helen Spaulding, Faye Walker, Pauline Kilby, Jesse Jr., Jerry and Homer Walsh. (2) Sarah Arivona (1900) married Grover C. Johnson. Their children are: Mildred Woodruff, Devola Walsh, Edward, Ernest Johnson and Marjorie Garner. (3) Thomas Irving (1903) married Sally Severt. Their sons are Thomas Irving, Jr. and Robert Calvin Eller. (4) Tempa Lucinda (1905) married Robert DeGuerre. They had a daughter Roberta D. Wallace. Tempa's second marriage was to George Borland. (5) Annie Evelyn (1906) married Thomas R. Goodson (6) Willard Rayvaughn (1909-1978) married Gertrude Johnson. They have a daughter Jewell Christine Walker and grandson Glenn Rayvaughn Walker. (7) Lafayette "Fate" Bennet married Elmina Roope. Their son is Kenneth Doyle Eller. (8) Edgar Eugene (1919) married Marie Joines. They have four children: Danny, Dianne, Wayne and Michael Eller.

Sources: Wilkes County census, family Bibles, grave markers, and interviews with family members.

— Christine Eller Walker

LEE WALSH
1064

This blue-eyed son of Wales and Ireland was born and raised in and around the mountains of western Wilkes. He married the beautiful Dinah Goforth, whose parents and grandparents had accumulated large land holdings in this area. Lee and Dinah either bought or were given a beautiful tract at the upper reaches of Hessian branch near the head of the hollow that became known as Goforth Hollow.

They still talk of the music that once reverberated down Goforth Hollow when the family of Lee and Dinah Goforth Walsh fiddled and sang at their home near the branch. When the hard, back-breaking work of living was done and it was twilight and supper past, then they gathered and joined in song. In song they

expressed their joys and their sorrows — their ambitions and frustrations — and music and song made life bearable and added substance to the lives of those who participated or heard this mountain music.

The sons of this family were Jim Walsh (90), one of the truly sweet Christian spirits of the area and who lives now in Kernersville, N.C.; Jim Walsh, who went to live in West Virginia; Otis Walsh, who stayed home to look after his parents for their lifetime; and Dock Walsh, who went on to become one of the first mountain music recording stars of the 1920's and 1930's. Daughters of Lee and Dinah were Dorothy, who married Hayes Foster; Lizzie, who married Hayes' brother F.O. Foster; Elziney, who married Arthur Triplett. Lizzie lives now in the Congo community with two of her daughters, Viono and Mildred, and retains her zest for fun and life at age 92. Lee and Dinah were buried just across the ridge from their home at Lewis Fork Baptist Church cemetery.

Sources: Personal knowledge.

— Roy Foster, Jr.

MR. and MRS. C.P. WALTER
1065

Charles Preston Walter was born in Frederick County, Virginia 10 November 1870, the son of Philip Andrew Walter, born 26 May 1844, died 6 June 1926, married 20 November 1866 to Mary Jane Cooper, who was born 25 December 1837, died 11 November 1902.

The ancestors of C.P. Walter, mainly German in origin, were early settlers in the upper Shenandoah Valley of Virginia. They were staunch believers in establishing churches and schools.

His father, Philip A. Walter served in the 33rd Virginia Infantry under the command of General "Stonewall" Jackson and was twice wounded. He sustained a body wound at Gettysburg and was shot through the hip during the Battle of the Wilderness.

The Walter family moved to Berkeley Springs, West Virginia where Charles Preston went to school with and later married on 17 November 1891, Carrie Mary Hovermale, the daughter of James William Hovermale, who was born 25 April 1848, died 3 June 1918 and married 3 March 1870 Sarah Ann Brown, who was born 6 March 1848, died 1 February 1904.

In Berkeley Springs, C.P. Walter gained his first knowledge of the tanning business at the Deford Tanning Company. In November 1897 he came with his wife and five year old daughter, Agnes, to North Wilkesboro where he became associated with the C.C. Smoot and Sons Company tannery as yard foreman. He later became assistant superintenzent; then superintendent in 1912. He retained this position when the tannery was bought by the International Shoe Company until his retirement in December 1939.

The Walter family, though members of the United Brethren, immediately attended the Methodist Episcopal Church South. They later joined this church and were faithful members. He served at one time as Sunday School super-

Mr. and Mrs. C. P. Walter.

intendent and teacher. Mrs. Walter served as treasurer of the Ladies Aid when the first brick church was built.

Mrs. Walter with the late Mrs. J.R. Marlow, spent much time in administering to the needy in the community before any welfare efforts were organized. Mrs. Walter was also a charter member of the Friday Afternoon Book Club.

C.P. Walter was a very devout Mason and a member of the York Rite of Freemasonry which is known as the Christian Rite of Masonery. He was Past Master of the North Wilkesboro Lodge #407, Past High Priest of North Wilkesboro Chapter #78, Past Patron of Wilkes Chapter #42 order Eastern Star; a member of Zabud Council #16, Royal and Select Masters, Winston-Salem, a member of Piedmont Commandery #6 Knights Templar, Winston-Salem. He was a member of Oasis Temple, Charlotte. In March 1955, he was presented posthumourly the Royal Arch Medal as the outstanding York Rite Mason in the Grand Justidiction of North Carolina, only one of these medals being presented each year by the General Grand Chapter, Royal Arch Masons International.

He was a director in the now North Wilkesboro Savings and Loan for 24 years. During World War II he served as Chairman of the Rationing Board, having started out with OPA in 1942.

The only child of the Walters, Agnes Mae, was born 4 November 1892, died 26th September 1969 and married 15 June to Dr. Charles Sheldon Sink. They became the parents of two children, Mary Lelia and Charles Shelton Sink, Jr.

The Walters reared in their home a foster daughter, Minnie Queen, who later married John Samuel Bennett. He, for 44 years was Director of Operations at the University of North Carolina at Chapel Hill.

Their home was always open to family, friends and even strangers. To the neighborhood children they were "Aunt Caddie" and "Uncle Pres." To the grandchildren, who

spent unlimited time in their home, they were "Nanny" and "Papa," and the friends of the grandchildren were always as welcome as they. Holidays were especially happy times there with fun and good food in abundance.

Both retained to old age a youthful attitude toward life, and they were always interested in the well-being of others. Charles Preston Walter died 27 January 1951 and Carrie Walter died 10 August 1963.

Sometime after her death, a great-grand child who had the privilege of knowing her, remarked, "If there's a stove in Heaven, I guess Nanny is up there baking sugar cookies."

Sources: Bible records, *North Carolina, Vol. IV*, 1928, newspaper accounts and personal knowledge.

— Mary S. Smithey

CHARLIE NATHAN WARD
1066

Charlie Nathan Ward, son of Levan A. Ward and grandson of Nathan Ward, was born in Wilkes County March 19, 1896. He and his two brothers grew up on their father's Yadkin River farm. He helped with the farm work and enjoyed going fishing. Charlie went to Oak Grove School, a country school with one room and one teacher.

After graduation, Charlie went to work in his Uncle Elbert (Dick) Wallace's clothing store in North Wilkesboro. He would ride his bicycle up the railroad to North Wilkesboro, board there for the week and then ride home on Saturday night.

Charlie Nathan Ward married Esther Riddle, born November 27, 1897, on July 30, 1916 and Rev. Jim Burchette performed the ceremony. Charlie and Esther had grown up in the same community and gone to the same school.

After our wedding, we made our first home in Winston-Salem and in January 1917, we moved to Hopewell, Va. Charlie worked in the E.I. Dupont Powder Plant making gunpowder through World War I. Our first child, a son, was born there. Soldiers were training at Camp Lee and they would march from Camp Lee through Hopewell to City Point to get on the ship going acorss the ocean to serve their country in World War I. Charlie and others would watch them with sad hearts. On November 11, 1918 all were so thankful the war was over. The powder plant closed down and we came home to Wilkes County. It seemed good to be back to this peaceful place. There were very few trucks or cars in Wilkes at that time.

We bought the house in which I still live. Our home was happy and soon full of children. We were blessed with five sons and three daughters: Norman Asbery (February 19, 1917), Dorothy Edna (May 31, 1919), Jesse Charles (October 30, 1921), James Lee (September 15, 1923), Robert Clifton (November 28, 1925), Saverna Elaine (April 1, 1928), Juanita Lavon (May 21, 1931), Muncie Sherrill (April 9, 1933).

Charlie owned and operated a little country store for a few years. He always had a willing mind and a helping hand. He bought a T-Model

Ford which was the only car in the community and he often used it to help his neighbors. The night never got too late or the weather too bad for him to carry anyone to the doctor or help in some emergency.

Charlie worked for the state awhile helping build bridges in different counties and then came the depression. It was a trying time and work was scarce, but we were fortunate to have our farm. We truly lived off the land and had plenty.

Charlie was an excellent hunter. He was an especially good bird hunter and became famous as a bird dog trainer. Men came from far and near to bring their dogs for him to train.

His next regular job was at Forest Furniture Co. where he worked until World War II when he went to Baltimore to work on ships which were being loaded to go to Europe.

We had one son in the fighitng of World War II. Cpl. James Lee Ward served in the 276th Armed Field Artillery of the U.S. Army under General George Patton in Europe. He went in the army in April, 1943 and was discharged on March 29, 1945.

The land for Arbor Grove Baptist Church and cemetery was given by Charlie N. Ward. This church began as a brush-arbor where Sunday School and preaching services could be held during the summer months only. The first frame building was started in 1934 and completed in 1935. The present brick building begun in 1956 and the first service there was January 31, 1957. God has blessed this Church.

Charlie was foreman in the cabinet room at American Furniture Co. and was still employed there when he became sick on March 15, 1955. He underwent surgery and was found to have a maligant tumor of the brain. He passed away June 13, 1955 and is buried in Arbor Grove Baptist Church cemetery.

Sources: Family Bible, personal knowledge and memory.

— Esther R. Ward

LEVAN ASBERY (L.A.) WARD
1067

Levan Asbery (L.A.) Ward, born September 14, 1850, the son of Nathan and Mary S. Foster Ward, died December 18, 1927. On February 7, 1894 he married Elizabeth (Bettie) Alexander (April 13, 1862 — January 31, 1953).

Levan's wife, Elizabeth (Bettie) Alexander Ward was the daughter of Jerry Alexander and Catherine Caroline Porter Alexander. Jerry Alexander owned land which he inherited from his parents Jesse T. and Elizabeth Alexander (August 18, 1801 — August 25, 1888. This Elizabeth Alexander was Elizabeth (Bettie) Alexander Ward's grandmother. . . She was buried at White Plain Baptist Church at Roaring River. Her husband, Jesse T. Alexander was a Confederate soldier from Wilkes First Regiment-Infantry, Company B. Private Jesse T. Alexander enlisted May 1, 1861, was wounded at Malvern Hill, and captured May 12, 1865. He never returned home, nor was he heard from again.

Leven Asbery Ward received his education at Traphill Seminary Methodist School. After finishing school he went to Wilkesboro and worked in a store which, as well as selling other merchandise, bought and sold locally-made legal whiskey. He was bonded to buy this whiskey and transport it by wagon to Salisbury, N.C. where it could be sent by train to buyers. At that time no train came closer to Wilkesboro. On the back of the bed of the covered wagon he had a feed trough in which to feed the horses. He would spend the night sleeping under the wagon both going and re-turning from Salisbury. He brought back a full wagon load of goods for the store as this was the only way to get many needed items.

While working at the store and making the wagon trips, Levan rented the Yadkin River farm he had inherited. This farm was located at the present site of Abitibi. He always had corn put in a crib on the farm and once he found out someone was stealing his corn so after closing the store, he walked the nine miles from Wil-kesboro to the farm taking his shotgun with him. When he found more corn had been stolen, he rigged the shotgun up in position so that if anyone opened the corn-crib door the gun would shoot. He went back to Wilkesboro to his sister's where he boarded and he began studying about the gun and fearing that some innocent person might open the door to the corn-crib and be killed; he walked the long way back down the river to the farm that night. He removed the gun, put it under his arm and made the walk back to Wilkesboro exhausted but knowing now he could lay down and go to sleep without worrying about someone getting shot.

When Levan married at age 44, he and his wife went to live on the farm. He had a big yoke of oxen to plow and make his crop. His large farm provided an abundance of food and his watermelon patch was quite well known be-cause he grew extra nice, sweet, juicy ones.

Levan Ward was a Methodist, a good Chris-tian and a friend to all.

Levan's wife, Elizabeth (Bettie) was sickly when her children were small. She was 32 years old when she and Levan married. Her first born were twins which died at birth. Also when Elmer was born his twin sister was born dead. She was hurt and depressed over the loss of those little ones and she got it in her mind that if she were left in the room alone that she would die. For years Levan hired extra help to care for her and the small boys. One day she was sitting in the chair and she picked up the Bible. It opened and she began to read, and she felt that God said to her, "Thou fool, why die before your time?" She decided that she wouldn't die until her time came and that cured her. In looking back, she said, "I was hippoed, all in my mind." She lived to be 90 years old.

Levan Asbery and Elizabeth (Bettie) Alexan-der Ward reared three sons:

Charlie Nathan Ward (March 19, 1896 — June 13, 1955) married Esther Riddle and they had five sons and three daughters. (See his story)

Jesse Clyde Ward (February 1, 1898 — March 24, 1980) married Blanche Lowe. They

reared four sons and six daughters. Clyde worked for the Southern Railroad Co.

James Elmer Ward (July 6, 1902) married Lula Duncan, had a daughter and a son and was a merchant. Elmer had a heart attack and died on the street at North Wilkesboro on March 3, 1965.

Sources: Wilkes County records; tombstones; personal records, knowledge and memories.

— Esther R. Ward

NATHAN WARD
1068

Nathan Ward, father of Levan A. Ward, and grandfather of Charlie Nathan Ward was born November 11, 1809 in Rowan County. He died February 2, 1873. The exact year he came to Wilkes from Rowan is unknown, but it is known that on August 17, 1837 Nathan Ward and Mary S. Foster were married in Wilkes County.

Mary S. Foster Ward (February 9, 1816 — September 15, 1885) was the daughter of John Foster (July 9, 1782 — June 14, 1860) and Ann Vannoy Foster (November 4, 1790 — May 21, 1873). John and Ann Foster were married January 8, 1809. They reared fifteen children of their own and adopted one son. They owned a plantation which is now known as the Henderson's Farm. A family cemetery is on this property where John and Ann Foster, their son, Thomas Foster and his wife, Bar-bara, and Nathan and Mary S. Foster Ward and others are buried.

In John Foster's will he gave a Negro girl, Lucendia, and sons, Larkin, Godwin, and Albert to his daughter, Mary, upon her mar-riage to Nathan Ward. Lucendia spent her life in the Ward home helping with the cooking and caring for the children. They all loved her and called her Aunt Cindy. Years later two men from South Carolina came to Nathan Ward and wanted to buy Lucendia's son, Larken. They offered Nathan $2,000 for him. Nathan told the men, "No amount of money can buy Larken. He will stay with his family." He did stay with Nathan and family, but that fall he took typhoid fever and died. Nathan said, "He died at home and with his family."

Nathan and Mary S. Foster Ward lived on their own farm on the Yadkin River, two miles west of Roaring River. Nathan was a good farmer. They had nine children. Listed in the order of birth with all available information, they were: (1) William F. Ward married Mary Caroline Foster on October 19, 1865. They had four sons, Thomas, Frank, Ackie, and Robert. (2) Frances Elizabeth Ward married a Smith. (3) Sarah Jane Ward married James P. Warren on December 26, 1866. (4) John Ward died in Tennessee in 1891. (5) Frances Matilda Ward (March 22, 1848— December 15, 1928) mar-ried Elbert Wallace (July 4, 1847 — March 10, 1914). They had two children. (6) Levan Asbery Ward (September 14, 1850 — Decem-ber 18, 1927) on February 7, 1894 married Elizabeth (Bettie) Alexander (April 13, 1862 — January 31, 1953). They reared three sons: Charlie, Clyde, and Elmer. (7) Nathan Ander-son Ward (Ance), (October 12, 1853 — April 29, 1929) married Mary (Molly) Alexander

(November 24, 1859 — July 8, 1943). They had five children: Dock, Ada, Ed, Will, and Mamie. (8) Edmond Ward lived in Blowing Rock, N.C., married and had at least two chil-dren. (9) Mary Ellen Ward married a Sims. After their daughter Abigail was born he died and Mary Ellen later married Elbert Pardue and they reared a family.

Nathan Ward was an outstanding citizen and an active Christian. Records show that he was elected in 1854 as a class leader for New Bethel Methodist Church at Roaring River, with 34 white and 20 colored attending. Also at a con-federance held in March, 1853 Nathan Ward was appointed to serve as Superintendent for the summer at New Bethel Methodist Church. There were no winter services at the church because they had no way to heat the building.

An election was held on September 21, 1865 to elect members to the North Carolina State Convention, all of whom were citizens of Wilkes County and prominent both before and during the Civil War. Nathan Ward was one of the three elected from Rock Creek Township to serve.

Sources: Rowan County Records, cemetery tomb-stones, *The Foster Family Book* and *The Land of Wilkes*.

— Esther R. Ward (Mrs. Charlie N.)

WILLIAM THOMAS PAISLEY WARD
1069

W.T.P. Ward was born 29 July 1866 in Stokes County, died 16 January 1903 in North Wilkesboro, married 20 February 1896 Nancy Sophronia Absher, born 18 March 1878, died 2 March 1909, daughter of William Matthew and Nancy Jane (Reynolds) Absher. He was a son of Samuel Marion David and Mary Ann Ruth (Hutcherson) Ward of Donnaha, Forsyth County, N.C.

He came to Wilkes County when the town of North Wilkesboro began to be built. He was

William Thomas Paisley Ward.

Nannie Absher Ward.

mayor of the town three terms — 1893, 1895, 1899 and was a charter member of the First Methodist Church of North Wilkesboro. He was a merchant, being one of the three who organized the W.M. Absher Company in 1896 and the same year married the daughter of Mr. Absher. At the time of his death he owned Ward Brothers, a mercantile business.

He and "Nannie" had one son, Dewey, born 8 April 1898, died 14 June 1899. He is buried with his parents in the North Wilkesboro Cemetery on Sixth Street. W.T.P. Ward was my mother's brother.

Sources: Bible Record, obituary in *Chronicle* Newspaper, personal knowledge.

— Ruby Tuttle Absher

THE JEWEL OWEN WATERS FAMILY

1070

Jewel Owen Waters was born January 20, 1894, in Prairie County, Arkansas. He was the third child of Robert Franklin Waters and Margaret Anderson Staggs Waters.

Owen was born and lived on the same farm all of his life with the exception of a few months while a problem with the property ownership was settled. The 80 acre farm is located 13 miles North-Northeast of Carlisle, Arkansas, in Prairie County. It was originally homesteaded by Ezekial Staggs, Margaret Anderson Waters' first husband.

Owen's formal education was only that of the third or fourth grade for he had to help his father on the farm. However, he was an avid reader and enjoyed reading his Bible and other publications such as National Geographics. He didn't have a lot of "booklearning" but he was one of the most interesting people you could ever meet.

On November 21, 1920, Owen married Miss Vera Pearl White, daughter of George Henry White and Annie Augustus Nichols White.

(George Henry White and Annie Nichols were originally from Wake County, North Carolina) Owen and Pearl were married at the Walter's Chapel Church, seated in a buggy in the churchyard. Pearl was the youngest child of thirteen.

Owen worked for the Arkansas Rice Milling Company in Carlisle, Arkansas in the maintenance department. He worked there and also farmed until he retired in September of 1967. He then devoted his time to farming and woodworking — a talent that he had inherited from his father.

Owen and Pearl were members of the Crossroads Baptist Church where he served as Deacon and taught Sunday School for many years.

Owen also inherited his fathers sense of humor and love for practical jokes. He would have rather pulled a prank on someone than to eat a good dinner, and was widely known around the area for doing just that! His favorite "toy" was a "Mongoose" — this consisted of a squirrels tail attached to a red rubber ball that was on a spring loaded lid on a wooden "cage" — you poked around at the ball with a pencil until you really had the attention of your "victim" and then let you go of the top and the tail comes flying out at you with the greatest of ease — this one little trick has caused many a grown woman to have an "accident" or a grown man to nearly break his neck trying to get away from the "Mongoose." Then there was the time that there was a newcomer to the family — she had married a cousin and was evidently very "citified" and didn't take to country ways at first — so just to be onery, Owen named one of his mules after her.

George Robert Waters, first child of Owen and Pearl, was born January 27, 1922, in Prairie Country, Arkansas. He married (1) Nell Johnson, daughter of Raymon M. Johnson and Myrtle Maronay Johnson. They were married in Carlisle, Lonoke County, Arkansas on August 6, 1949. Two children were born to this marriage: Irma Kay, born July 29, 1950, in Little Rock, Arkansas and Barbara Jane, born April 2, 1955, also in Little Rock. Robert was married (2) to Linda Miller Culver, January 24, 1971, in Pulaski County, Arkansas. George Robert Waters was named after both Grandfathers.

Audrey Sybil was the second child of Owen and Pearl's — she was born September 29, 1926. She was married first to Bryant Holloway of Des Arc, Arkansas, and they had one son — Bryant Edmon who was born September 27, 1951. Sybil married second Mr. Joe D. Harrington, of Little Rock, Arkansas.

Gene Owen was born March 14, 1936. He married Margaret Kaucher, daughter of Mr. & Mrs. Ted Kaucher. They ware married on June 14, 1958, at Walters Chapel Church under the same tree that Owen and Pearl were married — and by the same minister. Gene and Margaret have two children, Sharon Sue, born March 24, 1959, and Robert Owen, born November 10, 1962. Both were born in Little Rock, Arkansas.

Pearl White Waters died December 18, 1970, while seated at her sewing machine, making pillows from the old feather bed. They

were to be for her grandchildren for Christmas. She suffered a fatal heart attack. Owen had never lived alone and made a valiant effort and really surprised a lot of folks. He learned to cook and even to make homemade biscuits. He devoted most of his time to his woodshop and raising a few cows. Owen had a very deep sense of family pride — he knew all there was to know about his family and had all sorts of interesting little treasures that had belonged to one or the other of his ancestors. This unquenchable thirst for knowledge about his forebears is how this author first got hooked on doing family research.

Owen died on December 30, 1978, and is buried next to Pearl in the Carlisle Cemtery, Carlisle, Arkansas.

He is — my most unforgettable character.

Sources: Owen Waters, Robert Waters, Gene Waters, Sybil Harrington, Lonoke County, Arkansas Marriage Records.

— Kay Waters Sakaris

JOEL and REBECCA FERGUSON WATERS

1071

Joel Waters was born in Wilkes County about 1795. He was the son of Moses Waters. According to the marriage bond records, he was married April 1, 1826 to Rebecca Ferguson.

Rebecca was born about 1801. She was the daughter of Richard and Verlinda Triplett Ferguson. Rebecca and Joel ahd twelve known children.

(1) Willis, born about 1828, (2) Fanny Caroline, born about 1828, (3) Anna Emeline, born Sept. 1829, died Dec. 17, 1918, married William Triplett on March 21, 1850, (4) Amelia E. (Milly), born about 1834, married Martin Triplett, (5) William, born about 1835, (6) Mary (Polly), born about 1836, (7) Alice, born about 1839, (8) John, born about 1840, married Martha Wheeler, (9) Elizabeth, born about 1842, married Dec. 4, 1856 to Solomon Kees (Keys), (10) Lewis, born about 1843, (11) Sarah or Linah, born about 1844, (12) Malinda, born about 1846.

Sources: Census Records, Marriage Bonds, *Triplett* by Mrs. Hortense Abbott, and Wills.

— Mrs. J. Arnold Simpson

MOSES WATERS

1072

Moses Waters was born on May 15, 1753 in Baltimore County, Maryland. At the age of 18, about 1771, he moved to Wilkes County. Here he remained until his death at the age of 85 in 1838.

He served in the Revolutionary War. He entered service in June 1776 in the Militia under Captain Francis Hargrave and was at Holmans Fork and Lewis Fork.

Several land transactions are recorded, beginning as early as our first Land Entry Book in 1778. His land is shown to be on both sides of Stony Fork, the waters of Elk Creek and on some lesser known branches. He owned about 550 acres by 1788 in District 10. By 1790 he is listed in District 12 and in 1793 in District 11. The districts may have changed boundaries.

We can account for ten children, three sons and seven daughters. (1) Isaac, married Feb. 4, 1806 to Peggy Land, (2) Lewis, (3) Mary, born about 1780/84, married Feb. 1, 1803 to Jeremiah Hampton, (4) Elizabeth, born about 1788, (5) Hannah, married Nov. 2, 1819 to Jacob Lewis, (6) Rachel, married Dec. 20, 119 to Joseph Morris, (7) Leah, married Jan. 31, 1822 to Benjamin Greer, (8) Joel, born about 1795, married April 1, 1826 to Rebecca Ferguson, (9) Nancy, married Oct. 25, 1831 to Henry Main, (10) Aley Jane, born Mar. 8, 1803 married Oct. 23, 1827 to John George Spencer.

Little is known of his wife. She appears to have been living with him at the time of the 1830 Census and is shown in the same age bracket as Moses, between the ages of 70 and 80.

His estate indicated that he was a farmer with livestock holdings and farm tools. He evidently was educated and owned a number of books including a Bible and a dictionary. He is found in court records as serving as a juror, and was appointed Superintendent of Elections to elect a representative to Congress in 1796. He qualified as a Justice of Peace on Feb. 1, 1796 and was also appointed to return the list of taxable property in Capt. Dula's District. It appears that he was interested and involved in civic affairs.

Sources: Tax list, court minutes, land grants and deeds, marriage bonds, Revolutionary War records and census records.

— Mrs. J. Arnold Simpson

WILLIAM HICKS WAUGH
1073

William Hicks Waugh, was born in Ashe County, North Carolina in 1861, the son of Nathan Harris and Elizabeth Gentry Waugh. His mother died when he was four years old and his father remarried the next year.

When a young man, William Waugh worked as a bookkeeper in various mercantile establishments. In 1890 he married Eudora M. Howell, also of Ashe County. William and Eudora had eight children: William H.H., Ruth, Anna, Mayme, Edwin, Grace, Beulah, and Richard. All were born in Ashe County, except Richard.

William Waugh moved his family to North Wilkesboro in 1908 and took a job with A.M. Church and Sons. He later worked for S.V. Tomlinson operating the brick yard, located near what is now West Park Shopping Center.

About 1909 William Waugh moved his family into their new house on Trogdon Street. I remember this home as a place of fun and laughter. Every Sunday, true to the Southern custom, all the children and grandchildren came home. It was a special time of visiting, making homemade ice cream, slicing watermelon, and eating homemade pound cake.

Holidays and summer vacations, all the children and grandchildren, again, came home. One summer my Uncle Ed, who lived in New York City, rode his motorcycle all the way from New York to North Wilkesboro. This was quite an accomplishment in the 1920s, for in those days motorcycles and roads were not what they are today.

One of my earliest memories is of "Papa" shaving off his mustache. It was a Saturday night and Papa had been to the barbershop. While having his hair cut, he impulsively decided to have his mustache shaved. He returned home quite pleased with his new look. The rest of the family made favorable comments, but I, his namesake, screamed loudly when he picked me up. "Why little Bill!" he said. Everyone tried to encourage me by saying, "It's Papa. It's Papa." I remained unconvinced. Needless to say, the mustache was grown back in record time.

Both Grandfather and Grandmother were active members of the First Baptist Church in North Wilkesboro. Grandfather was a deacon for over 20 years and Grandmother was active in the Woman's Missionary Society. Grandfather was also a Mason and a member of the Liberty Lodge.

Grandfather and Grandmother became sick about the same time and died within a year of each other, William in 1926 and Eudora in 1927.

Sources: Obituaries and family tradition.

— Billie Johnson Stringfield

THE WELCH FAMILY
1074

William Welch came to America from Ireland. He married Elizabeth Roper and they were the parents of three sons; William Pleasant, Austin (unmarried), and Jasper (Jap).

Their son William Pleasant Welch was born at High Point, NC. He first married a Davis and had one daughter, Estella Welch, who married Niece Davis. He married for the second time Margaret Elizabeth Bradley who was born in Wilkes County, the daughter of George and Cindy Payne Bradley. William P. and Margaret had eight children: (1) Wm. George Washington who married Ida St. Claire Luther on December 31, 1885; (2) Mary Cornelia who married Larkin Keller; (3) Charles Edward who married twice — to Nancy Michael and to Margaret Baird; (4) Julia Emma who married George Greene; (5) Arthur Monroe who married Dora Wooten; (6) James Franklin who married Celia Church; (7) Martha Ann who married Thomas Hopkins and (8) John Quincy Adams who married Lilly Owens.

Ida St. Clair Luther, who married Wm. G.W. Welch, was born in Wilkes County June 16, 1870. She was the daughter of Jesse Elihu and Amelia Matilda James Luther, the grand daughter of Wm. Augustus and Nancy Loflin Luther of Randolph County and the great, granddaughter of Godfrey and Betsy Luther. The J.E. Luthers and the Welch's lived on adjoining farms. Ida and Bill were married at home in Yuma and from there went by horseback to Elk Park. They lived there a couple of years before moving back to Yuma.

They had eleven children. (1) Roscoe Horton, born at Yuma (now known as Deep Gap) on April 26, 1888, married Lena Mary Schumn on May 17, 1911. R.H. Married his second wife, Ollie McDowell Mar. 22, 1926; (2) Minnie Ida, born April 12, 1890 married Jesse Bynum Triplett Dec. 22, 1915. They had one child, Boice Elton Triplett, born July 12, 1917 who married Holly Greene in June of 1940; (3) Winifred (Jack) George, born Aug. 22, 1892 at Yuma, married Elizabeth Kathryn Nelson, Jan. 16, 1922 in Williston, North Dakota; (4) Lettie Alice, born Mar. 26, 1895, married Grady O. Triplett Dec. 24, 1914. They had two children — Lane William and Mable Violet; (5) Winnie Leota, born Nov. 22, 1897 at Yuma, married Clinton Morris Miller on Sept. 30, 1918. They have 3 children; (6) Viola May, born May 24, 1900 at Yuma, married Coy Edgar Beshears. They have six children; (7) Ola Ruth, born May 29, 1903 at Mt. Zion, married Conrad Hill Jones Nov. 27, 1924. They have 2 children — Gwyn Welch Jones and Fred Charles Jones; (8) Rex Ray, born Aug. 23, 1905 at Mt. Zion, married June 27, 1929 Mary Margaret Robinson. They have 2 daughters; (9) Connie Fay, born Oct. 4, 1908 at Mt. Zion, married Walter Glenn (Bob) Shepherd. They have 3 children — Glenda Laverne who married Raymond Winfield Huffman, Johnny Welch Shepherd and Linda Rea Shepherd; (10) Ruby Rea born Apr. 10, 1911 at Mt. Zion, married Edward Calvin Hodges. They have one son, Welch Edward. (11) Iris Ima, born July 16, 1916 at Mt. Zion, married Heggie Hamilton Phillips. They have seven children: Jessie Nell, Norma Rebecca, James Byrom, Jewel Loleita, Wade Ray, Wayne Grey and Madge Kay.

Bill Welch was a blacksmith who worked with leather goods and also made shoes. He was the one that neighbors called on when they needed help of any sort. Ida, too, was on hand to help friends and neighbors who had troubles or sickness. Ida's father lived to be 103 years old and Ida lived to be 102. She died on May 2, 1972. Her husband, Bill Welch, died of pnuemonia on Jan. 25, 1923. Both are buried at Mt. Zion Church in Wilkes County.

Sources: Personal knowledge and family legend.

— Mrs. Conrad Jones

WELLBORN
1075

The names of the early Wellborn's first appear on the passenger list of the Sea Adventure from Swenea, Wales in 1610. John, Jonatha, William, Samuel. Roberts and Matthew Wellborn (Welborn) appear among the records of Accomac County, Virginia as early as 1637.

The families of this immediate section were descendants of John and Jane McGee Welborn. Captain John McGee's wife was Martha McFarlane. After his death Martha married William Bell and as Martha Bell shs is recognized as a heroine during the Revolutionary War. She was the great grandmother of Elisha M. Wellborn of Wilkes County who married Margaret F. Clark of Randolph County. Their home was at the old General Wellborn homeplace near the airport where Stoneman camped. They at one time ran the hotel in Wilkesboro, now Smithey Hotel. They had nine children: Mrs. C.V. (Jessie) Davis, Mrs. F.L. (Davie) Greene Parks, Mrs. Hettie Morgan, Mrs. Lafayette (Belle) Pharr, Mrs. Ada Spears, Miss Lillian Wellborn, J.T. Wellborn, A.C. Wellborn, and W.S. Wellborn.

The E.M. Wellborn grandchildren from Wilkes County are: Miss Laura Gray Greene, Mrs. Stace (Louise) Alexander, Mrs. Wm. M. (Mary) Alexander, Mrs. M.T. (Ida) Hipps, Mrs. R.L. (Eleanor) Elam, David L. Parks, and Harold W. Parks.

Mrs. E.M. (Margaret) Wellborn told of the night Stoneman camped on their homeplace. She said when Stoneman's raid was nearing Wilkes, people (scouts) were stationed all along the Yadkin River reporting as Stoneman and troops neared. They quickly tried to hide all the corn possible and put many shelled bushels in an improvised attic in the barn. They had killed many hogs also and had much meat ready for sale and to eat that winter. They dropped all they could in between the siding in the barn and other places. When Stoneman and his troops decided to camp at Mrs. Wellborn's place with a rolling large field and yard, they immediately took over all the house but allowed the family to move up to the attic room and helped carry the children up. They found all the corn and meat they could find and asked, ''Is this all?'' Mrs. Wellborn said, ''yes,'' but a young negro girl spoke up and said, ''Law, Miss Margaret, you know we piled all that corn in that barn roof and meat in the sides.'' That took care of all the meat and corn and after the troops moved on the family picked up all the ham bones and what meat had been left on the bone and used it that lean winter. They took all the family's horses, but after much begging, Mrs. Wellborn said General Stoneman let her keep one much loved mare that she always rode.

That winter was very cold. Mrs. Wellborn told of sending ''hands'' to cut wagon loads of very thick ice blocks from the Yadkin River and storing much in an underground ice house to be used all summer. Mrs. Wellborn said although Stoneman's troops took everything they had in the way of food that they were polite and even played ''jumpsticks'' with the children. Thus, I believe, must have been what we call jumping rope now.

Many references were made to the terror of the time.

Sources: Family knowledge.

— Miss Laura Gray Greene

WELLBORNS OF STONY FORK
1076

Records indicate that the Welborns who settled in Wilkes County on the waters of Stony Fork Creek are descended from James Wilborne, who received a Granville Grant in Rowan County May 10th, 1762. This James Wellborn was born about 1731 and married Isabell Teague, born about 1742, the daughter of Moses and Elizabeth (Loftin) Teague. They had at least seven sons: Moses, Aaron, William, James, Jr., Isaac, Gideon and Samuel.

James Wellborn, Jr., son of James and Isabell, was born about 1764 in Rowan Coun-

Front row, left to right: John T. Wellborn, William Richard Wellborn, Lewis Johnson Wellborn, George Washington Wellborn, James Larkin Wellborn
Back row, left to right: Daniel L. Wellborn, Andrew J. Wellborn, Mary C. Wellborn Glenn, Thursa Rebecca Wellborn Brown, Celia Elizabeth Wellborn Watson, Alexander E. Wellborn

ty, married Rebecca Younger and died in either Stokes or Rowan County before 1800. They were the parents of at least three daughters and two sons, but only the sons have been identified. (1) James Wellborn, III, born 1782, died after 1860 in Wilkes County, married February 18, 1813 in Wilkes County, Rebecca Johnson; (2) Daniel Wellborn born 1784, died March 3, 1834 in Wilkes County, married June 13, 1803 in Stokes County, Sarah Douglas.

James Wellborn, III, son of James Jr. and Rebecca Younger Wellborn, married Rebecca Johnson, possibly a daughter of Lewis Johnson. They had six children: (1) Jane, born 1815, who married as his second wife, John Russel; (2) Daniel, a minister, born 1817, married February 11, 1836, Susannah Deal; (3) Fanny, born 1820, married April 25, 1836 as his second wife, Wright Earp; (4) Lewis Johnson, born May 19, 1824, died April 18, 1909, married December 16, 1848 Susan Miranda Watson; (5) James, born October 1828, married Martha Russel and (6) Rebecca born 1835.

Lewis Johnson Wellborn, son of James III and Rebecca (Johnson) Wellborn, married Susannah (Susan) Miranda Watson, born June 6, 1829, died July 12, 1885 in Watauga County on Stony Fork Creek. Both are buried in the Stony Fork Baptist Church Cemetery. They had ten children: (1) George W. born November 8, 1849, in Wilkes County, died July 2, 1926 in Wilkes County, married Mary Jane Hendrix; (2) James Larkin, born Nov. 5, 1851, died Sept. 13, 1925, married Jan. 6, 1876 Jane America Blackburn. They lived on Stony Fork in Watauga County. (3) William Richard, born May 27, 1853, died Sept. 4, 1927, married Rebecca M. Keys. He is buried in the Welborn Cemetery in Wilkes County. (5) John Thomas, born Dec. 13, 1856, died Feb. 3,

1917, married first, Sarah Yates, second, Mamie L. Dula (?) and third Mattie Holsclaw. He is buried in the Stony Fork Baptist Church Cemetery in Watauga County. (5) Alexander Elihue, born July 27, 1859, died Sept. 18, 1952, married first Jula A. and second C. Hampton. (6) Elizabeth, born 1860. (7) Rebecca, born Nov. 1863 (8) Mary, born 1865, died after 1900 unmarried (9) Andrew J. born Jan. 1867 and (10) Daniel L. born March 29, 1872, died November 1954, married Dec. 31, 1891, Martha Green.

George W. Wellborn, son of Lewis Johnson and Susannah Miranda Watson Wellborn, was born Nov. 8, 1849, in Wilkes County, died July 2, 1926 in Wilkes County. He married Mary Jane Hendrix, daughter of Wilson Hendrix, born Jan. 26, 1851 and died Feb. 19, 1934. They were both buried in the lower Mt. Zion Baptist Church Cemetery. They had nine children: (1) Margaret, born April 5, 1873, died Feb. 13, 1948, married Lewis W. Triplette. (2) Oma, born Dec. 25, 1876 and died Feb. 24, 1899. (3) Ila, born Aug. 14, 1879, died Sept. 25, 1929, married Thomas M. Hawkins. (4) Betty, born Oct. 16, 1881, died Jan. 16, 1981, married W. O. Barnett. (5) Julia, died an infant. (6) Jody (7) Benjamin F. born 1887, died 1966, married Artie Wagoner. (8) Jacob Wilson, born April 6, 1889, died Aug. 25, 1967 married Ila McNeil. (9) David, born Sept. 14, 1891 and died March 8, 1900.

John Thomas Welborn, son of Lewis Johnson and Susannah Miranda (Watson) Welborn and his first wife, Sarah Yates, born July 7, 1859 and died Dec. 25, 1892, is buried in Stony Fork Church Cemetery in Watauga County, had two children: (1) Rebecca born Nov. 1879, married George F. Hall and (2) Green L. born Dec. 25, 1882, died March 28, 1960 and married Sept. 26, 1907 to Nellie

Culver, who was born April 1888. He had five sons: John, Dick, Ray, Henry and Jack.

John Welborn and wife Vivian live at Boone, N.C. and have six children.

Dick Welborn, son of Green L. and Nellie Culver Welborn was born Aug. 21, 1910 in Wilkes County. He married Etolia Foster and has four children: (1) Paul Eugene, married Anne Lott and has two sons, Paul, Jr. and Andy. (2) Bobby Gene, married Dorothy Osborne and has three children, Gregory, Randy and Angelia. (3) Dickie Lee, married Gail Elledge and has three children: Donna, Darrell and Derick. (4) Mary Nell, married John Moloney and has one son, Jason.

Ray Welborn, son of Green L. and Nellie Culver Welborn was born Aug. 13, 1912. He married Annie Ruth Welch and has two sons: (1) Bill, married Tempa Hemric, and has two sons Danny and Mark. (2) Tommy, married Anne Garrett, and has two daughters Wendy and Kristen. Ray Welborn has served several terms as Wilkes Register of Deeds.

Henry Welborn, son of Green L. and Nellie Culver Welborn was born Nov. 23, 1914. He married Elizabeth Grayson and has two sons: (1) H. G. married Jo Ann Hayes and has two children; Lori and Dustin. (2) James A. married Betsy Kearns and has two sons: Michael and Christopher.

Jack Welborn, son of Green and Nellie Culver, was born June 24, 1927. He married Madeline Church and has two daughters: (1) Derry Lynn, married Kendall Hendrix and has one daughter Kendra Lynn. and (2) Sharon Kay.

Sources: The Family Bible Record, grave stones, Wilkes and Watauga County marriage and birth records, personal knowledge and memories.

— Ray Welborn
and Annie Cline B. Payne

THE WEST FAMILY

1077

The earliest known ancestor of the West families of Wilkes County was Alexander West.

It is thought he settled in Surry County, N.C. sometime before the American Revolution. He was born about 1720, and came from Virginia. He was still living as late as 1790 in Burke County.

He first settled on the north side of the Yadkin River, somewhere in the vicinty of the village of Ferguson. He later sold his claim to this place to William Triplett. Alexander West I, seems to have lived for a few years in Stony Fork, but after the close of the Revolution, removed to Burke County, and settled on Upper Little River.

Alexander West I had sons Alexander II, John, Isaac, and William, and some daughters.

John West married Margaret and removed to upper South Carolina, where he died. His widow returned to Wilkes County to live near her relatives in the same general neighborhood where Alexander West I had lived prior to his settlement on Upper Little River. Her name appears in 1810 in Wilkes County, with three children living with her, one son (Baylis), and

two daughters. Mrs. Peggy West was born about 1760 and died in the 1840's when she was past eighty years of age, in the home of her son Baylis West.

Baylis West was born about 1798 in South Carolina, but was raised in Wilkes County. He married Mary Swanson, the daughter of William Swanson and Elizabeth Stations, in the year 1818. Bondsmen were John Hooper and W. W. Martin.

For some years they continued to live in the same section where Baylis was raised, between Elkville and Ferguson, until sometime in the 1840's, when Baylis West purchased a small farm on the south fork of Lewis Fork.

Baylis and Mary West had nine children, as follows: (1) Franklin (1818-1897) married Cynthia Holder (1824-1919), the daughter of James Holder and Elizabeth Paisley, in 1844. They are the parents of the following children; Martha Carolina (1848); Sarah E. (1854); Thomas (1859) who married Bethinia Triplett; Julia Ann (1859-1937) who married L. F. Hendrix in 1883, and James H. Franklin and Cynthia Holder West are buried at the Mt. Zion Baptist Cemetery at Stony Fork. (2) Margaret (1828) married Wilson Hendrix. (3) Alexander B. (1828) married (1851) Nancy Land of Stony Fork. He was a licensed Baptist preacher. On 28 Feb. 1862, he enlisted in Company K, 53rd North Carolina Regiment, Confederate States Army, was promoted to Corporal, was wounded at Gettysburg 3 July 1862 and killed 19 September 1864. (4) William (1830) married (1855) his cousin Nancy West, daughter of Thomas West of Caldwell County, and died in the Civil War, leaving three children — Selena, Genlia, and William. (5) Melinda West (1832). (6) Elizabeth (1835). (7) Mary Ann (1837-1917) married Hamilton Barnett (1844-1902). They are buried at Mount Zion Baptist Church Cemetery at Stony Fork. (8) John Witherspoon (1840) married his cousin Catharine West of Caldwell County. (9) Lucy (1842).

Sources: Family members, Census Records, Wilkes County Court House Records, Family Bible.

— Irene Hendrix Basey

CANDIS RASH WEST

1078

Candis Rash West was an unusual character in many respects. She was born Aug. 29, 1886 to Martha Rash (Rhoades), Martha Rash was a daughter of Matilda (Tilda) Bumgarner and Joe Rash. She died Feb. 1, 1973.

Sometime in early life she sustained a severe injury resulting in a deformed hip and leg, but her handicap did not keep her from her independence. For years she cared for her grandmother, Matilda. Some years after her grandmother's death, she, by correspondence, met and married C.W. West from Harnett County, and resided there for six years during which time she helped care for a sister and brother of her husband who were deaf and mute. After her husband's death, she returned to Wilkes County to care for her mother for several years. After her mother's death, she lived alone until a short time before her death when it became necessary to have someone

with her because she lost her eyesight.

Despite her difficulties, she was always able to make it on her own; and she did more than her share in caring for her loved ones. She would go to any length for those she cared for, but she would have nothing to do with those she considered her enemies. She asked no quarter from anyone and expected none. One would have had to know her to appreciate her unique qualities.

Source: Gravestone, family tradition, and personal knowledge.

— Sidney Johnston

THE CARLYLE WESTON FAMILY

1079

William Carlyle Weston was born May 4, 1921 in Iredell County to Wesly Oren and Esther Cross Weston. He graduated from Scotts High School and served three and one half years in the military during World War II. After the war he helped his father on the dairy farm and did carpenter work. He married Edna Genevieve Andrews on March 5, 1948. She was born November 9, 1920 to Nelson and Ollie Andrews of Wilkes County. They started housekeeping in Iredell County. Carlyle worked on his family's farm and Edna continued nursing at Davis Hospital in Statesville.

The Weston's first two children were born in Iredell County. Gloria Kay born December 17, 1955 and Dan Carlyle born January 30, 1958. In 1959 Edna's Mother was killed in a car accident and Edna and Carlyle decided to move back to the Andrews homeplace to assist her father, Nelson with the farm. Their third child, Glenn Oren was born September 12, 1960.

Gloria Kay graduated from Wilkes Central High School with honors in 1974. She attended the U.N.C. at Greensboro and graduated from Wilkes Community College. She married Jerry Alexander Kilby May 23, 1975 and they have a daughter, Sara Elaine, born August 18, 1979. They are members of Little Rock Baptist Church, and are both employed by Broyhill Furniture Company in Lenoir.

Dan Carlyle graduated from Wilkes Central High School in 1976 and from Wilkes Community College in 1978. His height of over six feet aided the basketball teams in high school and college. Dan enjoys baseball and plays with the Little Rock Church Team. He is employed on the family farm. Glenn Oren graduated from Wilkes Central High School in 1978. His hobbies all center around the out doors: camping, fishing, frog gigging, and opossum hunting, to name a few.

Sources: Personal knowledge and Wilkes Co. records.

— Edna Andrews Weston

WHEATLEY (WHITLEY) FAMILY

1080

George Wheatley, Sr. (George II) son of George and Mary Wheatley came from Fauquier County, Virginia into Surry County with his 2nd wife, Diana Darnell, as early as 1771. George Wheatley II, in 1779, was granted 305 acres on Roaring River. He died there between 1800 and 1810.

George Wheatley, Sr. (George II) had three children by his first wife, Sara Williams, daughter of Jonas and Honour Williams: two daughters, Elizabeth, and Honor, who married, 28 May 1771, Peter Hord in Fauquier County, Virginia, and remained in Virginia; son, George III, was called "Esquire" in the Wilkes County records.

George Wheatley, Esquire (George III), was born about 1750. He served as a Private in the Rev. War. He married, 5 May 1774, Mary Poor. They settled in the Cane Creek Area on the South Fork of Roaring River. He was Clerk of the Court of Wilkes County, beginning 1781 and served many years. He died, 24 December, 1828, and Mary, his wife, died, 12 August, 1843.

There were three sons born to George III and Mary Poor Wheatley: (1.) Moses, born, 30 March, 1777; (2.) George IV, born 16 June, 1779, married, Mary Turner; (3.) William, born about 1792/3, married Elizabeth Kilby. He inherited his father's homeplace on Cane Creek and later sold it to his nephew, Martin H. Wheatley, and moved to Reddies River. There were at least four daughters: Sally, born 12 May, 1775; and Nancy, born 9 Aug., 1784, married Joshua Smith and removed to Monroe County, Tennessee.

George Wheatley IV, also, known as Esquire, born 16 June, 1779, died 6 July, 1854. He married, Mary L. Turner, born 22 August, 1780, and died 24 February, 1854.

George IV and Mary Turner Wheatley were the parents of nine children: 1. Millie, born about 1799, married Elisha McDaniel; 2. Martin H., born 12 April, 1801, died in 1860, in Missouri. He married, 12 June, 1821, Polly or Maryan Johnson. He married, 2nd, Frances or Franky Johnson Chote, a widow; 3. Sally, born 4 August, 1803/4, married Eli Johnson; 4. Polly, born about 1806, married her widowed brother-in-law, Elisha McDaniel and moved to Missouri; 5. William W., born 20 April, 1808, died, 30 March, 1862, in Missouri. He married, 24 December, 1829, Mary Cleveland; 6. Thomas, born about 1813. He married Elizabeth Sprinkle, moved to Missouri; 7. Betsy, born 11 July, 1816, died, 3 Sept., 1881, in Missouri. She married John Stull; 8. Nancy born about 1817, married Reuben Hayes. They remained in Wilkes County; 9. George, born about 1820, died 25 Sept., 1860, in Missouri, unmarried.

Sarah Williams Wheatley, wife of George Wheatley II, died before 10 Feb., 1760, when George II, married Diana Darnell in Fauquier County, Virginia.

George II and Diana Darnell Wheatley had sons: Mason, John, James and Joseph, and three daughters.

Mason Wheatley married a Mary. He died on Roaring River about 1807 and left several daughters and a son Daniel, who later sold out and left the County.

John Wheatley lived and died on Roaring River. John is believed to have had a son Willis Whitley, born about 1795, married 6 Jan. 1818, Nancy Matilda Robins. This branch of the family used the Whitley spelling of the

name. The story is told that a school teacher came into the area and told the family the way they pronounced the name it should be spelled "Whitley", and the family changed the spelling.

James Wheatley, acted as a witness for his father in 1794.

Joseph Wheatley, born about 1775, married Mary Brown, daughter of Walter and Mary Brown, lived on Roaring River until 1809, sold and his land moved to Gallatin County, Kentucky. Joseph and Mary had a son George W. Wheatley, who died in Owen County, Kentucky.

Willis Whitley, son of John Wheatley, married, 6 Jan., 1818, Nancy Matilda Robins, born about 1800. They are known to have had ten children: (1.) John, born 1822; (2.) Willis H., born 1826, married, Matilda Alexander; (3.) Winny Matilda, born 1828; (4.) George, born 1823; (5.) Sarah or Sally, born 1831; (6.) Thomas, born 1832; (7.) Daniel, born 1835; (8.) Nancy A., born 1837; (9.) Angus A., born, 9 April, 1838, married Martha Jane Alexander; (10.) Sol. A. F. or Doctor, born 1841.

Sources: Fauquier County, Virginia; Wilkes County; and Johnson Co. Mo. Records; Pension application of George Wheatley III.

— Verl F. Weight

THE JOSEPH HUBERT WHICKER FAMILY
1081

Mr. and Mrs. Joseph Hubert Whicker, Sr., and their three children, Joseph Hubert, Jr., Jane Adelaide and Charles Finch, moved from Winston-Salem to North Wilkesboro in September 1926, at which time Mr. Whicker opened a law office. Two more children were born to them, Thomas Austin in 1926 and Ann Elizabeth (Betty) in 1933. Mr. and Mrs. Whicker and their eldest son, J. H., Jr. spent their lives in North Wilkesboro and are all buried in Mount Lawn Memorial Park Cemetery.

Joseph Hubert Whicker, Sr. was born in Forsyth County December 19, 1887, son of Joseph H. and Mary Lee Bodenheimer Whicker, who resided in the Sedge Garden community near Kernersville. He was educated at Wake Forest College where he graduated from law school in 1911 and began to practice law in Winston-Salem until he came to Wilkes County. He was counselor of the 23rd Judicial District for a number of years and served as president of the Wilkes and District Bar Associations. He was senior member of the law firm of Whicker, Whicker, and Vannoy with son J. H., Jr. and Gary Vannoy. He practiced law for 57 years until his death November 24, 1968.

Mr. Whicker was a life deacon in the First Baptist Church, sang in the choir and taught the Berean Men's Bible Class for 38 years. Was active in the civic life of the community, serving twice as president of the Kiwanis Club which he had helped organize while a member of the Kiwanis Club in Winston-Salem. A leader in the Republican Party, he presided over numerous conventions in the county. In 1946, he was candidate for Congress. He was a member of the Masonic Lodge.

Mr. And Mrs. Whicker were married on September 5, 1914 in High Point, N.C. She was the former Adelaide Finch McKnight, daughter of Edward and Adelaide Finch McKnight, and was born June 13, 1892 in Winston-Salem. She attended Salem Academy and graduated from Salem College in 1914. She was interested in genealogy and belonged to several historical organizations. Was a member and served as Regent for the Rendezvous Mountain Chapter, DAR. She belonged to the United Daughters of the Confederacy and the Governor John Archdale Chapter, Colonial Dames of the Seventeenth Century. She was a member of the North Wilkesboro Woman's Club and attended the First Baptist Church. She died July 12, 1981 at the age of 89.

Joseph Hubert Whicker, Jr. was born November 4, 1915 in Winston-Salem. He attended North Wilkesboro city school and graduated from U.N. C. Law School in 1938. He joined his father's law firm and was active in the firm until his death from cancer May 14, 1969. He was attorney and court solicitor for the Town of North Wilkesboro, served as counsel for the city schools, Carolina Mirror Corp. and Key City Furniture Co.; was director and attorney for North Wilkesboro Savings and Loan Association. He was past president of the Wilkes Bar Association and held other posts in the legal profession. J.H. was a member of the First Baptist Church, serving as Sunday school teacher. A past president of the Lion's Club, member of the Elks Club, Junior Order and Oakwoods Country Club. His two hobbies were golf and flying. He earned a pilot's license and was a member of Civil Air Patrol.

J.H. Jr. married June 14, 1938 Miriam Durrett of Greenwood, Miss. whom he met when they were students at Chapel Hill. They had two sons, James Hubert, an ear, nose and throat specialist in Raleigh, and Joseph Lenieu, who lives in Greenwood, Miss.

Dr. Charles Finch Whicker, an Obstetrician and Gynecologist in North Wilkesboro, was born February 15, 1921 in Winston-Salem. He attended high school in North Wilkesboro and graduated from U.N.C. Chapel Hill in 1943. He served three years in W.W. II. He completed two years medical training at UNC and graduated from Temple University School of Medicine. He served his internship and residency at Rex Hospital, Crawford Long Hospital in Atlanta, Norfolk Hospital, and Sacred Heart Hospital in Penna. He came to North Wilkesboro in 1958 and became a member of staff of Wilkes General Hospital. He is a member of First Baptist Church. His hobbies include automobiles, music, and photography.

Dr. Thomas Austin Whicker was born November 12, 1926. After finishing school he served two years in the U. S. Navy. He attended Wake Forest College and Emory Dental School in Atlanta, graduating in 1952. He lives in Thomasville and has practiced dentistry for 30 years. He married Betty Goolsby of Atlanta. They have two children, Marcus and Charles.

Jane Adelaide Whicker, born September 20, 1917, graduated from Greensboro College with an AB degree and UNC-Greensboro with a MA degree. After her marriage to Harry D.

Kellett from Greenville, S.C., in 1938, she has lived in Greensboro where they have been active in church, civic and educational affairs. Jane has recently finished compiling a book for NSDAR in N.C. She is a past Regent of Rachel Caldwell Chapter DAR, past president of Earl of Shaftesbury Chapter Colonial Dames, and a member of Virginia Dare Chapter, Daughters of American Colonists. She was recently awarded an alumnae award from Greensboro College. She and her husband have four daughters, all Phi Beta Kappa graduates of Duke University.

Ann Elizabeth (Betty) Whicker was born February 13, 1933. She married Don Reins in December of 1950. She maintains a home in Annandale, Virginia, commuting to North Wilkesboro where she is office manager and assistant to her brother, Dr. Whicker. They have a daughter Donna Reins, who is married.

Sources: Family Bible, and personal recollections.

— Jane Whicker Kellett

FAMILY of JOHN W. WHITE, M.D.
1082

John Wesley White, M.D., was a physician and surgeon at Wilkesboro for Almost half a century. He was born on a farm in Yadkin County, near Hamptonville March 9, 1861. He was the oldest son of William and Sarah Nicholson White.

His people have lived in this section of North Carolina for several generations. His father was a building contractor. Among other structures, he erected the old court house at Yadkinville. Because of his advanced age, he was unable to enlist in the Army of the Confederacy, so he became a member of the Home Guard. William White married Sarah Nicholson, who was born at Eagle Mills, in Iredell County, North Carolina.

At her husband's death in 1867, she was left a widow with three small children: John Wesley, George Anderson and Charles Henry. She continued to live on the farm. George was associated with C. E. Jenkins Hardware Company of North Wilkesboro, and later moved to the state of Idaho. He bought a ranch near Idaho Falls and lived there until he came to Wilkes County in 1935, where he remained until his death in 1936: Charles graduated from Peabody College in Nashville, Tenn., the University of North Carolina, and Harvard University. He was a professor of mining and metallurgy at Harvard for a number of years, and later was employed by mining companies to test ore in mines in Yugoslavia and South Africa. He died in San Francisco, Calif. in 1953.

After teaching in the schools of Yadkin County for a few years, Dr. White entered Jefferson Medical College at Philadelphia, from which he graduated in 1889. He located at Wilkesboro in 1890. In 1906 he established a small hospital in Wilkesboro which for a number of years was the only hospital in the county. Dr. White was a member of the State Medical Society and the Wilkes County and Tri-State Medical Societies, and was vice-president of the N.C. Medical Society. He took a keen interest in schools and education and was for many years a member and chariman of the Wilkesboro School Board. He also served as mayor of Wilkesboro.

He was on the building committee and board of trustees when the present Wilkesboro United Methodist Church was built in 1896, and served on the Board of Stewards for over 25 years. For the last 10 years of his life he was County Health Officer for Wilkes County. He died in 1932.

As a daughter, I feel that an account of my father's life would be incomplete without writing something of the personal side of his life. Several years after coming to Wilkesboro, he suffered a stroke which left him slightly crippled for the rest of his life. He practiced medicine for many years before the days of good roads and automobiles, sometimes traveling for miles on horseback, or by horse and buggy. Day and night, cold or hot, and without inquiring whether the pay would be ready when the service was performed, my father answered the calls for his service, regardless of from whom or where they came. He had a ready wit, and thoroughly enjoyed a good joke. Above all, I remember his gentleness, kindness, and never-ending patience.

Dr. White married Pearl Sydnor who was born near Richmond, Va. She was a daughter of John Lincoln and Nellie Catlin Sydnor. She was very active in her church and civic affairs of the town. She died in 1960. They had two children, Nellie Katherine and John Wesley. Nellie married Julius C. Hubbard in 1923, who later became publisher of The Journal-Patriot. He died in 1972. Their children are Nell White, Julius C. III, and John White. Nell married Corneal L. Domeck, Jr. of Louisville, Ky. They have four children, Corneal III, Anne Winifred, Amanda Katherine and Julia Hubbard. Corneal III married Nancy Lindahl of Louisville, and Anne married James Burke. They live in Galveston, Texas. Corneal and Nancy have two sons Corneal IV, and Robert Craig. Julius III married Dorothy Shiver of Charlotte. Their children are: Frances Shiver, Julius C. IV, and Ellen (Nellie) White. John married Rebecca Shiver, sister of Dorothy. They have three children: John White, Jr., Caroline Elizabeth, and Charles Noble. John W. White, Jr. married Helen Jones of Kenansville. He worked for R. J. Reynolds Tobacco Company as a salesman, and was division manager for Kentucky for many years. Because of ill health, he retired in the late forties, and came back to Wilkes County to make his home. He died here in 1976. Their children are: John Wesley, III, and Helen Sydnor. John married Joy Judd of Nashville, Tenn., and they have two children, Julia, and John W. IV. Helen married William Mac Stephens and they live in Greensboro. Their children are: William Wesley and Robert Mark.

Sources: Personal knowledge, History of North Carolina North Carolina Biography.

— Nellie White Hubbard

THE WHITTINGTON FAMILY
1083

The surname Whittington appears to be locational in origin, and is believed to be associated with the Welsh, and English meaning, "one who came from Whittington." Although bearers of the old and distinguished Whittington name comprise a small fraction of the population, there are a number who have established for it a significant place in history. They include: Johannes Whittington (1379) whose residency is listed in the "Poll Tax Records" of Yorkshire; Sir Richard (Dick) Whittington (1359-1423), famous citizen of London who was thrice elected Lord Mayor of the city and noted as being a distinguished benefactor of the public; Robert Whittington, an English grammarian and Latin poet in about 1480; Thomas Whittington whose name is recorded in the register of the University of Oxford as residing in Hereford County in 1590; and Richard Whittington, the son of John Whittington, whose baptism is recorded in Saint Peter in Cornhill in 1713.

Sir William Whittington came to America from England sometime in the middle 1700's and settled in Halifax County, North Carolina. He married Catherine Halifax and they had three sons and five daughters. The family moved to Wilkesboro and established their residence. One son moved to Yadkin County; one son moved to Yancy County; and one son named Leonard remained in Wilkes.

According to county records, William Whittington was appointed in 1784 to do road work from the fork above the courthouse to the ford at Thomas Holman's. William was listed in the 1790 census as a landowner and head of household in Wilkes County. There was also a John Whittington listed as a head of a household in the 1790 census. It is unknown whether or not John was William's brother, but is reasonable to assume that he was.

Leonard Whittington was born July 24, 1770 and died February 12, 1856. He married Sarah Kilby, born October 20, 1780, the daughter of William and Frances Kilby. Leonard and Sarah settled near Tumbling Shoal Branch on Reddies River. Leonard purchased 200 acres of land in 1803 from William Kilby along Reddies River.

Leonard and Sarah reared ten children in a small cabin in a hollow by Tumbling Shoal Branch. Their children and their spouses included: Allen A., born 1801, died in 1900, first married to Elizabeth Lenderman, daughter of Leonard Lenderman, second marriage was to Mary (Polly) Eller, daughter of Simeon and Fanny McNeil Eller, his third wife was Mariah Vannoy; John, born 1802, married Frankie Yates; James A., born 1805, first married Polly Lenderman, daughter of Leonard Lenderman, second marriage was to Nancy Welch; William, born 1807, married Ann Gilreath; Carolina married Absolum Faw; Alexander, born 1811, died 1890, married Susannah Vannoy; Jesse, born 1814, married Sarilda James; Polly, married Henry Lenderman, son of Leonard Lenderman; Elizabeth, born 1804, married John Barker; Anne, born 1828, married Jack Johnson.

Leonard, his wife Sarah, and some of his children are buried in a small family cemetery on a hill facing his old homesite on Tumbling Shoal Branch. The graves are well maintained and marked with soapstone markers.

The children grew up, married and settled in the Reddies River and Parsonsville areas of Wilkes County.

They were farmers, road builders, distillers, gristmill operators, and storekeppers. In later years major occupations of Whittingtons have included public school and college teachers and administrators, Department of Transportation workers, poultry processors, cattle and poultry farmers, small business operators, ministers, and at least one medical doctor.

For the most part, they were devout Baptists. Almost without exception, Whittington families belonged to, and supported the Democratic Party.

According to county records, male members of the Whittington family served as school committeemen, Justices of the Peace, constables, jury members to oversee and lay out roads, and on the Board of Equalization for county taxes. They were public spirited citizens in every respect. One school and one corn and flour mill were named for the Whittingtons in the Reddies River section of Wilkes County.

Records indicate that Whittington males served their nation very well in times of war. Many were killed or wounded from the Civil War to the Vietnam War. There were many non-commissioned officers and at least one colonel in the Civil War.

Allen A. Whittington was the oldest son of Leonard and Sarah Kilby Whittington. As a youngster, he worked on his father's farm and helped him build roads. In later life Allen operated a large farm and a country store. Allen married Elizabeth Lenderman on December 18, 1826. He settled near his birthplace in the bend of Reddies River. Elizabeth died on July 13, 1838. She bore the following children to this union: William R. born in 1830; James born in 1832; Mariah E. born in 1834; and Thomas C.B. born in 1836.

Allen married Mary (Polly) Eller, daughter of Simeon and Fanny McNeil Eller on December 13, 1838. Mary died on May 16, 1894 when Allen was ninety-three years of age. To this union four children were born as follows: Emily born in 1839; Elvira born 1843 and died 1931; Lee (Leander) born in 1846; and Benjamin F. born 1850 and died 1888. Shortly after Mary's death, Allen married Mariah Vannoy. Needless to say, there were no children born from this marriage.

According to family members, Allen had to be helped on his horse to go courting prior to his last marriage. His children questioned him about getting married at the age of ninety-three. He said, "Surely to God I will live ten more years." He lived until he was ninety-nine.

Sources: Halbert's *Coat of Arms,* family Bible, interviews with family members, grave stones.

— Rex W. Whittington

BENJAMIN F. WHITTINGTON FAMILY

1084

Benjamin F. Whittington was born February

Ben and Rachel Whittington.

3, 1850 and died July 15, 1888. He was the youngest son of Esquire Allen A. Whittington and Mary (Polly) Eller Whittington.

Ben married Rachel Colvard, who was the daughter of Wade and Phebe Vannoy Colvard and the granddaughter of Rev. Jesse Vannoy. Rachel was born on January 23, 1846 and died June 22, 1891.

Ben and Rachel's children, spouses and their children include the following: A. Monroe, born 1871, died 1937, married Dora Whittington; children: Clayton, Tolbert, Roxie, Vallie, Paul, Edna, Rachel, Kate, and Richard. Octavia, born 1874, died 1955, married Zebulan McNeil; children: Raymond, Elihu, Flossie, Mamie, and Quincy. Hansford, born 1876, died 1899, married Octavia Welch; children: Ben and Mitch. Spainhour, born 1878, died 1964, married Ila Whittington; children: Terry, Virginia, Dolly, and Gwyn. Sallie, born 1880, died 1972, married Enos Barre, second husband, Newton Miller; children: Thurmon, Audrey, Eula, Blane, Otis, Curtis, and Corine. Virginia, born 1883, died 1950, married Fred Shumate; children: Murray, Ode, Johnnie, and Mable. John C., born 1885, died 1969, married Etta Kilby; children: Grant, Grace, Vernice, Andrew, and Rex. Dollie, born 1888, died 1979, married John Staley; children: Roscoe.

Ben worked on the farm, helped his father build roads, and also worked some at at corn and flour mill. Since he was the youngest son of Allen A. Whittington, he took care of his daddy and mother until his death.

Ben fell off a load of hay and died at the early age of thirty-eight. Rachel died three years later at the age of forty-five. Their children lived with Grandaddy Allen until his death in 1900. At that time John, Dollie, Virginia, and Sallie moved in with A. Monroe Whittington, their oldest brother. He and his wife, Dora, raised the four children in addition to their own.

Sources: Wilkes Genealogical Society Collection, Family Bible, Interviews with family members, and Grave Stones.

— Rex W. Whittington

JOHN C. WHITTINGTON FAMILY

1085

John C. Whittington was born on November 23, 1885 and died February 13, 1969. He married Etta Kilby on November 23, 1910, which was his twenty-fifth birthday. To this union were born five children: Thomas Grant, born 1911, married Ella Mae Burgess; Grace, born 1913; Vernice, born 1915, married H. L. Eller; James Andrew, born 1918, married Mattie Ashley; and Rex W., born 1926, married Aline Hayes. Andrew was killed in action on November 3, 1944 in World War II.

John's father died when he was two years old, and his mother died when he was five. So, practically his whole childhood was spent with his Grandfather Allen Whittington and his brother, A. Monroe and his wife, Dora, and their children.

John attended the Old Reddies River School through the seventh grade. He then worked on the farm until he went to West Virginia with his brother, Spainhour. They worked in a general store in the coal fields for about two years. He then returned home and worked for Giant Lumber Company on Reddies River until he married. He married Etta Kilby and moved in with her parents, John J. and Martha McNeil Kilby. They were up in years and needed to be taken care of during World War I.

In 1920, John and Etta bought a seventy-one acre farm from the John A. Faw heirs. This farm was located one mile east of Millers Creek, and about three miles from the John J. Kilby place on Reddies River. Grandpa and Grandma Kilby moved with the John Whitting-

L. to R. first row: Vernice Eller, Etta Kilby Whittington, Grace Whittington. L. to R. second row: Grant Whittington, John C. Whittington, Rex W. Whittington.

ton family to Millers Creek. Grandpa Kilby died in 1925 and Grandma Kilby died in 1931.

During the early years of the depression (1921-1933) John ran a store in Millers Creek. He also worked as a carpenter and operated a farm. About the middle of the depression John took a job with the International Shoe Company in North Wilkesboro. He worked there as yard foreman until the 1940 flood, when the Shoe Company was destroyed by the flood.

During World War II John worked for Isaac Eller's Feed Store and Tomlinson's Feed Store in North Wilkesboro. After the war he did construction work building church buildings. He was working as shop foreman with Eller's Lumber Supply when he retired in 1956.

John served as a deacon in Pleasant Home Baptist Church for over fifty years. He also was Sunday school superintendent and song leader for several years. He was elected Constable in Reddies River Township in 1920. He also served as a Millers Creek School district committeeman from 1931 to 1943.

John's main sport or recreation was fox hunting. He also loved baseball. His favorite team was the New York Yankees. As a young man he loved to hunt quail and rabbits. He also loved to go swimming in Reddies River. This was a treat in the summertime when the children had helped work in the corn and hay fields. In the winter evenings, he loved to listen to the radio to Amos and Andy, and Lum and Abner. In later years his favorite television program was Marshall Matt Dillion.

John Whittington was never a man to sit around and do nothing. After his retirement he worked everyday on the farm or in the garden. He also cleaned creek banks, cleared land, hauled off rocks from the pasture, worked on the road, and cut firewood. He continued to be active by raising a few beef cattle and growing hay for sale until his death by a heart attack when he was eighty-four years of age.

John's devoted and faithful wife, Etta, was always a homemaker. She not only raised five

children, but she also took care of Grandpa and Grandma Kilby until they passed away. She took care of Grant's two children during World War II while he and his wife and Grace worked in Baltimore on defense work. She also took care of Rex and Aline's children while Rex was in college and his wife was working. Etta is better known as "Mommie" to family and friends. She is presently ninety-one years of age. She attends church every Sunday, has lunch at the Holiday Inn, and goes to the grocery store and beauty shop once per week. She and Grace still reside at their homeplace in Millers Creek.

Sources: Family Bible, "Land of Wilkes", personal memory.

— Rex W. Whittington

THE ODELL WHITTINGTON, SR. FAMILY

1086

Odell Whittington, Sr. was born July 14, 1895, the son of John Lin Whittington (1847-1932) and his second wife, Mary Jane Vannoy (1862-1946). Other children of this marriage were Eugene (1888-1949), Ben F. (1889-1931), Otto (1893-4-8-65), Walter (1897), a retired Baptist minister, John Allen (1900), Claude (1905-1908), and Anna.

John Lin Whittington, the son of William (Billy) Whittington (1807-1850?) and grandson of Leonard Whittington (1770-1856), was first married to Henrietta Vannoy (1847-1882). Children of this marriage included Ethel (1880), Ellen (1873), Belle (1877), Mary Ann, Sarah Jane and Nancy. John Lin was active in church and community affairs throughout his life.

Whittington School was built for use by the children of Wilbar around 1900. Odell, Sr. and siblings attended Whittington School for the lower grades, but a trip to North Wilkesboro was necessary for high school (1910). Odell,

Sr. attended Appalachian for two years, driving a team and wagon to provide transportation for himself and others.

In 1916, Odell went to West Virginia to work in the mines. Soon after arriving, he and his friend, Arthur Holder from Mountain View, were intrigued by the promises of a Marine recruiter. In June 1917, they found themselves on board a ship bound for France and WWI. In June 1918, Odell, Sr. was wounded four times in the Battle of Belleau Woods.

Odell, Sr. returned to the Reddies River in 1920 and began working in the family corn and flour mill — a mill that had been in the family for over 100 years. On December 25, 1921, he married Edna Irene Whittington (1900). Odell, Sr. operated the mill until he opened a service station in 1928 (the first between North Wilkesboro and West Jefferson). In 1932, he was appointed road overseer for the area. In 1933, he was hired as school system bus mechanic for Wilkes. In 1936, Sheriff Claude Doughton selected Odell, Sr. as his Chief Deputy. He continued in that position until he became the mail carrier for Wilbar, Route 1. He retired in 1965.

Since joining Union Township Baptist Church in 1913, Odell, Sr. has served as the church spokesperson in the Stone Mountain Association. He was at one time moderator of the association. Odell has taught Sunday School for over 60 years, was Sunday School Superintendent for 20 years, and has served as representative for the Association to the Baptist Home for the Aging for 20 years.

Besides church work, his activies have included member and chaplain of the Master Mason Lodge at Mt. Pleasant, member of the York Rite Masons, member of the Shriners, township chariman for the Democratic party, charter member of the V.F.W., organizer and commander of the WWI veterans, president of the local chapter of Retired Federal Employees, charter member and president of the Civitan Club, president of the Wilkes Farm Board for 10 years, member of the Junior Lodge at New Hope, president of the Community Improvement Group, member of the organizational committee for Wilkes Rural Telephone Cooperative, and Master of the Reddies River Grange for 31 years.

Family life has played a large role in Odell, Sr.'s life. (1) Odell, Jr. (1922) is currently Vice-President of Vehicle Maintenance with Holly Farms Poultry. He was chosen National Fleet Executive of the Year in 1982. Odell, Jr. married Grace Dean Rhodes in 1944. Their son, Richard Odell was born October 14, 1945. Their daughter, Nancy Susan was born April 26, 1950.

(2) John Allen was born to Odell, Sr. and Edna in 1924. He survived the attack on the aircraft carrier *Hornet* in 1942. He is employed by Holly Farms. John Allen married Martha Shepherd in 1957. Their daughter, Sonja Teresa was born November 21, 1958. Their son, Mark Allen was born April 7, 1966.

(3) Van Hubert was born in 1927. He served in the U. S. Navy Medical Corps during both WWII and the Korean conflict where he received training in x-ray technology. He is now a technologist at Wilkes General Hospital.

Hubert married Maxine Sidden in 1960. Tena Van was born February 4, 1962, Hugh Sidden was born February 12, 1965 and Regis Lynn was born June 28, 1971.

Since Odell, Sr.'s retirement, his pet project has been the maintenance of the Reddies River Primitive Baptist Church cemetery. He was instrumental in the establishment of a trust fund for the perpetual care of the cemetery.

Odell and Edna Whittington have lived a long and fruitful life in the Reddies River community. Their example of community involvement and family commitment is a standard for us all.

Sources: Family Bible; Wilkes County marriage records and tax lists; Family Members.

— Susan Whittington

REX W. WHITTINGTON FAMILY

1087

Rex W. Whittington was born March 5, 1926, the youngest son of John C. and Etta Kilby Whittington of Millers Creek. He married Aline Hayes, the daughter of James Henry and Esther Felts Hayes, on September 6, 1947. They have four children: Sandra Jean, born February 22, 1949, married Danny K. Smith; children: Michael Scott. They are divorced. Sandra attend Wilkes Community College and works in Ashe County. Susan Diane was born June 13, 1953. Susan took her Bachelor's degree from Appalachian State University and her Master's degree from San Francisco State University. She lives and teaches in San Francisco. Richard David was born January 26, 1959. He graduated from West Wilkes High School and joined the army for four years, which he spent in Hawaii. During his army tenure he visited Korea and New Zealand. He also found time to train as a scuba-diving instructor. He married Beth Marie Brown from California on December 7, 1980. They reside in Wahiawa, Hawii where he works in a scuba diving shop. Janie Lynn Whittington was born March 23, 1963. She attended Wilkes Community College. She married Gene Allen Kilby on May 8, 1982. They reside in Millers Creek.

Rex W. Whittington grew up in the Millers Creek community. He graduated from Millers Creek High School, received his Bachelor's, Master's, and Specialist's degrees from Appalachian State University. He did additional graduate study at UNC-Chapel Hill and Virginia Tech.

He is a member of Pleasant Home Baptist Church where he serves as a deacon and assistant Sunday school teacher.

Rex belongs to the Veterans of Foreign Wars, Phi Delta Kappa, Retired Teachers Association, and is a life member of the North Carolina Association of Education, and the National Community Education Association. He served in the United States Army in Europe during World War II. He held the rank of Platoon Sergeant when he was discharged.

After the war, Rex returned home and began work with Church Music Company. After getting married, he changed jobs to Eller's Lumber Company. Since he particularly didn't like either job for a permanent livelihood, he en-

Rex W. Whittington family. L. to R: Susan, Sandy, Janie, Aline, Richard and Rex.

tered college in the fall of 1949. He graduated in 1952 and began a teaching career, which he followed for five years at Wilkes Central and East High School.

Rex was named principal of C.C. Wright Elementary School and continued in that position for the next nine years. In 1966, he was named Associate Superintendent of Wilkes County Schools. He served in this position until his retirement in 1979.

There were three significant accomplishments that Rex W. Whittington was primarily responsible for during the fourteen years that he served as Associate Superintendent of Wilkes County Schools: developed and directed the Title I program for educational handicapped students in the school system; organized and directed the pupil personnel department for the school system; developed and directed the Community School program for the county. These three programs are still going strong in Wilkes County under very capable leadership.

Hunting, fishing, and sports have been an integral part of the leisure time of Rex's life. He had good bird dogs and hunted every winter for many years. Likewise, he fished in the spring and summer months. In sports, Rex participated in baseball and basketball in high school and college. He coached baseball and basketball in high school. Now that he is retired he follows high school, college, and professional sports very closely, with college basketball being his favorite.

Another interest since Rex's retirement is family history and genealogy. He has written an autobiography and assists with the Whittington family history. He expects to do more research and writing on various topics in the future.

Since Rex and Aline have children and/or family members in several states, travel is very important to them. They have visited their family members in Delaware, Nevada, California, and Hawaii in recent years. It is their desire to continue to do this.

Aline Hayes Whittington has always been a

loyal wife and good mother to her children. She has given birth to four children while working before, between, and after each child was born. She helped send Rex to college and kept the family going when he was a patient in the Veterans Hospital.

She is very active in church, participating in the Womens Missionary Society, teaching an adult Sunday school class, singing in the church choir, and serving as Bible School Director. She is totally involved in Extension Homemakers, serving on the county and state level as an officer.

In addition to her community service, Aline is a full time bookkeeper with Holly Farms as well as a dedicated homemaker. Aline enjoys cooking a big meal on Sundays and having our children and both our parents for lunch. We are a very close family and I am thankful.

Sources: Family memories, Family Bible, and Personal knowledge.

— Rex W. Whittington

T. GRANT WHITTINGTON FAMILY

1088

My granddaddy, Thomas Grant Whittington, was born September 25, 1911, the first born of John C. and Etta Kilby Whittington. Grant was named after Grant Cothren, a baptist preacher and family friend of the Rock Creek Community.

Grant Whittington and his parents lived on the John J. Kilby place on Reddies River. Due to the mail route, the family mail box was located across the river. The family crossed the river by means of a swinging bridge. In 1916 a flood washed the bridge away. So Grant usually waded across the river. During the winter of 1917-18 the Reddies River became frozen due to the cold weather. Grant walked across the frozen river on several occasions before the river finally thawed. The family lived on the Reddies River until 1920 when John and Etta Whittington bought a seventy-

462

T. Grant Whittington family.

been a loyal wife to Grant, a good mother to Thomas and Ella Jean, and a good grandmother to me. She has worked hard at several jobs over the years until her retirement in 1980. She still does sewing in the home and occasionally does part-time work. Over the last two years she has concentrated on caring for my granddaddy who has cancer. We all hope and pray that my granddaddy's health will improve in the days ahead.

Sources: Interviews with family members, family Bible, and personal knowledge.

— Alan Grant Whittington

THE WILES (WILDS) FAMILY
1089

On August 5, 1820, Abraham Wiles (Wilds) applied for his pension as a former soldier of the American Revolutionary War. Wiles attested his age to be 58 years at this time. Wiles enlisted in the Delaware infantry on August 2, 1776, which was less than a month after the signing of the American Declaration of Independence. Possibly the name change from "Wilds" to "Wiles" was a result of an error within his military records. Abraham was totally illiterate, and therefore, would not have recognized the error.

Within his affidavit of 1820, Wiles declared that he was at the capture of Cornwallis at the Town of Little York in Virginia; that he was in a skirmish and wounded on Goose Creek in South Carolina; and that on his return home, the wagon he was driving ran over his feet and disabled him so that he could march no further, this being the reason he remained in North Carolina.

Wiles further attested that he presently owned 150 acres of poor land for which six years ago he paid only $20 and that sum in cattle. Also, he owned one small horse creature and a colt; two calves, two cows, and two yearlings; fifteen hogs — but for the two or three months passed, he has seen only three of them; a few sheep; one good pot and a few old chairs; a water pail and a milk piggin; five pewter plates, five delft plates, an old pewter dish; and one old table.

Wiles listed his occupation as that of farmer and breaker or dresser of flax. His children totaled six — three girls and three boys, namely: Betsy and Suekey, of age; William, age 15; Rachel, age 13; Evan, age 11; and Thomas, age 9. We must assume that his wife, Winnie, had died prior to 1820.

We know that Abraham Wiles was a native of Kent County, Delaware. His mother was named Mary and his father was also named Abraham. Abraham is believed to have married Winnie Auberry. Wiles died after 1837 and was buried in the family cemetery which is located in present-day Wiles Ridge in Wilkes County.

William Wiles was b. 1805, the eldest son of Abraham and Winnie Auberry Wiles. William married Nancy Richardson, daughter of Joseph Richardson. William and Nancy had children as follows: Sarah Wiles Brewer; Winnie Wiles Walters; Nancy Wiles Gillispie; Wilborn Wiles; and William Wiles, Jr., who was killed during the Civil War at Hanover Court-

one acre farm in Millers Creek.

In 1917 Grant attended Oak Grove School. He went to school five days a week and often rode to school in a wagon. In 1919 when Grant was about to enter the third grade, Oak Grove School and Millers Creek consolidated into Millers Creek School. Grant went to school until 1926, completing one half year of the ninth grade.

In 1926 Grant went to work at Oak Furniture Company in North Wilkesboro. He rode to work in his Dad's T-Model Ford. For the next several years Grant worked at different jobs, taking each job because it would pay more than the job he presently had.

In September 1929, while attending the Wilkes County Fair, Grant met Ella Mae Burgess, born February 13, 1915, the fourth child of George W. and Maro A. Burgess of the Mulberry Community. Grant and Ella Mae got married in York, South Carolina on June 21, 1930. To this union was born two children: (1) Thomas Ray, born July 24, 1932 at the John C. Whittington homeplace in Millers Creek. He married Nancy Carol Woodruff; children: Alan Grant and Diane Carol; (2) Ella Jean, born November 22, 1934, at the Maro A. Burgess Wyatt homeplace in Mulberry. She married William Kyle Eller; children: Gregory Alan and Lee Ann.

In 1939 Grant built his first home on a one acre section of land his daddy let him have. The house cost $350 to build. The land was not deeded until 1942 when Grant sold the house and land to his brother Andrew.

From 1939 to 1942 Grant worked as a mechanic at Gaddy Motor Company in North Wilkesboro. In 1942 Grant and Ella Mae bought a house in Millers Creek from the Gilbert Foster Family. They lived in that house for thirty-one years until 1973 when they bought a newer house just next door, owned by their son Thomas R. Whittington.

When World War II began Grant decided to do defense work. In 1943 he went to Newport News, Virginia and in 1944 he went to Baltimore, Maryland until the war ended in 1945. While Grant was away doing defense work, Ella Mae stayed home and cared for the children. She did so for a year and then she decided to join Grant in Baltimore so she left the children, Thomas Ray and Ella Jean with John C. and Etta K. Whittington.

When the war ended, Grant and Ella Mae returned home. Grant got a job as a mechanic at the Millers Creek Motor Company. He held this job for one year. In September 1946 he was hired as Service Manager at Motor Service Sales Company in North Wilkesboro. He held this job until his retirement in December of 1976.

Just before his retirement in December 1976, the management of Motor Service Sales Company honored Grant with a dinner to recognize his thirty years of service to the company. Grant was praised for his work and received many gifts, including a gold watch.

Since my granddaddy's retirement, he has kept himself busy. He enjoys working around the house, working in the garden, he goes fishing occasionally and he enjoys helping family members and friends with odd jobs. Granddaddy and Grandmother enjoy going to Myrtle Beach once each summer.

On June 21, 1980, Grant and Ella Mae celebrated their 50th wedding anniversary. This was a very big event for our family. I guess it seemed more like a family reunion because almost everyone related to the Whittington and Burgess families attended, including five living generations of the Whittington family. They are: Etta Kilby Whittington, 1891; T. Grant Whittington, 1911; Thomas R. Whittington, 1932; Alan G. Whittington, 1954; and Sarah A. Whittington, 1979.

Ella Mae Burgess Whittington has always

Robert M. and Angeline Wheatley Wiles daughter, Beatrice; granddaughter, Estelle.

house in Virginia.

William Wiles was active in organizing the first public school in his district. In 1841, he was named to the 32nd District School Committee of Wilkes County. The enrollment in the school was 32 students. William later taught school in Wilkes County. Wiles died in 1862, possibly a victim of the Civil War as was his son, William, Jr.

Wilborn Wiles (1830-1897), married Mary Ann Walker (1833-1874). The marriage of Wilborn and Mary Ann yielded children as follows: Robert M. Wiles (1857-1932), married Angeline Wheatley (1858-1929); Alice Caroline Wiles (1866-1924), married Columbus Walker; Jessie Franklin Wiles (b. 1861), married Francis Pamelia Springer. This marriage resulted in 14 children. Jessie and his family lived in Boone County, Texas and Lowry, Arkansas; James Oscar Wiles (1865-1942), married Martha Ann Walker; Joseph Thomas Wiles (1869-1946), married Rebecca Jane Waddell; and Ambrose Wiles (1871-1949), married Alice Prevette. Wilborn Wiles is buried in the New Covenant Baptist Church cemetery at Hays, North Carolina.

Robert M. Wiles (1857-1932) married Angeline Wheatley (1858-1929) on January 27, 1877. Ths couple grew up as children of the Civil War era. Robert (Bob) Wiles was a very articulate man. He took great pride in keeping his buggy and other possessions in immaculate condition. Children born to Robert and Angeline were as follows: Mary Ann (1878-1953), married Issac Wintfry Pruitt (1869-1942); Martha Ann (b. 1879), married Charlie Pruitt; Beatrice (b. 1899), married Granville Billings; Cicero (b. 1881), married Dora Blackburn and Pearl Viola Garris (b. 1888) married Walter Gentry; Lura (b. 1886), married Luther Chipman; and Dora (b. 1884), married James Wood.

Sources: Wilkes County records, personal knowledge and interviews with family members.

— G. Rex Barker

ABRAHAM WILES
1090

Abraham Wiles was born 1760, birth place unknown. From the Delaware Archives a payroll account of Captain Mathew Manlove lists Abraham Wiles as a private in the Flying Camp Battalion of the Delaware Blues of the Delaware Line. From the records it appears that Abraham's father was also Abraham Wiles and his mother was Mary. Mary Wiles signed for Abraham as his guardian for his pay.

Abraham Wiles first appeared in Wilkes County census, living on Little Elkin Creek. He owned a small farm there but sold it and moved to the Wiles Ridge area south of Traphill. He was crippled near the end of the war and after that was never able to do hard work. He hired out as a flax breaker for extra income.

He applied for a pension in 1818 and was awarded a Bounty Land Warrant for 640 acres of land. He was put on the rolls to receive 96.00 per year pension.

Abraham's wife was Winnie Auberry, probably the daughter of either Thomas or John Auberry. Abraham died after 1837 and is buried on his farm in the family cemetery in an unmarked grave and at this time there is no visible sign of a graveyard there.

Abraham and Winnie had the following children: (1) Elizabeth born 1800, married Charles Adams December 8, 1835. She had three children before she married Charles Adams; (2) John married a Sarah or a Nancy; (3) William, born 1803, died 1862, married Nancy Richardson, daughter of Joseph Richardson; (4) Rachel, born 1807, married Levi Waddell April 1, 1828; (5) Evan born August 10, 1809, married Mary Prevette, daughter of Williford and Susanah Durham Dawson Prevette; (6) Susanna born 1804, married Thomas Burchfield November 14, 1821; (7) Thomas married Elizabeth Ellis.

Evan Wiles, son of Abraham and Winnie Wiles was born August 10, 1909, married Mary Prevette December 6, 1830, daughter of Williford and Susanah Prevette. Susannah had first married William Dawson who died after three years, leaving her with a small son. Williford Prevette was appointed guardian to this son after their marriage.

Evan and Mary lived on Roaring River below the present Bethany Ford bridge. They had a small farm and a mill, but a flood washed the mill away. He deserted his family in the late 1860s and was said to have gone to some western state to never return, leaving Mary to rear her family alone. Mary was born November 10, 1809, and died September 19, 1894. She is buried in the Bethel Baptist Church cemetery near Hays.

Evan and Mary had the following children: (1) Elizabeth, born 1831, died February 23, 1916, buried in the Coffey Cemetery near Hays, who married Jeremiah Salmons and they had several children; (2) Ambrose, born August 25, 1832, died February 14, 1913, who married Rebecca Garner, daughter of William and Sarah Lee Garner, and had a family and are buried in Bethel Church cemetery, Hays; (3) Elvira, born February 10, 1835, died

1927, married Spencer Blackburn, born 1831, died 1919, who lived in the Rock Creek community near Hays and had a family; (4) Malinda born 1837, died June 6, 1891, married James Brewer, son of Joel and Nancy Adams Brewer and had a family, and after James' death, she married John Emerson and had one son; (5) Emoline, born June 5, 1840, married Elisha Porter, and had two children, and after Elisha was killed in the Civil War Emoline married his brother, William Porter and moved to Ashe County; (6) Hirum, born April 30, 1843, died September 10, 1914, married Sarah Ann Brewer, daughter of Joel and Nancy Adams Brewer, of whom both are buried at Liberty Grove Baptist Church east of North Wilkesboro; (7) Alexander A. born 1845, died December 1, 1926, married Martha James and lived in Ashe Country on Horse Creek where they are buried, and had a son, Wiley; (8) John W., born 1853, died 1929, married first Martha Emerson and had two children, after which he went to Ashe County and married Elizabeth Wilcox, and fathered seven more children.

Sources: Family papers, Wilkes County records, Revolutionary War accounts, Delaware Archives.

— Samuel E. Sebastian

DOCTOR GORDON WILES
1091

Our grandfather, Doctor Gordon Wiles, was born December 28, 1877 to William Callaway (1854-1904) and Elizabeth Johnson Wiles (1845-1917). He had three brothers; Adam (1879-1956), Eli (1883-1956), and Crealy (1885-1955). Mr. Wiles was not actually a physician but was named for a country doctor.

Doctor Gordon Wiles was united in marriage with Nancy Caroline Myers, daughter of Reverend and Mrs. William Waters Myers, on August 16, 1905. To this union nine children were born, six of whom survive; Elsie Wiles Felts, Cecil, Mable Wiles Meadows, Edna Wiles Winters, Lois Wiles Handy, and Clarence "Doc". Deceased are Syble who died at the age of two, Polly Anna who died of pneumonia at eleven years of age, and Cyrus Gordon, who died at the age of fifty-six.

Our grandfather attended the public schools of Wilkes County and later entered the Georgia-Alabama Business College of Macon, Georgia, where he graduated March 4, 1902. Following his graduation he taught school in Wilkes County for several years.

Grandfather Wiles moved in 1907 from Hays, N.C. to North Wilkesboro and resided there until his death November 15, 1923. For thirteen years he served his fellow man as a postal clerk having served as a rural and letter carrier. Perhaps his most interesting time was spent as he served as a railway mail clerk sorting the mail while riding the train from North Wilkesboro to Washington, D.C. In this capacity he was faithful, trustworthy, and efficient. During bad weather he rode horseback or walked, and in 1914 he bought a T-Model to help in the mail delivery. At that time, he was one of the few people in North Wilkesboro to own a car. He used his T-Model not only for

Doctor Gordon Wiles.

delivery of the mail but also to transport family and friends in their times of need.

At the age of twenty, Grandfather Wiles became a Christian, uniting with the Covenant Baptist Church at Dockery. Later he moved his membership to the First Baptist Church of North Wilkesboro. He was faithful to his church in every way, never missing a service, and always taking his family. He was a member of the choir, a teacher in Sunday School, and general secretary of the three young people's unions.

He was one of North Wilkesboro's most popular citizens and was beloved by all who knew him. He was also highly respected as a government official. Grandfather Wiles was a member of Lodge No. 67, Knights of Pythias, and at his death was laid to rest with Pythian honors.

Sources: *CARTER'S WEEKLY,* (1922) family records and family memories.

— Freida Felts Matthews

Ernest and Maude Combs Wiles (1912).

ERNEST WILES FAMILY
1092

My daddy, Ernest Wiles, was born on November 16, 1892 in Wilkes County to William Calvin and Julia Bauguess Wiles. He was a brother of Oid, Millard, Grant, and Sina Combs Wood. Their homeplace and a portion of the land is presently owned by Edsel Wiles.

His formal education was in a one-room school, the main learning tool was the *Blue Back Speller,* and all of his written work was done on slate with a slate pencil.

My daddy married Maude Ellen Combs, born September 19, 1894, of the Shepherd's Crossroads community. My mother always fondly remembered getting married in a buggy on November 5, 1911 and then proceding directly to Rachel Baptist Church for church service. They lived for a short time with my grandfather Wiles before "setting up house-keeping" across the hill from him.

Daddy was a versatile man with many abilities. He built all of his buildings, did repair work, and farmed to provide for our family. His main source of income was from tobacco, wheat, corn, peas, and eggs. Our farm produced everything we needed except salt, sugar, coffee, clothings, gas, and oil. We had a variety of fruit trees, grapes, and vegetables. We kept cows, hogs, chickens, turkeys and bees. Our workhorse "Dave" helped to provide for our family, as well as being a pet. He was retired after daddy got his tractor.

Everyone had to work hard, and social life consisted of church, "corn shuckings," "bean stringings," "molasses making" and vigils at the tobacco barn. "Ice cream suppers" were a big event, having to travel to North Wilkesboro to purchase the large containers packed in ice, and since there was no electricity you had to eat it that day. All the

neighbors were invited to share this rare treat. One year, a hail storm destroyed our tobacco crops and we had enough hailstones to make homemade ice cream.

When the threshing machine traveled through the neighborhood, the men helped each other work, feeding grain through the machine and stacking straw, while the women cooked to fill large tables with food. A person was considered a big eater if he could eat as much as a thresher.

Although daddy was primarily a farmer, in his early years of marriage, he worked at Chatham Manufacturing Co. and at R.J. Reynolds Tobacco Co. Travel was a hardship due to poor roads, lack of transportation, and distance. He usually had to walk to Elkin and travel by train to Winston-Salem after walking to Roaring River. He also carried mail to North Wilkesboro in Model T Ford on his return brought back mail to be delivered. Usually someone would want to ride with him or send for something they needed. When the roads were impassable, he rode a mule.

Christian Home Baptist Church was an important part of my parents' life. My mother was a charter member when the church was organized in 1937. My father was a deacon and served as Sunday School teacher, church clerk, and choir leader.

Daddy lived most of his life in the northern fork of Roaring River. Mother and daddy moved to the Mountain View Community in January 1955 where he was a poultry farmer until he was 77 years of age. Shortly afterwards, his health began to fail and he died on October 30, 1973. Our family and mother still own the original homeplace and 106 acres of land. Our mother, at 87, does her housework and enjoys crocheting and reading.

My parents raised seven children all of whom live in Wilkes:

(1) William Dean Wiles, born July 23, 1915, married Gladys Prevette; had two sons, Rex and Aldean;

(2) Walter Claude Wiles, born July 4, 1918, was fatally injured in an automobile accident on June 23, 1940.

(3) Julia Nina Wiles, born September 18, 1920, and died as an infant in January 1921.

(4) Hazel Maude Wiles, born December 14, 1921, married Beuford T. Sawyer; had three daughters, Marion, Sheila, and Debra, and one son, Bobby.

(5) Brady Ernest Wiles, born April 19, 1925, served in the U.S. Navy during World War II, married Mary Richardson; had three daughters, Brenda, Janice, and Renee.

(6) Boyce Sherman Wiles, born June 27, 1929, served in the Korean conflict U.S. Army, married Billie Sue Baker; had two children, Brian and Susan.

(7) Doris Eileen Wiles, born April 2, 1935, married R.L. Melton; had two sons, Randy and Steven.

Sources: The Wiles Family Bible, personal knowledge and memories and interviews with our mother.

— Doris Wiles Melton

WILLIAM CALVIN WILES
1093

William Calvin Wiles was born in Wilkes County on April 21, 1857 to Joseph (1832-1914) and Diana Combs Wiles (1823-1916). Calvin had three brothers and three sisters: Lanzie J., born 1861, died 1939, married Rausie Ingool; Wilborn born 1867, died 1939, married Janie Prevette; Ambrose born 1874, died 1939, married Rhoda Holloway; Rebecca "Becky," born 1871, died 1958, married Ransom Luffman; Cora, born 1865, died 1946, married J.W. "Bud" Holloway; Mary Ann, born 1861, died 1892, married J.T. Byrd.

Calvin married Tilda Bauguess and one child, Sina, who married Sherman Combs. Shortly after Tilda died, he married her sister Julie Bauguess, who was born October 15, 1860 and died February 18, 1918. Their children were:

Millard born August 3, 1884, died April 4, 1928, married Fannie Stiller (1885-1925). They had four children: Egbert, Aldean, Wallace, and Edna. After Fannie's death, Millard married Alice Absher and had Mildred and Jarvis.

Oid, born January 6, 1891, died March 1976, married Florence Myers and had children: Paul, Van, Edward, Larry, Mary, Ray and May (twins). Oid served as register of deeds of Wilkes County for one term and was deputy sheriff during the term of Bill Somers.

Ernest, born November 16, 1892, died October 30, 1973, married Maude Combs. Their children were Dean, Claude, Julia, Hazel, Brady, Boyce and Doris.

Grant born 1902, died 1964, married Faye Harrold and had: Mina, Coleen, Carol, Benny, Reggie, Danny and Sammy.

My grandfather lived all of his life on the north fork of Roaring River and worked on the land he loved. He was a hard worker and a humorous man.

Sources: Cemetery markers, memory and interviews with family members.

— Doris Wiles Melton

C. Glenn Williams.

THE C.G. WILLIAMS FAMILY
1094

Columbus Glenn Williams was the youngest child of Michael Columbus and Susanna Greenwood Williams. He was born May 21, 1900. He attended a private school in North Wilkesboro. When he was only 16 years old his father died. He keenly felt the responsibility for the care of his mother. He remained on the farm and helped with this operation.

The farm was in a beautiful valley on the Yadkin River with large river bottoms that grew some of the best corn found anywhere. There was also good pasture land for cattle and horses to graze. This area is covered with water from the Kerr Scott Reservoir now. Large patches of watermelons were also grown. They were the sweetest, best melons you can possibly imagine.

Glenn grew to be a handsome, young man with wavy, brown hair and was a much sought after young man. His choice was Frances Agnes Jones, the daughter of Robert and Mollie Jones. They were married on April 5, 1923 by the Reverend Milton McNeil.

They built a home on the farm in Goshen and here they reared their two daughters:

Mary Susanna was born July 14, 1928. She attended W.C.U.N.C. and upon graduation married Louis Brown Dula, Jr. They live on a farm on the James River in Amherst Co., Va. They have three children: Louis Brown Dula III who now lives in California; Susanne, who is married to Bo Saunders and lives in Washington, DC; and Michael Williams Dula who graduated from Dartmouth College and is presently getting his Doctor's Degree at the Univ. of Va.

The other daughter, Nancy Ruth is written up in the J. Arnold Simpson family story.

Glenn enjoyed hunting in his younger years. Later, he found fishing to be an enjoyable sport. He especially enjoyed the cattle he grew on his farm.

Frankie Jones Williams.

He was a very kind and generous man to all who knew him. He adored his grandchildren and visited them almost every day. One of his favorite gifts for them was a pony complete with cart. He was an honest man and trusted others.

It pained him deeply to see his beautiful farm flooded with water and on June 5, 1962 he died from a heart attack.

Frankie grew up in the Mt. Pleasant and Lewis Fork Communities. She attended Mt. View Institute and later Lenoir Rhyne College. She has been an outstanding teacher in Wilkes County. She started her teaching career in 1922 and taught every year but one until she retired in 1969. She probably has the longest teaching career of anyone in Wilkes County with her 46 years of teaching. She was a most dedicated person to her profession. During this career she taught the first through the fifth grades in a one teacher school at Goshen. She also has taught at Denny, Ferguson and North Wilkesboro.

Her other interest include playing the piano. At one time she was the organist in her church. She also taught Sunday School. She loves flowers and seems to have a green thumb as they respond to her touch.

She has a warm personality and is very devoted to her family. Many friends will attest how faithful she is in visiting and caring for those who are ill or in need.

She presently lives in her home in the Goshen Community.

Sources: Personal knowledge.

— Mrs. J. Arnold Simpson

JOHN BIDWELL WILLIAMS
1095

John Bidwell Williams, son of William Vance and Mary Ann Dula Williams was born in Iredell County 1892 and died 1959. Bid came to Wilkes County as a young man to work in the post office. Later he became conductor on the Watauga and Yadkin Railroad.

In 1919 he became secretary-treasurer of the North Wilkesboro Building and Loan Association. During that period he was also engaged in the insurance business and was a member of the Insurance Service and Credit Corporation.

Bid was associated with many organizations and civic groups. He helped organize The Wilkes Chamber of Commerce and was the first president.

He was a charter member and first secretary of the North Wilkesboro Kiwanis Club and later served as president. He was a Mason, member of Junior Order Knights of Pyhias, Dokies Club and First Baptist Church. He was a member for 24 years of North Wilkesboro School Board. He was also a leader in securing the 100-bed Wilkes General Hospital.

He married Susie E. Hutchens from Georgia. They had one daughter, Mary Margaret, who died at an early age. His wife, Susie, and three sisters, Nellie Powell, Jetta Dykstra and Della Holt are still living.

Sources: Family Bible, newspaper and personal knowledge.

— Dorothy Powell Gray

THE M.C. WILLIAMS FAMILY
1096

Michael Columbus Williams was born June 23, 1852 to Michael and Anne E. Boggs Williams. The family moved from Randolph Co. when Lum (as he was called) was about two years old in 1854. The farm they purchased on the Yadkin River is now covered by water from the Kerr Scott Reservoir.

Lum was not a large man in build. He was probably about 5'10'' in height. In later years he had a moustache.

He married a beautiful young girl, Susanna Greenwood on Jan. 24, 1882. She was the daughter of John and Sarah Money Greenwood.

Susanna and Lum were the parents of six children. Walter J. was born April 5, 1883 and died when two years old on Aug. 25, 1885.

Ida Lily was born Nov. 10, 1884. She married Walter Blume Carlton Nov. 6, 1901. Their two daughters were named Sue and Agnes. Most of their married life was lived in Winston-Salem. Ida died Aug. 19, 1955.

Mary Anna (Mamie) was born Aug. 15, 1886. She married Dr. Frank H. Gilreath on Nov. 5, 1902. They had one son, Esmarch, who was head of the Chemistry Dept. of Washington and Lee University. Mamie died on Feb. 10, 1975.

Louis Michael was born Sept. 5, 1889. He remained unmarried and died Dec. 8, 1947.

Nannie Naomi was born Aug. 24, 1893. She graduated from the Univ. of NC in Greensboro (present name), taught school at Goshen and cared for her mother in her later years. She married Andy Roberts. She died Nov. 29, 1975 and was a much loved person by her nieces.

Columbus Glenn was born May 21, 1900. On April 5, 1923, he married Frances Agnes (Frankie) Jones. Glenn died June 5, 1962. They had two daughters, Mary Sue and Nancy.

Michael Columbus was adored by the grandchildren who knew him. Sue and Agnes Carlton remember visiting him on his farm each summer. He allowed them to pick their choice of his calves. When the calf was sold, the money was theirs to enjoy. He loved children and must have enjoyed this tradition as much as they did.

He had a good sense of humor and it was hard to get the best of him with a joke. He was an honest, honorable man, well thought of and respected in his community. He and his family belonged to the Methodist Church.

His wife, Susanna, was fairly tall and quite slender. She was rather quiet and a very gently and genteel lady. She was both considerate and thoughtful of others. Her daughter-in-law, who lived next door, is highly complimentary of her. She was very patient and even-tempered and was never heard to raise her voice.

Mr. and Mrs. M.C. Williams.

As M.C. died on Oct. 28, 1916, Susanna had quite a responsibility in looking after the large farm they owned. She was an excellent manager.

Esmarch Gilreath, her grandson who spent his life among highly educated and brilliant college professors, paid her a high compliment. When asked to describe her he replied, "She was the most intelligent woman that I have ever known."

As a grandchild who lived next door and only knowing her as a child would know her, I had seen her as a grandmother who enjoyed reading nursery rhymes and stories to my sister and me. She was truly a remarkable and courageous woman with a quiet, unassuming but dignified manner.

She died March 19, 1945 and both she and my grandfather are buried in the Williams Family Cemetery in the Goshen Community.

Sources: Personal knowledge.

— Mrs. J. Arnold Simpson

MICHAEL WILLIAMS FAMILY
1097

Michael Williams was born April 7, 1800 in Randolph County. He was the son of Daniel and Nancy E. Cole Williams and the grandson of William and Mary Williams and Stephen and Sarah Cole of Randolph County.

He married his first wife, Martha Miller in 1823. They had one son Jesse A. (1829-1879) before Martha's death.

On Oct. 12, 1842, Michael married again. He chose Evanna (Anna E.) Boggs as his second wife. She was born Nov. 15, 1814, the daughter of John and Martha Mendenhall Boggs. She was named Evanna for her grandmother, Evanna Springer (daughter of Uriah and Margaret Springer) who married John Boggs, Sr.

Michael and Evanna lived on the Uwarie River. Their first six children were born in Randolph and the last two were born in Wilkes. They moved to Wilkes in 1854. The farm they purchased in the Goshen area must have reminded them of the one they had left. They had moved due to an out break of malaria and thought Wilkes would be healthier for their family.

Their children were Nancy Emily (July 24, 1843 — June 30, 1905); Benjamin Franklin (Oct. 28, 1844 — April 19, 1921) married Mary Ann Barlow; Sarah Mahaley (Aug. 28, 1846 — Feb. 8, 1913); Martha Jane (Aug. 14, 1848 — Mar. 3, 1924) married Thomas Greenwood; Daniel Whitson married Mary Powell; Michael Columbus (June 23, 1852 — Oct. 28, 1916) married Susanna Greenwood; Mary Elizabeth (1854) married first Jones Roberson, second Robert Shuping; Susan married Callaway Parlier.

Michael died at the age of 74 on Nov. 9, 1874. Anna died at the age of 79 on Jan. 8, 1894. Both are buried in the Williams Family Cemetery at Goshen.

Sources: Marriage bonds, census records, family knowledge, Rev. War records, deeds and wills.

— Mrs. J. Arnold Simpson

PATRICK MURPHY WILLIAMS FAMILY
1098

Pat Williams was a master-salesman with a repetoire of jokes and an affinity for telling them. He was close to his God and conversed with Him regularly, both privately and publicly.

Patrick Murphy Williams.

He never missed church on Sunday mornings and was known as a great Sunday School Teacher and a "keeper-of-the-time" during the sermon. (At 12:01 "Mr. Pat" would leave the church!) He was a curious blend of the intellectual and the earthy. It was debatable whether he was happier working in his vegetable garden, clad in khaki pants, suspenders and a big towel to mop his brow, or picking blackberries while listening to his beloved beagles chase a rabbit.

Well known in Wilkes County for attending the high school football games and planting walnut trees in memory of his deceased friends, Pat Williams was an outspoken teetotaler, an enthusiastic square dancer, a person who could laugh at himself, and one who could make any stranger feel at home. Without a doubt, Pat Williams added much "local color" to the Wilkes County of his time.

Patrick Murphy Williams was born Feb. 6, 1884 at Taylors Bridge, Sampson Co., N.C. He was one of twelve children born to Lou Murphy and Charles Judson Williams. His maternal great, great-grandmother and father, Elizabeth Kelso and Patrick Murphy came to the U.S. in 1774 from the Isle of Aaron, Scotland. His paternal great, great-grandmother and father, Philadelphia and John Williams arrived in the U.S. in 1783 and settled in Chatham Co., N.C.

Pat graduated from the University of N.C. in 1908 following which he taught school in Burgaw, N.C. for 3 years. In 1912, he joined his older brother, Charlie, in working for Moore Dry Kiln Co., in Jacksonville, Fla. which manufactured equipment for drying lumber. Pat first came to North Wilkesboro in 1914 to install dry kilns for Forest Furniture Co.

While attending the Presbyterian Church he met Mary Louise Finley. In 1916 they were married in the Presbyterian Church by Rev. C.W. Robinson. They lived all their married life at the corner of E and 10th Street. Pat was selling dry kilns to furniture and lumber manufacturers in the Atlantic States. In 1917, Pat was commissioned a 1st Lt. in the Army and was assigned the job of building dry kilns for the Army in France. After the war, Pat returned to his profession and lived in North Wilkesboro until his death in 1962.

The descendants of Louise and Patrick M. Williams are:

Mary Gwyn Williams (1918-1975) married Frederick C. Hubbard Jr. Their children are: Frederick C. Hubbard III, born 1939, married first Lorraine Henderson, and second Joan; His children are Richard Scott born 1965, Joel Todd born 1967; Jeffrey McRae born 1972; Richard Finley Hubbard born 1945; Ann Gwyn Hubbard born 1948, married James H. Carter and has Julia Gwyn born 1978; and James Calloway born 1979. Michael Williams Hubbard born 1949.

Patrick Murphy Williams, Jr. born 1921, married Dorothy Skinner. Their children are: Ann Bryant born 1950 married Robert A. Brinson and has Robert Williams Brinson born 1981; Mary Gwyn born 1952 married Peter S. Levy; Patrick Murphy III, born 1954 married first Jane Terry; Susan Skinner born 1963.

Charles Judson Williams III, born 1925, married first Jacqueline Chalmers. They have Charles Judson, IV. born 1951, John Chalmers born 1953, married Peggey Sue Lamb; David Finley born 1956, married Lisa Olsen; Robert Wood born 1959, married second Estelle Jones 1973.

Sources: Personal knowledge.

— Pat M. Williams

WILLIAM VANCE and MARY DULA WILLIAMS
1099

William Vance Williams was born in Iredell County September 5, 1860, the son of O.G. Williams and Mary Chenault.

William Vance married Mary Ann Dula, daughter of Lowery and Martha Jane Harris Dula of the Ferguson Community, Wilkes County. To this marriage 13 children were born, of whom 9 lived.

(1) John Bidwell, born 1892 married Susie E. Hutchens. They had one daughter, Mary Margaret who died very young. Bidwell died 1959. (2) Lowery Dula born 1896, died 1920. (3) Beulah Jane born 1897, married Steel Frazier Horton. They had four daughters: Doretha, Mary, Betty and Jean. Steel died 1926. Beulah later married Arnold Gettle. She died 1972.

(4) Nellie Vance born 1900, married James Wright Powell. To them was born one son, Jay Wright and two daughters, Dorothy Lee and Martha Bidwell. Nellie Vance still lives in Wilkesboro. (5) Jetta Mae born 1902, married Ralph Laxton and John Dykstra. Jetta lives in Gastonia, N.C. (6) Mary Lucy born 1906, married Paul Withers. Mary Lucy died 1978.

(7) Crystal Syler born 1907, married

Carolyn Taylor. They had one son, John. Crystal died 1965. (8) Della and Ella were born 1911. Ella died when she was 4 months old. Della married Ed Hulse. They had one son, Ed, and one daughter, Mary. Della later married Seaton Holt, Jr. (9) Malvina Isadore born 1916, married Fred Hankerson. She died 1968 in St. Louis, Missouri with burial in Mountlawn Cemetery.

William Vance and Mary Ann moved to Wilkes County in 1901. They lived in North Wilkesboro until 1914 when they moved to Ferguson. He ran a country store and was depot agent for Wachovia and Yadkin Railroad Company. They moved back to North Wilkesboro after the 1916 flood.

William Vance died at his home on C Street, North Wilkesboro 1920. Mary Ann died at her home on D Street, North Wilkesboro 1940. William Vance and Mary Ann are buried in the Greenwood Cemetery in North Wilkesboro along with their children, Bidwell, Lowery, Ella and Crystal.

William Vance and Mary Ann had 11 grandchildren (10 still living), 19 great-grandchildren and 6 great-great-grandchildren. One granddaughter, Dorothy Powell Gray, one great-grandson, William C. Gray, Jr. and one great-great-grandson, William C. Gray, III are living in Wilkes County.

Sources: Family Bible, newspapers and personal knowledge.

— Dorothy Powell Gray

TOM, NANCY and TOMMY WILLIAMSON
1100

Thomas Clay Williamson, Sr. was born 6 Sept. 1942 in Thomasville, N.C., son of Alex Graham and Mary Valentine Williamson. His parents moved to Clinton, Sampson County, N.C. in 1944, where Tom grew up. After graduation from Taylor's Bridge-Ingold High School in 1960, he joined the U.S. Air Force. While serving in the Air Force, he married 16 Sept. 1962 Nancy Scott Snipes. They lived in Roswell, N. Mex. In 1964 they returned to Clinton, N.C.

Tom attended Fayetteville Technical Institute from 1965 through 1968, graduating with an Associate of Applied Science Degree in Civil and Sanitary Engineering Technology. He was employed by the Sampson County Health Department in 1968. In 1972 he was employed by the then N.C. State Board of Health Services as a District Milk Sanitarian. In 1973 they moved to Millers Creek, where they presently live.

Nancy is the daughter of Archie Johnson and Beulah Mae Scott Snipes. She was born 12 July 1942 in Wilmington, N.C., graduated from Taylor's Bridge-Ingold High School in 1960, and is currently employed by the Wilkes County Board of Education as a teacher's aide.

On 31 May 1964, Thomas Clay Williamson, Jr. was born while they were living in New Mexico. Tommy, an honor graduate of West Wilkes High School in 1982 has been active in extracurricular activities including student council representative, vice-president of student council, and photographer on the annual staff. He was a member of the baseball and basketball teams. He enjoys music and has played the saxophone in the West Wilkes Band for seven years. He was drum major his senior year and received the annual Arian award.

Tommy will enter at N.C. State University in the Fall of 1982 and plans to major in mechanical engineering.

Tom, Nancy and Tommy are members of the Millers Creek United Methodist Church and are active in both school and community activities.

Sources: Personal knowledge.

— Thomas C. Williamson, Sr.

WINKLER FAMILY HISTORY
1101

Three brothers came to the United States from Germany and settled in or near Terra Haute, Indiana. Seven years later, about 1785, John Winkler, one of the three, came to Wilkes County. There is no record that states where the other brothers, Thomas and Walter, settled. Some family records indicate that one Winkler was in the Battle of Kings Mountain.

John Winkler married Mary Pennel. They had seven children. They were (1) Abraham who married Polly Matney; (2) Joshua who married Sarah Caroline Pearson; (3) Betsy, who married a Pipes; (4) Sallie who married H. Wheeling; (5) Anderson who married Mattha Matney; (6) Walter; (7) Wiley A. who married Lucinda Dula.

Wiley A. Winkler was born June 26, 1836 and died September 19, 1919. He married Lucinda Dula, born April 25, 1858, died May 8, 1920. They lived on a large farm three miles from Wilkesboro, on the north side of the Yadkin River. During the 1916 flood they had to go up the upstairs of their house because of the rising waters, where neighbors rescued them. Lucinda had their money and valuable papers tied in a bandana handkerchief. The 1940 flood then destroyed most of the house. They are buried in Union Methodist Church cemetery.

Wiley and Lucinda had two sons; John who died at age fifteen and is buried on a hill on Winkler property, near where the house stood. William Carter Winkler who was born August 22, 1858, died August 15, 1939, married Mary Louisa Bower, born November 17, 1866 in Happy Valley section of Caldwell County, died July 5, 1928.

William Carter Winkler attended Moravian Falls Academy, and she attended Davenport College in Lenoir. Carter managed his farm, inherited from his parents and also two farms in Caldwell County belonging to his wife's family. At one time he manufactured locust pins used on the telephone poles as insulators.

When they were married they moved in their new home, built in 1892 one block from the courthouse in Wilkesboro, which still stands and is occupied by a daughter, Elizabeth Winkler Perkins. The original house was remodeled some years later.

Carter and "Lou" as she was called, had five children: (1) Annie Bower Winkler, married Carson Parlier, son of Calvin and Eliza Ferguson Parlier. They had two sons, William of Charlotte, N.C. and Harry who is deceased. (2) Mildred Louise Winkler, married William Blair Miller, son of Claude and Minnie Smith Miller. William Blair Miller was one of the first twelve Wilkes men to volunteer for service in World War I. They had two children: William Garland, who was killed in Italy in World War II, and Mary Elizabeth who lives in California. (3) John Carter Winkler, married Latha Rhoades. They had five children: Louise, who lives in West Virginia; J.C. who lives in Chicago; Jeanette who lives in Oklahoma; Nancy and Carol who lives in West Virgina. (4) Elizabeth Pauline Winkler, married Bon S. Perkins, son of Dr. S.L. and Flora Shultz Perkins. They had one son, Bon Carter Perkins, who married

Carter Winkler home, Wilkesboro. L. to R: Mamie Wallace Deal: Carter Winkler: Annie Winkler: Lou Bower Winkler: Mary Brown, maid: Matilda Ward Wallace.

Carol Hardin, daughter of Edward and Codie Cooper Hardin. (5) Helen Horton Winkler, married Ray Andy Kennedy, son of Bulo J. and Laura Honeycuut Kennedy.

Sources: Records of Carter Winkler, cemeteries and family Bibles.

— Helen Horton Winkler Kennedy

JOSEPH EDWIN WINKLER
1102

Joseph Edwin Winkler was born 1877 and died in 1927. He was the son of John and Aurelia Vannoy Winkler. He was a Justice of the Peace, Postmaster of Straw P. O., farmer, mechanic and veteran of the Spainish American War.

John and Aurelia Vannoy Winkler also had Blanche Winkler Miller, Bertha Winkler Carr, Finley Winkler and Harrison Winkler.

J. Edwin Winkler married Mollie Stroud (1880-1965) daughter of Thomas and Catherine Sparks Stroud. Their children were: (1) Lella (1903-1923), married Archie McNeil; (2) Nellie married James K. Menefee and had Catherine Menefee (Price) and Mattie Menefee (Rhoades); (3) Walter Edwin Winkler (1906-1977), married Ruth Booker (1909-1981) and had Nancy Winkler (Wilson), Walter Edwin Winkler, Jr. and Thomas Booker Winkler; (4) John Hubert Winkler (1910-1969), married Annie Finley and had John Hubert Winkler, Jr., who married Alice Conway Lucas; Robin Winkler (Naughton), Molly Winkler (Good), and James Gordon Winkler.

Sources: Family records; *Finleys of Wilkes*.

— Annie Finley Winkler

THE WITHERSPOON FAMILY
1103

The Witherspoon's were early settlers and landowners of Wilkes. They settled in Elkville, one mile west of Ferguson. The house still stands, and the Clyde Wheeling family resides there.

My great-grandfather, William Pettigrew Witherspoon, married Nancy Curtis Montgomery, widow of John Montgomery, in April Of 1845. Children of this marriage were:

(1) Sidney Witherspoon, who married Ellen Ballou, daughter of Napoleon Bonaparte Ballou and sister of Jerome Uriah Ballou. After Sideny's death, she married Jesse Davis. Their daughter married Howard Caudill of Ashe County.

(2) Larkin Witherspoon settled in Texas.

(3) William Harrison Witherspoon married Clarissa Pennell of Wilkes County and moved to Ashe County.

(4) Lucius Leroy Witherspoon married Martha Hale of Wilkesboro. Lucius was a noted jurist, having practiced in Newton and Murphy. Their son, Donald, was also a lawyer.

(5) My grandmother, Mary Jane Witherspoon, married Jerome Uriah Ballou of Ashe County, son of Napoleon Ballou, grandson of Owen Meredith Ballou, and great-grandson of Colonel William Ballou, who was sent from England to protect the colonists from the Indians. They lived at the Ballou homeplace on the North Fork of the New River in Crumpler, NC. To this union, fourteen children were born. The youngest son was my father, Victor Eugene Ballou.

(6) Theodosia Witherspoon married A.R. "Dick" Little of Ashe County.

My grandmother, Mary Jane Witherspoon Ballou, told us of many incidents in her young life.

During the Civil War, the Witherspoons had managed to save numerous valuables in burying and hiding them. Livestock had been taken into the mountains to roam and were tended daily by the family. When Reconstruction began, the Witherspoons were invaded by marauding bands of Carpetbaggers who took the family's meats, food, and many other valuables. Aunt Dosia, who had been quite ill for several days, was even picked up from her sickbed and deposited on the floor so the Carpetbaggers could take her bedsheets, pillows, and quilts.

Grandmother also told of Laura Foster's coming by to borrow a saddle. Grandmother thought that the Witherspoons were the last people to see Laura before she journeyed to her tragic death.

I married W. Eugene Shepherd and reside one mile from the Witherspoon home. When I visit there, fond memories of my heritage return.

Sources: Family knowledge.

— Mary Amelia Ballou Shepherd

CURTIS WOODS FAMILY
1104

John Wood, Sr., b. 1775, probably the son of Joseph Wood, Sr., was the father of Anderson Wood of Traphill. He was born in 1803. He was a farmer. He married Agnes Burchette, who was born in 1803. They have five children who settled in the Traphill area: (1) Thomas Wood, b. 1837; (2) Bethania, b. 1839, (3) Hesakiah Anderson, b. 1841; (4) Ruth, b. 1843; (5) Polly, b. 1845.

Hesakiah (Tease) married Nancy Harriet Poplin, whose father was a Money. "Tease" was a blacksmith and a mail carrier. He was well known as a very kind and generous man. He was a large blond man. Tease and Nancy had four children: (1) John Wesley Wood, b. 10/10/1865; d. 5/13/1946, married Alice Pruitt, b. 9/26/1886; d. 6/22/1941. They had four children who were all school teachers: (a) Bertha Bumgarner; (b) Pearl Lyons; (c) Maude Hayes, (d) Orabelle Wagoner. (2) Rhoda, b. 9/25/1868; d. 2/13/1964, married John Wood, son of Wilson Wood, but had no children. (3) Fannie, b. 11/29/1873; d. 10/1/1957. She married Gordon Hutson, who was a merchant in North Wilkesboro. They had no children. She was the stepmother of Queenie Caudill Douglas of North Wilkesboro. (4) Charlie William (Will), b. 10/26/1880; d. 11/20/1967, married Nelia Elizabeth Wood, b. 10/20/1889; d. 1/15/1958. She was the daughter of John Wood and great granddaughter of Samuel Wood.

Will was a farmer, blacksmith, carpenter and occasionally carried the mail for his father.

He also got traveling in his blood and went to Idaho to herd cattle and sheep. He spent about a year there and returned home. They had seven children: (1) Louise Wall; (2) Esta Patterson Zimmerman; (3) Grace Joan English; (4) Ila Wiles; (5) Fred Woods; (6) Mary Landreth; and (7) Curtis L. Woods.

Curtis married Mary Edith Byrd, daughter of Brady and Vesta Wood Byrd of Rock Creek area of Wilkes County. She was also the great, great, great granddaughter of Samuel Wood. Curtis was born 8/4/27. Edith was born 2/10/1928. They were married 10/8/1947. They both attended Mountain View High School and Curtis graduated from Clevenger College in 1950. He is now a self-employed accountant and operates Curtis L. Woods Publishing Company and Star Record Company. He is the composer of numerous gospel and country songs and, at the present, is writing his third book of poetry. He also had the honor of being nominated for Poet Laureate of North Carolina in 1981 and came out second place.

Curtis and Edith have three children: (1) Dennis, who first married Claudia Hagaman and had one child, April (Taylor). He then married Rebecca Osborne and they have three children: Danna, Laura, and Tara. (2) Dalton Woods married Linda Whitley and they had one son, Derek Shaun (Edwards). (3) Mary Elizabeth (Libby) married Albert W. Triplett, Jr. and they have four children: (1) Shari, (2) Albert, Jr. (Sonny), (3) Sally, and (4) Brian.

Sources: Bible record, census.

— Curtis L. Woods

SAMUEL WOOD
1105

Samuel Wood was born 1797, died 7/28/1881, probably the son of John, Sr. and the grandson of Joseph Wood, Sr. He married Elizabeth Naler (Nale) (b. 1795, d. 2/5/1866) on November 20, 1821. Samuel Wood was a very large landowner in the Rock Creek Township area. He also was a slave owner.

Samuel was an early member of Briar Creek Church and in 1821 he and Hardwick Johnson, a minister, and others, requested authorization from Briar Creek Church to start another church known first as Johnsons' Church and then Mountain Church. This church is thought to have been held in a small building at the foot of Little Mountain. Also, the members of this church were the beginning of Rock Creek Church as Samuel was a member of Rock Creek and is also buried there.

Samuel had nine children: (1) Milly Wood, b. 1820; d. 1899; (2) Milicent (Melisa), b. 1824, d. 1910; was mother of Randal Wood; father was Randolph Alexander. She later was married to Alexander Hall. (3) Johnny Wood, b. 1823; (4) Henry Wood, b. 1832, (5) Wilson Wood, b. 1834; (6) Margaret (Peggy), b. 1835, (7) Elizabeth, b. 1849; (8) Rachel, b. 1852; and (9) Leland, b. 1855.

Johnny Wood married Elizabeth (Betsy Lyons) September 17, 1848. She was born 8/25/1824; died 5/31/1906. They were buried at Bethany Church. Johnny was the father of Daniel Wood, who married Frankie Cothren and they had two sons: (1) Thomas Wood; (2) Leander Marshall Wood. Thomas Wood married Mary Elizabeth (Betty) Martin and they had eight children. Thomas was a devout member of Bethany Church and a deacon for many years. He was also considered one of the best carpenters of his day. His daughter, Vesta, married Brady Byrd in March of 1921 and they had eight children. Their daughter, Edith, married Curtis L. Woods, who also is a great, great grandson of Samuel Wood.

Henry Wood, born 1832, married Alvira. They had one daughter, Elizabeth.

Wilson Wood, born 1834, married Mary McCurry and they had three children: (1) Ellen (Sis), b. 12/14/1861, mother of Garfield Wood, whose father was Martin Myers. Sis died 4/13/1897. (2) John Wood; (3) Daniel.

John Wood (son of Wilson Wood), b. 12/3/1865; d. 3/21/1940, married Louisa Brown, b. 1867; d. 4/13/1903. John was a farmer, merchant, and owned a mill. They had six children: (1) Nelia; (2) Lawson; (3) Monroe; (4) McKinley; (5) Mary Roberts; (6) Tempie Garris.

John married Rhoda Wood, b. 9/25/1868; d. 2/13/64 after the death of his first wife. They had no children. Nelia Elizabeth, daughter of John Wood and Louisa Brown was born 10/20/1889; d. 1/15/1958, married Charlie William (Will) Wood, b. 10/26/1880; d. 11/20/1967. He was the great grandson of John Wood, Sr., father of Anderson Wood (See John Wood, Sr.). They had seven children: (1) Louise Wall; (2) Esta Patterson Zimmerman; (3) Grace Joan English; (4) Ila Wiles; (5) Fred Woods; (6) Mary Landreth; (7) Curtis Woods.

Curtis L. Woods, b. 8/4/1927, married Mary Edith Byrd, b. 3/10/1928, and they have three children. Curtis is an accountant, writer and composer. See Curtis L. Woods Family.

Sources: Family Bible, Wilkes records, census reports.

— Curtis L. Woods

THE WRIGHT FAMILY
1106

William Williams Wright was born 26 February 1791, in Surry County, the fifth child of Thomas and Mary Clanton Wright. He was 16 years of age when his father Thomas, served as State Senator from Surry County, 1807-1808, then again from 1810-1817. At the age of 24 he married his 1st cousin, Sarah/Sally Martin, the daughter of Dr. Robert and Amelia Wright Martin, of Wilkes County, Sarah/Sally, was born 15 September 1794, and was 21 at the time she married William Williams. The family of William Williams appears on the Wilkes County Census Roll 1820, listing four children in his household.

Sometime druing the next few years (Probably around 1823) William Williams and his wife and five young sons (David Ralph was born in 1822) journied to Madison County, Alabama. Proof of this family having been in Madison County, Alabama, is evidenced by a deed, dated 2 April 1827, in which Dr. Robert Martin of Wilkes County, (father of Sarah/Sally) deeded "my negro girl Rachel and the heirs of her body, the wife of William W. Wright of

Madison County, Alabama." (Madison County Deed Book L, p. 105).

William Williams and his family appear on the Madison County Census Roll of 1830. By this time he has two more children, Amelia Matilda, born 1824, and James William, born 1826.

William Williams and Sarah/Sally were back in Wilkes County by 1840, as his family appears on the Wilkes County Census Roll, listing 5 children: James William, John, Thomas, William M, Amelia Matilda, and 1 female between 5 and 10, presumabbly his niece, Sarah M., granddaughter of Dr. Robert Martin.

On 11 September 1842, William Williams's father-in-law, Dr. Martin, made his will. (Wilkes County Will Book 4, pps 279-81). "I give and beguaeath unto my daughter Sarah Wright my tract of land known by the name of the squire Parker Tract, whereon Mary Standley now lives, supposed to contain 160 acres to be hers and not to be at the disposal of her husband W.W. Wright and after her death to be equally divided amongst her children together with what I have already given her." It was on this tract of that William Williams and Sarah/Sally built their home where four generations were to live.

William Williams and Sarah/Sally had seven children. 1) Robert Martin, born 8 January 1816, Surry County. Married Amelia Susanna Bell in 1838. Died 9 September 1871, in Wilkes County. 2) John Luther, born 21 September 1817, Surry County. Married Mary Shoffe/Shoaf, 7 June 1838. John died 20 March 1892. 3) Thomas W., born 22 May 1818, Surry County. Married Dianah (Dicy). Died 5 January 1899 in Wilkes County. 4) Williams Martin, born 3 June 1820, in Surry County. Married Adelaide Cauble in 1850. Died 18 April 1899 in Ashe County. 5) David Ralph, born 30 Mary 1822 in Surry County. Died at age of 16, 27 August 1838 in Wilkes County. 6) Amelia Matilda, born 18 April 1824 in Madison County, Alabama. Married 8 October 1850, John M. Brotherton, in Wilkes County. Amelia died 11 January 1903 and is buried in Wilkes County. 7) James William, born 28 February 1826, in Madison County, Alabama. He married Frances Almeda Transou in 1861. Died 31 January 1865, buried at Point Lookout, Maryland.

William Willliams died 4 December 1870. He is buried in the Wright family cemetery at Edgewood Baptist Church, Wilkes County. Sarah/Sally died 13 July 1864, at Hunting Creek, and is buried beside her husband in the family cemetery at Edgewood Baptist Church.

No will has been found for William Williams Wright, the Hunting Creek Plantation passed to his youngest son, James William Wright. The other sons having been married and probably owning land of their own.

Sources: *Frosts and Related Families of Bedford County Tennessee* by Wright W. Frost p. 88. Wilkes County Census Rolls. Tombstone inscriptions. Family Bibles and Wills.

— Mary Doris Wright Gooch

CHARLES CALVIN WRIGHT
1107

Charles Calvin Wright, often known as "Charley Wright," was the only son of James William and Frances Almeda Wright. He was born 14 August 1862, at Hunting Creek, on the farm where he lived until his death in 1933.

Charles Calvin taught school in his home district at Hunting Creek when he was seventeen for the salary of eleven dollars a month, and boarded himself, doing his own cooking. He continued to teach various country schools until he became county superintendent. School terms were from six weeks to three months in length at that time, and the salary was always less than twenty-five dollars a month. He taught two years at Dellaplane in 1895 and again in 1897.

He was appointed postmaster at Hunting Creek before he was twenth-one, but resigned because of his youth. He was elected justice of the peace when he was twenty-one and served ten years. He early became a leader in church work at Edgewood Baptist Church and remained active until his death.

Charley Wright's father died during the Civil War when he was only three years old. The future superintendent of schools was very poor as a boy, and as he was an only child, had to help his mother on the farm. He was educated in the then inadequate public schools, and the private schools of Wilkes. His life was spent almost entirely in school work. Farming had been one of his principal avocations.

As a boy and young man, he was a member of the group known on Hunting Creek, and celebrated in song and story as the "Big Four." Clint Jarvis, widely-known singing school teacher; Andrew Mitchell, school teacher, clerk of the Brier Creek Association and supposed to be the tallest man in Wilkes County; Resen Bell and C.C. Wright composed Hunting Creek's "Big Four". They went to church and to singings, to exhibitions and to parties, to corn shuckings and quiltings and went courting all over the county.

At that time young Wright would teach school in some remote district and escort the girls from his boarding place three or four miles through the snow to an exhibition (the old-fashioned name for a commencement), then always held in February. When he arrived at the entertainment where his talents were known, he would be asked to appear on the program and would respond with an address, an oration or with negro dialogues.

Charles Calvin Wright was Superintendent of Wilkes County Schools for thirty-four years, was elected vice-president of the Brushy Mountain Association for twenty-eight years, superintendent of the Edgewood Baptist church for twenty-six years and held an indeterminable catalogue of other important offices.

Charles Calvin Wright married Jane, Jennie, Catharine Land 23 September 1891. She was the daughter of Col. James Calvin Land of Mount Zion. Charley died 14 July 1933 at Hunting Creek and is buried at Edgewood Baptist Church. Jennie lived with her son, James Thomas Carr Wright in Boone, N.C. until her

L. to R. seated: Charles Calvin Wright, Jr.; Clyde Robert Wright. standing: Charles Calvin Wright, Sr., Jennie Land Wright; David Ralph Wright; James Thomas Carr Wright.

Source: Wilkes County Will Book 5, pg 421-422. Military records, Sexton of Point Lookout, MD. Confederate graveyard. Family Bible. NC Archives, Raleigh, NC. N.C. Troops. Yadkin Co. Will Bk 1 p. 7.

James William made his will and went to Greenville, Pitt County, North Carolina, to join the North Carolina Troops. He was enlisted by Capt. Jarrott, 20 March 1863, for 3 years or the war; 26th Regiment, Company C, as a private, known as The Wilkes Volunteers, or "The Boys from Wilkes".

James William fought with Colonel Robert E. Lee's Army of Northern Virginia, in the defense of Petersburg. He was captured at the Battle of Burgess Mills, 27 October 1864. Transferred to City Point Hospital and then to the Point Lookout Prison for Confederate Soldiers, Maryland. He died 31 January 1865, and is buried in the Confederate soldier cemetery at Point Lookout, Maryland.

James William and Frances had one child, Charles Calvin Wright who inherited the plantation at Hunting Creek.

Frances Almeda died May 18, 1907, and is buried in the Wright Family plot at Edgewood Baptist Church, Wilkes County., NC.

— Mary Doris Wright Gooch

death 20 October 1943. She is buried in the family plot at Edgewood Baptist Church.

Charles Calvin and Jennie Land Wright had five children, as follows: Mary Dorris Wright, born June 30, 1892, Hunting Creek, died April 10, 1913 Wilkesboro, is buried family plot Edgwood Baptist Church. She died of pneumonia while home on Christmas vacation from school in Winston-Salem, N.C. The Doris Wright Memorial fund at North Carolina College for Women at Winston-Salem was instituted by friends in her memory.

James Thomas Carr Wright was born 22 May 1894 at Hunting Creek, married Sinesca Mastin, daughter of Edward Olin Mastin of Wilkes County on 31 May 1917 in the home of Rev. McNeil of Wilkesboro. Carr Wright taught for thirty-four years at Appalachian University in Boone, N.C. and died 14 July 1963 and is buried at Mount Lawn Cemetery, Boone. Carr and Sinesca had three children: Charles Olin of Winston-Salem; Thomas Carr, of Smithfield; and Mary Doris of Winter Park, Fla. Mrs. Wright now resides in Winter Park, near the home of her daughter.

David Ralph Wright, born 3 May 1896 on Hunting Creek, married 1920 Eula Bumgarner. David died April 20, 1966 at North Wilkesboro and is buried in the family plot at Edgewood Baptist Church. David and Eula had two sons, David Ralph, Jr. born 1921, died 1974 and Rev. John Rowland Wright, born 1925 and now resides with his family in Cottondale, Florida.

Clyde Robert Wright, born Apil 12, 1901 at Hunting Creek, married 27 November 1929 Willie Elizabeth Woodruff of Elkin. Clyde died January 1978 and is buried in Elkin. Clyde and Bill had two sons, James Robert, born April 27, 1934, married Elizabeth Johnson. They have three daughters, Sabrina Elizabeth, born August 23, 1957, married Stephen Gregory and have Jeremiah B., born March 25, 1891; Shawn Leigh born February 7, 1968, and Nichole, born June 25, 1970. Joseph Wood-

ruff Wright was born 23 June 1939, married Sandra Shaw. They have a son, Christopher Shaw born May 21, 1968.

Charles Calvin Wright, Jr. was born February 1911 at Hunting Creek, married 19 July 1935 Evelyn Juanita Wilborn of Wadesboro. They were married at Polkton. They have a daughter, Nancy Carole, born October 9, 1942 who married Jerry Ray Blackburn December 19, 1961. Nancy Carole and Jerry Ray have two children, Charles Grant born September 16, 1962, and Charlotte Arden born April 5, 1968. Charles Calvin and Evelyn Juanita Wright live at Elkin, N.C.

The Hunting Creek house of Charles Calvin Wright, Sr. was sold in the early 1940s and burned several years later.

Sources: *Frosts and Related Families of Bedford County, Tennessee* by Wright W. Frost, p. 88; family Bible records; tombstone inscriptions at Edgewood; North Wilkesboro newspaper article by Ruth Linney, family knowledge.

— Mary Doris Wright Gooch

JAMES WILLIAM WRIGHT
1108

James William was the seventh child, and the youngest son of William Williams and Sarah/Sally Wright. He was born in Madison County, Alabama, 28 February 1826. By 1837 or 1893, he returned with his parents to Wilkes County, North Carolina. In 1852 he received a bequest of $150.00 from his Uncle John Wright, which was at that time a very substantial amount of money.

At the age of 35 he married Frances Almeda Transou, born 10 June 1839, daughter of James and Mary Rousseau Transou, of Wilkes County. James William married in 1861, nine years before his father William Williams died (1870), and just as the call to arms rang through both the North and the South . . . the tragic break had come . . . the North and the South had parted and the flames of war crackled ominously.

JOHN McKEE — JOHN WRIGHT FAMILIES
1109

John McKee was born in Ireland in 1766 and fought with Wellington in the Battle of Waterloo in Belgium in 1815. His daughter, Mary, born 23 Sept. 1803, married John Wright (1800-1860) in the Cathedral of Armaugh in North Ireland 10 Aug. 1831. They lived in the parish of Doughall, County of Armaugh. Three children were born in Ireland: Ann Wright Gaither, 30 May 1832; Mary Jane, 20 Nov. 1834; and Joseph, 13 May 1836.

The Wright family with John McKee left Penny Coose, Ireland 10 May 1839. They traveled to Wilmington, N.C., thence through Fayetteville and on to Wilkes County arriving in August or September, 1839. They settled on a 640-acre farm at Millers Creek, lying on both sides of the road running from Wilkesboro to Jefferson in Ashe.

The burial of John McKee on the grounds of what is now Millers Creek United Methodist Church on 17 April 1848 may be considered the beginning of the history of Friendship Church. The five acres of land on which the church was built was donated by his daughter, Mrs. Mary McKee Wright about 1 Dec. 1867. She died in 1892 and a picture of her hangs in Millers Creek Church.

Two Methodist churches, Friendship and Millers Creek, united in Oct. 1952 to form the present Millers Creek Methodist Church which is located on this site about five miles west of North Wilkesboro.

Sources: History of Millers Creek United Methodist Church.

— Mary Edna Gaither Faw

DAVID WYATT FAMILY
1110

As the daughter of a native of Miller's Creek, North Carolina, I have pursued the history of my father's family, James Fred Wyatt. I have been able to establish records of the family back to around 1800.

My great-great grandfahter, David Wyatt, received deeds of land, part of which were land grants on the north fork of Reddies River during 1831, 1837, 1853 respectively, totaling 255 acres. It was in what is called the Vannoy section of Wilkes County.

I am not certain who David's father was or where he came from, but there were families with the surname of Wyatt living Wilkes County as early as the 1780's.

David Wyatt (born ca. 1800), married Amelia "Milly" Wingler on Apr. 22, 1824. Their children were: Leonard Wyatt (born May 24, 1825, died Sept. 26, 1897) married Susanah Owens on Nov. 25, 1865; James Wyatt (born ca. 1826); Wilburn Wyatt (born ca. 1831) married Leonna ?; Sarah Wyatt (born ca. 1831); David Wyatt (born ca. 1833); John Wyatt (born ca. 1835); Franklin Wyatt (born ca. 1831) married Sibbie Dancy (Franklin was my great-grandfather); Jordan Wyatt (born ca. 1839); Malvina (born ca. 1841) married T.J. Royall on Apr. 12, 1867; Sidney Wyatt (born ca. 1843) married Cathy Miller on Aug. 18, 1860; Nathan Wyatt (born ca. 1845); Mary Wyatt (born ca. 1845) married Thomas Handy on July 3, 1864; Milly Wyatt (born ca. 1849).

David Wyatt was a very religious man and he was active in the church on Seed Tick Hill, started by the Reddies River Baptist Church in March 1802. In 1830 David and his wife, Amelia, were baptised and joined the church. In 1848, he contributed substantially to the church for furnishings and repairs. In 1850 he helped build a new church on the north fork of Reddies River called Reddies River Baptist Church. After the civil war, different denominations began to emerge, causing this church to be concerned over loss of members. About 1880 the Union Baptist Church came into existence and the church became known as Reddies River Primitive Baptist Church. In 1891, a new church building was built for the Primitive Baptists, and in July 1891, it was voted to use the church also as a public school.

My great grandfather, Frankling Wyatt, seventh child of David Wyatt, was a private in the Confederate Army during the Civil War. He was wounded and captured at Gettysburg, Pa. on July 5, 1863 and confined to Fort Delaware July 7-12, 1863.

Franklin married Sibbie Dancy of Wilkes County and they had the following children: John D. Wyatt (born ca. 1863); Fanney Wyatt (born ca. 1867) married Troy Miller; Martha Wyatt (born ca. 1870) married Wiley Wingler; Sarah Wyatt (born ca. 1871); James Calvin Wyatt (born ca. 1872) (who is this writer's grandfather). Alexander Wyatt (born ca. 1874) married Plina Woodie; Alvy Wyatt (born 1877) married Smith Dancy; Mary Wyatt (no dates known).

Franklin continued living in the same mountain area above the north fork of the Reddies River as did his father. His home was near Robbins Branch and Orr Knob. Two of his living grandsons can remember the log cabin he lived in, after his wife Sibbie died in 1917. Their graves are marked today in the abandoned Wyatt cemetery on the mountain near his cabin.

Sources: 1780 North Carolina State Census, 1830-1840-1850-1860 U.S. Censuses, Wilkes County Courthouse records, Reddies Church Records, gravestones, family traditions.

— Velna Ilene (Wyatt) Crouthers

JAMES CALVIN WYATT FAMILY
1111

My grandfather, James Calvin Wyatt, (born ca. 1872) fifth child of Franklin Wyatt built a home along the middle fork of Reddies River at the foot of the mountain where his father lived along old North 16 highway. My father vividly remembers his dad, James Calvin, traveling through the mountains as a "revenuer" breaking up moonshine stills.

Grandfather Calvin Wyatt married Julie Dillard, Dec. 30, 1893, at the home of S. J. Dancey. Calvin and Julie had eight children: Queenie Victoria (born May 11, 1896, died Aug. 17, 1978 in Wilkes County). She married Wade Ross. Clarence Freeman Wyatt (born May 5, 1898) married Laura Sheets. They moved to Delta, Pennsylvania about 1935, where they presently live. John Thurman Wyatt (born June 16, 1900) married Cordie Ashley (born June 4, 1891). She died in 1981. Cordie is buried in a family cemetery behind their home. Thurman still lives along Reddies River on old 16 highway. One has to cross the river on a foot bridge to get to his home, where his lived all his married life. Thurman was a miller for many years, grinding corn and wheat for the people of the vicinity. I can remember Uncle Thurman grinding corn when I was six years old. The old mill is still standing, but dilapidated. Wiley Thomas Wyatt (born Sept. 22, 1902) married Jane Ashley. For many years Thomas and Jane lived on the mountain behind Thurman's home and raised their children. After Jane died, Thomas married Odessa Cleary. Cora Lea Wyatt (born May 3, 1904) married David Ross later in life. They had no children. Elizabeth Louella Wyatt "Lizzie" (born Aug. 23, 1908) never married. Twins, Julie and Robey Wyatt (born Feb. 1911) died along with their mother a few days after birth.

Calvin's second wife was Dora Ashely, whom he married in November, 1911. Calvin and Dora then had five additional children: Philmore Wyatt (born Aug. 9, 1912) married Maggie Dancy. Philmore died Nov. 9, 1981 He retired from working many years in the cotton mills in Kannapolis, North Carolina. Gaither Pete Wyatt (born Mar. 21, 1914) married Ruth Eller. Gaither has also retired from working in the cotton mills in Kannapolis, N.C. Nancy Sibbie Wyatt (born Mar. 13, 1916) married Tam Roten on Oct. 12, 1937. Sibbie and Tam's home is on the site of my grandfather James Calvin's home. James Fred Wyatt (born Jan. 14, 1918) married Annie Elizabeth Jones on Dec. 17, 1937 (my parents); Robert Odell Wyatt (born Jan. 2, 1920) married Iris Mae Holbrook. Besides being a revenue officer, Calvin was a farmer, living off the land to support his family. He lived his entire life in Wilkes County along the middle fork of Reddies River on old highway 16, and is buried up the mountain from his home. He died May 24, 1942.

My father, James Fred Wyatt, moved to Delta, Pennsylvania, as a young man looking for work after the depression. He met and married my mother, Annie Elizabeth Jones, daughter of a Regular baptist preacher in Forest Hill, Maryland. The Jones family was originally from Ashe County, N.C. and had ties with the same churches in North Carolina. My grandfather, Henry Jones, helped start Baptist View Church in Forest Hill, Maryland, of which my family has remained active. My parents, Fred and Annie, have been active in the rebuilding of Baptist View Regular Baptist Church, of which my father is also a deacon.

My parents had two children: I am Velna Ilene Wyatt (born Sept. 8, 1938); Connie May Wyatt (born Sept. 12, 1941) married William Chester Quesinberry of Madonna, Maryland, onApril 7, 1962, at Bethel Presbyterian Church in Madonna, Maryland.

My father James "Fred" Wyatt is now a retired construction worker, spends much time doing for others and doing much of whatever needs to be done at church.

My first cousin, James Fred Wyatt, named after my father and the son of Clarence Freeman Wyatt, is now an ordained minister and pastor of the same church, Baptist View. He was ordained Aug. 4, 1962.

The line of Baptist doctrine has carried through six generations: My children and I today are also members of Bethel Free Will Baptist Church in Crystal City, Missouri.

I (Velna) was reared and educated near Forest Hill, Maryland where my parents spent most of their married life. I graduated from North Harford High School in 1956, Pylesville, Maryland, attended Towson State University for 3 years, just outside Baltimore. I married Bill J. Crouthers on June 6, 1959. Bill and I taught school in Baltimore County, Maryland. On Feb. 28, 1960 twin girls were born, Janet Lynn and Arlen Gale Crouthers. We decided to move back to my husband's hometown and state, Sikeston, Missouri. I went back to college and got my degree from Arkansas State University in 1964. We taught school in Sikeston for six years and when our children, Janet and Arlen were ready for first grade, we moved near St. Louis and taught school in Arnold, Mo. where we are presently teaching. I received my master's degree in 1976 from Webster College in Webster Groves, Mo. Janet and Arlen graduated from Crystal City High School in 1978 and are presently seniors at the University of Missouri School of Nursing.

My family still has relatives living in Miller's Creek that we visit, giving us strong ties to Wilkes County.

Sources: Wilkes County court records, family Bible records, family traditions and personal interviews.

— Velna Ilene (Wyatt) Crouthers

473

THE YALE FAMILY

1112

The Yale family of North Carolina, primarily the Wilkes County area, descends through Vallet Yale, only child of Joseph and Lois Hitchcock Yale. This family, early settlers in Connecticut, descends from Thomas Yale, son of David and Anna Lloyd Yale of Chester, Wales. The lineage from there can be traced back to the Tudor kings of early England.

Thomas Yale, of New Haven, Ct., married Mary Turner, daughter of Captain Nathaniel Turner. Capt. Turner immigrated to America in 1630 with the first Winthrop Fleet. In 1632 he moved to Lynn, Massacusetts and served as constable. He served in the 1637 campaign against the Pequots. In 1646 he set sail for England with seventy people aboard. His ship was never heard from again.

Among the children of Thomas and Mary Turner Yale was Thomas who married Rebecca Gibbards in 1667. They were the parents of Theophilus who married Susannah Abernathy in 1736. Their son, Amasa married Anna Richards in 1768. Their son, Joseph Yale, born October 7, 1770 in Cheshire, Ct. he married Lois Hitchcock March 4, 1800 in Cheshire.

Their only child, Vallet Yale, left home at an early age. He journeyed by horse boat, possibly to England, and at least down into Virginia. There he was befriended, finished his schooling and possibly taught school for awhile. He then became an early peddler and carried the wares of his New England family over the mountains of North Carolina and Tennessee. In Burke County, N.C. he met and fell in love with Susannah Pennell. They were married there September 24, 1829. The Pennell family was from the Warrior Creek area of Burke County.

Letters arrived from Vallet's mother, asking the young couple to come to Connecticut, but whether because his bride was hesitant to meet her new relatives or he was well content with his southern life, they niver visited his former home or family.

Vallet and Susannah moved to Wilkes County early in their marriage and all of their children were born there. Vallet taught school, farmed a bit, and in 1838 served in the Third Regiment of the Volunteers from North Carolina in the war against the Cherokees. Their known children were: Joseph Elias who died age eleven in 1884; Lois Elmira born in 1835; Jesse Tiry, born April 28, 1839 and married Francis (Fanny) Spicer; Fanny Elvira who died at the age of two in 1846; Susan born in 1841; Sarah Orilla . .Croline born in 1847; Vallet Columbus Lafayette born June 30, 1849 and married Millie Spicer. Both are buried at Old Roaring River Bapotist Church cemetery at Traphill. Mary J. was born 1853 and married James Patterson.

The Yale line of Rockford Bauguess of Seattle, Wa., Charles Ivan Bauguess of Woodbridge, Va. and Ruth Bauguess Pruitt of Traphill descends through Jesse Tiry Yale to Elihu York Yale, his son, and thence to Ella Yale Bauguess who still lives in Traphill.

Jesse Tiry Yale married Francis Spicer,

Elihu York Yale.

daughter of Harvey, on March 25, 1866. Among their children was Sarah Elmira born January 7, 1867 who married first Henry Talton Sidden and second Rufus Lewey; Nancy Susanna born January 16, 1869 and married to Abraham Sidden; Margaret Ann born May 22, 1871 and married Joe Tyre McBride; Elihu York born October 28, 1873; Abraham Columbus born December 24, 1874. He married first Carrie Walker and second Fonzie Byrd, and lived to the age of ninety five, dying in November 1970; John Hardin was born October 29, 1876 and married three times, his wives being Samantha De Borde, Sally Johnson and Thelma Truitt; John Wesley born January 21, 1890 married Delia Lyons; Lois Almedia, born August 1, 1886 married first Winfrey Holbrook who was killed by lightning and second, Claude Y. Miller; Frances Elizabeth born May 13, 1882 and married John Aaron Truitt.

Elihu York Yale married Mary Jane Bauguess born September 12, 1880 to John A. and Susan Childress Bauguess. They were married October 28, 1894 in Wilkes County and made their home there all their life. Mary Jane died on December 5, 1962 preceding her husband in death. He lived until November 13, 1966.

Both were good citizens of the community, loving parents and grandparents, and faithful members of their church. Both are buried in the church cemetery at Old Roaring River Baptist Church, Traphill, N.C.

Their three children were Robert Mostella, born June 20, 1897. He married Perna Martin. They made their home in Traphill as farmers and storekeepers. His wife survived him at his death on March 29, 1970. Elihu and Mary Jane had two daughters, Ella and Fanny. Ella is the widow of John Perly Bauguess. Fanny was married to Derry Brinegar. Of the three children, only Ella survives.

Nearly four centuries after the first descendents of the Yale family came to America, their descendants still reflect the sturdy independence and strength of their ancestors.

Sources: Yale Genealogy of 1850; Connecticut Vital Records; Census Records; Cemetery Records; Family history.

— Willmetta Bauguess (Mrs. Rockford Baugess)

DAVID YATES

1113

David Yates, son of John, Sr. and Jemima (Roper) Yates, was born in 1792 and died in November 1851 in Wilkes County. He first married 22 October 1814, Nancy Hayes, a daughter of Jesse and Nancy Ann (Dickerson) Hayes of Warrior Creek area.

David Yates was a farmer. Sometime after his marriage he moved to a farm on Mulberry Creek, known today as the Doughton farm on the road to Hays, N.C. He and Nancy are supposed to be buried on this farm in unmarked graves. It has been told that Nancy was very obese, weighing almost five hundred pounds. She died prior to 1850. Six months before he died, David Yates married Millie Lunceford on 17 May 1851. She remarried Reuben Riley Hall in December 1851.

David and Nancy were the parents of six known children, including two daughters who married the Siamese Twins. Stories have been told that the Yates home was always open to friends and a great deal of entertaining took place there. When Eng and Chang came to Wilkes County, they were impressed with the warmth of the Yates family and spent much of their time in their home. The Siamese twins became United States Citizens and legally had the surname Bunker added to their names while living in Wilkes County, N.C.

The children of David and Nancy were: (1) Alston, born 1816, died 15 January 1898 at Boomer, married Elizabeth Holbrook, (2) Jesse, born 1818, died in Surry County, (3) Letha, born 1821, died 24 January 1810 at the home of Abner Caudill in the Rock Creek township, where she made her home. She married 13 November 1840, Samuel J. Bauguss, but they were divorced in 1852, (4) Sarahann, born 18th December 1822, died 29 April 1892 in Surry County, married 13 August 1843, Wilkes County, Eng, a Siamese twin. She is buried on the Eng Bunker farm in Surry County, (5) Adelaide, born 11 October 1823, died 21 May 1917 in Surry County, married 13th April 1843 Chang, a Siamese twin. She is buried at White Plains Churchyard in Surry County, (6) Jerusha, born 1828, died about 1900, married about 1844 Robert Yates, her first cousin, son of John Jr. and Elizabeth (Cleveland) Yates. They lived and died at the Robert Cleveland homeplace on Lewis Fork and are buried in unmarked graves at the old barnsite behind the house.

Alston Yates, son of David and Nancy (Hayes) Yates, married 12 October 1852 Elizabeth Holbrook, born 5 March 1838, died 15 March 1918, daughter of Caleb and Mary (Winfrey) Holbrook. Alston had some strange ways, according to his obituary. He often carried a blanket into the woods near his home, built a fire and curled up to sleep there rather than sleep in his house. He was a farmer and lived in the Boomer community. He and Elizabeth had only two children: (1) Robert Pearce, born March 1860, died 20 August 1933, married 17 February 1883, Martha Jane Phillips, born 2 October 1856, died 28 January 1945, daughter of Elisha B. and Mary (Ferguson) Phillips. (2) Mary J. married 1 August 1888, John McGlamery.

Robert Pearce Yates was active in the political life of the county, being a county commissioner at one time. He and Martha were the parents of six children: (1) Robert Alston, born December 1883, (2) one who died young, (3) Elisha Thomas, born January 1888. (4) Lula Pansy, born March 1890, married J.D. Phillips, (5) Ruby F., born 6 September 1892, died 27 January 1973 in Guilford County, N.C., married 26 May 1914 by O.C. Fortenberry, Dr. William Frederick Jones. (6) Pearl P., born May 1899, married Johnson Cardwell.

Sources: Wilkes County deaths, marriage, *Chronicle* newspaper, census.

— Mrs. W. O. Absher

HUGH YATES, SR.
1114

Hugh Yates, Sr., son of John Sr. and Jemima (Roper) Yates, was born 5th February 1786, Wilkes County, died 13 July 1871, Ashe County, married Sarah Vannoy, born 1785, died after 1850, Wilkes County, daughter of Andrew Vannoy. Hugh Yates, Sr. was a farmer and lived in Job's Cabin township. Eight of their eleven children have been identified: (1) Jemima, born 27 December 1809 died 21 December 1880, married, 1st. 29 March 1828 William Phillips, 2nd. Isaac Brown (2) John D. born 31 October 1811, died 26 June 1876 in Ashe County, married 27 April 1840 Alice Wilcox (3) Couzanna, born 1813 (4) Frances, born 1815, married 5 February 1846 John W. Whittington (5) Hugh, Jr. born 1818, married 1st 23 March 1840 Sarah Miller, 2nd Mrs. Emaline McQuire, 3rd. 17 November 1897 in Watauga County, Lucinda Bradley. This third marriage was just before his death. (6) Sarah Isabella, born 1820, married 19 February 1847, Thornton Kilby (7) Elizabeth Caroline, born 1823, married 6 August 1842 Hugh Hamby (8) Squire Allen, born 4 April 1824, died 8 April 1895 in Ashe County, married Elizabeth Ann Miller.

Jemima Yates married first, William Phillips, born 17 March 1806, died 9th May 1857, son of Peyton & Rebecca Phillips, lived near Phillips Gap on the now Blue Ridge Parkway. They were the parents of eighteen children: (1) Elijah born 1829 (2) Peyton, born 2 February 1830, died 1 May 1904, married Rebecca Miller, removed to Wise County, Tennessee (3) Hambleton, born 1831, married 14 April 1853 Mary Mickel (4) Martha, born 27 December 1832, died 3 December 1922 in Ashe County, married Edmond Leroy Blackburn, Jr. (5) Hugh, born 27 December 1833, married 20 October 1857 Fanny Caroline Fairchild (6) Caroline born 1834 (7) Nancy born 1836, married 3 January 1855 Daniel D. Woodruff (8) Nathan (9) Frances, born 1839 (10) Sarah born 1840 (11) Mary A. born 1842, married 1 December 1859, Larkin Walsh (12) America,

born 1844, married Alexander Mikel (13) Hannah, born 1845, married 29 January 1862 J.T. Goforth (14) Amanda, born 1846 (15) William born 1847, married Elizabeth Phillips (16) George, born 1848 (17) Adalaide born 1851 (18) Jemima Emeline, born 1852, married Alexander Kimberlin.

Martha Phillips, the fourth child of William and Jemima (Yates) Phillips, married about 1849 in Wilkes County, Edmond Leroy Blackburn, Jr. born 1 January 1825, died 3 December 1906 in Ashe County. He was one of the twelve children of Emond Leroy, Sr. and Frances (Hodges) Blackburn. They lived for a few years in Wilkes County, but moved over into Ashe before 1860, living in the Blue Ridge Mountains. They were members of Beaver Creek Church in Wilkes County.

They were the parents of seventeen children (1) Elizabeth Evaline born 11 May 1850, died 16 March 1907, married 26 December 1867, John D. Cheek (2) Laura Virginia, born 26 March 1852, died 25 December 1945, married 23 May 1872 James F. Church (3) Hiram Marshall, born 1 December 1853, died 27 October 1925, married Juliette Calloway (4) Sarah Camilla, born 8 February 1855, died 21 November 1939, married William Beshears (5) Delphia Alzena, born 19 November 1856, died 28 February 1910 unmarried (6) Jane America, born 9 May 1858, died 27 December 1932 on Stony fork in Watauga County, married 6 January 1876 James Larkin Welborn (7) Mary Alice, born 2 March 1860, died 31 March 1915, married Levi Tomlinson.

Also, (8) William Pinkney, born 27 October 1861, died 6 January 1892, married Fanny Brown (9) Martha Ellen, born 23 February 1863, died 30 April 1911, married Thomas Church (10) Frances Malinda born 19 April 1866, died 25 January 1931, married 13 December 1887, Leander Whittington (11) Thomas Marion, born 15 April 1867, died 13 March 1900, married Amelia Church (12) Edmond Leroy III, born 11 February 1868, died 19 October 1953, married 12 June 1890, Judy Bishop (13) Lawrence Decatur, born 27 November 1869, died 13 November 1937, married 27 July 1898, Kate Calloway (14) Joseph Franklin, born 22 February 1871, died 9 October 1953, married 1st. Myrtle Phillips, 2nd. Lola Bare. (15) Julia Ann, born 22 Nov. 1872, died 13 November 1969, married 13 November 1890 William Gaither Parsons (16) Lillie Belle, born 1 June 1875, married 11 May 1890 L. Decatur Whittington (17) James Monroe, born 10 May 1878, died 14 April 1963, married 23 December 1900 Mary Jane Keys.

Sources: Family Bible records, old family papers, marriage records, tombstone inscriptions.

— Sarah Payne Absher

JOHN YATES, SR. and JR.
1115

John Yates, Sr. was in the Wilkes County area of North Carolina as early as 1776 when he entered the services of the United States in the Revolutionary War. He was born in March 1754 in Pittsylvania County, Virginia and possibly had come from that county as a young,

single man. He returned to Caswell County, North Carolina, where he married on the 8th March 1779, Jemima Roper, and brought her back to Wilkes County. They settled on the north fork of Lewis Fork Creek, where he acquired more than four hundred acres of land.

John Yates, Sr. died 16 December 1835. Jemima, born in 1755 in Virginia, died by 2 May 1853. Both John and Jemima drew Revolutionary Pensions. They were the parents of eight known children. all born on Lewis Fork in Wilkes County: (1) John, Jr. born 1780, died 6 February 1875, married 1st, Elizabeth Cleveland, 2nd. Fannie Lamira Laws. (2) Hugh, born 5 February 1786, died 13 July 1871 in Ashe County, married Sarah Vannoy (3) David, born 1790, died in November 1851, married first, Nancy Hayes, 2nd. Milly Lunceford (4) a daughter who married Jesse Harwood (5) Louisa, born about 1792, married 2 March 1822 Abraham Johnson, left Wilkes (6) Salvy, born 1795, married 10 July 1816 Jacob Michael, who died in 1827 Wilkes county, after which time Salvy went to Polk or Cherokee County and died there. (7) Sarah, born 1798, married 15 August 1823, John Hamby (8) Tillman, born 1801, died by 22 February 1856, married 15 April 1831, Mary Ann Bumgarner.

John Yates, Jr. married 13 May 1803, Elizabeth Cleveland, born 15 July 1783, died 4 November 1850. He bought 804 acres of the Robert Cleveland land, including the old home, from his brothers-in-law, Jesse and Presley Cleveland. He and Elizabeth lived in the old Cleveland home until they died and both are supposed to be buried in unmarked graves in the Cleveland cemetery. John Yates, Jr. was a farmer. They had eight children, all born on Lewis Fork: (1) Sarah, born 1804, died 27 March 1877, married 31 October 1820 George McGlamery from Burke County (2) Presley, born 1806, died 1878 in Caloosa County, Georgia, married Rachel Thedford (3) David, born 1808, died March 1860 by hanging himself, married 5 January 1847, Elizabeth Church (4) Barnard, born 1810, died November 1854 in Caloosa County, Georgia, married 1st. in Wilkes County 26 November 1834, Mary Vannoy, 2nd. in Wilkes County 21 September 1847, Nancy Eller (5) Frances born 1815, died before 1850, married Peter Eller (6) Jesse, born 4 March 1817, died 6 June 1891, married Sarah Caroline Eller (7) Eli C., born 1820, died by 6 January 1886 in Ashe County, married 1st. Nancy Spencer, 2nd. 23 February 1871 Rosa Deboard (8) Robert, born 1822, died 12 July 1894, married his first cousin, Jerusha Yates, daughter of David and Nancy (Hayes) Yates.

Jesse Yates, son of John and Elizabeth (Cleveland) Yates, was a school teacher and a farmer. After his marriage 18 June 1848 to Sarah Caroline Eller, born 14 June 1831, died 27 May 1919, daughter John and Sarah (Vannoy) Eller, he moved to Walker County, Georgia where he was soon joined by his wife and where their first two children were born. They returned to Wilkes County by 1853.

In a letter Jesse wrote to his wife from Georgia before she joined him, he told of his feelings that his parents had not given him as much as they had the other children, a feeling that perhaps stayed with him. After the death of his father, he repeatedly tried to get the old Cleveland-Yates home from his step-mother, but to no avail.

Jesse and Caroline had thirteen children: (1) Elizabeth born 1849 in Georgia died during Civil War (2) Finley Gordon, born 16 November 1850 in Georgia, died 8 April 1936 Wilkes County, unmarried. (3) *Leander* Carmichael, born 6 January 1853 died 14 June 1922, married 5 March 1890 in Ashe County, Jestine Martha Phipps (4) Lelia Jane, born 1856, died during Civil War (5) Jesse Vannoy, born 6 March 1857, died 1 February 1926, married 15 August 1880, Sarah Jane Miller (6) Alice born 1860, married Manley Watts (7) John Morgan, born 30 August 1862, died 27th July 1951, married 1st. 11 March 1900 Annie Huffman, 2nd. Lillian Alzena Dyer (8) Alpha Caroline, born 1865, married 27 September 1892, Eli H. McNiel (9) James Madison, born 19 December 1868, died 18 January 1945, married Pearl Howard (10) Thomas Jefferson (twin to J.M.) born 19 December 1868, died 9 December 1951, married Alpha Elizabeth Fletcher (11) William *Leander* born 22 December 1864, died 14 March 1959, married 16 November 1901 Mrs. Julia Cox Howard (12) Isaac Call, born 1872, married Annie Harmon, died in West Virginia. (13) Presley C. born 1874, married Alice Noland, died in West Virginia.

John Yates, Jr. married about 1851 Fanny Lamira Laws, born July 1823, died December 1912, daughter of Levi and Margaret (Church) Laws. They lived in the Robert Cleveland home where their three children were born: (1) Margaret Virginia born 1852, died 1864 (2) Elizabeth, born 18 February 1855, died 21 September 1948, married Lowery Eller (3) Angeline, born 1857, married Murchison Church.

Elizabeth Yates married about 1875, Lowery Eller, born 6 June 1855, died 19 November 1912, son of George and Mary (Minton) Eller. They are buried at Mt. Pleasant Churchyard. They were the parents of nine children: (1) John Porter born 6 June 1877, died 1967 in Roanoke, Virginia (2) Margaret Virginia, born 15 July 1879, married a Bolling (3) Romulus Lamar, born 1 March 1881, died 26 January 1971, married Mary Hamby (4) Dosky Geneva, born 13 December 1882, died 7 December 1974, unmarried (5) Polly Lois, born 30 November 1885, died 1918 (7) Rose Lela, born 27 July 1890, married Hall Triplett (8) Beulah Lillian, born 18 March 1892, died 1971, married "Bud" Walsh (9) Winnie Northy, born 11 August 1894, married John Wallace.

Sources: *Cleveland* Genealogy, Wilkes County deeds, wills, court minutes, old letters in N.C. Archives, Federal Census, family Bibles, living relatives, marriage records, gravestone inscriptions.

— Mrs. W. O. Absher

THE YOUNGER FAMILY
1116

The Youngers settled in Wilkes County in the late 1700's when Joseph Younger settled in an area near the mouth of the small branch at the upper end of Flanerys Bottom. In 1797 Joseph received a Grant from the State for 50 acres on the North Side of the Yakin River and then in 1804 he bought 200 acres on the waters of Swan Creek situated with a sawmill and a grist mill. This grit mill in later years became the property of O.G. Bagley and was known as the Bagley Mill.

A person can stand near the location of the original Younger Mill and almost hear the waters as they run over the wheel that powered the mill which kept the local residents supplied with flour and meal.

In 1786, it became necessary for Joseph Younger to secure a Bondsman, an Alexander Gordon, as a paternity suit was brought against him by Zeannah Phillips.

Records show that Joseph was an active leader in his community; in 1786 he was a member of a road jury to view the Big Road against John Bowlands across the river at an Island near Widow Guinn, leading into the road that leads to Adninum Allen's Mill. In 1796 Joseph was ordered to be overseer of a road in place of Richard R. Gwyn, who resigned.

On Feb. 6, 1790 Joseph married Elizabeth Gray, who was the daughter of James Gray Sr. Joseph and Elizabeth had six children: Nancy, Susannah, Unknown Male, William, Harrison and Joseph Jr.

In 1823 Joseph died leaving a will. The inventory of the estate of Joseph Younger leaves us a quite picture of our ancestry. The estate lists: Four Negros, Four Horses, Nine Cattle, Twenty Four Hogs, Nine Sheep, Sixteen Gees, Four Beds, Seven Chairs, One Cupboard, One Chest, two wheels, one clock reel, one loom, one table, two pots, two ovens, seven pewter plates, two pewter Basons, one pewter dish, Six Earthen Plates, two mattocks, two plows, four hoes, one cart, one cross cut saw, one froe, one iron wedge, two sets of geers and Two Guns.

Sometimes between 1833 and 1835 Joseph Younger, Jr., moved to Ky. and then between 1839 and 1841 moved to Switzerland County, Indiana. Joseph's wife name was Tabitha and they had a total of nine children: Martin, Fleming, Caroline, John, Arminda, Joseph, William, Nancy and Jennie. Perhaps the lure of the opportunities of the west was pulling them in this direction.

On Sept. 12, 1857 John, the third oldest son of Joseph and Tabitha, moved to Henry County, Ky. and married Margaret Hall. Margaret was widowed and had one son named Anis when she married John. Margaret's maiden name was Southern. John and Margaret had twelve children: Anis, William, John, Harriet, Margaret, Lucy, George, Mary, Josephine, Milton C., Sarah and Rose. Census records show John as being deceased in 1880, meaning he died before the age of 41, leaving Margaret with five children (and) the home.

Milton C. Younger moved to Franklin Co., Ky. and married Nannie B. Romans around 1891. Milton and Nannie had seven children: Milton, Jr, Willie, Ada, John, Ella, Daisy and Margaret. Milton C. was a small man who always sported a mustache. Milton and Nannie later moved to Indiana where they lived out their lives as farmers, enjoying the pleasures that go with working and nurturing the sweet earth.

In 1913 Milton Younger Jr. married Stella Jane Bain in Woodford County, Ky. Milton and Stella have seven children: Rosie, Elva, Juanita, Willie, Roy, Milton and Thelma. In 1942 Stella died of tuberculosis and in 1945 Milton remarried to Margaret L. Korb in Franklin, Indiana. Milton and Margaret had three children: Carolyn, Francis and Larry. As of this writing, Rosie, Elva, Juanita, Roy, Carolyn, Francis and Larry are still living.

On Jan. 12, 1946, in Franklin County, Ky. Roy Younger married Mary Helen Perkins. Roy and Mary Helen have four children: Franklin, Cole, Patricia, and Michael.

On April 29, 1972, Michael married Vicky L. Wells of Cincinnati, Ohio and today they reside in Florence, Ky. Michael and Vicky have two children: Sherry and Robert. Sherry and Robert are the eight generation of Joseph Younger, Sr., of Wilkes County, North Carolina.

What great dream we can all have because of the knowledge of our ancestry and of those who lived and died before us.

Sources: Wilkes County courthouse records, federal census records, Family records, Mrs. W.O. Absher, G. R. S. and personal records.

— Michael L. Younger

A Special Tribute:
Pictorial Honor Pages

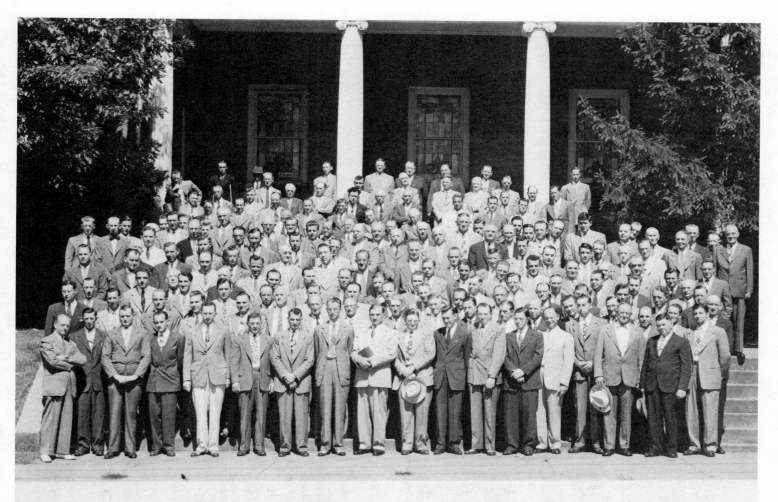

JOINT MEETING AT FIRST BAPTIST CHURCH OF MEN'S BIBLE CLASSES OF
BAPTIST CHURCH OF WILKESBORO · METHODIST CHURCH OF WILKESBORO · EPISCOPAL CHURCH OF WILKESBORO
FIRST METHODIST CHURCH · FIRST PRESBYTERIAN CHURCH.

September 12, 1948

PHOTO BY BEN A. STIMSON

In Honor of William Oliver Absher

William Oliver Absher was affiliated with the Dodge Automotive Agency for thirty-six years, selling his interest and retiring in 1971. He is a Deacon Emeritus of the First Baptist Church, vice-chairman of the Board of Directors of the North Wilkesboro Federal Savings and Loan, chairman of the Board of Trustees of the Wilkes General Hospital, president of the Medical Center of Wilkes, Incorporated, an honorary life member and past president of the North Wilkesboro Lions Club, a charter member and one of the original directors of the Wilkes Chamber of Commerce, a charter member of Oakwoods Country Club, a charter member of the Elk's Club, a Shriner and Scottish Rite Mason. He is a former town commissioner and mayor pro tem, and a life long resident of the town of North Wilkesboro, having been born at the corner of Third and C Streets.

Matthew Niel Brooks (1981).

Mary Elizabeth Absher Brooks, Leonard L. Brooks, Jr., Matthew Niel Brooks and Laura Elizabeth Brooks (1981).

Laura Elizabeth Brooks (1982).

Happiness Is
Children and Grandchildren

William Gray Absher (1981).

Henry Gray Absher, Sarah Jane Payne Absher, William Gray Absher and Elizabeth Barnhardt Absher (1980).

Elizabeth Barnhardt Absher (1979).

In Honor of William Matthew Absher
(1852-1903)

William Matthew Absher was the wealthiest man in the county, and was prominently connected with the banking, manufacturing and mercantile interest of this section. He was president of the W.M. Absher Company, vice-president of the Deposit & Savings Bank, a stockholder in various other enterprises, and probably owned more real estate than any other man in the county. For several years he was chairman of the board of county commissioners, a member of the county board of education, and served several terms as mayor of North Wilkesboro, being one of the founders of the town. Mr. Absher was a prominent and influential member of the First Baptist Church and for a number of years was Moderator of the Brushy Mountain Baptist Association. He was worshipful master of the Masonic lodge here. Obituary in the *North Wilkesboro Journal* — Thursday, December 1903.

The Hensford Ball Family

Hensford and Ann Ball.

Enie and Arlie Ball home, Ball's Mill Road, Brushy Mountain.

Ann Transou Ball's Beauty Parlor, Conover, N.C.

Hensford Ball (son); Arlie and Enie Ball; Effie Hayes (foster daughter).

Brenda Ball.

Durant Ball, Virginia Wildlife Artist.

Durant, Lucia, Kathryn, Julie and Daryl Ball.

Kay Ball.

The Dancy Family. Seated: David, Chere, Linda Ball, Andrea, Tisa and Mark. Back Row: Brad and Chad (twins).

Michael David Dancy.

A Tribute to the Bauguess Family

Robert J. Bauguess (1823-1914).

John and Letty Brooks Bauguess (1853-1936) (1860-).

John A. and Susan Childress Bauguess (1858-1945) (1861-1940).

Ella Yale Bauguess (1899-living).

Pearlie Bauguess (1886-1969).

The Millard F. Brown Family

Millard F. Brown.

M.F. Brown homeplace, Mulberry, N.C.

Alice Holbrook Brown.

Maud Brown Osborne.

John McKinley (Mack) Brown.

Bessie Brown Neel.

Ex-sheriff Presley E. Brown.

Rosalie W. Brown.

Millard F. Brown.

Alice Holbrook Brown.

In Honor of
D. Vernon Deal

In Memory Of
Isaac Prevette Duncan
1914-1978

— The Duncan Family

Dr. A.J. Eller Family

Dr. Albert J. Eller

Mrs. Albert J. Eller.

Andrew H. Casey.

Seated: Mrs. Eller and Dr. Eller. Standing: Wayne, Vera and Chelcie.

Wayne V. Eller.

Vera Eller Casey.

Thelma Holland Eller.

Cora Holland Eller.

Chelcie Baird Eller.

In Honor of Roy G. Foster, Sr.

William Hayes Foster: wife, Dorothy Walsh Foster: sons, Roy and Charlie (1905).

L to R: Roy G. Foster, Jr., William Hayes Foster II, Roy G. Foster, Sr., Roy G. Foster, III (1978).

Roy G. Foster, Jr., Roy G. Foster Sr., Virginia Foster Thurston (May 1964).

Seated: Roy G. Foster, Sr. L. to R.: William Hayes Foster II, Terri Leigh Foster, Roy G. Foster, Jr., Parkie Camp Foster, Roy G. Foster III (Sept. 1980).

The Family of Mack M. Goforth

John E. Goforth Family — Seated: John E. and Nancy Messick Goforth. Standing l. to r.: Curnel, Ola, Lillie, Kinney, Lonnie, Rayvon, Turner, Mack, Cyndi, Gertie, Charlie, Effie, Rex.

Bertie and Mack Goforth before marriage.

Mack and Bertie Dunnagan Goforth soon after marriage.

William Goforth (10/9/1792 — 1/13/1858) was a Baptist minister in Wilkes Co. for over 30 years. He married Sarah B. Foster (12/16/1789 — 3/11/1883). Their children included Samuel Smith Goforth (4/25/1831 — 12/28/1922) who was also a Baptist minister; he married Jane Walker (8/24/1834 — 8/29/1905). They lived in Somers Township on 265 acres along Little Hunting Creek. Their children included John E. Goforth (5/10/1870 — 9/4/1959) who married Nancy Jane Messick (5/20/1972 — 1/6/1950). John was a farmer and one of the few builders who travelled around the county helping build new homes. They had 13 children: Curnel R., Charlie C., S. Turner, Lillie, Gertrude, Effie, Mack McKinley, Robert M., Cynthia, Lonnie, Rex, Ola and Rayvon.

Mack McKinley Goforth was born May 8, 1902. He spent his early life working on the family farm in Wilkes. At age 23 he moved to Winston-Salem and went to work for R.J. Reynolds Tobacco Co. He married Bertie Dunnagan (3/3/1899 — 6/5/1972). They had four children:

1) Gloria Bernice, whose children are — Gloria Ann Lounsbury (m. James E. Wampler — sons James David and Benjamin George); David Robert Lounsbury, Jr. (m. Lois Ann Schaefer — daughter Rachel Deonne); Cathy Jean Lounsbury (m. Daniel James Gohlke); and Daniel Curtis Lounsbury (m. Carolyn Diane Ferguson). Gloria Bernice married, second, Cabel Franklin Lemons.

2) Mack McKinley, Jr. married Rebecca Godfrey.

3) Norma Inez married Harmon White — sons Dennis Ray (m. Sandra Chapell — sons Dennis Ray, Jr. and Jesse Chapell) and Bruce Glenn.

4) Wilbur Harrell married Jane Mason — sons Stephen Harrell and Mark Andrew.

Mack M. Goforth, Sr. married, second, Roxie Swaim in 1973. They live in Winston-Salem and organize the Goforth family reunion there each June.

Bertie and Mack M. Goforth.

Children of Mack and Bertie Goforth: Mack, Jr., Bernice, Norma and Wilbur.

Mack M. and Roxie Swaim Goforth.

60th Wedding Anniversary of John E. and Nancy Jane Messick Goforth — eleven of their thirteen children are pictured.

In Memory of
C.C. and Ida Huffman Hayes

C.C. and Ida Huffman Hayes
on their Golden Wedding Anniversary, 1950.

— by their children

In Memory of
Mr. and Mrs. Clarence Hayes
and Blake Curtis Hayes

**Clarence Hayes
1895-1974**

Clarence Hayes was born March 20, 1895 in the Brushy Mountain Community of Wilkes County, N.C. to Melver Lloyd Hayes and Martha Jane Johnson, both of Wilkes County. He attended local schools and was a farmer and orchardist until his mid 20's. At this time in his life he moved into town and worked in local factories a couple of years and later went into the plumbing business which became his life's work. He worked over twenty years for Wilkes Plumbing Co. and later was self employed until his retirement in 1960. Clarence Hayes was a member of the Hinshaw Street Baptist Church where he was Treasurer and Deacon for several years. He died November 5, 1974 of a heart attack at the age of 79.

**Emma Lenora Walker Hayes
1905-1968**

Emma Lenora Walker Hayes was born March 22, 1905 in the Brushy Mountain Community of Wilkes County. She was the daughter of Harvey Columbus Walker of Mecklenburg County, N.C. and Lenora (Nolie) D. Hendren of the Brushy Mountain Community of Wilkes County, N.C. She attended local schools and worked at the telephone company early in her life, prior to her marriage in 1924 to Clarence Hayes. She was a devoted mother, a christian, and loved by her neighbors and friends. She died June 24, 1968 of a heart attack.

Clarence and Emma Hayes had 9 children: Blake Curtis, Willa Jean, Hoover Harvey, Willard Lee, John and Don (twins), Clarence Lloyd who died in infancy, Nancy Grace, and Nora Ann.

Blake Curtis Hayes was the oldest child of Clarence and Emma Walker Hayes. He was born on his mother's birthdate, March 20, 1925. Blake attended elementary and high school in North Wilkesboro. He was drafted into the Marine Corps in 1943 and served in the South Pacific, Okinawa theater and other campaigns during World War II. He was honorably discharged in 1945. After his tour of duty, Blake was self employed in a service station business, a trucking business, and partners with his father in Hayes Plumbing Co. At the time of his death in 1972, he was a construction supervisor for Holly Farms. He passed away of a heart attack on November 20, 1972 in Mocksville, N.C. while on the job. Blake was active in the Masons, was Grand Master two different times and held several high degrees in the North Wilkesboro Lodge. He played a big part in the construction of the Lodge Hall, built a few years before his death. Blake was married to Mary Katherine Dancy on June 7, 1953 and had one son, Blake Curtis Hayes, Jr.

**Blake Curtis Hayes
1925-1972**

In Honor of the Sons of John A. Holbrook I

J. Sam Holbrook (1912).

J. Sam and John A. II
Holbrook (1918).

John A. Holbrook II (on horse — 1917).

Dr. J. Sam Holbrook (1940).

John A. Holbrook II (1930s).

Bob, Nan and Joe Holbrook (children of J. Sam).

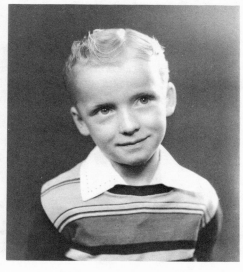

John A. Holbrook III (son of John A. II).

Lindsey Mansfield and Eulora Henderson Jarvis Family, 1939

Front: L to R: Vena Leah Johns, Eulora May Henderson Jarvis, Lindsey Mansfield Jarvis, Sr., Doretha Mozelle "Zelle" Pegg, Lindsey Mansfield Jarvis, Jr. Back: L to R: Ruby Ethel Mathis, James Shadrick Jarvis, Annie Marie (Greene) Inscore, Jay Franklin Jarvis, Letita Pauline (Henderson) Clark, Eula May (Sale) Correll.

Grace Lomax Kilby
(7 Feb. 1898 — 22 Jan. 1978)

Andrew Franklin Kilby
(10 Sept. 1886 — 22 June 1977)

In Memory of
Richard Tipton McNeil, Sr.
1897-1955

R.T. "Tip" McNeil was one of the original owners of the North Wilkesboro Coca-Cola Bottling Company, Inc. He was plant manager and president of the company at the time of his death. He was a member of the North Wilkesboro First Baptist Church, having served several terms as a member of the Diaconate. He was a Kiwanian. He served on the original committee to plan for and initiate the building of the Kerr Scott dam and reservoir. As former mayor of North Wilkesboro he served six terms from 1934 to 1947 and two terms from 1949 to 1953.

In Memory of
Chal Odell McNiel
1894-1955

Chal Odell McNiel was one of the original owners of the North Wilkesboro Coca-Cola Bottling Company, Inc. and its only secretary-treasurer until his death. He was a deacon and an active member of the North Wilkesboro First Baptist Church. He was an active democrat, chairman of the Wilkes County Board of Education for many years, a director of The Northwestern Bank and a member of the North Wilkesboro Kiwanis Club. He was one of the citizens who planned and worked for the building of the Kerr Scott Dam and Reservoir. — by Mrs. W.O. Absher

Robert Hayes McNeill
1926-1972

Town of North Wilkesboro

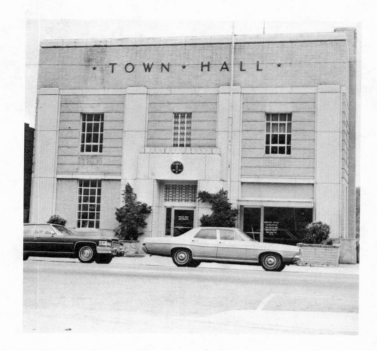

Seated l. to r.: Commissioner/Mayor Pro Tem Richard G. Brame, Mayor Neil G. Cashion, Jr., and Commissioner Homer W. Brookshire. Standing l. to r.: Town Manager Charles B. Lott, Commissioner George S. Forester, Jr., Commissioner Robert L. Johnson, Commissioner Don G. Jarvis, and Town Attorney E. James Moore.

The Neel Family

James W. and Bessie Brown Neel.

Elizabeth Neel Lowe.

Mr. and Mrs. Arthur C. Lowe, Sr.
and Elizabeth N. Lowe.

Arthur C. Lowe, Sr.

Rebecca Lowe Whicker.

Arthur C. Lowe, Jr.

Rosalie Osborne Creedmore.

In Tribute To

Hattie Little Smithey
Born April 1882

N.B. (Nike) Smithey
Aug. 11, 1880 — Sept. 3, 1953

— by their daughter, Margaret Smithey Hayes

The Vincent Spicer Family

Vincent Spicer Home, Traphill, N.C.

John and Ernest Spicer (1910).

Johnson Shafter and Verna Spicer Joines (Dec. 24, 1919, Green River, Wyo.)

Lee Roy, Vernon, Mattie, and William Brinegar and Friend.

Wesley II and Carrie Spicer Joines, Guy Joines, Ima Joines DeJournette, Ruby Joines Smith.

Verna Spicer Joines, Maude Spicer McBride Marion Ernest Spicer, Mattie Spicer Brinegar.

Front: L to R: Ruth Stevens Spicer, Eldon M. Spicer, Ernest Spicer. Back: L to R: John A. Spicer, Carol Spicer Luntey, Kathleen Spicer Allen.

Reunion in Green River, Wyoming (1957) Seated: L to R: Ernest Spicer, Maude Spicer McBride, Verna Spicer Joines, Mattie Spicer Brinegar.

Maude Spicer and Ed McBride with daughters: Mabel, Mary and Virgie.

Descendants of William Spicer, Revolutionary War Soldier

L. to R.: Gideon Spicer (1832-1914) son of William Spicer, Jr. and his wife Nancy Frederick Spicer (9-7-1835 — 5-7-1915.)

Son of William Spicer, Jr.: John Thomas Spicer (8-8-1869 — 10-8-1922).

Second wife John Thomas Spicer: Carrie Elizabeth Hicks Spicer (9-3-1879 — 10-3-1975).

Son Benjamin Spicer: grandson William Spicer, Rev. War. L. to R.: William Spicer (3-14-1816) (6-28-1896) wife Lucinda Pruitt (born Jan. 1823).

Son of Samuel Spicer (1784-1849); grandson William Spicer, Rev. War: Roger Spicer (1819-1901).

Daughter of Gideon and Nancy Frederic Spicer: Elizabeth Spicer (1871-1925).

Son William Spicer and Lucinda Pruitt: Major Frederick Spicer (Born 1855).

Circuit rider, minister, educator — Founder Randolph Academy (later Trinity College; then Duke): Brantley York (1-3-1805) (10-7-1891).

Methodist Minister-Educator: Dr. William Adrian Jenkins (2-11-1879) (1-26-1968).

William Kent, Sr. and Madge Linney Sturdivant

William Kent Sturdivant, Sr. became a member of the North Wilkesboro First Baptist Church in 1926. He served as B.T.U. director for ten years, finance chairman for thirty years, a deacon for forty years, and is now a deacon emeritus. He was on the building committee for the present church building.

He has been a member of the board of trustees of Wilkes General Hospital since its beginning, with the exception of a few years. A member of the Wilkes Y.M.C.A. building committee and board member from its beginning, a member of the Kiwanis Club for more than 50 years, serving a term as president, a member of the Chamber of Commerce Board, and a member of the Wilkes Library Board.

He served on the Old Hickory Council of Boy Scouts serving as president for a term, receiving the Silver Beaver Award in scouting.

He is a member of the endowment committee of Wilkes Community College, a member of Wilkes Chapter 42 Order of the Eastern Star and served five terms as Worthy Patron. He is a member of the Masonic Lodge No. 407 and past master, a York Rite and Scottish Rite Mason and a Shriner.

He has been president of N.C. Burial Association and served in other capacities, being president of N.C. Cemetery Association. A member of the board of trustees for Meredith College, Raleigh, N.C. and a member of board of advisors for Mars Hill College.

He is listed in Who's Who in the South and Southwest 1967-68 edition. Also listed in Personalities of the South in 1970.

Mr. and Mrs. Alvin A. Sturdivant

Alvin Alexander Sturdivant and wife, Rosalyn Caldwell came to Wilkes County from Rootstown, Ohio in 1930. They were married February, St. Valentines Day, 1924. Their children are A.A. Sturdivant, Jr., Harold James Sturdivant, and Anne Marie Sturdivant Nichols.

Alvin was a member of Wilkesboro Baptist Church where he served as a deacon and was chairman of the church building committee.

He was a member of Wilkesboro Professional and Business Mens Club, a Wilkes County commissioner for two terms and worked with Sturdivant Life Insurance Company for ten years.

He was a York Rite and Scottish Rite Mason, and a Shriner. Was past master of the Wilkesboro lodge, served as N.C. District Deputy and a member of the Eastern Star as Worthy Patron, O.E.S. 42.

Alvin Alexander Sturdivant died July 20, 1971.

North Wilkesboro Kiwanis Club

Organized April 5, 1923

"Taking Time to Care"

STRONG KIWANIS CLUB IS ORGANIZED IN CITY — Winston-Salem Sponsors Club and Elkin Sends Large Delegation for the event.

At a banquet in the Wilkes Commercial club rooms Tuesday night a strong Kiwanis Club for North Wilkesboro was organized, which is sponsored by the Winston-Salem Kiwanis Club and which marks a new epoch in the history of this growing city of the mountains, and links Winston-Salem and Elkin, at which place a Kiwanis Club was formed last week, and North Wilkesboro closer together than before in the Kiwanian spirit and in an effort to develop this section along the line of greater citizenship.

The North Wilkesboro Club has a membership of 57 and is composed of the city's leading business men. Last Friday night a temporary organization was made and Tuesday night this organization was made permanent and the following officers and directors were elected for the ensuing year:

President, C.C. Smoot, III; Vice-President, W.R. Wilkins; Secretary, J.B. Williams; Treasurer, R.W. Gwyn; District Trustee, J.B. Norris; Directors, J.L. Clements, H.C. Landon, R.D. Grier, J.B. McCoy, J.B. Mulligan, J.C. Reins and E.E. Eller. Following is a complete list of the newly formed North Wilkesboro Kiwanis Club:

F.D. Hackett, Eugene Trivette, J. Palmer Horton, T.S. Barnes, W.R. Wilkins, Edward G. Finley, J.G. Hackett, J.B. Norris, Sargent D. Duffield, Carl S. Coffey, J.C. Smoot, Jr., C.C. Smoot, 3rd., Joseph Parkin, W.F. Blair, E.M. Long, J.R. Hix, W.A. Fender, H.C. Landon, Ben B. Nicholl, R.M. Brame, E.M. Blackburn, Genio Cardwell, Charles H. Cowles, Horace Sisk, Clarence Call, W.A. McNeill, J.B. Williams, Clem Wrenn, P. Ward Eshelman, R.W. Gwyn, W.A. Bullis, J.D. Moore, Richard G. Finley, E.E. Eller, R.N. Pendley, J.R. Finley, J.P. Mulligan, J.L. Clements, Lee Hemphill, F.D. Forester, C.W. Robinson, T.B. Finley, R.D. Grier, P.M. Williams, J.B. McCoy, James F. Johnson, Johnson J. Hayes, W.F. Jones, J.E. Spainhour, Henry Reynolds, Wm. R. Spainhour, S.V. Tomlinson, D.J. Carter, J.C. Reins, E.M. Hutchens, Russell G. Hodges and R.P. Casey. (Carter's Weekly — 1923)

Members of the North Wilkesboro Kiwanis Club in 1982:

Allred, Joe	Davis, Eric	Love, James
Anderson, Jack F.	Davis, John L.	McLachren, William B.
Andrews, Alfred E. Jr.	Davis, Ralph	McClesky, J. Lawrence
Applefield, Bryan M.	Eller, Chelsie B.	McMahan, Thomas K.
Ashburn, Michael A.	Evans, Samuel C.	McNeil, Richard
Barker, John J.	Ferree, Max	Moore, Larry
Battle, John	Forester, George	Newton, Paul
Bauguess, John A.	Freeman, J. Max	Nye, William E.
Benson, William	Gabriel, Bill G.	Ogburn, Thomas
Billings, Hubert C.	Gardner, Edd F.	Ogilvie, Gordon F.
Bowman, Thomas	Green, E. Hal	Oliver, John
Brame, Dr. Phillip M.	Gresham, Aubrey R.	Osborne, Paul
Brame, William A.	Grier, Wm. C.	Peterson, Elof
Brewer, Joe O.	Guffey, Clifton H.	Prevette, Clifton
Brooks, Leonard	Hall, John E.	Priester, J.R.
Canter, Edwin J.	Hamilton, Paul	Redding, Earl
Casey, William E.	Hawkins, Hal B., M.D.	Richardson, Douglas
Caudill, Bryce J.	Hayes, Allie	Reeves, George F., Jr.
Caudill, H.D.	Hayes, Kyle	Rousseau, Julius A., Jr.
Church, Anderson M.	Hege, Robert III	Sale, George S.
Church, Mark S.	Hemric, S. Gregg	Sebastian, Kenneth E.
Clifton, Stanley	Hicks, William T.	Shealy, C. Frank
Coe, Millard H.	Horton, John P., Jr.	Shepherd, J. Greene
Coffey, Carl G.	Hubbard Fred C. (Life Memb)	Sloan, Elihu E.
Cohn, Ernest	Hubbard, Julius	Strader, Howard
Conley, John R.	Idol, John	Stroud, Sturdivant, W.K.
Connor, Buddy W.	Joyce, Dennis R.	Templeton, Bradley
Cossens, Kenneth	Kenner, Gaither N., Jr.	Thomas, David L.
Craig, Ben	Kilby, Larry S., MD	Underwood, Frank
Crook, D.L.	Kneece, Judson	Watson, Jerry F., M.D.
Culler, Don T.	Knox, Dr. James M.	Wayland, John T.
Currin, Walt	Landon, Dr. H.C. 3rd	Williardson, John S.
Daniel, David E.	Laney, Robert P.	Winslow, Douglas

North Wilkesboro Lions Club
Organized April 5, 1938

Past Presidents

H.B. Smith 1938

L.L. Carpenter '38-'39
Richard B. Johnston '38-'40
Blair Gwyn '40-'41
Hampton McNeil '41
Emmett C. Johnson '41-'42
Paul L. Cashion '42-'43
Jas. M. Anderson '43-'44
D. Vernon Deal '44-'45
Jule S. Deans '45-'46
W.O. Absher '46-'47
W.C. Marlow '47-'48
J.H. Whicker, Jr. '48-'49
W.D. Jester '49-'50
C.J. Swofford '50-'51
E.S. Finley '51-'52

Boyd E. Stout '52-'53
C.C. Faw, Jr. '53-'54
Joe Zimmerman '54-'55
J.H. Sowder '55-'56
Shoun Kerbaugh '56-'57
W.R. McNeil '57-'58
Don T. Culler '58-'59
R.G. Taylor, Jr. '59-'60
Wayne M. Coffey '60-'61
Sam Ogilvie '61-'62
Roy Crouse '62-'63
Edward P. Bell '63-'64
David Parks '64-'65
Neil Dalrymple '65-'66
J. Tom Ray '66-'67
Bennie Anderson '82-'83

Harry N. Baldwin '67-'68
Ralph Beaver '68-'69
Edward McEntire '69-'70
E. James Moore '70-'71
Conley Call '71-'72
Homer W. Brookshire '72-'73
Conrad A. Shaw '73-'74
R.W. Hoggard, Jr. '74-'75
Reginald F. Hill '75-'76
Joe Alan Gambill '76-'77
Bob C. Thompson '77-'78
John Myers '78-'79
James S. Hartley '79-'80
J. Arnold Simpson '80-'81
Kenneth P. Welborn '81-'82

Blue Ridge Shrine Club

Wilkes County and Elkin Area

Chartered November 14, 1968

an affiliate of

OASIS TEMPLE

AAONMS

Charlotte, North Carolina

We serve the crippled and burned child through
SHRINERS' HOSPITALS

P.O. Box 1504 — North Wilkesboro, North Carolina 28659

In Honor of
Rendezvous Mountain Chapter of D.A.R.

Rendezvous Mountain was once a soldiers' training camp. Three long tremendous blasts of a huntsman's horn crashed through the crisp stillness of a morning in the mountains. The hunter, for he appeared to be a veritable giant of a man, took the great horn from his lips and cast his gaze down the valley in the wake of the reverberations. His eyes lighted with pleasure.

From his high vantage point on the top of Rendezvous Mountain he could see the magic of his horn at work. A fawn appeared-two-three-dozen-and in the dim distance scores of men rushed from mountain huts and leaped to their saddles.

The gigantic figure atop the mountains turned slowly, training his horn in a second direction. The mountain slopes become alive with men and horses. In a third direction the immense blast pealed out and echoed, re-echoed and reverberated, finally breaking against Blowing Rock, 30 miles away.

Ten companies of soldiers assembled at Rendezvous Mountain in answer to the blasts. The horn, described as "the greatest ever seen," was used by Colonel Ben Cleveland when he was a comparatively small man of only 300 pounds. He later weighed 450 pounds. He was almost worshipped by his mountain soldiers of the Revolutionary period for his prodigious strength and daring. He trained them on the flat top of the mountain and later led them, a regiment of sharpshooters, against the British at King's Mountain.

The mountain and the men have become inextricably merged in the traditions which have existed on the hills and in the valleys in the "State of Wilkes" for generations. The mountain's name, "Rendezvous," comes from the mere fact that Cleveland's men gathered there in answer to his powerful blasts.

The story of the man is seductive to the romantic instincts, and that of the mountain is no less so. On its great green flanks are the rhododendron, the laurel, the azalea and sturdy primeval forests. Its ice-like springs gush with crystal water, its amphi-theatre was apparently scooped by the hand of some beneficient and bedecked with shrubs by the fairies. And from its summit are views that invite the eyes to sweeps of entrancing beauty.

Rendezvous Mountain is at the tip of a spur of the Blue Ridge chain which reached to a point nine miles from Wilkesboro.

A Prayer for Genealogists

Lord, help me dig into the past
And sift the sands of time
That I might find the roots that made
This family tree of mine.
Lord, help me trace the ancient roads
On which my fathers trod
And led them through so many lands
To find our present sod.

Lord, help me find an ancient book
Or dusty manuscript
That's safely hidden now away
In some forgotten crypt;
Lord, let it bridge the gap that haunts
My soul when I can't find
The missing link between some name
That ends the same as mine.

CURTIS WOODS

Wilkes County Government

Wilkes County Courthouse
Wilkesboro, N. C.

Wilkes County Board of Commissioners

Left to right: Hoke Wiles, Rev. Sherrill D. Wellborn, C.C. ''Jack'' Combs, chairman, R. Tracy Walker, vice chairman and Max Bauguss.

Liberty Lodge No. 45
A.F. & A.M.

Chartered 10 December 1904

School Street
Wilkesboro, North Carolina 28697

Traphill Masonic Lodge No. 483
A.F. & A.M.

Chartered 13 January 1897

Traphill, North Carolina 28685

North Wilkesboro Lodge No. 407
A.F. & A.M.

Chartered 11 January 1888

203 Temple Street
North Wilkesboro, North Carolina
28659

Mt. Pleasant Lodge No. 573
A.F. & A.M.

Chartered 12 January 1910

(Champion)
Route 1
Wilkesboro, North Carolina 28697

Index to Family Histories
(Indexing refers to article numbers, not page numbers.)

—A—
Abbott, 541
Abercrombie, 753
Abernethy, 498, 1112
Abraham, 1057
Absher, Abshire, 300, 301,
302, 303, 304, 305, 306,
307, 352, 357, 374, 383,
401, 415, 417, 425, 445,
453, 458, 459, 488, 494,
499, 524, 566, 621, 634,
688, 721, 722, 727, 731,
737, 741, 810, 817, 906,
951, 954, 955, 957, 962,
999, 1013, 1069, 1093,
1114, 1115
Adams, 301, 304, 306, 308,
309, 310, 311, 316, 317,
349, 352, 360, 361, 369,
418, 432, 440, 444, 445,
447, 453, 456, 458, 500,
524, 532, 566, 592, 613,
635, 664, 676, 685, 688,
692, 703, 715, 727, 761,
870, 901, 902, 904, 945,
947, 951, 957, 959, 968,
970, 1011, 1013, 1027,
1044, 1059, 1060, 1090
Adkins, 589
Akers, 635
Albers, 1057
Albert, 868
Alderfer, 472
Alderidge, 844
Aldrid, 715
Alexander, 312, 313, 314,
352, 361, 363, 473, 609,
685, 689, 691, 694, 695,
710, 731, 735, 741, 877,
896, 928, 968, 971, 993,
994, 1019, 1027, 1061,
1067, 1068, 1075, 1080,
1105
Al(l)ford, 677, 701
Alfriend, 769
Allen, 366, 417, 628, 731,
826, 895, 929, 999, 1004,
1014, 1015
Alley, 941, 942
Allison, 478, 489, 780
Allwood, 769
Aloway, 491
Alsby, 532
Alspaugh, 1022
Altop, 1057
Alvis, 1002
Amburgey, 629
Ammons, 973
Anderson, 315, 316, 317, 319,
331, 332, 342, 345, 374,
389, 418, 419, 421, 422,

434, 440, 453, 467, 473,
474, 475, 478, 494, 522,
529, 566, 616, 636, 643,
645, 649, 715, 725, 739,
740, 761, 821, 845, 850,
855, 916, 947, 987, 1000,
1013, 1028, 1047, 1050,
1054
Andrews, 320, 363,. 541, 627,
662, 669, 741, 826, 901,
1079
Andrus, 332
Archer, 437, 598
Armfield, 670
Armstrong, 352, 484, 724,
946
Arndt, 989
Arnold, 407, 475, 484, 594,
768, 809, 843
Arrington, 600, 934, 936
Ashburn, 679, 871
Ashkettle, 603
Ashley, 321, 335, 363, 371,
482, 575, 782, 951, 1085,
1111
Atchley, 981
Atkins, 393, 482, 610, 613,
696, 721
Atkinson, 566, 782
Atwater, 558, 995
Atwood, 939
Auberry, 1089, 1090
Aubrey, 350
Austin, 471, 909
Autenrieth, 700
Auton, 542
Avery, 431, 648
Axom, 944
Aycoth, 641
Ayers, 453, 596
Azmon, 923

—B—
Babcock, 483
Back, 688
Bagby, 495, 823, 833
Bagley, 590
Bagwel, 742
Bailey(s), Baily, Bayley, 384,
388, 391, 395, 636, 746,
916, 917
Bain, 1116
Baird, 712, 1074
Baity, Beaty, 322, 322A-A,
323, 324, 325, 767, 849,
856, 898, 946, 947, 1048
Baker, 357, 429, 478, 528,
547, 687, 688, 701, 741,
842, 920, 951, 1018, 1027,
1051, 1052, 1057, 1092
Balabous, 687

Baldock, 509
Baldridge, 780
Baldwin, 326, 327, 464, 503,
516, 931
Bales, 469
Ball, 328, 330, 331, 332, 338,
434, 529, 530, 544, 856,
866, 892, 921, 936, 948,
1037
Ballard, 440, 456, 638, 644,
775, 863, 910, 993
Ballew, Ballou, 465, 1103
Bandy, 594
Barbard, 1010
Barber, 306, 333, 334, 392,
428, 443, 457, 616, 964,
979, 996
Barbre, 641
Bare, 301, 335, 446, 532,
533, 536, 731, 841, 872,
920, 1114
Barefoot, 543
Barker, 336, 337, 352, 417,
418, 460, 475, 602, 617,
743, 823, 937, 968, 1083
Barkley, 475
Barksdale, 746
Barlow, 338, 427, 537, 541,
689, 717, 877, 926, 955,
1011, 1058, 1097
Barnard, 323
Barnes, 321, 331, 339, 363,
387, 395, 427, 452, 490,
537, 554, 555, 562, 565,
909
Barnett, Barnette, 323, 374,
395, 463, 478, 501, 544,
645, 649, 653, 908, 928,
1027, 1028, 1028, 1076,
1077
Barnhardt, 306, 587, 905, 906
Barre, 1084
Barret, 1018
Barringer, 862
Barth, 598
Bartlett, 544, 564, 951, 1018
Barton, 553
Baskins, 687
Basey, 677
Bason, 1002
Bass, 636
Battle, 507, 643
Baugham, 719
Bauguess, Bauguss, Boggess,
309, 336, 340, 341, 393,
394, 460, 685, 693, 694,
739, 790, 791, 793, 797,
878, 928, 959, 993, 1004,
1007, 1008, 1009, 1092,
1093, 1112, 1113
Baxter, 466, 547, 777

Beach, 619, 740
Beacham, 794
Beamon, 342, 495, 496, 553,
566
Beasley, 502, 1023
Bean, Beane, 417, 418, 488
Beaver, 306
Bebber, 371, 372, 384, 386,
388, 743
Becket, 640
Beckham, 716, 782
Becknell, 617, 892
Belk, 897
Bell, 329, 344, 362, 405, 491,
520, 634, 696, 738, 777,
817, 831, 842, 856, 886,
954, 974, 1075, 1106, 1107
Benbow, 932, 1034
Bendenbaugh, 489
Benfield, 320, 668, 817
Benge, 345, 568, 854, 1048
Benley, 346
Bennett, 348, 859, 1065
Bentley, 325, 357, 371, 382,
385, 391, 584, 655, 743,
744, 906, 911, 945, 1038
Benton, 725, 799, 912, 928,
1052
Berrier, 645
Berry, 351, 470, 491, 746
Berryford, 427
Beshears, 348, 398, 503, 841,
842, 891, 903, 907, 917,
920, 1006, 1074, 1114
Bezold, 307
Biddix, 326
Biggers, 1057
Biggs, 469, 487
Billings, 309, 313, 349, 350,
351, 352, 398, 417, 447,
460, 500, 536, 685, 695,
718, 744, 781, 791, 795,
797, 881, 937, 975, 993,
1005, 1011, 1027, 1052,
1089
Bingham, 353, 354, 355, 356,
357, 430, 728, 762, 811,
839, 840, 844, 936, 994,
995, 996, 997, 999
Binne, 764
Binter, 554
Birdsong, 395
Birdwell, 917
Bishop, 358, 400, 410, 661,
678, 715, 814, 871, 872,
876, 907, 938, 962, 1114
Bivens, 495, 1011
Black, 817, 1054
Blackburn, 309, 311, 340,
349, 352, 359, 360, 361,
440, 459, 528, 638, 666,

685, 692, 719, 720, 722,
791, 795, 796, 844, 865,
907, 917, 920, 953, 969,
970, 971, 1008, 1076,
1089, 1090, 1107, 1114
Blackweielder, 681
Blackwell, 499, 756
Bladesinger, 612
Blair, 362, 457, 465, 498,
550, 561, 702, 733, 835
Blanchard, 496
Blankenship, 363, 453, 1038
Blansett, 487
Blatt, 554
Blayton, 462
Bledsoe, 358, 667
Blevins, 336, 349, 350, 364,
385, 434, 471, 475, 553,
592, 613, 668, 671, 685,
727, 741, 784, 935, 959,
991, 993
Blossimgame, 459
Blue, 774
Blunt, 395
Boaz, 365, 366, 537, 832
Bockman, 312, 609
Bodenheimer, 590, 596, 597,
1081
Boggs, 422, 952, 1096, 1097
Bolden, 897
Boldwin, 894
Bolick, 1018
Bolling, 1115
Bollinger, 306
Bolt, 475
Boman, 633
Bondurant, 362
Booke, 526
Booker, 365, 1047, 1102
Boon(e), 410, 424, 487, 492,
532, 628, 678, 699
Boren, 420
Borland, 523, 1063
Bost, 481
Bottoms, 473
Bouchelle, 557, 833, 1019,
1037
Bourne, 456, 575, 727, 731,
733, 734, 735
Bower(s), 309, 335, 349, 352,
363, 392, 395, 461, 489,
617, 641, 685, 692, 713,
719, 742, 829, 861, 1101
Bowie, 911
Bowland, 1116
Bowles, Boles, 306, 425, 617,
714, 816, 834
Bowling, 999
Bowman, 312, 521, 589, 609,
642, 746, 841, 971
Boychuk, 731

Boyd, 351, 523, 566, 794, 1057
Boyer, 769
Bradburn, 948
Bradford, 750, 1022
Bradley, 342, 548, 906, 1074, 1114
Bradshaw, 300, 594, 829
Brady, 486, 570
Brame, 362, 367, 619, 683, 728, 1002, 1020
Brandon, 328
Branham, 796
Brannon, 326, 487
Brantley, 764
Braswell, 824
Bray, 384, 388, 418, 858
Brazeal, 623
Breedlove, 365
Brenden, 487
Brewer, 308, 309, 352, 361, 369, 416, 417, 425, 521, 575, 666, 692, 695, 791, 860, 993, 1021, 1061, 1089, 1090
Brice, 674
Brickey, 1057
Bridge(s), 331, 395, 846
Briggs, 363
Bright, 496
Brinegar, 352, 696, 791, 1008, 1112
Brinkley, 549, 1046
Brinson, 1098
Brittain, Britton, 596, 597, 1027
Britts, 654
Broadway, 366
Brock, 321, 346, 357, 370, 371, 372, 485, 743, 744, 940, 945
Brockland, 1002
Brooks, 306, 307, 317, 325, 340, 342, 349, 373, 374, 376, 395, 443, 460, 514, 553, 596, 597, 671, 688, 696, 721, 722, 739, 797, 878, 908, 937, 951, 965, 1008, 1014, 1041
Brookshire, 377, 387, 415, 439, 655, 839, 908, 1007, 1025
Bronson, 887
Brosius, 351
Brotherton, 317, 323, 674, 1106
Brown, 300, 301, 302, 307, 309, 316, 317, 336, 346, 349, 352, 355, 357, 364, 366, 378, 379, 380, 381, 382, 383, 391, 393, 400, 401, 403, 405, 422, 439, 460, 467, 472, 473, 474, 478, 486, 489, 495, 518, 521, 528, 532, 536, 546, 565, 580, 584, 592, 604, 614, 616, 623, 634, 638, 649, 657, 679, 680, 687, 692, 696, 704, 710, 714, 715, 720, 721, 722, 723, 727, 731, 733, 734, 739, 741, 745, 757, 758, 761, 781, 783, 785, 786, 789, 791, 796, 797, 818, 824, 830, 833, 844, 863, 865, 867, 891, 895, 898, 906, 914, 926, 936, 951, 966, 968, 986, 993, 1008, 1011, 1013, 1016, 1056, 1065, 1080, 1087, 1105, 1114
Browning, 993
Broyhill, Brayhill, Broughill, 319, 320, 321, 347, 382, 384, 385, 386, 387, 388, 389, 390, 391, 404, 611, 641, 743, 784, 785, 896, 901, 960, 1043, 1062
Bruce, 698
Bruno, 487
Bryan, 340, 393, 394, 438, 480, 505, 578, 645, 686, 688, 691, 694, 696, 746, 823, 861, 895, 896, 897, 915, 1007, 1037
Bryant, 326, 339, 565, 663, 911, 933
Bryson, 362, 973
Buchanan, 459
Buckner, 395

Buecker, 761
Buinn, 952
Bullen, 463
Bullis(on), 308, 317, 396, 397, 398, 412, 414, 482, 513, 568, 572, 721, 809, 875, 877, 879, 880, 899, 922, 938, 939, 947, 962
Bumgarner, 344, 358, 373, 376, 397, 399, 400, 401, 403, 404, 405, 406, 407, 408, 409, 410, 411, 412, 413, 414, 415, 448, 482, 490, 500, 514, 522, 536, 599, 644, 655, 668, 698, 732, 757, 759, 761, 762, 782, 794, 796, 809, 824, 846, 853, 871, 875, 877, 878, 879, 881, 892, 894, 901, 904, 908, 911, 923, 939, 955, 958, 962, 991, 1013, 1033, 1045, 1049, 1051, 1052, 1054, 1078, 1104, 1107, 1115
Bunch, 469, 1022
Bundy, 927
Bunker, 1113
Buntley, 366
Bunton, 568
Burcham, 309, 360, 566, 731, 752, 793
Burchette, 326, 352, 566, 853, 861, 1066, 1104
Burchfield, 1090
Burger, 829
Burgess, 751, 778, 842, 1085, 1088
Burke, 338, 514, 564, 641, 709, 1008, 1047, 1082
Burkett, 456, 471, 472, 616
Burleson, 1027
Burnett, 399
Burney, 392
Burrus, 777
Burton, 305, 313, 703, 723, 935, 1014, 1057
Bush, 829
Butcher, 1057
Butler, 691, 712
Butner, 598
Buttery, Buttrey, 300, 306, 341, 352, 417, 717, 740, 741, 792, 861, 931, 957, 993, 1004, 1012
Byers, 503, 539, 742, 806, 847, 891
Byrd, 309, 418, 440, 453, 493, 505, 521, 528, 613, 622, 648, 704, 706, 715, 792, 799, 825, 826, 931, 947, 997, 1003, 1093, 1104, 1105, 1112

— C —
Cabe, 363
Caccamise, 722
Cady, 1058
Caffey, 881, 1024
Cain, 553, 938
Caldwell, 510, 764, 1021
Call, 315, 322, 322A-A, 323, 325, 419, 420, 421, 422, 423, 432, 433, 445, 507, 669, 672, 715, 724, 832, 833, 849, 901, 932, 988, 989
Calloway, Callaway, 330, 392, 424, 458, 471, 529, 532, 533, 644, 657, 672, 710, 764, 814, 833, 1114
Cameron, 483, 550, 554
Campbell, 324, 325, 328, 347, 369, 397, 425, 462, 463, 478, 569, 606, 649, 665, 670, 674, 704, 706, 774, 790, 806, 862, 863, 998, 1027, 1028, 1052, 1057
Canady, Cannady, Etc. 308, 752, 753, 1014
Canner, 363
Cannon, 411, 801, 901, 962
Cannoy, 647
Canter, 390, 505, 507, 508, 509, 661, 811, 917, 1000
Cantrell, 471
Capehart, 463
Cardwell, 367, 586, 881
Carey, 347
Carlton, 319, 387, 389, 390,

426, 427, 428, 596, 597, 610, 619, 768, 911, 1025, 1058, 1096
Carmichael, Carmical, 392, 424, 713, 714, 748
Caroon, 738
Carothers, 487
Carpenter, 684, 779, 1030
Carr, 1102
Carrick, 974
Carrico, 352, 862, 993
Carrier, 731
Carrigan, 594, 743, 817
Carrington, 813
Carroll, 321, 355, 404, 429, 430, 548, 660, 928
Carser, 823
Carson, 311, 321, 393, 456, 694, 733, 734, 833, 1027
Carter, 431, 432, 433, 434, 465, 500, 569, 619, 636, 641, 676, 677, 679, 702, 746, 790, 806, 825, 826, 882, 921, 932, 968, 970, 1063, 1098
Carty, 927
Case, 357, 585
Casey, Cacey, 435, 436, 520, 685, 696, 792, 864
Cashion, 437, 778, 1059
Casperi, 731
Cass, 473, 578, 585, 929
Cassanda, 676
Cassel, 710
Castevens, 438, 495, 548
Cate, 695
Catlin, 1082
Catt, 1057
Caudill, Caudle, 301, 307, 311, 312, 322, 360, 361, 362, 379, 434, 439, 440, 441, 442, 443, 444, 475, 525, 534, 566, 609, 638, 659, 661, 666, 685, 690, 692, 693, 695, 731, 741, 743, 753, 761, 792, 813, 842, 861, 921, 971, 993, 1028, 1103, 1106, 1113
Cautheran, 951
Chadwick, 466
Chalmers, 1098
Chamberlain, 536, 1033
Chambers, 318, 473, 536, 717, 719, 849, 860, 881, 1019
Chandler, 363, 383, 402, 729
Chaney, 719
Chapman, 324, 351, 604
Chappell, Chapel, 401, 530, 725, 930
Chatburn, 323
Chatham, 422, 710, 816, 833
Chavers, Chavis, 636
Cheek, 336, 685, 687, 792, 847, 1114
Chewning(s), 841, 873
Childers, 321, 352, 349, 549, 685, 743, 832, 894, 1038
Childress, 326, 340, 352, 361, 371, 417, 478, 521, 541, 575, 692, 1012, 1013
Chilsa, 570
Chilton, 644, 810, 814, 1054
Chipman, 638, 825
Chipwood, 1089
Chisom, 885
Chittye, 939
Choate, Chote, 661, 734, 1080
Christianson, 974
Christy, 782, 805
Church, 302, 304, 347, 352, 363, 383, 398, 413, 415, 421, 445, 446, 447, 448, 449, 450, 452, 453, 454, 478, 482, 484, 493, 513, 514, 518, 528, 536, 547, 568, 576, 649, 655, 656, 662, 715, 717, 718, 732, 737, 743, 758, 803, 804, 806, 809, 816, 841, 847, 849, 871, 872, 874, 876, 877, 900, 901, 902, 903, 906, 907, 908, 909, 915, 917, 920, 922, 923, 925, 935, 939, 947, 965, 1027, 1030, 1051, 1052, 1056, 1074, 1076, 1114, 1115
Clanton, 363, 743, 786, 1062, 1106

Clark, 455, 463, 478, 488, 491, 522, 588, 643, 719, 761, 793, 817, 843, 852, 950, 951, 1000, 1033, 1075
Clayton, 864
Cleary, Clary, 352, 456, 493, 552, 563, 575, 622, 685, 809, 830, 824, 969, 1008, 1111
Clemens, 500
Clements, 362, 457, 703, 843
Clemmer, 958
Cleveland, 317, 447, 458, 459, 464, 465, 466, 527, 612, 628, 709, 775, 796, 811, 823, 936, 951, 1011, 1012, 1014, 1022, 1051, 1080, 1113, 1115
Clifton, 1041
Cline, 396
Clingman, 748
Cloaninger, 854
Clodfelter, 363
Clonce, 469
Clontz, 621
Coats, 527, 809, 811, 819
Coble, 497
Cochran, 436, 461, 560, 1002
Cockerham, 336, 337, 340, 418, 460, 679, 731, 808, 860
Cody, 610
Coffey, 352, 362, 374, 458, 459, 462, 463, 464, 465, 466, 491, 492, 499, 507, 560, 619, 631, 639, 640, 642, 643, 677, 809, 1025
Cofield, 558
Cohen, 352
Colbert, 1037
Coldiron, 307, 335
Cole(s), 351, 404, 414, 1038, 1039, 1047, 1097
Coleman, 321, 328, 467, 1037
Collier, 537, 538, 688, 696, 796
Collins, 429, 430, 440, 468, 469, 660, 679, 753, 792, 858, 859, 928, 1062
Colvard, Colvert, Cavert, 470, 471, 472, 524, 644, 755, 763, 814, 1011, 1051, 1052, 1055, 1056, 1084
Colver, 755
Combs, 349, 354, 378, 473, 474, 519, 594, 685, 692, 795, 849, 865, 912, 1003, 1005, 1037, 1092, 1093
Comer, 704, 848
Compton, 397
Conant, 958
Connel, 1008
Connelly, 895
Conner, 908
Cook, Cooke, 349, 352, 363, 420, 475, 496, 631, 651, 670, 674, 685, 688, 705, 794, 889, 899, 951, 993, 1016
Coone, 321, 371
Cooper, 352, 406, 414, 415, 458, 476, 563, 601, 710, 759, 806, 871, 938, 974, 978, 1009, 1065, 1101
Coots, 468
Copeland, 395
Corbin, 796
Corker, 707
Cornelius, 462
Cornett(e), 352, 920, 993
Corpening, 823
Correll, 719
Corum, 462
Cosby, 472
Costner, Costiner, 453, 478, 649
Cothren, 418, 440, 685, 722, 794, 797, 798, 832, 919, 1088, 1105
Cottrell, 491, 492
Couch, 393, 394, 418, 480, 766, 767, 998, 1037
Council, 705
Courtney, 615
Covington, 714
Cowan, 764
Cowles, 429, 481, 560, 640, 641, 660, 1079

Cox, 463, 472, 475, 487, 542, 545, 548, 549, 568, 624, 691, 715, 731, 792, 896, 1016, 1043
Crabb, 352, 771, 937, 1005
Crabtree, 475, 782
Craig, 958
Crane, Crain, 482, 568, 1019
Cramer, 677
Cranfield, 427, 686
Cranor, 483, 587, 606, 801
Crater, 484, 843, 864, 1059
Craven, 309, 373, 416, 453, 485, 486, 745, 747, 749, 947
Crawford, 487, 524, 547, 615, 963
Crawley, 720, 722, 775
Creasman, 494
Creed, 326
Creedmore, 891
Creekmore, 489
Creson, 707
Crews, 455
Crisp, 385, 391
Critz, 570
Critzer, 883, 885
Cromwell, 1051
Crooks, 640
Crosby, 521
Cross, 329, 427, 463, 685, 1022, 1079
Crouch, 770
Crouse, 305, 309, 530, 685, 688, 692, 695, 720, 722, 791, 937, 965
Crouthers, 1111
Crow, 462, 746
Crowder, 843
Crowell, 974
Crowson, 657, 1054
Crump, 446
Crumpton, 462
Crysel, Crystel, Etc., 347, 441, 490, 584, 590, 698, 843, 908, 938, 1026
Culbreth, 600
Culler, 490, 593, 719
Culver, 1070, 1076
Cummings, 799, 917
Cunningham, 366, 716, 746
Curley, 1045
Current, 657
Curry, 315, 423, 724, 725, 744, 799, 911, 1057
Curtis, 398, 478, 591, 631, 830, 881, 902, 911, 912
Cuthbert(son), Cubertson, Cutbirth, 301, 424, 532, 533, 958, 1002

— D —
Dacons, 704
Dagenhart, 503
Daileyon, 689
Dalecki, 881
Dalton, 463, 619, 683, 919
Dancy, 300, 315, 338, 400, 477, 493, 500, 553, 568, 622, 647, 662, 721, 722, 755, 809, 811, 814, 842, 865, 903, 914, 917, 939, 1011, 1013, 1110, 1111
Daniel(s), 478, 679, 997
Danielson, 489
Darden, 496
Darnell, 434, 460, 462, 484, 779, 791, 794, 971, 1080
Dautel, 719
Davenport, 350
Davidson, 621, 786
Davis, 322A-A, 351, 354, 356, 357, 358, 362, 384, 388, 391, 475, 501, 537, 548, 566, 576, 612, 617, 640, 658, 670, 679, 743, 761, 784, 786, 794, 817, 836, 841, 843, 873, 904, 935, 960, 962, 963, 1000, 1014, 1018, 1022, 1051, 1052, 1056, 1058, 1074, 1075, 1103
Dawson, 1090
Day, 479, 488, 495, 496, 612, 644, 675, 678, 813, 874, 899, 926, 1005, 1020
Deal, Diehl, 300, 443, 497, 498, 670, 836, 847, 1023, 1076

Dean(s), 499, 601, 619, 641
Dearing, Derring, 496, 789
Debord(e), Deboard, 328, 731, 1112, 1115
Decker, 731
Deeds, 731
Degan, 1051
Degueere, 523, 1063
Dejournette, 1008
Dehart, 441, 444, 973
Deitz, 338
Dekirmenjian, 848
Demoss, 612
Dempsey, 346
Denning, 487
Dennis, 717, 968
Denny, 629, 716
DePriest, 1041
Dequosie, 903
Derreberry, 676
Deshazo, 449
Devereau, 443
Deviney, 752
Dew, 906
Dial, 743
Diamond, 478
Dick, 519, 523, 889, 890, 921
Dickenson, Dickinson, 433, 556, 733, 1113
Dickey, 487
Dickson, 710
Dilbeck, 462
Dillard, 416, 500, 518, 544, 923, 951, 993, 1111
Dimmet(te), 794, 832
Dine, 1057
Dirr, 973
Dishart, 935
Dishman, 1000
Disslin, 533, 534, 535
Divan, 712
Diviney, 536
Dix, 339
Dixon, 331, 598, 751, 1016
Dobbins, 418, 484, 712, 713
Dockery, 452, 501, 545, 761, 996
Dodson, 616, 703, 729
Doggett, 547
Dolinger, 475, 1016
Doll, 436
Domeck, 709, 1082
Donalson, 1021
Donnely, 649, 721
Dorsett, 726
Dorsey, 921, 1058
Doss(e), 663, 876, 887, 1051, 1052
Dotson, 323, 469
Doughton, 552, 726, 895
Douglas, 349, 1076
Douthit, 986
Dove, 797
Dowell, 309, 425, 440, 467, 616, 617, 713, 724, 758, 785, 848, 928
Downey, 764
Downing, 487
Downs, 578, 640, 746, 1020
Draper, 1021
Draughn, 460
Dresser, 750
Duchamel, 1057
Dudley, 349, 849, 895, 896
Dueson, 832
Dugger, 623
Dula, 316, 402, 487, 502, 503, 504, 545, 561, 570, 577, 578, 589, 623, 624, 625, 632, 707, 746, 768, 990, 1027, 1042, 1076, 1094, 1095, 1099, 1101
Dumbell, 367
Dunbar, 465
Duncan, 372, 392, 488, 505, 506, 507, 508, 509, 510, 511, 529, 530, 643, 738, 743, 774, 797, 945, 947, 1067
Dunlap, 679, 746
Dunmore, 487
Dunn, 338, 912
Durham, 336, 460, 692, 791, 792, 794, 931, 1028
Durrett, 1081
Duvall, 481, 590, 635, 817
Dyer, Dier, 310, 705, 709, 710, 962, 1045, 1115
Dykstra, 1095, 1099

— E —

Eads, 564
Eager, 331
Eagleton, 341
Earnest, Ernest, 475, 746, 1015, 1016, 1017
Earp, 318, 320, 347, 372, 384, 388, 391, 485, 521, 542, 627, 744, 809, 933, 976, 1058, 1076
Easley, 862, 863
Eastridge, 512, 530, 531
Eaton, 829, 976
Echard, 1031
Eddins, 762, 933, 951, 1013
Edminston, Edmiston, 316, 475, 513, 662, 707, 743, 912, 1013
Edner, 340
Edsel, 371, 372, 786, 983
Edwards, 340, 349, 359, 360, 447, 487, 530, 563, 635, 648, 679, 685, 741, 883, 888, 915, 980, 985, 986
Egy, 700
Ekholm, 619
Elam, 693, 694, 896, 1075
Eldridge, 840, 844, 858
Elias, 681
Elkins, 351
Elledge, 309, 352, 374, 390, 401, 514, 515, 516, 518, 544, 553, 601, 717, 720, 721, 744, 805, 877, 956, 957, 962, 1013, 1043, 1076
Eller, 304, 318, 322, 323, 343, 373, 397, 400, 401, 435, 436, 441, 442, 447, 450, 453, 454, 455, 477, 516, 517, 518, 519, 520, 521, 522, 523, 524, 525, 526, 527, 532, 536, 562, 568, 572, 574, 586, 595, 617, 624, 642, 644, 655, 656, 657, 661, 663, 685, 692, 707, 730, 804, 806, 811, 814, 816, 824, 839, 847, 871, 872, 873, 876, 880, 881, 890, 904, 908, 911, 923, 925, 932, 936, 938, 951, 958, 962, 975, 987, 1011, 1013, 1033, 1046, 1056, 1063, 1077, 1083, 1084, 1085, 1088, 1111, 1115
Elliot, 467, 473, 499, 654, 722, 821, 1000, 1057
Ellis, 309, 311, 315, 350, 501, 518, 542, 572, 602, 670, 672, 673, 751, 799, 899, 921, 923, 926, 957, 960, 1045, 1090
Elmore, 934, 936
Elrod, 528, 596, 695
Emerson, 369, 644, 692, 997, 1019, 1090
Englebert, 1052
English, 552, 809, 1104, 1105
Ennis, 769
Erickson, 752
Erskin, 802
Erwin, 831
Eskew, Esque, 305, 685
Estep, 324, 331, 529, 530, 531, 650, 651, 652, 850, 853, 945, 1037
Estes, 548, 700, 1002
Evans, 458, 564, 605, 761, 816, 951, 973
Ewals, 796
Eysenbach, 1052

— F —

Fairchild(s), 521, 572, 576, 803, 812, 844, 1042, 1114
Fanclier, Fansler, 914
Fann, 462
Farlow, 436
Farmer, 354, 475
Farrington, 373, 910
Farthing, 912
Fasanella, 792
Faulkner, 619, 822
Faust, Foust, 324, 776, 939, 1023
Faw, Pfau, 318, 400, 412, 442, 513, 519, 532, 533, 534, 535, 590, 622, 697, 715, 717, 727, 737, 754,
817, 847, 849, 853, 875, 881, 903, 908, 938, 979, 1011, 1047, 1083, 1085.
Fehler, 782
Feltyberger, 621
Felts, 309, 339, 363, 467, 537, 538, 539, 546, 653, 665, 679, 727, 765, 766, 794, 816, 826, 863, 864, 865, 994, 1087, 1091
Fender, 401, 512, 662, 905
Ferguson, 501, 506, 509, 511, 541, 542, 543, 545, 546, 547, 548, 549, 555, 568, 570, 577, 619, 636, 639, 641, 642, 683, 705, 710, 744, 847, 855, 894, 934, 1040, 1042, 1044, 1071, 1072, 1113
Fhilyaw, 909
Fields, 418, 462, 688, 696, 791
Finch, 1081
Finger, 351, 367
Finke, 438
Finley, 362, 374, 481, 483, 550, 551, 552, 553, 554, 555, 556, 557, 558, 559, 560, 561, 609, 615, 636, 670, 683, 725, 833, 868, 883, 885, 886, 888, 890, 1098, 1102
Finney, 792
Fitzherbert, 565
Fletcher, 302, 311, 339, 505, 546, 562, 755, 817, 833, 848, 934, 1115
Flinchum, 326
Flynt, Flint, 336, 1036, 1037
Fonville, 534
Foote, 563, 895
Forcume, 396
Ford, 521, 564, 685, 743, 1027
Forehand, 367
For(r)ester, 340, 366, 367, 447, 488, 494, 524, 565, 566, 598, 670, 735, 818, 837, 843, 900, 911, 928, 1047, 1048, 1054
Forsyth, 800, 883, 887, 889, 890
Fortenberry, 1113
Fortner, 542, 567, 982
Forvendel, 435
Foster, 381, 396, 409, 416, 443, 456, 482, 485, 487, 500, 501, 516, 541, 542, 544, 568, 569, 570, 571, 572, 573, 575, 576, 577, 578, 579, 581, 582, 583, 584, 585, 586, 587, 588, 589, 608, 662, 663, 702, 711, 715, 730, 734, 744, 746, 756, 778, 797, 799, 806, 816, 832, 848, 872, 873, 877, 887, 890, 901, 902, 938, 946, 975, 1023, 1027, 1031, 1041, 1042, 1045, 1047, 1051, 1052, 1063, 1064, 1067, 1068, 1076, 1088
Fowler, 470, 471, 828, 830
Fox, 649
Fraker, 1057
Francis, Frances, 365, 421, 434, 445, 575, 881, 938, 1060
Francisco, 849
Franklin, 459, 521, 613, 702, 735, 741, 834
Frankum, 430
Frazier, 385, 478, 566, 568, 596, 709, 786
Fredrick, 648
Freel, 1053
Freeland, 988, 989
Freeman, 328, 385, 418, 619, 692, 974
Freeze, 385, 784
French, 1000
Freys, Frye, 849, 869, 1037
Fribell, 1022
Friend, 411
Frith, 715
Fritts, 490
Fropeck, 474
Frost, 619
Fugit, Fugate, 313, 695, 906

Fulcher, 570, 979
Fulks, 782
Funkhousen, 841
Fyffe, 569, 927

— G —

Gabriel, 455, 494
Gadberry, Gatbery, 617, 714
Gage, 333
Gainer, 990
Gaines, 755
Gaither, Gather, Gator, 373, 435, 520, 590, 761, 911, 1109
Galbraith, 951
Gallimore, 843
Gallion, 778
Galloway, 973
Gambill, Gamble, Gambrel, 313, 352, 358, 364, 381, 456, 459, 566, 575, 592, 598, 628, 685, 688, 696, 727, 733, 734, 735, 743, 755, 796, 818, 901, 955, 993
Gander, 829, 1037
Gant(t), 488, 687, 794
Gardner, 490, 593, 779, 974
Garner, 523, 607, 718, 719, 729, 1063, 1090
Garnett, 570, 583
Garret(t), 909, 1057, 1076
Garris, 692, 1089
Garrison, 418, 703
Garvey, 708, 912
Garwood, 794, 712, 817
Gauthy, 806
Gelettie, 740
Gent, 1008
Gentle, 310, 832
Gentry, 305, 306, 337, 459, 460, 559, 592, 644, 694, 790, 793, 895, 971, 1004, 1007, 1023, 1024, 1089
George, 662
German, 523, 595, 596, 597, 619, 640, 671, 744, 926
Gessing, 455
Gettle, 1099
Gibbards, 1112
Gibbs, 443, 598, 605, 710
Gibson, 362, 395, 469, 637, 771, 782
Gilbert, 947, 963
Gilbraith, 600
Giles, 1002
Gilland, Gillerland, 486, 751
Gillean, 499
Gillespie, 459, 1089
Gilliam, 941, 971, 1051, 1052
Gillie, Gilley, 849, 858
Gilmore, 352
Gilreath, 384, 406, 410, 493, 578, 599, 600, 601, 602, 616, 670, 674, 709, 710, 746, 855, 899, 945, 996, 1083, 1096
Ginnings, 431, 449, 700, 1002
Gish, 681
Givhan, 1002
Glandon, 641
Glascock, 565, 978
Glass, 717, 718, 730, 737, 740, 799, 830, 856
Glenn, 367
Goddard, 399, 870
Godfrey, 894
Goff, 338, 715
Goforth, 418, 453, 568, 571, 572, 578, 585, 797, 799, 981, 982, 984, 1058, 1064, 1114
Goins, 696
Gold(s), 426, 484, 513, 843, 896
Golier, 1007
Gooch, 724, 829
Goode, 523, 962, 1102
Goodman, 982
Goodnight, 597
Goodnow, 603
Goodson, 523, 1063
Goodwin, 499, 519, 731
Goolsby, Goosby, 720, 722, 1081
Gordon, 350, 480, 550, 556, 557, 558, 560, 604, 618, 636, 838, 948, 963, 1116
Gore, 969

Goss, 417, 1016
Goswick, 817
Gowins, 469
Gragg, 447
Graham, 453, 750
Grant, 317, 605, 654, 657, 659, 663, 704, 819, 849
Graves, 458, 459, 463
Gray, Grey, 306, 484, 495, 561, 571, 606, 607, 608, 609, 644, 718, 719, 730, 766, 797, 814, 833, 839, 843, 991, 1040, 1042, 1044, 1051, 1052, 1055, 1099, 1116
Graybeal, 456, 814, 1016
Grayson, 755, 835, 1076
Green, Greene, 312, 409, 478, 482, 513, 522, 609, 625, 660, 719, 723, 793, 861, 863, 896, 906, 911, 981, 990, 1037, 1074, 1075, 1076
Greenlee, 558
Greenstreet, 695
Greenwood, 610, 677, 868, 971, 1094, 1096, 1097
Greer, Grier(son), Grear, 430, 521, 558, 588, 596, 597, 611, 615, 626, 710, 746, 808, 933, 951, 964, 1072
Gregg, Greig, 503, 612
Gregor(son), 612
Gregory, 309, 471, 511, 543, 613, 622, 685, 935, 1000, 1107
Gresham, 614, 702, 869
Greter, 484
Grieder, 478
Griffin, 312, 358, 367, 482, 609, 845, 881
Grimes, 432, 514, 616, 816, 968
Grindstaff, 624
Grinton, 570, 636
Grist, 437, 886
Gritchellis, 403
Grittie, 532
Grizzle, 796
Grohse, 469
Gross, Groce, 309, 685, 688
Grundmann, 742
Gruneau, 794
Gryder, 478, 739, 1059
Guigou, 362
Gullet, 879
Gulley, 838
Gunter, 753
Gurley, 742
Guzal, 764
Gwaltney, 425, 1027
Gwyn, 362, 368, 551, 552, 556, 559, 604, 617, 683, 714, 1116

— H —

Hackett, 618, 657, 677, 1019
Hackman, 816
Hackney, 486, 833
Hadley, 1054
Hagaman, Hagerman, 632, 649, 869, 1028, 1104
Hagler, 487, 541, 578, 619, 620, 705
Hagopian, 521
Haigwood, 347
Hairston, 770
Hale, 393, 503, 733, 1103
Halifax, 1083
Hall, 302, 305, 309, 326, 340, 342, 351, 352, 500, 513, 514, 521, 584, 613, 621, 622, 623, 624, 625, 626, 632, 666, 692, 710, 720, 721, 725, 745, 749, 751, 768, 839, 849, 946, 947, 948, 951, 956, 957, 963, 970, 974, 975, 984, 993, 1008, 1063, 1105, 1037, 1076
Halsey, 335
Ham, 320, 434, 475, 546, 627
Hamby, 316, 501, 528, 536, 568, 645, 662, 791, 847, 871, 872, 903, 921, 938, 962, 975, 1022, 1045, 1114, 1115
Hamilton, 462, 525, 616, 881
Hammon(s), Hammond, 575,

513

628, 629, 630, 688, 695, 729, 733, 735, 761, 937
Hammontree, 462
Hampton, 310, 388, 392, 495, 505, 612, 624, 625, 626, 631, 632, 633, 679, 713, 895, 1072, 1076
Hamrick, 719
Hancock, 936
Handy, 308, 309, 336, 352, 363, 460, 592, 613, 634, 635, 643, 687, 727, 731, 741, 774, 789, 821, 898, 953, 955, 1091, 1110
Hankerson, 1099
Hanks, 361, 490, 662, 731, 793, 993
Hansen, 418
Harbin, 541, 1040, 1042, 1044
Harbison, 558
Hardgrave, 612
Hardin, Harding, 804, 1002, 1101
Hardison, 617, 714
Hardman, 722
Hardwick, 729
Hargis, Hargas, 628, 630, 688, 693
Haire, Hare, 418, 523, 525, 595
Harless, 616, 654, 883, 886
Harmon, 309, 383, 911, 962, 974, 1115
Harpe, 336, 794
Harper, 488, 750, 778, 890, 911
Harrington, 771, 1070
Harris, 314, 316, 369, 435, 436, 456, 487, 496, 505, 575, 636, 637, 640, 642, 644, 710, 717, 740, 789, 790, 792, 797, 808, 865, 868, 870, 916, 1002, 1003, 1051, 1058, 1073, 1099
Harrison, 368, 458, 628, 754, 823, 824, 895, 1075
Harrold, Harrill, Etc., 309, 392, 397, 440, 514, 532, 638, 646, 706, 970, 1027, 1060, 1093
Harry, 848
Harshaw, 503
Hart, 410, 475, 810, 917, 990
Hartin, 894
Hartley, 347, 507, 619, 639, 640, 641, 642, 643, 644, 645, 814, 873, 926, 1041, 1045
Hartzog, Hartsoe, Hartsock, 335, 575, 927, 1051
Harvel(l), Harville, 596, 707, 743
Harwell, 347, 356
Hash, 307, 714, 1016
Haulk, 528
Hauser, 748, 909, 978
Havener, 957
Hawkes, 362
Hawkins, 308, 316, 350, 422, 514, 617, 644, 645, 685, 699, 714, 720, 782, 792, 846, 859, 897, 962, 1008, 1076
Hawley, 681
Hawthorne, 689, 900
Hayes, Hays, 308, 310, 315, 322A-A, 323, 325, 347, 374, 399, 400, 408, 414, 416, 429, 439, 453, 463, 464, 465, 478, 493, 513, 522, 525, 529, 530, 565, 566, 568, 587, 594, 605, 631, 644, 646, 647, 648, 649, 650, 651, 652, 653, 654, 655, 656, 657, 658, 659, 660, 661, 662, 663, 664, 672, 692, 712, 717, 722, 732, 737, 752, 764, 792, 806, 809, 814, 819, 830, 842, 850, 853, 854, 855, 856, 871, 872, 876, 877, 880, 912, 921, 924, 925, 952, 953, 954, 955, 966, 989, 1000, 1024, 1026, 1027, 1028, 1033, 1037, 1048, 1053, 1055, 1059, 1076, 1080, 1085, 1087, 1104, 1113, 1115
Head, 832

Heard, 995
Heath, 307, 552
Heckenlively, 487
Hedgepeth, 883, 886
Heff, 521
Hefner, 669
Hellard, 668, 851
Helms, 301, 822
Helton, 385
Hemmerich, 723
Hemphill, 667, 710, 990
Hemric, 1076
Henderson, 360, 440, 719, 725, 796, 1000, 1057, 1098
Hendren, 382, 389, 425, 522, 596, 597, 601, 652, 658, 668, 669, 670, 671, 672, 673, 674, 799, 851, 897, 899, 1027, 1028, 1037, 1059
Hendrix, 319, 320, 355, 361, 440, 490, 597, 623, 632, 645, 675, 676, 677, 678, 679, 685, 712, 768, 791, 812, 1015, 1017, 1076, 1077
Henkle, 683
Henley, 367
Henry, 619, 1057
Henson, 453, 486
Herbert, 313, 314
Herlocker, 751
Herman, 498, 631
Herndon, 451, 604
Herron, 1027, 1028
Hester, 368, 643
Hethcock, 932
Hewitt, 932
Hiatt, 649
Hickerson, 617, 714, 823, 838, 895, 899, 915, 951, 1051, 1053, 1054
Hicks, 336, 418, 917
Higgins, 309, 340, 352, 363, 440, 492, 536, 543, 545, 547, 592, 685, 692, 731, 758, 781, 799, 830, 874, 928, 947, 976
Highsmith, 511
Hill, 641, 731, 1052
Hillery, 352
Hilton, 594
Hincher, 304, 336, 404, 409, 566, 594, 648, 680, 792, 951
Hines, Hinds, 361, 400, 609, 1007
Hinshaw, 484, 489, 521, 692, 910
Hinton, 946, 949
Hipps, 521, 609, 896, 1075
Hire, Hyre, 533, 534, 535
Hisle, 992
Hitchcock, 976, 1112
Hix, 367, 619, 681, 682, 683
Hoag, 619
Hoagland, 1027
Hobb(s), 643, 701
Hobson, 896
Hodge(s), 316, 645, 684, 945, 1016, 1042, 1074, 1114
Hodgson, 598
Hof(f)man, 532, 543, 958
Hogan, 500
Hogg, 771, 829
Hohman, 722
Holbrook, Halbrook, Etc., 302, 305, 309, 313, 314, 318, 336, 340, 349, 351, 352, 361, 379, 380, 381, 393, 438, 456, 603, 613, 622, 628, 629, 630, 685, 686, 687, 689, 690, 691, 692, 693, 694, 695, 696, 718, 731, 735, 741, 791, 792, 796, 797, 867, 937, 971, 976, 993, 1007, 1009, 1111, 1112, 1113
Holcomb, 373, 418, 662, 663, 877, 921
Holdaway, 414, 698, 880
Holden, 443
Holder, 453, 676, 697, 875, 880, 898, 1007, 1038, 1057, 1077
Holderman, 548
Holland, 463, 517, 526, 651, 652, 725, 731, 855, 862, 863, 915, 1026

Holler, 363, 704, 861, 908
Holliday, 341
Holloway, 311, 336, 340, 361, 434, 440, 468, 685, 1070, 1093
Holman, Holeman, Holdman, 453, 487, 546, 699, 700, 936, 1002, 1010, 1015, 1017, 1083
Holmes, 731
Holsclaw, 1076
Holt, 407, 513, 1095
Honeycut(t), 719, 799, 1101
Hood, 372, 395, 782
Hooks, 869
Hooper, 750
Hoots, 366, 418, 797, 1009
Hoover, 558
Hopkins, 705, 763, 782, 1074
Hopper, 701, 838
Hord, 1080
Hori, 523, 1063
Horn, 368
Horton, 397, 469, 500, 557, 561, 566, 702, 704, 746, 844, 869, 979, 1099
Houck, 398, 851, 852, 1013
Houghton, 635
House, 731
Hovermale, 979, 1065
Howard, 391, 436, 504, 567, 605, 619, 703, 704, 705, 706, 864, 848, 1115
Howe, 496
Howell, 397, 427, 499, 502, 503, 504, 513, 545, 549, 681, 683, 707, 708, 710, 770, 912, 952, 990, 996, 1016, 1037, 1073
Howland, 483
Hoyle, 376
Hubbard, 374, 396, 431, 512, 572, 573, 579, 587, 616, 621, 654, 683, 709, 710, 711, 755, 762, 770, 776, 779, 786, 787, 933, 967, 979, 996, 1018, 1045, 1082, 1098
Hudler, 622
Hudson, 352, 395, 640
Hudspeth, 610
Huf(f)man, 308, 349, 478, 631, 647, 701, 730, 821, 881, 903, 929, 932, 1027, 1074, 1115
Hufft, 487
Huggins, 536, 816
Hughes, 491
Huie, Huey, Hughey, 333, 685, 692, 809, 993
Hulcher, 594, 712, 750, 1020
Hulse, 1099
Humber, 789
Humphries, 443, 539, 707, 710
Hung, 528
Hunt, 427, 447, 470, 477, 487, 563, 602, 617, 712, 713, 714, 716, 738, 917, 1019
Hunter, 410, 530, 720, 722, 733
Hurd, 490, 593, 1057
Hurst, 340, 610
Hurt, 418
Hussey, 992
Hutchens, Hutchins, 715, 719, 834, 901, 905, 1099
Hutchinson, Hutcherson, Hutcheson, Etc., 306, 309, 395, 418, 421, 440, 471, 594, 685, 692, 696, 720, 722, 951, 970, 993, 1054, 1069
Hutson, 1104
Hutton, 791

— I —

Iantoni, 829
Icard, 498
Idol, 972
Iles, 353
Inge, 1051
Ingle, 963
Ingool, 1093
Ingram, 368, 373, 495, 712, 714, 716
Inscore, 419, 445, 672, 719, 724

Iredell, 740
Irvin, 347, 392
Irwin, 917, 923, 1019
Isbell, 705
Isenhour, 824
Israel, 385
Ivey, 566, 586

— J —

Jacks, 663, 817
Jackson, 429, 467, 596, 597, 756, 844, 1011, 1015, 1017
Jacob, 564, 590
James, 471, 755, 762, 784, 1010, 1054, 1074, 1083, 1090
Jarvis, 473, 566, 653, 662, 687, 704, 717, 747, 780, 894, 947, 1011, 1021, 1037, 1058, 1107
Jeffries, 393
Jenkins, 351, 381, 402, 405, 460, 472, 486, 580, 584, 647, 860, 918, 921, 958
Jennings, 301, 302, 304, 305, 317, 341, 342, 352, 374, 382, 410, 431, 439, 484, 673, 692, 720, 721, 722, 723, 727, 761, 770, 835, 836, 864, 951, 957
Jester, 1008
Jobe, 778
Johns, 719
Johnson, 301, 302, 304, 308, 309, 311, 313, 315, 317, 325, 326, 328, 339, 349, 356, 360, 363, 364, 369, 378, 388, 393, 405, 419, 422, 432, 438, 440, 447, 456, 459, 465, 473, 474, 478, 484, 489, 492, 503, 516, 523, 525, 529, 530, 543, 553, 568, 569, 570, 575, 584, 592, 594, 610, 612, 613, 622, 628, 638, 649, 650, 651, 652, 658, 662, 668, 680, 685, 693, 694, 704, 708, 715, 719, 724, 725, 726, 727, 728, 730, 731, 732, 733, 734, 735, 736, 741, 774, 789, 798, 799, 829, 833, 849, 850, 853, 856, 862, 863, 865, 879, 891, 903, 912, 924, 928, 930, 937, 951, 957, 965, 968, 979, 987, 1007, 1011, 1013, 1028, 1038, 1047, 1063, 1070, 1076, 1080, 1083, 1091, 1105, 1107, 1115
Johnston, 376, 507, 514, 521, 532, 643, 717, 730, 738, 739, 740, 776, 849, 927, 1010, 1019
Joines, Joynes, 300, 313, 338, 340, 347, 364, 371, 372, 374, 379, 381, 388, 417, 513, 523, 524, 592, 694, 721, 731, 741, 742, 743, 786, 892, 893, 894, 947, 983, 1008, 1011, 1013, 1063
Jolly, 793, 860
Jones, 353, 392, 417, 434, 443, 456, 459, 467, 478, 486, 493, 521, 522, 523, 568, 570, 572, 575, 578, 583, 585, 596, 602, 612, 622, 626, 641, 666, 679, 688, 696, 705, 708, 712, 731, 733, 734, 735, 738, 744, 745, 746, 747, 748, 749, 751, 755, 764, 771, 823, 838, 887, 890, 931, 939, 949, 962, 969, 977, 978, 979, 984, 986, 1019, 1039, 1051, 1074, 1082, 1094, 1096, 1111, 1113
Jordan, 326, 336, 348, 360, 463, 688, 696, 752, 797, 929
Joyce, 670
Joyner, 367, 496, 601, 832
Judd, 701, 755, 911, 1082
Justice, 420, 432

— K —

Kaczor, 363
Kales, 481

Kanatzar, 981
Kastelburg, 490
Kastin, 641
Katz, 542
Kaucher, 1070
Kaylor, 595
Kazee, 796
Keener, 547
Keeter, 489, 621
Keever, 761
Keithley, 395
Kelso, 1098
Keller, 489, 645, 750, 1074
Kellermeyer, 677
Kellet, 1081
Kelly, 392, 494, 499, 796
Kemp, 717, 742
Kendall, 487, 541, 546, 578, 585, 619, 746, 820, 1052
Kennedy, 410, 685, 741, 748, 753, 794, 1101
Kennett, 1057
Kent, 443, 1053
Kerbaugh, 346, 666
Kerley, 325, 363, 640, 649, 725, 784, 983, 1038
Kern, Kearn(s), 447, 519, 710, 1076
Kerr, 525
Kesler, 505, 602
Kessinger, 731
Key(s), Keye, Kees, 613, 631, 841, 842, 859, 917, 1071, 1076, 1114
Kid, 610
Kijek, 536
Kilby, 301, 338, 342, 352, 373, 381, 383, 397, 398, 400, 415, 472, 493, 522, 523, 532, 533, 687, 715, 726, 750, 755, 756, 757, 758, 759, 760, 761, 762, 779, 781, 784, 786, 809, 811, 814, 815, 818, 835, 853, 861, 874, 880, 903, 921, 924, 933, 938, 983, 1011, 1012, 1013, 1023, 1032, 1033, 1051, 1060, 1063, 1079, 1080, 1083, 1085, 1087, 1088, 1114
Killian, 908
Kimbell, 554, 802
Kimberlin, 1114
Kincaid, 481
Kindley, 488, 494
King, 326, 462, 522, 715
Kinnaird, 564
Kinyoun, 500, 569
Kirby, 641, 774, 1002
Kirk, 563
Kirkpatrick, 989
Kiser, 478, 903
Kitt, 395
Kleinschmidt, Kleinsmith, 487, 503
Klinkosum, 763
Knight, 528
Knowles, 764
Knox, 342, 466, 648, 764, 974
Kobayashi, 462
Kokot, 521
Koonts, 566, 817
Korb, 1116
Kroeckel, 677
Kulynych, 396
Kunkel, 526
Kurfees, 750
Kyle(s), 555, 619

— L —

Lackey, 649, 774, 932, 1041, 1045
Lacy, 885
Ladd, 765, 766, 767, 864
Lafayette, 826
Lafoon, 441, 444, 697
Lail, 363
Lake, 885
Lakey, 780
Lamb, 1098
Lambert, 485, 486, 558, 715, 745, 829
Lamony, 774
Lance, 648
Land, 547, 678, 768, 838, 900, 936, 958, 1072, 1077, 1107
Landenberger, 829
Landon, 769

Landquest, 367
Landreth, 727, 806, 1016, 1104, 1105
Landtrip, 805
Lane, 347, 370, 382, 490, 946, 947, 1037
Lang, 857
Lanier, 307
Lansdown, 623
Lanzl, 881
Largen, 366
Laster, 336
Latham, 568
Lawrence, Lorance, 453, 528, 588, 794, 826, 1016
Lawry, 845
Laws, 316, 318, 347, 410, 545, 631, 632, 633, 707, 743, 770, 771, 772, 773, 786, 881, 903, 906, 908, 960, 1038, 1062, 1115
Laxton, 427, 596, 619, 1099
Leach, Leitch, 621, 744, 750, 774
Leckie, 500, 569
Ledbetter, 958
LeDoux, 487, 732
Lee, 528, 909, 935
LeGrand, 563
Leinback, Leinbachs, 1037
Lemmons, 939
Lenderman, 371, 397, 900, 989, 1011, 1083
Leonard, 974
Letting, 842
Leventhorpe, 392
Levine, 521
Levy, 436
Lewey, 1112
Lewis, 355, 356, 411, 431, 473, 474, 475, 534, 660, 679, 704, 707, 738, 776, 782, 923, 926, 994, 1000, 1008, 1016, 1019, 1072
Lies, 438
Lincoln, 620
Lindahl, 709, 1082
Lindley, 751
Lindsay, Lindsey, 462, 679, 722, 782
Link, 881
Linney, 570, 777, 778, 823, 875, 1021
Lippard, 1054
Lipps, 844, 906
List, 395
Little, 637, 834, 958, 989, 1103
Livengood, 649, 819
Livingston, 426, 536
Llewellyn, 746
Lloyd, 976, 1112
Locket, 466
Lockey, 838
Lodin, 677
Loflin, 1074
Loftis, 437
Lomax, 756, 779
Long, 301, 302, 436, 438, 441, 618, 698, 731, 740, 743, 917, 1057
Longbottom, 780
Loomis, 692
Looney, 395
Lott, 1076
Love, 419, 473, 474, 513, 662, 758
Lovelace, 565, 780
Lovette, 318, 398, 399, 519, 648, 656, 661, 781, 782, 806, 853, 877, 881, 921, 1022, 1047
Lovill, 594
Lovin(g), 363, 469
Lowdermilk, 455
Lowe, Loe, Loo, Low, 372, 381, 385, 391, 443, 455, 495, 505, 567, 612, 621, 743, 782, 783, 784, 785, 787, 788, 857, 867, 944, 950, 983, 1057, 1067
Lowery, 995
Lucas, 1102
Luce, 829
Luffman, 336, 402, 665, 727, 789, 790, 792, 959, 1063, 1093
Lugar, 592
Lumpkin, 702

Lunsford, Lunceford, 314, 864, 1113, 1115
Lusk, 466
Luther, 747, 1074
Luttrell, 883, 888
Lutz, 649
Lyall, 456
Lyle, 619
Lynch, 911
Lyndon, 982, 985, 986
Lyon(s), 349, 361, 410, 418, 685, 692, 791, 792, 793, 794, 795, 796, 966, 993, 1104, 1105, 1112
Lytch, 744

— Mc —
McArthur, 776, 792
McArver, 896
McAuley, 764, 776, 792, 896
McBride, 537, 679, 797, 1008, 1112
McCall, 974
McCampbell, 392
McCann, 336, 459, 798, 826, 965
McCarter, 309, 730, 739, 799
McCarty, 340, 341, 351, 694, 826
McChuson, 819
McClelland, 1053
McCloud, 731
McClure, 989
McCollum, 485, 486, 819
McConnel, 817
McCord, 951
McCoy, 602, 786, 860
McCrary, 311, 350, 723, 809, 836
McCulley, 817
McCullough, 733, 824
McCurry, 1105
McCutchen, 551
McDaniel, 1080
McDonald, MacDonald, 747, 800, 883, 884, 1056
McDiarmid, 961
McDowell, 1074
McEachin, 522
McElroy, 311
McElwee, 362, 483, 776, 801, 896
McEwen, 358, 802, 837
McFarland, McFarlane, 465, 1018, 1075
McFerrin, 594
McGee, 316, 320, 454, 546, 596, 726, 744, 803, 804, 1075
McGhennis, 387
McGill, 805
McGimsey, 431
McGinnis, 316, 541
McGlamery, 406, 415, 455, 532, 536, 561, 647, 758, 806, 833, 841, 847, 881, 904, 938, 1047, 1113, 1115
McGrady, 308, 515, 690, 693, 694, 720, 721, 722, 723, 741, 807, 808
McGregor, MacGregor, 612
McGuines, 595
McGuire, 463, 662, 750, 817, 1016, 1114
McGuirt, 570
McHargue, 1015, 1017
McIntosh, Mackintosh, 363, 619
McKee, 396, 443, 590, 717, 733, 761, 786, 974, 1021, 1081, 1109
McLaughlin, 565
McLean, McLain, 490, 509, 534, 752, 761, 809, 812, 898, 988, 1007, 1035, 1051, 1052
McMahan, 881
McMenamin, 692
McMichael(s), McMickle, 610, 837, 1051
McMillian, 302, 470, 616, 817, 895
McMurray, 837
McNiel, McNiell, McNeil, McNeill, 302, 303, 317, 352, 358, 397, 400, 404, 406, 407, 409, 412, 415, 430, 439, 441, 447, 452, 476, 477, 493, 495, 503,

513, 518, 519, 522, 524, 527, 546, 566, 568, 572, 573, 592, 594, 644, 645, 653, 654, 657, 659, 663, 686, 689, 717, 750, 762, 804, 806, 809, 810, 811, 812, 813, 814, 815, 816, 818, 819, 821, 839, 840, 844, 853, 874, 881, 900, 905, 922, 923, 935, 936, 938, 939, 962, 969, 975, 1011, 1013, 1016, 1051, 1052, 1054, 1055, 1058, 1060, 1063, 1076, 1083, 1084, 1085, 1094, 1102, 1115
McPherson, 643
McQuery, 309
McRary, 498
McReynolds, 731
McRorie, 528
McShane, 546, 820
McWhirter, 1033

— M —
Mabe, 318
Maddox, 731
Madison, 500, 537, 665, 666, 692, 863
Magnuson, 846
Mahaffey, 309, 685, 928, 931, 1061
Maine(s), 307, 429, 925, 1072
Malcolm, 611
Malone(e), 616, 1002
Manard, Maynard, 309, 351, 361
Mann, 1045
Manus, 478
Manwaring, 598
Marable, 553
Margaro, 698
Marion, 821, 939
Markland, 881
Marley, 316, 513
Marlow, 329, 330, 331, 382, 385, 391, 466, 473, 474, 529, 530, 619, 650, 651, 652, 658, 666, 683, 692, 717, 737, 853, 856, 1027, 1065
Marsh, 648, 761, 822, 824, 935, 1011
Marshall, 570, 598, 635, 740, 782
Martin, 309, 311, 313, 392, 403, 458, 462, 469, 519, 561, 563, 578, 607, 613, 617, 707, 713, 714, 718, 735, 743, 823, 824, 825, 860, 895, 939, 962, 985, 986, 1027, 1105, 1106, 1112
Martinez, 1021
Marvel, 769
Mash, 917
Massey, 478
Mast, 471, 647, 906
Mastin, Marston, 326, 418, 420, 827, 828, 829, 830, 831, 832, 833, 987, 1010, 1037, 1107
Matherly, 663
Matheson, Mathison, 715, 1018
Mathias, 554, 829
Mathis, 304, 318, 418, 459, 667, 719, 724, 930, 951, 982, 1011, 1021
Matlock, 1062
Matney, 786, 1101
Matthews, 539
Maury, 666
Maxey, 469
Maxwell, 963, 1051, 1052
Mayberry, 349, 427, 484, 703, 756, 1000, 1021
Mayes, May(s), 343, 733, 834, 901
Meade, 927
Meadows, 425, 723, 846, 911, 933, 1091
Measmer, 342
Medaris, 660
Mehauolic, 410
Melton, 312, 418, 523, 609, 1063, 1092
Mendenhall, 969, 1097
Menefee, 1102

Mengel, 1008
Meredith, 743
Merritt, 518, 710
Merrymon, 548
Messic(k), 912, 1048
Michael, 752, 853, 896, 1074, 1115
Mikeal, Mickle, 513, 521, 594, 610, 817, 1045, 1114
Milam, 398, 402, 405, 416, 842
Miles, 309, 422, 649, 685, 692, 797, 861, 865, 1028
Miller, 300, 323, 325, 354, 356, 357, 377, 414, 417, 422, 447, 455, 472, 475, 484, 485, 505, 521, 522, 524, 536, 558, 566, 570, 575, 585, 602, 608, 624, 663, 700, 701, 726, 731, 741, 751, 761, 768, 811, 822, 831, 837, 838, 839, 840, 841, 843, 844, 873, 881, 912, 917, 920, 921, 922, 935, 936, 938, 951, 996, 1016, 1027, 1033, 1042, 1053, 1057, 1074, 1077, 1084, 1097, 1101, 1102, 1110, 1112, 1114
Milliken, 912
Mills, 392, 578, 746, 845
Miner, 816
Millsaps, 324, 345, 649
Milner, 931
Mimmo, 1019
Mims, 484, 843
Minton, 350, 358, 400, 472, 482, 490, 513, 521, 545, 576, 580, 619, 641, 697, 730, 742, 743, 819, 846, 847, 849, 872, 873, 875, 877, 879, 880, 901, 902, 904, 907, 938, 946, 947, 989, 1022, 1028, 1115
Miser, 469
Mitchell, Michell, 346, 347, 395, 478, 558, 586, 598, 605, 612, 636, 649, 674, 715, 764, 770, 833, 848, 901, 919, 1000, 1107
Mize, Mise, 780, 855
Moak, 612
Mobley, 1028
Mode, 319
Moffett, 766
Moloney, 1076
Moltase, 486
Monday, 453, 514, 741
Money, 610, 780, 854, 860, 1051, 1052, 1096, 1104
Monier, 829
Monin, 1029
Montgomery, 352, 458, 844, 1010, 1019, 1103
Moody, 568
Moon, 689
Mooney, 462
Moore, 301, 318, 322 A-A, 323, 324, 325, 330, 331, 333, 393, 472, 478, 519, 529, 530, 531, 536, 549, 566, 601, 610, 640, 651, 668, 683, 717, 730, 737, 740, 741, 805, 813, 850, 851, 852, 854, 855, 856, 999, 1014, 1020, 1027, 1028, 1048
Mooreman, 467
Moose, 594, 654
Moran, 997
Morehouse, 857
Moreland, 631, 743
Morgan, 318, 330, 366, 493, 495, 496, 498, 628, 630, 667, 908, 1013
Mori, 507, 643
Moring, 457
Morley, 590
Morphew, 918
Morrah, 741
Morrill, 857
Morris, 352, 471, 566, 926, 1072
Morrison, 521, 790, 792, 802, 858, 859, 860, 974, 981, 982, 984, 985, 1045
Morton, 822, 1021
Mosely, 615, 679
Moser, 509, 649

Mott, 487
Moxley, 692, 1000
Mullinax, 462
Mullins, Mullens, 468, 469, 619, 705, 1040, 1044
Mullis, 651, 674, 861, 863, 921, 1012
Munster, 1037
Murdock, 596, 802
Murphy, 340, 726, 911, 949, 974, 1098
Murray, Murry, 351, 352, 522, 586, 642, 734, 1063
Myers, 317, 322 A-A, 345, 352, 369, 379, 381, 417, 435, 436, 440, 444, 447, 452, 484, 500, 536, 575, 606, 670, 688, 692, 696, 703, 704, 728, 731, 744, 767, 790, 806, 860, 861, 862, 864, 865, 876, 904, 957, 969, 971, 1001, 1007, 1012, 1045, 1091, 1093, 1105

— N —
Nab, 318
Naler, 1105
Nall(s), 694, 796
Nance, 331, 473, 866, 1037
Nanney, 368
Napier, 363
Nash, 463
Naughton, 1102
Naylor, 953
Neal, Neel, 307, 381, 679, 867, 891
Neatherly, 620
Necessary, 381, 891
Neeley, Neely, 395, 715, 771
Neilson, 427
Neisler, 997
Nelson, 456, 560, 731, 747, 868, 914, 1074
Nelville, 454
Netherland, 946, 948
Nethey, 928
Newman, 858
Newton, 494, 614, 702, 869
Ney, 563
Nichols, 399, 400, 403, 404, 406, 408, 409, 411, 414, 415, 441, 448, 453, 469, 482, 513, 514, 516, 527, 532, 576, 590, 648, 659, 680, 697, 698, 715, 732, 761, 803, 806, 814, 819, 846, 871, 872, 873, 874, 875, 876, 877, 878, 879, 880, 881, 901, 902, 908, 922, 925, 938, 979, 984, 1000, 1007, 1070
Nicholson, 467, 752, 1052, 1082
Nickelow, 521
Nicole, 826
Niddrie, 731
Nisbet, 915
Nixon, 460, 794
Noble, 642
Noel(l), 503, 521
Noland, 625, 1115
Nooe, 974, 1053, 1054
Norman, 471, 490, 537, 538, 707, 779, 791, 794, 897, 969
Norris, 356, 395, 809, 844, 900, 1016

— O —
Oakley, 813
Oates, 801
O'Brian, 1043
Ogburn, 431, 882
Ogilvie, 558, 584, 800, 883, 884, 885, 886, 887, 890
Oliver, 537, 1027
Olsen, Olson, 700, 1002, 1098
O'Melia, 948
Osborne, 305, 349, 380, 381, 503, 596, 647, 809, 842, 867, 891, 908, 921, 1076, 1104
O'Sullivan, 960
Overcash, 349
Owen(s), 307, 308, 348, 417, 439, 447, 508, 622, 665, 721, 723, 739, 741, 744,

751, 838, 892, 893, 1074, 1110
Owenby, 969
Owings, 761, 847
Oxford, 972

— P —

Pace, 705
Padgett, 473, 894
Pafford, 598
Paige, Page, 455, 778
Paisley, Peasley, 525, 872, 1077
Palmer, 342, 363, 374, 487, 782
Pardue, 308, 336, 352, 364, 411, 447, 648, 665, 696, 710, 717, 747, 792, 832, 894, 921, 957, 1052, 1068
Paris, 911
Parker, 315, 318, 322, 362, 368, 397, 431, 459, 473, 474, 512, 528, 590, 651, 661, 664, 673, 679, 716, 725, 843, 847, 848, 849, 854, 862, 863, 869, 870, 969, 1027, 1037, 1038, 1053
Parks, 315, 326, 366, 392, 563, 602, 629, 651, 664, 724, 725, 729, 796, 801, 823, 895, 896, 897, 913, 915, 916, 951, 958, 963, 1043, 1051, 1057, 1075
Parlier, Perleir, Purlear, 347, 371, 430, 542, 594, 635, 641, 723, 744, 761, 898, 899, 1032, 1097, 1101
Parsons, 358, 386, 387, 407, 410, 416, 525, 548, 549, 586, 715, 725, 741, 768, 786, 797, 819, 834, 841, 847, 875, 900, 901, 902, 903, 904, 907, 958, 962, 975, 1016, 1048, 1056, 1114
Parteet, 561
Passmore, 695
Paster, 1011
Patrick, 891, 914
Patterson, 485, 816, 1027, 1112
Patton, 408, 655, 844, 951, 958, 1054
Paxton, 1057
Payne, 304, 306, 368, 395, 452, 503, 570, 670, 891, 905, 906, 907, 940, 973, 1114
Peak, 620
Pearson, 316, 372, 373, 423, 455, 513, 522, 541, 545, 546, 642, 707, 738, 761, 778, 786, 788, 857, 878, 908, 945, 950, 967, 1022, 1054, 1101
Peden, 333
Pegg, 719
Pegram, 490, 593
Pender, 351, 514
Pendergrass, 739, 809
Pendley, Penley, 339, 452, 462, 537, 909, 926
Pendry, 680, 692, 910, 932, 993
Pennell, 344, 382, 402, 405, 491, 542, 586, 590, 591, 708, 797, 836, 911, 912, 1101, 1103, 1112
Pennington, 432, 434, 477, 523, 700, 872, 968
People(s), 500, 569
Peppers, 993
Perkins, 400, 778, 913, 1037, 1101, 1116
Perrell, 643
Perry, 395, 434, 475, 521, 705, 769, 796, 914, 928, 965
Persons, 630
Peters, 321
Peterman, 341
Pet(t)erson, 487, 679
Petro, 1057
Petters, 459
Pettit, 462
Petty, 563, 895, 915, 916
Pfaff, 1037
Pfohl, 817

Pharr, 605, 990, 1075
Pheiffer, 912
Phelps, 819
Philbeck, 751
Phillips, 349, 389, 410, 423, 446, 455, 463, 493, 521, 528, 545, 549, 654, 685, 761, 771, 779, 786, 800, 809, 811, 817, 841, 842, 848, 873, 881, 899, 900, 907, 917, 918, 919, 920, 923, 947, 971, 993, 1016, 1029, 1051, 1052, 1074, 1113, 1114, 1116
Phipps, 475, 635, 695, 817, 1016, 1051, 1115
Pickard, 421, 925, 962
Pickel, 475
Pickens, 746
Pickett, 931
Pierce, Pearce, 301, 326, 392, 397, 448, 449, 521, 527, 532, 663, 761, 872, 876, 921, 922, 923, 924, 925
Piles, 701
Pilgrim, 302, 305
Pilkington, 383, 1058
Pinner, 478
Pinnix, 664
Pipers, 568
Pipes, 645, 926, 1101
Pitcher, 1057
Pittman, 507
Pitts, 411
Plampin, 742
Plexico, 581
Plonk, 776, 801
Plumlee, 487
Plummer, 622
Poe, 894
Poetker, 719
Poindexter, 743, 988, 989
Polk, 541, 750
Pollard, 307, 558
Poole, 777, 778, 929
Poor, 1080
Poplin, 410, 460, 861, 1051, 1052, 1104
Porter, 327, 352, 358, 447, 473, 683, 692, 710, 733, 734, 847, 861, 914, 927, 928, 951, 954, 1000, 1011, 1067
Posey, 921
Post, 799
Poteat, 453, 669, 672, 674, 881, 929, 930, 1063
Potter, 338
Potts, 742, 805
Pound, 992
Powell, 302, 358, 463, 507, 586, 606, 619, 643, 703, 720, 721, 723, 724, 841, 903, 917, 920, 932, 1023, 1095, 1097, 1099
Powers, 475, 528, 621, 946, 1027
Pratt, 337
Presley, 459
Presnell, 354
Preston, 410
Prevette, Privette, 304, 321, 360, 361, 369, 411, 440, 467, 507, 522, 685, 704, 725, 744, 790, 833, 931, 932, 959, 1089, 1090, 1092, 1093
Preysz, 566
Price, 362, 367, 385, 391, 453, 457, 475, 578, 723, 744, 782, 835, 836, 853, 855, 933, 1058, 1102
Priddy, 719
Pries, 1048
Priester, 756
Prince, 365
Prine, 521
Pritchard, 353, 995, 1057
Proctor, 581
Proffit, 353, 357, 364, 613, 768, 816, 840, 934, 935, 936, 975, 1022
Province, 754
Pruitt, Pruett(e), 336, 340, 349, 352, 374, 438, 475, 619, 685, 688, 693, 694, 696, 731, 791, 792, 793, 825, 832, 837, 1027, 1089, 1104, 1112

Puckett, 612
Pugh, 843
Pullen, 719

— Q —

Queen, 317, 318, 558, 673, 770, 779, 826, 899, 935, 1028, 1065
Quesinberry, 1111
Quilici, 744, 997

— R —

Raby, 973
Ragsdale, 370, 371, 372, 782, 1039
Ramsey, 700, 859, 883, 884, 887, 890
Randolph, 917
Raper, 806
Rariden, 1057
Rash, 373, 376, 395, 414, 415, 441, 444, 467, 518, 534, 751, 755, 759, 762, 806, 809, 821, 824, 864, 925, 938, 939, 1060, 1078
Rasmussen, 455
Rauch, 990
Ray, 575, 679, 684, 908, 945, 950, 1049, 1051, 1054
Raymer, 524, 570, 1002
Rea, 764
Read, 782, 800
Reagan, 940
Reavill, 987
Reavis, 324, 347, 370, 529, 661, 681, 684, 784, 788, 941, 942, 943, 944, 945, 950, 1027, 1051, 1052
Rector, 459
Redd, 616
Reddick, 916
Redding, 547, 616, 666, 832
Reddish, 521
Redmon, 962
Redwine, 751
Reece, Reese, 610, 792, 1036
Reeder, 731
Reep, 842
Reeves, 314, 462, 521, 647, 726, 731, 739, 817, 829, 853, 892, 1007
Regan, 459, 906
Reiches, 1037
Reid, Reed, 469. 565, 800, 929, 1027, 1047
Reinhardt, 362, 606, 1055
Reins, Rains, 500, 569, 580, 584, 621, 631, 726, 744, 946, 947, 948, 949, 991, 1054, 1058, 1081
Renninger, Renegar, 366, 846
Rex, 670
Reynolds, 300, 302, 308, 317, 459, 500, 519, 520, 537, 538, 544, 552, 566, 636, 796, 928, 951, 956, 993, 1069
Rhoades, Rhodes, 302, 308, 373, 415, 417, 420, 500, 514, 515, 522, 524, 532, 592, 621, 648, 685, 707, 715, 721, 728, 862, 928, 939, 951, 952, 953, 954, 955, 956, 957, 958, 1032, 1078, 1086, 1101, 1102
Rhymer, 1059
Rhyne, 521, 900, 958
Rice, 457, 808, 932
Rich, 372, 410, 908
Richards, 1112
Richardson, 307, 350, 418, 456, 470, 665, 685, 727, 731, 733, 734, 739, 790, 798, 830, 831, 959, 962, 1028, 1089, 1090, 1092
Richter, 395
Rickenbacker, 990
Rickert, 744
Rickman, 973
Ricks, 503, 891
Riddle, 653, 1066
Rider, 700
Riggs, 586, 782, 814
Riggsbee, 349
Riley, 410
Ritchie, 364, 996, 1043
Rittenburg, 741
Rivers, 912
Rives, 344, 366

Roach, 609
Roane, 491
Robbins, Robins, 392, 400, 578, 585, 702, 755, 762, 888, 926, 1000, 1013, 1080
Robbs, 459
Roberts, Robards, 301, 338, 393, 463, 475, 509, 514, 537, 542, 617, 685, 687, 717, 718, 719, 740, 741, 849, 901, 951, 966, 985, 1000, 1011, 1013, 1022, 1029, 1058, 1096
Rober(t)son, 352, 523, 525, 586, 621, 656, 704, 770, 772, 806, 807, 921, 955, 960, 1062, 1097
Robinett(e), 447, 519, 536, 578, 768, 951
Robi(n)son, 321, 621, 671, 769, 801, 813, 961, 1047, 1074, 1098
Roden, 462, 1008
Rogers, 397, 628, 744, 961, 1057, 1062
Roland, Rowland, 739, 740, 973, 981, 1063
Roller, 782
Roloff, 418
Roloson, 352
Romans, 1116
Roope, O'Roop, 358, 523, 644, 813, 962, 1063
Roper, 973, 1074, 1113, 1114, 1115
Rose, 340, 745, 832, 1042
Roseman, 747
Rosenberg, 1058
Rosenblat, 492
Ross, 1111
Rosser, 528
Roth, 710
Rothchild, 537
Roughton, 679
Rousseau, 340, 843, 895, 963, 964, 1036, 1037, 1108
Royal(l), 349, 412, 501, 791, 911, 914, 965, 966
Rucker, 463
Rudy, 861
Ruffy, 1027
Ruley, 590
Rushing, 700
Russel, 349, 513, 549, 644, 746, 967, 1063, 1076
Rutledge, 729

— S —

Sakurai, 487
Sale(s), 374, 418, 561, 605, 704, 719, 766, 823, 864, 929, 951
Sallee, 484
Salmons, 546, 951, 1090
Sampson, 553
Sander(s), Saunders, 466, 495, 678, 764, 805, 891, 908, 965, 966, 1040, 1044, 1094
Saner, 427, 709, 710
Sater, 705
Saterwhite, 640, 935
Satterfield, 974
Saufley, 465
Sauvage, 362
Sawyer, 307, 700, 1092
Saxon, 459
Saylor, Salyer, 925, 927
Scarboro, 496
Scarlett, 832
Scha(e)fer, 351, 709, 748
Schiveley, 487
Schmoyer, 993
Schnackenberg, 416
Schulz, 670, 1037
Schumn, 1074
Schuyler, 466
Scott, 309, 316, 407, 513, 521, 797, 817, 912, 1051, 1052, 1100
Scritchfield, 610
Scroggs, 710, 895
Seabright, 862
Seagle, 440
Sealey, 464
Seamster, 434
Sears, 816
Sebastian, 301, 304, 308, 311, 360, 361, 369, 383,

432, 441, 500, 514, 638, 666, 696, 722, 843, 861, 968, 969, 970, 971, 1014
Seehorn, 946
Segraves, 771
Self, 463, 481
Senarius, 990
Senter, 1015
Settle, 321, 336, 794, 1046
Setzer, 695
Severt, 523, 648, 917, 1063
Sexton, 418
Shackelford, 782
Shafford, 922
Sharp(e), 829, 863, 908, 1057, 1063
Shartzer, 801
Shatley, 779
Shaver, 349, 853, 923
Shaw, 696, 1057, 1107
Shearer, 487
Sheckles, 695
Sheets, 435, 475
Shell, 316
Shelton, 707
Shepherd, Sheppard, 309, 317, 323, 360, 379, 493, 527, 572, 575, 579, 586, 613, 673, 683, 721, 722, 745, 755, 797, 809, 811, 819, 832, 862, 875, 879, 880, 917, 922, 923, 925, 935, 972, 973, 993, 1011, 1013, 1049, 1051, 1054, 1074, 1086, 1103
Sheridan, 1007
Sherman, 356
Sherril, 338, 462, 640, 988, 989, 1025
Shertzer, 1057
Sherwood, 487
Shew, 725, 730, 744, 930
Shields, 392, 843, 1053, 1054
Shinliver, 669
Shinn, 899
Shipwash, 369
Shiver, 709, 1082
Shoaf, 575, 911, 988, 989, 1106
Shobers, 1037
Shook, 784, 983
Shore(s), 315, 340, 418, 766, 796
Short, 950
Shoumaker, Shomaker, 816, 894, 975, 1048
Shouse, 463, 696, 919
Show, 927
Shropshire, 592
Shuford, 899, 1002
Shultz, 913, 921, 1057, 1101
Shumate, 301, 302, 304, 308, 309, 321, 374, 441, 444, 453, 478, 592, 613, 622, 634, 692, 715, 721, 729, 741, 861, 865, 934, 954, 955, 956, 970, 976, 993, 1000, 1084
Shuping, 1097
Siamese Twins, 691, 694, 797
Sidden, 685, 692, 797, 910, 951, 976, 1086, 1112
Sigman, Sigmon, 435, 436, 520
Sikes, 868, 877
Silver, 637, 1046
Simcox, 463
Simmons, 450, 454, 520, 521, 528, 685, 745, 747, 790
Simpkins, 808
Simpson, 368, 608, 633, 782, 977, 1072, 1094
Sims, Simms, 1027, 1068
Singletary, 566
Singleton, 363
Sink, 534, 748, 869, 978, 979, 1065
Sisk, 769
Sizemore, 468
Skinner, 496, 1098
Skridulis, 822
Slater, 423
Slaybaugh, 993
Sleetman, 1037
Sloan, 363, 769, 799
Sloop, 368, 485, 641, 710, 962
Sluder, 806
Smith, Schmidt, 311, 321,

516

336, 339, 349, 362, 385, 397, 411, 423, 427, 434, 440, 459, 462, 463, 487, 489, 503, 522, 529, 537, 542, 548, 549, 570, 578, 586, 618, 640, 687, 689, 691, 709, 710, 715, 722, 727, 743, 744, 771, 777, 778, 779, 780, 784, 786, 794, 797, 808, 812, 819, 829, 838, 846, 854, 871, 872, 894, 899, 919, 950, 960, 965, 966, 980, 981, 982, 983, 984, 985, 986, 1008, 1038, 1039, 1054, 1058, 1068, 1080, 1087, 1101

Smithey, 326, 473, 478, 505, 530, 570, 647, 668, 715, 748, 890, 906, 950, 979, 987, 988, 989, 1035

Smoak, 364, 504, 833, 948, 990, 991

Smoot, 328, 349, 352, 447, 500, 551, 552, 553, 613, 622, 685, 688, 692, 696, 741, 792, 992, 993

Smyre, 498

Snell, 1054

Snider, Snyder, 700, 921, 923, 1013, 1015, 1017, 1048

Snipes, 1100

Snow, 1016

Soloman, 470, 471

Somers, 333, 356, 473, 537, 647, 710, 719, 744, 939, 994, 995, 996, 997, 998, 999, 1000, 1020, 1047

Soots, 352, 1028

Sorrels, 463

Southard, 340

Souther, 704, 761, 799, 934, 1000, 1058

Southwell, 344, 1001

Spaar, 533

Spainhour, 301, 409, 436, 670, 700, 754, 768, 895, 1002

Spangler, 309

Sparks, 317, 340, 341, 349, 361, 417, 685, 687, 688, 692, 693, 694, 696, 743, 765, 791, 792, 795, 796, 897, 931, 937, 993, 1003, 1004, 1005, 1047, 1102

Spaugh, 467

Spaulding, 523, 1063

Speaks, 334, 817

Spears, 471, 482, 841, 847, 871, 872, 917, 947, 1006, 1036, 1058, 1075

Speas, Speece, Speece, 451, 854

Speigal, 351

Speight, 496

Spencer, 610, 637, 683, 764, 1072, 1115

Spicer, 313, 314, 340, 430, 438, 639, 685, 687, 690, 691, 694, 696, 731, 797, 812, 863, 867, 937, 959, 976, 993, 1007, 1008, 1009, 1052, 1112

Spires, 455

Spivey, 700

Splawn, 369

Spraker, 720, 722

Springer, 564, 1089, 1097

Sprinkle, 345, 470, 495, 496, 537, 726, 929, 949, 1080

Spurlin, 476

Squire, 800

St. Clair, Saint Clair, 829, 833, 945, 983, 1010, 1053, 1054

St. John, Saint John, 356

Stacey, 771

Stafford, 447, 609

Staggs, 317, 1070

Stahl, 723

Staley, 321, 323, 338, 352, 417, 447, 458, 493, 521, 607, 669, 717, 718, 737, 739, 740, 744, 752, 797, 819, 861, 901, 903, 947, 971, 993, 1011, 1012, 1013, 1084

Stamper, 302, 308, 349, 432, 475, 635, 721, 968, 1014

Stanley, 331, 332, 512, 529, 853, 855, 866

Stan(s)berry, 475, 528, 699, 1015, 1016, 1017

Starbird, 722

Starling, 503

Starnes, 492

Stations, 1077

Steadman, 611

Steagall, 1039

Steele, 490, 507, 619, 640, 643, 808, 869, 912, 933, 1058

Steelman, 523, 586, 692, 731, 848, 894, 902, 943, 944, 1041

Stenguist, 496

Step, 464

Sterling, 348

Stevens, Stephens, 443, 710, 1008, 1082

Stevenson, 602, 620, 1018

Steventon, 563

Stewart, Stuart, 363, 432, 541, 866, 946, 1027, 1038

Stiller, 691, 1093

Stokes, 581, 582, 602, 618, 619, 712, 730, 738, 1010, 1019

Stoll, 767, 864

Stoltz, 518

Stone, 326, 445, 715, 928

Stonecipher, 491

Story, 367, 396, 619, 640, 683, 712, 999, 1020

Stout, 400, 416, 441, 484, 657, 751, 812, 816, 819, 877, 935, 975, 1013

Stover, 722

Strader, 911

Street, 610

Strikeleather, 972

Stringer, 417

Stringfield, 728

Stroud, 517, 526, 1102

Stubblefield, 366

Stubbs, 363

Stull, 1080

Stultz, 761

Sturdivant, 778, 813, 817, 994, 1021

Sturgill, 412, 414, 434

Stutz, 317

Styles, 487

Styvasent, 620

Sudde(r)th, 974, 1053, 1054

Sullivan, 686, 1009

Summerlin, 576, 762, 872, 901, 906, 1022

Summers, 569, 756, 1023, 1024

Sumter, 1053

Surbaugh, 338

Surratt, 710

Swaim, 349, 422, 703, 858, 1053

Swan(n), 333, 483

Swanson, 320, 427, 541, 542, 546, 782, 1025, 1077

Swift, 395

Swim, 858

Swink, 1053

Swisher, 696

Switzer, 710

Sydnor, 700, 1002, 1082

— T —

Taggart, 1057

Talbor, 951

Tanner, 934

Tarlton, 586

Tart, 568

Tate, 557, 561

Tatum, Tatem, 1016

Taylor, 301, 309, 368, 400, 416, 436, 440, 470, 475, 483, 524, 590, 670, 673, 674, 692, 726, 731, 741, 792, 806, 809, 817, 853, 932, 935, 993, 997, 1002, 1016, 1028, 1037, 1053, 1054, 1063, 1099

Teague, 525, 587, 786, 787, 1076

Tedder, 322A-A, 325, 331, 332, 395, 478, 512, 530, 658, 664, 1026

Teem, 320

Teeters, 316, 561

Temple, 481

Templeton, 605, 799, 929

Terry, 1098

Tevepaugh, 584, 649, 744, 1027, 1028, 1059

Tharpe, 504, 731, 861, 863, 865

Thedford, 1115

Thixton, 1057

Thomas, 560, 563, 681, 733, 764, 826, 827, 895, 932, 935

Thompson, 313, 314, 366, 368, 393, 417, 436, 459, 462, 475, 498, 542, 545, 549, 578, 610, 694, 741, 744, 746, 754, 761, 771, 990, 999, 1029, 1030

Thornburg, 651, 856

Thornton, 418, 670, 731, 792

Thurman, 365, 366, 578

Thurston, 581, 587, 1031, 1051

Tidline, 808

Tilley, 460, 548, 731, 853

Tinsley, 383, 818, 957, 1032

Toburen, 368

Todd, 829, 1027

Toernie, 597

Tolbert, 455, 522, 1033

Tolliver, Tollivar, 1014, 1016

Tomlinson, 505, 750, 920, 951, 953, 963, 988, 989, 1034, 1035, 1114

Tompkins, 934

Tonski, 776

Torrence, 669

Totty, 782

Townes, 320, 627

Townsend, 302, 311, 720, 721, 723, 957, 974

Tracy, 1057

Transau, Transou, Transeau, 833, 1036, 1037, 1106, 1108

Treadway, 363, 854, 1038, 1039

Trib(b)le, 770, 832, 1022

Triece, 905, 906

Triplett(e), 316, 349, 354, 356, 377, 402, 416, 417, 429, 438, 451, 455, 482, 513, 521, 541, 544, 545, 546, 568, 572, 594, 602, 608, 610, 619, 624, 625, 632, 642, 643, 645, 659, 678, 732, 737, 740, 751, 778, 803, 839, 847, 926, 935, 972, 975, 976, 1019, 1037, 1040, 1042, 1044, 1056, 1064, 1071, 1074, 1076, 1077, 1104, 1115

Tritt, 784, 786

Trivett(e), 307, 472

Trotter, 483

Troutman, 1027

Truitt, 741, 993, 1008, 1112

Tryon, 471

Tucker, 475, 619, 1016, 1046

Tugman, 338, 808, 906

Tulbert, 524, 537, 546, 1047

Turnbull, 940

Turner, 322, 417, 432, 522, 528, 544, 550, 590, 664, 677, 751, 776, 779, 833, 968, 1009, 1048, 1080, 1112

Turpening, 609

Turpin, 558, 701, 1063

Tuttle, 303, 306, 374, 704, 715, 810, 814

Tysinger, 408

— U —

Ullrich, 521

Umphrey, 548

Underwood, 619, 670, 843

Uzzle, 845

— V —

Valentine, 1100

Vance, 424, 657, 743

Van Eaton, 558

Van Hoose, 619, 620

Van Hoy, 703

Van Looven, 582

Van Noose, 541

Vannoise, Venois, 1049

Vannoy, 302, 307, 338, 363,

364, 379, 381, 400, 403, 425, 450, 452, 454, 459, 470, 471, 472, 493, 519, 520, 521, 524, 527, 565, 568, 569, 570, 575, 585, 606, 644, 722, 733, 738, 755, 761, 762, 808, 809, 811, 819, 847, 877, 906, 908, 918, 946, 949, 951, 965, 974, 975, 1010, 1011, 1013, 1049, 1050, 1051, 1052, 1053, 1054, 1055, 1056, 1068, 1081, 1083, 1084, 1086, 1102, 1114, 1115

Varner, 649

Vaught, 490

Vermillion, 465

Verser, 429

Vestal, 336, 990

Viars, 917

Vickers, Vickas, 328, 331, 727, 782, 819

Vickery, 948

Vines, 496

Viny, 917

Vlk, 368

Voglers, 1037

— W —

Wachter, 1052

Waddell, 309, 336, 340, 349, 417, 438, 613, 685, 692, 731, 739, 741, 764, 849, 928, 993, 1089, 1090

Wade, 518, 617

Wadkins, 951

Wag(g)oner, 366, 438, 456, 695, 731, 768, 819, 839, 914, 965, 1076, 1104

Wainwright, 333

Waites, 951

Walding, Walden, 380, 381, 744

Walker, 302, 304, 306, 316, 349, 352, 417, 440, 441, 444, 478, 493, 500, 523, 537, 547, 575, 622, 629, 638, 685, 688, 692, 705, 720, 722, 724, 725, 729, 730, 733, 735, 736, 759, 793, 842, 863, 902, 908, 920, 947, 956, 957, 975, 993, 1021, 1027, 1028, 1037, 1057, 1058, 1059, 1060, 1061, 1063, 1089, 1112

Wall, 762, 767, 778, 864, 1104

Wallace, Wallis, 372, 373, 384, 397, 426, 427, 443, 498, 523, 602, 770, 772, 863, 887, 960, 982, 1062, 1063, 1066, 1068, 1115

Walsh, 339, 342, 385, 402, 513, 523, 536, 542, 566, 570, 571, 572, 579, 582, 587, 594, 613, 625, 642, 656, 676, 678, 693, 694, 809, 901, 935, 936, 1028, 1045, 1047, 1063, 1064, 1114, 1115

Walter, 979, 1065

Walters, 493, 525, 590, 597, 603, 645, 693, 796, 817, 1089

Walton, 719, 754

Wanless, 654

Ward, 306, 326, 422, 443, 491, 569, 932, 1054, 1066, 1067, 1068, 1069

Warden, 366, 456

Warhold, 508

Warlick, 368

Warner, 313

Warren, 317, 327, 336, 363, 405, 415, 449, 456, 546, 685, 692, 704, 715, 733, 744, 847, 911, 938, 962, 1028, 1068

Washburn, 677

Washington, 563

Wassum, 979

Waters, 317, 462, 546, 624, 631, 632, 633, 660, 820, 873, 1006, 1042, 1070, 1071, 1072

Watkins, 309, 459, 597, 616, 785, 894, 962, 1045, 1062

Watson, 367, 457, 489, 490, 501, 543, 545, 626, 662, 751, 803, 855, 917, 918, 920, 936, 1021, 1058, 1076

Watts, 397, 513, 731, 836, 846, 908, 946, 1009, 1051, 1052, 1058, 1115

Waugh, 495, 557, 636, 708, 728, 771, 778, 833, 857, 867, 1073

Way, 742

Wayne, 628

Weaner, 854

Weatherman, 825, 826

Weaver, 434, 436, 575, 792, 982, 985

Webb, 589, 623, 625

Weber, 849, 986

Weddle, 1057

Weight, 731

Weinstein, 821

Weisner, 368, 657, 662

Weiterner, 558

Wel(l)born, Wil(l)burn, 336, 495, 513, 537, 563, 596, 609, 645, 648, 704, 710, 744, 761, 895, 906, 908, 929, 935, 951, 964, 989, 1010, 1027, 1054, 1075, 1076, 1107, 1114

Wellington, 761, 1109

Wellons, 591

Wells, 720, 1000, 1116

Welsh, Welch, 440, 453, 527, 747, 829, 903, 973, 1053, 1074, 1076, 1083, 1084

Wentworth, 418

West, 316, 336, 456, 489, 508, 536, 594, 676, 677, 678, 731, 761, 838, 859, 860, 1058, 1077, 1078

Westmoreland, 853

Weston, 320, 1079

Wheaton, 1057

Wheeler, 693, 782, 796, 1016, 1049, 1071

Wheeling, 619, 641, 1101, 1103

Whicker, 655, 867, 1081

Whisenhut, 321

Whistant, 586

White, 343, 467, 510, 617, 631, 661, 683, 704, 709, 710, 719, 746, 777, 805, 809, 829, 863, 930, 979, 985, 1002, 1057, 1058, 1070, 1082

Whitfield, 993

Whitley, Wheatley, 305, 309, 311, 349, 350, 383, 432, 458, 638, 725, 726, 731, 733, 734, 755, 762, 883, 888, 954, 955, 956, 1080, 1089, 1104

Whitlock, 352

Whitlow, 354

Whitmore, 909

Whitney, 374, 553

Whitsett, 654

Whitson, 413

Whitt, 908

Whittaker, 395, 613, 715, 826, 929, 937

Whittington, 304, 338, 400, 447, 471, 482, 493, 504, 534, 647, 653, 662, 714, 715, 731, 755, 757, 761, 762, 781, 806, 830, 862, 876, 900, 903, 917, 922, 923, 947, 976, 1011, 1012, 1051, 1052, 1056, 1060, 1083, 1084, 1085, 1086, 1087, 1088, 1114

Wienges, 620

Wiggins, 900

Wilcox(son), 333, 397, 400, 430, 715, 721, 743, 757, 762, 811, 881, 1090, 1114

Wiles, Wilds, 349, 350, 353, 361, 369, 407, 417, 425, 440, 493, 514, 539, 603, 649, 666, 685, 706, 744, 790, 861, 937, 970, 971, 1052, 1089, 1090, 1091, 1092, 1093, 1104, 1105

Wiley, 393

Wilhelm, 935

Wilkerson, 338, 521

Wilkes, 731

Wilkins, 778, 997
Wilkinson, 436
Williams, 469, 478, 503, 532,
    539, 554, 563, 601, 610,
    617, 649, 651, 669, 674,
    709, 710, 751, 752, 754,
    773, 854, 856, 899, 917,
    930, 953, 960, 977, 1058,
    1080, 1094, 1095, 1096,
    1097, 1098, 1099
Williamston, 784, 1100
Wills, 958
Willyard, 343
Wilmouth, 336
Wilson, 322, 323, 395, 407,
    410, 435, 436, 520, 524,
    619, 659, 701, 716, 756,
    782, 811, 904, 911, 1020,
    1102
Wimbish, 700
Windson, 864

Winfrey, 361, 693, 1113
Wingate, 726, 1021, 1027
Wingler, 301, 352, 407, 410,
    518, 1047, 1110
Winkler, 355, 429, 430, 436,
    913, 926, 1101, 1102
Winslow, 427
Winters, 976, 1091
Wiseman, 363, 780, 974
Withers, 958, 969, 1099
Witherspoon, 606, 704, 911,
    1103
Wolfe, 463
Wolford, 465
Womack, 395
Wood, Woods, 360, 361, 434,
    496, 519, 536, 538, 539,
    613, 653, 666, 692, 917,
    954, 992, 1089, 1104, 1105
Woodall, 550, 969
Woodbridge, 565

Woodie, Woody, 302, 493,
    692, 715, 847, 849, 880,
    917, 1110
Woodrine, 786
Woodruff, 339, 393, 394, 405,
    447, 523, 537, 679, 795,
    1007, 1063, 1088, 1107,
    1114
Woodward, 336, 1014
Woolfolk, 313, 314
Wooten, 935, 1047, 1074
Worley, 453
Wornimenh, 939
Worth, 333, 481
Wrenn, 882
Wright, 323, 362, 393, 396,
    397, 432, 433, 459, 544,
    563, 590, 710, 744, 761,
    768, 778, 812, 823, 829,
    912, 915, 986, 1037, 1057,
    1106, 1007, 1108, 1109

Wyatt, 352, 400, 434, 439,
    441, 453, 458, 634, 715,
    717, 721, 739, 758, 792,
    809, 847, 877, 908, 911,
    914, 938, 940, 947, 953,
    955, 1013, 1047, 1058,
    1088, 1110, 1111
Wynne, 702

— Y —
Yale, 340, 362, 797, 976, 993,
    1112
Yarbough, 370
Yates, Yeats, 340, 446, 459,
    510, 521, 647, 693, 755,
    881, 920, 1011, 1022,
    1030, 1076, 1083, 1113,
    1114, 1115
Yeakle, 424
York, 346, 434, 610, 613,
    647, 729, 860, 874, 1000,

1011
Yoshimura, 809
Young, 333, 641, 751, 789,
    1057
Younger, 1076, 1116
Yount, 533, 534, 535
Youtsey, 696
Yow, 911
Yuk, 969
Yunt, 534

— Z —
Zarembo, 681
Zealy, 402
Zimmerman, 1104, 1105
Zink, 978
Zody, 1057
Zwier, 829

Roy G. Foster Construction Co., 1920s.

Our Gen

great great grandfather	_great great grandfather_
great great grandmother	_great great grandmother_
great great grandfather	_great great grandfather_
great great grandmother	_great great grandmother_
great great grandfather	_great great grandfather_
great great grandmother	_great great grandmother_
great great grandfather	_great great grandfather_
great great grandmother	_great great grandmother_
great grandfather	_great grandfather_
great grandmother	_great grandmother_
great grandfather	_great grandfather_
great grandmother	_great grandmother_
grandfather	_grandfather_
grandmother	_grandmother_

Father   Wife   Mother

(your name)

Wife's Brothers and Sisters
Listed Below

married to

children

married to

married to

children

children

married to

Our Ch

married to

children

marri

married to

children

chile

children

children